What does a zebra have to do with **psychology**?

In the case of **THIS** zebra . . . it's here to remind us that not everything is black and white.

McGraw-Hill Connect Student Quick Tips for Blackboard Users

Use this McGraw-Hill Connect Student Quick Tips for Blackboard Users guide for a quick and easy start with your assignments within McGraw-Hill Connect or ConnectPlus. You'll get valuable tips on doing assignments, accessing resources, and support.

"Register Now" or "Sign In"

TIP: To start using Connect assignments within Blackboard, you will be asked to "Register Now" or "Sign In" the first time you click on a Connect assignment. Consider these points as you make your selection:

- If this is your first experience with a McGraw-Hill Connect assignment in Blackboard, select "Register Now" and follow the prompts to establish an account

- If this is not your first experience with a McGraw-Hill Connect assignment, simply select "Sign In" and enter the email address and password that you used for previous McGraw-Hill Connect assignments

- Enter the Connect Access Code purchased with your new textbook or choose "Buy Online" to purchase access online.

TIP: If you are creating a new account with McGraw-Hill, please choose your Security Question and Answer carefully. We will ask you for this information if you forget your password.

TIP: If you do not have an access code, or have not yet secured your tuition funds, you can click "Free Trial" during registration. This trial will provide temporary Connect access (typically three weeks) and will remind you to purchase online access before the end of your trial.

Home (Assignments)

TIP: If you are unable to begin an assignment, verify the following:

- The assignment is available (check start dates and due dates)

- You have not exceeded the maximum number of attempts for the assignment

- You have not achieved a score of 100%

NOTE: If an assignment contains questions that require manual grading, you can attempt to complete the assignment again if your instructor has enabled multiple attempts; however, you won't receive credit for the manually graded questions until the instructor reviews and enters a grade.

Do More

TIP: If you are unable to complete your assignment in one sitting, utilize the "*Save & Exit*" button to save your work and complete it at a later time. Once you have completed your assignment, utilize the "*Submit*" button in order for your assignment to be graded.

TIP: There may be limitations on your assignment, based on your instructor's settings. You may encounter the following limitations when working on your assignment(s):

- Ability to "Print" an assignment

- Once you begin a timed assignment, the timer will not stop

Library

TIP: For shortcuts to various resources, go to the **My Connect Section** under the McGraw-Hill Higher Education link in the "Tools" area.

Higher Education

» **My Connect Section**

↱ **Go to My Connect Section**
Access the McGraw-Hill Connect section associated with this course.
Paired Connect Section: T,R 10-11:15[2905417]

ⓘ **Learn about McGraw-Hill Connect**
Learn more about McGraw-Hill Connect

» **Diagnostics**

ⓘ **Diagnostic Information**
Display diagnostic information.

- If you purchased ConnectPlus, you will see an eBook link, which can also be accessed from the course section information widget of the "Home" tab

- Recorded lectures can be accessed if your instructor is using Tegrity Campus to capture lectures. You may also access recorded lectures when beginning an assignment by clicking on the projector icon in the navigation bar

- Many McGraw-Hill textbooks offer additional resources such as narrated slides and additional problem sets, which are accessible via the "Student Resources" link

Do More

Grades

TIP: Your grades and results are available in the **Grade Book** immediately.

NOTE: Your instructor has the ability to limit the amount of information (e.g. questions, answers, scores) you can view for each submitted assignment

Need More Help with Connect Assignments?

CONTACT US ONLINE:

Visit us at:

www.mcgrawhillconnect.com/support

Browse our support materials including tutorial videos and searchable knowledge base. If you cannot find an answer to your question, click on Contact Us to send us an email.

GIVE US A CALL

Call us at:

1-800-331-5094

Our live support is available:
Mon-Thurs:	8 am – 11 pm CT
Friday:	8 am – 6 pm CT
Sunday:	6 pm – 11 pm CT

SECOND EDITION

Perspectives & Connections

Gregory J. Feist
San Jose State University

Erika L. Rosenberg
University of California, Davis

PSY 101
Introduction to Psychology
Northern Arizona University - Flagstaff

McGraw Hill Education

1 2 3 4 5 6 7 8 9 0 DIG DIG 14 13 12

ISBN-13: 978-1-259-17056-0
ISBN-10: 1-259-17056-X

Learning Solutions Consultant: Adam Poston
Associate Project Manager: Elizabeth Topp
Cover Photo Credits: 106429262 © Stefano Lunardi
87608715 © Jupiterimages
110900780 © ginosphotos
155024043 © Suprijono Suharjoto
138199389 © chupacabra
136324748 © zhang bo
104732037 © Tyler Olson
134135932 © Maridav
158788566 © Shikhar Bhattarai
78631152 © Jupiterimages
152138240 © Jon Snyder
156889009 © Maridav
145198351 © Sophie Ledeme-Goodman
160103432 © Flashon Studio

To our most precious collaborative work,
Jerry and Evan

About the Authors

Gregory J. Feist

Gregory J. Feist is Associate Professor of Psychology in Personality and Adult Development at San Jose State University. He has also taught at the College of William & Mary and the University of California, Davis. He received his PhD from the University of California, Berkeley, and his undergraduate degree from the University of Massachusetts–Amherst.

Dr. Feist is widely published in the psychology of creativity, the psychology of science, and the development of scientific talent. One of his major goals is establishing the psychology of science as a healthy and independent study of science, along the lines of the history, philosophy, and sociology of science. Toward this end, Dr. Feist has published a book titled *Psychology of Science and the Origins of the Scientific Mind* (2006, Yale University Press), which was awarded the 2007 William James Book Prize by the Division of General Psychology, American Psychological Association (APA). In addition, he is the founding president of the International Society for the Psychology of Science and Technology and the founding editor-in-chief of the peer-reviewed *Journal of Psychology of Science & Technology.*

A second major focus for Dr. Feist is the identification and development of scientific talent, as seen in finalists of the Westinghouse and Intel Science Talent Search. His paper (co-authored with Frank Barron) "Predicting Creativity from Early to Late Adulthood: Intellect, Potential, and Personality" won Article of the Year for 2003 in the *Journal of Research in Personality.* His research in creativity has been recognized by an Early Career Award from the Division for Psychology of Aesthetics, Creativity and the Arts (Division 10) of the American Psychological Association (APA). Dr. Feist is past president of APA's Division 10 and has served on the editorial boards of the *Review of General Psychology, Journal of Research in Personality,* and *Psychology of Aesthetics, Creativity and the Arts.* His teaching efforts have been recognized by outstanding teaching awards at both UC Berkeley and UC Davis. Dr. Feist is also co-author with his father, Jess Feist, of the undergraduate text *Theories of Personality.*

Married to Erika Rosenberg, Dr. Feist is the father of Jerry and Evan.

Erika L. Rosenberg

Erika L. Rosenberg is an emotions researcher, health psychologist, and teacher of meditation. Her research on emotion has examined how feelings are revealed in facial expressions, how social factors influence emotional signals, and how anger affects cardiovascular health. Dr. Rosenberg received her PhD in psychology from the University of California, San Francisco, where she studied with Paul Ekman. Dr. Rosenberg served on the faculties at the University of Delaware and the College of William & Mary and currently is at the Center for Mind and Brain at the University of California, Davis, where she is a senior investigator on the Shamatha Project (at UC Davis), a multidisciplinary study of how intensive meditation affects cognition, emotion, and neurophysiology. She is a co-author of studies from this project, which are published in *Psychological Science, Emotion, and Psychoneuroendocrinology*.

Dr. Rosenberg is a world-renowned expert in facial expressions measurement using the Facial Action Coding System (FACS). She consults with scientists, artists, and the entertainment industry on the use of FACS in a variety of contexts, including her role as scientific consultant on the Fox TV show *Lie to Me*. She teaches FACS workshops worldwide.

A longtime practitioner of meditation, Erika Rosenberg serves on the faculty of Nyingma Institute of Tibetan Studies in Berkeley, where she teaches meditation courses and workshops for working with emotions in daily life. Recently, Erika helped develop a secular compassion-training program with Geshe Thupten Jinpa, PhD, at the Center for Compassion and Altruism Research and Education at Stanford University, where she is a senior teacher. Recently, Dr. Rosenberg presented this program to His Holiness the Dalai Lama and taught the program at Google and throughout the Bay Area. Dr. Rosenberg is a senior fellow at the Mind and Life Institute.

Dr. Rosenberg and her husband, Greg Feist, have two sons, Jerry and Evan. They live in the San Francisco Bay Area.

Brief Contents

Contents

3 The Biology of Behavior 74

8 Learning 304

16 Treatment of Psychological Disorders 628

Foreword by Paul Ekman

Perhaps it was because I had never taken Introductory Psychology that I became a psychologist—or so I used to quip at the start of undergraduate lectures. Fifty years ago the textbooks for introductory courses were a turn-off. Most were dry and segmented. The only reason to read them was to pass Introductory Psychology in order to get to the higher-level courses you really wanted to take. It was an obstacle you had to jump over. Things have changed!

This textbook—I hesitate to use the word—is fun to read, enlightening, useful, and provocative. I recommend it to anyone—not just undergraduates— who wants a contemporary overview of psychology. In fact, people with no intentions of studying psychology will find this book engaging and interesting, and useful to their life. Wow.

Make no mistake—this is not a how-to book. It is not going to tell you how to get rid of whatever bothers you or find a mate or choose a career or become the most charming person in the world. But it will fascinate you; in each chapter you will learn about the cutting edge of knowledge, how science is done, what it means, and why it is important to understand that most complex of all subjects—why we do what we do and when and how we do it.

My own specialty for 40 years has been the study of facial expressions, and in the last decade or so I have reached out to develop a theory about emotion itself and how to lead a better emotional life. So I was surprised to find that when I read Chapter 11, "Motivation and Emotion," I learned something new. This is a comprehensive book; the coverage, even from a specialist's view, is amazing. And in each chapter the reader learns about both the breakthrough discoveries that have fundamentally altered the field of psychology and those scientists responsible for them.

I still find it a bit amazing that I should be ending a foreword to a text-book with the phrase "have fun."

Don't Believe Everything

Virtually all of our students enter Introductory Psychology with a full set of preconceived notions—many of them incorrect. *Psychology: Perspectives and Connections* is designed to move students beyond what may seem obvious to them, to have them reevaluate the thoughts and beliefs they bring to the course.

Students often think they already "know" psychology. They sometimes *think* "psychology is just common sense." Perhaps they *believe* that human behavior is simply a by-product of heredity. Or perhaps they think that all they need to know about psychology is best learned by reading words on a page or a screen.

With this in mind, we challenge our students: *Don't believe everything you think.* We encourage students to question preconceived notions, putting their ideas—and the ideas of others—to the test. Through text that is one component of a rich, digital environment (fully integrated with BlackBoard® and including LearnSmart™, a powerful adaptive, metacognitively driven learning system described below), we *engage* students in thinking critically. We continually demonstrate the importance of challenging assumptions and experiences—whether as a student or as a researcher—to understand that *no one perspective tells the whole story.*

CHALLENGING ASSUMPTIONS

Psychology: Perspectives and Connections helps students understand the path to discovery by challenging their assumptions, moving beyond "black and white" thinking. With this in mind, each chapter begins with "Challenge Your Assumptions." We pose assertions such as "Pulling an all-nighter is a good way to study for an exam," or "Eyewitness memories are usually accurate," prompting students to question their own perspective and begin to understand the importance of thinking critically.

Challenge *Your Assumptions*

TRUE OR FALSE?

- Elephants can learn to paint paintings.
- Humans and lab rats basically learn in the same way.
- Pulling an all-nighter is a good way to study for an exam.
- Children are not affected by watching violent cartoons or movies.

GROUNDBREAKING RESEARCH: THE ULTIMATE DON'T BELIEVE EVERYTHING YOU THINK MOMENTS

Most truly groundbreaking scientific discoveries occur beyond the limits of conventional thinking.

In *Breaking New Ground*, students follow real researchers on their quest for knowledge, seeing how questions were posed and assumptions challenged on the way to some of the most noted discoveries in science. Consider the classic study by Ivan Pavlov, a Russian physiologist researching not learning or conditioning, but digestion and gastric function in dogs (Chapter 8). Through the course of his study, Pavlov noticed something unexpected: His dogs were salivating before coming into contact with food. This insight caused Pavlov to ask questions and test his own assumptions, leading to one of the most important findings in psychology: classical conditioning.

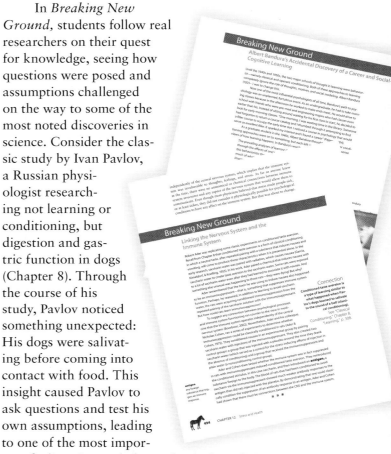

Fast-forward 80 years to Robert Ader and Nicholas Cohen (Chapter 12). While conducting an extension of Pavlov's experiments, Ader and Cohen were surprised to find a connection between the nervous system and the immune system. Although this connection ran counter to the views of the medical community, Ader and Cohen continued to test their ideas and eventually discovered an important link between mind and body that changed the face of modern medicine.

We also explore new cutting-edge studies in epigenetics (Chapter 3), mirror neurons (Chapter 8), and new theories on neuropsychoanalysis (Chapter 13) to

You Think

further illustrate that psychology is a growing science affecting our world today.

METACOGNITION

How many students *think* they know what they know but struggle on the first exam? LearnSmart, McGraw-Hill's adaptive learning system, identifies students' metacognitive abilities and limitations, identifying what they know—and more importantly, what they don't know. Using Bloom's Taxonomy and a highly sophisticated "smart" algorithm, LearnSmart creates a customized study plan, unique to every student's demonstrated needs. With virtually no administrative overhead, instructors using LearnSmart are reporting an increase in student performance by one letter grade or more.

USING ONLINE TOOLS TO FOSTER EXPERIENTIAL LEARNING

McGraw-Hill's Connect Psychology offers a wealth of interactive course materials for both instructors and students. Videos, interactive assessments, and simulations invite engagement and add real-world perspective to the Introductory Psychology course. Detailed reporting helps the student and instructor gauge comprehension and retention—*without adding administrative load.*

IS SOCIAL MEDIA REALLY MAKING US MORE SOCIAL?

Social media is now ingrained in our culture. But how are text messaging and social media sites impacting our everyday lives and behavior? Each chapter of *Psychology: Perspectives and Connections* provides a discussion of cutting-edge studies exploring the effects these technologies are having on our thoughts, experiences, and real-world interactions. Consider Cristin Norine's Public Isolation Project. In 2010 Norine lived without physical human contact for one month. Her only form of communication was through the Internet. Although we may *think* social networks are very "social," we explore how they are changing our relationships and the world around us.

TESTING ASSUMPTIONS THROUGH THE RESEARCH PROCESS

Overcoming preconceptions through an understanding of the research process is often one of the biggest challenges students face in Introductory Psychology. *Research Process*, appearing in Chapters 2 through 16, demystifies research by providing a step-by-step, visual approach to the scientific method. Students are presented with the basic structure of a contemporary study, walking through the "story" of how the research was conducted. In Chapter 3, for example, students are led through the methodology chosen by a researcher exploring whether different parts of the brain are responsible for imagining and seeing faces, versus only imagining.

MOVING BEYOND BLACK AND WHITE THINKING

Psychology: Perspectives and Connections pays careful attention to multiple causality, moving students beyond "black and white" or "either/or" thinking.

"Nature & Nurture" annotations appear throughout each chapter, highlighting the sometimes unexpected connections between biology and environment, and the resulting effect on behavior. The concept is further explored in coverage of emerging science, including infant brain development (Chapter 5), neuroplasticity (Chapter 3), and epigenetics (Chapter 3).

"Connections" annotations appear throughout the text, reinforcing the interrelatedness of subfields of psychology. In Chapter 8, for example, we explore the relationship between mirror neurons, learning, and socioemotional development.

PSYCHOLOGY IN EVERYDAY LIFE

By connecting psychology to students' own lives, concepts become more relevant and understandable.

Powered by McGraw-Hill's Connect, "Newsflash" exercises tie current news stories to key psychological principles and learning objectives. After interacting with a contemporary news story, students are assessed on their ability to make the connection between real life and research findings. Many cases are revisited across chapters, encouraging students to consider multiple perspectives. In Chapter 3, students visit the case of Congresswoman Gabrielle Giffords, who suffered a brain injury in a 2011 shooting. The case is revisited in Chapter 9, "Language and Thought."

"Research to Real Life" takes a key concept and asks students to think about it in context of their own lives, sparking a connection and deeper engagement with the content. The example in Chapter 6 shows students how to research the impact of sleep deprivation in their own lives, approaching the subject much like a research psychologist.

Created by a team of instructional designers, "Concept Clips" help students comprehend some of the most difficult concepts in Introductory Psychology. Colorful graphics and stimulating animations break down core concepts in a step-by-step manner, engaging students and aiding in retention. Powered by Connect, "Concept Clips" can be used as a presentational tool for the classroom or can be used for student assessment.

APPLYING THE SCIENTIFIC METHOD TO THE REAL WORLD

McGraw-Hill's NEW PsychInteractive allows students the opportunity to experience the scientific method as they learn to observe data, formulate and test a hypothesis, communicate their findings, and apply their understanding of psychology to the world. PsychInteractive is available through Connect.

MCGRAW-HILL/BLACKBOARD/ DO MORE

Through McGraw-Hill's partnership with Blackboard, *Psychology: Perspectives and Connections* offers a seamless integration of content and tools:

- Seamless gradebook between Blackboard and Connect
- Single sign-on providing seamless integration between McGraw-Hill content and Blackboard
- Simplicity in assigning and engaging your students with course materials

CHAPTER-BY-CHAPTER CHANGES

Psychology: Perspectives and Connections includes nearly 2,300 research citations, with one quarter of them coming from 2009 or later. This represents an increase of more than 600 research citations from the first edition.

But research is only part of the story. *Psychology: Perspectives and Connections* also reflects substantial chapter-by-chapter contents and begins with "Challenge Your Assumptions" questions.

Chapter 1: Introduction to Psychology

- New chapter opening vignette on the effects of technology
- New section: "No One Perspective Tells the Whole Story"
- New material on applying the field of psychology to real life
- New material on how introductory psychology can change your life
- New coverage of "softwiring": the notion that the human brain is neither hardwired nor tabula rasa, but rather the interaction of both
- Updated material on studying electronic social interactions
- Updated material on industrial/organizational psychology

Chapter 2: Conducting Research in Psychology

- Expanded and reorganized coverage of descriptive statistics and inferential statistics
- New coverage of IQ and normal distribution
- New material that applies the notion "Don't believe everything you think" to student lives
- New meaningful graphic on independent and dependent variables

Chapter 3: The Biology of Behavior

- New coverage of brain–computer and brain–machine interfaces
- New coverage of gray matter and white matter
- New coverage of diffusion tensor imaging
- New coverage of genes, environment, and family
- New coverage of "softwiring"; e.g., human brains are softwired and predisposed to certain traits
- Expanded coverage of epigenetics
- New research process coverage on distinct brain regions for perceiving faces and places

Chapter 4: Sensing and Perceiving Our World

- New coverage of echolocation
- New coverage on how political beliefs, motives, and emotions affect perception
- New material on color vision in humans and other animals
- Expanded coverage of the "Halle Berry neuron"
- Updated coverage of hearing loss in the age of the iPod

- New coverage of modern 3-D technology and the 3-SUV illusion
- New coverage of pruning and synesthesia

Chapter 5: Human Development

- New coverage of coming of age online
- New and expanded coverage of adolescence and emerging adulthood
- New coverage of rejection and social development of teens
- Expanded coverage of middle adulthood
- New coverage of digital technology's impact across every stage of human development
- Expanded coverage of identity, personality change, and delayed marriage and parenting
- New research process on the development of object permanence
- New coverage of Vygotsky
- New coverage of infant imitation and mirror neurons
- Reorganized coverage of Erikson

Chapter 6: Consciousness

- Reorganized coverage of hypnosis
- New coverage of REM sleep
- Expanded coverage of calling and texting while driving
- Updated research on meditation and the brain
- New coverage of sleep deprivation and daily functioning
- New coverage of sleep and neural growth
- New coverage of night terrors
- New coverage of multitasking

Chapter 7: Memory

- New coverage of hyperthymestic syndrome (the ability to remember nearly every single day of one's life)
- Updated coverage of H. M.
- New coverage of flashbulb memory
- New coverage of emotion in memory
- Revised coverage of forgetting
- New meaningful graphic on three types of memory

Chapter 8: Learning

- New coverage of elephant learning and painting
- New coverage of using operant conditioning to change personal behavior
- New section on applications of operant conditioning to treat disorders
- Revised coverage of primary reinforcer
- New nature and nurture coverage of animals being primed to learn
- New coverage of how sleeping facilitates learning
- Expanded coverage of Bandura and social learning
- Reorganized coverage of taste aversion

Chapter 9: Language and Thought

- New coverage of language and perception
- New coverage of language and nature and nurture
- New coverage of hormones and thinking
- Updated and expanded coverage of nonrational decision making
- Expanded coverage of brain and language development

Chapter 10: Intelligence, Problem Solving, and Creativity

- New coverage of limitations of conventional intelligence
- Expanded coverage of Sternberg and intelligence
- Expanded coverage of different forms of intelligence
- Connection made to emotional intelligence (Chapter 11) and crystallized and fluid intelligence (Chapter 5)
- New coverage of intelligence and nature and nurture
- New coverage of brain activity and creativity
- Updated coverage of Intel Science Talent Search
- New meaningful graphic on creativity and intelligence

Chapter 11: Motivation and Emotion

- New section on motivation and the workplace
- New coverage of emotions as powerful motivators
- Reorganized coverage of Ekman's expression research
- New coverage of "emotional intelligence"
- New coverage of why dieting does not work
- New coverage of appraisals
- Additional coverage of emotion and gender differences
- New meaningful graphic on needs and drives

Chapter 12: Stress and Health

- Expanded coverage of life stresses
- Revised coverage of immune system
- New coverage of stressors
- New meaningful graphic on emotion and stress process

Chapter 13: Personality: The Uniqueness of the Individual

- New section on neuropsychoanalysis
- Revised coverage of personality and Alzheimer's disease
- New coverage of inferiority complex
- New coverage of career interest and personality
- New meaningful graphic on nature and nurture of personality

Chapter 14: Social Behavior

- Updated coverage of social exclusion
- New coverage of the social psychology of social networks
- Updated coverage of media violence and aggression

- Revised coverage of implicit bias
- New coverage of implicit prejudice

Chapter 15: Psychological Disorders

- New section on somatoform disorders
- New coverage of compulsive hoarders
- Updated coverage of autism and Asperger's syndrome
- Expanded and updated coverage of Internet addiction
- New research process on gene–environment interaction in depression
- New coverage of the discovery of dopamine
- New coverage of the prevalence of psychological disorders
- New coverage of culture and psychological disorders
- Expanded coverage of suicide, with two new figures
- New meaningful graphic on brain size and neglect

Chapter 16: Treatment of Psychological Disorders

- New coverage of brain stimulation and depression
- New section on technology-based therapies such as therapy online, avatar therapy, and virtual reality with PTSD
- New coverage of the distinction between psychoanalytic and psycho-dynamic, and the effectiveness of psychodynamic therapy
- New discussion of how to choose a therapist
- Updated coverage of schizophrenia treatments
- Updated coverage of depression
- New coverage of changing unwanted habits
- New section on preventing disorders
- New meaningful graphic on hierarchy of exposure

REVIEWERS

Eileen Achorn, University of Texas–San Antonio

Andreas S. Anastasiou, Mary Baldwin College

Roxanna Anderson, Palm Beach State College

Cynthia Arem, Pima Community College

Michael Babcock, Montana State University

Ted A. Barker, Northwest Florida State College

James Becker, Pulaski Technical College

Kathleen Bey, Palm Beach State College

Stephen Blessing, University of Tampa

Tracie Blumentritt, University of Wisconsin–Lacrosse

Greg Bohemier, Culver–Stockton College

Stephen Brasel, Moody Bible Institute

Jennifer E. Breneiser, Valdosta State University

Eric Bridges, Clayton State University

Josh Burk, College of William & Mary

Kathryn Caldwell, Ithaca College

Dustin Calvillo, California State University–San Marcos

Janell Campbell, Colorado State University–Pueblo

Sandra Carpenter, University of Alabama–Huntsville

Jenel Cavazos, Cameron University

Mike Colbert, Camden County Community College

John V. Connor, Daytona State College

Mark Cushman, Peace College

Mark F. Daddona, Clayton State University

Lee W. Daffin, University of Idaho

Myra Darty, North Idaho College

Deanna DeGidio, Northern Virginia Community College–Annandale

Wendy Domjan, University of Texas–Austin

Cecil Duncan, Southern University

Russell Eisenman, University of Texas–Pan American

Thomas Fischer, Wayne State University

Roy Fish, Zane State College

Lauren Fowler, Weber State University

Alisha L. Francis, Northwest Missouri State University

Gleb Furman, Baruch College

Erica J. Gannon, Clayton State University

Laura Gaudet, Chadron State College

Rachel H. Gentry, Ball State University

Amy Goldberg, Elmhurst College

Ethan Gologor, Medgar Evers College

J. Sabine Griego, Luna Community College

Rodney J. Grisham, Indian River State College

Vivian M. Grooms, Jackson State Community College

Robert Guttentag, University of North Carolina Greensboro

Sidney E. Hardyway, Volunteer State Community College

Bridgette D. Harper, Auburn University–Montgomery

Lisa Harrison, California State University–Sacramento

Janice Hartgrove-Freile, Lone Star College–North Harris

Sheryl Hartman, Miami-Dade College

William J. Hauselt, Southern Connecticut State University

Debora S. Herold, Indiana University–Purdue University–Indianapolis

Julian Hertzog, William Woods University

Karen Hoblit, Victoria College

Chiquita D. Howard-Bostic, Blue Ridge Community & Technical College

Charles J. Huffman, Piedmont Virginia Community College

Rachel Hull, Texas A&M University

David P. Hurford, Pittsburg State University

Benetha G. Jackson, Angelina College

Jenny Jellison, Waynesburg University

James J. Johnson, Illinois State University

Patricia Johnson, Craven Community College

Deborah Jones, Kent State University–Stark

Todd Allen Joseph, Hillsborough Community College

Charles E. Joubert, University of North Alabama

Katherine Judge, Cleveland State University

Katrina Kardiasmenos, Bowie State University

Don Kates, College of DuPage

Deena Amy Kausler, Jefferson College

Serena King, Hamline University

Elizabeth A. Klopcic, Illinois Valley Community College

Monika Kosior, Baruch College

Aarre Laakso, University of Michigan–Dearborn

Arlene Lacombe, St. Joseph's University

Richard A. Lambe, Providence College

Andrea Lassiter, Minnesota State University–Mankato

Cynthia Lausberg, University of Pittsburgh

Etta Lee, Abraham Baldwin Agricultural College

Sue Leung, Portland Community College

Judith Levine, Farmingdale State University

Regan Lookadoo, Georgetown College

Lianggang Lou, Grand Valley State University

Don Lucas, Northwest Vista College

Mark Mach, Dodge City Community College

Randall Martinez, Cypress College

Chandra D. Mason, Mary Baldwin College

Cindy Lou Matyi, Ohio University–Chillicothe

BOARD OF ADVISORS

SYMPOSIA ATTENDEES

Every year McGraw-Hill conducts several Introductory Psychology Symposia for instructors from across the country. These events offer a forum for instructors to exchange ideas and experiences with colleagues they might not have met otherwise. They also provide an opportunity for editors from McGraw-Hill to gather information about the needs and challenges of instructors of Introductory Psychology. The feedback we have received has been invaluable and has contributed—directly and indirectly—to the development of *Psychology: Perspectives and Connections*.

2009: January 29–February 1, Naples, FL

Douglas L. Chute, Drexel University

Laurie L. Couch, Morehead State University

David T. Hall, Baton Rouge Community College

Jeff Love, Penn State University

Debra Rowe, Oakland Community College

Donna Love Seagle, Chattanooga State Technical Community College

Barry Silber, Hillsborough Community College

Peggy Skinner, South Plains College

Chris Smith, Tyler Community College

Margot Underwood, Joliet Junior College

Martin Wolfger, Ivy Tech Bloomington

2009: February 26–March 1, La Jolla, CA

Scott C. Bates, Utah State University

Ginette Blackhart, East Tennessee State University

Jack Chuang, San Jacinto College

Laura Duvall, Heartland Community College

Jerry Green, Tarrant County College

Barbara Kennedy, Brevard Community College

Sean Meegan, University of Utah

Shawn Mikulay, Elgin Community College

Michelle D. Miller, Northern Arizona University

Joel Morgovsky, Brookdale Community College

Alan Roberts, Indiana University

2009: March 5–8, San Antonio, TX

Diane Davis Ashe, Valencia Community College

David E. Baskind, Delta College

Aileen M. Behan-Collins, Chemeketa Community College

Michaela DeCataldo, Johnson & Wales University

Greg J. Feist, San Jose State University

Debra L. Frame, University of Cincinnati–Raymond Walters College

Robert L. Gordon, Wright State University

Lora Harpster, Salt Lake Community College

Lea Ann Lucas, Sinclair Community College

Karen Marsh, University of Minnesota Duluth

Kathleen Mentink, Chippewa Valley Technical College

Phyllis Rundhaug, San Jacinto College

Eva Szeli, Arizona State University

Helen Taylor, Bellevue Community College

2009: September 24–27, San Antonio, TX

Shirley Bass-Wright, St. Philip's College

Joan Batelle Jenson, Central Piedmont Community College

David Echevarria, University of Southern Mississippi

Bonnie Gray, Scottsdale College

Ericka Hamilton, Moraine Valley Community College

Barbara Kennedy-Stein, Brevard Community College–Palm Bay Campus

Yuthika Kim, Oklahoma City Community College

Eric Landrum, Boise State University

Ladonna Lewis, Glendale Community College

Wade Lueck, Mesa Community College

Wayne S. Stein, Brevard Community College/Melbourne Campus

Karen Tinker, NorthWest Arkansas Community College

Andrew Walters, Northern Arizona University

2009: October 15–18, Key West, FL

Carol Anderson, Bellevue College

Carrie Canales, West Los Angeles College

Jessica Carpenter, Elgin Community College

Jack Chuang, San Jacinto College Central

Barbara Etzel, Finger Lakes Community College

Jeff Green, Virginia Commonwealth University

Paul Grocoff, Scottsdale College

Robert Guttentag, University of North Carolina, Greensboro

Traci Haynes, Columbus State Community College

Diane Martichuski, University of Colorado at Boulder

Patricia Nation, Bluegrass Community and Technical College

Jeff Neubauer, Pima Community College, Northwest Campus

Cynthia K. S. Reed, Tarrant County College

Andrew Woster, South Dakota State University

2010: February 4–7, Tucson, AZ

Melissa Acevedo, Westchester Community College

Tamara Brown, University of Kentucky

Anne Marie Donohue, Montgomery County Community College

Ellen Furlong, Ohio State University

Mayte Insua-Auais, Miami Dade College–North Campus

Margaret Jenkins, Seminole State College

Robin Joynes, Kent State University

Kathy Morrow, Wayne County Community College

Traci Sachteleben, Southwestern Illinois College

Elizabeth Sheehan, Georgia State University

Rick Stevens, University of Louisiana at Monroe

Shawn Talbot, Kellogg Community College

2010: February 25–28, La Jolla, CA

Steven Barnhart, Middlesex County College

Jennifer Beck, Austin Community College

Andrea Ericksen, San Juan College

Beth Finders, Saint Charles Community College

Sam Gosling, University of Texas, Austin

Mark Griffin, Georgia Perimeter College

Brett Heintz, Delgado Community College

Linda A. Jackson, Michigan State University

Mary Lewis, Oakland University

Jeff Parsons, Hunter College–CUNY

Frank Provenzano, Greenville Technical College

Steven Ross, Owens Community College

Sheila E. Ten Eyck, Pittsburgh Technical Institute

Matt Yeazel, Anne Arundel Community College

2010: March 18–21, Naples, FL

Erskine Ausbrooks, Dyersburg State Community College

Brad Brubaker, Indiana State University

Lore Carvajal, Triton Community College

Doreen Collins-McHugh, Seminole State College of Florida

Penny Edwards, Tri-County Technical College

Dan Fawaz, Georgia Perimeter College

Lynne Gabriel, Lakeland Community College

Rose Hattoh, Austin Community College

Sean P. Jennings, Valencia Community College

Glenda Nichols, Tarrant County College–South Campus

Eileen O'Brien, University of Maryland, Baltimore County

Tanya Renner, Kapi'olani Community College

Genevieve Stevens, Houston Community College–Central

Richard Suplita, University of Georgia

Isabel Trombetti, Community College of Rhode Island

Martin Wolfger, Ivy Tech Community College Bloomington

2010: September 23–26, San Francisco, CA

Andrew Berns, Milwaukee Area Technical College–Milwaukee

Thomas Brandon, University of South Florida–Tampa

Robert Dunkle, Ivy Technical Community College of Indiana–Indianapolis

Lena Ericksen, Western Washington University

Kevin King, University of Washington

Irv Lichtman, Houston Community College–Northeast College

Eileen O'Brien, University of Maryland Baltimore County

Jeffrey Pedroza, Santa Ana College

Pam Simon, Baker College–Flint

Brian Sims, North Carolina A&T State University

Randi Smith, Metropolitan State College of Denver

William Winter, Kingsborough Community College

Steve Withrow, Guilford Technical Community College–Jamestown

Jill Yee, City College of San Francisco

2010: October 14–17, Key West, FL

Ted Barker, Northwest Florida State College

Holly Beard, Midlands Technical College

Deanna DeGidio, Northern Virginia Community College–Annandale

Anne Garcia, Washtenaw Community College

B. Sarah Haynes, St. Petersburg College

Bert Hayslip Jr., University of North Texas

Charles H. Jones, Wayne County Community College

Edie Sample, Metro Community College

Catherine Strathern, University of Cincinnati

Suzanne Valentine-French, College of Lake County

Tom VanderMolen, Allan Hancock College

Lori Van Wallendael, University of North Carolina at Charlotte

Kacy Welsh, University of Georgia

2011: January 27–30, Amelia Island, FL

Erskine Ausbrooks, Dyersburg State Community College

Penny Devine, Florida State College at Jacksonville

Ray Huebschmann, Georgia Perimeter College

Mark W. Hurd, College of Charleston

Heather Jennings, Mercer County Community College

Kiesa Getz, Kelly Tennessee State University

Ken Luke, Tyler Junior College

Amy Osmon, Daytona State College

Joe Reish, Tidewater Community College

Nancy Simpson, Trident Technical College

Berta Ward, Pellissippi State Community College

2011: February 3–5, Pasadena, CA

Karen Beck, Rio Hondo College

Gidget Brogdon, California State University Northridge

Kimberley J. Duff, Cerritos College

Susan Hornstein, Southern Methodist University

Mark Laumakis, San Diego State University

Kristie L. Morris, SUNY Rockland Community College

Karina R. Sokol, Glendale Community College

Clarissa A. Thompson, University of Oklahoma

Tom Vasile, Bakersfield College

Gordon Whitman, Tidewater Community College

William C. Williams, Eastern Washington University

Craft your teaching resources to match the way you teach! With McGraw-Hill Create, **www.mcgrawhillcreate.com,** you can easily rearrange chapters, combine material from other content sources, and quickly upload content you have written, such as your course syllabus or teaching notes. Find the content you need in Create by searching through thousands of leading McGraw-Hill textbooks. Arrange your book to fit your teaching style. Create even allows you to personalize your book's appearance by selecting the cover and adding your name, school, and course information. Order a Create book and you'll receive a complimentary print review copy in 3–5 business days or a complimentary electronic review copy (eComp) via e-mail in about an hour. Go to **www.mcgrawhillcreate.com** today and register. Experience how McGraw-Hill Create empowers you to teach *your* students *your* way.

Tegrity Campus is a service that makes class time available all the time by automatically capturing every lecture in a searchable format for students to review when they study and complete assignments. With a simple one-click start and stop process, users capture all computer screens and corresponding audio. Students replay any part of any class with easy-to-use browser-based viewing on a PC or Mac. Educators know that the more students can see, hear, and experience class resources, the better they learn. With Tegrity Campus, students quickly recall key moments by using Tegrity Campus's unique search feature. This search helps students efficiently find what they need, when they need it, across an entire semester of class recordings. Help turn all your students' study time into learning moments immediately supported by your lecture.

This text is available as an eTextbook at **www.CourseSmart.com.** At CourseSmart your students can take advantage of significant savings off the cost of a print textbook, reduce their impact on the environment, and gain access to powerful Web tools for learning. CourseSmart eTextbooks can be viewed online or downloaded to a computer. The eTextbooks allow students to do full text searches, add highlighting and notes, and share notes with classmates. CourseSmart has the largest selection of eTextbooks available anywhere. Visit **www.CourseSmart.com** to learn more and to try a sample chapter.

Support Materials

Psychology: Perspectives and Connections is supported by a highly collaborative and integrated digital program for instructors teaching and students studying Introductory Psychology. Our suite of tools and resources will help instructors connect to students and students connect to the material.

FOR INSTRUCTORS

All of the instructor ancillaries described below can be found on the password-protected instructor's side of the text's Online Learning Center at www.mhhe.com/feist2e. Contact your local McGraw-Hill sales representative for log-in information.

- **Instructor's Manual by Alisha Janowsky, University of Central Florida, and Martha Hubertz, Florida Atlantic University:** This manual provides all the tools and resources you need to deliver and enhance your course instruction. The Instructor's Manual includes chapter outlines, key terms, Innovative Instructions suggestions, and video resource lists, including suggested YouTube clips relevant to each chapter. Each marginal Nature & Nurture and Connection call-out is reinforced and expanded on in this manual to facilitate teaching psychology as an extensively connected discipline.

- **Test Banks:** Comprised of more than 2,400 questions, the test banks are designed to test factual, applied, and conceptual understanding. Each question and set of possible answers were created and methodically vetted by a team of subject matter experts for accuracy, clarity, effectiveness, and accessibility. In addition, each is annotated for level of difficulty, and Bloom's Taxonomy. The test questions build on the study skills gained through the Student Study Guide and online quizzes and are keyed to major concepts in Introductory Psychology.

- **PowerPoint Presentations by Jason Spiegelman, Community College of Baltimore County:** These slides cover the key points of each chapter and include charts and graphs from the text. The PowerPoint presentations serve as an organization and navigation tool and can be used as is or modified to meet your needs.

- **Image Gallery:** The Image Gallery features all the figures from the text. These images are available for download and can be easily embedded in your PowerPoint slides.

Acknowledgments

Writing *Psychology: Perspectives and Connections* has been an enormous undertaking of hard work and love. We have felt privileged by the opportunity to delve into the literature of so many areas of psychology in depth, something for which career academics rarely have time. We have also been fortunate to have had the commitment of a vast team of collaborators, to whom we offer our profound gratitude. We thank the wonderful professionals at McGraw-Hill who have had utter confidence in this project from day one: Mike Sugarman, as our publisher, has been a man of vision and always said the right things when we needed encouragement and support the most. Krista Bettino, our executive editor, jump-started our new vision for the second edition and shepherded it through the intense revision schedule. Art Pomponio, as our developmental editor, has been invaluable in helping shape new and crisper language and updating concepts. We also want to acknowledge the developmental editor on the first edition, Judith Kromm, who acted like a third author in crafting text, interpreting reviews, and helping us learn that strong substance can co-exist with simple and clear writing. Sheryl Adams, as executive market development manager, always has her finger on the pulse of the people for whom we wrote the book—instructors and students. As midcareer authors, we sometimes forget how 19- and 20-year-old students think and will respond to the information we are presenting. Sheryl always kept us in line in this regard. Dawn Groundwater, as director of development, was instrumental in keeping the project on task and developing new ideas for how to best package the unique qualities of the book. Julie Kuljurgis and Chantelle Walker, the editorial coordinators at McGraw-Hill, have been a tremendous help in managing the everyday details to keep a project as big as this one running smoothly. Finally, we would like to thank Sarah Colwell, digital development editor, who was instrumental in developing Newsflash, Concept Clip, and PsychInteractive, and Julia Flohr, executive marketing manager, whose energy and enthusiasm helped launch this project.

Our thanks also go to the Editing, Design, and Production team: Production Editor Catherine Morris, who guided us through the copyediting and composition stages of production; and Designers Jeanne Schreiber and Cassandra Chu; Photo Research Manager Alex Ambrose; and Art Manager Robin Mouat, whose talent and creativity are visible throughout this beautiful book. We also must thank freelance editors Sue Ewing, Barbara Conover, and Carolyn Smith, who, along with copyeditor Joan Pendleton, offered invaluable advice in helping to craft the language and clarify text based on reviewer feedback. Finally, we want to acknowledge the wonderful enthusiasm and support that Steve Debow, as President of Humanities, Social Sciences, and Languages at McGraw-Hill Higher Education, has shown for this project ever since we first presented our ideas. We also have been honored to have the invaluable input of our friends and colleagues—all experts in their fields—on various topics in the book. In particular we are grateful to Paul Ekman, Elissa Epel, Jess Feist, David Galin, Mary Gomes, Lee Huntington, Allen Kanner, Alan Kaufman, James Kaufman, Lee Kirkpatrick, Katherine MacLean, Clifford Saron, Valerie Stone, and Mary True, who contributed her expertise to important revisions in Chapter 5.

We have also benefited from having research support from our students, Sarah Greene, Adam Larson, Yvette Szabo, and Jessica Vandeleest. Yvette wrote a wonderful new piece for Chapter 1 on what Introduction to Psychology has meant for her. We also thank our parents—Sandra Rosenberg and Jess and Mary Jo Feist—for their love and unending support throughout the writing of the first edition. Mary Jo unfortunately passed away in September 2009 and was not around to see the second edition. She still lives on in our hearts. We also want to give our special and heartfelt thanks to our two wonderful boys, Jerry and Evan. They have been real troopers throughout our work on both editions. Although they sometimes lost us both for weekends or evenings, they also came to appreciate the positives of this project: like getting to attend sales meetings in New Orleans, team meetings in New York, or a national teaching of psychology conference at a beach resort in Florida.

We are in an unusual situation for ending this acknowledgments section. Often, authors end by thanking their spouses. In this case, spouse also means co-author. More than one person we have told about this project has said, "Wow! And you're still married!" Not only are we still married for the second edition, but this project has also deepened our marriage. Projects as big, complex, and difficult as this one test the mettle of any relationship. By affording us the opportunity to work creatively together, this project has strengthened the bond between us. We learned how to play to each other's strengths, balance viewpoints and expertise, and compromise. We were able to work through things late at night, even when one of us did not feel like it. We wonder how other co-authors of introductory psychology textbooks manage to work out the complex problems that arise while writing something this big without such convenience and intimacy as our relationship provides. We are grateful for each other.

Introduction to Psychology

1

Chapter Outline

Challenge *Your Assumptions*

TRUE OR FALSE?

- Psychology is all about curing mental illness.
- Intro to Psychology will give you the single perspective you need to explain your own thoughts and behaviors.
- Genetic influences on our thoughts and actions can't be changed.
- Psychologists are not all trained the same way to study the same things.

Answers can be found at the end of the chapter.

One summer afternoon in 2010, five psychology professors entered the wilderness, leaving their laptops and cell phones behind. They wanted to see what would happen when they distanced themselves from technology to hike, kayak, and sit around the campfire instead. One of them in particular believed that our frequent use of technological gadgets, though stimulating and informative, impairs our ability to focus on a task for an extended period of time and to reflect deeply—and may create an underlying sense of anxiety.

In their conversations, the scientists pondered the effects of technology—and of being in nature—on their minds. After five days, they found they'd settled down, listened better (to the crickets, the stream), and were more relaxed. One man, who had been a bit panicky on Day 1 over missing an e-mail about a multi-million-dollar grant, said that by the time he got back he realized "it didn't really matter that much" whether he found out about the grant immediately. Some felt transformed; others just felt restored. They all came back to their normal lives committed to understanding the effects of technology and rest on the brain (Richtel, 2010, p. A10).

A few months later, Cristin Norine set out to explore similar questions by very different means. She started *The Future of Socializing,* an "art piece" in which she isolated herself in a glass gallery on an urban street corner for 30 days; her only contact with other people came through social media. Her purpose was to see how these media change the way we communicate. Although people occasionally peered through her window, she didn't interact with them; her entire social world consisted of Facebook, Twitter, Skype, texting, and blogging.

A look at Cristin's Twitter feed while she was in the glass house reveals posts about the importance of human touch and the use of meditation and yoga to keep her sanity, a preoccupation with the mental health effects on adolescents of being "constantly connected," and statements such as "I don't think I would volunteer for this again" (Norine, 2010, November 23). She concluded that the main benefits of electronic social interaction were helping people stay in touch (she spoke with her father over Skype more than ever before). The main costs of the interactions were confusion (such as misunderstanding tone of voice in a text), and anxiety/exhaustion over what she felt was an expectation that she respond immediately to all texts (Seigneur, 2010). She missed physical touch. Recent research supports some of her conclusions, noting that with all social media, our friendships are in a state of decline and people are losing many of the benefits of direct human touch (Bauer et al. 2010).

Although they went about it in different ways, both of these real-life cases pursued questions such as these: Does technology make our attention scattered, or does it improve our ability to do more than one thing at a time? What happens to social interactions when they become primarily electronic? Do the depths of our friendships increase or decrease through social media? These are important questions; our interactions, social connections, or *networks,* can influence everything from opinion to eating patterns to one's likelihood of quitting smoking (Christakis & Fowler, 2007, 2008). Do Facebook and other social networks operate in ways that resemble real-world networks? What are the consequences of electronic interaction for our social lives? Each of these questions centers on understanding the effects of technology on thought, feeling, and behavior.

You might assume that social networks only enhance social life. The surprise from psychological science is that social networking both improves and impairs our relationships (Garrett & Danziger, 2008). People use "friending" on social networks to widen their social circles, which can translate into real-life social benefits (P. G. Lange, 2008). These media help us reach people we might not otherwise communicate with at all (such as long-lost cousins). Yet social networking can also reduce interactions with close friends to short electronic statements and lessen the amount of face-to-face time we have with our friends. In addition, technology in general increases our likelihood to multitask, which makes it harder for us to engage in any one task deeply (Bowman et al., 2010; Foerde et al., 2006). As psychology begins to identify the pros and cons of this overlap between real and virtual worlds, the ways to navigate this realm in a healthy manner become clearer.

You may be wondering why we are opening a book about psychology with a discussion of people's use of technology in its many forms. The answer is that technology involves people thinking, behaving, and interacting, which is what psychology is all about. ■

WHAT IS PSYCHOLOGY?

In one sense, you have been a psychologist for most of your life. Every time you ponder why you think and feel in particular ways, you are thinking psychologically. And every time you try to explain what someone else is doing—and why—you are thinking psychologically. You do it when you say your friend dominates conversations because he is self-absorbed. You also do it when you conclude that your big sister is bossy because she is older and always gets what she wants. We think and live psychology every day.

Psychology Defined

Many fields of study aim to understand people's thoughts and actions. Literature helps us understand people through storytelling, character exploration, development of setting, and use of imagery. History helps us understand people through description and analysis of past events and artifacts. Anthropology is the study of human culture and origins. Sociology seeks to understand people in terms of large-scale social forces and group membership rather than individuals. Psychology is unique in that it is the *science* of understanding individuals—animals as well as people. Formally defined, **psychology** is the scientific study of thought and behavior. The root word *psyche* comes from the Greek for "mind," but modern psychology is as likely to study brain and behavior as it is the "mind."

psychology
the scientific study of thought and behavior.

You might be thinking, "Don't psychologists treat people with mental illness or try to help us figure out how our parents messed us up?" Yes, they do these things too. Some professional psychologists practice, or *apply*, psychology to diagnose and treat problems of thought and behavior. In fact, psychology is both a clinical practice and a science. The clinical practice side encompasses the services provided in therapists' offices, schools, hospitals, and business. Without fail, when we (the authors of this text) tell someone that

After all our online chats, it's great to finally meet you in person.

Same here.

© 2000, Randy Glasbergen. Used by permission.

we are psychologists, they immediately think we are clinical psychologists and are analyzing their every move, looking for hidden meaning in everything they do.

You can also find popular psychology in homes, on radio talk shows, Internet news sites, and TV news reports. What sets scientific psychology apart from popular psychology—known as *folk psychology*—are the methods used in each. As you will see in Chapter 2, "Conducting Research in Psychology," and again in Chapter 16, "Treatment of Psychological Disorders," the methods of scientific and clinical psychologists are quite different from those of lay folk, who sometimes draw from an unreliable body of knowledge known as *common sense.*

Perhaps because of the ubiquity of popular psychology, most people you talk to on the street don't think of psychology as a science; rather, they probably think of it only as a clinical practice. The editors of *Scientific American,* for instance, commented that "whenever we run articles on social topics, some readers protest that we should stick to 'real science'" ("The Peculiar Institution," 2002, p. 8).

As we will see throughout this book, not only is psychology a science, but it is also considered a core science, along with medicine, earth science, chemistry, physics, and math (Boyack, Klavans, & Börner, 2005). Core sciences are those that have many other disciplines organized around them.

Why Should You Study Psychology?

Reasons for studying psychology vary from person to person. Maybe your advisor suggested it would be a good course to take, or maybe you're taking the course because it satisfies a general education requirement. Psychology is considered part of a good general education because its content is useful to many fields. It is also relevant to your life.

Adopting a scientific perspective on human behavior helps you develop a curiosity for how behavior works. It also fosters an appreciation for how much of human thought and behavior cannot be explained from one perspective. As you move through this book, you will find that many of the concepts you learn, such as memory, often have several definitions depending on how you look at it. Memory, for instance, can refer either to a specific recalled event (such as your memory of last summer's vacation) or to the process by which we recall such information.

Why do people act the way they do? That's what psychologists want to know.

Studying psychology not only makes you more aware of how people work in general, but it also makes you more aware of how *you* work—very practical knowledge to have in many settings. Understanding others' thoughts, feelings, and motives—as well as your own—may help you be a more effective doctor, lawyer, businessperson, or friend. Understanding how children learn, think, reason, and play will help you if you become a parent or a teacher. To learn how one recent college graduate has applied her knowledge of psychology in her life, read the "Psychology in the Real World" box on p. 8.

The study of psychology is as old as the human species. Before people wondered about the stars, rocks, and planets, no doubt they tried to figure out themselves and others. They did, after all, form relationships, have children, and protect their families. Human babies could not survive without others to care for them. Perhaps that is why people fascinate us. From our very first days, we humans are inherently interested in other humans—for survival. Newborns prefer faces to almost any other object. Our very existence is social, and as you will learn, our brains have evolved mechanisms and structures that allow us to understand others in a remarkably complex way (Dunbar, 1996; Frith & Frith, 2010).

As you begin your study of psychology, you will learn just how broad the field is. You may even find a subfield that dovetails with another interest you have already developed.

Quick Quiz 1.1: What Is Psychology?

1. Psychology is best defined as the scientific study of
   a. human behavior
   b. mental illness
   c. neuroses
   d. human thought and behavior

2. As a field, psychology is
   a. a social science
   b. the practice of diagnosing and treating mental illness
   c. a biological science
   d. all of the above

3. How does psychology differ from the related field of sociology?
   a. Psychology studies systems; sociology studies cultures
   b. Psychology studies cultures; sociology studies people
   c. Psychology studies individuals; sociology studies groups
   d. Psychology studies groups and cultures: sociology studies human behavior

Answers can be found at the end of the chapter.

SUBDISCIPLINES OF PSYCHOLOGY

As a science and a practice, psychology is divided into various areas of investigation. Just as this book consists of chapters on different topics in psychology, the field of psychology is divided into more than 25 distinct, but increasingly interrelated, subdisciplines. Figure 1.1 gives a breakdown of the percentages of doctorates awarded in 2008 in each of the major subdisciplines we discuss.

FIGURE **1.1**

PERCENTAGE OF PhDs AWARDED IN THE SUBFIELDS OF PSYCHOLOGY IN 2008. (Adapted from Mulvey & Grus, 2010, August)

Psychology in the **Real World**

Why Psychology Is Important to My Life

Yvette Szabo, San Jose State University

For me, studying psychology has meant so much more than learning concepts for an exam. Every day I see how it applies to my life. Material from class and the textbook come alive in my daily encounters. For instance, I now understand what affects my own productivity and what increases my motivation. I know that stress sometimes serves as a major stimulant for me and activates me to work, but it also wears down my immune system. Also, too much stress impairs the quality of my work. From Intro Psych, I've learned that these experiences are consistent with what research on motivation, stress, and health tells us.

I have also noticed how patterns of behavior repeat themselves within families or groups of friends. When I learned about the effects of birth order on personality, for example, I was able to connect the concept to my sister and me. I am the younger sister, and I am more rebellious and open to new ideas. In contrast, my elder sister is more agreeable and has a more cautious personality. When I learned in Intro Psych that younger-born children are "born to rebel" [see Chapter 13], I was amazed to discover that the pattern I see with my sister and me is a common one. This has helped put my own life in a larger context of human behavior.

As a curious student, I always enjoy understanding something new. One thing I appreciated with this class is how all of the fields of psychology overlap and interconnect. For example: Different people see and perceive events differently. In other words, social and personality psychology are closely connected to memory, sensation, and perception. What we perceive and remember overlaps with our social environment and our personality. Perceiving and remembering is almost like a camera lens, but the lens has filters—your personality and previous experiences filter what you take in, what sense you make of it, and what you recall.

Additionally, for me, connections between the subfields are clearer when I look at an area that interests me—diagnoses and treatments for depression. In order to understand both the causes of and treatments for depression, you need to appreciate how the biological origins of depression, such as hormones and neurotransmitters, are affected by life experiences, such as stress and trauma. If we don't integrate the biological and social approaches to understanding disorders, then we won't be very successful at diagnosing and treating them.

Moreover, psychology often explores the roles of nature and nurture in shaping behavior and personality. This book in particular does a great job of emphasizing how nature and nurture work together to create who we are and who we become. I have seen this firsthand. My cousin, adopted by my uncle and his wife, developed mannerisms similar to those of her family members. And yet, I've also learned in class that twins separated at birth will likely have similar interests and characteristics. These examples both show that nature and nurture are intertwined.

---

cognitive psychology
the study of how people perceive, remember, think, speak, and solve problems.

Cognitive psychology is the study of how we perceive information, how we learn and remember, how we acquire and use language, and how we solve problems. For example, a researcher who is concerned with how people visualize objects in their minds is studying cognitive psychology. Those who do research on cognition and learning are often referred to as *experimental psychologists* because they conduct laboratory experiments to address their research questions.

Developmental psychology explores how thought and behavior change and show stability across the life span. This developmental perspective allows us to appreciate that organisms—human or otherwise—change and grow. Developmental psychologists ask such questions as these: How do our reasoning skills

developmental psychology
the study of how thought and behavior change and remain stable across the life span.

8 CHAPTER 1 Introduction to Psychology

My knowledge of psychology provides constant explanations for the kinds of relationships I see all around me. For example, as I learned in my psychology courses, research shows that children who were bullied at home will be more likely to befriend someone meek so they can achieve dominance. Sure enough, a close friend of mine recently admitted she was a bully in grade school because it was the one place she was tougher than those around her. At home she was picked on, and so she wanted to dominate when she could at school. Psychology allowed me to better understand this not-so-desirable behavior in my friend. Similarly, I learned that people who do not receive much human contact and were not held as children will likely have difficulty forming bonds and close attachments as adults. I have seen this play out among numerous friends and acquaintances. Both of these cases show the importance of caregiving behavior in the formation of social relationships.

By turning what I learn in my classes outward, I can better understand the actions of others. I am more effective at motivating others and myself, because I better understand individual differences and different types of motivation that stem from internal and environmental sources. I am more conscious about what motivates me. Sometimes I am more motivated by an internal source, such as when I participate in a sport because I enjoy the game. Other times, I am more motivated by external sources, such as when I work to earn a high grade in a class.

Most importantly, the things I learned in Introductory Psychology have laid a foundation for all my future studies in psychology and even other courses. As I have studied more about the clinical applications of psychology, I have become more conscious of the role of a listener and speaker and have greatly improved my listening skills. Psychology has taught me techniques for learning, like scheduling study time over several days, getting a good night's sleep, rehearsing material, and making information personal and relevant. Intro Psych can help you not only to understand other people but also to do well in college.

Psychology has helped me so much in my everyday life that I want to continue to take as many psychology classes as I can and then pursue a doctoral degree in psychology. My motivation to learn more than what is required originated from the sampling of fields covered in introductory psychology. It is only in Intro Psychology where you learn about everything in psychology—from the brain and genetics to learning, memory, and perception; from development and aging to social groups and disorders of the mind. Intro Psych has been a wonderful foundation for understanding my own and other people's thought and behavior—and after all, isn't that what psychology is all about?

or emotional skills change as we age? How does parent–infant bonding affect adult relationships? Does old age bring wisdom?

behavioral neuroscience the study of the links among brain, mind, and behavior.

Behavioral neuroscience studies the links among brain, mind, and behavior. Neuroscience cuts across various disciplines and subdisciplines of psychology. One can study brain functions involved in learning, emotion, social behavior, and mental illness, to name just a few areas. The more general subdiscipline of **biological psychology** includes research on all areas of connection between bodily systems and chemicals and their relationship to behavior and thought. An example of research in biological psychology appears in Chapter 12 where we discuss the effects of stress on hormones and behavior. Neuroscience

biological psychology the study of the relationship between bodily systems and chemicals and how they influence behavior and thought.

The woman wearing the goggles and headgear is being prepared for a neuroimaging exam in a neuroscience lab.

and biological psychology overlap substantially. The latter is an older term that is being replaced by *behavioral neuroscience* in contemporary psychology. Using noninvasive advanced imaging techniques and electrical recordings, behavioral neuroscientists study the structure and functions of the living brain.

Personality psychology considers what makes people unique as well as the consistencies in people's behavior across time and situations. Personality research addresses questions such as whether our personal traits and dispositions change or stay the same from infancy to childhood to adulthood. A question from this area, for example, might be whether the tendency to be friendly, anxious, or hostile affects one's health, career choice, or interpersonal relationships, and whether a friendly or anxious child will necessarily have those same characteristics as an adult.

personality psychology
the study of what makes people unique and the consistencies in people's behavior across time and situations.

Social psychology considers how the real or imagined presence of others influences thought, feeling, and behavior. Research on prejudice and racism, for example, looks at how a person of one group perceives and treats people in other groups. Social psychologists ask such questions as these: How does the presence of other people change an individual's thoughts, feelings, or perceptions? Why is someone less likely to help a person in need when there are many people around than when there is no one else around? Why are we attracted to particular kinds of people?

social psychology
the study of how living among others influences thought, feeling, and behavior.

clinical psychology
the diagnosis and treatment of mental, emotional, and behavioral disorders and the promotion of psychological health.

Clinical psychology focuses on the diagnosis and treatment of mental, emotional, and behavioral disorders and ways to promote psychological health. Some clinical psychologists also conduct research and teach. Clinical psychologists work in universities, medical settings, or private practice. As you can see from Figure 1.1, clinical psychology is the single largest subdiscipline in psychology. In the United States, since the late 1940s, the main approach to training in psychology has been the scientist-practitioner model, in which PhDs in clinical psychology should be both therapists and researchers—or at least be trained to be both (Benjamin, 2007). Indeed, psychology is a practice as well as a science.

A related field is *counseling psychology*. Counseling psychologists tend to work with less severe psychological disorders than clinical psychologists. They treat and assess relatively healthy people and assist them with career and vocational interests. Training for counseling psychologists is more likely to occur in schools of education than in psychology departments (Norcross et al., 1998).

Other professionals who provide therapy include clinical psychologists who have obtained a PsyD (a professional degree oriented toward nonresearch clinical careers); social workers; marriage and family therapists (who generally have master's degrees); and psychiatrists. Psychiatrists have training in medicine and an MD degree; in addition to offering therapy, they can prescribe drugs.

Connection
Why are people in crowds less likely to help a person in distress than people who witness such an event while alone? Research on the *bystander effect* answers this question.
See "Social Relations," Chapter 14, "Social Behavior," p. 569.

health psychology
the study of the role psychological factors play in regard to health and illness.

Health psychology examines the role of psychological factors in physical health and illness. Topics in health psychology range from studies of how stress is linked to illness and immune function to studies on the role of social factors in how people interact with health care professionals. Some health psychologists work in disease prevention, treatment, and rehabilitation; thus, this area involves clinical practice as well as research.

Educational psychology draws on several other areas of psychology to study how students learn, the effectiveness of particular teaching techniques, the dynamics of school populations, and the psychology of teaching. This field also attempts to understand special populations of students such as the academically gifted and those with special needs. Educational psychologists are usually academics, theorists, or researchers. *School psychology* is a related field that is generally practiced by counselors in school settings. Approximately 9% of the doctorates in psychology were awarded in educational or school psychology in 2005–2006.

educational psychology
the study of how students learn, the effectiveness of particular teaching techniques, the social psychology of schools, and the psychology of teaching.

industrial/ organizational (I/O) psychology
application of psychological concepts and questions to work settings.

Industrial/organizational (I/O) psychology is an applied science, meaning it involves understanding real-world rather than laboratory behavior (Aamodt, 2010). The industrial and organizational sides focus on two distinct sets of problems. The *industrial* side involves matching employees to their job and uses psychological principles and methods to select employees and evaluate job performance. For this reason, the industrial side of I/O psychology is also sometimes referred to as personnel psychology. The *organizational* side of I/O aims to make workers more productive and satisfied by considering how the work environment and management styles influence worker motivation, satisfaction, and productivity. I/O is one of the fastest-growing subdisciplines in psychology, with a nearly 50% increase in the number of PhD programs between 1986 and 2004 (Rogelberg & Gil, 2006).

Two of the smaller and newer disciplines in psychology are sports psychology and forensic psychology. **Sports psychology** examines the psychological factors that affect performance and participation in sports and exercise (R. S. Weinberg & Gould, 2007). For instance, sports psychologists might focus on improving athletic performance through techniques such as relaxation and visualization. **Forensic psychology** is a blend of psychology, law, and criminal justice (Adler, 2004). Forensic psychologists make legal evaluations of a person's mental competency to stand trial, the state of mind of a defendant at the time of a crime, the fitness of a parent to have custody of children, or allegations of child abuse. Occasionally they develop criminal profiles of the type of person who might have committed a particular crime.

sports psychology
the study of psychological factors in sports and exercise.

forensic psychology
field that blends psychology, law, and criminal justice.

As you study the chapters of this text, you may find that one area of psychology especially excites you. Keep in mind, however, that psychology is about how humans think and behave. Thus, all of the topics are useful, many of them are closely intertwined, and there are many reasons for studying psychology, even if you don't become a psychologist. The field of psychology is the outcome of millions of years of humans' interest in their fellow human beings (Feist, 2006). As we will see next, however, the formal history of the field is not quite so old.

Quick Quiz 1.2: Subdisciplines of Psychology

1. What subdiscipline of psychology examines how thoughts, feelings, and behaviors change over the life span?
   a. developmental psychology
   b. cognitive psychology
   c. personality psychology
   d. educational psychology

2. A psychologist has conducted a series of studies on what part of the brain is most active during a memory task. She is probably
   a. a developmental psychologist
   b. a behavioral neuroscientist
   c. a cognitive psychologist
   d. an industrial/organizational psychologist

3. The main difference between a clinical and counseling psychologist is that counseling psychologists treat
   a. people with more severe psychological disorders
   b. children more than adults
   c. people with less severe psychological disorders
   d. people with learning disabilities only

Answers can be found at the end of the chapter.

THE ORIGINS OF PSYCHOLOGY

In this section, we look briefly at the origins of the two main forms of psychology: clinical practice and science. The practice of psychology has deeper roots in human history than does the science of psychology. The prehistoric record offers evidence of efforts to heal people's suffering from disturbances of the mind, often in ways we now find alarming. The foundations for psychology as a science date back to the ancient Greeks, and the modern science of psychology originated in the 1870s (D. N. Robinson, 1995). First, we consider the practice of psychology.

A Brief History of the Practice of Clinical Psychology

Disorders of thought and behavior are no doubt as old as humans—indeed, there is evidence that primates (monkeys and apes) are afflicted with psychological disorders such as depression, anxiety, repetitive and functionless behaviors, and self-injuries (Maestripieri et al., 2006; Novak, 2003; Troisi, 2003). Thus, research suggests that these behaviors go back to the ancestors of both species, in this case approximately 6 million years.

Prehistoric Views   As far back as the Stone Age (7,000 years ago and maybe even as long as 50,000 years ago), humans tried to cure one another of various mental problems. Most prehistoric cultures had medicine men or women, known as **shamans,** who would treat the possessed by driving out the demons with elaborate rituals, such as exorcisms, incantations, and prayers. Occasionally, some of these shamans appeared to practice the oldest of all known surgical procedures, trephination.

Trephination involves drilling a small hole in a person's skull, usually less than an inch in diameter (Alt et al., 1997; Weber & Wahl, 2006). Some of these surgeries may have been for medical reasons, such as an attempt to heal a brain injury. Some may also have been performed for psychological reasons, to release the spirits and demons that possessed the afflicted person. Anthropological evidence suggests that a surprisingly large percentage of people survived such surgeries—which today's scientists can confirm by

shamans
medicine men or women who treat people with mental problems by driving out their demons with elaborate rituals, such as exorcisms, incantations, and prayers.

identifying bone growth after the procedure—and the surgeons must have had moderately sophisticated knowledge and understanding of the brain (Alt et al., 1997; Weber & Wahl, 2006).

Ancient Views

Around 2600 BCE (Before the Common Era), the ancient Chinese moved away from supernatural explanations toward natural and physiological explanations of psychological disorders (Tseng, 1973). Specifically, they made connections between a person's bodily organs and emotions. The heart housed the mind; the liver, the spiritual soul; the lung, the animal soul; the spleen, ideas and intelligence; and the kidneys, will and vitality.

The ancient Egyptians and Greeks also sought natural explanations for psychological disorders. For example, in the second century BCE, the ancient Egyptians apparently used narcotics to treat pain (Finger, 1994). The Greek physician Hippocrates (460–377 BCE) was the first to write about a man suffering from a phobia of heights—what we now call acrophobia.

Medieval to Early Modern Views

In Europe during the Middle Ages, which lasted from approximately 400 to 1400 CE (Common Era), psychological disorders were again attributed to supernatural causes. In the worldview that dominated this era and the Renaissance (from about 1400 to the early 1600s), people were possessed by demons, spirits, and the devil—not by physical disorders. These views were taken to an extreme during the Inquisition, when the Catholic Church investigated witchcraft and heresy as part of a broad campaign to eliminate dissent from established Church dogma. Some witchcraft practices were viewed as harmless and even beneficial, but others were branded as the work of the devil. In order to distinguish the good witchcraft from the bad, Church officials held inquisitions and trials, employing several techniques to determine whether a person was a witch (D. N. Robinson, 1995). Sometimes the accused was prodded with a metal pole and spears; if she felt no pain, she was protected by the devil and therefore was a witch. In another common method, the *float test,* the woman's hands and feet were tied, and she was thrown into a lake or river. If she floated, she had to be guilty because only the devil could make someone float; if she sank, she was innocent—but had drowned (D. N. Robinson, 1995). The most common punishment for the infrequent survivor of the float test—deemed to be a witch—was being burned at the stake. To be fair, numerous writers during the 14th to 16th centuries argued that witchery was caused not by spirits and supernatural elements but rather by natural ones, such as hallucinations or "melancholia"—what we would now call depression (D. N. Robinson, 1995; Veith, 1965).

During the witch hunts of the 16th and 17th centuries, the first facilities for the mentally ill—called **asylums**—were built throughout Europe. The most famous, or infamous, of these was located at St. Mary of Bethlehem in London, England. Although it had served as a hospital for the mentally ill and others since the 1300s, Henry VIII designated it as a hospital for the insane in 1547. It was really no more than a storage house for the mentally ill and other social

The hole in this skull may have been created by trephination, a prehistoric practice believed to release spirits or demons responsible for psychological disturbances.

asylums facilities for treating the mentally ill in Europe during the Middle Ages and into the 19th century.

In the Middle Ages, people who were judged to be witches could be burned at the stake. Some of them may have had psychological disorders that caused them to behave strangely.

castaways. For the most part, early efforts to "treat" mental illness focused on removing afflicted people from society rather than helping them adjust to society. The conditions were deplorable and chaotic—patients were put in windowless and filthy rooms and were chained and shackled to the walls. The local population, including William Shakespeare, called the place *Bedlam,* a shortened version of "Bethlehem," and that is how the term came to be associated with chaotic and noisy conditions.

moral treatment
19th-century approach to treating the mentally ill with dignity in a caring environment.

In response to these inhumane conditions, reform movements in support of **moral treatment** emerged in Europe and the United States. The main idea was to provide a relaxing place where patients would be treated with dignity and care. The first major proponent of humane therapies was the Frenchman Philip Pinel in 1783. Dorothea Dix pioneered moral treatment in the United States. After visiting a prison in 1841 and witnessing the abhorrent and inhumane treatment of the inmates, some of them suffering from psychological disorders, Dix vowed to change these conditions. Over the next 40 years, she helped open 30 homes throughout North America (Nolen-Hoeksema, 2007). Moral therapies were among the first forms of treatment that regularly helped people get better.

Modern Views   The last decades of the 1800s also saw the emergence of the first truly modern view of psychological disorders—the idea that they are simply one form of illness and should be treated as medical conditions, with appropriate diagnosis and therapy. In the 1880s and 1890s, the German psychiatrist Emil Kraepelin collected data on the various kinds of psychological disorders and began systematically classifying and diagnosing them (Shepard, 1995). He popularized the term *dementia praecox* (premature dementia), which he later changed to *schizophrenia,* to refer to the major thought disorder known previously as "split mind." He was also the first to distinguish thought disorders (schizophrenia) from the mood disorders of melancholia (depression) and manic depression (bipolar disorder) (Jablensky & Woodbury, 1995). In short, his views were a major influence on diagnostic categories formulated during the 20th century.

Sigmund Freud

Around the turn of the 20th century in Austria, Sigmund Freud developed a form of therapy called psychoanalysis. A clinical approach to understanding and treating psychological disorders, **psychoanalysis** assumes that the unconscious mind is the most powerful force behind thought and behavior and that dreams have meaning and are the most direct route to the unconscious mind (Freud, 1900/1953). It also assumes that our experiences during childhood are a powerful force in the development of our adult personality. Psychoanalysis assumes that people use psychological defenses to protect themselves against threatening impulses, thoughts, feelings, and fantasies. Lastly, it assumes that the unconscious blocking, or repression, of disturbing thoughts and impulses—especially sexual and aggressive impulses—is at the heart of all maladaptive adult behavior.

psychoanalysis
a clinically based approach to understanding and treating psychological disorders; assumes that the unconscious mind is the most powerful force behind thought and behavior.

By the middle of the 20th century, three of the major modern developments in clinical psychology had emerged: psychotherapy, drug therapy, and modern criteria for diagnosing mental disorders. For example, one common form of modern therapy—cognitive-behavioral—focuses on changing a person's maladaptive thought and behavior patterns by discussing and rewarding more appropriate ways of thinking and behaving. Although we will consider the modern diagnostic criteria in detail in Chapter 15 and *psychotherapy* (psychological assessment and treatment by a trained therapist) and drug therapy in detail in Chapter 16, it is appropriate to conclude our discussion of the history of psychology as a clinical practice with a brief introduction to the classification system that guides the diagnosis of psychological disorders today.

Connection

Deviance, distress, and dysfunction must be present for the diagnosis of psychological disorders. The *DSM* describes specific symptoms of more than 250 different disorders.

See "Defining Psychological Disorders," Chapter 15, "Psychological Disorders," p. 589.

Psychotherapy techniques, including psychoanalysis, focus on the client's mental state.

When diagnosing psychological disorders, psychologists use the *Diagnostic and Statistical Manual*. Currently in its fourth edition (though the fifth edition is due out soon), this standardized reference is referred to as the *Diagnostic and Statistical Manual*, 4th edition, Text Revision—or *DSM-IV-TR* (American Psychiatric Association, 2000). Originally published in 1952, the *DSM* includes diagnoses for more than 250 psychological disorders. The various editions of the *DSM* have incorporated new findings and added new disorders, objectively describing the behaviors and symptoms of each disorder so that psychologists from all perspectives could agree on a single diagnosis for an individual with a given set of symptoms. You might find it surprising to know, however, that this goal of universal agreement often is not achieved so that different clinicians hold different views about what constitutes a mental disorder. Occasionally, the authors have removed behavior patterns (such as homosexuality, which was deleted from the list of disorders recognized by the American Psychiatric Association in 1973) that do not meet updated diagnostic criteria. Further, practitioners from the various subfields do not always agree with each other about definitions of a given disorder. Cognitive-behavioral practitioners view depression, for example, as the patient's distorted thinking ("I am worthless"), whereas psychodynamic practitioners might consider the same person's depression (and expressed thoughts) as the result of unconscious disturbing family relationship patterns that need to be made conscious. Clearly, perspective matters when it comes to psychological treatment, and we must continually question what we know from the perspective we are adopting.

A Brief History of Scientific Psychology

As with all sciences, scientific psychology can claim philosophy as one of its parent disciplines. By the middle of the 1800s, however, psychology grew away from philosophy to become a science. Let's look briefly at this history.

The Philosophy of Empiricism
Perhaps the most important philosophical question for psychology is the nature of knowledge and how human beings create knowledge. Does knowledge come from reflection and thinking or from experience? In the 4th century BCE, the Greek philosopher Plato argued for the former and his student Aristotle for the latter. In the 17th century CE, however, the English philosopher John Locke established the view that knowledge and thoughts come from experience, a point of view known as **empiricism.** Specifically, Locke argued that the mind begins as a *tabula rasa,* or blank slate, onto which experience writes the contents of the mind (Locke, 1690/1959).

> **empiricism**
> the view that all knowledge and thoughts come from experience.

This view that the mind simply receives what our sensory organs—eyes, ears, nose, skin, and tongue—take in from the outside world is very important in philosophy and psychology. In contrast to scientists, however, philosophers do not collect data to test their ideas. Psychology gained its independence from philosophy when researchers started to examine and test human sensations and perception using scientific methods. Psychology as a modern empirical science tests predictions about behavior with systematic observations and by gathering data. In the mid- to late 1800s, many German universities were starting scientific laboratories in physics, chemistry, and medicine. In the 1870s they opened the first laboratories in psychology.

The Psychophysics of Human Perception
Because of the profound influence of the empiricists, the first researchers in psychological science developed the field of **psychophysics** to examine the subjective experience of physical sensations. If the mind consists only of what we sense, then understanding the senses will lead to a direct understanding of the mind. German psychophysics researchers in the 1860s focused on the sensations of touch, vision, hearing, and smell. Whereas physicists study the physical properties of light and sound, psychophysicists study human perception of light and sound.

> **psychophysics**
> the study of how people psychologically perceive physical stimuli such as light, sound waves, and touch.

One important principle of psychophysics is that perception of physical properties is not the same as the physical properties themselves. To demonstrate, let's consider the classic question, What weighs more, a pound of feathers or a pound of bricks? You might be thinking "How dumb do they think I am? I've heard that so many times. They weigh the same! A pound is a pound." Maybe . . .

for that answer is true only for the objective, physical property of weight. The *perceived* weight of the two—a psychological property—would be very different. Researchers found that when people's estimates of the weights of both items are empirically tested, contrary to common sense, people think a pound of bricks weighs 2 to 3 times as much as a pound of feathers (Benjamin, 2007). If you don't believe us, try it for yourself. *Psychophysics* is all about this relationship between the physical and psychological worlds.

In essence, the scientists who first developed psychophysics were the first experimental psychologists. Ernst Weber (1795–1878) did some of the first research in perception and laid the groundwork for what later became known as psychophysics. For instance, he investigated the smallest change in weights or length that people could discern. Building on the work of his mentor, Weber, Gustav Fechner (1801–1889) had a sudden realization in 1850 that one could study the psychological and physical worlds. Fechner coined the term psychophysics for this new discipline, and he went on to refine some of Weber's principles of perception (Fancher, 1996).

A physician and physicist, Hermann von Helmholtz (1821–1894) not only made important contributions to the study of memory, physiology, and color vision, but also made key contributions to the laws of conservation in physics and to music theory, meteorology, and geometry; he designed a workable telephone years before Alexander Graham Bell (Benjamin, 2007). In addition, he was the first to calculate the speed of a nerve impulse at about 90 feet per second. With the work of these pioneers, psychophysics took the first steps toward establishing psychology as a science.

Wilhelm Wundt

Psychology blossomed into a full-fledged science with the help of Wilhelm Wundt (1832–1920). In 1879 (remember this date!), Wundt set up a psychology laboratory in Leipzig, Germany, now considered the birthplace of experimental psychology. Although others went before Wundt, he is credited with giving psychology its independence from philosophy and physiology (Benjamin, 2007; Fancher, 1996). He did so by applying the scientific methods of physiology to questions of philosophy (Benjamin, 2007). Before Wundt, people evaluated the question of how the mind worked only by way of argument, not by scientific investigation. By establishing a laboratory, Wundt created a place where the best young minds could learn the science of psychology. And come to learn they did. Wundt single-handedly trained more than 180 students in his laboratory. Of these, more than 100 came from countries other than Germany and then returned to their native countries, taking their knowledge of experimental psychology with them.

William James

An American, G. Stanley Hall (1844–1924), went to Germany to learn from Wundt. At Harvard, Hall also studied with William James, who is considered the founder of American psychology. Hall holds the distinction of earning the first PhD (1878) in psychology in the United States as James's student. He opened the first psychology laboratory in the United States at Johns Hopkins University in Baltimore, officially establishing psychology as a science in this country. He also founded the American Psychological Association (APA) and became its first president in 1892. Hall started the first scientific journal in American psychology, the *American Journal of Psychology*. Finally, he was able to persuade both Sigmund Freud and his famous protégé Carl Jung to make their only journey to the United States and give lectures at Clark University in Massachusetts in 1909. G. Stanley Hall was also the teacher and mentor of Francis Cecil Sumner (1895–1954), the first African American to earn a PhD in psychology (1920). From 1928 until his death in 1954, Sumner chaired the psychology department at Howard University, where he conducted research on equality and justice.

Another of William James's students, Mary Whiton Calkins (1863–1930), became the first female president of APA in 1905. Harvard was an all-male university until 1920, and the male students did not want to have a woman in class, so she and James had to conduct their coursework in James's home. Calkins went on to complete the requirements for the PhD, although Harvard would not grant her the degree simply because she was a woman (Benjamin, 2007). Nevertheless, Calkins had an accomplished academic career. She taught at Wellesley College and conducted research on dreaming, gender issues, and self-image (Furumoto, 1981). James acknowledged her to be among the best students he had ever encountered (Benjamin, 2007).

Structuralism and Functionalism   During its early decades as a science, psychology weathered its first major debate, with two different perspectives on how to study thought and behavior. The field was divided over whether it was more important to study the *elements* or the *functions* behind human thought and behavior. Focus on the former led to the school of thought known as structuralism, whereas focus on the latter led to the school of thought known as functionalism. Edward Titchener (1867–1927), a British American psychologist trained by Wilhelm Wundt, coined both phrases.

According to **structuralism,** breaking down experience into its elemental parts offers the best way to understand thought and behavior. Structuralists believed that a detailed analysis of experience as it happened provides the most accurate glimpse into the workings of the human mind. Their method was **introspection,** looking into one's own mind for information about the nature of conscious experience. Structuralists divided each experience into its smallest elements. Wundt, the chief proponent of structuralism, wanted to describe human experience in terms of the elements that combined to produce it (Benjamin, 2007). For example, structuralists, like chemists describing elements, would not describe a peach as "a good peach," but rather would describe their experience with the peach as sweet, round, slightly orange, fuzzy, wet, and juicy.

Influenced by Charles Darwin's theory of natural selection, psychologists who supported **functionalism** thought it was better to look at why the mind worked the way it did, rather than to describe its parts. The functionalists asked "Why do people think, feel, or perceive, and how did these abilities come to be?" Functionalists used introspection as well. William James, the most famous functionalist, relied on introspection as a primary method of understanding how the mind worked.

James's and Wundt's methods of introspection were impressive attempts to describe the conscious mind. Eventually, however, introspection failed as a method of science because of difficulties in reaching a consensus as to the nature of certain experiences. Moreover, the rise of psychology as the science of *observable* behavior led to the complete rejection of the study of the mind. It also gave way to the rise of behaviorism.

structuralism
19th-century school of psychology that argued that breaking down experience into its elemental parts offers the best way to understand thought and behavior.

functionalism
19th-century school of psychology that argued it was better to look at why the mind works the way it does than to describe its parts.

introspection
the main method of investigation for structuralists; it involves looking into one's own mind for information about the nature of conscious experience.

behaviorism
a school of psychology which proposed that psychology can be a true science only if it examines observable behavior, not ideas, thoughts, feelings, or motives.

Behaviorism

In 1913, a little-known 34-year-old psychologist, John Watson, directly challenged the use of introspection. He founded **behaviorism,** which asserts that psychology can be a true science only if it examines observable behavior, not ideas, thoughts, feelings, or motives. In Watson's view, mental experiences are hypothetical concepts, for they cannot be directly measured. As long as psychology focused on such internal states, it would forever be a false science, according to Watson. Behaviorism is an extreme form of environmentalism, the view that all behavior comes from experience interacting with the world. It is the school of psychology that most clearly expresses John Locke's ideas about our minds being a blank slate at birth.

Connection

People learn by making associations, by being rewarded and reinforced, and by watching others succeed or fail.
See "Conditioning Models of Learning," Chapter 8, "Learning," p. 307.

A decade or so after behaviorism emerged, it became the dominant force in experimental psychology. Its most famous figure, B. F. Skinner (1904–1990), was largely responsible for making behaviorism the major approach in experimental psychology, a position it held for nearly 50 years. Skinner modified Watson's ideas and argued that consequences shape behavior.

Humanistic and Positive Psychology

During the first half of the 20th century, the two major schools of thought in psychology were split along the divide between practice and science. On the therapeutic side were psychoanalysis and Freud, and on the scientific side were behaviorism and Skinner. In the 1940s and 1950s, Abraham Maslow and Carl Rogers presented an alternative to both of these perspectives. They argued that both psychoanalysis and behaviorism ignored people at their best, and neither approach considered what it meant to be psychologically healthy. Maslow and Rogers proposed an alternative called **humanistic psychology,** which promoted personal growth and meaning as a way of reaching one's highest potential.

The humanistic movement waned by the late 1970s, mostly because it had moved away from its research and scientific base. It surfaced again in the late 1990s, however, when Martin Seligman and Mihaly Csikszentmihalyi started the positive psychology movement (Seligman & Csikszentmihalyi, 2000). **Positive psychology** shares with humanism a belief that psychology should focus on studying, understanding, and promoting healthy and positive psychological functioning. It does so with a better appreciation than humanistic psychology for the importance of studying well-being from a scientific perspective. As you will see in this book, much of contemporary psychology embraces the positive psychological view.

This dolphin is being trained by means of shaping, a behaviorist technique that rewards animals for small changes in behavior as they learn a desired behavior pattern, such as leaping out of the water on cue.

Connection

Humanistic and positive psychologists strive to understand people who are psychologically healthy, happy, and compassionate.
See "Humanistic-Positive Psychological Theories," Chapter 13, "Personality: The Uniqueness of the Individual," p. 525.

Cognitivism

After Watson banished thoughts, feelings, and motives as the focal point of the modern science of psychology in the 1910s, research into these topics nearly disappeared from the field for almost 50 years. Two events kept them in the minds of psychologists, however. First, in the 1920s and 1930s, a movement in Germany called Gestalt psychology attracted worldwide attention. Led by Max Wertheimer (1880–1943), **Gestalt psychology**

humanistic psychology
a theory of psychology that focuses on personal growth and meaning as a way of reaching one's highest potential.

positive psychology
scientific approach to studying, understanding, and promoting healthy and positive psychological functioning.

Gestalt psychology
a theory of psychology that maintains that we perceive things as wholes rather than as a compilation of parts.

460–377 BCE
Hippocrates describes a patient suffering from mental disorder

1860
Gustav Fechner publishes *Elemente der Psychophysik,* establishing the discipline of psychophysics

1890
William James publishes *Principles of Psychology,* a text in 2 volumes

1860   1870   1880   1890

5,000 BCE
Trephination is used to release the spirits and demons from the mind

1879
Wilhelm Wundt opens first psychology laboratory in Leipzig, Germany

1690
John Locke proposes that the mind is a blank slate to be written on by experience

proposed that in perception a unified whole is more than a compilation of parts. As the Gestaltists suspected, our brains actively shape sensory information into perceptions. For an example of this phenomenon, look at Figure 1.2. You see a triangle within three circles, but no triangle actually exists. The brain, however, organizes your perception of the markings on the page into the shape of a triangle.

Second, mental processes returned to psychology full force in the 1950s and 1960s—just when the influence of behaviorism was at its peak. The new emphasis was really a forgotten focus on the processes that fascinated Fechner, Wundt, and Helmholtz in the 19th century: sensation, perception, and mental processes. The term *mental,* however, had lost its appeal. Instead, a new word for thought and mental processes appeared: *cognition* (Benjamin, 2007; H. Gardner, 1987).

By the 1960s the field of cognitive science was born, with a focus on the scientific study of thought (H. Gardner, 1987). In addition to freeing itself from the label *mental,* cognitive science made use of a new modern metaphor for the human mind—the computer. A fairly recent innovation at the time, the computer seemed to have a lot in common with the human mind. Computers store, retrieve, and process information, just as the brain stores, retrieves, and processes sensations, memories, and ideas. Sensation was the input; perception was the interpretation and processing of the input; and behavior and thoughts were the output. By the 1980s, cognitive science combined many disciplines in addition to psychology—namely, linguistics, philosophy, anthropology, artificial intelligence, and neuroscience (H. Gardner, 1987).

Some of the thinking in this new cognitive movement was based on a book by the British psychologist Frederick Bartlett (1886–1969). Bartlett wrote that memory is not an objective and accurate representation of events but rather a highly personal reconstruction based on one's own beliefs, ideas, and point

FIGURE 1.2
A DEMONSTRATION OF GESTALT PSYCHOLOGY.
You see a triangle even though no triangle actually exists.

1900
Sigmund Freud introduces his psychoanalytic theory of behavior with the publication of *Interpretation of Dreams*

1920
Francis Cecil Sumner becomes first African American to earn PhD in psychology

1932
Frederick Bartlett lays the foundation for cognitive science with his book *Remembering*

1900   1910   1920   1930   1940

1905
Mary Whiton Calkins becomes first female president of APA

1912
Max Wertheimer develops the principles of Gestalt psychology

1913
John B. Watson establishes behaviorism to study observable behavior

1892
G. Stanley Hall, a founding father of American Psychological Association (APA), becomes its first president

1938
B. F. Skinner publishes *The Behavior of Organisms*, outlining his version of behaviorism

FIGURE **1.3**
KEY FIGURES AND EVENTS IN THE HISTORY OF PSYCHOLOGY.

of view. For example, racial–ethnic stereotypes are frameworks that can alter memory (Graham & Lowery, 2004). If a witness to a crime holds a bias about how likely a crime is to be perpetrated by a person of a certain racial–ethnic background, the witness may misremember the appearance of the accused. This example illustrates that, as Bartlett argued, when people remember, they reconstruct experience in terms of what is most relevant to them rather than providing an unbiased account of events. Bartlett showed that our cognitive frameworks organize how we experience the world. This view is now well accepted in psychology, though Bartlett's insights were unappreciated in the United States for decades (Benjamin, 2007).

Evolutionary Psychology and Behavioral Neuroscience
By the 1980s, more and more psychologists became receptive to the ideas that who we are, how we got here, and what we do and think are very much a result of brain activity, are influenced by genetic factors, and have a long evolutionary past. The roots of this approach lie in many related fields. For example, behavioral neuroscience, behavioral genetics, and evolutionary psychology are each a blend of two or more other disciplines. Evolutionary psychology was jump-started in 1992 when John Tooby and Leda Cosmides (1992) published "The Psychological Foundations of Culture" in a seminal book on evolutionary psychology. These developments all began to shift psychology toward a more complex view of the origins of human thought and behavior, enhanced by new brain imaging techniques and the sequencing of the human genome.

Our review of the history of psychological science, summarized in Figure 1.3, has only scratched the surface of how psychologists think about human thought and behavior, about mind,

Connection
Our genetic code is not set in stone at birth. Genes are turned on or off by experiences we have, foods we eat, and even foods our mothers ate while pregnant with us.
See "Epigenetics: How the Environment Changes Gene Expression," Chapter 3, "The Biology of Behavior," p. 80.

1953
Abraham Maslow's *Motivation and Personality* outlines the stages of growth leading to personal fulfillment

1950
Karen Horney published *Neurosis and Human Growth* outlining her psychoanalytic social theory as an alternative to Freud's psychosexual theory

1965
Jean Piaget publishes *The Child's Conception of Number*

1998
Martin Seligman starts the positive psychology movement with Mihaly Csíkszentmihalyi to study and promote psychological well-being

1950	1960	1970	1980	1990	2000

1951
Carl Rogers publishes *Client-Centered Therapy,* advocating a new humanistic approach emphasizing personal growth

1974
Eleanor Maccoby and Carol Jacklin publish a seminal book on gender, *The Psychology of Sex Differences*

1992
John Tooby and Leda Cosmides publish a landmark chapter "The Evolutionary Foundations of Culture" that jump-starts evolutionary psychology

body, and experience. Debates and theories about how and why we think and act the way we do go back thousands of years. Some of the key debates remain unresolved to this day, primarily because in many cases no one perspective explains the whole story for how things work. These systems of thought have profoundly influenced the development of psychology. Let's now consider the major ways of thinking about mind, body, and experience that have shaped modern psychological science.

Quick Quiz 1.3: The Origins of Psychology

1. What perspective in psychology assumes the unconscious is the most powerful force behind most behavior?
   a. trephination
   b. cognitive psychology
   c. structuralism
   d. psychoanalysis

2. _____ argued that thoughts, feelings, and motives are unimportant in understanding human behavior.
   a. Behaviorists
   b. Psychoanalysts
   c. Functionalists
   d. Gestalt psychologists

3. Positive psychology is a modern form of which school of thought?
   a. structuralism
   b. humanism
   c. functionalism
   d. introspectionism

Answers can be found at the end of the chapter.

WAYS OF THINKING ABOUT MIND, BODY, AND EXPERIENCE

The topics covered by psychology sit in the middle of age-old debates and theories about the origins of human thought and behavior. Three major ways of thinking about human experience continue to influence the field today: the nature–nurture debate, the mind–body problem, and evolutionary theory.

The Nature–Nurture Debate

For millennia thinkers have argued over what determines our personality and behavior: innate biology or life experience (Pinker, 2004). This conflict is known as the *nature–nurture debate*. The nature-only view is that who we are comes from inborn tendencies and genetically based traits.

Consider this scenario. You are at a restaurant, and you see a young family trying to eat a meal. A 2-year-old girl is running in circles around a table and won't sit down, despite her parents' best efforts. You mention to the parents that she is quite active. The exhausted mom answers meekly, "Yes, she was born that way!" Other patrons of the restaurant might quietly disapprove of the parents' inability to control the child. Chances are, though, the mom is right. The girl was probably always active, and there may be little they can do to get her to sit down. In fact, a great deal of evidence indicates that our personalities are influenced by genetic factors and remain consistent across the life span (Plomin & Caspi, 1999).

The nurture-only side states that we are all essentially the same at birth, and we are the product of our experiences. As we have already considered, John Locke (1690/1959) popularized the idea that the newborn human mind is a blank slate on which the experiences of life are written. This accumulation of experiences makes us who we are. This view means that anything is possible. You can be anything you want to be. This notion is a very Western, very North American idea. It stands as the cornerstone of democracy, free will, and equality (Pinker, 2002).

Pitting nature against nurture, however, gets us nowhere. It creates a false split, or false dichotomy, that hinders our understanding of the mind and behavior. Almost nothing in psychology can be categorized as either nature or nurture— not learning, not memory, not cognition, not emotion, not even social behavior! These forces work together almost all the time; they are interdependent.

Throughout this book, we will point out many cases in which environmental and genetic forces work together to shape who we are (Rutter, 2002). For example, in the processes of learning and remembering, certain genes in the brain are turned on or off by what happens to us (Kandel, 2006). New connections between brain cells result from these changes in the genes. Consequently, the brains of people and animals reared in richly stimulating environments differ from the brains of people reared in understimulating, neglectful, or abusive environments.

Given how much biological and environmental forces interact and influence each other, we introduce the term *softwire* to reflect this new way of thinking about nature and nurture. **Softwiring,** in contrast to hardwiring, means that biological systems involved in thought and behavior—genes, brain structures, brains cells, etc.—are inherited yet are still open to modification from the environment (Herbert & Rich, 1999; Ottersen, 2010). Much of who we are is more softwired than hardwired.

softwiring
in contrast to hardwiring, means that biological systems—genes, brain structures, brain cells—are inherited but open to modification from the environment.

Here's an example of softwiring: Research reveals that people whose mothers developed certain infections during pregnancy are more likely to develop schizophrenia than people whose mothers were healthy during pregnancy (Brown, 2006). Risks of this disorder in offspring increase sevenfold in mothers infected with the flu virus and 10–12-fold in mothers infected with rubella, the virus that causes German measles (Boska, 2008; Brown, 2006). Evidence suggests that the crucial event here may be the fact that the mothers are mounting an immune response against an infectious agent during key stages of neural development in pregnancy (Fruntes & Limosin, 2008). A baby of the same genetic makeup who was not exposed to the virus and immune response would be less likely to develop the disorder.

These examples illustrate how what we are born with and what we are exposed to interact to create thought and behavior. For decades, many psychologists have shied away from the idea of an interrelationship, clinging to the nature–nurture debate. Old habits die hard. But to fully appreciate human behavior, we must take a broader view. All creatures are born with genetic instructions, but from the beginning, even before birth, environmental factors alter the ways in which genes are expressed. And throughout life, genetic factors assert themselves, such as a familial predisposition toward anxiety. Rather than pitting nature against nurture, we prefer the phrase **nature through nurture,** whereby the environment—be it the womb or the world outside—interacts continuously with biology to shape who we are and what we do (Begley, 2007; Pinker, 2004; Ridley, 2003).

nature through nurture the position that the environment constantly interacts with biology to shape who we are and what we do.

Mind–Body Dualism

How is the mind related to the body and brain? Are they one and the same or two distinct entities? Since its inception, psychology has been burdened by that question, known as *mind–body dualism*. In the 17th century René Descartes, a French philosopher and mathematician, offered proofs of many important concepts in mathematics (Crump, 2001). But he proposed one idea that crippled the social sciences for years. Descartes stated that the mind and the body are separate entities. This idea is often referred to as *mind–body dualism*. From this perspective, the mind controls the body. The body can occasionally control the mind too, but mainly when we abandon good judgment, such as in the throes of passion. Mostly, in Descartes' view, mind and body are separate.

Dualism, or separation of mind and body, allows for many ideas central to Western thinking: for example, that a soul survives bodily death, the mind is separate from the brain, humans are superior to animals. Like nature versus nurture, mind–body dualism represents a false dichotomy—in the sense of being either–or. Mind and body are both useful concepts, but they are exquisitely intertwined. That which we call *mind*, our thoughts, feelings, ideas—our entire mental world—results from the functioning of our *brain,* which is indeed part of the body.

Both the nature–nurture and mind–body dichotomies have influenced Western thought and the development of psychology as a field. Notice that we have been talking about *Western* thinking. Indeed, modern psychological science grew from the marriage of Western philosophy and physiology, with Wundt's laboratory in Leipzig as the first child. In contrast, systems of thought from elsewhere in the world—especially Eastern philosophy—have long emphasized the interdependence of body and mind (Begley, 2007; Tulku, 1984). But there are other perspectives still. In much of Eastern thought, body and mind are very much seen as part of one whole. Psychological science is, at last, beginning to arrive at this same conclusion, but it has taken over a century to get there.

The Evolution of Human Behavior

One principle that plays an important role in understanding human behavior is evolution. The basics of this theory are more complex than most of us realize. Here we briefly explain the fundamental processes of evolution.

Evolution means "change." With respect to biological species, **evolution** is the change over time in the frequency with which specific genes occur within a breeding species (Buss, 1999). What does the frequency of gene transmission have to do with behavior? Our genes contain instructions for making all the proteins in our bodies. Proteins, in turn, make up a lot of what we are: cell membranes, hormones, enzymes, and muscle tissue, to name just a few examples. These constituents carry out our intentions, in our brains, in our bodies. Thus, behaviors have genetic bases that are affected by many environmental factors. Human interaction with the world influences which genes are passed on to future generations, and these in turn shape human behavior. These changes take place by *natural selection*.

evolution
the change over time in the frequency with which specific genes occur within a breeding species.

First described by the 19th-century English naturalist Charles Darwin (1809–1882), **natural selection** is formally defined as a feedback process whereby nature favors one design over another, depending on whether it has an impact on reproduction. This process takes a long time to work, but it ultimately shapes who we are and how species evolve. Charles Darwin's genius and great contribution was not the theory of evolution itself but rather his explanation of *how* evolution works, that is, by natural selection.

natural selection
a feedback process whereby nature favors one design over another because it has an impact on reproduction.

Natural selection occurs by chance. Every once in a while, genes change for no apparent reason. Spontaneous changes in genes, called *chance mutations*, can alter the design of a structure or a set of behaviors. Let's suppose, for example, that a chance mutation in a population of green beetles results in a brown beetle. If the brown beetle is less visible to predators, it might have more success in surviving and reproducing, as Figure 1.4 shows. When it reproduces, the brown beetle passes on its "brown" genes to its offspring.

The brown offspring have a better survival rate, which means they are more likely to reproduce. Eventually, this physiological trait becomes common among members of the species. The complete change takes many generations, but eventually the entire beetle species will be brown (Tooby & Cosmides, 1992). The key in natural selection is that the behaviors have to increase reproductive success, because reproduction and gene transmission drive the whole process.

adaptations
inherited solutions to ancestral problems that have been selected for because they contribute in some way to reproductive success.

The accumulation of chance mutations underlies evolutionary change. Each generation is a product of beneficial modifications from its evolutionary past. Natural selection creates structures and behaviors that solve adaptive problems. Among the adaptive problems that our early human ancestors faced were avoiding predators, choosing nutritious foods, finding a mate, and communicating effectively with others. **Adaptations** are inherited solutions to ancestral problems that have been naturally selected because they directly contribute in some way to reproductive success (Tooby & Cosmides, 1992). Adaptations evolved to solve problems in past generations—not current ones. In other words, we are living with traits and tendencies that benefited our ancestors. Even though these tendencies might not seem to enhance our fitness in today's world, eons spent in harsher environments have left us predisposed to perform certain social behaviors when a situation calls forth ancient patterns. Consider, for example, our preference for fatty foods. In our evolutionary past, eating fat was a good strategy. Early humans, as hunter-gatherers, did not know when they would find food. If they found fat, they ate it, because fat could be stored in the body and used later when food might be scarce. For this reason, humans evolved to like fat. Modern society, however, offers easy access to food. Now eating fat is not the best strategy, because we don't need to store it for future use. More food will be available when we need it. So we eat fat, store it up, and carry it around as extra weight. Human cravings have not changed much, even though our environments have.

Evolutionary psychology is the branch of psychology that aims to uncover the adaptive problems the human mind may have solved in the distant past and the effect of evolution on behavior today. Rather than just describing what the mind does, evolutionary psychologists are interested in the functions of the human mind (Tooby & Cosmides, 1992). Evolutionary changes in organs and bodily structures—or color, as in our beetle example—are not difficult to understand. But how do human behaviors evolve?

Let's consider the emotions as an example of a behavioral adaptation. In Chapter 11, we discuss emotions in detail and explore those feelings that move us powerfully. For now, imagine that you are driving on the highway and the car in the lane next to you has just cut you off. You have to slam on your brakes to keep from smashing into it! You are shaking with fright. The possible car accident is an immediate cause of your fear.

But why do you experience this intense bodily reaction called fear in the first place? The answer, from an evolutionary perspective, is that fear was naturally selected to solve an adaptive problem. What we call fear—including the way it moves our bodies, impels us to act, and makes our hearts race—evolved because it helps us deal quickly and efficiently with danger

evolutionary psychology
the branch of psychology that studies human behavior by asking what adaptive problems it may have solved for our early ancestors.

To understand how Darwin's idea of evolution works, consider a population of beetles:

1 There is variation in traits.
Some beetles are green and some are brown.

2 There is differential reproduction.
Since the environment can't support unlimited population growth, not all individuals get to reproduce to their full potential. In this example, green beetles tend to be eaten by birds and thus do not reproduce, while brown beetles survive to reproduce. There are now fewer green beetles.

3 There is heredity.
The surviving brown beetles have brown baby beetles because this trait has a genetic basis.

Early hunters, like the ones portrayed in this ancient rock painting from the Tadrart Acacus of Libya, ate fat when it was available, and their bodies stored the excess in order to survive when food was scarce. This adaptation has persisted for thousands of years, even though for most people access to food is not a problem.

(Ekman, 2003). Eons ago, a genetic variation occurred in a human that somehow led to a specific way of responding to threatening circumstances—quick action to avoid being killed—and the human was able to avoid harm and reproduce more readily; that is, it had an advantage. Without thinking about it, the ancestor who recognized a beast who could kill her while she was picking berries just wanted to get out of harm's way. Experiencing fear, she was more likely to escape death. This woman survived, reproduced, and passed on a genetic tendency to experience fear to the next generation. Thus, emotions are behavioral adaptations. They are quick and ready response patterns that tell us whether something is good or bad for our well-being (Ekman, 2003; R. S. Lazarus, 1991).

Not all products of evolution are adaptations. Sometimes things evolve because they solved one problem and they just happen to solve another one too. These structures or features that

4 There is the end result.

The more advantageous trait, brown coloration, allows the beetle to have more offspring and becomes more common in the population. If this process continues, eventually, all individuals in the population will be brown.

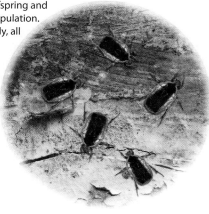

FIGURE **1.4**

HOW NATURAL SELECTION WORKS. Natural selection is one of the basic mechanisms of evolution. This hypothetical example shows how natural selection might change the predominant color of a population of beetles from green to brown.

Nature & Nurture

One of the best examples of the intricate interplay between our bodies and the environment (nature and nurture) is evolution by natural selection. Experiences and events over millions of years change our brains and bodies and hence our minds.

perform a function that did not arise through natural selection are often called *by-products* or, more technically, *exaptations* (Buss, 1999; S. J. Gould & Vrba, 1982). An example of a by-product is feathers. Feathers probably evolved for insulation in flightless dinosaurs, but they turned out to be useful for flight in birds, the dinosaurs' descendants. Because feathers did not evolve for that purpose, they are considered by-products ("Exaptations," 2006).

Similarly, humans didn't evolve to speak in fully grammatical sentences or to do scientific research, but once they started doing so, there were legitimate adaptive reasons to continue. Thus, language and science are not adaptations but are by-products of adaptations (Feist, 2006; Pinker, 1994).

Nothing illustrates more vividly than evolution how nature and nurture work together. Depending on how they enable organisms to respond to their environment, certain characteristics of animals predominate or not—like the brown color of the beetle and the fear response in humans. Nature and nurture work together to create our bodies (including our brains) and behavior. They are interdependent—that is, they depend on and interact with each other.

Quick Quiz 1.4: Ways of Thinking About Mind, Body, and Experience

1. Which phrase most accurately reflects a modern perspective in psychology?
   a. nature versus nurture
   b. nature over nurture
   c. nurture over nature
   d. nature through nurture

2. Charles Darwin's great contribution was the theory of
   a. how evolution works (natural selection)
   b. evolution

   c. psychoanalysis
   d. adaptations

3. Mind–body dualism proposes that
   a. the mind and body are one
   b. the mind influences the body and the body influences the mind
   c. the mind and body are separate
   d. the mind and body are both adaptations

Answers can be found at the end of the chapter.

NO ONE PERSPECTIVE TELLS THE WHOLE STORY IN PSYCHOLOGY

As we have seen in this chapter, in order to fully appreciate the complexity of human thought and behavior, one must consider a wide variety of perspectives—no one perspective tells the whole story. Throughout this book we highlight diverse explanations of human thought and behavior. This variety of perspectives raises the question: How does one resolve the various views? There are two strategies for answering this question: by using science and critical thinking and by making connections.

Don't Believe Everything You Think

First, the methods of science and critical thinking help us choose among various explanations for thought and behavior. Science tests our assumptions against observation from the real world. Think about it: People thought the world was flat until explorers began to map out the surface of the earth. Because it is based on skepticism, the scientific view encourages critical thinking—that is, not believing everything we think. By comparing our assumptions with real-world observation, science helps us choose among competing explanations of behavior. For example, one recent popular theory has been that something in childhood vaccines caused autism. Over the last 10 years, scientists have conducted many studies testing the vaccine-autism explanation and have found no support for it. Indeed, as we discuss in the research ethics section of Chapter 2, the original study on which the argument was based turned out to be fraudulent; that is, it consisted of false data.

Although collecting observations and conducting research helps us choose one viewpoint over another, sometimes more than one perspective can be correct. Consider, for example, the psychological disorder of schizophrenia. For years people attributed the development of this disorder mostly to upbringing, arguing for a pure "nurture" explanation. Then biological explanations, such as an imbalance of particular neurotransmitters, became fashionable. The most recent research suggests that schizophrenia emerges from an interaction of biological and environmental influences—so, in a very real sense, elements of both explanations are correct (Moffitt, Caspi, & Rutter, 2005). The more open we are to diverse perspectives, the better able we will be to explain the whole and often surprising picture of human behavior.

We believe strongly that modern psychological science tells us that we must combine multiple perspectives in order to come to a complete understanding of human thought and behavior. One of the overarching themes of multiple perspectives is the proverbial nature–nurture question. Psychological science shows that almost every fundamental aspect of human behavior—whether it is brain development, learning, intelligence, perception, personality, social behavior, or psychological disorders—develops from a complex interplay of biological and environmental forces. Whenever relevant and salient, we bring your attention to this combined perspective with "Nature and Nurture" callouts in the margins of the chapters (for example, see page 28).

Research can also lead us to surprising findings, sometimes challenging our most basic assumptions. For example, a young neuroscientist named Helen Mayberg parted paths with most of her colleagues and did not focus on drug therapies to treat depression. She focused instead directly on the brain. In so doing she stumbled on a surprising and counterintuitive discovery: A particular part of the brain is overactive in depressed people (Mayberg, 1997, 2003). She went on to pioneer treatment for depression by stimulating the part of the brain that was overactive.

As a way of highlighting research that challenged assumptions and took science in a new direction, we have developed a "Breaking New Ground" feature for every chapter. Each story not only lays out the groundbreaking research, but it also makes clear how personal acts of discovery and creativity are so often behind scientific research. There is a psychology behind the science of psychology, and there are personal stories for every discovery (Feist, 2006). Seeing the dynamic and often personal side of psychological science leads to a better appreciation of how

Connection

Area 25 is a brain region in the front of the brain and is overly active in people with depression. A therapy known as "deep brain stimulation" can calm this area down and lead to a sudden decrease in depressed symptoms for some people.

See "Breaking New Ground," Chapter 16, "Treatment of Psychological Disorders," p. 638.

psychological science came about and may help you challenge assumptions that break new ground.

We also hope that while reading you learn to adopt the attitude of not believing everything you think and that these chapters will foster your own desire to discover how or why you and other people do what you do. Along these lines we have developed in every chapter a "Research to Real Life" segment, in which we ask you to take an idea from the chapter and research it in your own life. In Chapter 16, for instance, we ask you to conduct a little study on your own life by making note of any undesirable habit or behavior you might have and then trying to change it.

Connections Within and Between Chapters

Second, to bring together the various perspectives, we also explicitly connect theories and findings throughout the book. Seeing connections is a creative act, and psychological ideas and research findings are connected sometimes in obvious ways and sometimes in surprising ways. Learning to synthesize and bring together ideas is an important part of being educated and learning to think critically. To facilitate this skill, we connect concepts both within and between chapters, as we just did with deep brain stimulation and depression. We do so by means of a "Connections" note in the margin, in which we provide chapter, section, and page number to facilitate easy access to these related ideas. By regularly returning to ideas from the same or different chapters, we can put them in a different context.

Finally, as a way of reviewing and connecting all of the important topics in each chapter, but in an applied way, we end each chapter with a section titled "Bringing It All Together." In this section, we explore one topic that brings together most of the main concepts and ideas in the chapter. For example, in this chapter, we consider how psychologists in different subfields of psychology have begun to study the effects of electronic social interactions on human behavior.

Research to Real Life

Psychology is the scientific study of thought and behavior. You have just read a bit about the field in general, as well as a few specifics about the various subdisciplines in psychology. With this general background in mind, look around you: at your life, your immediate environment, your friends, your relationships with others—or simply observe other people. Do you see psychology in action? Can you notice how one person's actions affect another? or how your behavior might be contingent on certain consequences or rewards? Maybe you are more likely to text friends who text you back, and the ones who don't eventually get less of your attention.

Connecting Psychology to Your Life: Try to find at least three instances (observations or experiences) from real life that demonstrate psychology in action. Try to notice what aspect of psychology they might reflect. Are social relationships involved? What do you observe about people's behavior? Do you see the effects one person has on another? How might people's impressions be motivated by their expectations of what might happen? Think about it.

Bringing It All Together
Making Connections in Psychology
Studying Electronic Social Interactions

There are nearly a dozen different ways a person can interact with others electronically—via e-mail, blogs, cell phones, chat rooms, texting, instant messaging, audio or video chats, gaming (either solo or multiplayer), videos, photos, bulletin boards, and social network sites (SNSs) (Subrahmanyam & Greenfield, 2008). Humans have taken to electronic forms of interaction like fish to water. As a form of behavior that is evolving at a rapid pace, electronic social interaction holds great interest for psychologists in all of the subfields you read about in this chapter. Let's consider how psychologists from some of these different areas might study electronic communication and its effects on human behavior and thought.

Cognitive Psychology

Cognitive scientists typically are interested in how we learn, remember, think, or reason. They are also interested in attention. The widespread use of cell phones has sparked a number of research questions. The most obvious one concerns how drivers can pay attention to driving while talking on a cell phone. Researchers who have examined the effect of talking on a hands-free cell phone while driving report that a person's ability to operate a car while doing so is similar to the ability to drive while drunk (Strayer et al., 2006). In addition, college students who most overestimate their actual driving experience while using a cell phone are most likely to use one while driving (Schlehofer et al., 2010).

Developmental Psychology

Developmental psychologists study how we change over the life span. They might ask questions like these: At what age is a person too young to form electronic social networks? At what age does participation in Internet social networks peak? Will they always be for the younger generation? Will people 60 and older use them? Does gender affect interest and participation in SNSs? How have cell phones and other electronic methods of communicating changed the way teenagers interact with others?

Researchers have already given us answers to some of these questions. For example, some research suggests that older teenage girls and young women are more likely to participate in social networking sites than are boys and young men (Boyd, 2007; Hargittai, 2008). The reason electronic interactions are so popular with adolescents has a lot to do

with psychological factors: identity, autonomy, intimacy, and sexuality (Subrahmanyam & Greenfield, 2008). One reason the popularity of electronic interactions declines with age may be that these issues decline in importance as one moves from early adulthood to middle and late adulthood (Erikson, 1982).

Social Psychology

More than just about any other area of psychology, social psychology lends itself to a rich set of research questions regarding electronic interactions. One of the first applications of the Internet for social purposes was online dating services. Such forms of electronic interaction may be a preferred method of contact for people with high social anxiety (Stevens & Morris, 2007). Although most people who use online dating services tend to be over 30, college-age teens and young adults are increasingly using them as well (Stevens & Morris, 2007; Valkenburg & Peter, 2007). Contrary to what some people originally thought, however, electronic interactions cannot easily be used to hide one's "real personality" and to avoid ever having real face-to-face contact with others. Research on this phenomenon suggests that people use the Internet not simply to interact with others from afar but also to arrange real face-to-face meetings (Couch & Liamputtong, 2008).

Electronic interactions have led to new behaviors and language as the boundaries between public and private have broken down. For instance, being *privately public* means connecting with many other people, while being relatively nonpublic about revealing who you are. Being *publicly private* means you disclose a lot of details of your private life and may or may not limit access to your site (P. G. Lange, 2008). Cristin Norine, who was profiled at the beginning of the chapter, was publicly private—she did everything except shower and go to the bathroom in a glass house while connected to thousands of people via Twitter, Facebook, and blogging.

Another electronic behavior is the concept of "friending." When others allow you access to their site, they have "friended" you. This in turn raises ancient issues of being "popular," socially excluded, rejected, and accepted. In one tragic case of online rejection, a 13-year-old girl was so distraught over being rejected by a boy online that she committed suicide. The even greater tragedy, however, was that the boy did not exist: A neighbor's mother allegedly made him up to get back at the girl for making disparaging remarks about her daughter.

Personality Psychology

A personality psychologist could ask many questions about electronic interaction and presentations. For example, Are people who interact extensively with other people via Facebook more or less outgoing than those who do not? Whose tube is YouTube anyway (Hargittai, 2008)? Moreover, how much of people's personality is reflected in their Facebook profiles? One somewhat counterintuitive finding is that Facebook profiles reflect more accurate portrayals of a person's personality than one would think (Back et al., 2010). Facebook profiles, in fact, are not idealized images of who we want to be or who we want others to ideally perceive us to be, but rather are more in tune with the personalities that we and our close friends actually perceive.

There is also the psychologically interesting phenomenon of creating an alternative personality, or avatar, in the gaming world. People sometimes take on personalities that are very different from their own in an online world that allows them to express and say things they would not in direct face-to-face contact. Indeed, this ability to be people we are not has allowed psychotherapists to use avatar personality games such as Second Life® to help people overcome their social anxieties in real life (Gottschalk, 2010; Lisetti et al., 2009).

Health Psychology

A very innovative and at least partially successful application of electronic media is using the cell phone to access health information and symptoms of various diseases. For example, a program in San Francisco, California, has phone numbers for people to call if they suspect they might have a particular disease, often a sexual disease. The embarrassment of having to ask questions face-to-face is taken away when one can call up or text a phone number to obtain a health diagnosis anonymously.

Clinical Psychology

When do SNSs and other electronic interactions become a problem? Can one become "addicted" to such behavior, and can such interactions become dangerous to those involved? One of the main criteria for a mental illness is that it interferes with everyday life and functioning. If one is online for 10–12 hours a day, is that healthy? What about the danger involved in meeting someone in person whom you know only from online interaction? Sexual predators use these connections to meet victims. They contact potential victims through chat rooms, instant messages, and e-mail. According to one study, 1 in 7 teens (ages 10–17 years) have been sexually solicited online (Ybarra & Mitchell, 2008). One psychological question is whether people with particular personality traits or syndromes are more likely to be solicited than others.

Connection

Can a person actually become addicted to online activities? What does it mean to be addicted to electronic interaction?

See "Psychology in the Real World: Can Internet Use Become an Addiction?" Chapter 15, Psychological Disorders," p. 598.

We hope this chapter has helped you to appreciate the richness and excitement of psychology as a clinical practice and as a science. But more than appreciating the material, we hope it encourages you to become an active and critical student of human behavior: Don't believe everything you think, and question how conclusions are drawn—even conclusions in this book. We hope that, as a first step toward active learning and investigating, you are at this point asking, How do psychologists know all of this? How do they do research? In the next chapter, we discuss the techniques by which psychological scientists study mental processes and behavior. Welcome to the fascinating world of psychology.

Quick Quiz 1.5: No One Perspective Tells the Whole Story in Psychology

1. Which of the following is a technique we argue for integrating the many perspectives in psychology?
   a. using not believing everything you think
   b. using the scientific method
   c. making connections within and between chapters
   d. all of the above

2. What area of psychology has reported findings that driving while using a hands-free cell phone is much like driving while being drunk?
   a. behavioral neuroscience
   b. cognitive psychology
   c. developmental psychology
   d. social psychology

3. Dr. Porsche is a psychologist who conducts research on whether hands-free phone use distracts drivers and leads to more accidents. Dr. Porsche is probably what kind of a psychologist?
   a. cognitive
   b. developmental
   c. personality
   d. clinical

Answers can be found at the end of the chapter.

Chapter **Review**

WHAT IS PSYCHOLOGY?

- Psychology is the scientific study of thought and behavior. We can see psychology all around us—in our own thoughts and feelings, in the behavior of our friends and relatives, and in how we interpret others' behaviors. As a field, it prepares us well not only for life in general, but also for a wide variety of professions in which social interaction plays a key role.

- As a discipline, psychology is both a practice and a science. Clinical psychologists and counselors treat mental, emotional, and behavioral disorders and promote psychological health. Clinical psychologists also conduct research on psychological disorders and health. They practice psychology. As a science, psychology is the field of study in which researchers examine how the mind works and the rules that govern behavior within and between individuals.

SUBDISCIPLINES OF PSYCHOLOGY

- As a broad field, psychology comprises several subdisciplines, or areas of focused study, including cognitive, developmental, social, personality, health, educational, and industrial/organizational psychology. Neuroscience explores the links among brain, mind, and behavior and thus cuts across other subdisciplines.

THE ORIGINS OF PSYCHOLOGY

- The practice of psychology goes back to prehistoric times. Thousands of years ago humans drilled holes in the skull to treat brain injury and perhaps mental anguish as well. In the Middle Ages, the mentally ill were often treated as if possessed by demons. A few hundred years later, asylums served as storage houses for the severely mentally disabled.

- The late 1800s and early 1900s witnessed the beginning of more humane and more sophisticated treatment of people with psychological disorders. Around the turn of the 20th century, Sigmund Freud developed psychoanalysis to treat people suffering from disorders. By the middle of the 20th century, modern diagnostic criteria for mental disorders, psychotherapy, and drug therapy had emerged.

- The history of psychology as a science is not nearly as old as that of clinical practice, although its origins in philosophy go back to the ancient Greeks. Psychological science emerged from a tradition of empiricism and observations of the world. John Locke's 17th-century view of the mind as a blank slate on which experience writes the contents influences psychology to this day.

- The first psychological scientists did experimental work in perception and laid the groundwork for psychophysics. Only when laboratories started to empirically examine and test human sensations and perception did psychology gain its independence from philosophy and become a science.

- Wilhelm Wundt opened the first laboratory in experimental psychology in Leipzig, Germany, in 1879. Key figures in the birth of scientific psychology in the United States include William James and G. Stanley Hall.

- The biggest development in psychological research in the United States was the birth of behaviorism in the early 20th century. According to behaviorism, all behavior comes from experience. Founded by John Watson, behaviorism reached its pinnacle with B. F. Skinner.

- Behaviorism proved a very useful model for developing methods of studying learning in humans and animals, but it left the unobservable world of the mind unexplained. This all changed with the cognitive revolution of the 1950s and 1960s. Initially, cognitive science used the computer as a model for the way the human mind processes and stores sensations, memories, and ideas.

- Many fields that have older origins came together in the psychology of the 1980s and 1990s: neuroscience, behavioral genetics, and evolutionary psychology.

WAYS OF THINKING ABOUT MIND, BODY, AND EXPERIENCE

- Psychological science in the 21st century has reintegrated biological and environmental explanations of human thought and behavior. The fully modern view squares explanations of behavior with the principles of evolution. It also surpasses old absolutes like the nature–nurture debate and mind–body dualism.

NO ONE PERSPECTIVE TELLS THE WHOLE STORY IN PSYCHOLOGY

- Multiple perspectives are often needed to fully explain the complexity of human thought and behavior. To integrate these multiple perspectives, it helps to use the methods of science and critical thinking and to integrate and connect related ideas and concepts.

BRINGING IT ALL TOGETHER: MAKING CONNECTIONS IN PSYCHOLOGY

- The world of electronic interaction provides a context for research in many subdisciplines of psychology. For example, personality psychologists have examined which types of people are more likely to use social networking sites (SNSs); social psychologists have studied whether SNSs operate like real-life social networks; and developmental psychologists have begun to explore how the use of e-mail, SNSs, and texting varies by age and gender.

Key Terms

adaptations, p. 25

asylums, p. 13

behavioral neuroscience, p. 9

behaviorism, p. 19

biological psychology, p. 9

clinical psychology, p. 10

cognitive psychology, p. 8

developmental psychology, p. 8

educational psychology, p. 11

empiricism, p. 16

evolution, p. 25

evolutionary psychology, p. 26

forensic psychology, p. 11

functionalism, p. 18

Gestalt psychology, p. 20

health psychology, p. 11

humanistic psychology, p. 19

industrial/organizational (I/O) psychology, p. 11

introspection, p. 18

moral treatment, p. 14

natural selection, p. 25

nature through nurture, p. 24

personality psychology, p. 10

positive psychology, p. 19

psychoanalysis, p. 15

psychology, p. 5

psychophysics, p. 16

shamans, p. 12

social psychology, p. 10

softwiring, p. 23

sports psychology, p. 11

structuralism, p. 18

Quick Quiz **Answers**

Quick Quiz 1.1:   1. d   2. d   3. c   Quick Quiz 1.2:   1. a   2. b   3. c   Quick Quiz 1.3:   1. d   2. a   3. b
Quick Quiz 1.4:   1. d   2. a   3. c   Quick Quiz 1.5:   1. d   2. b   3. a

Challenge Your Assumptions **Answers**

- Psychology is all about curing mental illness. **False. See pp. 5–6.**
- Intro to Psychology will give you the single perspective you need to explain your own thoughts and behaviors. **False. See pp. 28–30.**
- Genetic influences on our thoughts and actions can't be changed. **False. See pp. 21, 23.**
- Psychologists are not all trained the same way to study the same things. **True. See pp. 7–11.**

Conducting Research in Psychology

2

Chapter Outline

Challenge *Your Assumptions*

TRUE OR FALSE?

- Psychology is not a science.
- Eating sugar does not make you hyperactive.
- Knowing what you're looking for in an experiment has no effect on the outcome.

Answers can be found at the end of the chapter.

You are at your apartment near campus one summer day when the police knock at your door. After they confirm your identity, they say that you are being arrested on suspicion of armed robbery. The cops then handcuff your hands behind your back, put you in the police car, and take you down to the police station. There you are booked, fingerprinted, and placed in a detention cell. You are then blindfolded and driven to a nearby prison, where you are stripped, sprayed with a delousing agent, and made to stand nude and alone in the cell yard. Finally, you are given a uniform, photographed, and assigned to a prison cell. Yet you have done nothing, and the people who arrested you knew this.

This scenario may seem far-fetched, but it actually happened to 10 male college students in the summer of 1971 in Palo Alto, California. Granted, they had recently agreed to participate in a "psychological study on 'prison life' in return for payment of $15 a day" (Haney, Banks, & Zimbardo, 1973, p. 73). Yet the officers who arrested them said nothing about a connection between their arrest and their agreement to participate in such a study. Philip Zimbardo conducted this study— now known as the Stanford Prison Experiment—to examine whether normal people might behave in extreme ways when thrust into situations that place extreme demands on them. In this case, they readily took on roles that made them powerful or powerless (Haney et al., 1973). Zimbardo chose 21 carefully screened male student volunteers and assigned them to be either "guards" or "prisoners" in a simulated prison environment for 2 weeks. All were briefed beforehand about what conditions would be like in the mock prison. All the students signed a form consenting to participate. Six days into the simulation, however, the experiment had taken such an unexpected turn that Zimbardo had to end the study—the students were playing their roles too well. Prisoners went back and forth between plotting riots and having emotional breakdowns—getting sick and crying, for instance. Guards became extremely authoritarian, restricting the prisoners' personal freedom almost completely. They dehumanized the prisoners by referring to each one only by his assigned number— never by name. They put anyone suspected of "disobeying" and being "a bad prisoner" in solitary confinement. The line between fiction and reality, between assigned role and true identity, blurred. In fact, half of the "prisoners" had to be released ahead of schedule because they were experiencing extreme emotional distress as a result of their "incarceration."

Zimbardo's study served as a springboard for additional research on group behavior, and it provided a strong incentive for prison reform. Interest in this study continues today, and it takes on new significance in light of recent cases of prisoner abuse, such as the mistreatment of Iraqi prisoners by American soldiers following the 2003 U.S. invasion (Zimbardo, 2007). Still, the Stanford Prison Experiment also provoked great concern about the treatment of human participants in research. What hypothesis was Zimbardo testing? Were the scientific gains worth the trauma caused to these young men? These are questions of research ethics, one of many topics of research methods in psychology covered in this chapter. We will first look, however, at psychology as a science and the methods of scientific inquiry applied in psychological research. We will then turn to the subject of how psychologists collect, analyze, and interpret data—processes that become the building blocks of knowledge in the field. ■

THE NATURE OF SCIENCE

Science is about testing intuitive assumptions regarding how the world works, observing the world, and being open-minded to unexpected findings. Some of science's most important discoveries happened only because the scientist was open to surprising and unexpected results. Fundamentally, science entails collecting observations, or *data*, from the real world and evaluating whether the data support our ideas or not. The Stanford Prison Experiment fulfilled these criteria, and we will refer to this example several times in our discussion of research methods, measures, and ethics.

Common Sense and Logic

Science involves more than common sense, logic, and pure observation. Although reason and sharp powers of observation can lead to knowledge, they have limitations. Take common sense—the intuitive ability to understand the world. Often common sense is quite useful. Don't go too close to that cliff. Don't rouse that sleeping bear. Don't eat food that smells rotten. Sometimes, though, common sense leads us astray. In psychology, our intuitive ideas about people's behavior are often contradictory or flat-out wrong. For example, most of us intuitively believe that who we are is influenced by our parents, family, friends, and society. But it is equally obvious, especially to parents, that children come into the world as unique people, with their own temperaments, and people who grow up in essentially the same environments do not have identical personalities. To what extent are we the products of our environment, and how much do we owe to heredity? Common sense cannot answer that question, but science can.

Logic is also a powerful tool in the scientist's arsenal. But it can tell us only how the world *should* work. Sometimes the world is not logical. A classic example of the shortcoming of logic is seen in the work of the ancient Greek philosopher, Aristotle. He argued that heavier objects should fall to the ground at a faster rate than lighter objects. Sounds reasonable, right? Unfortunately, it's wrong. For two thousand years, however, the argument was accepted simply because the great philosopher Aristotle wrote it and it made intuitive sense. It took the genius of Galileo to say, "Wait a minute. Is that really true? Let me do some tests to see whether it is true." He did and discovered that Aristotle was wrong (Crump, 2001). The weight of an object does not affect its rate of speed when falling. Science combines logic with research and experimentation.

> **Connection**
>
> **How do psychologists tease apart the question of how much of a trait is due to genetics and how much is due to environment? A common approach is to study twins (both identical and fraternal) who are reared apart or reared together.**
>
> See "Genes and the Environment," Chapter 3, "The Biology of Behavior," p. 79.

The Limits of Observation

Science relies on observation, but even observation can lead us astray. Our knowledge of the world comes through our five senses, but our senses can be fairly easily fooled, as any good magician or artist can demonstrate. Even when we are not being intentionally fooled, the way in which our brains organize and interpret sensory experiences may vary from person to person.

Another problem with observation is that people tend to generalize from their observations and assume that what they witnessed in one situation applies to all similar situations. Imagine you are visiting another country for the first

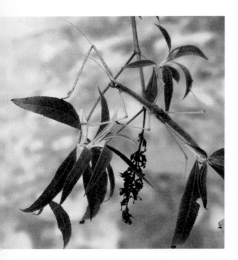

Can you spot the insect in this picture? The walking stick shown here relies on its natural camouflage to make itself appear invisible and thus deceive predators, demonstrating that observation isn't always a reliable guide to reality.

time. Let's say the first person you have any extended interaction with is rude, and a second briefer interaction goes along the same lines. Granted, you have lots of language difficulties, but nevertheless you might conclude that all people from that country are rude. After all, that has been your experience. But those were only two interactions, and after a couple of days there you might meet other people who are quite nice. The point is that one or two cases are not a solid basis for a generalization. Scientists must collect numerous observations and conduct several studies on a topic before generalizing their conclusions.

What Is Science?

Is physics a science? Few would argue that it is not. What about biology? What about psychology? What about astrology? How does one decide? Now that we have looked at some of the components of science and explored their limitations, let's consider the larger question: What *is* science? People often think only of the physical sciences as "science," but science comes in at least three distinct flavors: physical, biological, and social (Feist, 2006). As we mentioned in Chapter 1, psychology is a social science (see Figure 2.1).

The physical sciences study the world of things—the inanimate world of stars, light, waves, atoms, the earth, compounds, and molecules. These sciences include physics, astronomy, chemistry, and geology. The biological sciences study plants and animals in the broadest sense. These sciences include biology, zoology, genetics, and botany. Finally, the social sciences study humans, both as individuals and as groups. These sciences include anthropology, sociology, economics, and psychology.

Science is as much a way of thinking or a set of attitudes as it is a set of procedures. **Scientific thinking** involves the cognitive skills required to generate, test, and revise theories (Koslowski, 1996; Kuhn, Amsel, & O'Loughlin, 1988; Zimmerman, 2007). What we believe or theorize about the world and what the world is actually like, in the form of evidence, are two

scientific thinking process using the cognitive skills required to generate, test, and revise theories.

economics

anthropology

Social Science
people

sociology

psychology

chemistry

geology

Natural Science
things

physics

astronomy

biology

Biological–Life Science
plants & animals

botany

genetics

zoology

FIGURE **2.1**
SIMPLIFIED MAP OF THE SCIENCES: THE STUDY OF THINGS, PLANTS, ANIMALS, AND PEOPLE.

Dr. Andrew Wakefield published a scientific paper in 1998 that claimed that autism was often caused by vaccines for measles, mumps, and rubella. There were many problems with the paper from the outset, not the least of which was its small and unrepresentative sample size (12 children). Many scientists and medical panels could not confirm the results and were highly skeptical of Dr. Wakefield's findings. Unfortunately, the paper created quite a bit of publicity, and many parents ignored standard vaccination schedules, leading to numerous deaths from preventable diseases. In January 2011, the original 1998 paper was deemed fraudulent in a 7-year investigation by the *British Medical Journal*. The investigation concluded that Dr. Wakefield altered the results of his study to make vaccines appear to be the cause of autism.

Don't believe everything you think

FIGURE **2.2**
Science is an attitude that requires we keep open eyes and minds to exploring phenomena.

different things. Scientific thinking keeps these two things separate, whereas nonscientific thinking sometimes confuses them. In other words, scientists remember that belief is not the same as reality. They don't believe everything they think.

In short, science begins with questioning and rejecting authority—including scientific authority. The first attitude of science, therefore, is to *question authority*. Be skeptical (see Figure 2.2). Don't just take the word of an expert; test ideas yourself. The expert might be right, or not. That advice extends to textbooks—including this one. Wonder. Question. Ask for the evidence. Be a critical thinker. Also be skeptical of your *own* ideas. Our natural inclination is to really like our own ideas, especially if they occur to us in a flash of insight. But as one bumper sticker extols: "Don't believe everything you think." Believing something does not make it true.

to **Real Life**

Research

As recently as 10 years ago, one of your authors (GJF) did not believe that evolution was relevant to explanations of current human thought and behavior. In the process of writing a book on the psychology of science, however, he changed his mind and saw the richness and importance of an evolutionary perspective when explaining how humans came to do science.

Connecting Psychology to Your Life: Think about one assumption or idea or belief you once had that you no longer hold.
What made you change your mind? Did you observe certain things that contradicted your belief, or did someone convince you with the logic of an argument?

As expressed by cosmologist and astrophysicist Carl Sagan (1987), the second attitude of science is open skepticism. Scientists must be skeptical by default. The French philosopher Voltaire put scientific skepticism most bluntly: "Doubt is uncomfortable, certainty is ridiculous." But skepticism for skepticism's sake is also not scientific, but stubborn. Scientists are ultimately open to accepting whatever the evidence reveals, however bizarre it may be and however much they may not like or want it to be the case. For example, could placing an electrical stimulator deep in the brain, as if it were a switch, turn off depression? That sounds like a far-fetched treatment, worthy of skepticism, but it does work for some people (Mayberg et al., 2005). Be skeptical, but let the evidence speak for itself.

Connection

As a neuroscientist working on Parkinson's disease, Helen Mayberg found something unexpected about brain circuitry. Initially she was skeptical. But because she was also curious and open to the evidence, she decided to pursue it further. Her curiosity and openness led to her discovery that placing an electrical stimulator deep inside the brain could turn off depression.

See "Biological Treatments for Psychological Disorders," Chapter 16, "Treatment of Psychological Disorders," p. 630.

theory
a set of related assumptions from which scientists can make testable predictions.

hypothesis
a specific, informed, and testable prediction of the outcome of particular set of conditions in a research design.

The third scientific attitude is *intellectual honesty*. When the central tenet of knowing is not what people think and believe, but rather how nature behaves, then we must accept the data and follow them wherever they take us. If a researcher falsifies results or interprets them in a biased way, then other scientists will not arrive at the same results if they repeat the study. Every so often we hear of a scientist who faked data in order to gain fame or funding. For the most part, however, the fact that scientists must submit their work to the scrutiny of other scientists helps ensure honest and accurate presentation of results.

All science—whether physics, chemistry, biology, or psychology—shares these general properties of open inquiry that we have discussed. Let's now turn to the specific methods scientists use to acquire new and accurate knowledge of the world.

The Scientific Method

Science depends on the use of sound methods to produce trustworthy results that can be confirmed independently by other researchers. The **scientific method** by which scientists conduct research consists of five basic processes: Observe, Predict, Test, Interpret, and Communicate (O-P-T-I-C); see the Research Process for this chapter (Figure 2.3). In the *observation* and *prediction* stages of a study, researchers develop expectations about an observed phenomenon. They express their expectations as a **theory,** defined as a set of related assumptions from which testable predictions can be made. Theories organize and explain what we have observed and guide what we will observe (Popper, 1965). To put it simply: theories are not facts—they explain facts. Our observations of the world are always either unconsciously or consciously theory-driven, if you understand that theory in this broader sense means little more than "having an expectation." In science, however, a theory is more than a guess. Scientific theories must be tied to real evidence, they must organize observations, and they must generate expectations that can be tested systematically.

A **hypothesis** is a specific, informed, and testable prediction of what kind of outcome should occur under a particular condition. For example, consider the real-life study that suggests that caffeine increases sex drive in female rats (Guarraci & Benson, 2005). The hypothesis may have been phrased this way: "Female rats who consume caffeine will seek more couplings with male rats than female rats who do not consume caffeine." This hypothesis predicts that a particular form of behavior (coupling with male rats) will occur in a specific group (female rats) under particular conditions (under the influence of caffeine). The more specific a hypothesis is, the more easily each component can be changed to determine what effect it has on the outcome.

To *test* their hypotheses (the third stage of the scientific method), scientists select one of a number of established research methods, along with the appropriate measurement techniques. Selecting the methods involves choosing a design for the study, the tools that will create the conditions of the study, and the tools for measuring responses, such as how often each female rat allows a male to mount her. We will examine each of these elements in the section "Research Methods in Psychology" on page 46.

In the fourth step of the scientific method, scientists use mathematical techniques to *interpret* the results and determine whether they are significant (not

scientific method
the procedures by which scientists conduct research, consisting of five basic processes: observation, prediction, testing, interpretation, and communication.

Research Process

Observe
Researchers working with rats observe their behavior.

1

Communicate

5 Publish findings of "Caffeine and mating behavior in female rats" via peer review process.

Predict

2 Propose a hypothesis based in theory: Caffeine will make female rats seek more couplings with males.

Test

3 Collect data: how often do females on caffeine allow males to mate and how often do females not on caffeine allow males to mate?

Interpret

4 Analyze resulting data to confirm or disconfirm the theory-prediction.

FIGURE **2.3**

THE SCIENTIFIC METHOD. The scientific method consists of an ongoing cycle of observation, prediction, testing, interpretation, and communication (OPTIC). Research begins with observation, but it doesn't end with communication. Publishing results of a study allows other researchers to repeat the procedure and confirm the results.

just a matter of chance) and whether they closely fit the prediction. Do psychologists' ideas of how people behave hold up, or must they be revised? Let's say that the caffeine-consuming female rats coupled more frequently with males than did nonconsuming females. Might this enhanced sexual interest hold for all rats or just those few we studied? Statistics, a branch of mathematics that we will discuss shortly, helps answer that question.

The fifth stage of the scientific method is to *communicate* the results. Generally, scientists publish their findings in a peer-reviewed professional journal. Following a standardized format, the researchers report their hypotheses, describe their research design and the conditions of the study, summarize the results, and share their conclusions. In their reports, researchers also consider the broader implications of their results. What might the effects of caffeine on sexuality in female rats mean for our understanding of caffeine, arousal, and sex in female humans? Publication also serves an important role in making research findings part of the public domain. Such exposure not only indicates that colleagues who reviewed the study found it to be credible, but also allows other researchers to repeat and/or build on the research.

replication
the repetition of a study to confirm the results; essential to the scientific process.

Replication is the repetition of a study to confirm the results. The advancement of science hinges on replication. No matter how interesting and exciting results are, if they cannot be duplicated, the original findings may have been accidental. Whether a result holds or not, new predictions can be generated from the data, leading in turn to new studies. This is why the process of scientific discovery is cumulative. Previous knowledge builds on older knowledge.

What Science Is Not: Pseudoscience

Do you believe that the planets and stars determine our destiny, that aliens have visited Earth, or that the human mind is capable of moving or altering physical objects? Astrology, unidentified flying objects (UFOs), and extrasensory perception (ESP) are certainly fascinating topics to ponder. As thinking beings, we try to understand things that science may not explain to our satisfaction. In fact, many of us are willing to believe things that science and skeptics easily dismiss. For example, based on a survey of 1,574 U.S. adults done in 2002, the National Science Foundation (2002) reported the following:

- Sixty percent believed that some people possess psychic powers or extrasensory perception (ESP).

- Thirty percent believed that some reported objects in the sky are really space vehicles from other civilizations.
- From 1991 to 2001 the number of adults who believed in haunted houses, ghosts, communication with the dead, and witches increased by more than 10%; for example, 29% believed in haunted houses in 1991, whereas 42% believed in them in 2001.
- Thirty percent read astrology charts at least occasionally in the newspaper.
- Forty-eight percent thought humans lived at the same time as the dinosaurs.

pseudoscience
claims presented as scientific that are not supported by evidence obtained with the scientific method.

People often claim there is "scientific evidence" for certain unusual phenomena, but that does not mean the evidence is truly scientific. There is also false science, or *pseudo*science. **Pseudoscience** refers to practices that appear to be and claim to be science, but in fact do not use the scientific method to come to their conclusions. What makes something pseudoscientific comes more from the way it is studied than from the content area. Pseudoscience practitioners (1) make no real advances in knowledge, (2) disregard well-known and established facts that contradict their claims, (3) do not challenge or question their own assumptions, (4) tend to offer vague or incomplete explanations of how they came to their conclusions, and (5) tend to use unsound logic in making their arguments (Derry, 1999; see Figure 2.4).

1 Lacks the cumulative progress seen in science

2 Disregards real-world observations and established facts/results and contradicts what is already known

3 Lacks internal skepticism

4 Only vaguely explains how conclusions are reached

5 Uses loose and distorted logic

FIGURE **2.4**
THE CHARACTERISTICS OF PSEUDOSCIENCE. Skepticism is the best approach to claims that aren't supported by hard scientific evidence.

Philosophy, art, music, and religion, for instance, would not be labeled pseudoscience because they do not claim to be science. Pseudoscientific claims have been made for alchemy, creation science, intelligent design, attempts to create perpetual motion machines, astrology, alien abduction, psychokinesis, and some forms of mental telepathy.

Perhaps the most pervasive pseudoscience is astrology, which uses positions of the sun, moon, and planets to explain an individual's personality traits and to predict the future. There simply is no credible scientific evidence that the position of the moon, planets, and stars and one's time and place of birth have any influence on personality or one's life course (Shermer, 1997). And yet 30% of respondents to the National Science Foundation (2002) survey said they look at the horoscopes in the newspaper at least occasionally.

Overall, telekinesis, astrology, alien abduction explanations of UFOs, and creation science, to name a few, meet the criteria for pseudoscience. But in all fairness, there have been some reliable observations of UFOs and some scientifically sound evidence for telepathy (Bem & Horonton, 1994; Rosenthal, 1986). Reading the scientific literature on these two topics, one has little choice but to conclude that some of these experiences have some validity. Remember, open skepticism is the hallmark of science. If there is scientifically sound evidence for something—even if it is difficult to explain—and it has been replicated, then we have to accept it. The key is to know how to distinguish sound from unsound evidence.

1. The scientific method consists of
   a. observing, predicting, testing
   b. observing, predicting, trying
   c. observing, predicting, testing, communicating
   d. observing, predicting, testing, interpreting, communicating

2. Which of the following is NOT a characteristic of science?
   a. It is cumulative.
   b. It is a search for truth.
   c. It is an attitude.
   d. It requires intellectual honesty.

3. Scientific theories are
   a. a set of related assumptions that guide and explain observations and allow testable predictions to be made
   b. educated guesses
   c. hunches
   d. hypotheses

4. What distinguishes science from pseudoscience?
   a. use of statistics
   b. content area studied
   c. open skepticism
   d. the search for truth

Answers can be found at the end of the chapter.

RESEARCH METHODS IN PSYCHOLOGY

Science involves testing ideas about how the world works, but how do we design studies that test our ideas? This question confronts anyone wanting to answer a psychological question scientifically.

Principles of Research Design

research design
plans of action for how to conduct a scientific study.

Like other sciences, psychology makes use of several types of **research designs**—or plans for how to conduct a study. The design chosen for a given study depends on the question being asked. Some questions can best be answered by randomly placing people in different groups in a laboratory to see whether a treatment causes a change in behavior. Other questions have to be studied by questionnaires or surveys. Still other questions can best be answered simply by making initial observations and seeing what people do in the real world. And sometimes researchers analyze the results of many studies on the same topic to look for trends.

In this section, we examine variations in research designs, along with their advantages and disadvantages. We begin by defining a few key terms common to all research designs in psychology.

A general goal of psychological research is to measure change in behavior, thought, or brain activity. A **variable** is anything that changes or "varies" within or between individuals. People differ from one another on age, gender, weight, intelligence, and level of anxiety and extraversion, to name a few psychological variables. Psychologists do research by predicting how and when variables influence

variable
a characteristic that changes or "varies," such as age, gender, weight, intelligence, anxiety, and extraversion.

THE FAR SIDE® BY GARY LARSON

© 1985 FarWorks, Inc. All Rights Reserved/Dist. by Creators Syndicate

one, two... Testing... one, two... Hey!.. Hey, you! You little bug-eyed greasy sardine! Let me tell you Something about your sister!... Hello, hello... Al, is this thing on?

The Far Side® by Gary Larson © 1985 FarWorks, Inc. All Rights Reserved. The Far Side® and the Larson® signature are registered trademarks of FarWorks, Inc. Used with permission.

Testing whether fish have feelings

each other. For instance, a psychologist who is interested in whether girls develop verbal skills at a different rate than boys focuses on two variables: gender and vocabulary.

All researchers must pay careful attention to how they obtain participants for the study. The first step is for the researchers to decide the makeup of the entire group, or **population,** in which they are interested. In psychology, populations can be composed of, for example, animals, adolescents, boys or girls of any age, college students, students at a particular school. How many are older than 50 or younger than 20? How many are European American, African American, Asian American, Pacific Islander, or Native American? How many have high school educations, and how many have college educations?

Can you think of a problem that would occur if a researcher tried to collect data directly on an entire population? Because most populations are too large to survey or interview directly, researchers draw on small subsets from each population. Subsets of the population are called **samples.** A sample of the population of college students, for instance, might consist of students enrolled in one or more universities in a particular geographic area. Research is almost always conducted on samples, not populations. If researchers want to draw valid conclusions or make accurate predictions about the population, it is important that their samples accurately represent the population in terms of age, gender, ethnicity, or any other variables that might be of interest. When polls are wrong in predicting who will win an election, it is often because the polled sample did not accurately represent the population.

population
the entire group a researcher is interested in; for example, all humans, all adolescents, all boys, all girls, all college students.

samples
subsets of the population studied in a research project.

Researchers often work with a small sample of the population they're interested in.

Descriptive Studies

Many, if not most, creative ideas for studies start with specific experiences or events—one person being painfully shy; a news report of someone rushing onto the train tracks to rescue a person who had fallen in front of an ongoing train; or, as actually happened in a famous case, a young woman being stabbed to death in public with no one coming forward to help her. In the last case, which occurred in Queens, New York, in 1964, the victim was Kitty Genovese. The attack occurred in an apartment complex in which 38 other people later confessed that they either heard or saw the attack. Only one of the 38 did as much as call the police.

The Genovese case was so shocking that it drove two psychologists—Bibb Latané and John Darley—to conduct research on what they later called "the bystander effect."

descriptive designs
study designs in which the researcher defines a problem and variable of interest but makes no prediction and does not control or manipulate anything.

The point is that single events and single cases often lead to new ideas and new lines of research. When a researcher is interested in a particular question or topic that is relatively new to the field, often the wisest approach may be to use a descriptive design. In **descriptive designs** the researcher makes no prediction and does not try to control any variables. She simply defines a problem of interest and describes as carefully as possible the variable of interest. The basic question in a descriptive design is, What is variable *X*? For example, What is love?

Connection
The "bystander effect" explains why individuals in crowds may not help others in need. When in a group, individual responsibility is diffused and people tend to think that helping is someone else's responsibility.
See "Social Relations," Chapter 14, "Social Behavior," p. 569.

FIGURE 2.5

CHARACTERISTICS OF DESCRIPTIVE STUDIES.

In descriptive studies, researchers look for patterns that might help them create testable hypotheses.

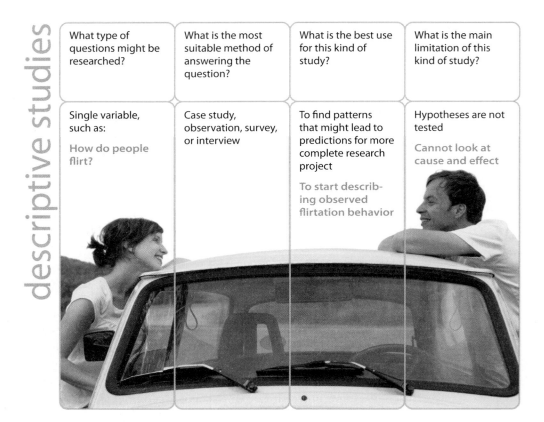

descriptive studies

What type of questions might be researched?	What is the most suitable method of answering the question?	What is the best use for this kind of study?	What is the main limitation of this kind of study?
Single variable, such as: **How do people flirt?**	Case study, observation, survey, or interview	To find patterns that might lead to predictions for more complete research project **To start describing observed flirtation behavior**	Hypotheses are not tested **Cannot look at cause and effect**

What is genius; What is apathy? The psychologist makes careful observations, often in the real world outside the research lab. Descriptive studies usually occur during the exploratory phase of research in which the researcher is looking for meaningful patterns that might lead to predictions later on; they do not involve testing hypotheses. The researcher then notes possible relationships or patterns that may be used in other designs as the basis for testable predictions (see Figure 2.5). Three of the most common kinds of descriptive methods in psychology are case studies, naturalistic observations, and interviews/surveys.

case study
a study design in which a psychologist, often a therapist, observes one person over a long period of time.

Case Study   Psychotherapists have been making use of insights they gain from individual cases for more than 100 years. A **case study** involves observation of one person, often over a long period of time. Much wisdom and knowledge of human behavior can come from careful observations of single individuals over time. Because they are based on one-on-one relationships, often lasting years, case studies offer deep insights that surveys and questionnaires often miss. Sometimes studying the lives of extraordinary individuals, such as van Gogh, Lincoln, Marie Curie, Einstein, or even Hitler can tell us much about creativity, greatness, genius, or evil. An area of psychology called *psychobiography* examines in detail the lives of historically important people and provides an example of the richness and value of case studies (Elms, 1993; Runyan, 1982; Schultz, 2005). Like other descriptive research, case studies do not test hypotheses but can be a rich source for them. One has to be careful with case studies, however, because not all cases are generalizable to other people. That is why case studies are often a starting point for the development of testable hypotheses.

naturalistic observation
a study in which the researcher unobtrusively observes and records behavior in the real world.

Naturalistic Observation   A second kind of descriptive method is **naturalistic observation,** in which the researcher observes and records behavior in the real world. The researcher tries to be as unobtrusive as possible so as not to influence or bias the behavior of interest. Naturalistic observation is more often the design of choice in comparative psychology by researchers who study non-human behavior (especially primates) to determine what is and is not unique about our species.

Developmental psychologists occasionally also conduct naturalistic observations. For example, the developmental psychologist Edward Tronick of Harvard University has made detailed naturalistic observations of infants of the Efe people in Zaire. He has tracked these children from 5 months through 3 years to understand how the Efe culture's communal pattern of child rearing influences social development in children (Tronick, Morelli, & Ivey, 1992). Although the traditional Western view is that having a primary caregiver is best for the social and emotional well-being of a child, Tronick's research suggests that the use of multiple, communal caregivers can also foster children's social and emotional well-being.

The advantage of naturalistic observation is that it gives researchers a look at real behavior in the real world, rather than in a controlled setting like a laboratory where people might not behave naturally. Few psychologists use naturalistic observation, however, because conditions cannot be controlled and cause-and-effect relationships between variables cannot be demonstrated.

Primatologist Jane Goodall is famous for her observational studies of chimpanzees in the wild.

Interview and Survey   Two related and widely used techniques for gaining information about people's thoughts and behaviors are interviews and surveys. They both involve asking people directly or indirectly what they think, feel, or have done. They also both involve specific questions, usually asked in precisely the same way to each respondent. Answers can be completely open-ended, allowing the person to answer however she or he wants. More often than not, however, the possible answers are restricted to some kind of rating scale, such as 1 for "completely disagree," 3 for "neither disagree nor agree," and 5 for "completely agree." Historically, interviews were conducted mostly face-to-face, but now both interviews and surveys are more often carried out over the phone or the Internet. Researchers may thus survey thousands of individuals on almost any topic, such as abortion, sex, capital punishment, voting, or gay marriage.

Collecting data via large-scale interviews and surveys has many pitfalls, the two most obvious being the inclusion of people who are not representative of the group at large and biased responses. Think about your own response when you are contacted via phone or e-mail about participating in a scientific survey. Many of us don't want to participate and ignore the request. So how does a researcher know that people who participate are not different from people who don't participate? Maybe those who participate are older or younger, have more education or have less education. In other words, we need to know that the information we collect comes from people who represent the group in which we are interested, which is known as a **representative sample** (see Figure 2.6).

The well-known Kinsey surveys of male and female sexual behavior provide good examples of the strengths and weaknesses of survey research (Kinsey, Pomeroy, & Martin, 1948; Kinsey et al., 1953). Make no mistake—just

representative sample a research sample that accurately reflects the population of people one is studying.

Research Methods in Psychology   **49**

FIGURE **2.6**

SAMPLING. For practical reasons, research is typically conducted with small samples of the population of interest. If a psychologist wanted to study a population of 2,200 people (each face in the figure represents 100 people), he or she would aim for a sample that represents the makeup of the whole group. Thus, if 27% of the population was blue, the researcher would want 27% of the sample population to be blue, as shown in the pie chart on the left. Contrary to what many students think, representative does *not* mean all groups have the same numbers.

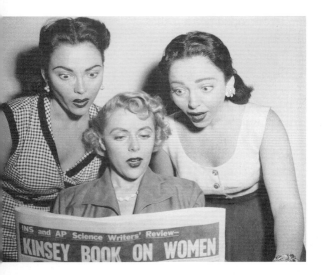

Americans were shocked by Alfred Kinsey's initial reports on male and female sexual behavior. Kinsey was the first researcher to survey people about their sexual behavior. For better or worse, his publications changed our attitudes about sex.

publishing such research caused an uproar in both the scientific community and the general public at the time. Kinsey reported, for instance, that up to 50% of the men and only about half as many (26%) of the women interviewed had had extramarital affairs. Another widely cited finding was that approximately 10% of the population could be considered homosexual. The impact of Kinsey's research has been profound. By itself it began the science of studying human sexuality and permanently changed people's views. For example, Kinsey was the first to consider sexual orientation on a continuum from 0 (completely heterosexual) to 6 (completely homosexual) rather than as an either–or state with only two options. This approach remains a lasting contribution of his studies.

But by today's standards, Kinsey's techniques for interviewing and collecting data were rather primitive. He didn't use representative sampling and oversampled people in Indiana (his home state) and in prisons, for example. In addition, he interviewed people face-to-face about the most personal and private details of their sex lives, making it more likely they would not be perfectly honest in their responses.

Correlational Studies

Once an area of study has developed far enough that predictions can be made from descriptive studies, a researcher might choose to test hypotheses by means of a **correlational design,** one that measures two or more variables and their

correlational designs studies that measure two or more variables and their relationship to one another; not designed to show causation.

relationship to one another. In correlational designs, the basic question is, "Is *X* related to *Y*?" For instance, "Is sugar consumption related to increased activity levels in children?" If so, how strong is the relationship, and is increased sugar consumption associated (correlated) with increased activity levels, as we would predict, or does activity decrease as sugar consumption increases? Or is there no clear relationship?

Correlational studies are useful when the variables cannot be manipulated—that is, controlled by the experimenter. For instance, it would be unethical to raise one group of children one way and another group another way in order to study parenting behavior. But we could use a good questionnaire to find out whether parents' scores related to their parenting behavior are consistently associated with particular behavioral outcomes in children. In fact, many questions in developmental psychology, personality psychology, and even clinical psychology are examined with correlational techniques.

The major limitation of the correlational approach is that it does not establish whether one variable actually causes the other or vice versa. Parental neglect might be associated with antisocial behavior in adolescence, but that does not necessarily mean that neglect causes antisocial behavior. It might, but it might not. Some other variable (e.g., high levels of testosterone, poverty, antisocial friends) could be the cause of the behavior. We must always be mindful that correlation is necessary for causation but not sufficient by itself to establish causation (see Figure 2.7).

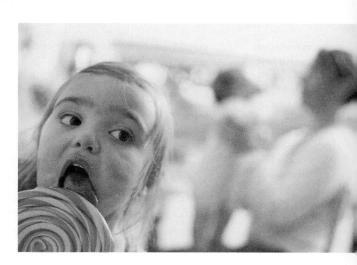

Is there a connection between sugar and children's activity level?

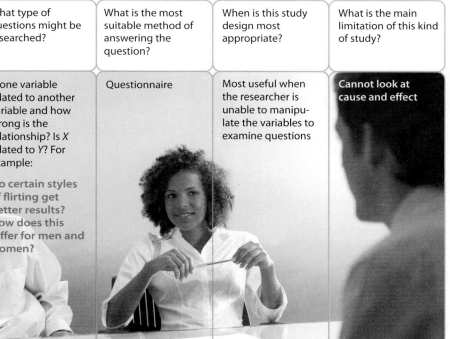

correlational studies

What type of questions might be researched?	What is the most suitable method of answering the question?	When is this study design most appropriate?	What is the main limitation of this kind of study?
Is one variable related to another variable and how strong is the relationship? Is *X* related to *Y*? For example: Do certain styles of flirting get better results? How does this differ for men and women?	Questionnaire	Most useful when the researcher is unable to manipulate the variables to examine questions	**Cannot look at cause and effect**

FIGURE **2.7**
CHARACTERISTICS OF CORRELATIONAL STUDIES. These studies measure two or more variables and their relationship to one another.

correlation coefficient
a statistic that ranges from −1.0 to +1.0 and assesses the strength and direction of association between two variables.

Psychologists often use a statistic called the correlation coefficient to draw conclusions from their correlational study. **Correlation coefficients** tell us whether two variables relate to each other and the direction of the relationship. Correlations range between −1.00 and +1.00, with coefficients near 0.00 telling us there is no relationship between the two variables. In other words, a 0.00 correlation means that knowing about one variable tells you nothing about the other. As a correlation approaches +1.00 or −1.00, the strength of the relationship increases.

Correlation coefficients can be positive or negative. If the relationship is positive, then as a group's score on X increases, its score on Y also increases. Height and weight are positively correlated—taller people generally weigh more than shorter people. For negative correlations, as one variable increases, the other decreases. Alcohol consumption and motor skills are negatively correlated—the more alcohol people consume, the more their motor skills deteriorate.

To further demonstrate correlation, let's consider the positive correlation between students' scores on the midterm and final. By calculating a correlation, we know whether students who do well on the midterm are likely to do well on the final. Based on a sample of 76 students in one of our classes, we found a correlation of +.57 between midterm and final exam grade. This means that, generally, students who did well on the midterm did well on the final. Likewise, those who did poorly on the midterm tended to do poorly on the final. The correlation, however, was not extremely high (.80 or .90), so there was some inconsistency. Some people performed differently on the two exams. When we plot these scores, we see more clearly how individuals did on each exam (see Figure 2.8). Each dot represents one student's scores on each exam. For example, one student scored an 86 on the midterm, but only a 66 on the final.

When interpreting correlations, however, it is important to remember that a correlation does not mean there is a causal relationship between the two variables. *Correlation is necessary but not sufficient for causation.* When one variable causes another, it must be correlated with it. But just because variable X is correlated with variable Y, it does not mean X causes Y. In fact, the supposed

FIGURE **2.8**

EXAMPLE OF SCATTERPLOT OF POSITIVE CORRELATION: STUDENTS' SCORES ON A MIDTERM AND FINAL EXAM.
The correlation between scores on the midterm and final is +.57, which means that in general the students who do well on the midterm tend to do well on the final. It also means that students who do poorly on the midterm tend to do poorly on the final. Each circle is a particular student's scores on the midterm and final. For example, one student scored an 81 on the midterm (vertical dashed line) and an 84 on the final (horizontal dashed line). Students above the diagonal line did better on the final than expected. Students below the diagonal line performed worse on the final than expected. For example, one student scored an 86 on the midterm but only a 66 on the final.

cause may be an effect, or some third variable may be the cause. What if hairiness and aggression in men were positively correlated? Would that imply that being hairy makes a man more aggressive? No. In fact, both hairiness and aggressiveness are related to a third variable, the male sex hormone testosterone (Simpson, 2001; see Figure 2.9).

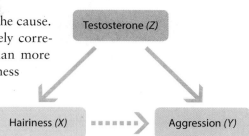

Experimental Studies

Often people use the word *experiment* to refer to any research study, but in science an experiment is something quite specific. A true **experiment** has two crucial characteristics:

FIGURE **2.9**

CORRELATION IS NOT CAUSATION. Hairiness (*X*) and aggression (*Y*) may be correlated, but that does not mean hairiness causes aggression. In reality, a third variable (testosterone, *Z*) is the cause of both of them (Simpson, 2001). Solid lines imply cause and dashed line implies correlation.

1. Experimental manipulation of a predicted cause—the independent variable—and measurement of the response, or dependent variable.

2. Random assignment of participants to control and experimental groups or conditions—meaning that each participant has an equal chance of being placed in each group.

The **independent variable** in an experiment is an attribute that the experimenter manipulates under controlled conditions. The independent variable is the condition that the researcher predicts will cause a particular outcome. The **dependent variable** is the outcome, or response to the experimental manipulation. You can think of the independent variable as the "cause" and the dependent variable as the "effect," although reality is not always so simple. If there is a causal connection between the two, then the responses *depend* on the treatment; hence the name *dependent variable*.

Earlier we mentioned the hypothesis that sugar consumption makes kids overly active. In this example, sugar levels consumed would be the independent variable and behavioral activity level would be the dependent variable. Recall the study of the effect of caffeine on sex drive in rats. Is caffeine the independent or dependent variable? What about sex drive? Figure 2.10 features other examples of independent and dependent variables.

Random assignment means that the method used to assign participants to different research conditions guarantees that each person has the same chance of being in one group as another. Random assignment is achieved with either a random numbers table or some other unbiased technique. Random assignment is critical because it ensures that *on average* the groups will be similar with respect to all possible variables, such as gender, intelligence, motivation, and memory when the experiment begins. If the groups are the same on these qualities at the beginning of the study, then any differences between the groups at the end of the experiment are likely to be the result of the independent variable.

Experimenters randomly assign participants to either an experimental group or a control group. The **experimental group** consists of those participants who receive the treatment or whatever is thought to change behavior. In the sugar consumption and activity study, for example, the experimental group would receive some designated amount of sugar.

The **control group** consists of participants who are treated in exactly the same manner as the experimental group, but with one crucial difference: They do not receive the independent variable or treatment. Instead, they often receive

experiment
a research design that includes independent and dependent variables and random assignment of participants to control and experimental groups or conditions.

independent variable
a property that is manipulated by the experimenter under controlled conditions to determine whether it causes the predicted outcome of an experiment.

random assignment
the method used to assign participants to different research conditions so that all participants have the same chance of being in any specific group.

experimental group
a group consisting of those participants who will receive the treatment or whatever is predicted to change behavior.

dependent variable
in an experiment, the outcome or response to the experimental manipulation.

control group
a group of research participants who are treated in exactly the same manner as the experimental group, except that they do not receive the independent variable, or treatment.

no special treatment or, in some cases, they get a **placebo,** a substance or treatment that appears identical to the actual treatment but lacks the active substance. In a study on sugar consumption and activity level, an appropriate placebo might be an artificial sweetener. So the experimental group would receive the treatment (sugar), and the control group would be treated exactly the same way but would not receive the actual treatment (instead, the control group might receive a food flavored with an artificial sweetener).

placebo
a substance or treatment that appears identical to the actual treatment but lacks the active substance.

Experimental and control groups must be equivalent at the outset of an experimental study so as to minimize the possibility that other characteristics could explain any difference found after the administration of the treatment. If two groups of children are similar at the start and if one group differs from the other on activity level after receiving different amounts of sugar, then we can conclude that the treatment caused the observed effect. That is, different levels of sugar consumption caused the differences in activity level.

You want to know the effect of X on Y

In our hypothetical study on sugar and activity, for instance, we would want to include equal numbers of boys and girls in the experimental and control groups and match them with respect to age, ethnicity, and other characteristics, so that we could attribute differences in activity level following treatment to differences in sugar consumption only. Suppose we didn't do a good job of randomly assigning participants to our two conditions, and the experimental group ended up with 90% boys and the control group had 90% girls. If, after administering the sugar to the experimental group and the placebo (sugar substitute) to the control group, we found a difference in activity, then we would have two possible explanations: gender and sugar. In this case, gender would be a **confounding variable**—that is, an additional variable whose influence cannot be separated from the independent variable being

confounding variable
variable whose influence on the dependent variable cannot be separated from the independent variable being examined.

Number of people present (X) and likelihood of helping someone in distress (Y)

Independent variable:
Number of people present

Dependent variable:
Likelihood of helping

Hours of sleep (X) and performance on a test (Y)

Independent variable:
Number of hours asleep

Dependent variable:
Test grade

FIGURE **2.10**
INDEPENDENT AND DEPENDENT VARIABLES.
Remember: The response, or dependent variable (DV), depends on the treatment. It is the treatment, or independent variable (IV), that the researcher manipulates.

experimental studies

What type of questions might be researched?	What is the most suitable method of answering the question?	What is the best use for this kind of study?	What is the main limitation of this kind of study?	FIGURE **2.11**
Does the independent variable cause the dependent variable? Does *X* cause *Y*? Do smiles with raised eyebrows versus those without lead to more offers of dates?	Random assignments of participants, controlled experimental conditions in a lab setting	Most useful for the researcher to infer cause	Results cannot always be applied to the real world	**CHARACTERISTICS OF EXPERIMENTAL STUDIES.** With experiments, researchers may find cause and effect based on the independent and dependent variables.

examined (sugar). As most of the people in the sugar group were also male, we do not know whether male gender or sugar consumption was responsible for the difference in active behavior. These two variables are confounded and cannot be teased apart.

The power of the experimental design is that it allows us to say that the independent variable (or treatment) caused changes in the dependent variable, as long as everything other than the independent variable was held constant (see Figure 2.11). Random assignment guarantees group equivalence on a number of variables and prevents ambiguity over whether effects might be due to other differences in the groups.

In addition to random assignment to control and experimental groups, a true experiment requires experimental control of the independent variable. Thus, researchers must make sure that all environmental conditions (such as noise level and room size) are equivalent for the two groups. Again, the goal is to make sure that nothing affects the dependent variable besides the independent variable.

In our experiment on sugar consumption and activity level, the researcher first must randomly assign participants to either the experimental group (in which participants receive some amount of sugar) or the control group (in which participants receive some sugar substitute). The outcome of interest is activity level, and so each group might be videotaped for a short period 30 minutes after eating the sugar or sugar substitute. But what if the room where the experimental group was given the sugar was several degrees warmer than the room where the control group

Relaxation training (X) and blood pressure (Y)

Independent variable:	Dependent variable:
Relaxation training	Blood pressure

Research Methods in Psychology **55**

received the sugar substitute, and our results showed that the participants in the warmer room were more active? Could we feel confident that sugar led to increased activity level? No, because the heat in that room may have caused the increase in activity level. In this case, room temperature would be the confounding variable.

Any knowledge participants and experimenters have about the experimental conditions to which participants have been assigned can also affect outcome. In **single-blind studies,** participants do not know the experimental condition to which they have been assigned. This is a necessary precaution in all studies to avoid the possibility that participants will behave in a biased way. For example, if participants know they have been assigned to a group that receives a new training technique on memory, then they might try harder to perform well. This would confound the results.

Another possible problem can come from the experimenter knowing who is in which group and unintentionally treating the two groups somewhat differently. This could result in the predicted outcome simply because the experimenter biased the results. In **double-blind studies,** neither the participants nor the researchers (at least the ones administering the treatment) know who has been assigned to which condition. Ideally, then, neither participants nor those collecting the data should know which group is the experimental group and which is the control group. The advantage of double-blind studies is that they prevent experimenter expectancy effects. **Experimenter expectancy effects** occur when the behavior of the participants is influenced by the experimenter's knowledge of who is in which condition (Rosenthal, 1976, 1994).

single-blind studies
studies in which participants do not know the experimental condition (group) to which they have been assigned.

double-blind studies
studies in which neither the participants nor the researchers administering the treatment know who has been assigned to the experimental or control group.

experimenter expectancy effects
result that occurs when the behavior of the participants is influenced by the experimenter's knowledge of who is in the control group and who is in the experimental group.

Breaking New Ground

Robert Rosenthal and the Discovery of Experimenter Bias

You don't have to be a scientist to understand that it would be wrong and unethical for an experimenter to tell participants how to behave and what to do. Even for the participants to know what group they are in or what the hypotheses of the study are is bad science and biases behavior. But can what the experimenter knows change the behavior of the participants? The answers to these questions might surprise you.

Robert Rosenthal

In a classic case of scientific serendipity, Robert Rosenthal conducted an experiment to complete his PhD at Harvard University in the 1950s. He hypothesized that people who believed they were successful would be more likely to see success in others. To test this idea, he conducted an experiment in which he told one group of participants that they had done well on an intelligence test and another group they had done poorly on an intelligence test. Rosenthal randomly assigned participants to be in one of these conditions (there was also a neutral control condition where participants received no feedback on the intelligence test). Then he asked all groups to look at photographs of people doing various tasks and rate how successful they thought the people in the photos were. He reasoned that people told they did well on an intelligence test should see more success in photographs of people doing various tasks than people who were told they did not do well on the test.

As a good researcher should, Rosenthal compared the average test scores of the participants assigned to different conditions before giving them any feedback on their performance—that is, before the experimental treatment. The reason is simple: If the treatment causes a difference in behavior for the different groups, the researcher needs to make sure the groups started out behaving the same way before treatment. To Rosenthal's dismay, the groups did differ before receiving treatment. And they were also different in exactly the way that favored his hypothesis! How did this happen?

Given random assignment, the only difference in the groups at the outset was Rosenthal's knowledge of who was in which group. Somehow, by knowing who was in which group, he created behaviors that favored his hypothesis. He was forced to conclude that even when trying to be "scientific" and "objective," researchers bias results unintentionally in their favor by subtle voice changes or gestures. Instead of having a wonderful "aha moment" of scientific discovery, Rosenthal had more of an "oh no" moment: "What I recall was a panic experience when I realized I'd ruined the results of my doctoral dissertation by unintentionally influencing my research participants to respond in a biased manner because of my expectations" (Rosenthal, personal communication, April 18, 2010).

Rosenthal decided to systematically study what he came to call experimenter expectancy effects. Through several experiments, he confirmed that experimenter expectancies can ruin even the best-designed studies. Also, he discovered that two other surprising factors can change the outcome of the study as well. First, if the study involves direct interaction between an experimenter and participants, the experimenter's age, ethnicity, personality, and gender can influence the participants' behavior (Rosenthal, 1976). Second, Rosenthal stumbled upon a more general phenomenon known as the **self-fulfilling prophecy.** A self-fulfilling prophecy is a statement that changes events to cause a belief or prediction to become true. If you say "I am going to fail this exam" and then do not study, then that belief has become self-fulfilling when you do fail the exam.

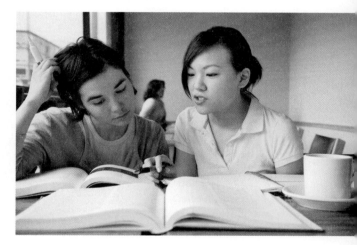

self-fulfilling prophecy
a statement that affects events to cause the prediction to become true.

Ten years after Rosenthal's first publication on experimenter expectancy effect, more than 300 other studies confirmed Rosenthal's results (Rosenthal & Rubin, 1978). Such expectancies affect animal participants as well as humans (Jussim & Harber, 2005; Rosenthal & Fode, 1963). Rosenthal's demonstration of experimenter expectancy effects and self-fulfilling prophecies also led to the development of double-blind procedures in science. Think about it: If what experimenters know about a study can affect the results, then they'd better be as blind to experimental conditions as the participants are. All of this, because he "messed up" his dissertation!

■ ■ ■

Meta-Analysis

Often researchers choose to stand back and analyze the results of the numerous studies on a given topic. For example, a researcher interested in the effects of media violence on children's aggressive behavior might want to know what all of

meta-analysis
research technique for combining all research results on one question and drawing a conclusion.

the research—not just one or two studies—suggests. **Meta-analysis** is a quantitative method for combining the results of all the published and even unpublished results on one question and drawing a conclusion based on the entire set of studies on the topic. To do a meta-analysis, the researcher converts the findings of each study into a standardized statistic known as effect size. **Effect size** is a measure of the strength of the relationship between two variables or the magnitude of an experimental effect. The average effect size across all studies reflects what the literature overall says on a topic or question. In short, meta-analysis tells us whether all of the research on a topic has or has not led to consistent findings and what the size of the effect is.

effect size
a measure of the strength of the relationship between two variables or the extent of an experimental effect.

Quick Quiz 2.2: Research Methods in Psychology

1. Dr. Lovejoy wanted to do research on real-world conditions that lead to aggression in 10-year-old children. She defined aggression as "intent to harm another person" and went to a local elementary school and videotaped a 10-minute recess period. She and her trained coders then coded the behavior of every child and counted the number of times each child acted aggressively. This is an example of what kind of research design?
   a. descriptive
   b. correlational
   c. case study
   d. experimental

2. If Dr. Lovejoy wanted to examine whether certain personality traits make aggression more likely, she would most likely use what kind of research design?
   a. descriptive
   b. correlational
   c. interview
   d. experimental

3. Researchers have consistently found that married men live longer than single men. From this finding, we can conclude that
   a. if a man gets married he adds years to his life
   b. marriage causes men to live longer

   c. being single causes men to die earlier
   d. marriage correlates with longer life

4. In research on whether sugar causes hyperactivity, researchers randomly assign children to receive no sugar, small amounts of sugar, or large amounts of sugar. They then observe and code activity levels. In this case, the sugar level is the
   a. outcome variable
   b. dependent variable
   c. independent variable
   d. control condition

5. In contrast to other kinds of research designs, a true experimental design must have two things:
   a. random assignment of participants to conditions and statistical analysis
   b. random assignment of participants to conditions and manipulation of an independent variable
   c. manipulation of an independent variable and dependent variable
   d. hypothesis testing and observation

Answers can be found at the end of the chapter.

COMMONLY USED MEASURES OF PSYCHOLOGICAL RESEARCH

measures
the tools and techniques used to assess thought or behavior.

When psychologists conduct research, they rely on a vast array of tools to measure variables relevant to their research questions. The tools and techniques used to assess thought or behavior are called **measures.** Measures in psychological science tend to fall into three categories: self-report, behavioral, and

Self-reports

Behavioral measures

Physiological measures

	Description	Use	Limitations
self-reports	Participants' written or oral accounts of thoughts, actions, feelings	Interviews and questionnaires	Social desirability bias Lack of clear insight into one's own behavior
behavioral measures	Objective observation of actions in either natural or lab settings	Small-scale studies on behavior	Time required to train coders and conduct coding Participants may modify their behavior
physiological measures	Data collection of bodily responses under certain conditions	Studies to determine the magnitude of physiological change	Specialized training on expensive equipment, on how to collect measurements, and on data interpretation
multiple measures	Several measures combined to acquire data on one aspect of behavior	Offset limitation of any single measurement Complex behaviors to study	Expensive and time-consuming

FIGURE **2.12**
COMMONLY USED MEASURES IN PSYCHOLOGY.

physiological. To study complex behaviors, researchers may employ multiple measures (see Figure 2.12).

Self-Report Measures

self-reports
written or oral accounts of a person's thoughts, feelings, or actions.

Self-reports are people's written or oral accounts of their thoughts, feelings, or actions. Two kinds of self-report measures are commonly used in psychology: interviews and questionnaires. In an interview, a researcher asks a set of questions, and the respondent usually answers in any way he or she feels is appropriate. The answers are often open-ended and not constrained by the researcher. (See the section on "Descriptive Studies," p. 47, for additional discussion on interviews.)

In a questionnaire, responses are limited to the choices given in the questionnaire. In the Stanford Prison Experiment, for example, the researchers used several questionnaires to keep track of the psychological states of the prisoners and guards. They had participants complete mood questionnaires many times during the study so that they could track any emotional changes they experienced. Participants also completed forms that assessed personality characteristics, such as trustworthiness and orderliness, which might be related to how they acted in a prison environment (Haney et al., 1973).

Self-report questionnaires are easy to use, especially in the context of collecting data from a large number of people at once. They are also relatively inexpensive. If designed carefully, questionnaires can provide important information on key psychological variables. A major problem with self-reports, however, is that people are not always the best sources of information about themselves. Why? Sometimes, as a reflection of the tendency to social desirability we discussed earlier, people do not want to reveal what they are thinking or feeling to others for fear of looking bad. Presented with questions about social prejudice, for example, respondents might try to avoid giving answers that would suggest they were prejudiced against a particular group. Another problem with self-reports is that we have to assume that people are accurate witnesses to their own experiences. Of course, there is no way to know exactly what a person is thinking without asking that person, but people do not always have clear insight into how they might behave (Nisbett & Wilson, 1977).

Behavioral Measures

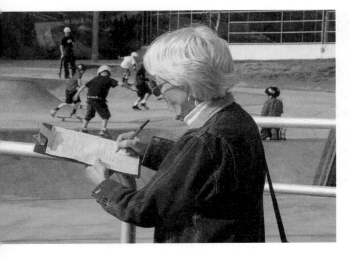

Behavioral measures involve the systematic observation of people's actions either in their normal environment (that is, naturalistic observation) or in a laboratory setting. For example, a psychologist interested in aggression might bring people into a laboratory, place them in a situation that elicits aggressive behavior, and videotape the responses. Afterward, trained coders would observe the videos and, using a prescribed method, code the level of aggressive behavior exhibited by each person. Training is essential for the coders so that they can evaluate the video and apply the codes in a reliable, consistent manner.

Behavioral measures are less susceptible to **social desirability bias** than are self-report measures. They also provide more objective measurements, because they come from a trained outside observer, rather than from the participants themselves. This is a concern for researchers on topics for which people are not likely to provide accurate information in self-report instruments. In the study of emotion, for example, measuring facial expressions from video reveals things about how people are feeling that they might not reveal on questionnaires (Rosenberg & Ekman, 2000).

One drawback of behavioral measures is that people may modify their behavior if they know they are being observed, watched, and/or measured. The major drawback of behavioral measurement, however, is that it can be time-intensive; it takes time to train coders to use the coding schemes, to collect behavioral data, and to prepare the coded data for analysis. As a case in point, one of the most widely used methods for coding facial expressions of emotion requires intensive training, on the order of 100 hours, for people to be able to use it correctly (Ekman, Friesen, & Hager, 2002)! Moreover, researchers can collect data on only a few participants at once, and therefore behavioral measures are often impractical for large-scale studies.

behavioral measures measures based on systematic observation of people's actions either in their normal environment or in a laboratory setting.

social desirability bias the tendency toward favorable self-presentation that could lead to inaccurate self-reports.

Physiological Measures

Physiological measures provide data on bodily responses. For years, researchers relied on physiological information to index possible changes in psychological states—for example, to determine the magnitude of a stress reaction. Research on stress and anxiety often measures electrical changes in involuntary bodily responses, such as heart rate, sweating, and respiration, as well as hormone changes in the blood that are sensitive to changes in psychological states. Some researchers measure brain activity while people perform certain tasks to determine the speed and general location of cognitive processes in the brain.

We will look at specific brain-imaging technologies in Chapter 3. Here we note simply that they have enhanced our understanding of the brain's structure and function tremendously. However, these technologies, and even more simple ones, like measurement of heart rate, often require specialized training in the use of equipment, collection of measurements, and data interpretation. Further, some of the equipment is expensive and can cost millions of dollars to buy and maintain. Outside the health care delivery system, only major research universities with medical schools tend to have them. In addition, researchers need years of training and experience in order to use these machines and interpret the data they generate.

Quick Quiz 2.3: Commonly Used Measures of Psychological Research

1. An advantage of self-report questionnaires is that they are easy to administer to large numbers of participants. A disadvantage of questionnaires is that
   a. they cost too much
   b. people do not always accurately report their true thoughts or feelings
   c. scoring responses is subjective
   d. they have low reliability

2. One advantage of behavioral measures compared to self-reported measures is that they
   a. are less prone to social desirability bias
   b. are less time-intensive

   c. are always more valid
   d. cost less

3. A psychologist who is interested in how brain activity relates to behavior will most likely use which kind of measure?
   a. interview
   b. questionnaire
   c. behavioral
   d. physiological

Answers can be found at the end of the chapter.

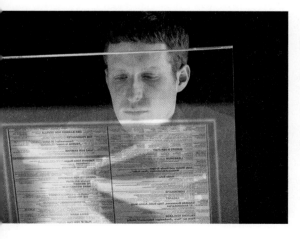

MAKING SENSE OF DATA WITH STATISTICS

Once researchers collect data, they must make sense of them. Raw data are difficult to interpret. They are, after all, just a bunch of numbers. It helps to have some way to organize the information and give it meaning. Scientists use **statistics,** mathematical procedures for collecting, analyzing, interpreting, and presenting numerical data, to make sense of their data. For example, researchers use statistics to describe and simplify data and to understand how variables relate to one another. There are two classes of statistics, descriptive and inferential.

Descriptive Statistics

descriptive statistics
measures used to describe and summarize research.

median
the score that separates the lower half of scores from the upper half.

standard deviation
a statistical measure of how much scores in a sample vary around the mean.

normal distribution
bell curve; a plot of how frequent data are that is perfectly symmetrical, with most scores clustering in the middle and only a few scores at the extremes.

Researchers use **descriptive statistics** to describe, summarize, and organize data. One useful way to describe data is by calculating the center, or average, of the scores. There are three ways to calculate an average—the mean, median, and mode. The **mean** is the arithmetic average of a series of numbers. It is calculated by adding all the numbers together and dividing by the number of scores in the series. An example of a mean is your GPA, which averages the numeric grade points for all of the courses you have taken. The **median** is the middle score, which separates the lower half of scores from the upper half. The **mode** is simply the most frequently occurring score.

Sometimes scores vary widely among participants, but the mean, median, and mode do not reveal anything about how spread out—or how varied—scores are. For example, one person's 3.0 GPA could come from getting B's in all his courses, while another person's 3.0 could result from getting A's in half of her classes and C's in the other half. The second student has much more variable grades than the first. The most common way to represent variability in data is to calculate the **standard deviation,** a statistical measure of how much scores in a sample vary around the mean. A higher standard deviation indicates more variability (or more spread); a lower one indicates less variability or less spread. So in the example above, the student with all B's would have a lower standard deviation than the student with A's and C's.

Another useful way of describing data is by plotting or graphing their frequency. **Frequency** is the number of times a particular score occurs in a set of data. A graph of frequency scores is known as a distribution. To graph a distribution we place the scores on the horizontal or X-axis and their frequencies on the vertical or Y-axis. And when we do this for many psychological variables, like intelligence or personality, we end up with a very symmetrical shape to our distribution, which is commonly referred to as either a **normal distribution** or a "bell curve"—because it looks like a bell (see Figure 2.13).

Let's look at a concrete example of a normal distribution with the well-known intelligence quotient (IQ). If we gave 1,000 children an IQ test and plotted all 1,000 scores, we would end up with something very close to a symmetrical bell-shaped distribution. That is, very few children would score 70 or below, and very few children would score 130 and above. The majority of children would be right around the average, or mean, of 100. In fact, right at two-thirds (68% to be exact) would be within 1 standard deviation (15 points) of the mean. Moreover, about 95% would be within 2 standard deviations, or between 70 and 130.

mean
the arithmetic average of a series of numbers.

mode
a statistic that represents the most commonly occurring score or value.

frequency
the number of times a particular score occurs in a set of data.

FIGURE **2.13**

BELL CURVE. Psychological variables, such as intelligence, show a normal distribution, which is represented by a bell curve.

How do we know this? We know it, because we know the exact shape of a normal distribution in the population. Knowing the shape of the distribution allows us to make inferences from our specific sample to the general population. For example, because a normal distribution has a precise shape, we know exactly what percentage of scores is within 1 standard deviation from the mean (68%) and how many are within 2 standard deviations of the mean (95%). This is why we know that a mean IQ score of 70 or lower or 130 or higher occur only five times in 100—they are very unlikely to occur by chance. It is this quality of allowing conclusions or inferences to be drawn about populations that is the starting point for the second class of statistics, inferential statistics.

Inferential Statistics

inferential statistics
analyses of data that allow us to test hypotheses and make an inference as to how likely a sample score is to occur in a population.

Inferential statistics allow us to test hypotheses and make an inference as to how likely a sample score is to occur in a population. They also allow us to determine how likely it is that two or more samples came from the same population. In other words, inferential statistics use probability and the normal distribution to rule out chance as an explanation for why the group scores are different.

But what is an acceptable level of chance before we say that a score is not likely to be chance? Five in one hundred (5%) is the most frequent choice made by psychological researchers and is referred to as the *probability level*. So if we obtain two means and our statistical analysis tells us there is only a 5% or less chance that these means come from the same population, we conclude that the numbers are not just different but statistically different and not likely by chance.

Researchers use many kinds of statistical analyses to rule out chance, but the most basic ones involve the comparison of two or more means. To compare just two means, we use a statistic known as the **t-test.** The basic logic of t-tests is to determine whether the means for your two groups are so different they are not likely to come from the same population. If our two groups are part of an experiment and one is the experimental group and the other the control group, then we are determining whether our treatment caused a significant effect, seen in different means. In short, t-tests allow us to test our hypotheses and rule out chance as an explanation.

t-test
statistic that compares two means to see whether they could come from the same population.

Let's look at an example, by returning to a question we considered earlier: Does sugar cause hyperactive behavior in children? We will make the common-sense prediction that sugar does cause hyperactive behavior. We randomly assign 100 children to consume sugar (experimental group); another 100 children do not consume sugar (control group). We then wait 30 minutes—to let the sugar effect kick in—and observe their behavior for an additional 30 minutes. We video record each child's behavior and code it on number of "high activity acts." If sugar causes activity levels to increase, then the sugar group should be higher than the no-sugar group. Our data show that the experimental (sugar) group exhibited an average of 9.13 "high activity" behaviors in the 30 minutes after taking the sugar, and the control (no-sugar) group exhibited an average of 7.91 such behaviors. On the face of it, our hypothesis seems to be supported. After all, 9.13 is higher than 7.91. However, we need to conduct a statistical test to determine whether the difference in the number of hyperactive behaviors between our groups of kids who ate sugar versus those who did not really represents a true difference between these two different populations of kids in the real world.

The t-test is the test to use in this case, the purpose of which is to determine whether the difference between the two means $(9.23 - 7.61 = 1.62)$ is a chance

Beware of Statistics in Advertising

Learning about research methods plays a crucial role in understanding psychological science, but it offers huge practical advantages as well. You can learn how to look at claims in the news and advertisements with a critical eye to challenge your assumptions about things that matter to you in your own life. Much of what you learn in this class may be forgotten not long after you leave college. But you are bombarded with advertisements dozens of times each day, something that will continue throughout your life. So let's look briefly at three scenarios that will help you to be a more critical and intelligent consumer of information.

> Scenario 1
> A billboard advertising a popular hybrid vehicle: "The car more people would buy again."

That sounds great! Not only is the car good for the environment (which is one reason to get it), but it also gets great mileage (which will save you money), and people like it (they must if they say they would buy it again). Are you sold yet?

Wait a minute. What did the ad actually say? The car more people would buy again. More than what? The meaning of this claim depends entirely on what this vehicle is being compared to. The implication is that more people would buy this car again than would buy any other car. But what did they actually compare it to?

> other hybrids?
> all other cars?
> a horse and buggy?

These are things you need to know. Otherwise, you can't judge what the statement means. Advertisers regularly leave such information out and hope you will fill in the blank with what helps them most. In this case, they hope and assume you fill in the blank with "all other cars."

> Scenario 2
> In an ad in the morning paper, Company B reports on a recent lab study showing that just a half ounce of its new drug—let's call it "No-Cold"—killed 37,202 germs in a test tube in less than 15 seconds! (adapted from Huff, 1954)

The implication is that "No-Cold" is a great cold medicine—perhaps better than others—on the basis of these hard scientific data. Let's take this claim apart though. Can you see what is wrong with this statement? Here are a few things to consider:

1. The fact that a substance works well in a test tube does not mean it will work in the human throat or respiratory tract. The test tube is a controlled environment, whereas a host of factors interact in the human body. Temperature, moisture, other bacteria, the human immune system, and phlegm are just a few examples of such factors.

2. The ad doesn't say what kind of germs "No-Cold" killed. Were they the kind that cause colds? In fact, medical researchers still have little idea of the specific viruses (germs) that cause colds, though some of them have

occurrence or not. If we calculate our t-test and find out that the probability (p-level) these two means came from the same population is .55, then we cannot rule out chance as an explanation. Because there is a 55% chance our two means came from the same population, we conclude the means are not significantly different from each other; children who eat sugar are no more active than those who do not. In this case, our hypothesis is *not* supported, and we are forced to conclude that we have no evidence that sugar actually increases activity level. By the way, these figures are hypothetical but completely consistent with the actual literature on the topic of sugar and activity level (Kanarek, 1994; Krummel, Seligson, & Guthrie, 1996).

FIGURE **2.14**

BILLIONS OF DOLLARS SPENT ON EDUCATION. If you wanted to persuade someone that education spending is out of control, which graph would you use to make your case?

been isolated. Were these germs even relevant to colds? Were they even viruses, for that matter? (The common cold is caused by a variety of viruses.) Can you identify any other problems with the ad?

Scenario 3
Graphic displays of data can be misleading.

Consider Figures 2.14a and 2.14b, both of which depict the billions of dollars spent on education over a 1-year period. Figure 2.14b seems to show a much bigger increase in spending on education than Figure 2.14a. If you look

closely, however, both depict a $2 billion increase in spending over a 1-year period. The information contained in each picture is exactly the same, but the slopes of the lines differ dramatically. This difference stems from how the illustrations' vertical axis is segmented. If you want to imply that the spending increases in education are insufficient, then you might graph them as shown in Figure 2.14a. Figure 2.14a has $2 billion increments, so it shows a gradual increase across the year. Figure 2.14b, on the other hand, uses $0.2 billion increments. Businesses, journalists, and politicians can mislead people all the time by graphically distorting data.

Rejecting a hypothesis is never fun. We may have really wanted sugar to be a cause of activity level, and in fact most parents believe this. But it is not what the evidence shows, and we have to conclude that sugar does not cause hyperactive behavior regardless of what we want to believe. This is a perfect example of a very widely held assumption being false. Scientists keep a distance from their ideas; they don't believe what they think—at least not until it can be confirmed and replicated.

As useful and helpful as statistics are to help us understand our results, be aware, however, that they also can be and are used to mislead people. To see how, read "Psychology in the Real World: Beware of Statistics in Advertising."

Quick Quiz 2.4: Making Sense of Data With Statistics

1. If two sets of scores have the same mean, then
   a. they must have the same variability
   b. they must have similar variabilities
   c. they must have different variabilities
   d. their variabilities could be the same or they could be different

2. Why is GPA a good example of the statistic *mean*?
   a. because it is calculated by adding scores and dividing by the number of scores
   b. because it is a good measure of how well a student is doing
   c. because it measures the spread or variability of a student's performance
   d. because we can plot it on a graph

3. Scores that are widely spread apart have a
   a. high standard deviation
   b. low standard deviation
   c. high mean
   d. low reliability

Answers can be found at the end of the chapter.

In the Stanford Prison Experiment, college students assigned to the role of either a prison guard or a prisoner acted their parts so well that the distinction between reality and the world created for this study disappeared. The extreme distress experienced by some of the prisoners forced the researchers to end the simulation earlier than planned.

RESEARCH ETHICS

Due to ethical guidelines, some of the most important classic studies in psychology could not be performed today. One of them is the Stanford Prison Experiment, which you read about at the beginning of this chapter. This experiment subjected participants to conditions that so altered their behavior, the researchers had to intervene and end the study early. When this study was done, in 1971, there were few ethical limitations on psychological research. Since then, and partly as a consequence of studies like the Stanford Prison Experiment, professional organizations and universities have put in place strict ethical guidelines to protect research participants from physical and psychological harm.

Ethics are the rules governing the conduct of a person or group in general or in a specific situation, or, stated more simply, ethics are standards of right and wrong. What are the ethical boundaries of the treatment of humans and animals in psychological research? In psychology today, nearly every single study conducted with humans and animals must pass through a rigorous review of its methods by a panel of experts. If the proposed study does not meet the standards, it cannot be approved.

Another notable example of research that would violate current ethics guidelines was a classic series of studies by Stanley Milgram in the early 1960s. Milgram's landmark research on obedience is discussed in more detail in Chapter 14, but we mention it here for its pivotal role in the development

ethics
the rules governing the conduct of a person or group in general or in a specific situation— or more simply, standards of right and wrong.

of ethical guidelines for human psychological research. Milgram, like many other social psychologists of the mid–20th century, was both fascinated and horrified by the atrocities of the Holocaust and wondered to what extent psychological factors influenced people's willingness to carry out the orders of the Nazi regime. Milgram predicted that most people are not inherently evil and argued that there might be powerful aspects of social situations that make people obey orders from authority figures. He designed an experiment to test systematically the question of whether decent people could be made to inflict harm on others.

Briefly, Milgram's studies of obedience involved a simulation in which participants were misled about the true nature of the experiment. Thinking that they were part of an experiment on learning, they administered what they thought were electrical shocks to punish the "learner," who was in another room, for making errors. In spite of protest from the "learner" when increasingly intense shocks occurred, the experimenter pressured the "teachers" to continue administering shocks. Some people withdrew from the study, but most of the participants continued to shock the learner. After the study, Milgram fully explained to his participants that, in fact, the "learner" had never been shocked or in pain at all (Milgram, 1974).

Milgram's study provided important data on how easily decent people could be persuaded by the sheer force of a situation to do cruel things. What is more, Milgram conducted many replications and variations of his findings, which helped build knowledge about human social behavior. But was it worth the distress it exerted on the participants? One could ask the same of the Stanford Prison Experiment. The prison study, though dramatic, created much publicity but did not generate a great deal of scientific research. Although the prison experiment led to some reform in U.S. prisons, it is hard to know whether the deception of the participants and the emotional breakdowns some of them experienced was worth it. What do you think?

Connection

Social psychologists have demonstrated both in the lab and in the real world that otherwise normal folks can be pressured to do cruel things, such as give people shocks to the point of knocking them unconscious (or so they believe).

See "Obedience," Chapter 14, "Social Behavior," p. 552.

Ethical Research With Humans

The Milgram study is one of the most widely discussed studies in the history of psychology. A number of psychologists protested it on ethical grounds (Baumrind, 1964). The uproar led to the creation of explicit guidelines for the ethical treatment of human subjects. Today all psychological and medical researchers must adhere to the following guidelines:

1. *Informed consent:* Tell participants in general terms what the study is about, what they will do and how long it will take, what the known risks and benefits are, and whom to contact with questions. They must also be told that they have the right to withdraw at any time without penalty. This information is provided in written form and the participant signs it, signifying consent. If a participant is under the age of 18, informed consent must be granted by a legal guardian. Informed consent can be omitted only in situations such as completely anonymous surveys.

2. *Respect for persons:* Safeguard the dignity and autonomy of the individual and take extra precautions when dealing with study participants, such as children, who are less likely to understand that their participation is voluntary.

3. *Beneficence:* Inform participants of costs and benefits of participation; minimize costs for participants and maximize benefits. For example, many have argued that the Milgram study was worth the distress (cost) it may have caused participants, for the benefit of the knowledge we have gained about how readily decent people can be led astray by powerful social situations. In fact, many of the participants said that they were grateful for this opportunity to gain knowledge about themselves that they would have not predicted (Milgram, 1974).

4. *Privacy and confidentiality:* Protect the privacy of the participant, generally by keeping all responses confidential. Confidentiality ensures that participants' identities are never directly connected with the data they provide in a study.

5. *Justice:* Benefits and costs must be distributed equally among participants.

In Milgram's study, participants were led to believe they were taking part in a learning study, when in fact they were taking part in a study on obedience to authority. Is this kind of deception ever justified? The answer (according to the American Psychological Association, APA) is that deception is to be avoided whenever possible, but it is permissible if these conditions are met: It can be fully justified by its significant potential scientific, educational, or applied value; it is part of the research design; there is no alternative to deception; and full debriefing occurs afterward. **Debriefing** is the process of informing participants of the exact purposes of the study—including the hypotheses—revealing any and all deceptive practices and explaining why they were necessary to conduct the study and ultimately what the results of the study were.

Debriefing is required to minimize any negative effects (e.g., distress) experienced as a result of the deception. Deception comes in different shades and degrees. In the Stanford Prison Experiment, all participants were fully informed about the fact that they would be assigned the roles of a prisoner or a guard. In that sense there was no deception. But they were not informed of the details and the extent to which being in this study would be like being in a real prison world. They were not told upfront that if they were assigned to the "prisoner" role, they would be strip-searched. When they were taken from their homes, the "prisoners" were not told this was part of the study. Not informing participants of the research hypotheses may be deceptive, but not telling participants that they might experience physical pain or psychological distress is a much more severe form of deception and is not ethically permissible. Not revealing the hypotheses to participants beforehand not only is permissible but also is necessary to prevent biased and invalid responses.

Today, to ensure adherence to ethical guidelines, **institutional review boards (IRBs)** evaluate proposed research before it is conducted to make sure research involving humans does not cause undue harm or distress. Should Milgram's study have been permitted? Were his procedures ethical by today's standards? To this day, there are people who make strong cases both for and against the Milgram study on ethical grounds, as we have discussed. It is harder to justify what Zimbardo did in the prison experiment.

Ethical Research With Animals

Human participants are generally protected by the ethical guidelines itemized above. But what about animals? They cannot consent, so how do we ethically treat animals in research?

debriefing
the explanation of the purposes of a study following data collection.

institutional review boards (IRBs)
organizations that evaluate research proposals to make sure research involving humans does not cause undue harm or distress.

The use of nonhuman species in psychological research is even more controversial than is research with humans. There is a long history in psychology of conducting research on animals. Typically, such studies concern topics that are harder to explore in humans. We cannot, for instance, isolate human children from their parents to see what effect an impoverished environment has on brain development. Researchers have done so with animals. The subfields of biological psychology and learning most often use animals for research. For instance, to determine what exactly a particular brain structure does, one needs to compare individuals who have healthy structures to those who do not. With humans this might be done by studying the behavior of individuals with accidental brain injury or disease and comparing it to the behavior of normal humans. Injury and disease, however, never strike two people in precisely the same way, and so it is not possible to reach definite conclusions about the way the brain works by just looking at accidents and illness. Surgically removing the brain structure is another way to determine function, but this approach is obviously unethical with humans. In contrast, nonhuman animals, usually laboratory rats, offer the possibility of more highly controlled studies of selective brain damage. For example, damage could be inflicted on part of a brain structure in one group of rats while another group is left alone. Then the rats' behaviors and abilities could be observed to see whether there were any differences between the groups.

Strict laws and ethical standards govern the treatment of animals used in research.

Animals cannot consent to research, and if they could, they would not likely agree to any of this. Indeed, it is an ongoing debate as to how much animal research should be permissible at all. Because animal research has led to many treatments for disease (e.g., cancer, heart disease), as well as advances in understanding basic neuroscientific processes (such as the effects of environment on brain cell growth), it is widely considered to be acceptable. Animal research is acceptable, that is, as long as the general conditions and treatment of the animals is humane.

If informed consent is the key to ethical treatment of human research participants, then humane treatment is the key to the ethical use of animal subjects. The standards for humane treatment of research animals involve complex legal issues. State and federal laws generally require housing the animals in clean, sanitary, and adequately sized structures. In addition, there are separate IRBs to evaluate proposals for animal research. They require researchers to ensure the animals' comfort, health, and humane treatment, which also means keeping discomfort, infection, illness, and pain to an absolute minimum at all times. If a study requires euthanizing the animal, it must be done as painlessly as possible.

Despite the existence of legal and ethical safeguards and the importance for medical research in humans, some animal rights groups argue that any and all animal research should be discontinued, unless it directly benefits the animals. These groups contend that computer modeling can give us much of the knowledge sought in animal studies and eliminates the need for research with animals. In addition, current brain imaging techniques, which allow researchers to view images of the living human brain, reduce the need to sacrifice animals to examine their brain structures (P. F. Thompson et al., 2000).

As is true of all ethical issues, complex and legitimate opposing needs must be balanced in research. The need to know, understand, and treat illness must be balanced against the needs, well-being, and rights of participants and animals. Consequently, the debate and discussion about ethical treatment of humans and animals must be ongoing and evolving.

Quick Quiz 2.5: Research Ethics

1. When conducting research with humans, researchers
   a. never have to obtain informed consent if it interferes with the research
   b. almost always must obtain informed consent
   c. always must obtain informed consent
   d. used to be required to obtain informed consent, but this requirement has been discontinued

2. Current guidelines on research ethics state that when studying humans, deception
   a. must be avoided whenever possible
   b. can be used only if it's of the research design
   c. must be followed by debriefing
   d. must be fully justified
   e. all of the above

3. Ethical guidelines for research with nonhuman animals state that
   a. informed consent is always required
   b. ethical and humane conditions must exist throughout the entire research process
   c. computer modeling must always be tried before research with animals
   d. deception can be used if fully justified

Answers can be found at the end of the chapter.

Bringing It All Together:
Making Connections in Psychological Research
Can Experience Change the Brain?

Can enriching experiences actually improve brain function and/or make the brain grow faster? By looking at different research approaches to answering this question and at some of the ethical issues involved, we can see why certain methods are chosen over others and get a sense of the cumulative nature of science.

In the early 1960s a group at the University of California, Berkeley, decided to study the effects of different environments on the brains of rats (Bennett et al., 1964; Rosenzweig et al., 1962). In numerous experimental studies, the researchers randomly assigned genetically similar rats to either enriched or impoverished environments for up to 30 days. The enriched environments included many opportunities and apparatus for play and activity, such as running wheels and tubes to climb, as well as food and water. The impoverished

environments provided only food and water. As you might have guessed, the independent variable in these experiments was how enriched the environment was; the dependent variables were change in brain size and/or changes in the growth of brain cells. The researchers found that rats raised in enriched environments showed evidence of growth in brain tissue compared to the animals reared in the impoverished environments. They also replicated their basic finding many times. By doing so, they established that rats raised in the enriched conditions did indeed develop more brain tissue and thicker cortexes. Moreover, because this

Nature & Nurture

The fact that a stimulating environment results in greater neural growth than an impoverished environment is an example of how nurture and nature interact.

finding was based on an experimental design with random assignment—the groups of rats were equivalent at the beginning of each experiment—we can conclude that enriching experience actually caused their brains to grow more.

These experiments all involved true experimental designs, in which the animals were randomly assigned to different environmental conditions, all aspects of the study were tightly controlled, and the animals were euthanized afterward to allow for detailed study of brain structure. One of the main reasons we study these phenomena in animals is to learn how these processes work in humans, but ethical limitations prevent human research. Thus, the animals serve as models for how human brain organization and function might be modified by experience in humans.

But do rats serve as good models for how things happen in humans? Although rat and human brains have many similarities, they also have a multitude of anatomical differences. This suggests that rat brain organization is not a perfect model for understanding human brain organization.

Research on humans is necessary to know whether environmental enrichment causes changes in the human brain, but the ways in which we can study such processes in humans are limited. Clearly it would be unethical even to randomly assign babies to live in either enriched or impoverished environments for several years so that we could assess differences in their behavior or brain activity. Which research designs might be appropriate to address these questions with humans?

quasi-experimental design

research method similar to an experimental design except that it makes use of naturally occurring groups rather than randomly assigning subjects to groups.

Probably the most rigorous design that one could apply in this context is a **quasi-experimental design,** which is much like an experimental design except that it makes use of naturally occurring groups rather than randomly assigned ones. For example, some humans grow up in more enriched environments than others, benefiting perhaps from specialized training or unique experiences.

Several quasi-experimental studies have focused on people who received intensive musical training—something beyond the normal level of experience or enrichment. According to studies of brain images, people who have received intensive musical training, especially those who started it before age 7, have a thicker corpus callosum (the band of nerve fibers that connects the two halves of the brain) than nonmusicians (Schlaug et al., 1995). This finding means that musicians have more communication between the two sides of the brain than people who have not had such training. Further, brain imaging studies comparing the brains of experienced musicians with those of nonmusicians reveal increased brain growth relative to control subjects in regions associated with music-related skills (Schlaug et al., 1995). Another recent

Early musical training not only develops a child's appreciation for music, but also correlates with increases in brain size relative to children who don't learn to play an instrument at a young age.

study reported that musicians have a larger cerebellum (an area involved in motor coordination) than nonmusicians (Hutchinson et al., 2003).

These findings suggest that musical training can change the brain, but because the researchers relied on naturally occurring groups and the groups were not matched, the results are correlational, *rather than* causal. That is, we cannot conclude that musical training causes brain growth in particular areas of the brain. Only true experiments, with random assignment, allow us to draw conclusions about cause and effect, so any group differences observed in a quasi-experimental design cannot be attributed to a specific cause. Remember that correlation is not causation, but causation does require correlation.

Quick Quiz 2.6: Bringing It All Together: Making Connections in Psychological Research

1. What is an enriched environment?
   a. a living situation that provides ample opportunity for play and activity
   b. a living environment that provides optimal nutritional enrichments as well as adequate sleeping space
   c. a living space with room and plenty of water
   d. a living situation with all of the latest toys and games

2. What is the most rigorous study design that can be used to study the effects of enrichment on brain development in humans?
   a. experimental design
   b. case study
   c. correlational design
   d. quasi-experimental design

Answers can be found at the end of the chapter.

Chapter **Review**

THE NATURE OF SCIENCE

- Science is about empirically testing our ideas and learning whether our understanding of the world is correct.

- The key attitudes of science are skepticism, openness to new ideas based on evidence, and intellectual honesty.

- The scientific method by which research is conducted can be summed up by OPTIC: Observing, Predicting, Testing, Interpreting, and Communicating. Scientists start with observations of the world, make predictions once they see a pattern, devise a study to test predictions, interpret results with the aid of statistics and decide whether the prediction was correct or not, and publish their work to clearly describe findings to others. These new findings lead to new predictions, and the whole process begins anew.

- Pseudoscience lacks cumulative progress, disregards empirical facts, lacks skepticism of its own assumptions, and vaguely describes how it came to its conclusions, which often stem from loose and distorted logic.

- In experimental designs, researchers randomly assign participants to conditions and carefully manipulate the predicted cause (independent variable), then look for differences in outcome (dependent variables). True experiments address the question "Does X cause Y?"

RESEARCH METHODS IN PSYCHOLOGY

- Psychologists use three types of research designs to test their ideas: descriptive designs, correlational designs, and experimental designs.

- In descriptive designs, researchers simply observe and describe what they see. They address the question "What is X?" They don't manipulate anything or have any real predictions to test.

- In correlational designs, researchers measure two or more things carefully to see whether or not they are related. They address the question "Is X related to Y?" These designs use correlational statistics to interpret the results and to make and test hypotheses, but do

not allow researchers to draw any conclusions about causality.

- Researchers use correlation coefficients to assess the strength and direction of association between two variables.

- In experimental designs, researchers randomly assign participants to conditions and carefully manipulate the predicted cause (independent variable), then look for differences in outcome (dependent variables). True experiments address the question "Does X cause Y?"

COMMONLY USED MEASURES OF PSYCHOLOGICAL RESEARCH

- Psychological researchers draw on several types of tools to measure variables relevant to their research questions. These measures fall into three major categories: self-report, behavioral, and physiological.

- Self-reports are people's written or oral accounts of their thoughts, feelings, or actions.

- Behavioral measurements involve systematic observation of people's actions in either their normal life situations (naturalistic observation) or laboratory situations.

- Physiological measures include various types of measures of bodily responses. Each measure has strengths and weaknesses. By employing multiple measures, researchers offset the limitations of any given measure.

MAKING SENSE OF DATA WITH STATISTICS

- Descriptive statistics organize data for interpretation and help researchers evaluate their hypotheses. The mean is the arithmetic average of a set of data. The median is the score that separates the lower half of scores from the upper half.

- Variability is the spread between the lowest and highest values in a set of data. Variability is measured in terms of the standard deviation around the mean.

- Inferential statistics go beyond describing data and allow researchers to test hypotheses and rule out chance as an explanation for the findings.

RESEARCH ETHICS

- Ethics are standards of right and wrong that guide people's behavior.

- Professional ethics have been developed to protect the rights of humans and animals who participate in psychological research. Researchers must obtain informed consent from human participants before a study begins. Animals cannot provide informed consent, but strict ethical guidelines exist to ensure humane living conditions and treatment.

BRINGING IT ALL TOGETHER: MAKING CONNECTIONS IN PSYCHOLOGICAL RESEARCH

- Research on environmental enrichment and brain growth using experimental designs with animal models

and correlational studies with humans illustrates how numerous methodological issues unfold in a given research area.

Key **Terms**

behavioral measures, p. 60
case study, p. 48
confounding variable, p. 54
control group, p. 53
correlation coefficient, p. 52
correlational designs, p. 50
debriefing, p. 68
dependent variable, p. 53
descriptive designs, p. 47
descriptive statistics, p. 62
double-blind studies, p. 56
effect size, p. 58
ethics, p. 66
experiment, p. 53
experimental group, p. 53
experimenter expectancy effects, p. 56
frequency, p. 62

hypothesis, p. 42
independent variable, p. 53
inferential statistics, p. 63
institutional review boards (IRBs), p. 68
mean, p. 62
measures, p. 58
median, p. 62
meta-analysis, p. 58
mode, p. 62
naturalistic observation, p. 48
normal distribution, p. 62
physiological measures, p. 61
placebo, p. 54
population, p. 47
pseudoscience, p. 45
quasi-experimental design, p. 71
random assignment, p. 53

replication, p. 44
representative sample, p. 49
research design, p. 46
samples, p. 47
scientific method, p. 42
scientific thinking, p. 40
self-fulfilling prophecy, p. 57
self-reports, p. 59
single-blind studies, p. 56
social desirability bias, p. 60
standard deviation, p. 62
statistics, p. 61
theory, p. 42
t-test, p. 63
variable, p. 46

Quick Quiz **Answers**

Quick Quiz 2.1: 1. d 2. b 3. a 4. c **Quick Quiz 2.2: 1. a 2. b 3. d 4. c 5. b** **Quick Quiz 2.3: 1. b 2. a 3. d**
Quick Quiz 2.4: 1. d 2. a 3. a **Quick Quiz 2.5: 1. c 2. e 3. b** **Quick Quiz 2.6: 1. a 2. d**

Challenge Your Assumptions **Answers**

- Psychology is not a science. **False. See pp. 40–42.**

- Eating sugar does not make you hyperactive. **True. See pp. 50–56.**

- Knowing what you're looking for in an experiment has no effect on the outcome. **False. See pp. 56–57.**

The Biology
of Behavior

3

Chapter Outline

Challenge *Your Assumptions*

TRUE OR FALSE?

- Learning can change the size of your brain.
- Traits that are genetically influenced are set and unchanging after conception.
- In people who are blind, vision areas of the brain do not function.
- You can't easily learn a new language as an adult.

Answers can be found at the end of the chapter.

T ake a look at the painting in Figure 3.1. It is pleasing, colorful, and nicely done. It features realistic color, perspective, and shadowing. It seems, perhaps, not extraordinary—except by virtue of its maker. He cannot see at all.

Born blind to an impoverished family in Turkey, Esref Armagan started drawing at a young age; later he began painting with oils and acrylics. Armagan has been actively painting for over 30 years. His work strikes us not only for its beauty but also for how it depicts objects in a way that a sighted person would see them. How can someone who has never seen anything in his life create beautiful paintings that depict realistic images? It seems as if his brain is doing something that his eyes cannot.

You can find a hint of how this is possible at the Tactile Dome, part of the Exploratorium in San Francisco. Once there, you enter a room full of common, recognizable objects such as a cheese grater, an egg carton, and a sieve. You look at them and feel them.

Then you proceed through a pitch-black tunnel. As you find your way through it by touch, you feel the common objects that you saw earlier. When you reach the end, you are prompted to think back and remember your way through the tunnel. Surprisingly, the memory of what you encountered along the path in the dark with your hands is visual! Your brain has taken a tactile experience and unwittingly converted it into a visual memory. How?

The Tactile Dome and the skills of Esref Armagan both suggest that our experience of the world is not a direct representation of what is out there. The brain can change our experiences— give us visual memories for tactile experiences. The brain is both fixed and flexible in how it acts. While most of us use the rear portion of our brains to process visual information, Esref Armagan uses that area when he paints by the feel of his hands.

In this chapter and the one that follows, we will explore what is known about how the brain works, how it supports behavior, and how it is transformed by experience. Our main task in this chapter is to introduce the biological systems that are most relevant to a basic understanding of psychology. In so doing, we will look at the role of heredity and evolution in shaping the brain and behavior, explore the workings of the nervous system, and learn of the relationship between chemicals called hormones and behavior. Given how much biological and environmental forces interact and influence each other, we use the term *softwire* to reflect this new way of thinking about nature and nurture. As mentioned in Chapter 1, softwiring, in contrast to hardwiring, means that biological systems involved in thought and behavior—genes, brain structures, brain cells, etc.—are inherited but open to modification from the environment (Herbert & Rich, 1999; Ottersen, 2010). Much of who we are is more softwired than hardwired. ■

FIGURE **3.1**

BLUISH VASE BY ESREF ARMAGAN, A BLIND PAINTER. Besides being beautiful to look at, Armagan's vivid, realistic paintings and drawings challenge conventional thinking about the brain and its ability to adapt and overcome limitations imposed on it.

GENES AND BEHAVIOR

We seldom have trouble accepting the idea that heredity is responsible for outward family resemblances, such as the shape of the nose and face, height, and the color of hair and skin. But when it comes to behavior, many of us are uncomfortable with the idea that heredity might determine what we think and do. Yet heredity very much affects behavior and experience, although it does not operate on thought and behavior in a simple, deterministic way.

Before we can explore how heredity and behavior interact, we must know something about the structures and mechanisms involved in heredity. A **chromosome** is a cellular structure that holds our genetic information in threadlike strands of DNA. Humans have 23 pairs of chromosomes in the nucleus of each cell of the body, except red blood cells, which do not have nuclei. **DNA (deoxyribonucleic acid),** the genetic material that makes up chromosomes, is a large coiled molecule that contains genes. **Genes** are small segments of DNA that contain information for producing proteins. These proteins in turn make up most chemicals and structures in the body (see Figure 3.2). Genes influence specific characteristics, such as height or hair color, by directing the synthesis of proteins. All of the genetic information contained in our DNA makes up our **genome.**

The fact that the individuals in a population are different from one another on a given trait—such as eye color, height, or personality—is a result of genetic

DNA (deoxyribonucleic acid)
a large molecule that contains genes.

genome
all the genetic information in DNA.

chromosome
a coiled-up thread of DNA.

genes
small segments of DNA that contain information for producing proteins.

The human body contains 100 trillion cells.

Each human cell (except red blood cells) contains a nucleus. Each body cell nucleus contains 46 chromosomes arranged in 23 pairs.

Each parent contributes one chromosome to every pair.

Each chromosome contains numerous genes, segments of DNA that contain instructions to make proteins—the building blocks of life.

FIGURE **3.2**

DNA, CHROMOSOMES, AND THE HUMAN CELL. Every cell in the human body contains the same genetic material distributed in 23 pairs of chromosomes.

differences. More specifically, genes within a population, or entire species, often take different forms. These different forms are known as **alleles** (W. R. Clark & Grunstein, 2000; Starr & Taggart, 2004). Individuals inherit one allele from each parent. Sometimes both alleles have the same form, but not always. Each gene in an allele pair can produce different characteristics. Take eye color, for example. The allele inherited from one parent may produce brown eyes, but the allele inherited from the other parent may produce blue eyes. Brown eyes result from a dominant gene. **Dominant genes** show their effect even if there is only one copy of that gene in the pair. So if you have one brown eye allele and one blue eye allele, chances are you will have brown eyes.

A **recessive gene** shows its effects only when both alleles are the same. Consequently, a person will have blue eyes only if he or she inherits an allele for blue eyes from each parent.

To understand how heredity affects behavior, psychologists turn to the science of **behavioral genetics** (J. L. Fuller & Thompson, 1960). Four principles of behavioral genetics are especially relevant in psychology:

1. The relationship between specific genes and behavior is complex.
2. Most specific behaviors derive from dozens or hundreds of genes—not one or two.
3. By studying twins and adoptees, behavioral geneticists may disentangle the contributions of heredity and environment to behavior.
4. The environment influences how and when genes affect behavior.

Let's consider each of these principles in turn.

The Complex Connection Between Genes and Behavior

The connection between genes and behavior is complex. To understand how genes influence behavior, we must abandon the notion of simple causation (Rutter, 2006). Genes seldom make behaviors a certainty. For example, no single gene causes anxiety. Both genetic and environmental factors make anxiety more likely to trouble some people than others.

In a few cases, having a specific gene guarantees an outcome—such as the incurable neuromuscular disease called Huntington's disease—but these outcomes are primarily physical, not behavioral. Typically, a specific gene plays only a small part in creating a given behavior, and genetic influence itself is only part of the story. Environmental events such as smoking during pregnancy, early childhood experiences, stress or trauma, and enriched environments all interact with genes to make specific behaviors more or less likely.

Polygenic Influence on Behavior

The second principle of behavioral genetics states that traits tend to be influenced by many genes (W. R. Clark & Grunstein, 2000; Hamer & Copeland, 1998). Relatively few human traits result from single genes. And, as stated above, they tend to be physical rather than behavioral characteristics. The hereditary passing on of traits determined by a single gene is known as **monogenic transmission.** Huntington's disease is an example of monogenic transmission.

Connection
Genetic influence accounts for about 50% of the differences in performance on intelligence tests, leaving about the same amount to be explained by nongenetic influences.
See "The Nature and Nurture of Human Intelligence," Chapter 10, "Intelligence, Problem-Solving, and Creativity," p. 402.

However, the number of potential outcomes for most traits and behaviors is not small. There is wide variation in intelligence, for example. Numerous genes contribute to intelligence. When many genes interact to create a single characteristic, the process is known as **polygenic transmission.** Other examples of polygenic traits include skin color, mental disorders, personality traits (such as whether a person is likely to be adventurous), height, and weight (W. R. Clark & Grunstein, 2000; Ebstein, 2006; Evans et al., 2007).

Genes and the Environment

A third principle of behavioral genetics is that teasing apart and identifying genetic and environmental influences on behavior requires special techniques. The extent to which a characteristic is influenced by genetics is known as **heritability.** Researchers use twin-adoption studies and gene-by-environment studies to study heritability.

In order to tease apart the role of genes and environment on behavior experimentally, researchers would have to hold one of these factors constant while varying the other one. That is hard to do because, for obvious ethical reasons, researchers cannot assign people to grow up in the same or different environments. Nor can researchers assign people to be either genetically alike or different. Fortunately, nature does both of these things for us. Researchers take advantage of genetically similar and different people by studying twins, siblings, and unrelated individuals reared together or apart.

Twin-Adoption Studies   **Fraternal twins** develop from two different eggs fertilized by two different sperm, as are any two siblings born at separate times. Thus, genetically speaking, fraternal twins are no more alike or different than are nontwin brothers and sisters. **Identical twins** develop from a single fertilized egg that splits into two independent cells. As a result, identical twins develop from two embryos with identical genetic information. Fraternal and identical twins provide a natural population for research to determine how much of a trait is due to genetics and how much is due to environment.

The best way to untangle the effects of genetics and environment is to study twins who are adopted, which is what **twin-adoption studies** do. The logic of the twin-adoption approach is simple yet powerful. Identical twins are 100% alike genetically, whereas fraternal twins, like all siblings, share only 50% of their genes. Adopted children and their adoptive

Actors Maggie and Jake Gyllenhaal inherited their blue eyes from their parents. Blue eyes are a recessive trait, which means that each parent must possess at least one allele for blue eyes.

parents and siblings share no genes. If genes play a strong role in a trait, then the greater the genetic similarity, the greater the similarity on the trait should be. That is, similarity should be strongest in identical twins reared together and next in identical twins reared apart. It should be modest in siblings reared together and biological parent–offspring. Similarity should be weakest in adopted siblings and adoptive parent–offspring. As we will see in later chapters, this pattern holds for intelligence, mental disorders, and even personality, suggesting a moderately strong genetic component to these outcomes.

Gene-by-Environment Studies   A second technique in the study of heritability, **gene-by-environment interaction research,** allows researchers to assess how genetic differences interact with environment to produce certain behavior in some people but not in others (Moffitt, Caspi, & Rutter, 2005; Thaparet et al., 2007). Instead of using twins, family members, and adoptees to vary genetic similarity, gene-by-environment studies directly measure genetic variation in parts of the genome itself and examine how such variation interacts with different kinds of environments to produce different behaviors. Individuals do not differ in whether or not they have a gene, but rather in the form that gene takes. For example, the same gene in different people might vary in the number of particular DNA sequences it has. Some DNA sequences are long in some people and short in others. Differences in the length of DNA sequences represent a *genetic marker.* Through gene-by-environment studies, researchers have learned that genetic markers interact with a stressful environment to make depression more likely in some people (short DNA sequence) than in others (long DNA sequence) (Caspi, Sugden, et al., 2003; Kendler et al., 2005).

Connection

How do stress and growing up in an abusive environment work together with genetic vulnerability to make depression more likely?

See "Depression and Its Causes," Chapter 15, "Psychological Disorders," p. 600.

gene-by-environment interaction research method of studying heritability by comparing genetic markers; allows researchers to assess how genetic differences interact with environment to produce certain behaviors in some people but not in others.

Epigenetics: How the Environment Changes Gene Expression

A fourth—and, in many ways, the most important—principle of behavioral genetics is a relatively new one: The unique and incomparable **genotype,** or genetic makeup, that each of us is born with is not the end point but the starting point of gene expression. Genes can be switched off by many different things, and our experiences and environmental exposure, starting in the womb, are among the off switches. This principle is seen most clearly in **epigenetics** (Meaney, 2010; Rutter, 2006). Epigenetics is the study of changes in the way genes are expressed—that is, are activated or deactivated—without changing the sequence of DNA. This means that experience (nurture) shapes our nature. More specifically, chemical tags attach to the double-helix structure of DNA and different patterns of tags turn off a gene or leave it on (see Figure 3.3). The incredible fact is that whether these tags get activated or "turned on" is determined by environmental events such as diet, drinking, and even exercise (Watters, 2006; I. C. G. Weaver et al., 2004).

The food we eat, the drugs we take, and our exposure to certain chemicals in the environment, among other things, can have epigenetic consequences. Contrary to what many people think, genes are not destiny. They are simply the starting point for biological structures. Many things—including experience—can turn genes on or off. Epigenetic effects have been demonstrated in a host of psychological traits from attention deficit hyperactivity disorder (ADHD) and aggression to dementia, obesity, and anxiety—just to name a few (Curley et al., 2010;

genotype the entire genetic makeup of an organism.

epigenetics study of changes in the way genes are turned on or off without a change in the sequence of DNA.

The field of study known as epigenetics examines how experience can turn genes on or off. Studies with rats suggest that parental nurturing may turn off genes that make a child vulnerable to stress.

Gluckman & Hanson, 2008; Mill & Petronis, 2008; Sweatt, 2010).

What is even more amazing is that these environmentally produced tags can be inherited—passed on from parent to offspring. In other words, genetics is not the only way inheritance works. It also works via epigenetics (Meaney, 2010; Zimmer, 2008). For example, a gene that is "on" in your grandparent but gets turned off environmentally in one of your parents can be inherited by you as turned off. This secondary form of inheritance via epigenetics is sometimes referred to as *soft inheritance* to contrast it with traditional genetically based inheritance (Graff & Mansury, 2008). The term *soft inheritance* is similar and related to *softwiring*—both express the fact that nature and nurture work side-by-side.

Epigenetics offers one explanation for why identical twins—whose genome is 100% alike—end up being not completely identical on numerous traits. Indeed, they do not have identical fingerprints. Recent longitudinal research shows that differences in epigenetic tags in identical twins already exist in early to middle childhood and that these differences can be related to personality differences in twins (Kaminsky et al., 2008; Wong et al., 2010). In short, although identical twins share 100% of their genotype, their **phenotype**—or their observed characteristics—may be subtly different because different epigenetic tags are turning different genes on or off.

FIGURE **3.3**

THE EPIGENOME: METHYL GROUPS TAG DNA TO TURN GENES OFF.
Methyl groups are tags that attach to DNA itself. These tags act as off switches and silence a particular gene. Incredibly, these methyl group tags come about purely by what happens to us—our diet, drugs, or exposure to certain chemicals. Genes, therefore, are not destiny, but simply a starting point for biological structures.

What a pregnant mother does and is exposed to can change which genes get turned off in the body of her baby.

phenotype
the organism's observed characteristics.

Quick Quiz 3.1: Genes and Behavior

1. Genes occur in pairs, or alternate forms of each other, called
   a. chromosomes
   b. alleles
   c. base-pairs
   d. ribosomes

2. Why are twin-adoption studies powerful ways to untangle the effects of genes and environment on thought and behavior?
   a. because they allow both genetic and environmental similarity to be compared and contrasted
   b. because twins share genes

   c. because of epigenetics
   d. because they allow researchers to experimentally manipulate genetic and environmental similarity

3. Nurturing behavior in rats can produce calmer, less-stressed offspring because genes that are involved in stress reactions are turned off. This is an example of
   a. epigenetics
   b. genetic engineering
   c. recessive genes
   d. dominant genes

Answers can be found at the end of the chapter.

central nervous
system (CNS)
the part of the
nervous system
that comprises the
brain and spinal
cord.

peripheral
nervous system
the part of the
nervous system
that comprises
all the nerve cells
in the body outside
the central nervous
system.

somatic nervous
system
nerve cells of the
peripheral nervous
system that trans-
mit sensory in-
formation to the
central nervous
system (CNS) and
those that transmit
information from
the CNS to the
skeletal muscles.

THE NERVOUS SYSTEM

The human genome contains an estimated 20,000–25,000 genes (National Human Genome Research Institute, 2010). At least half of these genes code for proteins in the brain, where they play a central role in seeing, hearing, thinking, memory, learning, movement, and all other behavior. The brain mediates all of our experiences and orchestrates our responses to those experiences.

The nervous system controls all the actions and automatic processes of the body. Ultimately, everything we experience and do results from the activity of nerve cells, which are organized in a net of circuits far more complex than any electrical system you could imagine. Let's look at the organization and basic elements of the nervous system and at how the nervous system transmits information.

Organization of the Nervous System

The human nervous system has two main parts and several components, as depicted in Figure 3.4. It is divided into the **central nervous system (CNS),** which includes the brain and spinal cord, and the **peripheral nervous system,** which consists of all the other nerve cells in the body. The peripheral nervous system includes the somatic nervous system and the autonomic nervous system. The **somatic nervous system** transmits sensory information to the brain and spinal cord and from the brain and spinal cord to the skeletal muscles. The **autonomic nervous system (ANS)** serves the involuntary systems of the body, such as the internal organs and glands.

Autonomic means "self-governing," and to a large extent the structures served by the autonomic nervous system control bodily processes over which we

autonomic
nervous system
(ANS)
all the nerves of
the peripheral ner-
vous system that
serve involuntary
systems of the
body, such as the
internal organs and
glands.

NERVOUS SYSTEM

- Central nervous system (CNS)
  - Brain
  - Spinal cord
- Peripheral nervous system (PNS)
  - Somatic nervous system (voluntary)
  - Autonomic nervous system (involuntary)
    - Sympathetic nervous system (arousing)
    - Parasympathetic nervous system (calming)

FIGURE **3.4**

THE NERVOUS SYSTEM. The central nervous system processes incoming information and crafts a response if one is needed. The peripheral nervous system transmits information between the external environment and internal systems of the body and the central nervous system.

sympathetic nervous system
the branch of the autonomic nervous system that activates bodily systems in times of emergency.

have little conscious control, such as changes in heart rate and blood pressure. The ANS has two main branches: the **sympathetic nervous system** and the **parasympathetic nervous system.** The nerves of these systems control muscles in organs such as the stomach, small intestine, and bladder and in glands such as the sweat glands. The sympathetic branch of the ANS is responsible for what the physiologist Walter Cannon (1939) labeled the *fight-or-flight response*; that is, it activates bodily systems in times of emergency. The main function of the sympathetic nervous system is activating the body, for example, by increasing the heart rate, dilating the pupils of the eyes, or inhibiting digestion. The function of the parasympathetic branch of the ANS is largely one of relaxation, or returning the body to a less active, restful state. All of the systems that are aroused by the sympathetic nervous system are relaxed by the parasympathetic nervous system (see Figure 3.5). Because of its effects on these various bodily

parasympathetic nervous system
the branch of the autonomic nervous system that usually relaxes or returns the body to a less active, restful state.

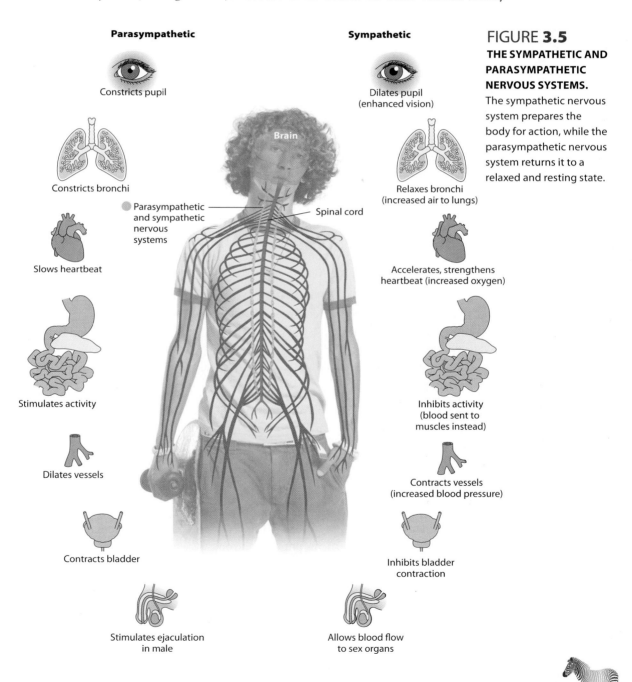

FIGURE **3.5**
THE SYMPATHETIC AND PARASYMPATHETIC NERVOUS SYSTEMS.
The sympathetic nervous system prepares the body for action, while the parasympathetic nervous system returns it to a relaxed and resting state.

Parasympathetic
Constricts pupil
Constricts bronchi
Slows heartbeat
Parasympathetic and sympathetic nervous systems
Stimulates activity
Dilates vessels
Contracts bladder
Stimulates ejaculation in male

Brain
Spinal cord

Sympathetic
Dilates pupil (enhanced vision)
Relaxes bronchi (increased air to lungs)
Accelerates, strengthens heartbeat (increased oxygen)
Inhibits activity (blood sent to muscles instead)
Contracts vessels (increased blood pressure)
Inhibits bladder contraction
Allows blood flow to sex organs

systems, the ANS produces many of the physical sensations we experience during emotional arousal, such as a racing heart or sweaty palms.

The Cells of the Nervous System: Glial Cells and Neurons

Without a nervous system, we would have no sensory experiences—no seeing, hearing, touching, tasting, smelling, or feeling. We would also have no thoughts, memories, or emotions. Everything we sense or do is accomplished by means of nerve cells.

The central nervous system is made up of two types of cells: glial cells and neurons. *Glia* is the Greek word for glue. Indeed, **glial cells** serve the primary function of holding the CNS together. Specifically, they provide structural support, promote efficient communication between neurons, and remove cellular debris (Kandel, 2000b). We now know that they also play an important role in communication between neurons, produce the material that insulates neurons (myelin), aid cell metabolism, help form the blood-brain barrier, and play a key role in the control of breathing (Ballanyi, Panaitescu, & Ruangkittisakul, 2010; Eroglu & Barres, 2010; Pfrieger, 2002).

Neurons are the cells that process and transmit information throughout the nervous system. Within the brain, neurons receive, integrate, and generate messages. By most estimates, there are more than 10 billion neurons in the human brain. Each neuron has approximately 10,000 connections to other neurons, making for literally trillions and trillions of neural connections in the human brain (Hyman, 2005; Nauta & Feirtag, 1979). Thus, it is understandable that some scientists consider the human brain to be one of the most complex structures in the known universe. Over the last 125 years, three major principles of neuroscience have emerged concerning the neuron and how it communicates with other neurons (Kandel, 2006):

1. Neurons are the building blocks of the nervous system. All the major structures of the brain are composed of neurons.
2. Information travels within a neuron in the form of an electrical signal by action potentials.
3. Information is transmitted between neurons by means of chemicals called **neurotransmitters.**

Let's explore each of these principles to better understand the mechanisms of brain function and behavior.

The Structure and Types of Neurons

Whereas most cells in the body have a round shape, neurons are spidery, with long branches and projections. Neurons are so small they cannot be seen with the naked eye, and only a strong microscope can magnify them enough to be viewed and described. In the late 1800s, the Spanish anatomist Santiago Ramón y Cajal deciphered the precise nature and structure of nerve cells, which he named neurons. It was Ramón y Cajal who identified the three major parts of the neuron: cell body, dendrites, and axon.

As in other cells, the cell body, or **soma,** of the neuron contains a *nucleus* and other components needed for cell maintenance and function (see Figure 3.6). The genes that direct neural change and growth lie within the nucleus itself. Extending from the soma is a long projection called the **axon,** which transmits electrical

glial cells
central nervous system cells that provide structural support, promote efficient communication between neurons, and serve as scavengers, removing cellular debris.

neurons
the cells that process and transmit information in the nervous system.

neurotransmitters
chemicals that transmit information between neurons.

soma
the cell body of the neuron.

axon
long projection that extends from a neuron's soma; it transmits electrical impulses toward the adjacent neuron and stimulates the release of neurotransmitters.

dendrites
fingerlike projections from a neuron's soma that receive incoming messages from other neurons.

myelin sheath
the fatty substance wrapped around some axons, which insulates the axon, making the nerve impulse travel more efficiently.

synapse
the junction between an axon and the adjacent neuron, where information is transmitted from one neuron to another.

terminal buttons
little knobs at the end of the axon that contain tiny sacs of neurotransmitters.

sensory neurons
nerve cells that receive incoming sensory information from the sense organs (eye, ear, skin, tongue, nose).

motor neurons
nerve cells that carry commands for movement from the brain to the muscles of the body.

mirror neurons
nerve cells that are active when we observe others performing an action as well as when we are performing the same action.

Soma

Dendrites

Nucleus

Axon

Myelin sheath
surrounding the axon

Sending Neuron

Axon

Terminal button

Axon

Receiving Neuron

FIGURE **3.6**

STRUCTURE OF THE NEURON. When an electrical impulse is received at the dendrites, it moves through the axon to the terminal buttons. There it triggers the release of neurotransmitters, which carry the impulse across the synapse to the dendrites of the receiving neuron.

impulses toward the adjacent neuron. On the other side of the soma are the **dendrites,** fingerlike projections that receive incoming messages from other neurons.

The axons of some neurons are wrapped in a fatty **myelin sheath.** Just like rubber around an electrical wire, the myelin sheath insulates the axon so that the impulse travels more efficiently and strengthens the connection to adjacent neurons. The process of *myelination* is a gradual one that starts before birth and continues into early adulthood (R. D. Fields, 2008). The glial cells myelinate axons throughout the nervous system (Nave, 2010). The junction between the axon and the adjacent neuron is known as the **synapse.** At the end of the axon, at each synapse, is a **terminal button** containing tiny sacs of neurotransmitters. When an electrical impulse reaches the terminal button, it triggers the release of neurotransmitter molecules into the gap between neurons, known as the *synaptic cleft*. The neurotransmitter carries the signal across the synaptic cleft to the next neuron.

There are three kinds of neurons: sensory neurons, motor neurons, and interneurons. **Sensory neurons** receive incoming sensory information from the sense organs (eyes, ears, skin, tongue, and nose). Any sensation you receive—anything you see, hear, touch, taste, or smell—activates sensory neurons, which take the message to the brain for processing. **Motor neurons** take commands from the brain and carry them to the muscles of the body. Each time you move any muscle in your body, intentionally or not, motor neurons are at work. Recently, researchers have identified motor neurons that are active when monkeys observe others performing an action as well as when the monkey itself undertakes the same action (Rizzolatti et al., 1996). Neurons that behave this way are called **mirror neurons,** and they appear to play an important role in learning (Rizzolatti & Craighero, 2004). The most

Connection
Mirror neurons support learning by imitation as well as empathy.
See "The Developing Infant and Child," Chapter 5, "Human Development," p. 178; "Imitation, Mirror Neurons, and Learning," Chapter 8, "Learning," p. 336; and "Prosocial Behavior," Chapter 14, "Social Behavior," p. 572.

Sensory and motor neurons working in concert with the brain make this sprinter's elegant strides possible.

definitive work on mirror neurons has been conducted on monkeys—because it has been possible to record directly from single neurons deep in their brains. So far this has not been done with humans, but there is indirect evidence of groups of neurons acting as mirrors in humans (Debes, 2010). The discovery of mirror neurons has changed the way we understand a wide range of human experience, including how we feel empathy toward others.

interneurons neurons that communicate only with other neurons.

Interneurons communicate only with other neurons. Most interneurons connect neurons in one part of the brain with neurons in another part. Others receive information from sensory neurons and transmit it to motor neurons for action. So if you touched a sharp object, interneurons in the spinal cord would receive pain information from sensory neurons in your fingers and communicate it to motor neurons in the muscles of your arm so that you could pull your hand away. Interneurons are the most common kind of neuron in the brain, outnumbering sensory and motor neurons by at least 10 to 1 (Nauta & Feirtag, 1979).

Neural Communication: The Action Potential

Neural communication is a two-step process. First, an impulse travels one way from the dendrites along the axon and away from the soma, a process that is both electrical and chemical. Second, the impulse releases chemicals at the ends of the neurons, which are released into the synaptic cleft to transmit the message to another neuron. The first process is known as an action potential, and the second is *neurotransmission,* which we discuss in the next section.

action potential the impulse of positive charge that runs down an axon.

The **action potential** is the positively charged impulse that moves down an axon. This happens by virtue of changes in the neuron itself. The neuron, like all cells in the body, is surrounded by a membrane. This membrane is somewhat permeable, which means that it lets only certain particles move through it. The fluid inside and outside the cell contains electrically charged particles called **ions.** Positively charged sodium and potassium ions and negatively charged

ions chemically charged particles that predominate in bodily fluids; found both inside and outside cells.

chloride ions are the most common. Channels in the membrane of the neuron allow ions to flow between the inside and outside of the cell. Some of these channels are always open. Others, called *voltage-dependent channels,* open only when certain electrical conditions are met, as we will discuss shortly.

Due to the flow of ions into and out of the neuron, there is a difference in charge inside the cell compared to outside the cell at all times. In the resting state, there is an excess of negatively charged particles inside the axon. The fluid outside the axon has a positive charge. This charge difference between the inside and outside of the neuron is known as a *potential*. When a neuron is at rest, the charge difference between the inside and the outside of the axon is −70 millivolts (mV). This value is the **resting potential** of the neuronal membrane (see Figure 3.7a).

Neurons do not stay at rest, however. An incoming impulse—which may have been stimulated by events as different as pressure to the skin and the thought of a loved one—can temporarily change the potential. How does this happen? A message received from sense receptors in the skin or from other neurons changes the axonal membrane's permeability, especially to positively charged sodium ions. If an incoming impulse increases the positive charge inside the neuron to a certain threshold, the neuron becomes *depolarized* and fires an action potential. The sodium channels at the top of the axon fly open and positively charged sodium ions pour into the cell. The influx of sodium leads to a brief spike in positive charge, raising the membrane potential from −70 mV to +40 mV. This surge in positive charge is the action potential (see Figure 3.7b).

Once initiated, the action potential causes sodium channels to close and potassium voltage-dependent channels to open (see Figure 3.7c). As positively charged potassium ions flow out of the cell, the membrane potential returns to its resting state of −70 mV. While the neuron is returning to its resting state, it temporarily becomes super negatively charged. During this brief period, known as the **refractory period,** the neuron cannot generate another action potential.

We can summarize the electrical changes in the neuron from resting to action potential to refractory period and back to the resting state as follows (see also Figure 3.7d):

1. Resting potential is −70mV.
2. If an incoming impulse causes sufficient depolarization, voltage-dependent sodium channels open and sodium ions flood into the neuron.
3. The influx of positively charged sodium ions quickly raises the membrane potential to +40 mV. This surge in positive charge inside the cell is the action potential.
4. When the membrane potential reaches +40 mV, the sodium channels close and potassium channels open. The outward flow of positively charged potassium ions restores the negative charge inside the cell.

This process repeats all along the axon, as the impulse moves toward the synapse. As the action potential subsides in one area, it immediately depolarizes the next portion of membrane, causing sodium channels to open there, continuing or *propagating* the action potential. Like a wave, the action potential travels along the axon, until it reaches the terminal buttons. In myelinated neurons, the action potential travels faster still, as depolarization occurs only at gaps in the myelin sheath and the action potential jumps from gap to gap (see Figure 3.6).

resting potential
the difference in electrical charge between the inside and outside of the axon when the neuron is at rest.

refractory period
the span of time, after an action potential has been generated, when the neuron is returning to its resting state and the neuron cannot generate an action potential.

(a) Resting potential: Time 1.
In the resting neuron, the fluid outside the axon contains a higher concentration of positive ions than the inside of the axon, which contains many negatively charged anions (A–).

(b) Action potential: Time 2.
An action potential occurs in response to stimulation of the neuron. Sodium channels in the axonal membrane open, and positively charged sodium ions (NA+) pour into the axon, temporarily raising the charge inside the axon up to +40 mV.

(c) Resting potential restored: Time 3.
As the impulse moves on down the axon, potassium (K+) channels open, allowing more K+ to flood out of the cell, restoring the negative resting potential (–70mV).

A touch or squeeze from a friend will generate an action potential.

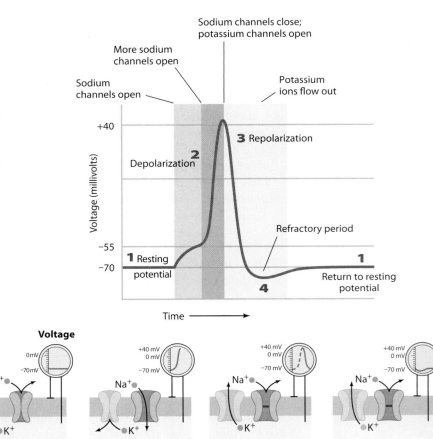

FIGURE **3.7**

MEMBRANES AND VOLTAGE CHANGES IN ACTION POTENTIALS.

Each change in membrane potential corresponds to specific changes in the axonal membrane.

(d) This graph depicts the electrical changes that occur during each stage of an action potential (resting, depolarization, repolarization, refractory period). The top portion shows changes in voltage over time as measured by direct recording from single neurons in animal research. The lower four pictures show the membrane changes that correspond to each stage. The electrical changes of an action potential occur in a few thousandths of a second. During the refractory period, no new action potential can be generated.

How fast are action potentials anyway? In the 1920s, Edgar Douglas Adrian recorded individual action potentials of sensory neurons and confirmed a speed of about 100 feet per second (Kandel, 2006). Adrian's work also confirmed the existence of thresholds—a point of no return. Once the charge inside the neuron exceeds threshold (and *only* if it exceeds threshold), the action potential fires. This is known as the **all-or-none principle;** that is, either an action potential fires or it does not.

Communication Between Neurons: Neurotransmission

The arrival of an action potential at the terminal buttons of a neuron triggers the second phase in neural transmission—the release of neurotransmitters into the synaptic cleft to pass on the impulse to other neurons. Neurotransmitters are packaged in sacs called **synaptic vesicles** in the terminal button. When an action potential reaches the terminal button, the vesicles fuse with the cell membrane of the terminal and release neurotransmitter molecules into the synaptic cleft, where they may be taken up by receptors in the dendrites of adjacent neurons (J. H. Schwartz, 2000).

Neurotransmitters bind with receptors in the receiving, or *postsynaptic,* neuron in a lock-and-key type of arrangement (see Figure 3.8). There are different types of neurotransmitters, each of which binds only with a specific receptor. For example, some receptors bind only with the neurotransmitter acetylcholine. If other neurotransmitters come in contact with acetylcholine receptors, they will not bind to them and no signal will be transmitted.

Not all of the neurotransmitter molecules that are released into the synaptic cleft bind with receptors. Usually, excess neurotransmitter remains in the synaptic cleft and needs to be removed. There are two ways to remove excess neurotransmitter from the synaptic cleft. One involves destruction by enzymes. In this process of **enzymatic degradation,** enzymes specific to that neurotransmitter bind with the neurotransmitter and destroy it. The second method, called **reuptake,** returns excess neurotransmitter to the sending, or *presynaptic,* neuron for storage in vesicles and future use. Even the neurotransmitter that binds to the dendrites of the *postsynaptic* neuron does not stay there. Eventually it disengages from the receptor and floats away. This excess neurotransmitter must be removed as well.

After a neurotransmitter binds to a receptor on the postsynaptic neuron, a series of changes occurs in that neuron's cell membrane. These small changes in membrane potential are called **graded potentials.** Unlike action potentials, these are not "all-or-none." Rather, they affect the likelihood that an action potential will occur in the receiving neuron. Some neurotransmitters, called *inhibitory* neurotransmitters, create graded potentials that decrease the likelihood of a neuron firing. One such neurotransmitter is GABA (gamma-aminobutyric acid). In contrast, *excitatory* neurotransmitters create graded potentials that *increase* the likelihood of an action potential. **Glutamate** is the most common excitatory neurotransmitter in the brain.

The excitatory potentials bring the neuron closer to threshold, while the inhibitory potentials bring it further away from threshold. The soma in the postsynaptic neuron *integrates* the various graded potentials in the postsynaptic neuron. If the integrated message from these graded potentials depolarizes the axon enough to cross the threshold, then an action potential will occur.

all-or-none principle
the idea that once the threshold has been crossed, either an action potential fires or it does not.

synaptic vesicles
tiny sacs in the terminal buttons that contain neurotransmitters.

enzymatic degradation
a way of removing excess neurotransmitter from the synapse in which enzymes specific for that neurotransmitter bind with the neurotransmitter and destroy it.

reuptake
a way of removing excess neurotransmitter from the synapse, in which excess neurotransmitter is returned to the sending, or presynaptic, neuron for storage in vesicles and future use.

graded potentials
small changes in membrane potential that by themselves are insufficient to trigger an action potential.

Connection
Many drugs used to treat depression directly affect reuptake to allow some neurotransmitters that affect mood to stay in the synapse longer.
See "Drug Therapies," Chapter 16, "Treatment of Psychological Disorders," p. 631.

glutamate
a major excitatory neurotransmitter in the brain that increases the likelihood that a postsynaptic neuron will fire; important in learning, memory, neural processing, and brain development.

(a) The neural impulse from the presynaptic neuron travels down the axon toward dendrites of the next neuron.

Soma

Dendrites

Direction of nerve impulse

Presynaptic Neuron

Terminal button

Axon

Postsynaptic Neuron

(b) In the terminal button, the impulse triggers the release of neurotransmitters into the synaptic cleft.

Terminal button

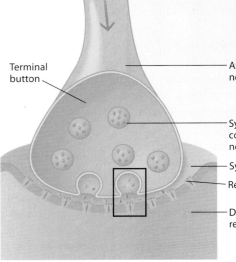

Axon of sending neuron

Synaptic vesicle containing neurotransmitters

Synaptic cleft

Receptor site

Dendrite of receiving neuron

(c) At a receptor site on the dendrite of the receiving (postsynaptic) neuron, the neurotransmitter causes channels to open and changes the membrane potential.

Neurotransmitters

Channel (open)

Synaptic vesicle releases neurotransmitters.

Neurotransmitters attach at receptor site; channel opens.

(d) Receptors will bind only with specific neurotransmitters. If no binding occurs, no action potential is generated in the postsynaptic neuron.

Transmitter will not fit receptor; channel remains closed

Transmitter will fit receptor; channel opens and ion can pass

Receptor molecules in postsynaptic membrane

FIGURE **3.8**

HOW SYNAPSES AND NEUROTRANMSITTERS WORK. In (a) two neurons connect, a presynaptic neuron and a postsynaptic neuron. They do not touch, but terminal buttons in the presynaptic neuron form a synaptic cleft with the postsynaptic neuron. In (b) the synaptic cleft has been enlarged to show the synaptic vesicles that carry neurotransmitters. They release neurotransmitters into the cleft where they bind to receptor sites on the postsynaptic neuron. In (c) we see a further enlargement of the neurotransmitters being released into the synaptic cleft and binding to receptor sites in the postsynaptic neuron. To the left is a three-dimensional artistic interpretation of neurons in the brain. In (d) we see how each receptor site binds to only one specific kind of neurotransmitter.

	Major function
Acetylcholine	Slows ANS activity; eating, drinking, neuromuscular junction; involved in learning, memory, sleeping, and dreaming
Dopamine	Plays an important role in arousal, mood (especially positive mood); oversupply correlates with schizophrenia; voluntary muscle control
Epinephrine	Increases ANS activity; fight-or-flight response
Norepinephrine	Affects CNS activity; plays role in increasing alertness, attention
Serotonin	Plays role in mood, sleep, eating, temperature regulation; undersupply correlates with anxiety and depression
GABA	Is the major inhibitory neurotransmitter in the brain; slows CNS function; correlates with anxiety and intoxication
Glutamate	Is the most common excitatory neurotransmitter in the brain; involved in learning and memory; may be involved in schizophrenia

FIGURE 3.9

NEUROTRANSMITTERS AND THEIR FUNCTIONS. Neurotransmitters can be excitatory, increasing the likelihood of an action potential, or inhibitory, decreasing the likelihood of an action potential.

Common Neurotransmitters

Within the past century, researchers have discovered at least 60 distinct neurotransmitters and learned what most of them do. Of the known neurotransmitters, the ones that have the most relevance for the study of human thought and behavior are acetylcholine, epinephrine, norepinephrine, dopamine, serotonin, GABA, and glutamate (see Figure 3.9). Neurotransmitters are found only in the brain. They are synthesized inside the neuron for the purpose of neurotransmission.

The neurotransmitter **acetylcholine (ACh)** controls muscle movement and plays a role in mental processes such as learning, memory, attention, sleeping, and dreaming. Whether ACh excites muscles or slows them down depends on what kind of receptor receives it. Furthermore, researchers have discovered that the degenerative memory disorder called Alzheimer's disease results at least partly from a decrease in ACh activity and that drugs that enhance ACh aid memory. ACh enhancers are now used to treat memory disorders such as Alzheimer's disease, and they seem to slow the progression of memory loss (Czech & Adessi, 2004; Selkoe, 2002).

Dopamine is involved in voluntarily controlling your muscles and is released during feelings of pleasure or reward. Eating a good meal, doing well on an exam, having an orgasm, or drinking a glass of water when really thirsty—each of these behaviors stimulates dopamine activity in the brain (Hamer & Copeland, 1998). Because dopamine activity makes us feel good, many drug addictions involve increased dopamine activity. For instance, cocaine blocks the reuptake of dopamine into the presynaptic neuron, leaving it in the synaptic cleft for a longer period of time before it binds to receptors in the postsynaptic neuron (Bradberry, 2007). The result is a feeling of euphoria and pleasure.

acetylcholine (ACh)
a neurotransmitter that controls muscle movement and plays a role in mental processes such as learning, memory, attention, sleeping, and dreaming.

dopamine
a neurotransmitter released in response to behaviors that feel good or are rewarding to the person or animal; also involved in voluntary motor control.

Recently both of your authors went to their own family reunions. What struck us was seeing relatives we hadn't seen in years and seeing how cousins, aunts, and uncles remind us of ourselves, our siblings, and our parents. The shape and color of their eyes, their voice, their laugh—we could see right away a common lineage. But there were differences too. Some from the same family were thin, some were not; some siblings looked like one parent, while other siblings looked like the other parent.

Connecting Psychology to Your Life: Think about your own extended family and the physical traits they share in common and on which they differ. Start with those most genetically related, your parents and your siblings. Then move to grandparents, uncles, aunts, and cousins. What traits do you share and on what traits do you differ? Can you see how genes and environment have shaped these traits in your family?

epinephrine
also known as adrenaline, a neurotransmitter that arouses bodily systems (such as increasing heart rate).

serotonin
a neurotransmitter with wide-ranging effects: involved in dreaming and in controlling emotional states, especially anger, anxiety, and depression.

GABA (gamma-aminobutyric acid)
major inhibitory neurotransmitter in the brain that tells postsynaptic neurons *not* to fire; it slows CNS activity and is necessary to regulate and control neural activity.

Epinephrine and **norepinephrine** primarily have energizing and arousing properties. (Epinephrine was formerly called "adrenaline," a term that is still widely used in everyday speech—"Wow! What an adrenaline rush!") Both epinephrine and norepinephrine are produced in the brain and by the adrenal glands that rest atop the kidneys. Epinephrine tends not to affect mental states, whereas norepinephrine increases mental arousal and alertness. Norepinephrine activity also leads to physical arousal—increased heart rate and blood pressure. People who suffer from ADHD have unusually low norepinephrine levels, and treatment sometimes includes drugs to increase norepinephrine levels (Barr et al., 2002).

Serotonin plays a role in a wide range of behaviors, including dreaming and controlling emotional states such as anger, anxiety, and depression. People who are generally anxious and/or depressed often have low levels of serotonin (Caspi, Sugden, et al., 2003; Frokjaer et al., 2009; Kendler et al., 2005). Drugs that block the reuptake of serotonin in the synapse are used to treat anxiety and depression.

People who are consistently angry and/or aggressive (especially males) often have abnormally low levels of serotonin as well. The administration of serotonin reduces aggressive behavior in monkeys (Suomi, 2005). The street drug ecstasy (MDMA), which makes people feel social, affectionate, and euphoric, stimulates extremely high levels of serotonin. Ironically, however, ecstasy ultimately interferes with the brain's ability to produce serotonin, and so depression can be an unpleasant side effect of the drug (de Win et al., 2004).

Gamma-aminobutyric acid, or **GABA,** is a major inhibitory neurotransmitter in the brain. Remember that inhibitory neurotransmitters tell the postsynaptic neurons *not* to fire. GABA slows CNS activity and is necessary for the regulation and control of neural activity. Without it, the central nervous system would have no "brakes" and could run out of control. In fact, one theory about epilepsy is that GABA does not function properly in people who suffer from the disorder (Laschet et al., 2007). Many drugs classified as depressants, such as alcohol, increase GABA activity in the brain and lead to relaxing yet ultimately uncoordinated states. Because GABA inhibits much of the CNS activity that keeps us conscious, alert, and able to form memories, large amounts of alcohol consumption can lead to memory lapses, blackouts, loss of consciousness, and even death (A. M. White, 2003).

norepinephrine
a neurotransmitter that activates the sympathetic response to stress, increasing heart rate, rate of respiration, and blood pressure in support of rapid action.

Connection

Common treatments for depression, which may result in part from a deficiency of the neurotransmitter serotonin, block the reuptake of serotonin at the synapse, making more of it available for binding with postsynaptic neurons.

See "Drug Therapies," Chapter 16, "Treatment of Psychological Disorders," p. 631.

Touring the Nervous System and the Brain

GOALS OF THE TOUR

1 **The Neuron and Synapse.** You will be able to identify parts of the neuron and synapse and describe how they communicate information.

2 **The Resting Potential and Action Potential.** You will be able to describe the membrane changes involved in maintaining the resting potential and in producing the action potential.

3 **Structures and Functions in the Human Brain.** You will be able to identify the brain's key structures and functions.

4 **Lobes of the Cerebral Cortex.** You will be able to identify the location and describe the function of the four lobes of the cerebral cortex.

5 **Visual Information in the Split Brain.** You will be able to describe hemispheric lateralization and communication in the brain.

6 **Central and Peripheral Nervous Systems.** You will be able to identify the parts of the central and peripheral nervous systems and describe the body functions they control.

The Neuron and the Synapse

1 Identify parts of the neuron and synapse and describe how they communicate information.

Presynaptic Neuron

1a **Neuron**
Stimulus to a neuron causes a neural impulse to travel down the axon toward dendrites of the next neuron.

Direction of nerve impulse

Postsynaptic Neuron

1b **Synapse**
In the terminal button, the impulse triggers the release of neurotransmitters into the synaptic cleft.

Axon of the presynaptic neuron

Terminal button

Vesicle containing neurotransmitters

Synaptic cleft

Receptor with binding site

Dendrite of postsynaptic neuron

The Resting Potential and Action Potential

Direction of nerve impulse

Axon | Membrane | Sodium channel | Potassium channel

Na⁺   K⁺   Na⁺   A⁻   A⁻   A⁻   Na⁺

2a Resting Potential

In the resting neuron, the fluid outside the axon contains a higher concentration of positive ions than the inside of the axon, which contains many negatively charged anions (A–).

Describe the membrane changes involved in maintaining the resting potential and in producing the action potential.

2

2a Action Potential

The action potential is an impulse of positive charge that sweeps down the axon.

Electrical property

Axon at time 1

Time 2

Time 3

The graph below depicts the electrical changes that occur during each stage of an action potential (**1** resting potential, **2** depolarization, **3** repolarization, and **4** refractory period).

Sodium channels open

More sodium channels open

Sodium channels close potassium channels open

Potassium ions flow out

+40

Repolarization

Depolarization

Voltage (millivolts)

−55

1 Resting potential

1

Refractory period

Return to resting potential

−70

Time

Voltage

0mV
−70mV

Na⁺

K⁺

1 Resting potential

Structures and Functions of the Human Brain

3 Identify the brain's key structures and functions.

3a Brain Stem Structures

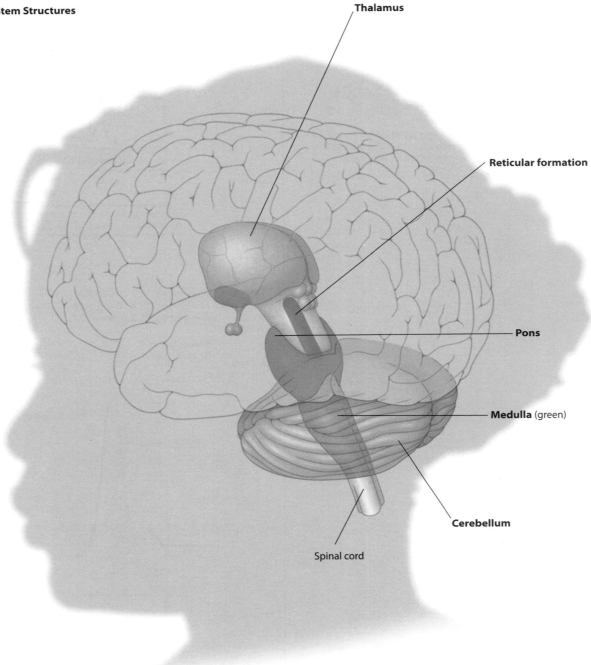

Thalamus

Reticular formation

Pons

Medulla (green)

Cerebellum

Spinal cord

Lobes of the Cerebral Cortex

Identify the location of the lobes of the cerebral cortex and describe their primary function.

4

Parietal lobe body sensation

Frontal lobe cognition, recent memory, planning of movement, and some aspects of emotion

Temporal lobe hearing and advanced visual processing

Occipital lobe vision

Visual Information in the Split Brain

5 Describe hemispheric lateralization and communication in the brain.

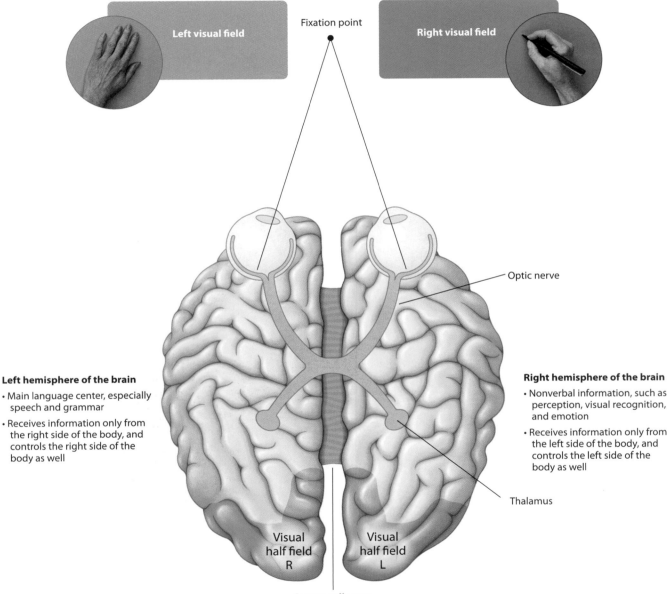

Fixation point

Left visual field

Right visual field

Optic nerve

Left hemisphere of the brain

- Main language center, especially speech and grammar
- Receives information only from the right side of the body, and controls the right side of the body as well

Right hemisphere of the brain

- Nonverbal information, such as perception, visual recognition, and emotion
- Receives information only from the left side of the body, and controls the left side of the body as well

Thalamus

Visual half field R

Visual half field L

Corpus callosum

A thick band of axons that connect brain cells in one hemisphere to the other. In healthy brains, the two sides engage in a continuous flow of information via this neural bridge and share information.

Central and Peripheral Nervous Systems

6a The Central Nervous System

⬤ Central nervous system

⬤ Brain

⬤ Spinal cord

Identify the parts of the central and peripheral nervous systems and describe the body functions they control.

6

ANSWERS

1. THE NEURON AND SYNAPSE

The *neuron* consists of a *soma, dendrites,* and an *axon.* The soma is the structure of the neuron that contains the nucleus, which consists of the genetic material including the chromosomes. The dendrites are branches of the neuron that receive information from other neurons. The axon sends information away from the soma to other neurons or cells.

When a neuron fires, it sends an electrical impulse down the axon, known as the *action potential.* When the impulse arrives at the axon terminal buttons, it causes the release of *neurotransmitter* molecules into the *synapse.* The synapse is the gap junction between two neurons. Neurons communicate with one another by means of chemical signals provided by neurotransmitters that cross the synapse.

The neurotransmitter released by the sending neuron enters the synaptic gap and attaches to a *receptor* on the postsynaptic neuron. The receptor site contains a channel that is typically closed when the receiving neuron is in the resting state (*resting potential*). When the neurotransmitter binds to the receptor site, the receptor channel opens to allow a particular *ion* to enter or leave the neuron. If a neurotransmitter causes channels for a positively charged ion like sodium (Na^+) to open, the postsynaptic neuron will become less negative in charge. The entry of sodium will cause a change in the electrical charge (potential) of the receiving neuron that may make it more likely to generate its own action potential.

2. THE RESTING POTENTIAL AND ACTION POTENTIAL

The neuron maintains electrical properties called an *electrical potential,* which is a difference in the electrical charge inside and outside of the cell. This charge difference is maintained because the membrane of the neuron is *selectively permeable.* This means some molecules can pass through the membrane more freely than others. The membrane is not permeable to large negatively charged protein molecules that are trapped inside the neuron. Inside and outside the neuron are electrically charged particles called *ions* that vary in concentrations. The ions that play an important role in the function of the neuron are sodium (Na^+), potassium (K^+), and chloride (Cl^-). These ions enter or leave the neuron through special channels provided by protein molecules that line the neuron.

The *resting potential* is the electrical property of the neuron when it is not stimulated or not sending a nerve impulse. In a typical neuron this is seen as a -70 mV charge inside relative to the outside of the membrane. During the resting potential, the sodium channels are closed, leaving a higher concentration of sodium ions outside of the neuron membrane. The negative charge of a neuron during the resting state is largely maintained by the negatively charged protein molecules trapped inside the neuron and by the inability of positively charged sodium ions to cross the membrane into the neuron.

If the neuron receives enough excitatory messages to surpass the threshold level, an *action potential* will occur, sending the nerve impulse down the axon. Positively charged sodium ions enter the neuron, and potassium ions move out. The action potential jumps from one space in the axon's myelin sheath to the next, changing membrane qualities at each space. Membrane channels for sodium close to keep sodium ions out of the neuron and potassium channels open to allow potassium to move into the neuron, restoring the resting potential.

3. STRUCTURES AND FUNCTIONS IN THE HUMAN BRAIN

The brain stem structures are embedded within the core of the brain and provide a number of vital functions for survival. These include the medulla, pons, cerebellum, reticular formation, and the thalamus.

The *medulla* is a brain structure just above the spinal cord. It controls a number of life-sustaining reflexes and functions including breathing, coughing, vomiting, and heart rate. The *pons* lies just above the medulla and is particularly involved in sleep and arousal. The *cerebellum* is a large structure at the base of the brain with many folds. It is traditionally known to be involved in motor coordination and balance but also plays a role in attention of visual and auditory stimuli and the timing of movements. The *reticular formation* is an elaborate diffuse network of neurons that runs through the core of the medulla and pons to the base of the thalamus. It plays a role in arousal, attention, sleep patterns, and stereotyped patterns such as posture and locomotion. The *thalamus* is a central structure in the brain that relays auditory, visual, and somatosensory (body senses) information to the cerebral cortex.

The limbic system comprises a number of brain structures involved in motivation, emotion, and memory. The *hypothalamus* is a small structure that is located just below the thalamus. It controls the autonomic nervous system as well as the release of hormones from the pituitary gland. It is involved in a number of functions including eating, drinking, and sexual behavior, and plays an important role in the expression of emotions and stress responses. The *hippocampus* is located in the temporal lobe and plays a role in learning and memory. Adjacent to the hippocampus is the amygdala, which is involved in fear and anxiety. The *cingulate gyrus,* a beltlike structure in the middle of the brain, is involved in attention and cognitive control.

The *cerebral cortex* is the outer layer of the brain and is involved in higher order functions such as thinking, learning, consciousness, and memory.

4. LOBES OF THE CEREBRAL CORTEX

The *cerebral cortex* is anatomically divided into four lobes: occipital lobe, parietal lobe, temporal lobe, and frontal lobe. The *occipital lobe* is located in the posterior end (back region) of the cortex and is involved in processing *visual information.* The *parietal lobe* makes up the top rear section of the cortex. The parietal lobe is involved in *bodily senses.* The area just in front of the parietal lobe is the *somatosensory cortex.* It is the primary target for the *touch senses* of the body and information for muscle-stretch receptors and joint receptors. The *temporal lobe* is the large portion of each hemisphere near the temples and lies behind the frontal lobe and below the *lateral fissure.* It is the primary region of the cortex that processes *auditory information.* The *frontal lobe* extends from the central sulcus to the anterior limit (forward region) of the brain. The region of the frontal lobe immediately adjacent to the central sulcus is called the *motor cortex* because it controls *fine movements.* The most anterior region is called the *prefrontal cortex;* it is involved in higher brain functions including *cognition* (thought processes), recent *memory,* the *planning of movement,* and some aspects of *emotion.*

5. VISUAL INFORMATION IN THE SPLIT BRAIN

Lateralization refers to the division of labor between the two cerebral hemispheres of the brain. The *left hemisphere* receives sensory information from and controls the movements in the right side of the body. Likewise, images of objects in the right visual field are projected to the left half of the retina of each eye, which in turn sends the information to the visual cortex in the left hemisphere. The left hemisphere also contains the main language area involved in the comprehension and production of language.

The *right hemisphere* receives sensory information from and controls the movements in the left side of the body. Likewise, images of objects in the left visual field are projected to the right half of the retina of each eye, which in turn sends the information to the visual cortex in the right hemisphere. The right hemisphere processes nonverbal information, such as perception, visual recognition, and emotion.

In the healthy brain the two cerebral hemispheres share information with each other across the broad band of axons called the *corpus callosum.* In some instances the corpus callosum is surgically cut, resulting in what is called a *split brain.* In the split brain, information in one cerebral hemisphere is confined to that side of the brain.

6. CENTRAL AND PERIPHERAL NERVOUS SYSTEMS

The nervous system is made up of the *central nervous system* and the *peripheral nervous system.* The central nervous system is comprised of the brain and the spinal cord. The peripheral nervous system consists of all nerve fibers outside of the brain and spinal cord. The peripheral nervous system is made up of two major divisions: the *somatic nervous system* and the *autonomic nervous system.*

The *somatic nervous system* consists of nerve fibers conveying information from the brain and spinal cord to skeletal muscles; this information controls movement and sends information back to the brain via the spinal cord from sensory receptors located in various parts of the body.

The *autonomic nervous system* controls the glands and muscles of the internal organs such as the heart, digestive system, lungs, and salivary glands, and it consists of the sympathetic and the parasympathetic branches. The *sympathetic branch* arouses the body, mobilizes its energy during physical exercise and in stressful situations, and activates the adrenal gland to release epinephrine into the bloodstream. The *parasympathetic branch* calms the body and conserves and replenishes energy.

The street drug known as ecstasy stimulates the release of high levels of the neurotransmitter serotonin, which makes people temporarily feel euphoric and affectionate. By interfering with the body's ability to produce serotonin, however, ecstasy eventually may cause depression in some people.

Connection

Glutamate does not function properly in people with schizophrenia, and so they become confused. Restoring glutamate function is the focus of new treatments for schizophrenia.
See "Schizophrenia," Chapter 15, "Psychological Disorders," p. 607, and "Drug Therapies," Chapter 16, "Treatment of Psychological Disorders," p. 631.

Glutamate, the brain's major excitatory neurotransmitter, is important in learning, memory, neural processing, and brain development. More specifically, glutamate facilitates growth and change in neurons and the migration of neurons to different sites in the brain, all of which are basic processes of early brain development (Nadarajah & Parnavelas, 2002). It also amplifies some neural transmissions so that a person can tell the difference between important and less important information. For example, which is more important? To notice that a car is skidding out of control in front of you or that your shoes are still the same color they were when you put them on this morning? Glutamate boosts the signals about the car. The physiologically stimulating effects of nicotine in tobacco stem from glutamate synapses (Guillem & Peoples, 2010).

Summary of the Steps in Neural Transmission

We have considered the complex phenomena of action potentials and neurotransmission and described the neurotransmitters involved in human thought and behavior. Before we discuss the major structures of the brain, let's take time to summarize the process of neural communication.

- The information in neural transmission always travels in one direction in the neuron—from the dendrites to the soma to the axon to the synapses. This process begins with information received from the sense organs or other neurons, which generate a nerve impulse.
- The dendrites receive a message from other neurons. That message, in the form of an electrical and chemical impulse, is then integrated in the soma.

- If the excitatory messages pass the threshold intensity, an action potential will occur, sending the nerve impulse down the axon. If the inhibitory messages win out, the likelihood that the postsynaptic neuron will fire goes down.

- The nerve impulse, known as the action potential, travels down the axon, jumping from one space in the axon's myelin sheath to the next, because channels are opening and closing in the axon's membrane. Ions pass in and out of the membrane—mostly sodium and potassium.

- This impulse of opening and closing channels travels like a wave down the length of the axon, where the electrical charge stimulates the release of neurotransmitter molecules in the cell's synapses and terminal buttons.

- The neurotransmitters are released into the space between neurons known as the synaptic cleft. Neurotransmitters released by the presynaptic neuron then bind with receptors in the membrane of the postsynaptic neuron.

- This binding of neurotransmitter to receptor creates electrical changes in the postsynaptic neuron's cell membrane, at its dendrites. Some neurotransmitters tend to be excitatory and increase the likelihood of an action potential. Others tend to be inhibitory and decrease the likelihood of an action potential.

- The transmission process is repeated in postsynaptic neurons, which now become presynaptic neurons.

Quick Quiz 3.2: The Nervous System

1. Which branch of the nervous system is responsible for the fight-or-flight response?
   a. the parasympathetic nervous system
   b. the somatic nervous system
   c. the sympathetic nervous system
   d. the central nervous system

2. The fingerlike projections on neurons that receive input from other neurons are called
   a. dendrites
   b. nuclei
   c. axons
   d. terminal buttons

3. What property of the neuron is most directly responsible for the changes that lead up to an action potential?
   a. sodium ions outside the cell
   b. its permeable membrane
   c. chloride ions inside the cell
   d. the flux of potassium ions

4. What is the most common excitatory neurotransmitter in the brain?
   a. GABA
   b. serotonin
   c. glutamate
   d. acetylcholine

Answers can be found at the end of the chapter.

THE BRAIN

The brain is a collection of neurons and glial cells that controls all the major functions of the body; produces thoughts, emotions, and behavior; and makes us human. This jellylike mass at the top of the spine has been mapped and described in astonishing detail. Here we consider the evolution of the brain, look at key brain regions, and explore what is currently known about their specialized functions. At this point, the picture is still far from complete, and neuroscientists continue to piece it together.

Evolution of the Human Brain

Evolution provides a fundamental example of how biology and environment interact. As we discussed in Chapter 1, over long periods of time, nature selects traits and behaviors that work well in a given environment. Recall the example of the beetle population becoming more brown than green as brown beetles blended into their surroundings better and were more likely to survive and reproduce. This natural selection process gradually leads to big changes in living forms and structures—from cells to muscles to brains to new species.

The human brain has been shaped, via natural selection, by the world in which humans have lived. It is worth noting here that brains do not fossilize to allow a present-day analysis, but the skulls that hold them do. By looking at the size and shape of skulls from all animals and over very long time periods, scientists can glean something about how and when human brains evolved. The evolution of the human brain is a fascinating story. Although the details lie well beyond the scope of this book, we can consider a general outline of brain evolution (Dunbar, 2001; Jerison, 2000; Klein, 1999; Striedter, 2005).

Flatworms, whose species dates back about 500 million years, were probably the first organisms with brains. Still, the flatworm brain consists of scarcely more than a bundle of nerve cells. Within a few million years, the first primitive vertebrates (animals with backbones) appeared. They were jawless fish, and they had a bigger mass of nerve cells than flatworms (Jerison, 2000). The first land animals came into existence around 450 million years ago and the first mammals around 200 million years ago. Land animals had more than a bundle of neurons above the spinal cord; they had complex brains with numerous structures.

The first primates lived around 55 million years ago—10 million years after the dinosaurs went extinct (Jerison, 2000). Compared to other mammals, birds and reptiles, and fish, primates have relatively large amounts of brain cortex, allowing more complex thinking and problem solving. The earliest ancestors of humans appeared in Africa about 6 million years ago. One of our closest evolutionary relatives, the Neanderthals (*Homo neanderthalensis*), lived from about 350,000 to 28,000 years ago, when they were replaced by our species (*Homo sapiens*). Neanderthals had brains slightly larger on average than those of modern humans (see Figure 3.10). Nevertheless, these early humans did not produce highly complex tools, may have possessed very rudimentary language, and never made symbolic pieces of art, at least none that have been found. In other words, their brains were modern in

From Neanderthal fossils, scientists have determined that this close ancestor of modern humans had a less complex brain along with many other distinctive anatomical features.

Australopithecus
(4 million years ago)

The brain capacity ranges from 450 to 650 cubic centimeters (cc).

Homo erectus
(1.6 million to 100,000 years ago)

Further development of skull and jaw are evident and brain capacity is 900 cc.

Neanderthal
(350,000 to 28,000 years ago)

The human skull has now taken shape: the skull case has elongated to hold a complex brain of 1,450 cc.

Homo sapiens
(200,000 years ago to present)

The deeply convoluted brain reflects growth in areas concerned with higher mental processes (1,300 cc).

FIGURE **3.10**

EVOLUTION OF THE HUMAN BRAIN OVER THE LAST 4 MILLION YEARS. An early form of pre-human, *Australopithecus,* had a brain about one third the size of the modern human (*H. sapiens*) brain. In general, the overall brain size has grown over the course of 4 million years. But note that Neanderthal's brain size was slightly larger than ours. Just as important as overall size for modern human thought and behavior is the relative enlargement of the frontal lobe area. This can be seen in the less sloped forehead of modern humans compared to their earlier ancestors.

size but not modern in function. It is possible, therefore, that the modern human brain took up to 100,000 years to become fully wired and complex, all the while staying the same overall size.

Overview of Brain Regions

In evolutionary terms, then, the human brain is the result of a few hundred million years of natural selection. The three major regions of the brain, in order from earliest to develop to newest, are the hindbrain, the midbrain, and the forebrain (see Figure 3.11). By comparing the relative size of each region in distinct kinds of animals that vary in evolutionary age (see Figure 3.12), we gain an appreciation of how these regions evolved. When we compare brains from these different groups, we see an increase in size of the forebrain in humans and other primates (Jerison, 2000).

— Forebrain

— Midbrain

Pons
Cerebellum } Hindbrain
Medulla

FIGURE **3.11**

THREE MAIN BRAIN STRUCTURES: HINDBRAIN, MIDBRAIN, AND FOREBRAIN. The hindbrain regulates breathing, heart rate, arousal, and other basic survival functions. The midbrain controls eye muscles, processes auditory and visual information, and initiates voluntary movement. The forebrain controls cognitive, sensory, and motor function and regulates temperature, reproductive function, eating, sleeping, and emotions.

FIGURE 3.12

THE BRAIN STRUCTURE OF MAMMALS. Mammals have many of the same brain structures, but of different relative sizes. Notice how much larger the cerebral cortex is in the human than in chimpanzees, cats, and rats. Also notice the increase in brain folds in primates.

medulla
a hindbrain structure that extends directly from the spinal cord; regulates breathing, heart rate, and blood pressure.

reflexes
inborn and involuntary behaviors—such as coughing, swallowing, sneezing, or vomiting—that are elicited by very specific stimuli.

pons
a hindbrain structure that serves as a bridge between lower brain regions and higher midbrain and forebrain activity.

cerebellum
a hindbrain structure involved in body movement, balance, coordination, fine-tuning motor skills, and cognitive activities such as learning and language.

Hindbrain   The oldest brain region is the hindbrain, the region directly connected to the spinal cord. Hindbrain structures regulate breathing, heart rate, arousal, and other basic functions of survival. There are three main parts of the hindbrain: the medulla, the pons, and the cerebellum.

Extending directly from the spinal cord, the **medulla** regulates breathing, heart rate, and blood pressure. It also is involved in various kinds of reflexes, such as coughing, swallowing, sneezing, and vomiting. **Reflexes** are inborn and involuntary behaviors that are elicited by very specific stimuli (Amaral, 2000). **Pons** means "bridge," and the pons indeed serves as a bridge between lower brain regions and higher midbrain and forebrain activity. For instance, information about body movement and various sensations gets relayed from the cortex via the pons to the cerebellum. The **cerebellum,** or "little brain," contains more neurons than any other single part of the brain. It is responsible for body movement, balance, coordination, and fine motor skills like typing and piano playing. The cerebellum is also important in cognitive activities such as learning and language (Amaral, 2000; Stroodley & Schmahmann, 2009).

Midbrain   The next brain region to evolve after the hindbrain is the smallest of the three major areas, the midbrain. Different parts of the midbrain control the eye muscles, process auditory and visual information, and initiate voluntary movement of the body. People with Parkinson's disease have problems with midbrain functioning, due to the loss of neurons that use dopamine there, and so they shake uncontrollably. The midbrain, the medulla, and the pons together are sometimes referred to as the *brain stem*.

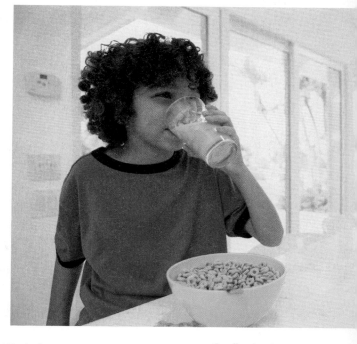

Swallowing is one of a number of inborn reflexes and is controlled by the medulla.

reticular formation

a network of nerve fibers that runs up through both the hindbrain and the midbrain; it is crucial to waking up and falling asleep.

A network of nerves called the **reticular formation** runs through both the hindbrain and the midbrain (*reticular* means "netlike"). The reticular formation plays a key role in wakefulness. Among the first neuroscientists to study the reticular formation were Giuseppe Moruzzi and Horace Magoun. In a classic study, Moruzzi and Magoun electrically stimulated the reticular formation of a sleeping cat, and it immediately awoke. When they *lesioned*, or damaged, its connection to higher brain systems, the cat went into a deep coma from which it never recovered. No kind of pinching or loud noises would arouse the cat (Moruzzi & Magoun, 1949).

Forebrain   The last major brain region to evolve was the largest part of the human brain, the forebrain. It consists of the cerebrum and numerous other structures, including the thalamus and the limbic system. Collectively, the structures of the forebrain control cognitive, sensory, and motor function and regulate temperature, reproductive functions, eating, sleeping, and the display of emotions. Most forebrain structures are *bilateral*; that is, there are two of them, one on each side of the brain.

thalamus

a forebrain structure that receives information from the senses and relays it to the cerebral cortex for processing.

From the bottom up, the first forebrain structure is the **thalamus,** which receives input from the ears, eyes, skin, or taste buds and relays sensory information to the part of the cerebral cortex most responsible for processing that specific kind of sensory information. For this reason, the thalamus is often called a sensory relay station. In fact, olfaction (the sense of smell) appears to be the only sense that does not have a thalamic relay (Kay & Sherman, 2007).

The Limbic System   In the middle of the brain directly around the thalamus lies a set of structures, traditionally referred to as the *limbic system* (see Figure 3.13). These are the hypothalamus, the hippocampus, the amygdala, and the cingulate gyrus. Together, the limbic system structures are important in emotion

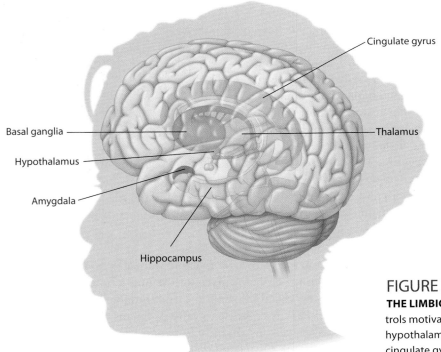

FIGURE **3.13**

THE LIMBIC SYSTEM. The limbic system controls motivation and emotion. It includes the hypothalamus, hippocampus, amygdala, and cingulate gyrus.

and motivation. However, there is some debate as to whether these structures work together as a system, so some neuroscientists suggest the term limbic system should be abandoned altogether (LeDoux, 2003).

The structure directly below the thalamus is the hypothalamus. In fact, *hypo* simply means "below." The **hypothalamus** regulates almost all of our major drives and motives, including hunger, thirst, temperature, and sexual behavior. It also controls the pituitary gland, which is responsible for producing and controlling the hormones our body produces. Researchers in the 1940s discovered the role the hypothalamus plays in eating: lesioning one part of it produced overeating and obesity in animals, whereas lesioning another part of the hypothalamus led to undereating (Kupfermann, Kandel, & Iversen, 2000). The hypothalamus is also involved in sexual arousal (Brunetti et al., 2008; Karama et al., 2002).

Wrapped around the thalamus is the **hippocampus,** which plays a vital role in learning and memory. Sensory information from the sense organs goes to the hippocampus. If these events are important enough, they are processed in the hippocampus and eventually established as lasting memories.

As we will see throughout this book, learning and memory change the brain, another example of softwiring. The brain structure most open to such change is the hippocampus. To get a feel for the kind of research that demonstrates this capacity, let's look at recent research conducted with taxicab drivers in London. Why study taxi drivers? Their work requires a tremendous amount of spatial and geographic knowledge, and they have to pass a difficult driving test (Maguire, Woollett, & Spiers, 2006). They must know where all the streets are relative to other streets. Neuroscientists examined images of the hippocampus and found that the hippocampi of taxi drivers was larger than that of other drivers. Moreover, the stress and frequency of driving did not account for these hippocampal size differences. Compared to bus drivers, taxi drivers had larger hippocampi (Maguire et al., 2006). Why? Bus drivers drive the same route every day, so they need to learn much less about the spatial layout of the city than taxi drivers. As this study suggests, learning changes the brain.

The **amygdala** is a small, almond-shaped structure located directly in front of the hippocampus. Anatomically, the amygdala connects with many other areas of the brain, including the structures that are involved in emotion and memory: the hypothalamus, which controls the autonomic nervous system; the hippocampus, which plays a crucial role in memory; the thalamus, which contains neurons that receive information from the sense organs; and the cerebral cortex. By virtue of its prime location, the amygdala plays a key role in determining the emotional significance of stimuli, especially when they evoke fear (Öhman, 2002; Phelps & LeDoux, 2005).

hypothalamus
a limbic structure; the master regulator of almost all major drives and motives we have, such as hunger, thirst, temperature, and sexual behavior; also controls the pituitary gland.

hippocampus
a limbic structure that wraps itself around the thalamus; plays a vital role in learning and memory.

Connection

Psychologists learned how essential the hippocampus is in memory and learning through a case study of Henry Molaison (H. M.), who had this structure surgically removed on both sides of the brain.
See "Three Types of Memory," Chapter 7, "Memory," p. 269.

amygdala
small, almond-shaped structure located directly in front of the hippocampus; has connections with many important brain regions and is important for processing emotional information, especially that related to fear.

How does this picture make you feel? The structures of the limbic system play a key part in emotion and motivation.

One of the special functions of the amygdala is to recognize situations for which fear is an appropriate response.

Studies in animals and humans show how important the amygdala is to emotions, especially fear. Electrical stimulation of the amygdala in cats makes them arch their backs in an angry-defensive manner, a response suggesting that anger and aggression involve the amygdala. Moreover, when aggressive monkeys had this region of the brain surgically lesioned, they became tame and non-aggressive. They also became fearless; for instance, rather than fleeing from snakes, they approached them (Klüver & Bucy, 1939; Meunier & Bachevalier, 2002). Similarly, in cases of disease, injury, or surgery to the human amygdala, people often lose their aggressive tendencies. They become mild-mannered, yet they also become fearless. Additionally, our ability to recognize certain emotional expressions on other people's faces—especially fear—involves the amygdala (Adolphs, Gosselin, et al., 2005; J. S. Morris et al., 1996). Without the amygdala, we cannot learn appropriate emotional responses, especially to potentially dangerous situations. The amygdala, along with the hypothalamus and other brain structures, is also activated during sexual arousal (Fonteille & Stoleru, in press; Hamann et al., 2004; Karama et al., 2002).

The **cingulate gyrus** is a beltlike structure in the middle of the brain. Portions of the cingulate gyrus, in particular the front part, play an important role in attention and cognitive control (Botvinick, Cohen, & Carter, 2004). For instance, when people are first trying to figure out a difficult problem and preparing to solve it, parts of the cingulate gyrus are activated (Kounios et al., 2006; Qiu et al., 2010). In contrast, this area seems to malfunction in people with schizophrenia, who do have major difficulties in focusing their attention (Carter et al., 1997).

The **basal ganglia** are a collection of structures surrounding the thalamus involved in voluntary motor control. Several movement-related neurological disorders, including Parkinson's disease and Huntington's disease, affect the functioning of neurons in this region. Individuals who have these disorders suffer from jerky, often uncontrollable movements. Often considered part of the limbic system, the basal ganglia reside on both sides of the thalamus and above the limbic system. They connect with the cerebral cortex, thalamus, and brain stem (Kopell et al., 2006).

The Cerebrum and Cerebral Cortex

The uppermost portion of the brain, the **cerebrum,** is folded into convolutions and divided into two large hemispheres. When most of us think about the human brain, we typically envision the outer layer, with all of its convolutions. This outer layer is called the **cerebral cortex.** The cortex is only about one tenth to one fifth of an inch thick, yet it is in this very thin layer of brain that much of human thought, planning, perception, and consciousness takes place. In short, it is the site of all brain activity that makes us most human.

Connection
The amygdala plays a significant role in emotions, especially fear.
See "Emotion and the Brain," Chapter 11, "Motivation and Emotion," p. 462.

cingulate gyrus beltlike structure in the middle of the brain that plays an important role in attention and cognitive control.

basal ganglia a collection of structures surrounding the thalamus involved in voluntary motor control.

cerebrum each of the large halves of the brain that are covered with convolutions, or folds.

cerebral cortex thin outer layer of the cerebrum, in which much of human thought, planning, perception, and consciousness takes place.

The cerebrum is composed of four large areas called *lobes*, each of which carries out distinct functions. These lobes are bilateral, which means they are located on both the left and right sides of the brain. The four lobes are the frontal, temporal, parietal, and occipital (see Figure 3.14). The *frontal lobes,* in the front of the brain, make up one-third of the area of the cerebral cortex. One important region of the frontal lobe, descending from the top of the head toward the center of the brain, is the *primary motor cortex.* One of the earliest discoveries about the brain's frontal lobes involved the motor cortex. In the 1860s, the German physiologist Eduard Hitzig had noticed while caring for wounded soldiers that touching the surface of a specific side of the brain caused the soldier's body to twitch on the opposite side. The researchers then discovered that as they moved the stimulation along this strip of cortex and stimulated one small region at a time, different parts of the soldier's body would move. More importantly, they were the first researchers to discover and study something that few believed: Different parts of the cortex are responsible for different functions—a phenomenon known as *cortical localization* (Finger, 1994).

Lobes of the brain

Frontal lobe

Parietal lobe

Occipital lobe

Temporal lobe

FIGURE **3.14**

FOUR LOBES OF THE CEREBRAL CORTEX. Each of the four lobes has a counterpart on the opposite side of the brain. Most important for thinking, planning, and integrating the brain's activity are the frontal lobes. The parietal lobes integrate the sensation and perception of touch. Hearing is the main function of the temporal lobes, and visual information is processed in the occipital lobes.

The frontal lobe carries out many important functions, including attention, holding things in mind while we solve problems, planning, abstract thinking, control of impulses, creativity, and social awareness (Miller & Cummings, 1999). The frontal lobes are more interconnected with other brain regions than any other part of the brain and therefore are able to integrate much brain activity. This integration allows for insight and creative problem solving (Furster, 1999). For example, connections between the frontal lobes and the hippocampus and temporal lobe facilitate tasks involving language and memory, respectively. More than any other part of the brain, the frontal lobes are what make humans human. They are also the "youngest" brain systems to evolve and the last to fully develop in individuals. The frontal lobes continue to develop until the early 20s. One reason why children and teenagers act more impulsively than adults is that their frontal lobes are not fully developed.

Probably the most famous story in neuroscience comes from the first case study of frontal lobe involvement in impulse control and personality (Macmillan, 2000). In September 1848, a 25-year-old railroad foreman, Phineas Gage, was laying railroad ties. While hammering a tamping iron (an iron bar), Gage accidentally ignited gun powder used to lay the track and it exploded. The iron bar shot upward, entered Gage's left cheek, and exited through the top of his skull after passing through his frontal lobe (see Figure 3.15). The iron bar was traveling so fast that it moved cleanly through Gage's head and landed 25 feet away. Miraculously, not only did Gage survive—he never even lost consciousness!

FIGURE **3.15**
PHINEAS GAGE'S ACCIDENT. Miraculously, Gage survived, but his personality changed dramatically as a result of the injury to his frontal lobe.

Although not mortally wounded, Gage suffered immediate and obvious changes to his personality. Before the accident, he had been a mild-mannered but clever businessman. After the accident he was stubborn, impulsive, and argumentative, and at times he would say offensive things. Gage's accident was one of the first documented cases of marked personality change following an injury to the frontal lobes, suggesting that these areas play a key role in regulating social behavior.

The *parietal lobes*, which make up the top and rear sections of the brain, play an important role in the sensation and perception of touch. The frontmost portion of the parietal lobes is the *somatosensory cortex*. When different parts of the body are touched, different parts of this strip of cortex are activated. The somatosensory cortex lies directly behind the motor cortex of the frontal lobe. In fact, these two regions are "twins." The areas of the motor and somatosensory cortexes that govern specific parts of the body are parallel to and directly next to each other (see Figure 3.16). For example, the part of the motor cortex involved in moving the lips is directly opposite the region of the sensory cortex where we sense that our lips are being touched. Neural signals from the motor cortex can communicate with computers to control robotic arms or artificial limbs, as we explain in "Psychology in the Real World."

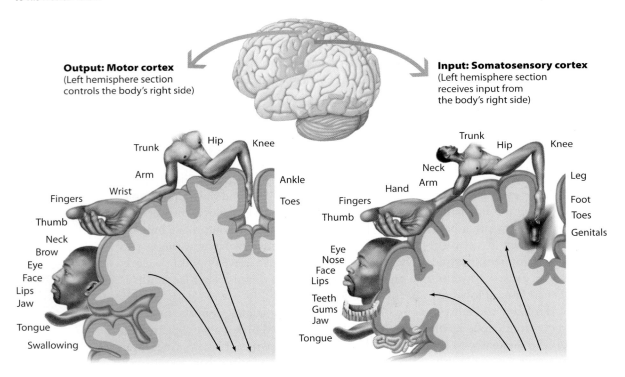

Output: Motor cortex
(Left hemisphere section controls the body's right side)

Input: Somatosensory cortex
(Left hemisphere section receives input from the body's right side)

FIGURE **3.16**

MOTOR AND SOMATOSENSORY CORTEXES OF THE BRAIN. Note that the regions of the motor and somatosensory cortexes are "twins." The face, lips, or toes, for example, activate the same areas of both cortexes. The arrows going down into the lower brain region represent motor neurons, and the arrows coming up into the somatosensory cortex correspond to sensory neurons.

The *temporal lobes* lie directly below the frontal and parietal lobes and right behind the ears. The temporal lobes have many different functions, but the main one is hearing. The temporal lobes house the *auditory cortex,* where sound information arrives from the thalamus for processing. Here, we "hear" our mother's voice, a symphony, an approaching car, or any other sound. The temporal lobes also house and connect with the hippocampus and amygdala, and so are also involved in memory and emotion.

The *occipital lobes* occupy the rear of the brain. The optic nerve travels from the eye to the thalamus and then to the occipital lobes—specifically, to the *primary visual cortex.* Visual information is processed in the visual cortex; it is here where we "see" and "imagine." Neuroscientists have discovered that different neurons in the visual cortex are activated when we see horizontal lines, diagonal lines, and vertical lines. In other words, individual neurons are specialized for the many different aspects of vision, including shape, color, shadow, light, and orientation (Wurtz & Kandel, 2000a).

The **insula** is a small structure that resides deep inside the cerebrum, in the area that separates the temporal lobe from the parietal lobe. The insula is active in the perception of bodily sensations, emotional states, empathy, and addictive behavior (Damasio, 2000; Naqvi et al., 2007). It communicates with structures of the limbic system and higher brain areas involved in decision making. The insula also plays a key role in our awareness of our body as our own (Tsakiris et al., 2007).

Cerebral Hemispheres

The human cerebrum is divided into two equal *hemispheres.* Although they look similar, the hemispheres differ in shape, size, and function. In general terms, the left hemisphere processes information in a more focused and analytic manner, whereas the right hemisphere integrates information in a more holistic, or broader, manner (Beeman & Bowden, 2000; Beever & Chiarello, 2009). Insights and solutions to ideas are more likely to occur in the right hemisphere.

The hemispheres do not operate independently, however. The **corpus callosum,** a thick band of nerve fibers connecting the two hemispheres of the brain, provides a channel for extensive communication between hemispheres in both logical and creative tasks.

Perhaps the best-known and biggest functional difference between the cerebral hemispheres is in language. Speech and language comprehension involve two separate regions in the left hemisphere. The French physician Paul Broca is credited with being the first "neuropsychologist." He deserves this title because his work in the early 1860s demonstrated for the first time that specific parts of the brain controlled particular behaviors (Kandel, 2006). Broca studied a man who had suffered a stroke. This man could understand language, but he could not speak in grammatical sentences. He had a type of **aphasia,** a deficit in the ability to speak or comprehend language. After the man died, Broca performed an autopsy and found that a cyst had damaged the man's left hemisphere. A small region in the left frontal lobe had been damaged, and Broca inferred that this area must be responsible for a person's ability to speak. Broca went on to discover similar damage in eight other aphasia patients (Pinker, 1994). These clinical findings have been confirmed by modern brain imaging techniques: People with aphasia often have damage or lesions in the same region of the left frontal lobe. This region is commonly referred to as **Broca's area,** and this type of aphasia is known as Broca's aphasia. Broca's area is responsible for the ability to produce speech.

insula
small structure inside the cerebrum that plays an important role in the perception of bodily sensations, emotional states, empathy, and addictive behavior.

corpus callosum
nerve fibers that connect the two hemispheres of the brain.

aphasia
deficit in the ability to speak or comprehend language.

Broca's area
area in the left frontal lobe responsible for the ability to produce speech.

Brain–Computer and Brain–Machine Interfaces

Think about how incredible it is that we can use our thoughts to control voluntary movement. We think "I want to scratch my nose," and then we can almost instantaneously lift an arm and move a finger to scratch the nose. When injury cuts connections between the CNS and the skeletal muscles, a person's intention to move a limb—say, to pick up a coffee cup—cannot affect the muscles needed to lift the cup. Thoughts cannot lead to action.

In recent years, researchers have combined technology and neuroscience to help people who are not able to move their limbs. With the development of brain–computer interfaces and brain–machine interfaces, people can learn to control computers or machinery with only their thoughts. How does this work? These machines convert neural activity (action potentials, see p. 86) into digital signals that can control a prosthetic or paralyzed limb (Fetz, 2007). These machines can then execute the neural instructions, such as "lift the arm."

What is needed so that thoughts can control an artificial limb that cannot be felt? First, we'd need to know which neurons in the motor cortex controlled intentional movement. Such mapping of individual neurons can be done in a surgical lab setting (most of these cases have been done in monkeys) (Pohlmeyer et al., 2009). Also, it would be important to know that some kind of mental representation of an action—such as imagining a movement—activates the same motor neurons necessary to make the movement happen. This creates the thought–action link. Neurons in the motor cortex that are instrumental in generating movement can also be activated when people simply imagine movement but do not actually move (Jeannerod, 1995).

Once we've identified the neurons that control movement and that we can mentally activate, we need a device for translating neural signals into instructions to be sent to a machine that can move a prosthetic or paralyzed limb. Computers convert the neural signal information into instructions that can then be sent to an artificial limb or robotic arm. The computer is the *interface* between your thoughts and the arm. The computer can control either an external device (an artificial or robotic arm) or a device that can electrically activate paralyzed muscles. In one seminal study, a paralyzed patient learned to use his intentional thoughts toward movement to control a computer cursor or a robotic arm (Hochberg et al., 2006).

Wernicke's area an area deep in the left temporal lobe responsible for the ability to speak in meaningful sentences and to comprehend the meaning of speech.

About 20 years after Broca found the area of the brain now named for him, a German physiologist, Carl Wernicke, discovered that damage to another region of the left hemisphere created a different language problem. This area of the left temporal lobe, now called **Wernicke's area,** is responsible for speech comprehension. Wernicke's aphasia, in contrast to Broca's aphasia, results in fluent, grammatical streams of speech that lack meaning. For instance, a patient with this disorder who was asked why he was in the hospital responded: "Boy, I'm sweating. I'm awfully nervous, you know, once in awhile I get caught up, I can't mention the tarripoi, a month ago, quite a little, I've done a lot well, I impose a lot, while, on the other hand, you know what I mean, I have to run around, look it over, trebbin and all that sort of stuff" (as quoted in Pinker, 1994, p. 316).

Communication Between the Hemispheres As we have seen, the two hemispheres of the brain do not operate independently. Information moves between both sides of the brain by way of the corpus callosum. All communication between one side of the brain and the other travels across the corpus callosum.

Forearm electrical stimulation (FES) is used to stimulate forearm muscles with fixed instructions from a computer (Peckham et al., 2001). FES can create movements in paralyzed limbs, but the actions generated are fixed and limited to only what the computer can instruct the arm to do. Ideally, one would have flexibility as with a normally functioning arm; that is, people could choose what movements to make.

Pohlmeyer and his colleagues (2009) took an important step toward creating more flexibility in moving paralyzed limbs. After putting implants deep into the brains of two monkeys to record signals from neurons in the motor cortex, they used nerve-blocking drugs to temporarily paralyze the animals' arms. Then they wanted to see whether they could use a brain–machine interface to have these neural signals stimulate muscles in the monkeys. The monkeys—in spite of almost completely paralyzed wrists—were able to use this cortically controlled FES system to control the contraction of four forearm muscles.

More recent research employs less invasive techniques—such as brain imaging with fMRI—to control machines (Min, Marzelli, & Yoo, 2010). These new systems allow for a bidirectional line of communication between the brain and

The monkey's real arms are constrained below (white cover at bottom), and a prosthetic arm is attached next to the shoulder and to microelectrodes in the motor cortex of the brain. The monkey learns to control the prosthetic arm much the same way it does its real arm—by sending neural signals from the motor cortex to the arm. Here the monkey is using the prosthetic arm to feed itself. (Source: Velliste et al., 2008)

the computer. That is, feedback from a computer can be used to modulate brain activity. Such computer-to-brain interfaces might even make possible brain-to-brain interfaces in the future (Min et al., 2010).

In the early 1960s a former prisoner of war from World War II developed epileptic seizures as a result of a failed parachute jump. The seizures were so severe that his doctor approached Roger Sperry, a local researcher who had begun to do research on the corpus callosum, for help (Finger, 1994).

Previous medical evidence had suggested that cutting the bundle of nerves between the two hemispheres could stop epileptic seizures. Because the war veteran's seizures had become life threatening, he underwent the surgery under Sperry's guidance and it was very successful. Not only did the man's seizures stop, but there was also no noticeable change in his personality or intelligence. However, Sperry and his colleagues soon discovered a fascinating problem. The man could not name things that were presented to his left visual field, but he could do so with things presented to his right visual field. Why?

Recall that language—both speech and comprehension—resides in the left hemisphere of the human brain. In addition, information from our right visual field (the right portion of the visual scope of each eye) goes to the left occipital cortex, while information from the left visual field (the left portion of the

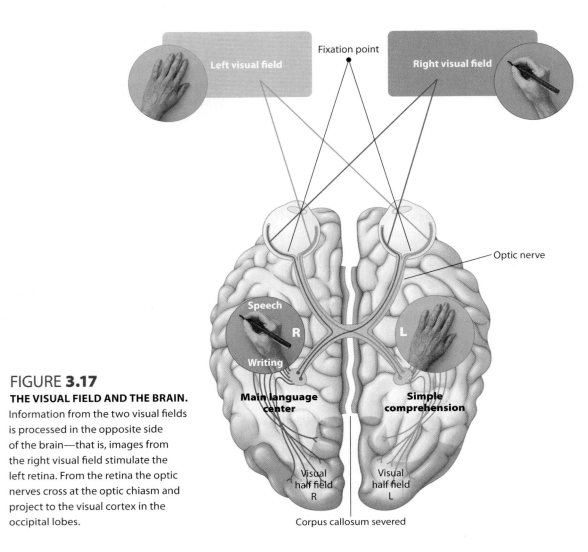

Fixation point

Left visual field

Right visual field

Optic nerve

Speech

R

L

Writing

Main language center

Simple comprehension

Visual half field R

Visual half field L

Corpus callosum severed

FIGURE **3.17**

THE VISUAL FIELD AND THE BRAIN.
Information from the two visual fields is processed in the opposite side of the brain—that is, images from the right visual field stimulate the left retina. From the retina the optic nerves cross at the optic chiasm and project to the visual cortex in the occipital lobes.

visual scope of each eye) goes to the right occipital cortex (see Figure 3.17). But, because the war veteran had had his corpus callosum cut, the information from the left visual field could not get transferred to the language centers in the left hemisphere. He could, however, consistently pick up with his *left* hand the image he saw! Thus, because the right hemisphere (where the image was projected) controls the left side of the body, he could move his hand to the correct object (see Figure 3.18). This *split-brain research* shows that we can know something even if we cannot name it (Sperry, Gazzaniga, & Bogen, 1969).

Brain Plasticity and Neurogenesis

When scientists began mapping the brain in the late 19th century, they did so by stimulating various brain regions in animals and observing the behavioral changes that such stimulation caused; they then diagrammed the locations of functions in the cerebral cortex (Kandel, 2006). Such mapping contributed to the notion that brain function was fixed. Certain brain regions had certain functions and that was that. But as far back as the early 20th century, researchers had stimulated different places on the motor cortex in several different monkeys and had found that maps generated from such stimulation varied from monkey to monkey. They were as individual as fingerprints.

Picture of hairbrush flashed on screen

(a)

"What did you see?"

"I don't know."

(b)

"With your left hand, select the object you saw from those behind the screen."

(c)

FIGURE **3.18**

PERCEPTION AND LANGUAGE IN A SPLIT-BRAIN PATIENT. In (a) a person who has had an operation to cut the corpus callosum is shown an object (hairbrush) to her left visual field. In (b), when asked what she saw, she cannot say, because her language production center (Broca's area) is in her left hemisphere. Because the image is shown to her left visual field, only her right visual cortex perceives it. With a split corpus callosum, there is no way for that information to cross from the right hemisphere to the left. So she is unable to say what she saw. In (c), however, she is able to pick up the object she saw with her *left* hand. Why her left hand? Because it is controlled by her right hemisphere, which did in fact perceive the brush.

neuroplasticity
the brain's ability to adopt new functions, reorganize itself, or make new neural connections throughout life, as a function of experience.

Connection

If a person is not exposed to language much before mid- to late childhood, the ability to speak is limited because the brain loses some of its plasticity as we age.
See "Language Development in Individuals," Chapter 9, "Language and Thought," p. 350.

In the early 20th century, other neuroscientists mapped the motor cortexes of several monkeys many times during a 4-month period. They found that neural areas corresponding to the movement of specific fingers changed to reflect changes in the animal's patterns of movement over that time period (Jenkins et al., 1990).

By the 1970s, there was evidence that learning occurs through synaptic change. These findings were only the tip of the iceberg. Since the 1990s, numerous principles of brain plasticity have emerged (B. D. Perry, 2002). First and most generally, **neuroplasticity** is the brain's ability to adopt new functions, reorganize itself, or make new neural connections throughout life, as a function of experience. Second, almost every major structure of the neuron is capable of experience-based change. Third, not all regions of the brain are equally plastic. For example, the part of the brain most involved in learning, the hippocampus, is more plastic than just about any other part of the brain. And fourth, brain plasticity varies with age, being strongest in infancy and early childhood and gradually decreasing with age. Contrary to popular belief, at no time in our lives does the brain lose its ability to grow new neurons. Neuroplasticity occurs in all stages of life, though the different parts of the brain are not equally plastic at all times.

The four principles of brain plasticity are summarized in Figure 3.19. Experience-based change in the nervous system occurs in several ways. Most common are the formation of new neurons, the growth of dendrites

FIGURE **3.19**
FOUR PRIN-CIPLES OF BRAIN PLASTICITY.

- Neuroplasticity is the brain's ability to adopt new functions, reorganize itself, or make new neural connections throughout life, as a function of experience.

- Almost every major structure of the neuron is capable of experience-based change, although we focus only on the three major ones: the neuron itself, dendrites, and synapses.

- Although the brain is plastic, not all regions are equally plastic.

- Brain plasticity varies with age, being strongest in infancy and early childhood and gradually decreasing with age.

neurogenesis
the development
of new neurons.

synaptogenesis
the formation
of entirely new
synapses or con-
nections with other
neurons.

in existing neurons, and the formation of new synapses. The process of developing new neurons is known as **neurogenesis.** The growth and formation of
new dendrites is called **arborization** (from the Latin *arbor*, or "tree"), because
dendrites are like branches on a tree. Probably the best-known example of neuroplasticity, however, is the process known as **synaptogenesis,** the formation
of entirely new synapses or connections with other neurons that is the basis of
learning. All of these neuroplasticity examples are forms of softwiring—biological systems being modified by input from the environment.

arborization
the growth and
formation of new
dendrites.

Although these principles of neuroplasticity are universal—that is, apply
to everyone—some of the strongest evidence for them comes out of research on
people with different kinds of sensory deficits, such as blindness or deafness. It
is in deafness and blindness that we see most clearly how flexible the brain really
is. Brain function and localization vary considerably on the basis of the experience of the individual brain.

In most hearing people, the area that is called the *auditory cortex* processes sound. Although it is labeled by its function, anatomically the auditory
cortex is actually a section of the temporal lobe. It is called the auditory cortex
because the sensory neurons from the inner ear come here.

But if those neurons don't pick up any sounds, what does this area
of the brain do? Nothing? What a waste of brain tissue that would be.
For centuries scientists and ordinary people have observed that deaf
people see better than hearing people and that blind people hear
better than sighted people. The neuroscientist Helen Neville
always thought there must be truth to these observations. In the process of testing these assumptions,
she discovered that—overall—blind people are
not better at hearing. They are not more sensitive
to softer sounds than sighted people. Similarly,
deaf people do not excel at all kinds of vision,
nor are they able to see fainter images than do
hearing people.

What Neville found, how-
ever, was that deaf and blind people
are more expert in peripheral sensory experiences. That is, deaf people
have better *peripheral* vision than sighted
people—they are better at seeing things "out
of the corner of their eyes" (Bavelier et al.,
2000). They have better motion detection
as well, and this also seems to be processed by the auditory cortex. Just as deaf
people see better at the periphery, those
who are blind don't hear better overall,
but their *peripheral* hearing—hearing for
things around the edges of a sound field
(rather than the center)—is better than
that of sighted people. And these peripheral sounds are processed by the visual cortex
(Bavelier et al., 2000). According to Neville,
"This was some of the first evidence that
brain specializations such as auditory cortex are

In blind people, the brain
compensates for deficits
in vision by reorganizing
and rewiring the visual
cortex to process sound.
The brain shapes behav-
ior, and behavior shapes
the brain.

To compensate for deafness or blindness, the brain
reorganizes and rewires the part normally dedicated to
hearing or vision for other uses. Marlee Matlin, shown
here with her dance partner from *Dancing With the Stars,*
is an Oscar-winning actress with limited hearing.

not anatomically determined" (Neville, as quoted in Begley, 2007, p. 84). In short, by virtue of its natural plasticity and softwiring, the brain compensates for deficits in one sensory modality by reorganizing and rewiring unused regions to take on new functions. Once again, we see how psychological research leads to startling changes in our assumptions.

Quick Quiz 3.3: The Brain

1. This region of the brain was the last to evolve. It is also the biggest part of the brain.
   a. cerebellum
   b. forebrain
   c. hindbrain
   d. pons

2. Which limbic structure plays a crucial role in fear?
   a. hypothalamus
   b. basal ganglia
   c. amygdala
   d. hippocampus

3. Where is the somatosensory cortex?
   a. in the occipital lobes
   b. in the frontal lobes
   c. in the temporal lobes
   d. in the parietal lobes

Answers can be found at the end of the chapter.

Breaking New Ground

Neurogenesis in the Adult Brain

Neurons are unique cells in the body. Unlike many other cells, including hair, blood, or skin cells, nerve cells do not grow and die on an hourly basis. Nor do they divide. Because of these two facts, discovered by the Spanish physician and Nobel Prize winner Santiago Ramón y Cajal more than 100 years ago, the prevailing wisdom was that neurons are incapable of growth, at least after early childhood.

These observations led Ramón y Cajal to put forth the *neuron doctrine,* which declared that neurons do not regenerate. Until the 1990s, researchers and physicians alike accepted the idea that once a region of the brain was damaged, its function was lost forever. All neural growth and change were understood to be limited to fetal and childhood development, and the adult brain did not change.

Early Evidence of Neurogenesis in Adults

By the early 1960s, however, an accumulation of evidence began to suggest that adult brains do change. Perhaps the first empirical demonstration of neurogenesis occurred when neuroscientists detected evidence of cell division (evidence of growth) in the brains of adult rats (Bryans, 1959).

In the early 1960s, Joseph Altman published a series of groundbreaking studies with adult rats and cats. Armed with a new cell-labeling technique, Altman found evidence of the growth of new neurons—neurogenesis—in several brain areas that are crucial for learning and memory (Altman & Das, 1966; C. G. Gross, 2000). Even though his reports appeared in prestigious journals, however, Altman's findings were almost completely ignored or discounted. Why? He was working alone, and he was a little-known researcher who violated the dogma, or strongly accepted view.

As often happens with ideas that radically challenge basic assumptions and long-held beliefs, neuroscientists and others either trivialized or ignored Altman's findings of adult neurogenesis. What does it take for a movement to change a well-entrenched, century-old idea? In this case, three scientific events took place during the 1980s and 1990s that finally turned the tide of belief.

First, a series of studies on birds showed exceptional neural growth in many areas of the adult avian brain, including the hippocampus (Nottebohm, 1985). Second, there was increasing evidence for the formation of new synaptic connections in the brains of rats when they were raised in enriched environments, more so than normally occurs with development (Comery et al., 1996). For example, rats that lived in cages with playmates and wheels to run on and toys showed more dendritic growth than those who lived alone in sparse cages (Rosenzweig & Bennett, 1969). Third, in the 1990s, researchers began to find solid evidence for neurogenesis in one particular region of the hippocampus in adult rats, monkeys, and humans. Neurogenesis was no longer something seen only in birds and rats. There was no more denying that neural growth occurs in humans.

Key Figures in the Discovery of Neural Growth in Adults

The person most responsible for demonstrating neurogenesis in humans is Fred "Rusty" Gage (ironically, a cousin of the famous Phineas Gage who had the iron rod blast through his skull) (Gage, 2002; Gage, Kemperman, & Song, 2008). But how is this research done in humans, since researchers cannot train humans and then slice open their brains to see if neural growth occurred? Indeed, the brain imaging techniques that we currently use cannot detect the growth of new cells. Gage got together with his researchers, some of whom did medical research, and they hit up on the solution that allowed them to detect new neural growth in humans. It involves injecting people with a substance called BrdU, which is incorporated into dividing cells so that they can be identified.

But there is a problem with BrdU: You can't simply inject humans with it because it is radioactive. But—and here was the big breakthrough—some people have to have it injected for medical reasons. Gage and his colleague Peter Erikkson knew that some cancer patients receive this injection as part of their therapy. Because it identifies new cells, it is used to track how aggressively cancerous tumors are growing. After some patients

Animals reared in natural-istic settings have higher rates of neurogenesis than those reared in cages.

who had been injected with BrdU died, Gage and Erikkson examined their hippocampus tissue. Based on the presence of BrdU, they found new cells in the adult human hippocampus (Begley, 2007; Erikkson et al., 1998). In fact, it was the same part of the hippocampus that earlier had shown the greatest neuronal growth in rats and monkeys.

Another of the key figures in demonstrating new neural growth in adult primates has been Elizabeth Gould (Glasper, Leuner, & Gould, 2008). She and her colleagues have compared rates of neurogenesis and synaptic growth in the brains of primates living in naturalistic settings with those living in lab cages. The naturalistic settings simulated a wild environment, with natural vegetation where the animals could search for food, among other activities. The brains of the animals that lived in these environmentally complex settings showed brain growth in areas important for thinking and feeling. They also had higher rates of neurogenesis and more connections between neurons than the animals reared in cages. In other studies, Gould and her colleagues found that stress and impoverished environments resulted in less neurogenesis in mammals (Mirescu & Gould, 2006; Mirescu et al., 2006).

Because of the onslaught of findings demonstrating neurogenesis in adult animals during the 1990s, the dogma of no new neural growth finally died. Now we know that neurons and their dendrites and synapses change, grow, and die in both young and old animals—including humans—depending on the kind of stimulation they receive from the outside world. Indeed, when we learn anything, and even when we exercise, neurons in our brain are changed.

Connection

Learning results in new synapses, dendrites, and even new neurons in certain regions of the brain. Regular exercise also stimulates neural growth.

See "Synaptic Change During Learning," Chapter 8, "Learning," p. 337, and "Research on Health-Relevant Behavior," Chapter 12, "Stress and Health," p. 500.

Quick Quiz 3.4: Neurogenesis in the Adult Brain

1. The brain's ability to adopt new functions, reorganize itself, and make new neural connections is known as
   a. neuroplasticity
   b. neurogenesis
   c. the neuron doctrine
   d. localization of function

2. In what region of the human brain is there the most evidence of neurogenesis?
   a. frontal cortex
   b. hypothalamus
   c. amygdala
   d. hippocampus

Answers can be found at the end of the chapter.

■ ■ ■

MEASURING THE BRAIN

To be able to look into the brain as it is working was a long-time dream of philosophers and scientists. In the last few decades, realizing this wish has become possible. At least three distinct techniques are now commonly used to measure brain activity in psychological research.

Electronencephalography

Researchers use **electroencephalography (EEG)** to record the electrical activity of the brain. The procedure involves placing electrodes on a person's scalp. The electrodes, metal disks attached to wires, are usually mounted in a fabric cap that fits snugly over the head. Typically, the person is conducting certain

electroencephalography (EEG) a method for measuring brain activity in which the electrical activity of the brain is recorded from electrodes placed on a person's scalp.

FIGURE 3.20

ELECTRO-ENCEPHALOG-RAPHY (EEG). One of the authors (Erika) in an EEG cap for a study on brain activity and facial expression of emotion. The dots on her face allow for video motion capture of facial expression changes.

tasks while electrical activity is recorded. EEG is superior to other brain imaging techniques in showing *when* brain activity occurs. It is not very accurate at indicating precisely *where* activity occurs (see Figure 3.20).

The **event-related potential (ERP)** is a special technique that extracts electrical activity from raw EEG data to measure cognitive processes. To examine ERPs, one gathers electrical recordings from an EEG cap on research participants who are performing cognitive or emotional tasks, such as trying to attend to an object on a computer screen, remember a list of words, or view emotionally charged slides. Typically, raw EEG data provide a summary of all the electrical activity in the brain that happens at a particular time. Generally this level of detail is fine for measuring states of wakefulness, for example. But you need more temporal precision if you want to see a brain reaction, say, to a particular stimulus, such as a flashing light or a line. To examine ERPs, researchers use a special averaging process that allows them to filter out all electrical activity except the activity that is related to the stimulus the person is processing in a controlled experiment.

Because they are based on EEG, ERPs provide excellent temporal resolution (they show brain activity linked with psychological tasks almost immediately in time) but poor spatial resolution. Spatial resolution involves how tiny an area can be pinpointed as being active at a certain time. Two other techniques provide better spatial resolution than EEG: MRI and PET.

event-related potential (ERP) a special technique that extracts electrical activity from raw EEG data to measure cognitive processes.

Magnetic Resonance Imaging (MRI) and Functional MRI (fMRI)

magnetic resonance imaging (MRI) brain imaging technique that uses magnetic fields to produce detailed images of the structure of the brain and other soft tissues.

MRI stands for **magnetic resonance imaging.** MRI uses magnetic fields to produce very finely detailed images of the structure of the brain and other soft tissues. In MRI, the patient lies on a platform or bed that slides into a tube surrounded by a circular magnet. The magnet, along with radio waves, is used to produce a signal that is then processed by computer. The computer then produces an image with an amazing level of detail (see Figure 3.21). MRI provides static pictures, and it is very useful for looking at structures and abnormalities in structures, such as when someone is injured. MRI does not tell us anything about activity, just structures.

A variation on MRI, **functional MRI (fMRI),** does, however, tell us about brain activity. Images from fMRI tell us where activity in the brain is occurring during particular tasks by tracking blood oxygen use in brain tissue, as shown in Figure 3.21. In this way, researchers can see which areas of the brain are using the most oxygen (and presumably are most active) during certain tasks (Casey, Davidson, & Rosen, 2002; Lagopoulos, 2007). When people perform different tasks while they are being scanned, the researchers can distinguish from high-resolution images which areas are active during the task. These are indirect images of activity based on how the brain uses oxygen rather than a direct "readout" of nerve impulses.

functional magnetic resonance imaging (fMRI) brain imaging technique that uses magnetic fields to produce detailed images of activity in areas of the brain and other soft tissues.

FIGURE 3.21

BRAIN IMAGING TECHNOLOGY. MRI equipment (right) takes very clear, detailed images of soft tissue, including the brain, but it doesn't record brain activity. Both PET scans and fMRI, in contrast, highlight brain activity.

MRI scan   PET scan   fMRI scan

Although fMRI provides a much better measure of *where* activity occurs than EEG does, it is not without drawbacks. For one thing, it is very expensive. Also, it does not provide very precise measures of *when* activation occurs in response to a particular stimulus or task. It is not entirely clear exactly how directly fMRI images reflect underlying neural activity (Lagopoulos, 2007). Some studies suggest a fairly direct correlation with processing in certain cortical areas (Logothetis et al., 2001). As a result, fMRI findings should always be interpreted with care. The Research Process for this chapter illustrates the use of fMRI to study how people perceive faces (see Figure 3.22).

Positron Emission Tomography (PET)

positron emission tomography (PET)
brain imaging technique that measures blood flow to active areas in the brain.

Positron emission tomography (PET) measures blood flow to brain areas in the active brain (see Figure 3.21). From these measurements researchers and doctors can determine which brain areas are active during certain situations. PET involves injecting the participant or patient with a harmless radioactive form of oxygen (or glucose). The brain then takes up the oxygen during cell metabolism. Thanks to the radioactive *label* on the oxygen, scanners and computers can be used to create images of the brain regions using that oxygen during a certain task.

Research Process

1 Research Questions

Is any part of the brain dedicated to seeing faces and no other object? Likewise, is there a part of the brain dedicated exclusively to perceiving places (such as buildings)? If so, are these brain regions equally active when you imagine a face or place and when you actually see one?

2 Method

Previous research had found one distinct part of the brain activated when we see a face (the fusiform face area, FFA) and a different area of the brain (the parahippocampal place area, PPA) activated when we see a place or a building. O'Craven and Kanwisher (2000) wanted to confirm this result and extend it by seeing whether the activity was as strong when just imagining faces or places as it was when seeing these images.

Eight participants were placed inside an fMRI machine (see image) and then viewed images of either famous faces or familiar buildings on their university campus. For the imagining condition, participants were read the names of famous names and places and asked to close their eyes and form a "vivid mental image" of each one.

A young boy being prepped for a brain imaging procedure in an fMRI machine.

3 Results

Results confirmed the FFA showed high activity (% signal change) for faces but low activity for places, whereas the PPA showed the opposite (see figure). Moreover, the results for imagining faces and places showed the same pattern of results, only less strongly.

4 Conclusion

Different regions of the brain are dedicated to very specific kinds of visual stimuli. We know this only because fMRI technology allows us to see specific areas of brain activity when we are shown different kinds of objects and given different kinds of tasks.

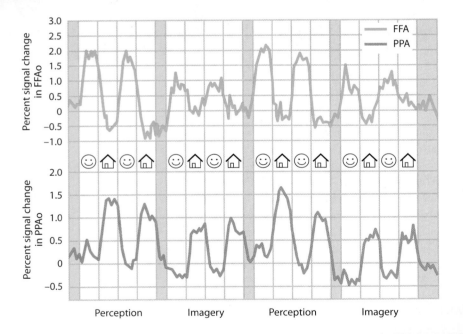

FIGURE **3.22**

DISTINCT BRAIN REGIONS ARE INVOLVED IN IMAGINING AND PERCEIVING FACES AND PLACES. Source: "Mental Imagery of Faces and Places Activates Corresponding Stimulus-Specific Brain Regions," by K. M. O'Craven and N. N. Kanwisher, 2000, *Journal of Cognitive Neuroscience, 12,* 1013–1023. doi:10.1162/08989290051137549

Although the results are very informative, the use of radioactive substances means PET is not risk-free. fMRI is a much safer way to image metabolism in the brain.

The imaging techniques we have discussed so far focus on measuring the structure or activity of clusters of somas of neurons. What is known as the *gray matter* is the brain tissue composed of neuron cell bodies, because the soma or cell body is where cell metabolism takes place (and thus oxygen is used by the cell). But information is communicated among different areas of the brain via long fibers of myelinated axons, which are not typically well imaged by MRI or PET. Because these fibers are covered with myelin, they are called *white matter*. Several methods have been developed for better imaging white matter, or neural fibers. These include *diffusion tensor imaging*, which is a special kind of MRI that is adapted for better imaging myelinated fibers and *tracts* (collections of myelinated fibers). This type of imaging is important for studying the connectivity among brain areas (Hua et al., 2009).

Quick Quiz 3.5: Measuring the Brain

1. Which brain measurement technique best shows *when* neural activity has occurred?
   a. PET
   b. MRI
   c. EEG
   d. fMRI
2. Betty has an injury to a particular part of her brain and suddenly has trouble imagining, recognizing, and interpreting faces. What region of the brain was likely affected and which technology told us this?
   a. parahippocampal place area (PPA); MRI
   b. parahippocampal place area (PPA); fMRI
   c. fusiform face area (FFA); MRI
   d. fusiform face area (FFA); fMRI

Answers can be found at the end of the chapter.

THE ENDOCRINE SYSTEM

endocrine system
system of glands that secrete and regulate hormones in the body.

pituitary gland
the master endocrine gland of the body that controls the release of hormones from glands throughout the body.

adrenal glands
endocrine structures that release hormones important in regulating the stress response and emotions.

In the nervous system, neurons communicate information electrochemically by means of membrane changes and neurotransmitters released into the synaptic cleft. In the **endocrine system,** glands secrete chemicals called **hormones,** which travel through the bloodstream to tissues and organs all over the body and regulate body functions. Hormones also play a crucial role in regulating metabolism, growth, reproduction, mood, and other processes. Figure 3.23 depicts some of the major endocrine glands of the body.

The hypothalamus, shown in Figure 3.23, is a brain structure that controls the pituitary gland. The **pituitary gland** is known as the master gland of the body, because it secretes hormones that control the release of hormones from glands elsewhere in the body.

The *thyroid* gland sits in the neck region and releases hormones that control the rate of metabolism. Metabolism is the process by which the body converts nutritional substances into energy. The *pancreas* releases hormones, including insulin, that play a vital role in regulating blood sugar levels. The sex glands (ovaries and testes) release sex hormones that lead to development of sex characteristics (such as body hair and breast development), sex drive, and other aspects of sexual maturation.

The **adrenal glands,** which sit atop the kidneys, release hormones in response to stress and emotions. They also help regulate heart rate, blood pressure, and blood sugar. In addition, the adrenal glands produce **catecholamines,** a class of chemicals that includes the neurotransmitters dopamine,

hormones
chemicals, secreted by glands, that travel in the bloodstream and carry messages to tissues and organs all over the body.

catecholamines
chemicals released from the adrenal glands that function as hormones and as neurotransmitters to control ANS activation.

FIGURE **3.23**

THE ENDOCRINE SYSTEM. The endocrine system consists of numerous glands found throughout the body. The pancreas, for example, releases insulin, which is important in transporting sugars (glucose) from the bloodstream into the cells. Cells then use the glucose as their energy source. The thyroid gland regulates metabolism.

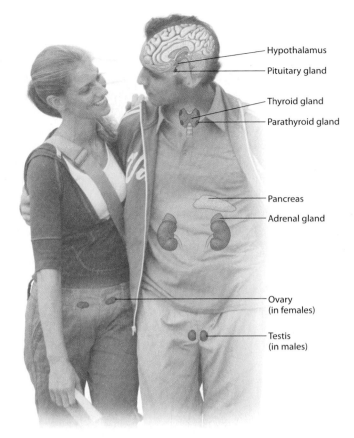

- Hypothalamus
- Pituitary gland
- Thyroid gland
- Parathyroid gland
- Pancreas
- Adrenal gland
- Ovary (in females)
- Testis (in males)

norepinephrine, and epinephrine, which control ANS activation. Norepinephrine activates the sympathetic nervous system, increasing heart rate, rate of respiration, and blood pressure in order to support rapid action of the body. The adrenal glands also release stress hormones such as **cortisol,** which is responsible for maintaining the activation of bodily systems during prolonged stress.

The endocrine system works in conjunction with the nervous system and in a dynamic relationship with the brain. An example is its control of the female menstrual cycle. Each month, the hypothalamus sends signals to the pituitary to release hormones that stimulate a woman's ovaries to develop (mature) an egg. As part of the process, the ovary itself releases hormones that prepare the womb to receive a fertilized egg. If the egg is fertilized, the ovaries send hormonal feedback to the hypothalamus, so that it will not stimulate further egg development.

cortisol

stress hormone produced by the body to ensure that the body gets enough fuel during emotional arousal and stress.

Quick Quiz 3.6: The Endocrine System

1. How do hormones differ from neurotransmitters?
   a. Hormones are proteins; neurotransmitters are fats.
   b. Hormones carry messages in the bloodstream; neurotransmitters carry messages across synapses.
   c. Hormones have no effect on mood; neurotransmitters do.
   d. all of the above

2. What is the name of the stress hormone released by the adrenal glands?
   a. catecholamine
   b. insulin
   c. thyroxin
   d. cortisol

Answers can be found at the end of the chapter.

Bringing It All Together
Making Connections in the Biology of Behavior
What Esref Armagan's Story Reveals About the Brain

This chapter opened with a profile of the blind artist Esref Armagan. Besides being a fine example of someone creatively overcoming a disability, Armagan's story offers us a way to connect much of the material in this chapter. Let's take a closer look.

When Armagan paints, he uses a Braille stylus (writing instrument) to sketch out his drawing by laying down bumps on paper. With his other hand, he follows the raised bumps to "see" what he has put down (Motluk, 2005). He then transfers this sketch to canvas and applies acrylic paint with his fingers, one color at a time. Armagan waits for each color to dry before applying another so that they will not blend or smear too much. No one helps him when he paints, and his paintings are entirely his own creations.

Armagan has learned much from talking with other people, such as what the typical colors of certain objects are. He always keeps his paints lined up in the same order so that he can find the right color. His sense of perspective is harder to explain. He portrays perspective with uncanny realism, far beyond what any other blind painter has ever achieved (Kennedy & Juricevic, 2006). He says he learned this from talking with others as well as from feeling his way in the world ("Biography," n.d.).

Armagan's skill appears to have at least some inborn basis, given how early he started without receiving any instruction. Before age 6, he would draw in dirt and scratch drawings on the furniture in his home. His parents, wanting to save their furniture, finally gave him drawing materials (Kennedy & Juricevic, 2006; Motluk, 2005)—something not usually offered to blind children. This early, automatic, and almost compulsive behavior suggests that something about how his brain was wired drove young Esref to draw, and genetics likely played a role.

What senses does Armagan use while painting? Like many blind people, Armagan relies mostly on his sense of touch. Interestingly, he needs total silence while working. In many blind people, the so-called visual centers of the brain are used to process hearing (Röder, 2006). Maybe Armagan needs silence because he cannot afford to devote the precious resources of his mind's eye to hearing.

How can we explain Armagan's act of painting in the context of the nervous system? As Armagan moves the stylus to create bumps on paper and moves his fingers over those bumps, the sensations from his fingertips stimulate his sensory neurons. These neurons, in turn, stimulate interneurons in different regions of the brain (discussed below), which eventually stimulate motor neurons to move his hands and fingers in precise ways to execute his painting.

Throughout this entire process, millions of neurons are firing. As Armagan moves his hands and fingers and begins to paint, the neurons send impulses to other neurons. Some of the messages are excitatory; some are inhibitory. If a neuron receives a preponderance of excitatory impulses and the membrane potential changes sufficiently, it will fire in an all-or-none fashion. At this point, the cell membrane opens channels letting potassium out and sodium in. The wave of opening and closing channels moves the impulse down the axon and stimulates the release of neurotransmitters in vesicles that are in the terminal buttons. The neurotransmitters are released into the synaptic cleft, where they bind with receptor sites in postsynaptic neurons, get taken back up into the presynaptic neuron, or degrade. The message is then relayed to the next (postsynaptic) neurons.

What neurotransmitters are most likely to be involved in painting? As Armagan sketches and paints, he voluntarily moves his arms, hands, and fingers. Voluntary motor

Esref Armagan with some of his paintings.

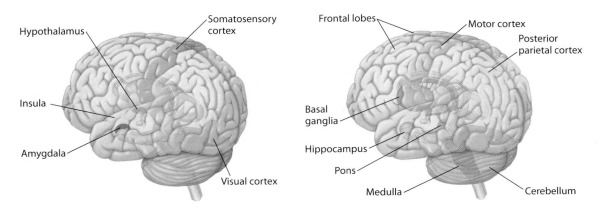

FIGURE **3.24**

SOME OF THE BRAIN REGIONS INVOLVED WHEN ESREF ARMAGAN PAINTS. When he is drawing or painting, Armagan uses many different regions of the brain. Most interestingly, Armagan's visual cortex is active in forming images of what he paints. These images do not stem from his visual system (eyes) but rather from his sense of touch (fingers). When Armagan touches something, his occipital lobes are as active as a sighted person's occipital lobes are when seeing something. In other words, he forms visual images, but they come from touching rather than seeing.

movements of muscles use synapses involving dopamine and acetylcholine. His attention and focus while painting, and his blocking out of auditory stimulation, increase his levels of norepinephrine as well. Additionally, the learning and memory needed for his artistry involve the effects of acetylcholine and glutamate in various parts of the brain.

There is activity throughout his brain, in brain stem structures as well as in the forebrain. As Armagan paints, as is true for anything he does, his breathing, heart rate, body temperature, and even consciousness are regulated by the medulla (see Figure 3.24). Armagan's thalamus transfers and relays most of the sensory information coming into various parts of the brain for different kinds of processing. And there is so much information to process! As he develops new ideas for what he wants to paint, his hippocampus is active in sending those ideas to the frontal lobes for memory or to various cortexes for more permanent storage.

In order to paint, Armagan needs to plan and execute the actions of painting. The frontal lobes play a key role in planning and keeping in mind the tasks needed to paint. His motor cortex controls movement of his legs, arms, hands, and fingers. His basal ganglia help carry out the commands to move the various parts of his body. Perhaps Armagan decides to put his fingers in the paint container to his left. The parietal lobes get involved in orienting his body in space, and the frontal lobes plan the action to reach for the paint pot to his left. When he is ready to move his hand, the signal from these cortical areas travels to the cerebellum to control fine movement, then to the pons, medulla, and finally to the

spinal cord to the nerves that control the muscles in his hand and arm. All this occurs in an instant. His brain gets feedback on the position of the hand and makes needed adjustments: a complex interplay among the somatosensory cortex (which receives sensory input from his fingers and arms as he paints), the insula, and the cerebellum.

Armagan is one of the few blind people with the ability to accurately portray depth and perspective in his drawings and paintings. When asked to draw a cube and then rotate it once and then once again, he draws it in perfect perspective, with horizontal and vertical lines converging at imaginary points in the distance (Kennedy & Juricevic, 2006). This ability to render perspective accurately in three dimensions is processed in the parietal lobes near the top and back of his brain. The visual images that Armagan forms from his sense of touch activate the same region of the brain that is active when sighted people see something: the occipital lobe.

When sighted people imagine something, their visual cortex (in the occipital lobe) is active—but in a much weaker way than when they actually look at something. When Armagan imagines an object, his visual cortex is even less active than that. But when he paints, his occipital cortex becomes so active that it cannot easily be distinguished from a sighted person's visual cortex as he actually sees something (Begley, 2007; Motluk, 2005). Armagan's brain appears to be seeing.

Because Armagan has been blind since birth, his visual cortex has never received any visual input (light). But that part of his brain didn't merely die or stop functioning. In many blind people, the visual cortex takes on hearing functions, enabling them to hear certain types of sounds better than sighted people can (Röder, 2006). Armagan's occipital cortex indeed is very active when he paints, but he is receiving tactile (touch) and not visual input.

Furthermore, in most blind people who read Braille, the visual cortex is active in processing tactile and verbal memory function. But Armagan can't read Braille and his visual cortex is not recruited for any aspect of language. In fact, his memory for language is rather poor. He is a very "visual" person, but his visual images are built from tactile information—just as images are during a walk through the Tactile Dome. There is evidence from neuroscientists who study blind people in general that this plasticity of the occipital lobes is the norm—it usually processes tactile information, verbal information, or both for blind people (Amedi et al., 2005). Armagan's life, abilities, and brain illustrate that the brain is both highly plastic *and* specialized (Begley, 2007). The so-called visual part of his brain found something to do.

Chapter **Review**

GENES AND BEHAVIOR

- At least four principles of behavioral genetics are important for psychology: (1) The relationship between specific genes and behavior is complex. (2) Most specific behaviors derive from many genes. (3) Behavioral genetics employs studies of twins and adoptees to disentangle the contributions of heredity and environment to behavior. (4) The environment influences how and when genes affect behavior.

- The extent to which a characteristic is influenced by genetics is known as heritability. Researchers use twin-adoption studies and gene-by-environment designs to study heritability.

THE NERVOUS SYSTEM

- There are two kinds of cells in the central nervous system: glial cells and neurons. Glial cells provide structural support, among other important functions.

- Neurons transmit information throughout the nervous system by means of action potentials. Messages are received by the branchlike dendrites and cell bodies of neighboring neurons; these messages create changes in the membrane of the receiving neuron. If the right conditions are met, that neuron fires in an all-or-none fashion. Action potentials move down the length of the axon as channels in the membrane open and close, allowing ions to move in and out of the axon. The action potential stimulates the release of neurotransmitters from the terminal buttons into the synaptic cleft.

- Neurotransmitters bind to receptor sites on the dendrites of postsynaptic neurons, allowing an action potential to be generated if the charge threshold is surpassed. Excess neurotransmitter is either taken back into the original neuron or broken down in the synaptic cleft.

THE BRAIN

- The brain is divided into three major regions: the hindbrain, midbrain, and forebrain.

- The topmost brain structures are the cerebrum and cerebral cortex, which are the seat of abstract reasoning, planning, and higher-order thought.

- The cerebrum comprises four lobes: the frontal lobes are involved in abstract reasoning, self-control, and motor control; the temporal lobes house the auditory cortex; the parietal lobes process tactile and spatial information; and the occipital lobes house the visual cortex.

- The left and right hemispheres of the brain carry out somewhat different functions. The biggest difference between the hemispheres is language, which is usually controlled by the left hemisphere.

- One major shift in our understanding of the brain over the last 15–20 years is how much neurons and brain structures are shaped by experience. New neurons form, new dendrites grow, and new synapses are created across the life span, especially in infancy and early childhood.

MEASURING THE BRAIN

- Various methods offer glimpses into the brain and its functions. Electroencephalography (EEG) measures electrical activity from scalp readings. Magnetic resonance imaging (MRI) measures blood flow changes in the brain without the added risk of the radioactive dyes used in PET scans. The adaptation of MRI to functional MRIs (fMRI) allows researchers to determine which brain areas are active during specific tasks.

THE ENDOCRINE SYSTEM

- In the endocrine system, glands secrete chemicals called hormones, which travel in the bloodstream to tissues and organs all over the body. The pituitary gland, called the master gland of the body, controls the release of hormones from other glands in the body. The adrenal glands secrete hormones involved in sympathetic nervous system responses and stress.

BRINGING IT ALL TOGETHER: MAKING CONNECTIONS IN THE BIOLOGY OF BEHAVIOR

- The story of Esref Armagan offers a glimpse of the brain in action. For example, as Armagan moves his hands and fingers and begins to paint, the neurons send impulses to other neurons. Activation occurs in many regions of the brain. The cerebellum fine-tunes his movements by attending to whether his body is moving appropriately with the right amount of effort. The visual images that Armagan forms from his sense of touch activate the same region of the brain that is active when seeing people see something: the occipital lobe.

Key **Terms**

Quick Quiz **Answers**

Quick Quiz 3.1: 1. b 2. a 3. a   Quick Quiz 3.2: 1. c 2. a 3. b 4. c   Quick Quiz 3.3: 1. b 2. c 3. d
Quick Quiz 3.4: 1. a 2. d   Quick Quiz 3.5: 1. c 2. d   Quick Quiz 3.6: 1. b 2. d

Challenge Your Assumptions **Answers**

• Learning can change the size of your brain. **True. See pp. 99 and 109–111.**

• Traits that are genetically influenced are set and unchanging after conception. **False. See p. 80.**

• In people who are blind, vision areas of the brain do not function. **False. See pp. 108 and 118–119.**

• You can't easily learn a new language as an adult. **True. See p. 107.**

Sensing and Perceiving Our World

4

Chapter Outline

Challenge *Your Assumptions*

TRUE OR FALSE?

- Blindness is permanent and cannot be reversed.

- The experience of "seeing sounds" or "hearing colors" occurs only under the influence of drugs.

- iPods can damage your hearing.

- Seeing is done as much with the brain as with the eyes.

Answers can be found at the end of the chapter.

123

When Ben Underwood was 3 years old, he had both eyes removed. He had a rare and malignant eye cancer, and removing the eyes altogether was his best shot at survival. When he woke up from the surgery, he said, "Mom, I can't see you anymore, Mom." But his mother said, "Yes you can see me. You can see me with your hands. You can see me with your ears. You can see me with your nose. I said baby, you can still see" ("Extraordinary People," 2007). Ben's mother wanted him to think of himself as normal, and he did. He not only thought of himself as normal, but he also acted normal, learning to ride a bike, shoot basketball, walk everywhere. He did all of these things without any aid whatsoever, other than a clicking tongue and his ability to "echolocate" (use differences in pitch when sounds bounce off objects of different sizes and distances). No one taught Ben how to echolocate. He taught himself. When he was 4, he was in the car with the window rolled down listening to the passing sounds. He astonished his mother by saying "Mom, do you see that big building out there?" She said, "Yeah, I can see that big building but how can you see it?" ("Extraordinary People," 2007). He was "seeing" the buildings by the different sounds the building made compared to open spaces or other kinds of buildings.

Tragically, when Ben was 16 the cancer returned, and he died in 2009. Yet Ben's legacy lives on. Inspired by Ben, and with the aid of echolocation proponent Daniel Kish, schools for the blind in Scotland and Israel are teaching their students to use echolocation to help them maneuver and get around (Kloosterman, 2009; Macaskill, 2008).

Ben's ability to "see" with sound is but one fascinating example of the flexibility in how humans sense and perceive their world. Every moment of every day we are bombarded with stimulation—sights, sounds, tastes, smells, and textures. In this chapter we examine the interface between the outer world and our inner experience by looking at how we sense and perceive external stimuli. Sometimes there is a one-to-one correspondence between the kind of stimulation our sense organs receive (such as light) and our perceptual experience (sight). Other times, one sense can replace another (as in Ben's case). For each of the major sensory systems, we will examine how physical information is transformed into neural signals, how the brain processes that information, and how our knowledge and expectations can shape our sensory experiences. ■

THE LONG STRANGE TRIP FROM SENSATION TO PERCEPTION

Is there a rainbow at the end of this road? We depend on sensation and perception together to detect, organize, and interpret stimuli in the world around us.

The better animals can sense what is happening in the world around them, the better they can survive and reproduce. Yet the apparently simple act of interpreting the sound vibrations hitting your ear as someone's calling your name, for example, is a complex process involving the sense organs and the brain. The sense organs transform information from its physical form (light or sound waves or chemicals) into a nerve impulse and transmit it to the brain, which organizes that information, interprets it, and then initiates a response. And it all happens in an instant and without effort on our part.

This interplay between taking in information from the outside world and interpreting it is what sensation and perception are all about. **Sensation** is the

sensation
a physical process: the stimulation of our sense organs by features of the outer world.

stimulation of our sense organs by the outer world. Our sense organs detect different features of our surroundings: Eyes are sensitive to light waves, ears to sounds, skin to touch and pressure, tongues to tastes, and noses to odors.

Yet sensing does not automatically translate into perceiving. Our brains have to receive the sensory input and then compare it to everything else it already knows, remembers, feels, and thinks. **Perception** is the act of organizing and interpreting sensory experience. It is how our psychological world represents our physical world. If you, for example, had not been taught to read, the words on this page would not be words. They would be shapes. You read and make sense of them because you spent years learning to speak English and then to read it. Your brain transforms the raw sensory experience of black and white marks into meaningful concepts that—we hope—will inspire you to learn and investigate further. The fact that different people can experience the same physical object in different ways is just one expression of how we can have different experiences of the real world and of how things are not always what they seem.

As we mentioned in Chapter 3, the brain organizes and interprets sensory experience to give it meaning. Before the brain can create meaning from sensory information, our sense organs transform physical stimuli from the outer world to a form that the brain can use—action potentials. Let's consider how basic sensory processes transform stimuli into neural information.

perception
a psychological process: the act of organizing and interpreting sensory experience.

Basic Sensory Processes

Imagine that you were constantly aware of the sensations that bombard your sense organs, such as the sound of the air conditioner, clock, traffic, and radio; the sight of the chair you're sitting on, the ceiling light, the rug on the floor; the smells in the air; and the feel of your clothing against your skin. If you were constantly sensing all this, you would suffer from sensory overload. Our sensitivity diminishes when an object constantly stimulates our senses, a process known as **sensory adaptation.** Sensory adaptation ensures that we notice changes in stimulation more than stimulation itself.

Once we know that a physical stimulus is something to attend to, the sense organs convert it into action potentials. This conversion of physical into neural information is called **transduction.** Transduction happens when cells in the retina change light waves to neural energy, when hair cells in the inner ear change sound waves to neural energy, when chemicals in the air bind to receptors in the nose, when food chemicals stimulate taste buds on the tongue, and when pressure and temperature stimulate nerve cells in the skin.

sensory adaptation
the process by which our sensitivity diminishes when an object constantly stimulates our senses.

transduction
the conversion of physical into neural information.

Principles of Perception

Some of the earliest experiments in psychology were in the field of *psychophysics,* the study of how people psychologically perceive physical stimuli such as light, sound waves, and touch (see Chapter 1). Some basic principles of perception have emerged from over a century of research in this area, including absolute threshold, signal detection theory, difference thresholds, and perceptual set. We outline these principles briefly in this section.

Absolute Thresholds   What is the smallest object you can see from a distance? What is the softest sound that you can hear? These questions refer to **absolute thresholds,** the lowest intensity level of a stimulus we can detect half

absolute threshold
the lowest intensity level of a stimulus a person can detect half of the time.

of the time. A common way to assess absolute thresholds is for a researcher to present stimuli (light, for example) of different intensities to a research participant. The intensity level that the participant can see 50% of the time is that person's absolute threshold for light. For example, imagine that six light intensities are presented 10 times each. The six intensity values are 150, 160, 170, 180, 190, and 200. Of these values, the participant detects the 180 value 50% of the time. Then 180 is this person's absolute threshold for this light stimulus (Goldstein, 2007).

Psychologists have made some general conclusions about thresholds of perception (see Figure 4.1). For example, researchers determined under ideal laboratory conditions that an average person on a very clear night could detect a single candle from 30 miles away or could distinguish 2 gallons of water with only 1 teaspoon of sugar as being different from 2 gallons of pure water (Galanter, 1962).

Signal Detection   There are a few problems, however, with measuring absolute thresholds. First, when a sensory stimulus is near absolute threshold,

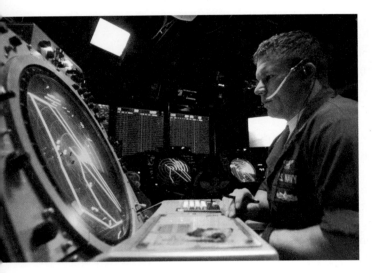

People whose jobs demand careful attention to sensory stimuli may be more aware of low-intensity signals than the rest of us. They may also be more likely to say they saw or heard something that wasn't there.

some people are more likely to say, "Yes, I perceive it," and others more likely to say, "No, I don't." Put differently, detecting sensations is a matter not only of intensity of the stimulus, but also of the decision-making process of the person in a particular context. **Signal detection theory** takes into account both stimulus intensity and the decision-making processes people use in detecting a stimulus.

Consider the situation in which there are serious consequences if you miss detecting a visual or auditory stimulus. A nurse in emergency medicine, for example, would not want to miss a slight change in a vital sign of a severely injured patient. An air traffic controller would not want to miss a bleep on the screen—it might make the difference between averting a midair collision or not. In such situations,

signal detection theory
the viewpoint that both stimulus intensity and decision-making processes are involved in the detection of a stimulus.

FIGURE **4.1**
ABSOLUTE SENSORY THRESHOLDS. These are the smallest amounts of a stimulus that most humans can perceive (Smith, 1998).

A candle flame seen at 30 miles on a clear night

The tick of a watch under quiet conditions at 20 feet

	Participant's Response	
	"Yes"	*"No"*
Stimulus Present	Hit	Miss
Stimulus Absent	False alarm	Correct rejection

FIGURE **4.2**

POSSIBLE OUTCOMES IN SIGNAL DETECTION RESEARCH. In signal detection theory, the participant's responses create a profile of hits, misses, false alarms, and correct rejections.

people may be more sensitive to sensory input, so much so that they might say they saw or heard something that was not there.

In signal detection research a low-intensity stimulus is presented on some occasions and not presented on other occasions (Green & Swets, 1974; Swets, 1964; Wickens, 2002). Instead of having a 50% detection line, signal detection experiments present only a single low-intensity stimulus. Let's use hearing as an example. A participant has 100 chances to detect a soft tone. During the 100 chances, the tone is either present or not. In signal detection, there are four possible outcomes: a *hit* is correctly detecting a stimulus that is there; a *miss* is failing to detect a stimulus that is there; a *false alarm* is saying that a stimulus exists when it does not; and a *correct rejection* is not reporting a stimulus that is not there. Figure 4.2 summarizes the possible outcomes in signal detection theory. In a signal detection study, the participant's responses create a profile of hits, misses, false alarms, and correct rejections. Using the classic method of absolute threshold, a person's threshold is assumed to be constant (for example, light intensity of 180). But in signal detection, it is assumed that a person's absolute threshold fluctuates, sometimes being more sensitive and other times being less sensitive.

Connection

Attention helps prevent sensory overload by filtering out sensory stimuli that aren't important.

See "Attention: Focusing Consciousness," Chapter 6, "Consciousness," p. 230.

The wing of a fly falling on your cheek from a distance of 1 centimeter — Touch

Vision

Hearing

A drop of perfume diffused into the entire volume of air in a six-room apartment — Smell

Taste

One teaspoon of sugar in 2 gallons of water

Difference Thresholds In addition to the principle of absolute threshold, another principle is evoked in answering the question, What is the smallest amount of change between two stimuli that a person can detect half of the time? This threshold is known as a **difference threshold.** Difference thresholds are also referred to as *just noticeable differences* (JND) because they involve the smallest difference that is noticeable. Being able to perceive slight differences is essential to a piano tuner, for example, who has to be able to distinguish the slightest change in pitch to tune the instrument.

The laws of just noticeable differences in sensory perception go back to Ernst Weber, who in 1834 discovered that the size of the JND is a constant fraction of the intensity of the stimulus. This is known as **Weber's law.** To put this more concretely: If you are given two weights, and one weighs 100 grams and the other weighs 103 grams, you would probably be able to say "Yes, these two objects are different in weight." But you might not be able to detect the difference between a 100-gram object and a 102-gram object. In this case, 3 grams, or 3%, is the JND. In fact, classic research demonstrated that 3% is the JND for weight perception (Canter & Hirsch, 1955). This means, then, that even if you had much heavier objects, say of 100 and 102 *kilo*grams, you would not perceive a difference in their weight.

Perceptual Set We have already made clear that perception happens in the brain, after transduction of the stimulus at the sense organ. So our experience of seeing or hearing or tasting is primarily a result of brain processing. Other things going on in the brain at the time of sensory processing can influence perceptual experience. In particular, our frame of mind, which is ultimately coded in the brain, can impact how we perceive things. The effect of frame of mind on perception is known as **perceptual set.** Figure 4.3 reproduces an image from a classic study of perceptual set. Bruner and Minturn (1955) showed two groups of research participants this image. The two groups, however, each saw a different set of items before viewing the image. One group saw a series of numbers; the other saw a series of letters. Of those who saw the numbers first, the vast majority said that this image was the number "13." For those who saw letters first, the vast majority saw the figure as a "B." Thus, what people had seen prior to the test image created an expectation, or perceptual set, for how they perceived what came next.

Beliefs, motives, culture, and emotions all act as perceptual sets when perceiving events in the world. As many people have pointed out, "We see what we want to see and hear what we want to hear." Such biased perception happens regularly in the political arena. People who hold particular political beliefs will perceive any one event in a way that is consistent with those beliefs (Blais et al., 2010; Munro, Lasane, & Leary, 2010; Richardson, Huddy, & Morgan, 2008). Political jokes, airport security, presidential debates, and news releases are among the many situations that are perceived one way by liberals and another way by conservatives. In one study, people differed in their perceptions of a biracial candidate's skin color depending on whether they were likely to vote for that candidate or not (Caruso, Mead, & Balcetis, 2009). As

difference threshold the smallest amount of change between two stimuli that a person can detect half of the time.

Weber's law the finding that the size of a just noticeable difference is a constant fraction of the intensity of the stimulus.

perceptual set the effect of frame of mind on perception; a tendency to perceive stimuli in a certain manner.

FIGURE **4.3**
A DEMON-STRATION OF PERCEPTUAL SET. People who saw this figure after a series of letters perceived it as a "B." Those who saw it after a series of numbers perceived it as a "13." (Source: Bruner & Minturn, 1955)

Connection
Memories of events, especially emotional events like crimes, are very selective, and our frame of mind (perceptual set) influences what part of an event we are likely to recall.
See "Three Types of Memory," Chapter 7, "Memory," p. 269.

we will discuss in Chapter 14 ("Social Behavior"), many attitudes and opinions we hold can influence how we perceive and interpret information that we bring in from the world around us.

Quick Quiz 4.1: The Long Strange Trip From Sensation to Perception

1. The conversion of physical into neural information is called
   a. conduction
   b. transduction
   c. perception
   d. adaptation

2. Which of the following may act as a perceptual set in constructing our visual experience?
   a. mood
   b. expectation
   c. knowledge of how the world works
   d. all of the above

Answers can be found at the end of the chapter.

VISION

Most mammals rely on smell over all other senses, but humans are visual creatures. We rely so much on our sense of sight that we often ignore other types of information. Why is vision so important? In terms of evolution, being able to see helps us know where we are, what other people might want from us, and whether there is danger nearby. We evolved as hunter-gatherers. In hunting, vision is critical for locating prey and avoiding danger. So is hearing, which is the sense we rely on the most after vision. In gathering food, we use vision to locate the foods we can eat, and we also rely on our sense of smell to know whether a food is safe. But vision is king, and it starts with the eye.

Sensing Visual Stimuli

What does the eye do? It bends light, converts light energy to neural energy, and sends that information to the brain for further processing. The eye is the gateway to vision, but very little of what we experience as vision actually happens in the eye. Visual experience happens in the brain, with input from the eye. Before we explore the more complicated matter of how the brain sees, let's look briefly at the organ of the eye itself and how it converts light energy to neural energy.

Vision and the Eye Light enters the eye at the **cornea,** a clear hard covering that protects the lens. It then passes through liquid until it reaches a hole called the **pupil.** Light enters the interior of the eye through the pupil. The colored part of the eye, the **iris,** adjusts the pupil to control the amount of light entering the eye. The light then passes through the **lens,** which bends the light rays. Muscles around the lens alter its shape, depending on the distance of an object, to allow it to focus light on the retina. The process by which the muscles control the shape of the lens to adjust to viewing objects at different distances is known as **accommodation.**

The **retina** is a thin layer of nerve tissue that lines the back of the eye. The retina consists of several layers of cells. As indicated in Figure 4.4, the light that hits the retina travels through several cell layers before processing begins. Note how the image hits the retina upside down. The brain reorients the inverted image so that our world is right side up.

cornea
the clear hard covering that protects the lens of the eye.

pupil
the opening in the iris through which light enters the eye.

iris
the muscle that forms the colored part of the eye; it adjusts the pupil to regulate the amount of light that enters the eye.

lens
the structure that sits behind the pupil; it bends the light rays that enter the eye to focus images on the retina.

accommodation
the process by which the muscles control the shape of the lens to adjust to viewing objects at different distances.

retina
the thin layer of nerve tissue that lines the back of the eye.

FIGURE **4.4**

THE EYE AND ITS RECEPTOR CELLS. In (a) we see all the main structures of the eye. Notice that the image of the butterfly is projected upside down on the retina in the back of the eye. In (b) we see the layers of cells in the retina, including the photoreceptors (rods and cones). In (c), an enlarged view of the retina shows the layers of the cells involved in processing light. Light hits the retina and is processed first by the photoreceptors (deepest layers), then by the *bipolar cells,* which send it to the ganglion cells.

The deepest layer of cells, where processing of light energy begins, is the layer of **photoreceptors** (see Figure 4.4). The two types of photoreceptors in the retina—rods and cones—convert light energy into neural impulses.

Rods play a key role in night vision, as they are most responsive to dark and light contrast. They work well at low illumination. We have all experienced rods in action. Consider what happens when someone turns out the lights. At first, everything is completely dark. Then, with a bit of time, you begin to see shapes and forms, although you cannot really see colors. The process of adjustment to seeing in the dark, known as **dark adaptation,** reflects the rods at work. This process of adapting to dark can take up to 30 minutes (Rushton, 1961). Rods are very sensitive, however, and sudden exposure to light can quickly cancel out their effectiveness.

photoreceptors
cells in the retina (called rods and cones) that convert light energy into nerve energy.

dark adaptation
process of adjustment to seeing in the dark.

rods
photoreceptors that function in low illumination and play a key role in night vision; responsive to dark and light contrast.

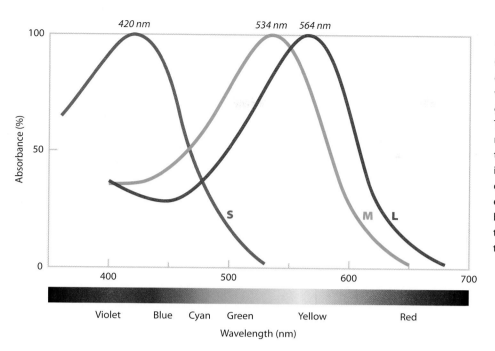

FIGURE **4.5**

THREE TYPES OF CONES IN HUMAN COLOR VISION. Humans have three different cones sensitive to different wavelengths of light: blue (short), green (medium), and yellow-red (long). The long-wavelength cone is actually most sensitive in the yellow range of the wavelength (about 565 nm), but is referred to as red. Most people with color blindness and most mammals except primates are sensitive only to blue and green wavelengths. That is, they are either missing or have insensitive red cones.

cones
photoreceptors that are responsible for color vision and are most functional in conditions of bright light.

visual acuity
the ability to see clearly.

Cones, on the other hand, are responsible for color vision and are most functional in conditions of bright light. They act much more quickly than rods. Upon exposure to light, cones reach maximum effectiveness in about 5 minutes or so, because the chemicals involved in their function replenish quickly (Rushton, 1961). The **fovea,** a spot on the back of the retina, contains the highest concentration of cones in the retina. We see images with the greatest clarity when they are focused on the fovea. So **visual acuity,** or our ability to see clearly, depends on our cones. Those animals with the best acuity have the most cones.

Humans and other primates are unique when it comes to vision in mammals. Primates—humans included—have three kinds of cones: those that are sensitive to red, green, and blue wavelengths of light (Jacobs & Nathans, 2009). Humans therefore are trichromatic (sensitive to three colors) (see Figure 4.5). The millions of colors we see are simply combinations of different intensities of these three wavelengths. All mammals except primates are sensitive to only

fovea
spot on the back of the retina that contains the highest concentration of cones in the retina; place of clearest vision.

How do 3-D glasses alter the way we perceive a movie?

FIGURE **4.6**

TEST YOUR BLIND SPOT. Locate the blind spot in your left eye by shutting the right eye and looking at the upper cross with the left eye. Hold the book about 15 inches from the eye and move it slightly closer to and away from the eye until the circle on the left disappears. At this point the circle occupies the blind spot on the left eye. If you then look at the lower cross, the gap in the black line falls on the blind spot and the black line will appear to be continuous. (Source: Wurtz & Kandel, 2000a, who adapted it from Hurvich, 1981)

two pigments—they are dichromatic, sensitive only to blue (short) and green (medium) wavelengths. Most nocturnal animals are sensitive to only one wavelength. Birds, reptiles, and many fish, however, have cones sensitive to four different wavelengths of light (Goldsmith, 2006; Jacobs & Nathans, 2009). They are usually sensitive to wavelengths longer than red—that is, infrared light. So not only do birds see more colors than we, but they also far surpass humans in visual acuity.

Vision and the Brain

After transduction at the photoreceptor layer, visual information is processed by different layers of cells in the retina. One of these layers is made up of the *ganglion cells,* the axons of which make up the optic nerve. The **optic nerve** transmits signals from the eye to the brain. The point at which the optic nerve exits the eye is the *blind spot* of the retina because this location has no receptor cells and therefore nothing is seen. Figure 4.6 offers a demonstration of the blind spot.

optic nerve
structure composed of the axons of ganglion cells from the retina that carry visual information from the eye to the brain.

Another interesting detail about the focusing of the visual image on the retina concerns how well we see. In people with normal vision, the lens projects the image to hit just on the retina. In people who are nearsighted (myopic), the image focuses slightly in front of the retina (see Figure 4.7). This means that nearsighted people can see close objects clearly, but distant objects are fuzzy. In people who are farsighted (hyperopic), the image actually focuses behind the retina. This means they can see distant objects clearly, but close objects are fuzzy. As people age, the lens becomes less flexible, and it is more likely that the visual image will focus behind the retina. This is an age-related form of farsightedness (presbyopia).

Exactly what happens when visual information arrives in the brain? The optic nerve carries impulses to the thalamus and, ultimately, to the visual cortex of the occipital lobes. This journey is *not* straightforward. As you can see from Figure 4.8, the information from the left visual field is processed in the brain's right hemisphere, and the information from the right visual field is processed in the brain's left hemisphere. How the visual information gets to these hemispheres is a bit complicated. Let's look at this process more closely.

In Figure 4.8, notice that in each eye, each half of the retina (the area at the back) sends out its own axons. So each optic nerve has two strands. One strand

Uncorrected

In **nearsightedness,** the lens focuses the image in front of the retina.

Corrected

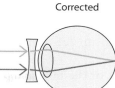

In **nearsightedness,** with a minus lens for correction, the image focuses directly on the retina.

Uncorrected

In **farsightedness,** the lens focuses the image past the retina.

Corrected

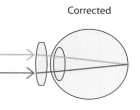

In **farsightedness,** with a plus lens for correction, the image focuses directly on the retina.

FIGURE **4.7**

NEARSIGHTEDNESS AND FARSIGHTEDNESS. In nearsightedness, the uncorrected lens of the eye focuses the image short of the retina. In farsightedness, the uncorrected lens focuses the image past the retina. With corrective lenses, the image is accurately projected on the retina.

FIGURE **4.8**

THE VISUAL PATHWAYS IN HUMAN VISION. In (a) we see how input from the right visual field is sensed by the left side of the retina of each eye. This input then travels along the optic nerve to the optic chiasm and then to the thalamus (lateral geniculate nucleus). The same happens to input from the left visual field, except it is sensed by the right side of the retina of each eye (blue). From the thalamus, nerve fibers transmit visual information to the visual cortex of the occipital lobes (green). In (b) we see a side view of the path that visual stimulation takes from the retina via the optic nerve and the thalamus to the visual cortex.

from each eye contains axons that travel from the retina to the thalamus and on to the visual cortex of the *same* side of the brain as the eye from which the axons come. The other strand crosses to the *opposite* side of the brain in an area called the **optic chiasm.**

optic chiasm
the point at which strands of the optic nerve from half of each eye cross over to the opposite side of the brain.

The first stop in the brain for most of the fibers of the optic nerve is the thalamus. If the pathways to the thalamus are cut, visual perception is not possible, beyond some crude ability to detect the presence of a stimulus (Wurtz & Kandel, 2000a). As we discussed in Chapter 3, the thalamus serves as a relay station for most of the major sense inputs to the brain, taking information from the sense organs and sending it to the relevant area of the cerebral cortex for processing. The thalamus does more than just relay information, however. Real visual processing occurs there. A cluster of the neuron cell bodies in the thalamus forms the *lateral geniculate nucleus* (LGN). Visual information creates a point-by-point representation on the tissue of the LGN. What this means is that patterns of neural firing that correspond to the shape projected on a specific region of retina affect a similar layout of cells in the LGN. So the retina and the LGN represent visual information in similar ways (Wurtz & Kandel, 2000a).

Fibers from the LGN in the thalamus then travel to the visual cortex in the occipital lobes. Neurons in the visual cortex analyze the retinal image in terms of its various patterns, contrasts, lines, and edges. Different cortical cells handle different aspects of this analysis, as a breakthrough discovery by Hubel and Wiesel demonstrated.

Vision and Specific Neurons

Researchers had known for decades that after leaving the retina, optic fibers go to the visual portion of the thalamus (the LGN) and then travel to the visual cortex in the occipital lobes. The work of Hubel and Wiesel—for which they won the Nobel Prize in 1981—showed something astounding. Their work showed us that individual neurons fire only because of very specific visual information. They provided the first evidence that the neurons of the visual cortex are highly specialized for detecting specific features of visual stimuli. They were able to record specialized activity of individual cells in the brain's vision area by implanting electrodes into the visual cortex of cats. As a result, they discovered neurons called **feature detectors** in the visual cortex, which analyze the retinal image and respond to specific aspects of shapes, such as angles and movements (Hubel & Wiesel, 1962, 1979).

feature detectors
neurons in the visual cortex that analyze the retinal image and respond to specific aspects of shapes, such as angles and movements.

More specifically, Hubel and Wiesel described three types of neurons in the visual cortex that act as feature detectors. Simple cells respond to very specific information, such as a bar of light oriented at a particular angle. Some simple cells respond to only one angle or orientation, other simple cells respond to other angles of orientation, and still others to edges. As seen in Figure 4.9a, a particular simple cell might be receptive only to a diagonal line of a particular orientation. As seen in Figure 4.9b, recordings from this one simple cell show activity only to lines that match its receptive field, which in this case is a diagonal line from about 11 o'clock to 5 o'clock (\). The cell begins to fire more often as the stimulus (line) approaches the angle to which the cell is most responsive. As the stimulus passes that orientation on its way back to horizontal, the cell fires less and less often. This is the activity of just one simple cell. Other simple cells are responsive to other orientations, shapes, and sizes of lines.

A simple cell responds only to visual stimuli that stay still or are in the middle of its receptive field. Other cells, called complex cells, receive input from many different simple cells and are receptive to particular stimuli in different

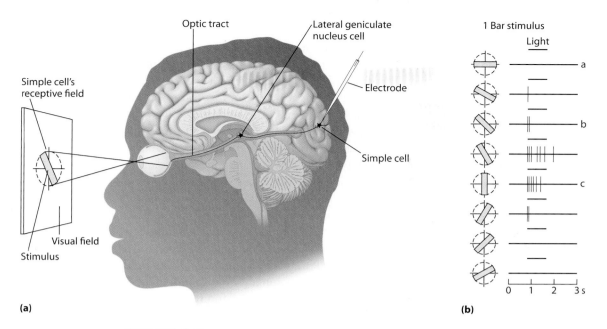

Optic tract

Lateral geniculate nucleus cell

Electrode

Simple cell

Simple cell's receptive field

Visual field

Stimulus

(a)

1 Bar stimulus

Light

a

b

c

0   1   2   3 s

(b)

FIGURE **4.9**

NEURAL ACTIVITY OF A SIMPLE CELL THAT IS RECEPTIVE TO ONE PARTICULAR DIAGONAL ORIENTATION. In (a) we see the stimulus on a visual field and how this particular simple cell is receptive to lines tilted from about 11 o'clock to 5 o'clock as if it were a clock face. In (b) each vertical line to the right of the stimulus represents a neural impulse. The cell begins to fire more often as the stimulus (line) approaches the angle to which the cell is the most responsive. As the stimulus passes that orientation on its way back to horizontal, the cell fires less and less frequently. Otherwise, this particular cell does not fire. (Adapted from Wurtz & Kandel, 2000a, p. 534)

parts of the receptive field. Unlike simple cells, complex cells are also sensitive to the movement of an image and respond if it appears anywhere in the visual field. In addition, hypercomplex cells receive inputs from many complex cells, and so they fire in response to patterns of lines. To give a concrete example: If some simple cells are responsive to / and others to \, then the hypercomplex cells are sensitive to the entire configuration of \/\/.

If the images and objects are broken up into horizontal and vertical lines, edges, colors, faces, hands, and shapes by the visual cortex, how is it that we ever see whole and integrated images? Reassembling the pieces occurs partly in hypercomplex cells in the visual cortex, but integration mostly happens when the visual cortex sends the images to other parts of the brain, such as the frontal or parietal lobes (Perry & Zeki, 2000; Wurtz & Kandel, 2000b). Thus, the cortex does not passively accept the nerve impulses from the retina and thalamus. The cortex actively transforms the signals by first breaking them down and then putting them back together.

Hubel and Wiesel made an even more monumental discovery when they closed one eye of a newborn cat. In the first weeks in a cat's life, when its brain is growing most rapidly, visual experience is critical for brain structures to develop all the necessary neural connections needed to see well. If a cat is blinded or has its eyes closed for a week or more during this important stage of development, its visual cortex does not develop properly and the animal's vision is forever stunted. If one eye is closed early in life for an extended period of time, the part of the brain receiving messages from the closed eye soon begins to receive and process visual messages from the one good eye. Moreover, it is not merely light that the developing brain needs if vision is to properly develop, but also lines, shapes, and colors—the full visual experience. Contrary to common sense, we see as much with our brain as with our eyes. In a very real sense, we have to learn to see.

A dramatic demonstration in humans of the principle of the brain needing to develop in order to see comes from the case of Mike May and others like him. May lost his vision at age 3. Four decades later, he had surgery to repair his eyes, in which doctors replaced the corneas (the clear outer layer of the eye) and other tissues. The surgery gave Mike working eyes. Mike May could not miraculously "see" right after his surgery. He could barely make out vague shapes, colors, and light. It took him months to learn how to see again. Finally, three years after the surgery, Mike's vision started to approach normal. Many formerly blind people never fully recover their vision, especially if they have been blind since birth (Kurson, 2007). Seeing requires the right environmental stimulation (in this case, light) and neurons specialized for vision. It requires both sensation and perception, which involve a complex dance of environmental input and biology, of nature and nurture. In short, visual perception is softwired and requires input from the environment in order to develop.

Breaking New Ground

Discovery of the "Halle Berry Neuron"

After Hubel and Wiesel's work, other researchers continued to find different cortical cells that fire in response to certain visual stimuli. Some, for example, respond to faces. If some cells fire when they are stimulated with faces in general, what happens when cells are stimulated with a specific face? The answer may surprise you.

Do you have a Halle Berry neuron?

In 2005 Rodrigo Quian Quiroga and his colleagues decided to test how selective individual neurons were (Quiroga et al., 2005). They took advantage of surgical procedures already being conducted on people with epileptic seizures to test the activity of individual neurons. The brains of these patients were already being probed with electrodes that measured activity of single neurons, and so Quiroga and colleagues piggybacked onto that procedure to examine whether single neurons fired to specific images of famous and nonfamous people, animals, and buildings. Famous people included Bill Clinton, Jennifer Aniston, and Halle Berry. Results of the study were stunning and surprising: As Quiroga put it, "The first time we saw a neuron firing to seven different pictures of Jennifer Aniston—and nothing else—we literally jumped out of our chairs" (Martindale, 2005, p. 22). The same thing happened with photos

Connections

In many areas of development, such as language and learning, there are sensitivity periods when the brain is optimally receptive to environmental stimulation. One researcher found this out when newly hatched goslings (geese) mistook him for their mother.

See "Imprinting," Chapter 8, "Learning," p. 335, and "Language Development in Individuals," Chapter 9, "Language and Thought," p. 350.

25 spikes/sec

1000 ms

FIGURE **4.10**

THE ACTIVITY OF A SINGLE "BILL CLINTON" NEURON. This figure shows the activity of a single neuron in the medial temporal lobe as it processes 12 different visual images. Below each image is a bar graph showing the neural activity. The higher the bar, the greater the neural activity. This particular neuron fired quite a bit to images of Bill Clinton (upper left boxed area) but hardly at all to other faces, shapes, buildings, landscapes, or animals. The light-gray regions extending upward in the bar graphs are the time when the image was being shown to the person. (Source: Kreiman, 2007)

Nature&
Nurture

Neurons are shaped by experience and "learn" to respond only to very specific faces, buildings, or animals.

of Clinton and Berry and famous buildings such as the Sydney Opera House and the Tower of Pisa. In Figure 4.10, we see the firing of a single neuron sensitive to images of Bill Clinton but no other faces, shapes, buildings, or animals.

This finding has been dubbed the "Halle Berry neuron" even though it applies to more than just Halle Berry. Recent research has extended this finding and has demonstrated that just thinking about Halle Berry (not actually seeing a picture of her) is enough to stimulate the "Halle Berry neuron" (Sanders, 2009).

Does that mean we are born with Halle Berry neurons? No. What it does mean is that based on our exposure and interest in certain things or people, *single cells* can come to represent a category of things, such as all things Halle Berry-ish. It also means that neurons are not passive switches, but rather are more like computers or even "thinking" cellular organisms.

■ ■ ■

Perceiving Visual Stimuli

So far we have followed visual information from light entering the eye to impulses sent to the thalamus and then on the visual cortex, where cells fire in response to very specific features of a visual stimulus. How do we move from detecting edges to perceiving shapes, from noticing lines to identifying objects? A number of processes work together to help us recognize objects in the world. These involve motion, depth, size, grouping, and color perception.

Perceiving Motion   Feature detectors play a role in how we perceive movement and form. We perceive movement when an image moves across the retina. Simple and complex cells respond to either the orientation or direction of moving images. Sometimes these moving images truly reflect movement in the world around us. As we view any scene, several factors contribute to how we perceive movement. One factor is the background against which an object moves, and another factor is the size of the object. When an object moves across a complex background, it appears to move faster than when it moves across a simple background. For example, a deer running across a field with mountains and trees in the background will seem to move faster than one running across a wide open plain, simply because the background objects provide references that help us note the change of position in the deer. The human visual system is quite sensitive to changes in the position of objects, a sensitivity that appears to decline a bit with age (P. J. Bennett, Sekuler, & Sekuler, 2007).

Size matters too. Smaller objects appear to move faster than larger objects, when all else is equal. If we see a domestic rabbit and a mule deer run across a wide open plain, the rabbit will appear to be running at a faster speed because of its size. In fact, these two animals run at about the same speed.

We can also be fooled into thinking something is moving when it is not. We refer to this illusion as *apparent motion* because our brains interpret images that move across our retinas as movement. The "moving" lights on a movie theater marquee are a rapid succession of bulbs lighting up in a row. Even though we know the lights are not moving, we still interpret this illusion as movement.

Here's another interesting question. If you press on your eyelid when your eye is open and look straight ahead, you will notice the image shaking around. Yet, you do not perceive this effect as an earthquake. Why? According to research on monkeys, there are neurons that respond only when the image itself moves and not when the eye moves. So when you press on your eye, these neurons that detect image movement, called *real movement neurons,* do not fire. When the image itself moves without eye movement, they do fire (Galletti & Fattori, 2003). This is one way the brain can determine the difference between real and false movement.

Depth Perception   We take for granted that we see things in three dimensions and can discriminate what is near from what is far; this is what we call **depth perception.** This skill is remarkable, given that the image projected on the retina is two-dimensional. So how does this work? Two major aspects of human visual anatomy and processing allow for depth perception: binocular and monocular depth cues.

depth perception
the ability to see things in three dimensions and to discriminate what is near from what is far.

Binocular Depth Cues   **Binocular depth cues** rely on input from both eyes. One key binocular cue to depth comes from the fact that the eyes are separated by a few inches, so the images from each eye provide slightly different viewpoints. The difference, or *binocular disparity,* in these retinal images plays a key role in our ability to perceive depth. To see how this works, hold a finger out in front of you. Close one eye, and then close the other eye: You will see how the image shifts slightly to one side, depending on which eye is closed and which eye is opened. The brain integrates these two slightly different two-dimensional images into a single three-dimensional image. Many animals are capable of depth perception, but this quality depends on the location of the eyes in the head.

binocular depth cues
aids to depth perception that rely on input from both eyes.

FIGURE **4.11**

TRADITIONAL TECHNOLOGY FOR THREE-DIMENSIONAL TELEVISION AND MOVIES. Two cameras, each with a different colored filter, record the action. Once a movie is made and projected, the moviegoer wears blue and red glasses. The blue eyepiece filters out the blue and leaves only the red image; the red eyepiece filters out red and leaves only the blue image. Each eye, therefore, sees only one image. The brain then integrates these two slightly different images so that we see them as being three-dimensional. (Source: Brain, 2003)

Three-dimensional TV and movies make use of binocular depth cues for their effect. Just as humans have two eyes slightly apart, 3-D movies are filmed with two cameras slightly apart. Traditionally, one camera films with a red filter and the other camera with a blue filter. On the screen both images are projected, but when the moviegoer puts on red and blue glasses, each eye sees only the image from one camera and not the other (see Figure 4.11). In other words, each eye is seeing only one of the two separate images. The brain then integrates these two images into one, and the effect is perceived as three-dimensional. Rather than using color to filter the images, modern 3-D technology in movie theaters uses polarizing filters to do the same. Each camera has a different polarizing angle (usually horizontal or vertical), and each eyepiece of the glasses has one polarizing angle or the other. The effect is the same: Each eye sees only one perspective, which is merged in the brain as three-dimensional.

monocular depth cues

aids to depth perception that do not require two eyes.

Monocular Depth Cues We derive a great deal of information about depth from the numerous **monocular depth cues** (*monocular* meaning "one eye") that do not require two eyes to be effective. These cues allow people who are blind in one eye to perceive some depth. Our knowledge of many of these cues derives from the seminal work of James Gibson (1950, 1966). Let's discuss some of the most common ones. *Linear perspective* involves parallel lines that converge or come together the farther away they are from the viewer. The more they converge, the greater distance we perceive. See Figure 4.12a for this classic effect in railroad tracks. *Texture gradient* is a monocular depth cue that causes the texture of a surface to appear more tightly packed together and denser as the surface moves to the background. These changes in textural information help us judge depth. Notice in Figure 4.12b that the red poppies are more tightly packed at the top of the picture, which makes us think that those flowers are farther away. Another cue, *atmospheric perspective*, comes from looking across a vast space into the distance in the outdoors. Anyone who has stood at the

(a) linear perspective

(b) texture gradient

(c) atmospheric perspective

(d) interposition

FIGURE **4.12**

MONOCULAR CUES TO DEPTH. It isn't necessary to have vision in both eyes to perceive depth using monocular cues.

edge of the Grand Canyon has seen atmospheric perspective at work. We are looking through air and particles in the air (more so when the air is polluted). Objects farther away appear more blurred and bluish as a result (see Figure 4.12c). A final monocular depth cue is called *interposition*, the partial blocking of objects farther away from the viewer by objects closer to the viewer, which happens when objects closer to the viewer often overlap with those farther away. This is a reliable cue to depth. Look at the image in Figure 4.12d of the lemons. The closer lemons hide part of the one behind them.

Perceptual Constancy We know what familiar objects look like, and we know that when they change position or distance in relation to us, they remain the same. Nevertheless, the images on our retinas change shape and size as objects move through space. The ability of the brain to preserve perception of such objects in spite of the changes in retinal image is known as **perceptual constancy.** We will look at two types of perceptual constancy: those of size and shape.

Size Constancy We see things as the same size regardless of the changing size of the image on the retina, because we know what the size of the object is. For example, if you see your friend Jayson, who is about 6 feet tall, walking away from you, the size of his image on your retina shrinks. Yet you do not suddenly think, "Oh no, Jayson is shrinking!" Rather, your knowledge of Jayson's height and your knowledge that people maintain their height even when they move away from you prevent you from interpreting the smaller retinal image as a smaller person. Also, distance cues, such as linear perspective, indicate that the road Jayson is walking on is in the distance, and your brain makes use of this information *plus* your knowledge of Jayson's size to keep his size constant in your mind.

A stunning demonstration of distortions in the perception of size is the Ames room. In the photograph shown in Figure 4.13a, the child on the right looks enormous compared to the one on the left. It turns out, however, that the room is not rectangular (as we expect it to be) but rather trapezoidal, and the girl on the right is standing much closer to the peephole through which the viewer looks (as depicted in Figure 4.13b). So the distance cues that we tend to rely on are not available, and we perceive the two people as equally far away, which makes the child on the right appear enormous.

Shape Constancy People know the shapes of common things just as they know their sizes. The brain uses this knowledge to override changing retinal images that might make the world very confusing indeed. Take a look

perceptual constancy
the ability of the brain to preserve perception of objects in spite of changes in retinal image when an object changes in position or distance from the viewer.

(a)

(b)

FIGURE **4.13**

THE AMES ROOM. The Ames room was designed to distort perceptions of size (a). When a person looks into the room through a peephole, it appears to be a normal rectangular room and hence the two people seem to be very different sizes: The one on the right is a giant compared to the one on the left. In reality, the two people are the same size. The room is built in such a way that the rear right wall is much closer to the viewer than the rear left wall, masking distance cues on which we tend to rely for size perception (b).

at Figure 4.14. When we see a door that is closed, it looks like a rectangle (and this is what the 2-D image on our retina looks like). A door that is partially open looks like a trapezoid. Still, we would not think that the door has suddenly changed shape. Again, the brain corrects our perception based on previous knowledge that doors retain their shape when they change position.

Organizing Visual Information: Gestalt Laws of Grouping

How is it that we recognize a set of black marks on a white page as a letter or a shape rather than just a bunch of markings? We know, for example, that the letter *E* is more than just one long vertical line segment plus three shorter horizontal line segments. The Gestalt psychologists recognized that often we perceive wholes as more than merely the sum of their parts. *Gestalt* is a German

FIGURE **4.14**

SHAPE CONSTANCY. Even though the two-dimensional retinal image of the door changes in shape from rectangular to trapezoidal when the door is opened, we know the door's shape hasn't changed.

Vision   **141**

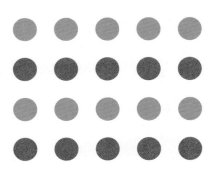

FIGURE **4.15**
GESTALT LAWS OF ORGANIZATION: SIMILARITY. People are more likely to see this figure as two rows of blue dots and two rows of red dots than as 20 dots, some red, some blue.

word that means "form," "pattern," or "shape." German researchers Max Wertheimer, Kurt Koffka, and Wolfgang Köhler studied visual perception in the early 20th century and described a set of principles or laws by which people organize elements of figures or scenes into whole objects. Let's examine the major Gestalt laws of visual organization: similarity, continuity, proximity, closure, and figure–ground.

What do you see when you look at Figure 4.15? Most people with normal color vision would report seeing two lines of blue dots alternating with two lines of red dots. You would not say, "Oh, 20 dots; some are red and some are blue." Instead, we group the elements that are like one another together into a perceptual unit—the red dots go together and the blue dots go together. This Gestalt tendency to group like objects together is known as **similarity.**

According to the Gestalt law of **continuity,** we see

similarity
Gestalt law that says we tend to group like objects together in visual perception.

continuity
Gestalt law that says we see points or lines in such a way that they follow a continuous path.

points or lines in such a way that they follow a continuous path. This sounds rather abstract, so let's look at an example. Consider the first drawing in Figure 4.16. We see a straight line running through a curved line. We do *not* see the first drawing as a result of combining the two pieces from the second drawing.

FIGURE **4.16**
GESTALT LAWS OF ORGANIZATION: CONTINUITY.

Connection
The Gestalt law of proximity makes use of the short-term memory technique called "chunking."
See "Short-Term or Working Memory," Chapter 7, "Memory," p. 272.

The Gestalt law of **proximity** says that we tend to group together objects that are near one another. Figure 4.17 shows a series of blue boxes. How would you describe what you see here? Most people say that they see four pairs of boxes, rather than eight boxes, because of the spacing. The first two are closer together than the second and third, and the third and fourth are closer together than the fourth and fifth, and so on.

proximity
Gestalt law that says we tend to group objects together that are near one another.

FIGURE **4.17**
GESTALT LAWS OF ORGANIZATION: PROXIMITY.

Take a look at Figure 4.18a. Most human observers see these figures as distinct shapes (a circle and two triangles) rather than as lines, curves, and spheres, even though they are incomplete. The **law of closure** occurs when we perceive a whole object in the absence of complete information. The drawing in Figure 4.18b provides another example of how our perceiving brain completes the drawing to see a duck.

law of closure
The tendency to perceive a whole object in the absence of complete information.

FIGURE **4.18**
GESTALT LAWS OF ORGANIZATION: CLOSURE. We see the figures (a) as distinct shapes. We see (b) as a duck, not as a bunch of curved line segments.

(a)

(b)

(a)

FIGURE **4.19**
FIGURE–GROUND EFFECTS.
In (a), is it a vase or two faces?
In (b), M. C. Escher's *Sky and Water I,* do you see fish or geese?

(b)

Another key Gestalt notion concerns how we separate things into *figure* and *ground*, where the figure is the thing that stands in front of a somewhat unformed background. Gestalt psychologists pointed out that we readily separate a figure from its background in order to perceive it. Perhaps the most famous example of figure–ground effects is the face–vase figure, a version of which is shown in Figure 4.19a. Notice that you can view the figure either as a blue vase against a light background or as two facial profiles (with blue space in between them). It is impossible to see both the vase and the faces at the same moment. Dutch painter M. C. Escher regularly used figure–ground effects in his paintings, one of which is also depicted in Figure 4.19b.

Numerous visual illusions stem from Gestalt figure–ground principles, many of which have hidden figures as in Figure 4.20. Once you know what to look for in the picture, the hidden object becomes figural and you cannot help but see it. Try it for yourself.

FIGURE **4.20**
FIGURE–GROUND EFFECTS IN SCENE PERCEPTION. What do you see in this image? See page 167 to find out what you may have missed.

FIGURE **4.21**

THE MÜLLER–LYER ILLUSION. Which line is longer?

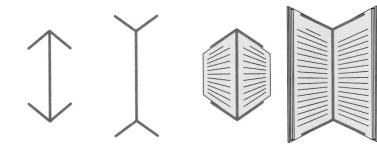

Other visual illusions make use of the way our brain interprets depth cues (see Figure 4.21). Which line is longer, the one on the right or the one on the left? If you take a ruler to the page you will find that both line segments are identical in length, but many people report that the one on the right looks longer. Why do we see it that way? This illusion, known as the Müller-Lyer illusion, results from our tendency to see the right line as the inside corner of a room and the left one as the outside corner of a room or building, making use of the monocular depth cue of linear perspective.

Another commonly experienced illusion results from monocular depth cues. Take a look at the three SUVs shown in Figure 4.22. Are they the same size, or is the one in the back larger than the other two? Distance cues (horizon) make objects look bigger than they are. More famously, the *moon illusion* occurs when the moon is closer to the horizon. At that time, it appears to be much larger than when it is in the sky. You can see the moon illusion in Figure 4.23. Of course, the moon is not any larger, so why does this happen? Scientists offer several different explanations for the moon illusion, and although no answer provides one true cause for the illusion, nearly all explanations involve cues to depth perception (E. B. Goldstein, 2007).

FIGURE **4.22**

ANOTHER ILLUSION OF SIZE AND DEPTH PERCEPTION. Which SUV is larger? Why don't you believe they are all the same size? Measure them and see for yourself. Like the moon illusion, this illusion comes about by our brain believing objects nearer the horizon are larger than those closer to us.

FIGURE **4.23**

MOON ILLUSION. Distance cues make the moon look bigger on the horizon.

144 CHAPTER 4 Sensing and Perceiving Our World

One explanation is that when the moon is near the horizon, we see it against other cues that indicate we are looking off into the distance (such as buildings interposed on the moon, possibly roads that offer cues to linear perspective, and so on). Another way to look at it is this: When the moon is in the middle of the night sky, there are no cues to distance, no objects with which to compare it, and it is surrounded by a huge sky. Relative to the sky, the moon does not look so big. When the moon is on the horizon, however, we view it against objects whose size we know. Relative to those earthly objects, the moon looks enormous, as it is (Baird, Wagner, & Fuld, 1990).

to Real Life

Research

We found websites that present some images that are fake, although many people perceive them as real. For example: http://www.youtube.com/watch?v=nipNsM4TDI4 or http://www.youtube.com/watch?v=jcjjGF_4jcg&feature=related

Connecting Psychology to Your Life: Do your own Web search and find two or three additional sites that present urban myths or fake images. Don't believe everything you see!

Visual Perception: Bottom-Up or Top-Down? Feature detection research suggests that visual perception is a process of building a visual experience from smaller pieces. We put the pieces together, and then we "see" the whole. This perspective is known as **bottom-up processing.** Yet we have also looked at how perceptual set and Gestalt principles can guide how we make visual sense of information. An implied familiar shape, such as that seen in Figure 4.3, overrides our perception of the elements. Processing in which perception of the whole guides perception of smaller elemental features is called **top-down processing.** These two processes would seem to work in opposition, so which is correct? It depends on the nature of the information being processed. Reading, for example, relies on both bottom-up and top-down processing. To recognize a vertical line segment intersected by a shorter line segment as a *t,* some building up of elemental features is required. But to make sense of the meaning of a *t* next to an *o* as the word *to,* some top-down processing takes over, including your knowledge of English and the function of a preposition in a sentence (Johnston & McClelland, 1974; Pelli, Farell, & More, 2003).

bottom-up processing idea that perception is a process of building a perceptual experience from smaller pieces.

top-down processing perception of the whole based on our experience and expectations, which guide our perception of smaller elemental features of a stimulus.

The Perception of Color

We tend to think of color as a property of the objects we see. "That rose is red" or "The sky is blue." You may be surprised to learn that color is not a property of objects—it is a property of us. Our perception of color depends on our photoreceptors, our brains, and the physical characteristics of the stimulus we look at. Let's start with the physical stimulus. Color perception is partly determined by wavelength, measured in billionths of a meter or nanometers (nm). The spectrum of color visible to humans ranges from 350 nm, which most of us perceive to be the color blue, to 750 nm, which most of us perceive as red. Light that we perceive as green is at 550 nm. Figure 4.24 shows the spectrum of light visible to humans.

Two Theories of Color Vision Psychological science has offered two main theories of color perception, each of which explains different aspects of how most humans see color. Let's consider the aspects of perception that each explains.

| Light violet | | Dark purple | Blue | Dark green | | Light green | Yellow | Orange | Red | | Wavelength (nanometers) |
| 350 | | 400 425 | 450 | 500 | | 550 575 | 600 | 650 | 700 | | 750 |

Visible spectrum

Light

Prism

FIGURE **4.24**

LIGHT WAVES AND THE ELECTROMAGNETIC SPEC-TRUM. The entire electromagnetic spectrum ranges from gamma waves at the smallest end to AC current at the largest end. Between these two extremes is a very narrow band of wavelengths visible to the human eye. Visible light ranges from about 300 nanometers (violet) to about 750 nanometers (red).

Young and Helmholtz developed their theory of color vision around the idea that people have three kinds of cones: red, green, and blue. We now know this is anatomically correct, but Young and Helmholtz did not. They inferred it from their experiments on color perception. They reasoned that all color that we experience must result from a mixing of these three colors of light, so they called their theory the **trichromatic color theory.** But mixing light is not like mixing paints. Mix red, green, and blue light together in equal amounts and you get white; with paints, you get a brownish muck. Light color mixing actually occurs inside the eye, in terms of how different kinds of cones respond to different wavelengths of light.

The human retina contains three kinds of receptor cones, each sensitive to different wavelengths of light. The red cones fire in response to longer wavelength light. Green cones respond to medium-wavelength light, and blue cones respond to shorter wavelength light. Different firing patterns of these various kinds of photoreceptors combine to help create our experience of a wide array of colors. How much each cone is stimulated determines the color we will see. For instance, for most people, the perception of yellow occurs with equal stimulation of red and green cones plus a smidgen of blue cone stimulation. So trichromatic color theory went a long way toward explaining how humans in fact see color. But it has limitations.

Even though trichromatic color explains how photoreceptors process colored light, it cannot explain some aspects of color vision. Take, for example, color afterimages. **Afterimages** are visual images that remain after removal of the stimulus. Figure 4.25 demonstrates a popular color afterimage. Stare at the white

trichromatic color theory
the theory that all color that we experience results from a mixing of three colors of light (red, green, and blue).

afterimages
visual images that remain after removal of or looking away from the stimulus.

FIGURE **4.25**

COLOR AFTERIMAGE. Stare at the white spot in the middle of the green and black flag for about 10 seconds, and then stare at the black dot in the white rectangle on the right. You will see, very briefly, a regular red, white, and blue American flag. Trichromatic color theory cannot account for this afterimage, but opponent-process theory can.

spot in the middle of the green and black flag for about 10 seconds and then stare at the black dot in the white rectangle, where you will see, very briefly, a regular red, white, and blue American flag. Trichromatic color theory cannot account for this afterimage, but opponent-process theory can.

Ewald Hering (1878) proposed **opponent-process theory** to explain color vision. He said that cones are linked together in three opposing color pairs: blue/yellow, red/green, and black/white. The members of the color pairs oppose one another, whereby activation of one member of the pair inhibits activity in the other. Opponent-process theory can account for the color afterimage of the American flag. This theory also helps to explain some types of color blindness, as well as why we never experience some colors, such as reddish-green or yellowish-blue.

Current research indicates that both theories account for how human color vision works. The trichromatic theory better explains color processing at the red, blue, and green cones in the retina. Opponent-process theory better explains how cells in the LGN of the thalamus and visual cortex process color information. In these brain areas, some cells are excited by red, for example, and inhibited by green stimuli (Lennie, 2000). Also, opponent-process theory can explain color afterimages, while trichromatic theory cannot.

opponent-process theory the theory that color vision results from cones linked together in three pairs of opposing colors, so that activation of one member of the pair inhibits activity in the other.

Deficiencies in Color Vision
There are many types of color blindness. Only about 10 people in a million actually fail to see color at all (Goldstein, 2007). More commonly, color blindness refers to a weakness or deficiency in perception of certain colors. Usually this results from an inherited pigment deficiency in the photoreceptors. The most common form, most often seen in men and boys due to the pattern of inheritance, occurs from a deficiency in cones sensitive to red (long-wavelength) and green (medium-wavelength) light. People with this disorder have trouble distinguishing some shades of green from red, may see green and brown as similar, or might have difficulty distinguishing blue and purple (purple has more red in it, so when a person cannot pick up on the red, purple and blue look alike).

Color blindness may be an evolutionary vestige of mammals most commonly being sensitive to only short and medium wavelengths rather than long (Jacobs & Nathans, 2009). Indeed, when mice had a gene introduced to them

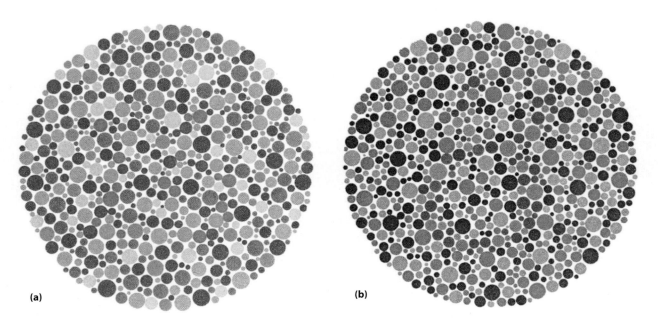

FIGURE **4.26**

EXAMPLES OF THE ISHIHARA COLOR BLINDNESS TEST. People with normal color vision can see the numbers embedded among the dots of both pictures. People with red–green color blindness can see the "16" in (a), but they cannot see the "8" in (b).

that made them trichromatic (sensitive to long wavelengths as well as short and medium wavelengths), they could suddenly distinguish colors the way trichromatic humans do (Smallwood et al., 2003). Figure 4.26 presents a color blindness test that taps into red–green weaknesses. Yellow–blue deficiencies are less common.

Quick Quiz 4.2: Vision

1. Neurons called _____ in the visual cortex analyze the retinal image and respond to aspects of shapes, such as angles and movements.
   a. subjective contours
   b. shape responsive cells
   c. feature detectors
   d. horizontal cells

2. How did Hubel and Wiesel discover that some cortical neurons responded to seeing lines of a specific orientation?
   a. by using fMRI to study cat brain function during visual tasks
   b. by inserting electrodes into single cells in the visual cortex
   c. through surgical removal of cortical tissue
   d. with EEG

3. After leaving the retina, what is the first stop in the brain for processing of visual information?
   a. the occipital cortex
   b. the parietal lobe
   c. the hypothalamus
   d. the thalamus

4. Which of the following is *not* a monocular depth cue?
   a. linear perspective
   b. 3-D movies
   c. texture gradient
   d. interposition

5. The ability of the brain to preserve perception of objects in spite of the changes in retinal image is known as
   a. interrelative consistency
   b. proximity
   c. visual stability
   d. perceptual constancy

Answers can be found at the end of the chapter.

HEARING

Theaters and concert halls are designed to reflect and absorb sound so that wherever you sit, you can hear the performance. For musicians, however, constant exposure to loud music can cause hearing loss.

We could clearly make the case that sight is the most important sense for humans. So much of our lives revolves around what we see. The science of vision is much more developed than the science of any other sense. And yet people who are both blind and deaf beg to differ. The deaf and blind American author Helen Keller put it most eloquently when she wrote:

> I am just as deaf as I am blind. The problems of deafness are deep and more complex, if not more important, than those of blindness. Deafness is a much worse misfortune. For it means the loss of the most vital stimulus—the sound of the voice that brings language, sets thoughts astir and keeps us in the intellectual company of man. (Helen Keller, as quoted in Ackerman, 1990, p. 191)

Just as vision starts when we sense light waves, hearing begins when we sense sound waves. Sound waves must travel through some medium or we cannot hear them. Sound waves can move through fluid or air, but most of the time we hear sound waves that travel through air. Sound waves travel much more slowly than light waves, which is why you hear thunder after you have seen lightning.

The Physics of Sound and the Psychology of Hearing

We perceive different shapes and sizes of sound waves as different sounds. Hearing is affected by three physical properties of the sound wave: its amplitude, frequency, and purity. The height, or *amplitude*, of the sound wave determines what we perceive as loudness. The taller the wave is, the louder the sound. The

Theaters and concert halls are designed to reflect and absorb sound so that wherever you sit, you can hear the performance. For musicians, however, constant exposure to loud music can cause hearing loss.

scale for a sound's loudness is decibels (dB). The scale starts with 0, which is the threshold for normal human hearing. The scale has no upper limit, but sounds above 150–170 dB are seldom registered anywhere.

To give you markers for loudness: A whisper is about 30 dB, a regular human conversation is about 55–60 dB, a jackhammer is about 90 dB, a very loud bar or nightclub is around 100–110 dB, a very loud rock concert is about 110–120 dB, and a jet airplane is about 130–140 dB. If you were to ever hear a sound at 160 dB, your eardrum would burst. Where might you hear such an incredibly loud noise? Believe it or not, car sound system competitions, such as "dB Drag Racing," regularly achieve sound in the 150–160 dB range. The record stands at 171 dB. Needless to say, these levels are strictly for competition, and no one is in the car during the competition.

The *frequency* of the sound wave, or how many waves occur in a given period of time, we perceive as the sound's pitch. Frequency is measured in units called *hertz (Hz)*, which is how many times the wave cycles per second. The higher the frequency, the higher the pitch. The higher keys on a piano—those farther to the right—are of higher pitch than the lower keys, for example. The range for human pitch perception is from about 20 Hz to about 20,000 Hz, but most people cannot hear sounds at either extreme. Sounds below 20 Hz are called *subsonic* and above 20,000 are called *ultrasonic*. Most sounds we hear are in the range of 400 to 4,000 Hz. The human voice generally ranges from 200 to 800 Hz, and a piano plays notes ranging from 30 to 4,000 Hz.

The third property of sound waves, *purity,* refers to the complexity of the wave. Some sound waves are pretty simple, made of only one frequency (see Figure 4.27). Most, however, are almost always a mixture of frequencies; how much of a mixture a sound is defines its purity. We perceive purity as timbre (pronounced "tamber"). Musicians often refer to timbre as the "color" of sound. Timbre allows us to distinguish a middle C (256 Hz) as being from either a piano or from a violin. They both are 256 Hz and may even be of equal loudness, but we have no trouble telling them apart because they produce waves of different purities.

Pure wave

Complex wave

FIGURE **4.27**

PURE AND COMPLEX SOUND WAVES. A pure sound wave consists of only one wave, whereas a complex wave is a mixture of more than one wave.

The Ear

The anatomy of the ear is relatively straightforward. First off, as the structures on the sides of our head, our ears have very little to do with hearing itself. These external structures, called *pinnae,* collect and funnel sounds into the passage called the *auditory canal.* Once inside this canal, sound vibrations travel to the eardrum, or **tympanic membrane.** The auditory canal and tympanic membrane make up the *outer ear.* The sound waves on the tympanic membrane set into motion the bones of the *middle ear:* the hammer, anvil, and stirrup (see Figure 4.28). These bones do more than just vibrate: They amplify the waves so that they have more than 20 times the energy they had entering the ear. The hammer hits the anvil, and the anvil moves the stirrup. The vibration of the stirrup, in turn, sets into motion a series of important changes in the *inner ear.*

The inner ear includes the cochlea and semicircular canals. The **semicircular canals** play a key role in maintaining a sense of balance. As the stirrup vibrates, it moves a membrane that covers the inner ear, called the *oval window.* The vibrations on the oval window send movement through the fluid-filled cavity

tympanic membrane the eardrum.

semicircular canals structure of the inner ear involved in maintaining balance.

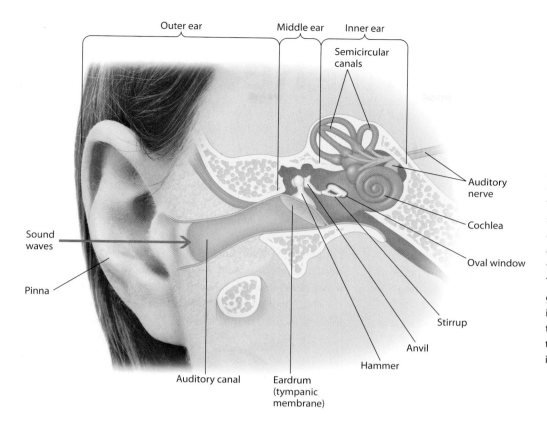

Outer ear   Middle ear   Inner ear

Semicircular
canals

Auditory
nerve

Cochlea

Oval window

Sound
waves

Pinna

Stirrup

Anvil

Hammer

Auditory canal   Eardrum
(tympanic
membrane)

FIGURE **4.28**

ANATOMY OF THE HUMAN EAR. Sound waves hit the outer ear and travel down the auditory canal, where they vibrate the eardrum, which sets in motion the bones of the middle ear (hammer, anvil, and stirrup). The bones vibrate and amplify the waves, where they vibrate the oval window. The vibrations cause fluid in the cochlea to bend the hair cells. Stimulation of the hair cells transduces sound vibrations into electrical impulses. These electrical impulses can generate an action potential in the auditory nerve, which is then sent to the brain's auditory cortex for processing and interpreting.

cochlea
a bony tube of the inner ear, which is curled like a snail's shell and filled with fluid.

of the cochlea. The **cochlea** is a bony tube, curled like a snail's shell, and filled with fluid. The **basilar membrane** runs through the cochlea. Within the basilar membrane of the cochlea are **hair cells,** which are the sensory receptors for sound just as the photoreceptors are for vision. As the vibrations move through the cochlear fluid, the basilar membrane vibrates, and this makes the hair cells bend. As they bend, the hair cells transduce the sound vibrations into electrical impulses, which may generate an action potential in the **auditory nerve.**

Hair cells vary in size depending on where in the cochlea they are. The smallest hair cells are nearest the oval window, and the largest hair cells are in the coiled-up center part of the cochlea. There is a one-to-one connection between the size of a hair cell and its sensitivity to different frequency of sounds. The smallest cells are sensitive to the highest frequencies (up to 20,000 Hz), and the largest hair cells are sensitive to the lowest frequencies (down to 20 Hz) (see Figure 4.29). The louder the sound, the bigger the vibration in the cochlear fluid, the more stimulation of the hair cells, the faster the rate of action potentials in the auditory nerve, and the louder the sound we perceive. If the hair cells in the inner ear become damaged, as can happen when a person is exposed to very loud noises once or moderately loud noises (such as machines) over long periods of time, the person can suffer irreparable hearing loss. For more information about hearing loss, see "Psychology in the Real World."

basilar membrane
a membrane that runs through the cochlea; contains the hair cells.

hair cells
inner ear sensory receptors for sound that transduce sound vibrations into neural impulses.

auditory nerve
the nerve that receives action potentials from the hair cells and transmits auditory information to the brain.

Hearing in the Brain

After the sound energy is changed to neural energy in the cochlea, the hair cells synapse with auditory neurons that transmit the sound impulses to the thalamus in the brain. From there, the neural impulses are relayed

Hearing Loss in the Age of the iPod

Most people take their hearing for granted, but there is a good chance that at some point in your lifetime you will suffer some degree of hearing loss. It could be minor, or it could be major. Studies often divide the causes of hearing loss into categories of age-related and noise exposure, but in fact these two are related. Being exposed to loud noise levels over long periods of time leads to a loss of hearing after 10–15 years.

Noise often leads to age-related hearing loss, especially in the high-frequency range of 5,000–15,000 Hz (Lutman & Spencer, 1991) (see Figure 4.30). For example, in a large-scale study of exposure to noise at work, middle-aged to older men (ages 45 to 70) have their threshold for hearing high-frequency sounds (4,000 Hz and higher) raised by 10 dB compared to men not exposed to such noise at work (Tambs et al., 2006). A 10 dB increase is sound that is 10 times as intense, which we perceive as twice as loud. Factory or machine workers exposed to noise at the 90 dB level for 8 hours a day, 5 days a week suffer permanent hearing loss after 10 years on the job (Bauer et al., 1991; Lutman & Spencer, 1991). Similarly, rock musicians—exposed to noise

levels from 95 dB to 107 dB—when tested before and after concerts, showed both temporary and permanent hearing loss (Gunderson, Moline, & Catalono, 1997).

But don't think that hearing loss affects only older people. MP3 players, including the iPod, have maximum decibel levels of around 115–120 dB, about the loudness of a rock concert. It is not a coincidence that during the "age of the iPod" (first released in late 2001) hearing loss of any kind in teens increased from 15% in 1988–1994 to 19.5% by 2005–2006 (Shargorodsky et al., 2010). As with older adults, hearing loss in teens is also most

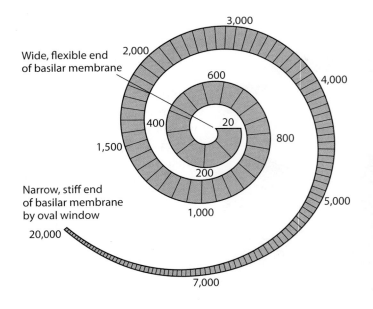

FIGURE **4.29**

DIFFERENT PARTS OF THE COCHLEA PROCESS DIFFERENT FREQUENCIES OF SOUND. The highest frequencies of sound stimulate the narrowest region of the cochlea. The small hair cells here are sensitive to high-frequency (high-pitch) sounds in the range of 15,000 to 20,000 cycles per second (Hertz). The largest hair cells are in the wide center portion of the cochlea. These hair cells respond to low-frequency (pitch) sounds in the range of 20 to 100 cycles per second.

likely in the high-frequency range (see National Institute of Deafness, 2008). Earbud-style headphones—which are very common—are the most problematic, as they let in the most ambient noise (Hodgetts, Szarko, & Rieger, 2009). Ambient noise comes from your surrounding environment; and when that is louder, you have to turn the volume up to hear the music. Most young people claim to understand the risks of hearing loss due to frequent MP3 player use, but it is not clear whether they act in accordance with that information (Danhauer et al., 2009). Here are some guidelines for listening to an MP3 player without causing long-term damage to your ears (Knox, 2007, April 26):

- Limit earphone listening to an hour a day, at a setting no greater than 6 on a 10-notch scale.
- If someone can hear earphone "leakage" from several feet away, it is too loud.
- If someone has ringing in the ears or a feeling of fullness in the ear, or if speech sounds muffled after a listening session, the music was too loud.
- Try over-the-ear headphones rather than earbuds.

FIGURE **4.30**

HEARING HIGH TONES. Knowing that older adults typically can't hear high-frequency tones, teenagers have downloaded high-pitched ring tones for the cell phones so that they can use them to send and receive text messages during class.

to various parts of the brain, including the brain stem and the temporal lobes, home of the auditory cortex. Recall that the visual pathways go through the LGN. The auditory pathways go from the cochlea to the *inferior colliculus* in the brain stem and from there to the *medial (middle) geniculate nucleus (MGN)* of the thalamus. It is in the brain that we organize and interpret sounds from the outside world. It is in the brain that hearing takes place.

Quick Quiz 4.3: Hearing

1. The _____ of a sound wave determines what we perceive as loudness.
   a. frequency
   b. shape
   c. amplitude
   d. width

2. Which structure is responsible for the transduction of sound vibrations into action potentials?
   a. the tympanic membrane
   b. cochlea
   c. stapes
   d. hair cells

Answers can be found at the end of the chapter.

THE BODILY SENSES

We feel things on our skin and in our bodily organs. The largest contact surface area any sensory input has with our bodies is the skin, and it is carefully mapped in the somatosensory cortex in the parietal lobe of the brain (Blakeslee & Blakeslee, 2007). Bodily senses also include knowing where our body parts are. In addition, we also sense things inside our bodies—organ pain, levels of heart rate, depth of breathing, to name a few. The senses based in the skin, body, or any membrane surfaces are known as the **bodily senses.** There are at least six distinct bodily or somatic senses: touch, temperature, pain, position/motion, balance, and interoception (perception of bodily sensations). Of these six senses, we will discuss touch and pain.

Connection

Figure 3.16 shows how the somatosensory cortex maps to specific regions of the body.

See "Overview of Brain Regions," Chapter 3, "The Biology of Behavior," p. 96.

bodily senses
the senses based in the skin, body, or any membrane surfaces.

Touch

Imagine that your eyes are closed and someone puts an object in your left hand. You feel it for a minute. You feel its weight, shape, hardness, and temperature. Then the person puts something in your right hand. You conclude, with eyes still shut, that the first was a screwdriver and the second was a pen. How were you able to do this?

The top layers of skin have receptor cells that are sensitive to different tactile qualities—some to shape, some to grooves, some to vibrations and movements. These receptor cells are known as **mechanoreceptors,** and they are like the photoreceptors in the eye or the hair cells in the ear. There are, in fact, four different kinds of mechanoreceptors, each of which has a unique profile of sensitivity. Some of the mechanoreceptors are slow to change, and others are fast to change with variations in tactile stimulation. Some are sensitive to fine details, whereas others are not sensitive. For example, slowly drag your fingertip over a quarter. You can feel the bumps and grooves, thanks to fine-detail receptors in your skin. Some mechanoreceptors also sense movement and vibration, such as when someone runs fingers over your forearm. It is important to point out that you have far fewer mechanoreceptors on the soles of your feet than on your fingertips. This is probably a good thing—it would be overwhelmingly uncomfortable to have extremely sensitive soles.

mechano-receptors
receptor cells in the skin that are sensitive to different tactile qualities, such as shape, grooves, vibrations, and movements.

Women have finer tactile sensitivity in their fingertips than men, but this appears to be due to smaller fingertip size in women (Peters, Hackeman, & Goldreich, 2009). The cells for tactile sensation are more densely packed in smaller fingers, and when men and women with equal-sized fingertips are compared, their tactile sensitivity is the same.

Like photoreceptors in the eye, mechanoreceptors mark only the beginning of the journey from sensation to perception. The sensory qualities (shape, size, hardness, and temperature) of the screwdriver and pen stimulate different kinds of mechanoreceptors in the skin, but the resulting sensory impulses must travel to the brain to be processed and interpreted. When something touches our fingertips, forearm, or shoulder, a dedicated region of cortex becomes active, and we perceive the sensation of being touched. Tactile sensations from our skin travel via sensory neurons to the spinal cord and up to the brain. The first major structure involved in processing bodily sensations is the thalamus, which relays the impulses to the somatosensory cortex in the parietal lobes.

Repeated sensory and motor tactile experience changes the amount of cortex involved in processing that particular sensation or movement. The general location in the somatosensory cortex stays the same, but areas of the cortex devoted to that experience or function grow (Jenkins et al., 1990; Ostry et al., 2010). The more one body region is touched or stimulated, the more sensory or motor cortex is used to process information from the mechanoreceptors. For instance, musicians who play stringed instruments such as a violin use the right hand to bow and the left hand to play the notes. Researchers have found that experienced violinists have larger representations, or *brain maps*, of the hand and finger regions of the somatosensory cortex than do nonmusicians (Pantev et al., 2001).

Connection

What are the benefits of touch for premature and low-birth-weight newborns?
See "Touch," Chapter 5, "Human Development," p. 195.

Pain

Pain is no fun, but we need it to survive. People born with no pain receptors can be severely injured or killed, because they don't know they have been harmed (Watkins & Maier, 2003). **Pain** is a complex emotional and sensory experience associated with actual or potential tissue damage (Merskey & Bogduk, 1994). It is usually very unpleasant, but people vary widely in their experiences of pain, what they think is painful, and whether they might even enjoy pain (Schwerdtfeger, 2007). In fact, some people feel no pain during great injury (such as soldiers in battle situations), and others feel pain when no tissue damage is present. The latter situation occurs with *phantom limb pain*, when people who have lost a limb feel pain in the missing arm or leg. Such cases dramatically show how pain is not just a direct result of tissue damage, but an experience in the brain as well. Pain also is enhanced by one's reaction to the injury. Often the emotional reaction to pain creates as much suffering as the actual tissue damage.

pain
a complex emotional and sensory experience associated with actual or potential tissue damage.

Pain is subjective, and the perception of pain varies from one person to another. Some people may perceive the experience of getting a tattoo as moderately uncomfortable. Others might find it to be quite painful.

Pain Perception   How do we sense and perceive pain? It's not merely touch gone too far. In fact, damage to the skin is only one kind of pain. Other forms include organ tissue and nerve damage as well as joint inflammation. Pain from skin damage is called *nociceptive pain*. The skin has pain receptors that are sensitive to heat, cold, chemical irritation, and pressure, all of which are kinds of *nociceptors* (Basbaum & Jessell, 2000). Heat, frostbite, chemical burns, and cutting or hitting your thumb with a hammer all hurt because these events stimulate nociceptors in our skin. The nociceptors send signals to the spinal cord

FIGURE **4.31**

THE BRAIN AND PAIN. The structures shown are activated during the perception of physical pain. The anterior cingulate cortex and the insula (located deep within the temporal lobe) are also activated by emotional pain.

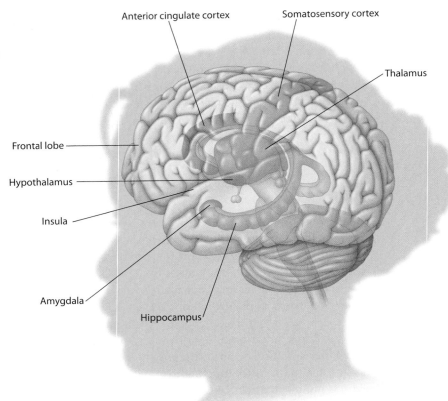

Anterior cingulate cortex

Somatosensory cortex

Thalamus

Frontal lobe

Hypothalamus

Insula

Amygdala

Hippocampus

and then to the brain, signaling that damage has occurred. Your brain can then initiate an appropriate response, such as pulling your hand away from the hot burner. You can now see why it is so dangerous not to experience pain!

Many brain structures are involved in the perception of skin damage alone. A partial list of brain structures activated by skin-based pain includes the thalamus, hypothalamus, limbic system, insula, and anterior cingulate cortex (see Figure 4.31; Goldstein, 2007). A somewhat surprising finding is that some of the same brain regions activated when we experience physical pain also are activated during emotional pain—especially when we are rejected by others or see others receive shocks (Eisenberger, Lieberman, & Williams, 2003; Singer et al., 2004). The brain regions active in both physical and emotional pain are the anterior cingulate cortex (ACC) and the insula (see Figure 4.31). Even more fascinating, as Singer and colleagues (2004) showed, when we observe a loved one being given a mild shock, only the ACC and the insula become active, not the somatosensory cortex, which is activated when we ourselves are shocked. So when we see someone we love hurt, the aspects of the pain circuit involved with emotion are active, but not the entire circuit.

In fact, emotion and pain systems interact considerably, as indicated by the well-established observation that emotional states can influence pain perception. Certain negative emotions—such as sadness—worsen the pain experience, while positive emotions can lessen the pain experience (Berna et al., 2010; Villemure & Schweinhardt, 2010). We are just beginning to understand the brain mechanisms involved in emotional modulation of pain. Apparently, in the transmission of pain signals between spinal cord and brain, there are many opportunities for communication with brain systems involved in emotion (Roy et al., 2009).

Touring the Senses

GOALS OF THE TOUR

1 Parts of the Eye. You will be able to identify the structures of the human eye and describe their functions.

2 Visual Pathways. You will be able to identify the pathways for visual stimulation and describe the brain's role in visual information processing.

3 Parts of the Ear. You will be able to identify the three areas of the ear and describe the key structures of the inner ear.

4 Parts of the Nose. You will be able to describe how the nose (olfactory sense) processes a smell.

Parts of the Eye and Visual Pathways

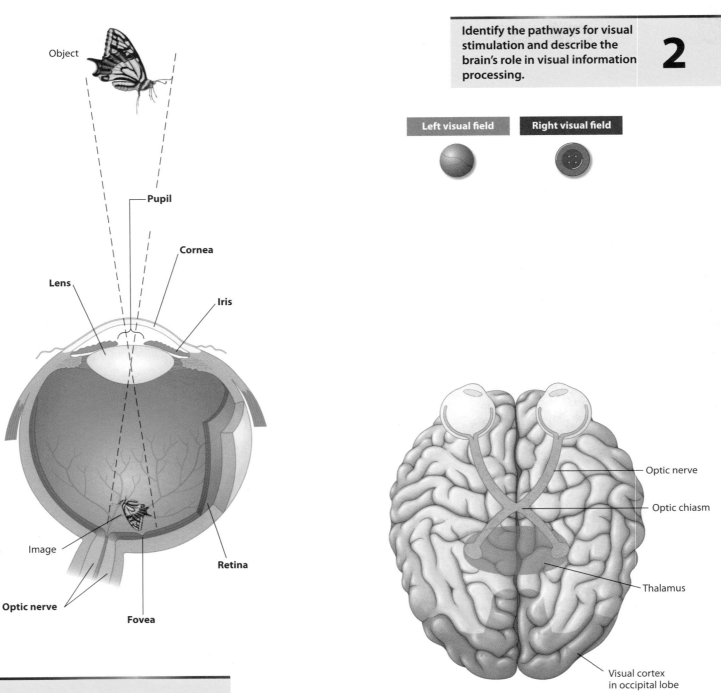

Object

Pupil

Cornea

Lens

Iris

Image

Optic nerve

Fovea

Retina

Identify the pathways for visual stimulation and describe the brain's role in visual information processing.

2

Left visual field   Right visual field

Optic nerve

Optic chiasm

Thalamus

Visual cortex in occipital lobe

Identify the structures of the human eye and describe their functions.

1

Parts of the Ear and Parts of the Nose

Pinna

Sound

Auditory canal

Eardrum

Hammer

Anvil

Stirrup

Semicircular canals

Auditory nerve

Cochlea

Identify the three areas of the ear and describe the key structures of the inner ear.

3

Describe how the nose (olfactory sense) processes a smell.

4

Olfactory nerve

Olfactory bulb

Nasal passage

1. PARTS OF THE EYE

The *retina* is made up of a layer of cells in the interior of the eye that contain the *photoreceptors*, the rods and the cones.

The *cornea* is the transparent membrane in the front of the eye that protects the eye and bends light to provide focus.

The *pupil* is the opening that allows light to enter the eye.

The *iris* is the colored muscle that surrounds the pupil and adjusts the amount of light entering into the eye through the pupil. It dilates (opens) or constricts (closes) in response to the intensity (brightness) of the light. It also dilates in response to certain emotions.

The *lens* focuses the image onto the retinal layer on the back surface of the eye. As in a camera, the image projected by the lens onto the retina is reversed.

The *fovea* is the region of the retina that is directly in line with the pupil and contains mostly cones, which are involved in color perception and visual acuity (sharpness).

The *optic nerve* receives inputs from the photoreceptors and sends information to the brain.

2. VISUAL PATHWAYS

Images of objects in the right visual field are projected to the left half of the retina of each eye, which in turn sends the information first to the thalamus for initial processing and then to the visual cortex in the left hemisphere where perception takes place. Likewise, images of objects in the left visual field are projected to the right half of the retina of each eye, which in turn sends the information to the thalamus and then to the visual cortex in the right hemisphere.

3. PARTS OF THE EAR

The *outer ear* is the visible portion of the ear and the auditory canal (ear canal) that funnels sound waves to the eardrum.

The *middle ear* includes the eardrum and three tiny bones (hammer, anvil, and stirrup) that transmit the eardrum vibrations to a membrane on the cochlea called the oval window.

The *inner ear* includes the snail-shaped tube called the *cochlea*, which translates sound waves into fluid waves, and the semicircular canals, which sense equilibrium.

4. PARTS OF THE NOSE

Airborne molecules (olfactory chemicals) enter the nasal passage and reach receptor cells located in the olfactory epithelium of the upper nasal passage. The receptors send messages to the brain's olfactory bulb and then onward to the primary smell cortex located in the temporal lobes.

Explaining Pain   One of the more influential explanations for pain is that proposed by Ronald Melzack and Patrick Wall (1965, 1988). Their **gate control theory of pain** proposes that the spinal cord regulates the experience of pain by either opening or closing neural channels, called *gates,* involved in pain sensations that get sent to the brain. Smaller neural channels are dedicated to pain sensations, and when they are activated, pain messages get sent to the brain. Activation of larger neural channels that are involved in the sensation of pain can inhibit the transmission of pain impulses to the brain. This mechanism explains why certain kinds of stimulation—such as acupuncture or even rubbing one's skin—can relieve sensations of pain. The signals from acupuncture may override other, even more intense sensations of pain, such as chronic pain from injury (White, 2006).

What is most interesting about the gate control theory of pain is the idea that inhibitory channels can actually come from the brain as well as the body. Messages sent by the brain itself can close channels in the spinal cord involved in pain sensations. Thoughts, feelings, and beliefs can affect pain sensations, which is one reason why people vary so much in their perception of pain. Different people experiencing the same level of pain may have completely different experiences of their pain.

Controlling Pain   In addition to thoughts and feelings that control the experience of pain, our bodies have natural painkillers called *endorphins* (for endogenous morphines). When we are hurt, our body responds by releasing these substances (Fields, 2009). Endorphins work by stimulating the release of neurotransmitters that interfere with pain messages in the spinal cord and brain. Endorphin release may explain why people initially experience no pain after a horrible injury from an accident. For example, soldiers and automobile accident victims often report no immediate sensations of pain (Warga, 1987). Only hours afterward or maybe the next day while in a hospital does the pain begin. Endorphins also play a role in acupuncture-based pain relief (Han, 2004).

If thoughts, feelings, and endorphins are not enough to control pain, there are drug treatments. For small aches and pains, many people take aspirin, acetaminophen, ibuprofen, or other similar drugs. Generally, these drugs work to control inflammation (Loeser & Melzack, 1999). For more severe pain, doctors may prescribe opioids. Opioids are a class of drug known as *analgesics,* meaning *without pain.* Morphine, heroin, oxycodone, and hydrocodone are all opioids. All but heroin are commonly prescribed for pain relief. They work to deaden or lessen pain by blocking neural activity involved in pain perception. Morphine, for example, is widely used before and after medical procedures and in the care of terminally ill patients. There is a high risk of dependency on opioids, so their use must be carefully monitored.

Connection

Opioids deaden pain and therefore have a high potential for abuse.

See "Opioids," Chapter 6, "Consciousness," p. 256.

Quick Quiz 4.4: The Bodily Senses

1. The receptor cells for touch that reside in the skin are called
   a. tactile cilia
   b. mechanoreceptors
   c. interoceptors
   d. receptive fields

2. Our bodies have natural painkillers called
   a. analgesics
   b. opioids
   c. endorphins
   d. acetaminophens

Answers can be found at the end of the chapter.

THE CHEMICAL SENSES: SMELL AND TASTE

Smell and taste are chemical senses, because they respond to contact with molecules from objects we encounter in the world. Smell and taste are very important survival-related senses, for they govern our choices about what we take into our bodies. As such, these senses are very sensitive, are heightened during pregnancy, and can trigger emotional reactions (Profet, 1992; Rolls, 2004).

Unlike receptors for other senses, receptors for chemical molecules are regularly replaced, because they are constantly exposed not only to the chemicals in food but also to dirt and bacteria that can impair function (Goldstein, 2007). Smell and taste receptors are replaced every few weeks.

Smell (Olfaction)

A small area high in the lining of the nasal cavity contains the **olfactory sensory neurons,** which are the receptors for smell (see Figure 4.32). These neurons contain hairlike projections called *cilia*, which are similar to the hair cells in the inner ear. The cilia convert chemical information in odor molecules into neural impulses.

When chemicals come in contact with the cilia, transduction occurs, and the olfactory message travels to the **olfactory bulb** in the forebrain. The olfactory bulb sends information either directly to the smell-processing areas in the cortex or indirectly to the cortex by way of the thalamus (Buck, 2000). The *primary olfactory cortex* resides in the temporal lobe; the *secondary olfactory cortex* is in the frontal lobe near the eyes.

Some fibers from the olfactory bulb go directly to the amygdala, which sends smell information to the hypothalamus, thalamus, and frontal cortex. You may recall that the amygdala plays a key role in emotional responses and also connects to memory areas like the hippocampus. These connections may explain why smells can instantly evoke an emotional memory (Herz, 2004). The smell of cedar wood, for example, immediately transports one of us (Greg) to his grandmother's attic in Kansas.

Just as there are specific photoreceptors for different primary colors, different odors stimulate different olfactory neurons. In fact, most mammals have hundreds and hundreds of different types of olfactory sensory neurons; these account for their highly discriminating sense of smell (Fleischer, Breer & Strotmann, 2009). Greater concentrations of odors will stimulate a greater number of sensory neurons: as a result, we perceive the same odor presented at different concentrations as being an entirely different smell. People differ considerably in their ability to sense odors. Some people lose the ability to sense smell with infection or injury, but usually this is short term.

FIGURE 4.32

OLFACTORY RECEPTORS IN THE NASAL CAVITY. The receptors in the nasal cavity, called cilia, are like the hair cells in the ear. They change chemical stimulation received from smells to nerve signals that are sent to the brain for processing and interpreting.

olfactory sensory neurons the sensory receptors for smell that reside high up inside the nose.

olfactory bulb a forebrain structure that sends information either directly to the smell processing areas in the cortex or indirectly to the cortex by way of the thalamus.

Animals have a heightened sense of smell compared to humans: We rely on dogs to sniff out suspects and bombs. Grizzly bears can locate dead animals from miles away and will readily feed on them ("Brown/Grizzly Bear," n.d.). Sharks can detect one drop of blood in 25 gallons of water (Marks, 2006).

Taste

papillae
textured structures on the surface of the tongue; contain thousands of taste buds.

taste buds
structures inside the papillae of the tongue that contain the taste receptor cells.

taste receptor cells
sensory receptors for taste that reside in the taste buds.

A close look at the human tongue reveals all kinds of ridges and bumps. These textured structures, called **papillae,** contain about 10,000 **taste buds.** The cells on the buds that process taste information are called **taste receptor cells.** There are dozens of taste receptor cells in each taste bud. The papillae in the central part of the tongue contain no taste buds and no taste receptor cells, so we do not taste from that region. Human experience of taste results from stimulation of taste buds on the front, sides, and rear of the tongue, as shown in Figure 4.33. When chemicals from food or liquid come into contact with the tips of these taste buds, a chain of events unfolds that leads to the experience of taste.

Because dogs have a keen sense of smell, humans often employ them to locate illegal drugs, explosives, criminals, and missing people.

Humans distinguish five basic taste qualities: bitter, sweet, salty, sour, and savory. There is increasing evidence that a sixth taste quality—fattiness—may exist as well, but further research is needed (Garcia-Bailo et al., 2009). Researchers once thought that receptors for the different tastes resided only in certain regions of the tongue, but we now know that these taste receptor cells are distributed in many regions (Buck, 2000). Although specific receptors exist for each type of taste, the savory experience—also known as *umami* from the Japanese word for "good flavor"—comes from the combined sensory experience of monosodium glutamate (MSG; a flavor enhancer, traditionally used in many Asian foods) and the perception of savory odors (Kawamura & Kare, 1987; McCabe & Rolls, 2007). The combined factors that produce the savory flavor point to the important roles both taste and smell play in our experiences of flavor in general.

Simply put, the experience of flavor results from the combination of taste plus smell (Goldstein, 2007). Have you ever noticed how dull food tastes when you have a cold? This is because your sense of smell is impaired. Try squeezing your nostrils shut while tasting an apple or any other food.

FIGURE **4.33**

LOCATION OF TASTE RECEPTORS AND TASTE BUDS ON THE HUMAN TONGUE. Different regions of the tongue generally contain taste buds for specific types of taste, although each region of the tongue has many different kinds of taste buds.

Notice the flavor. Then release your nostrils and take another bite. You will notice more intense "apple-ness" with your nostrils open, because food aromas contribute greatly to the experience of flavor (Lawless et al., 2004). When the nose is shut, olfactory receptors in the passage that connects the oral and nasal cavities do not get stimulated. As a result, less olfactory information is available, and taste is impaired. Also, the region of the brain most involved in flavor perception, namely the orbitofrontal cortex (OFC), receives inputs from brain areas involved in olfaction and taste, as well as from areas involved in touch and vision (Rolls, 2000). The OFC is where signals from taste and smell meet (Rolls, 2006).

The experience of flavor showcases the brain's ability to combine sensory information to produce a unique sensory experience. In some people, sensory experiences sometimes combine in even more unusual ways. The next section on synesthesia focuses on these cases.

Quick Quiz 4.5: The Chemical Senses: Smell and Taste

1. The primary olfactory cortex resides in which lobe of the brain?
   a. temporal lobe
   b. frontal lobe
   c. parietal lobe
   d. occipital lobe

2. Humans have taste receptor cells for what flavors?
   a. sweet, sour, salty, sharp, savory
   b. sweet, sour, bitter, salty, sharp
   c. sweet, sour, bitter, salty, savory
   d. sweet, sour, salty, sharp

Answers can be found at the end of the chapter.

SYNESTHESIA

synesthesia

an unusual sensory experience in which a person experiences sensations in one sense when a different sense is stimulated.

Many of us use expressions such as "he was green with envy" or "her anger was red hot." We use these colors metaphorically, knowing full well he is not really green and her anger is not really red. But what if we literally experienced numbers as colors or touch as tastes? A surprisingly large segment of the population—about 4%–5%—can do just that (Simner et al., 2006). They experience what is known as **synesthesia,** which occurs when a person experiences sensations in one sense when a different sense is stimulated (Cytowic, 1989; Ramachandran & Hubbard, 2003; Spector & Maurer, 2009). In short, synesthesia occurs when the senses get mixed up and don't stay separate. For example, some people with this condition experience yellow when they hear a tone such as middle C. Others taste shapes. Still others experience numbers as colors, such as 5s as green and 2s as red.

The most common form of synesthesia is this last one, in which people experience numbers or sometimes letters as colors (Ramachandran & Hubbard, 2003; Spector & Maurer, 2009). One way that scientists were able to discover that synesthesia was a real perceptual phenomenon and not just a learned association or merely an overly active sense of metaphor was to administer perceptual tests such as the one in Figure 4.34 (5s and 2s). In the figure on the left, there are a few 2s within the 5s. For most of us, they are hard to pinpoint, and it takes us a while to determine how many there are. But a person who sees 5s as blue and 2s as red, as shown on the right, has no trouble seeing that there are six 2s forming a triangle.

How does synesthesia happen? One explanation is that synesthesia results from a cross-wiring or cross-activation of sensory neurons in various parts of the brain (Hubbard & Ramachandran, 2005; Ramachandran & Hubbard, 2003;

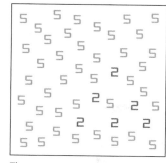

The way a person without synesthesia sees it

The way a person with synesthesia sees it

FIGURE **4.34**

SYNESTHESIA. People who perceive numbers as colors would have no trouble distinguishing the numbers 5 and 2 in the square on the left. They would see the numbers in color as shown in the example on the right. (Source: Ramachandran & Hubbard, 2003)

Spector & Maurer, 2009). Cross-activation occurs when two areas of the brain, normally kept separate, get activated at the same time by the same stimulus. In synesthesia, brain regions involved in color perception cross-activate with sensations of numbers. As it turns out, one region of the temporal lobe is active in processing both color sensations and numbers and is therefore the most likely area of cross-activation in this form of synesthesia (Hubbard & Ramachandran, 2005; Ramachandran & Hubbard, 2003). Some evidence suggests that this sensory cross-wiring is a result of unusual neural development (Spector & Maurer, 2009). Many infants have these cross-wired neurons connecting different sensory systems, but with age and experience they get pruned or eliminated. They do not appear to be pruned in people with synesthesia. Finally, certain hallucinogenic drugs can temporarily create synesthetic experiences, such as when people see musical sounds as colors. The brain mechanisms responsible for this kind of synesthesia are not well described (Weil & Rosen, 1998).

Bringing It All Together
Making Connections in Sensation and Perception
Differences Across Cultures

Throughout this chapter we have touched on ways in which people differ in sensory perception. For example, some people are more sensitive to bitter tastes than others. Individual differences in perception may result from differences in perceptual set, or frame of mind. Thus, it stands to reason that growing up in a certain environment, with particular beliefs, ways of viewing things, and physical settings might impact how one perceives the world. Culture and place can serve as perceptual sets. Most research on cultural influences on perception has focused on three sense systems: vision, olfaction, and pain.

Cultural Variation in Visual Perception
Differences exist across cultures in response to certain visual images that use monocular cues to depth. Look again at the

Müller-Lyer line illusion in Figure 4.21 (p. 144). Recall that linear perspective explains why people see the line on the right as longer than the one on the left, when the lines are in fact equal. The drawing on the right looks like the inner corner of a room, and the one on the left looks like the outer corner of a building. Do people who grow up in a world with no corners view these drawings the same way we do? Researchers have studied the effects of living in a *carpentered world*—an environment with constructed buildings with many right angles—on various people's perceptions of depth. Navajos who have lived at least 10 years in round huts are much less likely to see the lines of Figure 4.21 as differing in length, for they are not accustomed to rooms with edges (Pederson & Wheeler, 1983). A similar effect has been reported in studies of children living in Zambia, in a rural setting with few

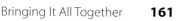

modern buildings (V. M. Stewart, 1973). But Navajos and Zambians who have lived in the presence of corners do experience the Müller-Lyer illusion (Matsumoto & Juang, 2004). Experience modifies perception.

Moreover, Hudson (1960) studied the perception of depth cues in the Bantu people of the Niger–Congo region of Africa. He showed people the picture depicted in Figure 4.35 and others similar to it. He then asked them to explain what was going on in the scene. When people from the United States, Europe, and India viewed such a picture, they said the hunter was going after the gazelle, as the elephant was clearly in the distance. Bantu people, however, said the hunter was attacking the elephant. So the Bantu do not appear to use relative size differences as cues to depth because they don't see the elephant as being in the background. Why? The Bantu people's response may result from not having much experience with two-dimensional drawings like the figure. Interestingly, Bantu who had been educated in European schools said the hunter was going for the gazelle (Matsumoto & Juang, 2004).

As we have just seen, different cultural backgrounds can impact how people make sense of and perceive their world. This is true not just for illusions and depth perception, but also for perceiving and attending to foreground and background.

Nature&Nurture

People who grow up in cultures without angular buildings do not experience the same visual illusions as those who grew up with angular buildings.

People from Eastern cultures tend to perceive the world more as a whole, with people, objects, and the context being connected and belonging together. Westerners, however, tend to focus most on foreground objects and less on background and the periphery (Nisbett et al., 2001). The Research Process for this chapter (see Figure 4.36) describes research on this question that found cultural influences in how people perceive and recall figural versus background information in visual scenes (Masuda & Nisbett, 2001). These findings are consistent with the more established observation that Eastern people view themselves as embedded in the larger world rather than as independent entities (Markus & Kitayama, 2001). In another example of top-down processing, one's orientation toward life and the world can shape visual perception and memory.

Cultural Variation in Olfactory Experience

Smell is an interesting sense to compare across cultures, in part because it is a highly emotional sense. Because smells elicit emotions so readily, cultures often develop strong rules or norms about which smells are okay and which ones aren't. That is, cultures differ widely on the acceptability of odors based on experience, climate, and cuisine. Also, different places vary in their standards for cleanliness and for what is acceptable body odor (Hannigan, 1995). Do people who are raised so differently with respect to what is typical to smell or what it is okay to smell like show differences in scent detection in controlled experiments?

A highly controlled experiment on scent detection with participants from the United States and Japan suggests

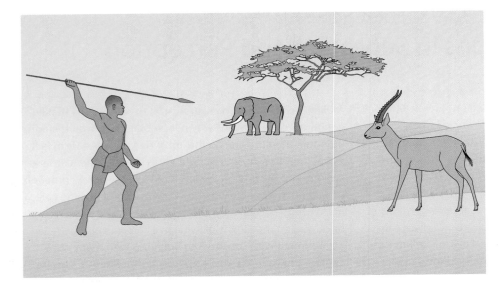

FIGURE **4.35**
PICTURE FOR DEPTH PERCEPTION TASKS TESTED ON BANTU. People from Europe, the United States, and India think the hunter is after the gazelle. Bantu tribespeople think he is after the elephant. (Based on Hudson, 1960)

Research Process

Japanese participant in perception study

1 Research Question

Do people from an Eastern culture (Japan) focus more on and have better recall for objects in the background and periphery of a scene than people from a Western culture (United States)?

2 Method

For this quasi-experimental study by Masuda and Nisbett (2001), participants came into the laboratory individually and sat down at a computer. They watched a 20-second video of the scene depicted here. The large fish are considered foreground. Plants, small fish, and the other nonmoving animals (rocks and snail) are considered background. Arrows indicate the direction in which the fish and other objects moved during the scene. After viewing the video, participants orally described what they had seen. Trained coders rated the number of statements they made about various aspects of the scene, such as foreground and background fish, the small stationary animals, and the plants.

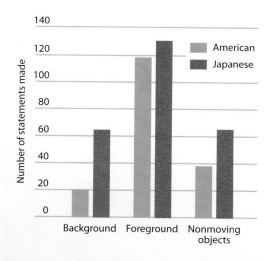

3 Results

As predicted, and consistent with cultural values and attitudes, the Japanese commented much more on the background and nonmoving animals (snail and frog) than the Americans did. There was no significant difference in how much people from each culture commented on the large fish in the foreground.

4 Conclusion

How we perceive everyday scenes is influenced by our culture. Our brains have been shaped by the assumptions and values of our society. In this case, people in Eastern cultures, such as Japan, tend to focus on background, foreground, and nonmoving objects, whereas those in Western cultures, such as the United States, tend to focus more on the foreground and moving objects only. This research is consistent with the more established observation that Eastern people view themselves as rooted in the larger world rather than as independent individuals.

FIGURE **4.36**

HOW CULTURE AFFECTS PERCEPTION OF FOREGROUND–BACKGROUND. Culture influences the perception of visual information. Japanese people view themselves as more embedded in the larger world and notice backgrounds more than Americans, who feel more independent from their settings. Source: "Attending Holistically Versus Analytically: Comparing the Context Sensitivity of Japanese and Americans," by T. Masuda and R. E. Nisbett, 2001, *Journal of Personality and Social Psychology, 81,* 922–934.

remarkable similarity across these two cultures in ability to recognize a wide variety of scents (Kobayashi et al., 2006). A few distinct differences, however, appear to be culturally based. Japanese were much better than Americans at detecting three of the 13 smells in final testing. Does that mean the Japanese have superior smell ability? Probably not. Each of these scents (such as condensed milk) is more common in Japan, and therefore these results help us to understand that smell recognition is a perceptual process guided by experience with the substances to which we are exposed. Other aspects of smell may be less susceptible to cultural effects. Consider gender differences in smell perception. Overall, women tend to be more sensitive to smells than men

Nature & Nurture

Different cultural backgrounds can impact how people perceive and understand their world.

(Brand & Millot, 2001). Scientists at the University of Pennsylvania wanted to know whether such gender differences in smell perception held across cultures and ethnic backgrounds. They tested how well native Japanese and Americans of African, European, and Korean descent could identify odors in a controlled laboratory setting (Doty et al., 1985). Korean Americans performed better than African Americans and White Americans on the odor detection tasks, and both of these groups performed better than the native Japanese. Across all the groups, however, women outperformed men.

Cultural Variation in Pain

Given the large role that subjective factors play in pain perception, many researchers have looked at cultural, gender, and ethnic differences in pain (Al-Atiyyat, 2009; Wickelgren, 2009). As we have discussed, there are big differences among people in pain tolerance, and we can even experience pain in the absence of any real tissue damage—remember phantom

Cultural differences in pain perception are evident in this photo, taken during the Hindu festival of Thaipusam in Malaysia.

limb pain? One general finding is that women tend to have a lower pain threshold than men; that is, they more quickly say a stimulus is painful as it becomes more intense (Wickelgren, 2009). Moreover, as the photograph on page 164 shows, there are clear cultural differences in tolerance for pain! In one of the most painful of human experiences, childbirth, we see widely differing perceptions of how painful it is. For example, the Yap who live in the South Pacific consider childbirth to be simply a part of everyday life. Yap women routinely work in the fields right up until childbirth and are often back at work the next day. What is even more interesting is that Yap fathers experience the pain of childbirth, and they are the ones who stay in bed to recover after the birth of the child (Kroeber, 1948). In the Huichol tribe of Mexico, so that fathers-to-be would go through their own painful birth process along with the mothers in labor, a string would be tied around the man's testicles. The woman in labor held the other end of the string and with each contraction she experienced, she would pull on the string (Cassidy, 2006)!

Quick Quiz 4.6: Bringing It All Together: Making Connections in Sensation and Perception

1. People who grow up in environments with few or no right angles and corners are less likely to be fooled by the _____ illusion.
   a. Ponzo
   b. moon
   c. Müller-Lyer
   d. apparent motion

2. Cultural differences in various kinds of sensory perception, which may stem from differences of belief and physical environments, point to the role of _____ in perceptual experience.
   a. top-down processing
   b. bottom-up processing
   c. elementalism
   d. perceptual constancy

Answers can be found at the end of the chapter.

Chapter **Review**

THE LONG STRANGE TRIP FROM SENSATION TO PERCEPTION

- Sensation is the stimulation of our sense organs by the external world. Perception is the process by which the brain organizes and interprets sensory experience.

- Stimulation of the sense organs involves taking in sensory energy from the outside world, whether it be sound waves, light waves, chemicals, or pressure. Our sensory system transforms the physical energy into neural energy in a process known as transduction. The brain then organizes the transformed information, interprets it, and initiates a response.

- Absolute thresholds are the lowest level of a stimulus that humans sense. Difference thresholds are the smallest amount of change in stimulus that a person detects.

According to Weber's law, the smallest detectable change is a constant proportion of the intensity of the original stimulus.

- Our frame of mind affects our perception of objects and is known as our perceptual set.

VISION

- The eye bends light, converts light energy into electrical energy, and sends that information to the brain for further processing.

- Vision happens in the brain, in the lateral geniculate nucleus (LGN) of the thalamus and in the visual cortex in the occipital lobes.

- Hubel and Wiesel demonstrated that single cells in the visual cortex act as feature detectors, and there are three kinds for vision: simple cells, complex cells, and hypercomplex cells. Integration of this feature information occurs in the parietal and temporal cortexes.

- Depth perception is the ability to figure out how far or near objects are. One cue for depth perception is binocular disparity, the fact that our two eyes provide slightly different viewpoints that our brains integrate into a single 3-D image. Monocular depth cues include linear perspective, texture gradient, atmospheric perspective, and interposition.

- The brain organizes visual sensations with Gestalt laws of similarity, continuity, proximity, and closure.

- Separating figures from backgrounds helps us organize visual sensations, but also makes us vulnerable to illusions.

- The retina contains two types of photoreceptor cells called rods and cones. Cones are sensitive to red, green, and blue light waves, whereas rods are sensitive to light and are responsible for dark adaptation.

- The trichromatic theory of color vision states that we perceive the full range of colors as different combinations of three colors. The opponent-process theory says that cones are linked together in three opposing color pairs: blue/yellow, red/green, and black/white.

HEARING

- Humans respond to three different properties of sound waves: We perceive amplitude as loudness, frequency as pitch, and purity as timbre.

- The receptor hair cells in the cochlea are sensitive to different frequencies of sound waves and convert the mechanical energy of sound into neural energy for processing in the auditory cortex.

THE BODILY SENSES

- The bodily senses include sensations of touch, temperature, pain, balance, position/motion, and interoception.

- The brain regions most involved in touch are the thalamus and the somatosensory cortex in the parietal lobes. Pain sensations are processed mainly by the insula and the anterior cingulate cortex in the frontal lobes.

THE CHEMICAL SENSES: SMELL AND TASTE

- Smell receptors in the nose contain olfactory sensory neurons, which convert chemical information into neural information. The olfactory message goes to the olfactory bulb and then to the primary olfactory cortex in the temporal lobe.

- Information about taste is processed in the taste buds of the tongue. Humans distinguish five basic taste qualities: bitter, sweet, salty, sour, and savory.

SYNESTHESIA

- Synesthesia occurs when one sensory system is activated by stimulation of a different sensory system, and the neurons are cross-activated in the brain.

- In the most common form of synesthesia, people experience letters or numbers as colors.

BRINGING IT ALL TOGETHER: MAKING CONNECTIONS IN SENSATION AND PERCEPTION

- Variations in experience across cultures influence the way people see, smell, and feel pain. Ethnic and cultural differences aside, women are more sensitive to smells than are men.

Key Terms

Quick Quiz **Answers**

Quick Quiz 4.1: 1. b   2. d   Quick Quiz 4.2: 1. c   2. b   3. d   4. b   5. d
Quick Quiz 4.3: 1. c   2. d   Quick Quiz 4.4: 1. b   2. c
Quick Quiz 4.5: 1. a   2. c   Quick Quiz 4.6: 1. c   2. a

Solution to Figure 4.20 on page 143:

Challenge Your Assumptions **Answers**

- Blindness is permanent and cannot be reversed. **False. See p. 136.**
- The experience of "seeing sounds" or "hearing colors" occurs only under the influence of drugs. **False. See pp. 160–161.**
- iPods can damage your hearing. **True. See pp. 152–153.**
- Seeing is done as much with the brain as with the eyes. **True. See p. 136.**

Human
Development

5

Chapter Outline

Challenge *Your Assumptions*

TRUE OR FALSE?

- Your personality begins to form in the womb.

- Learning to play an instrument makes you smarter.

- Parents are the main influence on development up through late adolescence.

- Pregnant women should eat their vegetables.

Answers can be found at the end of the chapter.

For ages the personal diary was a teenage girl's major confidant. School frustrations, relationships, friendships, crushes, and breakups could all be divulged there, and no one else would know about them. Most of us who had diaries kept them under lock and key, hidden from meddlesome little brothers or nosy parents. The diary never judged—it was just there to hear our every joy and woe.

Today, "Dear Diary" has been replaced by Internet blogs and social networking sites, which offer a similar but also very different forum for self-expression. Sure—they are always there, even very late at night. Compared to a hardbound diary with a key, however, the Internet "diary" is very public. Any personal revelations are shared with the online social world. As the largest group of online bloggers in the United States, teenage girls endure the brunt of this exposure, and they are more likely than boys to share content about their lives online than boys (Lenhart et al., 2010).

A key marker of adolescence is the movement away from family and toward friends for social support and influence. Online social sharing—whether in blogs or on networking sites—connects teens with a community of friends and acquaintances who see their posts. This activity feeds the major teen concern: the need for peer validation and social support. Although excessive use of the Internet for gaming and other solitary activities can degrade the quality of social relationships, online journaling and social networking may improve the quality of friendships, especially those with very close or "best" friends (Blais et al., 2008; Valkenberg & Peter, 2009).

The search for identity is a hallmark of adolescence, and the online social world helps young people explore who they are through shared content. By becoming fans of certain pages or groups, changing their profile pictures, altering the design of their sites, choosing their "avatars," and posting survey quizzes that ask "Which superhero are you?" teens experiment with different selves (Davis, 2010). The feedback they get from friends, family, and sometimes strangers shapes their own behavior and ultimately their development.

A look at the content of blogs or online posts by adolescent boys and girls offers a glimpse of the transitional state of this life phase (A. L. Williams & Merten, 2008). The blogs and postings by both girls and boys contain images and comments about parents, peers, athletics, substance use, sex, and profanity. Davis (2010) studied online blogs of 17–21-year-old girls over a 3-year period. These blogs revealed much of the drama and changes of adolescence. The writing and content matured, in ways that mirror the emotional and moral development in the late teens and early adulthood. Most notably, the girls' entries expanded outward from a focus on themselves to issues of relevance to the world—such as political causes and social issues.

Adolescence is one of the most dramatic phases of human development, but the entire life course is replete with other remarkable transitions as well. In this chapter, we look at the role of psychology in studying human development from conception to death. The study of **human development** is concerned with both change and continuity in a person across the life span. This process begins before birth, in the prenatal environment of the mother's womb. ■

human development the study of change and continuity in the individual across the life span.

THE DEVELOPING FETUS

From conception until birth, we grow from a single cell to a fully formed, but still developing, human. The brain is the first major organ to form. The heart develops about a week later. (It is strange to think we have a brain before we have a heart!) A little more than eight months later, when we are born, the brain has more than 100 billion cells.

We pass more biological milestones before birth than we will during the rest of our lives. Development in the womb is incredibly fast and complex and includes not only physical growth, but you may be surprised to learn, psychological development as well. Yes, personality and cognitive traits are already being shaped before we are born!

Stages of Prenatal Development

germinal stage
the first prenatal stage of development, which begins at conception and lasts 2 weeks.

Life before birth is commonly divided into three distinct stages: the germinal, embryonic, and fetal stages. The **germinal stage** begins at conception and lasts for 2 weeks. At conception, the fertilized egg is a single-celled **zygote.** This single cell starts dividing rapidly around 36 hours after conception. By day 7, the multicelled organism—now called a blastocyst—travels down the mother's fallopian tube and attaches to the uterine wall (see Figure 5.1). This process is far

zygote
single cell that results when a sperm fertilizes an egg.

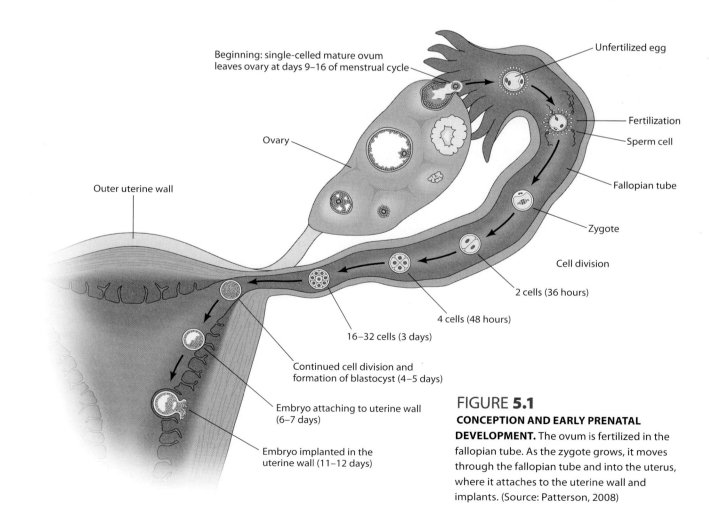

Beginning: single-celled mature ovum leaves ovary at days 9–16 of menstrual cycle

Unfertilized egg

Ovary

Fertilization

Sperm cell

Fallopian tube

Zygote

Cell division

2 cells (36 hours)

4 cells (48 hours)

16–32 cells (3 days)

Outer uterine wall

Continued cell division and formation of blastocyst (4–5 days)

Embryo attaching to uterine wall (6–7 days)

Embryo implanted in the uterine wall (11–12 days)

FIGURE **5.1**

CONCEPTION AND EARLY PRENATAL DEVELOPMENT. The ovum is fertilized in the fallopian tube. As the zygote grows, it moves through the fallopian tube and into the uterus, where it attaches to the uterine wall and implants. (Source: Patterson, 2008)

Life begins with the fertilization of an egg. In this highly magnified image, many sperm surround a single egg. Only one sperm will succeed in penetrating the egg.

from risk-free: between 30% and 50% of the blastocysts do not implant properly, and the pregnancy ends without the woman's having known she was pregnant (Gupta et al., 2007).

If implantation is successful, the second stage of prenatal development begins, at about two weeks after conception. At this point, the growing bundle of cells is officially an **embryo.** The **embryonic stage** is marked by the formation of the major organs: the nervous system, heart, eyes, ears, arms, legs, teeth, palate, and external genitalia. Embryonic development continues until about eight weeks after conception.

In Figure 5.2, we see the timetable for prenatal development. Each bar in Figure 5.2 shows when major structures develop and how long it takes. Notice that the central nervous system (brain and spinal cord) takes the longest amount of time to develop. Most major abnormalities occur only in the early stages of development, when exposure to environmental hazards such as drugs or illness can cause serious defects.

embryo
the term for the developing organism from 2 weeks until about 8 weeks after conception.

embryonic stage
the second prenatal stage, from 2 weeks to 8 weeks after conception, when all of the major organs form.

The key event that distinguishes the embryonic stage from the third stage, the **fetal stage,** is the formation of bone cells at 8 weeks after conception. By this time, all the major organs have already begun to form. Between 8 and 12 weeks into development, the heartbeat can be detected with a stethoscope. Organs continue to grow and mature while the fetus rapidly increases in size. Let's look at the important developments of this stage.

fetal stage
the third prenatal stage, which begins with the formation of bone cells 8 weeks after conception and ends at birth.

Brain and Sensory Development Before Birth

The brain is the first major organ to develop, and it is still growing rapidly at birth (see Figure 5.3). By the time an infant is born, its head has grown to 25% of its adult weight, whereas its body is only 5% of its adult weight (see Figure 5.4). During the fetal stage, the rate of new neural growth can be approximately 3 million neurons per minute at its peak (Purves & Lichtman, 1985). From months 3 through 5 of pregnancy, neurons move from one part of the brain to their more permanent home in a process known as **neural migration** (Nadarajah & Parnavelas, 2002). Factors that interfere with normal neural migration, such as prenatal exposure to certain toxins or viruses, can increase the risk of psychological disorders (Kandel, 2006).

neural migration
the movement of neurons from one part of the fetal brain to their more permanent destination; occurs during months 3–5 of the fetal stage.

Soon after the nervous system has started to form, the embryo begins to move its limbs. By 4 to 6 months after conception, the fetus's movements are noticeable (DiPietro et al., 1996). Mothers can feel the fetus moving as early as 16 weeks into pregnancy, although it may feel a little like abdominal gas or "butterflies." Generally, male fetuses are more active than females, suggesting their greater activity levels after birth may be inborn (DiPietro et al., 1996).

The major sensory systems develop at different times and at different rates. The neurons connecting the ear to the brain are complete around 18 weeks after conception, and the fetus begins to respond to sound around 26 weeks (6 months) after conception (Kisilevsky, Muir, & Low, 1992). A few weeks later, fetuses find their mother's voice soothing, and they prefer the sound of their

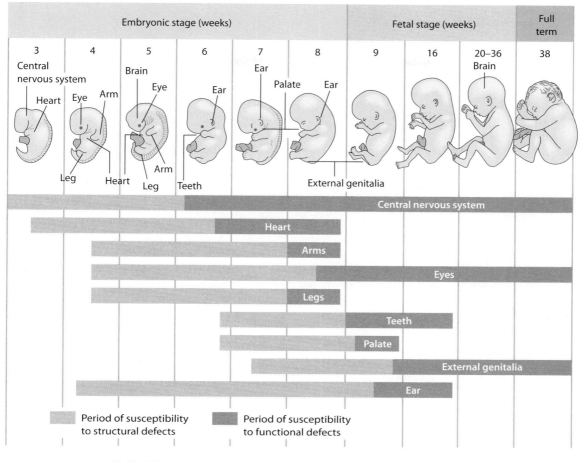

		Embryonic stage (weeks)						Fetal stage (weeks)			Full term

Period of susceptibility to structural defects

Period of susceptibility to functional defects

FIGURE 5.2

PRENATAL DEVELOPMENT TIMELINE. Each bar shows when major structures develop and how long it takes for development to be completed. Note that the central nervous system begins developing in the third week after conception and continues to develop nearly the entire time we are in the womb. The blue section of each bar indicates when major abnormalities can occur if growth goes awry. After that crucial period, minor abnormalities can still occur.

Kanye West or Mozart? Can a fetus hear the difference?

30 days
(4 weeks)

40 days
(6 weeks)

100 days
(14 weeks)

Five months

Six months

FIGURE 5.3

PRENATAL BRAIN DEVELOPMENT. The size and complexity of the brain increase dramatically in the weeks and months following conception. At birth, the baby's brain weighs about 25% of what an adult brain weighs. For comparison, a newborn weighs only about 5% as much as an adult. The photograph shows the brain at 44 days after conception. Note the well-developed blood vessels, which provide blood and oxygen to the rapidly developing brain.

mother's voice to other voices (DeCasper & Fifer, 1980; DeCasper & Spence, 1986). How can researchers possibly know what a fetus prefers? The researchers monitor the fetus's heart rate. Slowed heart rate indicates attention, interest, or orienting response, whereas an increased heart rate indicates fear or distress (Groome et al., 2000).

Taste and odor-related chemicals from the mother's diet are present in amniotic fluid (Mennella, Johnson, & Beauchamp, 1995). In turn, fetuses are sensitive to odors in the amniotic fluid before birth, and they remember these smells. When pregnant women consumed anise-flavored foods during the last stages of pregnancy, their newborns liked the smell of anise more than babies whose moms did not consume the anise flavor (Schaal, Marlier, & Soussignan, 2000).

Such studies suggest that our taste preferences may start in the womb (Beauchamp & Mennella, 2009; Hopson, 1998). By 13 to 15 weeks after conception, the taste buds of a fetus look very much like those of an adult (Bradley, 1972). Researchers do not know whether the fetus uses the taste buds, but babies born prematurely—who would otherwise still be developing in the womb—prefer sweet flavors to other flavors, suggesting that this taste preference exists in the womb (Beauchamp & Mennella, 2009; Mennella & Beauchamp, 1996).

	Newborn	2 years	4 years
Percentage of total weight			
Brain	25%	75%	90%
Body	5%	20%	20%

FIGURE 5.4

NEWBORN AND CHILD BRAIN AND BODY AS PERCENTAGE OF ADULT WEIGHT. The size and complexity of the brain increase dramatically in the weeks and months following conception.

Seven months

Eight months

Nine months

The sense that is least well developed in the fetus is vision (Hopson, 1998). Fetuses do not open their eyes. Also, as discussed in Chapters 3 and 4, vision perception occurs in the brain. The brain needs visual stimulation to develop the sense of sight (Ptito & Desgent, 2006). Because it is not receiving visual stimulation, the fetus's brain is not developing the appropriate neural connections in the visual cortex to respond to visual imagery. Thus, at birth, infants cannot see things clearly unless the objects are close to the face. Infants cannot see as well as adults until they are at least 6 months old, whereas their hearing is almost adultlike soon after birth.

Environmental Influences on Fetal Development

prenatal programming the process by which events in the womb alter the development of physical and psychological health.

teratogens substances that can disrupt normal prenatal development and cause lifelong deficits.

To a fetus, the mother's womb is its only "environment." Thus, what a pregnant mother eats, drinks, smokes, feels, and experiences plays an important role in fetal development. **Prenatal programming** refers to the process by which events in the womb alter the development of physical and psychological health (Coe & Lubach, 2008). Of particular concern in this context are **teratogens,** or substances that can cause permanent damage to the developing embryo or fetus.

Maternal Nutrition and Teratogens Doctors know that what a pregnant woman eats and drinks is important for the health of the fetus and even for the infant and child for years after birth. For example, both schizophrenia and antisocial personality disorder are more likely to occur if the mother is malnourished during pregnancy (Neugebauer, Hoek, & Susser, 1999; Wahlbeck et al., 2001).

As it turns out, the body may have a built-in toxin detector. It's called pregnancy sickness, commonly referred to as "morning sickness." Pregnant women often develop aversions to certain foods, and some women get nauseated and even vomit regularly during pregnancy (Profet, 1992). Pregnancy sickness is

Nature & Nurture

Chemical substances that a pregnant woman takes in or is exposed to shape the development of the fetus's brain and other bodily systems.

worst during the first three months of pregnancy, when the fetus's major organs develop and the embryo is most vulnerable to teratogens. Pregnancy sickness occurs most commonly with exposure to foods susceptible to molds (aged cheeses, mushrooms) and to bitter substances (such as coffee), possibly because these foods can cause birth defects (Keeler, 1983).

Maternal nutrition—a key part of the developing baby's environment— provides one of the most important examples of epigenetics, the study of how the environment affects gene expression (see Chapter 3). Certain kinds of maternal diet during pregnancy can lead to obesity in offspring—whether or not the mother is obese. In one study, researchers randomly assigned two genetically identical strands of female laboratory mice to receive two kinds of diet while pregnant (Dolinoy & Jirtle, 2008). One group—let's call them Group A—received a diet rich in substances that activate a gene that causes weight gain. The other group—Group B—received a diet rich in nutritional supplements (folic acid and B_{12}) that protect against such weight gain. Results showed that the *offspring* of the Group A mice that received the diet that turned on the weight gain gene became obese. The diet of the pregnant mother—not the diet of the animal after birth—led to obesity in the offspring. Equally noteworthy: The diets of Group B mice that are rich in vitamin B_{12} and folic acid appeared to protect against obesity in offspring (Dolinoy & Jirtle, 2008; Waterland & Jirtle, 2003).

Teratogens   Substances from the external environment impact fetal and infant development. Because all major body parts are forming and growing during the embryonic and fetal stages, the fetus is quite susceptible to birth defects. Known teratogens include viruses, such as those that cause rubella (measles) and the flu; alcohol; nicotine; prescription drugs, such as the antidepressants Prozac and Zoloft; and radiation. Viruses, for example, may have a major impact early in pregnancy and relatively little effect toward the end of pregnancy. More specifically, if a pregnant woman develops an infection, such as the flu, especially during months 4–6 of pregnancy, the risk of schizophrenia increases for the child later in life (A. S. Brown, 2006; Koenig, 2006).

Connection

Catching the flu while pregnant influences the way neurons grow in the developing fetus and increases vulnerability to schizophrenia later in life. How does this happen?
See "Schizophrenia," Chapter 15, "Psychological Disorders," p. 607.

Maternal substance use can also cause serious prenatal and postnatal problems. Pregnant women who drink alcohol take chances with their developing baby, as there is no known safe level of alcohol consumption during pregnancy (Centers for Disease Control and Prevention [CDC], 2007). The most serious effect of prenatal alcohol exposure is **fetal alcohol spectrum disorder (FASD),** which causes damage to the brain and central nervous system; mental retardation; low birth weight; physical abnormalities in the face, head, heart, and joints; and behavioral problems (Burd et al., 2007; May & Gossage, 2001; Medina & Krahe, 2008; Moore et al., 2007; Sen & Swaminathan, 2007; Uylings, 2006).

Another teratogen is nicotine, as exposure from maternal smoking interferes with the oxygen supply to the

fetal alcohol spectrum disorder

a consequence of prenatal alcohol exposure that causes multiple problems, notably brain damage.

Compared with the brain of a typical child (bottom), the brain of a child with FASD is clearly underdeveloped. Brain abnormalities caused by maternal alcohol use before giving birth result in mental retardation and behavior problems.

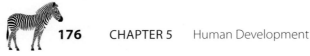

fetus. Such exposure can lead to premature and low-birth-weight babies as well as increased risk for stillbirth (delivery of a dead fetus) (CDC, 2007; Zigler, Finn-Stevenson, & Hall, 2002).

Prescription drugs pose other potential risks for the developing fetus. Many women take prescription drugs during pregnancy, especially if they were taking them before they learned they were pregnant. Some research on animals and humans indicates that the antidepressants Zoloft and Prozac can cause respiratory problems, increased risk of premature birth, and short-lasting effects on motor development, while other studies suggest such medications pose few risks to the developing fetus (Maschi et al., 2008; Moses-Kolko et al., 2005). The safest course of action, then, would be to avoid these drugs prior to pregnancy, if at all possible.

Prenatal Personality Development

Connection

Chronic stress creates a number of serious health problems, including a suppressed immune system, increased vulnerability to infection, and memory impairment.

See "Stress" Chapter 12, "Stress and Health," p. 476.

Before the 1990s, most people, including psychologists, thought that personality is something that starts to develop only after birth, maybe not until one is a toddler. But a surprising set of findings have revealed that temperament begins before birth. **Temperament** is the biologically based tendency to behave in particular ways from very early in life. In one study, Janet DiPietro and her colleagues (1996) showed that fetal activity and fetal heart rate predict temperament differences over the first year of life. In particular, a high heart rate in a 36-week-old fetus foreshadowed less predictable eating and sleeping habits at 3 and 6 months after birth. A high heart rate also predicted a less emotional infant at 6 months after birth.

What happens to the mother while pregnant may affect not only the temperament of the fetus, but the temperament and personality of the infant as well. As we discuss in more detail in Chapter 13, **personality** stems from temperament and is the consistently unique way in which an individual behaves over time and in many different situations. Mothers who are depressed or anxious or who experience a lot of stress during pregnancy are more likely to have infants who are temperamentally "difficult" and "fussy" (Austin et al., 2004; Gutteling et al., 2005). Thus, temperament and sensitivity to stress are set not only by our genes, but also by our mother's experiences.

temperament
the biologically based tendency to behave in particular ways from very early in life.

personality
the unique and relatively enduring set of behaviors, feelings, thoughts, and motives that characterize an individual.

Nature & Nurture

Infants born to mothers who experienced an unusual amount of stress during pregnancy tend to be more sensitive to stress throughout childhood and beyond.

Quick Quiz 5.1: The Developing Fetus

1. Life before birth is commonly divided into three distinct stages: the _____ , embryonic, and fetal stages.
   a. gestational
   b. seminal
   c. germinal
   d. cellular

2. How can researchers tell which sounds a fetus prefers to hear?
   a. by measuring the position of the fetus in the womb
   b. by measuring changes in fetal heart rate in response to sounds

   c. by taking a reading of fetal respiration
   d. It is not possible to measure fetal preferences.

3. Teratogens are
   a. substances that can cause birth defects
   b. genes that turn on or off with exposure to viruses
   c. inborn fetal taste preferences
   d. factors that influence the generation of fetal brain tissue

Answers can be found at the end of the chapter.

THE DEVELOPING INFANT AND CHILD

Because it's still developing, the newborn human brain is more responsive than that of other animals to its surroundings. This distinction allows nurture to shape human nature more than is the case for most animals.

Physical Development in Infancy and Childhood

Adults take for granted the ability to act at will, and yet when first born, humans are completely incapable of acting intentionally. Motor and sensory systems develop substantially in newborns. In this section, we explore how physical growth, motor skills, and sensory capacities develop in infancy and early childhood. We will examine how experience and the brain interact to shape early human experience.

Early Motor Development When we speak of motor development, we are referring to changes in physical movement and body control. Figure 5.5 outlines the major milestones of motor development during the first 15 months. Although the sequence is predictable, the exact age at which children reach each milestone varies. For example, our son Jerry did not crawl until he was 9 months old, but he walked at 10 months. Our son Evan, on the other hand, crawled at 7½ months and then started walking at about 12 months.

Early in infancy, babies start to show intentional movements. First, they look at their mother with an unfocused gaze, and then they turn their heads to look at her. By about 2 months of age, babies lying on their tummies can lift their

FIGURE **5.5**

MAJOR MOTOR DEVELOPMENT MILESTONES IN INFANCY AND TODDLERHOOD. Some children reach these milestones earlier than others, but most achieve them within the range indicated by the purple bars.

Walk alone easily

Stand easily

Pull self to stand

Stand with support

Sit without support

Prone, chest up, use arms for support

Age (months)
0 1 2 3 4 5 6 7 8 9 10 11 12 13 14 15

heads. A 3-month-old who is fascinated by a stuffed ring dangling in front of him will suddenly, though not very smoothly, grab for it. At 4 months, babies can hold objects. By 6 months, many can sit by themselves, without any help. By 7 months, babies can pull themselves up and hold on to furniture, and at about 8 to 9 months, they walk from sofa to coffee table by holding on to the furniture. Many babies take their first steps around their first birthday, though it may be some time before they settle into walking alone. Most babies walk without help by 17 months of age (Patterson, 2008).

Other motor responses are more specific. If you give a newborn baby your finger, she will grasp it. Tightly. If you stroke her cheek, she will turn her head, open-mouthed in expectation of a breast, a reflex called *rooting*. Grasping and rooting are among several reflexes present at birth—involuntary responses to very specific stimuli.

It takes a while before young children can turn knobs and pick up tiny objects. These *fine motor skills* involve the coordination of many smaller muscles, along with information from the eyes, in the service of some task. Fine motor development shows up, for example, in children's drawing skills. Two-year-olds typically show very crude crayon scribbles, but by age 3 or 4 children can make crude drawings of people, and by age 5 most kids can print letters, dress alone, and use silverware (H. Gardner, 1980; Patterson, 2008). In fact, training in fine motor skills actually aids kindergarteners' attention, especially in girls, showing just how joined cognition and action can be (Stewart, Rule, & Giordano, 2007).

Early Sensory Development

As noted earlier, the five major senses develop at different rates. Hearing is almost fully developed at birth, but a newborn's vision is only about 20-600, meaning infants see an object that is 20 feet away as indistinctly as an adult with normal vision would see an object 600 feet away (see Figure 5.6). Visual sharpness, or acuity, continues to improve during infancy, and by 6 months of age, vision is 20-100. By age 3 or 4, a child's vision is similar to an adult's (Banks & Salapatek, 1983). You may be surprised to learn that newborns do not see colors very well and are best able to see black and white edges and patterns (Fantz, 1963). Color vision approximates that of adults by 4 months of age (Kellman & Arterberry, 2006).

Experience is crucial in the development of vision, as it is in all aspects of human development. As noted earlier, the occipital cortex of the brain has to be stimulated by visual input so that it can develop the proper synaptic connections needed to process visual information. It is for this reason that young infants respond chiefly to visual stimuli within 8 to 12 inches of their faces.

All babies who have normal vision in both eyes and can crawl see the world in three dimensions. In a study that has become a classic, Gibson and Walk (1960) tested this question by creating the *visual cliff* to test depth perception in babies who have learned to crawl (see Figure 5.7). They placed clear Plexiglas (hard plastic) over one end of a crawl area to make it look as though there was a steep drop in the middle. They put a baby on one end of the crawl area and asked the mother to stand at the

FIGURE **5.6**
VISUAL ACUITY IN INFANTS.
These photographs are a computer simulation of what a picture of a human face looks like to a 1-month-old, 2-month-old, 3-month-old, and 1-year-old.

FIGURE **5.7**

THE VISUAL CLIFF. In a demonstration of depth perception, babies will stop at the edge of a clear sheet of plastic, rather than crawling over what appears to be a cliff.

end with the drop. The mother's role was to encourage the baby to crawl across the clear plastic surface to her. In this study, babies stopped crawling when they reached the visual cliff, indicating that at least by the time they learn to crawl, babies can perceive depth.

Early Brain Development Experiences such as eating, exercising, and learning mold our brains throughout life, but especially in infancy and childhood. With learning and experience certain synaptic connections strengthen, whereas those that don't receive stimulation from the environment die off. This process, known as **pruning,** is nature's way of making the brain more efficient (Baltes, Reuter-Lorenz, & Rösler, 2006; Greenough, Volkmar, & Juraska, 1973; B. D. Perry, 2002).

After birth, the brain continues to grow new neurons (see Figure 5.8). Contrary to scientific thought as recently as 15 years ago, brain

pruning
the degradation of synapses and dying off of neurons that are not strengthened by experience.

Connection
Experience is crucial in the formation of synaptic connections and the growth of neurons in the brain throughout the life span. Unused synapses are left to die. Pruning is nature's way of making the brain function more efficiently.
See "The Nervous System," Chapter 3, "The Biology of Behavior," p. 82.

FIGURE **5.8**

NEURAL GROWTH DURING THE FIRST 6 MONTHS OF LIFE. Neural growth in the human brain—in this case, the visual cortex—continues at a very rapid pace during the first year or two of life. After that, neurons and synapses that are not reinforced by learning die off by pruning. (Source: Reprinted by permission of the publisher from *The postnatal development of the human cerebral cortex, Vols. I–VIII,* by Jesse LeRoy Conel. Cambridge, Mass.: Harvard University Press. Copyright © 1939, 1941, 1947, 1951, 1955, 1959, 1963, 1967 by the President and Fellows of Harvard College. Copyright © renewed 1967, 1969, 1975, 1979, 1983, 1987, 1991.)

At birth   1 month   3 months   15 months growth continues throughout the life span. The rate of change slows down considerably after the age of 6, increases in early adolescence, and then settles again after adolescence (Chechik, Meilijson, & Ruppin, 1999; Sakai, 2005).

In some 9-year-old children showing early signs of puberty, gray matter in the prefrontal and parietal regions of the brain surprisingly *decreases* somewhat in volume (Giedd et al., 1999; Peper et al., 2009). Such decreases in gray matter volume suggest that pruning—in which unused neurons die—is still occurring late in childhood. Recall that gray matter consists of the cell bodies and is a measure of the number of neurons; white matter is made up of the axons and myelin (see Figure 5.9). The number of neurons (gray matter) starts to decline in adolescence, but white matter (axons and connectivity) continues to grow into one's 40s (Westlye et al., 2010).

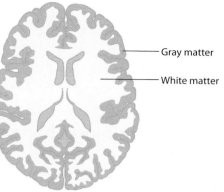

FIGURE **5.9**
WHITE AND GRAY MATTER IN THE HUMAN BRAIN.

Because pruning is based on input from the environment, the quality of the environments in which we are raised influences how our brains develop. Normal and enriched environments create more complex neural connections, while abusive, neglectful, and impoverished environments create less developed neural connections and fewer of them (Mirescu & Gould, 2006). An example of how experience can positively shape the brain is seen in the recent findings that physically fit children are also more cognitively fit; that is, they do better in reasoning tasks and school in general (Castelli et al., 2007; Hillman et al., 2009). "Psychology in the Real World" looks at another type of experience—musical training—that influences brain growth and cognitive development.

Neglect exists when caregivers fail to provide basic sensory experience and stimulation to a child during key periods of development (B. D. Perry, 2002). Timing is critical. A dramatic instance of the effect of neglect and abuse on the development of the human brain comes from research on children who spent their early years in Romanian orphanages, where they were confined much of the time to cribs and had very limited stimulation. Figure 5.10 shows a PET scan from one of the orphans alongside one from a typically developing child. The red to yellow areas in Figure 5.10a represent the active regions in the brain of a normal child. Figure 5.10b shows the brain activity of a Romanian orphan who was neglected from birth. As you can see, brain activity is greatly diminished in the

FIGURE **5.10**
BRAIN DEVELOPMENT IN A NORMAL CHILD COMPARED TO A DEPRIVED AND NEGLECTED CHILD. (a) In this PET scan of a typically developing child, the red and yellow areas indicate regions of high and moderate activity, respectively. (b) This PET scan of a child who experienced significant deprivation and neglect in a Romanian orphanage shows very little red and much more blue and black, indicating low activity. (Source: Cicchetti, 2001)

Musical Training Changes the Brain

The brain develops throughout life, and yet it is most responsive to stimulation during infancy and childhood. In other words, early in life there is more opportunity for experience to leave its mark on the brain (Cicchetti, 2001).

Learning to play a musical instrument is a good example of how experience changes the brain. If you want to learn guitar, you must learn fingering on the neck, how to hold your fingers and press the strings firmly enough to get a clear sound, and how the fingering movements relate to the notes on different musical scales. In Chapter 3, "The Biology of Behavior," we discussed how monkeys trained in a finger-tapping task showed substantial increases in the amount of somatosensory cortex devoted to the fingertips compared to both the amount they had before training and the amount in untrained monkeys (Jenkins et al., 1990). Can we see similar effects in the brains of string instrument players?

Researchers who were curious about this question applied a slight pressure to each finger on each hand of right-handed musicians and nonmusicians of various ages. Using fMRI, they mapped the brain's responses to this pressure. For musicians, the area on the somatosensory cortex devoted to those fingers on the side of the brain that controls the fingering left hand was bigger than the area that controls the nonfingering right hand. The somatosensory maps did not differ between sides in the brains of nonmusicians (Elbert et al., 1995). And musicians who started playing before the age of 12 showed the most pronounced differences. So musical training may change brain organization, especially for people who start training as children.

Musical training appears to shape the structure of the brain as well. People who have had intensive musical training have a thicker corpus callosum and more brain growth in regions associated with music-related skills than do non-musicians, and the difference is even greater if they started their training before age 7 (Schlaug et al., 1995). A thicker corpus callosum makes for greater communication between the two sides of the brain. Also, musicians have larger cerebellums (an area involved in motor coordination) than do nonmusicians (Hutchinson et al., 2003). Other research shows that the earlier musical training begins, the greater the degree of activation of the music-processing areas of the brain (left auditory cortex) when listening to music (Ohnishi et al., 2001). And other evidence indicates significant growth in brain regions of 6-year-old children after just 15 months of musical training compared to those without training (Hyde et al., 2009). Moreover, as the brain regions involved in

Nature & Nurture

Musicians have better communication between the two sides of the brain than do people who have not had musical training. This finding suggests that the skills of music training enhance connectivity—in white matter—between the hemispheres.

orphan (Cicchetti, 2001). Similarly, research shows decreases in brain size in children raised in severely neglectful homes. These deficits can be overcome if the children are removed from the neglectful environment—sooner rather than later, however. The longer they stay in the deprived environment, the less likely it is that they will recover (B. D. Perry, 2002).

Findings in neuroscience suggest that children's brains are more plastic and more sensitive to stimulation from the outside world than are the brains of older people. This is because young brains are more flexible because they have less myelin. In Chapter 3 we noted that many axons are covered with a myelin sheath, the fatty insulation that allows nerve impulses to travel faster. Few neurons are myelinated at birth; with age, myelination increases (R. D. Fields, 2008; Pepper et al., 2009). Figure 5.11 shows the relative increases in myelin over time from age 4 to age 20.

moving muscles and processing sound grew, the better the children's musical performance became.

The findings discussed so far are correlational. They suggest that musical training can shape the brain, but do not lead to the conclusion that musical training *causes* brain growth. One way to address the problem of correlation is to do an experiment. And this is what Alvara Pascual-Leone, professor of neurology at Harvard University, did. He taught people who had never before played piano a one-hand, five-finger exercise. They repeated the exercise in 2-hour practice sessions for 5 days, and then they were given a test. The test involved 20 repetitions of the exercise (responses measured by computer for speed, etc.). As skill improved, cortical representation for the finger muscles involved in the task increased (Pascual-Leone, 2001). Next, participants were randomly assigned either to continue daily practice of the exercise for 4 more weeks or to stop practicing. For those who stopped practicing, within 1 week, brain maps returned to the way they were before training. For those who continued practicing, brain map changes continued. In short, if you don't use it, you lose it!

Your parents may have wanted you to take music lessons "because it would be good for you." Well, there is

evidence, as difficult as it may be for you to believe, that your parents were correct about this. Musical training enhances cognitive skills beyond those directly related to music—skills such as verbal memory, verbal reasoning, nonverbal reasoning, and mathematical reasoning, as well as IQ in general (Forgeard et al., 2008; Ho, Cheung, & Chan, 2003; Schellenberg, 2004, 2006; Spelke, 2008). For example, music training is positively correlated with intelligence test scores in children and college students, and this relationship is strongest for people who have trained longer (Schellenberg, 2006).

Back   Forehead

Age 4   Age 8   Age 12   Age 16   Age 20

FIGURE **5.11**

MYELINATION IN THE DEVELOPING BRAIN. At birth the human brain has very little myelin around the neurons' axons. Over time, axons become more and more myelinated. Unmyelinated neurons appear yellow and orange. Myelinated neurons appear purple. (Source: Fields, 2008)

Myelin increases processing speed, but by strengthening commonly used neural connections, it may also limit a neuron's ability to grow and change. In short, myelination may close the window on the critical periods for such skills as learning language (R. D. Fields, 2008).

Early Cognitive Development

With brain growth comes advances in the ability to think, pay attention, reason, remember, learn, and solve problems. How do cognitive skills grow, and how can we study them in babies who cannot yet speak? The answer is that infants look at things longer when they are interested in them, and such looking can indicate preference. Researchers who study infants have come to rely on visual preference as their primary means of studying infant thought and attention (Richards, Reynolds, & Courage, 2010).

When infants from 4 to 7 months of age pay attention to something for more than a few seconds, brain activity narrows from many brain regions to more specific brain regions (Richards et al., 2010). This finding suggests that the brain is becoming more organized and efficient during the first 6 months of life, and this increased brain organization leads to increased ability to pay attention and focus on one thing during the first year of life (Richards et al., 2010).

If there is one important thing developmental psychologists have learned about infants over the last 20 years, it is that infants are smarter than we ever thought. Alison Gopnik recently summarized these findings in her book titled *The Philosophical Baby* (2009). Infant perception, knowledge of the world, and even problem-solving skills are much more sophisticated than previously thought. For example, research indicates that 8-month-old infants understand the basics of statistics and probability. To arrive at this finding, a researcher put mostly white but a few red Ping-Pong balls into a box. The researcher then reached into the box and pulled out a few white but many red balls (Xu & Garcia, 2008). The babies registered that this was very unlikely; they looked a lot longer at this situation than when the researcher pulled out many white and only a few red balls (Xu & Garcia, 2008). Psychologists therefore call babies "intuitive statisticians"—without any training, they know some events are very unlikely.

Jean Piaget

So we have learned from developmental science that infants and young children have many perceptual and cognitive skills that develop rapidly over time. The next question is, Are there any limits on how and when these skills develop? Jean Piaget's (1954) principles of cognitive development from birth throughout childhood outline stages at which certain cognitive capacities appear. Relying primarily on observations of his own three children, Piaget outlined four phases of cognitive development from birth through adolescence, which he called the sensorimotor, preoperational, concrete operational, and formal operational stages. Figure 5.12 summarizes Piaget's theory of cognitive development.

Piaget called the first stage of cognitive development the **sensorimotor stage** because it characterizes the way infants learn about the world through their senses and their own movements. Young children sense more than they "think." They come to understand the world by

sensorimotor stage
Piaget's first stage of cognitive development (ages 0–2), when infants learn about the world by using their senses and by moving their bodies.

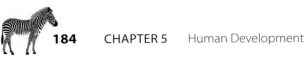

	Approximate age (years)	Core cognitive capacities
Sensorimotor	0–2	Knowledge is through senses (tasting, seeing, smelling, touching, hearing) Object permanence develops between 4 and 9 months
Preoperational	2–5	Verbal and egocentric thinking develop Can do mentally what once could only do physically Conservation of shape, number, liquid not yet possible
Concrete operational	6–11	Conservation of shape, number, liquid are now possible Logic and reasoning develop, but are limited to appearance and what is concretely observed
Formal operational	12 and up	Abstract reasoning—principles and ideals develop Systematic problem solving is now possible (no longer just trial and error) Ability to think about and reflect upon one's thinking (metacognition) Scientific reasoning

FIGURE **5.12**
PIAGET'S STAGES OF COGNITIVE DEVELOPMENT.

manipulating and moving through it. Piaget also observed that during the first 8 or 9 months, a child has no concept of **object permanence,** which is the ability to realize that objects still exist when they are not being sensed (Piaget, 1954). In other words, it is "out of sight, out of mind" for young infants. When an object is hidden from them, they will not look for it, even if they see someone hide it. Around 9 months of age, however, infants will move a cloth or look under something to find the hidden object. They have begun to remember that objects continue to exist even when they are not directly sensed. Mastering object permanence is a hallmark of the sensorimotor stage.

Renée Baillargeon and colleagues conducted intriguing research using a different technique that challenged Piaget's argument that infants develop object permanence at about 9 months (Baillargeon & DeVos, 1991). Their research design, results, and conclusions are depicted in the Research Process for this chapter (Figure 5.13).

At around age 2, with the emergence of symbolic thought, children move into Piaget's second stage of cognitive development—the **preoperational stage,** a period that lasts until about age 5 or 6. Symbolic thinking involves using symbols such as words or letters to represent ideas or objects. Cognitive limitations of the preoperational stage include animistic thinking, egocentrism, and lack of conservation.

Animistic thinking refers to the idea that inanimate objects are alive. For example, Piaget reported on a child in this stage who was asked whether the sun moved. The child answered, "Yes, when one walks, it follows." When the child was asked why it moves, he responded, "Because when one walks, it goes too." Finally, when the child was asked whether the sun was alive, he responded, "Of course, otherwise it wouldn't follow us; it couldn't shine" (Piaget, 1972b, p. 215).

Egocentrism is the tendency to view the world only from one's own perspective. Piaget and Inhelder (1967) designed the *three mountains task* to measure young children's egocentrism (see Figure 5.14). For this demonstration,

object permanence
the ability to realize that objects still exist when they are not being sensed.

animistic thinking
belief that inanimate objects are alive.

egocentrism
viewing the world from one's own perspective and not being capable of seeing things from another person's perspective.

preoperational stage
the second major stage of cognitive development (ages 2–5), which begins with the emergence of symbolic thought.

Research Process

1 Research Question

Can infants younger than 9 months remember that objects continue to exist after they stop seeing them; that is, do the infants understand object permanence?

2 Method

Baillargeon and DeVos (1991) measured infants' responses to both expected and impossible events. First, infants were shown an inclined track and a screen that was lowered or raised in front of the track. They learned that when a car rolls down the track, the car kept rolling behind the lowered screen and appeared on the other side of it. They were not surprised to see the car, even though it was hidden for a short time by the lowered screen. They were shown this event many times, until they got used to it—that is, until it became expected. In the next sequence, everything is the same except that the researchers place a toy mouse *behind* the track while the babies watch. Again, they are not surprised to see the car roll behind the lowered screen and appear on the other side of it. Then something impossible happened. The researchers placed the mouse *on* the track while the infants watched. When the screen was down, hiding the mouse from the infants' view, the experimenters removed the mouse.

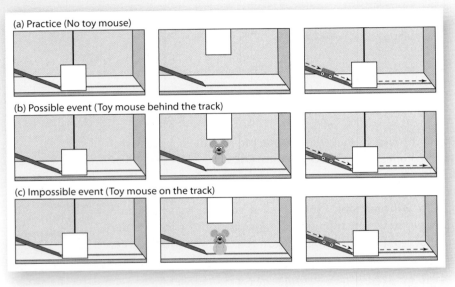

(a) Practice (No toy mouse)

(b) Possible event (Toy mouse behind the track)

(c) Impossible event (Toy mouse on the track)

To measure a baby's response to an impossible event, Baillargeon devised three scenarios. In (a) the screen is raised to show that there's nothing behind it, and a toy car rolls down the track behind the screen and appears on the other side. In (b), there's a toy mouse behind the car track, and again the car rolls down the track and keeps going. In (c) the impossible event occurs. The screen is raised to reveal the mouse sitting on the track, but again the car keeps going. By 4 months, most infants will stare at the impossible event longer than at the other two scenarios, as if surprised by what they saw. This behavior indicates that they have developed the concept of object permanence.

3 Results

When the car rolled down the track and kept rolling (impossible if the mouse were still on the track), the infants were quite surprised. How did they know that four-month-old infants who cannot talk were surprised? Baillargeon and DeVos studied their eyes. When things go as they expected, infants stop looking at the event—they get bored. But when they witness an impossible event—namely a car rolling through a solid object and continuing to move—their eyes widen and they keep looking at it.

4 Conclusion

Infants as young as 4 months of age, not 9 months, realize objects still exist even when they do not see them. In other words, Piaget was right about object permanence but wrong about the age at which it first happens.

FIGURE **5.13**

THE DEVELOPMENT OF OBJECT PERMANENCE.
Source: "Object Permanence in Young Infants: Further Evidence," by R. Baillargeon and J. DeVos, *Child Development, 62,* 1227–1246.

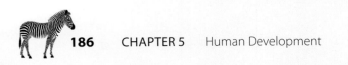

three mountains are placed on a small table. The child sits on one side of the table, and a doll is placed in a chair on the other side of the table. The experimenter asks the child to describe how the doll sees the three mountains. Typically, the three possible perspectives are drawn on a board and the child has to choose the correct perspective. Egocentric, preoperational children will choose the perspective from which *they* see the mountains—they cannot visualize them from the doll's point of view.

conservation
recognition that when some properties (such as shape) of an object change, other properties (such as volume) remain constant.

Conservation is the ability to recognize that when some properties (such as shape) of an object change, other properties (such as volume) remain constant. During preoperational thinking, the child cannot yet recognize that amounts stay the same when shapes change. Psychologists say that they are unable to conserve. Piaget used many objects and situations to examine conservation. Figure 5.15 shows a number of them.

Let's look at conservation of liquid as an example. This task involves filling two glasses of the same shape and size with equal amounts of water. The child confirms that

FIGURE **5.14**

PIAGET'S THREE MOUNTAINS TASK: EGOCENTRIC PERCEPTION OF PREOPERATIONAL CHILDREN. When asked to describe what the doll can see from the other side of the table, children in the preoperational stage can't visualize the scene from any perspective other than their own. (Source: Patterson, 2008)

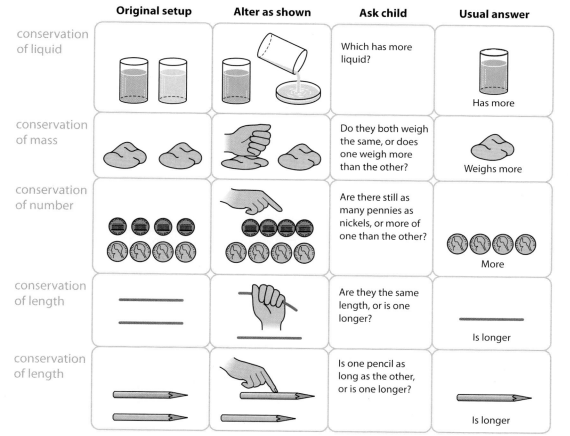

FIGURE **5.15**

DIFFERENT KINDS OF CONSERVATION TASKS. Children in the preoperational stage don't realize that the quantity of something doesn't change if it is rearranged. (Source: Seifert et al., 2000)

	Original setup	Alter as shown	Ask child	Usual answer
conservation of liquid			Which has more liquid?	Has more
conservation of mass			Do they both weigh the same, or does one weigh more than the other?	Weighs more
conservation of number			Are there still as many pennies as nickels, or more of one than the other?	More
conservation of length			Are they the same length, or is one longer?	Is longer
conservation of length			Is one pencil as long as the other, or is one longer?	Is longer

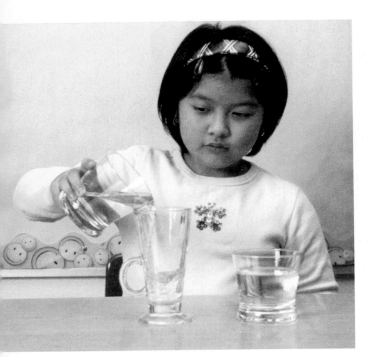

Conservation of liquid. Children in Piaget's preoperational stage of cognitive development typically say that there is more liquid in the taller container even though they saw that there was the same amount in the short, wide container before it was poured into the taller glass. Only when they reach the concrete operational stage do they understand conservation of liquid.

the two glasses contain the same amount of water. Then the child pours one of the glasses of water into a third container that is wider but shorter than the first two. The child does nothing to the second. When asked whether the two glasses contain the same amount of water, the child will say no if he or she lacks the ability to conserve. Usually, the child will say the tall, thin container has more water than the short, wide one.

During Piaget's third stage, called the **concrete operational stage** (ages 6–11), children can perform mental operations—on real, or concrete, objects and events—but they still have trouble with abstract ideas and reasoning. The ability to reverse events is one type of operation a child masters in this stage. One of the yardsticks that measures whether a child has moved from preoperational to concrete operational thinking is the ability to conserve. For example, the child can mentally pour the liquid back into the original container in the conservation of liquid task (a reversal) and realize that pouring liquid from one container into another doesn't change the amount. Notice that this is a logical conclusion: "It has to be the same—the amount of liquid does not change when the shape of the container changes." In this stage, logic remains concrete and limited to objects that a child directly observes. The child can reason that the amount of liquid she or he sees go from one glass into the other must remain the same, but would have trouble solving a problem of this type: "If Susan is half as old as Robert, and Robert is twice as old as Samantha, then Samantha is _____ compared to Susan."

With the onset of adolescence, children gain the ability to reason about abstract concepts and problems. Piaget called this phase of cognitive development the **formal operational stage** (Inhelder & Piaget, 1958; Piaget, 1972a). During this stage, formal logic becomes possible. Here is an example: "If Maria is a

concrete operational stage Piaget's third stage of cognitive development, which spans ages 6–11, during which the child can perform mental operations—such as reversing— on real objects or events.

formal operational stage Piaget's final stage of cognitive development, from age 11 or 12 on through adulthood, when formal logic is possible.

woman, and all women are mortal, then Maria is mortal." In addition, adolescents develop scientific reasoning and hypothesis-testing skills. We'll go into more detail about this stage of cognitive development in the section on adolescence (see p. 200).

The Russian psychologist Lev Vygotsky developed a more social view of cognitive development than Piaget. Vygotsky (1978), for instance, argued that cognitive development does not happen in a vacuum but rather must be understood in its social context. Other people can and do affect what we learn. More specifically, children can sometimes advance further with the aid of an adult than by themselves. Vygotsky coined the phrase **zone of proximal development** and defined it as the distance between what a child can learn alone and what that child can learn assisted by someone else, usually an adult. The idea of a zone of proximal development is that when a child is near his or her potential (in the zone), a more experienced person can aid the child in learning more and learning faster than the child would alone. Learning, therefore, is best understood as a social process.

zone of proximal development
the distance between what a child can learn alone and what that child can learn assisted by someone else, usually an adult.

Theory of Mind
The term **theory of mind** refers to our knowledge and ideas of how other people's minds work. Knowing and understanding what other people are thinking, wanting, or feeling is a critical skill in human society. The important questions from a development perspective are when and how does such a skill emerge, and how does it change with age?

Most adults know—especially those who learn to think critically—that people believe things that sometimes are not true. They may even come to realize their own beliefs may not always be true. Children under the age of 4 are cognitively incapable of understanding that people may believe things that are not true. Psychologists created the *false-belief* task to explore children's theory of mind and when they come to know that others may hold false beliefs (Wimmer & Perner, 1983).

For the false-belief task, a child between the ages of 3 and 5 sits with an experimenter at a table. The experimenter has cardboard cutouts of a story (see Figure 5.16). In the first cutout, Sally puts her marble in a basket. In the next

theory of mind
ideas and knowledge about how other people's minds work.

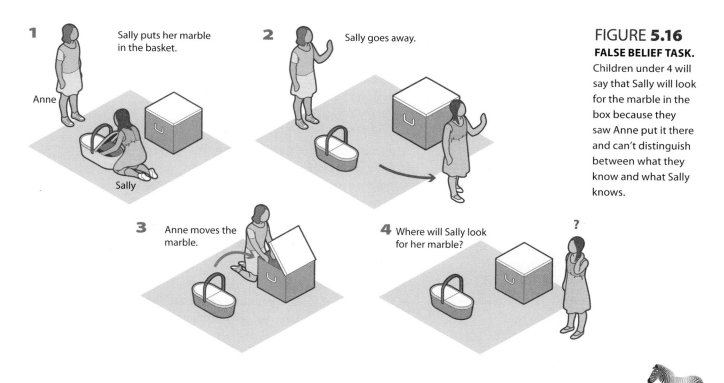

1 Sally puts her marble in the basket.
Anne
Sally

2 Sally goes away.

3 Anne moves the marble.

4 Where will Sally look for her marble?
?

FIGURE **5.16**
FALSE BELIEF TASK.
Children under 4 will say that Sally will look for the marble in the box because they saw Anne put it there and can't distinguish between what they know and what Sally knows.

picture, Sally goes away. In the next scene, Anne takes the marble from the basket and puts it in a box. In the final scene, Sally returns. The researcher asks this critical false-belief question: Where will Sally look for her marble, in the box or the basket? A 3-year-old will say that Sally will look in the box because a 3-year-old cannot distinguish what she or he knows from what Sally knows. Around age 4, however, children can disentangle their own beliefs from other people's beliefs and say, "Sally will look in the basket," because they understand that Sally doesn't know that Anne moved the marble (Gopnik, Meltzoff, & Kuhl, 1999; Sullivan, Zaitchik, & Tager-Flusberg, 1994; Wimmer & Perner, 1983).

Connection

Autism is a childhood disorder characterized by severe language and social impairment combined with repetitive habits and inward-focused behaviors. Autism appears to be related to both sensory organization in the brain and theory of mind.

See "Personality Disorders," Chapter 15, "Psychological Disorders," p. 616.

Development of Moral Reasoning

As children develop cognitive skills, social skills, and theory of mind, they also develop a sense of right and wrong. Most likely, social and cognitive skills work together to help the child make sense of the workings of the world.

The most well known account of the development of moral reasoning comes from Lawrence Kohlberg. Kohlberg (1981) studied the development of moral reasoning in children and adults by giving them a moral dilemma and recording the reasons they provided for their responses. Their responses were less important to him than was the reasoning behind them.

The dilemma Kohlberg commonly presented to his participants was the "Heinz Dilemma," as follows:

> A woman was near death from a special kind of cancer. There was one drug that the doctors thought might save her. It was a form of radium that a druggist in the same town had recently discovered. The drug was expensive to make, but the druggist was charging ten times what the drug cost him to produce. He paid $200 for the radium and charged $2,000 for a small dose of the drug. The sick woman's husband, Heinz, went to everyone he knew to borrow the money, but he could only get together about $1,000, which is half of what it cost. He told the druggist that his wife was dying and asked him to sell it cheaper or let him pay later. But the druggist said: "No, I discovered the drug and I'm going to make money from it." So Heinz got desperate and broke into the man's store to steal the drug for his wife. Should Heinz have broken into the laboratory to steal the drug for his wife? Why or why not? (Kohlberg, 1981)

Lawrence Kohlberg

After analyzing the reasoning that people of different ages gave in response to these questions, Kohlberg proposed a three-stage theory of moral reasoning. In Kohlberg's view, moral reasoning moves from being focused on the self to being increasingly focused on others, with a basis in clear personal principles of morality and ethics (see Figure 5.17).

In the first and least developed level of moral reasoning, the **preconventional level,** the responses tend to be something like this: "Heinz should not steal the drug because he will get in trouble and go to jail." The reasoning

preconventional level

the first level in Kohlberg's theory of moral reasoning, focusing on avoiding punishment or maximizing rewards.

behind the answer has to do with avoiding punishment or maximizing reward. Children obey rules because their parents tell them to comply.

In the second level, the **conventional level,** the person might respond with "Heinz should not steal the drug because stealing is wrong. Society cannot function if people steal all the time." At this level, the person values caring, trust, and relationships as well as social order and lawfulness.

In the third level of moral reasoning—the **postconventional level**—a person might respond, "Although it is legally wrong, Heinz should steal the drug to save his wife's life. But he also has to be willing to suffer the consequences and go to jail if need be." In this case, the person acknowledges both the norm and the law, but argues that there are universal moral rules that may trump unjust or immoral local rules. Therefore, disobeying the more local rule or law may be necessary. This is the principle of civil disobedience embraced by great moral leaders from Henry David Thoreau to Mahatma Gandhi to Martin Luther King, Jr., to Rosa Parks. These individuals exhibited well-developed moral codes for which they were willing to sacrifice their lives, if need be, to set right unjust and immoral laws and societies. When Rosa Parks refused to take a seat in the back of the bus and thus violated local law, she exhibited postconventional moral reasoning.

Research supports Kohlberg's argument that children tend to reason preconventionally and adults conventionally (Carroll & Rest, 1981; Lapsley, 2006). Moreover, research on moral reasoning in different cultures from all over the world offers support for the first two stages of Kohlberg's model, but challenges his argument for a third. Snarey (1985) reviewed 45 studies on the development of moral reasoning in 27 different countries and found universal support for the preconventional and conventional levels of moral reasoning. The postconventional level, however, appears to be limited to Western cultures. Western cultures place a strong emphasis on individual values, and postconventional moral reasoning is heavily based in a personal moral code, so this finding makes sense. In contrast, many non-Western cultures emphasize the importance of the group and community, so the highest level of moral reasoning would be likely to involve compassion and caring for others, altruism, and family honor, values that Kohlberg did not measure (Matsumoto & Juang, 2004). Other scholars say that Kohlberg's theory is a male-oriented perspective that values justice above caring. Women the world over tend to put more emphasis on caring than

conventional level

the second level in Kohlberg's theory of moral reasoning, during which the person values caring, trust, and relationships as well as the social order and lawfulness.

postconventional level

the third level in Kohlberg's theory of moral reasoning, in which the person recognizes universal moral rules that may trump unjust or immoral local rules.

	Motive–reasoning
pre-conventional	To avoid punishment Judgments are based on personal needs
conventional	Rules are rules and they are not to be broken Judgments are based on needs of society; individual needs serve group needs
post-conventional	Willing to break law—and suffer the consequences—if it is perceived as unjust or immoral Judgments balance needs of society with personal convictions

FIGURE 5.17

SUMMARY OF KOHLBERG'S STAGES OF MORAL REASONING. Kohlberg saw a possible progression through three stages of moral reasoning, but not everyone reaches the postconventional stage.

men, these scholars argue, and Kohlberg's theory, in effect, penalizes such an emphasis by including care for others in the conventional level, rather than in the higher postconventional level (Carlo, 2006; Gilligan, 1982).

Personality Development During Infancy

After birth, some infants soon settle into a predictable routine. Others do not. Some are generally happy, and others are fussy. And some infants have lower thresholds for stimulation than others. Based on their classic study of such differences, Alexander Thomas and Stella Chess (1977, 1996) developed an influential model of temperament with three general categories that is still widely accepted: the easy child, the difficult child, and the slow-to-warm-up child. The *easy child* is predictable in daily functions, is happy most of the time, and is adaptable. About 40% of children fell into this category. The *difficult child* is unpredictable in daily functions, is unhappy most of the time, and is slow to adapt to new situations. About 10% fell into this category. The *slow-to-warm-up child* is mildly intense in his or her reactions to new situations and mildly irregular in the daily patterns of eating, sleeping, and eliminating. Although his or her first response to new situations might be negative, after repeated exposures, he or she develops an approaching style. About 15% of the children fell into this category. About 35% of the children were not classified by these three dimensions.

Early Socioemotional Development

All mammals need warmth and contact to survive and flourish. Human babies need constant care in order to survive to early childhood. They seem programmed from birth to form close relationships with their primary caregivers. Thanks to some pioneering research that began in the mid–20th century, we know that the quality of those relationships can have lifelong implications.

Attachment Some animals, especially birds, follow and imitate the first large creature they see immediately after birth. This behavior is called **imprinting.** The newborn sees this creature as a protector. Usually this creature also happens to *be* the protector (mom or dad), so it is a good strategy (Lorenz, 1935, 1937). Newborn humans cannot follow around the first large creature they see, so they do not imprint. They *attach* (Kirkpatrick, 2005).

In everyday usage, *attachment* means "connectedness." In human development, **attachment** refers to the strong emotional connection that develops early in life to keep infants close to their caregivers. This relationship shapes the child's social and emotional development and forms the foundation for social relationships later in life.

Psychologist John Bowlby (1969) described the process of emotional attachment between infants and their caregivers and the emotional distress

imprinting
the rapid and innate learning of the characteristics of a caregiver very soon after birth.

attachment
the strong emotional connection that develops early in life between infants and their caregivers.

"During the next stage of my development, Dad, I'll be drawing closer to my mother—I'll get back to you in my teens."

that develops when they are separated. He proposed that the major function of this affection-based bonding system is to protect infants from predation and other threats to survival. In his observations of human infants and primates, Bowlby noted that they both went through a clear sequence of reactions—from protest, to despair, to detachment—when separated from their caregiver. Bowlby defined **separation anxiety** as the distress reaction shown by babies when they are separated from their primary caregiver (typically shown at around 9 months of age).

On the basis of such observations, Bowlby (1969, 1973, 1980) developed his *attachment theory,* which rests on two fundamental assumptions. First, a responsive and accessible caregiver (usually the mother) creates a secure base for the child. The infant needs to know that the caregiver is accessible and dependable. With a dependable caregiver, the child can develop confidence and security in exploring the world. The bonding relationship serves the critical function of attaching the caregiver to the infant, thereby making survival of the infant, and ultimately the species, more likely.

separation
anxiety
the distress reaction shown by babies when they are separated from their primary caregiver (typically shown at around 9 months of age).

Nature&
Nurture
Human attachment relies on an affection-based bonding system that protects an infant from threats to survival.

A second assumption of attachment theory is that infants internalize the bonding relationship, which provides a mental model on which they build future friendships and love relationships. Therefore, attachment to a caregiver is the most critical of all relationships.

In order for bonding to take place, infants must be more than a mere passive receptor to the caregiver's behavior. It is a bidirectional relationship—the infant and the caregiver respond to each other and influence each other's behavior.

Influenced by Bowlby's work, Mary Ainsworth and her associates (1978) developed a technique for testing Bowlby's assumptions about attachment of infant and caregiver. This procedure, known as the *strange situation,* consists of a 20-minute laboratory session that creates a mildly stressful situation for the baby. The strange situation is designed to see how much the caregiver (usually the mother) is a safe haven when the infant is distressed and a "secure base" from which to explore.

Here is how the strange situation works: After a brief 1-minute introduction, the mother and her 12-month-old infant are left alone in a playroom. Then a stranger comes into the room, and after a few minutes the stranger begins a brief interaction with the infant. The mother then leaves for two separate 3-minute periods. During the first period, the infant is left alone with the stranger. During the second period, the infant is left completely alone. Then mother and child are reunited. The critical behavior that Ainsworth and colleagues rated was how the distressed infant reacts when the caregiver returns.

From the behavior in this context, Ainsworth (1978) and others described one secure attachment style and three types of insecure attachment. In **secure attachment,** infants are happy and initiate contact when the mother returns. They will go over to her and want to be held. After they've been reunited with their mothers, they may return to their play. Securely attached infants are confident in the accessibility and responsiveness of their caregiver, and this security and dependability provides the child with the foundation for play and exploration when the caregiver is absent.

Connection
Attachment styles are stable throughout life and may set the blueprint for love relationships in adulthood.
See "Liking, Attraction, and Love," Chapter 14, "Social Behavior," p. 575.

secure
attachment
attachment style characterized by infants who will gradually explore new situations when the caregiver leaves and initiate contact when the caregiver returns after separation.

In all three kinds of insecure attachment, infants lack the ability to engage in effective play and exploration. The three types are insecure-avoidant, insecure-resistant, and insecure-disorganized/disoriented.

Insecure-Avoidant Attachment   The infant often shows little to no distress in the separation episodes, although physiological measures suggest that the infant is indeed under stress. When the mother returns, the infant tends to ignore and avoid her, focusing instead on something else in the room. The infant's avoidance on reunion may reflect the expectation that a bid for more contact would be followed by the parent's rejection. The avoidant classification is most common in Western cultures (15%–20% in the U.S. and Europe). In cultures such as Africa and Japan where infant care practices involve almost constant physical contact between mother and infant, the classification is rare (True, Pisani, & Oumar, 2001).

Insecure-Resistant The infant cannot be comforted by the mother on reunion and shows difficulty in returning to play. Some babies actively resist contact with the parents at this stage and others act more passive. The infant's resistance and distress during the reunion may reflect the infant's lack of confidence in being comforted. On average, only about 10%–15% of infants are classified as insecure-resistant (van IJzendoorn & Sagi, 1999).

Insecure-Disorganized/Disoriented These infants show odd, conflicted behaviors in the strange situation. They might approach the mother on reunion, but do so with their head averted. Or they might freeze in place for 50 seconds in the mother's presence (Main & Solomon, 1990). Theory and research suggest that these infants are frightened (Main & Hesse, 1990). In fact, kids who have been maltreated are more likely to be insecure-disorganized, and home observations suggest they are afraid of their parents. Not all parents of infants classified as disorganized/disoriented maltreat their infants (Hesse & Main, 2006). This classification is considered the most insecure because the infant's fear of their attachment figure inhibits the development of a strategy for effective regulation of stress.

The infant–caregiver relationship provides the first context for the development of love in the baby's life. Some research suggests that this initial relationship helps shape adult romantic love relationships because the attachment style from infancy brings something to bear on the ways one connects—or doesn't connect—with a romantic partner (Hazan & Shaver, 1987).

Breaking New Ground

Harlow's Discovery of the Importance of Physical Contact for Well-Being

One component of attachment is physical touch. Harry Harlow thought there might be more to infants' desire for contact than a need for nourishment. In his early work, Harlow (1958) noticed that baby monkeys whom he had separated from their mothers became very attached to cloth diapers that lined their cages. This strong attachment to cloth made Harlow think that a baby primate needs something soft to cling to. It reminded him of the attachment babies have for their blankets.

To test his hunch that the need for something soft to hold is as fundamental as the need for nutrition, Harlow and his colleagues carried out a series of studies with newborn monkeys whom they separated from their mothers. They housed them with two types of surrogate mothers constructed of wire and wood (see Figure 5.18). One was composed of just a wire frame with a crude head. The other was a wire frame covered with soft terry cloth. Both mothers were heated, and either could be hooked up to a bottle of milk.

In the first study, Harlow removed eight monkeys from their mothers shortly after birth. Cloth and wire mothers were housed in cubicles attached to the infants' cages. By random assignment, half the monkeys received milk from the wire mother; the other half got their milk from the cloth mother. Harlow used the amount of time spent with a surrogate mother as a measure of the affection bond. He found that contact comfort was much more important than the source of food in determining which surrogate mother the monkeys preferred. Regardless of whether a baby monkey nursed from the cloth mother or the wire mother, it spent most of its time with the cloth one (see Figure 5.19). Monkeys fed by wire surrogates would quickly get milk from the wire mom and then run over to the cloth mom to cuddle. Harlow's findings thus challenged the belief that feeding was the basis for the bond between babies and mothers. Harlow went so far as to say that contact is as essential a function of nursing in humans as is nutrition.

Yet having a cloth surrogate mother was clearly not as good as having a real mother. In follow-up research, Harlow found that monkeys raised without mothers (including some raised with cloth surrogates) were negligent and abusive mothers when they had their own babies. They failed to give their babies proper contact or even to feed them correctly (Arling & Harlow, 1967). One possible conclusion, then, is that they did not know how to behave with their offspring because they hadn't had a live mother themselves. And it would follow that real-life moms are more than a source of physical contact and nutrition. They are role models for future social relationships, especially caregiving.

■ ■ ■

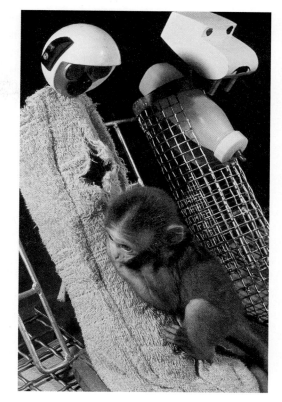

FIGURE **5.18**
THE CLOTH AND WIRE MOTHERS FROM HARLOW'S RESEARCH. The baby monkeys always spent more time on the cloth surrogate, going to the wire surrogate only for food.

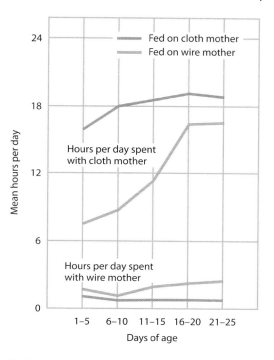

FIGURE **5.19**
TIME MONKEYS SPENT ON CLOTH VERSUS WIRE SURROGATE "MOTHERS." Whether the baby monkeys were fed by the wire mother or the cloth mother, all of them preferred the comfort of the cloth mother. (Source: Harlow, 1958)

Touch   Because of Harlow's work, physical contact came to be considered central to optimal human development. Yet, not all babies get enough of it. As researcher Tiffany Field noted, preterm human babies who spend weeks

FIGURE **5.20**

WEIGHT GAIN IN PREMATURE INFANTS WHO DID OR DID NOT RECEIVE TOUCH THERAPY. Note that the graph shows the amount of weight gained per day, in grams. Over time, the difference in the weights of the two groups could be expected to increase. Along with the added weight, the massaged babies gained better overall health. (Source: Field et al., 1986)

The benefits of touch and massage therapy for children with cerebral palsy include cognitive and social improvements as well as increased muscle control.

or months in special hospital beds, where they are kept warm, protected from infection, and monitored by the latest technology, are rarely touched.

What might be the effects of this deprivation among the neediest babies? To explore this question, Field and her colleagues (1986) tested the impact of touch on tiny premature infants. She randomly assigned 40 preterm infants from a hospital's newborn intensive care unit to either receive touch therapy (experimental group) or not (control group). All of the premature infants lived in isolettes, plastic-covered bassinets designed to prevent infection. The touch therapy involved gently stroking the baby with warmed hands (no gloves) through portholes in the isolette for 15 minutes, three times a day for 10 days. What Field and colleagues found was truly surprising: The regularly touched babies, who had the same diets as those who were not regularly touched, gained significantly more weight and were released from the hospital sooner (see Figure 5.20). Later research showed the same effect in weight gain when mothers touched their preterm infants (Field et al., 2004). And additional research found that touch also leads to reduced stress levels in premature babies and to less diarrhea (Diego et al., 2007; Jump, Fargo, & Akers, 2006).

Touch therapy has also been used to improve motor skills in children with *cerebral palsy,* a movement disorder caused by brain damage at birth (Hernandez-Reif et al., 2005). Moreover, it helps children with autism. A study of Qigong (a Chinese touch therapy) showed improvements in sensory, social, and basic living skills in autistic children (Silva et al., 2007). Finally, massage therapy improves the well-being, motor dexterity, sleeping, and overall health in kids with other disabilities (Barlow et al., 2008). In short, touch is more than just comforting—it can improve physical and mental health.

Developing Social Relationships and Emotions

It is no doubt frustrating at times to be a baby. Think about it: There are things you need and want, and you are not yet able to ask for them, other than by crying. Yet babies learn other ways to communicate their needs to their caregivers, even before they can talk. One way in which they do so is by facial expression. At just 7 hours old, newborns can imitate or *mimic* simple adult facial expressions (Meltzoff & Moore, 1977, 1983). By imitating others, infants learn to make certain facial expressions that help them to communicate their needs (Iacoboni & Mazziota, 2007). Such infant imitation may be a result of mirror neuron systems in the brain, although the brain mechanisms involved in imitation may extend beyond mirroring (Grossberg & Vladusich, 2010; Lepage & Théoret, 2007).

Connections

One way we learn is by imitating someone else's behavior. This type of learning, seen also in infant mimicry, may be based on mirror neuron systems in the brain.

To learn about these systems, see "The Cells of the Nervous System: Glial Cells and Neurons," Chapter 3, "The Biology of Behavior," p. 84; and "Imitation, Mirror Neurons, and Learning," Chapter 8, "Learning," p. 336.

Babies also seem to know at a very young age what the facial expressions of others mean. Four-month-olds show different patterns of visual attention to angry, fearful, and sad facial expressions in a peek-a-boo game (Montague & Walker-Andrews, 2001). Moreover, older babies know how to look to their primary caregiver, whom they know they can trust, for information about emotion and situations.

The visual cliff discussed earlier as a way of testing babies' depth perception has also been used to study whether babies look to their caregivers for information about safety (Sorce et al., 1985). If the mother showed fear or anger on her face, the baby did not move over the cliff. But most babies went willingly over the cliff when the mom smiled. What this means is that by the age of 1, children can make sense of their mother's emotional facial expressions and use them to know what to do. This ability to make use of social and emotional information from another person, especially a caregiver, is known as **social referencing** (Campos & Stenberg, 1981).

The research on social referencing shows that babies understand the meaning of some facial expressions much earlier than age 1. On the basis of studies measuring visual preference and brain activity, for example, we know that by 7 months babies can discriminate between fearful and happy faces. Babies of this age also understand the emotional meaning of the voice (intonation changes) that tends to go with certain emotional states, such as happy, angry, or sad (Grossman, Striano, & Friederici, 2006). Well before 1 year of age, then, babies possess a basic ability to interpret other people's emotions.

social referencing the ability to make use of social and emotional information from another person—especially a caregiver—in an uncertain situation.

Development of Emotions

Babies show emotions very early in life—though not with the subtle variations that adults do. They start with pleasure and pain after birth, and somewhat later they respond to mom's voice or face with a smile. This transition occurs between 2 and 3 months of age (Lavelli & Fogel, 2005). A month later, they laugh in response to playful social interaction.

Signs of anger in facial expression occur as early as 4 months. How do you make young babies angry? One way is to restrain their movement, simply by holding their arms firmly. Between the ages of 4 and 7 months, infants begin to show facial expressions similar to adult expressions of anger when restrained, and the more frustrated they get, the more they show it (Stenberg, Campos, & Emde, 1983).

Other studies tell us that babies may not be able to differentiate their emotions the way adults can (Bridges, 1932). There is evidence, for example, that babies use "anger faces" in situations where they might feel fear, such as when they see a noisy toy gorilla head. So it is not clear whether the anger faces at this age are specific to situations that generally provoke anger (Camras et al., 2007; Oster, 2005). With further development and experience, babies refine their emotional expressions.

Learning to regulate and control emotion is not easy for most children. **Emotional competence** is the ability to control emotions and know when it is appropriate to express them (Saarni, 1999; Trentacosta & Izard, 2007). The development of emotional competence starts as early as preschool and continues throughout childhood (Feng et al., 2008; Grolnick, McMenamy, & Kurowski, 2006; Saarni, 1984). Moreover, the better children do in school and the fewer stressful and dysfunctional situations they have at home, the more emotionally skilled and competent they become (Feng et al., 2008; Spinrad et al., 2006).

An aspect of emotional competence is learning to regulate one's emotional behavior. By the age of 9, children realize the impact of their reactions on other people's feelings. Carolyn Saarni (1984) conducted a classic series of studies to uncover how children learn to modify their emotional expressions in the presence

emotional competence the ability to control emotions and know when it is appropriate to express certain emotions.

of others. She gave first-grade (age 7), third-grade (age 9), and fifth-grade (age 11) children a task to complete and told them that afterward they would get a very desirable toy. The children, however, received a less-than-desirable toy either alone or in the presence of the experimenter. When alone, kids readily showed their disappointment. In the presence of the experimenter, the young children (age 7) readily showed their disappointment, but by the age of 9 they tried to inhibit facial expressions of negative emotion when receiving an undesirable gift so as not to hurt the experimenter's feelings. Such social smiling comes only with age and maturity (Simonds et al., 2007).

Peer Interaction

As children get older, their social world expands from the intimate environment of the home to include play with other children. Although attachment to the primary caregiver is important for the baby and young child, relations with other children have a big impact after early childhood (J. R. Harris, 1998). Indeed, in early childhood, children do not even interact much with other children, even if other children are playing nearby. Children begin to interact socially during play at about age 3 (Howes & Matheson, 1992).

Most people assume that parents are the biggest influence in a child's life. So they are surprised to learn that by mid- to late childhood, peers are probably an even bigger influence than parents on a child's development. Why? Peers share equal standing or status in terms of age, gender, skill, or power, so they are important role models. How early does peer influence begin? A study of over 100 British children shows that even 5-year-olds are sensitive to peer criticism. Kids who are more attuned to social and emotional information are more likely to display this sensitivity. Researchers have evaluated children's skills with social and emotional information by giving them tasks such as identifying facial expression of emotion or determining what a puppet in an acted-out scene or a character in a book might do or feel (Cutting & Dunn, 2002).

In peer interactions, children tend to sort themselves out by gender. First, even when not pressured by adults to do so, children flock to same-sex playmates (Maccoby & Jacklin, 1987). Second, these gender differences in play occur all over the world—in Europe, the United States, Asia, and Africa (Omark, Omark, & Edelman, 1973; Whiting & Edwards, 1988). Eleanor Maccoby (2000) has attributed this same-sex interaction preference to shared preferences for certain types of play. Boys prefer rough-and-tumble play, whereas girls opt for cooperative play (Green & Cillessen, 2008; Maccoby, 2000). Only in adolescence do boys and girls begin to move toward opposite-sex interactions.

Childhood Temperament and Personality Development

What does early childhood temperament predict about adult personality and behavior? One longitudinal study evaluated 1,000 New Zealand children over an 18-year

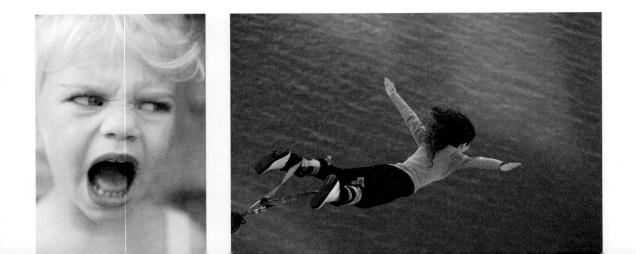

period to try to answer this question. The children were assessed on many temperamental, cognitive, medical, and motor dimensions at age 3 and then again about every 2 to 2.5 years until they were 21 years old (Caspi, 2000). Ratings by parents of their children at age 3 revealed three basic types of temperament: well-adjusted, undercontrolled, and inhibited.

Eighteen years after the initial assessment, the individuals whose parents had classified them as undercontrolled (impulsive and prone to temper tantrums) at age 3 were impulsive and likely to engage in thrill-seeking behaviors. Compared to well-adjusted kids, this group was also much more likely to be aggressive and hostile, to have more relationship conflict, and to abuse alcohol.

At age 21, the inhibited children were less likely to have social support and were more likely to avoid risk and harm, to be nonassertive and overcontrolled, and to suffer from prolonged depression. They also were somewhat more likely than well-adjusted individuals to attempt suicide or have problems with alcohol. Further, they were about as likely as well-adjusted types (and less likely than the undercontrolled individuals) to have committed a criminal offense. Finally, as adults, inhibited children reported the least amount of social, emotional, and financial support from others. In sum, our temperament at age 3 seems to continue shaping our personalities into adulthood (Kagan, 2003).

A separate study assessed 3- and 4-year-old children for openness to new experiences; that is, they were tested to how curious, exploratory, creative, and imaginative they were. These individuals were assessed again at ages 18 and 23 (Gjerde & Cardilla, 2009). Interestingly, the open and imaginative young boys tended to become self-assured, flexible, and resilient young adults. Results were rather different for the open and imaginative young girls. They tended to become relatively anxious and self-doubting young women. This finding may be explained by socialization differences whereby boys are more encouraged than girls to realize their cognitive potential (Gjerde & Cardilla, 2009). In sum, who we are as young children does foreshadow, sometimes in predictable and other times in unpredictable ways, who we become as adults.

Quick Quiz 5.2: The Developing Infant and Child

1. In the newborn infant, the sense of _____ is almost fully developed, but the sense of _____ continues to change and improve over the first few years of life.
   a. taste; hearing
   b. vision; taste
   c. vision; hearing
   d. hearing; vision

2. With learning and experience, certain synaptic connections grow stronger, while those that are not strengthened by experience degrade and die off. This process is known as
   a. neural efficiency
   b. honing
   c. pruning
   d. reductionism

3. People who have had intensive musical training have _____ than nonmusicians.
   a. thicker finger pads
   b. a thicker corpus callosum
   c. a thicker cerebellum
   d. a thicker caudate nucleus

4. Piaget's _____ stage of cognitive development begins when the child can conserve—that is, knows that the amount of a liquid or substance stays the same even when it changes shape.
   a. sensorimotor
   b. abstract–ideational
   c. logical operations
   d. concrete operations

Answers can be found at the end of the chapter.

The Developing Infant and Child   **199**

THE DEVELOPING ADOLESCENT

adolescence
the transition period between childhood and adulthood.

Adolescence is the transition period between childhood and early adulthood, beginning at about age 11 or 12 and lasting until around age 18. Adolescence is a tumultuous time, made both exciting and difficult by all the changes that have to take place in a relatively short period to turn a girl into a woman and a boy into a man.

Physical Development in Adolescence

puberty
the period when sexual maturation begins; it marks the beginning of adolescence.

Puberty, the period when sexual maturation begins, marks the beginning of adolescence. During puberty, major hormonal changes prepare the body for reproduction and stimulate changes in body size and proportions. On average, girls reach puberty at about age 11 and boys at about age 13. The changes that mark the beginning of puberty stem from the release of sex hormones. First, the pituitary gland sends hormonal signals to the sex glands, telling them to mature. The sex glands, or *gonads,* then release sex hormones (see Figure 5.21). The male gonads are called *testes;* the female gonads are the *ovaries.* The testes release the male sex hormone *testosterone,* which initiates the physical changes we associate with male maturation, such as facial and pubic hair, deepening of the voice, widening of the shoulders, and growth of the penis. The release of the female sex hormone *estradiol* from the ovaries transforms girls into women, with the growth of breasts, widening of hips, and an increase in body fat.

menarche
the first menstrual period.

In girls, breast development can start as early as age 10. The next major change is the onset of menstruation, known as **menarche.** You may be surprised to learn that menstruation is not solely a biological event; indeed, it is also affected by cultural and environmental events. The age of menarche is highly variable, but it often occurs by age 12. In most Western cultures, the age of menarche has dropped from about age 16 during the 1800s to 12 or 13 today. The beginning of

In the United States, girls start puberty about two years earlier than boys. African American girls begin maturing somewhat earlier than European American girls.

FIGURE
5.21
PHYSICAL DEVELOPMENT OF MALES AND FEMALES DURING PUBERTY.

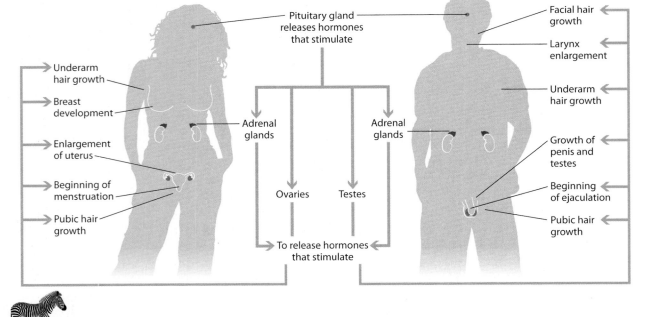

menstruation marks the beginning of fertility for a young woman, so this is an important developmental milestone.

spermarche
the first ejaculation.

In boys, the event that signals readiness to reproduce is **spermarche,** or the first ejaculation. Usually the first ejaculation is unexpected, and it occurs as a nocturnal emission or "wet dream." Once a male has ejaculated, technically he can father a child. This presents a primary problem of adolescence: In boys and girls, the body is ready for parenthood far earlier than the mind is.

Cognitive and Brain Development in Adolescence

As the body undergoes this dramatic transformation, changes continue to unfold in the brain. During adolescence, children gain the ability to reason about abstract concepts and problems. Recall that Piaget called this stage formal operational. In this stage, teens may show the ability to engage in scientific reasoning and hypothesis testing.

Adolescents and even adults do not all develop this reasoning ability to the same degree (Klahr, 2000; Kuhn, Amsel, & O'Loughlin, 1988; Kuhn & Pearsall, 2000; Wilkening & Sodian, 2005). The extent to which they do is related to their ability to think and solve problems systematically, rather than relying on the trial-and-error method that children use. It is also related to the ability to distinguish one's thoughts about how the world works from the evidence for how it really works (Kuhn & Pearsall, 2000). For example, believing that the position of the planets affects human personality does not make it so. Good scientific thinkers realize the world may or may not operate the way they think it does, so they devise step-by-step ways of testing their ideas. This requires the ability to think about alternatives and to question their own thinking.

With adolescence and formal operations, young people begin to ask abstract philosophical, religious, and political questions and form their own beliefs. Moreover, with abstract thinking comes the ability to consider alternatives—not just how things are, but how they could be. For instance, science fiction and Internet gaming appeal to adolescents because they involve abstract, imaginative, and alternative forms of thinking.

The cognitive developments of adolescence, such as abstract reasoning and logical thinking, are linked with the dramatic brain development occurring during this period. For instance, the frontal lobes are the last areas of the brain to fully develop, and they continue to mature until late adolescence or early adulthood (Fuster, 2002; Miller & Cummings, 1999; Sowell et al., 2001). The frontal lobes are involved in planning, attention, working memory, abstract thought, and impulse control. The onset of formal operational and scientific thinking occurs after the frontal lobes have developed more fully (Kwon & Lawson, 2000).

It is not so much that the frontal lobes and other brain regions are growing in size—but rather that they are growing in neural complexity. Complexity is seen in more myelin and white matter, greater neural coordination or synchrony, and neural pruning. In general, there is a direct relationship between cognitive development and brain development.

A multitude of changes occur in brain development throughout adolescence:

- The brain develops more myelin around the axons as well as more neural connections (R. D. Fields, 2008; Perrin et al., 2009; Sabbagh, 2006; Sakai, 2005; Shaw et al., 2006). As seen in Figure 5.11, myelination proceeds from the back of the brain to the frontal lobes during the period from childhood to adolescence. The rate and locations of myelination differ between boys and girls (R. D. Fields, 2008; Perrin et al., 2009; Schmithorst, Holland, & Dardzinski, 2008). In girls, this increased white matter organization is in the right hemisphere; in boys, it is in the left hemisphere (Schmithorst et al., 2008). This is one of numerous examples of developmental differences in the brains of boys and girls as they move into the teen years.

- *Neural synchrony,* or the ability of certain types of brain waves to work together to allow for coordinated activity in the brain, also increases throughout adolescence and possibly into early adulthood (Uhlhaas et al., 2009). Abnormal neural synchrony appears to play a role in such disorders as autism and schizophrenia (Uhlhaas & Singer, 2010).
- *Synaptic pruning* reaches its final stages, whereby rarely used synapses are allowed to die off to make the brain more efficient (deGraaf & Hadders-Algra, 2006; Paus, Keshavan, & Giedd, 2008).

How the brain develops and, in particular, how the cortex develops affects intelligence. Philip Shaw and colleagues (2006) periodically scanned the brains of more than 300 participants during childhood and adolescence and discovered something surprising. At age 7 the highly intelligent children had thinner frontal cortexes, but by mid-adolescence their cortexes had become thicker than those of the children with average intelligence. Moreover, by age 19 the thickness of the cortex in the two groups was the same (see Figure 5.22). So the cortex grows thicker into adolescence, and the brains of highly intelligent people are more elastic and trace a different developmental path.

But if so much brain growth is occurring, why do teens often seem absent-minded and/or prone to risky and impulsive behavior? The turmoil of puberty can make one a bit stupid. Research on other mammals offers some clues to this question. "Teen" mice taught how to learn a maze perform much more slowly than both prepubescent and adult mice. They also have an increased abundance of GABAnergic receptors in the hippocampus at that time, which impairs learning (Shen et al., 2010). Impaired hippocampus functioning, therefore, may be responsible for questionable and risky behavior seen in teen mice and, by extension, teen humans.

In teens, the frontal lobes become overloaded during complex and demanding tasks, whereas the workload is distributed more evenly throughout the brain in adults (Sabbagh, 2006). Moreover, although teenagers have the same basic reasoning skills as adults, the more sophisticated cognitive skills, such as the ability to plan ahead or evaluate the possible consequences of a decision, do not develop

FIGURE **5.22**

THE DEVELOPING BRAIN: CORTICAL THICKNESS AND INTELLIGENCE. The cortex is thinner in highly intelligent 7-year-olds than in 7-year-olds of average intelligence. At age 9, cortical thickness is the same in the two groups, but thereafter the cortex is thicker in the highly intelligent group. By age 19, the two groups are once again equal in cortical thickness. The changes are quite small (less than half a millimeter), but in the context of brain development, they are significant. (Source: Shaw, P., Greenstein, D., Lerch, J., Clasen, L., Lenroot, R., Gogtay, N., Evans, A., Rapoport, J., & Giedd, J. (2006). Intellectual ability and cortical development in children and adolescents. *Nature, 440,* 676–679. Reprinted by permission from Macmillan Publishers Ltd.)

until late adolescence or young adulthood (Steinberg, 2010). The tendency of teenagers to engage in impulsive and risky behavior, such as driving at excessive speeds and fighting, can be partly explained by these findings of brain development.

The active development of the teen brain—the growing brain structures, increased myelination, neural synchrony, and synaptic pruning—also helps explain why people are more vulnerable to brain-related dysfunctions and disorders during adolescence (Paus, Keshavan, & Giedd, 2008). When so many changes are happening in the brain, it is more vulnerable to toxins and diseases that affect the nervous system.

Social Development in Adolescence

The changes to the brain during adolescence influence social as well as cognitive behavior. Areas of the brain involved in how we interpret other people's faces, our understanding of emotion, and "theory of mind" are still developing into the teen years. These areas include the amygdala, portions of the temporal lobe, and the medial prefrontal cortex (mPFC) (Sebastian et al., 2010). For instance, teens use slightly different brain regions to process certain emotions than do adults, indicating that further change occurs during the teen years (Burnett et al., 2008).

As you may have noticed, teens are more sensitive than adults to rejection by others. In a laboratory task in which a teen is left out of simulated group play (a computer game with unseen partners) and then ostracized for it, the omitted teens showed a much stronger response to rejection than adults in the same situation. It may be that the sensitivity to rejection in teen years is related to the extended period of development in the prefrontal cortex that occurs over the course of adolescence, but more research is needed to confirm this hypothesis (Sebastian et al., 2010).

With the onset of puberty and adolescence, children begin to focus on the questions of who they are. Just as we try on clothes to see what fits, adolescents try on identities to see what looks good and feels comfortable. One way teens experiment with identity is in how they relate to groups, which groups they identify with, and how they present themselves to others more generally. Group identifications can be very important and long-lasting, and it can be quite distressing to teens if they are challenged (Lemay & Ashmore, 2004). For instance, one of your authors (Erika) ran track and cross-country in high school. Being a runner—an athlete—became an important part of her identity, as did relating to the community of runners at school. This identification lasted well through adulthood, in fact. Although identity development occurs across the life span, teens are more self-conscious about the changes associated with them and experience changes more intensely than do children or adults (Steinberg, 2005, 2010).

Connection

If you spend hours each day on Internet gaming and creating alternative realities and personalities (avatars), is that an addiction?

See "Psychology in the Real World: Can Internet Use Become an Addiction?" Chapter 15, "Psychological Disorders," p. 598.

Puberty brings profound changes not only in the body but also in relationships. Family becomes less central, and peer relationships become the focus of life. Having close, intimate friends during adolescence is associated with many positive social and emotional outcomes, such as self-confidence, better relationships with parents and authority figures, better performance in school, and even better overall adjustment and feelings of self-worth in adulthood (Bagwell, Newcomb, & Bukowski, 1998). In contrast, feeling isolated and lacking close peer relationships during adolescence is associated with poorer performance in school, more conflict with parents and authority figures, and lower self-esteem.

In the teen years, peers start to replace parents as a source of identification (Brown, 1990; Bukowski & Sippola, 2001; Pugh & Hart, 1999). In the search for who they are, adolescents look to their friends for answers. The values and social rules operating within different peer groups give teens "identity templates" that they use to define themselves (Pugh & Hart, 1999). Moreover, perceived pressure and criticism from others (mother and friends, for instance) foretell whether or not disordered eating might emerge in both male and female teens (Shomaker & Furman, 2009). Reactions from parents and peers also play a role in whether teens end up using alcohol and cigarettes (Kristjansson et al., 2010).

Compared to childhood, however, the most obvious change in adolescent social development is the emergence of sexual interest and sexual relationships. Teens not only become interested in sexual relationships, but sexual thoughts and feelings also occupy much of their attention and time. The average age for first sexual intercourse for men and women is around 17 years old, although there is quite a bit of variability (Chandra et al., 2005). A sexually mature body combined with a brain that is not fully developed can result in bad judgment, as shown in the high rates of unplanned pregnancy and sexually transmitted diseases in teens (CDC, 2005). Sexuality and sexual activity influence how teens think of themselves. Being sexually active increases self-esteem and enhances self-concept in both boys and girls, but it also can lead to an increase in risky behavior (Houlihan et al., 2008).

The teen years are also the time of sexual identity formation. Roughly 88% of teenagers describe themselves as predominantly *heterosexual* (interested only in the opposite sex), while about 1%–2% see themselves as either predominantly *homosexual* (interested only in the same sex) or *bisexual* (interested in both sexes). About 10% of teens say they are confused about their sexual orientation (Remafedi et al., 1992). Another survey showed that about 6% of teens are heterosexual with same-sex attraction/fantasy or behavior (Zhao et al., 2010).

Finally, adolescents explore their identity through experimenting with drugs and alcohol (Duncan, Duncan, & Strycker, 2006; Tang & Orwin, 2009). Both parental and peer behavior influence whether someone will start drinking and how their drinking behavior develops.

Personality Development in Adolescence Although many aspects of temperament and personality are stable over time, our personalities also grow

Experimenting with different styles of dress appeals to adolescents in the midst of identity formation.

and change as we age. Erik Erikson (1968) proposed a model of personality development with eight stages, each defined by an identity crisis or conflict (see Figure 5.23). According to Erikson, an identity crisis is an opportunity for adaptive or maladaptive adjustment. Each stage consists of a conflict from which a person may develop a strength or a weakness.

Erikson (1968) saw identity versus identity confusion as the conflict during adolescent personality development. Testing, experimenting, and trying on identities is the norm during adolescence. Experimenting allows a person to find out which identities work and which ones don't. Dating and sexual orientation, as well as testing of different belief systems, allow adolescents to resolve the identity conflict of this stage. The basic strength that develops in adolescence is fidelity, a sense of faith and commitment to a belief system.

Quick Quiz 5.3:
The Developing Adolescent

1. What event marks the beginning of adolescence?
   a. puberty
   b. formal operations
   c. growth of body hair
   d. all of the above

2. In which area of the brain does significant development occur during adolescence?
   a. occipital lobes
   b. hippocampus
   c. frontal lobes
   d. cerebellum

Answers can be found at the end of the chapter.

8 Old age
Wisdom
Integrity vs. despair, disgust

7 Adulthood
Care
Generativity vs. stagnation

6 Young adulthood
Love
Intimacy vs. isolation

5 Adolescence
Fidelity
Identity vs. identity confusion

4 School age
Competence
Industry vs. inferiority

3 Play age
Purpose
Initiative vs. guilt

2 Early childhood
Will
Autonomy vs. shame and doubt

1 Infancy
Hope
Basic trust vs. basic mistrust

FIGURE **5.23**
ERIKSON'S EIGHT STAGES OF PERSONALITY DEVELOPMENT. Each stage has a core strength (shown in bold type) and a crisis to resolve.

THE DEVELOPING ADULT

As adolescence draws to a close and people enter their 20s, the transition from high school to college or work increases independence. Many changes to behavior occur with the transition from the teens to the 20s, and even across the life span.

Early Adulthood

Major changes in thinking, feeling, and behavior occur during childhood and adolescence, but what happens when you turn 18? Are you suddenly grown-up and "all done"? Not by a long shot. By the time most young people have reached sexual maturity, their lives are still in great flux. Further changes associated with assuming responsibilities for one's own finances, housing, clothing, and career shape the time between adolescence and young adulthood. While some reliance on parents persists throughout college, when a person reaches adulthood, some threshold has been crossed. This threshold, however, is not defined by landmarks in physical and psychological development, as is the case for childhood and adolescence. Rather, the movement into adulthood entails successful passage through certain life transitions that end in near complete independence from one's parents.

emerging adulthood
the transitional phase between adolescence and young adulthood; includes ages 18–25 years.

Emerging Adulthood Arnett (2004) uses the term **emerging adulthood** for the phase between adolescence and young adulthood, which spans ages 18–25. Emerging adulthood is a phase of transition between the teen years and adulthood. Teens rely on their parents for food, clothing, and housing. By age 18, things change. Young people in their late teens know that soon they will have to assume greater responsibility for keeping themselves alive, and this has broad-reaching implications for behavior and thought.

As young people enter college or the workforce, financial responsibility starts to shift to their shoulders. They continue to try on many behaviors and self-concepts (just as teens do), but this experimentation is tinged by the realization that soon they will have to stabilize a bit and assume more responsibility for their own livelihoods. Not all young people go to college, of course, but many more do today than did 50 years ago ("Participation in Education," n.d.). Whether or not someone goes to college affects the timing of certain developmental milestones. Women who do not go to college, for example, marry and have their first child substantially earlier than those who do (Klein, 2004).

The key changes during emerging adulthood center on coping with increased responsibility and recognizing the need to make decisions about some of the things one has been exploring (Arnett, 2006). Figure 5.24 shows the key features of emerging adulthood.

Although much brain development has happened by the time of emerging adulthood, the brain continues to change and grow. The prefrontal cortex continues to develop and fibers there are increasingly myelinated, which facilitates neural communication. Brain structure changes as well (deGraaf & Hadders-Algra, 2006). For example, brain areas that organize incoming sensory information and help generate emotional responses change significantly from the early to late teen years (Bennett & Baird, 2006).

An emerging adult necessarily has an emerging identity. Numerous issues figure into identity formation, but we will discuss three: career identity, sexual identity, and ethnic identity.

Career Identity By the time young people are finishing high school, they need to start looking for a job or going to college to train for a career. These choices involve a great deal of soul searching about such questions as how to spend their time, what are their life goals, and what, exactly, might they offer the world (Porfeli, 2010).

Sexual Identity The age of first sexual experience varies by culture, ethnicity, and education, among other factors (Jordahl & Lohman, 2009). In this country, most people become sexually active during adolescence, on average by about age 17 for both men and women (Chandra et al., 2005). Although sexual behavior begins in the teens, issues surrounding psychological sexual maturation and experience occur also in the late teens and extend well into the early twenties. Although young men and women tend to begin sexual activity around the same time, men accumulate sexual encounters more rapidly between the ages of 16 and 26 than do women (Zimmer-Gembeck & Collins, 2008).

Gay couples still struggle with even more identity and acceptance issues than heterosexual couples.

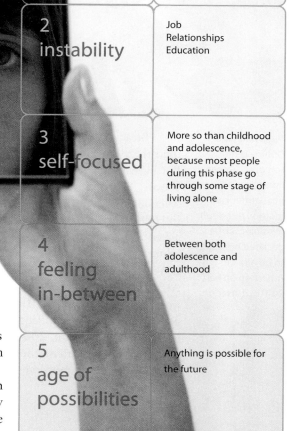

1 identity exploration	Who am I *really*?
2 instability	Job Relationships Education
3 self-focused	More so than childhood and adolescence, because most people during this phase go through some stage of living alone
4 feeling in-between	Between both adolescence and adulthood
5 age of possibilities	Anything is possible for the future

FIGURE 5.24
STATE OF EMERGING ADULTHOOD (Source: Arnett, 2004).

Adolescents experiment with relationships and partners. Fifty years ago, young people were expected to settle down with a single partner by their early 20s. Today, if you make a commitment to someone you have dated for a while in high school, it is considered a big mistake (Arnett, 2004).

Those who readily know they are heterosexual may have a hard enough time developing a sense of sexual identity during adolescence and emerging adulthood. But for those who are either confused about their orientation or identify as lesbian, gay, bisexual, or transgendered (LGBT), it is even harder. The additional pressure from and challenge of dealing with other people's negative attitudes toward their orientation and attempts to fit into a heterosexual identity that is not theirs are linked with depressed mood and even higher incidences of suicide than in heterosexual students (Spencer & Patrick, 2009). These young adults often experience a unique kind of "minority stress" that is different from the pressures experienced by other minorities: There's no guaranteed familial support. Hence the support from friends becomes even more important.

President Barack Obama is the son of an African father and a European American mother. Although he is biracial, he declared himself to be African American on his 2010 census form.

Ethnic Identity For people of mixed racial heritage, who constitute roughly 2% of the adult U.S. population, and a higher percentage of younger people (U.S. Census Bureau, 2009b), awareness of one's ethnic identity increases from adolescence to emerging adulthood (French et al., 2006; Syed & Azmitia, 2010). Each parent or grandparent may push for his or her identity as the prominent one, and the young person has to decide for him- or herself which one feels right. For example, Rosa is of Chinese and Mexican heritage. She says she feels more Chinese than Mexican, due to her mother's influence (Arnett, 2004).

Biracial people of all ages resist having to identify with one racial group over the other. Doing so can be stressful (Townsend, Markus, & Bergsieker, 2009). But even such mundane tasks as completing simple surveys may force them to choose. Recent versions of the SAT, for example, require students to complete a brief demographic questionnaire on their age, sex, ethnicity, and so on. According to Heidi Durrow (whose mother is Dutch and father is African American), when asked to identify her race, "The satisfactory answer usually isn't: I'm black *and* white. Other people want mixed-race kids to choose who they are" (*Reimagining*, 2010, March 2). The same debate followed President Obama—whose father was African and whose mother was European American—throughout the 2008 election and even onto his 2010 census form, where he selected African American as his racial identity. Indeed, biracial children often feel rejected by both groups (Crawford & Alaggia, 2008). Some biracial children—for instance, the child of an African American mother and a European American father—feel unsupported by parents who do not understand their dilemma.

young adulthood
development stage that usually happens by mid-20s when people complete the key developmental tasks of emerging adulthood.

Young Adulthood How do you know when you are an adult? At a certain point, some threshold has been crossed, but the criteria for adulthood vary from culture to culture (Cheah & Nelson, 2004). Though some cultures still have rituals of transformation, most modern technological societies rely on the assumption that certain responsibilities occur when the person reaches a certain age. Usually the transition to **young adulthood** occurs in the 20s, though certain life transitions represent more significant markers than does age (Arnett, 2004; see Figure 5.25). For instance, in young adulthood, financial and living arrangements have settled down, and many people marry or form other long-term partnerships (though this too is changing). These tasks all push the person to become increasingly engaged with the outside world (Burt & Masten, 2010).

Aberg and colleagues (2009) studied over a million Swedish men who had enlisted for military service at age 18, and examined data on intelligence, cardiovascular fitness, and muscular strength outcome measures. They found positive correlation between cardiovascular fitness (but not muscular strength) and better cognitive scores. Further, people whose cardiovascular fitness improved from 15 to 18 years of age had higher intelligence scores at age 18 years than those whose cardiovascular fitness declined over that time. What this means is that physical fitness and cognitive functioning are linked in young adulthood. Not only the middle-aged and elderly can benefit cognitively from being physical fit. Young adults can too.

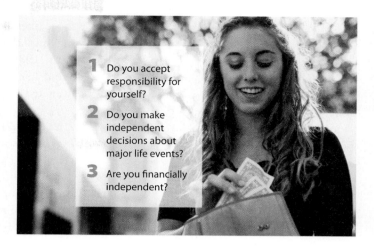

1 Do you accept responsibility for yourself?

2 Do you make independent decisions about major life events?

3 Are you financially independent?

FIGURE 5.25
ARE YOU AN ADULT?

Marriage   Over the past 50 years, the average age at which people marry has increased from the early 20s to the mid- to late 20s for both men and women, though women tend to marry a bit earlier overall (see Figure 5.26; Liu, Elliott, & Umberson, 2010; U.S. Census Bureau, 2009a). Why is marriage being delayed? One reason for the delay in settling down is due to more people pursuing higher education, a trend that accounts for the lengthening of young adulthood generally (Arnett, 2004). In addition, more people are living together prior to marriage, though according to survey research, living together before engagement does not predict better marital satisfaction down the line (Rhoades, Stanley, & Markman, 2009).

Parenthood   One clear marker of reaching adulthood is having a child, although about 15% of adults never have children, and many people consider themselves to be adults before they become parents (see Figure 5.27; Goodwin, McGill, & Chandra, 2009). The age at which people have their first child has increased steadily over the years, primarily because time spent in college and training means that it takes longer to settle down in industrialized nations (Kokko, Pulkkinen, & Mesiäinen, 2009).

Personality may also play a role in whether and when people become parents. For instance, shy men become fathers later than men who are not shy. By contrast, shy girls are more conventional and thus even

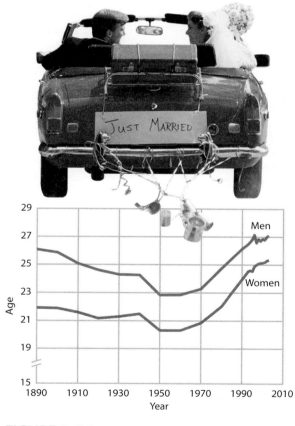

FIGURE 5.26

U.S. MEDIAN AGE AT FIRST MARRIAGE, 1890–2003. The median age of first marriage has always been above 23 for men and above 21 for women, except in the 1950s, when they were both lower. The median age now is higher than it has been in more than 100 years.

The Developing Adult   **209**

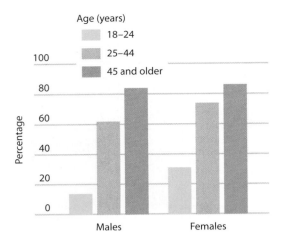

Age (years)

18–24

25–44

45 and older

FIGURE **5.27**

PERCENTAGE OF ADULTS AGES 18 AND OLDER WHO HAVE EVER HAD A BIOLOGICAL CHILD: 2000.

(Source: Goodwin et al., 2009)

intimacy

as defined by Erikson, the ability to fuse one's identity with another's without the fear of losing it.

more likely to parent early—less likely to be moving into the world of careers (Caspi, Elder, & Bem, 1988). Both men and women who tend to avoid harm and risk are less likely to have children at all (Jokela et al., 2010).

Early Adult Personality Development

Having a solid sense of self and identity is important for early adulthood—the period during one's 20s. In this stage, Erikson believed the primary conflict is between *intimacy and isolation.* Erikson defined **intimacy** as the ability to fuse one's identity with another's without the fear of losing it (Erikson, 1968). If an individual does not develop a relatively secure sense of identity as an adolescent, forming intimate relationships may not be possible during young adulthood. For example, before they have completely figured out who they are, people may develop very close love relationships and then let the relationship define who they are. Their identity gets lost in the relationship. Then, years later, the relationship may end—because as each person develops his or her own identity, differences surface. The core strength to emerge in young adulthood is *love,* which involves commitment, passion, cooperation, competition, and friendship (Erikson, 1982).

Erik Erikson

Middle Adulthood

After establishing a career and settling down in long-term relationships and, often, having children, one moves into middle adulthood—generally acknowledged to be the ages between 40 and 60 or 65 (Santrock, 2010). Like all developmental stages, middle adulthood has its own unique challenges, two of which involve sensory and physical development.

Sensory and Brain Development

Many people experience some loss of vision or hearing or both by middle adulthood. Most people need reading glasses sometime in their 40s, as the lens of the eye loses flexibility (E. B. Goldstein, 2007). For those who already wear glasses or contacts as adults, bifocals may become necessary as they enter their late 40s.

On average, about 10% of adults suffer from normal hearing loss, defined as difficulty in hearing normal conversation. But age, gender, and profession are the two biggest predictors of hearing loss (see Figure 5.28). A recent large-scale study found that as many as 50% of older adults (mean age of 67) experience some degree of hearing loss (Chia et al., 2007). Particular professions are much more prone to suffering hearing loss than others, with farming/agriculture, mining, construction, manufacturing, and certain forms of music being highest on the list (*Work-related hearing loss,* 2001). For instance, by age 50, 49% of miners have significant hearing loss, and by age 60 the figure is 70% (*Work-related hearing loss,* 2001). Exposure to loud sounds throughout life, such as rock concerts, heavy machinery, and overuse of headphones, accounts for many hearing problems in people over 40 (Wallhagen et al., 1997). Age-related hearing deficits can stem from problems with the ears, the auditory nerve, or various brain areas and are more common in men than women (Pearson et al., 1995; Tremblay & Ross, 2007). High-pitched, high-frequency sounds become harder to hear as people get older. Indeed, some people report that as they age, they can hear conversations but they cannot always understand them.

Some people also experience a loss of sensitivity to taste and smell, though these changes vary considerably among individuals. Taste buds lose sensitivity, although the ones affected—sweet, salty, bitter, or savory—vary from person to person. These changes do not seem to adversely affect appetite, however (Kremer et al., 2007). As many as half of the people over 65 demonstrate significant loss of smell (Doty et al., 1985).

In spite of the potential for sensory losses, the brain remains quite plastic and generative throughout adulthood (Leuner & Gould, 2010). Although the rate of neurogenesis tapers off in middle adulthood compared to young adulthood, in the hippocampus in particular, new neurons still form. The amount of neurogenesis depends on a number of factors. Opportunities for continued learning throughout life appear to aid neurogenesis, while stress and anxiety hinder it (Leuner & Gould, 2010; Morgenstern, Lombardi, & Schinder, 2008).

FIGURE **5.28**

PREVALENCE OF HEARING LOSS BY AGE GROUP AND GENDER. From childhood to middle age, men and women are equally likely to suffer hearing loss. After middle age, men far outnumber women in suffering from hearing loss.

Personality Development During Middle Adulthood

Carl Jung (1931/1960) argued that in midlife people are confronting the unfulfilled parts of their personality and ideally are developing them as a counterbalance to the other more fully developed parts of themselves. The process through which someone's personality becomes whole and full is what Jung called **individuation.** For instance, a very extroverted and masculine man might become more solitary and less focused on being "macho." But some middle-aged adults cling to their youth, deny their undeveloped selves, and spiral into a crisis of midlife. Jung believed that this midlife crisis is seen in higher divorce rates and more mental breakdowns during midlife than earlier in life.

Erik Erikson proposed that in midlife the crisis we confront is *generativity versus stagnation.* He defined **generativity** as the creation of new ideas, products, or people (Erikson, 1982). Parenting, starting a business, and creating a work of art are different ways of being generative. **Stagnation** occurs when the adult becomes more self-focused than oriented toward others and does not contribute in a productive way to society or family. The core strength of adulthood is *care*, being committed to and caring for the people, ideas, and products one has generated.

A very popular notion of midlife imagines that nearly everyone goes through some kind of "midlife crisis"—quitting their jobs, getting divorced, buying a sports car, contemplating the meaning of life, and becoming painfully aware of the passage of time and impending death. These ideas are in fact based on psychological theory, most notably the work of Jung and Erikson. Indeed, many people do experience crises and major life changes during middle adulthood. But the scientific evidence for a crisis being universal or widespread is

individuation
the process of a person's personality becoming whole and full.

generativity
a term Erik Erikson used to describe the process in adulthood of creating new ideas, products, or people.

stagnation
situation where the adult becomes more self-focused than oriented toward others and does not contribute in a productive way to society or family.

lacking (Freund & Ritter, 2009). Most people do not in fact change careers or take some other drastic action to change the course of direction in their lives.

Late Adulthood

The last stage of life begins around age 65 and is labeled "late adulthood." Of the many significant developmental changes occurring during late adulthood, we shall focus only on cognitive, personality development, and death.

Normal changes in the brain occur with age. Just as body mass gradually decreases with age, so does brain mass (Enzinger et al., 2005). Most normal cognitive decline with aging results in brain changes to the frontal lobes, the part of brain most involved in working memory, planning, and abstract reasoning (Braver & Barch, 2002; Raz, 2000).

The older brain does not change as rapidly as the younger brain, but it remains dynamic (Baltes et al., 2006). New experiences and mastery of new skills continue to give rise to neural branching and growth throughout life (Kemperman, 2006). Learning new skills, such as a new language, a new game, or a new computer activity, can lead to new neural growth (Cotman et al., 2007). Taking up a musical instrument can also stimulate brain growth (Pascual-Leone, 2001; see "Psychology in the Real World" earlier in this chapter).

People often complain about memory problems as they get older. Yet cognitive decline in adulthood is a complex topic. Some abilities, such as expertise in a given area, take time to develop and reach a peak in middle adulthood (Kim & Hasher, 2005). Verbal memory actually peaks after age 50 (Schaie, 1996). Declines do occur in other kinds of memory, however, especially the kind involved in processing information and maintaining information while making decisions. The rate of decline does not become noticeable until people reach their 60s or 70s. Even then, healthy older people in their 70s who receive training in memory skills show improvements not only in cognitive performance, but also in their ability to manage tasks of daily living, such as shopping, food preparation, managing finances, and household tasks (Willis et al., 2006).

In terms of intelligence we must first distinguish between two distinct kinds of intelligence—fluid and crystallized. **Fluid intelligence** involves raw mental ability, pattern recognition, and abstract reasoning and is applied to a problem that a person has never confronted before. Problems that require finding relationships, understanding implications, and drawing conclusions all require fluid intelligence. Neither culture nor vocabulary influence fluid intelligence. Knowledge that we have gained from experience and learning, education, and practice, however, is called **crystallized intelligence.** This form of intelligence is influenced by how large your vocabulary is as well as your knowledge of your culture. Being asked, for example, whether Dalmatian is to dog as oriole is to bird is an example of a problem that requires crystallized intelligence.

One of the clearest developmental changes in adult intelligence is the gradual decline in fluid intelligence beginning in middle adulthood, but the strengthening of crystallized intelligence (Schaie, 1996; see Figure 5.29). Only in very late adulthood do we see a leveling off in acquired knowledge and crystallized intelligence. How quickly one processes information, keeping things in mind while solving problems (working memory), and how well one recalls events are key components of fluid intelligence. These skills reach a peak in one's 20s and 30s and then begin to decline (Basak et al., 2008; Hedden & Gabrieli, 2004; Nilsson, 2003; Schaie, 1996).

fluid intelligence raw mental ability, pattern recognition, abstract reasoning that can be applied to a problem one has never confronted before.

crystallized intelligence the kind of knowledge that one gains from experience and learning, education, and practice.

For these aging Japanese baseball players, an active lifestyle has cognitive and social benefits as well as physical benefits.

Nature & Nurture

Mastering new skills stimulates neural growth and the formation of new synapses throughout the life span.

dementia
a loss of mental function, in which many cognitive processes are impaired, such as the ability to remember, reason, solve problems, make decisions, and use language.

One way to stave off, or at least reduce, cognitive decline with aging is to exercise. Older people who were previously inactive improved significantly in a wide range of cognitive tasks after aerobic exercise training compared to a control group that did not exercise (Colcombe & Kramer, 2003). Similarly, engaging in meaningful, challenging work can make a huge difference for thinking and the brain.

One cognitive benefit of aging is wisdom, the ability to know what matters, to live well, to show good judgment (Baltes & Smith, 2008). Wisdom comes with learning from the situations in which we find ourselves. The more we experience, the more we learn about what is important and how to manage our time (Carstensen, 2006). Wisdom also comes from learning not to take things too seriously.

Sometimes more than just normal forgetting occurs with aging. **Dementia** is an unusual degree of loss in cognitive functions and includes memory problems and difficulty reasoning, solving problems, making decisions, and using language. Age is a risk factor for dementia, but in and of itself, aging does not cause dementia (Fratiglioni, Winblad, & von Strauss, 2007).

FIGURE 5.29

COGNITIVE DEVELOPMENT OVER THE LIFE SPAN. Crystallized intelligence—intelligence based in experience—shows a steady increase from infancy to late adulthood. Fluid intelligence—raw intelligence independent of experience—increases until early to middle adulthood and then starts to decline.

Alzheimer's disease

a degenerative disease marked by progressive cognitive decline and characterized by a collection of symptoms, including confusion, memory loss, mood swings, and eventual loss of physical function.

Several neurological conditions, including stroke and **Alzheimer's disease,** can lead to dementia in the elderly. It may be impossible to determine which condition is responsible because they share symptoms. A *stroke* occurs when a blood vessel that serves the brain is blocked. As a result, the brain tissue served by that vessel does not receive the oxygen and nutrients it needs, and so the tissue dies. Multiple strokes are a common source of dementia in the elderly (Schneider et al., 2007). Dead brain tissue after a stroke makes for many little (or sometimes big) cognitive impairments, such as memory loss and confusion.

Alzheimer's disease is a degenerative disease marked by progressive cognitive decline with symptoms including confusion, memory loss, mood swings, and eventual loss of physical function (Figure 5.30). Alzheimer's accounts for 60%–70% of the cases of dementia among the elderly (Fratiglioni et al., 2007). Usually Alzheimer's affects older people, but not always. *Early-onset Alzheimer's* affects people younger than 65 (Alzheimer's Association, 2008).

Currently, the only way Alzheimer's can be diagnosed definitively is by examining brain tissue after death, although recent progress in brain imaging (such as MRI) may help identify early risk factors (Wermke et al., 2008). For the most part, physicians diagnose Alzheimer's by noting a collection of symptoms and structural brain changes (from brain imaging) that they cannot attribute to anything else.

The defining anatomical feature of Alzheimer's is the presence of patches of dead tissue in the brain, especially in the hippocampus and areas of the cortex (Kalat, 2007). As a result, the affected person experiences lapses in memory, confusion, and other cognitive impairments. In addition, low levels of the neurotransmitter acetylcholine inhibit memory formation in people with Alzheimer's (Akaike, 2006). Alzheimer's is progressive, which means that it worsens over time and eventually is fatal. Currently there is no cure for Alzheimer's, although some drugs do seem to slow the progression of the disease (Hansen et al., 2007).

Some evidence suggests that neurogenesis, the growth of new neurons, in the adult brain might offset or even prevent the kind of neural degeneration seen in Alzheimer's and other age-related brain disorders. One of the benefits of aerobic exercise—brisk physical activity that causes the heart and lungs to work harder to meet the body's increased need for oxygen—is that it appears to protect against a decline in higher mental processing and

- General confusion, disorientation to date, time, or place
- Apathy, irritability, depression, anxiety
- Problems with language, math, abstract thinking, and judgment
- Personality changes with strange quirks or inappropriate behaviors
- Wandering, hiding objects, problems with eating and sleeping
- Late in the disease, paranoia and delusions possible
- Toward the end, total loss of self and inability to control bodily functions

FIGURE **5.30**

TYPICAL SIGNS AND SYMPTOMS OF ALZHEIMER'S DISEASE. According to the Alzheimer's Association (2008), as many as 5.2 million people in the United States may be living with this fatal disease, most of them over 65.

Aerobic exercise can prevent mental decline in old age and may actually result in brain growth.

Nature&Nurture

Aerobic exercise appears to protect against a decline in higher mental processing among aging adults and may actually make the brain grow.

may actually make the brain grow (Colcombe et al., 2006; Colcombe & Kramer, 2003). Environmental enrichment is known to improve memory and learning, improve brain plasticity, and interact with genetic factors to reduce progressive degenerative diseases of the nervous system in rodents (Nithianantharajah & Hannan, 2006). It can also stimulate neurogenesis in humans and help counteract the cognitive effects of neural degeneration (Kemperman, 2006; Steiner, Wolf, & Kemperman, 2006).

Personality Development in Late Adulthood   The final stage of Erikson's theory of personality development is old age, starting around age 60 or 65. The conflict of old age is between *integrity and despair*. Integrity is the feeling of being whole and integrated. It is the sense that all one's life decisions are coming together. The core strength of old age is *wisdom*. Erikson defined wisdom as being informed and knowledgeable about life and yet having a detachment from it that comes only with old age, when one is no longer in the throes of establishing a family and career.

Death and Dying

Death can be defined in medical terms, though the criteria have changed. Physicians used to pronounce people dead when vital signs, such as heart rate and breathing, ceased. Today, medical technology can keep a body alive when the brain is no longer functioning. Brain death occurs when no measurable electrical activity in the brain is evident, but life support equipment may maintain vital signs long after the brain has stopped functioning.

In psychological terms, death is a complex event that marks the end of life. In Western culture, we don't emphasize talking about death. Some Eastern cultures take a different view. In Buddhism, for example, acceptance of death and of the fact that life is not a permanent condition is a touchstone against which life is evaluated. Knowing one has limited time on earth helps give meaning to daily life (Rinpoche, 1992). Some people with terminal illnesses report that knowing their time is limited helps them find meaning in their lives. Accessing such meaning seems to lessen their despair about dying (McClain, Rosenfeld, & Breibart, 2003).

People may move through a series of stages in dealing with the end of life. Based on her extensive talks with dying patients, Elizabeth Kübler-Ross (1969) detailed the stages people may move through after learning they are going to die. Initially they experience denial, a sense of utter disbelief that they are going to die. Next comes anger, in which the dying person feels the injustice of it all. At this stage, the dying person asks, "Why me?" In the bargaining stage, people start negotiating with God or whatever forces of nature they feel may control their fate to try to buy more time. Once the certainty of death sets in, depression may ensue. Finally, there is acceptance of death and the end of life. During this final stage people often come to terms with their own passing.

Increasingly, people in the United States and other Western countries prepare for death by resolving differences with family and friends and accomplishing their life goals. Some people prepare special rituals or events to mark the final stage of life or to say good-bye to friends and family (Bourgeois & Johnson, 2004). We have only so much control over when we die, but by preparing psychologically for it, not just for ourselves but also for the loved ones who will be left behind, we can bring comfort to many people. Palliative care and hospice are growing branches of medicine that are devoted to end-of-life care (Morrison et al., 2005). The main goal of palliative care is to ease suffering and to make the dying person as comfortable as possible rather than to cure or treat the patient. Similarly, hospice focuses on the overall needs of the patient and family members, such as physical comfort, emotional care, and a dignified death.

Quick Quiz 5.4: The Developing Adult

1. Which of the following enhances neural growth in adulthood?
   a. gingko biloba
   b. diet
   c. caffeine
   d. aerobic exercise

2. What is necessary for a definitive diagnosis of Alzheimer's disease?
   a. an fMRI
   b. an autopsy

   c. EEG
   d. psychological testing

3. As people age and become more aware of their limited time on earth, they become more _____ about how they expend their resources in personal and emotional relationships.
   a. selective
   b. anxious
   c. regretful
   d. concerned

Answers can be found at the end of the chapter.

Bringing It All Together
Making Connections in Human Development
Technology Across the Life Span

Technology is a fact of life in the modern world. From the moment we're born to the moment of our death, technology shapes who we are, how we behave, and with whom we interact. Computers, the Internet, video games, cell phones, iPods, social networking sites, and tablets like the

iPad pervade daily life. Psychological science has begun to examine how exposure to this much information and this many distractions affects the brain and behavior of people as they mature. In this "Bringing It All Together," we take a brief look at how technology influences development through all of the major life stages—infancy, childhood, adolescence, and early, middle, and late adulthood.

Infancy and Toddlerhood

It is not much of an exaggeration to say that even before birth, during, and immediately after birth, our development is influenced by technology—for example, the medical technology involved in hospital births. The first postnatal stage of life is infancy and consists of ages 0 to 12 months, followed by toddlerhood, which spans the ages 12 to 36 months.

Cognitive and Brain Development and Technology

If there is one important lesson we have learned from neuroscience over the last 20 years, it is that the brain is incredibly plastic, especially in infancy and early childhood. Early exposure to technology is no different—it changes the brain.

Television, because it is passive (the only action required to use it is viewing), is by far the most popular form of technology used in infancy. Although the American Academy of Pediatrics recommends children ages 0–2 *watch no TV or videos at all,* according to a recent survey, up to 20% of children ages 0–2 had TVs in their bedrooms, and 63% had watched television on the day before the survey was completed by a parent (see Figure 5.31; Vandewater et al., 2007). Only 4% of infants/toddlers had used a computer (Vandewater et al., 2007). When the question is "Has your child ever watched TV, used a computer, or played video games?" the percentages are a bit higher (see Figure 5.31; Kaiser Family Foundation, 2003).

Many technological tools have been developed to aid in preschool cognitive development and learning, from Leap-Pad to Baby Einstein. There are even some online programs for teaching infants and toddlers how to use the computer.

Percentage of children under 2 who have ever...

	Percentage
Watched TV	74
Watched videos/DVDs	70
Used a computer	11
Played video games	3

Data show that early computer use can both help and hinder cognitive development. There is some evidence that infants who learn to use the computer and do tasks other than play games are more likely to be able to read later on than children who use the computer just to play games (Calvert et al., 2005). Other findings, however, suggest that early media use is associated with having attention deficits later in childhood (Christakis et al., 2004). Recently, Disney has been required to revoke its claims that Baby Einstein is educational, because there are no data indicating it helps infants in any way (Lewin, 2009).

Childhood

Beginning at age 3, language is in full bloom, sentences are spoken, and children are quite mobile and able to get around. Their motor coordination allows them to draw, write, turn a TV on and off, and use a computer.

Cognitive and Brain Development and Technology

Most parents want more than anything for their children to be good learners—to learn to speak well, read, do math, make friends, and in general appreciate their world. The question is how to teach these skills, and for more and more parents the answer involves using some form of technology.

Ever since TV viewing became widespread in the 1950s and 1960s, parents and teachers have worried that watching the "boob tube" would create passive and inactive children and uncritical learners. It is true that children who watch the most TV tend to do slightly worse at school than children who watch little TV (Potter, 1987; P. A. Williams et al., 1982; Schmidt & Vandewater, 2008). But that is not the full picture. One of the central findings on early TV viewing and learning is that what children watch matters more than how much they watch. If they watch educational programs, they tend to do better in school, and if they watch noneducational programs they tend to do worse (Huston et al., 1999; Schmidt & Vandewater, 2008).

Certain kinds of video training may have positive effects on the brains of young children as well. With a simple attention-training computer program, children's brains show more efficient processing in the frontal lobes, where executive planning and attention and focus are most active (Posner & Rothbart, 2007). Moreover, researchers report that video games can in fact enhance cognitive skills such as mental rotation, visual tracking, and even certain kinds of problem solving (DeLisa & Wolford, 2002; Dye & Bevelier, 2004; Holmes, Gathercole, & Dunning, 2009; Schmidt & Vandewater,

FIGURE **5.31**

RESPONSES TO SURVEY ABOUT USE OF ELECTRONIC MEDIA BY VERY YOUNG CHILDREN.

2008). For example, one study reported that in low-income families, children who frequently use the Internet at home had higher scores on standardized tests than did children who used it very infrequently (Jackson et al., 2006). In a separate study, after just eleven 30-minute sessions playing *Tetris,* third-grade children improved on tests of mental rotation (DeLisa & Wolford, 2002). Mental rotation tasks require a person to mentally rotate a complex three-dimensional object to determine which one of three alternatives it is like. It is not clear, however, how or if these improvements on laboratory tasks and games might translate into better academic performance or real-world problem solving.

The news on technology and cognitive development, however, is not all positive. Researchers report that kids who heavily use TV, DVD, and computers tend to have problems with paying attention and keeping focus (Schmidt & Vandewater, 2008). More than 10 hours a week of electronic media use correlates with a lack of physical exercise and poor school performance (Schmidt & Vandewater, 2008; P. A. Williams et al., 1982). Heavy amounts of video gaming—but not TV viewing—were associated with being overweight in children (Vandewater, Shim, & Caplovitz, 2004).

Social–Emotional Development and Technology

Social networking is not very common in children: Because of concerns over safety issues, parents and most sites do not allow children of elementary school age to have accounts. In Australia, however, a recent social networking site has been developed for children ages 6 to 9—it is called "SuperClubsPLUS" (Masters & Barr, 2010). It is an online community for children that allows them to talk to current friends, meet new friends, publish their art or other articles, and participate in discussion groups. It is a safe community, because it is monitored by schools and all material is approved by teachers.

Adolescence

If there is an age group that has been most influenced by technology, it is adolescents. They are even referred to as the Net Generation or Digital Natives. For example, around 2005, nearly 30% of teens blogged (mostly on MySpace), but by the fall of 2009 nearly three-fourths of teens used social networking sites such as Facebook (Lenhart et al., 2010). Similarly, cell phone usage (and texting) has risen dramatically just in the last 5 or 6 years. In 2004 only 45% of teens had a cell phone, whereas by 2008 that figure had risen to 71% (Lenhart, 2009).

Cognitive and Brain Development and Technology

Most teens spend 10–15 hours a week on the Internet, gaming, or texting (Lehnart et al., 2010). What effect, then, does this have on their brains and cognitive development? There is not much research on the question of brain activity and computer/media use, but some studies suggest very distinct brain regions are activated with games containing aggression and violence, though not with other games (Mathiak & Weber, 2006). The anterior cingulate shows the strongest activity when exposed to violence.

How does the widespread "multitasking" in teens affect their attention, learning, or problem solving? Contrary to what many people believe, multitasking comes at a cost. For example, heavy multitaskers are in fact less able to filter out irrelevant information and are more likely to get distracted while working on problem-solving tasks than are light multitaskers (Ophir, Nass, & Wagner, 2009). Similarly, driving while using a hands-free cell phone distracts drivers enough so that their reaction time and coordination is on par with someone who is legally drunk (Strayer et al., 2006). Texting, which requires hand and thumb coordination as well as attention, appears to be even more dangerous while driving (LaPrecious et al., 2009). As novice drivers, teens require more attention to complete the tasks of safely operating and navigating a motor vehicle and are likely at even greater risk.

Social–Emotional Development and Technology

Recall that identity and identity confusion is the key conflict during adolescence (Erikson, 1968). More specifically, teens try to figure out who they are and what they like by exploring different experiences and people to sort out sexuality,

Connection

Can we really multitask **How does talking on the ce** **phone or texting affect you** **attention to driving? As w** **explain in the chapter on co** **sciousness, how you alloca** **your attention affects you** **ability to remembe**

See "Attention: Focusin Consciousness," Chapter "Consciousness," p. 23(

career, and ideology/belief systems. In our electronic world, adolescents use electronic interaction as part of this identity exploration and to connect with others.

Teens, more than any other age group, use social networking sites to nourish and maintain existing friendships, but also to obtain new friends (see Figure 5.32; Lenhart et al., 2010; Subrahmanyam & Greenfield, 2008). Teens are more likely than any other age group to use instant messaging, Twitter, and text messaging (Ling, 2010).

Both good and bad outcomes can and do result from these social networks. Negative outcomes include opening up to sexual predation, bullying, and harassment. Positive outcomes include gaining self-esteem, increasing social circles, and relieving social anxiety. For instance, research conducted in the 1990s reported that the more time teens spent in online interaction, the lower their degree of social connectedness and well-being (Valkenburg & Peter, 2009). Moreover, teens who form relationships with people they first met over the Internet are more likely to come from families where they have lots of conflict and troubled communication with their parents (Wolak, Mitchell, & Finkelhor, 2002).

Research conducted in the following decade, however, suggests that online communication bolsters and strengthens already-existing friendships more than it provides a venue for forming new relationships. Most adolescents use the Internet to talk to friends rather than strangers. Moreover, communicating online with friends increases closeness between friends (Valkenburg & Peter, 2007).

Just as is true in face-to-face friendships, online relationships can both enhance and lower a person's overall well-being and esteem. Take feedback on your profile as a case in point. When teens receive negative feedback on their online profiles, they experience lower self-esteem; but they get a rush of self-esteem when they receive positive feedback. Such changes in self-esteem, in turn, affect a person's overall sense of well-being (Valkenburg, Peter, & Schouten, 2006). Interestingly, introverted and socially anxious teens do prefer to disclose personal information more online than offline and seem to use the Internet to compensate for less comfortable face-to-face social skills to form new relationships (Peter, Valkenburg & Schouten, 2005; Pierce, 2009; Valkenburg & Peter, 2009). Extraverted teens, on the other hand, use online communication to enlarge their already large social network—to use the words of one group of researchers, "the rich get richer" (Peter et al., 2005).

Teens in particular use the Internet as a means of self-expression and as a way to indicate sexual interest (Subrahmanyam, Greenfield, & Tynes 2004; Subrahmanyam, Smahel, & Greenfield, 2006).

Easy access to sexual material, sometimes subtle and sometimes very explicit, also allows teens the opportunity to explore their sexuality, by discovering both what they like and what they don't like. Boys tend to enjoy explicit sex sites more than girls (Cameron et al., 2005). Sexting—sending provocative and sexy images of oneself to a girlfriend or boyfriend—is one high-profile example of teens exploring who they are sexually with the aid of technology. Oftentimes, sending such photos remains a private matter between two individuals. But all too often the person on the receiving end decides to forward these photos on to friends, and they become a public matter. Blackmail and harassment are not uncommon in these situations.

Cyberbullying has emerged as a serious pitfall of teen Internet use. **Cyberbullying** is the "willful and repeated harm inflicted through the medium of electronic text" (Patchin & Hinduja, 2006, p. 152). Cyberbullying can be more vicious and aggressive than offline bullying in many cases because of the anonymity of the hurtful language and insults. This enables more uninhibited insults—things someone would rarely say directly to a person's face. The profile of online bullies does not differ much from traditional

cyberbullying
the willful and repeated harm inflicted through the medium of electronic text.

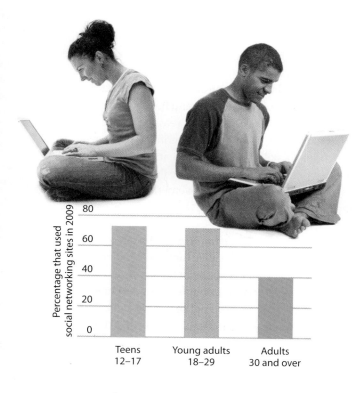

FIGURE **5.32**
TEENS AND YOUNG ADULTS CONVERGE IN ENTHUSIASM FOR SOCIAL NETWORKING SITES IN 2009 (Lenhart et al., 2010).

ones, except that more females practice online bullying than traditional bullying (Hinduga & Patchin, 2008; Ybarra & Mitchell, 2004). Online harassers tend to harass offline too, tend to have poor relationships with their parents, tend to have been heavily disciplined as children, are more likely to abuse drugs, and are not carefully looked after by their parent or guardian (Hinduja & Patchin, 2008; Twyman et al., 2009; Ybarra & Mitchell, 2004).

Emerging and Early Adulthood

Emerging adulthood covers ages 18 to 25 and early adulthood ages 25 to 40. Today's emerging adults have been dubbed "millennials," and this generation, like others, seems to have its own personality. When a survey asked what makes the generation unique, respondents' top answer was "technology use" ("The Millennials," 2010). To back that up, 75% have profiles on a social networking site, and 83% sleep with their cell phone near or on the bed.

Social–Emotional Development and Technology

Young adults are in the midst of two major life transitions: forming long-term romantic relationships and deciding on and entering a career. Technology is becoming more crucial for both of these tasks. Traditional ways of meeting potential life partners have begun to change over the last generation or two. Work, school, family, and friends still are the most common ways in which people meet life partners, with about two thirds of adults saying that is how they met their partners (Madden & Lenhart, 2006). The Internet, however, is gaining in popularity with each passing year, with roughly 11% of all adults and 18% of the millennial adults saying they had used online dating services in 2006 (Madden & Lenhart, 2006). By 2010, emerging adults were the most likely of all age groups to use online dating (Donn & Sherman, 2002; Madden & Lenhart, 2006).

Online relationship seekers share many things in common with traditional date seekers, but also have a few differences. Online daters place higher value on communication and physical attractiveness than offline daters (Rosen et al., 2007). How much emotion and self-disclosure an online ad reveals increases the chance of receiving a response (at least in women). For example, ads that used words such as "wonderful" or "excited" had more positive responses than ads that used milder words such as "fine" or "happy" (Rosen et al., 2007).

Middle Adulthood

Most developmental psychologists place middle adulthood between the ages of 40 and 60 or 65. This age group is also opening up to technology. In fact, in 2009 those from 35 to 55 years old were the fastest-growing group on Facebook (Smith, 2009).

The literature on use of social networks by middle-aged adults clearly points to the positive effects of having both face-to-face and electronic networks (Christakis & Fowler, 2009; Hogeboom et al., 2010; Lubben & Gironda, 1996). The bigger one's social support network is, the better able one is to cope with stress, depression, and relationship difficulties. Additionally, middle-aged adults who have the largest online social networks also have the largest face-to-face networks (Hogeboom et al., 2010). Perhaps a little later, but like their young adult counterparts, middle-aged adults are turning to the Internet for social networks and dating (Alterovitz & Mendelsohn, 2009; Thayer & Ray, 2006).

Late Adulthood

Late adulthood generally begins at age 65. Today's late adulthood generation did not come of age with computers, cell phones, and the Internet, but they nevertheless have taken up the call of these technologies, even if they are slower to adopt them.

Cognitive and Brain Development and Technology

By age 65, many people notice some degree of cognitive decline, especially in memory and selective attention, planning and cognitive control. Most of these processes are working memory and executive functioning processes and involve frontal lobe activity (Basak et al., 2008; Raz, 2000).

Training programs that stimulate the brain and help it to resist or at least slow down normal cognitive decline have become very popular (McArdle & Prindle, 2008; Willis et al., 2006). In one study, 70-year-old participants were randomly assigned to either an experimental condition or a control condition (Basak et al., 2008). The experimental condition consisted of training 70-year-olds for 7 to 8 weeks to learn a video game steeped in strategy and hence requiring executive functioning skills of planning, reasoning, attention, and working memory. Those in the experimental group improved their cognitive skills: They got faster at playing the game, and their problem solving was more flexible and capable of change; but the cognitive improvements were specific to the type of training received (Ball et al., 2002; Basak et al., 2008; McArdle & Prindle, 2008).

Apparently, video gaming is not the only electronic activity that improves cognitive function in older adults. Internet searching can keep the brain nimble as well. Small and colleagues (2009), for example, measured brain activation (using fMRI) during Internet searching and a text reading task. For experienced "searchers," Internet searching activated more brain areas than simple reading, especially those involved in decision making and reasoning.

1. Research on the effects of watching TV in children finds
   a. the more TV children watch, the worse they perform in school
   b. the more TV children watch, the better they perform in school
   c. TV viewing has no effect on school performance
   d. the kind of TV children watch affects school performance

2. Teens who multitask a lot
   a. can do everything well
   b. are better able to filter out irrelevant information compared to light multitaskers
   c. are less able to filter out irrelevant information compared to light multitaskers
   d. are no more prone to have accidents while driving compared to light multitaskers.

Answers can be found at the end of the chapter.

Chapter **Review**

- Human development is the study of change and continuity in the individual across the life span.

THE DEVELOPING FETUS

- Life before birth is divided into the germinal, embryonic, and fetal stages.

- Prenatal programming refers to a change in developmental trajectory for certain health outcomes that are established in the womb.

- Two common sources of prenatal programming are maternal nutrition and substances known as teratogens, which can harm the developing infant. Mild to profound changes in the brain and body of the fetus can result from diet and chemicals the pregnant mother takes into her body.

THE DEVELOPING INFANT AND CHILD

- The five major senses develop at different rates. Hearing is almost fully developed at birth, but vision is not.

- Learning and experience strengthen certain synaptic connections. Synaptic connections that are not reinforced and strengthened by experience degrade and ultimately die off. This process is known as pruning.

- Piaget proposed four major stages of cognitive development. The stage of cognitive development is the sensorimotor stage. The major accomplishment during the sensorimotor stage is object permanence. In the second stage, the preoperational stage, young children begin to think systematically. The third stage is the concrete operational stage, when school-age children master conservation, the knowledge that the total amount of something stays the same even when its shape or arrangement changes. The fourth stage is the formal operational stage. In this stage, adolescents begin to think logically and abstractly.

- The ability to know and understand what other people are thinking, wanting, or feeling is called theory of mind. Typically this skill develops around age 4, when children recognize that other people's beliefs may be different from their own.

- In human development, attachment refers to the strong emotional connection that develops early in life to keep infants close to their caregivers. Comfort and touch in infancy are crucial to healthy development.

THE DEVELOPING ADOLESCENT

- For girls, a major change during adolescence is the first menstrual period, known as menarche. For boys, the equivalent change is spermarche, the first ejaculation.

- Brain development continues in adolescence, with the frontal lobes being the last part of the brain to mature.

- Social relationships become paramount in adolescence. Girls tend to have one or two deep friendships and more intimate relationships than boys. Sexual maturity brings sexual behavior, with most adolescents being sexually active by age 18.

THE DEVELOPING ADULT

- Most sensory systems (for example, vision and hearing) gradually decline after middle age.

- Cognitive decline is complex and not inevitable in adults. Most decline begins in the late 60s or early 70s.

- Age is a risk factor for dementia, a loss of mental function in which many cognitive processes, such as the ability to remember, reason, solve problems, make decisions, and use language, are impaired.

- Alzheimer's disease is a degenerative condition marked by progressive cognitive decline, confusion, memory loss, mood swings, and eventual loss of physical function.

- Healthy aging is possible through physical exercise and cognitive training.

- One cognitive benefit of aging is wisdom, or the ability to know what matters, to live well, and to show good judgment.

- Infants and toddlers are more likely to use TV and video than any other form of technology.

- Educational technologies are widely used at home and school to help children learn to read, learn math, and socialize.

- Adolescents use new forms of technology that affect—both for good and for bad—their cognitive, social–emotional, and physical development.

- Social networking sites help foster friendships and relationships, but also run the risk of being used for cyberbullying.

- Emerging and young adults use online dating to help them find and maintain close intimate relationships.

- Middle-aged adults are likely to use technology to help them counteract their physical and sensory decline.

- Elderly adults are increasingly turning to computer training to stave off memory and cognitive decline.

BRINGING IT ALL TOGETHER: MAKING CONNECTIONS IN HUMAN DEVELOPMENT

- Technology affects development from cradle to grave.

Key **Terms**

adolescence, p. 200
Alzheimer's disease, p. 214
animistic thinking, p. 185
attachment, p. 192
concrete operational stage, p. 188
conservation, p. 187
conventional level, p. 191
crystallized intelligence, p. 212
cyberbullying, p. 219
dementia, p. 213
egocentrism, p. 185
embryo, p. 172
embryonic stage, p. 172
emerging adulthood, p. 206
emotional competence, p. 197
fetal alcohol spectrum disorder (FASD), p. 176

fetal stage, p. 172
fluid intelligence, p. 212
formal operational stage, p. 188
generativity, p. 211
germinal stage, p. 171
human development, p. 170
imprinting, p. 192
individuation, p. 211
intimacy, p. 210
menarche, p. 200
neural migration, p. 172
object permanence, p. 185
personality, p. 177
postconventional level, p. 191
preconventional level, p. 190
prenatal programming, p. 175

preoperational stage, p. 185
pruning, p. 180
puberty, p. 200
secure attachment, p. 193
sensorimotor stage, p. 184
separation anxiety, p. 193
social referencing, p. 197
spermarche, p. 201
stagnation, p. 211
temperament, p. 177
teratogens, p. 175
theory of mind, p. 189
young adulthood, p. 208
zone of proximal development, p. 189
zygote, p. 171

Quick Quiz **Answers**

Quick Quiz 5.1: 1. c 2. b 3. a   Quick Quiz 5.2: 1. d 2. c 3. b 4. d   Quick Quiz 5.3: 1. d 2. c
Quick Quiz 5.4: 1. d 2. b 3. a   Quick Quiz 5.5: 1. d 2. c

Challenge Your Assumptions **Answers**

- Your personality begins to form in the womb. **True. See p. 177.**
- Learning to play an instrument makes you smarter. **True. See pp. 182–183.**
- Parents are the main influence on development up through late adolescence. **False. See p. 198.**
- Pregnant women should eat their vegetables. **False. See pp. 175–176.**

Consciousness

6

Chapter Outline

Challenge *Your Assumptions*

TRUE OR FALSE?

- Multitasking allows you to perform many tasks well at the same time.
- Meditation practice can improve your attention.
- You can make up for lost sleep.
- You can't drink yourself to death.

Answers can be found at the end of the chapter.

On Super Bowl Sunday, January 30, 1994, our lives changed forever. David, the brother of Greg Feist, one of your authors, was hit by a car while riding his bicycle home from work. He crashed onto the windshield and then landed on the street. He was not wearing his helmet. Fortunately for David, within just a few minutes emergency workers whisked him off to one of the top trauma centers in the country. David had suffered a severe traumatic brain injury.

When we arrived at the hospital, David was in a coma. We asked the trauma nurse to explain just how comatose he was. She explained that they use a special scale to rate the degree of coma and nonresponsiveness. Scores range from 3 to 15. "Where was David on this scale?" we asked. She said David was a 4. We asked what a 4 meant in practical terms. The nurse picked up the small bottle of saline solution from David's bedside table. "You see this?" she asked. "This is a 3." David was barely alive.

Two weeks after the accident, David opened his eyes, but he was nonresponsive. Five months later, he emerged from his vegetative state and began responding to input from the outside world. Witnessing David's near miraculous recovery over the next year not only pushed the limits of our concepts of life and death but also illustrated just how delicate states of consciousness can be.

For a long time, the topic of consciousness—something that occupies the center of our psychological experience—was a neglected area in psychology. Thanks to the cognitive revolution, evolutionary psychology, and neuroscience, which all returned mental phenomena to the forefront of psychological research, the scientific study of consciousness is back. In this chapter, we review what the science of psychology has to say about consciousness.

In particular, we'll explore what consciousness is, examine how we know the contents of our own minds, look at how psychologists have studied the conscious mind, and consider how meditation, sleep, drugs, hypnosis, and mental exercises can modify consciousness. Finally, we return to the consciousness-altering effects of brain injury. ■

WHAT IS CONSCIOUSNESS?

Consider what happens if you walk out of a dark house onto a sunny porch. Many signals assault your brain: The bright light from the sky hits your eyes, which send information to visual processing areas in the thalamus and occipital cortex. The heat from the sun bathes your skin, and temperature sensors there send impulses to the thalamus, somatosensory cortex, and brain stem areas that regulate body temperature. The aroma from the orange blossoms in the yard wafts through your nostrils, quickly moving to the olfactory bulb and emotional centers in the brain, perhaps triggering pleasant memories of the orange trees that grew in front of your grandmother's house. The brain processes these signals instantaneously and simultaneously, and they come together into the experience of right now being on the front porch in the sun. They come together in your consciousness.

In spite of its central role in our experience, consciousness is not easily defined. Most simply, **consciousness** is the awareness of one's surroundings and of what is in one's mind at a given moment. It is our experience of a moment as we move through it. But consciousness also involves the capacity to take in and

consciousness
an awareness of one's surroundings and of what's in one's mind at a given moment; includes aspects of being awake and aware.

process information briefly before sending it to specialized areas for further use or storage. Consciousness can change very quickly and dramatically whenever new information arrives. Imagine the change in your experience if you step off the porch into a pile of dog droppings.

Consciousness acts as a stage for the "main event" of your brain at a given moment in time. Consider again the example of standing on the front porch with your brain receiving and processing sensory information from all around you. When the connections among the various processing areas of the brain areas become strong enough, a conscious experience occurs (Engel, Debener, & Kranczioch, 2006). The various sensory elements are brought together in what has been called the *global workspace* of consciousness (Baars, 1997; Baars & Franklin, 2003).

Still, as we will see more in the next few chapters, much of what we do does not require deliberate, conscious thought. That is, without thinking about it, we can lift our fingers, choose whom we prefer to talk with, and know how to tie our shoes (Bargh, 1997; Baumeister, Masicampo, & Vohs, 2011). If this is so, why do we need consciousness? Baumeister and his colleagues (2010, 2011)—who reviewed volumes of research in psychology on this question—argue that consciousness is required for any mental processes that involve imagining situations, such as planning future behavior. Also, consciousness is crucial for mental tasks that require working with sequences of information, such as counting, speaking and understanding languages, logical reasoning, and helping people share experiences (Baumeister & Masicampo, 2010; Baumeister et al., 2011).

Many studies have examined the processes of consciousness, including sleeping, dreaming, wakefulness, perception, sensation, responsiveness, and awareness. The subjective aspect of being a conscious human—*what it feels like* to be in love, see red, or have an idea—has eluded science. The focus of this chapter is on psychology's contribution to understanding conscious processes and to developing methods that may bring the subjective aspect of consciousness into clearer view.

Connection

How much information can we hold in consciousness before it is processed further, stored, or forgotten? Not as much as you might think, as we explain in our discussion of working memory.

See "Short-Term or Working Memory," Chapter 7, "Memory," p. 272.

TWO DIMENSIONS OF CONSCIOUSNESS: WAKEFULNESS AND AWARENESS

We defined consciousness as the extent to which we are aware of our surroundings and of what's in our mind at a given moment. But consciousness really has two aspects to it: the degree to which we are awake and the degree to which we are aware. **Wakefulness** refers to alertness, or the extent to which a person is awake or asleep. **Awareness** refers to the monitoring of information from the environment and from one's own thoughts (R. T. Brown & Ryan, 2003). Usually wakefulness and awareness go hand in hand, but they do not always work together. A person can be awake but not very aware, as is true in vegetative states or extreme drunkenness.

Variations in consciousness can be explained in terms of degrees of wakefulness and awareness (Laureys, 2007). Figure 6.1 shows that each component ranges from low to high and that all states of consciousness exist somewhere in this two-dimensional space. Coma, for example, is one extreme of consciousness and is characterized by very low wakefulness and awareness. The other extreme of consciousness is characterized by high wakefulness and awareness. In

wakefulness degree of alertness reflecting whether a person is awake or asleep.

awareness monitoring of information from the environment and from one's own thoughts.

FIGURE **6.1**

TWO DIMENSIONS OF CONSCIOUSNESS. Consciousness exists on a continuum from low to high wakefulness and from little to high awareness. Each state of consciousness exists somewhere in this two-dimensional space. Coma is one extreme of consciousness and is characterized by very low wakefulness and awareness. Conscious mindful wakefulness is the other extreme, characterized by high wakefulness and awareness. The vegetative state, in contrast, is wakeful but not very aware. (Source: Laureys, 2007)

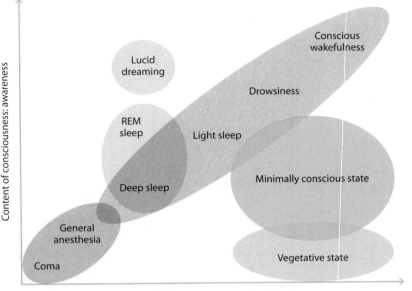

contrast, the vegetative state is wakeful but not very aware, as was the case when David opened his eyes but did not respond to the outside world. Let's look at variations in consciousness in more detail, starting with minimal consciousness and moving to moderate and full consciousness.

Minimal Consciousness

coma

a state of consciousness in which the eyes are closed and the person is unresponsive and unarousable.

If you have ever fainted, you have experienced a loss of consciousness. **Coma,** in which the eyes are closed and the person is unresponsive, is a much more severe and enduring loss of consciousness than fainting. People cannot be roused from a coma as they can be roused from sleep. Coma generally results from illness or brain injury that damages areas of the brain that control wakefulness—in particular, the reticular formation (Bernat, 2006). In fact, comatose people whose brains show normal sleep patterns are more likely to regain consciousness than are those who do not exhibit these patterns (Fischer, 2004).

FIGURE **6.2**

GLASGOW COMA SCALE. This scale is used to classify brain injuries as severe, moderate, or mild. Scores on each of the three sections are summed to provide a total score, which is used to predict chances of recovery in people with traumatic brain injury. (Source: Teasdale & Jennett, 1976)

Eye opening	
spontaneous	4
to speech	3
to pain	2
no reponse	1
Verbal response	
alert and oriented	5
disoriented conversation	4
speaking but nonsensical	3
moans/unintelligible sounds	2
no response	1
Motor response	
follows commands	6
localizes pain	5
withdraws from pain	4
decorticate flexion	3
decerebrate extension	2
no response	1

The medical community distinguishes different degrees of coma with the Glasgow Coma Scale, the instrument used to assess David's level of consciousness (Jain, Dharap, & Gore, 2008; Schutte & Hanks, 2010; Teasdale & Jennett, 1976; see Figure 6.2). The scale uses three factors to classify people on severity of injury: the degree of eye opening, verbal responsiveness, and motor responsiveness. People in the most severe coma have their eyes closed and do not respond verbally or motorically. Scores range from 3 to 15 and increase as each component improves. David initially was a 4—a score from which most people do not recover. We are glad to say that he has made a nearly full recovery.

In another form of minimal consciousness, the **vegetative state,** the eyes might be

vegetative state

state of minimal consciousness in which the eyes might be open, but the person is otherwise unresponsive.

open, but the person is otherwise unresponsive (Owen et al., 2006). The vegetative state has been defined as "wakefulness without awareness" (Bernat, 2006, p. 1181). Physicians used to think that anyone who was vegetative did not react to stimuli from the environment, primarily because of the lack of a behavioral response. We now know that this is not always the case.

A highly publicized case study offers insight into the responsiveness of the brain in a vegetative state (Owen et al., 2006). Researchers asked a young woman who was in a vegetative state to imagine a few things, such as walking through her house and playing tennis, while they scanned her brain using fMRI. Surprisingly, her brain showed activation in the same areas as did the brains of people who were conscious and asked to imagine the same things. Not only was this woman responsive while in a vegetative state—she was responding with her brain—but she could also exhibit intentional thought: She followed the researchers' instructions.

This patient may have been in transition from a vegetative state to a *minimally conscious* state in which the person is barely awake or aware but shows some deliberate movements (Laureys, 2007). People who are minimally conscious show signs of intentional behavior, but cannot communicate (Laureys, 2007). For example, whereas a vegetative person cannot intentionally track a person with the eyes, a minimally conscious person can.

How to determine a person's degree of awareness remains a complicated medical and ethical issue. Clearly these recent studies suggest that behavioral nonresponsiveness cannot be the sole determinant of someone's ability to interact with the world, if the brain is responding to input or even complicated instruction. Still, it is a big leap to infer conscious experience from neural firing (Busch, Fründ, & Hermann, 2009; Overgaard et al., 2009).

Moderate Consciousness

A great deal of mental activity occurs in the areas between a complete lack of consciousness and full consciousness. Freud used the term *preconscious* to refer to material that is potentially accessible but not currently available to awareness (Freud, 1933/1964). An example is the so-called *tip-of-the-tongue phenomenon* (Galin, 1994). We know a person's name, for example. We know we know it, but we can't come up with it. The experience of knowing that we know a name is conscious, even if we cannot bring the name into awareness. This state can be thought of as *moderate consciousness*.

When we sleep and dream we are moderately conscious. We may be roused by sounds that are important to us, while ignoring others. But while we sleep there is a perceptual wall in our consciousness that prevents us from perceiving most sensations of the outer world. Psychologists study many other processes that operate at the boundaries of awareness, several of which we discuss in Chapter 7.

Full Consciousness

Even when fully awake we experience fluctuations in consciousness—alertness ebbs and flows. There are periods when we are more alert and present than normal. We may be stimulated and even excited. Or we may become so involved in what we are doing that we lose a sense of time and forget where we are. Some psychologists have called this state *flow* (Csikszentmihalyi, 1990). Flow exists when we thrive in our ability to rise to the occasion of challenging tasks. Think of a sport or craft you really love to do and do well. Think of the times when you

mindfulness
a heightened awareness of the present moment, whether of events in one's environment or in one's own mind.

were involved in such an activity and everything "clicked" all at once—everything you did was just right. This is the flow state. Our attention is so focused and everything goes so smoothly that an hour may feel like a minute or a minute like an hour. We are so engaged with the experience that time does not matter at all.

Another state of full consciousness is **mindfulness,** a heightened awareness of the present moment, of events in one's environment and events in one's own mind. For example, when you are talking with a friend, you can be aware of what your friend is saying, how he looks, and how his words and tone of voice affect how you feel (R. T. Brown & Ryan, 2003; Kabat-Zinn, 1990). The more mindful person attends to all of these things; the less mindful person might notice only the friend's words. People vary considerably in how mindful they are, just as they differ in their personalities (Baer et al., 2006; R. T. Brown & Ryan, 2003). People can develop their mindfulness skills using techniques such as meditation.

Quick Quiz 6.1: Two Dimensions of Consciousness: Wakefulness and Awareness

1. Which brain region plays a key role in maintaining wakefulness?
   a. prefrontal cortex
   b. cerebellum
   c. amygdala
   d. reticular formation

2. _____ is a heightened awareness of the present moment, which can be applied to events in one's environment and events in one's own mind.
   a. Wakefulness
   b. Attention
   c. Mindfulness
   d. Optimism

Answers can be found at the end of the chapter.

ATTENTION: FOCUSING CONSCIOUSNESS

Being conscious—that is, being awake and aware—involves attending to particular parts of our world. So attention is a key aspect of consciousness; it is how we direct the spotlight of awareness.

attention
the limited capacity to process information that is under conscious control.

We can be aware of only a finite amount of material at a time. **Attention** is the limited capacity to process information that is under conscious control (Styles, 2006). For example, when you are in class, it is not possible to type a text message to your friend and also to pay attention to the lecture. If you are typing your thoughts to a friend, you cannot also listen carefully to what the professor is saying. There are several different types of attention. We will examine three attentional processes that help determine the contents of consciousness at any given moment in time: selective attention, sustained attention, and the shifting of attention through multitasking.

Selective Attention

selective attention
the ability to focus awareness on specific features in the environment while ignoring others.

Imagine being in a crowded room where several people are talking, although you want to listen to just one person. You filter out unwanted noise to focus on what you want to hear. If attention is a general process, then focusing conscious attention even more narrowly is selective attention. **Selective attention** is the ability to focus awareness on specific features in the environment while ignoring others. When your professor asks for your "undivided attention," then, she is really interested in your selective attention.

The classic scientific evidence for selective attention came from research on the dichotic listening task (Broadbent, 1954). In these studies, a participant received one message in one ear and another message in the other ear. Typically, researchers presented several messages to both ears and then told the participant to pay attention to just one ear (the attended ear). They then measured recall for items presented to both ears. Recall was much better for the attended ear. If, for example, people were instructed to attend to the left ear message, they showed little to no memory of the message presented to the right (unattended) ear (Broadbent, 1954; Styles, 2006).

In fact, however, if the material presented to the unattended ear is meaningful in some way, it can make its way into consciousness (Treisman, 1964). For instance, if you were at a large party trying to listen to a conversation in spite of a lot of background noise and someone in another part of the room mentioned your name, you would immediately become aware of the other conversation. Somehow you tuned out the background noise so that you could follow the first conversation, but now you cannot push that background information out of your awareness. The ability to filter out auditory stimuli and then to refocus attention when you hear your name is called the *cocktail party effect* (see Figure 6.3; Moray, 1959).

When we selectively attend, we focus so much on certain things that we are blind to other things. Focusing attention can create gaps in attention and perception. Many magic tricks take advantage of the fact that with attention diverted we can easily be fooled. In one study that clearly demonstrates gaps in attention, researchers showed people a video of two basketball teams, with one team dressed in white T-shirts and the other in black shirts (Simons & Chabris, 1999). They asked participants simply to count the number of times the players on the team wearing white T-shirts passed the ball. About half the participants were dumbfounded to learn afterward that they completely missed seeing a person dressed in a gorilla suit walk into the game, pause for a second to beat his chest, and then walk off screen. They were so focused on counting passes made by people wearing white shirts that they ignored everything else (see Figure 6.4). Attending closely to one thing can blind us to other events, even gorillas walking into a basketball game. This phenomenon by which we fail to notice unexpected objects in our surroundings is referred to as *inattentional blindness*.

If we can be inattentive in spite of efforts to attend, does that mean we can prevent the intrusion of unwanted information during concentration? For example, if you are reading an engrossing novel, is it possible to tune out the sounds of your roommate's TV? Can you apply your attention so intensely that nothing else can get in? The *perceptual load model* states that we do not notice potential distracters when a primary task consumes all of our attentional

FIGURE **6.3**

THE COCKTAIL PARTY EFFECT. The cocktail party effect is the ability to filter out auditory stimuli and then to refocus attention when you hear your name. This often occurs in noisy social situations, such as parties.

FIGURE **6.4**

MISSING THE OBVIOUS. How could anyone miss the gorilla in the middle of this picture? If you were asked to watch a video and count the number of people wearing white shirts, you might be one of the 50% who wouldn't notice the gorilla. (Source: D. J. Simons & C. F. Chabris, 1999)

capacity (Lavie et al., 2004). When a primary task is minimally demanding, however, distracters can capture your awareness. In a laboratory experiment on this phenomenon, participants were asked to view a drawing of a cross on a computer screen. The two arms of the cross were different colors, and one arm was subtly shorter than the other. In the low perceptual load condition, participants had to name the color of the arm. In the high perceptual load condition, participants had to say which arm was longer, a more difficult task. The researchers then introduced an irrelevant stimulus (a square) and looked at which group was more likely to see it. Those who were less busy—that is, the people in the low perceptual load condition—were more likely to see the square than those in the high perceptual load condition (Lavie, 2007). Perceptual load theory might explain why it is easier to ignore the TV when you are lost in an engrossing novel than when you are reading a boring chapter in a book. It might also explain why we might miss certain things when our mind is too busy. What might happen if you missed seeing a pedestrian while driving because you were texting while driving? See "Psychology in the Real World" for a discussion of the effects of phone use on attention in drivers.

Conscious attention occurs when neurons from many distinct brain regions work together—a process referred to as *synchronization*. Imaging techniques such as fMRI reveal synchronization in brain regions that are equally active. When synchronization occurs, we might have a conscious experience (Kranczioch et al., 2005). Imagine that you see an apple: Before you experience "apple," several areas of your brain are active, such as those responding to the object's shape (round) and color (red) and where the object is in your visual field. The synchrony of cell assemblies may be what binds together these separate experiences (of round and red, etc.) into the experience of an apple. This process harkens back to our earlier discussion of consciousness as a global workspace, and it shows how neuroscience is beginning to address how a moment of conscious experience actually occurs (Engel et al., 2006).

Sustained Attention

Staying focused on a task is difficult, especially if the task both requires a high degree of concentration and can have life-or-death consequences. For example, as we discussed in Chapter 4, air traffic controllers must focus on an airplane on a visual display. To do so, they must coordinate with other airplanes, controllers, and pilots to make sure that each plane lands where it should without crossing the paths of other planes that are landing or taking off. This ability to maintain focused awareness on a target is known as **sustained attention.**

What are the limits of people's abilities to sustain their focused attention on one task? The airlines need to know this, as do many other industries that

sustained attention
the ability to maintain focused awareness on a target or idea.

require careful attention on the part of their employees. Researchers study sustained attention using the Continuous Performance Test (CPT). Imagine having to detect the letter Y among other letters shown very rapidly, one by one, on a computer screen. The CPT requires that the participant maintain attentional focus for an extended period of time. Most people cannot perform well on CPT tasks for more than about 15 minutes, and their accuracy in detecting targets declines considerably after 5 to 7 minutes (Nuechterlein & Parasuraman, 1983; Parasuraman, 1998).

Multitasking: The Implications of Shifting Attention

Although everyone claims to multitask, you really cannot do more than one thing at a time. Instead, multitasking involves fast switching between activities so that one's attention gets broken up. You do not stay with one task for a long period of time; as a result, there is less sustained attention. Also, you lose time when you make the switch, especially for more complex tasks. So if you switch from simple task to simple task (like e-mail to Facebook) the amount of lost time is low, but if you move away from writing a paper or reading an article to Facebook and back, you lose more time. A study of office workers showed that once people multitasked away from their work to another activity, they forgot what they were doing prior to the distraction (Gonzalez & Mark, 2004). In order to compensate for interrupted work, people tend to work faster. The cost of this speeded-up, interrupted work, however, is more stress (Mark, Gudith, & Klocke, 2008). (If Internet distractions are a problem for you, apps, programs, and plug-ins are available that will allow you to set a given amount of time in which access to e-mail, Facebook, or Twitter is blocked.)

Multitasking compromises learning. Foerde and colleagues (2006) had students perform a weather prediction task. Half were randomly assigned to do the task with distraction (listening to beeps on headphones), half without the distraction. While both groups recalled what they learned with similar accuracy,

Hazards of Using a Cell Phone or Texting While Driving

People generally acknowledge the potential hazards of phone use while driving, yet the practice is widespread. Many states restrict cell phone use by drivers, but the laws vary. Some allow phone use on a hands-free device, others completely prohibit use among young drivers, and still others have no regulations (Governors Highway Safety Association, 2008). With the prevalence of texting, especially among young people, questions about the safety of texting while driving have also come to the forefront in the past few years.

In the view of psychologists, phone conversations and texting while driving are distracting, even when the hands are free. Talking on the phone or texting while driving diverts attention from the demanding tasks of safely operating and navigating a car. Think of all the things one has to manage while driving: scanning the road, operating the pedals and gears, watching for other cars and pedestrians, and remembering directions. There is much to attend to without the added task of having a phone conversation, or worse—typing a message.

A number of recent studies have looked at cell phone use in the car (Hafetz et al., 2010; Strayer & Drews, 2007). Most drivers with cell phones employ hands-free devices, based on the fact that most states approve the use of these tools. In fact, an analysis of studies looking at cell phone use during driving showed that the dangers while driving are similar for handheld and hands-free phones (Horrey & Wickens, 2006).

Strayer and Drews (2007) did several experiments with people in a driving simulator (see Figure 6.5). Some of the participants wore a hands-free headset and engaged in a conversation while doing a driving task; the others had no cell phone and simply drove. In the first study, the researchers inserted into the driving scene several objects that drivers were not told they'd need to attend to. Later they tested them on recognition of these objects. People talking on a phone saw half as many objects as those not on the phone—they were not fully paying attention to the driving situation. In another study (Strayer & Drews, 2007), researchers varied the objects inserted into the driving scene in terms of how important they were for driving safety. The hypothesis was that people talking on the phone simply do not attend to things that have little relevance to safety, but they do attend to things that matter. Some of the objects inserted into the driving scene were irrelevant to safety (such as billboards), and others were quite relevant (traffic signs, pedestrians). Later, when drivers were tested on

the distraction group members were less able to extrapolate what they learned from the task to another weather prediction simulation.

Quick Quiz 6.2: Attention: Focusing Consciousness

1. What term best describes not perceiving a person in a gorilla suit when asked to count the number of people playing basketball?
   a. inattentional blindness
   b. not paying attention
   c. absent-mindedness
   d. minimally conscious state

2. You are at a loud gathering talking to a friend. The noise of the chatter is nearly deafening, but all of a sudden you hear your name rise above the noise. This is known as the
   a. self-recognition effect
   b. cocktail party effect
   c. attentional effect
   d. divided attention effect

Answers can be found at the end of the chapter.

memory for seeing the objects, they were just as likely to miss safety-relevant objects as safety-irrelevant objects.

An fMRI study of people driving in a simulator while using a hands-free device showed that activity in regions of the brain involved in processing spatial information (the parietal lobe) decreased by 37% when people listened to sentences while driving, whereas activity in areas associated with language processing increased. Their driving was also worse. This result suggests that conversations divert attentional resources from the task of the driving (Just, Kellar, & Cynkar, 2008).

Clearly, talking on the phone while driving, even with a hands-free device, seriously impairs driver performance (Beede & Kass, 2006). Such effects may be particularly problematic for new drivers, who are less experienced, have more accidents, and tend to engage in more distracting activities while driving (Neyens & Boyle, 2007). In fact, using a phone while driving is similar to drunk driving in that the drivers follow other cars too closely, show slower braking reactions, and have more accidents (Strayer et al., 2006).

One experimental study showed that phone use, texting, and eating while driving all impaired performance on a driving simulator task, but texting leads to significantly

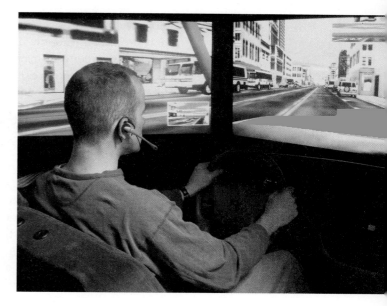

FIGURE **6.5**

RESEARCH PARTICIPANT IN A COMPUTERIZED DRIVING SIMULATOR. The simulator provides a 180-degree city street interactive driving display in a realistic car interior. The "driver" is wearing a hands-free cell phone headset.

slower reaction times than these other distracting activities (Cobb et al., 2010). Compared to a control condition, new drivers, while texting, made substantially more errors in shifting out of their lane and noticing traffic signs in a driving simulator task (Hosking, Young, & Regan, 2006). Even more frightening was that they spent 400% more time with their eyes off the road.

Think twice or three times before using a phone or texting while driving. The data are clear—it is dangerous.

TRAINING CONSCIOUSNESS: MEDITATION

Connection

Every time you make a memory or learn something new, you change your brain by strengthening synaptic connections or growing new neurons.

See "Synaptic Change During Learning," Chapter 8, "Learning," p. 337.

Any time you read, reason, solve problems, or learn something new, you are sharpening your mental skills. Some age-old techniques, however, are designed specifically to train the conscious mind. **Meditation** refers to a wide variety of practices that people use to calm the mind, stabilize concentration, focus attention, and enhance awareness of the present moment. There are many different types of meditation techniques with different goals. To improve concentration, for example, meditators might spend minutes or even hours sitting still, relaxed yet alert, focusing their attention on the sensations of breathing, noticing how the breath moves in and out of their mouths and noses. In this case, meditators attempt to keep their attention on the breath. If their minds wander, they bring their attention back to the breath. This simple, ancient practice calms the mind and stabilizes attention (Wallace, 2006).

meditation practices that people use to calm the mind, stabilize concentration, focus attention, and enhance awareness of the present moment.

Psychologists and neuroscientists study the effects of such meditative practices on mental processes, emotion, and brain function. This research illustrates the dynamic relationship between mental life and neural structure. Taken together, these studies show that meditation enhances mindfulness and well-being, improves attention, and is associated with changes in brain anatomy and activation.

Meditation and Conscious Experience

Many forms of meditation develop mindfulness, a fully conscious state of heightened awareness of the present moment. Unlike concentration techniques, mindfulness meditation encourages attention to the details of momentary experience, such as all the thoughts, feelings, and sensations available at present (Baer et al., 2006).

People with high scores on mindfulness questionnaires also score high on measures of well-being and optimism, are more in tune with their emotional states, and are less self-conscious and anxious. In addition, people who practice meditation consistently have higher mindfulness scores than those who do not (R. T. Brown & Ryan, 2003). Mindfulness-based meditation training appears to enhance well-being, reduce stress, decrease depression, improve physical health, and reduce pain (Anderson et al., 2007; Jung et al., 2010; Kabat-Zinn et al., 1998; Sahdra et al., 2011; Teasdale et al., 2000; Zeidan et al., 2011).

Meditation can improve attentional skills as well (Jha, Krompinger, & Baime, 2007; Kaul et al., 2010). In the first true experiment on this question, 64 experienced meditators were randomly assigned to a control group or to receive intensive training in concentration meditation (similar to the breathing technique described at the beginning of this section), which they practiced for several hours a day for 3 months. All participants were assessed before, during, and after the 3-month training. The Research Process for this chapter (see Figure 6.6) illustrates results from this study, showing that meditation improves attention (MacLean et al., 2010). Specifically, concentration meditation makes people perceive visual objects—lines at least—with greater sensitivity and helps them attend to such objects longer (which is an increase in sustained attention). These effects are akin to having sharper vision for a longer period of time.

The Joy of Tech: Geek Meditation Session. Geek Culture, www.geekculture.com.

Geek meditation session.

Meditation Training and the Brain

Meditation changes brain function and structure. For instance, after 8 weeks of mindfulness meditation training, people who had no previous meditation experience showed significant increases in EEG activity in the left frontal cortex (an area associated with positive mood) and decreases in negative mood, compared to those who received no training (Davidson et al., 2003). These EEG changes persisted for at least 4 months after training. Another study has linked meditation-related changes in brain activity with quicker performance in an attentional task.

Research Process

Study participant wearing EEG cap

① Research Question

Does intensive meditation training improve attention? MacLean and her colleagues (2010) hypothesized that intensive attentional training should improve the ability to attend to detail in visual stimuli and to hold that attention longer.

Longest "short" line
meditators perceived
pre-retreat

Reference line

Longest "short" line
meditators perceived
post-retreat

② Method

Participants—all experienced meditators—were randomly assigned to receive intensive meditation training (retreat group) or to wait for training until a later date (control group). The researchers asked all participants to perform many tasks pre- and post-retreat, in order to assess meditation-related changes in various skills. In one key task, participants viewed a series of lines—one at a time—on a computer screen. A long line was presented first, as a reference line. Participants were told they would see a series of lines and that they should click the mouse whenever they saw a line that was shorter than the reference line. Then they saw a long series of lines, many long, some short. In every trial the long line was the same. The short line changed in length across trials, but it was never as long as the reference line. The longest "short" line they perceived as different from the long line was their limit of perceptual sensitivity.

③ Results

The longer the line that participants perceived as "short," the greater their perceptual sensitivity. All participants improved in sensitivity over time, as indicated by an increase in the length of the short line on the graph. Those participants who underwent the 3-month retreat, however, improved more. That is, they became more sensitive to changes in line length. These improvements held at least 5 months after the retreat for people who continued with meditation practice. Also, when the control group had its own retreat, this effect replicated (not depicted here), and people were able to sustain their ability to make these distinctions much longer than they had before training.

Perceptual sensitivity

(Y-axis: Length of short line in degrees of visual angle: 3.0, 3.2, 3.4, 3.6, 3.8, 4.0, 4.2, 4.4; Legend: Control, Retreat; X-axis: Pre-retreat, Post-retreat)

④ Conclusion

Intensive meditation increases sensitivity to subtle changes in visual stimuli.

FIGURE **6.6**

HOW CONCENTRATION MEDITATION AFFECTS ATTENTION. A controlled experiment shows that intensive meditation training can improve attention to visual stimuli. Source: "Intensive Meditation Training Can Improve Attention to Visual Stimuli," by K. A. MacLean, E. Ferrer, S. Aichele, D. A. Bridwell, B. G. King, T. L. Jacobs, … C. D. Saron, 2010, *Psychological Science, 21*, 829–839.

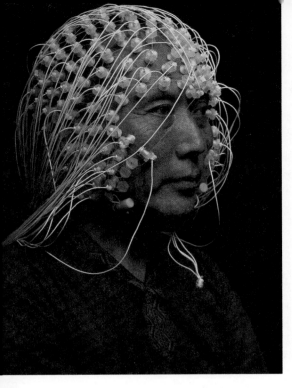

Meditation, an integral part of the Buddhist spiritual practice for thousands of years, develops concentration and mindfulness. Here a Buddhist monk is being outfitted with EEG electrodes for monitoring his brain during meditation.

Such findings help tell us whether measurable differences in brain activity really mean anything in terms of actual behavior (Lutz et al., 2009).

In another study, MRI scans revealed thicker brain tissue in areas of the cortex associated with attention, sensitivity to bodily sensations, and the processing of external sensory information in very experienced meditators versus a comparison group of nonmeditators (Lazar et al., 2005). Also, those who had meditated the longest showed the greatest cortical thickness in certain areas. The finding has since been replicated in a study of Zen meditators (Grant et al., 2010). Such correlational findings suggest that meditation can grow the brain, but an experimental design is required to uncover a causal link between meditation training and brain changes. A recent experiment studied people new to meditation. Compared to a control group, novices assigned to an 8-week meditation training program showed increases in growth in brain tissue in areas relevant to attention and emotion processing, which appeared to be linked with changes in emotional well-being over the 8-week period (Hölzel et al., in press).

Connection

What aspects of experimental designs allow for conclusions about cause and effect?

See "Research Methods in Psychology," Chapter 2, "Conducting Research in Psychology," p. 46.

Quick Quiz 6.3: Training Consciousness: Meditation

1. Which of the following does meditation appear to improve?
   a. mindfulness
   b. attention
   c. well-being
   d. all of the above

2. A study of brain images of experienced meditators and a comparison group of nonmeditators found that the experienced meditators' brains showed evidence of
   a. thicker cortex in brain areas associated with attention and sensitivity to sensory information
   b. more diverse synaptic connections throughout the cerebellum
   c. cortical thinning throughout motor areas, but thickening in frontal areas
   d. less synaptic death than nonmeditators

Answers can be found at the end of the chapter.

SLEEPING AND DREAMING

Meditation offers specific practices for working with consciousness. Yet consciousness varies constantly on a daily basis without much intervention, by virtue of our degree of wakefulness or our moods. In this section, we discuss two major sources of variation of consciousness: sleeping and dreaming.

Sleeping

A 5-year-old boy once described sleep as "when I go to my bed and I think about nothing." Typically, we think of sleep as a time of rest and relaxation, when we put out of our minds the day's events. Although our conscious experience of sleep may be of nothing and no time passing, it is in fact a very active process. We behave while we sleep—we move, we dream, sometimes we even talk and walk. The sleeping brain is very active, but it is only partially processing information from the outside world. Sleep has two essential features: There is a perceptual wall between the conscious mind and the outside world, and the sleeping state can be immediately reversed (Dement, 1999). Awareness of the outside world is greatly diminished in sleep, but not completely. The mind is still able to filter relevant from irrelevant stimuli: A baby's cry may awaken a parent, but much louder sounds (like a TV blaring in the room) may not. Moreover, because sleep is reversible, it is different from being in a coma.

Sleep and Circadian Rhythms

circadian rhythms

the variations in physiological processes that cycle within approximately a 24-hour period, including the sleep–wake cycle.

Sleep occurs in the context of a daily sleep–wake cycle, which follows a pattern known as a circadian rhythm. **Circadian rhythms** are the variations in physiological processes that cycle within approximately a 24-hour period. Many physiological systems, including the sleep–wake cycle, feeding, hormone production, and cellular regeneration, vary on a circadian basis (Refinetti, 2006). In Figure 6.7 we see how three different bodily processes—body temperature, the hormone melatonin, and alertness—fluctuate on a circadian cycle. Body temperature, for instance, peaks a few hours before bed and soon after waking up and then drops during sleep. That our bodies go through 24-hour cycles is the reason why we are sharper at some times of the day than others and why we experience jet lag. Shortening or lengthening our days by traveling across time zones throws the circadian cycles off, and it takes time for the body to readjust to the new daily cycle.

The body has an internal timekeeper located in the hypothalamus, called the suprachiasmatic nucleus. The *suprachiasmatic nucleus* (SCN) regulates physiological activity on daily cycles (Moore & Eichler, 1972; Weaver, 1998). When the retina in the eye senses light in the morning, it stimulates the SCN, which in turn signals the nearby *pineal gland* to decrease the amount of melatonin it releases (Itri et al., 2004). *Melatonin* is a hormone that plays a role in relaxation and drowsiness. In the evening, decreased activity in the SCN prompts the

FIGURE **6.7**

HUMAN CIRCADIAN CYCLES. Our body temperature (a), melatonin levels (b), and alertness (c) fluctuate regularly on 24-hour circadian cycles.

Sleeping and Dreaming **239**

secretion of melatonin, which increases relaxation. Because of its role in relaxation, melatonin can be taken as a drug to combat the effects of jet lag. Research suggests for some people it can be effective in reducing these disruptive effects of jet travel, but more when we travel ahead in time (east) than backward in time (west) (Atkinson, Reilly, & Waterhouse, 2007).

Sleep and the Brain Until the 1950s people assumed the brain was relatively inactive during sleep, except for dreaming. In the 1950s, Nathaniel Kleitman and Eugene Aserinsky were studying attention in children and noticed that when children lost attention and fell asleep, their eyes moved rapidly underneath their eyelids (Bulkeley, 1997). They suspected these movements were important in sleep and, after further research, discovered that they occurred in everyone throughout the night. Kleitman and Aserinksy coined the phrase **rapid eye movements (REM)** to describe these eye movements (Dement, 1999). Their discovery revolutionized the study of sleep and dreaming. The brain, as it turns out, is very active during sleep. With EEG technology, scientists have learned that sleep changes throughout the night and that distinct patterns of brain activity characterize these changes (Bulkeley, 1997; Dement, 1999). Let's consider what they have learned.

Each state of wakefulness and sleep has its own pattern of brain activity. When we are awake, brain activity is characterized by rapid, low-energy waves known as **beta waves.** When we are awake but relaxed and drowsy, our brain activity switches to slower and slightly higher energy waves known as **alpha waves.**

The second major form of sleep, called **non-REM,** has relatively few eye movements; those that occur are slow rather than fast. There are four stages of non-REM sleep, each marked by unique brain wave patterns (see Figure 6.8).

When we enter Stage 1 of sleep, our brain waves change to **theta waves,** which are slower and lower in energy than alpha waves. The precise moment

rapid eye movements (REM)
quick movements of the eye that occur during sleep, thought to mark phases of dreaming.

beta waves
pattern of brain activity when one is awake; a rapid, low-energy wave.

alpha waves
pattern of brain activity when one is relaxed and drowsy; slower, higher-energy waves than beta waves.

non-REM
form of sleep with few eye movements, which are slow rather than fast.

theta waves
pattern of brain activity during Stage 1 sleep; slower, lower-energy waves than alpha waves.

FIGURE **6.8**

TYPES OF BRAIN WAVES AND DIFFERENT STAGES OF CONSCIOUSNESS AND SLEEP. Each stage of wakefulness and sleep is marked by a unique pattern of brain wave. For the typical 7-hour night of sleep for an adult, there are about five cycles of sleep.

Relaxed-drowsy (alpha waves)   Stage 1 sleep (theta waves)

Sleep

1 second

FIGURE **6.9**

THE ONSET OF SLEEP. An EEG shows the abrupt transition from higher energy alpha waves typical of the drowsy but awake state to the lower energy theta waves of Stage 1 sleep. This transition occurs in a period of less than 10 seconds.

when we fall asleep is readily apparent on an EEG readout—we move from alpha to slower and lower energy theta wave activity (see Figure 6.9). Stage 1 sleep starts when the sensory curtain drops and we are no longer responsive to the outside world. However, Stage 1 sleep is a light sleep, and not much stimulation is needed to awaken us from it. After about 5–7 minutes in Stage 1, we move to Stage 2 sleep, when the theta waves now show short periods of extremely fast and somewhat higher energy *sleep spindles*. The other unique markers of Stage 2 sleep are sudden high-energy *K-complexes*. After a short period of time, we move from Stage 2 to Stage 3 sleep, which initially consists of theta waves with some higher energy **delta waves.** As we progress through Stage 3, more and more delta waves appear, and we have fewer and fewer sleep spindles and K-complexes. When the latter disappear completely, we have entered our deepest stage of sleep, Stage 4. Shortly after entering Stage 4 sleep, we start going back through Stage 3, Stage 2, and Stage 1. On return to Stage 1, our eyes begin to move rapidly underneath the eyelids. We are now in REM sleep and are actively dreaming. The night's first episode of REM sleep lasts for only about 8–10 minutes before the whole process starts over. With each progressive cycle, the non-REM periods are shorter and the REM periods longer (Dement, 1999). Adults move through about four to six different cycles of non-REM and REM sleep every night. Each cycle lasts roughly 90 minutes.

Full-blown dreams are less common during non-REM than REM sleep, but they do occur regularly during non-REM stages. Up to 70% of non-REM periods may involve dreaming. The dreams during non-REM sleep are different from REM dreams: They tend to be less detailed, less active, and more like regular thinking (Bulkeley, 1997; Foulkes, 1996; Kahan, 2001).

The Development of Sleep Over the Life Span

Newborns of many species, especially humans, spend more time in REM sleep than in non-REM sleep. In humans, REM sleep declines rapidly over the life span (see Figure 6.10). Although newborns typically sleep for only a few hours at a time—much to the chagrin of their sleep-deprived parents—they might spend a total of 8 hours in REM sleep and another 8 hours in non-REM sleep *per day*. The percentage of total sleep that is REM stays close to 50% for the first three months of life. By 8 months it falls to 33%, and by age 1 it drops to about 28%. During adolescence and adulthood, the amount of sleep that involves REM steadily decreases.

The fact that newborns and infants spend so much more time in REM sleep than adults has led some researchers to hypothesize that the main function of REM sleep is to assist in brain growth and development. The amount of

delta waves
type of brain activity that dominates Stage 3 sleep; higher energy than theta wave.

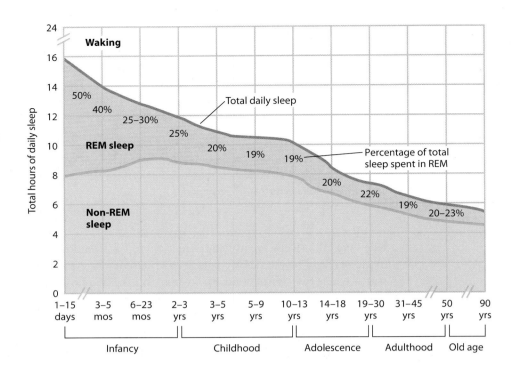

FIGURE **6.10**

SLEEP ACROSS THE LIFE SPAN. As this graph shows, infants and young children not only need more hours of sleep than do older children and adults, but also spend significantly more time in REM sleep. It may be that REM sleep supports brain growth and development.

REM sleep over the life span does correspond to the degree of brain plasticity and neural growth (Dement, 1999). Our brains are most plastic in infancy and childhood and less so in adulthood—precisely the pattern we see in REM sleep. REM sleep, just like new neural growth, continues throughout our lives—it just decreases with age.

The story of how rapid eye movements were discovered makes for a fascinating tale of how scientific discoveries often come from a combination of a good idea, good luck, and a lot of perseverance to result in an entirely new perspective on human experience. Some discoveries initially encounter resistance from other people, sometimes even the boss.

Breaking New Ground

The Discovery of REM Sleep

As early as the 1700s, some observers noticed eye movements under the lids of sleeping humans and animals. This observation, however, garnered little attention. By the late 1800s, however, some started to speculate that these movements might be related to dreaming. One scientist wrote, "I am inclined to believe that, in somewhat vivid visual dreams, the eyeballs move gently in their sockets, taking various positions induced by the retinal phantasms, as they control the dreams. As we look down the street of a strange city, for example, in a dream we focus our eyes somewhat as we should do in making the same observations when awake (Ladd, 1892, as quoted in Finger, 1994, p. 263). These observations and speculations had little scientific basis and were largely ignored until the early 1950s, after the electroencephalograph (EEG) had been discovered. Moreover, no one thought the brain was very active during much of sleep, except while dreaming.

One of the few sleep researchers in the world in the 1950s, Nathan Kleitman, took on a assistant by the name of Eugene Aserinsky, a 30-year-old graduate student who had never earned more than a high school diploma (Rock, 2004). Kleitman assigned Aserinsky the task that was ultimately going nowhere: observing infants while they slept to see whether blinking stopped gradually or suddenly. After working on this task for months to no avail, Aserinsky hit upon a different idea—namely, to observe a sleeping person's eye movements all throughout the night. No one had ever done this, and Kleitman didn't think it was a good idea (Rock, 2004).

Although remaining skeptical, Kleitman surprisingly did agree to the proposal. The project created two problems for Aserinsky: what machine to use to make the recordings of the brain and the eyes and whom to have as participants. He solved the first problem by finding an old unused polygraph machine in the basement of his research lab. The second problem was solved by having a willing participant in his 8-year-old son.

During the very first night of observations, Aserinsky saw results that were immediate and rather clear, but so unexpected that he assumed the machine was not working properly. But when he checked the machine and redid the observation on adults, he found the same thing. Every 90 minutes or so, the eyeballs began to move very quickly underneath the eyelids. He suspected these eye movements were associated with dreaming, and his hunch was confirmed when he woke up his participants and they almost always reported dreaming during these periods of eye movements.

Not surprisingly, when Aserinsky went to Kleitman with these results, Kleitman was quite skeptical (Aserinsky, 1996). But the findings had been replicated many times, and Kleitman could not ignore them. Before signing on to the results, however, Kleitman had to try the same study with his own daughter. Sure enough, he saw exactly the same results that his grad student did. The results of their paper were written up in 1953 and changed the field of sleep and dream research forever. Sleep is an active, not a passive mental state, and modern science could study this active sleep state.

Scientists had to change their minds about the absence of brain activity during sleep. Kleitman's willingness to overcome his skepticism and change his mind once the evidence was clear is the essence of the scientific mind. They could no longer believe what they once thought. A postscript and final irony to the story: Aserinsky died in 1998 at the age of 77 from an automobile accident. Reports said that he had fallen asleep at the wheel (Brown, 2003).

■ ■ ■

The Function of Sleep   Sleep supports three major restorative processes: neural growth, memory consolidation, and protection against cellular damage (see Figure 6.11). Each of these effects appears to be important for optimal function and well-being. Sleep deprivation has been shown to inhibit the growth of new neurons in rats (Guzman-Marin et al., 2003)—something to think about next time you consider staying up all night to cram for a test. In fact, children who experience chronic sleep disturbances show decreased connectivity and neuron loss in key memory areas of the brain, which has long-term implications for cognitive development (Jan et al., 2010).

Also, sleep helps us learn and remember better (Karni et al., 1994; Payne & Nadel, 2004; Stickgold & Walker, 2007). In a study of the effects of sleep deprivation on performance in a perceptual skills task, participants who had normal amounts of REM sleep performed better on the task afterward than did participants who were roused during REM sleep and

Nature & Nurture

Sleep increases neural growth in key memory areas of the brain. This is one reason why optimal sleep improves learning and memory.

FIGURE **6.11**

THE FUNCTION OF SLEEP. A good night's sleep before an exam may do more for your performance than an all-night cram session.

to restore neural growth

to consolidate memory

to produce enzymes that protect against cellular damage

missed some normal REM cycles (Karni et al., 1994). Neuroimaging studies of people learning to navigate a virtual maze show increases in activation in the hippocampus, the brain structure that is central to memory formation and learning (see Chapters 3, 7, and 8). If people sleep after this training, the same kind of hippocampal activity resurfaces during slow-wave sleep. The more hippocampal activation shown during slow-wave sleep, the better the person performs on the task the next day (Peigneux et al., 2004; Stickgold & Walker, 2007). In short, task learning is replayed in the brain during sleep, and this brain practice helps performance the next day. Napping after learning a task may improve performance as well (Wamsley et al., 2010).

Third, sleep fights cell damage. When our bodies use energy through the process of metabolism, some cells are damaged. Specifically, when we metabolize oxygen, by-products of this process known as free radicals damage cells, including brain cells (Harmon, 2006). Sleep aids cell function by triggering the production of enzymes that fight cell damage (Ramanathan et al., 2002). Similarly, sleep slows metabolism itself, thereby slowing the rate of cellular damage (Wouters-Adriaens & Westerterp, 2006).

What seems optimal for health is the right amount of sleep—more is not necessarily better. A recent meta-analysis of 16 prospective studies on sleep and mortality looked at the relationship between the amount of sleep people averaged nightly over their lifetimes and death (from any cause). People who slept between 6 and 8 hours a day lived longer than those who slept much less or more than that amount (Cappuccio et al., 2010).

Sleep Deprivation and Sleep Debt   Not only does sleep facilitate learning and memory, but it is also necessary for everyday functioning. Yet, 40%

of adults in the United States suffer from sleep deprivation (Dement, 1999). Are you one of them? You are probably sleep deprived if you need an alarm clock to wake up, if you sleep longer on the weekends than on weekdays, or if you fall asleep during lectures (Maas, 1998).

Recent surveys show that the typical adult gets about 6 hours and 40 minutes of sleep on weekdays and 7 hours and 25 minutes on weekends (National Sleep Foundation, 2008). Sleep expert William Dement (1999) developed the concept of *sleep debt* to represent the amount of sleep our brains owe our bodies. It is like a monetary debt that must be "paid back." Simply put, if you get 2 hours less sleep one night, then you owe your body 2 hours additional sleep the next night (or within a few days). Sleeping longer on weekends is a way to pay back a little bit of sleep debt accumulated during the week.

Most people don't pay back their sleep debt, so they pay in other ways: daytime drowsiness, use of stimulants such as caffeine and nicotine, lack of focused attention, and impaired learning and memory. The most dangerous payback comes in the form of accidents. A high percentage of automobile, airplane, boating, and job-related accidents are caused by sleep deprivation and sleep debt. As many as 30% of all automobile accidents can be attributed to drowsiness (Dement, 1999). When you realize that roughly 40,000 people die every year in this country from automobile accidents, that means more than 10,000 lives are lost due to sleep deprivation. (See Figure 6.12 for tips on how to get a good night's sleep.)

tips for better sleep

- Go to bed and get up at the same time each day.
- Avoid caffeine, nicotine, beer, wine and liquor in the 4 to 6 hours before bedtime.
- Don't exercise within 2 hours of bedtime.
- Don't eat large meals within 2 hours of bedtime.
- Don't nap later than 3 p.m.
- Sleep in a dark, quiet room that isn't too hot or cold for you.
- If you can't fall asleep within 20 minutes, get up and do something quiet.
- Wind down in the 30 minutes before bedtime by doing something relaxing.

FIGURE **6.12**

SLEEP BETTER. Everyone has trouble falling asleep occasionally. Following these simple suggestions can help you avoid persistent problems with sleeplessness. (Source: Calamaro, Mason, & Ratcliff, 2009; Higuchi et al., 2005; National Sleep Foundation, n.d.)

Not surprisingly, sleep deprivation affects mental health as well. Scores on measures of anxiety, depression, and paranoia increase with sleep loss (Kahn-Greene et al., 2007). In terms of daily sleep variations, the effects might not be immediate, and wear and tear might take a few days to show up. Consider this: Barber and colleagues (2010) asked students to complete a daily sleep log as well as online diaries of psychological symptoms and perceived stress in life over a 5-day period (Monday–Friday). They found that a few days of sleep deficiency early in the week, even when people try to offset this debt with subsequent sleep, can contribute to psychological strain later in the week (Barber et al., 2010). Not all sleep loss can be replenished, and inconsistent sleep patterns can wear us down.

Research to **Real Life**

Sleep deprivation seems to be a part of college life. Are you getting enough sleep? How can you tell whether you are getting enough sleep? What effects might the amount of sleep have on your sense of well-being, motor coordination, and ability to learn or remember certain information?

Connecting Psychology to Your Life: For one week, try keeping a sleep log. Each day, record how many hours of sleep you had the night before, and make some sort of ratings on your general mood (irritable or not? joyful or not?). You can make yourself a list of words and provide ratings on a 1–10 scale, if you like. Also make note of how well you did at school—paying attention in lectures, performance on any tests or assignments, and so on.

After one week, see if you notice any patterns. First, calculate the average amount of sleep you had each night by adding up your total for each night and then divide by the number of days for which you collected data (7 if you did a whole week).

Then look to see if you notice any obvious changes in mood or performance after days when you had less sleep than average. Or more. Are there any patterns? Are there other factors that might have played a role (such as exercise or stress?).

If you're not getting enough sleep, try some of these techniques for getting more sleep (Calamaro, Mason, & Ratcliff, 2009; Higuchi et al., 2005; National Sleep Foundation, n.d.):

1. Have a consistent bedtime and wake-up time throughout the week. Your body needs regular sleep–wake times to get into a natural cycle, making falling asleep and waking up easier.

2. Do not eat and drink too much close to bedtime, and especially avoid stimulating drinks like coffee late in the day. Also avoid nicotine and alcohol at night.

3. Get regular exercise, but not within 3 hours of bedtime.

4. Avoid naps, especially during the afternoon or early evening. Turn down the screen brightness on your computer screens, such as laptops, tablets (including iPad), or cell phones before bed. Bright computer screens may delay melatonin production, which signals your body to become drowsy and sleepy.

See Figure 6.12 for additional tips for getting better sleep.

Disorders of Sleep For most people, sleeping 6 to 8 hours a day is a welcome experience, notwithstanding the occasional nightmare or restless night. For an estimated 20% of the U.S. population, however, nighttime is often fraught with problems (Dement, 1999). Let's consider four disorders of sleep: insomnia, sleepwalking, narcolepsy, and hypersomnia.

insomnia
a sleep difficulty characterized by difficulty falling and staying asleep, as well as not feeling rested.

Insomnia is defined as taking more than 20 minutes to fall asleep, having trouble staying asleep, and/or not feeling rested after a night's sleep for two or more consecutive weeks (Krystal, 2005). Somewhere between 15% and 20% of U.S. adults suffer from insomnia (Pearson, Johnson, & Nahin, 2006). Some sleep experts consider insomnia more a symptom of other maladies than a disorder in its own right, although there is some debate on this matter (Dement, 1999). There are many possible causes of insomnia—for instance, restless leg syndrome, erratic hours, medical conditions, psychological disorders such as depression, and excessive use of alcohol (Dement, 1999; Roehrs, Zorick, & Roth, 2000). Iron deficiency may also cause insomnia. This fact might explain why women, who are more likely to be iron deficient, show higher rates of insomnia than men (Lee, 2006; Mizuno et al., 2005). Drug treatments for insomnia, such as the popular sleep aid Ambien, work by increasing the effects of GABA (gamma-aminobutyric acid), the neurotransmitter that decreases central nervous system activity. In this way, sleep aids produce a general feeling of relaxation. Several nondrug therapies, such as meditation and cognitive–behavioral therapy, help relieve symptoms of insomnia as well (Babson, Feldner, & Badour, 2010; Ong, Shapiro, & Manber, 2008). In fact, meditation may improve sleep even for people who do not experience insomnia (Kaul et al., 2010).

sleepwalking
sleep difficulty characterized by activities occurring during non-REM sleep that usually occur when one is awake, such as walking and eating.

Sleepwalking occurs when a person gets out of bed during sleep, usually during the first third of the sleep cycle, and engages in activities that normally occur during wakefulness, such as walking, eating, dressing, or bathing. People who sleepwalk are difficult to rouse and do not remember having been up after waking in the morning. Because sleepwalking occurs during non-REM sleep, the sleepwalker is not likely to be acting out a dream. Sleepwalking occurs in about 4%–15% of children and about 1.5%–2.5% of adults (Guilleminault et al., 2005).

narcolepsy
sleep disorder characterized by excessive daytime sleepiness and weakness in facial and limb muscles.

The main feature of **narcolepsy,** another sleep disorder, is excessive daytime sleepiness. People with this condition may fall asleep at inopportune times throughout the day, often with little to no warning. They may also experience *cataplexy*, a weakness of facial muscles and muscles in limbs (Nishino, 2007). The origin of narcolepsy may lie in disrupted nighttime sleep patterns. Narcolepsy is often a function of insomnia; EEG studies reveal that people who suffer from narcolepsy show some abnormality in sleep spindles and disruption of REM sleeping patterns. Narcolepsy appears to have a genetic basis. It is most often treated with amphetamines, which help prevent daytime sleepiness, and antidepressants, which can help with cataplexy. Neither treatment addresses the nighttime sleep disruptions (Nishino, 2007; Tafti, Dauvilliers, & Overeem, 2007).

hypersomnia
sleep difficulty characterized by sleeping more than 10 hours a day for 2 weeks or more; includes urge to nap during inappropriate times.

Hypersomnia exists when a person sleeps more than 10 hours a day for 2 weeks or more. Hypersomnia involves strong urges to nap throughout the day, often at inappropriate times such as during meals or in the middle of conversations. It can be caused by other sleep disorders such as apnea, brain injury, or depression. Adolescents who commit suicide are more likely to have suffered from hypersomnia than those who do not commit suicide (Goldstein, Bridge, & Brent, 2008).

Night terrors occur when a person, often a child, speaks incoherently and ultimately awakens suddenly in a terrified state from sleep; night terrors may also involve walking around in sleep (Smith, Comella, & Högl, 2008). The individual may scream, bolt upright from bed, and appear very confused and frightened. He or she may wake up sweating and breathing very fast, with dilated

Sleepwalking is more common in children than in adults, possibly because it occurs during non-REM sleep, and adults spend less time in non-REM sleep than children do.

night terrors
state that occurs when a person walks around, speaks incoherently, and ultimately awakens, terrified, from sleep.

pupils. The episodes generally last 10–20 minutes, and then the person returns to a normal sleep. The next morning the individual usually has no recollection of the event whatsoever. Although night terrors are rare in adults, those adults who do suffer from them tend to exhibit higher levels of depression, anxiety, and obsessive-compulsive traits than adults who do not suffer from them (Kales et al., 1980). To be clear, night terrors are *not* nightmares, which are typical dreams with a frightening plot. Night terrors do not occur during REM sleep and are not associated with dreams.

Dreaming

dreams
images, thoughts, and feelings experienced during sleep.

Dreaming is one of the most fascinating features of consciousness. But what are dreams exactly? **Dreams** are the succession of images, thoughts, and feelings we experience while asleep. The succession of images is loosely connected by unusual associations and not well recalled afterward. Most of us dream numerous times each night, and yet we rarely recall our dreams on waking. When people in sleep labs are awakened, they report dreaming almost always if they were in REM sleep and somewhat regularly if they were in non-REM sleep (Bulkeley, 1997; Dement, 1999).

Do dreams have real meaning, or do they simply reflect random activity of a complex brain? Psychologists from different perspectives disagree on what dreams are and what they mean.

Psychoanalytic Theory

In *The Interpretation of Dreams*, Sigmund Freud wrote that dreams are "the royal road to the unconscious" (1900/1953, p. 608). He argued that conflicting impulses, thoughts, feelings, and drives that threaten the waking mind are released as a visual compromise in distorted and disguised form by the sleeping mind. In this view, each dream is an attempt to fulfill unacceptable desires or satisfy unconscious wishes.

Connection

According to Freud, dream analysis is but one way to access the unconscious mind. Free association is another therapeutic technique used in Freudian psychoanalysis.

See "Psychoanalytic/ Psychodynamic Therapy," Chapter 16, "Treatment of Psychological Disorders," p. 642.

According to Freud's theory, dreams operate on two distinct levels of consciousness. The dream that we consciously recall after waking up is only the surface level, which Freud called the **manifest level.** The deeper, unconscious level, where the true meaning of a dream lies, he labeled the **latent level.** In his clinical practice, Freud used psychoanalysis to uncover the latent meaning of his clients' dreams, in order to help them resolve the hidden conflicts from which their problems arose.

manifest level
Freud's surface level of dreams, recalled upon waking.

latent level
Freud's deeper, unconscious level of dreams; their meaning is found at this level.

Biological Theory

One influential biological theory of dreams has been AIM theory, which argues that dreams are devoid of meaning and a result of random brain activity (Hobson, 2001, 2002). **AIM** stands for three biologically based dimensions of consciousness: Activation, Input, and Mode. *Activation* refers to the amount of neural activation and ranges from low to high activation. *Input* refers to whether stimulation is internal or external. Finally, *mode* refers to the mental state—from logical (wakeful) to loose-illogical (dreaming). These three dimensions (A-I-M) make up a cube, and all states of consciousness occupy a different space in this cube (see Figure 6.13). For example, waking is a highly active, external, and logical mode of consciousness residing in

AIM
three biologically based dimensions of consciousness— activation, input, and mode.

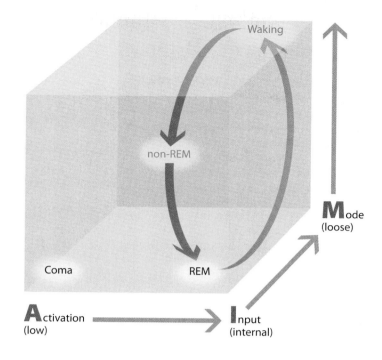

FIGURE **6.13**

HOBSON'S A-I-M MODEL OF CON-SCIOUSNESS. According to Hobson, the three dimensions of consciousness are activation, input, and mode. Activation ranges from low to high neural activation. Input ranges from internal to external, and mode ranges from loose to logical. All states of consciousness occupy a unique place in this three-dimensional space. Our days normally cycle between waking, non-REM, and REM sleep states of consciousness. (Source: Hobson, 2001)

the upper-back-right portion of the cube. Non-REM sleep is moderately active, external, and logical and resides in the middle of the cube. By contrast, REM sleep is highly active, internal, and loose and therefore occupies the lower-front-right portion of the cube.

Cognitive Theory   According to cognitive psychologists, dreams are not that different from everyday thinking. Research shows that some of the standard processes that we use during our waking life, such as imagery, memory, speech, and problem solving, operate in a similar manner during dreaming (Cavallero & Foulkes, 1993; Kahan, 2001). For instance, some people develop an ability to know when they are dreaming (lucid dreaming) and can therefore control the events and outcomes of the dreams (LaBerge, 1985). Others are able to reflect on and evaluate their experiences while dreaming (Kahan, 2001; Kahan & LaBerge, 1994). Also, recall that dreaming occurs during both REM and non-REM periods. Dreaming that occurs during non-REM sleep is closer to waking thought than is REM sleep dreaming—it is less visual, more verbal, and not as loose and unusual in its associations (Dement, 1999; Kahan, 2001).

Combined Theories   Some recent theories promote an integration of cognitive and biological perspectives on dreaming. One such cognitive–biological view suggests that dreams consolidate long-term memories first by strengthening the neural traces of recent events and then by integrating these traces with already stored memories. Dreams also keep existing memories stable even when new experiences attempt to interfere with older memories (Payne & Nadel, 2004). Particular hormones, such as cortisol, are involved in strengthening these neural connections to consolidate memory. Cortisol levels change throughout sleep stages, with peaks of cortisol matching REM stages of sleep (Payne, 2010; Payne & Nadel, 2004; Weitzman et al., 1971).

Quick Quiz 6.4: Sleeping and Dreaming

1. When a perceptual wall between our conscious mind and the outside world emerges and we are in a state that is immediately reversible, we are
   a. asleep
   b. unconscious
   c. vegetative
   d. minimally conscious

2. Research shows that sleep functions to
   a. give our cells some energy
   b. facilitate learning and memory
   c. facilitate neural growth
   d. both b and c

3. Dreaming is most active during what kind of sleep?
   a. non-REM
   b. REM
   c. Stage 3
   d. Stage 4

4. In lucid dreaming, people become aware that they are dreaming and can sometimes even control their dreams. Lucid dreaming is most consistent with which theory of dreams?
   a. psychoanalytic
   b. biological
   c. cognitive
   d. none of the above

Answers can be found at the end of the chapter.

HYPNOSIS

hypnosis
state characterized by focused attention, suggestibility, absorption, lack of voluntary control over behavior, and suspension of critical faculties; occurs when instructed by someone trained in hypnosis; may be therapeutic.

Although the Greek word root *hypnos* means "sleep," hypnotized people are very much awake. Yet they have little voluntary control over their own behavior. **Hypnosis** is a state of mind that occurs in compliance with instructions and is characterized by focused attention, suggestibility, absorption, lack of voluntary control over behavior, and suspension of critical faculties of mind (Raz & Shapiro, 2002; Stewart, 2005). People may be more easily hypnotized if they are relaxed, but they can be hypnotized without relaxation (Raz & Shapiro, 2002). Although about 65% of the population is mildly to moderately responsive to hypnotic suggestion, only about 15% are highly hypnotizable (Song, 2006; Hilgard, 1965). The rest are resistant to hypnosis.

The mention of hypnosis conjures up images of a performer putting audience volunteers into sleeplike trances and then instructing them to behave in

Hypnosis therapy has helped people to quit smoking. This group of smokers is being hypnotized to believe that cigarettes taste like vomit.

ways that are out of character. Yet hypnosis is a clinical tool and should not be confused with stage techniques. Numerous studies support the effectiveness of hypnosis for pain relief during childbirth, dental procedures, and surgery. Further, hypnosis may be effective in treating nicotine addiction, nausea, and vomiting related to chemotherapy and anxiety associated with certain medical procedures (Lang et al., 2006; Montgomery, DuHamel, & Redd, 2000; Patterson, 2004; Stewart, 2005). The therapeutic benefits of hypnosis are not fully understood, but the availability of brain imaging techniques has motivated efforts to document its effectiveness and to learn how it works to reduce pain (Flammer & Bongartz, 2003; Stewart, 2005). We now know that during hypnosis, cortical areas activated during normal pain situations (that is, during wakefulness) are not activated at all (Vanhaudenhuyse et al., 2009).

It is not easy to offer a general explanation for how hypnosis works, and theorists offer a range of different perspectives. First, some theorists consider hypnosis to be a state in which one part of the brain operates independently. Ernest Hilgard (1977) showed that under hypnosis one aspect of a person's mind can remain aware and open to stimulation from the outside (such as the hypnotist's voice), while other parts are cut off from external input.

A second theory maintains that hypnosis does not alter consciousness, nor do hypnotized individuals give up control of their behavior. Instead, they behave the way they think a hypnotized person would behave. In short, they are role-playing (Orne, 1959). For decades, this was the prevailing scientific view on hypnosis.

Neuroscientific research suggests a different, third, explanation, namely that hypnosis is not imitation but rather real brain activity. Neuroscientist Amir Raz and his colleagues have studied whether hypnosis might help to eliminate the **Stroop effect** (Raz, Fan, & Posner, 2005). The Stroop task tests visual selective attention; it measures how people deal with conflicting verbal and color information. In a typical Stroop test, participants view the names of colors, such as green, red, and blue, printed in different colors and must name the color in which the word is printed. People are slower to identify the color of words that are printed in a different color from the meaning of the word (such as when the word blue is printed in yellow ink) than words that are printed in the same color (blue printed in blue). The delay in reaction time caused by mismatching color words and the color in which the words are printed is known as the Stroop effect (Stroop, 1935; see Figure 6.14).

Raz and his colleagues (2005) hypnotized 16 people—eight who were highly hypnotizable and eight less hypnotizable. While hypnotized, the participants received instruction on a Stroop test that they would perform a few days later in an fMRI

Stroop effect delay in reaction time when color of words on a test and their meaning differ.

red	white	green	brown
green	red	brown	white
white	brown	green	red
red	white	green	brown
brown	green	white	red
white	brown	red	green
green	white	brown	red
red	brown	green	white

FIGURE **6.14**

THE STROOP EFFECT. Participants will name the color of the letters more rapidly when their color matches the meaning of the word compared to when there is a mismatch.

scanner. After the hypnosis session, all participants received a posthypnotic suggestion, which was a suggestive statement that a particular behavior will occur sometime in the future. Participants were told that during the test they would see gibberish words in different colors and they would have the task of pushing a button corresponding to the actual color of the letters. In fact, the words they saw during the test were names of colors.

Highly hypnotizable people who received the "gibberish" suggestion identified the colors faster than the less hypnotizable people who received the same suggestion. Brain scans taken during the Stroop test showed that highly hypnotizable people had less activity in the areas of the brain that normally process word meaning, and so these areas did not interfere with color recognition. Less hypnotizable people were not able to suppress the Stroop effect. In response to the posthypnotic suggestion, the highly hypnotizable people saw real words as gibberish and so they attended only to identifying the color of the letters. These findings support the idea that hypnosis is a real effect in the brain and not just imitation.

Another set of studies addresses the question of whether hypnosis involves role-playing (Derbyshire et al., 2004; Raij et al., 2005). Some participants were administered mild pain, others imagined pain, while yet a third group experienced hypnotized pain. Hypnotically induced pain activated the same brain circuit as did the real pain. Also, participants reported actually feeling pain for both real and hypnotically induced pain, but not for imagined pain. So both hypnotic pain and real pain activate the same brain regions and produce the same subjective feelings. Imagining pain (role-playing?) does not have the same effects. Hypnotic pain, then, is not just an imitation of the real thing. As far as the brain is concerned, it is the same thing.

Quick Quiz 6.5: Hypnosis

1. Scientific research has demonstrated that hypnosis
   a. is a real phenomenon
   b. is not real but learned
   c. is only an imagined state of mind
   d. is something everyone experiences

2. A groundbreaking area of research has recently demonstrated that under hypnosis
   a. hypnotically induced pain creates a subjective experience similar to real pain
   b. people had turned off the areas of the brain that normally process the meaning of words
   c. hypnotically induced pain activated the same brain circuit as real pain did
   d. all of the above

Answers can be found at the end of the chapter.

psychoactive drugs

naturally occurring or synthesized substances that, when ingested or otherwise taken into the body, reliably produce qualitative changes in conscious experience.

ALTERING CONSCIOUSNESS WITH DRUGS

Hypnosis creates profound alterations in consciousness for some people. Drugs can change consciousness too. In this section, we will focus on the type of drugs known as psychoactive drugs. **Psychoactive drugs** are naturally occurring or synthesized substances that, when ingested or otherwise taken into the body, reliably produce qualitative changes in conscious experience.

Psychoactive drug use is universal among humans. Every culture in every recorded age has used mind-altering substances. People use psychoactive drugs for many reasons: to aid in spiritual practice, to improve their health, to explore the self, to regulate mood, to escape boredom and despair, to enhance sensory experience, to stimulate artistic creativity and performance, and to promote social interaction (Weil & Rosen, 1998). Whatever the reason, habitual use of psychoactive drugs can lead to abuse.

Problems arise when people develop a *physical dependence* on the drug to maintain normal function and to cope with the challenges of daily life. For some drugs, repeated use causes tolerance, meaning people require more and more of the drug to get the effect from it that they desire. Withdrawal symptoms are the adverse effects people with physical dependence experience if they stop using a drug. The drugs that lead to physical dependence create the most severe withdrawal symptoms. Alcohol withdrawal for an alcoholic, for example, creates many unpleasant side effects—such as delirium tremens (often referred to as the DTs), the symptoms of which may include tremors, insomnia, irritability, seizures, confusion, hallucinations, nausea and vomiting, and agitation. In some cases the DTs lead to death.

Psychological dependence occurs when people compulsively use a substance to alleviate boredom, regulate mood, or cope with the challenges of everyday life. For example, people who regularly take sleeping aids to help them fall asleep at night may be unable to sleep without them even though they may not be physically dependent on them. The essence of a compulsive behavior is the inability to control or regulate it. **Addiction** results from habitual use or physical and psychological dependence on a substance (Taylor, 2009). People who are addicted continue to use a given substance in spite of knowing that it is harmful and often in spite of attempts to quit.

In this section we survey the behavioral, psychological, and neurological effects of the major classes of psychoactive drugs: depressants, stimulants, and hallucinogens (Figure 6.15). We will consider illegal substances as well as the most commonly used and abused legal ones.

addiction
condition that results from habitual use or physical and psychological dependence on a substance.

Depressants

Depressants slow down central nervous system activity. Alcohol, sedatives, and opioids (narcotics) are all depressants. In low doses, these drugs generally calm the body and mind. In high doses, they can slow down heart rate and brain activity to dangerously low levels. Alcohol and sedatives increase the activity of GABA, the main inhibitory neurotransmitter in the brain, and decrease the activity of glutamate, the main excitatory neurotransmitter in the brain. If taken during pregnancy, alcohol and sedatives can destroy developing neurons in the fetus's brain, leading to learning disabilities, poor judgment, or mental retardation (Farber & Olney, 2003). Additionally, combining alcohol with sedatives can be lethal. The opioids work differently, as we will see, but they can be equally dangerous. Let's look in more detail at each type of depressant.

depressants
substances that decrease or slow down central nervous system activity.

Alcohol   Alcohol is the most widely used depressant. How quickly alcohol is absorbed in the bloodstream depends on a variety of factors, including the amount of food in the stomach and the person's body mass. The amount of alcohol in the bloodstream is the common measure of inebriation known as blood alcohol concentration (BAC). BAC is measured in milligrams of alcohol per 100 milliliters of blood (milligrams %), so a BAC of .10 means that one tenth of

psychoactive drugs	Drug classification	Short-term effects	Risks
	Depressants Alcohol	Relaxation, depressed brain activity, slowed behavior, reduced inhibitions	Accidents, brain damage, liver damage, blackouts, birth defects
	Sedatives	Relaxation, sleep	Accidents, slowed heart rate, possible death
	Opioids	Euphoria, pain relief, bodily relaxation	Slowed heart rate and breathing, death
	Stimulants Caffeine	Alertness, nervousness, increased heart rate	Anxiety, insomnia
	Nicotine	Arousal, stimulation, increased heart rate	Cardiovascular disease, lung cancer risk with smoking
	Cocaine	Exhilaration, euphoria, irritability	Insomnia, heart attack, paranoia
	Amphetamines	Increased alertness, excitability, difficulty concentrating	Insomnia, paranoia, accelerated heart rate
	Ecstasy (MDMA)	Mild amphetamine and hallucinogenic effects, high body temperature and dehydration; sense of well being and social connectedness	Depression, mental deficits, cardiovascular problems
	Hallucinogens Marijuana	Euphoric feelings, relaxation, mild hallucinations, time distortion, attention and memory impairment, fatigue	Memory problems, respiratory illness, immune system impairment
	LSD	Strong hallucinations, distorted time perception, synesthesia	Accidents, insomnia

FIGURE **6.15**

COMMON PSYCHOACTIVE DRUGS, THEIR PRIMARY EFFECTS ON CONSCIOUSNESS, AND RISKS. Only caffeine, nicotine, and marijuana do not carry a risk of overdose resulting in death.

1 percent, or 1/1000th, of one's blood content is alcohol. Figure 6.16 shows the amount of alcohol one must consume to reach .08 BAC, which is currently the legal limit for driving in all states in the United States, for various body weights. The figure includes various effects for different BACs.

The more alcohol a person consumes, the more obvious the depressant effects become, sometimes leading to blackouts. These effects are counterintuitive to the loose feeling that many people get in the early stages of drinking alcohol. This apparently stimulating effect occurs because alcohol suppresses the higher social regulatory functions of the cerebral cortex, thereby lowering inhibitions.

Alcohol consumption creates numerous health hazards: accidents resulting in injury or death, usually caused by drunk driving; sudden death from binge drinking; blackouts; and increased risk of liver and throat cancers. Liver damage is one of the better known health effects of drinking alcohol. Over time, heavy drinking, which is defined as more than five drinks per day, leads to fat

Number of drinks per hour required to reach legal BAC limit of .08	
Weight in pounds	
120–140	3.0
140–160	3.5
160–180	4.0
180–200	4.5
200+	5.0

BAC .02 .05 .08 .10 .15 .20 .30 .40 .50

effects

Mellow feeling. Slight body warmth. Less inhibited.

Noticeable relaxation. Less alert. Less self-focused. Coordination impairment begins.

Drunk driving limit. Definite impairment in coordination and judgment.

Noisy. Possible embarrassing behavior. Mood swings. Reduction in reaction time.

Impaired balance and movement. Clearly drunk.

Many people lose consciousness.

Most people lose consciousness; some die.

Breathing stops. Many people die.

FIGURE **6.16**

BLOOD ALCOHOL CONCENTRATION (BAC) AND ITS EFFECTS ON THE CENTRAL NERVOUS SYSTEM. The legal maximum BAC for driving is .08, but even at lower levels our reflexes and judgment may be impaired. The number of drinks it takes to reach .08 BAC varies with weight.

Nature & Nurture

Excessive drinking can shrink the brain, and in the still-developing teen brain these effects are even more dramatic.

Connection

The brain continues to develop throughout adolescence, which makes it quite vulnerable to the effects of drugs and alcohol.

See "The Developing Adolescent," Chapter 5, "Human Development," p. 200.

accumulation and blocked blood flow in the liver. Without an adequate blood supply, liver tissue cannot function properly and dies. Chronic alcoholism causes *cirrhosis*, the accumulation of nonfunctional scar tissue in the liver, an irreversible and eventually fatal condition.

Heavy drinking over a prolonged period actually shrinks the brain. Brain tissue is lost, creating widespread deficits in cognition and behavior (Mechtcheriakov et al., 2007; Oscar–Berman & Marinkovic, 2003) (see Figure 6.17). For example, frontal lobe damage leads to deficits in planning, working memory, and abstract reasoning; and damage to the hippocampus leads to deficits in learning and memory. Neurons die from excessive alcohol. When a person is drinking heavily, reductions in both white and gray matter

Hypothalamus: hunger, thirst, and sexual motivation

Hippocampus: learning and memory

Cerebellum: movement and coordination

Frontal lobe: planning, abstract thinking, and reasoning

FIGURE **6.17**

BRAIN REGIONS MOST AFFECTED BY EXCESSIVE DRINKING. The main regions of the brain most affected by long-term and excessive drinking include the frontal lobes (planning and abstract thinking and reasoning); the hippocampus (learning and memory); the hypothalamus (hunger, thirst, and sexual motivation); and the cerebellum (movement and coordination).

can occur (Sullivan, Harris, & Pfefferbaum, 2010). With abstinence from alcohol, the brain recovers much of its lost volume, especially in the first month of abstinence (Gazdzinski, Durazzo, & Meyerhoff, 2005; Kubota et al., 2001).

Binge drinking is usually defined as at least five drinks in a row for men and four for women (Jackson, 2008; H. L. Wechsler, Lee, & Kuo, 2002). Some researchers argue, however, that not all binge drinkers are alike and that a distinction should be made between binge drinkers and heavy binge drinkers (seven or more drinks in a row for men and six or more for women) (Read et al., 2008). However defined, frequent episodes of consuming many drinks in a short period of time is an unhealthy pattern of behavior that is becoming increasingly common in college students. About 40% of college students binge drink, and the numbers are rising (National Institute on Alcohol Abuse and Alcoholism, 2005; H. L. Wechsler et al., 2002).

As dangerous and deadly as alcohol can be, mild to moderate alcohol intake appears to provide protective effects for cardiovascular health. Moderate alcohol consumption is generally defined as no more than two drinks a day. With moderate alcohol use, blood levels rise for the beneficial form of cholesterol (HDL), which has protective effects on the cardiovascular system (King, Mainous, & Geesey, 2008). Although these cardiovascular benefits were initially linked to red wine only, research now shows that many forms of alcohol convey the same advantages (Hines & Rimm, 2001; Sacco et al., 1999).

Sedatives   Sedatives create a feeling of stupor similar to that of alcohol intoxication. Prescription sedatives such as barbiturates and benzodiazepines slow the heart rate, relax skeletal muscles, and tranquilize the mind. Medically, barbiturates are used in anesthesia to calm people down during certain medical procedures and as a temporary sleeping aid. Examples of barbiturates are secobarbital (Seconal), pentobarbital (Nembutal), diazepam (Valium), and chlordiazepoxide (Librium). All these drugs have the potential for both physical and psychological dependence, can be lethal at high doses, and should be used only under strict medical supervision.

Opioids   Another class of depressants is the opioids (also called narcotics), a term that applies to all drugs derived from opium or chemicals similar to opium. Such drugs may be derived from natural sources (like morphine), may be partially synthetic (like heroin), or may be entirely synthetic (such as codeine). Modern synthetic opioids include oxycodone (Percocet or Percodan), which is prescribed for moderate to severe pain, and hydrocodone (Vicodin), which is prescribed for milder pain.

The effects of specific opioids vary, depending on the form and strength of the substance. Opioids depress central nervous system activity, slowing heart rate, respiration, digestion, and suppressing the cough center. In fact, pharmaceutical companies marketed heroin as a cough suppressant in the early 20th century. Prescription cough medicines today often include codeine, a safer alternative to heroin.

115–175

Michael Jackson died in June 2009 from a combination of long-term drug abuse and an anesthetic administered illegally by his personal physician.

Opioids have been used for centuries as pain relievers. These drugs make use of the body's own naturally occurring opioid systems. Our own bodies produce *endorphins*, opioid-like proteins that bind to opioid receptors in the brain and act as natural painkillers. The stronger opioids—opium, morphine, and heroin—produce feelings of overwhelming bliss, euphoria, and bodily relaxation. The feeling is so good that nothing else matters. As one intravenous heroin user said, "It's so good. Don't even try it once" (Weil & Rosen, 1998).

Generally, opioids (including the newer, widely prescribed synthetic opioids) have a high potential for abuse (Paulozzi, 2006). Contrary to the popular image, not all addicts are junkies on the street. Some people develop an addiction to opioids while being treated for chronic pain (Gallagher & Rosenthal, 2008). Opioids slow the heart and breathing; high doses can kill by stopping the heart and breathing (Hayes, Klein-Schwartz, & Doyon, 2008). For many of these drugs, the amount required to feel an effect may not be that much less than the amount that can be deadly, especially in people who have developed tolerance. Some newer therapeutic opioids, such as buprenorphine, can be taken at higher doses with less risk of overdose (Johnson, Fudala, & Payne, 2005).

Stimulants

stimulants
substances that activate the nervous system.

Stimulants activate the nervous system. Although many stimulants are illegal, two of the most widely used psychoactive drugs are the legal stimulants caffeine and nicotine.

Caffeine   If you drink coffee, tea, cocoa, or certain soft drinks (including energy drinks) regularly, you are a stimulant user (see Figure 6.18). Caffeine is the world's most commonly consumed psychoactive drug, ingested by 90% of North American adults on a daily basis (Lovett, 2005). The effects of mild to moderate caffeine intake are increased alertness, increased heart rate, loss of motor coordination, insomnia, and nervousness. Too much caffeine can make people jittery and anxious. Caffeine is also a diuretic, which means it increases urine output.

Caffeine in 8 oz of beverage (mg)

Beverage	Caffeine (mg)
Drip coffee	100
Espresso coffee*	100
Brewed black tea	60
Red Bull	53
Mountain Dew	36.7
Pepsi Cola	25
Coca-Cola	22.7
Green tea	15
Decaf coffee, brewed	3

FIGURE 6.18
CAFFEINE CONTENT, IN MILLIGRAMS (MG), OF SEVERAL POPULAR BEVERAGES. Is your favorite pick-me-up listed here?

* A single espresso is about 2 ounces rather than 8 ounces

While their owners sleep, nervous little dogs prepare for their day.

If regular caffeine users stop consuming caffeine, they can experience withdrawal symptoms, the most common of which is headache. Giving up caffeine can also lead to fatigue and decreased energy, depressed mood, and difficulty concentrating (Juliano & Griffiths, 2004). These withdrawal effects show that caffeine creates physical dependence. To eliminate these negative withdrawal effects, people who want to stop using caffeine should gradually reduce their consumption over time.

Nicotine The active drug in tobacco, nicotine is a powerful stimulant. Tobacco is used throughout the world. As of 2008, approximately 21% (45.1 million) of American adults smoked cigarettes regularly (American Heart Association, 2010).

Smoking tobacco puts nicotine into the bloodstream almost immediately; within 8 seconds of inhalation it reaches the brain. As a stimulant, nicotine increases heart rate and rate of respiration, and it creates a feeling of arousal. Over time, the cardiovascular arousal associated with nicotine use increases the risk of high blood pressure and heart disease. Ironically, many nicotine users report that cigarettes calm them down. This perception may stem from the fact that nicotine relaxes the skeletal muscles even as it arouses the autonomic nervous system.

Nicotine is extremely addictive. It creates high tolerance, physical dependence, and unpleasant withdrawal symptoms. The high that heroin creates is more intense than the feeling of arousal from cigarettes, and the disruption to daily life of the heroin addict is more extreme than that of the smoker; but in terms of how difficult it is to quit, nicotine ranks higher than heroin (Keenan et al., 1994).

There are many known health risks in smoking. Cigarette smoking reduces life expectancy on average by 10 years, increases the risk for lung cancer more than 10-fold, and triples the risk of death from heart disease in both men and women (CDC, 2001; Doll et al., 2004). The U.S. Surgeon General has reported that smoking is also conclusively linked to leukemia, cataracts, pneumonia, and cancers of the cervix, kidney, pancreas, and stomach.

Tobacco smoke contains many cancer-causing agents that trigger severe damage to DNA and can inhibit DNA repair in lung cells. Tobacco smoke also contains carbon monoxide, a toxic substance that displaces oxygen in the bloodstream, depriving tissues of needed oxygen. This is one reason why smokers often feel out of breath (CDC, 2001; Doll et al., 2004; Feng et al., 2006; Health & Human Services, 2004). Carbon monoxide from smoking also makes people look older than they are, because it reduces the blood supply to skin tissue. Tobacco smoking increases skin wrinkles even in young smokers (Koh et al., 2002).

Cocaine For centuries, South American Indians have chewed the coca leaf for its stimulant and digestion-aiding properties (Weil & Rosen, 1998). The most

Connection

Our moods are tightly linked to transmitter systems in the brain. Dopamine is released when we feel good, and serotonin affects how sociable and affectionate we feel.

See "Common Neurotransmitters," Chapter 3, "The Biology of Behavior," p. 91.

notable component in the coca plant is cocaine, a psychoactive substance that when isolated from the coca leaf is a much stronger stimulant than chewed coca. When snorted, cocaine increases heart rate and produces a short-lived, but intense rush of euphoria. It also can lead to a sense of invulnerability and power. Physiologically, cocaine induces a sense of exhilaration by increasing the availability of the neurotransmitters dopamine and serotonin in synapses (Mateo et al., 2004).

The brevity of the cocaine high helps explain why people abuse it—they keep chasing after a short-lived euphoria with even more cocaine. Some people inject (free-base) cocaine or smoke crack cocaine, a form of cocaine that is sold on the streets in pellets. Along with being extremely addictive, cocaine can cause other health problems, including increased heart rate and irregular heartbeat, increased risk of heart attack, and, occasionally, death (Weil & Rosen, 1998).

Amphetamines   Amphetamines are synthetically produced compounds that produce long-lasting excitation of the sympathetic nervous system, the part of the nervous system that keeps us ready for action. There are three main forms, all of which are pills: methamphetamine (meth), dextroamphetamine (Dexedrine), and amphetamine sulfate (Benzedrine, or "speed"). Methamphetamine is highly addictive. The street drug called crystal meth is a crystallized form of methamphetamine that is smoked. Most people who abuse amphetamines get them from health care providers. Common medical uses of amphetamines are to suppress appetite and to treat symptoms of attention-deficit hyperactivity disorder.

Amphetamines raise heart rate, increase motivation, and elevate mood. The effects vary with dosage and manner of use, but other short-term effects may include insomnia, stomach distress, headaches, decreased libido, and difficulty concentrating. Long-term use can lead to severe depression, paranoia, loss of control over one's behavior, and, in some cases, amphetamine psychosis, a condition marked by hallucinations. Withdrawal from chronic amphetamine use creates unpleasant symptoms, such as fatigue, anxiety and depression, hunger, overeating, and disordered thought and behavior.

Ecstasy   The psychoactive drug MDMA (3,4-Methylenedioxymethamphetamine), also known as ecstasy, is chemically similar to both methamphetamine and the active ingredient in psilocybin mushrooms, making it both a stimulant and a mild hallucinogen. At moderate to high doses, MDMA produces mild sensory hallucinations as well as physiological arousal. It is sometimes called "the love drug" because it produces feelings of euphoria, warmth, and connectedness with others. Among friends, it dissolves interpersonal barriers and produces feelings of affection and a desire to touch and hug. This effect may be why MDMA became popular in dance clubs.

The dangers of MDMA include increased risk of depression with repeated use, slower processing times on cognitive tasks, and greater impulsivity (J. H. Halpern et al., 2004). Long-term effects include persistent mental deficits, low mood, and serotonin deficiencies in certain areas of the brain (Thomasius et al., 2006). On the other hand, there may be some therapeutic applications of this drug as well. In a few studies, therapists introduce low doses of MDMA in the treatment of post-traumatic stress disorder, as it appears to help clients tap into hard-to-access emotional experiences (Bouso, 2008).

In light of marijuana's known effectiveness in treating certain medical conditions, a number of states have decriminalized marijuana use for medical purposes. California, where Jeff Braun runs a cannabis dispensary, allows patients with a doctor's recommendation to obtain marijuana for personal use.

Hallucinogens

hallucinogens substances that create distorted perceptions of reality ranging from mild to extreme.

The third major class of psychoactive drugs is the hallucinogens. As the name implies, **hallucinogens** create distorted perceptions of reality, ranging from mild to extreme. Sometimes, they also alter thought and mood. There are numerous hallucinogens, but we will discuss only marijuana, LSD, and psilocybin.

Marijuana Marijuana comes from the blossoms and leaves of the *Cannabis sativa* plant. People use the hemp fibers for clothing and other practical goods. They use the blossoms to alter consciousness and for medicinal properties. The active ingredient in cannabis is tetrahydrocannibinol (THC), a plant cannabinoid, which affects the brain and body when people eat or smoke it. Marijuana alters mood to create euphoria and changes perception, especially one's perception of time and food. It makes time appear to slow down and makes food more desirable (Crystal, Maxwell, & Hohmann, 2003; Nicoll & Alger, 2004). Marijuana is classified as a hallucinogen, although people rarely experience hallucinations when using low or moderate doses. Such experiences occur more readily when people eat it.

Marijuana is not addictive in the physiological sense; that is, it does not lead to physical dependence and withdrawal symptoms the way that nicotine and heroin do. But in the course of long-term habitual use, people develop cravings for marijuana when they are without it, and this craving has a physiological basis (Wölfling, Flor, & Grüsser, 2008). People can become psychologically dependent on marijuana or use it compulsively.

Many researchers have argued that regular marijuana smoking increases risk for lung cancer, as marijuana smoke contains many of the same cancer-causing agents as cigarette smoke (Tashkin et al., 2002). A large-scale study, however, found no increased risk of lung cancer among heavy marijuana smokers compared to nonsmokers, but researchers need to conduct more research on this topic (Tashkin, 2006). Heavy marijuana smoking does increase the likelihood of a variety of respiratory illnesses, can cause immune system impairment, and appears to lead to memory problems (Kanayama et al., 2004; Tashkin et al., 2002). Regular marijuana use is common in adolescents who later develop schizophrenia, which has led some people to suggest a link between marijuana use and schizophrenia in people who might be genetically predisposed to this disorder (Arseneault et al., 2004).

endo-cannabinoids natural, marijuana-like substances produced by the body.

Contrary to U.S. government reports that marijuana has no medical value, marijuana and the **endocannabinoids,** a class of marijuana-like chemicals produced by our own body, offer promise for medical treatment of various physical and even some psychological disorders ("Marijuana Research," 2004; Nicoll & Alger, 2004). For instance, marijuana is known for its effective prevention and treatment of nausea: It has been recommended and prescribed for people who suffer chemotherapy-related nausea or the involuntary weight loss due to AIDS. Research shows that marijuana may help people eat not by increasing appetite, but by making food appear more appealing (Nicoll & Alger, 2004). Additionally, marijuana and its derivatives may be helpful for the treatment of pain. Marijuana-activated receptors in brain areas modulate pain and may work more safely and more effectively than opioids (Hohmann et al., 2005). Cannabinoids such as marijuana and medical cannabis preparations reduce symptoms of neuropathic pain, one of the most common types of chronic pain (Rahn & Hohmann, 2009). As of 2011, fifteen U.S. states, plus the District of Columbia, have legalized marijuana for medical use.

LSD LSD (lysergic acid diethylamide-25), or "acid," is a synthesized form of lysergic acid, which is derived from the grain fungus ergot. People notice dramatic changes in conscious experience when they ingest LSD. These experiences include altered visual perceptions (such as seeing the tracks that your hand makes when you move it through the air or seeing the lines dance about on a page), enhanced color perception, hallucinations, and synesthesia, which is when we "see" sounds or "hear" visual images (see Chapter 4). Neurochemically, LSD appears to work by increasing the levels of the neurotransmitters dopamine and serotonin. Serotonin activity, in turn, increases the excitatory neurotransmitter glutamate, which may play a role in creating hallucinations (Marek & Aghajanian, 1996; Scruggs, Schmidt, & Deutch, 2003).

The known side effects from LSD include increased body temperature, increased blood pressure, insomnia, and psychosis-like symptoms in some people. Because it can temporarily separate a person from reality, for some people LSD use can lead to panic and negative experiences, known as bad trips. For other people, it can have the opposite effect and lead to very profound, life-altering experiences (Strassman, 1984; Weil & Rosen, 1998).

Psilocybin Psilocybin is the active ingredient of hallucinogenic mushrooms. Experimental studies on the use of psilocybin show that the trips can lead to profound spiritual experiences, even in studies where people were "blind" to what they were taking (Griffiths et al., 2006). What is more, the spiritual insights they experienced seemed to be fairly stable, as they endured 14 months following the drug exposure (Griffiths et al., 2008).

Quick Quiz 6.6: Altering Consciousness With Drugs

1. Even though it can make people feel more aroused in social settings, this popular drug is a depressant:
   a. alcohol
   b. heroin
   c. cocaine
   d. marijuana

2. This stimulant can be as addictive as heroin:
   a. caffeine
   b. ecstasy
   c. nicotine
   d. morphine

Answers can be found at the end of the chapter.

Bringing It All Together

Making Connections in Consciousness

Remember David? Today, nearly two decades after his brain injury, David functions pretty well. His most profound deficits are problems with consciousness that affect attention, memory, and learning. By revisiting David's situation and the effects of brain injury on consciousness in general, we can integrate many of the topics addressed in this chapter.

David moved through various stages of conscious awareness in his first year of recovery. He went from comatose to vegetative to responsive in 5 months, but even when he was responding to the outside world, he was minimally conscious. In some cases of brain injury this is a transitional state to full consciousness; sometimes it is a permanent state. Fortunately, in David's case, minimal consciousness eventually led to full consciousness. His brain gradually became more and more responsive. How does this happen? We do not know for sure. What we do know is that people with damage to lower brain regions that control basic functions, such as sleep–wake cycles, are less likely to regain consciousness than are people with damage to the cerebral cortex (Laureys, 2007). David had cortical damage.

David's consciousness bears permanent scars from his injury. For example, when he is working on a task, David can suddenly become distracted and forget what he is doing. We all experience this kind of distraction from time to time, but for David it can be disabling. He might be emptying the dishwasher and overhear someone saying something about baseball. Hearing the word baseball, David might look up and—as a fanatic about baseball statistics—suddenly have some thought about baseball. He will then ask Greg if he knew,

say, that Joe DiMaggio had a lifetime fielding percentage of .978. Then he'll head to his room to send an e-mail to his other brother about the same topic. Meanwhile, the dishwasher has yet to be emptied. By the time he's finished sending the e-mail, David has forgotten all about the dishwasher.

Such distractibility may be due to problems with selective attention. Indeed, David has a hard time staying on task and filtering out or setting aside information to deal with at a later time. As soon as he heard "baseball," David thought of Joe DiMaggio and simply had to talk about him. He couldn't set the topic aside briefly. As a result, he lost the ability to continue unloading the dishwasher. Distractibility is a common problem for people with brain injury. People with brain damage, especially to the frontal lobes, have trouble blocking out extraneous information and using selective attention to stay on task (Ries & Marks, 2005). Some studies show that such individuals perform poorly on the Stroop test, for example, possibly because it takes them longer to process information overall (Mathias & Wheaton, 2007). For David, a related problem is an inability to concentrate on one thing for any extended period of time. That is, he shows deficits in sustained attention. Research confirms that, in general, people with traumatic brain injury have deficits in sustained attention (Mathias & Wheaton, 2007).

Sleeping and dreaming may also change with brain injury. In fact, how people sleep while comatose or vegetative may be an important predictor of recovery. People in coma who show more organized EEG patterns during sleep have less disability later and a greater likelihood of survival than those whose brain patterns are less organized while sleeping (Valente et al., 2002). After they have regained consciousness, sleep and wakefulness may be disrupted. David's sleep is not normal. He suffers from hypersomnia, or excessive sleeping. Sometimes he sleeps 14 hours a day; other times he has trouble sleeping at night and naps frequently throughout the day. Insomnia and chronic fatigue are also common in people with traumatic brain injury (Ouellet, Beaulieu-Bonneau, & Morin, 2006; Ouellet & Morin, 2006).

Brain injury can also lead to disruptions in dreaming, probably as a consequence of disordered sleep, though this doesn't seem to be a problem for David. It may depend on the location of the brain injury. Some people who sleep normally following traumatic brain injury nevertheless have problems with dreaming, indicating that different areas of the brain may be responsible for sleeping and dreaming. People with damage to the areas of cortex involved in integration of sensory information and the limbic system and areas around it or the links between these areas show the greatest dreaming deficits and, in some cases, a total absence of dreaming (Domhoff, 2001; Solms, 2000). Although not dreaming might seem insignificant, often people who experience a total lack of dreaming due to brain injury also lack "initiative, curiosity, and fantasy" in waking life (Domhoff, 2001, p. 16).

Lastly, drug use and abuse can occur in people who are coping with the challenges of a brain injury. It is most common among those who experience depression and anxiety (Anson & Ponsford, 2006).

Quick Quiz 6.7: Bringing It All Together: Making Connections in Consciousness

1. Since his accident, David, like many people with brain injury, experiences an overwhelming need for sleep called
   a. somnambulism
   b. night terrors
   c. circadian flux
   d. hypersomnia

2. People with brain damage, especially to the frontal lobes, have trouble with selective attention. This problem leads to much _____ in daily life.
   a. fatigue
   b. distractibility
   c. amnesia
   d. confabulation

Answers can be found at the end of the chapter.

Chapter **Review**

WHAT IS CONSCIOUSNESS?

- Consciousness is an awareness of one's surroundings and of what's in one's mind at a given moment. It is also that limited portion of the mind of which we are aware at any given moment, sometimes called a global workspace.

TWO DIMENSIONS OF CONSCIOUSNESS: WAKEFULNESS AND AWARENESS

- Consciousness has two aspects: the degree to which we are awake and the degree to which we are aware.

- Three levels of consciousness stem from these two dimensions. First, minimal consciousness refers to states when people are barely awake or aware, such as coma and vegetative states. Second, moderate consciousness includes phenomena such as being preconscious, having words on the tip of the tongue, and sleeping and dreaming. Third, full consciousness is a high degree of wakefulness and awareness and ranges from normal waking states to states of flow and mindfulness.

ATTENTION: FOCUSING CONSCIOUSNESS

- Attention is focused awareness. Selective attention is the process by which we filter out unwanted stimuli while focusing on other stimuli. Selective attention can result in inattentional blindness, the failure to notice the unexpected. Sustained attention is the ability to stay focused on one thing.

TRAINING CONSCIOUSNESS: MEDITATION

- Meditation is a form of mental training that can be used to calm the mind, stabilize concentration, or enhance awareness of the present moment.

- Evidence from brain imaging studies suggests that meditation has lasting effects on mood, concentration, and learning.

SLEEPING AND DREAMING

- Four stages of sleep are characterized by different EEG patterns. We move through Stages 1–4 roughly once every 90 minutes during the night. Rapid eye movement (REM) sleep occurs only during Stage 1 sleep, when most dreaming occurs. Most sleep consists of non-REM sleep.

- Sleep is important for three major restorative processes: neural growth, memory consolidation, and the formation of enzymes that protect against cellular damage.

- Sleep disorders affect about 20% of the U.S. population. Insomnia, sleepwalking, narcolepsy, and hypersomnia are the most common sleep disorders.

- Dreams consist of images, thoughts, and feelings that we experience while we sleep. Freud maintained that dreams are attempts to fulfill unconscious wishes. A biological theory of dreams, AIM, argues that dreaming is the result of moderate levels of brain activation and internal focus, coupled with looseness of thought. The cognitive view argues that dreams do not differ greatly from normal waking forms of thinking, as seen most clearly in lucid dreaming.

HYPNOSIS

- Hypnosis is a state of mind that occurs naturally and is established by compliance with instructions. It is characterized by focused attention, suggestibility, absorption, lack of voluntary control over behavior, and suspension of critical faculties of mind.

- Research not only shows that hypnosis has a real physiological and neurological basis, but also points to ways that hypnosis may serve as a model for understanding attention.

ALTERING CONSCIOUSNESS WITH DRUGS

- A psychoactive drug is a naturally occurring or synthesized substance that produces qualitative changes in conscious experience. The three major categories of psychoactive drugs are depressants, stimulants, and hallucinogens.

- Depressants decrease central nervous system activity. Alcohol, sedatives, and opioids are all depressants. Typically, people develop tolerance for these drugs quickly, withdrawal is unpleasant, and the risk of overdose is high.

- Stimulants increase central nervous system activity. The most commonly used stimulants are caffeine and nicotine. Cocaine, amphetamines, and ecstasy all have stronger stimulant properties than caffeine and nicotine and carry a high risk of abuse and physical and psychological problems.

- Hallucinogens create altered sensations and perceptions. The two most widely known examples are marijuana and LSD. Heavy marijuana smoking increases the risk of respiratory ailments, impairs immune system functioning, and can lead to memory problems. Marijuana mimics the effects of endocannabinoids, pain-relieving substances produced in the body.

BRINGING IT ALL TOGETHER: MAKING CONNECTIONS IN CONSCIOUSNESS

- Brain injury can affect many different aspects of consciousness, depending on the location and extent of the damage.

- As happened to David, brain damage interferes with selective attention, creating difficulties with staying on task, as well as with sleep and dreaming.

Key Terms

Quick Quiz **Answers**

Quick Quiz 6.1: 1. d   2. c   Quick Quiz 6.2: 1. a   2. b   Quick Quiz 6.3: 1. d   2. a   Quick Quiz 6.4: 1. a   2. d   3. b   4. c
Quick Quiz 6.5: 1. a   2. d   Quick Quiz 6.6: 1. a   2. c   Quick Quiz 6.7: 1. d   2. b

Challenge Your Assumptions **Answers**

- Multitasking allows you to perform many tasks well at the same time. **False. See pp. 233–235.**
- Meditation practice can improve your attention. **True. See pp. 236–238.**
- You can make up for lost sleep. **True. See p. 245.**
- You can't drink yourself to death. **False. See pp. 255–256.**

Memory

7

Chapter Outline

Challenge *Your Assumptions*

TRUE OR FALSE?

- No one can remember every single day of his or her adult life.
- Emotional memories are easier to recall than nonemotional memories.
- We can know things we don't remember.
- Eyewitness memories are usually accurate.

Answers can be found at the end of the chapter.

Imagine being able to remember nearly every single day of your life, going back to childhood. Think about that for a second: every single day. All of the good things, the bad things, and even the trivial everyday things. Most of us are lucky to remember one or two things from a given month a few months back or perhaps a few things from a given year more than 10 years ago. But a very few people, and scientists have only confirmed the existence of about 20 such individuals, can remember some detail of every single day (Elias, 2009). The first known person with this ability, now termed *hyperthymestic syndrome* (*thymesis* means "memory" in Greek), is Jill Price (E. S. Parker, Cahill, & McGaugh, 2006).

Jill Price

Jill's ability extends back to 18 months of age, when she remembers being in her crib (E. S. Parker et al., 2006). But her ability to remember nearly every day did not begin until she was 8, and the ability to remember every day did not begin until she was 14 (1980). So if you name any day since 1980, she will have a memory for that day. But the truly remarkable thing is her memories are instantaneous—she doesn't have to work to recall them. They pop into her mind instantaneously. "*November 14, 1981,* a Saturday: My dad's forty-fifth birthday. That night a school group I was joining, the Rasonians, was initiating new members and taking us out in Westwood. *July 18, 1984,* a Wednesday: A quiet summer day. I picked up the book *Helter Skelter* and read it for the second time" (Price, 2008, p. 10). What is equally fascinating about Jill is that her IQ is only average and she is somewhat below average in memorizing lists of words or numbers.

Someone else with an incredible memory is Daniel Tammet, whose abilities have to do with numbers, not personal memories. Tammet memorized 22,514 digits of pi in just 3 weeks. Most people can recall perhaps 7–10 digits of pi without too much trouble (3.14159265…), but Tammet carried out this feat to more than 22,500 digits! What makes his accomplishment all the more amazing is that there is no pattern in pi, and he recalled the digits without a single mistake. It took him more than 5 hours to recite the numbers. His "trick" is an uncanny ability to see numbers as shapes and colors. As he described in his memoir, he would not remember numerals but rather a landscape of shapes and colors (Tammet, 2006). In fact, his rendition of how he sees the first 20 digits of pi is presented in Figure 7.1.

FIGURE **7.1**
EXTRAORDINARY NUMERICAL MEMORY.
David Tammet's description of how he sees the first 20 digits of pi; he memorized 22,514 digits in just 3 weeks.

Connection

Daniel's form of synesthesia is perhaps the most common form—seeing numbers as colors. Other forms include hearing smells, smelling touch, or tasting shapes. Synesthesia probably occurs because of a cross-wiring of neural connections in the brain.
See "Synesthesia," Chapter 4, "Sensing and Perceiving Our World," p. 160.

Needless to say, Jill and Daniel's memory abilities are anything but normal or typical. Scans of Jill's brain reveal two unusually large regions associated with kinds of memory, suggesting that her ability is based on the unique size of her brain structures (Elias, 2009). Daniel is on the autism spectrum and also suffered a severe epileptic seizure when he was 4 years old, after which his abilities with numbers and calculations began. Moreover, because he sees numbers as shapes and colors, he is also a *synesthete*, someone who experiences sensations in one sense when a different sense is stimulated.

And yet they both tell us important information about how normal memory works. Price's memories, for instance, are what psychologists refer to as long-term autobiographical memories, because they involve particular personal episodes or events from her life. These memories are different from recall of word lists or facts; they involve different parts of the brain. As we see later in the chapter, Tammet is using a mnemonic device, a method we all use to help us remember a series of things.

What psychological scientists do know about memory—both spectacular and mundane—is the topic of this chapter. These are the three main findings about memory:

1. There are three types of memory (sensory, short-term, and long-term) that last for different amounts of time.
2. Different memory systems involve different areas of the brain.
3. We reconstruct memories from our past experiences, rather than recording accurate images of what has happened. ■

THREE TYPES OF MEMORY

Until the 1950s, psychologists thought of memory as one thing. Either people remembered things or they didn't. As we've seen so often throughout this book, a single case in science changed our understanding and made it clear that there are different kinds of memory. The case involved Henry Molaison. When he was 9 years old, Molaison—who is better known to scientists as H. M.—was hit by a bicyclist (Squire, 2009). He suffered a brain injury that resulted in severe epileptic seizures. To stop these seizures, doctors removed the hippocampus on both sides of H. M.'s brain as well as the adjoining brain structures

Brenda Milner

Henry Molaison

(Figure 7.2). The seizures stopped, but at quite a cost: H. M. lost the ability to form new memories. He lived forever in the present. Brenda Milner, the neuropsychologist who examined H. M. regularly for more than 30 years, had to introduce herself each time they met! What makes H. M.'s story even more remarkable is that most of the memories he had formed prior to the surgery, at age 27, remained intact.

FIGURE **7.2**

PORTIONS OF H. M.'S BRAIN REMOVED DURING SURGERY.

The amnesiac patient H. M. had most of his hippocampus and the adjacent tissues in the temporal lobe removed from both hemispheres of his brain. (Source: Carey, 2008)

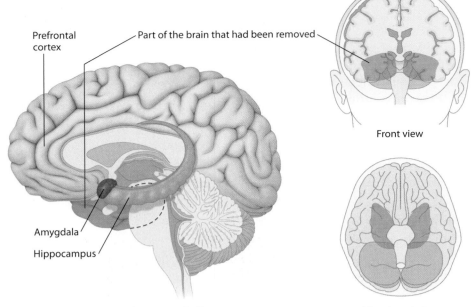

Prefrontal cortex

Part of the brain that had been removed

Front view

Amygdala

Hippocampus

Side view (brain cut in half)

View from below

Milner's (1962) work with Molaison provided the first documented evidence of distinct kinds of memory in operation. For example, she gave him a standard learning task, in which he had to trace inside the outline of a star while looking at the star in a mirror; see the Research Process for this chapter (Figure 7.3). This task is particularly difficult because the mirror image of every movement is reversed. True to Milner's expectations, H. M. had no recollection of doing this task even though he had been trained on it for days and even though he did it up to 10 times in one day. Each time he did it, H. M. said that it was a completely new task. Yet contrary to what you might expect, some part of his brain knew and remembered the task, because the drawings improved the more often he worked on them. Although Molaison may have lost the ability to form new memories of his experiences, some type of memory formation had to have occurred, or he would not have improved on the task.

How might one explain this contradictory finding? As H. M.'s case illustrates, being unable to consciously recall experiences doesn't mean there is no memory of an event. In fact, we humans are incapable of intentionally bringing into awareness much of what we remember, such as memories that have been put away for some time or memories for how to do things, like tie one's shoes or ride a bike. Many things we know are outside of conscious awareness. Most generally, **memory** is simply the ability to store and use information. It need not be a conscious recollection.

Some memories last much longer than others. The **three-stage model of memory** classifies three types of memories based on how long the memories last: sensory memory, short-term memory, and long-term memory (R. C. Atkinson & Shiffrin, 1971). **Sensory memory** holds information in its original sensory form for a very brief period of time, usually about half a second or less. **Short-term memory** temporarily stores a limited amount of information before it is either transferred to long-term storage or forgotten. Information stays in short-term memory for 2 to 30 seconds—about long enough to remember a

memory
the ability to store and use information; also the store of what has been learned and remembered.

three-stage model of memory
classification of memories based on duration as sensory, short-term, and long-term.

sensory memory
the part of memory that holds information in its original sensory form for a very brief period of time, usually about half a second or less.

short-term memory
the part of memory that temporarily (for 2 to 30 seconds) stores a limited amount of information before it is either transferred to long-term storage or forgotten.

Research Process

① Research Question

Can a person who cannot form new long-term memories learn to do a new task?

② Method

As part of her case study of H. M., who lost the ability to form new memories following the removal of his hippocampus, the neuropsychologist Brenda Milner (1962) asked H. M. to perform a mirror tracing task. The goal was to trace within the two lines of the star, while viewing only the reverse image of the star in a mirror. In other words, the image was inverted, so each time H. M. moved his hand in one direction, the movement of his hand in the mirror went in the opposite direction. H. M. was asked to perform this task up to 10 times each day for 3 days. An error was counted each time H. M. went outside the lines. H. M.'s drawings improved with time, even though he could not recall having done the task before.

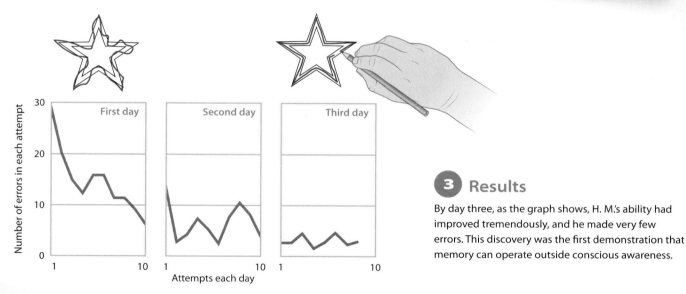

③ Results

By day three, as the graph shows, H. M.'s ability had improved tremendously, and he made very few errors. This discovery was the first demonstration that memory can operate outside conscious awareness.

④ Conclusion

Many different parts of our brain are involved in learning, and conscious awareness is not required for all learning.

FIGURE **7.3**

A CASE STUDY OF MEMORY WITHOUT RECOLLECTION. Although H. M.'s memory problems prevented him from recalling ever having completed this star tracing task, some part of his brain clearly did "recall" the task. He got better and better at it over time. Sources: From Kandel, E. R. (2006.) *In Search of Memory: The Emergence of a New Science of Mind*, p. 131, Fig. 8-6. Copyright © 2006 by Eric R. Kandel. Used by permission of W.W. Norton & Company, Inc. This selection may not be reproduced, stored in a retrieval system, or transmitted in any form or by any means without the prior written permission of the publisher. From Kandel, E. R., Kupferman, I., & Iverson, S. (2000). *Principles of Neuroscience,* 4th ed., p. 1230. © The McGraw-Hill Companies. Used with permission.

phone number before you dial it. **Long-term memory** has the capacity to store a vast amount of information for as little as 30 seconds and as long as a lifetime. Here reside the memories of your first pet and your knowledge of how to read. As the three-stage model suggests, memory formation is an active, dynamic process. Let's look at the stages of memory in more depth.

Sensory Memory

As we interact with the world, our sensory systems are stimulated—we may smell, taste, feel, see, or hear an experience. In fact, two or more sensory systems may contribute information about a single experience, as when we dig into a bag of buttery popcorn while watching a scary movie. In Chapter 4, we saw that sensory neurons respond to sensory stimuli by sending signals to the brain for processing. Sensory memory is made up of the brief traces of a sensation left by the firing of neurons in the brain. These traces last from less than half a second up to 2 or 3 seconds. Sensation is the first step toward the creation of a long-term memory.

Nature & Nurture

What we hear, see, touch, taste, and smell forms brief traces in our brain. If we attend to these sensory traces, they make lasting changes in our brain by becoming either short- or long-term memories.

Because seeing and hearing are key sources of information for humans, the two kinds of sensory memory that have received the most attention from memory researchers are iconic and echoic memory (Craik, 1979). *Iconic memory* is a brief visual record left on the retina of the eye, whereas *echoic memory* is short-term retention of sounds. In a simple laboratory demonstration of iconic memory, four digits, such as 5 4 7 1, are flashed on a computer screen for 30 milliseconds. (A millisecond is a thousandth of a second.) Then the screen goes blank. At 30 milliseconds, the information is barely perceived at all. Yet, when a blank screen follows the numbers, most people have no trouble recalling them. However, if the same four digits are followed on the screen by # # # #, people have a lot of trouble recalling any digits and often report that they did not see any digits at all (R. F. Thompson & Madigan, 2005). The presentation of the symbols interferes with the ability to recall the digits. This demonstration suggests that all sensory memory traces are preserved for very short periods of time and are very fragile.

Short-Term or Working Memory

We often need to stay focused on something temporarily to solve a problem or perform a task, such as getting to a restaurant soon after hearing the directions on the phone. To do so, we put our short-term memory to work. Because short-term memory is a place to temporarily store information we need while working on a problem, psychologists also refer to it as working memory. **Working memory** is the part of memory required to attend to and solve a problem at hand. When we no longer need the information, we forget it. Although we will use the terms *short-term memory* and *working memory* interchangeably, bear in mind that *short-term memory* emphasizes the duration of this type of memory, while the phrase *working memory* emphasizes its function.

Examples of tasks that involve short-term or working memory are reading, talking, and listening to someone speak. We use working memory to keep track of what we have just read or what we are about to say, but for only a brief period of time. Working memories can be transferred to long-term memory if they are practiced; otherwise, they are lost.

How good are you at remembering names of people after meeting them for the first time? Unless you rehearse them, names often don't make the transition to long-term memory.

Without working memory, we wouldn't be able to keep in mind the information needed to solve puzzles and other problems at hand.

Short-Term Memory Capacity

Most of us hear someone's phone number, repeat it a few times, and then place the call. The number of items that can be held in short-term memory is called short-term memory capacity, and it is limited to about seven items (Feldman-Barrett, Tugade, & Engle, 2004; G. A. Miller, 1956). It is not a coincidence that local phone numbers in this country contain seven digits. The short-term memory capacity of most people is between five and nine units of letters, digits, or chunks of information, but there are substantial individual differences in this capacity. Some people struggle with three or four bits of information, whereas others easily handle 11 or 12 (Baddeley, 2003).

chunking
the process of breaking down a list of items to be remembered into a smaller set of meaningful units.

One of the best ways to increase short-term memory capacity is to transform what you want to remember into a smaller set of meaningful units or chunks, a process known as **chunking** (R. F. Thompson & Madigan, 2005). For example, 4155557982 is much more difficult to remember than the chunks of (415) 555-7982. Social Security numbers follow the same idea: 555-66-8888 is easier to remember than 555668888.

How Short-Term Memory Works

One researcher, Alan Baddeley (2003, 2007), has suggested that working memory consists of three distinct processes: *attending* to a stimulus, *storing* information about the stimulus, and *rehearsing* the stored process to help solve a problem. In Baddeley's model, the first process, focusing and switching attention, is carried out by a master attentional control system. This attention system is supported by three

THE KIND OF THING YOU DON'T WANT TO HEAR HALFWAY THROUGH AN EXPERIMENTAL GAME OF MEMORY CHESS BETWEEN TWO OF THE WORLD'S MOST NOTED MEMORY EXPERTS

KING'S KNIGHT TO QUEEN THREE

AM I BLACK OR WHITE?

www.mrboffo.com

JOE MARTIN 5-13-05

FIGURE **7.4**

BADDELEY'S MODEL OF SHORT-TERM MEMORY. The four components of short-term memory are the central executive, which focuses attention, and three storage systems (visuospatial sketchpad, episodic buffer, and phonological loop). Once our attention is focused on something, we need short-term places to store the relevant information. Images and spatial relations are stored in one storage center; events and experiences in another; and language and sounds in another. (Adapted from Baddeley, A., 2003. Working memory: Looking back and looking forward. *Nature Reviews Neuroscience, 4,* 835. Reprinted by permission from Macmillan Publishers Ltd.)

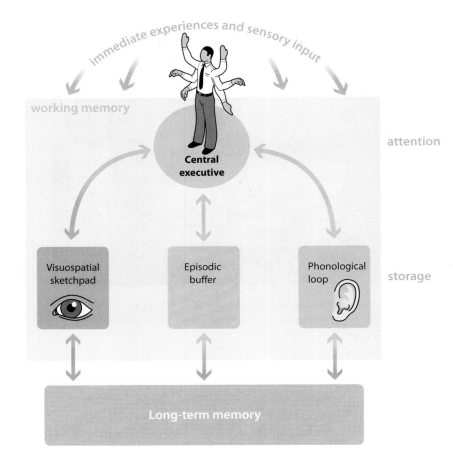

temporary storage systems, one for sounds and language (phonological), one for images and spatial relations (visuospatial), and one that provides temporary storage for specific events (buffer) (see Figure 7.4).

The *central executive* decides where to focus attention and selectively hones in on specific aspects of a stimulus. Attention allows us to focus on the task at hand and develop a plan for solving a problem. We are bombarded by dozens of sensations every second. How do we know which are important and deserve our attention and which we can ignore? According to Baddeley's model, children and people with brain injuries (at least those with frontal lobe damage) have a difficult time screening out irrelevant information because they lack well-developed or fully functioning central executives. Once information is taken in and we attend to it, it is sent to a temporary store: the *phonological loop* if it is sound or linguistic information, the *visuospatial sketchpad* if it is visual or spatial information, or the *episodic buffer* if it is a specific event or experience. The *phonological loop* assists the central executive by providing extra storage for a limited number of digits or words for up to 30 seconds at a time. The storage system allows us to hold memory traces for a few seconds before they fade.

The *visuospatial sketchpad*, as the name implies, briefly provides storage for visual and spatial sensations, such as images, photos, scenes, or three-dimensional objects. Like verbal information stored in the phonological loop, a visual image created on the visuospatial sketchpad lasts only seconds before it fades—unless we attend to it and process it more deeply. Normally we can hold a small number of images (three or four) in short-term storage. An example would be a cognitive map that you visualize while someone is giving you directions to an unfamiliar location. If you are going to actually find your way there, however, you have to move this map from sensory memory to short-term memory by verbalizing and rehearsing the directions ("left at the stop sign, right at the Quicki-Mart . . ."). Depending on how complex the directions are, you might even move them to long-term memory. The *episodic buffer* is a temporary store for information that will become long-term memories of specific events. You can think of the episodic buffer as being like a buffer in your computer software. When you type something in a word processing program like Microsoft Word, the letters typed reside in a temporary store until you save the material. That temporary store is a buffer. It will not be saved to your hard disk unless you tell Word to save it. Saving it transfers the material from the buffer into long-term memory.

The three storage systems each require rehearsal if the information is to be remembered for any length of time. **Rehearsal** is the process of reciting or practicing material repeatedly. The rehearsal system enables us to repeat the information to ourselves as long as we need to retain it. Storing and recalling a shopping list is an everyday example of the function of the phonological loop. When we want to remember the list long enough to use it, we typically rehearse it by repeating it to ourselves. As long as we keep rehearsing it, we will be able to recall it. If we continue rehearsing it, after more than a minute or two, the information might make the transition to long-term memory. Otherwise, it will be lost.

rehearsal

the process of repeatedly practicing material so that it enters long-term memory.

The Serial Position Effect

In the late 19th century, Mary Whiton Calkins observed an interesting phenomenon of short-term memory. When learning a list of items, people are better able to recall items at the beginning and end of the list; they tend to forget the items in the middle (Calkins, 1898; Madigan & O'Hara, 1992). This effect is known as the **serial position effect.**

In studies of the serial position effect, participants might be presented with a list of 15 words read at 1-second intervals. They would be told in advance that they would be asked to recall as many as they could, in any order. Typically, about 50% of the participants recall the first two words on the list, about 50%–75% recall words near the end of the list, and about 90%–95% of participants recall the last two words on the list. So recall for the beginning and end of the list is pretty good, but only about 25% of the participants recall words in the middle of the list. The tendency to preferentially recall items at the beginning of a list is known as the *primacy effect*, whereas recall for items at the end of a list is known as the *recency effect* (see Figure 7.5).

serial position effect

the tendency to have better recall for items in a list according to their position in the list.

The main explanation offered for the primacy effect is that the items in the beginning of the list are quickly rehearsed and transferred to long-term memory storage. So they are remembered. The items in the middle of the list haven't made that trip to long-term memory yet. The recency effect results from those items at the end still being held in short-term memory. They are therefore accessible. The items in the middle cannot be rehearsed as more and more items are being added to the list. These new items interfere with rehearsal of those presented before, which can prevent long-term storage. For instance, if people hear 15 words and are asked to say three digits immediately after the 15th word is read, then words in the 10th through 15th places are no better recalled than words in the 5th through 9th places (about 25% recall). Recall is superior without the interfering task (R. F. Thompson & Madigan, 2005). Recent neuroimaging data support the idea that the serial position effect results from both short-term and long-term memory processes and greater brain activation during early (primary)

FIGURE **7.5**

SERIAL POSITION EFFECTS AND RECALL. People have the best recall of items that are in the beginning of a series (primacy) or at the end of a series (recency). The recency effects go away if people are given a distracting task such as having to recall digits before recalling the words in a list. (Source: R. F. Thompson & Madigan, 2005)

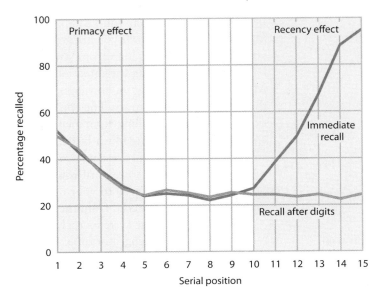

and late (recency) stages of perceiving stimuli (Azizian & Polich, 2007; Talmi et al., 2005).

Because of the serial position effect, we are more likely to remember the first and last parts of a book, TV program, movie, or commercial than to recall the middle. Writers, directors, and politicians all know about this tendency, either consciously or not, and try to place the most important information near the beginning and end of their works.

Long-Term Memory

In April 2006, during the centennial of the 1906 San Francisco earthquake, a 109-year-old survivor reported these two memories from that disaster: "I remember the smell of the smoke [from the fires afterward] . . . and the cow running down California Street with its tail in the air" (Nolte & Yollin, 2006). Memories that are 100 years old definitely qualify as long-term memories! Yet, according to our definition of long-term memory as "any information that is stored for at least 30 to 40 seconds and up to a lifetime," things that you remember from earlier today—the topic of a psychology lecture, for example—are also in long-term storage. So is information you remember for only a few weeks, such as material for your next midterm exam. Will you remember the material you learned in this course 20 years from now? That depends on a number of factors, but primarily it depends on how often you use or rehearse the information.

Long-term memory is what most people think of when they think of memory. Long-term memory is also the most complex form of memory: There are two distinct kinds and four distinct stages of processing.

Types of Long-Term Memory People often forget specific things, but they typically do not forget how to tie their shoes, ride a bike, or even how to add 6 to 12. How is it possible that a person could forget names but almost never forget skills such as simple arithmetic? The short answer is that there is more than one type of memory, and the types operate differently. At the broadest level, there are two types: implicit and explicit memory. How to ride a bike or add is implicit; where you left your car keys is explicit. H. M.'s case, described at the beginning of the chapter, is important partly because it helped psychologists change our long-held perspective on memory by distinguishing between implicit and explicit memory.

implicit memory
kind of memory made up of knowledge based on previous experience, such as skills that we perform automatically once we have mastered them; resides outside conscious awareness.

Implicit Memory When we know or remember something but don't consciously know we remember it, we are tapping into **implicit memory.** Implicit memory is also known as *nondeclarative memory,* because we cannot directly recall this type of memory. Instead, implicit memory is based on prior experience, and it is the place where we store knowledge of previous experience, such as skills that we perform automatically once we have mastered them—how to ride a bicycle, for instance. If asked to describe how we perform these skills, we can't do so very well. Although we can perform many skills automatically, we don't have ready access to the memory of the many steps they require (Kandel, Kupfermann, & Iversen, 2000).

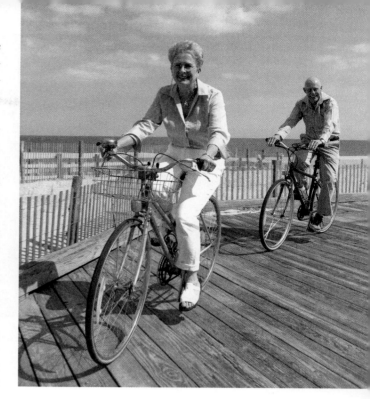

Once learned, skills for riding a bicycle become implicit memories that we recall without effort.

procedural memory
kind of memory made up of implicit knowledge for almost any behavior or physical skill we have learned.

Implicit memory includes procedural memory and priming. **Procedural memory** refers to knowledge we hold for almost any behavior or physical skill we learn, whether it is how to play golf, ride a bike, drive a car, or tie a shoe. The star-tracing task that H. M. worked on (Figure 7.3) is another example of procedural memory. Part of his brain remembered the mirror task because his performance improved each time he did it. The part of his brain responsible for conscious recall did not remember the task, however.

priming
a kind of implicit memory that arises when recall is improved by earlier exposure to the same or similar stimuli.

Priming is a kind of implicit memory that occurs when recall is improved by prior exposure to the same or similar stimuli. In one laboratory demonstration of priming, people with memory problems (amnesia group) were compared to individuals without such problems (comparison group) on a word-learning task.

When asked to recall a list of words they were exposed to, people in the amnesia group demonstrated much less recall than the comparison group (see Figure 7.6). But when they were given the first three letters of the words as a prime, or memory aid, the amnesia group performed at least as well as the comparison group (Squire, 1987). What is intriguing about this outcome is that the amnesia group had no conscious recollection of having seen the words before. Like H. M., who was primed by his previous learning of the star-tracing task, people with severe long-term memory problems show a remarkable ability to recall words if they have been primed.

FIGURE **7.6**

RECALL OF WORDS WITH AND WITHOUT PRIMING. With no priming, recall by people with memory problems is impaired. They recall only about 10% of the words compared to about 35% for those without memory problems. Those with memory problems, however, outperform those without memory problems after they have been primed (given the first three letters of the word). (Source: Squire, 1987)

Images associated with events like high school graduation are stored temporarily by the visuospatial sketchpad in short-term memory before making the trip to long-term memory. The emotions that accompany such occasions increase the likelihood that our memories of them will last a lifetime.

How do you spell _____? This spelling bee contestant is relying on her semantic memory to spell challenging words correctly.

Connection

Besides the ability to consciously recall a memory, what other forms of consciousness affect our behavior without our knowing it?
See "Two Dimensions of Consciousness: Wakefulness and Awareness," Chapter 6, "Consciousness," p. 227.

Explicit Memory **Explicit memory** is the conscious recall of facts and events. Explicit memory is sometimes called *declarative memory* because it refers to memories that can be deliberately accessed or *declared*. There are two distinct kinds of explicit memory: semantic and episodic (Tulving, 1972, 1985).

Semantic memory is our memory for facts and knowledge, such as what we learn in school. **Episodic memory** is our memory for the experiences we have had. Remembering that Baton Rouge is the capital of Louisiana is an example of semantic memory, whereas remembering your high school graduation would be an episodic memory. Episodic memories are more personal and autobiographical than semantic memories.

Stages in Long-Term Memory For sensory input to make the transition from sensory memory to short-term memory and then to long-term memory, it must go through four processing stages: encoding, consolidation, storage, and retrieval. Relatively few experiences survive this process, but those that do can become lifelong memories. These four stages occur for implicit and explicit memories alike, but they are more typical of explicit long-term memory, because we more consciously rehearse and retrieve this type of memory.

Encoding **Encoding** is the means by which we attend to, take in, and process new information. This phase is absolutely crucial for storage in long-term memory. Attention drives the encoding process. If we fail to pay attention or try to multitask, an experience is not going to be processed deeply enough to be stored for a long period. In general, we remember visual images more easily than verbal descriptions (Craik, 1979). Why? One explanation is that visual images create a richer and more detailed representation in memory than words and therefore are more deeply encoded (Craik, 1979).

explicit memory
knowledge that consists of the conscious recall of facts and events; also known as declarative memory.

semantic memory
form of memory that recalls facts and general knowledge, such as what we learn in school.

episodic memory
form of memory that recalls the experiences we have had.

encoding
the process by which the brain attends to, takes in, and integrates new information; the first stage of long-term memory formation.

Psychologists describe two kinds of encoding processes: one that happens with little effort and one that takes significant effort (Hasher & Zacks, 1979). **Automatic processing** happens with little effort or conscious attention to the task. Because these experiences are automatic, our recall of them does not improve much with practice. Furthermore, they are often not processed as deeply and are less likely to be recalled later. For instance, you most likely encoded what you ate for breakfast this morning without trying, but by this evening you may have trouble recalling what you ate hours earlier. Episodic memory involves this kind of automatic processing.

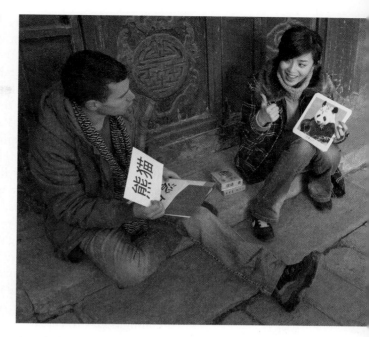

Associating images with information we want to remember, such as vocabulary words, helps to encode the material more deeply. Here, a man is trying to associate an image of a panda with its Chinese character.

Now think about what you learn in college. You read the textbook, attend lectures, take notes, and study those notes, usually multiple times. Before an exam, you then go over these materials again and again. Needless to say, this kind of learning takes work. **Effortful processing** occurs when we carefully attend to and put conscious effort into remembering information. Effortful processing is the basis of semantic memory. Effortful processing usually involves rehearsal of the information, so that it goes from short-term to long-term memory. Interestingly, advancing age tends to lessen recall for events and experiences that require effortful processing but not for those that involve automatic processing (Hasher & Zacks, 1979).

To review, memory formation starts with sensory input from the outside world (see Figure 7.7). If we do not pay attention to it, the sensation vanishes and the information is lost. If we pay attention to it, the sensation becomes a short-term memory. Once the sensation enters short-term memory, either it makes the transition to long-term memory within about 30 seconds or it disappears. If we repeat or rehearse the information actively, if we apply some other memory-enhancing technique, or if we experience a strong emotion and the information at the same time, the original sensation becomes a long-term memory.

The connection between encoding and remembering is at the core of the levels-of-processing approach to memory (Craik & Lockhart, 1972). The idea behind **levels of processing** is that the more deeply people encode information, the better they will recall it. Thomas Hyde and James Jenkins (1973) created a standard procedure for manipulating depth of processing in which they typically presented a list of about 28 words with a 5-second interval between words. To eliminate primacy and recency effects, the researchers ignored participants' recall of the first two and the last two words on the list. Excluding these four words left 24 possible words to be recalled. Participants heard beforehand that they would be given a list of words and should focus on a specific aspect of the words. Participants were not told that they would be asked to recall as many words as possible, so they were somewhat surprised when they were asked to name them.

Based on word-recall studies, researchers have identified three different levels of processing: structural, phonemic, and semantic (Craik & Tulving, 1975;

Hyde & Jenkins, 1973; see Figure 7.8). *Structural processing* is the shallowest level of processing. When studying structural processing, researchers might have directed participants to focus on the structure of the word by asking questions such as "Is the word in capital letters?" To study *phonemic processing*, or midlevel processing, they asked questions to focus participants' attention on the sound of the word, such as "Does the word rhyme with _____?" *Semantic processing* is the deepest level of processing. Participants in studies of semantic processing were asked to think about the meaning of the words and answer questions such as "Would the word fit the sentence: 'He met a _____ in the street?'

Results across many studies find the best recall when words are encoded more deeply and worse recall for words that are processed less deeply (Craik & Tulving, 1975; Hyde & Jenkins, 1973; Lockhart & Craik, 1990). Craik and Tulving (1975) conducted 10 different experiments in which they manipulated the participants' level of processing with target words (between 48 and 60 words) and found that the deeper the level of processing became, the better the recall was (see Figure 7.9). The take-away message here is that the more deeply you process material, the better you will remember it. We will come back to this point in our discussion of the role of memory in studying at the end of this chapter.

A common way to encode information deeply is to devise mnemonic (pronounced neh'-mon-ik) devices. A **mnemonic device** is a scheme that helps people remember information. Rhyming, chunking, and rehearsal are types of mnemonic devices. Others include imagery and acronyms. For example, imagery can be used to remember a set of words or a list of objects in a set order. Simply form a mental image of each word or object in a specific place along a route you know very well, such as from your home to your school. Rehearse this a few times. Then when you need to recall the word or object list, take a mental stroll along the familiar path and the visual images of the list should be relatively easy to recall (R. F. Thompson & Madigan, 2005). Remember our discussion of Daniel Tammet at the beginning of the chapter—the young man who could recall pi out to 22,514 digits by seeing the landscape of shapes and colors? These served as mnemonic devices for Tammet.

Acronyms are a type of mnemonic device. We usually create acronyms by combining the first letters of each word or object we need to remember. Acronyms work best when they form a word we can pronounce or some other

mnemonic device

a method devised to help remember information, such as a rhyme or acronym.

FIGURE **7.7**

THREE TYPES OF MEMORY. When our sense organs are stimulated, the nervous system forms a very brief image or trace of what we saw, heard, tasted, felt, or smelled (sensory memory). If we don't attend to it, we forget it immediately. If we do pay attention, the information is passed on to short-term memory. Here, if we attend to it only briefly, it will remain in short-term memory as long as we need it, but then will be forgotten. If we rehearse it over and over, the information is processed more deeply and passed on to long-term memory. If we encode the information deeply, it becomes a long-term memory. Some long-term memories fade or are forgotten over time. (Source: Atkinson & Shiffrin, 1971)

Sensory input

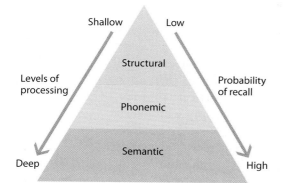

FIGURE **7.8**

LEVELS-OF-PROCESSING MODEL OF MEMORY AND RECALL. The level at which we process information affects the probability of recall. The deeper we process information, the more likely we are to recall it. Structural processing is the shallowest level of processing and also the least likely to be recalled. Semantic processing is both the deepest and the most likely to be recalled. (Source: Craik & Lockhart, 1972)

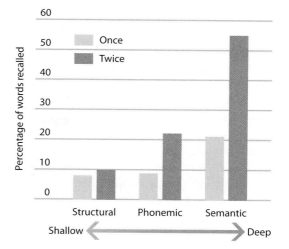

FIGURE **7.9**

RESULTS OF LEVELS OF PROCESSING AND RECALL. These results show that the more deeply people process information, the better they recall it. If people are presented the word list twice, the effect of depth of processing on recall is even stronger. (Source: Craik & Lockhart, 1975)

meaningful unit. For example, the acronym RADAR is easier to remember than "**Ra**dio **De**tection **a**nd **R**anging" and "ROY G. BIV" is easier to remember than the colors of the rainbow "red, orange, yellow, green, blue, indigo, and violet."

You might have your own favorite mnemonic devices to help you encode material that you need to know for an exam. If you have never tried this approach to studying, you might be surprised at how much it improves memory.

Consolidation   The second stage of long-term memory formation is **consolidation,** the process of establishing, stabilizing, or solidifying a memory (Kandel, 2006; McGaugh, 2000; Moscovitch, 2010). A consolidated memory is resistant to distraction, interference, and decay (Dubai, 2004). As we'll discuss in some detail shortly, new proteins are manufactured in the brain during

consolidation
the process of establishing, stabilizing, or solidifying a memory; the second stage of long-term memory formation.

long-term memory formation, and consolidation provides time for these proteins to develop. Once the proteins needed for consolidation have formed, a memory is beyond the effects of interference and decay.

Sleep plays an important role in memory consolidation. Psychologists have long known that we recall information better after we "sleep on it" than after the same amount of time if we stay awake. Recent findings indicate that not only does sleep stabilize the memory, but it also enhances memory and makes it stronger (Walker & Stickgold, 2006; Wamsley et al., 2010). Moreover, sleep deprivation has been shown to have a detrimental effect on memory (Stickgold, 2005). We can conclude, then, that cramming all night before an exam is not the best study strategy. (We'll consider better alternatives in the "Bringing It All Together" section at the end of this chapter.) In fact, research shows that learning over long periods of time and evenly spaced sessions leads to better recall (Kornell & Bjork, 2007; Kornell et al., 2010).

Storage   Once memories have been encoded and consolidated, they are ready to be stored. Storing a memory is akin to putting something—say, a birthday gift purchased months ahead of time—away in a special place where you can find it later. **Storage,** the retention of memory over time, is the third stage of long-term memory formation. We organize and store memories in at least three distinct ways: in hierarchies, schemas, and networks.

storage
the retention of memory over time; the third stage of long-term memory formation.

We use **hierarchies** to organize related information from the most specific feature they have in common to the most general. An example is the hierarchy human (specific), hominid (less specific), primate, mammal, and animal (general). Each step moves to a more general category in a hierarchy. They act as a filter through which we encode and organize information about our world.

hierarchies
a way of organizing related pieces of information from the most specific feature they have in common to the most general.

Schemas are mental frameworks that develop from our experiences with particular objects or events. They act as a filter through which we encode and organize information about our world. Once formed, schemas tell us how people, objects, or events are most likely to look or act. Because schemas help us organize and understand experiences, they can also aid memory and recall. For instance, if your favorite childhood pet was a Chihuahua, your schema of Chihuahuas would be a very positive one that predisposes you to expect other Chihuahuas to act as friendly and fun-loving as yours did. Because you had so many happy experiences with your Chihuahua as a child, when you see one now you are able to most easily remember the enjoyable experiences you had with your own pet. Likewise, because they do not fit your schema of the happy Chihuahua, you are less likely to remember the negative and aggressive experiences you may have had with your dog. For better and for worse, schemas bias our memory and perception.

schemas
mental frameworks that develop from our experiences with particular people, objects, or events.

Hierarchies and concepts bring order and organization to our perceptions and experiences. The psychological process that binds concepts together is *association*. Associations are linked together in networks by their degree of closeness or relatedness (Hopfield, 1982). An **associative network** is a chain of associations between related concepts. Each concept or association in a network is referred to as a *node*. The links between the nodes are associations. When people think of a concept, and its node is activated, they are primed and more likely to make an association to a nearby concept or node (Collins & Loftus, 1975). Figure 7.10 illustrates an associative network for the concept of fire engine. "Fire engine" activates both vehicle and color networks of association, and it may well activate others not shown here (such as emergency).

associative network
a chain of associations between related concepts.

Neural networks also use associations to explain how memory works. Unlike associative networks, *neural networks* are computer models that imitate

FIGURE **7.10**

ASSOCIATIVE NETWORK. Associative networks are chains of association between related concepts or nodes that get activated. The closer concepts are to each other, the more directly related they are and the more likely they are to activate the other node. The network for "fire engine" consists of a rich associative network of related concepts. (Source: Collins & Loftus, 1975)

the way neurons talk to each other (Chappell & Humphreys, 1994). Neural networks have nodes, too, but their nodes are not single concepts like a color or a vehicle. Rather, these nodes are information processing units. Neural networks are analogous to the nervous system, where the nodes in a network are single cells (neurons) that can process information. The more the nodes in a neural network communicate with each other, the stronger the link between nodes. As we will discuss later in this chapter and in the next, repeated connection between neurons leads to stronger connections, and stronger memories and learning (Hebb, 1949).

A well-known model of memory storage that integrates associative and neural networks is parallel distributed processing. *Parallel distributed processing* (PDP) models propose that associations involve the simultaneous activity of many nodes (McClelland, 1988; McClelland & Rogers, 2003; McClelland & Rumelhart, 1985). Many nodes can fire at the same time, spreading or distributing activation to other nodes in the network. This spread of activation can serve a priming function, making certain memories more likely than others to be stored. Recent work in neuroscience reveals that such PDP models may do a good job of explaining how neurons and genes actually work together to store new long-term memories (Mendelsohn, Furman, & Dudai, 2010; Miyashita et al., 2008).

retrieval

the recovery of information stored in memory; the fourth stage of long-term memory.

Retrieval   The work of encoding, consolidating, and storing memories would be wasted if we could not retrieve information when we needed it. **Retrieval** is the recovery of information stored in memory. It's remembering where you put that birthday gift that you bought early—or that you even bought one—when it comes time to present it to your friend. The ease of retrieval and the time frame over which we can recall a particular event or piece of knowledge is determined by the previous stages of memory. How did we encode it? Did we consolidate it? Did we store it where we can access it? Additionally, whenever we retrieve a memory, we need to focus our attention on remembering, which requires working memory. Retrieval, attention, and working memory are related activities.

Implicit memories, such as how to ride a bicycle, are retrieved without conscious effort. Explicit memories are the ones that require conscious effort for retrieval. An example would be the date of a friend's birthday—factual information that is encoded and stored for later recall. But factual information is not always properly encoded and stored, and we cannot always retrieve it at will. A common retrieval problem is the inability to remember the name of a person only minutes after meeting her, even if we repeated her name immediately after hearing it. What most likely happens in this situation is that we fail to pay enough attention to the person's name when we first hear it and focus instead on the whole social interaction. Consequently, we do not encode, consolidate, and store the name very deeply. When we try to retrieve it, we cannot. We'll explore retrieval problems in more detail when we talk about forgetting, and later the "Bringing It All Together" section outlines some strategies for improving retrieval.

Quick Quiz 7.1: Three Types of Memory

1. Suppose you met a person who could remember things that happened well before she had surgery, but who was now incapable of forming new long-term memories: What part of her brain would you say was most likely affected by the surgery?
   a. hypothalamus
   b. hippocampus
   c. insula
   d. amygdala

2. The brief traces of a touch or a smell left by the firing of neurons in the brain are examples of
   a. perceptual memory
   b. long-term potentiation
   c. implicit memory
   d. sensory memory

3. What kind of memory do we use to keep someone's phone number in mind right after we've learned it?
   a. working memory
   b. iconic memory
   c. long-term memory
   d. sensory memory

4. What sort of memory allows us to perform skills such as tying our shoes automatically once we have mastered them?
   a. explicit memory
   b. declarative memory
   c. procedural memory
   d. echoic memory

5. For sensory input to make the transition from sensory memory to short-term memory to long-term memory, it must go through four processing stages:
   a. encoding, consolidation, storage, and retrieval
   b. encoding, reconstruction, storage, and retrieval
   c. encoding, consolidation, storage, and remembering
   d. encoding, reconstruction, storage, and remembering

Answers can be found at the end of the chapter.

THE BIOLOGICAL BASIS OF MEMORY

At the beginning of this chapter we introduced H. M., who lost the ability to make new long-term memories after having his hippocampus and nearby brain sections removed. Why was he still able to retrieve memories stored before the surgery? And how was he able to learn the star-tracing task more and more rapidly each time it was presented, even though he didn't remember learning it before?

We can answer these questions only if we understand that memory consists of many different systems, each of which uses distinct regions of the brain (Poldrack & Foerde, 2008; Schacter & Tulving, 1994; Squire, 2009). As noted in the previous section, there are multiple long-term memory systems, and each system involves its own distinct brain regions (Eichenbaum, 2010). One anatomically based model of memory systems proposes three long-term memory systems: procedural-implicit, emotional, and declarative-explicit (see Figure 7.11).

Long-term memories begin with sensations being processed into output from cortical sensory association areas such as the auditory or visual association areas. Depending on the kind of memory system involved, the output goes to different brain regions. For instance, when we are learning to do things (implicit procedures), output goes mostly to the cerebellum and striatum. When we experience

FIGURE **7.11**

THREE LONG-TERM MEMORY SYSTEMS.
Memories begin with parallel output from cortical sensory association areas such as the auditory or visual association areas. Depending on the kind of memory system involved, the output goes to different brain regions. For instance, when we learn to do things (often implicit procedures), output goes mostly to the cerebellum and striatum. When we experience an emotional event, output goes to the amygdala. And when we remember explicit personal events (episodes), facts, and information, output goes mostly to the hippocampus. Those rehearsed and attended-to memories are then returned and stored in the cortical areas from which they came. Think of the hippocampus as being more like a librarian than a library. It processes, organizes, and directs memories and then returns them to the appropriate location in the cortex for long-term storage. (Source: Eichenbaum, 2010)

an emotional event, output goes to the amygdala. And when we consciously and explicitly remember personal events (episodes), facts, and information, output goes mostly to the hippocampus. After being processed by the hippocampus, however, the memory is stored back in the cortical association area from where it came.

H. M. had a very difficult time making new long-term explicit memories because of the damage to his hippocampus and surrounding areas. He could learn tasks like the star-tracing task, however, because his cerebellum and striatum, which are involved in implicitly learning to carry out procedures, were intact.

The overview of sensory, short-term, and long-term memory systems and the brain is this: Sensory memories are processed (encoded) in the various sensory cortexes; short-term memory is processed in the hippocampus and frontal lobes; and long-term memories are stored in different parts of the cortex and subcortex and retrieved with the help of areas associated with the **prefrontal cortex** (see Figures 7.12 and 7.13). The prefrontal cortex is the frontmost region of the frontal lobes. It plays an important part in attention, appropriate social behavior, impulse control, and working memory (Baier et al., 2010). Now that we know something about the three types of memory, we can explore the neuroscience of memory.

prefrontal cortex
the frontmost region of the frontal lobes that plays an important role in attention, appropriate social behavior, impulse control, and working memory.

The Sensory Cortexes

Our sensory memory system is fairly straightforward. As we saw in Chapter 4, sensory neurons carry information about external stimuli from our sense organs to different parts of the brain. First, the sensation travels to the thalamus, which then relays the sensory information to the cerebral cortex for further processing. Three of the five sensory systems have a dedicated sensory cortex for processing sensory stimuli. The visual cortex is located in the occipital lobes, the auditory cortex is in the temporal lobes, and the somatosensory cortex (touch) is in the parietal lobes. Taste and smell do not have their own processing regions, although a particular smell can elicit a very strong and immediate memory even if it's been decades since you were exposed to that particular scent.

Connection

Why do smells evoke particularly strong and specific memories?
See "Smell (Olfaction)," Chapter 4, "Sensing and Perceiving Our World," p. 158.

Pathways of Short-Term Memory in the Hippocampus and Prefrontal Cortex

The prefrontal cortex determines what information in the environment is worthy of our attention. Only then does a sensory memory make its way from the prefrontal cortex to the hippocampus. In other words, the encoding stage of memory formation activates the prefrontal cortex as well as the hippocampus, where the memory is consolidated through rehearsal and repetition (R. D. Fields, 2005; Kandel et al., 2000). The repeated firing of neural impulses necessary to convert a short-term memory into a long-term one occurs mostly in the hippocampus. Memory consolidation in the hippocampus may take hours, days, or sometimes weeks before the memory is transferred back to the cortex for permanent storage. Think of the hippocampus as being more like a librarian than a library—with aid from the frontal lobes, it processes, organizes, and directs memories and then returns them to the appropriate location in the cortex for long-term storage.

The hippocampus does not do all of the work in working memory, however. Attention and focus require the prefrontal cortex. Remember that a key function of working memory is to focus attention and to plan action. When we speak, read, solve problems, or make some other use of working memory, we rely on the prefrontal cortex to keep the crucial information accessible (Baddeley, 1998; Baier et al., 2010; Kandel, 2006; B. L. Miller & Cummings, 1999; Miyake et al., 2000).

The other main function of working memory is rehearsal. Auditory input is processed and rehearsed via the phonological loop from the prefrontal cortex to the language comprehension center (Wernicke's region) in the rear of the left parietal lobes (Paulesu, Frith, & Frackowiak, 1993; Schacter, 2001). The processing pathway for visual information and the visuospatial sketchpad goes from the prefrontal cortex to the temporal lobes (for spatial information) and then to the occipital lobes (for visual information; Baddeley, 2003). Figure 7.12 highlights the regions of the brain that play a role in short-term (working) memory.

FIGURE **7.12**

BRAIN REGIONS INVOLVED IN WORKING MEMORY. The prefrontal cortex focuses attention on sensory stimuli and holds information long enough for us to solve a problem and then transfers information to the hippocampus for memory consolidation. The temporal and occipital lobes, as well as Wernicke's area, are active in rehearsal of auditory and visuospatial information needed by working memory.

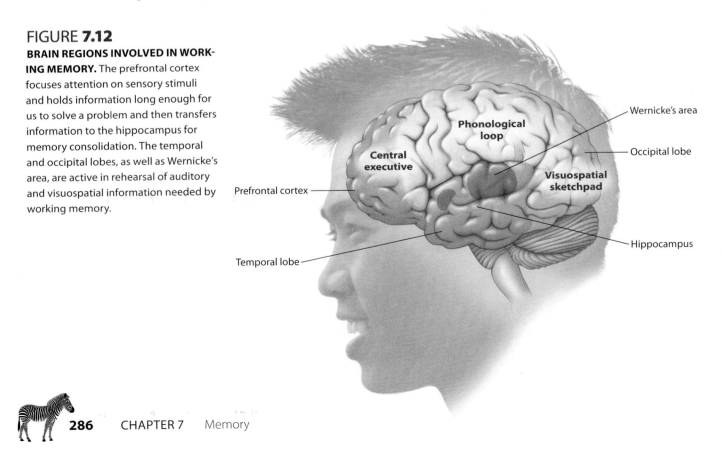

Long-Term Memory Storage in the Cortex

Most memories begin and end in the cortex, but in between, as we have seen, they are processed in the hippocampus, where some are converted to long-term memory. Because long-term memory is the most permanent form of memory, it is also the most complex when it comes to brain activity and location.

We store the different types of long-term memory in different places in the brain. Explicit long-term memories are stored in the cortex, specifically in the area where the original sensation was processed (Ji & Wilson, 2007). Implicit memories are stored in structures in the subcortex, specifically in the striatum (part of the basal ganglia), amygdala, and cerebellum (Kandel, 2006; see Figure 7.13).

When we actively try to recall information, especially words, from long-term memory, we use the prefrontal cortex (Gershberg & Shimamura, 1995; Mangels et al., 1996; R. F. Thompson & Madigan, 2005). Retrieving information requires attention and focus, and hence involves working memory, which is predominantly an activity of the prefrontal cortex.

Implicit memories are also processed and stored in different parts of the brain. Priming, for example, occurs mostly in the cortex. Procedural memories for skills and habits involve the striatum. The amygdala is crucial for associating particular events with emotional responses such as happiness or fear. So when we learn to associate a neighbor's house with a mean dog and we become afraid of going there, the amygdala is the part of our brain that is most involved.

Much of what we know in psychology comes from studying questions from different perspectives. Much of what psychologists have learned about memory and the brain has come not from studying normal brains but instead from studying people who have suffered brain injury. The different functions of the cortex and hippocampus in memory explain why some brain-injured people can remember skills and behaviors, but not knowledge, events, and facts. As we have mentioned, memories for behaviors and skills are implicit, and we process them mostly in the subcortex. Explicit memories for events and facts we process and store mostly in the cortex. This

Explicit Memory Storage

Implicit Memory Storage

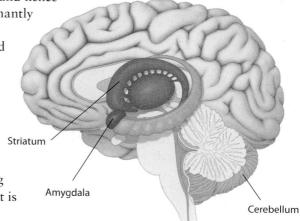

FIGURE 7.13

BRAIN REGIONS INVOLVED IN LONG-TERM MEMORY.
Many different brain areas are involved in memory. The hippocampus is involved in laying down and retrieving memories, particularly personal ones and those related to finding your way about. After being processed in the hippocampus, explicit long-term memories are returned to the cortex for storage in the area where the sensory information was processed originally. Implicit memories are processed and stored in the cortex, the striatum, and the amygdala. (Source: Kandel, E. R., 2006. *In search of memory: The emergence of a new science of mind*, p. 130, Fig. 8-7. Copyright © 2006 by Eric R. Kandel. Used by permission of W.W. Norton & Company, Inc. This selection may not be reproduced, stored in a retrieval system, or transmitted in any form by any means without the prior written permission of the publisher.)

can occur only if the hippocampus is intact and can pass them on for long-term cortical storage. Even if part of the hippocampus is removed, we cannot easily form new long-term memories.

Damage to areas of the cortex involved in processing particular kinds of information can lead to deficits in that knowledge system. For instance, damage to the temporal lobe often results in problems with one's sense of direction—that is, spatial problems. In Chapter 6 we introduced David, who suffered a major brain injury when hit by a car. David's injury involved portions of the left temporal lobe of his brain. Since his accident, David can get lost easily in almost any location except his immediate neighborhood, which he sees daily. Even there, if he wanders more than a few blocks down the street he knows he may become disoriented and lose his way.

So specialized knowledge in certain brain regions plays a role in memory for that kind of knowledge, such as spatial skills. This is just one example of the ways in which anatomy and function guide memory. Another example is emotion. Brain regions involved in memory are anatomically linked to those involved in emotion. Not surprisingly, emotion and memory are intimately connected.

Emotion, Memory, and the Brain

Why is it that you can remember in great detail the events of your first date but cannot recall what you ate for breakfast 3 days ago? Generally speaking, emotional memories are easier to recall than are factual ones. Emotions help us encode and retrieve memories. When emotions occur—especially negative ones—attention is focused and details are noted, because emotions usually are connected with events that have important implications for the individual.

As such, these events may be important to recall. From an evolutionary perspective, it makes sense for creatures to have better recall of anything that may have significance for well-being (as emotional events do).

How does emotion help memory? One way, as we'll see in more detail in the next section, is through biochemical and genetic processes. Emotional events switch on genes that build proteins that strengthen the synaptic connections between neurons. These proteins also stimulate the formation of new synapses and even new neurons (Kandel, 2006). All of these structures make the memory "stick" for a long period of time.

Additionally, emotion helps memory by way of anatomy. Important structures for memory, namely, the amygdala and hippocampus, are linked to key structures for emotion. These two structures lie next to each other in the brain and are connected by many nerve fibers. Indeed, these two structures become activated simultaneously during emotional experiences (Strange & Dolan, 2006). The amygdala is involved in assigning emotional significance to events and is crucial in encoding information relevant to emotional experiences, especially fear (Dolcos, LeBar, & Cabeza, 2005; Phelps & LeDoux, 2005; Sigurdsson et al., 2007). People remember the visual details of an object better if negative emotions were aroused while viewing it (Kensinger, Garoff-Eaton, & Schacter, 2007). One mechanism through which emotional arousal affects memory formation is the release of norepinephrine (Tully & Balshakov, 2010). This neurotransmitter makes synaptic connections between neurons more plastic—that is, changes their structure. Neural plasticity in turn is necessary for making the connection between synapses stronger; hence, an event becomes more memorable. In short, the release of norepinephrine is an essential connection making emotional events memorable.

In a study on memory, emotion, and sleep, evidence suggests that sleep helps consolidate memories, especially of emotional experiences (Payne & Kensinger, 2010). Participants were shown images that were either emotionally neutral or negative. An example of a neutral image would be a yellow car on a city street, whereas an emotionally negative image would be that same yellow car with a person lying injured after having crashed the car. Researchers then tested the recall of these images soon (30 minutes) after showing them to participants, and the participants recalled about 80% of the neutral objects and nearly 90% of the emotionally negative objects. Next, researchers waited 12 hours to retest the participants' memories. In one 12-hour condition, the participants were awake the whole time (it was during the day, from morning to night), and in the second condition participants slept for at least 6 hours (it was from night to the next morning). What the researchers found was quite interesting: Recall declined in three of the four conditions; the exception was emotional images after sleep (see Figure 7.14).

Connection

One of the primary functions of sleep is to consolidate memories and facilitate new neural growth.

See "Sleeping," Chapter 6, "Consciousness," p. 238.

Only when objects were emotionally charged and only after sleep did recall improve slightly. When the objects were neutral or after staying awake, recall declined. Sleep helps consolidate memories, at least if they are emotional memories.

The relationship between emotion and memory is far from perfect. Sometimes, emotions distort our memories. As we have just reviewed, emotion enhances memory in many different ways, but it is important to keep in mind that the accuracy of these memories is a different story. Indeed, emotional memories tend to be less accurate in their details than nonemotional memories (Phelps & Sharot, 2008). Emotional memories are often held with great confidence, but with blindness to their inaccuracy. In addition, in terms of autobiographical memories, when people look back over their lives they recall pleasant times rather than the negative. So there is a positive bias in autobiographical memory recall. The "good ole' days" are good partly because we remember the good more readily than we remember the bad (Walker, Skowronski, & Thompson, 2003).

No doubt there are certain, powerful events that you remember vividly. For instance, most people remember exactly what they were doing when two jets flew into the World Trade Center towers on September 11, 2001. Your authors also know exactly what they were doing when they heard John Lennon was killed

12 hours awake   12 hours sleep

FIGURE **7.14**

RECALL OF EMOTIONALLY CHARGED IMAGES IMPROVES AFTER SLEEP. Only people who get sleep and are exposed to emotional scenes consolidate their memories after a night's sleep. They not only maintain their memories compared to 30 minutes after initially being exposed to them, but also slightly improve them 12 hours later after sleep. The same emotional scenes, however, are not remembered well if the person stays awake. Moreover, uninteresting or neutral scenes are forgotten both with sleep and staying awake. (Source: Payne & Kensinger, 2010)

(Erika was doing her American History homework, in her red chenille bathrobe, when her brother told her of the announcement on Monday Night Football).

Such detailed, especially vivid memories of very specific, highly charged events are known as **flashbulb memories,** in reference to how they are experienced and recalled like snapshot pictures (Brown & Kulik, 1977). These recollections tend to be highly charged with emotion, which marks them for recall in some way. For years people thought flashbulb memories were more accurate than less emotional memories, but we now know that this is not true. Rather than being accurate representations of specific emotional events, the emotion makes every aspect of the event more susceptible to the memory reconstruction process, bringing irrelevant as well as relevant information into the recollection (Lanciano, Curci, & Semin, 2010). As such, flashbulb memories are really just special cases of emotional memories.

flashbulb memories
detailed, especially vivid memories of very specific, highly charged events.

Research to Real Life

Your authors will never forget the details of their wedding day, a sunny June day overlooking the Pacific Ocean. We will also never forget the call from the police department telling us Greg's brother had been in a serious accident and was in the hospital. The psychologist Abraham Maslow said, as an adult, "I can find no single glimpse of happiness in all of my memories [of childhood]."

Connecting Psychology to Your Life: Some people remember more negative experiences and others remember more positive experiences about their lives. What about you? Take a few minutes and write down 10 memories of your childhood. How many are positive? How many are negative? How many are neutral?

The importance of the amygdala in making emotional events memorable is seen in people with damaged amygdalas. They do not recall emotional events better than nonemotional events (Adolphs et al., 1997). In fact, there is evidence that amygdala damage can impair memories for the overall feeling of an event, but not for details. The details are still there, but the emotional accent is gone (Adolphs, Tranel, & Buchanan, 2005). Moreover, damage to the left amygdala results in deficits in verbally recalling emotional events (Buchanan et al., 2001).

Nature & Nurture

Thanks to the amygdala, memories of scary things are hard to shake, so we can change our behavior to avoid things that have been threats to us in the past.

We do not have normal recall of traumatic events—those that are extremely stressful or horrifying. We may recall such events quite vividly or not at all, or we may alternate between recollection and memory loss. Post-traumatic stress disorder (PTSD) is a condition in which a person who has experienced an extremely traumatic event, such as being a crime victim or a soldier in battle,

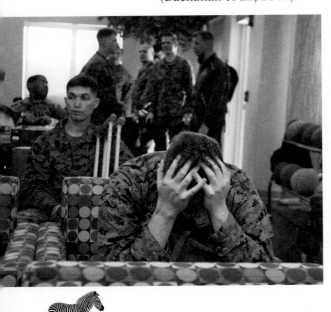

Not all battle scars are physical. Post-traumatic stress disorder (PTSD), a condition that forces sufferers to relive terrifying events over and over, makes readjusting to civilian life difficult for an increasing number of war veterans. After returning to the United States from Iraq, this soldier was diagnosed with PTSD.

relives the event over and over. But stress may both enhance the encoding of information and impair the retrieval of emotional memories (Buchanan & Tranel, 2008). Refugees who have endured extreme emotional stress show impaired recall of specific episodic memories; cancer survivors with PTSD show impaired semantic memory (Moradi et al., 2008). It is possible that loss of autobiographical memory is a way of regulating or coping with extreme emotional stress.

Breaking New Ground

Kandel's Discoveries of Memory and the Brain

In the first half of the 20th century, much of psychology ignored the biological basis of memory and learning, but not all psychologists did. Based on his studies of brain anatomy and behavior, Donald Hebb (1949) developed a theory of how neural connections form and how synaptic connections change with learning and memory. Hebb proposed that when the synapse of one neuron repeatedly fires and excites another neuron, there is a permanent change in the receiving neuron, the excitatory neuron, or both, which strengthens the synaptic connection. This strengthening process is called **long-term potentiation (LTP)** (Whitlock et al., 2006). When synapses fire more readily, learning becomes easier and more efficient.

long-term potentiation strengthening of a synaptic connection that results when synapse of one neuron repeatedly fires and excites another neuron.

Hebb further suggested that repeated stimulation of a group of neurons leads to the formation of *cell assemblies,* networks of nerve cells that persist even after stimulation has stopped. The more times synapses in these assemblies fire together, Hebb asserted, the stronger the network becomes, increasing the likelihood that they will fire together again. Simply put, *neurons that fire together, wire together.* What is now referred to as Hebb's law led to another important conclusion from his theory: *Use it or lose it.* If the cell assemblies are not stimulated repeatedly, eventually the synaptic connections weaken and we forget.

No one suspected a link between the hippocampus and memory formation, however, until a student of Hebb's, Brenda Milner, reported clinical observations of Henry Molaison (H. M). Her observations supported Hebb's theories (Milner, 1962; Milner, Corkin, & Teuber, 1968; Penfield & Milner, 1958). Moving beyond the case study approach of Milner, Eric Kandel and his colleagues were able to conduct systematic research into the biological basis of learning and memory.

Kandel decided to study memory and learning in the neurologically simplest animal he knew, the sea slug (*Aplysia*). Sea slugs have far fewer neurons than humans, and their neurons can also be seen with the naked eye. When Kandel's group administered a shock to the tail of the sea slug, it responded with a defensive posture. If the researchers administered the shock only once, the sea slug's defensive response persisted for only about 10 minutes. If administered four or five times in close succession, the sea slug exhibited the same defensive response to the shock days later. The sea slug had created a long-term memory of how to react to a shock (Pinsker et al., 1973). Kandel's conclusion: "Conversion from short-term to long-term memory storage requires spaced repetition—practice makes perfect, even in snails" (Kandel, 2001, p. 294).

In Kandel's study, the sea slug (*Aplysia*) created a long-term memory of how to react to shock.

Nature & Nurture

Experience changes the brain by strengthening and forming new synapses.

Following up on these findings, Kandel set out to learn just how repeated experience changes the brain. What he found provides an intriguing example of the interaction of nurture and nature. Kandel and his colleagues discovered that repeated stimulation of a neuron actually sends signals to the nucleus of the cell, where its DNA is stored. These signals trigger the production of *CREB,* a protein that switches on genes responsible for the development of new synapses. Repetition brings about the growth of new synapses that stabilize a new memory (see Figure 7.15). Both the timing and frequency of neural firing are crucial in

3 Cellular machinery translates genetic instructions into synapse-strengthening proteins that diffuse throughout the cell

Only a synapse temporarily strengthened by the original stimulus is affected by the proteins

Synapse strengthening proteins

Gene
CREB
Nucleus

Axon
Dendrite

Synapse

1 Strong repeated stimulation temporarily strengthens a synapse and somehow signals the nucleus to make the memory permanent

2 To strengthen the synapse permanently, a protein called CREB must be activated

Inside the cell nucleus, CREB activates select genes, causing them to be copied into versions that leave the nucleus

FIGURE **7.15**

HOW MEMORIES STICK. When we experience something emotionally important or an experience is repeated over and over, synapses fire repeated neural impulses as if to say "this is important; remember this event" (1). These repeated neural firings in turn strengthen the synapse by activating a protein called CREB (2). CREB then turns on certain genes that set into motion a process that builds other proteins that strengthen the synaptic connection (3). This process makes memories last in our minds, in effect "tattooing" the event in our brain. So timing and frequency of neural firings are crucial in making a memory permanent—an idea or thought needs to be rehearsed many times if it is to pass from short-term to long-term memory. (Source: R. D. Fields, 2005)

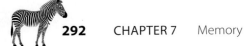

making a memory permanent. By repeatedly pulling away from a shock, the sea slug rehearsed and remembered a defensive behavior. Thus, experience from the outside world (repeated stimulation) changes genes and the way in which they are expressed (Kandel, 2006).

People, too, need to rehearse an idea or thought many times in order to create a long-term memory. Strong emotions also make memories stick. In the process, our brain literally grows more synapses, thereby strengthening the neural connections—it becomes a different brain. Experience changes our brain, and these changes then change how we respond to our environment.

Kandel found the link between behavior and long-term memory that Hebb had speculated about in his model. This work was so significant that Kandel was awarded the 2000 Nobel Prize in Physiology and Medicine. In the words of the Nobel Committee, "Since we now understand important aspects of the cellular and molecular mechanisms which make us remember, the possibilities to develop new types of medication to improve memory function in patients with different types of dementia may be increased." Kandel agreed: He helped start a pharmaceutical company to develop drugs for the treatment of Alzheimer's disease, an application described in this chapter's "Psychology in the Real World." Not only did Kandel succeed in what he started out to do—that is, to confirm Hebb's Law—but in so doing he came to the surprising discovery that what we experience affects genes in neurons to change the brain. Once again, psychological science challenges long-held beliefs.

Connection

Kandel's findings explain how and why the brains of mice reared in enriched environments are heavier and have more dendrites than the brains of mice reared in impoverished environments. See "Brain Plasticity and Neurogenesis," Chapter 3, "The Biology of Behavior," p. 106.

■ ■ ■

Quick Quiz 7.2: The Biological Basis of Memory

1. When we actively try to recall information, especially words, from long-term memory, we use the
   a. occipital cortex
   b. prefrontal cortex
   c. parietal cortex
   d. parahippocampal gyrus

2. Rehearsal makes memories stick. So does this kind of experience:
   a. drunkenness
   b. storage
   c. emotion
   d. fatigue

3. Complete this phrase: Neurons that _____ together, _____ together.
   a. grow; sow
   b. lie; die
   c. synapse; degrade
   d. fire; wire

4. One sea slug had frequent and closely-spaced-in-time puffs of air administered to it. Another had frequent puffs but they were not closely spaced. Yet another slug had one puff administered to it. Which one is most likely to remember this aversive event?
   a. The one with frequent and closely spaced air puffs
   b. The one with frequent, but not closely spaced, air puffs
   c. The one with one air puff
   d. They all are equally likely to remember the event.

5. CREB is a(n) _____ that switches on genes responsible for the development of new synapses.
   a. amino acid
   b. protein
   c. neurotransmitter
   d. enzyme

Answers can be found at the end of the chapter.

Psychology in the **Real World**

Memory in a Pill

Have you ever wished for a better memory? Forgetting things we once had no trouble recalling, especially as we age, is one of the more frustrating experiences in life. The transience of most memory is inevitable, but for some people memory loss represents the loss of identity, the loss of self, and ultimately the loss of life. Alzheimer's disease, for instance, robs people in their later years of their most valued treasure—their memories. Ultimately, this fatal disease destroys the brain's ability to maintain basic functioning. Therefore, there is a real medical need, as well as a psychological need, for therapeutic help for people with Alzheimer's and other severe memory deficits.

A number of memory-oriented biotech companies have started developing memory-enhancing drugs. In fact, the Food and Drug Administration (FDA) has approved two drugs for the treatment of Alzheimer's disease: Aricept and Reminyl. Both of these drugs boost levels of *acetylcholine*, a memory-enhancing neurotransmitter that is deficient in Alzheimer's patients.

Memory researchers Eric Kandel and Timothy Tully have joined the quest for new drugs to treat memory loss. Tully, a former academic researcher who became a pharmaceutical entrepreneur, and his colleagues demonstrated the power of the CREB protein in fruit flies. Flies bred to have an excess of CREB demonstrated super powers of memory: Instead of needing 10 trials to learn to avoid a scented room, they needed only one trial (Yin et al., 1995). Currently, Tully's team and others are researching drugs that stimulate the production of CREB and other memory-enhancing proteins in the brain (Xia et al., 2009). Clinical trials with humans are still at least a few years away.

FORGETTING AND MEMORY LOSS

So far we have discussed two of the three principles of memory: There are three types of memory, and different types of memory involve different areas of the brain. Here we examine the third principle: Memory and **forgetting** are much more of a subjective and reconstructive process than an objective one. It is all too easy to think of the mind as an objective recorder of events. But human memory is not an objective recorder of experience. In the process of remembering we select, distort, bias, and forget events (Levy, Kuhl, & Wagner, 2010; Schacter, 2001).

forgetting
the weakening or loss of memories over time.

Forms of Forgetting

interference
disruption of memory because other information competes with the information we are trying to recall.

One reason why we forget is **interference,** which occurs when other information competes with the information we are trying to recall. Interference can happen in one of two ways (Jacoby, Hessels, & Bopp, 2001). First, **retroactive interference** occurs when new experiences or information causes people to forget previously learned experiences or information. Memory's vulnerability to interference from information that follows immediately after an event has profound applications in the real world. For example, recall of a crime by an eyewitness, even if testimony is given only minutes after the event (which it usually is not), will be distorted by the events that occurred in those few minutes (or

retroactive interference
disruption of memory because new experiences or information causes people to forget previously learned experiences or information.

Herbal preparations that do not require or rely on the laborious, time-consuming, expensive, and bureaucratic process of developing drugs that require FDA approval are readily available now. Some of these alternative medicines have been in use for thousands of years.

One herbal medication, the ground-up leaves of the ginkgo biloba tree, does have a moderate amount of empirical support indicating that it is effective in mild to moderate cases of Alzheimer's disease. The effectiveness of ginkgo biloba seems limited to people with actual memory problems, such as in early to mid-level stages of Alzheimer's disease (Le Bars et al., 1997). It is not yet completely clear why and how ginkgo biloba enhances cognitive functioning, but one reason may be that it increases blood flow to the brain. Ginkgo biloba seems to have no effect on people with no memory problems (Solomon et al., 2002).

The science of memory has led to some promising treatments for problems with memory. Yet all "memory pills" are not equally effective. Be leery of pills that claim to "increase your mental power." One day, however, Alzheimer's disease and other memory problems may be a thing of the past.

proactive interference
disruption of memory because previously learned information interferes with the learning of new information.

hours or days or weeks) after the crime occurred. A second type of interference, **proactive interference,** occurs when previously learned information interferes with the learning of new information. Perhaps the serial position effect occurs because the process of remembering the first words interferes proactively with recall of the middle words.

Research on forgetting began in the 1880s with Herman Ebbinghaus, who found that recall shows a steady decline over time (Erdelyi, 2010). This decline is what we now call Ebbinghaus's **forgetting curve.** A classic demonstration of the forgetting curve comes from the work of Norman Slamecka and Brian McElree (1983). Participants in their research were given a long list of words to learn. Some saw the list once and others saw it three times. Moreover, some were asked to recall the list either immediately or one, two, three, or four days later. When Slamecka and McElree plotted the results, they produced the classic forgetting curve. Recall was between 70% and 80% immediately, but it declined steadily for each additional day between learning and recalling the word list (see Figure 7.16). It is noteworthy that seeing the list three times, compared to once, increased recall only a little bit.

forgetting curve
a graphic depiction of how recall steadily declines over time.

absent-mindedness
a form of forgetfulness that results from inattention.

Most normal forgetting occurs because we don't pay close attention when we first learn or experience something, and therefore we never encode or consolidate the memory very well. In contrast, **absent-mindedness** is a form of forgetfulness that involves attention as well as memory (Cheyne, Carriere, &

FIGURE **7.16**

THE FORGETTING CURVE. Forgetting happens in a predictable way over time. The "forgetting curve" shows that with each passing day, we remember less, though the rate of decline slows. (Source: Slamecka & McElree, 1983)

Smilek, 2006; Robertson, 2003). Consider this: Sandra is distraught over not being able to find her keys. After spending 10 minutes looking all over the house in all of the obvious places, she finally goes out the front door to the car only to discover the keys are still in the lock to the house. Such experiences happen when we do not pay close attention or divide our attention among different tasks.

Divided attention is likely to lead to absent-mindedness. Talking on your cell phone while writing an e-mail can only lead to poor encoding of either the phone conversation or the e-mail or both. You are much less likely to remember things if you try to multitask. Paying attention is crucial to long-term recall.

Absent-mindedness increases with age, but it typically is not a problem until people reach their 70s (Schacter, 2001). Due to slowing of processing speed and less ability to filter out irrelevant information with age, some degree of dementia or age-related memory decline is common in people in their 60s and 70s (Salthouse, 2000; Van Gerven et al., 2007). Yet as is true with all cognitive capacities, there are vast differences among individuals in memory decline with age. Some people show little decline into their 90s, and others begin to experience it in their 40s.

Education seems to have a positive effect on age-related decline. Schmand and colleagues (1997) discovered that when trying to recall a list of words 30 minutes after learning them, people in their early- to mid-80s with low education recalled less than 50% of the words, whereas those in the same age group with high education recalled about 60% of the words. One of the few cross-cultural studies to compare age-related memory decline across different cultures found no cultural differences in the effect (Crook et al., 1992). Age-related memory decline, in other words, appears to be universal (Matsumoto & Juang, 2004).

Another form of forgetting is **blocking,** or the inability to retrieve some information that we once stored—say, a person's name or an old phone number (Schacter, 2001). It simply won't resurface despite our efforts. One example of blocking is the frustrating *tip-of-the-tongue* phenomenon in which we can almost recall something but the memory eludes us. We might even know that the word begins with a particular letter. We say to ourselves: "I know it! It's right there. I can even see her face. Her name begins with an M." More often than not, it does begin with that letter. **Repression,** where retrieval of memories that have been encoded and stored is actively inhibited, is another example of blocking. Memories of a traumatic experience are more likely to be repressed than other memories. The implication is that under the right circumstances—during

Connection

Most people think they can multitask well. Research shows otherwise—especially when it comes to talking on the phone while driving.
See "Sustained Attention," Chapter 6, "Consciousness," p. 232.

blocking
the inability to retrieve some information once it is stored.

Forgetting is a normal part of the aging process and is quite natural. It also appears to be universal.

repression
the unconscious act of keeping threatening thoughts, feelings, or impulses out of consciousness.

psychotherapy, for instance—the person may suddenly remember the repressed event. We come back to this topic in the next section when we discuss "recovered memories."

A final form of misremembering or forgetting is **suggestibility,** which occurs when memories are implanted in our minds based on leading questions, comments, or suggestions from someone else or some other source. We are most prone to suggestions present in the interval between our original experience and when we are asked to recall it.

Elizabeth Loftus has conducted the most systematic research on two major types of memory distortion: eyewitness testimony and false and recovered memories. Her findings changed our understanding of how memory works. Eyewitness testimony may be the deciding evidence presented at a trial, and so the reliability of eyewitnesses' recall of what they saw is a central concern for judges, lawyers, and jurors. Historically, lawyers and jurors have been prone to believe the testimony of eyewitnesses unless it was contradicted by firm, hard evidence. Loftus and her colleagues, however, were among the first memory researchers to demonstrate that people's memories of events, even under the best of circumstances, are not very accurate and are susceptible to suggestion (Loftus, 1996, 2003). In one classic study, Loftus and her colleagues showed participants an event on videotape and then asked them to answer questions, some of which contained misleading suggestions about the event they had just witnessed. A misleading suggestion, for instance, might be about what a person on the tape was wearing. After answering these questions, participants were asked to recall specific details about the event they saw on videotape. Results showed that participants are likely to incorporate suggestions about the wrong clothing into their memory and even elaborate on them.

Another classic study from Loftus's lab indicates how changing the wording of a question impacts people's recall for events. People will estimate higher speeds of travel when asked "How fast were the cars going when they *smashed* into each other?" rather than "How fast were the cars going when they *hit* each other?" (Loftus, 2003). With the first question, people also are more likely to report seeing

suggestibility

problem with memory that occurs when memories are implanted in our minds based on leading questions, comments, or suggestions by someone else or some other source.

SPEED BUMP   Dave Coverly

By permission of Dave Coverly and Creators Syndicate, Inc.

Leading questions might influence how an eyewitness recalls a car accident. Did these cars "hit" each other or "smash" each other?

297

broken glass than with the second question, simply because one word in the question was different. This effect is unconscious: People have no idea and will even deny that they responded differently to the different wording in the questions.

The most fascinating, if not the most disturbing, example of suggestibility comes from research on false memories and recovered memories. **False memories** are memories for events that never happened, but were suggested by someone or something (Loftus, 1997; Loftus & Pickrell, 1995). With a false memory, an individual develops an actual memory, sometimes very elaborate and detailed, based on false information. Loftus pioneered the technique of suggesting falsely that subjects in her studies experienced some event and then later asking them about their memories of that event. To be sure, a majority of the subjects never recalled anything. But across eight studies, on average 31% of the participants did create false memories (Lindsay et al., 2004).

A **recovered memory** is one supposedly from a real event, which was encoded and stored and not retrieved for a long period of time, but then is retrieved after some later event brings it suddenly to consciousness. Recovered memories have been blocked or repressed for years. Recent research shows that people who suffered childhood sexual abuse do in fact have less specific autobiographical memories compared to people who have not suffered childhood sexual abuse (Raymaekers et al., 2010). That is, they are not likely to remember specific events on specific days from their childhood. Their memories tend to be general; for example: "when I was about 9, one summer our family took a trip to New York. But I can't recall any specific details of the trip." Interestingly, however, those who were abused and had continuous recall of the event (that is, did not have to recover the memory later), had equally poor specific autobiographical memories compared to those with recovered memories (Raymaekers et al., 2010). Traumatic events may alter how people store memories and as a defense make them less likely to be specific in their recall.

The topic of recovered memories, however, is controversial. Sometimes they are triggered while a person is under the care of a psychotherapist. Controversy arises when it is not clear whether the psychotherapist has helped a patient to recover a memory of an actual event or has unwittingly suggested an event that the client "remembers." If the event involves traumatic experiences, such as physical or sexual abuse, and people's lives are at stake, recovered memory becomes an explosive topic, as it did when the phenomenon first came to light in the early 1990s.

The 1990s saw the peak of the controversy over recovered memories. The so-called memory wars often pitted academic memory researchers against psychotherapists. The debate has died down somewhat, partly because everyone recognizes the truths on both sides: A large segment of the population really does experience abuse in childhood, and unprofessional suggestions by therapists can also lead to falsely recovered memories (Ost, 2009).

Memory Loss Caused by Brain Injury and Disease

When people forget due to injury or disease to the brain, we refer to the condition as **amnesia.** Two types of amnesia associated with organic injury or disease are anterograde amnesia and retrograde amnesia (Collinson, Meyyappan, & Rosenfeld, 2009). **Anterograde amnesia** is the inability to remember events and experiences that occur *after* an injury or the onset of a disease. People with anterograde amnesia fail to make new long-term memories. They recall experiences for only a short period of time, perhaps 10 minutes or less. H. M., whose case we recounted earlier in the chapter, had anterograde amnesia after his hippocampus had been

false memories
memories for events that never happened, but were suggested by someone or something.

recovered memory
a memory from a real event that was encoded, stored, but not retrieved for a long period of time until some later event brings it suddenly to consciousness.

amnesia
memory loss due to brain injury or disease.

anterograde amnesia
the inability to remember events and experiences that occur after an injury or the onset of a disease.

removed. **Retrograde amnesia** is an inability to recall events or experiences that happened *before* the onset of the disease or injury. The memory loss in this type of amnesia might involve only the incident that preceded it or might include years of memories. Accidents almost always result in retrograde amnesia of the event itself. Car accident victims, for instance, will usually say that they do not remember the accident.

David Feist's brain injury (from Chapter 6) resulted in problems with both anterograde and retrograde amnesia. A typical example of David's anterograde amnesia is that upon meeting friends who visit infrequently, David will forget having met them at all and say, "Have I told you about my memory problem?"

An example of the retrograde amnesia that David experiences is that he cannot remember anything that happened in the months before his accident, which includes completing a very difficult bicycle ride that he would have considered the "memory of a lifetime." His accident erased this event from his long-term memory, likely because the region of his cortex that stored those memories was permanently damaged or destroyed.

A severe form of age-related memory loss occurs in the organic brain disease known as Alzheimer's disease. Although it can affect people in their 40s or 50s, Alzheimer's disease usually strikes people in their 60s, 70s, and 80s (Toyota et al., 2007). It results in progressive memory loss, ending with complete memory loss. For instance, forgetting the death of a spouse is common among people who suffer from moderate to severe forms of Alzheimer's. They may go through the whole grieving process over and over, as if each time someone reminds them that their loved ones are gone, they are hearing the news for the first time. In Alzheimer's disease, experiences are lost due to anterograde amnesia, which can be caused by retroactive interference and absent-mindedness.

Savage Chickens by Doug Savage

I HAVE AN IRRATIONAL FEAR OF AMNESIA

I KNOW. YOU TOLD ME LAST WEEK.

www.savagechickens.com

Quick Quiz 7.3: Forgetting and Memory Loss

1. Sofia is fluent in Spanish and is now trying to learn French. Much of it comes easy to her. And yet she keeps forgetting some French words that are similar to and yet different from their Spanish equivalent. The kind of forgetting that Maria is suffering from is
   a. amnesia
   b. retroactive interference
   c. proactive interference
   d. blocking

2. The fact that changing the wording of a question impacts people's recall for events illustrates which kind of forgetting?
   a. retroactive interference
   b. traceability
   c. rephrasing
   d. suggestibility

3. Gwendolyn is 29 years old and is now convinced that she was abused as a child. From the time she was 9 until she was 28, however, she had no recollection of the abuse. We would say Gwendolyn has
   a. a false memory
   b. retrograde amnesia
   c. proactive interference
   d. a recovered memory

4. Jon was in an automobile accident. It has now been a month since his accident, and he has no recollection at all of the two days after the accident. He suffers from
   a. anterograde amnesia
   b. retrograde amnesia
   c. post-traumatic amnesia
   d. selective amnesia

Answers can be found at the end of the chapter.

Bringing It All Together
Making Connections in Memory
How to Study

One of the most common questions students have while learning about memory in Introductory Psychology is "How can I use this material to study more efficiently?" This question may come up after the first exam, especially from students who expected an A but got a C. "What did I do wrong? I re-read my notes, highlighted the book; how come I didn't do better?" It turns out that the things that worked for you in high school might not work anymore. To really master a lot of complex new material, you may have to adopt new study strategies. You can make psychological science work for you by using the years of research about memory to optimize how to learn new material and prepare for exams (Bjork, 2001; Kornell & Bjork, 2007; Kornell et al., 2010).

Consider that anything you hear in lecture or read in the book—after a brief stint in sensory memory—is in that vulnerable place called short-term memory. Your job is to move this information into long-term memory and to then retrieve it for an exam. In particular, the material you learn in any class—new facts, terms, processes, and so on—is semantic memory. Like all long-term memories, how well you remember this material begins with encoding.

1. *Go to class and pay attention.* Attending and paying attention in lecture is a first, very important step. If there is something you don't understand when the instructor first mentions it, ask a question about it right away. If you are too shy to do so in class or you can't get a word in edgewise with your instructor, note it in the margin of your notes so you can come back to it later. Consider that if you don't attend to it now, you'll forget it by the end of class. Why? Interference of new material presented afterward, the fact that your stomach is growling, and thoughts of getting to your next class in time will make it difficult for you to remember what you wanted to ask. If you don't rehearse or work with the material in some way—in this case, just the fact that you have a question about X and need to revisit it later—it will be gone. Then, by being in class and hearing in more detail what was posted on the lecture outline and what you read in the book, you give yourself another context in which to work with the material: engaging your attention. Avoid creating sources of interference, like talking with a friend, text messaging, or e-mailing during lecture. These activities will interfere with encoding and make it likely that

you are not paying attention. If you start optimizing how you encode material in class, you will be ahead of the game. If you can do this, you are much more likely to store the information in long-term memory and be able to retrieve it easily during the exam. Who knows, some of the information might even stay with you longer than that.

2. *Read the book before class.* To increase the odds of learning and remembering the material for a long period of time, it is important to read the material in the book. Reading the chapter before class helps you to establish a network of associations in which to fit the new material, so that when you hear your instructor talk about it, you have a place to put the information—you can make the associations. A related encoding tool is relating the new material you learn to things you have already experienced, so you begin to build more associations. What else can help at the encoding stage? Many professors post lecture outlines electronically before class, which, like reading the book in advance, gives you the opportunity to begin encoding and storing material from the upcoming lecture before you get there. Reading through both lecture material and book assignments before going to class *primes* you to process the lecture material in a deep and meaningful way.

3. *Study deep, not shallow.* In addition to the lecture and book information, you can improve the way you study the material outside of class. What you have learned from levels of processing theory can help you learn how to approach studying. According to depth of processing theory and research, the more deeply you process material, the better it is recalled. Re-reading notes and highlighting the book are both examples of shallow processing. They involve rote rehearsal. You want to process the material semantically, to work with the meaning of the material, which enhances your depth of processing and memory. Simply reading a definition of a term like *storage* over and over again is not all that different from repeating a list of nonsense words over and over. But if you attempt to work with the meaning of the material, you will remember it better. Think about it. *Storage* is a word we use a lot, and you only recently saw it related to memory. What does it mean in our everyday speech? To put something

away and keep it there. Like storing your memorabilia from high school in the attic of your parents' house. You put your yearbooks, varsity jacket, and track trophies into a box and bring them to the attic. You label the box and make a mental note—maybe even a cognitive map— of where you put the box, so that you will be able to retrieve it later. Memory storage is just like this. It is the process of putting something away and leaving it there for future use. If you can elaborate your understanding of concepts like storage in this way, you don't have to remember the word-for-word definition, because you understand what it means. That's good semantic processing. Add a few salient visual images to the mix—like the old bicycle and Darth Vader costume in the attic—and your depth of processing increases.

Also, the more different ways you work with material, the better you learn it. Connecting the concept of storage with your own experience—storing your high school things in a box—places *storage* into a semantic network of associations, with meaningful nodes in other networks: high school (friends, sports, classes, graduation), your parents' attic (and all the attic junk you know is up there), boxes and other forms of storage (file cabinets, closets). By making the material personally relevant—linking the concept of storage to fond memories from high school—you are adding the element of emotional significance, which research shows strengthens the associations. Moreover, every time you succeed in getting information stored deeply and permanently in long-term memory, you are actually changing your brain. Proteins in your neurons are activating genes that promote the growth of new dendrites and synapses.

Recent research on student study habits shows that spacing out study activities is also important. Students tend to cram right before an exam, and they often think this is the most effective approach to learning. Yet spacing things out and covering topics or chapters in separate study sessions, using both studying and self-testing of that material, is much more effective for long-term memory (Kornell & Bjork, 2007; Kornell et al., 2010).

4. *Form a study group.* Another way to increase depth of processing is to form a study group. Getting together with a few other students to review and discuss material before an exam can be enormously helpful, as long as you prepare before getting together. Meeting with your peers to discuss course material adds new information, fills in gaps, and helps build up new semantic networks, but most importantly, it offers a context in which to talk about the material. This is an excellent opportunity to see whether you know the material—by talking about it with others. You might also have a peer who can explain a concept in a way that your instructor did not. Study groups foster discourse, social interaction, and the need to make another person understand you. This requires semantic processing, preparation, and some emotional charge, because you don't want to look like an idiot in study group. It is also important to have time between meeting with the study group and taking the test, so that you can go over any lingering questions that may have arisen during study group and consolidate your learning. To be sure that the material you are studying becomes consolidated or firmly established, make a point of sleeping well after studying.

5. *Devise meaningful mnemonics.* Will you be able to access the information you learned when you need it? What can you do while studying to facilitate retrieval? Reviewing material with the study group is like a practice test, which is a nice evaluation of retrieval ability. Also, using an easy-to-remember mnemonic device during encoding may make it easier to retrieve information later. If you make a concept personally relevant and integrate it into a semantic network, you can provide yourself with labels or tags as memory prompts. So, for example, to remember the meaning of memory *storage,* you can just think *attic* and you will activate that whole network of associations.

Quick Quiz 7.4: Bringing It All Together: Making Connections in Memory

1. In terms of studying your course material, re-reading notes and highlighting the book are both examples of _____ processing.
   a. depth of
   b. staged
   c. shallow
   d. retroactive

2. Which of the following study approaches is most effective for long-term memory?
   a. rote rehearsal
   b. studying large amounts of material in a few sessions
   c. re-reading the chapter
   d. spacing out your study sessions to cover different topics in several sessions

3. Which of the following helps you process new material more deeply?
   a. making the material personally relevant
   b. building up associations with new concepts
   c. discussing the material
   d. all of the above

Answers can be found at the end of the chapter.

Chapter **Review**

- Memory, the ability to store and recall information, is the foundation of all intelligence, learning, and thought.

- Three major principles of memory state that (1) memories persist for different lengths of time, (2) memories are processed and stored in different parts of the brain, and (3) memory is very much a reconstructive process.

THREE TYPES OF MEMORY

- Memory systems are classified as sensory, short-term (working), and long-term.

- Sensory memory is the brief trace of a sensory experience that lasts from less than half a second to 2 or 3 seconds. Iconic memory is the trace memory of a visual sensation. Echoic memory is short-term retention of sounds.

- Short-term memory holds a limited amount of information for between about 2 seconds and 30 seconds, or as long as we continue to rehearse it, before we either transfer it to long-term memory or forget it. Baddeley's model of working memory describes how we are able to hold information in short-term memory while solving a problem.

- The serial position effect is a phenomenon of short-term memory whereby we most likely remember information that comes first and last in a series.

- Long-term memory is the repository of any material that we retain for between 30 seconds and a lifetime. It includes implicit memory, where skills, behaviors, and procedures that we don't consciously retrieve are stored, and explicit memories of events and facts stored for conscious recall.

- Long-term memory is divided into four stages: encoding, consolidation, storage, and retrieval.

- Encoding results from automatic processing or from effortful processing, such as rehearsal. The more deeply we encode information, the more likely we are to recall it. Mnemonic devices such as acronyms aid the encoding process.

- During consolidation, memory becomes firmly established and resistant to distraction, interference, and decay.

- Storage is the retention of information over time. Information can be stored via hierarchies, schemas, or association networks. According to parallel distributive processing (PDP) models, associations and neural processing result from the synchronized activity of many units or nodes.

- Retrieval is the recall of stored information from long-term memory.

THE BIOLOGICAL BASIS OF MEMORY

- Different memories are processed in different areas of the brain. Sensory memories are processed primarily by their respective sensory cortexes. Short-term memories are processed mostly by the hippocampus and frontal lobes. Long-term memories are stored for the most part in the areas of the cortex where they were processed as sensory memories.

- Repetition and sometimes strong emotion initiate neural activity that converts short-term memories into long-term memories. In long-term memory formation, proteins activate genes that turn on the production of new dendrites and synapses.

- In short-term memory, existing synapses grow stronger with rehearsal, but no new ones form.

FORGETTING AND MEMORY LOSS

- One form of forgetting is interference, which can happen in one of two ways. Retroactive interference occurs when new experiences or information causes people to forget previously learned experiences or information. Proactive interference occurs when previously learned information interferes with the learning of new information.

- The two most serious effects of suggestibility are false memories and recovered memories. A false memory is a recollection of an event that never happened, whereas a recovered memory resurfaces after it was completely forgotten.

BRINGING IT ALL TOGETHER: MAKING CONNECTIONS IN MEMORY

- Going to class and paying attention to lectures help you to encode lecture material deeply.

- Reading the book before a lecture will help build a richer network of associations of the lecture material.

- You can process the material deeply by rehearsing and spacing out your studying.

- Forming a study group also facilitates deeper processing of the material because you have to learn by generating information, not simply reading or hearing it.

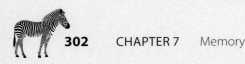

Key **Terms**

absent-mindedness, p. 295

amnesia, p. 298

anterograde amnesia, p. 298

associative network, p. 282

automatic processing, p. 279

blocking, p. 296

chunking, p. 273

consolidation, p. 281

effortful processing, p. 279

encoding, p. 278

episodic memory, p. 278

explicit memory, p. 278

false memories, p. 298

flashbulb memories, 290

forgetting, p. 294

forgetting curve, p. 295

hierarchies, p. 282

implicit memory, p. 277

interference, p. 294

levels of processing, p. 279

long-term memory, p. 272

long-term potentiation, p. 291

memory, p. 270

mnemonic device, p. 280

prefrontal cortex, p. 285

priming, p. 277

proactive interference, p. 295

procedural memory, p. 277

recovered memory, p. 298

rehearsal, p. 275

repression, p. 296

retrieval, p. 283

retroactive interference, p. 294

retrograde amnesia, p. 299

schemas, p. 282

semantic memory, p. 278

sensory memory, p. 270

serial position effect, p. 275

short-term memory, p. 270

storage, p. 282

suggestibility, p. 297

three-stage model of memory, p. 270

working memory, p. 272

Quick Quiz **Answers**

Quick Quiz 7.1: 1. b 2. d 3. a 4. c 5. a
Quick Quiz 7.2: 1. b 2. c 3. d 4. a 5. b
Quick Quiz 7.3: 1. c 2. d 3. d 4. a
Quick Quiz 7.4: 1. c 2. d 3. d

Challenge Your Assumptions **Answers**

- No one can remember every single day of his or her adult life. **False. See p. 268.**
- Emotional memories are easier to recall than nonemotional memories. **True. See p. 288.**
- We can know things we don't remember. **True. See p. 271.**
- Eyewitness memories are usually accurate. **False. See p. 297.**

Learning

Chapter Outline

Challenge *Your Assumptions*

TRUE OR FALSE?

- Elephants can learn to paint paintings.
- Humans and lab rats basically learn in the same way.
- Pulling an all-nighter is a good way to study for an exam.
- Children are not affected by watching violent cartoons or movies.

Answers can be found at the end of the chapter.

In a remote area of Thailand you will find an elephant preserve, inside of which a most curious thing is occurring: Elephants are painting. They hold brushes in their trunks and carefully paint pictures—mostly portraits of other elephants in various poses. As you can see, some of the paintings are quite lovely, almost like Chinese brushwork. If you Google "painting elephants," you'll find many videos of elephants engaged in these artistic activities.

Drawing by a Thai elephant.

Obviously, elephants don't come by painting naturally. How do they *learn* to paint? Like most of human learning, elephant learning is a combination of physical attributes, intelligence, ability, and training (Komar & Melamid, 2000). First of all, elephants are quite intelligent, and second they have a trunk that is both very strong and capable of refined movement. The muscles at the tip of the trunk allow them to easily hold a paintbrush. Just as with humans, not all elephants take to painting. To find out which elephants might be able to paint, trainers use a screening process to determine which ones have both interest and ability. Trainers use rewards (food) at each step to teach the elephants to hold the brush and to be at the correct distance from the easel. Then the elephants learn to make specific strokes on the canvas and finally to shape specific objects, such as flowers or elephants, as you see here. Each step along this training process is accomplished by the relationship between the behavior (such as making a stroke) and some reward for it. Behaviors that are not desired (such as flicking the paint all over the canvas) are not rewarded.

In short, elephants learn to paint in very much the same way that humans learn certain new skills. Learning is not a simple process, as we will see in this chapter. We examine the three major theories of learning—classical conditioning, operant conditioning, and social learning theory. We also explore the role of evolution in learning and how learning both emerges from and changes the brain. ∎

BASIC PROCESSES OF LEARNING

learning
enduring changes in behavior that occur with experience.

Psychologists define **learning** as enduring changes in behavior that occur with experience. This definition sounds simple, but there are many forms of learning—from an elephant learning to paint to a child developing a preference for certain foods to a student learning a foreign language. As we try things out in the world, changes in sensation, perception, behavior, and brain function alter who we are, what we know, what we feel, and what we can do. The essence of learning involves acquiring new knowledge, skills, values, or behaviors.

Learning and memory work together. Without learning and memory, we could not process, retain, or make use of new information. Learning occurs when information moves from short-term to long-term memory. During this process, new knowledge is stored in networks in the brain. For this reason, we don't have to learn to ride a bicycle every time we want to go for a spin. Once we have mastered the skill of riding a bicycle, that knowledge can be retrieved from memory, and we can pedal away without thinking about it.

Habituation and the Orienting Response

Some phenomena fit the definition of learning as "enduring changes in behavior that occur with experience" much more clearly than others. For example, if a dim light were presented to you in a dark room, you would look at it immediately. This automatic shift of attention toward a new stimulus is known as the *orienting response*. After a while, if the brightness and location of the light remained the same, you would no longer respond to it. In fact, you might not notice it at all. This phenomenon, called *habituation,* is a sensory process by which organisms adapt to constant stimulation. The result is a change in your response (from seeing a spot of light to not seeing it) stemming from experience. The change is a fairly short-lived one, however. As soon as the stimulus is varied even slightly, the orienting response occurs, and the process begins again.

Habituation is a change in behavior due to experience, but is it learning? An argument can be made that neither habituation nor the orienting response fits our definition of learning, because each disappears immediately with a slight change in the stimulus. Still, habituation is often regarded as learning in its simplest form (Carew & Kandel, 1973).

Connection

Right now you are habituated to dozens of stimuli—including the feel of clothing on your skin. Now you are sensitized to it. How so?
See "The Long Strange Trip From Sensation to Perception," Chapter 4, "Sensing and Perceiving Our World," p. 124.

Association

Every time we feed our cats, Scooter and Belle, we first take the can opener out of the drawer in the kitchen. Ever since they were kittens, Scooter and Belle have heard the sound of someone opening a drawer at feeding time. So the sound of the drawer opening has signaled to them that food was coming. Now, every time anyone opens a kitchen drawer, the kitties come running while meowing eagerly. Frequently it is a false alarm (sometimes the drawer is opened for other reasons), but the connection, or association, between the sound of a drawer opening and being fed is very strong for them.

An **association** occurs when one piece of information from the environment is linked repeatedly with another and the organism begins to connect the two sources of information. Associations form simply as a result of two events occurring together, whether or not the relationship between them makes any sense. Eventually, the repeated association results in the events becoming linked in the individual's memory. By virtue of their association, one event may come to suggest that the other will occur. Learning by association is a simple but powerful form of learning.

association
process by which two pieces of information from the environment are repeatedly linked so that we begin to connect them in our minds.

Scooter and Belle—the authors' cats.

conditioning
a form of associative learning in which behaviors are triggered by associations with events in the environment.

CONDITIONING MODELS OF LEARNING

Conditioning is a form of associative learning in which a behavior becomes more likely because the organism links that behavior with certain events in its environment. Scooter and Belle, for example, are *conditioned* to the sound of the drawer opening because they have come to associate the sound with food. Sometimes the sound means that food will come; sometimes it does not. But the association is strong because feeding is always preceded by the sound of a drawer opening.

Psychologists distinguish between two types of conditioning: classical and operant. Both are forms of associative learning. In classical conditioning, organisms learn from the relations between stimuli. In operant conditioning, organisms learn from the consequences of their behavior. Let's look at these two forms of learning in more detail.

Classical Conditioning

In **classical conditioning,** learning occurs when a neutral stimulus becomes associated with a stimulus to which the learner has an automatic, inborn response. Exactly how this works will become clearer if we consider the pioneering example of Ivan Pavlov and his dogs.

classical conditioning form of associative learning in which a neutral stimulus becomes associated with a stimulus to which one has an automatic, inborn response.

Pavlov's Dogs   Ivan Pavlov received the Nobel Prize in Medicine in 1904 for his research on saliva and digestion. While he was studying digestion in dogs, Pavlov (1906, 1928) discovered classical conditioning quite accidentally—a famous example of how scientists looking at one thing inadvertently discover another. As often happens, luck, keen observation, and serendipity (making important discoveries by accident) led to this important scientific discovery.

In order to examine digestive enzymes in the dogs' saliva, Pavlov and his technicians placed tubes in their mouths to collect their saliva. Then they placed meat powder in their mouths, which naturally produces salivation. After doing this for a while, Pavlov noticed that the dogs would begin to salivate even before the meat powder was presented, when the laboratory technician who fed them prepared the apparatus to collect their saliva. It was as though the sounds of the technician manipulating the apparatus signaled to the dogs that meat powder was about to come (Fancher, 1996). Pavlov guessed that the dogs had formed an association between the sounds of the apparatus and the meat powder, just as our cats formed an association between the sounds of a drawer opening and being fed.

Pavlov reasoned that the dogs had formed an association between a stimulus that had no inherent food value (the sound of the apparatus) and one that did (the meat powder). Could he teach a dog to salivate to something else? He designed a laboratory experiment that mimicked the conditions in which the dogs salivated to sounds made by the technician. Working with different dogs, Pavlov presented a neutral stimulus (a bell sound) just before showing them the meat powder. The dogs

Pavlov and his dogs.

had no previous experience with the bell, but they salivated to the meat powder, because dogs always salivate to meat powder, from the first time they smell it. Salivation is a reflex, an automatic response to a particular stimulus (food) that requires no learning.

Pavlov presented the bell along with the meat powder to the dogs over and over again. The dogs salivated. Then he tried presenting the bell alone to see if the dogs might now link the bell with the meat powder in the way the first dogs linked the noise of the apparatus with the meat powder. Bingo! The dogs salivated to the bell alone. By virtue of the association made during repeated pairings with meat powder, the nonappetizing bell had come to signal "meat powder" to the dogs. The dogs had learned that they would get meat powder after the bell sounded.

How Classical Conditioning Works

Pavlov called the kind of learning he'd observed the *conditioning of reflexes*, and we now call it *classical conditioning*. He coined the term **unconditioned response (UCR)** to describe the automatic, inborn response to a stimulus. In this case, salivation is the UCR. *Unconditioned* simply means "unlearned." Pavlov used the term **unconditioned stimulus (UCS)** to refer to the environmental input (meat powder) that always produced the same unlearned response (salivation). Without learning, the UCS always produces the UCR; in Pavlov's experiment, meat powder—the UCS—always leads to salivation—the UCR.

Food makes you salivate, pressure on your eye makes you blink, and a tap just below your kneecap will cause your leg to jerk forth. These reflexes are unlearned, fixed responses to specific types of environmental stimuli. Pavlov defined reflexes, such as salivation in response to food, as fixed stimulus–response patterns. Classical conditioning is the modification of these stimulus–response (S–R) relationships with experience. Pavlov presented the neutral stimulus (bell) right before the UCS (meat powder). Salivation in the presence of meat powder was the UCR.

After repeated pairings of the bell with meat powder, when the bell alone led to salivation, the bell would be called a conditioned stimulus. A **conditioned stimulus (CS)** is a previously neutral stimulus that an organism learns to associate with the UCS. If salivation occurred in response to the CS (as it did in Pavlov's experiment), it would then be called a conditioned response. A **conditioned response (CR)** is a behavior that an organism learns to perform when presented with the CS alone. Figure 8.1 shows how classical conditioning works.

Notice that Figure 8.1 shows the neutral stimulus being presented just before the UCS. This process is known as *forward conditioning*. One can also present the neutral stimulus and the UCS simultaneously. When the neutral stimulus follows the UCS, a process called *backward conditioning*, conditioning is less successful. An example of backward conditioning would be sounding the bell after presenting the food to Pavlov's dogs. Based on repeated, painstakingly careful experimentation, Pavlov laid out certain criteria for stimulus–response conditioning to succeed (Pavlov, 1906, 1928). Two of the most fundamental criteria are as follows:

1. Multiple pairings of UCS and neutral stimulus (CS) are necessary for an association to occur and for the CS to produce the conditioned response.

2. The UCS and CS must be paired or presented very close together in time in order for an association to form.

unconditioned response (UCR) the natural automatic, inborn reaction to a stimulus.

unconditioned stimulus (UCS) the environmental input that always produces the same unlearned response.

conditioned stimulus (CS) a previously neutral input that an organism learns to associate with the UCS.

conditioned response (CR) a behavior that an organism learns to perform when presented with the CS.

Nature & **N**urture

Through classical conditioning, innate responses—like salivation—can become associated with and changed by almost any experience.

When a behavior has been conditioned to occur in the presence of a given stimulus (such as when Scooter and Belle meow because they hear the kitchen drawer opening), it may also increase in the presence of similar stimuli. The cats come running to the kitchen not only when they hear the kitchen drawer opening, but also when they hear us open a cabinet or make almost any sound related to food preparation. This phenomenon, known as **stimulus generalization,** is the extension of the association between UCS and CS to a broad array of similar stimuli. The opposite of stimulus generalization is **stimulus discrimination,** which occurs when a CR (such as salivation) occurs only to the exact stimulus to which it was conditioned. For example, if Pavlov's dogs did not salivate to a buzzer but only to a bell, they would discriminate the conditioned stimulus (bell) from other stimuli (buzzers, clicks, and so on).

Can a conditioned response be unlearned? Would you expect Pavlov's dogs to continue salivating indefinitely in response to the bell alone? It turns out that the dogs gradually stopped salivating to the bell (CS) once they learned that the bell wasn't accompanied by meat powder (UCS). This weakening and disappearance of a conditioned response is called **extinction,** and it occurs when the UCS is no longer paired with the CS. It can be difficult to extinguish behaviors. Sometimes it takes 100 or more presentations of a CS without the UCS to achieve extinction, and still the behavior might return. For example, consider the case of a young man who had a bad experience with a bee sting when he was 4 years old. Thereafter, he had an extreme reaction to the sight of bees. Psychologists can treat this kind of abnormal fear reaction using extinction. Exposing the man repeatedly to bees in situations in which he does not get stung helps him learn that they will not always sting. This experience reduces the extreme fear reaction he has to bees (see Figures 8.2 and 8.3).

The sudden reappearance of an extinguished response is known as **spontaneous recovery** (see Figure 8.3). One real example of spontaneous recovery comes from a colleague who was involved in a car accident. His car was sideswiped as he was making a blind turn from a campus parking lot. After the accident, he would have a panic attack whenever he passed that parking lot, and so he couldn't park there. Several months later the attacks stopped, and he started parking in the lot again.

stimulus discrimination restriction of a CR (such as salivation) to only the exact CS to which it was conditioned.

stimulus generalization extension of the association between UCS and CS to include a broad array of similar stimuli.

extinction the weakening and disappearance of a conditioned response in the absence of reinforcement.

spontaneous recovery the sudden reappearance of an extinguished response.

before conditioning

UCS

UCR

Neutral stimulus

No response

during conditioning

Neutral stimulus   then   UCS

UCR

Then, one day as he approached the parking lot, he had an unexpected panic attack. A learned response he thought had been extinguished suddenly came back. It is clear from recent research on spontaneous recovery that extinction never completely eliminates the response, only suppresses it (Moody, Sunsay, & Bouton, 2006). After the response has been extinguished, it is quite common for the response to reappear spontaneously if a person returns to the original setting where the conditioning took place.

Why does classical conditioning—the ability to associate innate stimulus–response patterns with novel stimuli—work? It may be adaptive in an evolutionary sense. We need to be able to associate certain types of stimuli with potential harm and to respond quickly to new stimuli that present threats. For instance, we might not be hardwired to see long, sharp metal objects as dangerous; but once we see that pressing one of them against the skin causes bleeding, then we know it is dangerous. Most animals can learn such things readily, and it helps them survive and reproduce. It is by virtue of experience and association that many objects acquire their meaning for us. That knives are dangerous is something we learn. The fact that classical conditioning is a powerful learning device for nearly all creatures suggests that it has advantages for survival.

The Conditioning of Little Albert

Pavlov's work caught the attention of young psychologists in the United States in the early 20th century. They saw in Pavlov's research the first systematic account of a scientific procedure for studying behavior. One American psychologist, John Watson, felt strongly that classical conditioning could be used to shape human behavior:

> Give me a dozen healthy infants, well-formed, and my own specified world to bring them up in and I'll guarantee to take any one at random and train him to become any type of specialist I might select—doctor, lawyer, artist, merchant-chief, and yes, even beggar-man and thief, regardless of his talents, penchants, tendencies, abilities, vocations, and race of his ancestors. (J. B. Watson, 1925, p. 82)

Watson's complete faith in the ability to mold human behavior seems naïve today, and some would even call it dangerous. Yet Watson and his view of the infant as a blank slate helped push psychology—which Watson defined as "the study of behavior"—forward as a science. To Watson, classical conditioning offered a model for transforming the field.

In a classic study of the power of conditioning techniques, Watson conditioned a baby known as Little Albert to fear white rats and other white fluffy objects. When Watson and his colleague Rosalie Rayner first met Albert, they

after conditioning

CS

CR

FIGURE **8.1**

CLASSICAL CONDITIONING. A dog's natural reflex is to salivate to food. The food is an unconditioned stimulus (UCS), and salivation is an unconditioned response (UCR). Before conditioning, a dog will not salivate when a bell rings. During conditioning, the bell is presented right before the food appears. The dog salivates (UCR) because of the food (UCS). After repeatedly hearing the ringing bell right before being presented with the food, the dog will begin to salivate. Now the ringing bell has become a conditioned stimulus (CS), and salivation to the sound of the bell alone has become a conditioned response (CR).

FIGURE **8.2**

CLASSICAL CONDITIONING IN THE REAL WORLD. A person who suffered a painful bee sting continues to fear all bees for a long time. After enough exposure to bees without being stung, however, the person can learn to not react with fear. At this point, the conditioned response (fear) is extinguished.

Unconditioned stimulus: bee sting

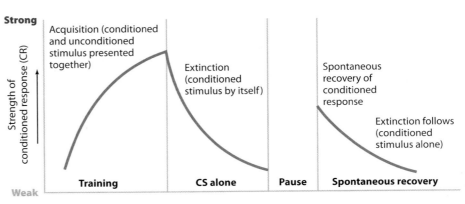

brought out a white rat and showed it to Albert. He was curious, but not afraid of it. Then Watson and Rayner (1920) paired the presentation of the rat with a very loud noise (the sound of a hammer striking a steel bar right behind Albert's head). Naturally, the loud sound (a UCS) startled Albert (the UCR), and he got very upset.

After repeated pairings of the loud sound with the rat, seeing the rat alone (the CS) upset Albert. Upon further testing, Albert's fear grew to include an intense emotional response not only to white rats but also to many other white, fluffy items, including John Watson's fake white beard. This is an example of stimulus generalization.

Regrettably, Little Albert did not undergo deconditioning (J. B. Watson & Rayner, 1920). Controversy surrounded this case for years, and it is still not clear what happened to Little Albert. We see in this case that psychology in its infancy lacked clear ethical guidelines for research. Watson's "experiment" raised many ethical issues, particularly about the need to safeguard the rights of individuals who cannot give informed consent to participate in research. Still, Watson is remembered as the father of behaviorism for his role in establishing psychology as the study of behavior.

Little Albert with Rosalie Rayner and John B. Watson.

Connection

The ethics of human research today would not allow Watson to do his research on Little Albert.

See "Ethical Research With Humans," Chapter 2, "Conducting Research in Psychology," p. 67.

Operant Conditioning

Unlike Little Albert's fear of white rats and other reactions that people can elicit from others, some behaviors occur spontaneously. In the late 19th century, Edward L. Thorndike (1905) noted that rewarding consequences can make a

FIGURE **8.3**

ACQUISITION, EXTINCTION, AND SPONTANEOUS RECOVERY IN CLASSICAL CONDITIONING. The graph shows how a conditioned response (CR) gradually becomes stronger during conditioning, then weakens when the conditioned stimulus (CS) is no longer paired with the UCS, and disappears (extinction). Following a pause during which the CS is not presented, spontaneous recovery of the CR may occur briefly before it is extinguished again.

Strong

Strength of conditioned response (CR)

Acquisition (conditioned and unconditioned stimulus presented together)

Extinction (conditioned stimulus by itself)

Spontaneous recovery of conditioned response

Extinction follows (conditioned stimulus alone)

Weak

Training   **CS alone**   **Pause**   **Spontaneous recovery**

Unconditioned response: pain, which can lead to fear

2

Conditioned response: fear of bees

3

Extinction: repeated exposure to bees without getting stung may reduce fear of bees.

4

spontaneous behavior more likely to occur again. He found, for example, that a cat would escape from a specially designed cage if left to its own devices for a while, not necessarily because it figured out how to get out, but because certain motions eventually were rewarded by the door opening (see Figure 8.4). This reward made it more likely that the specific behavior that led to the door opening would happen again if the cat were again confined in the same cage. In the same way, you might come back to a café you casually walked into if you found out that it had free wireless Internet service and gave out tasty samples of its pastries. Thorndike labeled this principle the **law of effect.** Briefly, the law of effect

law of effect
the consequences of a behavior increase (or decrease) the likelihood that the behavior will be repeated.

FIGURE **8.4**

THE LEARNING CURVE. Depicted here is the box from which Thorndike's cats learned to escape. Thorndike found that a cat would escape from a specially designed cage if left to its own devices for a while, not necessarily because it figured out how to get out, but because certain motions eventually were rewarded by the door's opening. This reward of the opening door made it more likely that the specific behavior that led to the opening door would happen again if the cat were again confined in the same cage. The graph shows the amount of time it would take the cat to escape. Initially, it took more than two minutes, but after just a few trials, the cat could consistently escape in about 10 seconds.

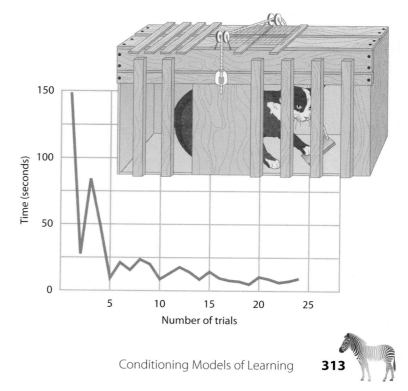

means that the consequences of a behavior increase (or decrease) the likelihood that the behavior will be repeated.

Like Thorndike, B. F. Skinner viewed the consequences of an individual's actions as the most important determinants of behavior (Skinner, 1938, 1953). Skinner set out to explain the environmental factors that led Thorndike's cat to learn to open the cage (or you to return to the Internet café). Skinner wanted to know how disorganized, spontaneous behavior becomes organized. And exactly what role do the consequences of an action play in the organization of the response? Figure 8.5 shows how consequences may increase behavior in real-life examples.

B. F. Skinner

Skinner (1938) coined the term *operant* to refer to behavior that acts—or operates—on the environment to produce specific consequences. **Operant conditioning** is the process of modifying behavior by manipulating the consequences of that behavior. According to Skinner, a behavior that is rewarded is more likely to occur again. For example, if a hungry animal does something that is followed by the presentation of food, then the animal is more likely to repeat the behavior that preceded the food presentation. If a café gives you free wireless access, you might come back. In contrast to classical conditioning, which modifies an involuntary behavior (such as salivation), operant conditioning works when voluntary behavior is made more likely by its consequences.

operant conditioning the process of changing behavior by manipulating the consequences of that behavior.

FIGURE **8.5**

THREE EXAMPLES OF HOW CONSEQUENCES CAN INCREASE OR REINFORCE BEHAVIOR.

Reinforcement and Punishment When the consequences of a behavior increase the likelihood that a behavior will occur again, the behavior is reinforced, or strengthened. A **reinforcer** is any internal or external event that increases a behavior. When a baby sees he can get a big smile from his mother when he smiles at her, he is likely to smile more often (Adamson & Bakeman, 1985). The mother's smile in response to the infant's is a reinforcer that increases the frequency of smiling by the baby, because parental smiles are inherently rewarding to babies. This is a key point. Reinforcers have to be things that the learner wants in order for them to influence the likelihood that a behavior will occur again. For example, you will continue getting paid on a regular basis if you do your job. You want the money, so you keep working hard. But if your employer gave you paper clips for your hard work, you'd quit. Similarly, if your credit card company suddenly offered iTunes credits for using your card, you might use it more often. This last case shows how corporations apply principles of operant conditioning to make a profit. All of these examples differ from classical conditioning in which two things become linked because they occur together, whether or not they are inherently rewarding.

With operant conditioning, Skinner developed a programmatic approach to using schedules of reinforcement for modifying behavior. This basic system has been applied widely with much success in education, animal training, and numerous behavioral treatments for everything from weight loss and smoking cessation to the treatment of autism in children.

> **reinforcer**
> an internal or external event that increases the frequency of a behavior.

Research to Real Life

You might want to use reinforcement to change something in your life. The following guidelines could be helpful.

Connecting Psychology to Your Life: Pick an activity such as losing weight, learning an instrument, or beginning a workout regimen. It's up to you. Set aside 15 minutes a day to start working on it. Then implement these steps:

1. Pick a target amount of time that you would like to work up to (say, 30 minutes).

2. Try to shape the goal by reinforcing yourself for a smaller increment of time (say, 10 minutes). That is, the first time you spend at least 10 minutes at your activity, give yourself some reinforcement (see below about choosing a reinforcement).

3. After doing this for a while (say, a week or two), require 15 and then 20 minutes, and so on, with progressively longer chunks of time before rewarding yourself with the reinforcement.

Choose a reinforcer that is pleasing to you but not excessive—such as rewarding yourself with a refreshing beverage or talking with a friend. Of course, you will also have the added reinforcement of noticing you are getting better at the skill, and that will drive you along. With a bit of work and reinforcement, you will have learned a new skill.

> **primary reinforcers**
> innate, unlearned reinforcers that satisfy biological needs (such as food, water, or sex).
>
> **secondary (or conditioned) reinforcers**
> reinforcers that are learned by association, usually via classical conditioning (such as money, grades, and peer approval).

There are two kinds of reinforcers: primary and secondary. **Primary reinforcers** are not learned. They are innate and often satisfy biological needs. Food, water, sex, and even artificial sweeteners with no food value are primary reinforcers (Vaughan, 2009). **Secondary (or conditioned) reinforcers** are learned by association, usually via classical conditioning. Money, grades, and peer approval are secondary reinforcers. A potential reinforcer may acquire pleasant characteristics if it is associated with something that is inherently reinforcing (such as food or sex). Advertisers regularly take advantage of this fact. Consider ads for sports cars, for instance. If a sports car is always shown in commercials or photo advertisements with attractive individuals, then it becomes linked in memory with something that is inherently desirable. The car itself becomes a secondary reinforcer due to its association with sex.

Reinforcement can be positive or negative—not in terms of being good or bad, but in terms of whether a stimulus is added to a situation (positive) or taken away (negative). **Positive reinforcement** occurs when the presentation or addition of a stimulus to a situation increases the likelihood of a behavior. Giving extra credit points for turning in homework on time would be positive reinforcement if it led to students submitting their assignments on time. We use the term **negative reinforcement** to refer to the removal of a stimulus to *increase* behavior. Frequently, the stimulus removed is something unpleasant. As an example, consider the beeper that sounds in your car until you fasten your seat belt. Those beepers are designed to be annoying, and fastening the seat belt stops the beeping noise. So in this case, the *removal* of the beeping is negative reinforcement for fastening the seat belt.

Is the distinction between positive and negative reinforcement important? Some behavioral psychologists have argued that it is unnecessary and, at times, difficult to make (Baron & Galizo, 2006; Michael, 1975). Here is an illustration of how this distinction can be confusing. Let's say you drink coffee to wake up. From one perspective, the wakefulness induced by the caffeine is positive reinforcement for drinking coffee. But are you really increasing wakefulness or decreasing fatigue (which would be negative reinforcement for drinking coffee)? Either way, the consequence for behavior is the same—you drink more coffee.

Negative reinforcement is often confused with **punishment,** which is any stimulus that *decreases* the frequency of a behavior. Like reinforcement, punishment can be positive or negative. Remember, however, that punishers *decrease* the frequency of behavior. By definition, negative reinforcers *increase* desired behaviors, and so they cannot be punishers.

Typically, when most people think of punishment, they think of **positive punishment,** the addition of a stimulus that decreases behavior. A classic example of a positive punisher is spanking. Spanking a child (adding a stimulus) is positive punishment if it decreases the undesirable behavior. Similarly, if you are fined for parking in the faculty lot and stop parking there, you have received positive punishment. **Negative punishment** decreases behavior by removing a stimulus, usually a desirable stimulus.

positive reinforcement
the presentation or addition of a stimulus after a behavior occurs that increases how often that behavior will occur.

negative reinforcement
removal of a stimulus after a behavior to increase the frequency of that behavior.

punishment
stimulus that decreases the frequency of a behavior.

positive punishment
the addition of a stimulus that decreases behavior.

negative punishment
the removal of a stimulus to decrease behavior.

A smile is inherently rewarding for babies. According to the principles of operant conditioning, the more often the baby is rewarded with a smile for smiling at mom, the more likely he will continue to smile at her.

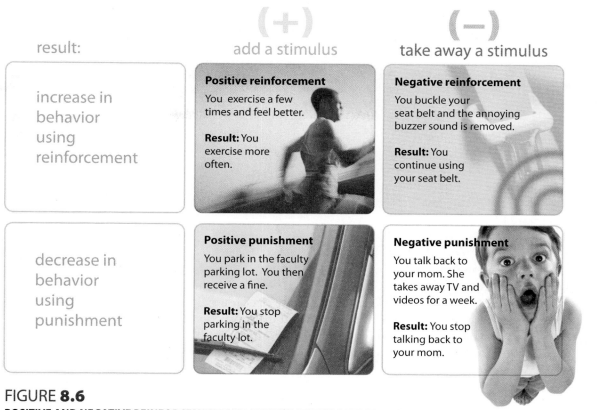

result:	(+) add a stimulus	(−) take away a stimulus
increase in behavior using reinforcement	**Positive reinforcement** You exercise a few times and feel better. **Result:** You exercise more often.	**Negative reinforcement** You buckle your seat belt and the annoying buzzer sound is removed. **Result:** You continue using your seat belt.
decrease in behavior using punishment	**Positive punishment** You park in the faculty parking lot. You then receive a fine. **Result:** You stop parking in the faculty lot.	**Negative punishment** You talk back to your mom. She takes away TV and videos for a week. **Result:** You stop talking back to your mom.

FIGURE 8.6

POSITIVE AND NEGATIVE REINFORCEMENT AND PUNISHMENT IN OPERANT CONDITIONING. It is the actual result, *not* the intended result, that matters. For example, if an intended punisher does not decrease the behavior, it is not a punishment.

For example, revoking a child's TV-watching privileges for repeatedly hitting a sibling is a form of negative punishment if it stops the hitting. Figure 8.6 summarizes positive and negative forms of punishment and reinforcement.

Skinner emphasized that reinforcement is a much more effective way of modifying behavior than is punishment (Skinner, 1953). Specifically, using reinforcement to increase desirable behaviors works better than using punishment in an attempt to decrease undesirable behaviors. Let's say a girl hit her brother because he took away her toy. Instead of punishing the girl for hitting her brother, the parents could reinforce more desirable behaviors for dealing with the stolen toy—such as the girl's telling her brother that it upset her that he took the toy and suggesting that if he would please give it back, they could share it for a while. When the little girl acts in this preferable way, the parents could commend her, perhaps give her special privileges (like more play time). This, in turn, would increase the likelihood of the girl's using something more appropriate than physical retaliation to deal with theft. Punishment, as it focuses on decreasing or eliminating behaviors, doesn't tell kids what they should be doing, only what they shouldn't be doing. Reinforcement offers them an alternative.

How Operant Conditioning Works

In classical conditioning, organisms learn about the relationships between stimuli; in operant conditioning, organisms learn from the consequences of their behavior. The basic idea behind operant conditioning is that any behavior that is reinforced becomes strengthened and is more likely to occur in the future. Behaviors are reinforced because they are instrumental in obtaining particular results.

FIGURE **8.7**

THE SKINNER BOX. This modern Skinner box provides a small space in which the rat can move and a lever to press that delivers food as a reinforcer. A small region of the floor can be set up to deliver a shock as a punisher. The rats learn through punishment to avoid that region of the floor.

Labels: Speaker; Signal lights; To food dispenser; Lever; Food pellet; Electric grid; To shock generator

Substance use and abuse can be learned through operant conditioning. When people try a substance such as alcohol or nicotine for the first time and it makes them feel elated (a positive reinforcer) or removes their fears (a negative reinforcer), they will be more likely to use that drug again in the future. The problem with many drugs (especially alcohol and nicotine) is that the body adjusts to their presence, and more and more of the drug is required to get the desired effect. When increasing amounts of the drug are required to obtain reinforcement—to get "high"—then the behavior of taking the drug increases even more. This is one reason why drug addictions are so powerful and hard to overcome.

To test his conditioning principles, Skinner created the **Skinner box,** a simple chamber in which a small animal can move around, with a food dispenser and a response lever to trigger food delivery (see Figure 8.7). The Skinner box has been modified in recent years to allow for computer collection of responses, but many laboratories still use chambers very similar to Skinner's original device.

How exactly does someone do operant conditioning? How can you get a rat to press a lever? Rats have no inherent interest in lever pressing. You might give the rat a food pellet for pressing the lever, but how do you get the animal to press the lever in the first place?

Skinner trained a rat to perform a desired behavior (such as lever pressing) by reinforcing behaviors that occurred when the rat came closer and closer to pressing the lever. If you put a rat in a Skinner box, sooner or later—as a function of its random movements—it will come closer to the lever. When it does, you reinforce that behavior by giving it some food.

Eventually the rat makes an association between getting closer to a particular region of the chamber and food appearing. More specifically, the rat learns that the appearance of food seems to be contingent on getting over to that region of the chamber. The researcher then increases the requirements for food presentation. Now brushing up against the lever will be reinforced with a food pellet. Finally, the rat has to press the lever to get the food.

Gradually reinforcing behaviors that come closer and closer to the target behavior will eventually produce the target behavior. The reinforcement of successive approximations of a desired behavior is called **shaping.** Shaping behavior is a bit like shaping clay, for the idea really is that an organism can be molded to do things that it typically wouldn't do. Professional trainers rely on shaping to get animals to perform tricks or to be guide dogs to assist people with disabilities.

Does shaping work with humans? Let's say you're trying to teach your friend how to drive a car with a stick shift. The first time he tries, even if he makes a

Skinner box
simple chamber used for operant conditioning of small animals.

shaping
the reinforcement of successive approximations of a desired behavior.

few mistakes and stalls a few times, you might give him lots of encouragement and praise. Later, when you're trying to get him to master changing gears smoothly, you give praise only when each movement is done correctly. You are reinforcing successive approximations of the desired behavior, and as your student gets closer and closer to the desired behavior, the criteria for reinforcement become more stringent. By the 15th attempt, bucking forward a few feet before stalling gets no praise.

Through shaping and reinforcement, pigeons can learn to discriminate colors.

In operant conditioning, extinction occurs when a behavior stops being reinforced. So if a rat presses the lever and repeatedly gets no food, the lever-pressing behavior will decrease and eventually disappear. If you keep leaving phone messages for someone you want to ask on a date, but he or she never returns your calls, eventually you will stop calling. The phone calling behavior has been extinguished. Figure 8.8 compares classical and operant conditioning.

Applications of Operant Conditioning

Operant conditioning also offers a powerful method for modifying behavior in the treatment of several disorders in humans, such as phobias (severe, specific fears), nicotine addiction, and learning disabilities (Anthonisen et al., 2005; Lamb et al., 2004; Lovaas, 1987). Treatment programs based on operant methods effectively reduce self-harming behaviors in adults with intellectual deficiencies (Chowdhury & Benson, 2011) and in suicidal teens with borderline personality disorder (Klein & Miller, 2011).

One important application of operant conditioning is in the treatment of autism (Beadle-Brown, Murphy, & Wing, 2006; Lovaas, 1987; Soorya, Carpenter, & Romanczyk, 2011). Applied behavioral analysis (ABA), developed by Ivar Lovaas at UCLA, uses reinforcement to increase the frequency of adaptive behaviors in autistic children and, in some cases, punishment to decrease the likelihood of maladaptive behaviors. The intensive program involves ignoring harmful or undesirable behaviors such as hand flapping, twirling, or licking objects, as well as aggressive behaviors. It also involves reinforcing desirable behaviors, such as contact with others and appropriate toy play. ABA appears to be quite effective in reducing many harmful and aggressive behaviors in young autistic children, though it appears to be a bit less effective in improving the socioemotional deficits of autism (Beadle-Brown et al., 2006).

Schedules of Reinforcement

Reinforcers can be arranged (or scheduled) to follow behavior under a variety of conditions or rules that can be termed *schedules of reinforcement*. Although schedules of reinforcement are a powerful tool in the laboratory, it is sometimes difficult to describe complex human behavior in terms of simple reinforcement schedules. Nonetheless, there are some parallels.

Reinforcers may be presented every time a behavior occurs or only occasionally. **Continuous reinforcement** means rewarding a behavior every time it occurs. Giving a dog a biscuit every time it jumps is continuous reinforcement. **Intermittent reinforcement** does not occur after every response.

Intermittent reinforcement produces a stronger behavioral response than continuous reinforcement does. Why? The explanation has to do with memory and expectation. If an animal gets a food pellet every time it hits the lever, it will

continuous reinforcement reinforcement of a behavior every time it occurs.

intermittent reinforcement reinforcement of a behavior—but not after every response.

Conditioning Models of Learning   **319**

	Classical conditioning	**Operant conditioning**
basic principle	Learning to associate a conditioned stimulus (CS) and a conditioned response (CR).	Reinforcement increases the frequency of a behavior. Punishment decreases the frequency of a behavior.
nature of behavior	The behavior is based on an organism's involuntary behavior: its reflexes. The behavior is elicited by the unconditioned stimulus (UCS) or conditioned stimulus (CS).	The behavior is based on an organism's voluntary action. The consequence of the behavior creates the likelihood of its increasing or decreasing the behavior.
order of events	Before conditioning occurs, a UCS leads to a UCR. After conditioning, a CS leads to a CR.	Reinforcement leads to an increase in behavior. Punishment leads to a decrease in behavior.
example	A bee stings a boy (UCS). The boy feels pain (UCR) from the sting. He then develops a strong fear (CR) when he sees bees (CS).	Buckling a seat belt removes the annoying buzzer, so you're more likely to buckle the seat belt again. **Negative reinforcement** A child who misbehaves and loses TV and video for a week is less likely to repeat that behavior again. **Negative punishment**

FIGURE 8.8
DIFFERENCES BETWEEN CLASSICAL AND OPERANT CONDITIONING.

remember and expect that food will appear each time it presses the lever. But if it sometimes receives food after one lever press and other times it takes 5 or 10 presses, the animal will not learn a predictable pattern. It will keep responding as fast as possible in hope that eventually it will receive food, because it is not sure when food will come.

It is well documented that intermittent reinforcement produces stronger responses— in terms of both rate of responding and resistance to extinction— than does continuous reinforcement (Ferster & Skinner, 1957). Think about your own behavior: How often do you check e-mail each day? Maybe you check it several times a day. Some people are essentially "addicted" to e-mail and check

FIGURE 8.9

SCHEDULES OF REINFORCEMENT. Workers who are paid for the number of units produced are reinforced on a fixed ratio schedule. Winnings from playing slot machines vary in amount and in the interval between payoffs (variable ratio). An example of fixed interval reinforcement would be going to class right before a scheduled exam and not attending lecture after taking an exam. Continuing to redial a friend who doesn't respond to "call waiting" until you get an answer illustrates a variable interval reinforcement schedule, because the number of times you have to redial varies over time.

it dozens of times a day. This behavior is very easy to explain in terms of operant conditioning. Occasionally a very important or interesting (reinforcing) e-mail arrives. But we don't know when the next one will come (intermittent), so we check and we check, each time hoping for that important e-mail. This behavior is shaped by intermittent reinforcement.

Skinner identified four patterns of intermittent reinforcement, which he called **schedules of reinforcement** (see Figure 8.9). These schedules can be distinguished on the basis of whether reinforcement occurs after a set number of responses or after a certain amount of time has passed since the last reinforcement.

In a **fixed ratio (FR) schedule,** reinforcement follows a set number of responses. The pattern becomes predictable, and so the response rate is not steady. Typically, there will be a pause in response immediately after reinforcement occurs, and then the response rate will increase. The FR schedule produces a steep, stepwise pattern of response, as shown in Figure 8.10. An example is being paid by the number of units a worker produces, whether the units are pajama sets or pizzas delivered. A worker whose wages or tips depend on the number produced will work faster, possibly risking injury, to make more money.

schedules of reinforcement
patterns of intermittent reinforcement distinguished by whether reinforcement occurs after a set number of responses or after a certain amount of time has passed since the last reinforcement.

fixed ratio (FR) schedule
pattern of intermittent reinforcement in which reinforcement follows a set number of responses.

FIGURE 8.10

EFFECT OF DIFFERENT SCHEDULES OF REINFORCEMENT ON LEARNING. Different schedules of reinforcement lead to different rates of response. Each hash mark indicates when a reinforcer is administered. Ratio schedules of reinforcement result in more of the reinforced behavior being performed over a given amount of time (the two steep slopes) than interval schedules of reinforcement (the two flatter slopes). Also, the fixed interval schedule leads to the classic "scallop" effect, which indicates that responses decrease immediately after the reinforcer is administered and then increase again as the next reinforcer draws near.

variable ratio (VR) schedule
a pattern of intermittent reinforcement in which the number of responses needed for reinforcement changes.

A **variable ratio (VR) schedule,** in which the number of responses needed for reinforcement varies, produces a very steady rate of response, because the individual is not quite sure how many responses are necessary to obtain reinforcement (see Figure 8.10). VR schedules produce reinforcement around a mean number of responses, but the exact ratio differs for each trial. So the mean may be set at 10 responses, but some trials may require 10 responses for reinforcement, some 20, some 5, some 7, and so on. An example of a device that delivers reinforcement on a VR schedule is the slot machine. The player cannot know how many pulls of the slot machine arm it will take to win. On one occasion it might take just one pull to win a small jackpot. Other times dozens of quarters might be spent before winning. Casinos make a lot of money capitalizing on the steady rate of response produced by a variable ratio schedule—gamblers do not.

In a **fixed interval (FI) schedule,** reinforcement always follows the first response after a set amount of time—say, every 4 seconds. This produces a response pattern in which the rate of response immediately following reinforcement is low. The response rate accelerates as the time of reinforcement approaches. A graph of the FI schedule produces a scalloped pattern, as seen in Figure 8.10. An example of the effects of a fixed interval schedule of reinforcement might be studying behavior before and after a test. If tests are given every four weeks, students learn that immediately after the test their performance will not be evaluated, so we would expect to see a drop in rate of studying at that time. The same is true of class attendance before and after exams.

fixed interval (FI) schedule
pattern of intermittent reinforcement in which responses are always reinforced after a set period of time has passed.

In a **variable interval (VI) schedule,** the first response is reinforced after time periods of different duration have passed. The researcher sets a mean interval length around which the intervals will vary. For example, the mean interval may be 5 seconds, but sometimes reinforcement occurs after 10 seconds, sometimes after 1 second, sometimes after 5 seconds, and so on. The variable nature of the interval makes it difficult for the subject to predict when reinforcement will occur. Variable interval schedules therefore produce a steady, moderate rate of response (see Figure 8.10). Suppose, for example, you are trying to reach a good friend on the phone, but every time you call you get her voice mail. You can tell she is on the line already. So you keep calling back every few minutes to see if she is off. Her conversation can last only so long. Eventually, she will pick up the phone (your reward), but the wait time is unpredictable. In other words, reinforcement follows a variable interval schedule.

variable interval (VI) schedule
a pattern of intermittent reinforcement in which responses are reinforced after time periods of different duration have passed.

Success! The variable interval schedule paid off.

Challenges to Conditioning Models of Learning

Traditional learning theory assumes that the principles of conditioning are universal. That is, classical conditioning and operant conditioning each work pretty much the same way in different species of animals. In fact, Skinner maintained that given the proper reinforcement, almost any animal could be taught to do almost anything.

Skinner's faith in universal principles of learning was so strong that he was convinced that what he learned about a rat or pigeon in a conditioning chamber was representative of most species' learning in any context. In one sense Skinner was correct. The biochemical processes involved in learning and memory are the same in slugs as in humans (Kandel, 2006). Skinner was also suggesting that we could understand learning by training behavior, not because it is inherently interesting to us or to the animal, but rather because trained behavior is easily

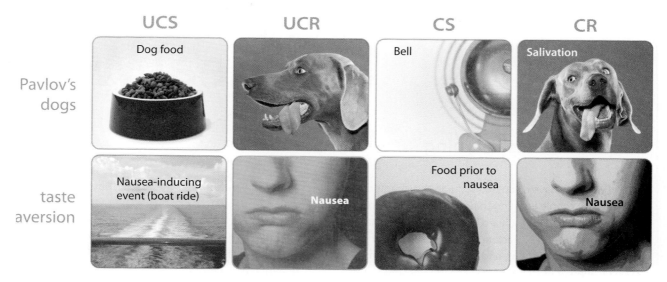

	UCS	UCR	CS	CR
Pavlov's dogs	Dog food		Bell	Salivation
taste aversion	Nausea-inducing event (boat ride)	Nausea	Food prior to nausea	Nausea

FIGURE **8.11**

CLASSICAL CONDITIONING MODEL OF TASTE AVERSION.

observed. The specific species or the behavior does not make a difference. As we are about to see, however, some of the basic assumptions of conditioning models of learning did not go unchallenged. Three domains of research challenged traditional learning theory:

- Conditioned taste aversion
- Instinctive drift
- Latent learning

Conditioned Taste Aversion

One of your authors—Erika—once took an ocean voyage despite a susceptibility to motion sickness. As she boarded the ship, someone served chocolate doughnuts and Erika grabbed one. Unfortunately, only 30 minutes after setting off, she was turning green and soon was vomiting. So uncomfortable was this experience that for 10 years afterward she could not eat chocolate doughnuts. This sea misadventure was a case of **conditioned taste aversion,** the learned avoidance of a particular taste when nausea occurs at about the same time as the food (Garcia, Kimeldorf, & Koelling, 1955). Whether or not the food actually causes the sickness, it is experienced that way in future encounters.

Traditional learning theory would explain conditioned taste aversion as a special case of classical conditioning, in which a neutral or even pleasant taste is linked with the unconditioned causes of nausea. This learned association (say, between a doughnut and nausea) is not much different from the one made by Pavlov's dogs (see Figure 8.11). The catch is that classical conditioning requires repeated pairings of the CS and the UCS to create and maintain a conditioned response. But in the case of the chocolate doughnut, the doughnut (the CS) acquired the ability to induce nausea (CR) after a brief pairing with the motion of the boat (UCS), more than 30 minutes after the doughnut was eaten.

The person responsible for describing and discovering this new kind of learning was John Garcia. In the 1950s Garcia and his colleagues wondered whether rats in their laboratory had developed a taste aversion for the food and water they had consumed while they received radiation for one of the lab's experiments. He and his colleagues (1955) at the U.S. Naval Laboratory decided to look more closely

cconditioned taste aversion the learned avoidance of a particular taste or food.

Sleep Facilitates Learning

Much of what we have discussed so far in this chapter concerns very simple learning that may not sound directly relevant to how you might learn in school. To learn material in a class, you have to pay attention, take in new information, form new associations, and then store it in a form that can be recalled or used later. The processes of consciousness, memory, and learning all come together in classroom learning. Our topic in this section is simple—you need sleep to do all of these things.

Few college students get the sleep required to help their brain learn at an optimal level. It's almost regarded as a rite of passage for college students to "pull all-nighters" before exams and term papers. Sleep deprivation is rampant during the transition from high school to college and among college students (Buboltz et al., 2006; Carskadon & Davis, 1989).

A growing scientific literature shows that sleep plays an important role in learning. Beginning in infancy, better sleep is associated with increases in cognitive functioning—it enhances and consolidates what we learn during the day (Bernier et al., 2010; Karni et al., 1994; Payne & Nadel, 2004; Stickgold & Walker, 2007). During childhood and adolescence, sleep enhances performance in the classroom. For instance, college students who have the most and best quality sleep have higher course grades in psychology and higher overall GPAs than those who have disruptive and disturbed sleep (Beebe, Rose, & Amin, 2010; Gilbert & Weaver, 2010; Howell et al., 2004). Pulling all-nighters is associated with a lower GPA (Thacher, 2008).

In addition to overall academic performance, sleep facilitates learning specific tasks and procedures (Ellenbogen et al., 2007; Gaab et al., 2004; S. C. Mednick et al., 2009; S. C. Mednick, Nakayama, & Stickgold, 2003; McKenna et al., in press; Payne & Kensinger, 2010; C. Smith & MacNeill, 1994). For example, motor skills such as typing are approximately 20% faster after a night's sleep compared to before sleep (Kuriyama et al., 2004). In another study on recall,

students were shown photographs but were not told they would be asked to recall the details of the photographs (Walker & Stickgold, 2006). Participants were assigned to either a sleep-deprived condition (2 nights without sleep) or a normal sleep condition (8 hours). Both groups were unexpectedly (to them) tested on how much they could recall about the photographs they had been shown 36 hours earlier. The normal sleep group recalled 40% more details about the photographs than the sleep-deprived group (see Figure 8.12).

There are several possible means by which sleep facilitates learning, but one of the main mechanisms involved is the spontaneous replay and consolidation of daily events during sleep. Evidence for this conclusion comes from both animal and human research (Ji & Wilson, 2007; O'Neill et al., 2010; Wilson & McNaughton, 1994). A fascinating example of this finding involves research with rats (Ji & Wilson,

FIGURE **8.12**

SLEEP DEPRIVATION AND RECALL OF EMOTIONAL PHOTO-GRAPHS AFTER 36 HOURS. After being randomly assigned to one of two sleep groups, students' recall for visual images is increased by 40% if they sleep normally, compared to the group that is sleep-deprived. (Source: Walker & Stickgold, 2006)

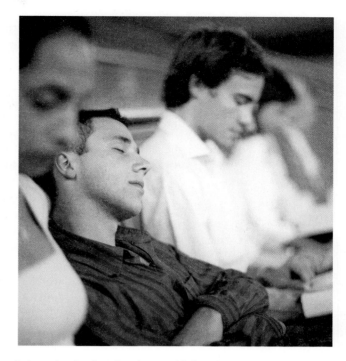

A sleep-deprived student has trouble learning.

2007). Before running a maze, rats had very thin electrodes painlessly implanted in their hippocampus (learning and memory center) to measure activity patterns of specific neurons. When the mice were running the maze, a particular pattern of neural firing was observed. Much to the researchers' surprise, while these rats slept, a *very* similar pattern of brain activity was replayed in the hippocampus and the visual cortex. In other words, while they slept their brain spontaneously and without effort was rehearsing and consolidating what it learned during the day. In fact, the phenomenon of "sleeping on" a problem and working it out spontaneously during the night and having a solution suddenly appear in the morning is probably related to rehearsal and replay of learned experience (Walker & Stickgold, 2006). Dozens of human studies support a strong role for sleep in memory consolidation and learning (Diekelmann, Wilhelm, & Born, 2009).

Even the most basic processes of learning—classical and operant conditioning—are affected by sleep. The eyeblink can be conditioned to occur in response to a neutral stimulus (such as a sound). This is textbook classical conditioning. In a study of sleep-deprived and non-sleep-deprived college students, those who missed out on REM sleep show serious deficits in even this simple kind of conditioning (Ohno et al., 2002). It seems that adequate REM sleep, in particular, is even crucial for basic motor learning (Smith, Aubrey, & Peters, 2004).

If sleep facilitates learning and memory—and yet college students are notoriously sleep-deprived—then what can you do to help combat this problem without resorting to drugs such as caffeine and other addicting stimulants? To simply implore you to get more sleep is a bit unrealistic and vague, and yet it is the single most helpful thing you can do to overcome the sleep-deficit effect on learning. We offer a few specific recommendations on how you can use sleep to improve your school performance.

First, get more sleep the night or two before an exam. Studying for hours and hours all through the night is not very efficient, because what you try to learn has no time to replay and consolidate in your brain. Second, short mid-day naps enhance learning, alertness, and memory (S. C. Mednick & Ehman, 2006; Waterhouse et al., 2007). If you can steal a 20–30-minute nap during the day, then this will help with alertness, attention, and memory (not to mention physical performance as well). Finally, if you have trouble getting a good night's sleep, try exercising more. Aerobic exercise provides the best benefits to neural growth, learning, attention, and alertness (Hillman, Erickson, & Kramer, 2008; Marks et al., 2007; Pereira et al., 2007). Even a brief period of exercise (10 minutes) can temporarily increase alertness, memory, and performance (Horne & Foster, 1995; Sallinen et al., 2008). Regular and longer periods of exercise are associated with both better sleep and better performance in school (Brand et al., 2010; LeDuc, Caldwell, & Ruyak, 2000). The connection between exercise and sleep is simple: Students who exercise more tend to sleep longer and have better quality sleep.

at this phenomenon. They would try to condition rats to develop an aversion to a taste they liked—saccharin water. They began with the following questions:

1. Could taste aversion to saccharin water occur by pairing the taste with radiation (a UCS for nausea)?
2. How long would the taste aversion last without repeated exposure to radiation (the UCS)?

John Garcia

Garcia's team varied the type of fluid presented during a radiation period (plain water or saccharin water) and the radiation exposure level (none, low, or moderate dose). One control group had access to plain water during a 6-hour period of exposure to radiation (irradiation). Another control group received saccharin water and no radiation. In the experimental conditions, rats received saccharin water during periods of low or moderate irradiation. According to traditional classical conditioning, UCS and CS must be paired very closely in time—typically no more than a few seconds apart. But in some cases, several minutes passed between the time when the rats were irradiated (UCS) and when they drank the fluid (CS).

Following the conditioning period in which rats were irradiated or not, all rats were housed in cages with two drinking bottles, one containing plain water and one with saccharin water. At this time, taste aversion was measured, and the dependent variable was how much saccharin water the rats consumed.

There were no changes in the control groups' water preferences, but in the two experimental groups aversion occurred (see Figure 8.13). Regardless of radiation level, rats that had been drinking saccharin water during irradiation consumed significantly less saccharin water after conditioning. This result answered the first question the researchers posed: Rats could be conditioned to avoid a taste they previously liked. Also, the drop in intake of saccharin water lasted for at least 30 days. This finding answered the second question about how long such conditioning might last.

FIGURE **8.13**

CONDITIONED TASTE AVERSION. Compared to rats that received no radiation, rats exposed to radiation (UCS) while drinking saccharin water (CS) developed a long-lasting aversion to saccharin water (CR). Water intake did not vary much among the control and experimental groups, but the amount of saccharin water consumed by the irradiated rats was significantly less than the amount consumed by the control group. (Source: Garcia, Kimeldorf, & Koelling, 1955)

Percentage of fluid intake after radiation

Legend:
- No radiation
- Low radiation
- Moderate radiation

Fluid during irradiation: Water, Saccharin

FIGURE **8.14**

LIMITS ON CONDITIONED TASTE AVERSION. Contrary to predictions from traditional learning theory, taste aversion conditioning depends on the stimulus. Conditioned taste aversion occurs only to the kind of stimulus that makes biological sense. For example, nausea produces aversion to taste, but not to noise and light, as shown in the graph on the left. Pain produces aversion to frightening stimuli, such as noise and bright lights, but not to saccharin water, as shown in the graph on the right. (Source: Garcia & Koelling, 1966)

Garcia's subsequent research derailed another assumption of traditional learning theory: that reflexive responses (such as nausea) could be conditioned to any kind of stimulus. Garcia and Koelling (1966) varied the type of aversive stimulus (UCS) to which rats were exposed and the type of neutral stimulus (CS). Nausea (the UCR) was induced by exposure to X-rays, whereas pain (the other UCR) was induced by electrical shocks sent through the floor of the cage. When the rat licked the drinking tube, it received the CS of either saccharin water or "bright-noisy water" (plain water accompanied by a light and a buzzer that went on when the rat touched the drinking tube). The UCS for half the rats was irradiation-induced nausea. The other half received a shock. The irradiated rats avoided the sweet water but not the bright-noisy water (Figure 8.14), whereas rats that received a mildly painful shock avoided the bright-noisy water but not the sweet water (Figure 8.14). The researchers described the first response as "conditioned nausea" and the second as "conditioned fear."

The key finding here is that contrary to the predictions of traditional learning theory, an organism cannot be conditioned to respond to just any "neutral" stimulus paired with an unconditioned stimulus. We can learn certain things only under certain conditions. In other words, nausea can be conditioned to a taste but not to a light, because taste is relevant to eating and light is not.

As another example of how research can radically change what we think we know, Garcia's research on taste aversion undermined two key assumptions of classical conditioning: (1) that conditioning could happen only if an organism was exposed repeatedly within a brief time span to the UCS and CS together and (2) that organisms can learn to associate any two stimuli. With respect to the first assumption, Garcia showed in other research that the CS and UCS could be separated by as much as 75 minutes and still lead to conditioned taste aversion (Garcia, Ervin, & Koelling, 1966). With respect to the second assumption, the "bright-noisy water" findings showed that only certain stimuli could be conditioned to produce nausea (Garcia & Koelling, 1966). More specifically, you cannot make someone be nauseated by a sound or a sight as easily as by a taste.

Instinctive Drift   Many studies of conditioning used different species in learning experiments. Also, results from rats were readily assumed to be relevant for humans. But are species really interchangeable? And is learning to press a bar equivalent to learning to play the piano? Over many years, it has become clear that the notion of the equivalence of species and tasks is problematic. As it turns out, there are limits to what different species will learn and how they will learn it.

Ironically, this conclusion stemmed from the research of two of Skinner's students, Keller Breland and Marian Breland. Initially, the Brelands (1961) successfully applied traditional operant conditioning principles to shaping all kinds of behaviors in many kinds of animals. In fact, they successfully conditioned 38 different species and more than 6,000 animals.

When they turned their attention to species whose learning behavior had not been studied, however, they began to experience failures. For example, when they tried to condition different animal species to insert poker chips into a vending machine, raccoons rubbed them instead of putting them in the slot machine, pigs rooted them with their snouts, and chickens pecked at them. When describing the raccoons' "problematic behavior," Breland and Breland wrote,

> The rubbing behavior became worse and worse as time went on, in spite of non-reinforcement. . . . These egregious failures came as a rather considerable shock to us, for there was nothing in our background in behaviorism to prepare us for such gross inabilities to predict and control the behavior of animals with which we had been working for years. (Breland & Breland, 1961, p. 683)

Initially the Brelands considered such behavior misguided and even titled their article "The Misbehavior of Organisms." Once again, new science topples old assumptions to offer new perspectives. With research, it became clear to the Brelands that these behaviors were not "misbehaviors" but normal expressions of innate instincts. It seems that raccoons naturally wash, pigs root, and chickens peck. Breland and Breland (1961) called this effect **instinctive drift,** which they defined as learned behavior that shifts toward instinctive, unlearned behavior tendencies.

Instinctive drift challenges the behaviorist conviction that learning always results either from associating an event with an unconditioned stimulus or from shaping by reinforcement or punishment. The Brelands' findings imply that there are biological limitations, or constraints, on learning. According to the **biological constraint model** of learning, some behaviors are inherently more likely to be learned than others (Garcia, McGowan, & Green, 1972; Seligman & Hager, 1972). In other words, biology constrains, or limits, options so that the adaptive ones are more likely to occur than the maladaptive ones.

Constraints on learning have positive evolutionary implications: They guide organisms in a direction that speeds up learning and aids survival or reproductive success. This model serves to explain instinctive drift. Humans are geared to learn language—one could say we "instinctively drift" toward speaking. It is very easy for us to learn to speak, assuming we are simply exposed to

instinctive drift learned behavior that shifts toward instinctive, unlearned behavior tendencies.

biological constraint model a view on learning which proposes that some behaviors are inherently more likely to be learned than others.

Connection
Every human learns a language. Why is that?
See "Theories of Language Acquisition," Chapter 9, "Language and Thought," p. 353.

Nature&
Nurture
Animals are primed from birth to readily learn some things and not others. Humans, for example, are primed to talk.

language early in infancy and childhood. Reading, writing, and arithmetic, however, are not so easily learned, which is one reason why we need to go to school to learn these skills. We do not need to go to school to learn to speak. School might help with teaching us formal grammar and syntax, but we all use a grammar and kind of syntax.

Instinctive drift and biological constraints provide excellent examples of the limits nature places on nurture. Biology makes it possible for humans, but not chimpanzees, to talk. Experience interacting with the capacity for speech determines not only whether an individual learns to talk, but also the language learned. As we just learned, Garcia's groundbreaking research revised traditional thinking about classical conditioning within the limits of biology.

Latent Learning   Even before the Brelands studied biological constraints and learning, other psychologists challenged some of the basic assumptions of learning theory. One was Edward Tolman. Like many other learning researchers, Tolman ran rats through mazes. In one key study, hungry rats were randomly assigned to one of three groups (Tolman & Honzick, 1930). Rats in Group 1 were rewarded with food if they reached the end of the maze. Rats in this group became better and better at maze running, thanks to the reliable reinforcement of a food reward. Rats in Group 2 received no food for their work, and not surprisingly, they never ran the maze very well. They had no reinforcement. These results are what standard behaviorism would predict.

The rats in Group 3, however, received no reinforcement for running the maze—at least not at first. Like Group 2, they did not run the maze very well. But after a set of nonreinforced trials, they started being reinforced with food for their maze running. Suddenly, these rats started running the maze really well. It was as if they had been learning all along. In fact, the Group 3 rats even started performing better than the rats in Group 1.

latent learning
learning that occurs in the absence of reinforcement and is not demonstrated until later, when reinforcement occurs.

How might we explain this outcome? Tolman argued that the rats in Group 3 had been learning all along—they just didn't show it before they started being reinforced. This type of learning is called **latent learning,** which is learning that occurs in the absence of reinforcement and is not demonstrated until later, when reinforcement occurs. Tolman reasoned that these rats had formed internal *cognitive maps*—like pictures in their minds—of the maze from all the practice they had received. When they finally had rewards waiting for them, the rats could use these maps to run the maze more efficiently. It is difficult to know whether the rats really had maps of the maze in their minds. What is clear from these findings is that some learning can occur in the absence of reinforcement. Running the maze, even without rewards, helped the rats in Group 3 run much better when reinforcement was available.

Tolman's work was very important because it set the stage for future work on the role of thought in learning, something that Skinner (1990) and other behaviorists deemed irrelevant. Tolman's work also showed that prior experience—whether reinforced or not—aids future learning. Further, it suggested that motivation plays a part in learning. The idea of latent learning implies that learning sometimes stays hidden until the learner is motivated to perform.

Connection
People who cannot form new memories nevertheless learn. The body can learn things of which the conscious mind is not aware.
See "Long-Term Memory," Chapter 7, "Memory," p. 276.

Quick Quiz 8.1: Basic Processes and Conditioning Models of Learning

1. Using the definition provided in the text, which is the best example of learning?
   a. A plant moves toward the sun in order to get the best sunlight.
   b. A newborn baby automatically grabs a finger that is placed in its palm.
   c. A cat perks up its ears and looks toward a sound.
   d. Ten-year-old Jerry can snowboard down the mountain after practicing for a week.

2. Because we always use a can opener when getting their food, Scooter and Belle run into the kitchen each time they hear someone open the drawer where the can opener is kept. According to the text, the cats have _____ .
   a. remembered what cat food is
   b. made an association between the drawer opening and being fed
   c. habituated to noises in the kitchen
   d. none of the above

3. A rat presses a lever, resulting in food delivery. The rat then presses the lever more frequently. This is an example of
   a. punishment
   b. higher-order conditioning
   c. reinforcement
   d. extinction

4. In a typical classical conditioning experiment, a neutral stimulus is
   a. repeatedly paired with the UCR
   b. not paired with any other stimulus
   c. repeatedly paired with the CS
   d. repeatedly paired with the UCS

5. A reinforcer is anything that _____ ; a punisher is anything that _____
   a. makes a behavior less likely; makes a behavior more likely
   b. makes a behavior more likely; makes a behavior less likely
   c. is positive; is negative
   d. is shaped; is extinguished

6. A slot machine player cannot know how many pulls of the slot machine arm it will take to win. On one occasion it might take just 1 pull to win a small jackpot. Other times dozens of quarters might be spent before winning. This payout schedule is what kind of schedule of reinforcement?
   a. fixed interval
   b. fixed ratio
   c. variable interval
   d. variable ratio

Answers can be found at the end of the chapter.

SOCIAL LEARNING THEORY

We all look to others for clues on how to behave. Think about how you first learned to tie your shoes or even to swim. Did someone just explain the way to do it? Or did you try random motions and then get praise from your teacher every time you did something that was right? There may have been some random success, but chances are you learned the right movements by copying what your swim teacher or parent did. There is more to learning than associating one thing with another (classical conditioning) or doing something and then being reinforced for it (operant conditioning). Classical and operant conditioning explain many aspects of learning, but they neglect the powerful role of modeling in the learning process.

Obviously, people learn from their own experience, from their own successes and failures, and from trial and error. But if we had to learn everything that way, not only would the process take much, much longer, but it would also require reinventing what others have already learned, over and over again. Learning by observing others is much more efficient. Albert Bandura proposed that we learn both by doing and by observing. Bandura (1986) called learning by doing **enactive learning** and learning by watching the behavior of others **observational learning.**

enactive learning
learning by doing.

observational learning
learning by watching the behavior of others.

330   CHAPTER 8   Learning

Connection
Does watching violence in movies, on TV, and in video games lead to aggressive behavior? Overwhelmingly, the answer seems to be yes.
See "The Nature and Nurture of Aggression," Chapter 14, "Social Behavior," p. 569.

Breaking New Ground

Albert Bandura's Accidental Discovery of a Career and Social-Cognitive Learning

Until the 1940s and 1950s, the two major schools of thought in learning were behaviorist—namely classical and operant conditioning. Both of these approaches to learning completely ignore the role of thoughts, motives, and social modeling. Albert Bandura (1925–) was to change this.

Now one of the most influential psychologists of all time, Bandura's path to psychology was an unplanned, fortuitous event. As an undergraduate, he had to take morning classes because in the afternoon he worked to make ends meet. He would drive to school with friends who were pre-med and engineering majors who had classes even earlier than his. Instead of sitting around waiting for his first class to start, he decided to look for early-morning classes. "One morning, I was wasting time in the library. Someone had forgotten to return a course catalog and I thumbed through it attempting to find a filler course to occupy the early time slot. I noticed a course in psychology that would serve as excellent filler. It sparked my interest and I found a career" (Pajares, 2004).

As a graduate student in the 1940s, Albert Bandura thought the two major conditioning approaches were on to something, but each left out important commonsense views of how learning happens. In Bandura's words,

> The prevailing analyses of learning focused almost entirely on learning through the effects of one's actions [operant conditioning]. . . . I found this behavioristic theorizing discordant with the obvious social reality that much of what we learn is through the power of social modeling. I could not imagine a culture in which its language, mores, familial customs and practices, occupational competencies, and educational, religious, and political practices were gradually shaped in each new member by rewarding and punishing consequences of their trial-and-error performances. (Bandura, 2006, p. 51)

At the time, only one book had been written on learning that took a social perspective. It was *Social Learning and Imitation* by Neal Miller and John Dollard (1941). Bandura was more taken by this approach than by classical or operant conditioning, but he was not completely happy, however, with Miller and Dollard's view of social learning (Bandura, 2006). He believed it was too simplistic, and he soon developed his own views of how observing and imitating others is at the foundation of much of human learning. His dissatisfaction propelled him to develop his own view on social learning, or what he now calls social-cognitive learning. The theory was built upon two classic studies of aggression and learning—the so-called "Bobo-Doll Studies."

Albert Bandura

■ ■ ■

social learning theory
a description of the kind of learning that occurs when we model or imitate the behavior of others.

Bandura's **social learning theory** (1986) goes beyond traditional conditioning approaches to include observation and modeling as major components of

modeling
the imitation of behaviors performed by others.

learning. **Modeling** is Bandura's term for the process of observing and imitating behaviors performed by others. Modeling is everywhere. Younger children mimic the behavior of their older siblings. We pick up figures of speech and mannerisms from our closest friends. Modeling is more likely to occur in some people than in others, more likely after some behaviors than others, and more likely after some consequences than others.

Modeling is only one aspect of social learning theory. According to Bandura (1986), social learning also works through reinforcement. Remember from operant conditioning that the consequences of our behavior influence whether we repeat those behaviors. People learn best those things they are rewarded for doing, whether the rewards are external (such as praise, money, candy) or internal (such as joy and satisfaction). Bandura noted that reinforcement matters not only for the person carrying out the behavior, but also for those who watch. Advertisers make use of this phenomenon all the time. For example, when teenagers see young adults getting a lot of attention and having fun while they are drinking beer, they might be more likely to want to drink beer themselves. People will do things they see others doing, especially if the model's behavior is rewarded.

Bandura and his colleagues demonstrated the power of observational learning in a series of classic studies in the 1960s—the Bobo doll studies. They came up with clever experiments to show how two key elements of social learning—modeling and reinforcement—affect behavior. The first study focused on the power of observational learning on aggressive behavior (Bandura, Ross, & Ross, 1961). Children observed an adult either being aggressive or not with an inflatable doll, called a Bobo doll. Half saw the adult play politely with the Bobo doll. The others saw the adult sock the Bobo doll hard, hit it with a rubber mallet, and kick it around. Afterward, one at a time, the kids entered a room filled with toys (including the ones the model played with) and were allowed free play. Children who saw the adults act aggressively with the doll were much more likely to be aggressive when they had the chance to play with the Bobo than those who saw the adults play pleasantly with the doll. In fact, they adopted many of the same actions the adults used. So these initial studies demonstrated the power of modeling in the learning of aggression.

Children who observed an adult model being aggressive with a Bobo doll (top) in a study by Bandura tended to behave aggressively when given the opportunity to play with the doll (bottom).

Another key study showed how reinforcement works with modeling to lead to learning (Bandura, Ross, & Ross, 1963). Again using an experimental design, this time the researchers introduced another variable: What happened to the models after they behaved aggressively? Here's how they set it up. The children saw one of four films: one with no models, one with two adult men who interacted in a nonaggressive manner, and two films with adult men who played aggressively with each other, but in one the aggressive man was punished, whereas in the other he was rewarded. The first two films (no model and nonaggressive models) were control conditions, whereas the last two (aggression) were experimental conditions. In the films shown to the experimental groups, one man was aggressive toward the other man. The aggressive man hit the nonaggressive man with a rubber mallet and shot darts at him. He also roughed up the inflatable Bobo doll. A key element of this study is that

FIGURE **8.15**

EXPERIMENTAL DESIGN FOR BANDURA'S STUDY OF OBSERVATIONAL LEARNING AND AGGRESSION. Children viewed one of four films: one with no model, one with nonaggressive adult models, or one of two with an aggressive adult model where the model is either punished for being aggressive or rewarded for it. (Source: Bandura, Ross, & Ross, 1963)

Aggressive model

No model

Nonaggressive model

Punished for aggression

Rewarded for aggression

control films   experimental films

the films also showed what happened to the aggressive adult after the interaction. There were two possibilities. The aggressive adult was either punished (he lost the conflict and ended up cowering in the corner) or rewarded (he won the conflict and got to play with all the toys) for his aggression. The research design is summarized in Figure 8.15.

After seeing the film, the children had an opportunity to play with the Bobo doll and other toys they saw in the film. Just as in the previous set of studies, how the kids acted with the doll and other toys was the main dependent variable. The primary finding from the previous study was replicated: Those who viewed aggression were more aggressive with the doll than those who did not see aggression (see Figure 8.16). But the consequences for the model also mattered. The children who saw the aggressive adult rewarded for his aggression were more

Too much violent TV?

Social Learning Theory   **333**

FIGURE 8.16

EFFECT OF MODELING AND REWARD ON LEARNED AGGRESSIVE BEHAVIOR.
This graph depicts the number of imitative aggressive acts by children who viewed one of four film conditions. The children who saw the aggressive adults get rewarded for their aggression showed more aggressive acts, such as hitting the Bobo doll with a hammer or punching it, than did the children in the other three categories. (Source: Bandura, Ross, & Ross, 1963)

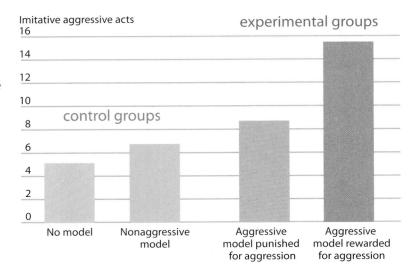

violent with the toys and Bobo doll than those who saw the aggressive adult get punished. Those who did not see an aggressive model did not show much aggression with the toys, nor did those who saw the adult punished. These studies show how modeling and reinforcement can work together to influence behavior. Kids are more likely to copy behavior that they see others being rewarded for.

The Bobo doll studies were pivotal in showing how children learn aggression and other violent behaviors from viewing aggression in others. The results, of course, have implications for the effect of violence on television, in movies, and in video games on children and teens. Numerous studies have demonstrated that kids behave more violently after exposure to violence in the media (Bushman & Anderson, 2001). Consider this startling real example: Two teenage lovers, Ben Darras and Sarah Edmondson, apparently under the influence of drugs and Oliver Stone's movie *Natural Born Killer,* went on a killing spree. The movie depicted two young lovers, on a wild and drug-filled rampage, callously killing and robbing people. After the copycat killers were arrested, they claimed they had also taken drugs and played Stone's movie in a continuous loop all night ("Natural Born Copycats," 2002).

Quick Quiz 8.2: Social Learning Theory

1. Barbara just started a new job, and she watches how her colleagues dress and act. The type of learning Barbara is doing is known as
   a. observational learning
   b. enactive learning
   c. operant conditioning
   d. reinforcement

2. The major finding(s) from Bandura's so-called Bobo doll experiments were that
   a. children learn to be aggressive by watching other people be aggressive
   b. children learn to be aggressive by observing reinforced aggression in others

   c. children learn to be aggressive only if they see someone of the same sex be aggressive
   d. both A and B are correct

3. Research generally shows that children
   a. are not at all likely to be aggressive after watching aggression on TV or in movies
   b. are likely to be aggressive after watching aggression on TV or in movies
   c. are more aggressive after watching aggression on TV or in movies only if they are from impoverished backgrounds
   d. know the difference between movies and real life and are not influenced by movie violence

Answers can be found at the end of the chapter.

THE INTERACTION OF NATURE AND NURTURE IN LEARNING

The early behaviorists refused to study anything that could not be directly observed, including mental processes and any potentially relevant biological structures. Watson and Skinner, in particular, took the position that all learning was a function of either stimuli (classical conditioning) or consequences (operant conditioning), both of which come from the outside environment. Although Skinner acknowledges the role of genetics in behavior, he and Watson ignored the role of cognitive and brain processes in learning, because these could not be observed (Skinner, 1938, 1990). Likewise, the behaviorists did not consider any form of instinctive behavior worthy of scientific study.

As we have seen, behaviorism sprang in part from a desire to study behavior in a measurable way. In behaviorism's heyday, there simply was no technology available for observing brain function or measuring its activity. When such technologies began to appear in the 1950s, the behaviorist model was challenged from various angles. Learning, it turns out, is not just an environmental process. It results from the constant interaction of the brain and the environment. Biology makes learning possible, and learning changes biology. Extreme forms of behaviorism paint a picture of learning resulting primarily from the experiences one has. It is an extreme environmental, or nurture-only, view. Few modern behaviorists agree with such a one-sided view. Here we will look at four learning processes that illustrate the dynamic interplay between nature and nurture in learning: imprinting, imitation, synaptic change, and brain growth with enrichment.

Imprinting

Not all forms of learning depend on reward and reinforcement. A good example is **imprinting,** the rapid and innate learning of the characteristics of a caregiver within a very short period of time after birth (Lorenz, 1935, 1937). Mammals and birds, which are born helpless, need to form a strong bond to a caregiver almost immediately after birth to avoid getting lost or being killed by a predator. We know this from **ethology,** the scientific study of animal behavior, and especially from the work of Austrian ethologist and winner of the 1973 Nobel Prize in Medicine, Konrad Lorenz. Lorenz studied imprinting extensively in birds. He observed that soon after they hatched, ducklings and goslings (baby geese) would learn to follow whomever they saw most, be it a mother duck or goose or, surprisingly, a human. This parent figure tends to be the first moving object the young

imprinting
the rapid and innate learning of the characteristics of a caregiver very soon after birth.

ethology
the scientific study of animal behavior.

Konrad Lorenz and goslings.

animal sees within the first few days of life. Usually this figure is the animal's mother, but it need not be, as Lorenz found out when he became an imprinted parent to a flock of goslings.

Imprinting provides clear evidence of a *sensitivity period* in learning: a period when a particular type of learning occurs very readily if an animal is exposed to a particular stimulus or situation. The brain seems to be primed at a particular time for a particular kind of learning. Once the animal has moved beyond that sensitivity period, it becomes much harder, if not impossible, to learn certain skills or make use of certain kinds of information. Once a "parent" has been imprinted on young ducks or geese, that learning is permanent and cannot be unlearned. Imprinting, in other words, can be learned soon after birth—or not at all. After a certain age, imprinting cannot be learned, unlearned, or relearned—it cannot be modified at all.

Although imprinting does not occur in humans, young babies do develop an important bond with their primary caregivers that serves much the same function (see Chapter 5). Imprinting and sensitivity periods in learning remind us that the mind is not a blank slate, able to learn anything at any time, given the right reinforcers and stimuli. The brain is structured in such a way that certain kinds of experiences are more or less easily learned at different periods in life; language learning by humans is one example, as discussed in Chapter 9.

Imitation, Mirror Neurons, and Learning

Humans imitate one another. Imitation is fundamental to the way in which human and nonhuman primates learn. As we discussed in the section on social learning theory, classical and operant conditioning do not take into account the powerful role of imitation in the learning process. Infants begin copying the behavior of adults and other children almost immediately. Babies as young as 7 hours old imitate simple adult facial expressions (Meltzoff & Moore, 1977, 1983).

Like father, like son. We learn by observing and imitating others.

Connection

Mirror neurons help explain why even newborn infants imitate adult behavior so easily.

See "Early Socioemotional Development," Chapter 5, "Human Development," p. 192.

Imitation by infants may be a result of mirror neuron systems in the brain (Lepage & Théoret, 2007). As discussed in Chapter 3, humans and other primates have mirror neurons that respond in much the same way while watching an action as they do while performing an action (Iacoboni & Mazziota, 2007; Rizzolatti et al., 1996); see the Research Process for this chapter (Figure 8.17). Simply put, for some neurons in the frontal lobe of the cerebral cortex, the experience of watching someone else do something is like doing it yourself. When a monkey observes another monkey or a human grab a peanut, the same neurons fire in the frontal lobe as fire when the observing monkey actually grabs a peanut (Fogassi & Ferrari, 2006). It is likely that mirror neuron systems are involved in imitation and social learning (Filimon et al., 2007; Iacoboni et al., 1999; Lyons, 2009). Autistic children, who have trouble imitating others' gestures, may have deficits in mirror neuron systems (Bernier & Dawson, 2009; Oberman & Ramachandran, 2007; Williams et al., 2006).

Synaptic Change During Learning

If you've ever tried to learn a second language, you know that if you don't use it for a while, you forget what you've learned. Similarly, you will probably forget much of the material you learn in this class soon after the exam, even if it is learned well to begin with. Why is that?

In Chapter 7 we saw what Hebb's work on learning and memory revealed about the plasticity of the brain: "Neurons that fire together wire together" and "Use it or lose it." We also discussed Kandel's studies on the sea slug *Aplysia*. Both areas of research provided experimental evidence of the neural basis of learning and memory (Kandel, 2006; Pinsker et al., 1973). Specifically, certain proteins become activated in short- and long-term memory formation and learning. These proteins change preexisting synaptic connections and cause the growth of new synapses (H. L. Fields, 2005; Kandel, 2001). What this means is that learning, in a real sense, *is* the growth of new synapses. Synaptic connections between neurons become stronger and even grow during long-term associative learning. The brain literally grows and changes as we learn. The development and frequent use of new synaptic connections in response to stimulation from the environment strengthens the associated memories and makes learning easier. So having experiences repeated over a short period of time is often essential for moving an experience from short-term to long-term memory—that is, for learning to take place. The saying "practice makes perfect" is quite relevant here. To learn and become proficient at something requires repeating the behavior over and over. Synapses need to grow and strengthen.

Yet these same synaptic connections will weaken if they aren't used regularly, resulting in forgetting and the loss of learning. So when we stop using learned information, the synapses that support our knowledge weaken and ultimately degrade—and we forget what we once knew. Practice, use, and rehearsal are important in retaining what we have learned.

If you play a musical instrument, you have experienced this phenomenon directly. The more you practice the scales on your piano or guitar, for example, the more synaptic connections you build and the stronger they become. The scales become easier and easier to play. The sensations and movements associated with the increased experience of playing occupy a greater area of your

Research Process

1 Research Question

Rizzolatti and colleagues (1996) were studying neurons involved in hand movements in monkeys, when they made an accidental discovery: The same motor neurons fired when the monkey observed an experimenter grabbing an object as when the monkey made a similar action itself. It made the researchers wonder: Does the brain contain neurons that rehearse motor actions during observational learning?

2 Method

In a descriptive study of two monkeys, the researchers monitored activity of individual neurons in the motor cortex. They implanted a wire electrode in the motor cortex (area F5) and measured the firing rate of a single neuron while the monkey either grasped a piece of food itself or saw the experimenter pick it up.

3 Results

The graph shows the results of firing patterns in area F5 when food is presented, when it is moved toward the monkey, when the researcher grasps food, and when the monkey grasps food. The peaks of the graph are taller when the firing rate in area F5 is faster. They are shorter when the firing rate is slower. Notice that there is minimal firing when the monkey simply looks at the food. The firing rates increase during observation of grasping and during grasping itself. More importantly, the pattern of firing is similar when action is observed and when action is made by the monkey itself. Neurons that fire during action and observation of similar actions are called mirror neurons.

4 Conclusion

Mirror neurons support the function of rehearsal during learning. By watching others' actions, we "exercise" the motor regions of the brain involved in making those actions. This, in turn, allows us to perform the same behavior more readily.

FIGURE **8.17**

THE DISCOVERY OF MIRROR NEURONS. Mirror neurons in the brain respond in much the same way while watching an action as they do when performing an action. Source: Rizzolatti, G., Fadiga, L., Gallese, V., & Fogassi, L. (1996). Pre-motorcortex and the recognition of motor actions. *Cognitive Brain Research, 3*, 131–141.

Practice makes perfect synaptic connections.

motor cortex and, in effect, change the mapping of touch information in your brain (Pascual-Leone, 2001). If you stop practicing, those connections weaken, the brain map changes, and the scales are harder to recall the next time you try to play.

Experience, Enrichment, and Brain Growth

As we have seen again and again, experience changes the brain. Recall the discussion in Chapter 2 of the classic work demonstrating that rats reared in enriched or normal environments grow more neural connections and learn to run mazes faster than genetically identical rats raised in impoverished environments (Bennett et al., 1964; Rosenzweig et al., 1962).

Building on this research, later experiments showed that animals did not have to be raised from birth in an enriched environment to benefit. Laboratory mice, for example, can have identical "childhoods" (the first 21 days of their lives) and then be randomly assigned to three different environments: no enrichment, short enrichment (68 days), and long enrichment (6 months). The longer they live in an enriched environment, the more neural growth there is in the hippocampus (Kempermann & Gage, 1999). More importantly, however, simply being in an enriched environment is not even the best way to stimulate the growth of new neurons: Being in an enriched environment that continues to have new and novel forms of stimulation is even better (Kempermann & Gage, 1999). Other research, in an effort to learn what it was about an enriched environment that caused the growth of new neurons (neurogenesis), compared the effects of social interaction, swimming, running, and maze learning (Pereira et al., 2007; van Praag, Kempermann, & Gage, 1999). Only the running condition led to neurogenesis. Similar enrichment effects on neuron growth occur in other species besides rats, including birds, primates, and humans (Doetsch & Scharff, 2001; Eriksson et al., 1998; Gould et al., 2001; Hillman et al., 2008).

Nature & Nurture

When we stop using what we've learned, the synapses that support that knowledge weaken, and ultimately we forget what we once knew.

Connection

Can experience and learning generate new neurons in an elderly person?

See "The Developing Adult," Chapter 5, "Human Development," p. 206.

1. Because Konrad Lorenz was the first and only animal they knew for the first few weeks of their life, baby geese thought Lorenz was their "mother." This kind of association is known as
   a. reinforcement
   b. imprinting
   c. learning
   d. conditioning

2. What biological structures or systems best explain why we cry along with characters in a sad movie?
   a. mirror neurons
   b. sensory neurons
   c. frontal lobes
   d. hypothalamus

3. Research on learning and the brain has shown that rats raised in impoverished environments
   a. learn just as quickly as rats raised in enriched environments
   b. have the same number of neurons in the hippocampus as the rats raised in enriched environments
   c. learn more slowly but have the same number of neurons and synaptic connections as rats raised in enriched environments
   d. learn more slowly and have fewer neurons and synaptic connections than rats raised in enriched environments

Answers can be found at the end of the chapter.

Bringing It All Together
Making Connections in Learning
Why Do People Smoke?

As you have probably figured out by now, human behavior is complex. So it should be no surprise that any given behavior may be acquired and maintained by means of several types of learning (classical, operant, and/or social), all operating in the context of a human being who has a personality and history. Consider, for example, cigarette smoking (see Figure 8.18). The acquisition of smoking behavior—how people become smokers in the first place—is perhaps best explained by social learning theory (Bandura, 1969, 1986). Think about it: The actual sensory qualities of cigarette smoking on first experience are anything but pleasant—coughing, dizziness, and nausea. But most smokers start smoking as teenagers, and most teens start smoking because they seek some of the rewards that appear to come with smoking: coolness, peer acceptance, looking like an adult. (All of these rewards are secondary reinforcers, which acquire their reinforcing characteristics by means of classical conditioning and operant conditioning.) Kids see that others who smoke get some of these rewards for smoking. Thus they might model smoking behavior in order to obtain these rewards themselves. They might view "being seen as cool"—a form of peer acceptance—as desirable, and so being seen as cool becomes a reinforcer for the smoking behaviors of others. "Whenever Mom gets stressed, she smokes a cigarette to relax—maybe that will work for me, too" is another example of social learning.

Once someone has become an established smoker, operant conditioning helps maintain smoking behavior. Smoking is bolstered by a number of positive reinforcers: arousal of the sympathetic nervous system (the "rush" of smoking), mild relaxation of the muscles, and, in some cases, increased peer acceptance. Smoking also has a number of negative reinforcers, such as the removal of stress, the removal of social isolation for some smokers, and a reduced appetite. The power of these reinforcers, combined with the physiologically addictive properties of nicotine, make it very difficult to quit smoking. Moreover, the potential punishers of smoking—a substantially increased risk of lung cancer and heart disease—are threats that are so far off in the future for teens that they tend to ignore them. It is for this reason

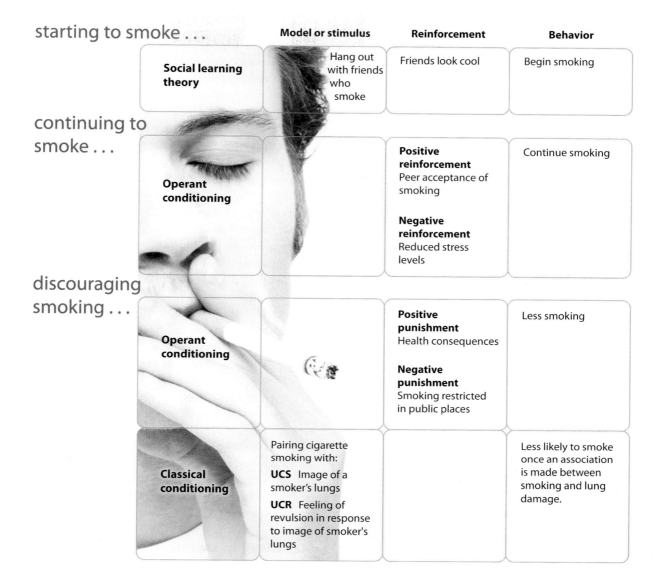

starting to smoke . . .	Model or stimulus	Reinforcement	Behavior
Social learning theory	Hang out with friends who smoke	Friends look cool	Begin smoking
continuing to smoke . . .			
Operant conditioning		**Positive reinforcement** Peer acceptance of smoking **Negative reinforcement** Reduced stress levels	Continue smoking
discouraging smoking . . .			
Operant conditioning		**Positive punishment** Health consequences **Negative punishment** Smoking restricted in public places	Less smoking
Classical conditioning	Pairing cigarette smoking with: **UCS** Image of a smoker's lungs **UCR** Feeling of revulsion in response to image of smoker's lungs		Less likely to smoke once an association is made between smoking and lung damage.

FIGURE **8.18**

HOW LEARNING THEORIES EXPLAIN SMOKING BEHAVIOR. Different theories of learning can explain why people start smoking and continue smoking. In addition, they provide treatment models for helping people to quit smoking. Here are some examples.

that some psychologists who are concerned with preventing smoking by teens have tried to link smoking with unpleasant images and effects (such as ugliness and social rejection). The hope is that by using both classical and operant conditioning, they can make smoking appear less rewarding. For example, in order to discourage smoking, some public health campaigns show pictures of diseased lungs or smokers who look older than they are. The idea is that by means of classical conditioning, people might associate smoking with negative outcomes. It is an effort to teach people to have an unpleasant association with a cigarette and therefore stop smoking.

But smoking, like many complex human behaviors, derives from numerous other influences besides conditioning. Gender, personality, and sociocultural characteristics are some of the factors that may interact with conditioning and biology to influence people to start smoking and affect whether they successfully quit.

Although numerous studies have found no evidence for gender differences in factors related to smoking, one large-scale study found that gender influences susceptibility to smoking, the way people work with their urges to smoke, and the ability to successfully quit (Ellickson, Tucker, & Klein, 2001). Whether friends smoke plays a stronger role in whether adolescent girls attempt and succeed at quitting smoking than it does in boys. In a study of the effects of smoking abstinence (and therefore nicotine withdrawal) on craving and cognitive performance in male and female adolescent smokers, girls reported greater tobacco cravings and symptoms of nicotine withdrawal than boys, but boys performed worse on two cognitive tasks during nicotine withdrawal than did girls (Jacobsen et al., 2005). Taken together, these studies suggest that gender may interact with social and cognitive factors to maintain smoking, both by influencing whether teens decide to attempt to quit (girls have more social pressures to try to quit) and the extent to which the effects of nicotine withdrawal are debilitating (the adverse effects on performance are worse for boys). These are just some of the factors that may explain why more boys smoke than girls, although the gap is narrowing (Robinson & Kleseges, 1997).

Other research shows that personality style predicts whether people start smoking and whether they try to stop,

Having friends who smoke increases the likelihood of smoking.

introducing yet another variable into this complex behavior. A study of personality and smoking found that people who are more sociable, impulsive, rebellious, hostile, and sensation seeking are more likely to start smoking and less likely to quit successfully than those who do not have these personal characteristics (Lipkus et al., 1994). This finding fits with established theory that extraverts are more likely to be smokers than introverts because extraverts have a physiological need for stimulation and therefore seek experiences that are physiologically arousing, such as smoking, drinking, and thrill-seeking feats (Eysenck, 1980). Furthermore, the lack of certain cognitive skills, including long-term thinking and planning abilities, in some adolescents may predispose them to smoke. Not having a long-term perspective, they fail to understand the negative effects of smoking on health (Dinn, Aycicegi, & Harris, 2004). This explanation makes sense if we consider the prevalence of health promotion efforts designed to discourage people from smoking. The urges or need for stimulation may combine with cognitive factors and social learning (modeling peer behavior) to make it very difficult for some people to resist smoking.

The presence of models for smoking (such as parents and friends) figures among the environmental factors that influence smoking behavior. A study of more than 6,000 seventh-grade girls and boys reported differences between African Americans and European Americans in their exposure to peer and parent role models for smoking, which may account for discrepancies in smoking rates in these groups (Robinson & Kleseges, 1997). Specifically, African American children were less likely to smoke than European American children, and they had fewer family members and friends who smoked. They also believed that smoking was less common than did European American children. These findings indicate that cultural variables (ethnic group), social factors (availability of role models), and basic principles of learning (observational learning) can all interact to influence whether young people start smoking (Ellickson et al., 2004).

Given the role that reinforcement plays in the acquisition of smoking behavior, it is not surprising that operant conditioning has been used to help people kick the smoking habit. **Behavior modification** techniques, which apply principles of operant conditioning to changing behavior, have been particularly effective in helping people quit smoking, especially when combined with nicotine replacement therapies (such as gum or the patch), which ease the symptoms of withdrawal. Smokers who participate in such programs are likely to live longer than those who don't (Anthonisen et al., 2005).

behavior modification
principles of operant conditioning used to change behavior.

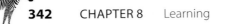

Quick Quiz 8.4: Bringing It All Together: Making Connections in Learning

1. Which model of learning best explains why people might start smoking?
   a. classical conditioning
   b. operant conditioning
   c. latent learning
   d. observational learning

2. Which model of learning best explains why people continue to smoke?
   a. classical conditioning
   b. operant conditioning
   c. latent learning
   d. both b and c

3. Which model of learning best explains how campaigns attempt to discourage smoking?
   a. classical conditioning
   b. sensitization
   c. latent learning
   d. observational learning

Answers can be found at the end of the chapter.

Chapter **Review**

BASIC PROCESSES OF LEARNING

- Learning is an enduring change in behavior that results from experience. It involves changes in sensation, perception, behavior, and brain function.

- Learning by association is a simple form of learning that links two pieces of information from the environment with one another because, in our experience, they repeatedly occur together.

CONDITIONING MODELS OF LEARNING

- Classical conditioning centers on stimulus–response (S–R) relationships. It involves the modification of reflexes with experience. A conditioned response occurs when a neutral stimulus (such as a bell) elicits what was previously an unconditioned response (such as salivation) to an unconditioned stimulus (such as food) when it is presented alone. After conditioning, the neutral stimulus is called a conditioned stimulus.

- In operant conditioning, the consequences of spontaneous behavior are manipulated in order to elicit the desired behavior. According to Skinner, certain consequences make a behavior more likely to occur again. When the consequences of a behavior increase the likelihood that a behavior will occur again, we say that the behavior has been reinforced. Reinforcement can be positive (something added) or negative (something subtracted). In contrast, punishment decreases the likelihood that a behavior will occur again. The stimuli used for reinforcement and punishment are unrelated to the target behavior. Shaping is the reinforcement of successive approximations of a desired behavior.

- Reinforcement may be presented every time a behavior occurs or only occasionally. Intermittent reinforcement, reinforcement that does not occur after every response, produces a stronger behavioral response than does continuous reinforcement. There are four schedules of reinforcement that dictate how an intermittent reinforcement might be implemented: fixed ratio, variable ratio, fixed interval, and variable interval.

- Conditioned taste aversion, the learned avoidance of a particular taste or food if sickness occurs at the same time as or shortly after exposure to it, can develop after only one exposure. The time lapse between exposure and getting sick may be an hour or more.

- Biological constraints limit the development of a conditioned response to a neutral stimulus that is relevant to the situation. For example, it is easier to make someone nauseated by a taste than by a sound or a sight.

- Biology limits behavioral options in order to make the adaptive ones more likely. The biological constraint model of learning suggests that some behaviors are inherently more likely to be learned than others. Instinctive drift, in which an organism fails to learn the target behavior because it conflicts with a stronger instinctive behavior, is a type of biological constraint.

- Latent learning occurs in the absence of reinforcement and is not demonstrated until later, when reinforcement occurs.

SOCIAL LEARNING THEORY

- Social learning theory takes into account the role of social influence in learning. Imitation or modeling plays a key role in how we learn, and it can work together with reinforcement to shape behavior. Bandura proposed that reinforcement makes learning more likely not only for the person doing the behavior but also for observers.

- Modeling is the process of observing and imitating behaviors performed by others, particularly behaviors that are rewarded in others.

THE INTERACTION OF NATURE AND NURTURE IN LEARNING

- Examples of the bidirectional relationship between learning and the brain include imprinting, the rapid and innate learning of the characteristics of a caregiver within a very short period of time after birth; sensitivity periods, when the brain is most receptive to learning certain skills; imitation; the growth and strengthening of synaptic connections in response to environmental stimuli; and environmental enrichment.

BRINGING IT ALL TOGETHER: MAKING CONNECTIONS IN LEARNING

- All of the major learning perspectives, as well as other factors, are needed to fully explain behaviors such as smoking.

- Applications derived from models of learning, such as behavior modification, may help people unlearn unwanted or undesirable behaviors, such as smoking.

Key **Terms**

association, p. 307
behavior modification, p. 342
biological constraint model, p. 328
classical conditioning, p. 308
conditioned response (CR), p. 309
conditioned stimulus (CS), p. 309
conditioned taste aversion, p. 323
conditioning, p. 307
continuous reinforcement, p. 319
enactive learning, p. 330
ethology, p. 335
extinction, p. 310
fixed interval (FI) schedule, p. 322
fixed ratio (FR) schedule, p. 321
imprinting, p. 335

instinctive drift, p. 328
intermittent reinforcement, p. 319
latent learning, p. 329
law of effect, p. 313
learning, p. 306
modeling, p. 332
negative punishment, p. 316
negative reinforcement, p. 316
observational learning, p. 330
operant conditioning, p. 314
positive punishment, p. 316
positive reinforcement, p. 316
primary reinforcers, p. 315
punishment, p. 316
reinforcer, p. 315

schedules of reinforcement, p. 321
secondary (or conditioned) reinforcers, p. 315
shaping, p. 318
Skinner box, p. 318
social learning, p. 331
spontaneous recovery, p. 310
stimulus discrimination, p. 310
stimulus generalization, p. 310
unconditioned response (UCR), p. 309
unconditioned stimulus (UCS), p. 309
variable interval (VI) schedule, p. 322
variable ratio (VR) schedule, p. 322

Quick Quiz **Answers**

Quick Quiz 8.1: 1. d 2. b 3. c 4. d 5. b 6. d
Quick Quiz 8.2: 1. a 2. d 3. b
Quick Quiz 8.3: 1. b 2. a 3. d
Quick Quiz 8.4: 1. d 2. b 3. a

Challenge Your Assumptions **Answers**

- Elephants can learn to paint paintings. **True. See p. 306.**
- Humans and lab rats basically learn in the same way. **False. See p. 328.**
- Pulling an all-nighter is a good way to study for an exam. **False. See pp. 324–325.**
- Children are not affected by watching violent cartoons or movies. **False. See pp. 332-334.**

Language and Thought

9

Chapter Outline

Challenge *Your Assumptions*

TRUE OR FALSE?

- French speakers understand the world differently than German speakers.
- Learning grammar is easy for everyone.
- Critical thinking involves seeing only the weaknesses and flaws in ideas.
- Most decisions we make are rational.
- Twenty-year-olds can learn to speak a second language without an accent just as easily as a six-year-old.

Answers can be found at the end of the chapter.

Susan had guests coming over and wanted the place to look nice. She wanted to have her new artistic bowl be the centerpiece of the table. As she was bringing it into the dining room, however, it slipped out of her hands and shattered on the floor. That one event, as it turns out, is described differently in different languages. English speakers would say, "She broke the bowl." But speakers of Japanese or Spanish would say, essentially, "The bowl broke itself." How we describe an event may affect our views of what caused it. English speakers, who use a more active voice, are more likely to blame the person in this situation. Japanese or Spanish speakers, on the other hand, use a more passive voice. They would be more likely to describe this as an unintentional act where no one is to blame (Begley, 2009).

Language influences our thoughts and perceptions. Another comparison between languages makes this clear. English is a bit unusual in one respect: It does not have gendered nouns. If you speak Spanish, you know about the masculine "el" and feminine "la"; or if you speak French, "le" and "la." Some languages even have three genders; for example, German has masculine ("der"), feminine ("die"), and neuter ("das"). Do you think these differences affect how speakers of these languages perceive the world?

Consider the case of the opening of the world's tallest bridge in France in 2004—the Millau Viaduct. The German press described it as breathtaking and elegant, whereas the French press described it as a concrete giant. One interesting difference between the languages is that in French "bridge" is masculine (*le pont*), but in German it is feminine (*die Brücke*) (Begley, 2009). Of course, we don't know for sure that the gender of the word affected the writers of these descriptions, but it may well not be a coincidence that they correspond to traditionally masculine and feminine traits. In short, the language we speak might influence how we think about and perceive the world.

Language is so much a part of being human that we forget it is possible to think without words. Yet when we dream, visually imagine something, or experience a strong sensation such as a touch or a smell, our thoughts are not initially word-bound. And surely the thoughts of young babies are not verbal. Still, most of our thoughts are translated into words. Even a smell is quickly labeled as a rose or a cake in the oven and so becomes a verbal experience as well as a sensory one. Language and thought develop side by side with few exceptions. One is not possible without the other, at least in adult humans.

This chapter introduces the psychology of language and thought, both separately and together. First we look at language by exploring its nature, evolution, and development in humans. Then we turn to current psychological research and theory concerning how we represent our thoughts visually and verbally. We will look at how people reason, form judgments, and make decisions. Finally, we bring all these topics together by examining how and when learning a second language changes our brain and affects our ability to reason, solve problems, and think flexibly. We will continue the discussion of thought in Chapter 10, where we discuss intelligence, problem solving, and creativity. ■

LANGUAGE

If you lived 300,000 years ago, before language was fully developed, how would you think? How would you communicate if everyone you met could only grunt and groan? Much like the other primates on the planet, you would communicate with other humans only about immediate, concrete states. Everything you knew would be experienced directly through smell, taste, hearing, sight, or touch. Your memory would be limited chiefly to events in the recent past; you would have no language with which to process events and store them in long-term memory. Culture and civilization as we know it could not exist without language. Without language, your ways of thinking, understanding, and transmitting knowledge would be limited to the here and now.

The Nature of Language

human language
a communication system specific to *Homo sapiens;* it is open and symbolic, has rules of grammar, and allows its users to express abstract and distant ideas.

Linguists define **human language** as an open and symbolic communication system that has rules of grammar and allows its users to express abstract and distant ideas (Bickerton, 1995). *Open* means that the system is dynamic and free to change. *Symbolic* means that there is no real connection between a sound and the meaning or idea associated with it. Sounds are parts of words that symbolize meaning and ideas. Words, in turn, are put together in ways that follow the rules of syntax and grammar. **Syntax** refers to the rules for arranging words and symbols in sentences (or parts of sentences), whereas **grammar** comprises the entire set of rules for combining symbols and sounds to speak and write a particular language and includes such things in English as subject–verb agreement, plurals, and use of possessives.

The easiest way to demonstrate the arbitrary nature of the connection between sound and meaning is to point out that we can say the exact same sentence in almost every language in the world, of which there are nearly 7,000. For example, "I am reading the book" can also be "*Ich lese das Buch*" in German," "*Estoy leyendo el libro*" in Spanish, "*Je lis le livre*" in French, and "*Я читаю книгу*" in Russian. Each language has its own distinct sounds for saying the same thing. Because this is true, ideas can often be directly translated—more or less—from one language to another, an idea we return to in "Bringing It All Together" at the end of the chapter.

Human language is unique because it is the only system capable of transmitting abstract ideas. Although most animals communicate, for the most part they are able to signal to other members of their species only their immediate and concrete states, such as being angry, threatened, hungry, hurt, or eager to reproduce

syntax
the rules for arranging words and symbols to form sentences or parts of sentences in a particular language.

grammar
the entire set of rules for combining symbols and sounds to speak and write a particular language.

If bonobos (pygmy chimps) could speak, what would these two be talking about? Bonobos do communicate with one another—not with words, but by leaving trail markers on the floor of the tropical forests where they live.

Language **349**

(Deacon, 1997). Yet humans using language can discuss not only immediate feelings and needs but also abstract and remote ideas or states of being, such as infinity, God, the afterlife, the universe—or whether Macs are better than PCs.

The Evolution of Language in Humans

As far as we know, earlier species of humans, such as *Homo erectus* and *Homo neanderthalensis*, had, at most, very rudimentary language, called **protolanguage,** or pre-language (Arbib, Liebal, & Pika, 2008; Givón & Malle, 2002). No one knows for sure when fully grammatical language first appeared, but archaeologists and linguists suggest that probably only our species *(Homo sapiens)* has used grammatical and syntactical language. If so, language is less than 150,000 to 200,000 years old.

protolanguage very rudimentary language; also known as pre-language; used by earlier species of *Homo.*

Because the development of fully grammatical language is such a big and unusual step, scientists think that evolution of language and evolution of the brain were intertwined. Anthropologists and psychologists suggest that the complexity of the human brain and the human ability to use language co-evolved. That is, as our ancestors moved from protolanguage to grammatical language, they required brains with greater working memory and the ability for abstract thought (Arbib et al., 2008; Deacon, 1997; Dunbar, 2001). As the human brain, and especially the frontal lobes, grew larger and larger, people became capable of thinking and communicating more and more complex and abstract thoughts. Increases in the size of human social groups may have triggered increased brain size as well. The more complex a group is, the greater the need for its members to communicate (Dunbar, 2001). Moreover, large group size led to a greater need to cooperate and help others. The needs for reciprocating and cooperating also played a role in the evolution of human language (Nowak & Sigmund, 2005). Finally, recent evidence also suggests that because language and music share much of the same structure and function, they may have evolved simultaneously (Roederer, 2009).

Nature & Nurture

The development of language, the evolution of the brain, and the development of culture are all connected.

Language Development in Individuals

If you have ever traveled to a country where you don't speak the language, you know that a foreign language can seem like a single, continuous string of sounds. It is hard to know where one word ends and the next one begins unless you have been hearing and speaking that language since early childhood. As young children develop their understanding of language, they learn that the sounds coming from the mouths of the people around them are meaningful units that form words.

In a child's language development, the ability to understand words develops before the ability to produce words (Fenson et al., 1994). We can easily observe that comprehension comes first because babies can do many things that are asked of them, such as pointing to their nose, long before they can say the words associated with those actions. Language comprehension, as we saw in Chapter 3, occurs in the left hemisphere of the brain, in the region called Wernicke's area, whereas language production is associated with the left-hemisphere region called Broca's area (see Figure 9.1). The fact that infants understand language before they start speaking suggests that Wernicke's area develops earlier than Broca's area.

Wernicke's area
(speech understanding)

Broca's area
(speech formation)

Occipital lobe

FIGURE **9.1**
WERNICKE'S AND BROCA'S AREAS AND THE OCCIPITAL LOBES. The occipital lobes are home to the visual cortex. As we'll see later, thinking involves both verbal and visual representations.

cooing
the first sounds humans make other than crying, consisting almost exclusively of vowels; occurs during first 6 months of life.

babbling
sounds made as a result of the infant's experimentation with a complex range of phonemes, which include consonants as well as vowels; starts around 5–6 months.

one-word utterances
single words, such as "mama," "dada," "more," or "no!"; occur around 12 months of age.

Stages of Language Development   The first speech sounds humans make consist almost exclusively of vowels, such as "aah, ee, ooh." Most infants begin uttering repeated vowel sounds, called **cooing,** during the first 6 months. Cooing sounds are universal: They vary little from hearing to deaf babies or among babies from all over the world.

Babbling overlaps with cooing, and it starts at around 5 or 6 months of age. **Babbling** refers to the infant's experimentation with a complex range of sounds, called phonemes, which include consonants as well as vowels. In babbling, however, the sounds are not yet recognizable as words. At first babies babble single syllables, such as "buh" and "duh"; later they utter "gibberish," which is simply a string of single syllables, such as "da, buh, ma, wee. . . ."

At first, babbling babies make many more sounds than they hear in their native language. Before babies' brains have been fully shaped by their native language, they can make many more sounds than their parents can. They can also hear more sounds than their parents (Jusczyk, 1997; Plunkett, 1997). Adults who speak certain Asian languages, which do not distinguish between "r" and "l" for example, do not perceive a difference between these two sounds. Yet their toddler children do. As children progress through the babbling stage, and with repeated exposure to the subset of sounds in their native language, they "prune" away sounds that are not used in that language and lose the ability to say or perceive nonnative sounds (Goto, 1971; Kuhl, Stevens, & Hayashi, 2006).

At the end of the babbling stage, usually at around 12 months, **one-word utterances** emerge. Now children first speak such classic words as "mama," "dada," "more," and the all-important "no!" One-word utterances are likely descended from protolanguage. Like toddlers, our ancestors probably made up sounds for objects (nouns) and actions (verbs) before they developed more complex sentences (Goldfield, 2000).

Whether a word is at the beginning, middle, or end of a sentence seems to be related to how likely young children are to learn that word. Children tend to acquire words that are spoken at the ends of sentences first. For example, in languages that are structured in the order of subject-verb-object, such as English, children acquire nouns earlier than verbs because objects are nouns. In languages that are structured subject-object-verb, such as Japanese and Mandarin, children acquire verbs earlier than nouns (Chan, Brandone, & Tardif, 2009; Clancy, 1985; Tardif, Gelman, & Xu, 1999). In English, for example, we say, "Maria read the book," whereas in Japanese people say, "Maria the book read." English-speaking children learn *book* before *read*, whereas Japanese-speaking children learn the Japanese version of *read* before *book*. This tendency to learn the last word in a sentence first may reflect the memory phenomenon called the *recency effect* discussed in Chapter 7.

Starting around 18 months, children make **two-word utterances** such as "my ball," "mo wawa" (more water), or "go way" (go away). During this phase of language development, parents often find themselves serving as translators because their children create unique ways of saying things. For instance, our youngest son, Evan, would say "ba" for any kind of water. Why? Because he had learned to say "ba" to mean "bottle of water." He extended "ba" to other types of water, such as a lake, pool, or bathtub, which we easily understood. Our babysitters did not, however, so we had to translate "Evanese" for them.

By age 2½ or 3, most children enter the third phase of language development—the **sentence phase**—in which they begin speaking in fully grammatical sentences. This transition happens so quickly that linguists usually have a tough time studying it. Linguist Steven Pinker uses Adam as an example. At age 2, Adam would say, "Play checkers. Big drum. I got horn." Less than a year later, at age 3, he would say, "I going come in fourteen minutes. You dress me up like a baby elephant. You know how to put it back together" (Pinker, 1994, pp. 273–274). These sentences may not always be what adults consider grammatically correct, but they are grammatical sentences.

In sum, children go through a very predictable sequence in acquiring language: from cooing to babbling, one-word utterances, two-word utterances, and finally adultlike sentence structure, a stage that is reached around age 3. These stages in speech development map remarkably well onto the growth in the child's overall brain size (see Figure 9.2). There is a steep rise in both brain growth and language between the ages of 1 and 3. The brain of a 3-year-old child has reached about 80% of adult size. At about this age children can form adult-like sentences.

The Sensitivity Period An important principle of language development is that if children are not exposed to any human language before a certain age,

two-word utterances
phrases children put together, starting around 18 months, such as "my ball," "mo wawa," or "go way."

sentence phase
stage when children begin speaking in fully grammatical sentences; usually age 2½ to 3.

By age 3, children begin to speak in fully grammatical sentences. Their brains are also nearly adult size.

FIGURE **9.2**

ASSOCIATION BETWEEN BRAIN GROWTH AND LANGUAGE DEVELOPMENT. As the child's brain approaches its final adult size, the onset and rapid development of language matches the rapid growth of the brain. At age 1, when the child's brain is less than 50% of its adult size, the infant is babbling and perhaps saying a few words. By age 3, when the brain is 75%–80% of its adult size, the child has progressed to two-word phrases and short sentences. (Source: Sakai, 2005)

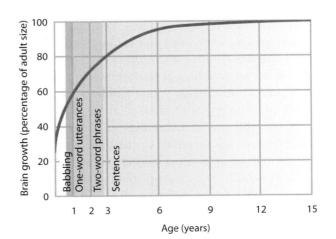

their language abilities never fully develop (Lenneberg, 1967; Newport, 2003; Uylings, 2006). This sensitivity period for language acquisition begins in the first years of life and ends at about age 12. It is the optimal time for learning language. Severe neglect and lack of exposure during this period cause permanent problems in language development. As Uylings (2006) points out, sensitivity periods end after neural pruning and neural wiring have reached their peak, at which point the plasticity of neural connections becomes less flexible.

One of the most dramatic examples of the importance of the sensitivity period in language development is the case of an abused and severely neglected girl known as "Genie." When she was 2 years old, a family doctor diagnosed Genie as being mildly retarded (Rymer, 1993). Her father, who was mentally unstable, interpreted this to mean that she was severely retarded and needed "protection." He tied her to a chair all day long and caged her in a crib at night. Moreover, he beat her every time she tried to speak and barked at her like a dog. This abuse lasted until Genie was 13½, when her mother finally ran away, taking Genie with her. The local social worker whose help they sought thought Genie was 6 or 7 years old because she was only 4 feet 6 inches tall and weighed 59 pounds. The social worker arranged for the state of California to take temporary custody of the child. At that time, Genie could speak only a few words, such as *stopit* or *nomore.*

At age 17, after 4 years of language training, Genie's language skills were still extremely delayed. She could communicate simple ideas, but her speech was limited mainly to ungrammatical sentences. She would say things like "Spot chew glove" or "Applesauce buy store" (*Transcripts,* 1997). In this sense, her language ability was at the level of a young child's. Her language comprehension, however, was much better than her language production. She understood much of what was said to her. Brain imaging revealed something most unusual about Genie's brain activity while speaking or listening: The activity was located mostly in her right hemisphere (Curtiss, 1977). Recall that language ability is located in the left hemisphere. The case of Genie suggests that left-hemisphere speech development requires stimulation from the environment during a certain sensitivity period if it is to develop properly.

As tragic as Genie's story is, it reveals something very important about language: We need verbal stimulation from others, and we need it while we are young children if we are to develop fully and completely the ability to speak. Now in her early 50s, Genie lives in supportive foster care. The movie *Mockingbird Don't Sing,* released in 2001, is based on her life.

Theories of Language Acquisition

Unless they suffer from some sort of disease or deficit, all humans learn to speak, including those who were born deaf. Many children who can't hear learn spoken language in order to communicate with hearing individuals, but many rely heavily on sign language as well. Sign language is every bit as complex and communicative as spoken language. This suggests that we have innate, genetically based structures in the brain that enable us to learn language. Yet the vast differences in how well each of us learns to speak illustrate the importance

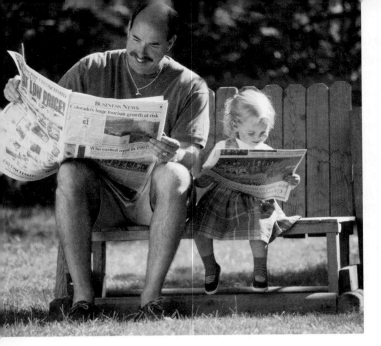

Imitating family members helps shape children's language and vocabulary.

of environmental stimulation. Different theories of language acquisition emphasize contributions of nature and nurture to language differently, but they all agree that both are involved.

Sociocultural Theories We learn language from the people around us. We acquire vocabulary by hearing others speak, and we figure out what they mean by the context (Hoff, 2006; Y. Zhang et al., 2008). Children who hear more total and unique words, and more complex sentences, develop their language faster and more richly than those who do not (Gathercole & Hoff, 2007; Huttenlocher et al., 2002; Pan et al., 2005). In a review of the evidence for how environment shapes and molds language acquisition, Erika Hoff (2006) provides a partial list of the environmental influences on language. They include culture, socioeconomic status, birth order, school, peers, television, and parents. Each of these influences has a rich research history demonstrating how sociocultural forces shape language development, particularly the timing of vocabulary development.

Much of what we learn comes from imitating family members. Imitation is doing exactly what you see someone else do, and with certain behaviors imitation is evident immediately after birth. Newborns as young as 50 minutes old will stick out their tongues or open their mouths when they see an adult do so (Meltzoff & Moore, 1983). At a slightly older age babies try to imitate the speech sounds they hear (Kuhl & Meltzoff, 1997). Adults, in turn, do many things to encourage imitation. For example, they speak in a higher pitch, raise and lower the volume of their voice, use simpler sentence structures, emphasize the here and now, and use emotion to communicate their messages (Fernald & Morikawa, 1993; M. L. Rice, 1989). These changes in adult speech patterns— which appear to be universal—are referred to as **child-directed speech.**

child-directed speech

changes in adult speech patterns— apparently universal—when speaking to young children or infants; characterized by higher pitch, changes in voice volume, use of simpler sentences, emphasis on the here and now, and use of emotion to communicate messages.

The richness of verbal stimulation from family members affects the timing of a child's vocabulary development (Hoff, 2006). For instance, the children of very verbally responsive mothers reach the 50-word vocabulary milestone a full 5 months earlier than do children of less verbally responsive mothers. More generally, much of the differences in the timing of the child's vocabulary development can be explained by three characteristics of the mother: her socioeconomic status, her vocabulary use, and her personality characteristics.

Although these are very social processes we have been discussing, they also demonstrate profound interdependence with brain processes, which is yet another example of the interplay between nature and nurture. Mirror neurons, the clusters of brain cells that fire not only when an individual performs some task (such as sticking out one's tongue), but also when an individual observes another person do the same task, facilitate social learning and imitation (Rizzolatti & Arbib, 1998; Rizzolatti & Craighero, 2004). Many human social skills, including speech, develop because our brains allow and foster such social learning.

Connections

One reason newborn infants are capable of imitating behavior immediately after birth is that humans and other animals have "mirror neurons." These were detected first after a chance observation in laboratory monkeys.

See "The Cells of the Nervous System: Glial Cells and Neurons," Chapter 3, "The Biology of Behavior," p. 84, and "Imitation, Mirror Neurons, and Learning," Chapter 8, "Learning," p. 336.

Conditioning and Learning Theory

B. F. Skinner (1957) believed that language is like any other behavior: something that exists because it is reinforced and shaped. He proposed that we speak not because we want to convey an idea or a feeling but, rather, because we have been reinforced for doing so. What are the conditions that bring about or reinforce verbal behavior? According to Skinner, children learn to speak a particular language because when they say anything that even comes close to a word, the parents smile and say things like "Wow! She said 'mama'!" The parents' reaction has a reinforcing effect, making the child more likely to say that word; that is, the reaction shapes her behavior.

As we just discussed, young children begin language development by cooing, then babbling, then uttering one and two words until they begin to say short phrases and sentences. Skinner explained this progression in terms of shaping, successive approximations, and reinforcement: The first approximation of a complex behavior will be reinforced. When, for instance, a toddler utters "mama," she gets more of her mother's attention and smiles than she does when she utters "baba." The child learns first that the word *mama* matters and soon thereafter learns what it means. In a short while the child is saying "mama go bye-bye." Each step is subsequently reinforced until the child reaches the final behavior, which, in this case, would be speaking in fully grammatical sentences—"Mommy is going away."

Nativist Theory

There is little doubt that language development, such as the acquisition of certain words, is shaped partly by parental responses. When a child correctly names an object for the first time—such as "doggy"—the parents lavish much praise and encouragement: "Yes, that's right! Spot is a doggy!" However, such reinforcement does not occur as consistently for other aspects of language development, such as syntax and grammar rules. Still, children seem to learn these aspects with little difficulty. In fact, children tend to overgeneralize language rules; for example, they may add *ed* to *run* to form the past tense because adding *ed* is the typical way of forming the past tense in English. Instead of saying "Spot ran," then, the child says "Spot runned." Reinforcement cannot explain this formation, because children most likely have never heard "runned" from their parents and so have not been reinforced for using it. In other words, it is impossible to learn novel utterances through imitation and reinforcement. One cannot use shaping to teach someone to say something no one has ever said. So Skinner's explanation of language acquisition cannot fully explain how we learn language.

Some linguists contend that we discover language rather than learn it, that language development is "native," or inborn. This is the main assumption of the **nativist view of language.** In this view, the brain is structured, or "wired," for language learning; indeed, as you have learned, Broca's and Wernicke's areas are dedicated to speech production and comprehension, respectively. The linguist Noam Chomsky (1972, 1986) has argued that humans are born with a **language acquisition device (LAD)**—an innate, biologically based capacity to acquire language. Just as birds are biologically built to fly, humans are biologically built to speak. It is part of our nature; hence the term *nativist*. Further, Chomsky (1972, 2000) has suggested that there is essentially a single universal

nativist view of language
the idea that we discover language rather than learn it, that language development is inborn.

language acquisition device (LAD)
an innate, biologically based capacity to acquire language, proposed by Noam Chomsky as part of his nativist view of language.

Language **355**

Noam Chomsky

grammar underlying all human languages; each individual language is simply a specific expression of this universal grammar.

Chomsky argues for a built-in language acquisition device partly because of how easily and automatically humans learn to do this most complex and difficult thing: speak in complete and grammatical sentences. It is universal. Moreover, it develops in children in about the same way and at the same time all over the world, regardless of which language they learn. Indeed, any child can learn equally easily any language as her or his native language. If you grew up in certain regions of Africa, you would be speaking Swahili; certain parts of Asia, Mandarin; certain parts of Europe, German.

Chomsky also argues that our biologically based language acquisition device must have *principles* of universal grammar that allow a child to learn any language as her or his native language (Chomsky, 2000; Radford, 1997). Universal grammar follows universal principles. For instance, a universal grammar principle might be "Languages have subjects, objects, and verbs." All languages have these components of speech, but they vary in where they can be put in sentences. As we have seen earlier in the chapter, English, for instance, is a subject-verb-object (S-V-O) language, whereas Japanese is a subject-object-verb (S-O-V) language.

Although there are universal principles for language, each specific language sets limits, or parameters, for what is correct. We learn these parameters as we learn to speak: Verbs go before objects in English but after them in Japanese. Limits, or parameters, make clear why it is relatively easy for a child to learn a particular language: Every language has rules that limit possible word orders

According to Noam Chomsky, regardless of where we are born or what language we are exposed to, we have no trouble learning it.

and other aspects of language. Once children learn those rules, or limits, of their particular language, forming grammatically correct sentences becomes relatively easy (Dunbar, 2001; Pinker, 1994). And they learn these rules easily because of a built-in language acquisition device.

Nature, Nurture, and Language Learning

As we have seen, different theorists emphasize different contributions of nature and nurture. Social and learning theorists argue for the importance of social input and stimulation, whereas nativist theorists argue for the importance of brain structures and genetic factors. Yet, once again, both perspectives are needed to fully explain language. Most scholars of language agree that acquiring language involves natural abilities that are modified by the language learner's environment (Hoff, 2006; Lidz & Gleitman, 2004; MacWhinney, 1999). Indeed, the phrase *innately guided learning* captures the interaction between nature and nurture very well (Elman et al., 1996). We learn to speak, but in doing so we are guided by our innate capacity for language learning. The importance of both nature and nurture is starkly illustrated by the case of Genie: She could speak, and even learned a few words as a child, but her environment was so barren that her language development was severely stunted.

Still, genetic factors and innate structures have a stronger influence on some aspects of language development, while environmental conditions have a greater influence on other aspects. For instance, grammar is more innate and genetically influenced than vocabulary, which is more strongly shaped by input from the environment (Dale et al., 2000; Hoff, 2006). Recall that one common way to determine how much of a trait is due to genetic influence is by comparing identical twin pairs to fraternal twin pairs (see Chapter 2). If a trait is strongly genetically influenced, it will show much stronger correlations in identical twins than in fraternal twins because identical twins are more genetically alike than fraternal twins. Dale and colleagues (2000) compared vocabulary and grammar skills in 1,008 identical twin pairs to those same skills in 1,890 fraternal twin pairs; all were about 2 years old. The children's parents assessed their vocabulary and grammar skills by completing questionnaires dealing with the kinds of words and sentences their children could say. Identical twin pairs were more similar in vocabulary and grammar than were fraternal twin pairs. Figures from the study show us that genetics influences about 25% of vocabulary development and about 40% of learning about grammar (Dale et al., 2000).

Moreover, brain systems not only are involved with language development, but the two also change together over time (Szaflarski et al.,

Nature & Nurture

The fact that you speak a language fluently means you made use of innately guided learning as a child. Your brain is set up to accept and respond to language.

Studies of twins, like these fraternal twins, suggest that grammar is more influenced by genetics than by the environment, whereas vocabulary is more influenced by the environment than by genetics.

FIGURE **9.3**

DEVELOPMENT OF LANGUAGE REGIONS IN THE BRAIN. Brain regions that decrease in activity from ages 5 to 11 are shown in A, whereas brain regions that gain in activity during language processing are shown in B. The regions that decrease are in the left insula, cingulate gyrus, and thalamus, whereas the regions that increase in activity are the well-known Broca's and Wernicke's regions of the left hemisphere. (Source: Szaflarski et al., 2006)

2006). Not surprisingly, between the ages of 5 and 11 years old, the brain regions associated with language (Broca's area and Wernicke's area: see Figure 9.3) increase in activity during language processing.

Animals of all kinds communicate with members of their own species. Birds sing songs to tell other birds where they are, that they want to mate, or that a predator is nearby; sometimes they sing just for the fun of it (Rothenberg, 2005). Whales sing long, melancholic (to human ears) tones that other whales hear from miles away. Bees dance to tell other bees where nectar can be found. Apes in the wild communicate only what they want other apes to do and not internal states or feelings or desires as humans often do (Tomasello & Hermann, 2010). But do these forms of animal communication represent the ability to use language as humans use it?

Can Other Species Learn Human Language?

For centuries it was argued that the capacity for language is what separates humans from other animals. Yet, if humans share almost all of their genes with chimps, and humans and apes share a common ancestor from roughly 6 million years ago, an obvious question is, Is it possible for apes to learn human language?

Chimps do not have a vocal apparatus that allows them to speak, so they are physically incapable of making the same range of sounds that humans can

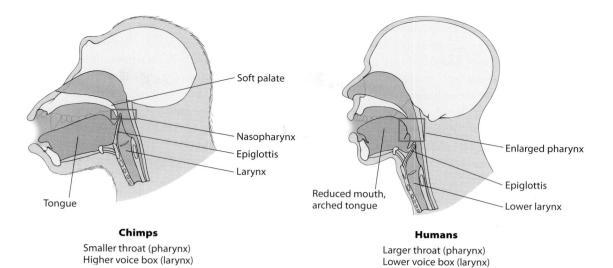

Chimps
Smaller throat (pharynx)
Higher voice box (larynx)

Humans
Larger throat (pharynx)
Lower voice box (larynx)

FIGURE **9.4**

VOCAL ANATOMY OF CHIMPS AND HUMANS. Vocal structures (throat, voice box, tongue) determine the kinds of sounds chimps and humans are capable of making. (Source: From Deacon, T. W. 1996. *The symbolic species: Co-evolution of language and the brain*, p. 356. Copyright © 1997 by Terrence W. Deacon. Used by permission of W.W. Norton & Company, Inc. This selection may not be reproduced, stored in a retrieval system, or transmitted in any form or by any means without the prior written permission of the publisher.)

(see Figure 9.4). The only way humans can teach apes to communicate is to use a nonvocal sign language, most often American Sign Language (ASL). A number of captive apes have learned ASL to different degrees and have been able to communicate with humans. Allen and Beatrix Gardner, for instance, have compiled more than 400 ASL signs that three chimps named Dar, Tatu, and Moja acquired in the course of extensive training (R A. Gardner, Gardner, & Van Cantfort, 1989). Their first chimp, Washoe, learned to sign almost 200 distinct words. Another chimp, Sarah, developed a vocabulary of about 100 words (Premack, 1971). Perhaps the most linguistically gifted ape to date is Kanzi, a bonobo chimp (Cohen, 2010; Rumbaugh, Beran, & Savage-Rumbaugh, 2003).

Kanzi was the son of Matata, who had been caught wild in Zaire. When Matata was an adult, linguist Sue Savage-Rumbaugh attempted to teach her sign language, with limited success. Kanzi was present during these training sessions but was not formally taught any signs. Savage-Rumbaugh soon discovered, however, that Kanzi had been paying attention to the signs being taught to his mother. Moreover, he learned more quickly and developed a larger vocabulary than his mother. The research team decided to compare Kanzi's language comprehension to that of a 2½-year-old human child, Alia. At the time, Kanzi was 7 years old. Both Kanzi and Alia were given 660 spoken requests to see whether they understood them well enough to carry them out. The requests were things like "Take the shoe to the bathroom," "Give Karen an apple," or "Put the pine needles in the refrigerator," and reversals such as "Make the doggie bite the snake" then "Make the snake bite the doggie" (Rumbaugh, Beran, & Savage-Rumbaugh, 2003, p. 411). Alia and Kanzi performed these commands at very similar levels of success— about 70%. Since then, Kanzi, now 27 years old, has learned to comprehend as many as 3,000 English words (Raffaele, 2006).

If apes can learn sign language, do they use it to talk with each other? The answer seems to be, Sometimes, in some circumstances, and in some species of ape. So what do apes sign to one another about? Fouts and colleagues (1984) analyzed the types of conversations five signing chimpanzees had among themselves. They found that 88% of the conversations were about social interaction, play, and reassurance, whereas the other 12% were about feeding, grooming, cleaning, discipline, and chimps signing, or "talking," to themselves (just as we humans talk to ourselves) (Fouts, Fouts, & Schoenfeld, 1984). More incredibly, one chimp, also named Washoe, spontaneously began teaching her adopted son Loulis how to sign (Fouts, 1997). Human trainers were careful not to sign around Loulis to ensure that he would learn only from Washoe. After just 8 weeks with Washoe, Loulis would regularly sign with humans, and after 18 months he had learned about 20 signs.

Taken together, however, even the most linguistically talented apes are limited compared to humans. First, the developmental sequence in which they acquire signs is slower than the sequence in which humans do so. For instance, a gorilla named Koko acquired signs at about half the speed of very young human children (Parker & McKinney, 1999), and Loulis learned only about one sign a month during his first 18 months of learning. In addition, apes seldom progress beyond two- or three-word combinations, which means that their highest level of language learning is equivalent to the level achieved by a toddler in terms of vocabulary and sentence structure. Adult apes may have vocabularies of 100 to 300 words, whereas an average high school student knows 60,000 words (Hauser, Chomsky, & Fitch, 2002; Parker & McKinney, 1999). Finally, nonhuman primates seldom either understand or consistently use correct word order

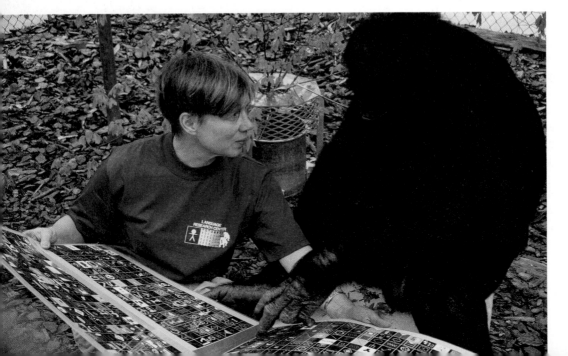

Kanzi, a bonobo who understands at least 3,000 English words, uses symbols to communicate with his teacher, linguist Sue Savage-Rumbaugh.

(syntax). For example, one chimp, named Nim Chimsky, after linguist Noam Chomsky, would alternate among "Banana give Nim," "Give Nim banana," and "Banana Nim give" (Terrace, 1987).

Given the successes and limits of language acquisition by apes, the scientific community is split on the question of whether apes really can use language to communicate with humans (Cohen, 2010). On the one hand, some researchers emphasize the linguistic abilities of apes. Often they have raised these apes like children of their own and taught them language. Such close relationships can also bias their perceptions—causing them to see things that may or may not be there. On the other hand, others, often linguists with little direct experience with apes, emphasize the linguistic limitations of apes. The main conclusion to draw from these opposing views is that the capacity for learning language in rudimentary form evolved from our early ancestors—ancestors common to both humans and apes (Deacon, 1997).

Language, Culture, and Thought

Does the language we speak cause us to see the world in a particular way? Can people who speak vastly different languages communicate effectively, even in translation? After we learn our native language, can we still learn about concepts that do not exist in our language but only in other languages?

According to the *Whorf-Sapir hypothesis,* language creates thought as much as thought creates language (Whorf, 1956). Anthropologists Benjamin Whorf and Edward Sapir, the authors of the Whorf-Sapir hypothesis, suggested that language shapes our thoughts and perceptions to such an extent that people who speak languages that lack a common foundation, such as English and Chinese, have difficulty directly communicating and translating their ideas from one language to the other. Taken to its logical conclusion, the Whorf-Sapir view leads to the **linguistic determinism hypothesis,** which states that our language determines our way of thinking and our perceptions of the world. In this view, if there are no words for certain objects or concepts in one's language, it is not possible to think about those objects or concepts.

An example offers support for the linguistic determinism hypothesis. The Pirahã, a very small tribe of only about 200 people that lives in the Amazon area of Brazil, are challenging some of science's most basic notions of language, numbers, memory, perception, and thought (Everett, 2005). The Pirahã have no words for the numbers higher than 2. As a result, it is nearly impossible for them to learn concepts such as 9 or 10. They even have difficulty learning simple arithmetic relationships, such as 3 + 1 (Gordon, 2004). This difficulty occurs not because they are unintelligent but, rather, because their language so strongly works against such concepts. They function very well without these concepts, and by adulthood learning them is rather difficult.

The most radical claim made by linguists studying the Pirahã is that the

linguistic determinism hypothesis the proposition that our language determines our way of thinking and our perceptions of the world; the view taken by Sapir and Whorf.

Support for the linguistic determinism hypothesis comes from studies of the Pirahã tribe in Brazil. The language of the Pirahã has no words for numbers higher than 2, and they have difficulty learning simple arithmetic relationships because they don't need them in their daily life.

Pirahã have no way to include one clause within another. They can construct only independent clauses. For example, they cannot say something like "When I finish eating, I want to speak to you." Instead, they must say two things: "I finish eating. I speak to you" (Bower, 2005). This claim is radical because it directly challenges the concept of a universal grammar. According to Chomsky, a cornerstone of universal grammar is that all languages embed clauses within clauses. The Pirahã, however, do not do this; they do not construct sentences that start with words like *when, before,* or *after,* and as a result they are limited to talking about the here and now and only about what is directly observable. Not surprisingly, they lack stories about the ancient past—they have no stories, for instance, of how the world began, and they refer only to known, living relatives.

Nonetheless, the view that language determines our thinking is almost certainly overstated. In fact, most research on the topic shows how language influences rather than determines our thinking (Boroditsky, 2001; Newcombe & Uttal, 2006; Regier & Kay, 2009; Regier et al., 2010). This position is known as *linguistic relativism.* A good example of linguistic relativism was reported in a study on how language affects color perception (Winawer et al., 2007). Russian has distinct words for lighter blues (*goluboy*) and darker blues (*siniy*). English has only "blue." When researchers presented 20 different shades of blue to both Russian and English speakers, they discovered Russian speakers were faster— by milliseconds—at discriminating between these two shades of blue that came from within the same category (either within *goluboy* or within *siniy*) than when they came from different categories of blue; see the Research Process for this chapter (Figure 9.5). For English speakers, however, who have no words for the different categories of blue, the category of blue made no difference. This is a typical finding on how language influences but does not determine thinking and perception.

As these examples illustrate, thought, memory, number, and perception are all tied to language. In fact, language is a close cousin to thought—humans rely on language for organizing, storing, and communicating ideas. Our ability to think, reason, and make decisions often takes verbal form. Let's therefore turn our attention to human thought, reasoning, and decision making.

Quick Quiz 9.1: Language

1. A language's particular rules for arranging words and symbols in a sentence or parts of a sentence is called
   a. grammar
   b. lexicon
   c. syntax
   d. representation

2. During which stage of language development do babies make many more sounds than they hear in their native languages?
   a. babbling
   b. cooing
   c. one-word utterances
   d. telegraphic speech

3. According to Skinner, children learn to speak a particular language because
   a. they possess an inherent ability to speak
   b. they engage in imitation of what they hear
   c. they have a language acquisition device
   d. they get reinforcement from their parents for various utterances

4. Which theory of language argues that if there are no words for certain objects or concepts in one's language, one is unable to think about those objects or concepts?
   a. nativist theory
   b. theory of innately guided learning
   c. linguistic determinism hypothesis
   d. Skinnerian theory of language

Answers can be found at the end of the chapter.

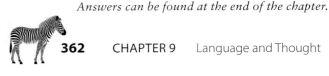

Research Process

1 Research Question

Is people's ability to discriminate colors altered by language? Unlike English, Russian has two distinct words for lighter blues (*goluboy*) and darker blues (*siniy*); English does not. Does knowledge of these different color categories affect how quickly a person can discriminate between different shades of blue?

2 Method

Winawer and colleagues (2007) designed a quasi-experiment to measure color discrimination performance in native English and Russian speakers in a simple perceptual task. Twenty color stimuli spanning the Russian *siniy/goluboy* range were used. The participants viewed colors arranged in a triad as shown above. Their task was to indicate as quickly and accurately as possible which of the two bottom color squares was identical to the top square.

The prediction was that for the Russian speakers the time it takes them to identify the color as matching the target would depend on whether the color was in the same category or a different one. For English speakers there would be no real difference in reaction times for blues that were in the same or a different Russian color category.

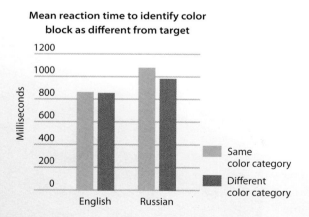

Mean reaction time to identify color block as different from target

3 Results

Russian speakers were faster at discriminating blues that came from different color categories than at discriminating blues that came from within the same category. For English speakers, response time did not differ for same versus different category of blue, because there is only one category of blue in English.

4 Conclusion

Knowledge of words for different categories of blue does affect how quickly people can discriminate between examples of blue. Notice, however, that the English speakers performed very well overall—in fact, they were faster than Russian speakers—but their performance was not affected by the different language categories. Language knowledge can influence thought.

FIGURE **9.5**

LANGUAGE AND COLOR DISCRIMINATION. Words for color influence our perception of thinking about those colors.
Source: J. Winawer, N. Witthoft, M. C. Frank, L. Wu, A. R. Wade, & L. Boroditsky, 2007, Russian blues reveal effect of language on color discrimination. *Proceedings of the National Academy of Sciences, 104,* 7780–7785.

Among other things, humans rely on language to communicate ideas about who we are and how we feel.

THINKING, REASONING, AND DECISION MAKING

What does it mean to know something? For instance, if our bodies just do something automatically, like breathing or digesting food, could we say that we know how to breathe and digest or that we just do it?

These questions and examples suggest that knowledge is distinct from instinct, and certainly it is. In this section we explore some questions about mental processes, such as how we come to know anything as well as how we know that we know anything. Psychologists use the word **cognition,** which means "to know," to refer to mental processes involved in acquiring, processing, and storing knowledge. **Cognitive psychology** is the science of how people think, learn, remember, and perceive (Sternberg, 2006a). Humans are unique in their ability to represent ideas and think abstract and symbolic thoughts.

In this section, we will consider three fundamental questions about cognition and reasoning:

- How do we represent thoughts in our minds?
- How do we reason about evidence?
- How do we make judgments and decisions?

cognition
mental processes involved in acquiring, processing, and storing knowledge.

cognitive psychology
the study of how people perceive, remember, think, speak, and solve problems.

How Do We Represent Thoughts in Our Minds?

Have you ever wondered, "Where exactly in my brain is a thought?" Cognitive psychologists and neuroscientists have and have even conducted research to find an answer. Cognitive psychologists, however, frame the question this way: How do we store or represent thoughts in our minds?

Even with the most up-to-date brain imaging technology, we cannot actually see inside the brain as it conjures up an image or comes up with a solution to a problem. Imaging techniques can only measure changes in blood flow, which suggest brain activity. We cannot and probably never will be able to actually *see* thoughts and ideas. Yet it is clear that we all have thoughts, memories, and ideas, so the question arises: How do we use our brains to store and maintain these mental processes?

Cognitive psychologists approach this question by proposing that we represent ideas, knowledge, or memories as *mental representations*. A **mental representation** is a structure in our mind—such as an idea or image—that stands for something else, such as the external object or thing (Thagard, 1995). In general, mental representations are frequently not about things we are currently sensing (seeing, touching, or smelling, for instance), but rather about things we sensed in the past. Mental representations, therefore, allow us to think about and remember things in the past or imagine

How does the brain store and maintain mental processes?

mental representation
a structure in our mind—such as an idea or image—that stands for something else, such as an external object or thing sensed in the past or future, not the present.

Connection

The occipital and parietal lobes of the brain develop before the temporal and frontal lobes. This pattern of growth partly explains why we see before we can talk. See "Physical Development in Infancy and Childhood," Chapter 5, "Human Development," p. 178.

visual imagery
visual representations created by the brain after the original stimulus is no longer present.

things in the future. They also allow us to think about abstract ideas that have no physical existence, such as love, truth, beauty, or justice. For the most part, we represent ideas and thoughts in our minds visually and verbally.

Visual Representation We think in both images and words. The visual system, located mostly in the occipital lobes (see Figure 9.1), is older in evolutionary terms than the verbal system. It also develops before verbal ability (Givón, 2002): We see before we talk. Consider how babies respond to picture books before they learn to talk.

Every animal with eyes perceives visual images, but only those animals with significant cortex are better able to keep and store visual sensations in mind after the sensory stimulation stops. Indeed, visual perception occurs while the stimulus is still present, as we learned in Chapter 4. **Visual imagery,** however, involves visual representations created by the brain after the original stimulus is no longer present (Kosslyn, 2005). The brain is active much the same way during visual imagery as it is during visual perception. Thus, you would have a hard time distinguishing between a brain image of someone actually perceiving something and a brain image of someone imagining seeing the same thing (W. L. Thompson & Kosslyn, 2000).

Being able to imagine things that are not currently being perceived is a very useful and complex skill, although about 2% of the population cannot do it at all (Kosslyn 2002). People clearly differ in their ability to imagine an event or object in their "mind's eye" (Ganis, Thompson, & Kosslyn, 2009; Kosslyn, Van Kleeck, & Kirby, 1990). If you have the ability to imagine outcomes, you can make them more likely to happen. For instance, if you first form a mental image of an ideal performance, such as hitting a home run or playing a piece of music without errors, you are more likely to perform that activity better (Hale, Seiser, & McGuire, 2005). Performance may be improved because the brain is primed by the images of success; that is, the pathways are activated in advance. Neuroscientists have shown that the brain is activated in much the same way while imagining a task as it is while performing that task (Bonnet et al., 1997). So, next time you are getting ready to play a game of tennis or perform a Mozart sonata, imagine doing your best. It can help you succeed.

Visual imagery and visual imagination can also be critical to many creative accomplishments, in both art and science (A. Miller, 1996). For example, Albert Einstein made it quite clear that words were not involved or came after the fact when he was developing his most creative ideas: "The words of the language, as they are written or spoken, do not seem to play any role in my mechanism of thought" (quoted in Calaprice, 2005, p. 279). When describing how he came up with his ideas for the theory of relativity, Einstein said, "These thoughts did not come in any verbal formulation. I rarely think in words at all. A thought comes and I may try to express it in words later" (quoted in Wertheimer, 1959, p. 228). He would often

Many successful athletes use visual imaging to improve their performance. Visualizing success can help to make it happen.

visually imagine certain thought experiments, such as riding on a light beam or traveling at the speed of light in an elevator. Other physicists have argued that Einstein's great creativity dried up when he could no longer produce such visual images (Feist, 2006).

The process of imagining an object rotating in three-dimensional space is known as **mental rotation.** Look at the shapes in Figure 9.6. The pairs are either the same or different, and your task is to decide which is which. If you are like most people, it will take you about 2.5 seconds for each pair to determine whether it is the same (a and b) or different (c).

Researchers examining gender differences in the performance of mental rotation tasks have reported moderate to large gender effects, with boys and men doing better than girls and women (Geary & DeSoto, 2001; D. Halpern, 2004; J. S. Hyde, 1990). Cross-cultural research has shown that these effects also appear in China, Ecuador, Ireland, and Japan (Flaherty, 2005; Geary & DeSoto, 2001).

Nature&**N**urture

Hormones affect our way of thinking. In both men and women, testosterone levels are associated with the ability to perform spatial and mental rotation tasks such as finding one's way around a new building or playing a three-dimensional video game.

One possible cause of this gender difference in spatial ability appears to be levels of the male sex hormone testosterone (Kimura, 2007). For example, female rats injected with testosterone during development perform better than non-injected female rats on spatial tasks (maze running) (Berenbaum, Korman, & Leveroni, 1995). The relationship in humans, however, between testosterone, gender, and spatial ability is complex and not linear (Ceci & Williams, 2010). In humans, it is females with relatively high levels and males with relatively low levels of testosterone who perform best on spatial tasks. So it is too simple to say that high levels of testosterone alone result in better spatial skills. In humans, this is true only for women. For men, actually having low levels of testosterone leads to better spatial skills (Ceci & Williams, 2010; Hines et al., 2003).

Verbal Representation   A major function of thought is to organize and classify our perceptions into categories. One way in which humans organize their environment is by naming things and giving them labels. We organize our sensory experience by putting like with like and then distinguishing that group of things from other groups of things.

We do this by first finding similar features and then forming concepts and building categories based on those similarities. Indeed, the most basic unit of knowledge is a **concept,** which is a mental grouping of objects, events, or people. The concept *fruit* includes yellow, red, blue, orange, and green fruit, and large and small fruit, but what an apple and banana have in common defines the concept *fruit:* the edible part of a plant that contains seeds.

Concepts help us organize our perceptions of the world. We can store and process these concepts in at least two ways: in a hierarchy and by parallel distributed processing, which we discussed in Chapter 7. A **concept hierarchy** lets us know that certain concepts are related in a particular way, with some being general and others specific. In so doing, it helps us order and understand our world.

FIGURE **9.6**

MENTAL ROTATION. In this example, figures on the right are always rotated 80 degrees compared to the figures on the left. It takes most people about 2.5 seconds to mentally rotate the figures. The pairs in (a) and (b) are the same, whereas the pair in (c) is different. (Source: Shepard & Metzler, 1971)

 (a)

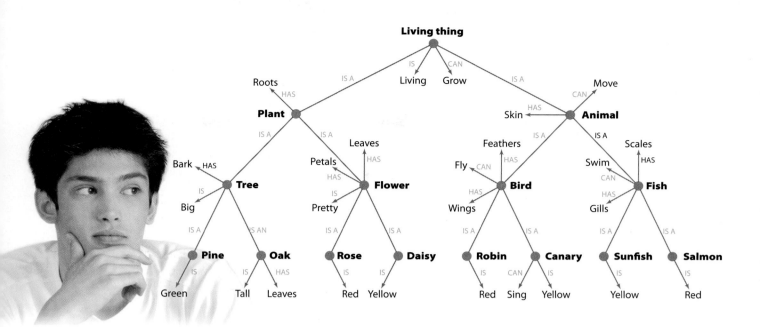

FIGURE **9.7**

PARALLEL DISTRIBUTED NETWORK OF THE VERBAL CONCEPT "LIVING THING." Concepts, printed in bold type, are represented by circles, or nodes, and are interconnected. Properties of concepts are depicted by arrows, which represent statements. Relationships are shown in CAPS. The concept Flower, for instance, HAS petals and leaves, IS pretty, IS a plant, and IS a rose or a daisy. The concept Plant is a more general concept, whereas Rose and Daisy are more specific ones. (Source: McClelland & Rogers, 2003)

A particular dog, Goldie, is a "Golden Retriever," which is a "dog," which is a "mammal," which is an "animal," which is a "living thing."

A more complex model of how we store and organize knowledge in our brain is *parallel distributed processing* (PDP). As you'll recall from Chapter 7, the PDP model proposes that associations between concepts activate many networks or nodes at the same time (McClelland, 1988; McClelland & Rogers, 2003; McClelland & Rumelhart, 1985). The nodes are neuronlike and involve patterns of activation over the network. Concepts are activated in the network based on how strongly associated or connected they are to each other. They are also arranged by similarity as well as hierarchy. For instance, animals such as *bird* and *fish* are closer to each other and farther away from plants such as trees and flowers. The location of a concept is based on its relation to other concepts. In the example in Figure 9.7, "living thing" is the most general conceptual category, of which there are two particular examples, "plants" and "animals." The relationship between nodes takes the form of

(b)

(c)

Thinking, Reasoning, and Decision Making   **367**

"CAN," "HAS," or "IS A." An animal, for instance, CAN move, HAS skin, and IS A bird or fish, whereas a plant HAS roots and IS A flower or tree. A fish, in turn, HAS scales and gills, IS A salmon, and CAN swim. We can use these relationships and networks to reason about things: If a bird can fly and a robin is a bird, then a robin can fly.

Connection
Parallel processing of concepts help us establish, maintain, and retrieve memories.
See "Long-Term Memory," Chapter 7, "Memory," p. 276.

category
a concept that organizes other concepts around what they all share in common.

A **category** is a concept that organizes other concepts around what they all share in common. For instance, all things that move and eat belong to the category "animals," whereas all living things that grow out of the earth and do not eat are in the category "plants." Categories can be either *well-defined* (e.g., triangles, cars) or *fuzzy* (e.g., good, consciousness). In addition, some examples of a category fit that category better than others. "Robin," for example, fits and represents the category "bird" better than does "ostrich," as ostriches cannot fly, are big, and have long legs. We refer to the best-fitting examples of a category as **prototypes** (Rosch, 1973). Thus, a robin is a better prototype for the category "bird" than an ostrich is.

prototypes
the best-fitting examples of a category.

Now that we have developed concepts and categories to help organize our mind's representations, how do we use them to make sense of our world and to reason about them? In the next section we'll consider an answer to this question as we talk about humans' reasoning ability.

How Do We Reason About Evidence?

Almost anytime we use the word *because*, we are reasoning (for example, "She is smiling at me because she likes me"). **Reasoning** is the process of drawing inferences or conclusions from principles and evidence (Sternberg, 2006). Sometimes reasoning allows us to draw sound, correct conclusions, yet this is not always the case. Consider the statement "The FBI and CIA are both out to get me because I always see people looking at me." The conclusion is not a sound one, for it is based only on the evidence that people are looking at you. In fact, it's probably not correct, either.

reasoning
the process of drawing inferences or conclusions from principles and evidence.

Cognitive psychologists distinguish between two kinds of reasoning drawn from formal logic: deductive and inductive. **Deductive reasoning** occurs when we reason from general statements of what is known to specific conclusions. The specific conclusion is always correct if the general statement is true. For instance:

deductive reasoning
reasoning from general statements of what is known to specific conclusions.

All humans are mortal (premise A).
Socrates is human (premise B).
Therefore, Socrates must be mortal (conclusion).

That Socrates is mortal is a logical conclusion that has to be true if the two premises are true. This form of reasoning, of course, leads to correct conclusions only when the general premises on which they are based are true. Consider the following:

All humans are green (premise A).
Socrates is a human (premise B).
Therefore, Socrates must be green (false conclusion).

This reasoning obviously leads to a false conclusion because it is based on false premise A. Even though the structure of the two arguments is exactly the same, one leads to a correct conclusion, and the other does not. When scientists make specific predictions from their general theories, they are engaging in deductive reasoning.

The second kind of reasoning is known as **inductive reasoning,** which is defined as drawing general conclusions from specific evidence. Conclusions drawn from inductive reasoning are less certain than those drawn from deductive reasoning because many different conclusions might be consistent with a specific fact. With deduction we can reach certain and necessarily correct conclusions. With induction, however, the best we can hope for are highly likely conclusions. An example of inductive reasoning is "All peaches I have eaten have been sweet; therefore, all peaches are sweet." All it takes is one unsweet peach to undermine that conclusion. A better inductive conclusion would be that *most* peaches are sweet. When scientists develop theories, they employ inductive reasoning because they offer general statements that explain many specific facts or observations. When we use inductive reasoning we often use **causal inferences,** judgments about whether one thing causes another thing (Koslowski, 1996). "Every time I get chilled, I catch a cold. So getting chilled must cause colds."

Inductive reasoning and causal inferences are related to a phenomenon that is often seen in most people, including scientists: confirmation bias. **Confirmation bias** is the tendency to selectively attend to information that supports one's general beliefs while ignoring information or evidence that contradicts one's beliefs. In the 1960s, Peter Wason conducted classic research to demonstrate the pervasiveness of the confirmation bias. Wason (1960) decided to find out whether people propose and test hypotheses systematically and, more to the point, whether they would be more likely to falsify or to confirm their own theories.

Wason gave students the task of determining the hidden rule behind a sequence of three numbers, known as a *triplet.* The students were asked to guess at the rule by writing down triplets that they thought conformed to it and the reason they selected them. They could make as many guesses and explanatory statements as they wished, until they thought they knew the rule. Then they wrote down what they thought the rule actually was. The experimenter, who knew the hidden rule, could answer only "yes" or "no" to the students' guesses and was not allowed to say whether their reasons were correct or incorrect. For instance, if the experimenter gave the students the triplet "2–4–6," the students might guess a triplet of "6–8–10" and state that the hidden rule is "continuous series of even numbers." In this case, the guess is right but the rule is incorrect, so the experimenter would say "yes" to the guess but "no" to the rule. The students would then have to keep proposing triplets to test other reasons until they come up with the specific rule.

Out of frustration, students might throw out a triplet with seemingly no pattern to it, such as "1-10-21." Imagine their surprise when the experimenter said "yes" to that seemingly nonsensical triplet! Yet the triplet "1-10-21" conformed to the rule the experimenter had in mind, because that rule was simply "three numbers that must ascend in order of magnitude." As this experiment shows, people are so inclined to test only ideas that confirm their beliefs that they forget that one of the best ways to test an idea is to try to tear it down—that is, disconfirm it. This is the foundation of the scientific method. Most people, though, look only for information that confirms what they already believe and seldom look for information that disconfirms what they think; that is, they fall prey to confirmation bias.

inductive reasoning
reasoning to general conclusions from specific evidence.

causal inferences
judgments about causation of one thing by another.

confirmation bias
the tendency to selectively attend to information that supports one's general beliefs while ignoring information or evidence that contradicts one's beliefs.

When writing a research or term paper, you probably look only for sources that confirm your main ideas or theses.

Connecting Psychology to Your Life: Think of a time either in high school or in college when you were given a writing assignment. When you started your research in the library or on the Internet, what did you do when you came upon studies or points of view that contradicted yours? Did you incorporate them or ignore them? Next term paper, try to find sources that challenge your beliefs.

Also, as you move through your life, take note of how you approach material that is either consistent with or contrary to your own viewpoint(s). Do you have a tendency to pay more attention to events or ideas that are consistent with your perspective and dismiss or ignore those that are inconsistent?

Critical Thinking

You've probably heard about "critical thinking" quite often, first in high school and now in college. Teachers are always talking about getting their students to think critically. So what exactly is critical thinking?

We can answer this question in part by examining the origin of the word *critical*. It comes from the ancient Greek word *kritikos* and means "to question, to make sense of, and to be able to analyze; or to be skilled at judging" (Chaffee, 1999, p. 32). Educator Paul Chance has provided a more complete definition of **critical thinking**: "The ability to analyze facts, generate and organize ideas, defend opinions, make comparisons, draw inferences, evaluate arguments, and solve problems" (Chance, 1986, p. 6). The core traits of critical thinking are sound analysis, evaluation, and formation of ideas based on the evidence at hand.

critical thinking process by which one analyzes, evaluates, and forms ideas.

First think

Know what you do and do not know

metacognitive thinking

FIGURE **9.8**
EVIDENCE THAT THE EARTH IS NOT FLAT. The drawing on the left shows how a ship would appear as it comes into view if Earth were flat. On the right we see the ship coming into view on a round Earth. Which view is correct?

In the late 1980s a group of educators, philosophers, psychologists, and biological and physical scientists organized a conference around the topic of critical thinking in education, and there they arrived at a consensus on what it means to be a good critical thinker. They were almost unanimous in identifying three activities or qualities that define critical thinking, and more than three quarters of them agreed on the next three (Facione, 1990):

What a Critical Thinker Does:

- Analyze
- Evaluate
- Make Inferences
- Interpret
- Explain
- Self-Regulate

If you become skilled in these activities, or at least in most of them, you will be able to think critically. In particular, you will be able to counter assertions that have little basis in reality, and you will know the difference between sound and faulty reasoning. For instance, the following argument was made by Charles Johnson, a former president of the International Flat Earth Research Society: "Nobody knows anything about the true shape of the world. The known, inhabited world is flat. Just as a guess, I'd say that the dome of heaven is about 4,000 miles away, and the stars are about as far as San Francisco is from Boston."

Instead of simply saying, "That's silly" or "That's stupid" or "That's just wrong," a critical thinker would examine the claim by analyzing, evaluating, and drawing conclusions based on the facts and evidence at hand. A great deal of evidence directly and clearly contradicts the belief that Earth is flat. Just consider these two pieces of evidence: (1) The top of a ship is the last thing we see as it sails out to sea because it is sailing on a sphere rather than on a flat surface (see Figure 9.8), and (2) images and photographs taken from spaceships and satellites show Earth as a round sphere with half of it shining in the light of the sun.

Critical thinking, and its cousin, scientific thinking, both involve being able to think metacognitively. **Metacognitive thinking** requires the ability first to think and then to reflect on one's own thinking (Feist, 2006; Kuhn & Pearsall, 2000). People who can think metacognitively are able to question their own thinking (see Figure 9.9). This ability is not universal, however. Without specific training, many people find it difficult to question their own thinking. If one were able to do so as a matter of course, one could more readily dismiss a line of thinking as wrong when it is not supported by evidence.

metacognitive thinking process that includes the ability first to think and then to reflect on one's own thinking.

Reflect on your thinking

FIGURE **9.9**

METACOGNITIVE THINKING. In an era marked by 24/7 information overload, we often leap to overly simplistic or incorrect conclusions based on what we think we "know." Accurately knowing what you do and do not know and the ability to monitor your thinking as you work on a problem are two hallmarks of metacognition.

Thinking, Reasoning, and Decision Making   **371**

Applying Critical Thinking Beyond the Classroom

Critical thinking is a necessary skill in almost every walk of life. We can apply it to any domain in which we form beliefs and opinions. Here is just a partial list: deciding whether someone committed a crime; evaluating the claims of a company advertising a product; deciding whether what we read or hear in the classroom, in the newspaper, in politics, or in our work environment is valid and what evidence it is based on.

To apply critical thinking skills we should ask ourselves, What is the evidence for this conclusion, and is it valid? Let's take just one example. Suppose you are on a jury in a murder trial. The primary evidence on which the case is based is eyewitness testimony: two people picked out the defendant from a lineup. The prosecutor offers no other concrete evidence, such as DNA findings, fingerprints, bloodstains, or ballistic (bullet) matching. Your job is to decide whether the defendant committed the murder. You will want to draw on your critical thinking skills, because in this situation ignoring evidence and basing judgments on bias can have costly, even deadly, consequences.

Unfortunately, many people, including adults, sometimes lack critical and scientific thinking skills (Ransdell, 2010). **Scientific thinking** is metacognitive thinking that is used to generate, test, reflect upon, and revise theories. Deanna Kuhn studied the connection between scientific and informal (everyday) reasoning in adults (Kuhn, 1993). She asked 160 people (teenagers and people in their 20s, 40s, and 60s) their theories on three topics: what causes prisoners to return to a life of crime, what causes children to fail in school, and what causes unemployment. After stating their theories, participants were asked for evidence on which they based their ideas. Only 40% of the participants could give actual evidence—that is, information that is based on actual observations that bear on the theory's correctness. For instance, a man in his 20s who theorized that poor nutrition causes

scientific thinking
process using the cognitive skills required to generate, test, and revise theories.

How Do We Make Judgments and Decisions?

Should I go to class or not? Should I wear a green shirt or the brown one? Paper or plastic? Can I make it across the street without getting hit by that car? Should I have a glass of water or a soda? We make hundreds of decisions every day, and each of those decisions is based on many different assumptions, judgments, and estimates. We also make judgments countless times each day. Every time we say things like "I decided . . . ," "Chances are . . . ," "It is unlikely . . . ," or "She probably did that because . . . ," we are judging how likely something is to happen.

heuristics
mental shortcuts; methods for making complex and uncertain decisions and judgments.

As it turns out, most often we use shortcuts to make decisions. These shortcuts, known as **heuristics,** are methods for making complex and uncertain decisions and judgments (Kahneman & Tversky, 1972). Consider, for example, the thought processes involved in deciding how to avoid being hit by a car when crossing a busy street. Instead of reasoning out each step systematically, we check oncoming traffic in both directions and quickly judge how fast the cars are moving and how fast we can get across. We base the decision to step off the curb or not on our quick judgment of the pace of the oncoming cars. We usually don't debate with ourselves for very long before making that decision. Heuristics allow us to come to quick and efficient decisions.

President Barack Obama and his chief advisors had to weigh a wide range of issues and options in considering the capture or killing of Osama bin Laden. The mission was very dangerous and the outcome was uncertain. Critical thinking was essential in weighing the possible costs and benefits in taking any action.

children to fail in school answered the question "What would show that?" with "[They would get poor grades because] they are lacking something in their body." He fails to understand what evidence is and how it is different from his beliefs. He simply restates his belief in a different way. When asked to come up with reasons their thinking may be wrong, many actively resisted. As one participant said, "If I knew from the evidence that I'm wrong, I wouldn't say what I am saying." Others were even more stubborn, saying things like, "They'll never prove me wrong." Scientific and critical thinking both require that we be open to evidence that bears on whether our ideas are correct or not, even if we are not happy with the evidence.

Developing critical thinking has consequences beyond the classroom and even beyond studies in psychology. To summarize:

> The ideal critical thinker is habitually inquisitive, well-informed, trustful of reason, open-minded, flexible, fair-minded in evaluation, honest in facing personal biases, prudent in making judgments, willing to reconsider, clear about issues, orderly in assessing complex matters, diligent in seeking relevant information, reasonable in the selection of criteria, focused in inquiry, and persistent in seeking results that are as precise as the subject and the circumstances of inquiry permit. Thus, becoming good critical thinkers means working toward this ideal. It combines developing critical thinking skills with nurturing those dispositions that consistently yield useful insights and that are the basis of a rational and democratic society. (Facione, 1990, p. 2)

Finding one item in a large supermarket is made easier by heuristics. If you're looking for cold juice, you can narrow your search to a few places where cold beverages are stored and ignore all the other aisles. Deciding on a specific juice drink might be harder.

We use many types of heuristics. Here we look briefly at the two most common types: the representativeness heuristic and the availability heuristic.

The Representativeness Heuristic

representativeness heuristic
a strategy we use to estimate the probability of one event based on how typical it is of another event.

The Representativeness Heuristic

We use the **representativeness heuristic** when we estimate the probability of one event based on how typical or representative it is of another event (Tversky & Kahneman, 1974). For example, consider this information about Joe: He is not overweight, wears glasses, and reads poetry. Now we ask you to answer this question: Is Joe more likely to be a truck driver or a professor of English at an Ivy League university? It's simply an *either-or* decision that most people get wrong: Joe is more likely to be a truck driver!

To understand why this is so, we need to be aware of base rates, or how common something is in the population as a whole. The concept of a base rate can be applied to people, events, or things. For example, 6 out of 100,000 people contract brain cancer in a given year; that is the base rate for brain cancer. Taking the four descriptors *truck driver, not overweight, wears glasses,* and *reads poetry,* let's consider the base rates for those segments of the U.S. population. First (assuming that by "truck driver" we mean drivers of semis), there are about 3 million truck drivers in the United States (*Trucking Stats and FAQ's,* n.d). Second, because about two thirds of adults in the U.S. population are overweight (see Chapter 11), we could use the figure 67% to determine how many truck drivers are overweight—about 2 million. This leaves us 1 million truck drivers who are not overweight. Third, about 50% of adults wear corrective lenses (National Eye Institute, 2002). Fifty percent of 1 million leaves us with 500,000 not-overweight glasses-wearing truck drivers. Last, it is difficult to estimate how many people read poetry, but even a very conservative figure of 1% of the population leaves us with 5,000 truck drivers who wear glasses, are not overweight, and read poetry. Once we have established that figure, we can simply ask ourselves whether there are more than 5,000 professors of English at the eight Ivy League universities. There are approximately 50 professors of English at each of the eight schools, meaning there are about 400 Ivy League English professors. So in fact, even though it goes against our prejudices, Joe is more likely to be a truck driver than a professor of English at an Ivy League university. The information (not overweight, glasses, poetry) is so *representative* of an English professor and not a truck driver that we ignored the base-rate differences when we made our initial decision. There are simply many more truck drivers than there are English professors.

The Availability Heuristic

availability heuristic
a device we use to make decisions based on the ease with which estimates come to mind or how available they are to our awareness.

The Availability Heuristic

The second major type of heuristic is the **availability heuristic,** which is a strategy we use when we make decisions based on the ease with which estimates come to mind or how available they are to our awareness (Tversky & Kahneman, 1974). One example of the availability heuristic occurs when people are asked whether they are more likely to be killed while flying in an airplane or while driving in a car. Some might answer that they are more likely to be killed in plane crashes, even though statistics show that far more fatalities are caused by auto accidents than by plane crashes. According to the National Safety Council (*The Odds of Dying From . . . ,* 2010), in 2006 the odds of dying in one's lifetime in an automobile accident was 1 in 85, whereas the odds of dying in a plane crash during one's lifetime was 1 in 5,682—a ratio of about 66 to 1. We may want to believe we are safer in cars than airplanes, but remember "Don't believe everything you think."

We may think we have a greater chance of dying in a plane crash because the thought of such a death conjures up dramatic images, which we refer to as *vividness*. Thoughts of large numbers of people dying violent deaths in plane crashes, therefore, are readily available because they are vivid. Vividness and availability lead us to overestimate how likely certain events are.

Additional research by Kahneman and Tversky revealed other areas in which people are less than rational in their decision making and judgments. For example, if people were rational they would realize that the odds of two events can never be higher than the odds of one of those events alone. To put it most simply, the odds of A and B occurring together can never exceed the odds of either A or B occurring separately. Let's consider a specific example: The odds of your both (A) winning the lottery and (B) getting a promotion on the same day can never be greater than the odds of either one of these events happening alone. Sometimes, though, we get information that can be so representative of a stereotype that it biases us, and we are likely to forget this simple rule of logic and make an error in our judgment. Take the classic example of Linda offered by Tversky and Kahneman (1983):

> Linda is 31 years old, single, outspoken, and very bright. She majored in philosophy. As a student, she was deeply concerned with issues of discrimination and social justice, and participated in anti-nuclear demonstrations.

Now you are asked the odds of each of the following: (A) that Linda is active in the feminist movement, (B) that Linda is a bank teller, and (C) that Linda is a bank teller and is active in the feminist movement. It is clear that A is more likely than B. But what about B compared to C? Remember that the combination of two events cannot be more likely than either event separately. Yet because what we are told about Linda is representative of feminists (A) and not of bank tellers (B), we are likely to say what 85% of the participants said—namely, that (C) is more likely than (B). In this case, the representativeness heuristic has led to an error known as the **conjunction fallacy,** which occurs when people say the combination of two events is more likely than either event alone.

conjunction fallacy
error in logic that occurs when people say the combination of two events is more likely than either event alone.

These findings and others like them point to the conclusion that people sometimes ignore base rates, sometimes are biased by stereotypes, and sometimes use shortcuts to arrive quickly, but not completely rationally, at their decisions and conclusions. In short, Kahneman and Tversky demonstrated that people bypass fully rational decision making and make use of automatic shortcuts in their reasoning and judgments.

Heuristics and their importance in decision making and judgments are relatively new concepts in psychology. These notions developed from research in the early 1970s by Daniel Kahneman and Amos Tversky. How they came up with the idea for carrying out this research provides an interesting glimpse into how psychologists are personally connected to their discoveries (see Breaking New Ground).

Quick Quiz 9.2: Thinking, Reasoning, and Decision Making

1. Structures in our mind—such as an idea or image—that stand for something else, such as the external object or thing, are known as
   a. memories
   b. mental representations
   c. mental rotation
   d. visions

2. Which of the following would be considered a prototype for fruit?
   a. kiwi
   b. tomato
   c. avocado
   d. apple

3. When we reason from general statements of what is known to specific conclusions, we are engaging in
   a. hypothesis testing
   b. inductive reasoning
   c. deductive reasoning
   d. logic

4. What distinguishes scientific thinking from nonscientific thinking?
   a. the ability to separate belief from evidence
   b. the ability to reason
   c. concept formation
   d. the use of heuristics

5. _____ are mental shortcuts for making complex and uncertain decisions and judgments.
   a. Categories
   b. Schemas
   c. Calculations
   d. Heuristics

6. Which of the following makes people believe they are more likely to die in a plane crash than while driving a car?
   a. the fear schema
   b. the availability heuristic
   c. concept formation
   d. the representativeness heuristic

Answers can be found at the end of the chapter.

Breaking New Ground

Nonrational Decision Making

Are the mental processes you use to make decisions based on reasonable, rational thought? Are you sure? Most of us like to think we are always reasonable and rational, and yet a Nobel Prize was awarded in 2002 for findings showing that people often make decisions that are not rational and reasonable, especially economic decisions. Simply put, most of us are not as rational as we would like to think we are.

For much of the 20th century, cognitive scientists and economists who studied human decision making believed that people generally make rational decisions. Specifically, it was thought that when given a choice between two or more options, humans will choose the one that is most likely to help them achieve their particular goals—that is, the rational choice. Economists called this *rational choice theory* (Scott, 2000).

Daniel Kahneman

As we saw in the case of confirmation bias, not all reasoning is rational. In the 1970s, Amos Tversky and Daniel Kahneman began to challenge rational choice theory with their research on human judgment and decision making. Their collaboration began when both were at the Hebrew University in Israel, where Kahneman was teaching a graduate seminar in applied psychology. "In what turned out to be a life-changing event," Kahneman writes, "I asked my younger colleague Amos Tversky to tell the class about what was going on in his field of judgment and decision-making" (Kahneman, 2002). In the seminar, Tversky demonstrated how people make judgments about the probability of events. He combined red and white poker chips in two different bags and in two different ratios as an example. He explained that people are generally rational in their judgments; that is, they take into account differences in base rates. Using his bags of poker chips, he demonstrated that the odds are higher that a red chip will come from a bag with a base rate of 70/30 red to white chips than from a bag with a base rate of 30/70 red to white chips.

Tversky's conclusion that people are rational and make use of base rate information, however, started a lively debate in the seminar, as Kahneman later described:

The idea . . . did not seem to fit with the everyday observation of people commonly jumping to conclusions. [Tversky] went in to the seminar believing in his findings that people are relatively rational judges but left with that belief shaken. . . . I do remember that Amos and I decided to meet for lunch to discuss our hunches about the manner in which probabilities are "really" judged. There we exchanged personal accounts of our own recurrent errors of judgment in this domain, and decided to study the statistical intuitions of experts. (Kahneman, 2002)

As Kahneman recently recounted, it was this back and forth in that seminar that led Kahneman to realize he and Tversky were an "exceptional team" (personal communication, October 1, 2010). From there, they went on to do research which demonstrated that people are often less than rational in their decision making. These conclusions changed psychology, economics, and philosophy (e.g., Tversky & Kahneman, 1974).

To some economists and philosophers, Kahneman and Tversky's findings were nothing short of revolutionary, although not everyone appreciated them. A well-known American philosopher once told Kahneman, who had started to describe some of his findings at a dinner party, "I am not really interested in the psychology of stupidity" and walked away (Kahneman, 2002).

By the late 1970s Kahneman and Tversky began to apply their ideas of decision making to economics (Kahneman & Tversky, 1979). They were particularly intrigued by situations that pitted people's intuitions against their rational choices. They discovered that people often make economic decisions based on intuition rather than rational choice. For example, which would you pick:

a. A coin toss (50–50) chance for $1,000
b. $460 for sure

Many of us are not rational consumers. The fact that we cannot afford to buy three pairs of shoes at a time does not mean that we do not buy them.

Most people choose the certain option (certainty effect). But what about these choices? Which would you choose?

   a. A 100% chance of losing $3,000
   b. An 80% chance of losing $4,000, and a 20% chance of losing nothing

Now, which would you choose?

   c. A 100% chance of winning $3,000
   d. An 80% chance of winning $4,000 and a 20% chance of winning nothing

Only 20% of the people chose d, whereas 92% of the people chose b (Kahneman & Tversky, 1979). People treat wins and losses differently. People are risk-averse when faced with the prospect of winning and risk-loving when faced with the prospect of losing. Put differently, people are more averse to losing money than attracted to winning it. Most people will not choose an option where they might lose $20 unless they have a chance of gaining at least $40. Notice the asymmetry in this. A $20 loss has to be balanced by a $40 gain, not $20. These results are not what standard (rational) economic theory would predict, but they are what Kahneman and Tversky's "prospect theory" predicted.

Amos Tversky

What Kahneman and Tversky were brilliant at was figuring out what most people would do based on what they themselves would do. If they both agreed on an option, they assumed most others would too. This saved them a lot of time. In the early phases of coming up with new ideas, rather than having to carry out studies to test them, they would simply go through the options themselves and assume their choices were the common ones (and in fact they were). As Kahneman put it: "I have always felt that seeing data instantly raised my IQ by 20 points: eliminating alternatives makes everything look clearer. Furthermore, waiting for results is actually harmful to good research, because it gives you time to become attached to your ideas, blind to their flaws and unwilling to give them up. Because Amos [Tversky] and I relied on our preferences as data we had none of these problems. We invented and dismissed hypotheses at top speed" (Kahneman, personal communication, October 2, 2010).

■ ■ ■

Bringing It All Together
Making Connections in Language and Thought
Learning a Second Language

Learning a second language involves many of the linguistic and cognitive principles we reviewed in this chapter. Bilingualism, or fluency in more than one language, is common, especially in India and Europe. As we consider bilingualism and how we can apply it to the topics in this chapter, we'll think about these questions: Is learning a second language essentially the same as learning one's first language? How much does it matter how old we are when we learn the second language? Finally, does learning a second language actually make you more creative?

Sensitivity Periods and Second-Language Acquisition

There is a sensitive period for second-language acquisition: Children learn second languages more quickly than adults do and speak them more fluently (Birdsong, 2006; K. H. S. Kim et al., 1997; Sakai, 2005; Uylings, 2006). By around age 7, learning a second language starts to become more difficult, and proficiency is reduced (Sakai, 2005). The sensitive period for learning to speak a second language without an accent appears to end in early adolescence (around age 13 to 15) (Birdsong, 2005; Flege, Munro, & MacKay, 1995; Long, 1990; Jiang et al., 2009; Oyama, 1976). For example, native English speakers evaluated the strength of the accent in English spoken by Italian immigrants to the United States (Oyama, 1976). The length of time the immigrants had been in the United States did not affect the strength or thickness of their accent, but the age at which they had moved to the United States did. If they were 6 when they immigrated and had been in the country for only 2 years, they had much less of an accent than if they were 30 years old when they learned the language but had been in the United States for 10 years. A systematic review of the literature by Long (1990) confirmed this finding from dozens of studies. Thus, as a time for learning to speak a second language without an accent, childhood is better than adolescence and adolescence is better than adulthood. Although the finding is robust that age of second-language acquisition affects the accent level of non-native speakers, there are numerous social factors that lessen this effect, such as continued education, amount of second language that is used, and gender (Flege, 1999; Flege, Munro, & MacKay, 1995; Hakuta, Bialystok, & Wiley, 2003).

Second-Language Learning and the Brain

People who are fluent in two languages apparently are capable of more efficient cognitive processing than those who speak only one language. Psychologists examined the ability of speakers of one and two languages to perform cognitive tasks (Bialystok, Craik, & Ryan, 2006). They found that those who spoke two languages performed better on these cognitive tasks and continued to do so later in life.

Learning another language may also have a long-term beneficial effect on the brain. When matched for age, gender, and other qualities, elderly speakers of two languages develop dementia more than 4 years later than do elderly speakers of only one language (Bialystok & Craik, 2010). What is most interesting about these results is they once again support the view that stimulation from the environment—in this case, learning another language—can enrich our brains and enable them to process information more efficiently.

Neuroscientists have begun to demonstrate the long-lasting effects of learning two languages even more

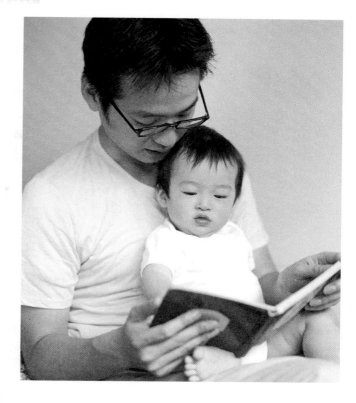

directly. First, compared to those of single-language speakers, bilingual speakers have a greater density of neurons in the language centers of the brain (Mechelli et al., 2004). Not only that, but neural density is also proportional to the age at which the person learned the second language. The earlier the second language is learned, the greater the neural density (Mechelli et al., 2004). These findings demonstrate yet again how the brain is shaped by experience.

Second, bilingual people exhibit differences in brain activation depending on when they learned their second language (K. H. S. Kim et al., 1997). What is most fascinating is that the brains of people who learn a second language early in life are more efficient at language processing and more similar when speaking in both languages than are the brains of people who learn a second language late in life. If someone learns a second language early in life, essentially at the same time that they learn their first language, the brain regions that are active during speech (production) overlap almost completely. On the other hand, if a person learns a second language years after learning the first language, the brain regions that are active during speech (production) are next to each other but hardly overlap (see Figure 9.10).

What is equally fascinating is that the same pattern does not hold for comprehension or listening. The brains of both early and late second-language learners show the same areas of activation when listening to their first and second language (K. H. S. Kim et al., 1997). Thus, the age at which a

**"Late" bilingual
posterior language area**

**"Early" bilingual
anterior language area**

R

- ■ Native (English)
- ▢ Second (French)
- + Center-of-mass

R

- ■ Native 1 (Turkish)
- ▢ Native 2 (English)
- ■ Common region
- + Center-of-mass

FIGURE **9.10**

ACTIVATION IN BROCA'S AREA FOR LATE LEARNERS AND EARLY LEARNERS OF A SECOND LANGUAGE. People who learn a second language later in life (after the age of 16) use different areas of the brain to produce speech in two languages, as shown by the images on the left. People who learn a second language in childhood show activation in overlapping areas of the brain when producing speech in two languages, as shown on the right. In other words, the brain of the early learner responds almost identically when speaking either language. Perhaps the reason why late learners are less fluent is that the brain treats the two languages differently. (Source: K. H. S. Kim et al., 1997)

person learns a second language is reflected in differences in the brain, but only in areas involved in producing rather than understanding speech.

Concept Formation and Translation Into Foreign Languages

Linguists have demonstrated that the more prototypical an idea is, the more easily it can be translated from one language to another (Gass, 1984; Kellerman, 1979). Recall that a robin is a more prototypical example of bird than is an ostrich. Ideas and concepts that are prototypical are easier to understand in a second language. For example, consider the phrases *to kick the ball* and *to kick the bucket*. With *to kick the ball,* the use of the verb *to kick* is prototypical and easily translated. The phrase *to kick the bucket,* which means "to die," does not yield an accurate literal translation because the use of the verb *to kick* in this phrase does not represent the prototypical concept of *to kick,* meaning "to use your leg and foot in such a way as to move an object quickly." Many such **idioms**—expressions that are unique to a particular language—do not make sense when they are literally translated.

Reasoning in a Second Language

It is difficult enough to get through a college entrance exam, such as the Scholastic Aptitude Test (SAT), in one's native

idioms
expressions unique to a particular language; usually their meaning cannot be determined by decoding the individual meanings of the words.

language. Imagine doing it in a second language in which you are not perfectly fluent. Each year thousands of foreign students seeking admission to American universities undertake this challenge. The SAT includes questions that require deductive reasoning, such as text comprehension. In research that compared students' deductive reasoning in their native language and their deductive reasoning in a second language, not surprisingly the students performed better in their native language (D'Anglejan, 1979). Therefore, it is quite possible that the validity of these tests for nonnative speakers is somewhat questionable and that the scores do not accurately portray the aptitude of the test takers.

Second-Language Acquisition and Metacognition

Accurately knowing what you do and do not know and the ability to monitor your thinking as you work on a problem are two hallmarks of metacognition. Because learning a second language requires one to think about one's thinking, some linguists and psychologists have proposed that bilingual children should be better at knowing what they know and monitoring their thinking than monolingual children (Jimenez, Garcia, & Pearson, 1994; Ruan, 2004; Tobias & Everson, 2002; Wenden, 1998). The findings of research on this question are mixed. It may be, however, that metacognitive thinking is more pronounced when one is first learning a second language than later, when one is rather fluent (Tobias & Everson, 2002).

Other studies have also reported at least partial support for the idea that speaking two languages facilitates creative, flexible, and original problem solving (Landry, 1973; Lasagabaster, 2000; Ricciardelli, 1992; L. Zhang, 2010). In a quantitative review (meta-analysis) of a large body of research, Ricciardelli reported that 20 out of 24 published studies found that bilingual students scored higher on creativity tasks than did monolingual students. Flexible and creative thinking thus is closely aligned with metacognitive thinking (Sternberg, 2004).

Quick Quiz 9.3: Bringing It All Together: Making Connections in Language and Thought

1. Kahneman and Tversky broke new ground in psychology by showing that people
   a. are not always rational in their decision making
   b. are almost always rational in their decision making
   c. often act like scientists in their decision making
   d. are motivated by self-interest and rational decision making

2. The sensitive period for learning to speak a second language without an accent appears to end at what stage of life?
   a. early childhood
   b. early teens
   c. young adulthood
   d. middle age

3. Compared to those of single-language speakers, the brains of bilingual speakers have
   a. greater density of neurons in the language center of the brain
   b. higher income
   c. higher intelligence
   d. fewer axons in the corpus callosum

4. Expressions that are unique to a particular language and do not make sense when literally translated are called
   a. axiomatic phrases
   b. tangential clauses
   c. idioms
   d. conjunctions

Answers can be found at the end of the chapter.

Chapter **Review**

LANGUAGE

- Human language is an open symbolic communication system that follows rules of syntax and grammar.

- Individuals develop language in a four-stage sequence, beginning with cooing and babbling in infancy. At about 12 months of age, toddlers start making their first one-word utterances. At around 18 months, babies progress to two-word utterances. By age 2½ to 3, most children enter the short-sentence phase. Continued language development requires stimulation from other people during a sensitive period between about the first 6 years of life and age 12.

- There are three major theories of language. Social–cultural theories propose that we learn vocabulary by hearing others speak and figure out what they mean by the context. Conditioning and learning theories argue that language is like any other learned behavior, something that occurs because it is reinforced and shaped. Nativist theories argue that humans possess a language acquisition device (LAD), an innate, biologically based capacity to acquire language that comes with a general and universal grammar.

THINKING, REASONING, AND DECISION MAKING

- Cognitive psychology is the scientific study of how people think, learn, remember, and perceive.

- We use visual and verbal representations in our mind as mental structures or processes for an image or idea. Concepts and categories are mental representations that we use to organize our world. Prototypes are the best-fitting examples of a category.

- We use reasoning to draw inferences or conclusions from principles and evidence. In deductive reasoning, we start with a general statement of what is known and draw specific conclusions from it. We use inductive reasoning to draw general conclusions from specific evidence. These conclusions are less certain because many different conclusions might be consistent with a specific fact.

- Confirmation bias is the tendency to selectively attend to information that confirms one's general beliefs while ignoring information or evidence that contradicts one's beliefs.

- Critical thinking uses sound reasoning when analyzing facts, generating and organizing ideas, defending opinions, making comparisons, drawing inferences, evaluating arguments, and solving problems.

- Scientific thinking is metacognitive thinking that is used to generate, test, reflect upon, and revise theories.

- Heuristics are shortcuts that we use in making judgments. We use the representativeness heuristic when we estimate the probability of one event based on how typical it is of another event. We use the availability heuristic to make estimates based on the ease with which we can bring an event or object to mind.

BRINGING IT ALL TOGETHER: MAKING CONNECTIONS IN LANGUAGE AND THOUGHT

- Children who learn a second language early, during a sensitive period that ends around age 7, speak it more fluently and with greater proficiency than do older children or adults.

- Bilingualism appears to enhance cognitive processing and is associated with a lower rate of dementia in the elderly.

- People who learn a second language in childhood process both languages in roughly the same area of the brain, whereas in later learners, processing of the two languages occurs in two scarcely overlapping areas.

- At least initially, learning a second language may enhance metacognition, knowledge of what we know and don't know, and foster flexible thinking and creative problem solving.

Key Terms

availability heuristic, p. 374
babbling, p. 351
category, p. 368
causal inferences, p. 369
child-directed speech, p. 354
cognition, p. 364
cognitive psychology, p. 364
concept, p. 366
concept hierarchy, p. 366
confirmation bias, p. 369
conjunction fallacy, p. 375
cooing, p. 351

critical thinking, p. 370
deductive reasoning, p. 368
grammar, p. 349
heuristics, p. 372
human language, p. 349
idioms, p. 380
inductive reasoning, p. 369
language acquisition device (LAD), p. 355
linguistic determinism hypothesis, p. 361
mental representation, p. 364
mental rotation, p. 366

metacognitive thinking, p. 371
nativist view of language, p. 355
one-word utterances, p. 351
protolanguage, p. 350
prototypes, p. 368
reasoning, p. 368
representativeness heuristic, p. 374
scientific thinking, p. 372
sentence phase, p. 352
syntax, p. 349
two-word utterances, p. 352
visual imagery, p. 365

Quick Quiz Answers

Quick Quiz 9.1:   1. c   2. a   3. d   4. c
Quick Quiz 9.2:   1. b   2. d   3. c   4. a   5. d   6. b
Quick Quiz 9.3:   1. a   2. b   3. a   4. c

Challenge Your Assumptions Answers

- French speakers understand the world differently than German speakers. **True. See p. 348.**
- Learning grammar is easy for everyone. **True. See p. 356.**
- Critical thinking involves seeing only the weaknesses and flaws in ideas. **False. See pp. 370–371.**
- Most decisions we make are rational. **False. See pp. 376–378.**
- Twenty-year-olds can learn to speak a second language without an accent just as easily as a six-year-old. **False. See p. 379.**

Intelligence, Problem Solving, and Creativity

10

Challenge *Your Assumptions*

TRUE OR FALSE?

- Intelligence is a single, general capacity.

- Genetic factors influence people's intelligence.

- If a person has very unique and original ideas, he or she is creative.

- People with very high IQs are geniuses.

Answers can be found at the end of the chapter.

In 1902, Ansel was born into an educated family in San Francisco. His father was a wealthy businessman; his mother, a socialite. Ansel was energetic—perhaps excessively so—and did not do well academically. In fact, he had trouble fitting in at school and was very shy. Eventually, he was taken out of school for an education based on home tutoring. Still, at an early age Ansel displayed an intensity of focus that would be necessary for genius-level attainment.

Then there was Charles. As a boy, he was competent but not outstanding in school, and he later performed poorly in his medical studies. In fact, his father—a wealthy physician—found his son's skills lacking. Even into the early part of his career, Charles's writings were quite ordinary. Up through his 20s, all signs pointed to a person who was destined to have a competent but unremarkable career. Only his passion for collecting bugs and keenly observing nature offered subtle hints of someone who might change all of science.

By any contemporary measure of intelligence, these two young men were not exceptional. But they became exceptional men. Ansel Adams revolutionized photography and became one of the most compelling artists of the 20th century. Charles Darwin developed the most dominant theory in the life and social sciences yet, and he became one of the most influential scientists of all time.

Both Adams and Darwin were smart enough, but not necessarily brilliant in the academic "book smart" sense. These two cases show us that conventional intelligence is inadequate to explain greatness and also raises questions about what intelligence is. Both topics are covered in this chapter. Are we born smart, or does this capacity grow with training? Is intelligence a single general skill or many different skills? Psychologists agree that there are capacities that shape how smart people are, and these constitute the three central topics of this chapter: intelligence, problem solving, and creativity. In this chapter, we will discuss what intelligence is and how it is measured, we will look at a practical ability called *problem solving*, and then we will examine the process of solving problems in unique ways known as *creativity*. Throughout the chapter, we aim to show how these topics overlap considerably, yet also reveal distinct capabilities of the human mind. ∎

INTELLIGENCE

Many people consider intelligence the primary trait that sets humans apart from other animals. But what is intelligence? Is it the same as being generally smart, or is it more complicated than that? Is it a single ability or many different abilities? Intelligence can be defined in a number of ways, and even the experts cannot agree on a definition. Over the years, groups of intelligence experts have convened for the purpose of defining intelligence (Neisser et al., 1996; Snyderman & Rothman, 1987; Sternberg & Detterman, 1986). Let's see what they have found.

Defining Intelligence

Intelligence may be our inherent potential for learning, how fast we are able to learn, or the body of knowledge we possess. It may also include the ability to do things in ways that other people have never tried. The definition of intelligence that we will use in this book encompasses all these qualities. According to the

Question	Theory	Summary
How intelligent are you?	Spearman's general intelligence (g)	Intelligence is a single general capacity.
How are you intelligent?	Thurstone's multiple factors	Intelligence consists of 7 primary mental abilities, including spatial ability, memory, perceptual speed, and word fluency.
How are you intelligent?	Cattell–Horn–Carroll (CHC) hierarchical intelligence	Intelligence can be broken down into 3 levels of ability: general, broad, and narrow.
How are you intelligent?	Sternberg's triarchic theory	Intelligence is made up of 3 abilities (analytical, creative, and practical) necessary for success.
How are you intelligent?	Gardner's multiple intelligences	Intelligence includes at least 8 distinct capacities, including musical intelligence, interpersonal intelligence, and bodily-kinesthetic intelligence.

FIGURE **10.1**
THEORIES OF INTELLIGENCE.
There are two principal views of intelligence. One considers intelligence as a single, measurable ability. The other looks at intelligence as comprising several distinct abilities.

intelligence
a set of cognitive skills that include abstract thinking, reasoning, problem solving, and the ability to acquire knowledge.

experts, **intelligence** is a set of cognitive skills that includes abstract thinking, reasoning, problem solving, and the ability to acquire knowledge. Other less-agreed-on qualities of intelligence include mathematical ability, general knowledge, and creativity (see Figure 10.1).

Theories of Intelligence

Theories of intelligence started sprouting up in the early 1900s, soon after the first modern intelligence tests appeared. Two distinct views dominate our understanding of intelligence. One view says that intelligence is a single, general ability; the other says that intelligence consists of multiple abilities.

Intelligence as One General Ability Charles Spearman (1904, 1923) developed the first theory of intelligence. He proposed that human intelligence is best thought of as a single general capacity, or ability. Spearman came to this conclusion after research consistently showed that specific dimensions, or factors, of intelligence—namely, spatial, verbal, perceptual, and quantitative factors—correlated strongly with one another, suggesting that they were all measuring pretty much the same thing. In other words, people who achieve high scores on the verbal section of an intelligence test are also likely to have high scores on the spatial, perceptual, and quantitative sections.

g-factor theory
Spearman's theory that intelligence is a single general (g) factor made up of specific components.

Spearman's theory is now known as a **g-factor theory** of intelligence because it describes intelligence as a single *general* factor made up of specific components. This theory influenced intelligence test construction for most of the 20th century. Most intelligence tests determine a person's overall intelligence score by his or her scores on specific subtests. G-factor theory implies that this single number accurately reflects a person's intelligence, the higher the better. A person who scores 115 on an intelligence test is generally more intelligent than a person who scores 100, for example. This perspective is illustrated by the question "How intelligent are you?" (see Figure 10.1).

Intelligence as Multiple Abilities   Critics of Spearman's theory argue that it does not do justice to the complexity of intelligence. They do not dispute that subtests of intelligence are moderately correlated, but they disagree on how such relationships should be interpreted. Early critics noted that the correlations are low enough to support arguments that verbal, quantitative, and other abilities are distinct dimensions of intelligence (Thurstone, 1938). Moreover, they insisted that test scores by themselves ignore important aspects of intelligence that the traditional tests don't measure. This view, the **multiple-factor theory of intelligence,** holds that the different aspects of intelligence are distinct enough that multiple abilities must be considered, not just one. This perspective is illustrated by the question "*How* are you intelligent?" (see Figure 10.1). The key difference, then, between g-factor and multiple-factor theorists is that g-factor theorists say a single test score accurately reflects a person's overall intelligence, whereas multiple-factor theorists say that it doesn't.

multiple-factor theory of intelligence idea that intelligence consists of distinct dimensions and is not just a single factor.

One of the first people to "break intelligence in two" was Raymond Cattell, with his notion of *fluid* and *crystallized intelligence* (Horn & Cattell, 1966). We introduced these terms in Chapter 5, "Human Development." Recall that fluid intelligence involves raw mental ability, pattern recognition, and abstract reasoning and is applied to a problem that a person has never confronted before. Fluid intelligence is not influenced by culture or the size of your vocabulary. Instead, it simply involves how fast you learn new things. So some children just learn to read, write, and do math more quickly and easily than others. One commonly used measure of fluid intelligence is the *Raven's Progressive Matrices Test* (see Figure 10.2). Matrix reasoning is fluid intelligence because it does not depend on acquired knowledge and involves the ability to find patterns. Fluid intelligence measures are *culture-free* because their solutions do not require culturally acquired experience.

By contrast, crystallized intelligence involves using skills, experience, and knowledge to solve problems. This form of intelligence stems from how large your vocabulary is as well as your knowledge of your culture. For example, understanding the meaning of a written paragraph requires crystallized intelligence, because it requires you to use your experience and knowledge to solve the problem. Vocabulary tests are also measures of crystallized intelligence.

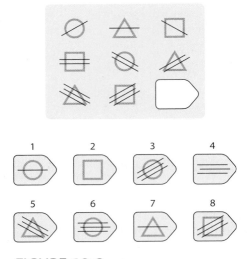

FIGURE **10.2**

EXAMPLE FROM RAVEN'S PROGRESSIVE MATRICES TEST. This sample problem requires fluid intelligence. It is nonverbal and requires pattern recognition, not prior acquired knowledge. For this reason, this test is often considered a "culture-free" test of intelligence. Can you figure out which of the numbered bottom figures would be next in the series of nine above? (Source: Simulated items similar to those in the Raven's Progressive Matrices. Copyright © 1998 by NCS Pearson, Inc. Reproduced with permission. All rights reserved. "Raven's Progressive Matrices" is a trademark, in the US and/or other countries, of Pearson Education, Inc. or its affiliates.)

Connection

As we go from young adulthood to middle adulthood, our experience-based intelligence (crystallized) continues to improve. Abstract and culture-free intelligence (fluid), however, peaks during our 20s.

See "The Developing Adult," Chapter 5, "Human Development," p. 206.

John Carroll (1993) further subdivided intelligence when he reviewed and integrated more than 450 sets of intelligence data published from the 1930s to the mid-1980s and concluded that the Cattell–Horn model of fluid and crystallized intelligence best fit the existing evidence. Carroll extended the model, however, arguing that intelligence actually consists of three levels,

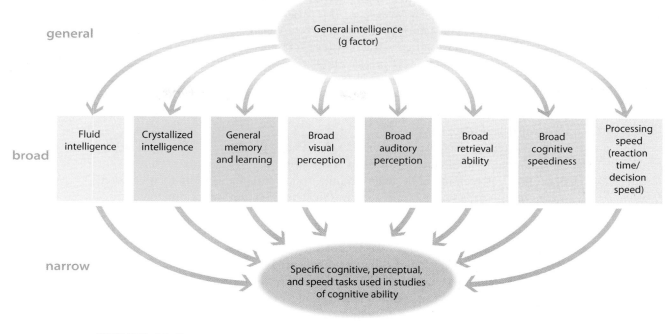

FIGURE **10.3**

THE CATTELL–HORN–CARROLL (CHC) MODEL OF INTELLIGENCE. This hierarchical model integrates the concept of a general intelligence with several broadly defined abilities, including fluid and crystallized intelligence. The broad categories consist of more specific abilities, such as speed of reasoning (fluid intelligence) and language comprehension (crystallized intelligence).

arranged in a hierarchy. At the top of the hierarchy is **general intelligence,** at the middle is **broad intelligence,** and at the bottom is **narrow intelligence.** General intelligence is very similar to Spearman's concept of "g." Broad intelligence consists of abilities such as crystallized and fluid intelligence, as well as memory, learning, and processing speed. Narrow intelligence consists of nearly 70 distinct abilities, such as speed of reasoning and general sequential reasoning for fluid intelligence and reading, spelling, and language comprehension for crystallized intelligence (see Figure 10.3). Because this model includes Cattell and Horn's crystallized and fluid intelligences, it has become known as the Cattell–Horn–Carroll (CHC) model of intelligence.

Robert Sternberg and Howard Gardner have proposed even more radical theories of multiple intelligence. Sternberg argues for a broader view of intelligence than is found in traditional g-factor theories. Most important, he focuses not simply on intelligence but on **successful intelligence,** which he defines as an integrated set of information-processing and cognitive abilities needed for life success (Sternberg, 2005, p. 104). Three interrelated but distinct abilities make up successful intelligence:

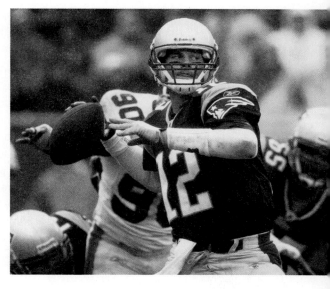

Athletes use practical intelligence to solve problems on the field.

analytic, creative, and practical intelligence (Sternberg, 1985, 2006b). Sternberg's three-part theory is known as the **triarchic theory of intelligence.**

triarchic theory of intelligence
Sternberg's three-part model of intelligence, including analytic, creative, and practical intelligence.

The first type of intelligence, *analytic intelligence*, involves judging, evaluating, or comparing and contrasting information (Sternberg, 1998). Analytic intelligence resembles the kind of academic intelligence that leads to high scores on tests of intelligence. For example, an analytic problem might require a person to decipher the meaning of an uncommon word from its context in a sentence, or it might ask the person to determine the next number in a series of numbers (Sternberg, 2003).

The second form of intelligence is *creative intelligence*. Creative intelligence involves coming up with fresh and useful ideas for solving problems. For example, a person might be given a number of cartoon images and then be asked to come up with a caption for each one (Sternberg, 2006b). Traditional measures of intelligence do not measure creative intelligence well. The third processing skill, *practical intelligence*, is the ability to solve problems of everyday life efficiently. Practical intelligence plays a role in knowing how to do one's job well and requires knowledge and skills that one learns "on the street" rather than in the classroom. A practical intelligence problem, for example, might ask people to come up with three solutions to a real everyday problem they are currently experiencing in their life, such as how to live on a fixed income (Sternberg, 2003).

Breaking New Ground

The Origins of Sternberg's Theory of Successful Intelligence

Robert Sternberg's ideas for different kinds of intelligence—analytical, practical, and creative—and how to measure them are themselves the result of his own creative and practical intelligence. These ideas have become some of the most influential ideas in modern conceptualizations of intelligence; and yet, according to Sternberg, all of his major research and theoretical ideas have come directly from his personal weaknesses. In his own words (personal communication, May 30, 2010):

> In my own case, almost all my ideas for research have emerged from areas in which I have weaknesses. I became interested in psychology because, as a child, I performed poorly on group intelligence tests. My performance was at a level such that, when I was in sixth grade, I was sent back to a fifth-grade classroom because the school authorities thought that the sixth-grade test would be too difficult for me. I have continued my study of intelligence even until the present day, still trying to figure out what went wrong when I took those tests. (I like to attribute my poor scores to test anxiety, although that may be a rationalization.) . . . So I recommend to you that, if you are bad at something, you use that as a basis to get new ideas about what you can study in psychology!

Robert Sternberg

Out of this experience with IQ tests in middle school, Sternberg grew to realize that people are intelligent in different ways, only one of which is measured by traditional IQ tests—namely, analytical intelligence. Analytical intelligence involves analyzing, comparing, contrasting, and judging.

Sternberg argues that in addition to being smart analytically, people can also be intelligent in ways not found on IQ tests: creatively and practically. Creative intelligence is the ability to generate new ideas, whereas practical intelligence involves putting these ideas into practice in everyday life and convincing others that these ideas are good ones. Overall, successful intelligence requires that people figure out their intellectual strengths and weaknesses and "make the most of their strengths while finding ways around their weaknesses" (personal communication, May 30, 2010).

He goes on to say how the other major areas of his research—love, wisdom, and creativity—similarly came from personal experiences of failure. For example, he became driven to understand creativity when after his first year in graduate school he had run out of ideas on which to do more research. In short, he turned a problem into a solution and studied the problem itself. From these potential failures, he became one of the most influential, widely published, and widely awarded psychologists over the last 50 years. Indeed, he made the most of his strengths and found his way around his weaknesses.

■ ■ ■

Howard Gardner is another scholar who has focused on the multifaceted view of intelligence. Gardner (1983, 1993) argues that intelligence consists of at least eight distinct capacities: linguistic, mathematical–logical, musical, bodily–kinesthetic, spatial, intrapersonal, interpersonal, and naturalistic. *Naturalistic intelligence,* for instance, is the ability to recognize, classify, and understand the plants and animals in one's environment. In cultures that have formal science, highly skilled people in this domain of intelligence are likely to become biologists, botanists, and animal scientists or veterinarians. In cultures without formal science, they are the most talented hunters, gatherers, and farmers. *Interpersonal intelligence* is the ability to perceive and understand other people's intentions, emotions, motives, and behaviors. Interpersonally intelligent people therefore work well with others and know how to get along with others. Interpersonal intelligence is very closely related to what other psychologists refer to as "emotional intelligence." See Figure 10.4 for a complete listing and definitions of Gardner's eight intelligences.

Howard Gardner

Connection

The concept of "emotional intelligence" is related to interpersonal intelligence and has blossomed as a complement to "intelligence" in the traditional sense. People who are emotionally intelligent do well in situations involving people and conflict. In fact, emotional intelligence can positively affect academic performance.
See "Emotional Intelligence," Chapter 11, "Motivation and Emotion," p. 466.

Scholars are strongly divided, however, over Gardner's theory. In fact, those who have the most problems with it tend to be psychologists. They see little value in calling skills like music, movement, and social skills "intelligence" and argue that Gardner has not provided tests of these intelligences. Moreover, there have been few direct empirical tests on Gardner's theory, and therefore some argue that his ideas are more theoretical than empirical. For some psychologists and many educators, however, Gardner's ideas address two real-world facts: (1) Different students learn in different ways, and (2) some students who have demonstrated ability in some areas fail academic subjects and do poorly on traditional intelligence tests (Kornhaber, Fierros, & Veenema, 2004). They may even drop out of school.

How should teachers nurture and teach these failing students—indeed, all students—given the fact that different students learn different material differently? Entire schools have been designed to enhance the "intelligences" of students. We describe a few of these programs in "Psychology in the Real World."

Intelligence	Definition	Representative Professions
linguistic	Ability to learn, understand, and use both spoken and written language	Poets, writers, lawyers, politicians
logical-mathematical	Ability to analyze information and problems logically and to perform mathematical operations	Scientists, engineers, accountants
musical	Ability in performing, composing, or appreciating musical patterns	Musicians, dancers, song-writers
bodily-kinesthetic	Ability to use one's body or parts of it to solve problems or create products	Athletes, dancers, mechanics, craftspeople
spatial	Ability to think about and solve problems in three-dimensional space	Navigators, pilots, architects, sculptors
interpersonal	Ability to understand and be aware of other people's intentions, motivations, thoughts, and desires; also the ability to work well with and get along with others	Psychologists, social workers, teachers, politicians
intrapersonal	Ability to be aware of, understand, and regulate one's own behavior, thoughts, feelings, and motivations	Psychologists, monks, priests
naturalistic	Ability to recognize, classify, and understand the plants and animals in one's environment	Naturalists, biologists, botanists, veterinarians, hunters, farmers

Measuring Intelligence

Like different theories of intelligence, tests of intelligence, commonly called IQ tests, are controversial. Some of the questions they raise are "How does someone interpret a person's score on an intelligence test?" "Where does a person stand compared to everyone else?" and "How do we know that a given test is any good at all?" The numerous attempts to answer these questions over the years have been based on the way intelligence was understood at the time the tests were devised, and so we begin our discussion with a bit of history.

Traditional Measures of Intelligence Intelligence tests were among the first psychological tests. The French scholar Alfred Binet deserves the most credit for developing the first true test of intelligence. In the early 1900s, the government hired Binet to identify students who would benefit most from special instruction techniques. For this purpose, Binet and a colleague, Theodore Simon, developed a test containing 30 problems of increasing difficulty. Their idea that ability to solve increasingly difficult problems depends on age became widely influential and has since become known as mental age. **Mental age** is the equivalent chronological age a child has reached based on his or her performance on an intelligence test. Children are given a mental age not according to how old they are in years, but rather according to the level or age group at which

mental age
the equivalent chronological age a child has reached based on his or her performance on an IQ test.

Bringing Multiple Intelligences to School

The chief motivation behind bringing multiple intelligences (MI) to the school setting is to avoid some of the limitations of traditional testing and teaching that discourage students who do not do well. Gardner (1999) realized that testing in the usual sense would have to be abandoned and classrooms would have to be arranged and equipped with materials that stimulate and foster each of the different forms of intelligence. Under this model, classrooms may be arranged with areas meant for dance, exercise, and construction. The materials may include board games, art and music materials, nature specimens (e.g., a fish tank), and natural objects.

An educational principle based on MI theory is that children should have some freedom to choose activities on their own. If they ignore certain kinds of activities, their teachers provide encouragement and "bridges" for them to try the neglected activities. For instance, if students are reluctant to tell stories, a teacher might encourage them to build a diorama (a three-dimensional model). The teacher would then ask the students to tell a story about what is happening to the people and animals in the diorama.

More than 40 schools in the United States have been designed to put into practice the development of all Gardner's forms of intelligences (Kornhaber et al., 2004; Kunkel, 2009). One example is the Key Learning Community in Indianapolis, Indiana. It opened in 1987 as a public elementary and middle school. Assessment takes place at the end of the school year, when each student presents a project based on any or all of the intelligences on which he or she has focused during the year. Students often present their project as a performance, such as a play, poetry reading, or artistic interpretation. They may also write papers on what they have learned. Each presentation is videotaped and put into the student's portfolio, which serves as a record of the student's cognitive and emotional development. Students in these schools still must take the local school district's standardized tests, and when they do, they do at least as well as students from other schools (*Key Learning Community,* n.d.; Kornhaber et al., 2004). Moreover, most of the schools adopting this model reported that the MI approach helped decrease disciplinary problems and increase parent participation. Finally, the performance of students with learning disabilities improved markedly when they attended MI schools.

In short, the MI schools teach to different learning styles and to their students' different intellectual talents. For some students at least, this alternative fosters academic achievement that might not occur in a traditional setting.

Evaluating the effectiveness of programs like the Key Learning Community is difficult in a culture dominated by test scores as the main criterion of success (Kunkel, 2009). This is especially true as MI-based programs emphasize community service, completion of projects, and apprenticeships. In a recent survey of Key students (among a community with a 73% poverty rate, which works against successfully completing school in traditional school settings), 88% of Key students graduate and 91% go on to further education or training after high school (Kunkel, 2009).

According to Gardner, naturalistic intelligence should be nurtured in the same way as mathematical skills, verbal ability, and at least five other kinds of intelligence.

they can solve problems. Mental age is a norm or average because it is based on what most children at a particular age level can do.

A few years after Binet developed the concept of mental age, a German psychologist, William Stern, introduced the *intelligence ratio,* in which mental age (MA) is divided by chronological age (CA) and multiplied by 100 to determine an intelligence score. The ratio of mental age over chronological age is commonly known as a person's *intelligence quotient,* or IQ. In other words, if a child had a mental age of 10 and was 10 years old, she had an IQ of 100 (10 ÷ 10 × 100). But if she had a mental age of 12 and was only 10 years old, she had an IQ of 120; if she had a mental age of 8 and was 10 years old, her IQ was 80. This ratio was very useful in the early years of IQ testing with children, but it is no longer used. Today IQ scores are based on how well a child does on tests relative to norms or standards established by testing children of the same age.

About 10 years after Binet published his first test, Lewis Terman, an American psychologist, translated the test for American students. Because Terman taught at Stanford University, he named the test the *Stanford–Binet test.* The most significant changes Terman made were to establish national norms and to adopt and apply the ratio score of MA ÷ CA to a widely used IQ test.

In the 1930s, David Wechsler created new intelligence tests to measure adult intelligence. Wechsler's test became known as the *Wechsler Adult Intelligence Scale,* or WAIS (Wechsler, 1944, 1958). Later he developed a test for children, the *Wechsler Intelligence Scale for Children* (WISC). At present, these two tests are the ones most frequently administered in the United States (Wasserman & Tulsky, 2005). To sample the kinds of problems included on one of these IQ tests, see Figure 10.5. The current versions of both the Stanford–Binet and the WAIS are based on modern theories about intelligence.

Modern Measures of Intelligence

For 50 years IQ tests were based on the assumption that intelligence is a single quality. The developers of both the Stanford–Binet and Wechsler tests failed to take into account Jean Piaget's work on cognitive development and newer findings from neuroscience. As discussed in Chapter 5, Piaget found that the cognitive abilities of young children and adolescents are fundamentally different and that cognitive development occurs in stages rather than gradually over time. Adolescents can reason abstractly, for example, but young children cannot. Yet IQ tests continued to give very similar problems to young children, teenagers, and adults, changing only the level of difficulty. Moreover, until the 1980s, IQ test developers ignored advances in neuroscience (Kaufman, 1979). In the late 20th century, a new approach to intelligence testing incorporated Piaget's ideas, findings from neuroscience, and learning style differences.

As advances in neuroscience led to greater understanding of how the brain solves problems, psychologists became increasingly aware of the limits of existing IQ tests. By the late 1970s, alternatives to the two dominant IQ tests (Stanford–Binet and Wechsler) began to be published. One of the best known of

Alan and Nadeen
Kaufman

these alternatives, developed by Nadeen and Alan Kaufman, is the *Kaufman-Assessment Battery for Children,* or K-ABC (Kaufman & Kaufman, 1983). The K-ABC differed from the Stanford–Binet and Wechsler tests in four ways. First, it was the first IQ test to be guided by theories of intelligence, in particular Cattell and Horn's concepts of fluid and crystallized intelligence

FIGURE **10.5**

verbal subscales

Similarities

An individual must think logically and abstractly to answer a number of questions about how things might be similar.

Example: "In what ways are boats and trains the same?"

Comprehension

This subscale is designed to measure an individual's judgment and common sense.

Example: "Why do individuals buy automobile insurance?"

nonverbal subscales

Picture Arrangement

A series of pictures out of sequence is shown to an individual, who is asked to place them in their proper order to tell an appropriate story. This subscale evaluates how individuals integrate information to make it logical and meaningful.

Example: "The pictures below need to be placed in an appropriate order to tell a story."

Block Design

An individual must assemble a set of multicolored blocks to match designs that the examiner shows. Visual-motor coordination, perceptual organization, and the ability to visualize spatially are assessed.

Example: "Use the four blocks on the left to make the pattern at the right."

FIGURE 10.5

IQ TEST PROBLEMS SIMILAR TO THOSE ON THE WECHSLER ADULT INTELLIGENCE SCALE (WAIS). The WAIS and the Wechsler Intelligence Scale for Children are the most widely administered intelligence tests in the United States. (Source: Simulated items similar to those found on the Wechsler Adult Intelligence Scale—Revised (WAIS-R). Copyright © 1981, 1955 by NCS Pearson, Inc. Reproduced with permission. All rights reserved. "Wechsler Adult Intelligence Scale" and "WAIS" are trademarks, in the US and/ or other countries, of Pearson Education, Inc. or its affiliates.)

and Piaget's theory of cognitive development. Second, influenced by Piaget, the Kaufmans included fundamentally different kinds of problems for children of different ages, as well as problems at varied levels of difficulty. Third, unlike older tests, the K-ABC measured several distinct aspects of intelligence. Finally, influenced by neuroscience and information processing theory, the K-ABC assessed different types of learning styles. In this sense, the K-ABC was the first of many intelligence tests informed by contemporary ideas about how the brain worked and developed (Kaufman & Kaufman, 1983).

Tests may still produce an overall IQ score, but now they also yield scores on as many as seven dimensions of intelligence. Influenced by the CHC model, the newest versions of both the WAIS (WAIS-IV) and the WISC (WISC-IV) include scores on four dimensions: verbal comprehension, perceptual reasoning, working memory, and processing speed (T. P. Hogan, 2007). Working memory, which holds information in mind for a short period so that

Connection

Working memory is another term for short-term memory. In general, people can retain only about seven bits of information in short-term memory.

See "Short-Term or Working Memory," Chapter 7, "Memory," p. 272.

FIGURE 10.6

SIMULATED EXAMPLES OF WORKING MEMORY TASKS ON THE WECHSLER SCALES OF INTELLIGENCE. The latest version of the WISC and the WAIS also assess verbal comprehension, perceptual reasoning, and processing speed. (Source: Simulated items similar to those in Wechsler Intelligence Scale for Children—Fourth Edition (WISC-IV). Copyright © 2003 by NCS Pearson, Inc. Reproduced with permission. All rights reserved. "Wechsler Intelligence Scale for Children" and "WISC" are trademarks, in the US and/or other countries, of Pearson Education, Inc. or its affiliates.)

Digit span

| Examiner says:
6 - 2 - 9 | Examinee repeats it back |
| Examiner says:
7 - 4 - 6 - 1 - 4 - 8 - 3 - 9 | Examinee repeats it back |

Letter-number sequencing

| Examiner says:
L - 7 - C - 3 | Examinee has to repeat the sequence with numbers in ascending order and then letters in alphabetical order
3 - 7 - C - L |

it can be used to solve a problem at hand, is one dimension that was missing before 1985. For examples of working memory tasks included in the Wechsler scales, see Figure 10.6.

Also influenced by the CHC model, the fifth edition of the Stanford–Binet assesses five different factors of general intelligence, each with verbal and non-verbal dimensions (Roid & Pomplun, 2005). In addition to assessing fluid and crystallized intelligence, the newest version of the Stanford–Binet assesses quantitative reasoning, visual–spatial processing, and working memory.

In sum, current intelligence tests reflect contemporary thinking about intelligence as a general quality with many dimensions. Since the development of the CHC model and publication of the first version of the K-ABC, all other major IQ tests have followed suit and developed more theory-driven and complex tests of at least five aspects of intelligence rather than just two or three.

to Real Life

Research

Intelligence tests boil down to combining different forms of intelligence (verbal, mathematical, spatial) to one number. The idea is that one number captures an individual's "general" intelligence. Other scholars, such as Sternberg and Gardner, however, argue that intelligence is more than one thing and expand the notion of intelligence to include creative, practical, interpersonal, and musical intelligences, among others.

Connecting Psychology to Your Life: What do you think? Does it make more sense to think about how intelligent you are overall or how you are intelligent in different areas of life? Try making a list of your own intellectual strengths and weaknesses. Do these intelligences cluster into one overall category, or are they distinct and different categories?

Reliability and Validity of IQ Tests

reliability
consistency of a measurement, such as an intelligence test.

Tests are meaningful only if they are both reliable and valid. **Reliability** refers to consistency of results. If a test is reliable, a person who takes the same test on two different occasions will obtain very similar scores on both occasions. Reliability over time is referred to as **test–retest reliability.** IQ tests tend to be extremely reliable over time. A second form of reliability exists when questions on a given subtest tend to

test–retest reliability
consistency of scores on a test over time.

internal reliability
characteristic of intelligence test in which questions on a given subtest tend to correlate very highly with other items on the subtest.

construct validity
the degree to which a test measures the concept it claims to measure, such as intelligence.

correlate very highly with other items on the subtest, meaning that the test's **internal reliability** is very high. So, overall, test makers have done a good job of creating reliable IQ tests (Gregory, 2007).

Validity requires that the tests really measure intelligence and not something else and that test scores predict real-world outcomes. The validity of a test is more difficult to establish than is its reliability. Although there is a great deal of evidence that the Wechsler and Stanford–Binet tests, among others, do provide valid measures of intelligence, many intelligence experts, notably Sternberg and Gardner, have argued that they measure only verbal, spatial, and mathematical forms of intelligence. The other forms that Gardner identified—social, emotional, musical, bodily, practical, and natural history—are not measured at all.

There are at least two distinct forms of validity: construct and predictive. **Construct validity** refers to what we have just discussed: that a test measures the concept, or *construct*, it claims to measure. **Predictive validity** addresses the question of whether the construct is related positively to real-world outcomes, such as school achievement or job success. IQ tests do predict certain real-world outcomes, the first and foremost being academic performance. IQ scores predict students' grades, school performance, and class rank in high school quite well. That is, after all, what they were meant to predict. For example, preschool scores on two IQ tests taken by children in the Head Start Program accurately predicted the children's academic achievement scores from kindergarten to sixth grade (Lamp & Krohn, 2001). Moreover, scores from the WAIS predict both one's academic class rank in high school and one's college GPA (Gregory, 2007). Even though IQ can predict the kind of job you will get and how much money you will make, it cannot predict how happy and satisfied you will be with your life or how well you will do in your job (Gow et al., 2005).

Are IQ Tests Biased? Given the differences among groups in average IQ scores, it is tempting to conclude that IQ tests are biased and unfair (Ford, 2008). Yet group differences on tests in and of themselves do not necessarily mean the tests are biased, but it may mean they are unfair. Whether a test is either biased or unfair or both involves two separate, though related, issues.

validity
the degree to which a test accurately measures what it purports to measure, such as intelligence, and not something else, and the degree to which it predicts real-world outcomes.

predictive validity
the degree to which intelligence test scores are positively related to real-world outcomes, such as school achievement or job success, and thus have predictive value.

Are IQ tests unfair to a particular group of individuals?

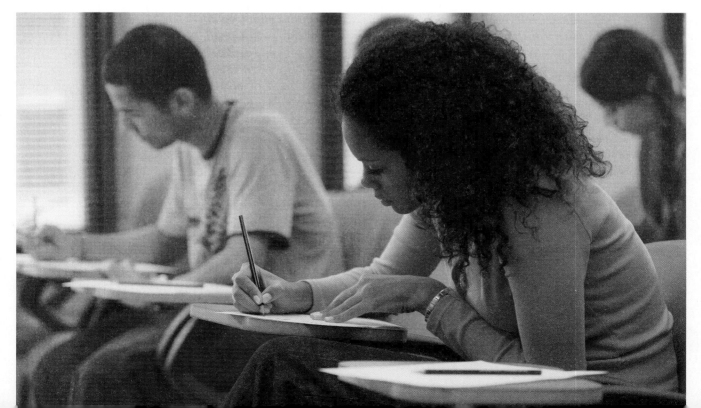

Let's first be clear about what each term means and then examine the evidence for each. The general public attaches a different meaning to *bias* than scientists do. The general public may use the term *bias* to refer to the notion that group differences in IQ scores are caused by different cultural and educational environments, not by real differences in intelligence. This view is known as **cultural test bias** (C. R. Reynolds, 2000). Given how complex and controversial the causes of intelligence are, there is quite a bit of disagreement in the general population about what causes group differences on IQ test scores. Even when different groups agree that IQ testing has cultural bias, the underlying causes are still disputed (see "Race–Ethnicity and Intelligence" later in this chapter).

cultural test bias hypothesis
the notion that group differences in IQ scores are caused by different cultural and educational backgrounds, not by real differences in intelligence.

When scientists refer to **test bias** in an IQ test, however, they refer to whether a test predicts outcomes equally well for different groups. A test is biased if it is a more valid measure for one group than for another. For example, if an IQ test predicts academic achievement better for Hispanics than for Asians, it is biased. Researchers have found, however, very little evidence for the existence of this kind of bias in IQ tests (R. T. Brown, Reynolds, & Whitaker, 1999; Hunter & Schmidt, 2000; C. R. Reynolds, 2000). Intelligence tests are developed using norms that reflect the makeup of the general population. Just because different groups score differently on a given test does not automatically mean that it is biased. If the test is equally valid for different groups and they still score differently on it, the test is not biased. It may be unfair, but it's not biased.

test bias
characteristic of a test that produces different outcomes for different groups.

test fairness
judgment about how test results are applied to different groups based on values and philosophical inclinations.

Test fairness, on the other hand, reflects values, philosophical differences, and the ways in which test results are applied (Gregory, 2007). Test results, especially IQ test results, are meant to be applied—often by people in education, the military, and business. Problems arise when people use IQ test results unfairly to deny certain groups access to universities or jobs. So test fairness, in this sense, concerns the application of the test results rather than the test itself. An unbiased test result could be applied unfairly.

Extremes of Intelligence

Intelligence varies in a very predictable way, which is most easily seen in the frequency of different IQ scores in the population. When one plots the scores on a graph, one sees a very clear bell curve, with most people falling in the middle and a few people at the high and low ends of the curve. This shape is referred to as a *bell curve* because it is shaped like a bell. Looking at the bell curve for IQ scores in Figure 10.7, we can see that 68% of test-takers will score between

FIGURE 10.7

NORMAL DISTRIBUTION OF IQ TEST SCORES (BELL CURVE).

The vast majority of people (95%) achieve scores between 70 and 130 on the Wechsler IQ scales. The norm is 100. The higher the standard score is, whether positive or negative, the further away the scores are from the norm. Only a small percentage are found at the extremes.

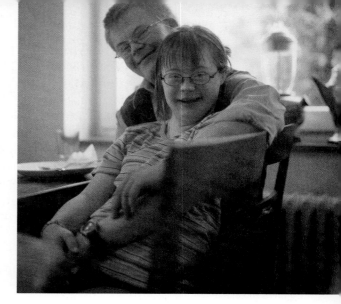

85 and 115 and almost all—99.7%—will score between 55 and 145. It is at the two ends of the curve, or distribution, that we find "extremes of intelligence"—specifically, mental retardation and giftedness.

Mental Retardation   To meet the criteria for **mental retardation,** an individual must show significant limitations in intellectual functioning as well as in everyday adaptive behavior, and these deficits must start before age 18 (American Association on Mental Retardation, 2002; American Psychiatric Association, 2000). Historically, retardation was defined and diagnosed solely on the basis of IQ, with 70 being the most common cutoff score.

Like this happy couple, many people with Down syndrome have full, productive lives in spite of their intellectual limitations.

There are four levels of mental retardation, depending on how adaptive the behavior or thinking is: mild (IQ of 50–70), moderate (35–50), severe (20–35), and profound (below 20). More recently, however, a different criterion, adaptive behavior, has been added to IQ as a determinant of mental retardation. **Adaptive behavior** is defined as how well a person adjusts to and copes with everyday life (T. P. Hogan, 2007). For example, how well can the person feed or dress himself or herself? Does the individual have the ability to tell time, make change, or read simple words? At a more complex level, one might ask whether he or she can take a bus or subway or follow the news on TV. Most current diagnoses of mental retardation emphasize adaptive functioning over IQ scores. They therefore measure a person's everyday abilities more than their academic performance.

The origins of mental retardation vary and are many, but there are at least three main causes:

- Chromosomal–genetic abnormalities (e.g., Down syndrome and Fragile X syndrome)
- Prenatal abnormalities (e.g., fetal alcohol syndrome)
- Environmental deprivation

In about 50% of cases, the cause of mental retardation is *organic*, meaning that it is genetic or the result of brain damage. **Down syndrome,** a disorder that results from a condition known as trisomy 21, in which a person has three rather than two number 21 chromosomes, is an example of chromosomal cause of mental retardation. The genetic cause of Down syndrome is not fully known, but it is related to maternal age. Children born to older women are more likely to develop trisomy-21 and Down syndrome ("What Causes Down Syndrome?" 2011). Fragile X syndrome is a disorder on the X chromosome and results in abnormal development of a gene involved in neural development. People with Fragile X syndrome often have stunted cognitive development and social interactions.

As we first discussed in Chapter 6, fetal alcohol syndrome occurs when the mother drinks while pregnant and is a prenatal cause of mental retardation (Streissguth et al., 1989). If the pregnant mother is also exposed to other chemicals—for example, lead, manganese or mercury—that affect brain development or is physically abused, the risk of mental retardation also increases (Dietrich et al., 1991; S. Jacobson & Jacobson, 2000; Mash & Wolf, 2010).

Finally, environmental deprivation, such as neglect and poor nutrition, is to blame for some cases of mental retardation. Sometimes called *familial–cultural*

mental retardation
significant limitations in intellectual functioning as well as in everyday adaptive behavior, which start before age 18.

adaptive behavior
adjustment to and coping with everyday life.

Down syndrome
a chromosomal disorder characterized by mild to profound mental retardation.

retardation, this type is more prevalent among people of low socioeconomic status, tends to occur in more than one family member, and tends to be mild (Kerig & Wenar, 2006; Mash & Wolf, 2010).

Giftedness

Giftedness lies at the high end of the intelligence spectrum. Starting in about the third grade in the United States, students who do very well in school and also do well on standardized tests of intelligence are sometimes placed in "gifted" programs. In most schools, children are admitted to such a program if they score 130–140 or above on a standardized IQ test like the WISC or Stanford–Binet. Extreme giftedness takes various forms, two of which are prodigies and savants.

Prodigies   A **prodigy** is a young person who is extremely gifted and precocious in one area, such as math, music, art, or chess, and is at least average in intelligence (Feldman, 2004). Most often, prodigies are people under the age of 20. Sometimes they possess extreme talent in more than one domain, such as math and language. Probably the world's most famous child prodigy was Wolfgang Amadeus Mozart, who was playing keyboard by age 3 and composing symphonies by age 8. Although they are relatively rare, some people display extreme early talent in visual arts. Akiane Kramarik is an example. She was sketching incredibly lifelike drawings by age 4 and producing world-class paintings by age 9. She loves drawing and painting so much that she wakes each morning at 4 a.m. to express herself on canvas (Kramarik, 2006). What makes Kramarik even more unusual is that she is also an accomplished and published poet. In short, she is both visually and verbally gifted.

In addition to documenting individual cases of intellectual prodigies, researchers have conducted large-scale studies of mathematical prodigies. The best known of these is the Study for Mathematically Precocious Youth (SMPY;

Akiane Kramarik is a gifted young artist who has been painting and drawing since she was a small child. With her parents' encouragement, Akiane has developed her natural creative abilities to an extraordinary level. She also writes poetry.

Stanley, 1996). Begun in 1971, the SMPY is a 50-year longitudinal study of extremely talented people, especially in math. To qualify for the SMPY, students had to score 700 on the SAT-Quantitative and 630 or higher on the SAT-Verbal *before* their 13th birthday. Only about one in 10,000 test-takers achieves a score of 700 or above (Lubinski et al., 2006). Students in the latter group go on to have very successful careers. Follow-up research 25–35 years later shows that many of them attended top universities at both the undergraduate and graduate levels and then went on to become successful scientists, mathematicians, engineers, and doctors (Lubinski & Benbow, 2006; Wai, Lubinski, & Benbow, 2009).

savant syndrome

a very rare condition in which people with serious mental handicaps also show isolated areas of ability or brilliance.

Savants   Since at least the 1700s, there have been reports of people with **savant syndrome,** a very rare condition characterized by serious mental handicaps and isolated areas of ability or remarkable giftedness (Treffert, 2006). Savants (the word *savant* comes from the French word for "knowing") have low overall intelligence, typically with an IQ below 70, and an incredible ability for calculating numbers, recalling events, playing music, or drawing. Often these individuals cannot speak at all or speak poorly.

Although it is difficult to know for sure, by some estimates, there are only about 100 savants in the world today, about 50% of whom suffer from autism and the other 50% from some other kind of psychological disorder, such as brain injury, epilepsy, or mental retardation (Treffert, 2006). Savant syndrome occurs most often in five major areas of talent: music (usually piano), art, math, calendar calculations, and spatial/mechanical skills (Treffert, 2006). A relatively common form is seen in individuals who can immediately calculate the day of the week on which a particular date in history fell. For example, if asked what day of the week June 15, 1899, was, they would correctly answer "Thursday." Others with savant syndrome can take apart clocks, toys, bicycles, and other machines and rebuild them with expert precision.

Connection

Daniel Tammet uses mnemonic devices, a memory tool, to help him remember the value of pi. He retraces the different shapes, colors and textures in his head and then just reads the number. How do mnemonic devices aid memory?

See "Long-Term Memory," Chapter 7, "Memory," p. 276.

In Chapter 7, we met Daniel Tammet, whose uncanny memory skills enable him to recall pi to 22,514 digits and calculate complex mathematical problems almost instantaneously. Tammet has savant syndrome as well as synesthesia, which, as you might recall from Chapter 4, occurs when a person experiences sensations in one sense when a different sense is stimulated. In Tammet's case, he sees each number as a distinct color and shape, and this is the secret behind his uncanny memory for numbers and calculations. For example, he finds the 762nd to 769th digits (a series of six 9s) of pi to be a beautiful "deep, thick rim of dark blue light" (Tammet, 2006, p. 179).

Another person with savant syndrome was Kim Peek. Although Peek was most famous as the inspiration for the movie *Rain Man*, starring Dustin Hoffman, his abilities went much further than the movie suggests. He was one of the world's only true speed-readers—he could read a page in about 3 seconds and retain essentially every word. Incredibly, Peek memorized about 9,000 books after reading them only *once*. He immediately provided biographical information about any of the U.S. presidents; could tell you the zip code of any city or borough in the United States; and identify who composed almost any piece of classical music and tell you where it was composed and when it was first performed. Like some other savants, he also could tell you more or less instantly the day of the week on which any date in history fell.

Given his phenomenal abilities, it is easy to forget that Peek was unable to do many basic things—such as dress himself. Indeed, his tested IQ was 73, which is in the range for people with severe autism. Socially he was very awkward, and he liked to repeat certain phrases, saying over and over again how great was the person he had just met. He also did not understand metaphors like "get hold of yourself." Instead, he interpreted everything literally. His adaptive functioning skills were poor, and his father had to take care of him on a daily basis. A scan of his brain revealed that Peek, like some other savants, had no corpus callosum and very little cerebellum (Treffert & Christensen, 2005). The absence of a corpus callosum means that information processed in one of the brain's hemispheres cannot be communicated to the other hemisphere.

The Nature and Nurture of Human Intelligence

If you want to start an argument, all you need to do is take a strong stance on one of the following positions: (1) A person's intelligence is determined almost completely by genetics, or (2) a person's intelligence is determined almost completely by the environment in which he or she is raised. Most people realize that intelligence results from a combination of "being born that way" and "being brought up that way" by our family and teachers. What is most remarkable is the complexity of the interaction between these two forces.

One way we see the interaction between environment and biological forces is in how the brain responds differently to different kinds of problems, intelligence problems among them. The region most often involved in various IQ tasks is the prefrontal cortex (Colom et al., 2009; DeYoung et al., 2009; Duncan et al., 2000; Haier et al., 2004; R. E. Jung & Haier, 2007). For instance, when a person is working on verbal tasks, only the left prefrontal region of the brain is activated. When an individual is working on spatial tasks, however, the prefrontal cortexes of both the left and right hemispheres, as well as the occipital cortex, are activated (see Figure 10.8; Duncan et al., 2000; Haier et al., 2004; R. E. Jung &

FIGURE **10.8**

BRAIN ACTIVATION WHILE WORKING ON IQ PROBLEMS. Red areas show activation during two different IQ tasks, a verbal task and a spatial task. The spatial task activates the frontal lobe in both the right and left hemispheres, whereas the verbal task activates only the left frontal lobe region (Broca's area). (Source: Duncan et al., 2000)

Spatial Task

Left Hemisphere   Right Hemisphere

Verbal Task

Left Hemisphere   Right Hemisphere

Haier, 2007). Moreover, the frontal lobe is more involved when an individual is performing fluid intelligence tasks, such as pattern recognition, than when the person is performing tasks that involve crystallized intelligence and learned experiences (Gray & Thompson, 2004).

Furthermore, twin-adoption and family studies demonstrate the interconnectedness of nature and nurture in intelligence. As we saw in Chapter 3, these kinds of studies allow researchers to hold one factor constant, while varying the other one. The more genetically related people are, the more similar they are in IQ, even if reared apart (see Figure 10.9). Identical twins reared apart are more similar in their levels of intelligence than fraternal twins reared together. Similarly, dozens of studies have shown that adopted children's

Separated at birth, the Malifert twins meet accidentally.
© 1981 Charles Addams. With permission of the Tee and Charles Addams Foundation.

overall intelligence is more similar to that of their biological parents than to that of their adoptive parents (Munsinger, 1975). Yet adoption—hence, the environment—can also enhance a child's IQ (van IJzendoorn & Juffer, 2005). Compared to orphans not adopted, adopted children tend to have higher IQs. In sum, genetic factors ("nature") account for about 50% of the variability in intelligence among individuals; environment ("nurture") accounts for about 40%; the remaining 10% is, as yet, unexplained (Grigorenko, 2000; Lynn, 2006; Plomin & Petrill, 1997).

The concept of reaction range provides further evidence for the interaction of biology and environment in determining a person's intelligence. A **reaction range** is the genetically determined range within which a given trait, such as intelligence, may fall; that trait's

Nature & Nurture

The concept of reaction range describes how biology and environment work together to produce a person's overall level of intelligence.

reaction range
for a given trait, such as IQ, the genetically determined range of responses by an individual to his or her environment.

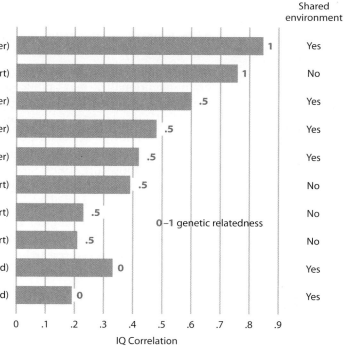

	Shared environment
Monozygotic twins (reared together) — 1	Yes
Monozygotic twins (reared apart) — 1	No
Dizygotic twins (reared together) — .5	Yes
Siblings (reared together) — .5	Yes
Parent-offspring (reared together) — .5	Yes
Dizygotic twins (reared apart) — .5	No
Siblings (reared apart) — .5	No
Parent-offspring (reared apart) — .5	No
Siblings (adopted) — 0	Yes
Parent-offspring (adopted) — 0	Yes

0–1 genetic relatedness

IQ Correlation

FIGURE **10.9**

GENETIC AND ENVIRONMENTAL EFFECTS ON IQ.
Numbers in orange represent genetic relatedness. Genetic relatedness of 1 means 100% genetic similarity; .5 means 50% genetic similarity; and 0 means no genetic similarity. Monozygotic twins are identical twins. Dizygotic twins are fraternal twins. (Adapted from Grigorenko, 2000, and Plomin & Petrill, 1997)

FIGURE **10.10**

REACTION RANGE AND INTELLI-GENCE. The concept of reaction range suggests that heredity places upper and lower limits on an individual's potential, but environment determines whether the individual reaches the upper limit or a point somewhere between the upper limit and the lower limit. This graph shows hypothetical reaction ranges for three children (A, B, and C) and how their surroundings could shape their IQs. With enriched environments, all three could reach their individual upper limit, as shown on the right side of the graph. (Source: Seifert et al., 2000)

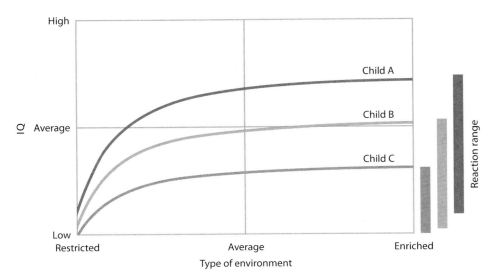

exact value, however, depends on the quality of the individual's environment (Scarr, 1981; Weinberg, 1989). For most people in most environments, the reaction range for IQ is about 25 points—meaning that a given person may end up scoring anywhere in a 25-point range on an IQ test, depending on the kind of environment in which he or she is raised (Weinberg, 1989). Being raised in an enriched environment means someone is likely to obtain an IQ score near the upper limit of his or her reaction range; being raised in an impoverished environment means one is likely to obtain a score near the lower limit; and being raised in a normal environment means one is likely to obtain a score in the middle of his or her reaction range (see Figure 10.10). The important point here is that genes do not determine behavior but, rather, establish the range of possible behaviors.

Environment, however, is a complex thing. Only part of the environmental influence on intelligence comes from being in the same household and sharing experiences. The other part comes from experiences that are not shared by family members—that is, the individual's unique environmental experiences. One such experience is the prenatal environment and what happens to the fetus during pregnancy. Toxins ingested by the mother, either intentionally or unintentionally, may influence the child's intelligence. Alcohol, drugs, and viral infections in a pregnant woman can seriously lower her child's overall intelligence (Dietrich et al., 1991; S. Jacobson & Jacobson, 2000; Ruff, 1999; Steinhausen & Spohr, 1998; Streissguth et al., 1989).

Other aspects of intelligence stem from the joint influence of biological and environmental factors. One such example is birth weight. For many years, researchers and physicians have known that insufficient birth weight—a sign of severe prenatal malnutrition—creates a high risk for cognitive impairment (and thus impaired intelligence) later in life. Only recently, however, has anyone

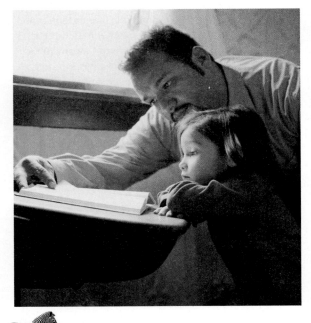

Reading to children regularly from the time they are very young as part of an enriched environment may actually enhance their IQ.

Nature& Nurture

What happens in the womb can permanently affect a person's measured intelligence.

examined whether birth weight matters for children born at a normal weight. Broekman and colleagues (2009) obtained birth weight, head measurement, and length information on over 1,500 children born in Singapore. All infants were born in the normal healthy weight/size range. After age 7, they conducted yearly intelligence testing on these children. Longer birth length, higher birth weight, or larger head circumferences within the normal birth size range (neither undernourished nor obese) are associated with higher IQ scores later in childhood; that is, the bigger children had higher IQs. Why might this be? Certain prenatal factors affecting fetal growth, such as maternal stress, also influence cognitive development. When a pregnant woman is under severe stress, her stress hormones might affect the growth of new neurons in the baby's brain (Oitzl et al., 2010).

Group Differences in Intelligence Scores

Given the importance of intelligence to success in life, the question of whether there are group differences in intelligence is bound to stir up controversy (Fancher, 1985). Research on this topic necessarily has political and social implications, and from time to time scientists who have studied group differences in intelligence have been harassed or threatened. If there are differences in intelligence between racial–ethnic groups or genders, what should we do as a society to compensate for those differences to level the playing field? Can that even be done?

Race–Ethnicity and Intelligence

In the 1960s and 1970s, Arthur Jensen received death threats for publishing research that not only reported differences in IQ among racial–ethnic groups, but also argued that because IQ is under genetic influence, racial–ethnic differences in IQ must be at least partly genetic in origin (Jensen, 1969). But it was another highly controversial book, published in the mid-1990s, that most recently ignited an academic, political, and cultural firestorm over intelligence. The book was called simply *The Bell Curve*, but its subtitle hinted at the more controversial contents: *Intelligence and Class Structure in American Life*. The book's authors, Richard Herrnstein and Charles Murray (1994), summarized the results of a study on racial–ethnic group differences, social class, and intelligence among 12,000 individuals. They concluded what many others had before and since: First, racial–ethnic groups vary on IQ scores; second, differences in IQ contribute to a large extent to differences in education and income (Gottfredson, 1997). Their conclusion suggested that group differences in IQ, and hence in education and income, can be explained in part by genetics.

After *The Bell Curve*, when all of the smoke cleared and tempers settled down, there was still no widely accepted and agreed-on explanation for racial–ethnic differences on IQ scores. There are a few schools of thought on the causes (in addition to the one that attributes the difference in part to genetics). Some experts maintain that racial–ethnic differences in IQ result from biases in IQ tests that favor people from certain cultural backgrounds over others (Ford, 2008; C. R. Reynolds, 2000). Others have argued that differences in IQ scores based on race–ethnicity are meaningless because race is mostly a social construct with little scientific support or biological foundation (Sternberg, Grigorenko, & Kidd, 2005). In addition, these psychologists also point out that heritability findings apply only within the group of people studied, not between groups. So it is a misinterpretation of heritability to argue that group differences are due to genetics even if IQ is heritable (Sternberg et al., 2005).

The conclusion that genetics influence intelligence is often interpreted—or misinterpreted—as implying that IQ levels are determined at birth or conception.

If this were so, then trying to change IQ levels with intervention programs such as Head Start would likely be unsuccessful (Herrnstein & Murray, 1994). Yet, such a conclusion is faulty for two reasons. First, genes interact with environmental forces, and therefore environment can shape gene expression. We saw this in Chapter 3 with the concept of epigenesis. Similarly, the concept of a reaction range makes clear the connection between genes and environment. Second, interventions have succeeded in changing IQ levels. Children raised under conditions of severe neglect and abuse who are adopted within the first few years of life showed tremendous growth in brain size and gains in IQ scores. Those adopted later in life or not adopted at all do not show increases in IQ scores (B. D. Perry, 2002). Moreover, one longitudinal study randomly assigned infants either to an early educational intervention program or to a control group. All children were from socially disadvantaged households. The intervention program lasted up until age 5 and focused on language, social, emotional, and cognitive stimulation. The children from both groups were studied again at ages 12, 15, and 21. The findings were clear: During adolescence and early adulthood, those who had been in the intervention program had higher IQ scores, performed better in school, and obtained higher-paying jobs than those in the control condition (F. A. Campbell & Ramey, 1995; F. A. Campbell et al., 2002). In short, both genetic and environmental forces play important roles in determining IQ scores.

Nature & Nurture

Early intervention with abused, neglected, and disadvantaged children raises IQ scores. Changes in environment can change brain structures that affect intellectual functioning.

Men and women may have their differences, but intelligence isn't one of them.

Gender and Intelligence Larry Hedges and Amy Nowell (1995) reviewed six nationally representative sets of IQ scores. Each set ranged from 12,000 to 73,000 participants altogether. They concluded that there are relatively few real differences between the sexes in cognitive ability; men and women are equally intelligent. Indeed, most research on overall intelligence and gender has reported no difference between men and women on average.

There is one area of variability in intelligence among men and women, illustrated in Figure 10.11. Men are more likely than women to score at either end of the range, especially in some areas.

FIGURE **10.11**

GENDER VARIABILITY IN INTELLIGENCE. Results from more than 80,000 Scottish children found that mean IQ scores were nearly identical. Mean IQ was 100.5 for boys and 100.6 for girls. Boys were much more likely to be at the two extreme ends of intelligence, however. They made up 58% of the scores at 60 and 140, whereas girls made up only about 42% of those scores. (Source: Deary et al., 2003)

Men more frequently score at the high or low end of the scale on tests of science, math, spatial reasoning, and social studies (Ceci & Williams, 2007; Gallagher & Kaufman, 2005). Women, however, tend to consistently do better than men in writing, reading comprehension, perceptual speed, and associative memory (Deary et al., 2003; Hedges & Nowell, 1995; Maccoby & Jacklin, 1974).

Non-Western Views of Intelligence

Ask people in the United States or Europe what it means to be intelligent. Then ask people in Kenya, China, Malaysia, and Bolivia. No doubt you will get very different answers. Western cultures emphasize verbal and cognitive skills first, whereas many African cultures see social skills, such as being socially responsible, cooperative, and active in family and social life, to be crucial aspects of intelligence (Ruzgis & Grigorenko, 1994; Serpell, 1982). Asian cultures have traditionally emphasized humility, awareness, doing the right thing, and mindfulness as important qualities of intelligence (Sternberg, 2000). Doing well in school and being quick to learn are not universally acknowledged to be essential qualities of intelligence. Sternberg and his colleagues have examined practical intelligence in cultures where academic intelligence is not valued as highly as it is in Western cultures. They have found that children in Kenya and Tanzania, for example, may not do well at solving "bookish" analytic problems but do very well at solving everyday, practical problems (Sternberg, 1998).

Problems that require intelligence are just one kind of problem we face. Problem solving pervades almost everything we do, from our choice of a major in college to our choice of friends, where we live, how we vote, and so on. Next we look at the psychology of problem solving.

Quick Quiz 10.1: Intelligence

1. Which of the following skills is NOT part of the definition of intelligence?
   a. abstract reasoning
   b. problem solving
   c. acquiring knowledge
   d. remote associations

2. Historically, a child's IQ was calculated by dividing _____ by chronological age and multiplying by _____. (Pick the best pair of words/numbers.)
   a. perceptual skill; 100
   b. mental age; 50
   c. perceptual skill; 50
   d. mental age; 100

3. The Kaufmans changed the field of intelligence testing by developing an IQ test that
   a. could be universally applied
   b. was grounded in psychological theory and knowledge of the brain
   c. was reliable and valid
   d. was culture-free and fair

4. _____ involves raw mental ability, pattern recognition, and abstract reasoning and is applied to a problem that a person has never confronted before.
   a. Crystallized intelligence
   b. Narrow intelligence
   c. Fluid intelligence
   d. General intelligence

5. Someone who is good at detecting whether or not a person is lying would be said to have high
   a. interpersonal intelligence
   b. naturalistic intelligence
   c. practical intelligence
   d. creative intelligence

Answers can be found at the end of the chapter.

PROBLEM SOLVING

None of us go through a day without having to solve a problem, because every time we face a task that we do not know how to carry out, we are confronted with a problem (Simon, 1978). On any given day, you may have to budget your time so that you can study for your test and go to a party with friends or figure out the most efficient route to drive to a place you have never visited.

Psychologists have examined how people go about solving problems, often by presenting research participants with problems and studying how they solve them. Take a few minutes to work on each of the following problems. Some are easy and others not so easy, but give them a try. We will return to each problem later in the section.

- How would you solve the problem of rising world temperatures?
- Pretend you have three jars (A, B, and C), each containing a set amount of water. Add or subtract the given amounts in each jar to come up with a set final amount. For instance, Jar A holds 21 units of water, Jar B 127 units, and Jar C 3 units. Using any of the jars, discard or add water as needed to end up with 100 units of water. Figure 10.12 shows some variations you can try.
- Figure 10.13 is a picture of a person in a room with two strings hanging from the ceiling. Also in the room are a book of matches, a pair of pliers, and some cotton. The task is to tie the two pieces of string together. The strings are too short for the person to hold on to one and grab the other. How would you go about tying the strings together?
- In Figure 10.14a, remove one match to make 7 squares.
- Look at the 9 dots in Figure 10.14b. Connect all the dots using only 4 straight lines without lifting up your pen or pencil from the paper once you've started.

Types of Problems

convergent thinking problems problems that have known solutions and require analytic thinking and the use of learned strategies and knowledge to come up with the correct answer.

Convergent thinking problems have known solutions, which can be reached by narrowing down a set of possible answers. Intelligence tests and college entrance exams include convergent problems. Figuring out how to operate a new coffee maker is another convergent problem. There is one right way to brew coffee with a given machine. Convergent problems require analytic thinking and crystallized intelligence—the problem solver has to analyze the problem and then apply learned strategies and knowledge to come up with the answer.

Some problems, however, may not have a known solution. Consider the question posed earlier: "How would you solve the problem of rising world temperatures?" There are many possible solutions to these problems, some of which work better than others. These kinds of problems are known as **divergent thinking problems.** To solve them, we must break away from our normal problem-solving strategies and make unusual associations to arrive at novel ways of thinking about a problem. Imagine that your new dorm mate snores so loudly you can't sleep. How would you solve this problem? Divergence may lead to redefining the problem in a way that makes finding a solution more likely. These kinds of problems require fluid and creative intelligence.

divergent thinking problems problems that have no known solutions and require novel solutions.

Solution Strategies

Psychologists describe three kinds of strategies that people use to solve different kinds of problems: algorithms, insight, and thinking outside the box. When you were solving the water jug problems in Figure 10.12, did you realize that the last two could be solved much more easily than the first five? If you are like about 75% of the population, you continued to use the solution pattern or algorithm you may have discovered in solving the first few problems. **Algorithms** are step-by-step formulas or procedures for solving problems. In this case, the algorithm is "Jar B − Jar A − Jar C (twice)."

algorithms
a step-by-step procedure or formula for solving a problem.

Not all solutions involve algorithms. Some occur with a flash of insight. One of the best known examples of insight occurred in ancient Greece, when the philosopher–scientist Archimedes solved the problem of how to determine whether a crown contained anything besides gold. The solution came to him in a flash when he saw the water level rise as he entered the public baths. Because gold is heavier than other metals, it will displace more water, so by seeing how much water it displaced, Archimedes would be able to determine whether the crown was pure gold without melting it down. The insight excited him so much that without pausing to dress, he ran out of the baths yelling *Eureka!* (in Greek, "I have found it!"). In honor of Archimedes, these kinds of sudden solutions are referred to as either **Eureka insights** or **insight solutions.**

Eureka insight or insight solutions
sudden solutions that come to mind in a flash.

A modern version of such a "Eureka solution" happened to George de Mestral, a Swiss engineer ("How a Swiss Invention Hooked the World," 2007). De Mestral would often go on hikes in the Alps with his dog. When they came home, he noticed that his clothes and his dog's fur caught thistle burrs, which he found on close inspection to have hooks on the ends. The dog's fur and his clothes contained loops that snagged the plants. In a flash, de Mestral realized that a fastener could be made to connect to loops. The best part about the hook-and-loop system was that it was easily reversible and could be fastened over and over again. De Mestral invented Velcro, which is now a common fastener of such things as shoe straps, backpacks, and clothing.

The solution to the two-string problem in Figure 10.13 often comes as a Eureka insight (Maier, 1931). You might have suddenly realized that the pliers could be used as a weight at the end of one string and then swung into motion. As

FIGURE **10.12**

WATER JAR PROBLEMS AND MENTAL SET. The task is to use any combination of jars A, B, and C, subtracting or adding jars of "water" to obtain the desired amount. Try it. (Source: Luchins & Luchins, 1970)

Problem	Jar A	Jar B	Jar C	Obtained the amount
1	21	127	3	100
2	14	163	25	99
3	18	43	10	5
4	9	42	6	21
5	20	59	4	31
6	23	49	3	20
7	15	39	3	18

FIGURE **10.13**

TWO-STRING PROBLEM. How do you connect two strings if you can't reach the second one without dropping the first one? (Answer appears at the end of the chapter.)

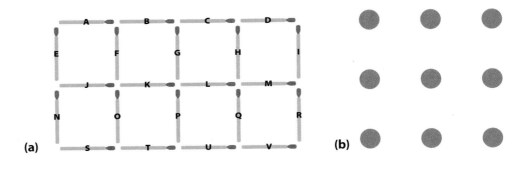

FIGURE **10.14**

PROBLEM SOLVING. (a) Remove one match to make seven squares. (b) Connect all 9 dots with 4 straight lines—without lifting your pencil. (Answer to b appears at the end of the chapter.)

(a)   **(b)**

"Never, ever, think outside the box."

you stand holding the other string, the weighted string swings over and you grab it and tie the two together.

The third problem-solving strategy is turning a problem around and thinking about it from a different perspective. If you have ever heard the phrase "thinking outside the box," you now know where it comes from—the 9-dot problem (Figure 10.14b). **Thinking outside the box** requires you to break free of self-imposed conceptual constraints and think about a problem differently in order to solve it. If you came up with a solution, it required that you go outside the self-imposed "box" that the 9 dots create in your mind. There is no such box there in reality, but you perceive one. Once you think outside the box, a couple of solutions may come to you rather easily (see the end of the chapter for the solution). Creative thinkers regularly think flexibly and differently about problems by challenging their own assumptions (Feist, 1999).

thinking outside the box

approach to problem solving that requires breaking free of self-imposed conceptual constraints and thinking about a problem differently in order to solve it.

Obstacles to Solutions

The difficulties people encounter in solving the 9-dot problem also point to some of the common obstacles we face in solving all kinds of problems. One of the biggest blocks to solving a problem is cognitive **fixation,** or the inability to break out of a particular mind-set in order to think about a problem from a fresh perspective. Fixation prevents many people from seeing possible solutions to the 7-square match problem (Figure 10.14a). It is difficult, for example, to see that you can simply remove match B, C, T, or U. If you take away match B, for instance, there are only 7 squares but the continuity in the upper row of squares is broken. This solution may not be obvious because people become fixated on a self-imposed mental set in which "all the squares must continue to touch each other." Note that the instructions do not require this—people unconsciously impose such rules themselves.

Solutions themselves can sometimes be an obstacle: For the jar problem, the algorithm used to solve the problem also created a **mental set,** which is a tendency to continue to use problem-solving strategies that have worked in the past, even if better solutions are available (Luchins & Luchins, 1970). This mental set probably made you miss the easier solutions to Problems 6 and 7 in Figure 10.12: Jar A − Jar C and Jar A + Jar C, respectively. Luchins and Luchins (1970)

fixation

the inability to break out of a particular mind-set in order to think about a problem from a fresh perspective.

mental set

a tendency to continue to use problem-solving strategies that have worked in the past, even if better solutions are available.

found that if Problems 1 to 5 were not given first, 100% of adults saw the direct solution. In contrast, if they first received Problems 1 to 5 and had to develop an algorithm, only 24% found the more direct solutions to Problems 6 and 7. Education and training also create mental sets. When we learn solution strategies in school and in the workplace, we learn how to solve problems. Sometimes these solutions are algorithms and sometimes insights. But strategies can blind us to more novel, efficient, and even creative solutions. It becomes hard to step back and see the problem from a fresh perspective.

functional fixedness

mind-set in which one is blind to unusual uses of common everyday things or procedures.

Another obstacle to successful problem solving is our tendency to be blind to unusual uses of common everyday things or procedures: This is known as **functional fixedness** (Duncker, 1945). A good example of functional fixedness occurs when people try to solve the two-string problem. People are used to thinking of pliers as tools for holding or gripping something so that it can be turned, twisted, or cut. But a pair of pliers can also be used as a weight at the end of a string to cause it to swing like a pendulum. Figuring out a new way to use pliers is an example of thinking outside the box to find a creative solution to a problem. As mentioned earlier, creative thinkers often think differently about how to solve a problem. We discuss this type of creative thinking and creativity in general next.

Quick Quiz 10.2: Problem Solving

1. What kind of problems require you to narrow down the range of possible solutions to arrive at the correct answer?
   a. simple problems
   b. convergent thinking problems
   c. algorithms
   d. divergent thinking problems

2. A child discovers that 2×2 is the same as $2 + 2$. He therefore wrongly concludes that 3×3 is the same as $3 + 3$. What tendency is affecting this child's problem-solving strategies?
   a. mental set
   b. divergent thinking

   c. test bias
   d. response bias

3. An inability to break out of a particular frame of mind in order to think about a problem from a fresh perspective is known as
   a. perpetuation
   b. mental set
   c. fixation
   d. functional fixedness

Answers can be found at the end of the chapter.

CREATIVITY

What was it about Leonardo da Vinci that made him so versatile as an artist and inventor? What was going on in the mind of Isaac Newton when he realized the significance of the apple falling from a tree? Why are some people able to paint magnificent landscapes while others can hardly draw a straight line? The answer is that these individuals are more creative than the average person.

The ability to think or act creatively is highly prized in our society (Feist, 1999; Sawyer, 2006; Simonton, 1999). All of society's advances—artistic, musical, industrial, governmental, legal, and scientific—happen because a person or group of people came up with a creative idea. Creative thinking is related to, yet distinct from, both intelligence and problem solving.

What Is Creativity?

Read the following two paragraphs, written by different people, and think about what each one means and whether they are equally "creative":

> They're all so different Boylan talking about the shape of my foot he noticed at once even before he was introduced when I was in the DBC with Poldy laughing and trying to listen I was waggling my foot we both ordered 2 teas and plain bread and butter I saw him looking with his two old maids of sisters when I stood up and asked the girl where it was what do I care with it dropping out of me and that black closed breeches he made me buy takes you half an hour to let down wetting all myself always with some brand new fad every other week. . . .

> This creation in which we live began with the Dominant Nature as an Identification Body of a completed evolutionary Strong Material creation in a Major Body Resistance Force. And is fulfilling the Nature Identification in a like Weaker Material Identification creation in which Two Major Bodies have already fulfilled radio body balances, and embodying a Third Material Identification Embodiment of both.

The first paragraph is an excerpt from James Joyce's great novel *Ulysses*. The second paragraph was written by a person who has schizophrenia and is an example of what is called *word salad*, a collection of words that are mixed up in sentences with no real meaning (R. White, 1964). These two paragraphs demonstrate an essential point about what creativity is and what it is not. It is not simply original thinking, for the paragraphs are equally original. They are both unusual, and both give voice to sentences that probably had not been uttered or written before these writers penned them. For something to be deemed creative,

The 2009 movie *Avatar* required many instances of novel and adaptive problem solving, or creativity.

however, it not only has to be original but must also be useful or adaptive and solve a problem. Joyce's paragraph does that because it's part of solving the problem of telling a story. The second paragraph is not creative because it is not useful and it does not solve a problem.

Creativity, then, is thought or behavior that is both novel–original and useful–adaptive (Amabile, 1996; Feist, 1999; MacKinnon, 1970; Simonton, 1999). The usefulness criterion requires that someone at some time sees real value and usefulness in the creative accomplishment. Truly creative works are often appreciated in the creator's lifetime, but not always. For instance, Vincent van Gogh sold very few of his paintings while alive. But his creative genius is now fully appreciated by novices and experts alike, and his paintings are worth millions.

Stages of Creative Problem Solving

Creative problem solving is a process that has distinct stages. Long ago, Graham Wallas (1926) identified four stages of creative problem solving: preparation, incubation, insight, and elaboration–verification. The first stage, *preparation,* involves discovering and defining the problem and then attempting to solve it. This leads to the second stage, *incubation,* or putting the problem aside for a while and working on something else. The third stage, *insight,* is a Eureka insight in which the solution comes immediately to mind. The fourth and final stage of creative problem solving is *verification–elaboration.* The solution, even if it has the feel of certainty, still needs to be confirmed. How it is confirmed depends on what kind of task is involved. The verification process is different for everyday problems and for problems in art, literature, music, science, technology, invention, or philosophy.

WHERE EARL GETS HIS IDEAS

Genius, Intelligence, and Creativity

What makes someone a genius? Is superior intelligence enough? Consider Marilyn vos Savant. Most people have not heard of her, although she does write a weekly nationally syndicated column for *Parade* magazine. She has the world's highest recorded IQ ever—an off-the-chart 228. Yet she has not created master works of note. Genius is not, as some have claimed, simply being smart or having a very high IQ (Simonton, 1999). Having an IQ of 130 or 140, which puts one in the top 1% or higher of the population, does not guarantee producing creative works of lasting influence.

Something other than intelligence must go into the making of a genius. **Genius** is high intelligence combined with creative accomplishments that have a tremendous impact on a given field (Simonton, 1999). The paintings, plays, buildings, novels, or

William Shakespeare

Virginia Woolf

Leonardo da Vinci

Isaac Newton

Albert Einstein

scientific discoveries of geniuses change their respective fields. Literature was never the same after Shakespeare or Virginia Woolf. Physics has not been the same since Newton, Einstein, and Marie Curie. Art has not been the same since van Gogh and Picasso. Music has not been the same since Bach and Beethoven. And art, medicine, anatomy, and invention have not been the same since Leonardo da Vinci. If people's accomplishments change their field, other people appreciate their importance sooner or later. Indeed, having a major impact on a field and being appreciated for the accomplishments is what distinguishes genius from genius-like IQ. For every Shakespeare, Beethoven, Leonardo, and Einstein, there are many more people with equally high intelligence who make no significant contributions to society. Moreover, there have been people of truly monumental creative accomplishment whose intelligence was only somewhat above average. As we suggested in the opening to this chapter, Charles Darwin, was—by his own admission—of only modestly high intelligence (Simonton, 1999). Yet his accomplishments have had as much impact on science and culture as those of just about any other person. By this standard, he was a genius.

Genius, by definition, and creativity are closely related. Surprisingly, however, IQ and creativity are not very strongly related (Albert & Runco, 1989; Sternberg & O'Hara, 1999). For example, a meta-analysis of 21 studies that included more than 45,000 participants reported an average correlation between creativity and intelligence of only +.17 (H. K. Kim, 2005). That is, knowing an IQ score tells us only a little bit about how creative someone may be. In addition, the relationship between IQ and creativity is not stronger for IQs below 120 than for IQs above 120, as researchers once proposed (R. E. Jung et al., 2009; H. K. Kim, 2005; Preckel, Holling, & Wiese, 2006).

Creativity and the Brain

Imagine what was going on in Newton's brain when he "discovered" gravity or in Einstein's when he came up with the theory of relativity. Of course, we'll never know what was going on in the minds of these geniuses from the past. But neuroscientists are beginning to uncover what happens in the brain when a typical person has a Eureka insight or when creative people solve problems compared to less creative people (R. E. Jung et al., 2010). The research has revealed three consistent findings: Creative insight increases frontal lobe activity. Insights occur in the right hemisphere rather than the left. And creative people solving creative problems show more balanced activity between their right and left frontal lobes.

Marie
Curie

J. S.
Bach

Ludwig
van Beethoven

Vincent
van Gogh

Pablo
Picasso

Creative Insight Results in Increased Frontal Lobe Activity

The frontal lobes are active in abstract reasoning, planning, focused working memory, and integrating sensory input. Creativity involves integrating ideas in novel and valuable ways. It is not surprising, therefore, that modern neuroscience supports the conclusion that creative problem solving and insights involve frontal lobe activity (Carlsson, Wendt, & Risberg, 2000; Chow & Cummings, 1999; Feist, 2004; Folley & Park, 2005; Mell, Howard, & Miller, 2003; Takeuchi et al., 2010). For instance, recent research examined whether greater neural connection in the frontal lobe is associated with greater levels of creativity. Takeuchi and colleagues (2010) measured creativity and neural connectivity in 55 college students. The creativity tasks involved generating unique ideas for how to use everyday objects. For example, students were asked such questions as "Other than reading, how can we use newspapers?" Neural connectivity was measured with an MRI technique that assesses the volume of neurons in a given region in the brain. The greater the neural volume, the greater the connectivity. Takeuchi and colleagues found a direct and positive relationship between the students' creativity scores and their neural connectivity, especially in the frontal lobe. Greater connectivity suggests more myelinated neurons and hence more efficient communication between the neurons. Recall from Chapter 3 that axons are often covered with myelin, which facilitates neural transmission. It may be that more creative people have both more connections between neurons and more myelin. Further research, however, is needed to confirm this idea.

Creative Insight and the Right Hemisphere   One kind of problem that has been used in creativity/brain research is a *remote association* word problem (Mednick & Mednick, 1967). Remote association problems display three words at one time to the participant, who must then come up with a single word that could be used with all three of the words. The single word could be added to each of the words to create a compound word, or it could modify one of the displayed words in some way. This requires the participant to form a non-obvious or "remote" association in order to solve the problem. For example, if the three words were *French, shoe,* and *car,* what one word could you think of that could be used with the other three? What if the three words were *pine, crab,* and *sauce?* (The answers appear at the end of the chapter.) Interestingly, people often solve these kinds of problems with Eureka insights.

In one set of studies, researchers presented remote association tests to either the right or left visual fields of participants. These participants were not selected

Connection

People who have had their corpus callosum severed cannot say what they see if the information is presented to their left visual field but can verbally label it if it is presented to their right visual field. Why?

See "Overview of Brain Regions," Chapter 3, "The Biology of Behavior," p. 96.

for high or low levels of creativity. The researchers presented the information to the individual visual fields because they wanted to control which hemisphere of the brain processed the information. Recall from Chapter 3 that information presented to the left visual field is processed in the right hemisphere of the brain and information presented to the right visual field is processed in the left hemisphere of the brain. When the problem was presented in the left visual field and processed in the right hemisphere, insight into the problems occurred much more frequently than when the problem was presented to the right visual field and processed in the left hemisphere (Beeman & Bowden, 2000; Bowden & Jung-Beeman, 2003). Moreover, when researchers took brain images using fMRI and EEG while people were solving insight problems, they found that sudden insights consistently activated the right hemisphere more than the left (Bowden et al., 2005). Similarly, patients with damage to the frontal region of their right hemisphere are less able to solve problems requiring insight than people without damage to their right hemisphere (L. A. Miller & Tippett, 1996).

Creativity and Balanced Activity Between the Hemispheres The third consistent finding from the neuroscience of creativity is that when solving problems, creative people have more balanced brain activity between the hemispheres than less creative people (Takeuchi et al., 2010). In particular, while solving problems, they show equally active areas in their right and left frontal lobes, which translates into a widening rather than a narrowing of attention and a greater flexibility in moving from one way of thinking to another (Carlsson, Wendt, & Risberg, 2000; Goel & Vartanian, 2005); see the Research Process for this chapter (Figure 10.15). Widening attention and being able to shift ways of thinking easily and flexibly are hallmarks of creative thinking (Feist, 2004; Martindale, 1999).

Cognitive Processes in Creative Thinking

Creative thinking entails unique cognitive processes. Psychologists who study the cognitive aspects of creative thought have focused on visual thinking, fluency, flexibility, and originality. Visual imagery occurs when we see a solution in our "mind's eye." Many scientists, artists, and writers solve problems by using creative mental images (A. Miller, 1996). Einstein, for example, often visualized a situation, such as riding in an elevator traveling at the speed of light. Imagining such a scenario and then thinking about what would happen to a light beam he emitted led to his discovery of the theory of relativity.

Cognitive psychologists have developed clever experiments to test people's ability to come up with creative mental images. They display images of letters or geometric shapes and ask participants to combine some of them in a creative way (Finke, Ward, & Smith, 1992). Figure 10.16a contains a set of such objects. Three of these images are chosen at random during each trial, and the participant's task is to assemble them in such a way as to create a recognizable shape or pattern. Various solutions are presented in Figure 10.16b.

The ability to produce many ideas is central to creative thought. This ability is termed **ideational fluency** (Guilford, 1967). Highly creative people usually come up with more ideas for a given problem than less creative people do. Not all the ideas will be equally useful, but having a large number of ideas increases

ideational fluency
the ability to produce many ideas.

Research Process

1 Research Question

Is brain activity of creative people different from the brain activity of less creative people while solving problems?

2 Method

Carlsson and colleagues (2000) selected participants who during earlier testing scored either high or low on creativity problems. They were grouped as "highly creative" or "less creative" based on these earlier results. Participants in these two groups were each given a noncreative and creative task to complete while in a brain scanner. Brain activity was measured by cerebral blood flow to compare the two conditions. Blood flow increases to brain areas that are active. The creative task consisted of having participants list as many possible uses of an everyday object (a brick) as they could think of. A noncreative task consisted of a simple request to count numbers aloud, starting with 1.

3 Results

Results showed more left than right frontal lobe activity in the less creative participants. Highly creative participants, however, showed a balance in right and left frontal lobe activity. Orange regions in the figure show areas of increased activity while solving creative problems compared to noncreative problems. Green regions show areas of decreased activity. The more creative participants (on the left) use both left and right hemispheres in the frontal region while working on creative problems, whereas the less creative participants (on the right) show increased activity only in their frontal lobe.

Highly creative participants   **Less creative participants**

4 Conclusion

Creative people make more balanced use of the parts of the brain involved in focused attention, abstract reasoning, and planning while solving problems than do less creative people. This finding may appear to contradict what we just said about the importance of the right hemisphere in creative problem solving, but it does not. The right hemisphere findings are from noncreative participants who are coming up with insight solutions. The balanced hemisphere result comes from comparing creative to less creative people. In both cases, right hemisphere activity is more pronounced in creative people than in less creative people.

FIGURE **10.15**

BALANCED BRAIN ACTIVITY IN CREATIVE PEOPLE. Source: I. Carlsson, P. Wendt, & J. Risberg, 2000, "On the Neurobiology of Creativity: Differences in Frontal Activity Between High and Low Creative Subjects," *Neuropsychologia, 38*, 873–885.

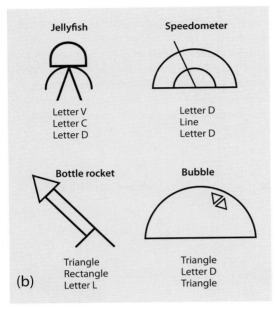

FIGURE 10.16

CREATIVE PROBLEM SOLVING USING MENTAL IMAGERY. (a) Three stimulus shapes at a time are presented to a person, whose task it is to combine them in any way to produce a single image or object. (b) These are some of the solutions created using shapes in (a). (Source: Finke et al., 1992)

the chance that any one of them will be a useful or adaptive solution to the problem at hand. J. P. Guilford developed the *Alternate Uses* test to measure creativity. In this test, participants are given a common object such as a brick or a pencil and asked to write down all the possible uses they can think of for the object within a limited amount of time. An ideationally fluent person can list many alternate uses for the object within a short period.

The ability to produce many ideas does not by itself guarantee that one can break out of one's mental set and think of unusual uses. A creative person can also come up with many different categories of ideas and think of other responses besides the obvious one. This ability is called **flexibility of thought** (Guilford, 1967). In the Alternate Uses test, flexibility of thought is gauged by the number of categories of response a person offers. For instance, if all the answers for the uses of a brick involve building something, the person is not displaying flexible thinking but remaining within one rather obvious category. In contrast, coming up with uses that involve building, painting, writing, weights, step stools, and ballasts means a person is a flexible thinker because those uses cut across many different categories.

A third cognitive process involved in creative thought is **originality,** which means thinking of unusual and novel ideas. In the Alternate Uses test, the test-taker's originality is scored by comparing his or her responses to a set of norms developed from the answers given by thousands of respondents who have taken the test previously. A person's answer is scored as original if it is rare or uncommon compared to the norms. Again using the brick as an example, a higher originality score is given to "step stool" than to "paperweight" because there are fewer instances of "step stool" in the norms. In this sense, an original response is the same as an infrequent response. But originality in itself is not enough to explain creative thought. Creative thinking occurs when a person combines all three cognitive processes at once—fluency, flexibility, and originality.

flexibility of thought
the ability to come up with many different categories of ideas and think of other responses besides the obvious one.

originality
the ability to come up with unusual and novel ideas.

The Creative Personality

We have seen how creative people differ from others by their brain activity and cognitive style. What about their personalities? Do creative people tend to have unique personalities; and if so, what personality characteristics tend to be found in highly creative people? The best way to answer this question is by looking at what all of the published studies on the topic say—that is, by conducting a meta-analysis.

Feist (1998) conducted such a meta-analysis by locating all of the published studies that reported personality qualities of artists and scientists (see also Batey & Furnham, 2008). Twenty-six studies on almost 5,000 participants had reported personality traits of scientists compared to norms and twenty-nine studies on almost 4,400 participants had reported the personality traits of artists compared to norms. Creative artists and scientists do share some common personality traits (see Figure 10.17). To highlight some of the most pronounced personality traits of creative artists and scientists: Openness to experience is the tendency to enjoy and seek out new experiences, new foods, new places, and new ideas. Highly creative people have this quality, which is not surprising given that creativity involves novel thoughts and behavior (Prahbu, Sutton, & Sauser, 2008). Also, they are unconventional and tend to have a firm belief that they possess a better way of doing things. In some, this comes off as self-confidence and in others as arrogance (Feist, 1993). Despite the similarities, artists are more emotionally sensitive and unstable than scientists (Feist, 1998; Ludwig, 1995).

Open to new experiences
Self-confident
Arrogant
Dominant
Hostile
Driven-ambitious
Impulsive
Not conventional or accepting of group norms
Not conscientious

Connection

Is there a connection between mental illness and creativity?

See "Bringing It All Together," Chapter 15, "Psychological Disorders," p. 622.

Quick Quiz 10.3: Creativity

1. Creative thinking or behavior is both novel and
   a. interesting
   b. artistic
   c. useful
   d. unusual

2. The four stages of creative problem solving include preparation, incubation, insight, and
   a. elaboration–verification
   b. validation
   c. discrimination
   d. resolution

3. When compared to less creative people, creative people show what pattern of brain activity while solving problems?
   a. asymmetry between the hemispheres
   b. balance between the hemispheres
   c. parietal lobe activation
   d. occipital lobe activation

4. What is measured by the task in which participants are asked to think of as many different uses for a brick as they can?
   a. originality
   b. flexibility of thought
   c. functional fixedness
   d. both a and b

Answers can be found at the end of the chapter.

Bringing It All Together

Making Connections in Intelligence, Problem Solving, and Creativity

Whiz Kids in Science

Perhaps you participated in science fairs in elementary or high school. Projects for these events might have been something you did because it was required. For some students, however, science fairs provide a means of expressing their interest in and passion for science, as well as an outlet for creativity. Especially creative teens who participate in science fairs may become finalists in the prestigious Intel Science Talent Search. Intel finalists possess in abundance and combine all three main topics of this chapter—intelligence, problem solving ability, and creativity.

First, let's examine the evidence for their high levels of intelligence and academic performance. Many finalists score in the top 1 or 2% in the quantitative portion of the SAT, and approximately 25% of the finalists score perfect scores on the SAT overall ("Teen Scientists," 2005). We also know from research on gifted students who become top scientists that they tend to achieve high scores on tests of both quantitative reasoning and spatial ability (Achter et al., 1999; Shea, Lubinski, & Benbow, 2001). Finalists are at or near the top of their high school class, and a very high percentage of them gain entrance to elite universities, such as Harvard, Stanford, MIT, and Yale (Berger, 1994; Feist, 2006; Subotnik, Duschl, & Selmon, 1993). Finally, about two thirds of the finalists go on to have careers in science, and the average IQ of scientists is high—about two standard deviations above average (130) (Feist, 2006; MacKinnon & Hall, 1972).

Becoming an STS finalist takes more than a high level of intelligence. It also requires an aptitude for solving difficult problems creatively. This involves devising a solution to a novel task that is both original and useful. For example, 18-year-old Erika DeBenedictis, first-prize winner in 2010, stated a real problem: Can we devise a way to use less fuel in spacecraft as they travel through the solar system? DeBenedictis not only clearly formed an interesting and important problem, but she also answered it simply *and* creatively. Her solution involved making use of existing gravitational forces of planets and other space objects to help propel spacecraft through space (Intel Science Talent Search, 2010). She challenged assumptions and thought outside the box and came up with a new way to propel spacecraft through space. If you doubt that Intel finalists are a creative bunch, consider this: Six finalists have gone on to win Nobel Prizes, and many others have had illustrious and award-winning careers in

science, math, and medicine (Feist, 2006; Kaye, 2001). For this reason, becoming an STS finalist is often referred to as winning the "Junior Nobel Prize."

Quick Quiz 10.4: Bringing It All Together: Making Connections in Intelligence, Problem Solving, and Creativity

1. Thinking back to Sternberg's model of intelligence and applying it to the Science Talent Search finalists, we would predict they are unusually talented in their
   a. analytic intelligence
   b. creative intelligence
   c. practical intelligence
   d. both a and b

2. A high percentage of STS finalists
   a. leave science careers
   b. have productive and creative careers in science, engineering, or math
   c. have unremarkable careers
   d. win Nobel prizes

Answers can be found at the end of the chapter.

Erika DeBenedictis

Chapter **Review**

INTELLIGENCE

- Intelligence is a set of cognitive skills that include abstract thinking, reasoning, problem solving, and the ability to acquire knowledge.

- There are two major theories of the nature of intelligence. The single-factor or general-factor theory argues that intelligence at its core is one overall ability. The other theory, the multifactor theory, says that intelligence consists of multiple abilities.

- Some of the factors of intelligence in the multifactor theory are crystallized and fluid intelligence, as well as analytic, practical, musical, and bodily–kinesthetic intelligence.

- Measures of intelligence, including the Stanford–Binet and the Wechsler Adult Scale of Intelligence (WAIS), tend to be reliable and predictive of certain outcomes (school achievement), but not others (happiness or satisfaction with one's job).

- Intelligence ranges widely on a continuum from very low to very high. On the extreme low end is mental retardation and on the extreme high end is giftedness.

- Group differences in IQ do exist for race and gender, and yet there is much debate concerning possible explanations for these differences.

PROBLEM SOLVING

- Two distinct kinds of problem exist. Convergent thinking problems have known solutions, which can be reached by narrowing down a set of possible answers. Divergent thinking problems have no known solution and require breaking away from our normal problem-solving strategies and making unusual associations to arrive at novel ways of thinking about a problem.

- People use different kinds of strategies to solve problems. Algorithms are formulas that guarantee correct solutions to particular problems. Thinking outside the box requires one to break free of self-imposed conceptual constraints and think about a problem differently in order to solve it. Eureka insights involve a sudden understanding of a solution.

- Obstacles to solutions include fixation, or inability to break out of a particular mind-set in order to think about a problem from a fresh perspective; mental set, the tendency to continue to use problem-solving strategies that have worked in the past; and functional fixedness, which is the tendency to be blind to unusual uses of common everyday things or procedures.

CREATIVITY

- Creativity is thought or behavior that is both novel and useful or adaptive.

- Genius is closely related to creativity in that it combines high intelligence with achievements that change entire fields (art, music, science, technology, business).

- Researchers have uncovered three principles of creative thinking and the brain: Creative insight increases frontal lobe activity; insights occur in the right hemisphere rather than the left; and creative people solving creative problems show more balanced activity between their right and left frontal lobes. Cognitive processes commonly associated with creative thinking are visual imagery, flexibility (coming up with many different categories of ideas), ideational fluency (the ability to produce many ideas), and originality (thinking of novel solutions).

- Creative people tend to be open to new experiences, self-confident, arrogant, and unconventional.

BRINGING IT ALL TOGETHER: MAKING CONNECTIONS IN INTELLIGENCE, PROBLEM SOLVING, AND CREATIVITY

- Science research, as exemplified by the Intel Science Talent Search, requires not just intelligence, but also the ability to identify and solve problems in a novel and useful way.

Key **Terms**

adaptive behavior, p. 399

algorithm, p. 409

broad intelligence, p. 389

construct validity, p. 397

convergent thinking problems, p. 408

creativity, p. 413

cultural test bias, p. 398

divergent thinking problems, p. 408

Down syndrome, p. 399

Eureka insight or insight solutions, p. 409

fixation, p. 410

Quick Quiz **Answers**

Quick Quiz 10.1: 1. d   2. d   3. b   4. c   5. a
Quick Quiz 10.2: 1. b   2. a   3. c
Quick Quiz 10.3: 1. c   2. a   3. b   4. d
Quick Quiz 10.4: 1. d   2. b

Solution to first remote association on p. 415 is "horn" and the second is "apple."

Challenge Your Assumptions **Answers**

• Intelligence is a single, general capacity. **False. See pp. 388–392.**
• Genetic factors influence people's intelligence. **True. See pp. 403–404.**
• If a person has very unique and original ideas, he or she is creative. **False. See pp. 412–413.**
• People with very high IQs are geniuses. **False. See pp. 413–414.**

Solution to Figure 10.13

Solution to Figure 10.14b. Can you think of any others?

Motivation
and Emotion

11

Chapter Outline

Challenge *Your Assumptions*

TRUE OR FALSE?

- Like animals, humans are driven by basic, biological needs.

- Even without a stomach, people still feel hungry.

- Most dieters would have been better off if they'd never dieted at all.

- People in different cultures have different facial expression of emotion.

- More money leads to greater happiness.

Answers can be found at the end of the chapter.

Thirteen-year-old Cari Lightner was walking to a carnival one afternoon in her hometown in California (Lightner & Hathaway, 1990). Suddenly, a car came careening from off the street, swerved, and hit Cari from behind with such impact she flew 125 feet in the air. Cari died instantly. The driver of the car, Clarence William Busch, had passed out behind the wheel because he was drunk. Not only that, Busch had four previous convictions for drunk driving and had been arrested just two days before killing Cari on another hit-and-run accident. He was out on bail for that offense.

Cari's mother, Candy, was so enraged by what had happened to her daughter that she vowed to stop these kinds of things from ever happening again to anyone else. "I promised myself on the day of Cari's death that I would fight to make this needless homicide count for something positive in the years ahead" (Hanson, n.d.). Four days after Cari's death, Candy Lightner founded Mothers Against Drunk Driving (MADD), whose primary goal is to change laws increasing penalties for repeat drunk drivers. MADD has been responsible for invoking many changes to curtail drunk driving. For one, MADD was instrumental in getting states to lower the legal drinking limit from .10 to .08 blood alcohol content (BAC).

Candy Lightner's anger drove her to make important, useful changes to society. Still, we know that anger does not always lead to constructive action. What if she had decided to seek vengeance instead? The world is changed—sometimes for the better and sometimes for worse—by emotions: fear, anger, disgust, sadness, joy, and happiness. These emotions change people and change lives. In other words, emotions are powerful motivators.

As we show in this chapter, motivation and emotion are related but distinct concepts. Motivation encompasses the forces that move us to behave or think the way we do, whereas emotions are responses to meaningful events in our lives—often threats or benefits to our well-being. Hunger, sexual desire, the need to belong, the urges to achieve and work are the primary motives we explore in this chapter. But as the MADD example shows us, emotions motivate behavior too. ◼

MOTIVATION

Consider what the following situations have in common:

  a baby seeking a nipple
  a girl studying for a math exam
  a homeless person searching for food in a garbage can
  a scientist conducting research
  a musician learning a new piece
  a couple having sex

motivation
the urge to move toward one's goals; to accomplish tasks.

These are all examples of motivated behaviors. **Motivation** is the urge to move toward one's goals, whatever they may be. Motivation provides an energetic push toward accomplishing tasks, such as getting dinner, getting rich, and getting lucky. Babies seek the nipple because they need contact and nutrition; a girl might study for a test because she finds the material fascinating. There might be various reasons for a behavior, but each involves motivation.

needs
inherently biological states of deficiency (cellular or bodily) that compel drives.

Needs, drives, and incentives all contribute to motivation. **Needs** are states of cellular or bodily deficiency that compel drives. These are what your body seeks. Examples include the needs for water, food, and oxygen. **Drives** are the perceived states of tension that occur when our bodies are deficient in some need. Such a deficiency creates a drive (thirst or hunger) to alleviate the state—to drink or eat. In this way, needs and drives push us. On a very hot day when we are extremely thirsty, we simply must get a drink of water! All our physiological needs have drive components. Figure 11.1 shows the drive components associated with various physiological and psychological needs. Motivated behaviors, therefore, result from needs and drives.

drives
the perceived states of tension that occur when our bodies are deficient in some need, creating an urge to relieve the tension.

incentive
any external object or event that motivates behavior.

If drives push us into action, then incentives pull us into action. An **incentive** is any external object or event that motivates behavior. In general, drives come from the body, whereas incentives come from the environment. For some people, money is a primary incentive, but for others winning a gold medal at the Olympics or getting a college diploma might be the main incentive behind their training or studying.

Models of Motivation

Psychologists propose many models, or explanations, for motivation. Some models of motivation focus more on internal drives, some more on external incentives, and others on both.

The Evolutionary Model

Evolutionary theory looks at internal drives to explain why people do what they do. Biologically speaking, the purpose of any living organism is to perpetuate itself. The processes of natural and sexual selection have shaped motivation over time to make all animals, including humans, want those things that help them survive and reproduce (D. M. Buss, 2003). As a result, the major motives all involve basic survival and reproduction needs and drives: hunger, thirst, body-temperature regulation, oxygen, and sex. Our bodies "know" they want food, water, oxygen, and—after adolescence—sex.

Desires, wants, and needs have been shaped over the course of human evolution to guide behavior either toward adaptive or away from maladaptive actions (D. M. Buss, 2003; G. F. Miller, 2000). In most cases, we are unaware that our behavior is related to these drives. We know only that we do something because it feels good and that we stop doing something if it feels bad. So one answer to the question of why we do what we do is that we do it to please ourselves or to remove some undesirable state. Often we are unaware of why we want what we do, but we are aware of what feels good or bad.

The Drive Reduction Model

Other psychologists argue that when our physiological systems are out of balance or depleted, we are driven to reduce this depleted state (Hull, 1943; McKinley et al., 2004; Weisinger et al., 1993). That's one explanation of what drive is—the perceived internal state of tension that arises when our bodies are lacking in some basic physiological capacity. Central to drive reduction is the idea of maintaining physiological balance, or **homeostasis** (Cannon, 1929).

homeostasis
the process by which all organisms work to maintain physiological equilibrium or balance around an optimal set point.

set point
the ideal fixed setting of a particular physiological system, such as internal body temperature.

The term implies that all organisms are motivated to maintain physiological equilibrium around an optimal **set point,** defined as the ideal, fixed setting of a particular physiological system. We have set points for hunger, thirst,

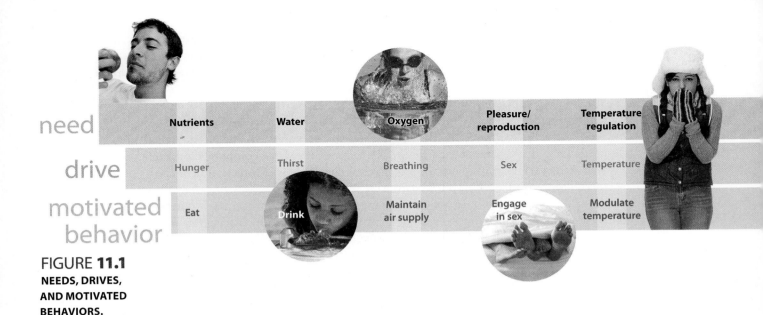

need	Nutrients	Water	Oxygen	Pleasure/ reproduction	Temperature regulation
drive	Hunger	Thirst	Breathing	Sex	Temperature
motivated behavior	Eat	Drink	Maintain air supply	Engage in sex	Modulate temperature

FIGURE **11.1**

NEEDS, DRIVES, AND MOTIVATED BEHAVIORS.

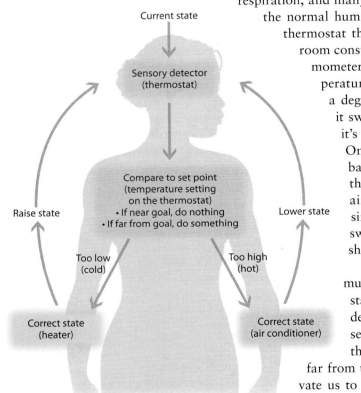

Current state

Sensory detector (thermostat)

Compare to set point (temperature setting on the thermostat)
• If near goal, do nothing
• If far from goal, do something

Raise state

Lower state

Too low (cold)

Too high (hot)

Correct state (heater)

Correct state (air conditioner)

respiration, and many other drives. For example, compare the normal human body temperature of 98.6°F to a thermostat that is set to keep a temperature in a room constant (see Figure 11.2). When the thermometer in the thermostat senses that the temperature in the room has fallen more than a degree or two lower than the set point, it switches on the heater. If it senses that it's too hot, the air conditioner comes on. Once the temperature has been brought back within the ideal set-point range, the thermostat turns off the heater or air conditioner. Our body behaves in a similar fashion: If we get too hot, we sweat to cool off. If we get too cold, we shiver to warm up.

For this system to work, our bodies must have sensors that detect its current state and any changes that cause it to deviate from the set point. Most of these sensory detectors are mechanisms in the brain. If our bodily states move too far from the set point, these mechanisms motivate us to take action—to raid the refrigerator,

FIGURE **11.2**

MODELS OF HOMEOSTASIS. Detectors in the brain stabilize the body's physiological state by comparing the current state (for example, blood sugar level, body fluids, body temperature) to a set point. If the body is far from the set point, the organism is motivated to correct the imbalance (for example, by seeking food or putting on a sweater). Sensory feedback to the brain tells it when the set point has been achieved, and the brain then tells the body to stop correcting. This feedback system keeps the body's physiological systems at their ideal set point. (Source: Berridge, 2004)

Optimal level of arousal	Knowledge/ understanding	Sensory experience	Belongingness/ social contact	Challenge
Beauty	Curiosity	Understand the world	Affiliate	Achieve
Create and appreciate	Explore	Build theories/ models	Interact with others	Succeed

for example. In other words, certain brain mechanisms evaluate the options and decide what to do to meet a biological need based on the information the brain is getting from our organs and tissues. *Homeostasis* is the term we use to describe this feedback loop.

The Optimal Arousal Model

Another model of motivation proposes that we function best at an "optimal level of arousal." This model rests on classic research by Yerkes and Dodson (1908), who showed that both low arousal and high arousal lead to poor performance, whereas moderate levels of arousal lead to optimal performance (Yerkes & Dodson, 1908). The finding is so common that it is now referred to as the **Yerkes–Dodson law** (see Figure 11.3).

The optimal arousal model of motivation argues that humans are motivated to be in situations that are neither too stimulating nor not stimulating enough. We know this, for instance, from research on sensory deprivation. Sensory deprivation research involves having a person lie down on a bed or in a sensory deprivation (salt water) tank. Classic research from the 1950s demonstrated that people could not remain in sensory deprivation for more than 2 to 3 days even if they were paid double their daily wage for each day they remained in the tank (Bexton, Heron, & Scott, 1954). Moreover, when they stayed for only a

Yerkes–Dodson law

the principle that moderate levels of arousal lead to optimal performance.

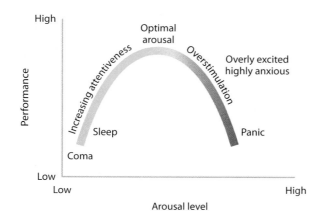

FIGURE **11.3**

YERKES–DODSON LAW. The Yerkes–Dodson law states that performance is best when we are optimally aroused. To be optimally aroused is to be moderately aroused. Performance is worst when we are not very aroused (asleep or not paying attention) or overly aroused (highly excited or anxious). (Source: Smith, 1998)

Nature&
Nurture

When the brain is deprived of sensory stimulation, the tissue in the brain region that processes that kind of sensory information actually shrinks.

few days, "pathology of boredom" developed (Heron, 1957). After long periods of sensory deprivation, people begin to hallucinate, their cognitive ability and concentration suffer, and they develop childish emotional responses. Sensory deprivation in rats actually shrinks the brain regions most involved in the senses that have been deprived—yet another example of the plasticity of the brain (Cheetham et al., 2007; Finnerty, Roberts, & Connors, 1999).

In the 1990s, Mihaly Csikszentmihalyi introduced the concept of *flow* to describe the fact that people perform best and are most creative when they are optimally challenged relative to their abilities (Csikszentmihalyi, 1990, 1996). Others have applied a similar model to explain learning and motivation (Day, 1982). According to this school of thought, needs such as curiosity, learning, interest, beauty-aesthetics, competence, challenge, flow states, and optimal experiences are motivated by the desire to be optimally aroused (Berlyne, 1960; Csikszentmihalyi, 1990; Deci & Ryan, 1985; Silvia, 2006).

The Hierarchical Model   Another model of motivation, which combines drives and incentives, is Abraham Maslow's hierarchy of needs (Maslow, 1970). The essence of Maslow's hierarchy is simple: Needs range from the most basic physiological necessities to the highest, most psychological needs for growth and fulfillment (see Figure 11.4). At the lowest level of the hierarchy are *physiological needs,* such as the needs for food, water, oxygen, and adequate body temperature. At the next level are *safety needs,* which include the needs for physical security, stability, dependency, protection, and freedom from threats such as war, assault, and terrorism. We need to be fed and out of danger's way before we can pay attention to higher level needs.

The third level in the hierarchy consists of the *love and belongingness needs,* including the desire for friendship, sex, a mate, and children, as well as the desire to belong to a family or social group. The fourth level in Maslow's hierarchy of needs is the *need for esteem*—that is, the need to appreciate oneself and one's worth and to be appreciated and respected by others. The top level in the hierarchy is the need for self-actualization. Maslow defined **self-actualization** as the full realization of one's potentials and abilities in life. Only when lower level needs have been satisfied can people focus on higher level needs. For example, hunger and safety needs must be met before self-actualization needs can be fulfilled.

Now we are ready to turn our attention to two very basic drive states: hunger and sex. In evolutionary terms, there is nothing more basic than the survival of the individual and the species.

Self-actualization

Esteem needs

Love and belongingness needs

Safety and security needs

Physiological needs

FIGURE 11.4

MASLOW'S HIERARCHY OF NEEDS. Lower level needs must be satisfied before we can focus on achieving self-actualization.

Connection

What motivates people to want the most out of life and to live life to its fullest? Learn about the qualities of self-actualizing people.

See "Humanistic–Positive Psychology Theories," Chapter 13, "Personality: The Uniqueness of the Individual," p. 525.

self-actualization
the inherent drive to realize one's full potential.

Hunger: Survival of the Individual

All animals need to replenish the energy continuously being used by their bodies. The rate at which we consume energy is known as *metabolism.* When our energy has been depleted, hunger drives us to replenish it by eating. Hunger is not just an internal biological process, however. It is the product of biological processes interacting with external, environmental ones.

The Biology of When We Eat Internal signals control the desire to eat or stop eating. From a drive reduction perspective, being hungry depends not only on how much food we have consumed recently but also on how much energy is available for organ function. Hunger has four biological components: the stomach, the blood, the brain, and hormones and neurochemicals.

Hunger involves internal biological processes interacting with external, environmental ones.

We've all noticed that when we get hungry, our stomach starts to growl. "Growling" results from gastric secretions that are activated by the brain when we think of, see, or smell food. Hunger can also cause the stomach to contract. Contractions occur when the stomach and small intestine have been relatively empty for about two hours. Although stomach contractions correspond with hunger pangs, they do not cause hunger. You might be surprised to learn that people who have their stomachs removed for medical reasons still feel hunger, as do rats in whom the nerves between the stomach and the brain have been severed (T. S. Brown & Wallace, 1980; Cannon & Washburn, 1912). So the stomach does not act by itself to produce feelings of hunger.

glucose

a simple sugar that provides energy for cells throughout the body, including the brain.

Blood sugar plays an important role in hunger. The most important source of energy for the body is cellular glucose. **Glucose** is a simple sugar in the blood that provides energy for cells throughout the body, including the brain. Although fat and protein provide their own forms of energy, some organs, including the brain, can use only glucose. Our blood sugar level drops when we go without eating for long periods. If this happens, the hypothalamus, which monitors glucose levels, triggers the drive to obtain food.

As with almost all behavior, many regions of the brain are involved in eating behavior. The hypothalamus regulates all basic physiological needs, including hunger. The body signals the hypothalamus about the nutritional needs of cells. In this way it acts as hunger's sensory detector. Different parts of the hypothalamus, in turn, send signals to different brain regions to either start or stop eating (Berthoud, 2002; Stellar, 1954).

Hormones and neurochemicals also play a role in hunger. Some of these substances stimulate appetite, and others suppress it (Rowland, Li, & Morien, 1996; G. Williams et al., 2004). At least four major hormones stimulate appetite: neuropeptide Y (NPY), orexin, ghrelin, and melanin (G. Williams et al., 2004). Neuropeptide Y (NPY) is released in the hypothalamus when an animal is hungry or underfed, and it stimulates appetite. Ghrelin sends signals of hunger to the brain and thereby stimulates hunger. Ghrelin levels rise when we are hungry and fall drastically after we eat. The endocannabinoids are naturally occurring neurochemicals that can increase appetite. Blocking receptor sites for endocannabinoids leads to a decrease in eating and to weight loss (Kirkham, 2005; Nicoll & Alger, 2004).

At least four hormones suppress appetite: insulin, leptin, peptide YY (PYY), and cholecystokinin (CCK) (G. Williams et al., 2004). For example, one of the most important hormonal effects on hunger comes from insulin, which is produced by the pancreas. Rising glucose levels stimulate insulin production; insulin, in turn, transports glucose out of the blood and into the cells. As a result, hunger decreases.

Connection
Endocannabinoids and their relative, marijuana, are used medically to treat cancer patients who are on chemotherapy, because they stimulate appetite.
See "Hallucinogens," Chapter 6, "Consciousness," p. 260.

The Psychology of What We Eat

Our body's internal signals concerning eating and hunger dictate *when* we eat. *What* we eat, however, is influenced by external factors, including the sight and smell of food and cultural preferences, or both.

Our choice of what we eat is driven by cultural exposure. That some people eat cows and others worms is, for the most part, culturally determined. Different cultures expose children to different flavors. Exposure does not immediately lead to preference, however (Pliner, 1982; Rozin, 1996). It often takes multiple exposures, perhaps eight to ten, before children will come to like a food that they initially disliked (Birch & Fischer, 1996; Birch & Marlin, 1982). Different cultures expose children to their unique flavor combinations, which means that

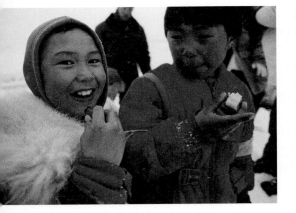

different cultures shape food preferences while people are young. For instance, people in very cold climates commonly eat raw animal fat: Icelanders eat raw whale blubber pickled in whey; the Inuit eat raw seal fat. In contrast, cow brains and tongue are commonly eaten in Mexico. The more often people eat certain foods, the more they like them. Once people develop a preference for a kind of food, they are motivated and even driven to eat that kind of food. If, for example, you develop a strong liking for Mexican food, but then spend a year studying in Europe or Asia, where there is little Mexican food, you will probably be driven to seek out and find any kind of burrito.

The Motive to Be Thin and the Tendency Toward Obesity

Fat provides a store of energy for future use. In our evolutionary past, this was important, in case food became scarce. But in modern industrialized societies with abundant food, fat is a liability. We no longer need to consume large quantities of food against the day when there isn't enough to eat.

Moreover, because our lifestyle generally is sedentary compared with earlier times, we need less food to be healthy. Even our ideas about beauty have been transformed as a result of having more food available than we need. Thinness has come to define attractiveness, and being thin has become a cultural obsession. For example, 70% of girls between the ages of 14 and 21 in the United States say they are on a diet (Hamer & Copeland, 1998). The obsession with thinness sometimes leads to the development of eating disorders.

At the same time, rates of obesity have increased dramatically over the last 50 years. How do we define obesity? Any definition of being overweight must consider both height and weight. Therefore, in evaluating an individual's weight, we use a measure termed the body mass index (BMI). BMI is determined by dividing weight by height to yield a weight-to-height ratio (see Figure 11.5). The ideal BMI range is between

Our preferences for particular foods have a biological basis—we crave foods that are essential but were scarce during early human evolution (fats, salts, and sugars)—but are shaped by experience and cultural preferences.

Connection
Anorexia nervosa and bulimia nervosa are the most common eating disorders in more affluent nations.
See "Defining Psychological Disorders," Chapter 15, "Psychological Disorders," p. 589.

Actress America Ferrera downplayed her own looks for her role in the TV series *Ugly Betty*. Her character presented a different kind of role model for U.S. girls growing up in a culture in which being thin defines attractiveness.

FIGURE 11.5

BODY MASS INDEX (BMI). To determine your body mass index, find your height in the left column and go across to your body weight. Then, at the top of the chart, locate the BMI for your height and weight.

BMI	Normal						Overweight					Obese									
Height (inches)	**19**	**20**	**21**	**22**	**23**	**24**	**25**	**26**	**27**	**28**	**29**	**30**	**31**	**32**	**33**	**34**	**35**	**36**	**37**	**38**	**39**
58	91	96	100	105	110	115	119	124	129	134	138	143	148	153	158	162	167	172	177	181	186
59	94	99	104	109	114	119	124	128	133	138	143	148	153	158	163	168	173	178	183	188	193
60	97	102	107	112	118	123	128	133	138	143	148	153	158	163	168	174	179	184	189	194	199
61	100	106	111	116	122	127	132	137	143	148	153	158	164	169	174	180	185	190	195	201	206
62	104	109	115	120	126	131	136	142	147	153	158	164	169	175	180	186	191	196	202	207	213
63	107	113	118	124	130	135	141	146	152	158	163	169	175	180	186	191	197	203	208	214	220
64	110	116	122	128	134	140	145	151	157	163	169	174	180	186	192	197	204	209	215	221	227
65	114	120	126	132	138	144	150	156	162	168	174	180	186	192	198	204	210	216	222	228	234
66	118	124	130	136	142	148	155	161	167	173	179	186	192	198	204	210	216	223	229	235	241
67	121	127	134	140	146	153	159	166	172	178	185	191	198	204	211	217	223	230	236	242	249
68	125	131	138	144	151	158	164	171	177	184	190	197	203	210	216	223	230	236	243	249	256
69	128	135	142	149	155	162	169	176	182	189	196	203	209	216	223	230	236	243	250	257	263
70	132	139	146	153	160	167	174	181	188	195	202	209	216	222	229	235	243	250	257	264	271
71	136	143	150	157	165	172	179	186	193	200	208	215	222	229	236	243	250	257	265	272	279
72	140	147	154	162	169	177	184	191	199	206	213	221	228	235	242	250	258	265	272	279	287
73	144	151	159	166	174	182	189	197	204	212	219	227	235	242	250	257	265	272	280	288	295
74	148	155	163	171	179	186	194	202	210	218	225	233	241	249	256	264	272	280	287	295	303
75	152	160	168	176	184	192	200	208	216	224	232	240	248	256	264	272	279	287	295	303	311
76	156	154	172	180	189	197	205	213	221	230	238	246	254	263	271	279	287	295	304	312	320

20 and 25, with 26 to 29.9 considered overweight and 30 or above considered obese. As of 2008, the CDC reported that more than one third of adult Americans were obese, one third were overweight, and less than one third were of ideal weight (Flegal et al., 2010). Moreover, rates of obesity have climbed rapidly over the last 20 years—from 12% in 1991, to 18% in 1998, to 34% in 2008 (Flegal et al., 2010; Mokdad et al., 1999).

Weight gain is clearly subject to environmental influence. This is not to say, however, that biological factors play no role in being overweight or obese. They do, as genes appear to be responsible for about 70% of adult weight (Allison et al., 1994; Hamer & Copeland, 1998). One study found that adults who had been adopted as children were much closer in weight to their biological parents than to their adoptive parents (Maes, Neale, & Eaves, 1997). In addition, in some obese people the gene that produces the leptin hormone, which normally suppresses appetite, has suffered a mutation and therefore does not function properly (Hamer & Copeland, 1998).

Genes also control the number of fat cells a person has: The number of fat cells a person has is set by childhood and adolescence and does not change much after that (Spalding et al., 2008). Each year about 10% of our fat cells die, but they are replaced by roughly the same number of new fat cells (Spalding et al., 2008). Dieting does not change this. When people diet, they are not decreasing the number of fats cells they have, but rather how much fat each cell stores. The stable number of adult fat cells may explain why it is so hard to keep off weight that has been lost. Indeed, a recent meta-analysis of 31 studies reported that losing

Fat cells.

Psychology in the Real World

Why Dieting Does Not Work—And What Does

Traci Mann

For all of you who have tried to lose weight by dieting, we have bad news for you: Dieting generally does not work—not in the long term at least. Despite what so many of us are led to believe from the countless diet books and diet-related advertisements and television shows to which we are exposed, gains from dieting almost never last. Traci Mann and colleagues (2007) conducted a meta-analysis of 31 high-quality published studies on the question of long-term weight loss from dieting and report the depressing news that diets work only for a small minority of the population. But the news is even worse: The authors concluded that dieters would have been better off in the long term if they had never dieted at all. Their weight would be the same, but their bodies would not have gone through the stressful yo-yoing in weight. Losing and regaining weight is associated with heart disease, stroke, diabetes, and altered immune function.

To be clear: people typically lose about 5–10 pounds within the first 6 months they start dieting (Mann et al., 2007). Within 2 to 5 years, however, the vast majority have not only gained all of the weight back, but many also end up weighing more than when they started dieting. In one study, for example, of more than 19,000 older men over a 4-year period, the single best predictor of weight gain was whether or not the men had lost weight on a diet soon before the study began.

What Does *Work for Keeping Weight Off? Lifestyle Change*

Health and social scientists have accumulated a fairly clear body of evidence for the kinds of lifestyle changes that are needed if someone is going to lose weight and keep it off for more than a year (CDC, 2009; Christakis & Fowler, 2009; Culvers, 2010; Murray, 2009):

- Eat slowly—it takes 20 minutes after eating before your brain knows you are full.

- Write down what you eat for at least one month.

- Monitor your weight regularly (at least a few times a month).

- Eat small meals throughout the day rather than a few big ones; snacking is fine, but choose low-fat and/or whole grain foods.

- Eat what you want but in moderation—eat "comfort foods" but eat them less often.

- Stop eating when you feel full.

- Drink lots of water—among other things, lots of water fills your stomach and decreases a tendency to overeat.

- Ensure at least moderate physical activity each day—totaling approximately 30 minutes (could be as short as three 10-minute sessions).

- Get support from your friends and family.

weight is relatively easy, but keeping it off is very difficult (Mann et al., 2007; see "Psychology in the Real World: Why Dieting Does Not Work—And What Does").

Sex: Survival of the Species

Without food, we would starve to death. Without sex, individuals would not die; but if everyone went without sex, our species would die. So the simplest answer

The last point deserves some elaboration. Recent research points to the remarkable power of our social groups to affect our overall health and lifestyle habits, including weight and weight gain (Christakis & Fowler, 2009). For example, a study by Wing and Jeffery (1999) recruited people who wanted to lose weight according to one of two groups: those who enrolled alone or those who enrolled with three other friends. These two groups in turn were randomly assigned to either receive social support or not. Social support training consisted of each team of four selecting a name for their team and then calling each other and providing social support (encouragement and coaching) throughout the treatment.

Results showed that only 23% of those who enrolled alone in the weight loss program kept the weight off 10 months after treatment (see Figure 11.6). Between 40% and 45% of those who either enrolled alone but who were assigned social support or enrolled with friends but without social support training kept the weight off for 10 months. And 66% of those who enrolled with friends and who received social support training kept off the weight for 10 months. On average, those who were recruited with friends lost 33% more weight than those who were recruited alone. Note, however, that this outcome is relatively brief—only 10 months—and hence we don't know what percentage of any group kept the weight off for 2 or more years.

Losing weight, therefore, is more about lifestyle change than dieting. Eating what you want but simply eating it less

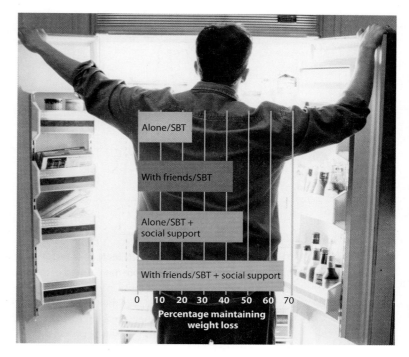

FIGURE **11.6**
PERCENTAGE OF PARTICIPANTS WHO MAINTAINED THEIR WEIGHT LOSS IN FULL 10 MONTHS AFTER TREATMENT. Note: SBT = standard behavioral treatment; alone = recruited alone. (Source: Wing & Jeffery, 1999, p. 37)

often or in smaller portions is a change in lifestyle, not a diet. In addition, losing weight is not just about changing the lifestyle of an individual or even a social group. It often also requires changing the whole society. The World Health Organization (WHO) recently reported some of the most effective policies for getting people to lose weight that operate at the public policy and government level (WHO, 2009). For example, in their meta-analysis of 937 diet studies and 776 physical activity studies from all over the world, they found the most effective interventions for weight loss and exercise were government policies that mandated healthier composition of foods and increased public recreation facilities.

to the question "Why do we have sex?" would be "To propagate the species." Such an answer is useful at the species level but not at the individual level. As individuals we have sex for the simple reason that it is enjoyable and feels good.

sexual behavior
actions that produce arousal and increase the likelihood of orgasm.

Human Sexual Response   Like many basic questions, "What is sex?" is more complex than it would appear. For the sake of clarity, we define **sexual behavior** as actions that produce arousal and increase the likelihood of orgasm.

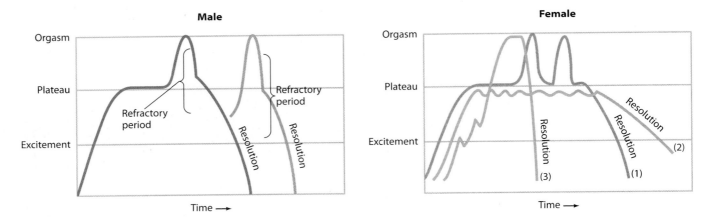

FIGURE 11.7

THE SEXUAL RESPONSE CYCLE IN MEN AND WOMEN. The four phases are excitement, plateau, orgasm, and resolution. Women are more varied in their sexual response than men. There are at least three distinct types of response in women. In (1) we see a response pattern much like men's, except that there is the possibility of multiple orgasm. In (2) we see a woman who gets aroused and stays at the plateau level, never reaching orgasm. In (3) we see a pattern where the woman gets aroused and excited, skips the plateau phase, and has a quick resolution phase. In men, there is only one pattern, though sometimes a second orgasm can occur after a refractory period. (Source: Masters et al., 1986)

Masters and Johnson (1966) were the first scientists to study the human sexual response systematically and directly. One of their major findings was that men and women go through four phases of sexual arousal, but do so somewhat differently (see Figure 11.7). The four phases are excitement, plateau, orgasm, and resolution. The major signs of the initial excitement phase are vaginal lubrication in the female and erection in the male. In the second phase, plateau, excitement level remains high but is preorgasmic. In men, the plateau phase might be rather short, but orgasm almost always follows. In women, the plateau phase often lasts longer than in men and is not necessarily followed by orgasm. In fact, some women stay in the plateau phase for a while and then pass to the resolution phase without achieving orgasm. These women also have a gradual resolution phase. An even more striking gender difference is the ability of women to have multiple orgasms. Men always have a refractory period immediately following orgasm in which erection is lost and orgasm is not possible, but women may go on to have multiple orgasms.

Updated models of female sexual arousal suggest that the initial sexual response in women involves more psychological processes than simply arousal and desire (Basson, 2000). Desire and arousal do not happen spontaneously in many women, who often require the right balance of thoughts and feelings dealing with intimacy, closeness, trust, and lack of fear and anxiety. Only if these conditions are met will arousal happen. These thoughts and feelings play off and feed arousal, which in turn leads to deeper feelings of intimacy and closeness. Arousal continues to increase and may or may not lead to orgasm, but arousal and excitement are important and meaningful even without orgasm (Basson, 2000).

The Biology of Sexual Behavior

This newer model of sexual response matches well with brain imaging research on sexual arousal and orgasm. Many brain regions involved in emotion, which we will discuss shortly, are also involved in the stages of sexual arousal prior to orgasm. As is true of many physiological drives, such as hunger, the hypothalamus plays a crucial role in sexual behavior (Dominguez & Hull, 2005; Melis & Argiolis, 1995). In humans, lesions to the back portion of the hypothalamus lead to a decrease in sexual behavior, whereas electrically stimulating the same region leads to an increase in sexual behavior, especially in males (Dominguez & Hull, 2005). In addition, the part of the hypothalamus involved in sexual behavior is larger in men than in women (Allen & Gorski, 2007).

Testosterone, the primary male sex hormone, also controls women's sex drive.

As you might expect, brain activity changes during orgasm—surprisingly, certain brain regions actually shut down. Gert Holstege and colleagues from the Netherlands took brain images of women while they were having an orgasm (being manually stimulated by their partners) and while they were faking it (Georgiadis et al., 2006). Achieving a real orgasm always involved deactivation of brain regions involved with fear and anxiety in the amygdala and hippocampus as well as parts of the cortex involved in consciousness. During faked orgasms, however, these brain regions remained activated. Men showed brain deactivation during orgasm, but only in the left amygdala (Holstege et al., 2003).

Testosterone, the major male sex hormone, controls sex drive in both men and women (N. M. Morris et al., 1987; Persky et al., 1978). The role of testosterone in the female sex drive was discovered accidentally when women whose adrenal glands were removed lost their sex drive (Waxenberg, Drellich, & Sutherland, 1959). The adrenal glands produce testosterone. Moreover, younger women have both higher levels of male sex hormones and more frequent sexual activity than do older women (Persky et al., 1982). Indeed, males and females with high baseline levels of testosterone are more sexually active at earlier ages and engage in sex more frequently than those with low baseline levels of testosterone. It's not surprising that testosterone treatments increase sex drive in both men and women (Bolour & Braunstein, 2005).

In most species, females are not continually receptive to males. Although women are not nearly as cyclical in their sexual desire as are females of other species, there is, in fact, some regular cyclical activity and interest in the course of the 28-day menstrual cycle. Female-initiated sexual behavior peaks around ovulation and again before and after menstruation (Bullivant et al., 2004; Ford & Beach, 1951; Udry, Morris, & Waller, 1973). The strongest cyclical effect for women, however, occurs in relation to their fantasies involving men other than their regular sex partner (D. M. Buss, 2003). As women approach ovulation, the frequency and intensity of their fantasies involving sex with men other than their partner increase (Bullivant et al., 2004). Such an increase in sex drive makes sense from an evolutionary and biological perspective, because a woman is most likely to become pregnant during ovulation. This is a case in which biological motives drive behavior.

Culture and Sexual Behavior

What is acceptable and normal sexual behavior varies from culture to culture. Perspectives on even this basic human experience are many and varied. In a classic study of sexual behavior and culture, Clellan Ford and Frank Beach (1951) studied attitudes toward sex before and after marriage in 190 different cultures. They identified three kinds of societies in terms of sexual attitudes: Restrictive societies restrict sex before and outside of marriage; semirestrictive societies place formal prohibitions on pre- and extramarital sex that are not strictly enforced; and permissive societies place few restrictions on sex. Thirty years later, Broude and Greene (1980) conducted a similar study of 141 non-Western cultures and found that for women, premarital sex was mildly to moderately disapproved of in 30% of the societies and strongly disapproved of in 26%. Extramarital sex was common among men in 69% of the cultures and among women in 57% of the cultures.

Gender and the Drive for Casual Sex
The belief that men are more promiscuous than women is widespread, but is it true? In a word, yes. Research consistently shows that men are more willing and interested in casual sex than are women (see, for example, M. J. Bailey, Kirk et al., 2000; D. M. Buss, 2003; R. D. Clark & Hatfield, 1989; Maticka-Tyndale, Harold, & Opperman, 2003). For instance, in a meta-analysis of 177 studies of gender and sexual attitudes and behavior published between 1966 and 1990, Oliver and Hyde (1993) reported that men, on average, have much more positive attitudes toward casual sex and are slightly more likely to approve of premarital or extramarital sex. Russell Clark III and Elaine Hatfield (1989, 2003) conducted a classic study on the question of gender differences and casual sex. Research assistants approached strangers of the opposite sex and asked them whether they would be willing to either go on a date, come over, or go to bed with them.

As you can see in the Research Process for this chapter (Figure 11.8), the results were striking. Three quarters of the men responded that they were willing to have sex with a stranger of the opposite sex, but not one woman was willing to do so!

Parental investment theory offers an explanation for the gender difference in attitude toward casual sex. If pregnancy results, the cost of having sex is quite different for men and women (Trivers, 1972). Biologically speaking, for men the only assured contribution to parenthood is the act of sex itself. If a woman becomes pregnant, however, her contribution includes 9 months of carrying the fetus, a good portion of which might involve pregnancy sickness; then there is the painful labor and delivery; and finally, there are approximately 18 years of caring for the child. It follows, therefore, that women would be less motivated to have sex with little emotional commitment—a single sexual encounter could have consequences that endure a lifetime.

Sexual Orientation
What drives most people to be attracted predominantly to the opposite sex, yet a significant minority to be attracted to the same sex? **Sexual orientation** is our disposition to be attracted to either the opposite sex (heterosexual), the same sex (homosexual), or both sexes (bisexual). Historically, sexual orientation was thought of as an either–or proposition: A person was either heterosexual or homosexual. But in the 1940s Alfred Kinsey proposed a now-standard view of sexual orientation: It exists on a continuum from exclusively heterosexual to exclusively homosexual (Kinsey, Pomeroy, & Martin, 1948). After interviewing thousands of individuals, Kinsey and his colleagues realized that sexual orientation was not either–or and devised a 7-point scale extending from 0 to 6. Zero was exclusively heterosexual and 6 exclusively homosexual. Most people fall between 0 and 2 but a consistent minority of people exist on the homosexual end of the scale. Between 1% and 5% of the adult male population and 1% and 3.5% of the adult female population classify themselves

sexual orientation
the disposition to be attracted to either the opposite sex (heterosexual), the same sex (homosexual), or both sexes (bisexual).

Research Process

1 Research Question

Are there differences between men and women in their interest in casual sex? The researchers hypothesized that men are more eager for casual sex than are women.

2 Method

Clark and Hatfield (1989) developed a brief survey to address the research question. Research assistants who were college students approached students of the opposite sex. After a brief introduction, the research assistant would ask each student one of these questions: "Would you go out with me tonight?" "Would you come over to my apartment tonight?" or "Would you go to bed with me tonight?"

Question	Percentage saying "yes"	
	Men	Women
"Would you go out with me tonight?"	56%	50%
"Would you come over to my apartment tonight?"	69%	6%
"Would you go to bed with me tonight?"	75%	0%

3 Results

This table gives responses to the various questions, by gender.

FIGURE 11.8

GENDER AND CASUAL SEX. A simple survey revealed gender differences in the interest in casual sex. When approached, most men will agree to casual sex with an opposite-sex stranger, while most women will not. Source: R. D. Clark III and E. Hatfield, 1989, "Gender Differences in Willingness to Engage in Casual Sex," *Journal of Psychology and Human Sexuality, 2,* 39–55.

4 Conclusion

Men and women were equally likely to agree to go on a date with someone they didn't really know. As the proposal became increasingly intimate, however, women backed off. Consistent with the hypothesis, men were much more likely than women to agree to have sex. This finding would be predicted by parental investment theory, which states that the cost of having sex is quite different for men and women.

as predominantly homosexual (LeVay & Hamer, 1994; Tarmann, 2002). For men, sexual orientation tends to be either–or, producing a dip between 2 and 4 on Kinsey's 7-point scale (the "bisexual" range). For women, however, there is a more gradual decrease from exclusively heterosexual to exclusively homosexual, with more women than men identifying themselves as bisexual (Diamond, 2008; Hamer & Copeland, 1998; Rahman, 2005).

Naturalistic observations of animals suggest that same-sex pairings may be much more common than previously thought. Same-sex sexual behavior is seen in numerous species, including beetles, penguins, and snakes (N. W. Bailey & Zuk, 2009). In the Laysan albatross, for example, a high proportion (more than 30%) of pair-bonded birds are female–female pairs who care for eggs and raise young together (Young, Zaun, & VanderWerf, 2008). Scientists are still at a loss to explain the prevalence of same-sex sexual or matelike behavior across different species, because the framework for understanding sexual behavior relies on sex being an adaptation to support perpetuating the species. If sex does not serve a reproductive goal, then what is its purpose (N. W. Bailey & Zuk, 2009)? We still do not know the answer to this question.

Many people wonder what causes a person to be sexually attracted to someone of the opposite sex or the same sex. The age-old nature–nurture question inevitably arises: Is sexual orientation more a result of biology or of upbringing and environment? Both are involved in sexual orientation, and in complex ways (M. J. Bailey, Dunne, & Martin, 2000). There is evidence that our first biological environment—the womb—exerts a long-term effect on our sexual orientation. Research has revealed that, to some extent, individuals exposed to relatively high levels of testosterone in the womb are more likely to be attracted to women, whereas those exposed to relatively low levels of testosterone are more likely to be attracted to men (K. M. Cohen, 2002; Ellis & Ames, 1987; Rahman, 2005). These findings are not fully replicated and more research is needed before people can draw conclusions about the role of prenatal testosterone exposure in sexual orientation.

The hypothalamus also seems to be involved in sexual orientation, which is not surprising, given its key role in sexual behavior. Intrigued by research

Sexual orientation is influenced by both nature and nurture.

showing that a small region in the hypothalamus involved in sexual behavior is about twice as large in men's brains as in women's, Simon LeVay (1991) decided to examine this structure in the brains of gay and straight men. He found that this region is substantially smaller in gay men than in straight men—it's about the size of women's. As a correlational study, we cannot know exactly what this means—whether overactivity in this brain region causes homosexuality or whether homosexual behavior shapes this region of the brain. This is yet another example of mutual interaction of biology and behavior.

Some studies point to other brain differences between homosexual and heterosexual men. A brain imaging study of men showed that a region of the corpus callosum (the band of myelinated neurons that communicates between the cerebral hemispheres) is thicker in homosexual than in heterosexual men (Witelson et al., 2008). Another study indicates that different neural circuits are activated in homosexual versus heterosexual men while watching erotic films (Hu et al., 2008). These findings are all quite new, and we are not sure whether they hold for women, but they do point to a biological basis for sexual orientation.

Genetic research suggests that sexual orientation is partly under genetic influence, at least in men. Studies of twins indicate that genetics play a bigger role in determining sexual orientation in men than in women. For women, environmental factors seem to have a strong influence on sexual orientation. Female twins raised in the same household are much more likely to have the same sexual orientation than are female twins raised in different households, regardless of whether they are identical or fraternal twins. For males, degree of genetic relationship seems to matter most in twin sexual orientation (M. J. Bailey, Dunne, & Martin, 2000; Demir & Dickson, 2005; Hamer & Copeland, 1998; J. S. Hyde, 2005; Rahman, 2005).

Scholars have also proposed a number of social–environmental theories to explain the origins of sexual orientation. These theories argue that sexual orientation is a social construction (Bell, Weinberg, & Hammersmith, 1981; Van Wyk & Geist, 1984). Some social–environmental theories of sexual orientation have argued, for example, that child play, early peer relations, differences in how parents treat boys and girls, and gender identity are important factors in the development of sexual orientation, both heterosexual and homosexual. For instance, many studies report that engaging in play more typical of the opposite sex early in childhood predicts a homosexual orientation later in life, in both men and women (M. J. Bailey & Zucker, 1995; K. M. Cohen, 2002). These environmental theories are quite consistent with biological ones. Biology could start the development of sexual orientation, which in turn would be strengthened or discouraged by environmental factors. The two sets of explanations work best in cooperation rather than competition.

Nature & Nurture

Who we are attracted to is influenced by a complex mix of biological and cultural factors.

The Needs to Belong and to Excel

As we saw in Maslow's hierarchy of needs, human needs extend beyond the physiological needs of hunger and sex. The need for social contact and belonging is a powerful and universal need. Psychologists call this the need for affiliation.

The need to excel, achieve, and be competitive with others is also a powerful and universal one. Psychologists call this the need for achievement.

The Need to Belong: Affiliation

Humans are inherently social creatures. We depend on other people our entire lives, especially at life's beginning and end. It is not surprising, therefore, that our need to belong and to be accepted by others is one of the strongest of all human needs (Adler, 1956; Baumeister & Leary, 1995; Murray, 1938/1962). Almost every close relationship in our lives is driven by this fundamental need to connect, a motivation common to social species from humans to cockroaches (Lihoreau, Brepson, & Rivault, 2009).

The opposite of being accepted is being rejected, which can be one of the more painful experiences in life. A lack of belongingness and being rejected lead to both physical and psychological problems, ranging from having more health problems to developing eating disorders, from being more depressed to being more likely to commit suicide (Baumeister & Leary, 1995). Moreover, being rejected makes people more prone to get angry, lash out, and be aggressive toward others (Leary et al., 2006). Many explosive violent episodes are preceded by the person's being fired from work or being rejected by peers, a lover, or a spouse (K. D. Williams & Zudro, 2001). For example, many of the school shootings over the last 12 years, such as Columbine and Virginia Tech, have been carried out by boys and men who were teased and rejected by their peers (Leary et al., 2003).

Connection

Affiliation with others is so important that social exclusion physically hurts and activates pain regions in the brain involved in physical pain.

See "Exclusion and Inclusion," Chapter 14, "Social Behavior," p. 559.

What makes Oscar run? Oscar Pistorius, a double-amputee sprinter from South Africa, won three gold medals at the 2008 Paralympics in Beijing. Determined to race against able-bodied runners in the Olympics, Pistorius competed in the 2008 Olympic trials, breaking a personal record but falling short of the qualifying time.

The Need to Excel: Achievement

Some people have a tremendous need to excel and to be the best at what they do. Many successful athletes, businesspeople, and politicians, for example, are driven by such a need. But in truth, almost everyone strives to overcome shortcomings and imperfections (Adler, 1956). In the process, some people compete fiercely with other people, whereas others compete more with themselves simply to do the best they can.

The motivation to succeed raises the question of how to define achievement and success. David McClelland and his colleague John Atkinson emphasized that **achievement motivation** is a desire to do things well and overcome difficulties and obstacles (D. C. McClelland, 1985). However, those obstacles can be measured only in terms of one's goals. When David Feist (whom you met in Chapter 6) was coming out of his vegetative state following his bicycle accident, lifting a finger was a tremendous achievement. Yet, for a highly driven, accomplished, and motivated athlete, a silver medal at the Olympics might be a crushing defeat.

Atkinson (1964) argued that the tendency to achieve success is a function of three things: motivation to succeed, expectation of success, and the incentive value of the success (see also D. C. McClelland, 1985). Let's apply Atkinson's model to a familiar example: your motivation to obtain a good grade

achievement motivation a desire to do things well and overcome obstacles.

in this introductory psychology course. Your motivation to succeed is the extent to which you really want to be successful. In a course such as introductory psychology, success will have different meanings for different students. For some, an A− might be a horrible failure, whereas for others a B+ might be a great accomplishment.

Expectation of success is an individual's evaluation of the likelihood of succeeding at a task. Your evaluation of your performance in this course consists of two different beliefs: whether you have the ability to do well and what the actual outcome is likely to be. These two beliefs may not match. For instance, some students may see themselves as quite capable, but due to other circumstances, such as missing several classes, they may not obtain a high grade for the course.

Incentive value stems from two factors. First, success at the task has to be important to you. Second, the more difficult the task and the lower the odds of succeeding at it, the more it will mean to you if you do succeed. Applied to taking this course, the incentive value for doing well differs depending on what a good grade in the course means to you. If you are a psychology major and the GPA in your major plays an important role in your class standing or whether you keep your scholarship, the grade in Intro Psych might have a higher incentive value than it would if you were a physics major taking the course to satisfy a general education requirement. In addition, the difficulty of a task plays a role in its incentive value. Succeeding at something that is very difficult means more to most people than succeeding at something they consider easy, because the easier task does not provide much feedback about ability. Likewise, failing at a difficult task may not provide much useful feedback concerning your abilities. Intuitively most people shy away from tasks that they perceive as very easy or very difficult and seek to tackle tasks that are moderately challenging.

Highly driven and accomplished athletes may view anything less than a gold medal as poor achievement.

Motivation in the Workplace

Soon you will be entering the workplace. What will push you in one direction versus another? What can keep you motivated to do well in a job? Industrial/ Organizational (I/O) psychologists study motivation and behavior in work contexts (Aamodt, 2010). Consider an I/O question very important to businesses: What motivates employees to work at their best?

Three Models of Employee Motivation
What would you prefer most in your job—money or interesting and enjoyable work? The most sensible answer is probably "both." And in fact, "interesting work," "good wages," and "job security" have been the top priorities among employees in surveys from the 1940s onward (Wiley, 1997).

From a behavioral perspective, the bottom line for business is productivity. Historically, many businesses and companies have operated using principles of operant conditioning to motivate workers to perform well—that is, good behavior is rewarded by pay increases, promotions, and incentives. More recently, however, some companies have questioned whether money and reward are really the best motivators and instead have emphasized supportive and pleasant work environment, autonomy, enjoyment, and challenge in their workers. There are at least three competing models of how to best motivate workers and make them more productive—namely, either through extrinsic motivation, intrinsic motivation, or organizational support for the well-being of employees (Aamodt, 2010; Deci, Koestner, & Ryan, 1999; Deci & Ryan, 1985; Eisenberger & Cameron, 1996; Hennessey & Amabile. 1998).

Extrinsic Motivation Some models, influenced by Skinner's discoveries of the power of reinforcement to shape behavior, argue that reward, money, and feedback are all important and powerful shapers of workplace behavior (Aamodt, 2010; Eisenberger & Cameron, 1996). This model is known as the extrinsic motivation model. **Extrinsic motivation** comes from outside the person (extrinsic) and usually involves rewards and praises. Essentially, extrinsic motivators are used to get people to do things they themselves wouldn't normally do or perhaps even don't like doing—such as when children get an allowance for cleaning their room and doing the dishes.

In capitalism, money is the major extrinsic reward in business. Companies, of course, want to make products of high quality, but it is money above all else that motivates the executives of all for-profit companies. As reported in Eisenberger and Shanock (2003, p. 121), Michael Eisner, then the CEO of Disney, once stated, "We have no obligation to make art. We have no obligation to make a statement. Our only obligation is to make money."

But when money becomes the sole motivator, then sometimes the big perspective can become lost—as happened during the recession of 2008–2009. Wall Street investment firms and banks lost all perspective because they participated in a bonus-greed culture, in which producing goods and helping people didn't seem to matter. Making money was the only thing that seemed to matter.

Psychological research offers much support for the power of reward and extrinsic motivation on behavior, including workplace behavior (Bandura, 1997; Eisenberger, Rhoades, & Cameron, 1999; Harackiewicz & Sansone, 1991; Skinner, 1971). Reward not only can increase a particular behavior but it can also increase performance and feelings of competency. For example, when rewards are connected directly to performance, workers will be more motivated to do a job well than when they simply receive positive feedback without a reward (Harackiewicz & Sansone, 1991).

And yet, extrinsic motivation does have its drawbacks (D'Ausilio, 2008). For example, it requires the reward to be constant. If the reward goes away, the motivation to continue goes away and the worker stops doing the rewarded behavior. Similarly, if the reward stays the same and doesn't increase, then motivation will drop. So it requires always raising the bar and getting more and more pay. In addition, reward has a way of narrowing focus, and so it works for simple tasks; but narrow focus hinders creative thinking and the expanded focus and ideas required to solve difficult problems. Finally, reward can sometimes remove a person's own desire to perform a task out of pure enjoyment. If people think or perceive that they are being controlled by others, then their own intrinsic interest in doing the task dwindles. The idea is that reward and evaluation by other people undercuts one's own pleasure in doing a task. For example, if you enjoyed reading in middle school and then your parents started paying you for every 25 pages you read, you might start reading for money rather than for

extrinsic motivation
motivation that comes from outside the person and usually involves rewards and praises.

pleasure. In this case, your intrinsic enjoyment of reading would have been destroyed by external reward.

motivation in the workplace

Intrinsic Motivation The rock musician Tom Petty recently summed up the second model of work motivation very well: "I think any time you're making a living at what you love to do, you're blessed. That's what I try to instill in my kids. Go after what you really love and find a way to make that work for you, and then you'll be a happy person" (Fong-Torres, 2010). **Intrinsic motivation** happens when you want to do something simply because you enjoy doing it. Intrinsic motivation, in fact, has four components (Amabile & Khaire, 2008; Amabile et al., 1994; Deci & Ryan, 1985; Miao et al., 2009):

Extrinsic motivation

Intrinsic motivation

intrinsic motivation motivation that comes from within a person and includes the elements of challenge, enjoyment, mastery, and autonomy.

- *Challenge:* How much do you enjoy the thrill and excitement of new challenges?
- *Enjoyment:* How much pleasure do you receive from the process of doing the task?
- *Mastery:* Do you gain a sense of accomplishment and pride in doing a difficult task?
- *Autonomy and self-determination:* Do you believe that you are free to determine much of what you do and how you do it?

Teresa Amabile and her colleagues argue that intrinsic motivators are key to helping employees to work creatively and productively (Amabile & Khaire, 2008; Amabile & Kramer, 2007). They present evidence that companies that most successfully motivate their employees and inspire their creativity are those that

- don't have executives who think they are the only source of good ideas but rather elicit and champion ideas from anyone in the company, as long as they are good, creative ideas
- open their organization to a diverse number of perspectives, based on ethnicity, gender, age, and experience
- have managers/executives who know when to put controls on the creative process (commercialization phase) and when not to (idea generation phase)
- create positive emotions in workers, such as satisfaction, pride, and elation because positive emotion is likely to make workers more creative, productive, and more committed to the company

Perceived support by supervisors and organizations

Two kinds of motivation in the workplace: extrinsic and intrinsic.

Intrinsic motivation is not a static and changeless attribute of a person. It changes as life circumstances change. We see this with the various components of intrinsic motivation (Miao et al., 2009). For example, the need for challenge in employees rises for those in their 20s to 30s but then drops as they move toward late middle age and the end of their career. However, enjoyment, which is the emotional component of intrinsic motivation, drops only a little over the course of one's career (see Figure 11.9).

FIGURE 11.9

TWO KINDS OF INTRINSIC MOTIVATION OVER THE LIFESPAN: CHALLENGE AND ENJOYMENT. The numbers on the left represent mean motivation score. (Source: Miao et al., 2009)

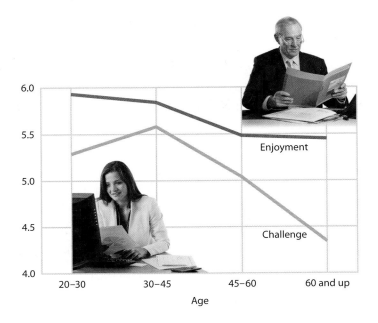

Enjoyment

Challenge

Age

Perceived Support by Supervisors and Organizations   Few things can be more deflating than working hard at something and then having it taken for granted or not appreciated by people whose opinions matter most to you. How much we believe our hard work is recognized and rewarded goes a long way in keeping us motivated in a particular job.

According to the competing models of intrinsic and extrinsic factors in employee motivation, how much employees believe the organization appreciates and supports their contributions and well-being, known as **perceived organizational support,** plays a big role in keeping them motivated and committed to working at that company (Allen, Shore, & Griffeth, 2003; Eisenberger et al., 2002; Kottke & Sharafinski, 1988; Shore & Wayne, 1993; Yoon & Thye, 2000). Eder and Eisenberger (2008), for example, reported research that supports the idea that when employees work at companies that support and care about their well-being compared to companies that do not, employees are happier at their jobs, experience less stress, and are more motivated to stay at their jobs. In addition, they are less likely to miss workdays, be late for work, or take long lunch breaks.

In another study, Allen, Shore, and Griffeth (2003) predicted that perceived organizational support would be positively related to both how committed employees were to their company and how satisfied with their jobs they would be. Two samples were studied: first, 264 salespeople at a large department store in the southeastern United States, and second, 442 insurance agents at a large national insurance company. Allen and colleagues found that perceptions of fairness and opportunity affect perceptions of organizational support, which affect the likelihood of staying with a company (see Figure 11.10).

Which Business Model Works Best at Motivating Employees?   Two of the three basic business models of how best to motivate employees—with money and incentives or with challenge, autonomy, and pleasure—appear to be in direct competition. One shows that extrinsic reward reduces intrinsic motivation, whereas the other claims that it increases intrinsic pleasure. But which one is correct and works best to motivate employees? There is some truth to both sides.

Sometimes extrinsic rewards work the best to motivate employees. Rewards are most effective when situations are relatively well defined and simple and it is

perceived organizational support

employees' beliefs about how much the organization appreciates and supports their contributions and well-being.

FIGURE 11.10
MODEL LINKING ORGANIZATIONAL SUPPORT TO COMMITMENT TO STAY WITH A COMPANY.
(Adapted from Allen et al., 2003)

clear that creative and innovative behavior itself will be rewarded (Eisenberger & Cameron, 1996; Eisenberger, Rhoades, & Cameron, 1999; Eisenberger & Shanock, 2003; Harackiewicz & Sansone, 1991). Eisenberger, Rhoades, and Cameron (1999), for example, reported that reward can actually enhance rather than undermine intrinsic motivation. The evidence shows that people have to believe that they will be rewarded specifically for creative behavior if rewards are to enhance their intrinsic motivation and creativity (Eisenberger & Shanock, 2003).

In other situations, however, intrinsic motivators work best to stimulate employee creativity and productivity. These situations tend to be job tasks that are complex and do not have clear solutions or outcomes (Amabile & Khaire, 2008; Amabile & Kramer, 2007; Deci, Koestner & Ryan, 1999; Hennessey & Amabile, 1998). For instance, Hennessey and Amabile found that reward increases creativity only if the task is very simple and laboratory based. Rewards do not work as well in stimulating interest in real-world or complicated tasks. Also, rewarding people for finishing or completing a task lowers their intrinsic enjoyment of doing the task. For example, in a meta-analysis of 128 studies, researchers reported that external rewards can undermine intrinsic motivation (Deci, Koestner, & Ryan, 1999).

The kind of motivation required to stimulate worker productivity and creativity may also vary depending upon how young or old a company is. In the early stages of a company's development, innovation, creativity, and flexible working conditions foster intrinsic motivation. By contrast, once a company is mature and fully established, incentives, rewards, and pay may be the most effective way to promote worker productivity and commitment. These conditions foster extrinsic motivation.

For example, when the computer company Apple was starting in the late 1970s and early 1980s, it quickly became known for its informal, jeans-only and democratic working environment (Schneider, n.d.). On its current website, Apple argues that it still maintains such an innovative and informal workplace: "A lot of big companies are about endless meetings. Massive bureaucracy. Executive parking spaces. And suits. We don't see what any of that has to do with great work. So we don't bother. This isn't your cushy corporate nine-to-fiver. Fortunately." (Corporate jobs, n.d.).

Similarly, during the early 2000s, Google set the industry standard by hiring very young, creative workers and fostering their free thinking. The company's hiring process is known for its very creative and difficult strategies to ensure that Google hires employees who are creative and flexible in their thinking. For example, during initial interviews potential applicants might be asked questions such as "Why are manhole covers round?" or "How many balls fit into a schoolbus?" ("15 Google Interview Questions," 2009). In addition, Google has implemented and still has what it calls "20 percent time" for its engineers ("The Engineer's Life at Google," n.d.). One day a week (20% of the work week), engineers are required to work on anything they want, as long as it is not their regular work project. Many of Google's more innovative products have come from work done during "20 percent time," such as Gmail and Google Suggests (where as you type a search, searches by other people with similar words are automatically suggested). In fact, one analysis that tracked the success of Google executives' ideas compared to employees' ideas found that the employees' ideas were the most successful (Amabile & Khaire, 2008).

Different motivation styles appear to be effective in different cultures throughout the world (DeVoe & Iyengar, 2003). Companies in North America rely mostly on extrinsic motivators of pay, bonuses, and promotions. Companies in Asia, however, tend to be more holistic and use both extrinsic and intrinsic motivators, whereas companies in South America use more intrinsic than extrinsic motivators.

The bottom line is that there are many different kinds of companies and business situations, and each one may have somewhat different incentives and ways to motivate its employees for its particular environment. Knowing which strategy to use when can mean the difference between a company's prosperity and its bankruptcy.

Quick Quiz 11.1: Motivation

1. Which model of motivation can be compared to the thermostat in your house?
   a. evolutionary
   b. drive reduction
   c. optimal arousal
   d. hierarchical

2. In addition to blood sugar (glucose) and the hypothalamus, and as discussed in this chapter, what is another important biological system involved in regulating hunger?
   a. adrenaline
   b. the liver
   c. hormones
   d. protein

3. Most research on weight loss has reported that
   a. losing weight is very difficult for most people
   b. losing weight is relatively easy initially, but keeping it off is very difficult
   c. keeping weight off is relatively easy for most people
   d. losing weight is relatively easy and so too is keeping it off

4. Brain imaging research has found that during orgasm
   a. some parts of the brain "shut down" and become deactivated
   b. most of the brain becomes very active
   c. only the brain stem is active
   d. the insula becomes very active

5. Researchers have found that a region of the _____ is about the same size in homosexual men and heterosexual women.
   a. amygdala
   b. hippocampus
   c. hypothalamus
   d. prefrontal cortex

6. Company A believes the best way to motivate its employees is through money and promotions. Company B believes the best way to motivate employees is by letting employees come up with their own ideas and creating challenging and interesting work. What model of motivation is each company arguing for, respectively?
   a. intrinsic; extrinsic
   b. extrinsic; intrinsic
   c. achievement; intrinsic
   d. extrinsic; perceived organizational support

Answers can be found at the end of the chapter.

EMOTION

Basic drives such as hunger and sex differ from emotions in important ways. First, drives are linked with very specific needs, whereas emotions are not (Tomkins, 1962, 1981). Hunger comes from a need for food, thirst from a need for water, physical desire from a need for sex. But joy can be associated with just about anything: smelling a rose, visiting a friend, reading a good book, or seeing a beautiful sunset. Also, emotions can override biological drives (Tomkins, 1962). We saw that sexual orgasm cannot occur unless the areas of the brain involved in fear and anxiety are shut down. Another example is how the emotion of disgust can easily override the fundamental drive of hunger. A sandwich is less appealing after a fly lands on it or if, on closer contact, it smells bad.

How can the emotion of disgust override a drive as strong as hunger? Disgust is important for survival. It arises when we come across something that is potentially toxic or harmful. Sometimes just thinking that something is disgusting, even when we know it's not, can override drives. Consider how you would react if you were asked to hold a piece of rubber that is joke vomit between your lips. How about a rubber eraser? Studies show that most people are disgusted by the fake vomit but would willingly put the eraser between their lips (Rozin & Fallon, 1987). We know they are made of the same substance and are equally sanitary, but the basic need to avoid contamination overwhelms our sense of reason. This fear of contagion appears in cultures all over the world (Nemeroff & Rozin, 1994; Rozin & Fallon, 1987).

Disgust is one of several basic emotions (Ekman, 1992; Rozin, Haidt, & McCauley, 2000). In this part of the chapter we explore what emotions are, why we have them, and how they affect our thoughts and bodily systems.

Defining Emotion

Emotions emerge from our interactions with the world around us. They are triggered by situations that are relevant to our personal goals, physical safety, or well-being. Because emotions stem from situations that are important to us, they reveal much about what makes us tick.

Types of Affect   Psychologists use the term *affect* to refer to a variety of emotional phenomena, including emotions, moods, and affective traits. **Emotions** are brief, acute changes in conscious experience and physiology that occur in response to a meaningful situation in the person's environment. Emotions make us pay attention, forcing us to set priorities and deal with life-relevant situations (Ekman, 1992; R. S. Lazarus, 1991; Levenson, 1994). They occupy the foreground of our consciousness, often dominating our awareness. In fact, emotions can impact memory, perception, attention, and decision making (Cohen, 2005; Phelps, 2006).

Moods are transient changes in affect that fluctuate throughout the day or over several days. We experience moods both physiologically and psychologically, and they tend to last longer than most emotions (Davidson, 1994; Ekman, 1984; Hedges, Jandorf, & Stone, 1985). Moods make certain emotions more likely to occur than others. An irritable mood, for instance, makes people more easily angered than usual. A slight inconvenience that would not ordinarily bother you, such as having to wait in line at the supermarket checkout, might cause you to act rudely toward the clerk.

emotions
brief, acute changes in conscious experience and physiology that occur in response to a personally meaningful situation.

moods
affective states that operate in the background of consciousness and tend to last longer than most emotions.

Emotion   **449**

Connection

Emotional events are remembered better than nonemotional events, almost as if they were seared into our brains.

See "Emotion, Memory, and the Brain," Chapter 7, "Memory," p. 288.

Affective traits are enduring aspects of our personalities that set the threshold for the occurrence of particular emotional states (Ekman, 1984; R. S. Lazarus, 1991; Rosenberg, 1998). Consider the example of being cut off in traffic. People who have the affective trait of hostility are most likely to feel anger. They aren't always angry, but they have hair triggers. For several minutes or likely even longer, these people will continue focusing on the event—how they were wronged—and they feel the emotion of anger. Then the event recedes from consciousness, and the feelings of anger go with it. Nonetheless, they may remain in a more diffuse, less focused, less pressing irritable mood. By the end of the day, they may still be in a bad mood but not even realize it.

affective traits
stable predispositions toward certain types of emotional responses.

Emotions, Basic Emotions, and the Dimensions of Affect   A small set of emotions seems to be common to all humans and a product of our evolutionary past (Ekman, 1992). These **basic emotions** are anger, disgust, fear, happiness, sadness, and surprise (see Figure 11.11). These emotions reflect fundamental emotional states that play a role in essential life tasks, such as protecting oneself and loved ones from harm (fear), progressing toward the realization of a goal (happiness), or experiencing irrevocable loss (sadness) (Ekman, 1992; R. S. Lazarus, 1991). Basic emotions are only a small set of the infinite variety of emotional states humans can experience.

basic emotions
set of emotions that are common to all humans; includes anger, disgust, fear, happiness, sadness, and surprise.

The basic emotions are not single states; rather, they are categories or groups of related emotions. Ekman (1992) describes such a grouping as an emotion family. For instance, the fear family may arise in response to a threat to physical safety. This family includes such emotions as anxiety, trepidation, and nervousness. The happiness family of emotions includes joy, contentment, elation, amusement, and exhilaration, among others.

Other theorists argue that all emotions are states that vary in their degree of pleasantness and arousal (L. A. Clark, Watson, & Leeka, 1989; Russell, 1980; D. Watson & Tellegen, 1985; Woodworth & Schlossberg, 1954). Figure 11.12 shows how these underlying dimensions of pleasantness and arousal might explain a number of emotions.

self-conscious emotions
types of emotion that require a sense of self and the ability to reflect on actions; they occur as a function of meeting expectations (or not) and abiding (or not) by society's rules.

Self-Conscious Emotions   The feeling of pride a child feels at learning how to ride a bike and the shame of being caught in a lie are examples of **self-conscious emotions,** which are emotions that occur as a function of how well

FIGURE **11.11**

BASIC AND SELF-CONSCIOUS EMOTIONS.
(Source: Ekman, 1992; Tracy et al., 2007)

Basic emotions
Anger
Disgust
Fear
Happiness
Sadness
Surprise

Self-conscious emotions
Embarrassment
Guilt
Humiliation
Pride
Shame

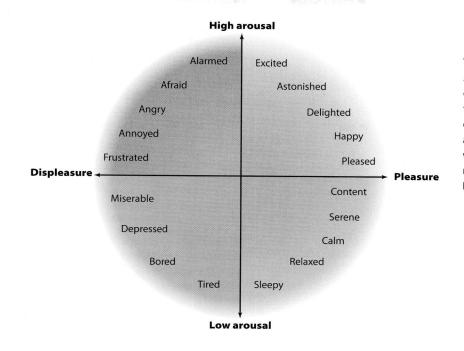

High arousal

Alarmed   Excited

Afraid   Astonished

Angry   Delighted

Annoyed   Happy

Frustrated   Pleased

Displeasure ← → **Pleasure**

Content

Miserable   Serene

Depressed   Calm

Bored   Relaxed

Tired   Sleepy

Low arousal

FIGURE **11.12**

MODEL OF EMOTIONS AS COMBINA-TIONS OF AROUSAL AND PLEASURE. According to Russell's (1980) model of emotion, all emotions can be placed in two dimensions, arousal and pleasure–displeasure. For example, being afraid is a state of high arousal and displeasure, whereas being happy is a pleasant and moderately aroused state. (Source: Russell, 1980)

we live up to our expectations, the expectations of others, or the rules set by society (see Figure 11.11; Tracy, Robins, & Tangney, 2007; Tangney, Stuewig, & Mashek, 2007). These emotions require a sense of self and the ability to reflect on one's own actions. They include shame, guilt, humiliation, embarrassment, and pride. Let's look at pride and embarrassment in detail.

Jessica Tracy and Rick Robins (2007) distinguish between two kinds of pride: authentic pride and hubristic pride. Authentic pride is the pride we feel in some sense of accomplishment, like finishing a task, completing a marathon, and the like. It is pride due to success in situations with controllable causes. It applies to a specific accomplishment. Hubristic pride is a more general sense of pride in oneself, such as "I won because I am great." It is the more puffed up, slightly arrogant version of pride. Indeed, hubristic pride seems to highlight differences in status between self and other (whereby the proud person has beaten out the other), especially when the other is perceived as weak (Oveis, Horberg, & Keltner, 2010).

Pride has a recognizable expression, which involves body movements, a smile, head tilted upward, with slightly expanded chest (see Figure 11.13). This expression is recognized as pride by children and adults in America and by people in a preliterate, socially isolated tribe in West Africa (Tracy & Robins, 2008). These cross-cultural recognition data from very diverse groups suggest that this pride expression may be common across the globe, but more data are needed to be sure. People show elements of this behavior

FIGURE **11.13**

THE EXPRESSION OF PRIDE. U.S. swimmer Michael Phelps shows the typical pride display after winning one of his eight gold medals at the 2008 Olympic Games in Beijing, China.

FIGURE 11.14

TYPICAL FACIAL EXPRESSIONS OF EMBARRASSMENT. The display of embarrassment involves a sequence of actions, each of which might serve a social function. First there is a smile, which may reflect amusement at one's own transgression. Then the eyes gaze away, as if to indicate a desire to escape the awkward situation. Smile control is an attempt to dampen the amusement, as well as looking downward and turning the head away. (Source: Keitner, 1995)

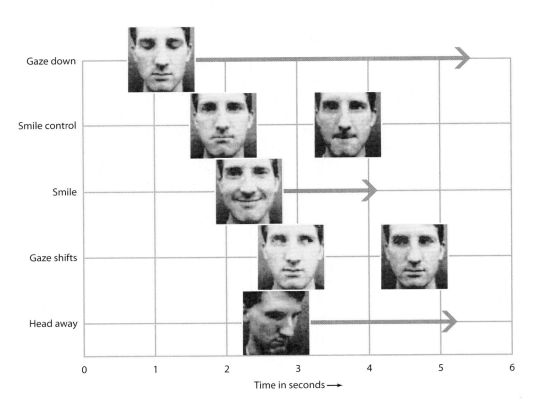

when in situations that produce pride, such as winning medals at the Olympics (Tracy & Matsumoto, 2008).

We all know quite well what it feels like to be embarrassed. You are admiring yourself in the mirror when you realize your roommate has walked in and caught you preening. Embarrassment involves unintentionally revealing something about yourself to someone else. Being embarrassed makes you feel self-conscious, as if you have violated some social rule (such as not admiring yourself in the mirror). People often get giggly when embarrassed and act as if they want to make amends for some sort of social transgression (Keltner, 1995; Tangney et al., 2007). Keltner (1995) describes the facial expression of embarrassment, which he argues serves to appease and placate those who have seen one's mistake. The embarrassment expression involves a sequence of facial and gestural actions, each of which may correspond to some sort of social function (see Figure 11.14).

Emotions as Evolutionary Adaptations

Why do we have emotions? From an evolutionary perspective, emotions are adaptations. That is, they evolved because they solved a particular problem in our ancestral past and thus contributed to survival and reproductive success (Tooby & Cosmides, 1990). According to one evolutionary view, emotions bring our physiological systems together to help us deal efficiently with critical situations (Levenson, 1988; Mauss et al., 2005; Rosenberg & Ekman, 1994). For example, when danger approaches, the heart pumps blood to the skeletal muscles to enable quick movement in case escape is necessary, the respiratory system works harder to bring in more oxygen, and the brain prioritizes attention so that we can figure out what we need to do to escape the dangerous situation. This view of emotions as organized responses illustrates the adaptive value of negative emotions, which enable people to respond efficiently to a significant challenge or obstacle.

broaden-and-build model
Fredrickson's model for positive emotions, which posits that they widen our cognitive perspective and help us acquire useful life skills.

Positive emotions, such as contentment, happiness, love, and amusement, solve different kinds of adaptive problems. According to the **broaden-and-build model,** positive emotions widen our cognitive perspective, making our thinking more expansive and enabling the acquisition of new skills (Fredrickson, 1998, 2001). Compared to negative emotions, which promote a narrow, vigilant way of looking at the world, positive emotions help us see the possibilities for new ways of responding to situations, which helps us to build new skills (Derryberry & Tucker, 1994). Play, for example, especially the rough-and-tumble play of animals and young children, is a kind of fun that helps develop physical and strategic skills that may be useful for hunting, escaping, or defensive fighting.

Several studies show that positive emotions broaden one's focus (Fredrickson & Branigan, 2005). For instance, when people are in positive moods they perform poorly on tasks of selective attention that require a narrow focus compared to people in sad or neutral moods, and they perform better on tasks that require a broader attentional focus (Rowe, Hirsch, & Anderson, 2007). Also, in a task in which people were instructed to think of as many uses as they could for a brick, people who had been put in a positive mood thought of more uses and more creative uses than those experiencing negative emotion (Isen, Daubman, & Nowicki, 1987; Rowe et al., 2007). In a perceptual task, positive emotions also enhance attention to visual information in the outer edges of a visual display, compared to the center (Wadlinger & Isaacowitz, 2006). This finding indicates that positive emotions might enable people to take more information from any given visual scene.

Emotion as a Process

Emotions create changes in experience, thought, physiology, and behavior. For decades psychologists debated which component of emotion best represents what an emotion is, whether a facial expression, an experience, or a physiological change. Researchers now recognize that we can best understand emotions by considering how the various aspects of emotion unfold—that is, by viewing emotion as a process (R. S. Lazarus, 1991; Levenson, 1994).

antecedent event
a situation that may lead to an emotional response.

An emotion begins with an **antecedent event,** a situation that may lead to an emotional response (see Figure 11.15). We use the word *may* because not everyone responds to the same situation in the same way. The person evaluates the event to determine whether it is potentially harmful or beneficial. Depending on the results of that appraisal, he or she may experience an emotional response.

FIGURE **11.15**

THE EMOTION PROCESS. Emotions start with an event that is appraised as relevant to one's goals. If deemed relevant, an emotional response begins, which consists of physiological changes, behavioral and expressive changes, and subjective changes in feelings. Changes in the body's physiology, behavior, and subjective feelings then feed back to the appraisal process and become inputs for experiencing new emotions. Attempts to regulate (modify, change, or suppress) emotion can occur early or late in the emotion process.

The emotional response, in turn, produces changes in physiology, behavior and expressions, and a subjective experience of the event. The direction of the arrows moving from left to right in Figure 11.15 is only part of the story. As the reverse-curved arrow suggests, the process can move in the other direction as well. That is, the activation of facial and physiological responses might enhance the emotion, becoming yet another kind of input for a new emotional experience. Levenson (2003) points out that in addition to the antecedent events that are external to us, there may be internal inputs into the emotion process, inputs provided by facial and physiological changes. In addition, once we generate emotions, we sometimes attempt to modify them, regulate them, or make them go away, which in turn involves new appraisals and new responses. To some extent, then, the emotion process moves in a loop rather than in a single direction.

Appraisal in the Emotion Process   Whether an event or situation leads to an emotion depends on how the person appraises it. **Appraisal** is the evaluation of a situation with respect to how relevant it is to one's own welfare (R. S. Lazarus, 1991). Appraisal need not be a conscious, deliberate thought process. Most of the time it probably occurs automatically, well outside awareness, and it may occur in an instant (Barrett, Ochsner, & Gross, 2007).

Appraisal drives the process by which emotions are elicited (Roseman, 1984; Scherer, Dan, & Flykt, 2006). It explains why, for example, the level of happiness expressed by Olympic athletes can be greater for winners of the bronze medals (third place) than for winners of the silver medal (second place) (Medvec, Madey, & Gilovich, 1995). Bronze medalists could easily imagine an alternative outcome: They may not have even placed. Compared to that outcome, third is great. Silver medalists, on the other hand, could easily imagine having won first place! Compared to that outcome, second might be felt as disappointing. Our own frame of reference influences the way we evaluate our situation, as do our personalities, personal histories, and goals.

Examples of appraisal dimensions include control (how much control you feel you have in a situation), agency (whether you or someone else made something happen), pleasantness, and fairness (Ellsworth & Scherer, 2003). The type of appraisal that occurs determines the type of the emotion generated. Fear, for instance, arises in situations of uncertainty and over which we feel we have little control (Arnold, 1960; Ellsworth & Scherer, 2003; R. S. Lazarus, 1991).

Although it may be impossible to study automatic appraisals as they happen, research on people's understanding of situations and their responses to them can inform us indirectly about appraisal (Smith & Ellsworth, 1987). To illustrate, Tong and colleagues (2009) conducted a set of studies on the relationship between situations and emotions, and how those relationships were linked to certain dimensions of appraisal. Students read brief stories describing common situations that can occur in students' lives (for example, how well another student managed the demands of an important class) and answered questions about how they would have responded to the situations if they had experienced them themselves. They also completed ratings of appraisal dimensions for each story. For instance, to assess the degree to which someone felt control over a situation, participants rated how much they agreed with comments such as "I feel that I can control what happens" (*Control*). Results showed that, as predicted, emotions resulted from specific appraisals of the situation. For instance, sadness was likely in stories in which the participants perceived that they had little control and were not responsible for the situation (that is, they had no agency).

Nature & Nurture

Our appraisal of events leads to emotional experiences, which in turn influence how we respond to new situations.

appraisal
the evaluation of a situation with respect to how relevant it is to one's own welfare; drives the process by which emotions are elicited.

to Real Life

Research

Did you ever notice how you and a friend might see the same movie, but one of you thinks it's hilarious while the other thinks it's boring?

Connecting Psychology to Your Life: Start paying attention to how your interpretation of situations dictates how you feel in response to them.

For the next few days, notice situations in which you experience emotions. How might the sense you made of that situation determine your emotions? Notice how a different interpretation of the situation might have made you feel differently. For instance, was someone who said something abrupt (thus causing you to feel insulted) really being aggressive, or was the person just in a hurry?

Regulation of Emotion People can intentionally or unintentionally change their emotions or the extent to which they experience certain emotions. The term **emotion regulation** refers to the cognitive and behavioral efforts people use to modify their emotions. Looking at the emotion process as depicted in Figure 11.15, you can see that attempts to regulate emotions may occur at the beginning or end of the emotion process (J. J. Gross, 1998; J. J. Gross, Richards, & John, 2006). An example of emotion regulation that can occur early in the emotion process is **reappraisal,** in which people reevaluate their views of an event so that a different emotion results. For example, rather than seeing your next midterm as an opportunity for failure, an outlook that might create fear or anxiety, you might reappraise the exam as a challenging opportunity to prove to yourself and others how much you have learned, an outlook that would lead to eager anticipation.

Another kind of emotion regulation operates when people want to make an unpleasant feeling go away. An example of this kind of strategy for regulating emotion is **expressive suppression,** the deliberate attempt to inhibit the outward display of an emotion (J. J. Gross et al., 2006). For instance, in order to avoid a confrontation, you might literally bite your lip rather than tell your roommates that they are slobs for letting the dishes pile up and waiting for you to wash them. Instructing people to suppress their negative emotions like this can decrease the experience of negative emotion, but it increases activation of the sympathetic nervous system and sustains the emotional response (J. J. Gross & Levenson, 1997).

The Emotional Response Whether processed consciously or automatically, emotional responses emerge from events appraised as relevant to one's safety or personal goals. As shown in Figure 11.15, the **emotional response** includes physiological, behavioral/expressive, and subjective changes. Here we will discuss each type of change.

Physiological Changes Emotions produce physiological changes, such as increases in heart rate and rate of respiration. The physiological system responsible

emotion regulation
the cognitive and behavioral efforts people make to modify their emotions.

expressive suppression
a response-focused strategy for regulating emotion that involves the deliberate attempt to inhibit the outward manifestation of an emotion.

reappraisal
an emotion regulation strategy in which one reevaluates an event so that a different emotion results.

emotional response
the physiological, behavioral/expressive, and subjective changes that occur when emotions are generated.

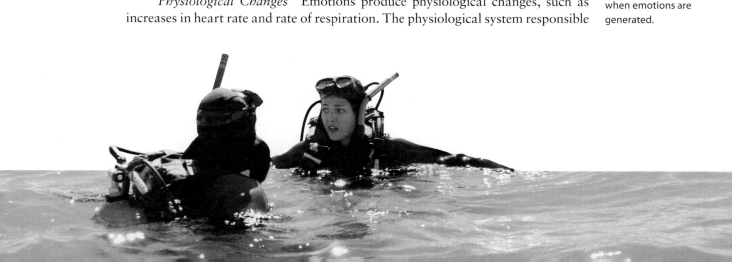

for changes during an emotional response is the autonomic nervous system (ANS). The ANS governs structures and processes over which we have little conscious control, such as changes in heart rate and blood pressure and the release of hormones. The ANS plays a crucial role in emotional response because it activates other systems that are needed for action, including the circulatory system and the respiratory system.

Once elicited, emotions engage the ANS almost immediately. For emotions that are concerned with survival and protection from harm, such as fear, the sympathetic branch of the ANS is activated. Sympathetic activity mobilizes body resources into an organized response to a real or imagined environmental threat. The heart pumps blood rapidly to the muscles; oxygen intake in the lungs increases; and processes that are not immediately necessary for action, such as digestion, shut down so that energy is conserved for more urgent body functions.

The patterns of ANS activity can vary, depending on the emotion elicited. Anger increases heart rate more than fear does; disgust slows the heart (Ekman, Levenson, & Friesen, 1983; Levenson, Ekman, & Friesen, 1990). Such autonomic nervous system changes appear to be common to people all over the world (Levenson et al., 1992; Tsai et al., 2002; Tsai, Levenson, & Carstensen, 2000). Cross-cultural data on the physiology of emotion support the view of emotions as evolutionarily old, as does evidence of emotion in nonhuman primates, other mammals, birds, and even fish (Paul, Harding, & Mendl, 2005).

Positive emotions engage the parasympathetic branch of the ANS. They apparently serve to return the body to a more relaxed, responsive state (Levenson, 2003). For example, Fredrickson and Levenson (1998) showed participants a fear-eliciting film and followed it with film clips known to elicit sadness, amusement, or contentment—or no emotions at all. They measured cardiovascular activity while participants viewed the films and again afterward. Cardiovascular activation elicited by the negative film returned to baseline levels more quickly in people who saw a pleasant film (amusement or contentment) after the fear film, than in those who saw films leading to sad or nonemotional conditions. This ability of positive emotions to "undo" the effects of negative emotional arousal by helping to return the body to a state of relaxation may result from parasympathetic nervous system activation.

Behavioral–Expressive Changes: Facial Expression Emotions create expressive changes in the face and voice, as well as behavioral tendencies toward particular types of action (Frijda, 1986). People show their emotions—knowingly or not—through both verbal and nonverbal means, such as changes in facial behavior and vocal intonation. Although researchers have studied both facial and vocal expressions of emotion, the most extensive body of research has focused on facial expressions.

Humans are predisposed to respond to faces. Newborn babies mimic the facial expressions of adults. At 5 months they can discriminate between different types of facial expressions of emotion; and by 1 year of age they rely on the faces of their caregivers to convey important information about how they might act (Meltzoff & Moore, 1977; Schwartz, Izard, & Ansul, 1985; Sorce et al., 1985). There are specialized neurons in the brain for responding to faces, and certain brain areas are specialized for particular facial expressions, such as fear (Adolphs et al., 1994, 2005; Kanwisher, 2000).

How do psychologists study spontaneous facial expressions? The **Facial Action Coding System (FACS)** is a widely used method by which coders score

Facial Action Coding System (FACS)
a widely used method for measuring all observable muscular movements that are possible in the human face.

all observable muscular movements that are possible in the human face (Ekman & Friesen, 1978). Using FACS, researchers have found that many different facial expressions recognized across cultures—such as anger, disgust, fear, happiness, sadness, and surprise—are also shown when people spontaneously experience emotions (Ekman & Rosenberg, 2005).

The most recognizable facial expression of emotion is the smile of happiness. Yet research using FACS shows that not all smiles are created equal. Only certain smiles indicate truly felt enjoyment. Other smiles are used for a variety of interpersonal reasons, such as to be polite in conversation or to mask negative emotions, as when one pretends to feel happy when, in fact, one does not. A smile that both pulls up the lip corners diagonally and contracts the band of muscles that circle the eye to create crow's feet and raise the cheeks is known as a **Duchenne smile.** A Duchenne smile is a genuine smile that expresses true enjoyment. When we smile for social reasons and are not genuinely happy, we use only the lips and not the band of muscles around the eye, which is called a non-Duchenne smile (Davidson et al., 1990; Ekman, Davidson, & Friesen, 1990). Figure 11.16 compares a Duchenne smile to a non-Duchenne smile.

Duchenne smile a smile that expresses true enjoyment, involving both the muscles that pull up the lip corners diagonally and those that contract the band of muscles encircling the eye.

Is Leonardo da Vinci's Mona Lisa smiling out of pleasure or merely posing a smile in her portrait?

Happiness is the emotion we most easily recognize, but what about other emotions? How do we know which expressions reveal which emotions? Much of what we know about facial expression of emotion was originally based on studies of people's ability to recognize emotion in the human face. Charles Darwin was the first modern thinker to formally propose that facial expressions reveal different emotions. In *The Expression of the Emotions in Man and Animals* (Darwin, 1872/1998), he described in detail how people and animals display emotions through their faces and bodies and offered a theory for the evolution of emotional expression; he also described such actions in animals.

It was not until the 1960s, however, that psychologists began conducting the research that directly addressed Darwin's claims. In his early studies of people's judgments of emotion in the human face, Silvan Tomkins showed participants

FIGURE 11.16
DUCHENNE SMILE VERSUS NON-DUCHENNE SMILE. Both photos depict a smile of the same intensity, but they differ in the involvement of muscles around the eye. Which one is a Duchenne, or true enjoyment, smile?

FIGURE 11.17
Most people recognize this face as an expression of fear. What do you think? (Source: Ekman, 1973)

universal
term referring to something that is common to all human beings and can be seen in cultures all over the world.

numerous photographs of European Americans posing different emotions and asked them to decide which emotion the person in the picture may have been feeling. Researchers obtained pretty strong evidence of agreement on the emotional meaning of those facial expressions, with roughly 70% or more of the respondents for each emotion recognizing the face as showing the same emotion. For instance, most agreed that the picture in Figure 11.17 showed fear (Tomkins & McCarter, 1964). Then Ekman and Friesen showed Tomkins's pictures to people in the United States, Japan, Argentina, and Chile and found a high degree of consensus on the meanings of a core set of facial expressions of emotion (Ekman & Friesen, 1969). At about the same time, Carroll Izard (1969) did a similar study and obtained similar results. Such high level of consensus on the meaning of facial expressions of emotion across numerous cultural groups in several studies supported Darwin's (1872/1998) assertion that the facial expressions of certain "basic" emotions are **universal,** that is, common to all human beings.

One problem with these studies on emotion recognition, however, is that all participants lived in literate, industrialized cultures. Maybe the findings of cross-cultural consistency in facial expression recognition reflected the spreading influence of the popular media rather than the existence of a universal human skill. That is, people in Japan and the United States might have agreed on the emotional meaning of certain expressions because they had seen portrayals of actors in movies. The only way to resolve this question was to collect data from preliterate people who were isolated from Western culture, which is what Ekman did by investigating a preliterate culture (see "Breaking New Ground").

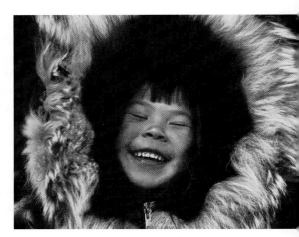

Breaking New Ground

Paul Ekman and Universality in Facial Expression of Emotion

By way of some fortunate connections with an anthropologist friend, Paul Ekman had the chance to study an isolated, preliterate group: the Fore tribe from Papua New Guinea. His plan was to show members of this tribe pictures of facial expressions of emotion—similar to those that had been used in other studies—and find out which emotions, if any, they saw in those faces. But how could he gather such data from a culture without a written language? After experimenting fairly unsuccessfully with a few different approaches, he settled on a technique that had been used with children who also do not have a written language. The method involved presenting stories about emotional situations to New Guineans and showing them a set of three photographed faces per story. Examples of stories include "He [she] is angry and about to fight" (which should lead participants to pick an "angry" face) or "She [he] is looking at something that smells bad" (for disgust). Then the experimenter would ask the listener which of the three faces matched the story. When Ekman used this method, the degree of consensus was much higher.

Both children and adult New Guineans consistently discriminated the "correct" face from other faces; that is, they consistently matched a given story with the face that would have been predicted, and the results matched the data from studies of people in literate cultures (Ekman & Friesen, 1971). Results of these two early studies from both literate and preliterate cultures show that the range of agreement was relatively high for five of the six basic emotions (Ekman et al., 1969; Ekman & Friesen, 1971). Follow-up research conducted 20 years later showed similar high-level agreement across 10 literate cultures (Ekman et al., 1987). For summaries of facial recognition data across several studies see Figure 11.18.

These studies are about the recognition of emotion expressions, usually ones that are posed by people for photographs. But do we see these expressions appear spontaneously on people's faces when they are experiencing emotions? The fact that people from all over the world recognize a core set of such expressions as particular emotions certainly suggests that we do (otherwise, how would so many people agree on their meaning?), but what about research on spontaneous emotion? Although there are fewer studies on facial expressions of emotion as naturally shown by people

Paul Ekman with children in Papua New Guinea, circa 1967. The boys are wearing Western clothing that they accepted as gifts for participating in Ekman's research.

Emotion	Percent agreement in 3 literate cultures[a] (Ekman et. al., 1969)	Percent agreement in a preliterate culture[b] (Ekman & Friesen, 1971)	Percent agreement in 10 literate cultures[c] (Ekman et. al., 1987)
Anger	63–82	82–87	67–84
Disgust	82–86	77–89	60–89
Fear	71–88	28–87	65–91
Happiness	87–97	90–100	69–98
Sadness	73–84	69–81	71–92
Surprise	82–91	64–71	78–94

FIGURE **11.18**
CONSISTENCY IN EXPRESSIONS OF BASIC EMOTION ACROSS LITERATE AND PRELITERATE CULTURES.

a = Brazil, Japan, United States
b = Papua New Guinea (Fore)
c = Estonia, Germany (West), Greece, Hong Kong, Italy, Japan, Scotland, Sumatra, Turkey, United States

(compared to recognition studies), several studies using FACS and other methods for measuring facial behavior from video show that many of the same expressions (and variations) as those recognized cross-culturally also occur in spontaneous behavior (Ekman & Rosenberg, 2005).

■ ■ ■

Behavioral Expressive Changes: Vocal Expression   The human voice also expresses emotion. Have you ever noticed how your voice can betray you? Consider the first time you ever gave a speech. You may have had your hair and clothes in fine order; perhaps your facial expressions showed great composure; and you knew your speech well, having practiced it over and over. But when the time came to start speaking, your voice quivered or even squeaked! Why did this happen? The voice is very sensitive to emotional arousal, because the autonomic nervous system has projections to the vocal chords. So nervousness leaks through the voice (Bachorowski, 1999; Scherer et al., 1991). In studies of actors' portrayals of emotions through spoken nonsense sentences, certain emotions (anger, fear, joy) were associated with higher pitch and volume, while sadness was associated with lower pitch and volume (Scherer et al., 1991).

We have discussed how people can recognize emotion from the face, but can you tell what someone is feeling simply by hearing vocal changes? Even though cross-cultural research reveals cultural variability in many aspects of vocal emotion recognition, the recognition of emotion from speech appears to be a basic human social skill (Scherer, Banse, & Wallbott, 2001). Research suggests that people do a fairly good job of recognizing emotion from the voice alone. When people are asked to provide what they think are vocalizations for each of 22 different emotional states, people who listen to the recordings can guess which emotion the speaker was trying to convey (Simon-Thomas et al., 2009). There may even be differences among positive emotion vocalizations (Simon-Thomas et al., 2009). For instance, laughter is a well-known vocal expression of emotion. Studies of people watching funny films show that there are several different types of laughs (Bachorowski, Smoski, & Owren, 2001). Some people grunt or snort, while others open their mouths with a big guffaw. Voiced laughs—those that involve vibration of the vocal fold and typically involve expelling air out of the mouth, such as when you talk—generate more positive ratings from people asked to evaluate them (compared to unvoiced laughs) on such features as likeability, sexiness, and friendliness (Bachorowski & Owren, 2001). Simply put, voiced laughs make people happy.

Vocal and facial responses systems can work together in emotion expression. The same vocalization can sound different, depending on the speaker's facial expression. This happens because lip movements affect vocal characteristics. For example, you can actually hear a smile or a frown, as people can reliably distinguish between laughs made with these various expressions on the face (Bachorowski, 1999).

People talk about different emotions differently as well (Habermas, Meier, & Mukhtar, 2009). For instance, people talk about negative emotions more specifically than they talk about positive emotions.

Emotions create expressive changes in the face and voice. What do you think Angelina Jolie's facial expression is expressing to her adversary?

This makes sense when you think about it. When people talk about their previous experiences being angry or upset, they are often trying to figure things out—what went wrong, how things could have gone differently, and how they might cope with the situation. Positive emotions rarely require as much processing. When is the last time you had a great time with a close friend in which you tried to figure out why you were so happy?

Subjective Changes   The third component of the emotional response is referred to as the **subjective experience of emotion,** which is the quality of our conscious experience during an emotional response. When people talk about how an emotion feels, they are referring to subjective experience. Each emotion creates a unique feeling: Anger feels different from sadness, which feels different from happiness. The subjective aspect of emotion draws on a person's experience of body changes as well as the effects emotions have on cognition, for emotions can activate associations with images and memories of significant events.

What produces subjective feelings of emotion? Perhaps the most influential theory was proposed by William James (1884) and Carl Lange (1885/1992). The **James–Lange theory of emotion** says that it is our perception of the physiological changes that accompany emotions that creates the subjective emotional experience. Without the perception of body changes, they argued, there is no emotional experience. Moreover, these changes that accompany different emotional states are unique. We experience fear as feeling different from sadness, for example, because we perceive different body changes for each emotion. In short, "I am trembling, and therefore I am afraid; or I feel a lump in my throat, and therefore I am sad."

Several lines of evidence support the James–Lange view. First, when people in many cultures are asked to identify the body sensations associated with emotions, they differentiate among several emotional states. For instance, "stomach sensations" are associated most strongly with disgust, far more so than with other emotions, and sadness with a lump in the throat (Breugelmans et al., 2005). Figure 11.19 presents an overview of the sensations that people participating in research studies report are associated with each emotion. In support of the idea that feedback from body sensations creates the subjective experience of emotion, people who pose on their faces the muscular movements of some emotion

subjective experience of emotion
the changes in the quality of our conscious experience that occur during emotional responses.

James–Lange theory of emotion
the idea that it is the perception of the physiological changes that accompany emotions that produces the subjective emotional experience.

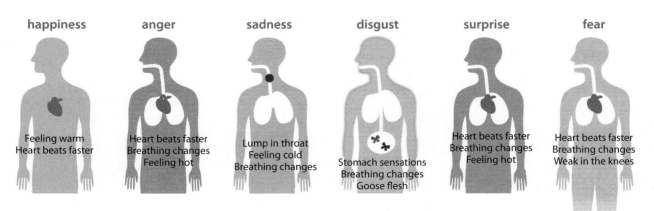

FIGURE 11.19
BODILY SENSATIONS ASSOCIATED WITH DIFFERENT EMOTIONS. (Source: Breugelmans et al., 2005)

expressions report feeling that emotion (Strack, Martin, & Stepper, 1988). Additionally, the better people pose facial expressions of emotion, the more intense the feeling (Ekman et al., 1983; Levenson et al., 1990).

Emotion and the Brain

So far we have examined the emotion process in detail, from the eliciting event to the appraisal mechanisms that bring forth the emotional response to the resulting changes in physiology, expression, and experience. Missing from this picture is the brain, which participates in every aspect of the emotion process.

Affective neuroscience, the field devoted to studying the brain's role in emotion, is a rapidly growing area of research. Most current evidence tells us that emotional information is processed in brain circuits that involve several brain structures, and emotional processing is highly interlinked with cognitive processing (Pessoa, 2008). Although there is no main emotion center in the brain, we can identify some key areas for emotion processing, including the amygdala and the prefrontal cortex (see Figure 11.20).

Anatomically, the amygdala has connections with many important brain regions, including structures that appear to be involved in emotion and memory: the hypothalamus, which controls the ANS; the hippocampus, which plays a crucial role in memory; the thalamus, which receives information from the sense organs; and the cerebral cortex. The amygdala appears to play a very important role in appraisal of the emotional significance of stimuli, with a specialized function for noticing fear-relevant information (Öhman, 2002; Phelps & LeDoux, 2005).

Much of the research on the amygdala has centered on its pivotal role in quick appraisals during threatening or fear-inducing situations (LeDoux, 1996, 2000). Along these lines, Joseph LeDoux and his colleagues have used classical conditioning of fear in rats as a model for studying emotion in the human brain (Wilensky et al., 2006). In their experiment, a rat is exposed to a tone, which is emotionally neutral at first. Then the tone is repeatedly paired with an aversive stimulus, an electric shock (the unconditioned stimulus, or UCS). After repeated pairings with the shock, the tone itself becomes a fear-eliciting stimulus (the conditioned stimulus, or CS). When the researchers examined the circuitry of fear conditioning in the rat brain, they found that the side and middle of the amygdala are most active in learning to be afraid of the tone (Wilensky et al., 2006).

There is evidence of the amygdala's role in fear in humans as well. People with damaged amygdalas do not show normal physiological reactions under fear conditioning. They tend to trust faces that most people find to be untrustworthy and have trouble recognizing facial expressions of fear, especially in the eyes (Adolphs et al., 1994, 2005; Adolphs, Tranel, & Damasio, 1998; Phelps & LeDoux, 2005). Brain imaging studies of people with intact brains reveal increased amygdala activation when they are exposed to fear faces, while the amygdala is not active when people view other facial expressions of emotion (Breiter et

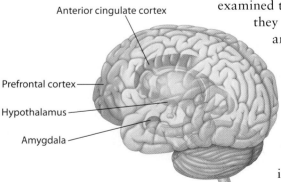

Anterior cingulate cortex

Prefrontal cortex

Hypothalamus

Amygdala

FIGURE **11.20**

FOUR MAIN REGIONS OF THE EMOTIONAL BRAIN. No single area of the brain is responsible for emotion, but the amygdala, prefrontal cortex, anterior cingulate cortex, and the hypothalamus play key roles in the way we experience emotion and remember emotional experiences.

al., 1996). Finally, although certain regions of the amygdala are more involved in fear, other regions are more involved in anger and rage (Panksepp, 2000). In fact, tumors of the amygdala have been found in violent criminals, such as in Charles Whitman, who climbed the tower at the University of Texas in 1966 and in a 90-minute shooting spree killed 19 people and wounded 38 (*Charles J. Whitman Catastrophe*, 1966, cited in Joseph, n.d.).

Connection

The prefrontal cortex plays a key role in working memory by evaluating sensory information and designating it for storage or disposal.

See "Pathways of Short-Term Memory in the Hippocampus and Prefrontal Cortex," Chapter 7, Memory, p. 286.

The case of Phineas Gage, the 19th-century railroad worker who survived a severe injury to his prefrontal cortex (see Chapter 3), provided early evidence of the importance of the prefrontal cortex in emotion and personality. Gage's prefrontal cortex injury transformed him from a relatively mild-mannered man into an impatient, easily enraged individual. More recently, studies show that the prefrontal cortex is one of the more active regions of the brain in the experience and appraisal of emotions. Damage to the left prefrontal cortex results in depression (P. L. Morris et al., 1996; Sackeim et al., 1982). According to EEG studies that measure cortical activity, clinically depressed people show less activity in the left prefrontal cortex than do nondepressed people (Davidson, 2001).

Moreover, due to its involvement in planning, impulse control, and working memory, the prefrontal cortex plays a role in the appraisal and reappraisal of emotion (B. L. Miller & Cummings, 1999; Miyake et al., 2000). Kevin Ochsner and his colleagues (2002) reported that the amygdala is more involved in determining whether a situation merits an emotional response at all, while the prefrontal cortex may be more involved in determining options for response or reappraisal. Given that there are neural connections between the prefrontal cortex and the amygdala, this finding and others like it may indicate that certain regions of the prefrontal cortex influence the emotional responses produced by the amygdala (Davidson, 2004; Pessoa, 2008; Pessoa, Padmala, & Morland, 2005).

Other regions of the brain are involved in emotions as well (Dalgleish, 2004). A meta-analysis of more than 55 brain imaging studies reports that the anterior cingulate cortex (ACC) is active when people either recall or imagine emotional experiences (Phan et al., 2002; also see Figure 11.20). The ACC is also the region of the brain that is active both in physical pain and in the pain of rejection or exclusion (Eisenberger et al., 2003).

What happens in the brain when we experience positive emotions? Several studies suggest that the left prefrontal cortex is more involved in positive emotions than the right (Davidson, 2004; Davidson et al., 1990). These regions are primarily involved in emotions that have approach components (emotions that impel the organism to move toward something or someone), which includes the negative emotion of anger as well as positive emotions (Harmon-Jones, 2003). The hypothalamus also appears to be a pleasure or reward center, because animals will forgo food and drink to receive stimulation there (Olds & Milner, 1954). Similarly, humans report feeling pleasure when this region is stimulated (Heath, 1975).

The neuropeptide oxytocin is well known for its role in lactation and bonding in mammals, especially females (A. Campbell, 2008). We now know that it plays a broad role in positive emotional states, especially those involving affiliation or connection with others (Lee et al., 2009). When adults are given doses of oxytocin, both males and females are more likely to want to be around other people (A. Campbell,

2008), to help others (Ebstein et al., 2010), to cooperate with others (Declerck, Boone, & Kiyonari, 2010), and to show greater generosity toward others (Zak, Stanton, & Ahmadi, 2007). Also, oxytocin makes people better at recognizing facial expression of happiness, but not the other emotions, especially for subtle expressions of happiness (which are harder to read). It's as if oxytocin enhances responsiveness to positive emotional states, especially when the information is subtle (Marsh, Yu, & Pine, 2010).

Connection

When you see someone you care about get hurt physically, it creates activity in the insula similar to the activity that occurs when you experience physical pain yourself.

See "Prosocial Behavior," Chapter 14, "Social Behavior," p. 572.

Finally, the insula is the brain structure most involved in interoception, or the perception of sensations arising within the body. As such, it plays an important role in emotional experience. In fMRI studies, the insula is active during the experience of pain and empathy for another's pain (Singer et al., 2004). This brain structure also appears to play an important role in disgust, which is an emotion associated with a high degree of internal bodily sensations. Visualizing disgusting scenes also leads to activation of the insula as well as the ACC (Schienle, Shafer, & Vaitl, 2008). Insular activity is reduced when women attempt to regulate their disgust with reappraisal (Goldin et al., 2008). In fact, certain areas of the insula are so specific to disgust that they show activation to facial expressions of disgust but not to those of distaste (von dem Hagen et al., 2009).

neurocultural theory of emotion

Ekman's explanation that some aspects of emotion, such as facial expressions and physiological changes associated with emotion, are universal and others, such as emotion regulation, are culturally derived.

How Culture Impacts Emotion Expression

The research on facial expression recognition from New Guinea led to an integration of the two competing perspectives, culture differences and universality. Soon after returning from New Guinea, Ekman (1972) proposed the **neurocultural theory of emotion** to account for the fact that certain aspects of emotion, such as the facial expressions and physiological changes of basic emotions, are similar in all humans, whereas other aspects, such as how people appraise situations and regulate their emotional expressions in front of others, vary from one culture to another.

Anthropologists have offered numerous examples of cultural variability in emotion expression—such as the case of Samurai women who smiled broadly after learning that their husband or son had died in battle (Ekman, 1973). Such examples suggest that facial expressions of happiness and sadness

Culture affects emotional expression in many ways. For many Japanese the inclination to refrain from the outward expression of certain painful emotions may have made it difficult for that nation to ask for or accept help from other nations in the wake of the tsunami-related devastation in 2011.

display rules
learned norms or rules, often taught very early, about when it is appropriate to express certain emotions and to whom one should show them.

are not universal. How can the findings on universality of facial expressions jibe with the fact that there are cultural differences in emotions? Ekman and Friesen (Ekman, 1972; Friesen, 1972) proposed the concept of display rules to address this dilemma. **Display rules** are learned norms or rules, often taught very early, about when it is appropriate to show certain expressions of emotion and to whom one should show them (Ekman, 1972). As it turns out, Samurai women were expected to be proud of a son or husband who had been killed in battle, and the society required them to display joy at the news. More mundane examples from daily life in the United States include the requirements that winners should not boast, losers should not mope, and men should not cry in public (although this last norm is changing).

The first empirical support for display rules came from a study comparing disgust expressions in American and Japanese students (Ekman, 1972; Friesen, 1972). Both groups viewed a film showing a very graphic medical procedure, but in two different conditions: in the presence of an authority figure and alone. When alone, both groups felt perfectly comfortable expressing the obvious response—disgust. When in the presence of an authority figure, however, the Japanese students did not show disgust, and they masked their responses with non-Duchenne (fake) smiles. American students, however, showed about the same level of disgust in both conditions. The expressive differences between groups emerged in a situation in which the cultures had very different norms about expression, but not in the solo viewing condition. More recent research on display rules and expression supports and extends these original findings (Matsumoto, Yu, & Fontaine, 2008). Overwhelmingly, however, people across many cultures show remarkably similar emotion displays in highly emotional situations—in the Olympics, for example (Matsumoto & Willingham, 2006).

Darwin (1872/1998) asserted that facial expressions evolved due to their functional role in survival. For instance, the expression of fear, with its raised brows and widely opened eyes, increased the scope of vision for someone looking for options for escape. Recent research shows that people posing fear faces actually see better in terms of tests of peripheral vision and quickness of eye movements. These appearance changes may actually reveal the function of the fear face hypothesized by Darwin—to enable people to respond more quickly to danger (Susskind et al., 2008).

There seem to be some universals in vocalizations of emotion, as well. Motherese, the sing-songy manner with which mothers speak to their babies, shows remarkable consistency worldwide and may be a unique adaptation particularly suited to infant perception (Fernald, 1992). Nonverbal vocalizations of emotions also seem to be recognized cross-culturally (Sauter et al., 2010). By nonverbal vocalizations we mean grunts, retching noises, laughs (for amusement). In a study using methods very similar to those Ekman used with preliterate New Guinea culture to classify facial expressions, Sauter and colleagues (2010) asked Namibians to match voices with the emotion stories that may have elicited them. Namibians and native English speakers made remarkably similar judgments, despite being from widely separate cultures.

In sum, when and how we express emotion on our face is determined both by innate, biologically determined factors and by culturally learned influences, such as display rules, that may vary from one culture to another. The evidence strongly suggests that all humans share a core set of basic facial expressions of emotion.

Nature&Nurture

When and how we express emotion is a function of both biological and cultural forces.

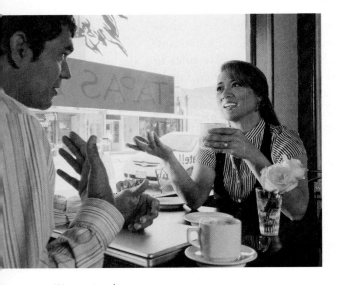

Women tend to talk about emotions more than men do, but there is little difference in the facial expressions of men and women during emotional experiences.

Gender and Emotion

If cultural factors can influence emotion expression, what about gender, which is both culturally and biologically driven? People all around the world think women are more emotional than men (Fischer & Manstead, 2000), but what do the data say? An overwhelming amount of data speak to no sex differences in emotion, but a few areas stand out as potential areas of difference: the verbal description of emotion, facial expression, and brain physiology.

The sexes differ in how they describe their emotional experiences in words. Women talk more about emotions than men do. In a study of older married couples discussing an area of conflict in their marriage, women were more likely to use words expressing distress and anger, whereas men were more likely to withdraw from conflict (Levenson, Carstensen, & Gottman, 1994). Women are more likely to describe their reactions to a particular experience with more refinement than men, using phrases such as "I felt angry and upset" rather than the more general phrase "I felt bad" (Barrett et al., 2000).

Women outperform men in accurately recognizing facial expressions of emotion, especially more subtle emotion expressions (Hall & Matsumoto, 2004; Hoffmann et al., 2010; Merten, 2005). This benefit may extend beyond just face recognition. Collignon and colleagues (2010) compared men and women in their processing of emotional information about fear and disgust from several channels of information: the face, voice, and both presented together. Women outperformed men in the recognition of emotion across all three modes of presentation. But this is emotion recognition. What about actual emotional behavior when one is experiencing emotions? In general, women smile more often than men (LaFrance, Hecht, & Paluk, 2003). Otherwise, there is very little evidence of consistent sex differences in the facial expression of emotion (J. J. Gross & John, 1998).

A few studies have noted sex differences in how the brain processes emotions. Exposure to pictures of animal or human attacks provokes greater amygdala activation in men than in women, which suggests a greater tendency toward aggressive action in men (Schienle et al., 2008). Also, during efforts to regulate emotion by cognitive reappraisal, men and women show different patterns of brain activation, which suggests men and women may use different brain areas to modulate their emotional responses (Domes et al., 2010). Further research is needed, however, to fully appreciate the meaning of these differences. Generally the similarities between the sexes in terms of emotion and the brain outweigh the differences (T. D. Wagner & Ochsner, 2005).

Emotional Intelligence

Culture and gender can shape emotional behavior, but there are individual differences in the way people use and regulate their emotions. These differences among people in emotional skills suggest the existence of an underlying emotional intelligence on which people vary, just as they vary in IQ.

In the mid-1990s Daniel Goleman published the book *Emotional Intelligence,* which popularized the idea that emotional skills are crucial in determining

emotional intelligence
the ability to recognize emotions in oneself and others, empathic understanding, and skills for regulating emotions in oneself and others.

how well one does in life—both professionally and personally. **Emotional intelligence** is the ability to recognize emotions in oneself and others, empathic understanding, and skills for regulating emotions in oneself and others, which may be at least as important to one's success in life as academic achievement. Goleman (1995) drew heavily on research by Peter Salovey and John Mayer, who introduced the concept of emotional intelligence in 1990 (Salovey & Mayer, 1990). The idea of emotional intelligence gained great popularity from Goleman's book, and psychologists quickly began to bring it into the real world.

One natural application of this work is in the field of education. Researchers have taught schoolchildren strategies for regulating emotion in order to reduce maladaptive behavior and improve academic performance; these strategies are referred to as *socioemotional learning*, or SEL (Conduct Problems Prevention Research Group, 1999a, 1999b; Kam, Greenberg, & Kusché, 2004). Typically, IQ is seen as the best predictor of school performance. We now know that training in emotional skills not only improves emotional behavior and functioning, but enhances cognitive performance and school performance as well (M. J. Hogan et al., 2010). One groundbreaking SEL program is PATHS (Providing Alternative Thinking Strategies), developed by Mark Greenberg and Carol Kusché (Greenberg & Kusché, 1998; Kusché & Greenberg, 1994). The PATHS program gives teachers a detailed curriculum for improving children's emotional awareness and regulation skills and enhancing their social competence. Research in which classrooms were randomly assigned to receive the PATHS curriculum or not (thereby continuing as usual) shows that PATHS leads to improvements in social and emotional skills in high-risk children, reduction of aggressive behaviors in both normal and special-needs children, fewer depressive symptoms in special-needs kids, and improvements in classroom functioning (Conduct Problems Prevention Research Group, 1999a, 1999b; Kam, Greenberg, & Kusché, 2004). Other prevention programs, such as Head Start, have also applied the theory and methods of emotion research to decrease behavior problems in schools, and initial results are promising (Izard et al., 2004).

More than a decade after the implementation of major SEL programs, it is possible to see how the development of socioemotional learning might be linked to academic success. A large-scale meta-analysis of more than 500 studies shows that SEL programs significantly improve children's academic performance (Durlak et al., 2007). Specifically, children who participate in these programs have better attendance and exhibit less disruptive classroom behavior; they like school more and have higher GPAs.

Emotional intelligence may be an enduring characteristic or skill—like other forms of intelligence, one that can be measured by questionnaire (much like IQ). There are even now several questionnaires designed to measure emotional intelligence, much as intelligence tests have traditionally been used to measure IQ. Two such instruments include the EQ-I (Bar-On, 2004) and the Mayer–Salovey–Caruso Emotional Intelligence Test, or MSCEIT (Mayer et al., 2003). With such tools, researchers can look at the relationship between emotional intelligence scores and other academic and nonacademic variables. Such trait measures of emotional intelligence correlate with higher GPA in adolescent boys and girls (M. J. Hogan et al., 2010), less job burnout in teachers (Platsidou, 2010), better coping with stress (Mikolajczak & Luminet, 2008), and improvements in mental and physical health (Schutte et al., 2007).

Quick Quiz 11.2: Emotion

1. The fact that sexual orgasm cannot occur unless the areas of the brain involved in fear and anxiety are shut down illustrates what basic feature of emotions versus drives?
   a. Drives have supremacy over emotions.
   b. Emotions can override biological drives.
   c. Emotions and drives serve similar masters.
   d. Drive must be resolved before emotions can motivate behavior.

2. Which of the following is *not* a self-conscious emotion?
   a. pride
   b. embarrassment
   c. resentment
   d. shame

3. According to the view of emotions as a process, _____ drive(s) the process by which emotions are elicited.
   a. emotional responses
   b. expressive changes
   c. physiological changes
   d. appraisal

4. Which of the following is not a basic emotion?
   a. fear
   b. happiness
   c. disgust
   d. shame

5. The social norm set forth by our culture which says that winners should not gloat is an example of a(n)
   a. display rule
   b. human universal
   c. affective trail
   d. antecedent event

6. The _____ appears to play a very important role in appraisal of the emotional significance of stimuli, with a specialized function for noticing fear-relevant information.
   a. amygdala
   b. hypothalamus
   c. prefrontal cortex
   d. insula

7. Which kind of emotion phrases are women more apt to use than men?
   a. more general comments, such as "I feel bad"
   b. more specific comments, such as "I am upset and angry"
   c. more affective imagery, such as "my fear is blue and cold"
   d. phrases such as "I will blow my top!"

Answers can be found at the end of the chapter.

life satisfaction
the overall evaluation we make of our lives and an aspect of subjective well-being.

subjective well-being
state that consists of life satisfaction, domain satisfactions, and positive and negative affect.

Bringing It All Together
Making Connections in Motivation and Emotion
Living a Satisfied Life

The word *happiness* often refers to a brief emotion, but it can also be used to mean a long-term sense of satisfaction with life. **Life satisfaction** is the overall evaluation we have of our lives (Diener et al., 1999). Psychologists consider life satisfaction to be a subset of **subjective well-being,** which also includes satisfaction in different domains, such as career, family, finances, and social networks. In this section

we discuss the pursuit of life satisfaction in the context of motivation and emotion.

Motivation and Happiness
Maslow's hierarchical model of motivation offers a useful framework for a discussion of motivation and happiness. Both basic and higher-level needs contribute to life satisfaction.

Basic Needs and Happiness

It is a well-known adage that money cannot buy happiness, but basic needs must be met for a person to be relatively satisfied with life. Accordingly, industrialized countries have higher levels of well-being than nonindustrialized countries, largely because those in industrialized nations, by and large, are more likely to have food and shelter (see Figure 11.21). In modern society, we require money to buy food, clothes, and shelter. But more and more money does not lead to more and more happiness. At a national level, in the early stages of a country's development, increased income makes people happier with their lives. After a relatively modest level of increased income, however, money makes little difference and may even be a hindrance to happiness. In general, the higher a country's GNP, the higher its well-being. But there are many exceptions, especially in Latin America. Countries like Mexico and Colombia are just as happy as countries like Denmark, Iceland, and Switzerland, in spite of having only half their per person GNP. Moreover, when absolute income rose in the United States from the late 1940s to the late 1990s, well-being and life satisfaction stayed constant (Diener & Seligman, 2004).

At the individual level, there is a modest and complex relationship between income and overall life satisfaction as well. Having more money does make people slightly happier, but this is true only for those driven by money (Diener et al., 1999; Nickerson et al., 2003). In fact, the relationship between spending money and happiness depends on whom you are spending for. In an experiment, people assigned randomly to spend money on others were happier than those who spend it on themselves (Dunn, Aknin, & Norton, 2008).

Diet and weight also relate to overall happiness in various ways. First, having a healthy diet is associated with high life satisfaction (Due et al., 1991; Valois et al., 2003). On the other hand, being overweight—having a body mass index higher than 25—is associated with low life satisfaction (Ball, Crawford, & Kenardy, 2004; Nieman et al., 2000; Sarlio-Lähteenkorva, 2001; Zullig, Pun, & Huebner, 2007). Second, long-term weight loss, which less than 10% of dieters are able to maintain, is related to increases in life satisfaction (Korkeila et al., 1998; Valois et al., 2003). Obese people who have had gastric bypass surgery experience enhanced well-being after their procedure (Bocchieri Riccardi, 2007).

Having a satisfying sex life can also be a source of overall happiness and well-being for people, just as problems in one's sex life can lead to overall problems in one's well-being. A worldwide survey of more than 27,000 men and women from 29 countries found a positive relationship between how happy people were in their lives in general and how happy they were in their sexual lives (Laumann et al., 2006). In general, subjective well-being and sexual satisfaction were highest in European and Western cultures (e.g., Germany, Austria, Spain, Canada, and the United States).

Higher Needs and Happiness

Once a person or a country crosses the $12,000 per person per year GNP, close relationships matter most for overall levels of happiness (Headey, 2008). This would explain why the Danes are consistently the happiest people on the planet. The Danish are a happy people who are more interested in fostering healthy relationships than in increasing their personal wealth or climbing the career ladder (Christensen et al., 2006).

Bruce Headey (2008) reported in a 20-year longitudinal study that people who value noncompetitive goals, such as spending time with a spouse, children, and friends, tend to

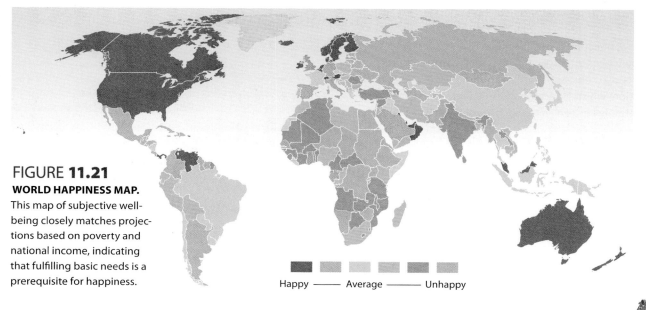

FIGURE 11.21
WORLD HAPPINESS MAP.
This map of subjective well-being closely matches projections based on poverty and national income, indicating that fulfilling basic needs is a prerequisite for happiness.

Happy ——— Average ——— Unhappy

become happier and more satisfied with life over time. However, people who most value competitive achievement goals, such as career advancement and material gains, actually decrease in happiness over time. Headey argues that when the main goal is monetary or advancing a career, all people have to look forward to after they achieve their goals is more competition and a greater pressure to achieve at an even higher level—not a recipe for happiness and well-being.

Another higher level need is the cognitive need to explore and understand the world. People who are curious and interested in exploring novel and challenging situations tend to be happier than people who would rather stick with what they know and not challenge themselves with new tasks and experiences (Diener et al., 1999; M. Gallagher & Lopez, 2007; Headey, 2008). This finding is consistent with the broaden-and-build model of positive emotion we discussed earlier, which assumes that positive emotional states lead to expansive thoughts and behavior rather than to a narrow focus. The connection between curiosity and openness to novel experiences on the one hand and life satisfaction on the other is also consistent with the optimal arousal theories of motivation, which assert that people seek out challenging and moderately arousing situations for optimal performance.

Emotions, Happiness, and Meaning in Life

A sense of well-being and satisfaction in life consists of the right balance of many different positive and negative emotions. In particular, the positive emotions can act as a buffer against long-term negative emotions. Happiness and life satisfaction are not about avoiding negative emotions, but rather about not dwelling on them. Sadness, anger, disgust, and even depression can happen to anyone. Some people are better able to regulate these emotions when they arise,

and not let negative moods persevere. In fact, people with higher scores on trait measures of emotional intelligence—part of which involves such skills in emotion regulation—tend to experience a greater sense of satisfaction in life, higher well-being, and even better mental health overall than those with lower scores on emotional intelligence (Schutte et al., 2010).

Psychological science shows that if we bring some degree of life satisfaction and positive emotions with us as we go through our more challenging life experiences, we are more likely to emerge happier and healthier than if we don't. For example, after the terrorist attacks in the United States on September 11, 2001, people who were resilient and prone to experience positive emotion and life satisfaction 6 months prior to 9/11 experienced more positive emotion in the weeks after the attacks and less depression in the months after the attacks (Fredrickson et al., 2003). Fostering positive emotion, even in the face of tragic and trying experiences, can reap long-term psychological and emotional benefits (Fredrickson & Joiner, 2002).

Similarly, people who find meaning in their lives in general and even in negative and tragic experiences are likely to be happier in life than those who do not see meaning and purpose in life's difficult and unpleasant experiences (L. A. King et al., 2006). Historically, the search for meaning has been associated with spirituality, which also appears to play a role in people's finding a lasting sense of well-being (Argyle, 2001; Holder, Coleman, & Wallace, 2010).

Digging deeper into what is really important seems key to finding happiness—whether you are spiritual or not. Exploring the important things in life implies stepping out of the daily humdrum and busy-ness of our daily existence and finding time for what really matters. Psychological science has recently turned its eye to what that entails, and a number of interesting findings are accumulating. One major theme is

"I've got the bowl, the bone, the big yard. I know I should be happy."
© 1992 Mike Twohy/The New Yorker Collection/cartoonbank.com

that if we stop and take stock of what we have to be thankful for, our sense of well-being improves dramatically over time. In fact, when both adults and adolescents are instructed to take a bit of time out each day to count their blessings, they become happier (Emmons & McCullough, 2003; Froh, Sefick, & Emmons, 2008). The key is to take out the time and notice—and to do this regularly.

As a nation we measure our wealth in terms of a statistic called the Gross National Product (GNP). GNP reflects the value in goods, services, and income produced by a country in 1 year. Worldwide, a high GNP is considered a sign of a country's economic success, but is it a good indicator of how successful a nation is? In 1972, the King of Bhutan decided to measure the wealth of his nation differently. In response to criticism that his country was poor, King Jigme Singye Wangchuk argued that, on the contrary, Bhutan is rich. This tiny Himalayan kingdom is steeped in spiritual practices that promote happiness and freedom from suffering for all beings. Although the king didn't intend to discount the role of economic growth, he emphasized that wealth ought to be measured in terms of happiness as well.

As an alternative to the GNP, King Wangchuk created the GNH, an indicator of Gross National Happiness. This measure reflects such national characteristics as access to health care, a clean nonpolluted environment, the amount of free time available for family, and other nonmonetary measures of well-being. GNH per person is measured by having people complete a survey to measure their sense of well-being in different contexts, from the workplace to the home. Imagine what it would be like to live in a country where the top priority was the happiness—not the financial wealth—of its citizens.

Quick Quiz 11.3: Bringing It All Together: Making Connections in Motivation and Emotion

1. Which of the following contribute to subjective well-being?
   a. negative emotions
   b. fulfillment of basic needs
   c. sexual satisfaction
   d. all of the above

2. People who are curious and interested in exploring novel and challenging situations tend to be
   a. about as smart as everyone else
   b. happier than those who have a narrow perspective
   c. smarter than narrow-minded people
   d. alienated from others

Answers can be found at the end of the chapter.

Chapter **Review**

MOTIVATION

- The psychology of motivation addresses the question of why people do what they do.

- Motivation encompasses needs, drives, and motivated behavior. Motives involve anything that energizes or directs behavior.

- Needs are states of cellular or bodily deficiency that compel drives, such as the need for water, food, and oxygen, while drives are the perceived state of tension that occurs when our bodies are deficient in some need—thirst, hunger, breathing.

- Maslow organized the various forces that drive human behavior in a vertical fashion, creating a hierarchy in which lower level biological needs are subordinate to higher level needs.

- Hunger is a basic drive that ensures that we take in sufficient nutrition to survive.

- Internal signals of hunger include sensations of the stomach and blood glucose levels, both of which are coordinated by sensors in the brain; external signals for hunger include the sight and smell of food as well as culturally influenced preferences.

- Eating disorders are complex and dangerous outcomes of a culture obsessed with thinness. At the same time, rates of obesity have increased dramatically over the last 50 years.

- Like all human motives, sexual desire results from a complex interplay of both biological and social forces.

- The hypothalamus plays an important role in sexual arousal.

- Hormones, especially testosterone, regulate sexual drive.

- Research on gender differences and casual sex tends to consistently find that males are more likely than females to engage in casual sex.

- Sexual orientation is a motive that involves both biological and social influences.

- One's tendency to achieve success is a function of three things: motivation to succeed, expectation of success, and the incentive value of the success.

- Motivation to work comes in three kinds: extrinsic motivators (rewards, money, positive feedback), intrinsic motivators (pleasure, joy, challenge, and autonomy), and organizational support (belief that the company cares about you and your well-being).

EMOTION

- Unlike the longer lasting moods and affective traits, emotions are acute, multifaceted responses to important events in our environment. Emotion can best be understood as a process that unfolds over time, beginning with exposure to an antecedent event, then appraisal. Appraisals determine whether an emotion occurs. Emotional responses include changes in behavior/expression, physiology, and subjective experience.

- Emotion regulation is an umbrella term for anything we do to try to change or otherwise manipulate the emotions we experience.

- From an evolutionary perspective, emotions function to organize body systems for a quick and efficient response to an important environmental event. This model applies best to negative emotions. Positive emotions, according to the broaden-and-build model, expand our thinking and help us develop knowledge and skills.

- The facial expressions of a set of basic emotions—anger, disgust, fear, happiness, sadness, and surprise—are recognized universally and appear to have evolutionary significance.

- Self-conscious emotions are a function of how well we live up to our expectations, the expectations of others, or the rules set by society and require a sense of self and the ability to reflect on one's own actions. Shame, guilt, humiliation, embarrassment, and pride are examples of self-conscious emotions.

- Display rules show how cultural factors can lead to differences in expression of emotion. Cultural variability is less apparent in the physiological changes associated with emotions.

- Physiological changes of negative emotions tend to be associated with higher arousal and activation of the sympathetic branch of the autonomic nervous system. Many physiological changes of positive emotions engage the parasympathetic nervous system to relax the body.

- Scientists are not sure what produces the subjective experience of emotion. The James–Lange theory holds that the perception of body changes plays an important role in a person's emotional experience.

- The brain is involved in every aspect of the emotion process, from appraisal to regulation. Although many brain structures appear to be crucial to emotions, the amygdala and the prefrontal cortex are major players.

- Men and women differ in how they talk about their emotional experiences, and women tend to smile more than men. The sexes, however, are much more similar than different in their emotionality.

- Emotional intelligence is the ability to recognize emotions in oneself and others, the development of empathic understanding, and skills for regulating emotions in oneself and others; it may be at least as important to one's success in life as academic achievement.

BRINGING IT ALL TOGETHER: MAKING CONNECTIONS IN MOTIVATION AND EMOTION

- Happiness, life satisfaction, and subjective well-being are not directly related to income. People who find meaning in their lives in general and even in negative and tragic experiences are likely to be happier in life compared to those who don't find meaning in the full range of human emotion.

Key **Terms**

Quick Quiz **Answers**

Quick Quiz 11.1: 1. b 2. c 3. b 4. a 5. c 6. b
Quick Quiz 11.2: 1. b 2. c 3. d 4. d 5. a 6. a 7. b
Quick Quiz 11.3: 1. d 2. b

Challenge Your Assumptions **Answers**

- Like animals, humans are driven by basic, biological needs. **True. See p. 427.**
- Even without a stomach, people still feel hungry. **True. See p. 431.**
- Most dieters would have been better off if they'd never dieted at all. **True. See p. 434.**
- People in different cultures have different facial expression of emotion. **False. See pp. 458–459.**
- More money leads to greater happiness. **False. See p. 469.**

Stress and Health

12

Chapter Outline

Challenge *Your Assumptions*

TRUE OR FALSE?

- Stress can make you sick.
- There is a gene for stress.
- Stress makes you age faster.
- People who are Type A are really anxious and high-strung.
- Exercising 10 minutes a day can change genes that increase your metabolism.

Answers can be found at the end of the chapter.

475

It seems that every semester when final exams roll around *something* happens to Dora's health. One year she had huge canker sore under her tongue and could hardly talk for a few days. Another time she had horrific headaches. Both problems occurred shortly after the most intense studying period of the semester, making it hard for her to concentrate on her exams.

Kyle has herpes, a virus that often remains dormant in the body but occasionally causes very painful and itchy sores. His outbreaks always seem to occur when he's been stressed out. Moreover, the more he worries about the possibility of an outbreak, the more likely he is to get one.

Estelle, 52, takes care of her 75-year-old mother who has advanced Alzheimer's disease. It is exhausting work, because her mother is losing the ability to perform many daily tasks (such as preparing food or bathing); and it is made worse because her mother's emotions have become very unpredictable. Confused from the disease, she yells at Estelle frequently and blames her daughter for her problems. Estelle has a hard time coping with this stress and finds herself drinking vodka for relief, far more often than she knows she should.

Each of these real-life cases highlights a kind of life stress and shows how stress might affect health. What causes stress, and what effects does stress have on us? Why do some people manage to see a situation as challenging rather than burdensome, while others don't? And can stress really make us sick?

In this chapter we examine the psychological and physiological nature of stress and the related topic of coping. We then survey some major topics in the field of health psychology, a discipline that emerged from an interest in the effects of stress on physical health. Throughout this chapter we will highlight how stress emerges from and modifies mental and physical processes, how differences in people's ability to deal with life's challenges influence the functioning of their bodies, and how these bodily responses can affect how people think and feel. Few other topics in psychology illustrate as clearly the interdependence of nature and nurture. ■

STRESS

The term *stress* can refer to a wide variety of phenomena. We speak of having a stressful life when the pressures of daily life interfere with our ability to maintain a sense of well-being. Sometimes people talk about "feeling stressed," as if stress were an emotional state, one that involves anxiety and exhaustion. Some people are "stressed" by minor events such as a parking ticket or a missed train, whereas others seem to sail through life amid a great number of demands—work, family, school—all the while maintaining a sense of well-being and balance.

stress
a response elicited when a situation overwhelms a person's perceived ability to meet the demands of a situation.

Stress occurs when a situation overwhelms a person's perceived ability to meet the demands of that situation. As with emotions, we evaluate our experiences of stressful situations and attempt to cope with the challenges they pose. Suppose, for example, you are doing poorly in a class, and you have the final exam in one week. At first, you feel stressed, but then you realize that with more review of the material, meeting with a study group, and more sleep, you could do better. You resolve to make these changes to improve your chances for a good final exam grade.

Driving, particularly in high-traffic urban areas, can elicit a stress response.

Stress as Stimulus or Response

Stress has different meanings in different contexts. We often think of stress as something that happens *to* us—that is, as situations that push us to the limit or threaten our safety or well-being. Or stress can be the relentless onslaught of difficulties, such as being late on a term paper, the car breaking down, realizing there is no money in the bank, and then getting into an argument with a roommate all in one week. We call these events that push us to the limit or exceed our ability to manage the situation at hand **stressors.** The focus on the situations that cause stress is known as the *stimulus view of stress.*

stressors
events that trigger a stress response.

In contrast, stress can be internal to us; we can think of it as the feeling we experience when events are too much to handle. The *response view of stress* focuses on the physiological changes that occur when someone encounters an excessively challenging situation. Later in the chapter, we explore Hans Selye's view of stress as a physiological response.

Clearly stress is much more than being in certain situations, and it is much more than physiological responses. Stress emerges from people's interpretations of the relevance of certain stressors to their lives and their ability to deal with them. This *relational view of stress* defines stress as a particular relationship between people and the situations in which they find themselves.

We will look briefly at the view of stress as a stimulus, which has dominated psychological research for many years. Then we will explore the relational view, before turning to the research on stress as a physiological response, which sets a foundation for our understanding of how stress can affect health.

Stress as a Stimulus   Some events demand an overwhelming amount of our energy and time. Any number of things can be stressors: unpleasant situations, such as divorce, financial troubles, or being sick; or pleasant situations, such as a wedding or the birth of a child. Psychologists measure stress as a stimulus by quantifying the number of stressors a person experiences during a given period. Two major categories of stressors are major life events and daily hassles.

Any situation that creates a major upheaval in a person's life might lead to stress. Indeed, one approach to measuring stress as a stimulus focuses on major life events. In the late 1960s, Thomas Holmes and Richard Rahe developed the Social Readjustment Rating Scale (SRRS), an instrument to quantify stress in terms of major life changes. This scale, shown in Figure 12.1, consists of a list of events that might be considered life changing; each is assigned a corresponding life change value. After a person has responded to the questions on the scale, a researcher can calculate the total amount of stress the respondent is experiencing by adding up relative stress values, which were derived from previous research, known as Life Change Units (Holmes & Rahe, 1967).

The SRRS is easy to administer and score, but it has some drawbacks. First, it ignores the fact that people view similar events differently. For instance, while some people might find marriage more stressful than a major work change, for others it may be vice versa (Scully, Tosi, & Banning, 2000). Second, by measuring stress in terms of life events, the SRRS fails to consider differences in people's emotional responses to stressors. Nevertheless, the SRRS is still widely used in research on stress and health, and it relates to measures of mental and physical health (Gottlieb & Green, 1984).

Life Event	Value
Death of spouse	100
Divorce	73
Marital separation	65
Jail term	63
Death of close family member	63
Personal injury or illness	53
Marriage	50
Fired from job	47
Marital reconciliation	45
Retirement	45
Change in health of family member	44
Pregnancy	40
Sex difficulties	39
Gain of a new family member	39
Business readjustment	39
Change in financial state	38
Death of a close friend	37
Change to a different line of work	36
Foreclosure of mortgage	30
Change in responsibilities at work	29
Son or daughter leaving home	29
Trouble with in-laws	29
Outstanding personal achievement	28
Wife begins or stops work	26
Begin or end school	26
Change in living conditions	25
Revision of personal habits	24
Trouble with boss	23
Change in residence	20
Change in school	20
Change in recreation	19
Change in church activities	19
Change in social activities	18
Change in sleeping habits	16
Change in eating habits	15
Vacation	13
Christmas	12
Minor legal violations	11

Sometimes little things really bother us. The accumulation of minor irritations—traffic, too much homework, relationship troubles—might wear us down, both mentally and physically. The Hassles and Uplifts Scale measures the frequency and intensity of minor irritations (hassles) and positive events of daily life that may counteract their damaging effects (Kanner et al., 1981). A number of studies report positive correlations between the frequency of daily hassles and self-reported health symptoms (DeLongis, Folkman, & Lazarus, 1988; Feist et al., 1995; Kohn, Lafreniere, & Gurevich, 1991). Some data indicate that hassles are more strongly related to health outcomes than are major life events (Kohn et al., 1991; Weinberger, Hiner, & Tierney, 1987).

A major limitation to measuring both major life events and hassles is that not all people view situations in the same way. For example, a poorly prepared student might dread an exam, but a student who has studied thoroughly might welcome it as a challenge. This example points to the ways in which people differ in their responses to situations. Using this logic, Lazarus and Folkman (1984) argued that because people do not view similar situations in the same way, it is misleading to examine stress solely in terms of the situations that may call it forth. We have to look at the person in relation to the situation.

FIGURE 12.1

SOCIAL READJUSTMENT RATING SCALE. Developed by Holmes and Rahe (1967), this scale quantifies stress in terms of major life changes. The higher the value, the greater the stress associated with an event.

Relationship Between Person and Situation

As we saw with emotion, when we first encounter a situation in our environment, we quickly appraise what it means for us. Lazarus and Folkman (1984) talk about two kinds of appraisal. **Primary appraisal** is an assessment of what a situation means to us. The outcome of this appraisal determines whether an emotional response might occur. If we view the event as personally irrelevant, we feel no emotion. If we view it as personally relevant, the event may be either contrary to or consistent with our goals or welfare. If we appraise it as contrary to our well-being, we feel a negative emotion, which might cause stress. If we appraise it as consistent with our well-being, we feel a positive emotion. Figure 12.2 on pages 480–481 depicts the process by which different appraisals lead to different emotional outcomes. Even though both pleasant and unpleasant *events* might lead to stress, stress emerges from negative emotional responses to events that we cannot get under control. Any kind of event—pleasant or unpleasant—might lead to such emotional reactions. For example, a wedding is a pleasant event that can be stressful.

Emotional events may escalate into stress when we cannot deal with the demands that the event entails. According to Lazarus and Folkman, we assess the resources available to cope with stress in a process called **secondary appraisal.** When we find ourselves in a stressful situation, we try to figure out what to do about that situation, how to resolve it, or how to make the unpleasant feeling it creates go away.

The Physiology of Stress

When we experience situations as stressful, physiological changes occur in our bodies. Most notably, the autonomic nervous system (ANS), the endocrine system, and the brain interact to create a range of changes in bodily systems.

The ANS, as discussed in Chapter 3, consists of all the neurons that serve the organs and the glands. Because it is linked to the body systems that support action, the ANS plays a crucial role in the stress response. These systems include the circulatory system, to pump blood to large muscle groups during times of emergency, and the respiratory system, to provide the oxygen required so that those muscles can function.

The second major system involved in stress is the endocrine system, which consists of the major hormone-releasing

primary appraisal
quick assessment of the meaning of a given environmental event for the individual.

Connection

Like stress, emotions are generated by our appraisals of events in our lives. How we evaluate the meaning of certain situations—whether a smile from a stranger or an upcoming exam—determines whether we feel threatened or joyful in response to that situation.
See "Emotion as a Process," Chapter 11, "Motivation and Emotion," p. 453.

Physiological changes that enable us to respond quickly during an emergency can take a toll on our bodies if stress persists.

secondary appraisal
self-assessment of the resources available to cope with stress.

FIGURE 12.2

THE EMOTION/STRESS PROCESS. When events are appraised as threatening, negative emotions occur. In this model, stress occurs only when negative emotion is sustained.

1 antecedent event

2 appraisal

neuroendocrine system
the hormonal systems involved in emotions and stress.

catecholamines
chemicals released from the adrenal glands that function as hormones and as neurotransmitters to control ANS activation.

glucocorticoids
hormones responsible for maintaining the activation of physiological systems during emergencies.

glands. The term **neuroendocrine system** refers to the hormonal systems involved in emotions and stress. The interactions among various organs, glands, and nervous system chemicals lay the groundwork for the dynamic interplay between psychological experience and physiological functioning.

The hypothalamus, the pituitary gland, and the adrenal glands are key structures in the neuroendocrine regulation of stress responses. The hypothalamus links the nervous system to parts of the endocrine system relevant to emotions: Hypothalamic neurons release chemicals that stimulate the release of hormones from the pituitary gland, which sits just beneath it and is connected to brain stem structures that control the ANS. The pituitary releases hormones that play a key role in the stress response. The adrenal glands, which sit atop the kidneys, release several stress-related hormones: the **catecholamines,** which control ANS activation, and the **glucocorticoids,** which maintain the activation of physiological systems during emergencies.

Once activated, the hypothalamus initiates a series of endocrine events that profoundly affect the body. Two major neuroendocrine pathways are activated: the adrenal-medullary system and the hypothalamus-pituitary-adrenal axis (see Figure 12.3). First in line is the **adrenal-medullary system,** in which

adrenal-medullary system
a major neuroendocrine pathway stimulated during stress, in which the hypothalamus activates the sympathetic nervous system.

FIGURE 12.3

THE HPA AXIS AND THE ADRENAL-MEDULLARY SYSTEM. During emotional arousal and stress, the hypothalamus activates the neuroendocrine system to prepare the body's response. The hypothalamus releases CRF, which stimulates the pituitary to release ACTH. ACTH then stimulates the cortex of the adrenal gland to release the "stress hormone" cortisol.

Stress

Hypothalamus

Corticotropin releasing factor (CRF)

HPA axis

Adrenal-medullary system

Pituitary gland

Autonomic nervous system (sympathetic division)

Adrenocorticotropic hormone (ACTH)

Adrenal medulla
Adrenal cortex

Secretion of cortisol
• Increases energy from storage
• Regulates immune system

Secretion of norepinephrine
• Increases heart rate
• Increases respiration
• Raises blood pressure

Beneficial to me → Positive emotion

Threatening to me →

③

Negative emotion → **stress**

Not relevant to me → No emotion

Connections

The sympathetic branch of the ANS activates the body; the parasympathetic branch calms the body. Both play a role in how the body responds to and recovers from stress.
See "The Nervous System," Chapter 3, "The Biology of Behavior," p. 82, and "Emotion as a Process," Chapter 11, "Motivation and Emotion," p. 453.

norepinephrine
a neurotransmitter that activates the sympathetic response to stress, increasing heart rate, rate of respiration, and blood pressure in support of rapid action.

hypothalamic-pituitary-adrenal (HPA) axis
a major neuroendocrine pathway relevant to the stress response involving the hypothalamus, pituitary gland, and the adrenal cortex.

cortisol
the stress hormone produced by the body to ensure that the body gets enough fuel during emotional arousal and stress.

the hypothalamus sends instructions to the brain stem to activate sympathetic neurons. Then sympathetic neurons tell the adrenal gland to release the important catecholamine **norepinephrine.** Norepinephrine activates the sympathetic response, increasing heart rate, rate of respiration, and blood pressure to make the body ready for action.

The sympathetic response evolved because rapid mobilization of the body's resources in emergency situations had clear survival and reproductive benefits. In cases of stress, however, this activation is prolonged. Moreover, if we live with prolonged stress-inducing situations, our body remains in "emergency mode" for long periods of time. Thus, a response that is adaptive in the short term can take a toll on the body in the long term, leading, for example, to sustained increases in blood pressure and heart rate. Think about how you feel when something startles you: Your heart races; you start breathing heavily; you're in a state of high alert. Now imagine what it would be like to remain in that condition for several days.

The other major neuroendocrine pathway in stress responses is the **hypothalamic-pituitary-adrenal (HPA) axis.** Recall that the hypothalamus releases substances, called releasing factors, that tell the pituitary when to release various hormones. During emotional arousal and stress, the hypothalamus releases a substance called corticotropin releasing factor (CRF), which stimulates the pituitary to release adrenocorticotropic hormone (ACTH). ACTH then stimulates the cortex of the adrenal gland to release **cortisol,** the major glucocorticoid produced in humans, which is commonly known as the "stress hormone." When the level of cortisol in the blood adequately meets the body's metabolic needs, the hypothalamus stops releasing CRF, thereby reducing the release of cortisol. This kind of negative feedback occurs throughout the neuroendocrine system.

Cortisol has many important functions. It plays a role in the breakdown of complex molecules into simpler ones to release energy and so plays an important role in ensuring that more glucose is available for fuel in the bloodstream (Rose, Vegiopoulos, & Herzig, 2010). Cortisol also regulates the immune system, by reducing the number of immune cells in the bloodstream. In so doing, cortisol can suppress the immune system's ability to protect the body against infection (Segerstrom & Miller, 2004).

The General Adaptation Syndrome (GAS) In 1946, Austrian physiologist Hans Selye proposed a three-stage model to describe the changes in physiology that occur during exposure to severe stressors. Selye believed that attempts to adapt to overwhelming stressors cause the body to wear down and eventually get sick. With homeostasis as his starting point, Selye viewed the changes that the body goes through when confronted with extreme situational demands as manifestations of adaptation to stress. He exposed animals to stressors such as extreme temperature change, severe electrical shock, radiation, or heavy exercise (Selye, 1976).

Selye proposed that all stress causes a generalized, nonspecific set of changes in the body—no matter what the type of elicitor. He measured hormones, metabolism, organ function, and other variables and observed a consistent pattern of responses regardless of the stressor. Selye (1946) coined the term **general adaptation syndrome** (GAS) to describe this general pattern of responses to prolonged exposure to stress.

The GAS consists of three stages: alarm, resistance, and exhaustion (see Figure 12.4). Upon exposure to a stressor, an animal enters into a state of physiological shock, called the **alarm stage,** which is the body's emergency response to a threat. The alarm stage mobilizes the body's resources to act via the effects of adrenal-medullary activation of the sympathetic nervous system. During this stage the HPA axis is active as well, and the sustained release of cortisol from the adrenal glands may move from being helpful (by making more fuel available) to being harmful in the long run (by suppressing certain aspects of immune function).

Animals, however, cannot persist in the alarm stage for long. With continued exposure to the stressor, they will either die or find other ways of coping with the enduring threat. When they develop other ways to cope, they enter the second stage of adaptation, the **resistance stage.** Resistance implies that the organism tries to manage the threat. This extended effort, however, takes its toll physically and psychologically by diverting resources from maintenance of normal body functions.

general adaptation syndrome (GAS) as defined by Hans Selye, a generalized, nonspecific set of changes in the body that occur during extreme stress.

resistance stage in the general adaptation syndrome, extended effort by the body to deal with a threat.

alarm stage the phase of the general adaptation syndrome in which all of the body's resources respond to a perceived threat.

FIGURE **12.4**

SELYE'S GENERAL ADAPTATION SYNDROME (GAS). In the alarm stage, the body's resources are mobilized in response to a stressor. Resistance occurs when the body can no longer sustain the emergency response and the organism must find other ways to ward off the threat. If the threat persists, eventually the body's resources become depleted, physical exhaustion occurs, and illness becomes much more likely.

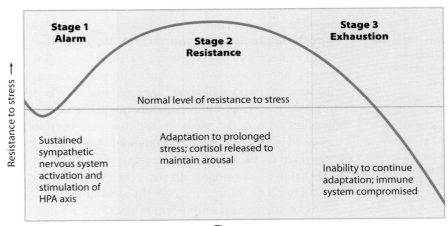

Stage 1 Alarm

Stage 2 Resistance

Stage 3 Exhaustion

Resistance to stress

Normal level of resistance to stress

Sustained sympathetic nervous system activation and stimulation of HPA axis

Adaptation to prolonged stress; cortisol released to maintain arousal

Inability to continue adaptation; immune system compromised

Time →

exhaustion
stage
the phase of the
general adapta-
tion syndrome
when all resources
for fighting the
threat have been
depleted and ill-
ness is more likely.

Resistance cannot be maintained indefinitely. With repeated exposure to a stressor, animals enter the **exhaustion stage.** At this stage, their resources for fighting off threats have been depleted, and illness becomes much more likely. Have you ever come down with a cold or other illness a week or so after final exams? You get the idea.

Selye's model laid the groundwork for research on the physiology of stress, but soon it became clear that his GAS model did not fit all stress responses. First, Selye studied extreme physical stressors, such as nearly freezing an animal to death or repeatedly exposing it to severe electrical shock, and subjected animals to these stressors for prolonged periods. Questions arose as to whether the body changes that occurred in response to such severe demands in animals provided a good model for enduring the stress of, say, divorce or financial troubles in humans. Second, some research-ers questioned the idea that a syndrome of body responses to stress occurred regardless of the type of stressor.

Stress isn't unique to humans. Other species, like this oil-covered survivor of Hurricane Katrina, also experience a physiological reaction in response to stressful situations.

Connection

Do you think an ethics review board would allow Selye to conduct his research on extreme stressors in animals today? Why or why not?
See "Ethical Research With Animals," Chapter 2, "Conducting Research in Psychology," p. 68.

In the 1970s, research challenged Selye's assumption that the stress response is a general one. Mason (1971, 1975) showed that an animal's response to a stressor differed depending on its psychological state. If the animal could anticipate a stressor, for example, it showed a less severe physiological response than an animal that could not anticipate a stressor (Mason, 1971). Further, research conducted during the 1980s showed that dif-ferent emotions produce different patterns of ANS activation, casting further doubt on Selye's idea of a generalized physiological response to any environmen-tal demand (Ekman, Levenson, & Friesen, 1983).

How We Adapt to Stress   Most accounts of the physiology of stress (such as Selye's) think of stress as a deviation from balance. Recovery from stress occurs when all systems return to normal. This view stems from the notion of homeostasis—the idea that unless we are being provoked by something, we are humming along at an even-keeled *baseline* state, and we return to that same state after the stress. Moreover, homeostasis implies that just one system in the body struggles to return to baseline at a time (*homeo-* means "same"). For exam-ple, suppose you are walking in a desert: The homeostasis view says that you would sweat to cool your body to return to an ideal temperature. If you think about it for a minute, you'll realize that this is not ideal. If your body did this, you would become dehy-drated (Sapolsky, 1998). So a new concept was needed to explain the more complex and dynamic changes that occur when the body is stressed.

Connection

The concept of homeosta-sis is key to drive theories of motivation. It is used to explain why and when people get motivated to eat, drink, or have sex. When your body is below an ideal point, you need more. When it is above, you need less.
See "Emotion," Chapter 11, "Motivation and Emotion," p. 449.

allostasis
process by which
the body achieves
stability through
physiological
change.

Some researchers offer an alternative explanation to how we adapt to stress. Rather than a state of balance, they say, our normal state is one of actively responding to the world around us. This more dynamic, responsive "resting" state is known as **allostasis,** which means that the body achieves stability through change (Schulkin, 2005; Sterling & Eyer, 1988). *Allo* means "different"

or "changing." Thinking of the baseline state as one of dynamic responsiveness makes it easier to understand the effects of stress on the body (Juster, McEwen & Lupien, 2010). Back to the example of walking in the desert: The concept of allostasis emphasizes that your body would respond in many ways, not simply by sweating. Your kidneys would start producing less; mucous membranes in your eyes and skin would dry out; even your veins and arteries would constrict to maintain blood pressure with a smaller volume of blood. The concept of allostasis makes clear that our bodies can respond adaptively to challenge for only a short period of time. If we are pushed too long, the body's active attempts to adapt are sustained, and we are taxed. The body starts to wear down. This is how stress causes illness.

Stress and the Brain

So far we have emphasized how stress affects a wide array of physiological responses, most of which involve systems outside the central nervous system. What about the brain? We tend to think of stress as being caused by processes within the brain, for it is our interpretations of the events in the world around us that trigger emotions. But the physiological activation triggered by stress also affects the brain. Cortisol has a profound effect on the hippocampus, a brain structure that plays a pivotal role in memory. It turns out that the hippocampus also contains one of the greatest concentrations of cortisol receptors in the brain (McEwen, De Kloet, & Rostene, 1986). Unfortunately, stress-related cortisol release causes hippocampal dendrites to shrink, which can interfere with several types of memory. Stress also reduces neurogenesis in the hippocampus, and it may inhibit the synaptic plasticity in the hippocampus and neocortex, impacting learning and memory formation (Artola, 2008; Wang et al., 2008). Animal research shows that excessive stress in a pregnant mother can affect the development of several brain areas— including the amygdala, hippocampus, hypothalamus, and corpus callosum—in her offspring (Charil et al., 2010).

Connections

The hippocampus, located deep inside the brain, is critical for memory formation. See "Overview of Brain Regions," Chapter 3, "The Biology of Behavior," p. 96; and "Pathways of Short-Term Memory in the Hippocampus and Prefrontal Cortex," Chapter 7, "Memory," p. 286.

Coping plays a big role in the duration of stress responses and whether they develop sufficiently to become harmful to the brain and body. In monkeys, more effective coping with stress increases neurogenesis in the hippocampus, which offers the hopeful suggestion that the adverse effects of stress on the brain may be reversible (Lyons et al., 2010). In a fascinating new study of rats, researchers found that increased experience with sex—even chronic exposure to sex—also increases neurogenesis in the hippocampus (Leuner, Glasper, & Gould, 2010)!

Stress and Genes

No single "stress gene" dictates how the body responds to stress in the way a cancer gene might turn cancer cells on and off. Instead, several complex processes involving stress, genes, and endocrines regulate the relationship between stress and disease (Cole, 2009, 2010). From this complex area of research, we can distill out a few key points. First, the effects of chronic social isolation on illness appear to be regulated by genetic factors (Cole 2010; Cole et al., 2007). Also, those genes associated with the human stress response seem critical to certain chronic diseases (Capri et al., 2006). Finally, genes appear to play a role in the relationship between the stress of social isolation and diseases that involve inflammatory processes, such as heart disease and cancer (Cole et al., 2010; Khatami, 2009; Miller et al., 2009).

Quick Quiz 12.1: Stress

1. According to the definition provided in the text, which of the following is the best example of stress?
   a. Maria is studying for one exam.
   b. Maria is studying for three exams on the same day, but she has a handle on all three.
   c. Maria is studying for two exams on the same day and feels unprepared for both of them.
   d. Maria is angry with her boyfriend.
2. This view of stress focuses on the physiological changes that occur when someone encounters an excessively challenging situation.
   a. Stimulus
   b. Response
   c. Relational
   d. Situational
3. The model of adaptation that says there is stability through change is the
   a. functional view
   b. physiological view
   c. homeostatic view
   d. allostatic view
4. Which part of the nervous system becomes most involved when we are feeling stressed?
   a. hypothalamic-pituitary-adrenal (HPA) axis
   b. temporal lobes
   c. hippocampus
   d. frontal lobes

Answers can be found at the end of the chapter.

COPING

coping
act of dealing with stress or emotions.

Generally, **coping** refers to anything people do to deal with or manage stress or emotions. When we walk away from someone who is making us angry or complain about our boss to a friend, we are coping with stresses in our lives. In this section we explore various ways people cope with stress.

Coping Strategies

People don't like feeling bad. So they try to get out of situations that create unpleasantness or look for ways to change their negative feelings. Psychologists Richard Lazarus and Susan Folkman (1984) differentiated between these two types of coping strategies, labeling them *problem-focused* and *emotion-focused* coping. Social support combines problem-focused and emotion-focused coping strategies. Figure 12.5 provides an overview of these three coping strategies.

problem-focused coping
way of dealing with stress that aims to change the situation that is creating stress.

Problem-Focused Coping   **Problem-focused coping** strategies aim to change the situation that is creating stress. For example, if your roommate plays a stereo loudly while you are sleeping, you might choose to discuss it with her, buy earplugs, or cut the speaker wires. Each of these choices is a form of problem-focused coping; each is geared toward changing the situation that created the stress. Examples of problem-focused coping strategies include devising a plan to solve the problem, seeking social support as a way to gather information, and taking assertive action. Problem-focused coping focuses attention on the stress-provoking situation, and we are most likely to use it when we think we can change the situation.

emotion-focused coping
way of dealing with stress that aims to regulate the experience of distress.

Emotion-Focused Coping   In contrast, **emotion-focused coping** aims to regulate the experience of distress. Lazarus and Folkman describe several forms of emotion-focused coping, including *reappraisal,* the reevaluation

Strategy	Example
problem-focused strategy	Solve the problem Seek social support Take assertive action	Roommate's stereo too loud: Focus on how to make it quiet. An assertive act might be to cut the stereo speaker wires.
emotion-focused strategy	Reappraise Distancing Use escape-avoidance Seek social support Exercise self-control Emotional disclosure	Breakup with a partner: Focus on how to feel better. An escape-avoidance act may be to take a vacation to get away from the former partner. Write about it to unburden emotions.
social support strategy	Combines problem-focused and emotion-focused strategies Develop social connectedness Seek advice from or talk with friends and loved ones	Support groups: Giving and showing support to other people may increase longevity.

FIGURE **12.5**

COPING STRATEGIES. We tend to apply problem-focused coping strategies to change a stressful situation and emotion-focused coping strategies in situations that we feel we cannot control.

of a situation in light of new information or additional thought; *distancing,* or attempting to separate oneself from an emotional experience; *escape–avoidance,* wishful thinking or doing something to get one's mind off the situation (such as going to the movies); *seeking social support* by talking with friends for purposes of emotional support; *self-control,* or trying to regulate one's feelings or actions regarding the problem; and *accepting responsibility,* acknowledging one's role in the stress-eliciting situation (Lazarus & Folkman, 1984).

When a situation is beyond one's control, certain types of emotion-focused coping—especially reappraisal—can be helpful in regulating the emotional aspects of stress. But other kinds of emotion-focused coping can be problematic. Willful suppression of upsetting emotions, which is a form of self-control, can lead to chronic physiological arousal and is associated with poor psychological adjustment (J. J. Gross & Levenson, 1993; J. J. Gross, Richards, & John, 2006). Moreover, some strategies that we use to reduce the experience of distress, such as drinking, smoking, and other forms of drug use, may be maladaptive (Hien & Miele, 2003).

It is widely believed that a good way to cope with stress is to "let it all out." James Pennebaker developed a technique known as **emotional disclosure** that enables people to unburden (Pennebaker, 1995). In a typical emotional disclosure task, people are instructed to write for about 15 minutes about a recent emotional experience—in particular, one that they have found troubling, that still bothers them from time to time, and that they haven't discussed much with other people. Participants in the control condition write for a similar amount of time about nonemotional events, such as what they did the day before. Emotional disclosure improves a number of health outcomes, including health variables related to HIV/AIDS, immune function, and cancer (O'Cleirigh et al., 2008; Petrie et al., 2004;

emotional disclosure

way of coping with stress through writing or talking about the situation.

Smyth, 1998; Stanton et al., 2002). A few studies, such as a recent large-scale study of women seeking fertility treatment, show that disclosure did not benefit health outcomes, however (Panagopoulou, Montgomery, & Tarlatzis, 2010).

How might writing about one's emotional experiences, especially traumatic ones, benefit health? There are several possible explanations. People in both Western and non-Western cultures believe that confession is beneficial. For the Ndembu of West Africa, for instance, public confession allows for the transformation of negative feelings into positive ones in the community, thereby promoting social harmony (Georges, 1995). It is also thought that *not* working through difficult emotions taxes the body, as research on the association between emotional suppression and ANS arousal suggests (J. J. Gross & Levenson, 1993). When confession or disclosure occurs, then, one should observe a decrease in sympathetic nervous system activation or a return to a more relaxed state. In fact, numerous laboratory studies have found that just talking about a traumatic event creates noticeable reductions in autonomic measures such as blood pressure and sweating (Pennebaker, 1995). Writing about positive experiences also benefits mental and physical health, presumably by other mechanisms, such as helping the person maintain a broader focus on life (Burton & King, 2009).

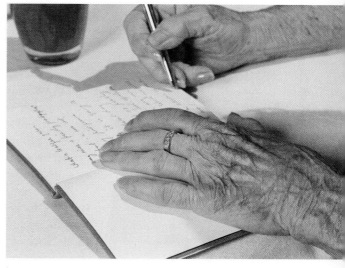

Writing about a stressful experience is one way of working through the negative emotions associated with it.

Connection

Emotion regulation is another term for the strategies we use to alter our emotional state and is similar to emotion-focused coping. Both terms refer to efforts to change the way we feel.

See "Emotion as a Process," Chapter 11, "Motivation and Emotion," p. 453.

Research to Real Life

You know how some days you feel really stressed? What does that really mean?

Connecting Psychology to Your Life: Start paying attention to what is going on and why you feel stressed. Is it simply because you have a lot of work, assignments, or tests coming up? Or is something important going on in your personal life (problems with boyfriend or girlfriend, money trouble)? Or is it all of these kinds of things? For one day, on your phone or a notepad, record what is going on when you feel stressed. What is the situation or stressor? Also, try to indicate what the "stress" feels like in terms of emotions, changes in your body, and so on. Are you anxious or irritated? Is your heart racing? Note these sorts of sensations.

At the end of the day, look back at these events and your reactions to them and see whether you could have responded differently to the stressor, in a way that might have had a different emotional effect. For instance, what if you interpreted (appraised) your professor's moving a test date up to Friday instead of Monday as an opportunity to have more free time on the weekend rather than as unfairly restricting your study time before the test?

If you check in with yourself, you can gain insight on what stresses you out, how stress makes you feel, and the opportunity for reappraising a situation when you encounter it next time so that it is not so stressful for you.

Social Support Social support is a coping strategy that combines problem- and emotion-focused coping. Our friends and loved ones provide advice, give hugs, or simply listen when we are under stress. Social support not only is one of the most frequently used ways of coping but also can benefit physical health. The *direct effects hypothesis* states that social support is beneficial to mental and physical health whether or not the person is under stress. Sheldon Cohen (2004) has pointed out that being part of a social network guarantees the availability of certain resources. Our social networks may offer guidelines for health-related behaviors, help us regulate our emotions, and give us a sense of identity. We may learn from friends, for instance, that running or jogging can help us feel better when we're stressed. Examples of social connectedness include being married, belonging to social groups such as churches or clubs, and having many friends. Friends provide an outlet for sharing emotional distress, offering comfort as well as advice.

Alternatively, social support may buffer the impact of stress. This is known as the *buffering hypothesis*, which states that social support works as a buffer only under certain conditions, such as a highly stressful life. In fact, one influential study found that regular participation in a support group in which members discussed their emotional difficulties improved well-being and extended survival in women with advanced breast cancer (Spiegel et al., 1989), though this finding has not replicated consistently (Edelman et al., 1999; Edmonds, Lockwood, & Cunningham, 1999; Goodwin, 2004; Goodwin et al., 2001).

How well a person is integrated into a *social network* influences health. A social network is simply a cluster of related people, such as family members, spouses, friends, coworkers, or neighbors. This web of friends and acquaintances is related to but not the same as an electronic social network, such as the kind you might have on Facebook. When people are well integrated into a social network, social support can buffer the effects of stress by providing interpersonal resources for emotional support and problem solving (S. Cohen & Wills, 1985). The health benefits of social connectedness include longer life and reduced susceptibility to colds (Berkman & Glass, 2000; S. Cohen et al., 2003). A recent study that followed more than 12,000 people over 32 years examined the role of social networks in quitting smoking (Christakis & Fowler, 2008). Social networks influenced the likelihood that a person would stop smoking, but not all social connections had the same effect. If a spouse stopped smoking, the chance the other spouse would also stop went up by 67%; if a friend stopped smoking, the chance another friend stopped went up by 36%; and if a coworker stopped smoking, the chance another worker stopped went up by 34%. So the effect of the other person's behavior on any given person depended to some extent on how close they were to each other.

Social networks may be harmful to health as well. For instance, in a study of 12,000 people, researchers looked at the influence of obesity in the same social network. The risk of obesity spread among people who were socially connected. In other words, if a person became obese (with a body mass index, or BMI, greater than 30), his or her friends, family members, spouse, or neighbors were more likely to become obese. As was true with smoking, however, not all social connections had the same effect. For instance, if a person's friend became obese over a given period of time, that person's chance of becoming obese increased 57%; if a sibling became obese, the chance increased 40%; and if a spouse became obese, the chance increased 37% (Christakis & Fowler, 2007). Moreover, gender mattered. Individuals of the same gender in a social network influenced same-sexed individuals more than opposite-sexed individuals. In another study, infectious diseases (such as the flu) spread more rapidly among connected individuals than they did among randomly studied groups of people (Christakis & Fowler, 2010). This undesirable aspect of social networks, however, might help in the detection and prevention of further outbreaks.

Social resources clearly play a role in health-related behavior and how we manage stress, but so do our own personal resources. Life is not just a course in stress management, but rather a daily journey through a series of joys as well as challenges.

The Positive Psychology of Coping

Traditionally, research on stress and coping has focused on how people respond to threatening situations and manage the distress associated with them. For years, however, some psychologists have argued that it is an oversimplification to assume that stress involves only negative emotions and their management (Folkman & Moskowitz, 2000; Lazarus, Kanner, & Folkman, 1980; Seligman & Csikszentmihalyi, 2000). This section discusses various ways in which positive psychological states have been studied in relation to stress and coping.

Positive Traits, Positive Emotions
Some people approach the world in a positive way, and as a result their experience of distress is reduced compared to that of others. *Optimists* tend to emphasize the positive, see the glass as "half full" rather than as "half empty," and believe that things will turn out well (Carver, Scheier, & Sergerstrom, 2010). *Pessimists,* by contrast, emphasize the negative; for them, the glass is always half empty and the future uncertain. Optimists are less likely to feel helpless or depressed, adjust better to negative life events, and show better general mental health than do pessimists (Chang, 1998; Smith, Young, & Lee, 2004). Optimism may also benefit physical health (Kubzansky et al., 2001). By seeing the world positively, optimists may appraise events in such a way that negative emotions are less likely and positive emotions more likely. They may be more likely to see potentially stressful situations as challenges rather than threats. Research shows that the more optimistic a person is, the less likely it is that he or she will die from cardiovascular disease (Giltay et al., 2004). Furthermore, changes in optimism are related to changes in positive emotion that predict immune function (Sergerstrom & Sephton, 2010). Surprisingly, believing that you have some control over situations in life, especially traumatic situations, can improve your psychological health (Taylor, 1989). Health psychologist Shelley Taylor has studied various groups of people suffering from chronic, debilitating, and often fatal diseases such as breast cancer, heart disease, and HIV/ AIDS. She has found that people who believe they have some control over their illness—in spite of medical evidence to the contrary—are actually happier and less stressed than less optimistic people with the same diseases (Hegelson & Taylor, 1993; Reed et al., 1994; Taylor, 1989). As it turns out, these perceptions of control provide the greatest benefits in situations that are severe or uncontrollable (Taylor et al., 2000). Positive emotions may facilitate recovery from the physiological effects of negative emotions. Fredrickson and Levenson (1998) showed participants a fear-eliciting film and followed it with a sad, pleasant, or neutral film and measured cardiovascular activity throughout the film-viewing and postfilm-viewing period. Cardiovascular activation elicited by the fear film returned

to baseline levels more quickly in people who saw the pleasant film after the fear film, but not in people experiencing the sad or neutral conditions. So positive emotions may help the body return to a state of calmness. In fact, research is pointing to a number of potentially beneficial effects of positive emotion on the body—such as lowering blood pressure and regulating cortisol—that we are just beginning to understand (Dockray & Steptoe, 2010).

Tugade and Fredrickson (2004) looked at how resilience affected people's ability to recover from stress. *Resilience* is a personality trait that means being more flexible and able to bounce back from difficult situations. Resilient people experience quicker recovery from stress-induced cardiovascular arousal, in part because they are more likely to find some positive meaning in a difficult situation (Tugade & Fredrickson, 2004).

Finding Meaning   Perhaps the key to psychological health is to be open enough to notice the other things going on in life, even in the midst of tragedy. Positive psychological traits and states do play a big role in whether people are able to find meaning in stressful and tragic events (Folkman, 1997; Folkman & Moskowitz, 2000; Park & Folkman, 1997; Tugade & Fredrickson, 2004). People with terminal illnesses who notice beauty amidst their pain and find opportunities for positive experiences are happier than those who don't, and they may even live longer (Folkman, 1997; Moskowitz, 2003). As we mentioned in Chapter 11, resilient people who managed to experience positive moods amidst their despair in the wake of the September 11, 2001, terrorist attacks were more likely to thrive and less likely to fall into depression than those who were less resilient (Fredrickson et al., 2003). A fascinating set of studies by Elissa Epel and her colleagues reveals some of the connections between biology and environment that play a role in people's responses to stress and their effects on health. In the next "Psychology in the Real World," we describe how Epel and her colleagues (2004; Jacobs et al., 2010) demonstrated that stress affects aging at the cellular level.

Nature & Nurture

Stress makes your cells age more rapidly.

Quick Quiz 12.2: Coping

1. You buy earplugs so you can sleep when your roommate plays loud music at 1:00 a.m. You have used what kind of coping?
   a. problem-focused
   b. emotion-focused
   c. stimulus-focused
   d. meaning-focused

2. Research has found that having a well-connected social network of friends, family, neighbors, and coworkers is _____ for health outcomes.
   a. never beneficial
   b. sometimes beneficial
   c. sometimes beneficial and sometimes harmful
   d. always beneficial

3. Seeing the "glass as half full," or being optimistic, is likely to have what kind of effect on a person's response to stress and illness?
   a. no real effect
   b. negative effect
   c. positive effect
   d. the same effect as being pessimistic would

4. Who would be most likely to bounce back quickly from a very stressful experience?
   a. a pessimist
   b. a young person
   c. someone who holds in his or her feelings and pretends the event did not happen
   d. a resilient person

Answers can be found at the end of the chapter.

Effects of Chronic Stress on Aging

Stress often makes people look worn out. As mentioned earlier, this is one of Selye's main ideas: Physiologically, long-term stress wears down the body, making a person more vulnerable to illness (the exhaustion stage). People often refer to the stresses of life as wearing them out or causing gray hairs. Is there any evidence, however, that this everyday logic has any basis in the physiology of aging? Can stress actually make you age more quickly?

In an innovative study of the physiological effects of stress, psychologist Elissa Epel and her colleagues examined indicators of cellular aging in healthy women who were biological mothers of either normal or chronically ill children. The mothers reported on the amount of stress they perceived in their daily lives, using a standard questionnaire.

The researchers derived indicators of cellular aging from tests on blood samples collected from each woman. In particular, they examined the telomeres of chromosomes in the DNA of certain white blood cells. *Telomeres* are part of the chromosome involved in replication during the process of cell division. With age, telomeres shorten; moreover, the activity of **telomerase,** an enzyme that adds DNA sequences to telomeres, decreases with age. Both of these variables are good measures of aging.

Epel and her colleagues measured stress not in terms of life conditions per se but in terms of the duration of stress a woman *perceived* in her life; results showed that the more stress a woman perceived, the shorter the telomeres and the lower the level of telomerase activity in her blood, conditions that imply older cells. In practical terms, these women's cells were "the equivalent of 9–17 additional years" older than those of women who perceived less stress (Epel et al., 2004, p. 17314). A different analysis of the same sample found a positive relationship between measures of cellular aging and the stress-relevant hormones norepinephrine and cortisol (Epel et al., 2006). Even though we do not yet know how cellular aging translates into body age and health changes, this research provides a fascinating example of how stress can wear down the body.

If stress can accelerate cellular aging, can engaging in practices that reduce stress or promote well-being

Ask any mother of young children how she feels. Chances are she'll tell you she's exhausted. Long-term stress that is perceived as severe can speed up the process of cellular aging.

enhance cellular health? A recent study of the psychological and physiological effects of intensive meditation training addressed this question. Positive psychological changes that occur during meditation training are associated with higher activity of telomerase (Jacobs et al., 2010). Specifically, increases in self-reported purpose in life and perceived control predicted greater telomerase activity. This is the first study to link positive changes in psychological status with changes in telomerase.

telomerase
 an enzyme that adds DNA sequences to telomeres.

HOW STRESS AND COPING AFFECT HEALTH

psychosomatic theory
the idea that emotional factors can lead to the occurrence or worsening of illness.

Our discussion so far has implied that stress increases a person's susceptibility to disease. This idea is one of the oldest expressions of the interplay between nature and nurture, and it forms the central tenet of **psychosomatic theory.** Even though people tend to use the term *psychosomatic* to refer to an illness that is "all in the head" or, by implication, "made up," this is a misconception of the actual theory. Rather, *psychosomatics* deal with how emotional factors can increase the likelihood of certain disorders occurring or worsening. Even the well-known link between stress and ulcers is not a matter of simple causality—stress increases the likelihood of ulcers by changing the chemical balance in the gut, but certain preconditions must be met for that internal environment to produce ulcers (Yoemans, 2011).

health psychology
the study of the role psychological factors play in regard to health and illness.

The field of health psychology grew out of psychosomatic medicine. **Health psychology** is the study of psychological factors related to health and illness. It includes disease onset, prevention, treatment, and rehabilitation and involves clinical practice as well as research. Research in health psychology ranges from studies of how psychological variables enhance health or increase susceptibility to disease to the role of social factors in doctor–patient communication. Two models can explain the relationship between stress and illness: Both illustrate the dynamic interplay among environmental situations, people's interpretations of them, and changes in body functioning. The **physiological reactivity model** examines how the sustained physiological activation associated with the stress response can affect body systems in such a way as to increase the likelihood that illness or disease occurs. As such, this model is rooted in psychosomatic medicine. By contrast, the **health behavior approach** focuses on the behaviors in which people engage, such as diet, exercise, or substance abuse, which may make them more susceptible to illness or may enhance health. These explanations are not mutually exclusive. For example, a person might experience sustained blood pressure elevation due to stress and drink heavily during a time of intense stress, both of which would affect the person's health.

physiological reactivity model
explanation for the causal role of stress-related bodily changes in illness.

health behavior approach
explanation for illness or health that focuses on the role of behaviors such as diet, exercise, or substance abuse.

Figure 12.6 depicts the physiological reactivity model. (We discuss the health behavior approach later in the chapter.) You will notice similarities between this and the emotion/stress process diagram in Figure 12.2: Each begins with the elicitation of negative emotion and stress. In the physiological reactivity model, however, the activation of the sympathetic nervous system persists and creates sustained physiological arousal (recall Selye's exhaustion stage). A wide array of body systems may be affected by sustained stress, but a few key systems have been the focus of much research.

The physiological reactivity model starts with sustained physiological arousal. Earlier we said that the sympathetic branch of the autonomic nervous system activates organ systems to enable an animal to respond to emergency situations. So the effects of sympathetic arousal on the heart and lungs (increasing pumping and oxygen intake) help the animal act quickly and thus survive. From an evolutionary perspective, these effects were advantageous because of their ability to enable a quick and efficient response. However, the same type of emotional response occurs in daily life, in most cases without an outlet for action—for example, when

Eating in response to stress may make us feel good, but it may also make us more susceptible to certain diseases.

Event
(possible stressor)

↓

Appraisal

↓ ↓

Positive/beneficial
(e.g., seeing an old
friend)

Negative/threatening
(e.g., rush-hour traffic jam)

↓ ↓

Positive emotion → Negative emotion → **Stress** → Sustained sympathetic → Increased
(Sustained activation weakens the body: susceptibility
sympathetic • Suppression of immune system to illness
activation) • Cardiovascular wear and tear

FIGURE **12.6**

PHYSIOLOGICAL REACTIVITY MODEL OF STRESS AND ILLNESS. Situations that people deem threatening evoke negative emotions, which in turn activate the sympathetic nervous system. Sustained sympathetic activation in conditions of stress weakens the body's defenses and increases the likelihood of illness.

you are stuck in traffic or annoyed with a coworker. So the activation persists for hours or days, or is elicited repeatedly in similar situations over many years. Under such conditions, you can become ill as a result of the recurring arousal produced by stress-related body changes (Sapolsky, 1998).

The **cardiovascular system,** which consists of the heart and all the blood vessels of the body, is especially susceptible to the effects of sustained arousal. During activation of the sympathetic nervous system, heart rate and blood pressure increase. In sustained physiological activation, heart rate and blood pressure remain elevated or are activated repeatedly over extended periods. Frequent blood pressure elevations can damage arteries by reducing their elasticity and increasing the likelihood of fatty buildup. These processes set the stage for heart disease.

The immune system suffers from the effects of sustained arousal, and impaired immune function increases susceptibility to disease. How does this work? Sustained activation of the HPA axis leads to sustained release of cortisol, which inhibits the production of certain immune cells. In the short term, suppression of immune cell production makes sense, because in an emergency immune cells might not be immediately necessary. Over the long term, however, immune suppression makes a person more susceptible to certain diseases.

cardiovascular system

the heart, blood, and all the blood vessels.

One way of assessing the risk of heart disease is to take a stress test, aptly named because it subjects the cardiovascular system to increasing physiological activation.

Psychological Processes and the Immune System

With the general adaptation syndrome, Hans Selye provided a framework for thinking about how stress might make the body vulnerable to disease, and he implied that this vulnerability might be due to the effects of stress on the immune system. No one knew whether psychological factors could affect the immune system until some groundbreaking research of the 1970s.

The job of the immune system is to defend the body against foreign substances. Before the 1970s, the prevailing view was that the immune system operated independently of the central nervous system, which implies that the immune system was invulnerable to thoughts, feelings, and stress. As far as anyone knew at the time, there were no anatomical or chemical connections between immune system structures and any aspect of the nervous system that would allow them to communicate. Even though most physicians believed that stress made people sick, or at least sicker, they did not consider it physiologically possible for psychological conditions to have any effect on the immune system. But that was about to change.

Breaking New Ground

Linking the Nervous System and the Immune System

Robert Ader was replicating some classic experiments on conditioned taste aversion. Recall from Chapter 8 that conditioned taste aversion is a form of classical conditioning in which a neutral taste, after repeated pairing with a substance that induces nausea and vomiting, will come to produce those characteristics when it is presented alone. In the early research, saccharin water was paired with radiation, which causes nausea (Garcia, Kimeldorf, & Koelling, 1955). In his work, Ader paired a chemical that induces nausea with saccharin water to create taste aversion to the saccharin water. Some rats were exposed to a lot of saccharin water even after they had learned to associate it with nausea. And something else unusual was happening to those rats—they were dying! But why?

Ader remembered that the toxin he was using to induce nausea also happened to be an immunosuppressant—that is, something that suppresses immune system function. Perhaps, he reasoned, in addition to learning to avoid saccharin water, the rats were acquiring conditioned immunosuppression from the repeated pairing of the saccharin solution with the immunosuppressant. But how could rats *learn* immunosuppression?

To suggest any connection between psychological processes and immune system functioning ran counter to the view in medicine that the immune system operates independently of the central nervous system (Boorboor, 2002). Nevertheless, Ader and his colleague, Nicholas Cohen, ran a series of experiments to determine whether immunosuppression could be classically conditioned in rats (Ader & Cohen, 1975). They conditioned nausea in an experimental group by pairing saccharin water with injections of the immunosuppressant. They also created two control groups: a group that was injected with a placebo around the time they drank saccharin water (which served as a control for the stress-inducing effects of injection in the absence of conditioning) and a group that received the immunosuppressant and plain water (a nonconditioning control group).

Ader and Cohen then tested whether the immune system was in fact suppressed in rats with immunosuppressant-induced conditioned taste aversion. They reintroduced the conditioned stimulus, in this case saccharin, and then introduced an **antigen,** a substance foreign to the body. The blood of rats that had been conditioned to avoid saccharin via the immunosuppressant showed much weaker antibody responses to the antigen than did rats injected with the placebo. By demonstrating that one could classically condition the suppression of an antibody response to an antigen, Ader and Cohen had shown that there must be connections between the CNS and the immune system.

■ ■ ■

antigen
any foreign substance that triggers an immune response.

Connection
Conditioned taste aversion is a type of learning similar to what happened when Pavlov's dogs learned to salivate to the sound of a bell (classical conditioning).
See "Classical Conditioning," Chapter 8, "Learning," p. 308.

The Birth of Psychoneuroimmunology

Not long after Ader and Cohen published their results on conditioned immuno-suppression, some important findings in biomedical science increased the credibility of their findings. In the late 1970s and early 1980s, scientists discovered that the ANS is linked to immune system structures such as the thymus gland and that immune cells have receptors for and can produce certain stress hormones (Smith & Blalock, 1988). There was now solid behavioral and biological evidence for what Selye and others had believed all along—that psychological processes and immune processes interact. The field of **psychoneuroimmunology (PNI),** the science of how psychological factors relate to immune changes, was born.

Today, the field of psychoneuroimmunology (PNI) examines the relationships among the brain, thought, feeling, endocrine changes, and immune system functioning. As a discipline, PNI is concerned with any kind of connection between psychological processes and the immune system. For instance, there are chemical linkages between psychological processes and immune system changes. Chemicals involved in the stress response, such as cortisol and norepinephrine, influence the number of immune cells produced in the body. This is a means by which stress can affect the immune system.

Furthermore, connections between the central nervous system and immune system are bidirectional. That is, just as stress can change immune function, certain immune changes (such as the release of chemicals called *cytokines,* which regulate immune response) can feed back and influence brain areas involved in mood regulation (Miller, Capuron, & Raison, 2005; Nishida et al., 2002).

Overview of the Immune System The human immune system defends the body against invasion by disease, inspects the body for cells that may take on dangerous mutations, and performs basic housekeeping functions such as cleaning up cellular debris after an injury. There are two basic lines of defense: natural immunity and acquired immunity. **Natural immunity** consists of a number of inborn processes that help remove foreign substances from the body. These responses typically are very quick, and they provide the first line of defense upon exposure to antigens. Forms of natural immunity include phagocytosis and inflammation. *Phagocytosis* is a process by which a white blood cell engulfs a substance (usually an antigen or another cell) and digests it or moves it to a place where it will be destroyed. *Inflammation* is a process by which tissues are restored following injury. After you cut your finger, for example, blood vessels at the injured area contract and dilate to increase blood flow to the area, creating warmth and redness. The damaged cells release enzymes to destroy invading microorganisms.

The immune system includes several kinds of white blood cells, including those responsible for phagocytosis. Other white blood cells, called *lymphocytes,* control acquired immunity. **Acquired immunity** involves a number of endocrine and cellular processes that recognize specific antigens and

psychoneuro-immunology (PNI) the science of how psychological factors relate to changes in the immune system.

A newborn's immune system is still developing. Antibodies present in the mother's breast milk protect the baby from infection until the infant's own immune system has matured.

natural immunity form of immunity that is the first response to antigens.

acquired immunity immunity provided by antibodies produced in the body in response to specific antigens.

then reproduce specialized cells or circulating proteins to fight those antigens. Acquired immunity is so called because it involves experience—an effective immune response occurs only after prior exposure to a particular antigen. For instance, every cold we get leads to an acquired immune response. As a result we are less likely to get sick if we encounter that particular virus again. Acquired immune responses take longer to initiate than natural immune responses, because the former involve recognition processes and duplication of cells. On subsequent exposure to a specific antigen, however, acquired immune responses can be rapid and efficient. Vaccines, for example, provide a safe initial exposure and an acquired immune response that protects us against disease.

Acquired immunity involves two classes of lymphocytes, called B and T lymphocytes. In response to specific antigens, *B lymphocytes* release antibodies into the bloodstream. Antibodies destroy antigens directly. The *T lymphocytes*, or "T cells," fight antigens not by releasing antibodies but by means of cellular processes, collectively known as **cellular immunity.**

cellular immunity
the immune response that occurs when the T lymphocytes (T cells) fight antigens

Research on Stress, Immune Function, and Health

The physiological reactivity model predicts that the physiological effects of stress, when sustained over time, will eventually weaken the immune system. Theorists have extended the model a step further, reasoning that *immunosuppression* increases susceptibility to disease by reducing the body's ability to fight invading bacteria or viruses or its ability to fight off potentially cancerous cells, or both. This is why psychologists, in collaboration with medical researchers, began conducting studies of stress and immune function. The basic idea is simple: If researchers can show that stress affects immune variables, it should follow that such immune system changes would leave the organism more susceptible to disease. In reality, many studies link stress with changes in immune system measures, but very few have shown that these changes affect susceptibility to disease. Let's look at some of the major research on stress and immune function in both animals and humans.

Results from animal research show that a variety of stressors can weaken responses to antigens, reduce the numbers of certain immune cells, and impair immune cell functions such as responses to vaccines (Glaser & Kiecolt-Glaser, 2005). Some of the stressors tested in animal studies are maternal separation, inescapable shock, abrupt temperature change, and loud noise. A few studies have manipulated stress in humans by randomly assigning people to participate in a stressful task, such as public speaking, or an emotion-evoking task, such as writing about a traumatic event (Pennebaker, Kiecolt-Glaser, & Glaser, 1988). The more common approach in human research, however, is to rely on naturally occurring stressors such as final exams, sleep deprivation, loud noise, bereavement, divorce, and caring for an Alzheimer's or AIDS patient. These studies use various measures of immunity as dependent variables. These include numbers of certain lymphocytes, tests of how effectively certain lymphocytes function either in a test tube or in a living person, the toxicity of tumor-fighting cells called *natural killer cells,* and the quantities of chemicals that regulate lymphocytes.

Research on the effects of stress on the human immune system often makes use of natural stressors, such as exam time.

Although the major finding in studies of humans is that stressors are associated with changes in various kinds of immune function, it is often difficult to know whether the observed immune changes have meaningful effects on health. A few studies address this concern by including measures of illness that are controlled by immune mechanisms. In a study of people caring for Alzheimer's patients, the caregivers and a matched comparison group (all volunteers for the study) received small puncture wounds. They then returned to the laboratory for wound healing assessments and blood tests to measure immune variables. Compared to the comparison group, the caregivers exhibited substantially slower healing of puncture wounds and reductions in chemicals involved in healing (Kiecolt-Glaser et al., 1995).

What about stress and the common cold, an infectious illness mediated by the immune system? Sheldon Cohen and his colleagues (1993, 2003) have studied the interplay of stress and social connectedness in people's susceptibility to the common cold. Susceptibility is the key issue here, as exposure to the cold virus does not guarantee a person will get sick. For example, you and your roommate might both spend time with a friend who is sick, but only one of you might catch the cold. In these studies, Cohen and his colleagues exposed people to a virus; measured perceived stress in some participants as well as external stressors and social networks; and clinically verified whether or not people got sick. They used a clever means by which to measure how sick people were, such as weighing tissues to approximate how much mucus they produced! As it turns out, that perception of stress—rather than the number of stressors to which people had been exposed—predicted whether or not people developed a cold (S. Cohen, Tyrell, & Smith, 1993). Further, having more meaningful social interactions in one's daily life reduces susceptibility to colds (S. Cohen et al., 2003). Perceiving oneself as lower in socioeconomic status also predicts susceptibility to the common cold in people exposed to the virus, independent of one's actual socioeconomic status (S. Cohen et al., 2008).

The relationship between stress and illness, then, is not driven by the situation as much as by how the individual evaluates that situation. In terms of susceptibility to the common cold, *perceived* stress mattered more than actual exposure to stressors; *perceived* low socioeconomic status mattered more than actual socioeconomic status. These results remind us of the importance of examining stress not just as a stimulus (number of stressors), but also in terms of how people respond to the stressors and cope with possible stress (transactional view). As discussed earlier, social support and connectedness might buffer the effects of stress by providing interpersonal resources for emotional support and problem solving (S. Cohen & Wills, 1985).

Nature & Nurture

Having plenty of meaningful social relationships can protect you from the common cold. How? Possibly by providing more resources to help buffer the effects of stress in your life or increasing your ability to face adversity.

Psychological Risk Factors for Heart Disease

Heart disease is the number one killer of both men and women in the United States (American Heart Association, 2005; Lethbridge-Cejku & Vickerie, 2005). We saw earlier that the physiological changes associated with negative emotions and stress affect the cardiovascular system. Research has identified a number of psychological risk factors for heart disease, including hostility, anger, and depression.

Type A and Anger   For centuries scientists have argued that personality and emotion play a role in the development of heart disease, but research on

Time urgency is a component of the Type A behavior pattern that does not predict heart disease after all.

this topic did not begin until the middle of the 20th century. In fact, it began in the waiting room of cardiologist Meyer Friedman's office in San Francisco. A janitor pointed out to Friedman that the upholstery on the chairs in his waiting room was wearing out much more quickly than that on chairs in other waiting rooms. He wondered whether Friedman's patients fidgeted a lot. Friedman said that he had noticed that many of his patients were tense and impatient. Friedman and his colleague Ray Rosenman decided to study the effects of such an emotional style on a person's risk of developing heart disease. They described a set of psychological characteristics that they believed put people at risk for heart disease: impatience, competitiveness, hostility, and time urgency. They named it the **Type A Behavior Pattern (TABP)** and explained that this pattern emerges when under conditions of challenge or stress. That is, Type A people are not always impatient and hostile, but when they find themselves in high-pressure situations they exhibit this pattern of behavior.

Type A Behavior Pattern (TABP) a way of responding to challenge or stress, characterized by hostility, impatience, competitiveness, and time urgency.

Friedman and Rosenman hypothesized that people who exhibit the TABP *under provocation* are at greater risk for heart disease than those who do not. After developing an interview to measure Type A behavior, they tracked 3,000 healthy White men for 8 years. They found that Type A behavior predicted the incidence of coronary heart disease, over and above such traditional risk factors as blood pressure, cholesterol, and age (Rosenman et al., 1964). This finding shocked the medical world—no one had anticipated that something psychological could affect heart disease! Other major studies replicated the finding that the presence of Type A behavior predicted the incidence of heart disease and extended it to women (French-Belgian Collaborative Group, 1982; Haynes et al., 1978).

Twenty-two years later, Rosenman and Friedman conducted a follow-up study on their original participants (Rosenman et al., 1975). Surprisingly, Type A did *not* predict death from heart disease in this group. Then another major study of men and women produced null findings as well (Shekelle et al., 1985). Could it really be that Type A did not affect the incidence of heart disease after all?

Remembering that Type A is a collection of various characteristics, Matthews and her colleagues (1977) decided to take a closer look at the follow-up interviews from Friedman and Rosenman's original sample. She reasoned that maybe certain aspects of Type A were still relevant to coronary health, even if the overall pattern did not predict death. Matthews studied how each component of the Type A pattern (hostility, time urgency, competitiveness, and impatience) related to coronary outcomes. As it turned out, *hostility* was the only component that predicted death from heart disease at a 22-year follow-up. As a result of Matthews's findings, the measurement of global Type A has been abandoned, for the most part, in favor of more specific measures of hostility.

Suddenly the focus changed to the study of hostility and cardiovascular health. In subsequent research, specific measures of hostility again positively correlated with the degree of arterial blockage and other cardiovascular conditions

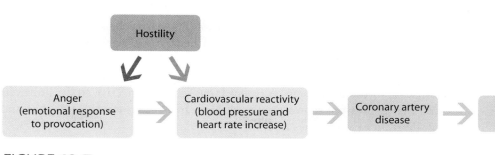

FIGURE 12.7

CARDIOVASCULAR REACTIVITY MODEL OF STRESS AND ILLNESS. This version of the physiological reactivity model links hostility and anger to heart disease. Repeated cardiovascular reactivity leads to coronary artery disease and heart disease.

much more so than general Type A behavior did (Suarez et al., 1993; Suarez, Bates, & Harralson, 1998; Suarez & Williams, 1989; R. B. Williams et al., 1980).

How might having a hostile personality put someone at greater risk for heart disease? Hostility is an affective trait, which some emotion theorists say sets a threshold for the likelihood of particular emotional responses (Ekman, 1984; Rosenberg, 1998). By this logic, hostile people would have a lower threshold for the elicitation of anger. To link hostility and anger to heart disease, we need to look at a special version of the physiological reactivity model known as the cardiovascular reactivity model (see Figure 12.7). In the **cardiovascular reactivity (CVR) model,** hostility can increase the likelihood of heart disease through at least two different causal routes. On one route, hostility makes the elicitation of anger more likely and more frequent (this route starts with the red arrow in Figure 12.7). Frequent episodes of anger lead to frequent cardiovascular reactivity. Over time, repeated cardiovascular reactivity sets the stage for the development of coronary artery disease. As coronary artery disease develops, the narrowed arteries deprive the heart of the blood it needs to function properly; thus, progressive coronary artery disease can lead to coronary heart disease. The yellow arrows in the diagram designate the transition between repeated cardiovascular reactivity and coronary artery disease and the later development of coronary heart disease. The second route, indicated by the blue arrow in Figure 12.7, is a direct path from hostility to how much cardiovascular reactivity certain people experience, without the need for anger.

In support of the first route, research shows that anger does affect cardiovascular outcomes. For instance, anger can lead to heightened and prolonged blood pressure reactivity (Schuler & O'Brien, 1997; Siegman et al., 1992). In coronary patients, the risk of heart attack increases significantly during the hour following an outburst of anger (Moller et al., 1999). A study of coronary patients undergoing the Type A Structured Interview found that episodes of insufficient blood supply to the muscle of the heart were more likely to occur when those patients displayed facial expressions of anger (Rosenberg et al., 2001).

Depression   A hostile disposition is not the only trait relevant to cardiac health. Depression, a mood disorder involving sadness and lethargy, is also associated with increased severity of symptoms and increased risk of death from coronary heart disease (Geerlings et al., 2002; Glassman & Shapiro, 1998). A large-scale meta-analysis reported that for people with coronary heart disease, being clinically depressed more than doubles the risk of death from the disease

cardiovascular reactivity (CVR) model
hypothesis that hostility can increase the likelihood of heart disease through at least two different causal routes.

(Barth, Schumacher, & Hermann-Lingen, 2004). Also, chemicals involved in inflammation that present a risk for coronary heart disease are present at higher levels in people who are depressed than in others (Barth et al., 2004; Empana et al., 2005). Studies such as these make it hard to know which comes first—the heart disease or the depression. A recent large-scale prospective study, however, showed that depression scores predicted death from cardiovascular disease and overall mortality (Nabi et al., 2010).

Research on Health-Relevant Behavior

Earlier we mentioned another pathway to illness called the *health behavior approach*. People engage in behaviors that increase risk for disease or help to prevent disease. Some health behaviors are conscious lifestyle choices, such as how and what to eat or whether or not to exercise. Others may begin as conscious choices but over time become habits with serious health implications, such as smoking, drinking alcohol, and taking other drugs. Sometimes, when stressed, people drink or take drugs to change their mood. This is emotion-focused coping. They may turn to tobacco, alcohol, or food to calm themselves down or cheer themselves up. Long-term use of some of these substances can create health problems and may increase the likelihood of major, sometimes fatal, illnesses.

Smoking   Many smokers say they have a cigarette when they are stressed because it calms them down. Yet nicotine, the drug component of cigarette smoke, is a stimulant. Nicotine activates the sympathetic nervous system, increasing heart rate and blood pressure. Nicotine relaxes the skeletal muscles, however, which is probably why some people find it calming. This calming effect is one reason that smokers tend to have a cigarette when stressed—they use nicotine for emotion regulation. But cigarette smoking is harmful to health in many ways. In fact, according to the U.S. Department of Health and Human Services (USDHHS, 2006), it is the single most preventable cause of death in the United States. Cigarette smoking reduces life expectancy by an average of 10 years, increases one's risk for lung cancer more than 10-fold, and triples the risk of death from heart disease in both men and women (CDC, 2001; Doll et al., 2004). Smoking also increases the risk of many other cancers, stroke, lung disease, emphysema, and male impotence (USDHHS, 2006). The increased risk of mortality associated with smoking is found in several cultures (Jacobs et al., 1999). Although the rates of smoking in the United States have dropped considerably in recent years, still about 20% of the U.S. population smokes cigarettes. With over 1,000 people a day under the age of 18 in the United States taking up smoking, this is a major health problem (USDHHS, 2006).

   We are exposed to *secondhand smoke* by being near someone who is smoking. Analyses of the composition of the smoke that is burned from the end of a cigarette indicate that it is high in carcinogens (sometimes higher than the smoke inhaled by the smoker) and is a health threat to those who inhale it passively. In fact, the person who breathes secondhand smoke regularly is at increased risk of all the same health problems that the smoker is (USDHHS, 2006).

Drinking Alcohol   Some people drink alcohol to calm down or loosen up. Alcohol is a depressant, which means it slows down central nervous system functions. Alcohol can cause liver damage, and severe alcoholism can lead to a serious liver condition known as cirrhosis. Heavy alcohol consumption also increases the likelihood of liver cancer and cancers of the digestive tract, not to mention an increased risk for accidents due to alcohol's effect on motor and cognitive performance. Not all the news regarding alcohol is bad, however. Considerable data indicate that regular but moderate alcohol consumption (one to two drinks), especially with food, may reduce the risk of coronary heart disease, the number one killer in the developed world (Guiraud et al., 2008; Renaud & de Lorgeril, 1992).

Diet and Eating

Eating well promotes health. Eating saturated fats, such as those found in meats and dairy products, increases risk for heart disease, while eating other essential fats, such as those found in certain kinds of fish and nuts, may have protective effects (Schaefer, Gleason, & Dansinger, 2005). The consumption of high-fiber, less fatty foods, such as whole grains and plenty of leafy green vegetables, may help protect against cancers of the colon and rectum, although the data are somewhat inconclusive (Cummings et al., 1992). It is well known that excessive weight gain is risky. Obesity increases a person's risk for heart disease, high blood pressure, adult-onset diabetes, and certain cancers (McTiernan, 2005). Increasingly we can see how diet, exercise, and lifestyle interact in ways that can profoundly impact health (Powell et al., 2010).

Eating and Stress Some people eat to cope with stress. In fact, sugary foods in particular help some people feel better and calm down. Research now supports the connection between eating and stress reduction: Stress increases eating and, in turn, eating reduces stress reactivity in the HPA axis (Dallman, Pecoraro, & la Fleur, 2005). When a person eats in response to stress, stress-related physiological activity decreases. So eating relieves stress for some people, which makes it likely they will continue to do such eating. When people eat in response to stress (especially sugary foods), reward pathways in the brain are stimulated. These areas release endorphins that make people feel better. So people eat under stress because they get a "good feeling" reward—like a drug high—from the brain (Adam & Epel, 2007).

But stress-induced eating is risky, as it increases fat in the abdominal area (compared to other places), which is a predictor of heart disease in men and women (Epel et al., 2000; Rexrode et al., 1998; Rexrode, Buring, & Manson, 2001). This is especially true if the stress-induced eating includes sugary junk foods (Kuo et al., 2007).

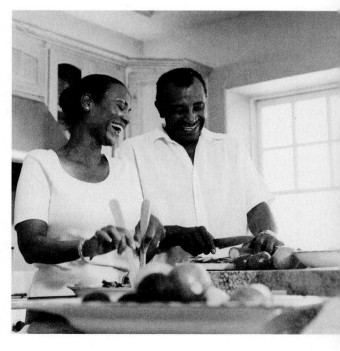

A healthy diet rich in fruits, vegetables, and whole grains and low in fat may protect against heart disease and certain cancers and prevent conditions associated with obesity, such as adult-onset diabetes.

Eating Disorders Sometimes a person's relationship with food becomes maladaptive. The two most prevalent eating disorders are anorexia nervosa and bulimia nervosa. People diagnosed with **anorexia nervosa** cannot maintain 85% of their ideal body weight for their height, have an intense fear of eating, and have a distorted body image (American Psychiatric Association, 2000). Moreover, they do not recognize that they are unusually thin or that they have an eating disorder. The other major

anorexia nervosa

an eating disorder in which people cannot maintain 85% of their ideal body weight for their height, have an intense fear of eating, and have a distorted body image.

eating disorder is bulimia. A person suffering from **bulimia nervosa** is prone to binge eating and feeling a lack of control during the eating session. Binge eating involves eating much more food at one time than the average person would, such as having a half gallon of ice cream as a late-night snack. A person with bulimia regularly engages in either self-induced vomiting, use of laxatives or diuretics, strict dieting or fasting, or vigorous exercise in order to prevent weight gain.

bulimia nervosa an eating disorder characterized by binge eating and a perceived lack of control during the eating session.

The causes of anorexia are unknown, although a number of factors appear to put people at risk for this disorder, such as reactivity to stress, genetics, and personality. Women are much more likely than men to develop anorexia or bulimia (Nolen-Hoeksema, 2007). Women with eating disorders show higher physiological reactivity to stress. A study of more than 31,000 fraternal and identical twin pairs (both male and female) from Sweden examined the genetics of anorexia nervosa (Bulik et al., 2006). By comparing twins raised apart to twins raised together, one can calculate how much of a trait is due to genetics and how much to environment. This study reported that 56% of the variability in whether or not people develop anorexia nervosa is attributable to genetic influence, with the remainder (38%) being attributable to the common environments shared by family members. Moreover, people who had demonstrated a proneness to anxiety, depression, and low self-esteem (as measured by the trait of neuroticism) later were more likely to develop anorexia. Other studies report that many personality traits distinguish anorexics. In addition to being higher in neuroticism, anorexics are also more conscientious, more introverted, and less open to new and novel situations than are non-anorexics (Bollen & Wojciechowski, 2004). Recent questionnaire data suggest that both men and women with eating disorders also seek approval from others and are more likely to have insecure attachments to their caregivers (Abbate-Daga et al., 2010).

Exercise Besides not smoking, one of the best things you can do for your health is to exercise regularly. Regular exercise reduces the risk of heart disease, stroke, and certain types of cancer (Noda et al., 2005; Thune & Furberg, 2001). Exercise helps keep diabetes under control and also slows the rate of bone loss in older women (Cussler et al., 2005). Data show that moderate exercise, even as little as walking 20–25 minutes a day three or four times per week, can extend life by 3 to 4 years (Franco et al., 2005). In addition, exercise offers a healthy way to regulate mood, as it reduces anxiety and depression (Barbour, Edenfield, & Blumenthal, 2007; Binder et al., 2004).

The best way to affect your metabolism, and as a result change your weight, is by exercising regularly. But did you know that introducing just a brief (10 minutes or so) exercise regimen can make a difference in your metabolism? Such metabolic changes can change your genes (Lewis et al., 2010). This lends credibility to the idea that you can change your set point with exercise and thereby eat less.

Exercise can also help your brain. One correlational study found that the most physically fit third- and fifth-grade children also performed the highest on standardized math and reading tests (Hillman, Erickson, & Kramer, 2008). Other research more directly suggests that exercise promotes the growth of new neurons (neurogenesis) in the hippocampus, the area of the brain most

Nature & Nurture

Physical exercise causes new neurons to grow in brain areas devoted to learning and memory.

involved in learning and memory (Pereira et al., 2007). Compared to mice that did not exercise, mice that exercised showed increased activity in their hippocampi after exercising for 2 weeks. They also developed new neurons in the same region of the hippocampus. Increased activity was directly related to neural growth. In fact, similar treadmill studies in rats show that exercise can offset age-related memory loss due to a reduction in neurogenesis in the hippocampus (Kim et al., 2010) and may decrease depressive-like behavior in chronically stressed rats (Marais et al., 2009). Similar effects have been found with humans as well; see the Research Process for this chapter (Figure 12.8). Being physically fit appears to make the brain fit, too.

Meditation for Stress Reduction and Health

We have already discussed how positive emotions can reduce the physiological activation caused by negative emotions and how higher positive affect may help people with diseases like AIDS live longer (Moskowitz, 2003). Given the harmful effects of stress, strategies designed to reduce stress can benefit both mental and physical health. One such strategy is meditation.

Mindfulness meditation involves both paying attention to the present moment and being aware that everything that may arise in one's mind, be it a thought, an emotion, or a sensation, will eventually fade away. The meditator is trained to note experiences as they occur, without clinging to or ascribing value to them. These skills allow one to keep thoughts and emotions in perspective and help prevent an unhealthy obsession with negative emotions (Kabat-Zinn, 1990).

Researchers have applied mindfulness meditation training to the treatment of stress reduction, pain relief, and physical disorders. Kabat-Zinn and his colleagues have developed and studied the effectiveness of a program called Mindfulness-Based Stress Reduction (MBSR) for treating a variety of physical and psychological conditions. MBSR training reduces self-reported pain and pain-related behaviors in people suffering from chronic pain (Kabat-Zinn, Lipworth, & Burney, 1985). Also, MBSR training leads to significant and substantial reductions in anxiety, depression, and fear in people who have various types of anxiety disorders (Kabat-Zinn et al., 1992).

Mindfulness training helps other health conditions as well, especially those that may worsen with stress. Consider the case of psoriasis, an annoying and often painful rash that can be exacerbated by stress (Chapman & Moynihan, 2009). Mindfulness training improves the rate of skin healing in people with psoriasis (Kabat-Zinn et al., 1998). Mindfulness meditation techniques appear to be effective in reducing the stress-related immune changes underlying skin outbreaks. Such meditation training appears to help in the treatment of eating disorders, recovery from substance abuse, and enhancing quality of life in people with multiple sclerosis (Grossman et al., 2010; Liehr et al., 2010; Masuda & Wendell, 2010).

Connection

Mindfulness meditation can improve well-being, cognition, and brain function.

See "Training Consciousness: Meditation," Chapter 6, "Consciousness," p. 235.

Research Process

1 Research Question

Will exercise increase brain activity and stimulate neural growth in humans?

2 Method

Having found that exercise was correlated with neural growth in the hippocampus of mice, Pereira and colleagues (2007) conducted a study to look for the same effects in humans. They recruited eleven adults (ages 21–45) with below-average cardiovascular fitness to take part in an exercise program 4 times a week for 12 weeks. Each session lasted about 1 hour and consisted of a combination of stretching, aerobic training, and cooling down. Brain images were made before and after the training with MRI to measure changes in blood volume, an indirect measure of neural growth.

The hippocampus is the brain region most involved in learning and memory, so participants' memories were tested before and after the program with a list of 20 words read by the experimenter, to find out whether there was any change in memory capacity. Participants were distracted with another word list and were then asked to recall as many words from the original list as they could.

Hippocampus

Brain activity (blood volume) in the hippocampus—an indirect measure of neurogenesis

Cognitive task performance

3 Results

MRIs performed before and after the exercise program revealed that cerebral blood flow increased after the program. In addition, participants improved their performance on a cognitive test after 12 weeks of exercise.

4 Conclusion

After exercising regularly, people who had been out of shape showed improvement in memory. This improvement is correlated with—and perhaps a consequence of—new neural growth in the region of the brain most involved in learning and memory, the hippocampus. Although we cannot conclude from the correlations revealed by this study that physical exercise causes improvements in memory, these findings suggest that exercise not only makes the body more fit, but it also makes the brain more fit.

FIGURE 12.8

EFFECTS OF EXERCISE ON THE BRAIN. Physical exercise is as good for the brain as it is the body. Source: "An In Vivo Correlate of Exercise-Induced Neurogenesis in the Adult Dentate Gyrus," by A. C. Pereira, D. E. Huddleston, A. M. Brickman, A. A. Sosunov, R. Hen, G. M. McKhann . . . S. A. Small, 2007, *Proceedings of the National Academy of Sciences, 104,* 5638–5643.

Quick Quiz 12.3: How Stress and Coping Affect Health

1. If a psychologist studies how diet and sleep affect overall health, which view would best match her research?
   a. physiological reactivity
   b. general adaptation syndrome
   c. health behavior approach
   d. homeostasis view

2. Martin is very prone to anger, impatient, and competitive; he is always in a hurry and feeling rushed. We would say Martin probably suffers from
   a. Type A behavior pattern
   b. Type B behavior pattern
   c. hostility
   d. high drive disorder

3. Which personality trait is most strongly related to the development of heart disease?
   a. anxiety
   b. hostility
   c. depression
   d. introversion

4. Exercise helps
   a. decrease stress
   b. improve cardiovascular health
   c. stimulate neural growth
   d. all of the above

Answers can be found at the end of the chapter.

Bringing It All Together
Making Connections in Stress and Health
The Health Psychology of HIV and AIDS

HIV/AIDS is an incurable, chronic, and sometimes fatal disease. The progression from infection to management of the illness to possible death presents a series of major psychological challenges. The course of HIV offers a good model for examining the psychological and physiological correlates of coping in a real-life context. Living with HIV is a serious challenge involving enormous stressors such as managing the symptoms of a chronic illness, dealing with the threat of death, and carrying out a complex treatment regimen. Those who care for people suffering from AIDS, which is less common these days, endure the extreme stress of caring for loved ones who are dying.

How does this disease work? The human immunodeficiency virus (HIV) enters the bloodstream and, latching on to T lymphocytes, inserts its own genetic information into the lymphocytes and then turns them into HIV replication factories (see Figure 12.9). If untreated, HIV wipes out the infected person's cellular immunity, making him or her vulnerable to many kinds of infections. AIDS is the disease that results from living with such an extremely deficient immune system. It may be characterized by a host of irritating infections; ultimately, the victim may die of rare forms of pneumonia or cancer. New drug treatments for HIV, however, have transformed it from a death sentence into a chronic, manageable

FIGURE **12.9**

T LYMPHOCYTE INFECTED WITH THE HUMAN IMMUNODEFICIENCY VIRUS (HIV). The virus (red) uses the lymphocyte (whitish green) to reproduce and prevents it from functioning normally.

disease for many people. But adhering to the complex drug regimen and dealing with the side effects are often stress provoking.

Susan Folkman

In the early to mid-1990s, before the more effective current treatments were widely available, Susan Folkman and her colleagues (1997) interviewed caregivers of men dying of AIDS. Many of the caregivers were themselves infected with HIV. The researchers were surprised to find that some of the caregivers managed to find beauty or meaning in the details of daily life despite the stress of caring for a partner who was dying of AIDS. Folkman argued that traumatic experiences often motivate people to find sources of positive emotion. This coping strategy may provide mental and physical health benefits, as we know that positive emotions can alleviate negative emotional arousal (Fredrickson & Levenson, 1998). According to Folkman, "The negative psychological state associated with significant and enduring stress may actually motivate people—consciously or unconsciously—to search for and *create* positive psychological states in order to gain relief, if only momentary, from distress" (Folkman, 1997, p. 1216).

Choosing to use a particular coping strategy in times of stress is also an indicator of coping ability. Reappraisal, especially reframing a situation in a positive light, is an adaptive coping strategy in chronic stress situations. Reappraisal can be thought of as any strategy that helps people see something difficult or unpleasant in a positive light. A study of people coping with the loss of a partner to AIDS found that engaging in reappraisal correlated with increases in positive mood (Moskowitz et al., 1996). Cognitive coping strategies

such as reappraisal seem more effective in reducing depression and anxiety in men with HIV than seeking social support and substance use (Kraaj et al., 2008).

Before effective drug therapies became available, some HIV-infected people did not manifest AIDS for years, while others died within months (Rutherford et al., 1990). How could this be? The physiological reactivity model would predict that people with HIV who experienced greater distress might be more vulnerable to disease progression than people who experienced less distress. Many researchers have investigated the role of emotions and coping in this general context. One study of men infected with HIV found slower disease progression in those who were happier (Moskowitz, 2003). Other research has found that depression appears to alter the functioning of certain T cells in both men and women infected with HIV (Kemeny et al., 1994; D. L. Evans et al., 2002, respectively). Also, chronic depression increases the risk of mortality in men infected with HIV (Mayne et al., 1996). Even in the presence of effective medications, psychosocial factors influence immune variables and disease progression in both men and women. In a longitudinal study of psychological factors in men and women infected with HIV, baseline self-reports of stress, depression, hopelessness, and avoidant coping predicted significant reductions in the kinds of T lymphocytes that are most dramatically targeted by HIV (Ironson et al., 2005). More stressful life events, more depressive symptoms, and less social support all correlated with a faster progression to AIDS in gay men infected with HIV (Leserman et al., 1999). Consistent with the findings on depression, apathy—or a lack of motivation or drive—is associated with thinning of the white matter in the brains of people who are HIV-positive (Hoare et al., 2010). A correlational study such as this makes it hard to know which came first (the apathy or

Once a week these women distribute condoms and educational leaflets about safe sex and AIDS in the Gauteng Province of South Africa. The AIDS epidemic has hit South Africa particularly hard, in part because of social instability, high levels of poverty, the low status accorded women, and the government's reluctance to acknowledge the extent of the problem and its causes.

the brain changes), but given that we know that HIV can lead to central nervous system damage, it is likely that the virus causes the brain changes that increase apathy.

Certain ways of coping with emotional trauma or distress may affect whether one becomes infected as well as the progression of HIV in those already infected. In a study comparing recently infected gay and bisexual men, the recently infected experienced more recent stressful events than a comparison group of uninfected men (Burchell et al., 2010). This difference may be due to the fact that more stressful events were linked with riskier sexual behaviors. Faster disease progression is associated with denial as a form of coping and with less satisfactory social support (Leserman et al., 2000). In another study of HIV and coping, patients with HIV were either asked to write about an emotional topic (disclosure condition) or assigned to a control condition; those in the disclosure condition showed a drop in HIV viral load (an indication of improved immune function) and an increase in T lymphocytes that are crucial to combating the virus (Petrie et al., 2004). These various studies—and others like them—suggest that stress and the ways in which people cope with it may impact HIV infection and disease progression directly by weakening the body's ability to fight infection or indirectly by increasing risky behaviors. Both may occur, of course.

Indeed, whether or not you engage in safe sex practices is probably the single biggest determinant of HIV risk, with intravenous drug use the next. So infection with HIV is largely a result of health-related behavior. Nevertheless, many people continue to practice unsafe behaviors (Weinhardt, 2005). Indeed, the health behavior approach is relevant not only to infection, but also to progression. Choosing to get tested early and taking the medications regularly are key to successful treatment; these are both voluntary acts where behavior can make the difference between life and death (Malta et al., 2010).

Quick Quiz 12.4: Bringing It All Together: Making Connections in Stress and Health

1. Human immunodeficiency virus (HIV) replicates by latching on to
   a. T lymphocytes
   b. B lymphocytes
   c. red blood cells
   d. antibodies

2. Which of the following reduces disease progression in men with HIV?
   a. depression
   b. optimism
   c. hostility
   d. happiness

Answers can be found at the end of the chapter.

Chapter **Review**

STRESS

- Stress results when we appraise the demands of a situation as exceeding our ability to cope with or manage those demands. Researchers often define stress in terms of events or our physiological responses to certain events.

- Primary appraisal is the initial evaluation of how threatening a situation is. Secondary appraisal involves evaluation of resources to manage the stressful situation or the feelings it generates.

- Most stress-related physiological changes are observed in the autonomic nervous system (ANS), especially the sympathetic branch.

- The adrenal-medullary system controls the release of catecholamines, chemicals that activate heart rate, respiration, and other responses that prepare the organism to deal with emergency situations.

- The hypothalamic-pituitary-adrenal (HPA) axis releases the hormone cortisol, which frees up glucose as a source of energy.

- The stress response is beneficial in short-term, emergency situations but not over the long term. When sustained over time, the stress response can weaken the body.

- Hans Selye proposed a three-stage model, the general adaptation syndrome (GAS), to describe how the body reacts and adapts to chronic, extreme stress. In the alarm stage, the body is in emergency mode and all body systems are activated for quick response. In the resistance stage, the body gradually adjusts to the high level of stress created by the demands of its environment. In the exhaustion stage the body is unable to sustain the response and becomes more susceptible to illness.

- Mason and others argued that Selye had overlooked the fact that people respond to different situations with different emotions and made a case for greater specificity in the stress response. Research shows that different emotions are indeed associated with different patterns of ANS response.

COPING

- Some strategies for coping are problem-focused, in that they address how to remedy or change the situation that called forth the stress response. Others are emotion-focused, aimed at reducing the emotional distress or unpleasant experience created by a stressful situation.

- Social support can profoundly improve mental and physical health. Social networks influence health behavior, both positively and negatively.

- Some people are more likely than others to believe that they have control over situations, and this belief may make them healthier.

- Some people experience positive affect, even in dramatically stressful situations. Positive affect, in turn, may facilitate recovery from the negative emotional arousal of stress.

HOW STRESS AND COPING AFFECT HEALTH

- There are two major approaches to studying how stress leads to illness: the physiological reactivity model and the health behavior model.

- The physiological reactivity model examines how the psychological effects of sustained stress make illness more likely.

- Psychoneuroimmunology (PNI) encompasses research on any type of connection between the CNS and the immune system.

- The work of Ader and Cohen on classically conditioned immunosuppression showed a relationship between psychological processes and changes in immune function.

- The immune system defends the body against disease. Immunity consists of natural and acquired aspects. When antigens are present, lymphocytes either release antibodies into the blood or bind directly with the antigen to disable it.

- Numerous studies have demonstrated the effects of stress on regulation of the immune system. The most convincing argument for a meaningful stress-immune connection comes from studies that measure the experience of stress, immune measures, and related illness outcomes.

- The Type A Behavior Pattern, a way of responding to demanding situations with hostility, time urgency, and competitiveness, can predict the later development of heart disease. The hostility component of the Type A pattern best predicts coronary heart disease.

- The cardiovascular reactivity model offers a perspective for understanding how hostility might increase risk for heart disease. Hostility increases the likelihood and frequency of the physiological effects of anger, which, over time, increases the likelihood of hardened arteries and, eventually, coronary heart disease.

- People engage in behaviors that enhance health as well as those that make them more susceptible to illness. Behaviors such as smoking and drinking alcohol increase risk for major illness such as heart disease, cancer, and liver disease. Eating in response to stress also imposes risks.

- Healthy diet and exercise can extend life and enhance brain function.

BRINGING IT ALL TOGETHER: MAKING CONNECTIONS IN STRESS AND HEALTH

- Living with HIV and possibly developing AIDS presents enormous challenges for patients and caregivers alike. Psychosocial variables, such as depression and coping, influence immune measures, disease progression, and mortality in people infected with HIV.

Key **Terms**

emotion-focused coping, p. 485

exhaustion stage, p. 483

general adaptation syndrome (GAS), p. 482

glucocorticoids, p. 480

health behavior approach, p. 492

health psychology, p. 492

hypothalamic-pituitary-adrenal (HPA) axis, p. 481

natural immunity, p. 495

neuroendocrine system, p. 480

norepinephrine, p. 481

physiological reactivity model, p. 492

primary appraisal, p. 476

problem-focused coping, p. 485

psychoneuroimmunology (PNI), p. 495

psychosomatic theory, p. 492

resistance stage, p. 482

secondary appraisal, p. 476

stress, p. 476

stressors, p. 477

telomerase, p. 491

Type A Behavior Pattern (TABP), p. 498

Quick Quiz **Answers**

Quick Quiz 12.1:   1. c   2. b   3. d   4. a
Quick Quiz 12.2:   1. a   2. c   3. c   4. d
Quick Quiz 12.3:   1. c   2. a   3. b   4. d
Quick Quiz 12.4:   1. a   2. d

Challenge Your Assumptions **Answers**

• Stress can make you sick. **True. See pp. 476, 492–493.**

• There is a gene for stress. **False. See p. 484.**

• Stress makes you age faster. **True. See p. 491.**

• People who are Type A are really anxious and high-strung. **False. See p. 498.**

• Exercising 10 minutes a day can change genes that increase your metabolism. **True. See p. 502.**

Personality: The Uniqueness of the Individual

13

Chapter Outline

Challenge *Your Assumptions*

TRUE OR FALSE?

- Your personality is determined mostly by your family environment.

- Our unique temperament does not start to show itself until early childhood.

- Freud's ideas are interesting but have no scientific support.

- Many different kinds of animals have personality in the sense that humans do.

- Your personality predicts what you major in or what career you go into.

- People can usually change their personalities if they try.

Answers can be found at the end of the chapter.

Jerry and Evan are young brothers—Jerry is 13, and Evan is 9. They have similar yet distinct personalities. Both are curious, intelligent, socially skilled, full of energy, and active. Jerry, however, the older of the two, knows it's better to stick to rules than break them, is bothered if an adult gets angry at him, and is socially skilled with boys but very shy around girls. In addition, he is gentle, yet afraid of spiders and the dark. He is a leader and competitive, but never aggressive with peers, and incredibly friendly. He would not go up and talk to a stranger if his life depended on it.

Evan, by contrast, is very artistic, dramatic, energetic, aggressive, and fearless. He loves breaking rules just for the fun of it and, without a shred of shyness, will ask a stranger a question or strike up a conversation. Moreover, he can easily tell you what he is thinking and feeling and describe the details of why something bothers him. All you get from Jerry is an "I don't know" or "Nothing" when he's asked what's bothering him or "good" and "fine" when he's asked how he liked something. Often during play, even if alone, Evan will pose intense anger and scowl at pretend enemies.

We, your authors, know these two children very well: They are our children! Although we highlight them here, Jerry and Evan could be any pair of brothers. This kind of contrast is more the rule than the exception among siblings. If you have brothers or sisters, this description, at least in outline form, probably rings true. How is it that two people—reared in similar environments by the same parents—can have such different personalities?

To answer this question, we must address what personality is, examine classic and current research on the nature and nurture of personality, review the major theoretical explanations for what personality is and how it develops, and describe how personality is measured. Lastly, we connect many of these topics by reviewing the issue of personality change. ■

DEFINING PERSONALITY

personality
the unique and relatively enduring set of behaviors, feelings, thoughts, and motives that characterize an individual.

When psychologists use the term **personality,** they are referring to the unique and relatively enduring set of behaviors, feelings, thoughts, and motives that characterize an individual (J. Feist & Feist, 2009; Roberts & Mroczek, 2008). The definition of *personality* includes two key components. First, personality is what distinguishes us from one another and makes us unique. Second, personality is relatively enduring, or consistent. Let's consider these key components in more detail.

The first major component of personality involves the uniqueness of an individual's thoughts, feelings, and behavior. People will respond to almost every situation in different ways. Consider what happens when one driver cuts in front of another. Some people react to such an incident with "road rage," while others take it in stride. A characteristic of personality—hostility—may determine whether someone responds with road rage or not. Personality, therefore, is about uniqueness, or *individual differences*. The concept of personality would not exist if everyone acted and thought alike. Research supports the strength of individual differences: Even when a strong authority figure creates extreme pressure to obey, not everyone will do so (Milgram, 1963). Personality psychology is concerned with the different ways people act in the same situation.

A second part of the definition of personality is its relatively enduring consistency: both across different situations and over time. Consistency across situations refers to the notion that a person behaves the same way in different situations and carries who he or she is into almost every situation. Consistency over time, in contrast, is the extent to which a person behaves the same way throughout the life span.

Bringing these two components of personality together, we label a person as "friendly," for example, only if we observe her behaving in a friendly manner in situations in which most others might not act friendly and she does so consistently over time and in many different situations. A friendly person might behave in a friendly manner at a party, while having coffee with friends, or when meeting someone for the first time. We would say that this person's friendly behavior is unique and consistent.

trait
a disposition to behave consistently in a particular way.

Friendliness is a personality **trait,** or a disposition to behave consistently in a particular way. Although traits make up a large part of an individual's personality, they are not quite synonymous with it. *Personality* is the broader term because it comprises traits but also motives, thoughts, self-concept, and feelings.

One important principle of personality traits is that they, like intelligence, are normally distributed in the population. Recall from Chapter 10 (Figure 10.7) that a normal distribution exists when the graph of all the scores is symmetrical and bell-shaped. A few people exist at both the extreme low and extreme high end of the distribution, but most people are average. Consider the traits of anxiety (or neuroticism), warmth, and extraversion. A few people, for instance, are barely anxious, and a few are extremely anxious, but most people are somewhere in the middle. The same is true for extraversion, warmth, and any other personality trait.

Connection
Would you shock someone to unconsciousness if an authority figure told you that you had no choice? Extreme situations can push people to behave in ways we would not expect from their personalities.
See "Obedience," Chapter 14, "Social Behavior," p. 552.

Another important principle of traits is that they are directly connected to behavior. They lower **behavioral thresholds,** or the point at which you move from not having a particular response to having one (Allport, 1937; Feist & Barron, 2003; Rosenberg, 1998). A low threshold means you are very likely to behave in a particular way, whereas a high threshold means you are not. To illustrate: Carlos is shy, which means he has a low threshold for feeling awkward. If he were introduced to a group of strangers, he would likely feel uncomfortable. In the same situation, however, Karen, who is outgoing, would probably feel comfortable because she has a much higher threshold for social awkwardness. Their optimal levels of arousal—or thresholds—are different. In short, traits lower behavioral thresholds and are directly connected to behavior.

behavioral thresholds
the point at which a person moves from not having a particular response to having one.

Quick Quiz 13.1: Defining Personality

1. Two characteristics of personality include
   a. uniqueness and instability in behavior
   b. uniqueness and consistency in behavior
   c. consistency in behavior and identity formation
   d. uniqueness and change in behavior

2. A statistical property of most personality traits is that they are
   a. unreliably measured
   b. randomly distributed
   c. normally distributed
   d. skewed distributions

Answers can be found at the end of the chapter.

THE NATURE AND NURTURE OF PERSONALITY

The forces of both nature and nurture shape personality. The interaction between the two can be seen in at least four lines of reasoning and research into personality: evolutionary theory, genetics, temperament and fetal development, and cross-cultural universality.

The Evolution of Personality Traits

Human personality traits evolved as adaptive behavioral responses to fundamental problems of survival and reproduction. Certain behaviors were useful for survival or reproductive success during early periods of human evolution, and these behaviors have been shaped by natural selection (D. M. Buss, 2008; D. M. Buss & Greiling, 1999; McCrae & Costa, 1999). The tendency to be sensitive to threats, for instance, may well have been adaptive in dangerous environments like those in which our ancestors lived. Heightened anxiety would provide a signal of danger and threat; its absence would quickly lead to extinction of the species. Consider a hunter on the savannah. He hears the growl of a large animal and becomes fearful. He drops back behind the bushes, before the animal becomes aware of his presence. If he did not feel anxious, he might not hide, with dire consequences for his safety and his likelihood of catching dinner. By the same token, the other extreme—hypersensitivity to threats—would be debilitating and disruptive to everyday functioning. If the same man who became fearful at hearing the growl of a large animal also became fearful with every rustling of leaves or every sound of the wind, he would have a hard time functioning in everyday life. Having some degree of fearfulness is adaptive, and people with that quality were more likely to survive, reproduce, and pass on that disposition.

Naturally selected traits are favored if they increase one's chances of survival and reproductive success. Sexually selected traits, on the other hand, make one more attractive to the opposite sex. For example, a study of over 400 individuals, many of whom were creative artists and poets, revealed a positive correlation between creativity and sexual success. That is, more creative people were also more sexually active (Nettle & Clegg, 2005). The researchers argue that their findings support the theory, first proposed by Darwin and more recently by Geoffrey Miller (2000), that human creative ability is a sexually selected trait because it is a quality that increases one's attractiveness to members of the opposite sex.

The evolution of personality traits demonstrates how environmental forces can shape our bodies, brain, and behavior over long periods of time. Nurture shapes nature.

Genetics and Personality

quantitative trait loci (QTL) approach
a technique in behavioral genetics that looks for the location on genes that might be associated with particular behaviors.

Recall from Chapter 3 that complex traits are almost never the result of a single gene and that our genome is the starting point, not the end point, for how our genes are expressed (our phenotype). There is no "smart" gene, "shy" gene, or "aggressive" gene. We discuss these two themes in detail later in this section, but first let's look at how *behavioral geneticists* study the relationship between genes and personality.

When studying behavioral genetics, researchers use two major methods to examine the relationship among genetics, behavior, and personality. With the first method, the **quantitative trait loci (QTL) approach,** they look for the

Connection

Many people think a single gene affects behavior—that we have a gene for "aggression," for example. Any given behavior or personality trait, however, is never the result of single genes but rather of many genes.

See "Genes and Behavior," Chapter 3, "The Biology of Behavior," p. 77.

location of specific bits of DNA on genes that might be associated with particular behaviors. In this sense, it is a search for "genetic markers" of behavior. The traits are quantitative because they are markers for behaviors that are expressed on a broad continuum, from very little to very much. For example, anxiety is a quantitative trait because some people are not at all anxious, most people are average, and a few are very anxious. The QTL method uncovers the location on particular genes that is associated with high or low levels of a trait. These locations are also known as "markers."

QTL research points to genetic markers for several basic personality traits, such as novelty- or thrill seeking, impulsivity, and neuroticism/anxiety (Benjamin et al., 1996; Hamer & Copeland, 1998; Lesch et al., 1996; Plomin & Caspi, 1999; Retz et al., 2010; Rutter, 2006). Consider the case of thrill seeking, a trait that entails risk taking. People with this trait may seek out highly exciting activities like bungee jumping, mountain climbing, or scuba diving. Thrill-seeking activities create a "rush" of excitement—a positive feeling that may be related to the release of dopamine, a neurotransmitter associated with physiological arousal. Given the possible connection between dopamine and thrill seeking, one theory suggests that people who are deficient in dopamine will tend to seek out exciting situations as a way of increasing their dopamine release and making up for deficient levels of dopamine.

In the mid-1990s, researchers presented the first genetic evidence to support this theory. The gene DRD4 is involved in dopamine production in the limbic system, and the longer the gene sequence, the less efficient dopamine production is. In other words, long versions of the DRD4 gene are associated with less efficient dopamine production. If the theory is correct, people who seek out thrills should have the longer form of this gene, and that is exactly what the research has shown (Ebstein et al., 1996; Hamer & Copeland, 1998). An exciting aspect of this finding is that it was the first to demonstrate a specific genetic influence on a normal (nonpathological) personality trait.

As discussed more fully in Chapter 3, the second method for examining the effect that genetics play in behavior and personality is the study of twins, both identical and fraternal, who have been raised together or apart. Twin studies have found that most basic personality traits have heritability estimates of between 40% and 60%. In other words, an individual's genetic makeup goes about halfway toward explaining his or her basic traits. For instance, the trait of extraversion, or outgoingness, often correlates around .50 for identical twins and around .24 for fraternal twins, which leads to a heritability estimate of 48% (see Figure 13.1). Likewise, between 50% and 55% of the differences in neuroticism and conscientiousness are due to genetics, and about 40% of differences in openness and agreeableness are due to genetics (Bouchard & Loehlin, 2001; Caspi, Roberts, & Shiner, 2003; Krueger & Johnson, 2008; Loehlin et al., 1998; Plomin & Caspi, 1999; Tellegen et al., 1988).

Such a figure leaves roughly 50% of the differences in personality to be explained by three nongenetic sources: shared environment, unshared environment, and error. Even the environment is not just one thing,

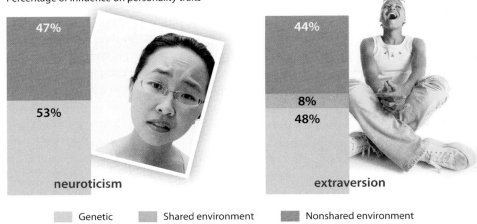

FIGURE **13.1**

NATURE AND NURTURE OF PERSONALITY: HERITABILITY OF FIVE TRAITS. Twin studies indicate that heredity (genetics) accounts for 50%–60% of most traits, slightly less for agreeableness and openness. What's surprising is that the influence of the shared environment (home and family) on these traits is small, compared with the influence of the nonshared environment. (Source: Plomin & Caspi, 1999)

Percentage of influence on personality traits

47%

53%

neuroticism

44%

8%

48%

extraversion

☐ Genetic ☐ Shared environment ☐ Nonshared environment

but needs to be broken into multiple parts. Shared environment consists of living conditions that siblings have in common, such as parents or household, whereas unshared environment consists of things like birth order, different friends, different teachers, and different social groups. Surprisingly, research indicates that the "unshared" environment—differences in birth order or peer groups or even changes in parenting style and attitudes over time—seems to matter most (see Figure 13.1) (Arseneault et al., 2003; Bouchard & Loehlin, 2001; Krueger & Johnson, 2008; Plomin & Caspi, 1999; Rutter, 2006). In short, personality is influenced by our environment, but surprisingly more by the experiences we do *not* share in common with our family members, such as peer group influences.

Temperament and the Fetal Environment

Recall from Chapter 5 that temperament is the biologically based disposition to behave in certain ways, which lays the foundation for later personality traits. Evidence suggests that temperament and personality differences are manifest even before birth. Apparently, fetal activity and heart rate can reveal something about temperament differences over the first year of life. In particular, a high heart rate at 36 weeks' gestation (nearly full term) foreshadowed less predictable eating and sleeping habits 3 and 6 months after birth and less emotionality at 6 months after birth. Having high activity levels at 36 weeks' gestation predicted being slow to adapt to new people or situations and having more irregular eating and sleeping habits at 3 and 6 months as well as being more difficult or fussy at 6 months (DiPietro et al., 1996).

The prenatal environment may play an important role in shaping personality. In fact, the amount of stress the mother experiences during pregnancy may alter the infant's own stress response. That is, infants born to mothers who have experienced an unusual amount of stress during pregnancy tend to have impaired stress function; higher baseline levels of stress hormones; and a faster, stronger, and more pronounced physiological response to stress, all of which persist into childhood (Barbazanges et al., 1996; A. S. Clark & Schneider, 1997).

Connection

Are some babies and toddlers temperamentally fussy and more difficult to care for than others? As we explain in the chapter on human development, with very little influence from the environment, some newborns are fussy, unpredictable, and get upset in new situations, whereas others are generally happy, predictable, and curious in new situations.

See "The Developing Infant and Child," Chapter 5, "Human Development," p. 178.

47% 14% 39% openness

58% 5% 37% agreeableness

44% 56% conscientiousness

Personality and Culture: Universality and Differences

Additional evidence that both nature and nurture shape personality comes from cross-cultural research on personality traits. If personality dispositions are part of our biology, we would expect the same personality dimensions or traits to appear in cultures all over the world. Environment and culture, however, might modify temperament and make certain traits more likely in some societies than in others. Indeed, there is evidence for both of these perspectives.

Researchers have investigated the personality traits of extraversion, neuroticism, agreeableness, openness to experience, conscientiousness, and psychoticism. Research confirms the existence of these personality traits not only in Western cultures (the United States, the United Kingdom, Germany, Australia, Iceland, Spain, Portugal), but also in Asian (China, Japan, South Korea), African (Zimbabwe), Middle Eastern (Iran, Israel), and Pacific Rim (Malaysia and the Philippines) cultures (Benet-Martinez & Oishi, 2008; McCrae, 2002; McCrae & Allik, 2002; McCrae & Costa, 1997). One measure of five major dimensions of personality, the NEO-Personality Inventory (PI), for example, has been translated into more than 40 languages, and the same five personality dimensions have emerged in every one (Rolland, 2002). In other words, people from vastly different cultural backgrounds exhibit these traits—evidence of their universal and biological basis.

Yet people in different cultures also differ on certain dimensions of personality. Once again, it is useful to appreciate behavior and personality from multiple perspectives. In particular, people in Asian cultures exhibit qualities that fit a dimension of "interpersonal relatedness" that is rarely seen in Western cultures. Interpersonal relatedness includes such behaviors and attitudes as a respectful, obedient demeanor toward others, a belief in saving "face" (that is, allowing a "losing" party to suffer a loss and yet maintain esteem and reputation), and an emphasis on harmonious relationships. This dimension of personality reflects how people in Asian cultures tend to be more concerned about the impact of their behavior on their family, friends, and social groups (known as *collectivism*), whereas people in Western cultures are more concerned with how their behavior will affect their personal goals (known as *individualism*) (Cross & Markus, 1999; Hofstede, 2001). Thus, an Asian employee who is offered a promotion that would require relocating to another city may be concerned

In Japan and other Asian cultures, respect for others and an emphasis on harmonious interpersonal relationships takes precedence over individual concerns. Interpersonal relatedness as a dimension of personality is rare in the West.

primarily with how the move would affect her family. On the other hand, the primary consideration of a Western employee might be how the move would increase her chances of someday becoming an executive in a major corporation.

Quick Quiz 13.2: The Nature and Nurture of Personality

1. The genetic marker for thrill seeking involves genetic differences in which neurotransmitter?
   a. dopamine
   b. acetylcholine
   c. serotonin
   d. norepinephrine

2. Researchers obtain estimates of how heritable personality traits are by
   a. studying biochemical markers of personality
   b. analyzing DNA in rats reared together

   c. documenting family histories
   d. studying twins

3. People in Asian cultures exhibit qualities that suggest a personality dimension of _____ that is rarely seen in Western cultures.
   a. anxiety
   b. interpersonal relatedness
   c. separation distress
   d. agreeableness

Answers can be found at the end of the chapter.

HOW DO THEORISTS EXPLAIN PERSONALITY?

Some people are calm and relaxed, and others are regularly nervous and anxious; some are warm and friendly, while others are hostile and aggressive; some people are organized, neat, and fastidious, while others are disorganized, sloppy, and scattered. How do we explain such differences in personality style? Let's take a look at the answers theorists have provided. The major explanations can be grouped into five distinct theoretical camps: psychoanalysis, humanism, social–cognitive learning, trait theory, and biological theory. As you will see, each offers a different perspective on the phenomenon of personality.

Psychoanalytic Theories

Psychoanalytic theories are all based on or are variations of Freud's seminal ideas.

Sigmund Freud Undoubtedly the most famous of all psychologists is Sigmund Freud (1856–1939). Freud not only proposed an overarching theory of personality and psychotherapy but also founded the movement known as psychoanalysis and in the process of doing so essentially invented the field of psychotherapy.

As we mentioned in Chapter 1, the starting point for Freud's theory of psychoanalysis is the idea that the unconscious is the most powerful force in our personality. More generally, Freud described three layers of consciousness: unconscious, preconscious, and conscious. The conscious layer is what we are aware of at any given moment in time, whereas the preconscious is just below the surface of awareness. It is not currently conscious but can become so relatively easily. Because the conscious and preconscious layers are less important in Freud's theory, we focus instead on the unconscious.

According to Freud, the **unconscious** contains all the drives, urges, or instincts that are outside awareness but nonetheless motivate most of our speech, thoughts, feelings, or actions. Before Freud, most people assumed that what we consciously think, feel, and believe is a relatively accurate and important source of information for explaining our behavior and personality.

Freud believed that much of what we do and the reasons that we do it are hidden from our awareness and revealed to us only in distorted forms, such as slips of the tongue and dreams (Freud, 1900/1953, 1901/1960). The technique of free association whereby people are encouraged to speak about anything on their minds without censoring their thoughts also provided access to the unconscious (see Chapter 16 for a discussion of free association). He developed an elaborate system for interpreting the meaning of dreams, because they were the best way to understand a person's unconscious.

Freud also developed the notion that the human mind has three distinct "provinces," or regions, that involve control and regulation of impulses. The first province—developed in infancy—is the **id,** and it is the seat of impulse and desire. The id is the part of our personality that we do not yet own; it owns or controls us. Its sole function is to seek pleasure; it is therefore founded in the "pleasure principle" and operates on the "do it" principle. By the end of the first year of life, a sense of self, or **ego,** begins to emerge. It is the only part of

unconscious
one of Freud's three levels of consciousness; it contains all the drives, urges, or instincts that are outside awareness but nonetheless motivate most of our speech, thoughts, feelings, or actions.

id
one of Freud's provinces of the mind; the seat of impulse and desire; the part of our personality that we do not yet own; it owns or controls us.

ego
one of Freud's provinces of the mind; a sense of self; the only part of the mind that is in direct contact with the outside world: operates on the "reality principle."

Connections
Cognitive psychologists refer to mental processes that occur outside awareness as "implicit" or "automatic." Much of what we learn and remember is implicit. See "Long-Term Memory Storage in the Cortex," Chapter 7, "Memory," p. 287, and "Basic Processes of Learning," Chapter 8, "Learning," p. 306.

Theories of personality, like all scientific theories, are based on theorists' observations and are used to generate research hypotheses. What observations about personality does this photograph bring to mind?

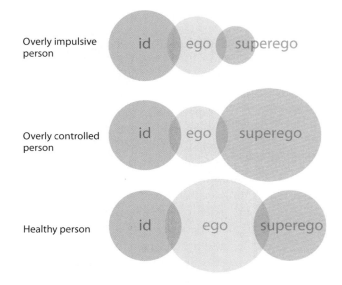

FIGURE **13.2**

THE RELATIVE INFLUENCES OF ID, EGO, AND SUPEREGO IN THREE TYPES OF PEOPLE. Freud argued that the relative sizes and strengths of the id, ego, and superego (as symbolized by the size of the circles) contributed to whether a person is overly impulsive, neurotically repressed and overcontrolled, or psychologically balanced and healthy. (Source: J. Feist & Feist, 2009)

superego
one of Freud's provinces of the mind; the part of the self that monitors and controls behavior; "stands over us" and evaluates actions in terms of right and wrong; hence, our conscience.

the mind that is in direct contact with the outside world, and it operates on the "reality principle." If the id wants pleasure, the ego makes a realistic attempt to obtain it. The last part of the mind to develop, around age 2 or 3, is the **superego,** the part of the self that monitors and controls behavior. The superego "stands over us" and evaluates actions in terms of right and wrong; hence, it is our conscience. It operates on the "moralistic principle" and gives us a sense of what we should and should not do. Thus, the superego is the control center of the personality and frequently applies the brakes to impulses of the id.

In a healthy person, the ego mediates this conflict between impulse and control. In fact, Freud believed that some people are mostly id-driven, whereas others are mostly superego-driven. People who are overly impulsive and pleasure seeking have an uncontrolled id. People who are overly controlling and repress their impulses have an exaggerated superego. The healthiest person is one in whom the ego is most developed and can control in a realistic and healthy way the conflict between impulse and control (see Figure 13.2).

Another of Freud's major contributions to psychology is the concept of psychological **defense mechanisms** (Freud, 1926/1959). Although Freud first described these mechanisms, his daughter, Anna, developed them further (A. Freud, 1946). Just as the physical body has the immune system to protect it from foreign substances, the mind also protects itself from harmful, threatening, and anxiety-provoking thoughts, feelings, or impulses. All defense mechanisms share two qualities: (1) They operate unconsciously; (2) they deny and distort reality in some way.

defense mechanisms
unconscious strategies the mind uses to protect itself from anxiety by denying and distorting reality in some way.

The most basic of all defense mechanisms is **repression**; it underlies all the other defense mechanisms. Repression is the unconscious act of keeping threatening or disturbing thoughts, feelings, or impulses out of consciousness. The impulses that are most likely to be repressed are sexual and aggressive impulses, because these are inherently the most threatening. Although repression may keep these impulses and thoughts out of awareness, they may be expressed in disguised or distorted form. In fact, they often reveal themselves—through dreams, slips of the tongue, or neurotic behavior.

repression
the unconscious act of keeping threatening thoughts, feelings, or impulses out of consciousness.

reaction formation
a defense mechanism that occurs when an unpleasant idea, feeling, or impulse is turned into its opposite.

Reaction formation occurs when an unpleasant idea, feeling, or impulse is turned into its opposite. This often results in exaggerated or compulsive feelings and behavior (Freud, 1926/1959). For example, a woman may resent and even hate her mother, but because these feelings are not acceptable to her or to society, she turns them into showy, exaggerated love. Homophobia is another example: Hatred and aggression toward homosexuals might well be a reaction against fear of one's own latent homosexual impulses.

In **projection,** people deny and repress their own particular ideas, feelings, or impulses and project them onto others. For example, a man may desire a married woman, but instead of recognizing his feelings, he projects his desire onto the woman and believes that she is seducing him. Another defense is **sublimation,** which involves expressing a socially unacceptable impulse in a socially acceptable and even desirable way. Freud believed that most creative achievements are motivated by sublimated impulses, usually sexual or aggressive. That is, unfulfilled sexual desire or aggressive impulses drive much creative output. Thus, for example, a man who is hopelessly in love with an unattainable woman may engage in sublimation, channeling his feelings into writing a novel whose main characters closely resemble him and the woman he desires.

Freud is one of the most complex figures in the history of psychology. His theories have had a significant and lasting influence on Western thought. Large segments of 20th-century art and literature were directly or indirectly influenced by Freud's views of human nature, from James Joyce's use of stream of consciousness to Salvador Dalí's surrealistic paintings (Adams & Szaluta, 1996; Brivic, 1980; Kimball, 2003). And yet over the last generation, many research-oriented psychologists have dismissed Freud as a pseudoscientist because he did not support his ideas with research that could be replicated. His status as a scientist is indeed questionable, but this does not mean that his insights as a clinician have no scientific merit. In fact, in the late 1990s, a group of neuroscientists began to argue that the latest evidence from neuroscience confirms certain of Freud's ideas. According to Antonio Damasio, a well-known contemporary neuroscientist, "we can say that Freud's insights on the nature of consciousness are consonant with the most advanced contemporary neuroscience views" (quoted in Solms & Turnbull, 2002, p. 93). Others argue that Freud's ideas about the power of the unconscious, the conflicting nature of motives, and the importance of early childhood experience on adult personality have had a lasting impact and have survived empirical testing (Weston, 1998).

For all of Freud's genius, however, he became dogmatic about his ideas after he had published them. Any followers who seriously challenged them might

projection
a defense mechanism in which people deny particular ideas, feelings, or impulses and project them onto others.

sublimation
a defense mechanism that involves expressing a socially unacceptable impulse in a socially acceptable way.

To honor Freud's contributions to psychology, his last home, in London, has been preserved as a museum. His patients would lie on this couch during treatment sessions.

be ejected from Freud's inner circle or official society. Some of these followers went on to develop their own theories of psychoanalysis. Among them were Alfred Adler, Carl Jung, and Karen Horney.

Alfred Adler   The first to break away from Freud, Alfred Adler (1870–1937) saw himself as Freud's colleague rather than follower. But when he disagreed with Freud on the major motives underlying behavior, he had to resign from the presidency of Freud's Vienna Psychoanalytic Society. Adler's first major assumption was that humans naturally strive to overcome their inherent inferiorities or deficiencies, both physical and psychological. This **striving for superiority,** not sex or aggression, is the major drive behind all behavior (Adler, 1956). Adler introduced the term *compensation* to explain how this process unfolds. All people, he pointed out, begin life as young, immature, and helpless. As they grow, they strive toward growth and completion. In the process, they attempt to compensate for their feelings of weakness or inferiority. Although all people do this to some extent, some develop an unhealthy need to dominate or upstage others as a way of compensating for feelings of inferiority—that is, they develop an **inferiority complex.**

striving for superiority according to Adler, the major drive behind all behavior, whereby humans naturally strive to overcome their inherent inferiorities or deficiencies, both physical and psychological.

inferiority complex an unhealthy need to dominate or upstage others as a way of compensating for feelings of deficiency.

Research to **Real Life**

Napoleon purportedly became grandiose and a world conqueror to overcome his unconscious feelings of being inferior.

Connecting Psychology to Your Life: Do you know anyone in your life who is very arrogant and cocky, but deep down probably doubts his or her abilities?

Another key idea in Adler's theory of individual psychology is the importance of birth order in influencing personality (Adler, 1931). Adler noticed consistent differences in the personalities of first-born, middle-born, and last-born

Adler observed that people's personalities are shaped by their birth order.

individuals. First-born children tend to have strong feelings of superiority and power. After all, by definition, first-born children are older and more mature than their siblings. First-borns can be nurturing of others, but they are sometimes highly critical and have a strong need to be right. Second children tend to be motivated and cooperative, but they can become overly competitive. Youngest children can be realistically ambitious but also pampered and dependent on others. Finally, only children can be socially mature, but they sometimes lack social interest and have exaggerated feelings of superiority.

Carl Jung   Though younger, Carl Jung (1875–1961) became more widely known than Adler. Jung's signature idea was that the unconscious has two distinct forms: personal and collective (Jung, 1918/1964). The **personal unconscious** consists of all our repressed and hidden thoughts, feelings, and motives. This is similar to Freud's notion of the unconscious. Jung also believed, however, that there is a second kind of unconscious, one that belongs not to the individual but to the species. He called it the **collective unconscious,** and it consists of the shared experiences of our ancestors—God, mother, life, death, water, earth, aggression, survival—that have been transmitted from generation to generation. Jung decided that there must be some kind of collective unconsciousness that would explain the many instances in which dreams, religions, legends, and myths share the same content even though the people who created them have never directly or even indirectly communicated with one another. The idea of a collective unconscious came naturally to Jung because he was extraordinarily well versed in world mythology, world religion, and archeology. However, he was less well versed in biological theory or genetics; thus, his understanding of the mechanisms involved was inconsistent and, at times, based on faulty assumptions, such as experiences being inherited from generation to generation.

The collective unconscious is made up of **archetypes:** ancient or archaic images that result from common ancestral experiences. Their content is made manifest most often in our dreams but also in fantasies, hallucinations, myths, and religious themes. Jung postulated many archetypes, including the shadow, anima, and animus. The **shadow** is the dark and morally objectionable part of ourselves. We all have impulses that are dark and disturbing; in fact, most often we project evil and darkness onto our enemies and deny that we ourselves are evil or capable of it. Shadow figures are found everywhere in politics, literature, and art, not to mention movies: Darth Vader of *Star Wars* clearly personifies the shadow figure.

The **anima** is the female part of the male personality, and the **animus** is the male part of the female personality. All people possess characteristics and traits—not to mention hormones—that are typical of both genders, but men tend to deny and repress their feminine side, or anima. Women likewise tend to deny or repress their masculine side, or animus. Full personality development requires acknowledging and being receptive to these unconscious or less-well-developed sides of one's personality.

collective unconscious according to Jung, form of consciousness that consists of the shared experiences of our ancestors—God, mother, life, death, water, earth, aggression, survival—that have been passed down from generation to generation.

archetypes ancient or archaic images that result from common ancestral experiences.

shadow according to Jung, the dark and morally objectionable part of ourselves.

anima according to Jung, the female part of the male personality.

animus according to Jung, the male part of the female personality.

personal unconscious according to Jung, form of consciousness that consists of all our repressed and hidden thoughts, feelings, and motives.

Darth Vader, the villain from the movie *Star Wars,* epitomizes Jung's shadow archetype of the dark, morally repugnant side of human nature.

Karen Horney   One of the first major female voices in the psychoanalytic movement was that of Karen Horney (pronounced "horn-eye"; 1885–1952). Compared to Freud, Horney focused more on the social and cultural forces behind neurosis and the neurotic personality, and indeed her approach is labeled "psychoanalytic social theory." The essence of Horney's theory is that neurosis stems from basic hostility and basic anxiety. *Basic hostility* is anger or rage that originates in childhood and stems from fear of being neglected or rejected by one's parents. Because hostility toward one's parents is so threatening, however, it is often turned inward and converted into *basic anxiety,* which Horney defined as "a feeling of being isolated and helpless in a world conceived as potentially hostile" (1950, p. 18).

Although basic anxiety in itself is not neurotic—it can give rise to normal behaviors—in some people it can result in neurotic behaviors. Horney argued that all people defend themselves against basic anxiety (isolation and helplessness) by developing particular needs or trends (see Figure 13.3). If these needs become compulsive and the person is unable to switch from one need to another as the situation demands, that person is neurotic. The three neurotic trends or needs are

1. *moving toward others* (the compliant personality)
2. *moving against others* (the aggressive personality)
3. *moving away from others* (the detached personality)

Neurotically moving toward others involves consistently needing or clinging to other people, belittling oneself, getting people to feel sorry for "poor little me," and almost completely repressing feelings of anger and hostility. Neurotically moving against others involves puffing oneself up in an obvious and public manner, "chest-beating," competing against others at almost everything, and being prone to hostility and anger. Finally, neurotically moving away from others involves developing a detached and "cool" demeanor—not responding emotionally, not caring, and being "above it all." One way to avoid feeling isolated and helpless is not to feel anything. Whenever someone tries to get close to a

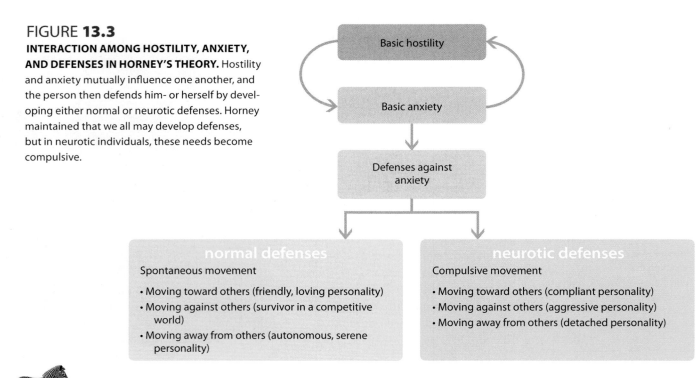

FIGURE 13.3

INTERACTION AMONG HOSTILITY, ANXIETY, AND DEFENSES IN HORNEY'S THEORY. Hostility and anxiety mutually influence one another, and the person then defends him- or herself by developing either normal or neurotic defenses. Horney maintained that we all may develop defenses, but in neurotic individuals, these needs become compulsive.

Basic hostility

Basic anxiety

Defenses against anxiety

normal defenses
Spontaneous movement

• Moving toward others (friendly, loving personality)
• Moving against others (survivor in a competitive world)
• Moving away from others (autonomous, serene personality)

neurotic defenses
Compulsive movement

• Moving toward others (compliant personality)
• Moving against others (aggressive personality)
• Moving away from others (detached personality)

detached person and open up to him or her, the detached person withdraws and closes up. Detached individuals are unwilling to make commitments, especially to long-term relationships (Horney, 1945).

Neuropsychoanalysis   One of the major criticisms of Freudian theory has been its lack of empirical or scientific foundation. Critics claimed that it was more "armchair speculation" than scientifically testable hypotheses (Crews, 1998). Although there is some validity to some of these criticisms, it is also true that certain Freudian assumptions—that unconscious motives affect our thinking and reasoning, and that dreams are mostly about repressed ideas—have received recent scientific support (Westen et al., 2006).

neuropsycho-analysis
a new scientific movement started in the late 1990s that combined Freudian ideas with neuroscientific methods.

In fact, **neuropsychoanalysis,** a new scientific movement that started in the late 1990s, combined Freudian ideas with neuroscientific methods. By combining the subjective insights into the mind made by Freud with the objective insights of the mind gained by neuroscience, neuropsychoanalysts are closing the divide that existed between Freud's ideas and science. Neuropsychoanalysts argue that at least seven core assumptions made by Freud have received recent scientific support (Solms, 2004; Westen et al., 2006; Westen, Gabbard, & Ortigo, 2008):

- importance of early childhood experience on later personality development
- unconscious motivation
- repression and defense mechanisms
- pleasure principle
- primitive drives
- dreams as wish fulfillment
- thinking and perception being guided by unconscious motives and emotions

For example, a recent study from a Freudian perspective examined the ways unconscious feelings and motives affect how people judge presidential candidates (Westen et al., 2006). The researchers found that people tended to gloss over contradictions made by their preferred candidate; that is, they didn't see them as real contradictions. They did, however, latch on to the contradictions of their nonpreferred candidate. Such a result is quite consistent with Freudian notion of repression, where people ignore or deny threatening ideas. In addition, neuroimaging results of the study showed that motivated reasoning involves different brain regions than nonmotivated reasoning. Motivated reasoning is reasoning that is influenced by our wishes and desires. To be more exact, both forms of reasoning involve the prefrontal cortex, but different regions. In addition, motivated reasoning activated regions of the brain involved in emotional responses (anterior cingulate cortex and the insula), whereas nonmotivated reasoning did not.

Humanistic–Positive Psychological Theories

A second major perspective explaining personality comes from a *humanistic approach,* which is optimistic about human nature, believing that humans are naturally interested in realizing their full potential. Humanists argue that psychology needs to study humans at their best as well as at their worst. As Abraham Maslow wrote (1968, p. 5), "Freud supplied us with the sick half of psychology, and we must now fill it with the healthy half." The term *humanism* is not commonly used today, mostly because many adherents of this approach did not conduct empirical research. Yet the movement has been rekindled since the late 1990s under a new label: *positive psychology.* Positive psychology embraces and generates empirical research, but its fundamental ideas come from two major thinkers in the humanistic tradition: Abraham Maslow and Carl Rogers (Seligman & Csikszentmihalyi, 2000).

Abraham Maslow   We discussed one of Abraham Maslow's (1908–1970) major ideas in Chapter 11: his hierarchy of needs. An important concept that followed from his theory of needs was that of self-actualization, which stood at the top of the hierarchy. This term refers to people's inherent drive to realize their full potential (an idea that was influenced by Adler's notion of striving for superiority; Maslow, 1970). Very few people attain this highest level of the hierarchy of needs because very few are "fully human"—that is, living life at its fullest and achieving their full potential.

Based on an examination of historical figures whom he considered self-actualizing, Maslow identified a set of characteristics that he believed to be more common in self-actualizing individuals than in other people (Maslow, 1970). He listed 15 characteristics, five of which we summarize here:

1. *Spontaneity, simplicity, naturalness:* Self-actualizing people sometimes can appear quite childlike in their ability to be spontaneous and straightforward; they do not pretend to be what they are not.

2. *Problem-centered (have a "calling"):* Self-actualizing people often experience moments of profound personal importance or personal meaning (what Maslow called "peak experiences"), and these experiences shape the rest of their lives. A sense of what they were meant to do with their lives is suddenly revealed to them, and they devote the rest of their lives to it. These individuals are focused and secure in who they are and what matters most to them—and often their concerns have great philosophical, spiritual, political, artistic, or scientific meaning.

3. *Creativity (self-actualizing rather than specialized):* Problems confront us dozens, if not hundreds, of times each day. Self-actualizing people are able to readily solve problems with originality

Connection
A truly starving person is not concerned with art and beauty. Maslow's hierarchy of needs describes how the basic needs (such as hunger, thirst) must be satisfied before one can pursue the higher needs, such as self-actualization.
See "Models of Motivation," Chapter 11, "Motivation and Emotion," p. 427.

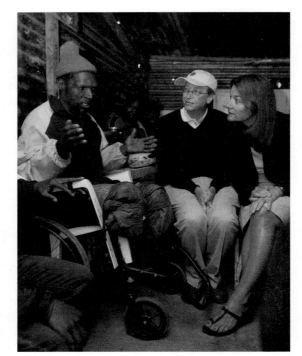

Does Bill Gates (center, with his wife Melinda Gates and a patient at a clinic in South Africa) fit Maslow's profile of a self-actualizing individual? In 1975 Gates founded the Microsoft Corporation and revolutionized the computing industry. Having left the day-to-day management of Microsoft to others, he now dedicates his efforts to eradicating AIDS and other diseases throughout the world, providing college scholarships for minority students, and funding other philanthropic endeavors through the Bill and Melinda Gates Foundation.

and novelty. By creativity, Maslow does not mean creativity as expressed in art or science (specialized creativity) but rather the kind of creativity that can be found in everyday life (self-actualizing creativity). Practical, everyday creativity is more important than professional achievement—although self-actualized people may be creative in their work as well.

4. *Deep interpersonal relations:* Self-actualizing individuals are likely to have few but profound relationships. They do not call 10 or 15 people their "best friends" or even "friends" but instead may have close relationships with only one or two people. These relationships, however, are intensely intimate—they share deep thoughts and feelings about themselves, each other, and the world.

5. *Resistance to enculturation:* Self-actualizing people are less likely than most people to be influenced by the ideas and attitudes of others. Their ideas are solidly their own; because they have a clear sense of direction in life, they don't look to others for guidance on what to think or how to behave.

Carl Rogers   Another key figure in the humanistic–positive psychology tradition was the psychotherapist Carl Rogers (1902–1987). Rogers developed a unique form of psychotherapy based on the assumption that people naturally strive toward growth and fulfillment and need unconditional positive regard for that to happen (Rogers, 1980). **Unconditional positive regard** is the ability to respect and appreciate another person unconditionally—that is, regardless of the person's behavior. This may sound easy, but in fact it is very difficult. It means that even if someone violates our basic assumptions of what it means to be a good, decent, and moral person, we still appreciate, respect, and even love him or her as a person. It requires that we separate person from behavior—which can be difficult even for parents and their children. To love people only when they do things that we want and like is to love them conditionally.

In contrast to Maslow, Rogers had a specific, measurable way of defining the self-actualizing tendency and psychological adjustment. To Rogers, all of us have two distinct ways of seeing and evaluating ourselves: as we really are and as we ideally would like to be. The first he called the real self and the second the ideal self (Rogers, 1959). Rogers then defined psychological adjustment as congruence between the real and ideal selves.

In the late 1990s a modern offshoot to humanism began under the name *positive psychology* (Seligman & Csikszentmihalyi, 2000). The core idea behind

unconditional positive regard acceptance of another person regardless of his or her behavior.

Carl Rogers (second from right) leads a group therapy session. His client-centered therapy approach is discussed in Chapter 16.

positive psychology is a focus on positive states and experiences, such as hope, optimism, wisdom, creativity, spirituality, and positive emotions (for example, happiness). In contrast to the humanistic psychologists, however, positive psychologists are more likely to base their ideas in research than in speculation, clinical practice, and observation.

Social–Cognitive Learning Theories

A third major category of personality theory is based on the social–cognitive learning perspective, exemplified by the research and writings of Walter Mischel. As we have seen, personality traits produce consistent behavior over time and across situations. A hostile person, for example, may be less hostile in one situation (for example, being run into by a child) than in another (for example, being cut off in traffic). Yet, compared to a nonhostile person, he or she is likely to be more hostile in many—but not all—situations. Mischel says that people are not consistent across all situations (Mischel, 2009; Mischel & Shoda, 1995, 1999), because it would be pathological not to change one's behavior when the situation changes. The qualities a person brings to each situation interact with the situation to make behavior change when the situation changes. Figure 13.4 illustrates how people and situations interact according to Mischel's theory. The figure presents the probabilities of two individuals (A and B) acting in a hostile manner across nine different situations. As you can see, Person A is more likely to be hostile in six of the nine situations, so we would label this person "hostile." But notice two things: (1) There are a few situations in which Person B is more hostile, and (2) Person B is more stable and consistent across all nine situations, whereas Person A is sometimes very hostile but at other times not hostile at all. This hypothetical situation demonstrates how the person, situation, and behavior interact.

Trait Theories

A fourth general perspective that explains personality is the trait approach, which assumes that traits or dispositions are the major force behind personality. But

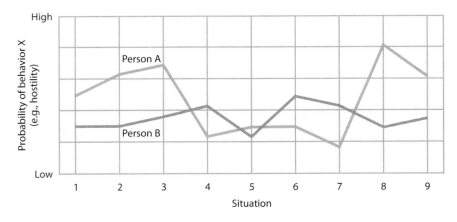

FIGURE **13.4**

HYPOTHETICAL PERSON–SITUATION BEHAVIOR INTERACTION. People respond to different situations differently, producing unique personality–situation profiles. Here, Person A is more hostile than Person B in the first three situations. They are roughly the same in the middle four situations. So saying that Person A is more hostile than Person B would be misleading and simplistic. It depends on the situation. (Source: Mischel & Shoda, 1995)

which traits are most important? Between the 1930s and the 1980s, dozens of different measures of personality were developed, but almost none of them measured the same personality traits. Some psychologists argued for the central importance of hostility, authoritarianism, introversion, intelligence, repression, and impulsivity, while others cited psychopathic deviance, tolerance, or psychological insight.

But until personality psychologists could reach a consensus on a set of traits that make up personality across cultures, no progress could be made in the study of personality, for it would mean different things to different people.

As far back as the 1930s, Gordon Allport (1897–1967) tried to figure out how many personality traits existed (Allport & Odbert, 1936). He began with the idea that language would be a good place to start looking. He argued quite simply that if a word exists for a trait, it must be important. He approached the problem by taking an English dictionary and combing through it page by page and counting each time a term described a person. After going through and counting all the personally descriptive words, he came away with nearly 18,000 words in English. A few problems arose, however. First, some of these terms—such as *sad, angry, bored,* or *annoyed*—described temporary states. Others were personal evaluations (*wonderful, unhelpful*) or described physical traits (*tall, heavy*). And finally, others were essentially synonyms, such as friendly and nice. When he fixed these problems, he still ended up with more than 4,000 English words that were personally descriptive. He went on to argue, however, that most individuals could typically be described with only about 10 or so central traits.

By the 1980s, personality researchers amassed evidence for the existence of five universal and widely agreed upon dimensions of personality (Costa & McCrae, 1992; Digman, 1990; John & Srivastava, 1999). This perspective is known as the **Big Five** or **five-factor model;** the five dimensions are openness to experience, conscientiousness, extraversion, agreeableness, and neuroticism (see Figure 13.5). An easy way to remember these is to use the acronym O-C-E-A-N or C-A-N-O-E.

The Big Five dimensions are more of a taxonomy, or categorization scheme, than a theory. They describe but do not explain personality. In the 1990s, Robert McCrae (1949–) and Paul Costa (1942–) proposed a theory around the Big Five personality dimensions. The two primary components of their theory are basic tendencies and characteristic adaptations (McCrae & Costa, 1996, 1999,

Big Five or **five-factor model**
a theory of personality that includes the following five dimensions: openness to experience, conscientiousness, extraversion, agreeableness, and neuroticism (OCEAN).

Dimension	Description
Openness (O)	How interested in new experiences or new ideas is someone? How imaginative, original, and curious is he or she?
Conscientiousness (C)	How planned, organized, orderly, hard-working, controlled, persevering, punctual, and ambitious is someone?
Extraversion (E)	How sociable, talkative, active, outgoing, confident, and fun-loving is someone?
Agreeableness (A)	How friendly, warm, trusting, generous, and good-natured is someone?
Neuroticism (N)	How anxious, worrying, tense, emotional, and high-strung is someone?

FIGURE **13.5**
BIG FIVE DIMENSIONS OF PERSONALITY. The acronym OCEAN (or CANOE) will help you remember the five dimensions.

2008). The Big Five personality dimensions, along with our talents, aptitudes, and cognitive abilities, are referred to as **basic tendencies,** and they have their origin in biological forces. In fact, McCrae and Costa take a clear but somewhat controversial stance in arguing that these basic tendencies are due solely to internal or biological factors such as genes, hormones, and brain structures.

Biological Theories

The fifth way of explaining personality theoretically, biological theory, does provide explanations for McCrae and Costa's scheme. The biological theories of personality assume that differences in personality are partly based in differences in structures and systems in the central nervous system, such as genetics, hormones, and neurotransmitters. Among the most important of these theories for personality is the one proposed by Hans Eysenck (1916–1997), who argued for the fundamental importance of biology in shaping personality. Eysenck (1947, 1982, 1990) proposed three, rather than five, fundamental dimensions of personality. Two are included in the Big Five, neuroticism and extraversion. The third, *psychoticism,* is a combination of the three other traits from the Big Five of openness, conscientiousness, and agreeableness. Psychoticism consists of traits such as "aggressive," "cold," "antisocial," "impulsive," "egocentric," "non-conforming," and "creative." All three personality dimensions are hierarchical; that is, neuroticism, extraversion, and psychoticism each comprise more specific traits, which in turn comprise even more specific traits (see Figure 13.6).

Eysenck developed a model in which differences in personality are caused by the combined influences of genes, neurochemistry, and certain characteristics of the central nervous system (Eysenck, 1997). The main idea behind Eysenck's model is that differences in individuals' genomes (DNA) create a different level of arousal and sensitivity to stimulation. These differences in genetics and levels of arousal and sensitivity lead to differences in the three primary dimensions of personality: psychoticism, extraversion, and neuroticism (P-E-N). Personality differences in dimensions, in turn, lead to differences in learning, conditioning, perception, and memory. These cognitive-perceptual-learning differences lead to differences in social behaviors such as sociability, criminality, sexual behavior, and creativity.

Evidence supports the connection between central nervous system arousal and personality traits, especially extraversion–introversion. Specifically, differences in cortical arousal and sensory thresholds lead to differences in extraversion–introversion. **Cortical arousal** refers to how active the brain is at a resting state as well as how sensitive it is to stimulation (Eysenck, 1997; Gale, 1983). Because they have higher baseline levels of cortical arousal, introverts require a lower stimulus

FIGURE **13.6**

EYSENCK'S HIERARCHY OF PER-SONALITY TRAITS FOR EXTRA-VERSION. For each of the three dimensions of personality, Eysenck developed a hierarchy of related traits and responses. (Source: Eysenck, 1990)

level to arouse them and reach their "comfort zone" than do extraverts. Eysenck argued that lower thresholds to arousal imply greater sensitivity to stimuli. Stimulation, whether it is a new place or new people, can easily become overwhelming for an introvert. Therefore, introverts consistently shy away from or withdraw from stimulating environments. By the same token, extraverts, with low cortical arousal and high thresholds of arousal, seek out and enjoy highly stimulating experiences (Eysenck, 1990, 1997). Introversion or inhibition can thus be seen as a way of coping with an inherently aroused and sensitive central nervous system.

As you see, a number of different approaches to understanding personality have been proposed by different theorists. The primary assumptions and key ideas of each of the five approaches are presented in Figure 13.7.

	Assumptions	Theorist	Key ideas
Psychoanalytic	Our personality resides in the unconscious and early childhood experiences lay the foundation for adult personality.	Freud	Unconscious, Preconscious, Conscious Id, Ego, Superego
		Adler	Striving for superiority Compensation Inferiority complex Birth order
		Jung	Personal unconscious, Collective unconscious Archetypes: shadow, anima, animus
		Horney	Basic hostility, basic anxiety, defenses against anxiety
Humanistic–Positive	We have a natural interest in becoming the best person possible.	Maslow	Strive to become the best possible person Self-actualization
		Rogers	Strive toward growth and fulfillment through unconditional positive regard Real self, Ideal self
Social–Cognitive	A person's behavior changes in different situations.	Mischel	Behavior results from the interaction of the cognitive and emotional qualities of the person and the particular situation he or she is in.
Traits	Traits are the major force behind personality.	McCrae/Costa	**O**penness to experience **C**onscientiousness **E**xtraversion **A**greeableness **N**euroticism Five-Factor Model includes: Basic tendencies—biologically based Characteristic adaptations—culturally based
Biological	We have a biological foundation for our personality traits.	Allport	Personality is a product of both heredity and environment.
		Eysenck	**P**sychoticism **E**xtraversion **N**euroticism Differences in genetics, neurochemistry, and CNS cause personality differences.

FIGURE **13.7**
SUMMARY OF FIVE APPROACHES TO PERSONALITY.

Quick Quiz 13.3: How Do Theorists Explain Personality?

1. Hatred and aggression toward homosexuals as a reaction to fear of one's own homosexual impulses would be an example of which Freudian defense mechanism?
   a. reaction formation
   b. psychosexual stages
   c. repression
   d. projection

2. According to Jung, the collective unconscious is made up of ancient or archaic images that result from common ancestral experiences called
   a. core-relational themes
   b. the animus
   c. the inferiority complex
   d. archetypes

3. The key assumption of humanistic theorists, such as Maslow or Rogers, is that people
   a. are driven by unconscious motives
   b. strive toward growth and fulfillment
   c. learn from observing others
   d. none of the above

4. The Big Five dimensions of personality are openness to experience, conscientiousness, extraversion, _____ , and _____ .
   a. depression; neuroticism
   b. agreeableness; neuroticism
   c. agreeableness; introversion
   d. anxiousness; introversion

Answers can be found at the end of the chapter.

Breaking New Ground

The Question of Animal Personality

Your authors recently adopted two 7-month-old kittens: "Scooter" (a male) and his sister, "Belle." These two kittens could hardly be more different in terms of their behavior. Scooter is absolutely curious and sociable. He explored every inch of his new home on the first day and forces himself into every one of our activities—eating, watching TV, working at the computer, and sleeping. Not once has he been afraid of any situation. He approaches everything with glee and wonder. Belle, however, has been anxious and shy from the beginning. It took her about 3 days to come out of hiding and become comfortable with her new home. She plays, but not so much with strangers, which we were for the first few days. She loves playing with her brother, however, and they regularly tease and chase each other. Now she hangs out with us and enjoys a good massage, but she is still skittish to sudden approaches.

To pet owners the question of animal personality seems to have an obvious answer: Of course, animals have distinct personalities. Just look at Scooter and Belle. But to psychologists the question might seem to be stretching the definition of personality too far. If we claim that animals have personality, might we simply be projecting human qualities onto them, what scientists term *anthropomorphizing*? Most people who have owned more than one cat or dog can identify differences in the personalities of their pets. Some pets are calm, while others are excitable; some are friendly and readily approach strangers, whereas others are more reserved and wary. But even if we can see evidence of personality in animals such as dogs and cats, can we see it in other animals? Do mice have personality? birds? reptiles? fish? worms? What do you think?

Until the 1990s, most psychologists would have argued that the term *personality* made sense only as applied to humans. But a graduate student at the University of California, Berkeley, changed this view. In the early 1990s Samuel Gosling was attending his required graduate seminar on personality psychology, which involved detailed discussion, readings, and debate about what personality means and how it should be defined. Here is his description of how he stumbled onto the question of animal personality:

> My undergraduate degree had been in philosophy and psychology so in the service of understanding what personality means, I tried to adopt a *reductio ad absurdum* [reduction to absurdity] strategy, pushing the term personality until it no longer made sense. I thought I'd take a case where it clearly made no sense to use personality and then work backward to find out where the limits of personality lay. Animals seemed like a good example of something that clearly didn't have personality so I decided to start there. But the more I thought about it the less I could generate arguments for why personality could not be applied to animals. (Gosling, personal communication, November 9, 2005)

Gosling's "aha moment" came when he questioned his own assumption of the absurdity of animal personality: animals, he and his colleagues were to discover, have personality traits quite similar to those of humans.

Gosling and Oliver John (1999) conducted a meta-analysis of 19 studies across 12 nonhuman species. They found evidence for at least 14 nonhuman species with personality traits that can be categorized along the same dimensions as human personality. The summary of these findings is presented in Figure 13.8. Keep in mind that the labels from the Big Five are general labels, and the specific ones used in these studies vary somewhat. For instance, neuroticism is sometimes called emotional stability, excitability, fearfulness, emotional reactivity, fear–avoidance, or emotionality. Agreeableness is sometimes labeled aggression, hostility, understanding, opportunistic, sociability, affection, or fighting–timidity. In addition, dominance–submission is a trait that is often seen and measured in nonhuman animals, but it does not fit into any of the Big Five categories. These ratings of animal personality were made by one of two behavioral observation techniques: either by animal trainers who had extensive knowledge of the individual animals or by trained observers with no history with the animals but who were trained until they could reliably evaluate the dimensions in question.

It may not surprise you that primates and other mammals tend to share the largest number of personality traits with humans (Weinstein, Capitanio, & Gosling, 2008). However, chimpanzees, our closest relative, share with humans a distinct "conscientiousness" dimension. Such a finding suggests that conscientiousness—which involves impulse control and therefore requires highly developed brain regions capable of controlling impulses—is the most recently evolved personality trait. Thus, with the exception of chimps and horses, animals other than humans do not possess the required brain structures to control impulse and organize and plan their activities in advance. Even with chimps, the conscientiousness dimension was somewhat narrowly defined as lack of attention, goal directedness, and disorganized behavior.

It may be surprising, however, to see wild birds, fish, and even octopus on a list of animals that possess humanlike personality traits. For instance, in a study of a European bird resembling a chickadee, when researchers placed a foreign object, such as a battery or a Pink Panther doll, into the cage, some birds were consistently curious and explored the novel object while others consistently withdrew and avoided the object (Zimmer, 2005; cf. Dingemanse et al., 2002). The researchers called these differences in birds "bold" and "shy." These differences are much like those psychologists observe when they place an infant in a room with a stranger. Approach–boldness and shyness–avoidance are also dimensions of human temperament.

	Neuroticism	Extraversion	Agreeableness	Openness	Conscientiousness
chimpanzee	✔	✔	✔	✔	✔
horse[a]	✔	✔	✔	?	✔
rhesus monkey	✔	✔	✔	✔	
gorilla	✔	✔	✔		
dog	✔	✔	✔	✔	✔[b]
cat	✔	✔	✔		✔[b]
hyena	✔		✔	✔	
pig		✔	✔	✔	
vervet monkey		✔			
donkey		✔	✔		
rat	✔		✔		
guppy	✔	✔			
octopus	✔	✔			
chickadee[c]				✔	

[a] Based on Morris, Gale, and Duffy (2002).
[b] Competence/learning is a mixture of openness and conscientiousness.
[c] Based on Dingemanse et al. (2002).

FIGURE 13.8

PERSONALITY DIMENSIONS ACROSS SPECIES. Ratings by trainers who know the animals or by trained observers produced these results, which suggest that animals do have personalities and that they share some of the same traits as humans. Note that domestic dogs and cats have a "competence" or "learning" dimension that is a mixture of openness and conscientiousness. Where no check mark appears, there is no evidence for that trait in that species. (Source: Gosling & John, 1999)

In summary, Gosling helped discover personality in a wide range of animals because he did not "believe everything he thought." He was able to question his assumptions that animals do not have personality and take that as a call to research rather than as a dead-end in his thinking.

■ ■ ■

Quick Quiz 13.4: Breaking New Ground: The Question of Animal Personality

1. Which of the human Big Five personality characteristics appears only in humans, chimpanzees, and horses?
   a. openness
   b. extraversion
   c. conscientiousness
   d. agreeableness

2. What is one real-world application of the work on animal personality?
   a. animal therapy
   b. dog show training
   c. selection of pets
   d. selection of seeing-eye dogs

Answers can be found at the end of the chapter.

HOW IS PERSONALITY MEASURED?

Defining and explaining personality are of prime importance, but you can define and explain only what you can measure. So how do psychologists measure and study personality? Four distinct methods are most common: behavioral observation, interviewing, projective tests, and questionnaires.

Behavioral Observation

The most direct and objective method for gathering personality data is to observe behavior and simply count specific behaviors that are associated with particular traits, such as aggression, hostility, friendliness, anxiety, or conscientiousness. However, collecting valid data is more difficult than it might seem. For instance, choosing to rate the fairly straightforward example of "aggression" raises many questions. What specific behaviors will count as aggression? Hitting? Insulting? Sarcasm? How does a researcher quantify each behavior—on a continuum from none to a great deal, or simply on the basis of whether it is present or not? Over what time period will the behavior be observed? Where will the behavior take place: in a real-world setting or in a laboratory? Who will rate the behavior? How do we know that different observers will view a given behavior in the same way?

These questions address the issue of measurement in general and reliability in particular. If two or more raters are to accurately rate and agree upon their ratings, there must be **inter-rater reliability.** The researchers must first establish an exact definition of the trait they wish to measure, identify the behaviors that make up that trait, and practice rating it against experienced, expert, and reliable raters. The new raters are deemed "reliable" if their ratings compare well with established norms or expert ratings, usually with a correlation of .80 or higher.

When children or others, such as animals, who cannot evaluate or report on their own personalities are being assessed, behavioral observations are required. The advantages of behavioral observations are that they do not depend on people's view of themselves, as self-report measurements do, and they are direct and relatively objective.

Despite these strengths, behavioral observations are costly and time-consuming. Moreover, not all personality traits can be observed by other people. Anxiety and depression, for instance, although they can be expressed through behavior, are often experienced internally and subjectively—external observations can't tell the whole story. For these kinds of personality traits a person's own reporting—that is, a self-report—is more reliable. Self-reports can be obtained in three ways: interviewing, projective tests, and questionnaires.

inter-rater reliability
measure of how much agreement there is in ratings when using two or more raters or coders to rate personality or other behaviors.

Interviewing

Sitting down with another person face-to-face is probably the most natural and comfortable of all personality assessment techniques. Interviewing is an ideal way to gather important information about a person's life. In fact, from the participant's perspective, interviewing is usually more engaging and pleasant than, for example, completing a questionnaire. The clear advantage for participants is the open-ended nature of the interview, in which they can say anything they wish in response to a question. Of course, this is also a drawback of interviewing. What does a response mean? How are responses scored and by whom? What criteria are used? These issues are similar to those associated with behavioral ratings, but with interviews the "behavior" is a verbal response to a question that must be coded reliably and accurately. Thus, the ease of interviews from the participant's perspective is offset by the difficulty of scoring responses reliably.

Projective Tests

projective tests personality assessment in which the participant is presented with a vague stimulus or situation and asked to interpret it or tell a story about what they see.

Projective tests present an ambiguous stimulus or situation to participants and ask them to give their interpretation of or tell a story about what they see. These techniques are based on the assumption, stemming from psychoanalysis, that unconscious wishes, thoughts, and motives will be "projected" onto the task. By interpreting an entire series of such answers, a psychologist can identify consistent unconscious themes. One of the most widely used projective tests is the Rorschach Inkblot Test.

In the **Rorschach Inkblot Test,** a series of ambiguous inkblots are presented one at a time, and the participant is asked to say what he or she sees in each one (see Figure 13.9). The responses are recorded and then coded by a trained coder (most often a psychologist or psychotherapist) as to how much human and nonhuman "movement," color, form, and shading the participant sees in each card (Exner, 1974; Masling & Borenstein, 2005). Not only is the test used to measure unconscious motives, but its supporters also claim that responses can help them diagnose various psychological disorders, such as depression, suicidal thoughts, pedophilia, post-traumatic stress disorder, or anxiety disorders (Guarnaccia et al., 2001; Nash et al., 1993; Ryan, Baerwald, & McGlone, 2008; Sloan, Arsenault, & Hilsenroth, 2002; Xiang, Shen, & Li, 2009).

Rorschach Inkblot Test a projective test in which the participant is asked to respond to a series of ambiguous inkblots.

FIGURE **13.9**

AN INKBLOT SIMILAR TO THOSE FOUND ON A RORSCHACH INKBLOT CARD. In the Rorschach Inkblot Test, a person is asked to interpret the inkblot however he or she wishes. After the participant has interpreted a dozen or more cards, psychologists can form ideas about what kinds of thoughts, feelings, and motives are consistently being "projected."

Personality Questionnaires

Because of the expense and time that behavioral ratings and interviews require, along with the relative unreliability of projective tests, the most common way of measuring personality is asking participants to summarize their own behavioral tendencies by means of questionnaires. **Personality questionnaires**

personality questionnaires self-report instruments on which respondents indicate the extent to which they agree or disagree with a series of statements as they apply to their personality.

consist of individual statements, or items; respondents indicate the extent to which they agree or disagree with each statement as it applies to their personality. Responses are usually arranged on a *Likert scale*, which attaches numbers to descriptive responses, such as 1, "completely disagree"; 3, "neither agree nor disagree"; and 5, "completely agree."

Questionnaires are developed with years of validation using either the rational or the empirical method. The **rational, or face valid,** method involves using reason or theory to come up with a question. For instance, if we wanted to develop a new measure of anxiety, we might include an item like "I feel anxious much of the time." This is a "face valid" item because what it measures (anxiety) is clear and can be taken at face value. A frequently used personality questionnaire that uses the face valid method is the NEO-PI (Costa & McCrae, 1992). The problem with such questionnaires, however, is that because the questions are transparent, participants might give socially desirable or false answers rather than honest ones. For example, for the item "I am anxious much of the time," someone might not want to admit to frequently feeling anxious and hence might not answer honestly.

The **empirical method** focuses instead on whether responses to various items differentiate between the groups it should (Gough & Bradley, 1996). For instance, if preliminary studies show that the statement "I prefer baths to showers" is answered a certain way by anxious people and a different way by non-anxious people (thereby discriminating between these two groups), it is used in a measure of anxiety. This method requires an outside criterion of who is anxious or not, such as a therapist's evaluation of the anxiety levels, to relate to such items. If the evidence shows that it does distinguish the two groups, then it is used in the questionnaire.

Two of the most widely used personality questionnaires were developed using the empirical method: the Minnesota Multiphasic Personality Inventory (MMPI) and the California Personality Inventory (CPI). The *MMPI* is used by psychotherapists to assess the degree and kind of a person's psychiatric personality traits, such as depression, paranoia, or psychopathic deviance (antisocial personality; Tellegen et al., 2003). The *CPI*, however, is a measure of nonpathological or normal personality traits such as sociability, responsibility, dominance, or self-control (Gough & Bradley, 1996). Both the MMPI and CPI consist of questions that target groups answer differently than does the general population. In "Psychology in the Real World," we describe how personality predicts college major, career interest, and job performance.

rational (face valid) method a method for developing questionnaire items that involves using reason or theory to come up with a question.

empirical method a method for developing questionnaire items that focuses on including questions that characterize the group the questionnaire is intended to distinguish.

Quick Quiz 13.5: How Is Personality Measured?

1. The most objective method for gathering information about personality traits is to
   a. observe behavior
   b. conduct interviews
   c. administer questionnaires
   d. do genetic testing

2. The Rorschach Inkblot Test is an example of which type of personality measurement?
   a. structure interview
   b. questionnaire
   c. projective test
   d. standardized test

3. Scales that use response categories ranging from 1 to 5 (with labels ranging from 1 for "completely agree" to 5 for "completely disagree") are called
   a. ratio scales
   b. Likert scales
   c. face valid
   d. dichotomous

Answers can be found at the end of the chapter.

Personality and Career Interest and Job Performance

Would you want a surgeon operating on you who is known for being anxious and nervous? How about having a police officer in your hometown who is violent and aggressive? Would you want to buy something from a shy and socially awkward salesperson? Personality is important when it comes to jobs.

If you go to your university or college career guidance counselor, they will very likely use personality tests in advising you in your career choices (Costa, 1996; Mount et al., 2005). Governments and organizations also rely on them to select the right people for particular jobs (Carless, 1999; De Fruyt & Murvielde, 1999). Indeed, Hammer and Macdaid (1992) provide a list of occupations most and least similar to one's personality. Among other things, personality traits predict the majors and careers we select, what kinds of employers select us, how people perform at jobs, and how likely they are to leave them once they get them.

Personality and Career and College Major Interest

The first stage of job selection—for college students at least—is picking a major. You may not be surprised to learn that different personality types are attracted to and interested in different kinds of majors. College majors are generally classified using three career codes, with the first one being primary (Emery, 2006). For example, psychology is SIE (Social-Investigative-Enterprising), economics is IAS (Investigative-Artistic-Social), and biology is IRE (Investigative-Realistic-Enterprising).

Personality research consistently shows that different personalities prefer different kinds of careers and college majors. Pulver and Kelly (2008) examined the association between personality and college major using a measure of personality based on Carl Jung's theory, the Myers-Briggs Type Indicator (MBTI; Myers, 1962). The MBTI consists of opposing types: Extraversion-Introversion, Thinking-Feeling,

Intuition-Sensing, and Judging-Perceiving. In other words, people are classified either as an extravert or an introvert, or as a thinker or a feeler, and so on. For example, Intuition-Sensing describes how people prefer to take in information—focused on what is real and actual (sensing) or on patterns and meanings in data (intuiting), whereas Thinking-Feeling describes how people prefer to make decisions—based on logical analysis (thinking) or guided by concern for their impact on others (feeling).

Pulver and Kelly (2008) found that extraverts preferred social and enterprising majors (such as psychology, social work, elementary education), whereas thinking types preferred realistic and investigative majors (such as mechanical engineering or archeology). Feeling types preferred artistic and social majors (such as art, music, and theater).

Similarly, Larson and colleagues (2010) examined whether personality scores reliably differentiated majors in 368 undergraduate students, but they used a different measure of personality. In this study, students completed the Multidimensional Personality Questionnaire (MPQ; Tellegen, 2000), a self-reported measure of personality that is scored on 11 primary personality traits, including social closeness, aggression (low agreeableness), harm–avoidance, and absorption.

Results showed that education majors scored higher than engineering majors on social closeness, whereas business majors scored significantly lower on agreeableness than humanities and architecture/design majors. In addition, architecture/design majors were more absorbed than business majors. Elementary education majors scored highest on harm avoidance (avoiding situations where one can get hurt) and social closeness out of the nine majors. Similar research reported harm–avoidance is negatively related to realistic interests and specifically interests in mechanical activities (Staggs et al., 2007). In other words, mechanical and athletic majors are not as likely as other majors to be afraid or driven to avoid harmful situations.

Personality–Environment Fit and Job Performance

Because so much research shows certain personalities matching certain majors and jobs, researchers have proposed a theory of fit between personality and job. Holland calls this idea "congruence," stating that "people find environments reinforcing and satisfying when environmental patterns resemble their personality patterns" (Holland, 1985, p. 53). I/O psychologists also refer to this notion of congruence as "person-organization fit," or how well matched the person is to his or her work environment (Kristof-Brown, Zimmerman, & Johnson, 2005). Numerous large-scale meta-analyses of over a thousand studies show that fit between personality and job does matter (Assouline & Meier, 1987; Kristof-Brown et al., 2005; Verquer, Beehr, & Wagner, 2003). The better the fit, the more satisfied people are with their jobs, the less likely they are to leave their jobs, and the more successful they will be.

Measures of fit and congruence allow employers not only to use personality measures to recruit/hire workers who best fit the job, but also to weed out people who might behave counterproductively. *Counterproductive work behaviors* can be defined as anything done by the employee that is intentionally negative for the organization (MacLane & Walmsley, 2010). Such behavior might include such major infractions as betraying company secrets or employee theft, but may also involve minor transgressions such as working nonproductively (spending too much time on Facebook or other Internet sites, for example).

What sort of personal characteristics have been linked with counterproductive workplace behavior? Of the traditional Big Five traits, people who are more conscientious, agreeable, and emotionally stable are less likely to engage in behaviors that harm their companies (Berry, Ones, & Sackett, 2007). In another study, a cluster of personality scales from the widely used California Psychological Inventory was able

Government and business organizations sometimes use measures of personality in screening job applicants. What kind of person do you think would make an effective police officer?

to reliably predict police officers who consistently used excessive force and provided drugs to inmates (Hargrave & Hiatt, 1989). More specifically, the problematic officers scored unusually low on the CPI's Self-control, Socialization, and Responsibility scales.

Personality and Switching Jobs

Personality traits also predict how long people stay in or switch their jobs. Two of the Big Five dimensions—openness to experience and agreeableness—appear to be most predictive of leaving jobs early in one's career. Recall that people with high openness to experience prefer new experiences over routine ones and that people high in agreeableness are warm, caring, and friendly. Researchers have reported that people high in openness and low in agreeableness are most likely to switch jobs and/or companies (Vinson, Connelly, & Ones, 2007; Wille, De Fruyt, & Feys, 2010).

In sum, people who are matched to their jobs make better, happier, more productive employees. Personality has wide-ranging influence over the kinds of careers we are interested in, how well various careers fit who we are, how long we stay, and how well we do in particular careers.

Bringing It All Together
Making Connections in Personality
Does Personality Change Over Time?

Personality is at the center of who we are. Recall our definition of personality at the beginning of the chapter: Personality is the unique and enduring manner in which a person thinks, feels, and behaves. Although it shows considerable stability over our lifetime, it also changes and develops between our infant and adult years. Hundreds of studies have looked at how personality traits change or don't change over the course of individuals' lives. Personality consistency and change illustrate many of the principles discussed in this chapter. Indeed, all definitions, theories, and measures of personality confront the question of consistency and change of personality.

Personality Consistency

In many ways, it is more difficult to change our personalities than we think. Much of who we are remains rather stable and consistent over our lifetimes. When we talk about personality consistency, however, we mean relative consistency. In fact, that is one of the lessons learned from Walter Mischel's work on how qualities and traits interact with specific situations to bring about different behavior across different situations (Kammrath, Mendoza-Denton, & Mischel, 2005; Mischel, 2009; Mischel & Shoda, 1999). No one is consistent all of the time or in all situations. Consistency is a matter of degree.

Longitudinal studies, those that examine the same people over a period of time, reveal high levels of stability of personality traits. Early in their collaboration, Costa and McCrae (1976) conducted a longitudinal study of personality, expecting to find that personality traits change over time. To their surprise, they found a high degree of stability over a 10-year period. Another set of longitudinal studies revealed very small changes in neuroticism, extraversion, and openness over a period of 6 to 9 years (Costa et al., 2000; McCrae & Costa, 2003).

Most parents or observers of infants and toddlers are quick to project subtle signs of their children's interest or talent into the future. But do our personality and traits at age 3 portend future outcomes such as employment, mental illness, criminal behavior, and quality of interpersonal relationships? Jack and Jeanne Block conducted some of the first long-term studies of human temperament and personality. They used most of the methods for assessing personality discussed in this chapter: interviews, behavioral observations, and personality questionnaires. They found, for instance, that children who were impulsive, aggressive, and tended to cry at age 3 were most likely to use drugs during adolescence (Block, Block, & Keyes, 1988).

Research from behavior genetics has demonstrated that personality stability between adolescence and adulthood is largely due to genetic factors (Blonigen et al., 2006; Krueger & Johnson, 2008; Takahashi et al., 2007). More specifically, genetics contribute to the personality consistency we see from adolescence to adulthood, whereas environmental factors contribute to both stability and change in personality traits (Takahashi et al., 2007).

Personality Change

We all like to think we can change—that we have the power to change our destructive habits and become a better person. But can we? Research does support some degree of personality change as we move from adolescence through adulthood and as we adapt to changes in life circumstances. First, we consider changes across the life span.

Typical Personality Change Across the Life Span

Recent research confirms that some degree of change in personality occurs normally from adolescence to adulthood and into old age (Allemand, Zimprich, & Hendricks, 2008; Lodi-Smith et al., 2009; Roberts & Mroczek, 2008). The most impressive evidence comes from a meta-analysis of 92

Connection
Children who are rated by their parents as being undercontrolled at age 3 are more likely than other children to have drinking problems, get in trouble with the law, and even attempt suicide by age 21.
See "The Developing Infant and Child," Chapter 5, "Human Development," p. 178.

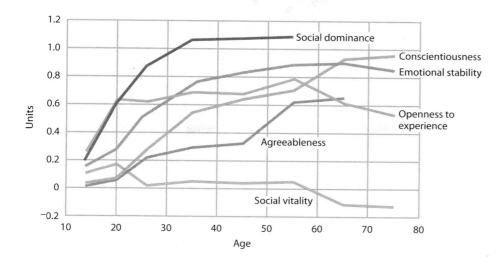

FIGURE **13.10**

PERSONALITY CHANGE FROM ADOLESCENCE TO LATE ADULT-HOOD. This graph shows the results of a meta-analysis of personality change on the Big Five dimensions across 92 studies and involving more than 50,000 individuals. The scale of change is measured in standardized units. 0 units means no change. Emotional stability is the opposite end of neuroticism. (Source: Roberts, Walton, & Viechtbauer, 2006)

studies that assessed personality change in over 50,000 individuals on the Big Five dimensions of personality (Roberts, Walton, & Viechtbauer, 2006). In general, people become steadily more agreeable and conscientious from adolescence to late adulthood (see Figure 13.10). In addition, people tend to become more assertive or dominant and emotionally stable from adolescence to middle adulthood and then level off on these personality dimensions. Finally, people generally become more sociable (social vitality) and open to new experiences from adolescence to early adulthood. These traits level off in adulthood and then decline in older adulthood. The same pattern of change is seen in cross-sectional research that examines personality differences in different age groups at the same time (Allemand et al., 2008). Together, these results make clear that personality is not set in plaster once we reach adulthood.

Personality Change After Changes in Life Circumstances

Not only does personality show some degree of change during normal life-span development, but it also is open to change when we experience drastic changes in our lives, such as becoming a parent, suffering a brain injury, or developing Alzheimer's disease. Let's consider each of these circumstances.

Parenting and Personality Change Few events change a person as much as becoming the primary caregiver for a totally helpless infant. How does such a major transition affect one's personality? The answer seems to be that it depends on many factors. Paris and Helson (2002) conducted a longitudinal study of female college seniors in their early 20s and followed them until they reached their 50s and 60s. They found that becoming a mother affected personality differently, depending on the woman's evaluation of motherhood.

That is, if a woman liked being a full-time mother, then having children led to an increase in her flexibility, self-esteem, adjustment, resourcefulness, and control and a decrease in her dependence and fearfulness. If, however, she did not especially enjoy being a full-time mother, the opposite personality changes were observed.

Other researchers report that parenthood affects the personalities of mothers and fathers differently. For example, although self-concept in general seems to stay the same for both mothers and fathers, self-esteem goes down and irritability goes up in mothers but not in fathers (Onodera, 2003). Similarly, the gender of the parent interacts with the temperament of the child. Compared to having a child with an "easy temperament," having one with a "difficult temperament" is more likely to increase the father's but not the mother's anxiety (Sirignono & Lachman, 1985). The biggest personality change seems to come from increases in a personal sense of control and mastery if parents have an "easy" child and decreases on these dimensions if they have a "difficult" child (Sirignono & Lachman, 1985). Having a child who is difficult undermines the belief that parents can truly control the life and behavior of their children.

Brain Injury and Personality Change Do you remember Phineas Gage from Chapter 3? He was the railroad foreman who had a tamping iron shoot through his cheek and out the top of his skull, forever changing his personality (Macmillan, 2000).

Current research on damage to the same part of the frontal lobes where Gage's injury occurred shows similar kinds of personality change. Based on ratings of personality (behavioral observations, Rorschach Inkblots, and semi-structured interviews), children and adults who suffer brain injury often lose the ability to control impulses, are socially inappropriate, have a temper, and are more prone to anger

Research Process

❶ Research Questions

Does Alzheimer's disease change an individual's personality? Do different observers agree on the nature of personality change after a person develops Alzheimer's disease?

Jack and Lucy before Alzheimer's diagnosis

❷ Method

Eleven elderly men and 11 elderly women (mean age = 72) who met the criteria for Alzheimer's disease, based on cognitive testing and brain images, participated in this correlational study by Strauss and colleagues (1993). The primary caregiver (most often a spouse) and a secondary good friend or family member each rated the patient's personality using the NEO-PI. The NEO-PI measures the "Big Five" personality dimensions of neuroticism, extraversion, openness, agreeableness, and conscientiousness. Raters were asked to remember when the symptoms of Alzheimer's first started and then pick a period of a few years prior to that and rate the person's personality at that time. Approximately two to three months later, each rater was asked to evaluate the patient's personality again, but this time as he or she was then—after the onset of Alzheimer's.

Lucy after diagnosis

Personality rating by Jack and his daughter

NEO personality rating

(Bar chart with y-axis labeled "Mean" ranging from 20 to 70, x-axis categories: Neuroticism, Extraversion, Openness, Agreeableness, Conscientiousness. Legend: Before, After)

❸ Results

Personality ratings of the person showed changes in three of the Big Five dimensions of personality after the onset of Alzheimer's disease. People were rated higher in neuroticism (anxiety) and lower in extraversion, openness, and conscientiousness. Agreeableness did not change. Independent ratings by secondary raters matched those of the primary raters and showed the same pattern.

❹ Conclusion

Primary and secondary raters agreed that after the onset of Alzheimer's disease people became more anxious, less extraverted, less open, and less conscientious. Other studies have replicated these general findings (Clark et al., 2000; Williams et al., 1995). Alzheimer's changes personality in predictable ways.

FIGURE **13.11**

PERSONALITY CHANGE AFTER ALZHEIMER'S DISEASE. Source: "Concordance Between Observers in Descriptions of Personality Change in Alzheimer's Disease," by M. E. Strauss, M. Pasupathi, & A. Chatterjee, 1993, *Psychology & Aging, 8,* 475–480.

(Mathiesen, Förster, & Svendsen, 2004; Max, Robertson, & Lansing, 2001; Max et al., 2006; Rao et al., 2008; Romain, 2008).

Alzheimer's Disease and Personality Change Alzheimer's disease is a major degenerative brain disease whose hallmarks are severe dementia and memory loss. It eventually affects personality and ultimately leads to death. Using the NEO-PI as a measure of the Big-Five personality dimensions, various studies have shown that neuroticism increases and openness and conscientiousness decrease after the onset of Alzheimer's disease (Chatterjee et al., 1992; L. Clark et al., 2000; Strauss, Pasupathi, & Chatterjee, 1993). Two studies have also reported a decrease in extraversion (Strauss et al., 1993; R. Williams, Briggs, & Coleman, 1995), and at least one study, described in the Research Process for this chapter, has reported a decrease in agreeableness (Chatterjee et al., 1992; see Figure 13.11). Most studies, however, report no change on the agreeableness dimension. Research using other measures of personality have reported that Alzheimer's patients became less kind, generous, enthusiastic, and self-reliant and more irritable and out-of-touch (Petry et al., 1989; Talassi et al., 2007). Some research has reported that personality

change can even precede the onset of the disease (Balsis, Carpenter, & Storandt, 2005). In other words, there is a biological basis for our personality. Changes in the brain are often accompanied by personality changes.

Quick Quiz 13.6: Bringing It All Together: Making Connections in Personality

1. Which personality trait tends to increase sharply from adolescence to adulthood but then taper off in late adulthood?
   a. social dominance
   b. neuroticism
   c. conscientiousness
   d. repression

2. People who suffer brain injury, especially to the frontal lobes, often show which kind of personality change?
   a. They become more agreeable.
   b. They become less able to control their impulses.
   c. The have lower self-esteem.
   d. They become more neurotic.

Answers can be found at the end of the chapter.

Chapter **Review**

DEFINING PERSONALITY

- Personality is the essence of who we are—both our uniqueness and our consistency. Personality traits function to change behavioral thresholds and make certain behaviors more likely and others less likely.

THE NATURE AND NURTURE OF PERSONALITY

- Personality is an expression of both nature and nurture. Personality traits have evolved through natural and sexual selection, in which genetic and environmental

forces work in tandem in shaping an individual's personality.

- Studies of infant temperament offer further support for a biological basis for adult personality. Infants make their way into the world with different and unique ways of behaving. Children may be temperamentally easy, difficult, or slow to warm up.

HOW DO THEORISTS EXPLAIN PERSONALITY?

- Theories of personality organize and explain observations and also stimulate testable hypotheses. Five perspectives explain personality differences and development.

- The first perspective, Freud's psychoanalytic theory, assumes distinct levels of consciousness. The most important of these is the unconscious, the level at which most thoughts, feelings, motives, and images reside.

- Freud developed the idea of psychological defense mechanisms, which defend us against psychological threats by unconsciously denying or distorting reality. Repression, for example, is the unconscious process of keeping disturbing thoughts, feelings, or impulses out of consciousness.

- Three followers of Freud broke their ties with him to establish their own views. Alfred Adler argued that striving for superiority is the primary motive underlying almost all behavior. Carl Jung introduced the idea of the personal unconscious and the collective unconscious. Karen Horney developed a psychoanalytic social theory centered on three neurotic trends: moving toward others, moving against others, and moving away from others.

- Contemporary research in neuroscience is beginning to provide empirical support for some of Freud's theories.

- The second perspective, humanistic theory, emphasizes psychological growth and health. Abraham Maslow developed a detailed concept of self-actualization— that is, the inherent tendency to strive to realize one's full potential. Carl Rogers developed the concept of unconditional positive regard to help people achieve self-fulfillment.

- The third perspective, the social–cognitive learning theory of Walter Mischel, is based on the belief that consistent personality characteristics interact with the environment to produce a person's unique behaviors.

- Trait theory, the fourth perspective, argues for a universal and stable personality structure that consists of five dimensions of personality: openness, conscientiousness, extraversion, agreeableness, and neuroticism (O-C-E-A-N). These traits are normally distributed in the population, with most people falling somewhere between the two extremes on each trait.

- The fifth perspective includes biological theories such as those of Hans Eysenck. Eysenck argued for three fundamental dimensions of personality: psychoticism, extraversion, and neuroticism (P-E-N). Eysenck's theory holds that differences in individuals' cortical arousal and sensitivity threshold lead to differences in introversion and extraversion.

- Confirming the importance of the biological basis of personality, personality psychologists and animal behaviorists have begun to explore the nature of animal personality. They have found not only that other primates and mammals exhibit many consistent and unique personality qualities but also that birds, fish, octopi, and even insects have personality traits that distinguish one individual from another.

HOW IS PERSONALITY MEASURED?

- Personality is measured in four major ways: observing and coding behavior; interviewing; administering projective tests; and administering structured personality questionnaires.

BRINGING IT ALL TOGETHER: MAKING CONNECTIONS IN PERSONALITY

- Most of the major topics in this chapter can be connected by highlighting research demonstrating the stability and change in personality over time. Genetic forces contribute to personality stability, whereas environmental factors contribute to both stability and change.

Key Terms

anima, p. 523

animus, p. 523

archetypes, p. 523

basic tendencies, p. 530

behavioral thresholds, p. 513

Big Five or five-factor model, p. 529

collective unconscious, p. 523

cortical arousal, p. 530

defense mechanisms, p. 520

ego, p. 519

empirical method, p. 537

id, p. 519

inferiority complex, p. 522

inter-rater reliability, p. 535

neuropsychoanalysis, p. 525

personal unconscious, p. 523

personality, p. 512

personality questionnaires, p. 536

projection, p. 521

projective tests, p. 536

quantitative trait loci (QTL) approach, p. 514

rational (face valid) method, p. 537

reaction formation, p. 520

repression, p. 520

Rorschach Inkblot Test, p. 536

shadow, p. 523

striving for superiority, p. 522

sublimation, p. 521

superego, p. 520

trait, p. 513

unconditional positive regard, p. 527

unconscious, p. 519

Quick Quiz Answers

Quick Quiz 13.1: 1. b 2. c
Quick Quiz 13.2: 1. a 2. d 3. b
Quick Quiz 13.3: 1. a 2. d 3. b 4. b
Quick Quiz 13.4: 1. c 2. d
Quick Quiz 13.5: 1. a 2. c 3. b
Quick Quiz 13.6: 1. a 2. b

Challenge Your Assumptions **Answers**

- Your personality is determined mostly by your family environment. **False. See p. 516.**
- Our unique temperament does not start to show itself until early childhood. **False. See p. 516.**
- Freud's ideas are interesting but have no scientific support. **False. See p. 525.**
- Many different kinds of animals have personality in the sense that humans do. **True. See pp. 533–534.**
- Your personality predicts what you major in or what career you go into. **True. See pp. 538–539.**
- People can usually change their personalities if they try. **False. See pp. 540–541.**

Social Behavior

14

Chapter Outline

Challenge *Your Assumptions*

TRUE OR FALSE?

- Being left out really hurts.
- I know whether I am prejudiced or not.
- People will sometimes risk their lives to help others.
- Attractive faces are anything but average.

Answers can be found at the end of the chapter.

547

Thalia and her closest friend from high school, Deidre, chose to go to the same university. They had always done everything together. The highlight of each year, according to Thalia, occurred when Deidre invited her to the family cabin to go skiing each winter. For years, Thalia took it for granted that she'd be going, even though she was always formally asked. In college, Thalia and Deidre had different roommates, but still saw each other frequently. Although their friendship felt a bit different, Thalia understood that they had different classes and some new friends. When winter rolled around that freshman year, Thalia asked Deidre when they'd be heading to the snow. Deidre said softly, "I invited my new roommate this year." Thalia—stunned—felt like she'd been kicked in the stomach.

Being rejected hurts. In fact, social exclusion creates physical pain. In one study on the neural basis for social pain, participants were brought into a lab with an fMRI scanner and were told they would be involved in an electronic ball tossing game called "Cyberball" (Eisenberger et al., 2003; Masten et al., 2009). Once inside the scanner, they could see, on a screen, a Cyberball game that was apparently in progress between two other research participants in scanners in different rooms. Unknown to the participant, there were no other people playing the game. After watching the "others" play for a few throws, the participant joined in. For a while, the three players continued playing Cyberball together. After seven throws, the other players stopped throwing the ball to the participant and resumed their game. In effect, the participant was left out, as Thalia had been. Participants reported being upset about their exclusion. What's more, the fMRI scans showed activation of brain circuitry involved in physical pain, especially those areas that are involved with how unpleasant pain feels. Indeed, this kind of *social pain* can be relieved by painkillers like Tylenol (DeWall et al., 2010) and may affect endocrine systems that support social connection (Maner et al., 2010). Also, people who are more sensitive to physical pain are more sensitive to the pain of rejection, and these differences may have a genetic basis (Eisenberger et al., 2006; Way, Taylor, & Eisenberger, 2009).

Why does it hurt to be excluded? Like other social animals, humans form important bonds with other members of our species. We depend on other people to raise us and to cooperate with us in the presence of threats (Neuberg & Cottrell, 2006). As a result, the ways in which we relate to others play a huge role in our lives, and the need to belong is ingrained in our biology (Way et al., 2009). In this chapter, we will discuss why belonging to a group matters to us, as well as other key aspects of social behavior, such as how the presence of other people influences our behavior, how we perceive our social world, how we form attitudes, and how we make friends. These topics are the focus of **social psychology,** which studies the effects of the real or imagined presence of others on people's thoughts, feelings, and actions. As we will show, the research in social psychology repeatedly reflects an important theme of this book, that no one perspective tells us everything there is to know about something. What is particularly interesting in social psychology is just how often our perspective on things is influenced in dramatic or subtle ways by others—often without our even being aware of it. ∎

social psychology
the study of how living among others influences thought, feeling, and behavior.

GROUP LIVING AND SOCIAL INFLUENCE

The social nature of human beings stems from the importance of group living in our evolutionary history. We are not solitary animals. Group living offered many advantages in human evolution, such as increased safety in the presence of danger, cooperation with others to complete challenging tasks (such as hunting), and child rearing (Brewer & Caporael, 2006; Melis & Summann, 2010). This heritage explains why people work to preserve group membership and why they modify their behavior when in the presence of others. In this section we examine how the presence of other people affects performance and one's willingness to go along with the group. As we will see, social factors can push people to do things they might not otherwise do.

You may have noticed that sometimes you perform a task better with others around and sometimes you do worse. Such effects are seen in animals as diverse as humans, chimps, birds, and even cockroaches (Gates & Allee, 1933; Klopfer, 1958). The effect of having others present can depend on the situation or task at hand, how easy or difficult the task is, and how excited you are. For example, some runners find that they run faster in groups than when running alone. **Social facilitation** occurs when the presence of others improves our performance. Over a century ago, Norman Triplett (1898) noticed that he bicycled faster when he rode with others. In a laboratory test of the idea that the presence of others improves performance, Triplett asked children to wind a fishing reel as fast as they could. He tested them alone and among other kids doing the same thing. Sure enough, they wound faster when other kids were present—they showed social facilitation. Social facilitation usually occurs for tasks we find easy, we know well, or we can perform well (Zajonc, 1965).

Social loafing is the opposite; it occurs when the presence of others causes individuals to relax their standards (Harkins, 1987). For example, if you are singing in a choir and there are dozens of other voices supporting yours, you are less likely to sing your heart out. You alone are not responsible for the sound, so the diffusion of responsibility alters your behavior (you loaf). If you were singing a solo, you might belt it out—because all responsibility would rest on your shoulders.

social facilitation phenomenon in which the presence of others improves one's performance.

social loafing phenomenon in which the presence of others causes one to relax one's standards and slack off.

Connection

Our level of arousal also affects our performance, according to the Yerkes–Dodson law. People perform better on an exam if they are slightly anxious than they would if they were either totally relaxed or very anxious.

See "Models of Motivation," Chapter 11, "Motivation and Emotion," p. 427.

Conformity

Social facilitation is a subtle way in which the presence of others changes our actions. More direct social factors also pressure us to act in certain ways. Society imposes rules about acceptable behavior, called **social norms.** Examples of social norms include "Boys don't cry," "Don't pick your nose in public," and "Don't be a sore loser." Norms vary by culture, too. Burping at the dinner table is considered rude in the United States, but in some parts of East Asia, belching is seen as a compliment to the chef.

Most of the time we conform to the social norms of our culture. **Conformity** occurs when people adjust their behavior to what others are doing or adhere to cultural norms. The reasons for conformity vary, depending on the situation. **Informational social influence** occurs when people conform to the behavior of others because they view them as a source of knowledge about what they are

social norms rules about acceptable behavior imposed by the cultural context in which one lives.

conformity tendency of people to adjust their behavior to what others are doing or to adhere to the norms of their culture.

informational social influence conformity to the behavior of others because one views them as a source of knowledge about what one is supposed to do.

In nomadic cultures, such as Mongolia, extended family groups have traditionally stayed together, sharing food, shelter, livestock, child rearing, and all other aspects of daily life. How might communal living in isolated surroundings affect an individual's behavior?

supposed to do. Consider the incoming freshmen who look to other students for information about where to hang out, how to behave in class, and the like. Informational social influence is most pronounced in ambiguous or novel situations. We rely on it all the time, especially as children. Chimps even look to other chimps to learn how to use unfamiliar tools (Whiten, Horner, & de Waal, 2005).

Normative social influence is the type of conformity that occurs when people go along with the behavior of others in order to be accepted by the group. A classic example is peer pressure, in which people engage in certain behaviors, such as drinking or trying drugs, so that they will be accepted by a particular social group. This phenomenon is widespread. Look at yourself and your peers. Do you wear the same kinds of clothes? How many of you have similar hairstyles? Consider a more subtle example of normative social influence. You emerge from the theater after going to a movie with friends, not sure whether you liked the movie or not, although everyone else in the group loved the film and is talking about it. By the end of the evening you may also be talking about what a great film it was and may have actually convinced yourself that you loved it. As you can see, we are not always aware of how other people shape our behavior and beliefs.

normative social influence conformity to the behavior of others in order to be accepted by them.

One of the classic studies of social psychology, conducted by Solomon Asch in 1951, demonstrates the power of normative social influence. Asch devoted his career to understanding situations in which perception is not a direct function of the physical properties of stimuli. For example, he found that our perceptions of the angle of a line can be biased by the frame around it (Witkin & Asch, 1948). Asch wondered whether the social world might also shape our perceptions. If pressured by the opinions of others, would people say they saw something that clearly wasn't there? Asch didn't think they would, but he was wrong.

FIGURE 14.1

STIMULUS LINES PRESENTED TO PARTICIPANTS IN THE ASCH CONFORMITY STUDIES. Each participant was asked to say which of the comparison lines (1, 2, or 3) matched the length of the standard line. The answers were always clear-cut; in this case, the answer is "2." The conformity manipulation involved the confederates in the group giving an obviously wrong answer (such as "1") and then seeing how the participant answered.

Standard line   Comparison lines

Asch assembled several groups of six to seven people in the lab and told them he was researching visual acuity. He was really interested in conformity, but didn't tell his participants what he was really researching in case the information influenced their behavior. Asch then showed the participants two cards—one with a standard line, the other displaying three lines of varying length. The participant's job was to pick the one line out of the three that matched the standard line. As you can see in Figure 14.1, the task was easy. This comparison process was repeated 18 times and, on each occasion, participants gave their answers out loud.

The one real participant didn't know that the other so-called participants were *confederates*, people who actually worked for the experimenter. The one real participant was always seated in the last chair and heard the judgments of all of the other group members before making a choice. On the first six trials everyone gave the obvious and correct answer. Starting on the seventh trial, however, the confederates started giving wrong answers. On the first of the rigged trials, the first confederate would glance at the cards and confidently say, "The answer is line 1," even when it clearly was not correct. The next confederate would nod in agreement and say, "Yes, it is line 1." After five or six people in a row gave the wrong answers—remember, this is a *very* easy task—it was the real participant's turn. Participants faced a choice: Agree with everyone else's clearly erroneous judgments or give the answer that they personally thought was correct.

While none of the participants agreed with the group all of the time, 76% of them went along with the group at least once when a group answer was clearly wrong. On average, participants answered incorrectly 37% of the time. Yet when left alone to do the task, participants made errors less than 1% of the time.

How does the design of this study make it a test of normative rather than informational social influence? Judging the lengths of the lines was really easy—there was no need for participants to look to others for information about the right answer. When participants worked alone, they rarely made errors. But in the situation just described, after all the confederates had given the same wrong answer, many participants conformed by also giving the clearly wrong answer.

groupthink
situation in which the thinking of the group takes over, so much so that group members forgo logic or critical analysis in the service of reaching a decision.

Indeed, sometimes people go to great lengths to do what the group is doing, when it does not make sense, especially when groups are engaged in decision making. This phenomenon, called **groupthink,** occurs when the thinking of the group takes over, so much so that group members forgo logic or critical analysis in the service of reaching a decision (Janis, 1983). Juries that are hard-pressed to reach a verdict sometimes engage in groupthink, as do governments under pressure. According to the Senate Intelligence Committee's report on intelligence failures leading up to the 2003 invasion of Iraq, the erroneous CIA assertion that Iraq possessed weapons of mass destruction—the primary justification for the invasion—was based on groupthink by an administration invested in finding a reason to attack Iraq (U.S. Senate, 2004).

Culture affects conformity as well. In collectivist cultures, groups matter more than the individual, so any group-preserving behavior (such as conformity) would be valued and encouraged. In Japan, for example, the company that one works for is elevated to the status of family. An employee is expected to make personal sacrifices for the company to preserve group unity (A. S. Miller & Kanazawa, 2000). In fact, cross-cultural replications of the Asch experiments reveal that people in collectivist cultures like Japan are more likely to conform than are people in individualistic cultures like the United States (Bond & Smith, 1996).

Neuroscience research sheds light on the brain mechanisms involved in conformity. When people are made aware that their beliefs differ from those of most other people in a group, a brain region active when we make an error becomes active (Klucharev et al., 2009). In other words, our brain acts as though we've made a mistake when we deviate from the group opinion.

Connection

In an individualistic culture, behavior is determined more by personal goals than by group goals, whereas in a collectivist culture, behavior is determined more by shared goals.

See "Personality and Culture: Universality and Differences," Chapter 13, "Personality: The Uniqueness of the Individual," p. 517.

Minority Social Influence

At times a single individual or small number of individuals can influence an entire group. In social psychology, a single person or small group within a larger group is called a *minority,* while the larger group is referred to as the *majority.* Just as the majority pushes for group unity, the minority can push for independence and uniqueness. After all, if people always conformed, how would change occur (Moscovici, 1985)? In order to change the majority view, however, the minority must present a consistent, unwavering message.

Most often, minority opinion shifts majority opinion by means of informational social influence. If a group encounters a situation in which the members are unsure of what to do and a minority carefully presents a well-thought-out position to the majority, then the majority might accept it. This is how juries can change course. Juries must provide unanimous decisions, and sometimes only one voice disagrees with the majority. If that minority of one offers a logical argument for the dissenting opinion, the majority view might be changed.

Obedience

obedience
a type of conformity in which a person yields to the will of another person.

Another kind of conformity, called **obedience,** occurs when people yield to the social pressure of an authority figure. Social psychological research on obedience emerged in response to real-life concerns in the aftermath of World War II. The horrific events of the Holocaust raised troubling questions: How could an entire nation endorse the extermination of millions of people? Were *all* Germans evil? Adolf Hitler did not act alone—a supporting cast of thousands was necessary to annihilate so many people. Former Nazi officers who testified in war trials after the war said they were "following orders." The same rationale was offered in 2004 by U.S. soldiers who humiliated and tortured Iraqi prisoners at Abu Ghraib.

Will people do horrible things if an authority figure orders them to do so? One psychologist spurred into action by the Nazi atrocities was Stanley Milgram. A Jew whose family left Europe before Hitler's rise to power, Milgram spent much of his early academic life trying to make sense of the Holocaust (Blass, 2004). With the support of his graduate advisor, Solomon Asch, Milgram decided to investigate whether people would conform even when their actions might harm others.

Stanley Milgram

Milgram recruited people from the community to participate in an experiment at Yale University. A participant arrived at the lab and sat down next to another supposed participant, who was a confederate. The experimenter, who looked very official in a white lab coat, told both individuals that they would be participating in a study on the effects of mild punishment on memory. He then assigned them to be either a teacher or learner by asking them to pull a note that said either "teacher" or "learner" from a bowl. The drawing was rigged so that the real participant always landed the "teacher" role and the confederate got the "learner" role. Then the experimenter showed both the teacher and learner to the room where the learner would sit. The learner's task involved learning and repeating lists of words. The learner was told that every time he made an error he would receive a mild electric shock, delivered by the teacher. With each mistake the shocks would increase in intensity. Both teacher and learner saw the chair where the learner would sit, which had restraints to make sure the electrodes had a good contact when he received the shock. The teacher then received a sample shock of very low voltage to get a sense of what the learner would experience. In actuality, this was the only real shock administered during the entire experiment.

Then they went to the teacher's room. The teacher sat at a table behind a panel of switches. Under each switch was a label indicating voltage level that ranged, in 15-volt increments, from 15 volts ("mild shock") all the way up to 450 (labeled "XXX"), with 315 volts designated as "Danger: Severe shock" (see Figure 14.2a). The teacher was reminded that if the learner made mistakes, he or she would have to deliver a shock and with each mistake would have to increase the level.

The experiment began uneventfully. Then the learner made occasional mistakes. At lower levels of shock, the learner gave no real response to the pretend shocks. As the teacher moved up the shock scale and the learner supposedly made more errors, the teacher and experimenter could hear a yelp of pain come from the learner with each shock. (In fact, the learner played a prerecorded tape of his responses to the shock.) At this point, many teachers asked the experimenter if they should go on, and he would say, "The experiment requires that you go on."

Connection

Do you think participants were treated ethically in the Milgram study? What are the obligations of researchers to ensure the ethical treatment of participants in research?

See "Research Ethics," Chapter 2, "Conducting Research in Psychology," p. 66.

Before beginning the experiments, Milgram polled experts to see how many "teachers" they thought would go along with the experimenter's demands to administer high levels of shock. One group of experts, psychiatrists, predicted that only about 30% would administer shocks as high as 150 volts, less than 4% would go to the 300-volt level, and only 1 person in 1,000 would go all the way to 450 volts. How far do *you* think most people would go in administering shocks?

The results differed drastically from these predictions. As shown in Figure 14.2b, at 150 volts, the point at which the learner yelled, "Get me out of here! My heart's starting to bother me! I refuse to go on! Let me out!" there was a drop in obedience—from 100% to about 83%. Some participants stopped, but many, although

(a) Control panel seen by the "teacher."

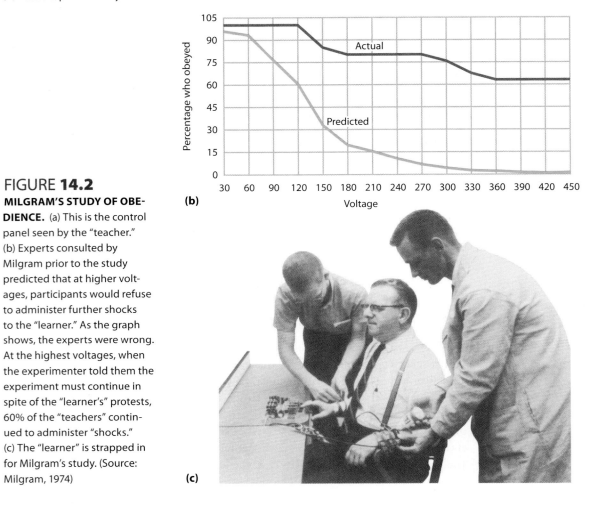

(b)

FIGURE 14.2

MILGRAM'S STUDY OF OBE-DIENCE. (a) This is the control panel seen by the "teacher." (b) Experts consulted by Milgram prior to the study predicted that at higher voltages, participants would refuse to administer further shocks to the "learner." As the graph shows, the experts were wrong. At the highest voltages, when the experimenter told them the experiment must continue in spite of the "learner's" protests, 60% of the "teachers" continued to administer "shocks." (c) The "learner" is strapped in for Milgram's study. (Source: Milgram, 1974)

(c)

visibly uncomfortable, continued with the experiment. What is alarming is how many people went all the way up to the end of the shock scale, despite the yells and protests (and eventual silence) of the learner. Twenty-six of the 40 participants in the original experiment (65%) went all the way to 450 volts (Milgram, 1963, 1974). Men and women were equally likely to reach the 450-volt level.

Milgram's experiments show that reasonable people may do things that seem cruel and unusual in the presence of powerful social influence. In fact, several "teachers" did protest and yet went on when the experimenter urged them to continue. When asked, "Who is going to take responsibility if that guy gets hurt?" the experimenter would say, "I have full responsibility, please continue." Somehow, the belief that someone else (the authority figure) was responsible for their actions alleviated feelings of guilt or concern in some of the participants. This is akin to former Nazi officers saying, "I was just following orders." But who really has the final responsibility?

Because participants clearly experienced mental anguish while taking part in the study, it sparked a fierce debate about ethics in research. Milgram contacted his participants later and asked whether they regretted having participated. Less than 2% did (see Figure 14.3).

Now that I have read the report, and all things considered...

Percentage of participants

1. I am very glad to have been in the experiment. — 43.5%
2. I am glad to have been in the experiment. — 40.2%
3. I am neither sorry nor glad to have been in the experiment. — 15.1%
4. I am sorry to have been in the experiment. — 0.8%
5. I am very sorry to have been in the experiment. — 0.5%

FIGURE 14.3
QUESTIONNAIRE RESPONSES OF PARTICIPANTS IN MILGRAM'S OBEDIENCE STUDY.
Despite the distress they experienced during the experiment, the majority of the respondents did not regret their involvement.

You might think that you would never administer those shocks or that people today would know better. Not so. In 2006, social psychologist Jerry Burger conducted a modified version of Milgram's original study with college students. An important change from the original study was that when the participants began to protest, they were told to continue rather than told that they *had* to continue. Also, once participants passed the 150-volt range, the experiment stopped. By making these changes, the researchers were able to obtain permission from the American Psychological Association to conduct the experiment, which otherwise would not meet current standards for ethical treatment of human participants. As in Milgram's experiment, Burger reported that two thirds of participants obeyed the authority figure and continued to administer shocks after the "learner" began protesting.

Quick Quiz 14.1: Group Living and Social Influence

1. Sometimes people perform better—for example, ride a bike faster—when they are in groups than when alone. Social psychologists call this
   a. the Yerkes–Dodson principle
   b. social loafing
   c. social facilitation
   d. conformity

2. People who are of a minority opinion in a group are most likely to change the opinion of the majority by
   a. getting them to conform to group pressure
   b. reason and logic
   c. trying to shame them
   d. presenting a well-formed persuasive argument

3. When put in a situation where an individual has to say something about the length of a

line that goes against what everyone else in the group has said, most people
   a. eventually conform at least once and go along with the group
   b. always conform and go along with the group
   c. never conform and go along with the group
   d. pretend not to be paying attention

4. In Milgram's study on obedience, under pressure from an authority figure, approximately what percentage of the participants gave the maximum punishment of 450 volts to the learner's incorrect answers?
   a. 25%
   b. 50%
   c. 65%
   d. 90%

Answers can be found at the end of the chapter.

SOCIAL PERCEPTION

Social processes not only influence our behavior but also guide our perceptions of the behavior of others. For example, we wonder why people do what they do. *Why does Maria wear those clothes?* We wonder whether we can believe what people say. *Is he lying to me?* We form impressions and attitudes about other people. *Ashan is smart.* These are all matters of *social perception*, the way in which we make sense of our social world.

Attribution

We often wonder why people do the things that they do (Kelley & Michela, 1980), and we try to explain their actions. **Attributions** are the inferences we make about the causes of other people's behavior.

attributions
inferences made about the causes of other people's behavior.

Social psychologist Fritz Heider (1958) made an important distinction between two types of attributions. Internal or *dispositional attributions* ascribe other people's behavior to something within them, such as their personality, motives, or attitudes. For example, let's say that Chris flunked a test. A dispositional attribution would be "Chris flunked the test because he is too lazy to study." The person making this attribution assumed that Chris's flunking is a result of something about him. But it is also possible that Chris's failing grade resulted from some external factor. Perhaps the test was too hard. People make external or *situational attributions* when they think that something outside the person, such as the nature of the situation, is the cause of his or her behavior. If Jake says that Chris failed because the exam was too hard, Jake has made a situational attribution for Chris's grade.

Connection
Cultural differences in big-picture versus detailed processing are seen in performance on visual perception tasks too.
See "Perceiving Visual Stimuli," Chapter 4, "Sensing and Perceiving Our World," p. 137.

We tend to evaluate our own behavior in different ways depending on whether we have succeeded or failed. For instance, it is likely that Chris would attribute his failure on a test to something about the situation—say, the test was too hard or the professor unfair—rather than to his own abilities. If Chris had aced the test, however, it is likely he'd attribute his success to his own skills. Making situational attributions for our failures but dispositional attributions for our successes is known as a **self-serving bias.**

self-serving bias
the tendency to make situational attributions for our failures but dispositional attributions for our successes.

People tend to explain other people's behavior in terms of dispositional attributions rather than situational ones, a bias in judgment known as the

Meeting potential mates in a group of singles might make some people seem shy. Would you make the fundamental attribution error in a situation like this and assume that shyness is a personality trait?

fundamental attribution error (Ross, 1977). This is not to say that dispositions don't matter, but rather that when making attributions of other people's behavior, we tend to think that dispositional characteristics matter the most. People living in Asian cultures, such as India and Japan, are much less likely to make the fundamental attribution error than are European Americans (Choi, Nisbett, & Norenzayan, 1999). This seems to be due to a cultural tendency for Asians to explain behaviors—even things as extreme as murder—in situational terms (M. W. Morris & Peng, 1994; Norenzayan & Nisbett, 2000).

Detecting Deception

One way that we try to figure out others is by judging whether or not they are being truthful. Most people think that they know when people lie to them. According to the research, however, most of us are not effective lie detectors. Most people perform no better than the accuracy rate of chance guessing in detecting deception from people's behavior (Ekman & O'Sullivan, 1991).

Why are we unsuccessful at catching liars? Most of us rely on misleading cues. We put too much weight on what people are saying, overinterpret ambiguous nonverbal cues (thinking any sign of nervousness means a person is lying), ignore relevant nonverbal information, and get fooled by signs of warmth and competence (Ekman & O'Sullivan, 1991). If people learn to focus instead on inconsistent behaviors (shaking the head while saying yes) and signs of emotion that don't match what people are saying, then they become better "lie detectors." There are no foolproof ways of detecting deception, however.

The best lie detectors attend to nonverbal information more than verbal information (Frank & Ekman, 1997). In a study of experts who should be good at catching liars, such as U.S. Secret Service agents, FBI agents, CIA agents, police, judges, and psychiatrists, only the Secret Service agents performed significantly better than if they had been guessing (Ekman & O'Sullivan, 1991). Psychologists with a special interest in deception have also been shown to do much better than others in detecting deceit (Ekman, O'Sullivan, & Frank, 1999).

Work on deception attracts much public interest. In 2009, Fox premiered the TV drama *Lie to Me,* based on the deception research of Paul Ekman. The protagonist, the fictitious Cal Lightman (played by Tim Roth; see photo below), and his colleagues read facial expressions and other nonverbal behaviors to determine whether people are lying in this crime-oriented drama. The science in the show was vetted by experts on deception and facial expression (Paul Ekman and Erika Rosenberg).

In the TV drama *Lie to Me,* the main character (played by Tim Roth) used the science of facial expression to root out liars in criminal cases.

557

Schemas

Whether we are trying to determine if people are lying or simply trying to make sense of simple actions, our own ideas of how the world works influence our perceptions of it. People develop models, or *schemas,* of the social world, which function like lenses through which we filter our perceptions. We first discussed schemas in Chapter 7 and defined them broadly as ways of knowing that we develop from our experiences with particular objects or events. In the area of social perception, schemas are ways of knowing that affect how we view our social world.

We rely on schemas when forming impressions of other people, especially when we encounter ambiguous information. Imagine you are invited to dinner and notice that one of the guests has slurred speech and walks shakily across the room. You assume—reasonably—that she is drunk. Later you learn that she has Parkinson's disease, a neurological condition that affects motor coordination. Slurred speech and shaky walking are common symptoms of this disorder. You assumed that the woman was drunk because the schema of drunkenness was much more *accessible* to you than that of Parkinson's disease.

What stereotypes do these images bring to mind?

Stereotypes

Schemas of how people are likely to behave based simply on the groups to which they belong are known as **stereotypes.** When we resort to stereotypes, we form conclusions about people before we even interact with them just because they are of a certain race–ethnicity or live in a certain place. As a result, we end up judging people not by their actions, but by our notions of how they might act.

stereotypes
schemas of how people are likely to behave based simply on groups to which they belong.

People resort to stereotypes because they allow for quick—but often inaccurate—impressions, especially if we do not know someone very well. The human mind has a tendency to categorize and understand all members of a group in terms of characteristics that are typical of the group (Rosch, 1975). So if we meet someone new and learn that they belong to a particular (racial–ethnic, social, political, or religious) group, we rely on what we think we know about that group to anticipate how this new person might behave. fMRI scans show that when people avoid thinking in this stereotyped way, the prefrontal cortex—an area involved in inhibiting inappropriate responses—is activated (De Neys, Vartanian, & Goel, 2008). This suggests that when you rely on stereotypes, you are not thinking carefully.

Take a look at a few of the common stereotypes that exist in U.S. culture:

Jocks are dumb.

Jews are cheap.

Middle Eastern men with beards might be terrorists.

With stereotypes, we have formed conclusions about people even before we interact with them. Stereotypes may originate in something that is factual but that does not characterize a whole group. The terrorists involved in the September 11, 2001, attacks in the United States, for example, were Middle Eastern men, many of whom had beards—but not all Middle Eastern men with beards are terrorists.

Connection
Another name for mental shortcuts we use in decision making is *heuristics*. Heuristics can be adaptive but also can lead to flawed thinking.
See "How Do We Make Judgments and Decisions?" Chapter 9, "Language and Thought," p. 372.

Social networks such as Facebook played a key role in the revolutions in the Middle East and North Africa in the spring of 2011.

rapidly than they would in a real-world social network. It is possible that the three degrees rule may not apply to SNSs or that the limits of influence may be wider. Also, surveys of Facebook use show that people of all ages share much more private information publicly than they realize (Brandtzæg, Lüders, & Skjetne, 2010). For instance, people readily disclose drug and alcohol use more freely on SNSs than they might in real-world public settings (Moran, Snelson, & Elison-Bowers, 2010).

Not everyone is equally interested in using SNSs, and people use them differently. Some users post frequently, while some prefer to read others' postings only. Not surprisingly, a number of personality factors relate to Facebook use. For instance, people who score higher on measures of conscientiousness have more friends; those who score higher on openness to experience are more expressive in their personal profiles; and those who score high on introversion have smaller social networks than extraverts (Amichai-Hamburger & Vinitzky, 2010). People who score either low or high on neuroticism share more information than people with moderate levels of neuroticism.

Although Facebook and Twitter are international, people in Asia use Asian SNSs more often: QQ in China, Cyworld in Korea, and Mixi in Japan (Ji et al., 2010). In spite of many similarities between cultures in how people use

SNSs, there are some differences in how they use SNSs to obtain what is known as *social capital*. Social capital refers to the value, or payoff (socially, professionally), one gains by connecting with others. Korean and Chinese users rely more on searching and friending functions to build bridges with others, while American users use direct communication (such as wall postings) to foster more intimate relationships with online friends in their networks (Ji et al., 2010).

Both real and virtual social networks spread information to large numbers of people in a short period of time—often to powerful effect. In February 2011, the people of Egypt protested the authoritarian government of Hosni Mubarak. Within a matter of days, early reports and images of police violence against peaceful protestors spread to millions of young Egyptians via Twitter and Facebook. This, along with other information, incited a successful revolution that ultimately led to Mubarak's resignation.

human evolution, these two needs were often intertwined. To be included in a social group meant you were fed, you were secure, and you could reproduce. Being excluded threatened not only survival but also the chance to reproduce (MacDonald et al., 2005). The need for connection runs so deep down the phylogenetic tree that you find it in social insects. When raised without social contact, cockroaches show behavioral deficiencies including poor mating skills, reduced willingness to interact with others, and impaired foraging (Lihoreau, Brepson, & Rivault, 2009).

Humans also form social groups through social networks, which are webs of people who share common interests, professions, or familial relations (Christakis & Fowler, 2009). Both real-life and electronic social networks play an important role in social life. See "Psychology in the Real World: The Social Psychology of Social Networks."

Prejudice and Discrimination

We have discussed many processes that affect group behavior and how we view others. Unfortunately, as people try to make sense of each other and rely on schemas to decide who is similar or who is different, they sometimes use stereotypes to unfairly categorize others, which can fuel prejudice and discrimination.

prejudice
a biased attitude toward a group of people or an individual member of a group based on unfair generalizations about what members of that group are like.

A **prejudice** is a biased attitude toward a group of people or an individual member of a group based on unfair generalizations about what members of that group are like (Allport, 1954). Prejudicial thinking often stems from stereotypes rather than from careful observation of people's behavior. Prejudices are generally negative and often based on insufficient information. Prejudices based on race–ethnicity are called *racism*; those based on sex are called *sexism*. If a business executive does not seriously consider a highly qualified female applicant for a high-level management job because he is convinced that women are not capable of leading a company, his thinking is prejudicial. More precisely, he is sexist. Not offering her an interview—even if she is the best-qualified applicant in the pool—is discrimination. **Discrimination** is the preferential treatment of certain people that is usually driven by prejudicial attitudes. Discrimination can also result from institutionalized rules, such as the requirement that flight attendants cannot be excessively overweight.

discrimination
preferential treatment of certain people, usually driven by prejudicial attitudes.

Prejudicial attitudes are learned early in life; and even if they are formally abandoned later in life, these reactions can become quite automatic (Banaji & Greenwald, 1995). Consider the case of Edith, a 21-year-old European American college student who is politically liberal and an activist for progressive causes. Yet, when Edith walks to her car at night, if an African American man is on the other side of the street, she becomes nervous without knowing why. She is not a racist! Why does this happen? Prejudices can operate outside conscious awareness, and they sometimes stand in stark contrast to one's conscious beliefs (Devine, 1989). Even a person who works hard at being fair may have a hard time overcoming biases that are automatic and deeply learned. There may also be an evolutionary basis for our automatic responses: The mechanism of recognizing group members may have evolved to preserve group harmony, cohesion, and close alliances (Melis & Summann, 2010; Neuberg & Cottrell, 2006).

Breaking New Ground

Discovering a Way to Measure Implicit Bias

Mahzarin Banaji

Anthony Greenwald

Prejudice operates both inside and outside a person's awareness. As in Edith's case, much racial–ethnic bias is unconscious and in conflict with consciously held views. Two social psychologists, Anthony Greenwald and Mahzarin Banaji, suspected there was a disconnect between people's conscious and unconscious views of prejudice and developed a way of measuring what they called *implicit bias*.

Social psychologists distinguish between *explicit* and *implicit* prejudice. Explicit ideas are plainly stated. Implicit views are indirect, perhaps unconscious. An explicit reference to a desire to have sex with someone is "I want to go to bed with you." An implicit reference would be "Why don't you come by my place and watch a movie with me?" Measuring implicit knowledge and beliefs presents a challenge.

A New Measure of Bias

Mahzarin Banaji and Anthony Greenwald had become interested in implicit social thought and attitudes but were unhappy about the lack of scientific measures of them (Greenwald & Banaji, 1995). Greenwald and his colleagues had developed a computer program that measured implicit cognitive attitudes towards flowers and insects.

There were four steps to the program. First, participants had to press a computer keyboard letter with their left hand for flowers and a different key with their right hand for insects. Second, they had to do the same for pleasant words (left hand) and unpleasant words (right hand). Third, flowers and pleasant words were combined (left hand), and insects and unpleasant words were combined (right hand). When Greenwald did this, he found these three tasks very easy and he did them very quickly. Things changed when he got to the fourth and final condition. Now flowers, which used to be left hand, and insects, which used to be right hand, were switched, but the pleasant and unpleasant words stayed on the same side. In other words, flowers were now paired with unpleasant words and insects with pleasant words. Greenwald was much slower at making these associations. He thought he could get better with practice and to his surprise he couldn't. There was no way to change the implicit association.

He quickly realized this might be the measure of implicit social attitudes they were looking for. In Greenwald's words,

> It was a relatively short step to construct a test in which the concepts of Black and White race (represented by well known names of Black and White celebrities) replaced flower names and insect names. I was again the first subject at this task. I was both distressed and elated to discover that my performance was much faster when White names and pleasant words had the same response (Greenwald, 2009).

When Banaji took the same test, she, too, was upset by the results, which looked about the same as Greenwald's. Banaji and Greenwald knew they were on to something. They dubbed the new test the *Implicit Associations Test (IAT)*.

Most famously, Greenwald and Banaji applied the IAT to concepts of race–ethnicity. Faster response times on the test indicate that people more readily associate two concepts; slower response times indicate a less automatic association. European Americans tend to respond more slowly to pairings of "Black" (words or faces) with positive words than they do to pairings of "Black" with negative words (Dasgupta et al., 2000; Greenwald, McGhee, & Schwartz, 1998). This holds even for people whose questionnaire responses indicate that they do not hold racist attitudes. The reverse is true for African Americans. They respond more slowly to pairings of "White American" with positive words than they do to pairings of "White American" with negative words. Banaji and Greenwald (1995) have also reported evidence of implicit gender bias using the IAT; female and male college students more readily associated "fame" with male names than with female names.

Reducing Implicit Bias

In just over 15 years since the IAT's publication, more than 600 published research papers, in areas ranging from marketing to neuroscience, have used the IAT technique. IAT scores predict suicidal tendencies, consumer preferences, political preferences, sexual orientation, and drug and alcohol use (Greenwald et al., 2009; Nock et al., 2010). Indeed, the IAT is an excellent teaching tool for anyone confronting his or her own implicit prejudice. As Banaji described it in an interview:

> The test is unusual in that it provokes a reaction of surprise, even astonishment. It is both a tool to understand what goes on invisibly in our minds, but is also a catalyst for insight.... We can ask "Am I leading my life the way I want to?" It is a unique test in that regard." ("Implicit Association Test," 2008)

Results from the test can be used to reduce prejudice and sensitize individuals and groups to the fact that these prejudices operate in subtle yet powerful ways. In 1998 Banaji, Greenwald, and Nosek established a nonprofit organization (Project Implicit) to help people apply the IAT technique.

Banaji lives by her own advice. She was so dismayed by her own performance on race- and gender-based IATs—in spite of being a minority woman herself—that she changed her behavior. In addition to the nonprofit work, she does little things to help undo her deeply held biases, such as displaying pictures of prominent Black men and women from history in her office.

■ ■ ■

Research to **Real Life**

Most people today like to think they are not at all biased or prejudiced toward people who differ from them in race–ethnicity, gender, or religion. Consciously, relatively few people think they are prejudiced. And yet, as we just saw with Greenwald and Banaji's discovery of implicit prejudice, most people nevertheless harbor subtle forms of prejudice.

Connecting Psychology to Your Life: If you'd like to find out whether you hold subtle and implicit prejudices, visit the website developed by Banaji, Greenwald, and Nosek (https://implicit.harvard.edu/implicit/demo/) and click on the link that says "Go to the Demonstration Tests." Read the general information and follow the "I wish to proceed" link. Choose one or more from many different forms of the IAT: race, religion, gender-science, sexuality, Arab-Muslim, age, and skin-tone. Each one takes only about 10 minutes to complete. After you complete one version of the test, you will be provided with general results of how you did.

Don't be surprised if your results show you hold some implicit prejudices. In fact, as Banaji has done in her own life, try to use this feedback to make changes in your attitudes and beliefs toward other people.

Quick Quiz 14.2: Social Perception

1. Our tendency to conclude that Alex must have an aggressive personality because we see him hit Bobby once on the playground is an example of
   a. a stereotype
   b. a prejudice
   c. deception
   d. the fundamental attribution error

2. "College professors are absent minded" is an example of
   a. an attitude
   b. an attribution
   c. a stereotype
   d. a prejudice

3. Out-group homogeneity is the tendency to
   a. see people outside our group as looking or acting alike
   b. see people inside our group as looking or acting alike
   c. believe people outside our group think the same way we do
   d. believe people inside our group think the same way we do

4. Brandon believes women are not very good at math. However, as a computer scientist, he has always been able to treat women the same way he treats men at work.
   a. Brandon is prejudiced against women.
   b. Brandon's behavior is an example of discrimination.
   c. Brandon's beliefs are based on stereotypes.
   d. Both a and c are correct.

5. Measuring how long it takes a person to pair positive or negative terms with particular ethnic groups is used in social psychology as a measure of
   a. explicit racism
   b. implicit racism
   c. stereotypes
   d. reaction time

Answers can be found at the end of the chapter.

ATTITUDES AND BEHAVIOR

attitudes
an individual's favorable or unfavorable beliefs, feelings, or actions toward an object, idea, or person.

People use the word *attitude* frequently, but what does it mean? Social psychologists define **attitudes** as a person's favorable or unfavorable feelings, beliefs, or actions toward an object, idea, or person (Olson & Zanna, 1993). Thus attitudes have affective, cognitive, and behavioral components. The *affective* component includes the feelings or emotions associated with the belief; the *cognitive* component consists of the rational thoughts and beliefs that make up the attitude; and the *behavioral* component includes the motive to act in a particular way toward the person or object of the attitude. Consider Elizabeth, who is a huge Giants fan (see Figure 14.5). She loves the team (affective), knows all about each starting player (cognitive), and has bought season tickets to their home games (behavioral).

Attitudes differ by how heavily each component is weighted. Some attitudes are more cognitive, such as your beliefs about the best way to slice a mango. Others may be more affective, such as your attitude about the death penalty. Our attitudes and beliefs stem from our history as a species as well as our history as individuals.

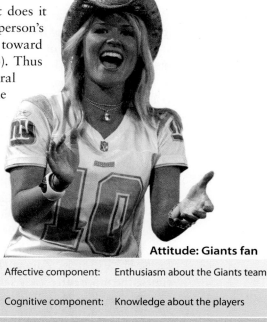

Attitude: Giants fan

Affective component:	Enthusiasm about the Giants team
Cognitive component:	Knowledge about the players
Behavioral component:	Goes to all Giants home games

FIGURE **14.5**
ATTITUDE COMPONENTS. For a sports fan, a positive attitude is sometimes the only way to get through a losing season.

The Nature and Nurture of Attitudes

Some of our most basic attitudes may be instinctive, while others are learned. Certain negative attitudes and emotional responses, such as fear of snakes or the nearly universal human revulsion for bodily waste and decaying matter, may be so important for human survival that they are part of our genetic heritage (Buss, 1999). Evolutionary pressures to preserve group membership favor

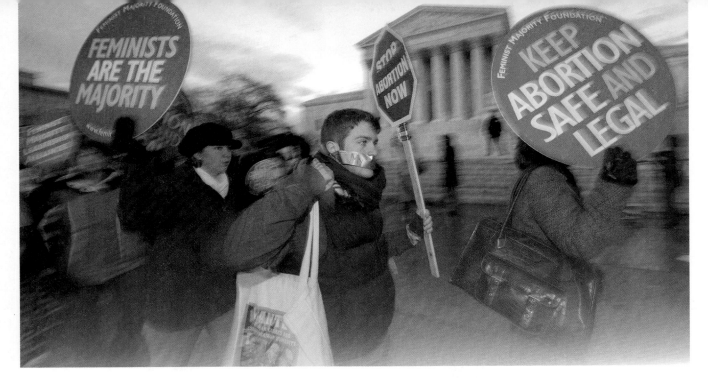

Strong attitudes about controversial issues, such as abortion, often reflect long-standing beliefs and consequently are difficult to change.

in-group bias (fear of those who are different). Because humans evolved in small social groups in threatening environments, it made sense for people to trust those who were most like them. In addition, the tendency to automatically make quick good–bad and like–dislike assessments is a fundamental cognitive process with clear evolutionary benefits: It helps people make quick decisions in life-threatening situations (Cunningham & Zelazo, 2006; Neuberg & Cottrell, 2006).

On the other hand, *many of our attitudes come from experience*. In some cases, we learn attitudes through both direct and indirect instruction by others. We may adopt the musical preferences of our friends, for example. Sometimes we like ideas or objects simply because they are familiar. *Mere exposure,* or direct experience with an object, idea, or person, increases our overall preference for it (Zajonc, 1968). The things that we come to like from exposure can be trivial, such as abstract symbols, or very meaningful, such as human faces. For example, Zajonc (1968) showed people nonsense words 5, 10, or 25 times; the more often they saw a word, the more they reported liking it.

Nature & Nurture

Evolutionary forces may explain certain inborn attitudes, but many of our attitudes come from culture and experience.

Attitude Change

Are people willing to switch attitudes based on evidence or a persuasive argument? What role do personality and persuasion play in our willingness to change attitudes? These are just some of the questions asked by social psychologists interested in attitude change. We examine two major reasons for changes in attitude: cognitive dissonance and persuasion.

cognitive dissonance
the feeling of discomfort caused by information that is different from a person's conception of himself or herself as a reasonable and sensible person.

Cognitive Dissonance

The theory of cognitive dissonance offers one explanation for why and how we change our attitudes. **Cognitive dissonance** is the feeling of discomfort caused by information that is at odds with one's conception of oneself as a reasonable and sensible person (Festinger, 1957). Because we don't like feeling uncomfortable, we are motivated to try to reduce the discomfort. Three options are available for decreasing the discomfort created by dissonance:

1. We can change our behavior to make it consistent with dissonant cognition.
2. We can attempt to justify our behavior by changing one of the cognitions to make it more consistent with our behavior.
3. We can add new cognitions that are consistent with the behavior and that therefore support it.

When people experience cognitive dissonance, they go to extreme lengths to reduce it. In this way, they reduce their discomfort and maintain self-esteem. People end up rationalizing or justifying their not-so-adaptive behavior in order to reduce cognitive dissonance.

Smoking offers a classic example of an irrational behavior in which many people engage. Smoking can cause lung cancer, emphysema, and heart disease. Still, many people continue to smoke. True, they are addicted. Cognitively, however, smokers must manage the conflict between their notion of themselves as rational beings and the fact that they engage in a very risky habit. To reduce the unpleasant feeling these dissonant thoughts and behaviors create, people who smoke may behave in one of the three ways that we just listed, as seen in Figure 14.6. People will work hard to rationally defend behaviors or strongly held positions in order to reduce the dissonance—the uncomfortable feeling—produced by opposing arguments.

persuasion
the act of attempting to change the opinions, beliefs, or choices of others by explanation or argument.

Persuasion   Persuasion changes attitude as well. **Persuasion** is an attempt by a person or group to change our opinions, beliefs, or choices by explaining or

change behavior

justify smoking by changing cognitions associated with it

change cognitions so as to justify smoking

Quit smoking.

"Smoking is not that harmful."

"Results of research on smoking and cancer are not as conclusive as people think they are."

"It makes me feel good, so it's worth it, whatever the risk."

FIGURE **14.6**

COGNITIVE DISSONANCE AND SMOKING. People smoke even though they know it's unhealthy. To reduce their cognitive dissonance, smokers might try one of these approaches, including quitting.

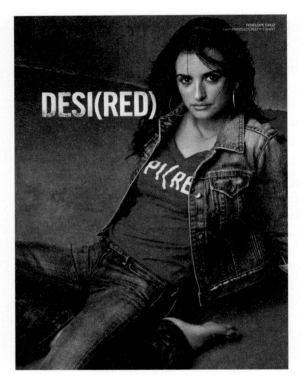

Which persuasion criteria are represented by this GAP ad featuring actress Penelope Cruz? At what audience do you think it is aimed?

arguing their position. Persuasion is all around us all the time; friends, family, teachers, politicians, salespeople, and advertisers often want to change our minds about something. The success of persuasion depends on three things: who the persuader is (source), the method used to convey the message, and who the receiver (audience) is (Lippa, 1994).

First, how trustworthy, prestigious, and likeable is the source of the message? The more prestigious and trustworthy the persuader, the more likely he or she is to succeed in persuading us. If the persuader is also attractive and familiar, so much the better. This is why people want to buy pain relievers promoted in commercials by famous TV doctors rather than unknown figures. The perceived credibility of the character enhances the credibility of the product.

Second, what methods of persuasion are used? Politicians often rely on fear to convince us to support their policies or candidacy. An example is the "Willie Horton" ad that was shown during the 1988 U.S. presidential campaign. When Democratic presidential candidate Michael Dukakis was governor of Massachusetts, he supported a weekend release program for prisoners. Willie Horton committed armed robbery and rape during such a weekend. A group supporting the Republican candidate, George H. W. Bush, ran a TV ad showing prisoners walking out of a prison yard with a voice-over about Horton. It ran regularly on stations across the country. It played on people's fears of dangerous criminals, and it linked that fear with Dukakis. That commercial is thought to have played a major role in Dukakis's loss to Bush.

Fear campaigns work only if they actually create fear in the audience (Witte & Allen, 2000). Most ads meant to scare us don't scare us enough to change our behavior. Simply citing statistics about the health risks of smoking is not very effective at getting people to change their behavior. People rarely believe that they will suffer the negative consequences implied by the ads.

Last, who is the targeted audience or receiver of the message? People are not equally malleable in their opinions or behavior. The more people know about a topic and the firmer their prior opinions are, the less likely they are to change their attitudes (Eagly & Chaiken, 1998). Political campaigners know this well. Candidates often focus their efforts—especially near election day—on swing states that either have voted inconsistently in the past or have a mix of party preferences. In regions that have voted Republican for years, say, campaigning by Democratic candidates may be a waste of time.

Quick Quiz 14.3: Attitudes and Behavior

1. Janice is a college student who is active in politics. She considers voting to be very important for everyone, especially young people. So she volunteers 5 hours a week to staff a table at the student union encouraging students to register to vote, for any political party. Her stance toward voting would best be described as a(n)
   a. belief
   b. attitude
   c. attribution
   d. bias

2. Levon considers himself to be a healthy person. He eats a healthy diet and exercises 4 days a week. Yet he is a smoker. His attitude toward smoking before he became a smoker was very negative. Now that he is a smoker, however, his attitude is not so negative. The change in his attitude is best explained by
   a. attribution
   b. persuasion
   c. mere exposure
   d. cognitive dissonance

3. Social psychologists have demonstrated that three things matter most in whether an argument will persuade other people or not. The three things are
   a. source, method, and audience
   b. source, believability, and audience
   c. logic, believability, and audience
   d. pressure to conform, source, and authority

Answers can be found at the end of the chapter.

SOCIAL RELATIONS

We constantly interact with other people. Sometimes these interactions lead to special connections with others that grow into friendship or even love. Other times we clash and find ourselves in conflict with others. In this section we discuss three different kinds of social interaction: aggression, helping, and attraction.

The Nature and Nurture of Aggression

Aggression is part of life. All animals compete with others, both within and outside their species, for survival. Almost every animal can be aggressive, and many animals kill others in order to survive. Humans are unique in that they often engage in aggression and violent behavior when their survival is not at issue.

Aggression refers to violent behavior that is intended to cause psychological or physical harm, or both, to another being. By definition, aggression is deliberate. A dentist who performs a root canal may hurt a patient, but we hardly would call that behavior aggressive. Aggression is often provoked by anger, but not always.

When aggression stems from feelings of anger, it is called *hostile aggression*. When aggression is a means to achieve some goal, it is called *instrumental aggression*. The hostile type of aggression is easy to understand. While you are driving, someone cuts you off on the road. You honk and, in response, the other driver makes an obscene hand gesture toward you. The hand gesture is an aggressive action.

An example of instrumental aggression occurs in football when a defensive lineman smashes down a ball carrier to prevent the opponent from scoring. The goal is to prevent scoring by the other team, not to hurt the ball carrier. In this case, the aggressive action is considered to be justified by its instrumental goal.

Where does aggression come from, and why are people aggressive? Some people are more prone to violence than others. An individual's genetic disposition may play a role, but genes by themselves are seldom enough to cause violent behavior (Miczek et al., 2007). Caspi and colleagues (2002)

Connection

How does hostility differ from anger? Hostility is a personality characteristic that sets the threshold for the emotion of anger.

See "Defining Emotion," Chapter 11, "Motivation and Emotion," p. 449.

aggression violent behavior that is intended to cause psychological or physical harm, or both, to another being.

found that when genetic factors combine with an abusive and neglectful environment, the likelihood of committing violence increases dramatically.

Moreover, research on murderers points to a cluster of traits shared by most of these individuals: being male, growing up in an abusive and neglectful household, having at least one psychological disorder, and having experienced some kind of injury to the head or brain (Pincus, 1999, 2001; Strueber, Lueck, & Roth, 2006–2007; Yang et al., 2010). Having only one of these traits is not enough—all must be present for a person to become antisocial and prone to violence. In other words, the person's disposition interacts with certain environmental influences to make aggressive behavior more likely.

Several brain areas are involved in aggression, including the hypothalamus, the amygdala, and the prefrontal cortex (Pincus, 1999). More specifically, the part of the prefrontal cortex responsible for impulse control often is functionally impaired in aggressive and violent people (Grafman et al., 1996). Amygdala damage is found frequently in murderers (DeLisi, Umphress, & Vaughn, 2009). Similarly, as a result of head injuries, psychopathology, or abuse, murderers may have moderate to severe problems with frontal lobe functioning, which involves impulse control, emotional intelligence, working memory, and attention (Strueber et al., 2006–2007) or reductions in size of the hippocampus (Yang et al., 2010). Living in a constant state of fear can lead to neural systems being primed for unusually high levels of anxiety, impulsive behavior, and vigilance, or a constant state of alertness (Bishop, 2007). These are all conditions that may bring about violent behaviors.

In addition to these brain structures, two hormones are consistently related to high levels of aggression: testosterone and serotonin. A number of lines of evidence point to testosterone's role. As the male sex hormone, it may be responsible for boys being more aggressive than girls at most ages (Maccoby & Jacklin, 1974). In adults, the great majority of people arrested for criminal offenses are men (Strueber et al., 2006–2007). Relatively high levels of testosterone, whether in men or women, correlate positively with a propensity toward violence. Among both male and female prisoners, naturally occurring testosterone levels are higher in criminals convicted of violent crimes than in those convicted of nonviolent crimes (Dabbs, Carr, & Frady, 1995; Dabbs & Hargrove, 1997). In an experimental study, giving testosterone reduces performance on an empathy task in women (University of Cambridge, 2011). Serotonin has a broad range of effects on behavior, one of which is keeping anger and anxiety in check. Research shows that low levels of serotonin make aggression more likely in humans and animals (Moffitt et al., 1998; Raleigh et al., 1991).

Nature & Nurture
Aggression stems from the interaction between genetic and social forces.

Social Influences on Aggression Situations that prevent us from reaching our goals are likely to make us aggressive. Moreover, the closer we are to our goal when we become frustrated, the more aggressive our response. A classic study by Harris (1974) demonstrated this effect. Confederates of the researchers cut in front of people in lines for movies or crowded restaurants. Sometimes they cut in front of the second person in line; other times they cut in front of someone farther back in line. The response of the person standing behind the intruder was much more aggressive when the confederate cut in front of the person second in line—closest to the goal.

Similarly, situations that lead to anger stimulate aggression, especially hostile aggression. Threats to our safety or the safety of our family fall into this category. Aggressive responses may be motivated by anger and/or fear. Road rage is a good example of such a situation, and aggressive driving is most likely to happen when people are angry (Nesbit, Conger, & Conger, 2007).

Observing aggressive people and the consequences of their actions can make us more aggressive. This is the fundamental idea behind Albert Bandura's *social learning theory*. Bandura's research demonstrated repeatedly that if children see adults punching an inflatable Bobo doll, they will do it too, especially if they see the adult being rewarded for the aggressive behavior.

Does violence in video games and other visual media increase the likelihood of aggressive behavior?

How does the Bobo doll research apply to real-life aggression? According to longitudinal studies of men and women, the more violence people watch on TV when they are children, the more violent behavior they exhibit as adults (Huesmann, Moise-Titus, & Podolski, 2003). This correlational result does not prove that TV is the cause of the aggressive behavior. However, more controlled experiments also suggest that watching TV violence leads to aggressive behavior in children. Liebert and Baron (1972) showed a violent TV program to a group of children. The control group saw an exciting but nonviolent sporting event that had the same running time. Children were randomly assigned to the two groups. After viewing the programs, each child was allowed to play in another room with a group of children. Those who had watched the violent program were far more aggressive in their play than those who saw the nonviolent show.

Until recently, the evidence was overwhelming that exposure to violent programs or video games increased aggression in kids (Bushman & Anderson, 2001; Kirsh, 2006). Results from a recent meta-analysis suggest, however, that the effects of watching violence on aggressive behavior have been exaggerated. It seems many of the studies fail to consider how other factors (such as sex, personality, family violence) may also play a role in aggressive behavior (Ferguson & Kilburn, 2009). There is clearly a relationship between viewing violence and aggression, but the size of the effects is a matter of great debate (Anderson et al., 2010; Ferguson & Kilburn, 2010).

Connection

Social learning theory offers an explanation of modeling, the kind of learning in which we imitate the behavior of others.

See "Social Learning Theory," Chapter 8, "Learning," p. 330.

Whether or not viewing violence increases aggressive behavior, repeatedly seeing or participating in violent action in a virtual world may make young people less sensitive to violence. In one study, researchers randomly assigned more than 250 male and female college students to play either a violent or a nonviolent video game for 20 minutes (Carnagey, Anderson, & Bushman, 2007). Then they measured the participants' physiological responses to films of real-life violence, such as courtroom outbursts, police confrontations, shootings, and prison fights. The students who played the violent video games showed less physiological arousal (as measured by heart rate and sweating) while watching films of real people being stabbed and shot than did the students who had played the nonviolent games. In a similar study, young men with a history of playing video games showed reduced brain activation to real-life violence, and this reduced brain activation correlated with aggression in a behavioral task (Bartholow, Bushman, & Sestir, 2006). Such nonreaction to violence is disturbing.

Prosocial Behavior

prosocial behavior
action that is beneficial to others.

Just as people can harm others through aggression, sometimes people can be extraordinarily kind to others. **Prosocial behavior** benefits others. In this section we will explore social processes that benefit others: altruism and empathy.

Sometimes humans do extraordinary things for others at great cost to themselves. Consider the case of Wesley Autrey. One morning in January 2007, Autrey and his two daughters were waiting for the subway in New York City. Suddenly a teenager standing nearby began convulsing and collapsed on the platform. Among the dozens of people there, only Autrey and a few women stopped to help the young man. They thought they had stabilized him, but the young man got up, tottered, and fell onto the tracks. The headlights of an oncoming train appeared, and in an instant Autrey jumped onto the tracks to help the young man. When Autrey realized that he could not pull the teen off the tracks before the train hit them, he lay on top of him and pressed him down firmly in a bear hug. The train went over both men without touching them.

Autrey heard the screams of onlookers. "We're okay down here," he yelled, "but I've got two daughters up there. Let them know their father's okay." He heard cries of wonder and applause (Buckley, 2007). When interviewed later, Autrey said he had done nothing heroic. He had simply decided to help someone in need. "I didn't want the man's body to get run over," he said. "Plus, I was with my daughters and I didn't want them to see that" (CBS News, 2007).

Would you jump in front of an oncoming train to help a complete stranger? How many people do you think would? What makes people help other people? Most evidence, both from real life and from laboratory studies, indicates that most people would not help a stranger, especially when many others are present and are doing nothing. Social psychologists have studied various factors that influence whether people will help others or not.

In 1964, Kitty Genovese was attacked and killed while residents of her Queens neighborhood, shown in this photo taken after the murder, ignored her screams. Subsequent research has shown that the more people who witness an emergency, the less likely it is that someone will offer help.

The Bystander Effect

Late one night Kitty Genovese walked from her parked car to her apartment building in New York City after coming home from her job as a bar manager. As she approached the building, a man accosted her and stabbed her in the back. She screamed, "Oh my God, he stabbed me! Help me!" Fearing that her cries for help would be heeded, her attacker ran away. Lights went on in the apartment building, and a few people looked out, but no one called the police or came to help her. The man returned and renewed his attack. Genovese's screams were heard by numerous people, but still no one came to help. The 28-year-old Genovese died from her wounds before someone summoned the police.

How could so many people ignore the screams of a young woman being brutally attacked? What kind of attribution—either dispositional or situational—best explains this behavior?

The Kitty Genovese case received tons of publicity, and it spurred a great deal of research in social psychology. John Darley and Bibb Latané (1968) used science to understand why no one came to Genovese's rescue. They did an experiment in which research participants heard another participant choking over an intercom (what they actually heard was an audiotape). The researchers led some of the participants to believe that they were the only ones hearing the person choking, while others thought many participants heard it. Of the participants who thought they alone heard the choking man, 85% tried to help. Of those who thought many other people also heard the man choking, only 62% tried to help. Here's the bottom line: The more people who witness an emergency, the less likely any one of them will help. Latané and Darley called this phenomenon the **bystander effect.**

One explanation of the bystander effect involves *diffusion of responsibility;* that is, when there are many people around, an individual's responsibility to act seems decreased. It makes sense when you think about it. When you alone witness an emergency, you know that you are the only source of aid. If several people are present, however, you might not regard it as your responsibility to help the person in need. Someone else might take care of it. Indeed, this is probably why no one helped poor Kitty Genovese. A lot of people were around, so everyone assumed "somebody else must have called the police."

Several factors influence whether or not someone will intervene in an emergency. One is whether people actually notice the event. When people are in a hurry, they are less likely to notice an emergency (Darley & Batson, 1973). Moreover, when many people are present and doing nothing, a person is less likely to interpret an event as an emergency. This is an example of informational social influence, because in this ambiguous situation people look to others for clues as to what should be done. If everyone else is doing nothing, then maybe there's no emergency after all.

Even if we notice an event and interpret it as an emergency, we must decide that it is our responsibility to do something. In addition to a diffusion of responsibility, people often do a cost–benefit analysis to determine whether helping is worth the cost. Sometimes it is dangerous to be helpful. If you get to this step and decide it is worth helping, you still might not know how to help. For example, if you witness someone having a heart attack and want to help, you might not know CPR. Even if you've passed all the previous hurdles, you may not be able to help after all, but you could still call 911.

Altruism   The term **altruism** refers to a selfless concern for and giving of aid to others. Because altruists often expose themselves to greater danger than those who selfishly protect themselves, helping poses risks to personal survival. For this reason, altruism makes no sense from an evolutionary perspective (Dawkins, 1989). So why do humans and other animals sometimes engage in altruistic behavior?

From an evolutionary point of view, true altruism has no clear survival advantage. What might explain altruistic behavior?

kin selection
the evolutionary favoring of genes that prompt individuals to help their relatives or kin.

Evolutionary theory offers two explanations for altruistic behavior: kin selection and reciprocal altruism. **Kin selection** is the evolutionary mechanism that prompts individuals to help their close relatives or kin so that they will survive to reproduce and pass on related genes to their offspring (Hamilton, 1964). For instance, a dominant macaque monkey will share food with a subordinate monkey only if the two are close relatives (Belisle & Chapais, 2001; Furuichi, 1983). Individuals who help close relatives may be risking their lives, but they are also increasing the chances that if they do not survive, at least some of their genes will survive in their relatives.

Kin selection is more common in social animals, such as bees. Greenberg (1979) bred bees to have varied degrees of genetic relatedness and then released them near a nest watched by guard bees. Because the nest was crowded, not everyone could get in. Guard bees more often let in the closely related bees than the distantly related bees. There is evidence for kin selection in humans too. Burnstein and colleagues (1994) asked people to specify whom they would be most likely to help in life-and-death situations and non-life-and-death situations. People reported they would be more likely to help a relative in life-and-death situations, but not in non-life-and-death situations. In fact, when people are rescuing others from a burning building, they are much more likely to look for relatives first (Sime, 1983).

reciprocal altruism
the act of helping others in the hope that they will help us in the future.

Another evolutionary explanation for altruistic behavior is **reciprocal altruism,** helping others in the hope that they will help you in the future (Trivers, 1971, 1985). It is easier for humans to survive when group members cooperate, and reciprocal altruism promotes such cooperation. That is, you might help another member of your group if you believe that you might benefit in some way as a result. From an evolutionary perspective, reciprocal altruism should be most common in species that are social, for only animals that live in groups have opportunities to benefit from reciprocal helping.

Some people have argued that these evolutionary mechanisms do not adequately explain all altruistic behavior. After all, what about Wesley Autrey? Some social psychologists argue that in our relations with others we try to maximize our gains and minimize our losses (Thibaut & Kelly, 1959). This is the essence of **social exchange theory,** a nonevolutionary explanation of altruistic behavior that says we help others because such behavior can be rewarding, but we will help only if the rewards will outweigh the costs. How can helping be rewarding? For one thing, helping someone in need relieves our own distress at witnessing suffering. Also, helping someone is an investment in the future, because it is possible that they will help us when we need help. In this sense, social exchange is essentially the same as reciprocal altruism.

social exchange theory
the idea that we help others when we understand that the benefits to ourselves are likely to outweigh the costs.

According to social exchange theory, truly selfless altruism does not exist. What about Wesley Autrey? Were his actions representative of selfless altruism? He did say that he didn't want his daughters to see the man die. Perhaps by helping, Autrey was protecting the psychological well-being of his kids (which is kin selection after all). Human and nonhuman primates may have both selfish and nonselfish motives for the helping (deWaal & Suchak, 2010). An example of a selfish motive would be helping a suffering person to ease the guilt of not helping. In nonselfish helping, the helper derives no personal benefit.

empathy
the ability to share the feelings of others and understand their situations.

Empathy   C. Daniel Batson (1991) has proposed that true selfless helping occurs only when there is empathy. **Empathy** can be defined as sharing feeling and understanding about another person's situation. According to Batson's

empathy–altruism hypothesis
the idea that people help others selflessly only when they feel empathy for them.

empathy–altruism hypothesis, people will offer selfless help only when they truly empathize with the victim. Consider the following example: A professor is talking with a student in his office. While pleading with the professor to postpone an upcoming test, the student begins to cry. Reacting to the student's distress, the professor becomes upset as well. The professor decides to help the student by postponing the test. Batson and his colleagues believe that two different motivations may underlie the professor's behavior.

The first motivation Batson calls the *egoistic motivation.* The professor may help the student in order to relieve the professor's own distress. This is not true altruism and would fit with social exchange theory, where the reward is reduction of distress. A second motivation, *empathic motivation,* holds that the professor's behavior may spring from an altruistic desire to reduce the distress of the person in need. Unlike the egoistic helper, the empathic helper serves another with the primary goal of helping the student through the crisis.

Clearly empathy plays an important role in helping, but what do we really know about empathy? In order to understand the brain mechanisms of empathy, Singer and colleagues examined brain activation during a person's real pain experience and when witnessing the pain of a loved one (Singer et al., 2004). They created an experiment to study the response to a loved one's pain in the confines of an MRI scanner. Singer obtained measures of functional brain activity in the female partner of a couple while the woman herself received a painful stimulus to her hand and then while she witnessed her male partner receiving the same painful stimulus; see the Research Process for this chapter (Figure 14.7). The actual pain stimulus, which was a mild electric shock delivered by an electrode attached to the hand, activated a well-known pain circuit in the brain, involving the somatosensory cortex, insula, anterior cingulate cortex (ACC), thalamus, and cerebellum. When her partner was experiencing pain, only those structures in the pain circuit that are triggered by the emotional aspect of pain showed activation, most notably the front region of the insula and the ACC. So when a partner experiences pain, people truly do feel it *with* their loved ones.

Nature&Nurture

Watching someone you love experience pain activates components of physical pain circuitry in the brain.

Liking, Attraction, and Love

What makes one person want to be with another? Is this process different for friends and lovers? What is love, anyway? In this section we will see how psychologists tackle a few questions of the human heart. Let's first examine how we come to like and be attracted to other people, and then we'll take a look at love.

Familiarity, Similarity, and Attraction   As we have seen throughout this chapter, research in social psychology shows that merely being exposed to an object, idea, or person causes you to like it more (Zajonc, 1968). The more often we see a face, the more we like it.

People with similar ideas, values, and interests are more likely to like one another and share satisfying, long-lasting relationships (Keller, Thiessen, & Young, 1996). For example, researchers randomly assigned male college students to be roommates in a certain dorm at the beginning of the year. Roommates who became real friends had common backgrounds, similar majors, and similar political viewpoints (Newcomb, 1961). People report that they like and want to help others who have similar personalities, attitudes, or beliefs (Wakimoto & Fujihara, 2004; Westmaas & Silver, 2006). Finally, people also tend to be attracted to

Research Process

1 Research Question

If empathy really is feeling what another person is feeling, are pain circuits in the brain activated similarly when someone feels pain and when empathizing with a loved one's pain?

2 Method

In a quasi-experimental study, Tania Singer and colleagues (2004) used fMRI to measure brain activation in women when they received a mild shock to the hand and also while they witnessed their partner receiving the same painful stimulus.

The partner sat next to the MRI scanner. The woman and her partner placed their right hands on a tilted board, which allowed the woman to see her and her partner's right hand with the help of a mirror. On a large screen the woman saw visual cues that indicated whether she or her partner would get low pain or high pain. When administered, the shock lasted for 2 seconds.

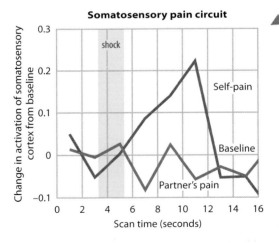

The experimental set up

3 Results

A mild shock was administered 3.5 seconds after the scan began, lasting for 2 seconds. The scans showed that self-pain activated all the structures in the pain circuit, while the partner's pain (the empathic pain condition) mainly activated the structures typically involved only in the emotional aspect of pain (anterior cingulate cortex, or ACC, and the insula). The graphs show brain activation for the women as a change from a baseline (pain-free) state.

▼ The similarity in patterns of activation in the ACC across these two conditions suggests that the women empathized with—that is, *felt*—their partner's pain.

▲ The difference in patterns of activation in the somatosensory cortex suggests that the women did not experience the same sensory aspects of pain when their partners received the shock as when they received the shock themselves.

Emotional pain circuit

Somatosensory pain circuit

Pain circuits in the brain

Anterior cingulate cortex (ACC)

Somatosensory cortex

Insula

Thalamus

Cerebellum

4 Conclusion

Experienced pain activates all pain networks in the brain (emotional and sensory), but empathic pain activates only the emotional pain network. When a loved one experiences pain, people truly do feel their loved one's pain, but that feeling may be more emotional than sensory.

FIGURE 14.7

FEELING ANOTHER'S PAIN. Empathy for a loved one's pain involves brain circuitry that is activated by real pain. Source: "Empathy for Pain Involves the Affective but Not Sensory Components of Pain," by T. Singer, B. Seymour, J. O. O'Doherty, H. Kaube, R. J. Dolan, & C. D. Frith, 2004, *Science, 303,* 1157–1162.

and partner with people of a similar level of attractiveness to themselves—a phenomenon known as *assortative mating* (Buss, 2004). There is a moderately strong correlation between the personality of one's ideal partner and one's own personality; married couples also have strongly correlated age, levels of intelligence, and imaginativeness (Botwin, Buss, & Shackelford, 1997; Keller et al., 1996).

Physical and Chemical Attractiveness

Humans worldwide value physical attractiveness in partners (Buss, 1999; Etcoff, 1999; G. F. Miller, 2000). But what, exactly, is considered to be attractive? In research on attractiveness, people rate average and symmetrical faces as more attractive than less average and less symmetrical faces. *Average,* in this case, does not mean "common." Rather, *average* means that the size, location, and shape of each feature of the face—nose, eyes, mouth, cheekbones—are mathematically average in the population. They are neither too big nor too small, neither too far apart nor too close together. Look, for example, at the faces in Figure 14.8. These faces were produced by computer technology that morphed images of several real faces together. The more faces averaged, the higher the attractiveness ratings. People rated the 8-face composite as more attractive than the 4-face composite; the 16-face composite as more attractive than the 8; and the 32-face composite as more attractive than the 16 (Langlois & Roggman, 1990; Langlois, Roggman, & Musselman, 1994). Although standards for beauty vary by culture, average faces are rated as most attractive all over the world (Langlois & Roggman, 1990). Furthermore, infants as young as 6 or 9 months of age also tend to prefer average faces over others, although they are too young for other people to have had much influence over their face preferences (Hoss & Langlois, 2003).

Averaged faces tend to be more symmetrical, and people seem to prefer symmetry when they rate faces for attractiveness (Etcoff, 1999). Moreover, symmetry is a rough indicator of genetic fitness; that is, symmetrical faces and bodies are signs of fewer genetic mutations (G. F. Miller, 2000).

Scent plays a role in attraction, but we are not talking about perfumes. Pheromones—scents produced by animals that have an effect on other members of the same species—are well-established modes of social communication among many species of animal. They are full of sexual and organizational messages, but whether they operate or even exist in humans has been a matter of debate (Brennan, 2010).

Apparently scent matters in humans as well, but not in the way you would think. In a clever experiment, researchers instructed men and women to wear a clean T-shirt to bed for two nights (Thornhill et al., 2003). The shirt had no perfumes and was not washed with deodorant soaps. The T-shirts were returned to the lab and sealed in zippered bags. An independent group of students rated the attractiveness of pictures of the people who wore the shirts. Another group of students smelled and rated the T-shirts on attractiveness of odor. Men preferred the scent of women in their fertile phase; fertile women preferred the scent of men who were most symmetrical.

In a similar study in which men smelled women's shirts, researchers measured men's testosterone levels in response to the smells. Men released more testosterone when exposed to the scent of ovulating women than when exposed to the scent of non-ovulating women (S. L. Miller & Maner, 2010).

sexual strategies theory
the idea that men and women face different problems when they seek out mates, and so they often approach relationships in very different ways.

Sexual Attraction and Mate Selection

What qualities do you look for in a prospective sexual partner? **Sexual strategies theory** suggests that men and women often approach relationships differently (Buss & Schmitt,

4-face composite

8-face composite

16-face composite

32-face composite

FIGURE 14.8

RATING PHYSICAL ATTRACTIVENESS. The more faces that are morphed into one image, the more they move toward having average features. As they become more average in features, the faces are perceived as increasing in attractiveness.

1993). In virtually all societies, men and women use both short-term matings (affairs, one-night stands) and long-term matings (marriages, extended companionships). Both are effective ways to increase one's reproductive fitness, but each strategy has strengths and weaknesses. Sex differences in attraction arise because *parental investment* is greater for women than for men (Trivers, 1972). Consequently, men devote a larger portion of their total mating effort to short-term mating than do women (Buss, 1999).

Connection
Men are more likely than women to be interested in casual sex.
See "Sex: Survival of the Species," Chapter 11, "Motivation and Emotion," p. 434, for an evolutionary explanation.

Love takes many different forms and means different things to different people. How might you characterize love that takes on such a public aspect? How might the feelings of millions of well-wishers around the world affect their relationship?

Buss (1999) found that men report wanting an average of 18 different partners throughout their lifetime, whereas women report wanting only four or five. Men value qualities that may signal fertility and accessibility (e.g., large breasts, wide hips compared to waist, youth), especially in short-term partners. This is less true in evaluating long-term partners. Women, in contrast, value men who can provide resources to support their offspring.

Mate selection factors might drive sexual partnerships, but these evolutionary pressures operate outside conscious awareness. Once people mate, it is the love that may develop between two people that keeps them together. But what is love?

Love As a concept, love is not easy to define. It takes many different forms and means different things to different people at different times in their lives.

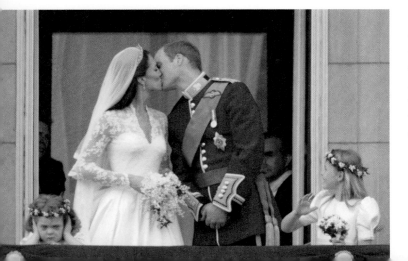

Types of Love Humans love in many different ways. We love our parents, lovers, friends, brothers and sisters, children, dogs, lattes, and music. How do we account for the variations? One well-known theory is Robert Sternberg's **triangular theory of love** (Sternberg, 1986). Sternberg proposed that three

triangular theory of love
Sternberg's idea that three components (intimacy, passion, and commitment), in various combinations, can explain all the forms of human love.

4-face composite

8-face composite

16-face composite

32-face composite

components—intimacy, passion, and commitment, in various combinations—can explain all the forms of human love (see Figure 14.9). *Intimacy* refers to close, connected, and bonded feelings in loving relationships. *Passion* refers to the drives that lead to romance, physical attraction, and sexual consummation and is accompanied by physiological changes and arousal. *Commitment* refers to both the decision to love someone—or not—and the decision to commit to love for the long term.

These three components are present in different amounts for different kinds of love. *Companionate love* exists when intimacy and commitment are high and passion is low. In *passionate love,* intimacy and passion are high and commitment is low. *Lust* is characterized by a lot of passion but no intimacy or commitment. In contrast, arranged marriages are all about commitment, at least in the beginning, with no intimacy or passion.

Love as Attachment Love is also closely connected to a well-known psychological phenomenon: attachment. Attachment, an important concept in human development, is an affection-based bond between infants and their primary caregivers that serves to protect infants from threats to their survival (Bowlby, 1969). Attachment researchers distinguish among secure, avoidant, and anxious/ambivalent attachment styles (Ainsworth et al., 1978).

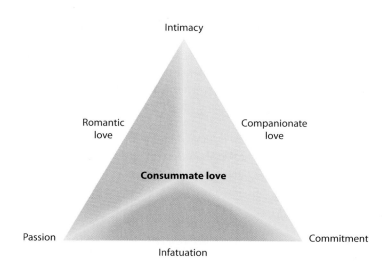

FIGURE **14.9**

STERNBERG'S TRIANGULAR THEORY OF LOVE. In Sternberg's model, all types of love are made up of three components: intimacy, passion, and commitment. Each type of love consists of a different balance of the three components. When all three exist in equal proportions, consummate love exists. (Source: Sternberg, 1986)

The attachment system established when we are infants forms a template for our adult relationships with others, including our intimate partners, according to Cynthia Hazan and Phillip Shaver (1987). Hazan and Shaver argued that the infant–caregiver attachment system underlies the important dynamics and individual differences in adult romantic relationships. By categorizing people's infant–caregiver attachment style based on an adult attachment interview, they found that securely attached adults report that they easily get close to others, readily trust others, and have more satisfying romantic relationships. Anxious/ambivalent adults tend to have less satisfying relationships, are more preoccupied with them, and fear that their partners do not want the intimacy they desire. Avoidant adults are uncomfortable being close to others and have less satisfying relationships (Hazan & Shaver, 1987).

As you can see, we have a partial understanding of how liking, attraction, and love work, but psychological science has yet to explain how these elements come together. Evolutionary psychology offers one integrative framework. In this view, for example, liking and loving both evolved to help ensure survival of the species.

Connection

Attachment is a bidirectional relationship requiring the active participation of infants and caregivers.

See "Early Socioemotional Development," Chapter 5, "Human Development," p. 192.

Bringing It All Together
Making Connections in Social Behavior
Analysis of the Jonestown Cult

The tragic mass suicide of hundreds of members of the People's Temple in Jonestown, Guyana, illustrates many of the social–psychological concepts discussed in this chapter. In late November 1978, under the direction of the Reverend Jim Jones, members of this cult fed a poison-laced drink to their children and then drank it themselves. More than 900 adults and children died; most were found lying together, arm in arm.

Most of the members of the People's Temple went willingly to their deaths. Why? After years of indoctrination and isolation from mainstream society, they had been led into complete commitment to Jones and the People's Temple. People's Temple had all the hallmarks of a cult. A **cult** is an extremist group led by a charismatic, totalitarian leader in which coercive methods are used to prevent members from leaving the group.

If we apply social–psychological theory to an analysis of these events, they become more comprehensible because we can see that the members of the People's Temple were not very different from us. Four principles of social psychology—persuasion, conformity, obedience, and cognitive dissonance—can shed light on the tragedy of Jonestown (Osherow, 1999).

Jim Jones and the People's Temple

Jim Jones founded the People's Temple in Indiana in 1958, preaching a message of brotherhood, racial integration, and freedom from poverty. His group helped feed and employ the poor. Jones presented a public image of a beloved leader who promoted a vision of racial harmony.

Throughout the 1960s, the group grew in size and popularity. Rumors surfaced that Jones used coercive methods to keep people from leaving the People's Temple. In the mid-1970s, after a great deal of bad publicity, Jones and his followers moved to a jungle outpost he called Jonestown in Guyana, South America. In 1978, U.S. Congressman Leo Ryan heard reports that the People's Temple was holding members against their will. He led a delegation of government officials, reporters, and concerned relatives to Jonestown to talk with residents about how they liked living there. Two families secretly informed Ryan that they wanted out. As Ryan's party and these two "defector" families tried to board their plane for the United States, Temple gunmen ambushed and killed five people, including Congressman Ryan. This ambush precipitated the mass suicide, an act that Jones and

cult
an extremist group led by a charismatic, totalitarian leader in which coercive methods are used to prevent members from leaving the group.

Jim Jones

his followers had rehearsed many times. It was their final act of rebellion against the system that they believed forced them into exile.

The Role of Persuasion

Jones was a charismatic figure. He sought out people who needed to hear his message: the urban poor, minorities, the elderly, ex-addicts, and convicts. Potential members of the People's Temple first encountered an almost idyllic scene in which Blacks and Whites lived, worked, and worshiped together in total harmony. Guests were greeted warmly and invited to share a meal. Jones also gave them miracles. He cured diseases;

he made predictions that came true with uncanny frequency. Members were motivated to believe in Jones; they appreciated the racial harmony, sense of purpose, and relief from feelings of worthlessness that the People's Temple provided.

Jones carefully managed his public image. He used letter writing and the political clout of hundreds of cult members to praise him and impress the politicians and reporters who supported the People's Temple as well as to criticize and intimidate its opponents. Most important, Jones limited the information available to members.

The Role of Conformity and Obedience

Conformity played a role in the People's Temple from the outset. Even getting into the group was not easy. People underwent a strict initiation process that actually drew members more firmly into the group. As they became increasingly involved in the People's Temple, they committed themselves more strongly to the group because they were required to donate their property and 25% of their income to the church. Before they entered the meeting room for each service, they wrote self-incriminating letters that were turned over to the church. If anyone objected, the refusal was interpreted as a "lack of faith" in Jones. All of these rules functioned to make the group more important than individuals, which makes conformity to the group all the more likely.

As he gradually increased his demands, Jones also exposed cult members to the concept of a "final ritual," mass suicide. Rehearsals of this ritual served to test followers and their faith in Jones. In essence, Jones was making use of what social psychologists call the *foot-in-the-door* technique

These are some of the victims of a mass suicide at Jonestown, Guyana, in 1978. People's Temple leader Jim Jones used his status as an authority figure to persuade, intimidate, and indoctrinate his followers over several years, apparently convincing them that death was the only alternative to being captured and separated from the group.

by getting people to agree to a moderate request (i.e., rehearsal). Once cult members had agreed to engage in frequent rehearsals of mass suicide, it became easier for them to go through with the real thing.

The suicides at Jonestown can be viewed as the product of obedience—people complying with the orders of a leader and reacting to the threat of force. In the People's Temple, whatever Jim Jones commanded, the members did. Jones was a forceful authority. By the early 1970s, the members of the People's Temple lived in constant fear of severe punishment—brutal beatings coupled with public humiliation—for committing trivial or even inadvertent offenses. Milgram's experiments show us that the power of authority need not be so explicitly threatening to create compliance with demands. Nor does the consensus of the group need to be coercive, as Asch's experiments on conformity indicate. Yet Jones's power was both threatening and coercive.

Jones used threats to impose the discipline and devotion he demanded, and he took steps to eliminate any behavior that might encourage resistance among his followers. As Solomon Asch found in his experiments on conformity, if just one confederate expressed an opinion different from that of the majority, the rate of conformity drastically declined. This is minority social influence. In the People's Temple, Jones tolerated no dissent, made sure that members had no allegiance more powerful than their loyalty to him, and tried to make the alternative of leaving the church unthinkable. Anyone who dared to dissent was terrorized as a traitor, thereby squelching the possibility of minority social influence.

How did Jones do this? He used informers who reported indiscretions, split families to prevent allegiances, and forced parents to give over their children to the Temple. He thereby created conditions in which kin selection could not promote helping between members. Similarly, Jones worked to dissolve marital bonds by forcing couples into extramarital relations (sometimes with Jones himself). "Families are part of the enemy system," Jones said, because they weakened the individual's dedication to the cause. Not surprisingly, it was very hard to leave the cult. Not being able to defect or escape from the group, people had little choice but to conform.

The Role of Cognitive Dissonance

Cognitive dissonance helps explain why cult members believed Jones to the end and why so few defected. People did not become cult members all at once. Rather, the process of justifying their choice and becoming committed to Jones unfolded slowly over the course of weeks and months, sometimes years. Jones knew what he was doing. Starting the process with harsh acts of initiation is a perfect way to get people to rationalize their otherwise embarrassing behavior. If people don't see the group they are about to join very

positively, how could they possibly justify going through such humiliation in order to get in?

Even so, how could members not seek to escape and accept killing themselves and their children so easily? These acts were the product of a situation that made dissent impossible and faith in Jones and the Temple absolute. Once they were isolated from the rest of the world at Jonestown, escape was impossible. When escape is impossible, people rationalize their predicament. The members of the People's Temple reduced their cognitive dissonance by changing their attitude to conform with their behavior. In this case, they told themselves that Jones was great and his message was wonderful. When the time to commit suicide finally arrived, most of the members clearly drank the juice quite willingly and by their own choice, so strong was their belief in Jones and his message.

Quick Quiz 14.4: Bringing It All Together: Making Connections in Social Behavior

1. Sam was driving his car and recklessly caused an accident that seriously injured a driver in another car. Susan insulted an acquaintance because she believed the acquaintance had questioned her honesty. According to the definition of aggression in the book, who behaved aggressively?
   a. Sam
   b. Susan
   c. both Sam and Susan
   d. neither Sam nor Susan

2. The bystander effect says
   a. the more people who observe a person in need of help, the less likely any one person will help
   b. the fewer people who observe a person in need of help, the less likely any one person will help
   c. people stand by and wait for help when they need it
   d. people are more likely to rescue people who are most closely related to themselves

3. The world over, faces that have _____ are perceived as the most attractive.
   a. the smallest nose
   b. blue eyes
   c. features that are average in their dimensions
   d. eyes farthest apart

4. The tragedy of Jonestown, where more than 900 committed mass suicide, can be explained by four principles of social psychology: persuasion, conformity, _____, and _____.
   a. attraction; aggression
   b. obedience; cognitive dissonance
   c. obedience; empathy
   d. discrimination; prejudice

Answers can be found at the end of the chapter.

Chapter **Review**

GROUP LIVING AND SOCIAL INFLUENCE

- Social psychology is the study of the effects of the real or imagined presence of others on people's thoughts, feelings, and actions.

- We act differently when other people are present than we do when we are alone. Sometimes our performance is improved when we are with other people; sometimes it is hindered. In addition, people adjust their behavior in order to conform to what others are doing or to adhere to the rules of their culture.

- An individual can change the majority opinion of a group, but doing so takes perseverance and consistency.

- Obedience to authority can and has led to numerous instances of people doing things they otherwise would not, from soldiers in Nazi Germany and Abu Ghraib prison in Iraq to participants in Milgram's studies.

SOCIAL PERCEPTION

- We are constantly drawing conclusions about why people do what they do; that is, we make attributions. Sometimes we say internal qualities of the person were the cause of their behavior. Other times we see outside forces in the environment as the cause of a person's behavior.

- When forming opinions about others, we use schema about individuals based on what they are like or are likely to do based simply on the group they belong to. Opinions formed this way are stereotypes. Similarly, a prejudice is an attitude toward a group of people or an individual member of a group based on unfair generalizations about that group. Finally, discrimination is preferential treatment of certain people that is driven by prejudicial attitudes.

- Applying stereotypes, prejudices, and discrimination to people based on their racial–ethnic group affiliations is racism. Racism operates both inside (explicitly) and outside (implicitly) our awareness.

ATTITUDES AND BEHAVIOR

- Psychologists define attitudes as a person's favorable or unfavorable beliefs, feelings, or actions toward an object,

idea, or person. People's attitudes and behaviors do not always match and are often resistant to change.

- One explanation for why and how people change their attitudes is cognitive dissonance, which is the feeling of discomfort caused by information that differs from one's conception of oneself as a reasonable and sensible person.

- Persuasion is another way in which attitudes can be changed.

SOCIAL RELATIONS

- People hurt other people, help other people, and are attracted to and love other people.

- Aggression refers to violent behaviors that are intended to cause psychological and/or physical harm to another being. Aggression stems from a complex interplay of genetic and social forces.

- The more people who witness an accident or crime, the more likely it is that no one will call for help or intervene. This phenomenon is the bystander effect.

- People also act in prosocial ways to help others in need. In life-and-death situations, kin selection explains why people are most willing to help those who are most closely related to them.

- Relationships that are bound by similarities in personality, attitude, intelligence, and attractiveness tend to last the longest.

- People all over the world rate as most attractive those faces that possess average and symmetrical features. Sexual strategies theory suggests that men and women face different problems when they seek out mates, so they often approach relationships in very different ways.

- Sternberg's triangular theory of love states that all of the different forms of love each have three components: intimacy, passion, and commitment. Romantic love, for example, exists when intimacy and passion are present but commitment is absent.

BRINGING IT ALL TOGETHER: MAKING CONNECTIONS IN SOCIAL BEHAVIOR

- The People's Temple was a cult, which is an extremist group led by a charismatic, totalitarian leader who uses coercive methods to prevent members from leaving the group.

- Methods used by Jim Jones to ensure obedience and conformity by his followers included persuasion, rigid discipline and punishment of dissent, isolation, separation from family, and forced marital infidelity. Cult members resolved cognitive dissonance brought on by their situation through rationalization, telling themselves that Jones was a great leader with a wonderful message.

Key Terms

Quick Quiz Answers

Quick Quiz 14.1:   1. c   2. d   3. a   4. c

Quick Quiz 14.2:   1. d   2. c   3. a   4. d   5. b

Quick Quiz 14.3:   1. b   2. d   3. a

Quick Quiz 14.4:   1. b   2. a   3. c   4. b

Challenge Your Assumptions Answers

- Being left out really hurts. **True. See p. 548.**
- I know whether I am prejudiced or not. **False. See pp. 562–564.**
- People will sometimes risk their lives to help others. **True. See pp. 573–575.**
- Attractive faces are anything but average. **False. See p. 577.**

Psychological Disorders

15

Chapter Outline

Challenge *Your Assumptions*

TRUE OR FALSE?

- Most people who suffer from mental illness are dangerous.
- Panic attacks often include heart palpitations.
- Extreme stress can make you depressed.
- Schizophrenia is a disorder of split personalities.
- All the great artists in history can be viewed as psychologically disturbed.

Answers can be found at the end of the chapter.

Langley and Homer Collyer were brothers who lived in a large three-story house in New York City (Frost & Steketee, 2010). In March 1947, police were called to their "mansion" because a neighbor reported that one of the brothers had died in the house. The police, however, could not enter through the front door or any other doors or windows on the first floor. All entrances were blocked with household items and appliances—newspapers, boxes, pianos, and car parts, to name but a few examples. When the fire department used ladders and finally gained entrance on the second and third floors, what they found (after workers spent a total of 3 weeks cleaning out the house) was astonishing: a car, a horse-drawn carriage, 14 grand pianos, a rusted bicycle, even a two-headed fetus. All in all, more than 170 tons (340,000 pounds) of stuff was removed from the house. The entire house was filled from floor to ceiling, and the only way to move around was through tunnels. As it turned out, the booby-trapped boxes the brothers had set up to prevent anyone from coming in had apparently caused Langley's death. Homer, however, was blind and relied on Langley to feed him; and so when Langley died, Homer gradually starved to death. The Collyer brothers were among the first widely publicized compulsive hoarders—people who collect stuff to the point that it interferes with everyday functioning.

Ted Bundy was a handsome, well-educated, and charming man, who also happened to be one of the worst serial killers in U.S. history—murdering somewhere between 20 and 100 women, though most likely about 35 (Keppel, 2005; Sullivan, 2009). Between 1974 and 1978, he charmed young female students between the ages of 15 and 25 with a story of being hurt and needing help to carry his books. Once they were in his car he would often batter them with a baseball bat or crowbar and sometimes have sex with the body.

Vincent van Gogh and Paul Gauguin—the artists—had an intense argument on December 23, 1888, a Sunday evening in the middle of winter. Over what they argued, we do not know. What we do know is how it ended: Van Gogh, in a fit of rage, took a razor and cut off the lower portion of his left ear. He then wrapped the earlobe in a newspaper and gave it to a prostitute named Rachel, telling her to "keep this object carefully" (Runyan, 1981).

That the Collyer brothers, Bundy, and van Gogh each had some kind of psychological disorder is apparent. What is not so easy to agree on, however, is how to define psychological disorder in general and how to specify the concrete criteria for particular disorders.

Clearly, these three examples are extreme cases, but behavior varies along a continuum from more to less disordered. In this chapter, we describe many psychological disorders and explain some of what is known about how they develop. As we discuss the causes of these disorders, we will focus on explanations that intertwine the biological with the environmental (Kendler, 2005; Moffitt, Caspi, & Rutter, 2005; Uher & McGuffin, 2010). We will begin by considering what it means for behavior to be disordered and how disorders are diagnosed. At the end of the chapter we will explore the topic of creativity and psychological disorders and consider whether artists are more likely than the general population to suffer from a psychological disorder. ■

DEFINING PSYCHOLOGICAL DISORDERS

Creative artists such as Vincent Van Gogh are different from most people. So too are spelling bee champs, Olympic athletes, and class valedictorians. Yet *different* does not mean *disordered*. Does a young child who has more than 5,000 baseball cards and can tell you something about every one of them suffer from a psychological disorder? What about people who wash their hands for 45 minutes 10 times a day? How do psychologists distinguish behavior that is simply different from behavior that is disordered?

Most psychologists agree on three criteria that qualify a behavior as disordered: It must be deviant, distressing, and dysfunctional (APA, 2000). *Deviant* literally means "different from the norm," or different from what most people do. This criterion allows for the fact that behavior which is considered deviant in one culture might be considered normal in others. *Distressing* behavior leads to real discomfort or anguish, either in the person directly or in others. The distressing element is one reason we say a person is "suffering" from a disorder. It causes pain to the person and/or other people, especially family members. *Dysfunctional* behavior interferes with everyday functioning and occasionally can be a risk to oneself or others. The term *dysfunctional* also implies it prevents one from participating in everyday social relationships, holding a regular job, or being productive in other ways. In sum, deviant behavior can be classified as disordered only if it is also both distressing and dysfunctional. Albert Einstein was deviant in his intelligence and creativity, but he was not suffering from a psychological disorder. Behaviors that possess only one or even two of these qualities are not typically classified as disordered.

Most people suffering from psychological disorders do not pose a risk to others, but some do. For instance, people who are sexually attracted to children (pedophiles) and individuals with violent impulse disorder could be a very real danger to others. Others may pose a risk to themselves; for example, people with severe depression are at heightened risk of attempting suicide (APA, 2000).

Van Gogh painted *Self-Portrait With Bandaged Ear* (1889) after cutting off part of his ear following a violent disagreement with his friend and fellow painter Paul Gauguin.

Looking at this photograph, we might think this person has a psychological disorder. However, behavior must be deviant, distressing to the individual, and dysfunctional to be classified as disordered.

589

Culture certainly plays an important role in the expression and diagnosis of what is considered a mental disorder and what is not. Some disorders are found only in certain cultures, and others are usually found in certain other cultures. For instance, anorexia nervosa is nearly nonexistent in most African and Asian cultures. Likewise, in some southeast Asian cultures, certain men suffer from *koro*, the debilitating belief that one's genitals are retracting into one's body. In parts of the Middle East, some people suffer from *zar*—the belief that they are possessed by spirits—and run around in fits of laughter, shouting, and singing (Watters, 2010).

How do mental health professionals determine whether someone is suffering from a psychological disorder? In the United States and some other Western cultures, the major tool for diagnosing psychological disorders is the *Diagnostic and Statistical Manual (DSM)* published by the American Psychiatric Association (APA). Beginning with the third edition and continuing in the fourth edition, the *DSM-IV-TR* (for "Text Revision"; APA, 2000), the *DSM* places disorders in one of two diagnostic classifications, or axes. **Axis I disorders** include the major clinical **syndromes,** or clusters of related symptoms that cause significant impairment to life functioning, such as anxiety, depression, bipolar disorder, and schizophrenia. These disorders tend to develop after adolescence, can wax and wane, and are not always permanent. **Axis II disorders** include personality disorders and mental retardation, which tend to appear in childhood or adolescence and usually last a lifetime. One main difference between Axis I and Axis II disorders is that Axis I disorders tend to be viewed by people suffering from them as inconsistent with their personality, and therefore they cause some degree of subjective stress. Axis II disorders are viewed as consistent with an individual's personality and therefore do not cause as much subjective stress as Axis I disorders. They are simply part of the person (APA, 2000).

To be sure, the *DSM* stems from an American–Western perspective of psychological illness, but this view is starting to spread to other cultures that historically have a very different way of conceptualizing mental illness (Watters, 2010). For example, historically in China anorexia nervosa has been extremely rare; when it was described, the fear of being fat was not a symptom. Sufferers most frequently complained of having bloated stomachs. However, a single widely publicized case of anorexia in 1994 that led to the death of a Hong Kong teenager suddenly made anorexia a much more commonly reported disorder—rates of the disorder increased dramatically by the late 1990s. Moreover, because the journalists in Hong Kong who were covering the story tended to use the American *DSM* to describe the disorder, with the increase in prevalence also came a change in symptoms. After the publicity surrounding this case, more and more Chinese people with anorexia began to complain mostly of their fear of being fat and not of bloated stomachs. In short, their disorder became more Americanized.

The *DSM-IV-TR* includes three additional axes, which list medical conditions and environmental factors that may contribute to an individual's psychological state or affect treatment. Figure 15.1 lists the five axes of the *DSM* classification system.

Psychological disorders are not uncommon (see Figure 15.2). In a given year, 26% of the population suffers from a diagnosable disorder. Over the course of their entire lifetime, almost half (46%) of the adults in the United States will suffer from at least one psychological disorder, and more than

Axis I disorders in the *DSM-IV-TR,* the major clinical syndromes that cause significant impairment.

syndromes groups or clusters of related symptoms that are characteristic of a disorder.

Axis II disorders in the *DSM-IV-TR,* the more long-standing personality disorders as well as mental retardation.

Connections

Dementia and Alzheimer's disease are cognitive disorders related to age. Other disorders, such as sleep disorders, can occur at any time in a person's life.

See "Late Adulthood," Chapter 5, "Human Development," p. 212, and "Disorders of Sleep," Chapter 6, "Consciousness," p. 246.

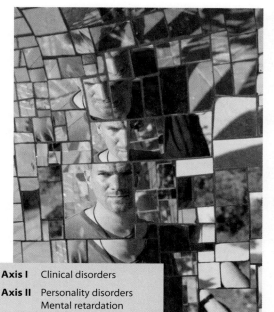

FIGURE **15.1**

DSM-IV-TR **AXES.** Axes I and II describe the disorders and their symptoms. Axes III, IV, and V take into account factors in an individual's background and environment that might affect the diagnosis or treatment of a psychological disorder. (Source: APA, 2000)

Axis I	Clinical disorders
Axis II	Personality disorders Mental retardation
Axis III	General medical conditions
Axis IV	Psychosocial and environmental problems
Axis V	Global assessment of functioning

half of those will suffer from two or more disorders (Kessler et al., 2005). The existence of two or more disorders at the same time is called **comorbidity.**

The *DSM* describes more than 250 Axis I disorders and more than 100 Axis II disorders. Figure 15.3 on page 592 lists the major ones. In this chapter, we examine anxiety disorders, mood disorders, schizophrenia, dissociative disorders, somatoform disorders, personality disorders, and childhood disorders.

comorbidity
occurrence of two or more disorders at the same time.

ANXIETY DISORDERS

For most of us, anxiety and fear are occasional, distressing, but necessary emotions that tell us something is wrong. For about 29% of the U.S. population, however, anxiety is out of proportion to the situation and interferes with everyday functioning. In this section we discuss seven of the more common forms of anxiety disorder (see Figure 15.4 on page 593).

Generalized Anxiety Disorder

Generalized anxiety disorder (GAD) is a common anxiety disorder, characterized by a pervasive and excessive state of anxiety lasting at least 6 months (APA, 2000). More women than men experience GAD (Kessler et al., 2005). Moreover, unlike those suffering from other anxiety disorders, people with GAD often have been anxious throughout their lives and cannot recall when they began to feel that way (Barlow, 2004). In everyday language, we might call such people "worrywarts"—or those who worry about anything and everything, often out of proportion to the actual threat. The writer, director, and actor

generalized anxiety disorder (GAD)
state of pervasive and excessive anxiety lasting at least 6 months.

Three or more disorders
17.3%

Two disorders
10.4%

53.6%
No disorder

18.7%

One disorder

FIGURE **15.2**

PERCENTAGE OF AMERICAN ADULTS WHO WILL EXPERIENCE A PSYCHOLOGICAL DISORDER AT SOME POINT DURING THEIR LIVES. Of the 46% of the population who will suffer a psychological disorder during their lifetime, more than half will suffer from at least two different disorders. (Source: Kessler et al., 2005)

FIGURE **15.3**

MAJOR PSYCHO-LOGICAL DISOR-DERS. Although *DSM-IV-TR* describes more than 250 Axis I disorders and 100 Axis II disorders, these are the most common. (Source: APA, 2000)

Axis I disorders	Description
Disorders usually first diagnosed in infancy, childhood, or adolescence	Attention deficit hyperactivity disorder, autistic spectrum disorders, learning disorders, conduct and oppositional disorder, separation anxiety disorder, and feeding, tic, and elimination disorders.
Anxiety disorders	Characterized by motor tension, hyperactivity and apprehensive expectation/thoughts. Include generalized anxiety disorder, panic disorder, phobic disorder, obsessive-compulsive disorder, and post-traumatic stress disorder.
Somatoform disorders	Occur when psychological symptoms take a physical form even though no physical causes can be found. Include hypochondriasis and conversion disorder.
Factitious disorders	Characterized by the individual's deliberate fabrication of a medical or mental disorder to gain medical attention.
Dissociative disorders	Involve a sudden loss of memory or change of identity.
Delirium, dementia, amnestic, and other cognitive disorders	Disorders involving problems in consciousness and cognition, such as substance-induced delirium or dementia related to Alzheimer's disease.
Mood disorders	Characterized by a primary disturbance in mood; include depressive disorders and bipolar disorder (sometimes called manic depression).
Schizophrenia and other psychotic disorders	Characterized by distorted thoughts and perceptions, odd communication, inappropriate emotion, and other unusual behaviors.
Substance-related disorders	Characterized by abuse or dependence on drugs, such as alcohol, cocaine, and hallucinogens.
Sexual and gender-identity disorders	Consist of three main types of disorders: gender-identity disorders (person is not comfortable with identity as a female or male), paraphilias (person has a preference for unusual sexual acts to stimulate sexual arousal), and sexual dysfunctions (impairments in sexual functioning).
Eating disorders	Include anorexia nervosa and bulimia nervosa (see Chapter 12).
Sleep disorders	Consist of primary sleep disorders, such as insomnia and narcolepsy, and sleep disorders due to a general medical condition, such as sleep apnea (see Chapter 6).
Impulse-control disorders not elsewhere classified	Include kleptomania, pyromania, and compulsive gambling.
Adjustment disorders	Characterized by distressing emotional or behavioral symptoms in response to an identifiable stressor.

Axis II disorders

Mental retardation	Low intellectual functioning and an inability to adapt to everyday life (see Chapter 10).
Personality disorders	Develop when personality traits become inflexible and maladaptive.
Other conditions that may be a focus of clinical attention	Include relational problems (with a partner, sibling, and so on), problems related to abuse or neglect (physical abuse of a child, for example), or additional conditions (such as bereavement, academic problems, and religious or spiritual problems).

Disorder	Major symptoms	Behaviors
Generalized anxiety disorder (GAD)	Pervasive/excessive anxiety lasting at least 6 months	Inability to relax
Panic disorder	Persistent worry about having a panic attack	*Panic attack:* Heart palpitations, trembling, dizziness, intense dread, and fear of dying *Panic disorder:* Prone to panic attacks, concerned about having a panic attack and about embarrassment of having a panic attack
Agoraphobia	Fear of not being able to escape or of help not being available if panic attack should occur in public place	Unwilling to leave home so as to avoid panic attacks
Post-traumatic stress disorder (PTSD)	Anxiety disorder triggered by a traumatic experience	(1) Possible flashbacks; nightmares about the traumatic event (2) Emotional numbness and avoidance of thoughts, feelings, and activities associated with the trauma (3) Irritability or outbursts of anger; hypervigilance and trouble sleeping
Social phobia	Persistent fear of humiliation in the presence of others	Highly anxious, extremely self-conscious about appearance or behavior or both, possibly housebound
Specific phobias	Undue anxiety response to particular objects or situations	Intense fear or panic when confronted with particular situations or objects or even when thinking about them
Obsessive–compulsive disorder	Preoccupation with unwanted thoughts and repetitive behaviors to control the anxiety caused by the distressing thoughts, which are often understood to be irrational	Cleaning and checking behaviors that may help to control the obsessive thoughts but that interfere with daily life

FIGURE **15.4**

MAJOR SYMPTOMS AND CRITERIA OF SPECIFIC ANXIETY DISORDERS. All of these disorders share the symptom of intense anxiety. (Source: APA, 2000)

panic attacks
brief episodes of anxiety associated with perceptions of threat and occurring because of fear of danger, inability to escape, embarrassment, or specific objects, for example.

panic disorder
an anxiety disorder characterized by panic attacks and persistent anxiety about having more attacks.

Woody Allen has made a career out of his pervasive tendency to worry. Allen says he uses filmmaking and writing as a creative distraction from his pervasive anxiety (Briggs, 2005). The constant anxiety of GAD can be debilitating, however, preventing many people who suffer from it from being able to work at all.

Panic Disorder With or Without Agoraphobia

Panic attacks are characterized by an overwhelming sense of impending doom, accompanied by heart palpitations, trembling, dizziness, intense dread, and even fear of dying. Such attacks are associated with perceptions of threat and can occur for a number of reasons: fear of danger, inability to escape, fear of embarrassment, or fear of a specific category of objects. Panic attacks usually last about 10 minutes. but sometimes come and go over a period of an hour or more. Due to their physiological effects, people undergoing a panic attack may believe they are having a heart attack or are "going crazy." People with **panic disorder** get panic attacks and experience persistent worry, embarrassment, and concern

Filmmaker Woody Allen uses writing, acting, and directing as a distraction from his own anxiety.

about having more attacks (APA, 2000). One key criterion for the disorder is the preoccupation and anxiety over having another attack, which creates an anxious mood, which then increases the likelihood of more worrisome thoughts and, ironically, another attack. Thus, panic disorder creates a positive feedback cycle, wherein anxiety about future attacks hijacks the body's emergency response system and catapults it out of control.

People who have only occasional panic attacks without intense anxiety or fear about the possibility of future panic attacks do not qualify for the diagnosis of panic disorder. Approximately 10% of the U.S. population has experienced a panic attack in the past 12 months, whereas only about 2% to 5% of the population has panic disorder (Grant et al., 2006).

Panic attacks are associated with agoraphobia in about one third of cases. **Agoraphobia** is intense anxiety and panic about being in places from which escape might be difficult or in which help might not be available should a panic attack occur (APA, 2000). It is the most severe of all phobias (Bouton, Mineka, & Barlow, 2001). Contrary to popular belief, the primary "fear" in agoraphobia is not of being out in public but rather of being in an inescapable situation. The fear of being unable to escape keeps people at home, where they feel safe. Agoraphobia typically begins when a person experiences a panic attack in a public place, such as a park or a crowd of people, and feels trapped and unable to escape.

Post-Traumatic Stress Disorder

Post-traumatic stress disorder (PTSD) is an anxiety disorder triggered by exposure to a catastrophic or horrifying event that caused serious harm or posed a dire threat to the person—such as experiences of war, attempted murder, rape, natural disasters, sudden death of a loved one, or physical or sexual abuse. Symptoms of PTSD are grouped into three categories: (1) re-experiencing the trauma; (2) avoiding thoughts, feelings, and activities associated with the trauma; emotional numbing and distancing from loved ones; and (3) increased arousal, such as irritability, sleeping, or exaggerated startle response (Duke & Vasterling, 2005). War veterans are at increased risk not only for PTSD but also for depression, drug abuse, and suicide after returning home. For example, upwards of 24% of the veterans from Iraq have developed PTSD (Renshaw, 2011; Roehr, 2007; Tanielian & Jaycox, 2008).

People of all ages can experience post-traumatic stress symptoms, including children who have experienced a serious trauma such as extreme domestic abuse (Nixon et al., 2010). Compared to healthy controls, children with post-traumatic stress symptoms show reduced brain activity in the hippocampus while performing a verbal memory task (Carrion et al., 2010). The hippocampus plays a central role in learning and memory, so these results suggest that post-traumatic stress interferes with learning.

Social Phobia (Social Anxiety Disorder)

A **phobia** is a persistent and unreasonable fear of a particular object, situation, or activity (APA, 2000). Some people suffer extreme anxiety when they have to interact with other people. **Social phobia,** or **social anxiety disorder,** a pronounced fear of humiliation in the presence of others, is marked by severe self-consciousness about appearance or behavior or both. People with social phobia are most afraid of embarrassing or humiliating themselves, of being evaluated

agoraphobia
an anxiety disorder involving fear of being in places from which escape might be difficult or in which help might not be available should a panic attack occur.

post-traumatic stress disorder (PTSD)
a type of anxiety disorder triggered by exposure to a catastrophic or horrifying event that poses serious harm or threat.

social phobia (social anxiety disorder)
an anxiety disorder: fear of humiliation in the presence of others, characterized by intense self-consciousness about appearance or behavior or both.

phobia
an anxiety disorder: an ongoing and irrational fear of a particular object, situation, or activity.

negatively by others, and of having their faults continually observed by everyone. Consider the case of "Sarah," who hates going to the grocery store: She would not dare ask anyone working there how to find an item, out of fear that she might look stupid for not being able to find it herself. She doesn't want anyone to know she is anxious about being in the grocery store. She is concerned that her voice might quiver when forced to say the obligatory "hello" to the cashier. This would make her seem really foolish, and everybody would stare at her foolishness.

People with social anxiety disorder are extremely self-conscious and fearful of embarrassing themselves in front of others.

Fear like Sarah's can be paralyzing, making it very difficult to go out into public situations, even though in most cases the person recognizes that these fears are irrational. Unfortunately, the high degree of anxious arousal produced by social phobia may lead the person to act very nervously and thus, in a self-fulfilling way, exhibit behaviors that do indeed attract other people's attention.

Specific Phobias

Only a few of us enjoy spiders, snakes, or heights, but most of us feel only mild levels of anxiety about such objects or experiences. Some of us, however, go beyond mild levels of fear. As many as 1 in 8 people will develop a *specific phobia* for a particular object or situation, such as spiders (arachnophobia), heights, flying, enclosed spaces (claustrophobia), doctors and dentists, or snakes (Kessler et al., 2005). Specific phobias are marked by an intense and immediate fear, even panic, when confronted with very particular situations or objects; even thinking about those situations or objects may set off the fear reaction. People with specific phobias are not generally anxious people, but they will do almost anything to avoid coming into contact with the feared object or experiencing the feared event. Megan Fox, Britney Spears, and Jennifer Aniston all fear flying. Aniston, for instance, has to perform the same ritual each time she boards a plane ("Jennifer Aniston Talks," 2009):

Actress Jennifer Aniston has spoken publicly about her fear of flying and the ritual she performs before each flight.

> If I walk onto an airplane, I always have to go on with my right foot first and tap the outside of the plane. I have always done it. For luck. Someone told me to do it and I don't remember when that was. But it's kind of stuck.

Connection

Anxieties or phobias associated with specific objects or situations (like flying or spiders) are much easier to treat than those that are more diffuse, such as GAD. See "Drug Treatments for Mood and Anxiety Disorders," Chapter 16, "Treatment of Psychological Disorders," p. 631.

obsessive–compulsive disorder (OCD) an anxiety disorder in which obsessive thoughts lead to compulsive behaviors.

Obsessive–Compulsive Disorder

Obsessive–compulsive disorder (OCD) is an anxiety disorder that is manifested in both thought and behavior. An **obsession** is an unwanted thought, word, phrase, or image that persistently and repeatedly comes into a person's mind and causes distress. People with OCD have thoughts that they cannot dismiss, especially negative thoughts that most people can disregard (APA, 2000).

obsession an unwanted thought, word, phrase, or image that persistently and repeatedly comes into a person's mind and causes distress.

compulsion
a repetitive behavior performed in response to uncontrollable urges or according to a ritualistic set of rules.

A **compulsion** is a repetitive behavior performed in response to uncontrollable urges or according to a ritualistic set of rules. In short, obsessions are thought disturbances, whereas compulsions are repetitive behaviors.

Obsessive–compulsive disorder most often involves either cleaning, checking, or counting behaviors that interfere with everyday functioning. A man who is obsessed with security might check that the front door is locked 15 or 20 times before being able to drive away; a woman who is obsessed with germs might wash her hands dozens or even hundreds of times throughout the day.

People who suffer from OCD often know that their thoughts are irrational, or at least that their compulsive behaviors are excessive, but they cannot stop themselves. In some cases, compulsive behaviors stem from superstitions. For example, a man might feel the need to tap the wall 65 times before leaving a room for fear that not doing so will mean that his parents will die. He knows rationally that there is no connection between wall tapping and the death of one's parents, but performs the ritual nevertheless.

impulse control disorder
an anxiety disorder related to obsessive–compulsive disorder in which a person feels an intense, repetitive desire to perform certain behaviors.

There may be a close link between some compulsive and some *impulsive* behaviors. *DSM-IV-TR* defines **impulse control disorder** as involving those behaviors that people cannot control and feel an intense, repetitive desire to perform (APA, 2000). Moreover, the behavior must interfere with everyday functioning. The behavior seems pleasurable but has unpleasant repercussions or creates impairments. Behaviors that develop into impulse control disorders in some individuals include gambling, shopping, hair pulling, and fire setting. Recently, mental health professionals have pointed to a great deal of similarity between OCD and impulse disorders, even to the point of suggesting that OCD spectrum disorders should be a separate category in *DSM* (Storch, Abramowitz, & Goodman, 2008). For a recent manifestation of a possible impulse control disorder, see "Psychology in the Real World."

Nature and Nurture Explanations of Anxiety Disorders

How do anxiety disorders develop? Like all animals, humans have evolved fear mechanisms to determine whether a situation is safe or not and whether we need to try to fight or flee (LeDoux, 2000). Additionally, as is true for most complex traits, some people are more genetically disposed to anxiety than others. Anxiety disorders—and most other psychological disorders—result from the interplay between biological and environmental factors. Instead of offering either biological or social theories of disorders, we present integrated nature–nurture explanations.

diathesis–stress model
explanation for the origin of psychological disorders as a combination of biological predispositions (diathesis) plus stress or an abusive environment.

Historically, this explanation has been called the **diathesis–stress model.** *Diathesis* is the Greek word for "predisposition," so the diathesis–stress view is that biological predispositions plus stress or abusive environments together produce psychological disorders. The diathesis–stress model is becoming more fully developed and refined based on the findings of research in such areas as behavioral genetics, epigenetics, and brain plasticity.

Three biological factors that make people vulnerable to anxiety disorders are deficiencies in the neurotransmitter GABA, their genetic heritage, and their personality. Researchers have discovered that people who are prone to anxiety are deficient in receptors for GABA, a major inhibitory neurotransmitter (Charney,

2004; Nikolaus et al., 2010). Deficiencies in GABA lead to excessive activation in certain brain regions, especially the limbic structures associated with fear. Moreover, the fact that major medications for treating anxiety disorders work on GABA receptors is further evidence for GABA's role in anxiety. Genetic heritability estimates for generalized anxiety, panic disorder, and agoraphobia range from 30% to 40% (Hettema, Neale, & Kendler, 2001; Maron, Hettema, & Shlik, 2010).

As for personality, people who are high in neuroticism—prone to worry, anxiety, and nervousness—are more likely to develop anxiety disorders than are people who are low in neuroticism (Eysenck, 1982; Hamer & Copeland, 1998). Degree of extraversion may play a role in some anxiety disorders as well. For instance, in panic disorder, people who are more introverted are more likely than those who are extraverted to avoid putting themselves in public situations (Rosellini et al., 2010).

In summary, people who have the bad luck of having a genetic predisposition to anxiety, low levels of GABA, or the personality trait of neuroticism *and* who also experience chronic stress or abuse are most likely to develop anxiety disorders. Those who have the biological predispositions *or* experience abuse are next most likely to develop these disorders, whereas those who have *neither* biological vulnerability nor chronically stressful experiences are least likely to develop these disorders.

How is hyperactivity in the brain related to OCD? Some scientists argue that the brain circuit that connects the caudate, the anterior cingulate cortex (ACC), and limbic structures (such as the amygdala and hypothalamus) is working overtime in OCD (Aouizerate et al., 2004; J. M. Schwartz, 1999a, 1999b). The overactive ACC creates a perpetual feeling that something is wrong, which the limbic system structures translate into anxiety. In turn, anxiety stimulates more intrusive thoughts, which sometimes become compulsive actions. These actions occur as behavioral responses aimed at reducing the tensions or anxiety generated by the situation (from the caudate nucleus). Relief may be experienced, but only briefly, before the anxiety returns. The cycle goes on endlessly, due to the hyperactivity of the brain circuit—which is stuck in the "on" position. So this circuit involving the ACC, caudate nucleus, and limbic structures supports the obsessive thinking and compulsive responding (Fitzgerald et al., 2005; Guehl et al., 2008).

In OCD, too many thoughts are held in awareness, too much importance is ascribed to all thoughts (rational or irrational), and thinking about one's thoughts is excessive (Janeck at al., 2003). Research on cognitive performance in people with OCD reveals a preoccupation with conscious thinking; it is hard for people with this disorder to keep certain ideas or information out of awareness. Consequently, people with OCD have trouble with implicit learning but not with explicit learning (Goldman et al., 2008; Marker et al., 2006).

An ambitious study that is changing the way psychologists view the interaction between biology and environment in the development of psychological disorders, including anxiety disorders, is the Adverse Childhood Experiences (ACE) Study. For the ACE

Connection

How does our first environment—the womb—shape the expression of our genes?

See "Epigenetics: How the Environment Changes Gene Expression," Chapter 3, "The Biology of Behavior," p. 80.

Connection

Development—language development, in particular—occurs rapidly during critical periods, when we are biologically most receptive to a specific kind of input from the environment.

See "Language Development in Individuals," Chapter 9, "Language and Thought," p. 350.

Nature & Nurture

Those most likely to develop anxiety disorders are people with a genetic predisposition to anxiety, low levels of GABA, or the personality trait of neuroticism *and* who also experience chronic stress environments or abuse.

Psychology in the Real World

Can Internet Use Become an Addiction?

In March 2010, police discovered that a couple in South Korea had starved their 3-month-old daughter due to neglect caused by their constant preoccupation with online gaming. The tragic irony is that the online game the parents played nearly round the clock involved raising a virtual baby. They let their real, live baby die so that they could take care of an electronic one ("South Korea couple," 2010)!

As this case demonstrates, some people just can't stay off-line. For many people, this, in itself, may not be a serious problem. In some cases, however, people are online all day; they check their Facebook or Twitter feeds dozens or even hundreds of times a day; and they cannot continue their work or activities around the home without logging on. For them, Internet use has become so intrusive that it adversely affects their professional and personal lives in the real world.

Mental health professionals do not agree on whether excessive Internet use is an addiction, a compulsion, or an impulse disorder; but they do recognize that one's relationship with the online world can become maladaptive. The word *addiction* is problematic, as it suggests a physiological dependence in which the body cannot function without a particular substance, as is the case with heroin or nicotine. Some researchers have suggested that some people do experience behavioral withdrawal symptoms, such as emotions of irritation and anger, when the computer or smart phone is not available (Block, 2008). Still, the addictive-like behaviors people develop with the online world are with

specific activities available on the Internet (e.g., chatting, networking, online gaming, news, porn), rather than the *Internet* itself (Van Rooij et al., 2010; see Figure 15.5). A group of clinical researchers in China has developed a set of diagnostic criteria for Internet addition, but these have not been formally adopted elsewhere (Tao et al., 2010).

Some psychologists argue that Internet problems may have more in common with other diagnostic categories that exist in the current version of the *DSM,* such as compulsive gambling. In fact, one of the terms recently proposed for this problem is "Compulsive Internet Use" (CIU), which seems to capture the uncontrollable urge to be online all day long (Van Rooij et al., 2010). However, it is more likely that problems of Internet use are compulsions or impulse disorders. As you've read, compulsions are uncontrollable behaviors that serve to control the anxiety created by the obsessions.

A primary criterion for whether a behavior is a disorder is the extent to which a behavior impairs normal, daily functioning. Clearly the case of the South Korean parents was dysfunctional. But what about more typical levels of intrusiveness or dysfunction? There can be little doubt that, for an ever-growing number of people, Internet use does interfere with everyday functioning and activities. In the United States, a large-scale telephone survey found that 4%–13% of teens and adults answered at least one question in a way that indicated problematic Internet use (Aboujaoude et al., 2006; Pallanti, Bernardi, & Quercoli, 2006). In Japan, Internet use

study, more than 17,000 participants have been interviewed about eight "adverse childhood experiences," including abuse, domestic violence, and serious household dysfunction (meaning that someone in the household abused drugs, had a psychological disorder, or committed criminal acts). Because participants had extensive medical histories on file at the hospital, researchers could correlate their adverse childhood experiences with health and mental health outcomes in adulthood.

The results were dramatic. The more adverse childhood experience participants reported, the worse the psychological outcomes. For example, someone who reported four or more adverse childhood experiences was two and a

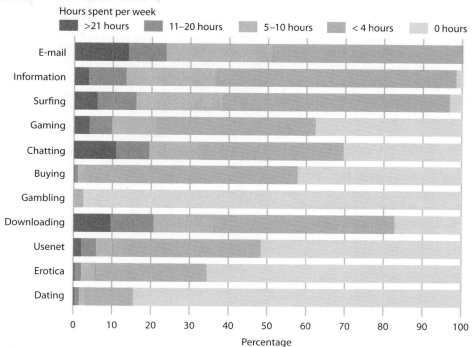

Hours spent per week

■ >21 hours   ■ 11–20 hours   ■ 5–10 hours   ■ < 4 hours   ■ 0 hours

E-mail
Information
Surfing
Gaming
Chatting
Buying
Gambling
Downloading
Usenet
Erotica
Dating

0   10   20   30   40   50   60   70   80   90   100
Percentage

FIGURE **15.5**

TIME SPENT ON INTERNET ACTIVITIES. Participants were Dutch adults who used the Internet for at least 16 hours a week and had home Internet access. Of the 1,000 e-mail users who received a request to participate, 447 completed the online survey. (Source: Meerkerk et al., 2006)

doubled between 2001 and 2006 (Nakano & Watanabe, 2009). In China in 2008, a wide-scale survey indicated that over 13% of youth met the criteria for "Internet addiction" (Block, 2008).

Perhaps the fastest growing areas of Internet use are social networking sites. A recent large-scale Dutch study shows a 20% increase between 2007 and 2008 in the percentage of teens who use social networking sites (Van Rooij et al., 2010). But how do we measure whether spending excessive amounts of time online is a disorder or not?

Indeed, many cases of problematic Internet use may be explained by other psychological or psychiatric disorders, such as depression (Block, 2008; Ceyhan & Ceyhan, 2008), which is one reason why there is not yet a diagnostic category for it in the *DSM*. In fact, a large-scale survey studying more than 2,000 Taiwanese teens on measures of attention deficit hyperactivity disorder (ADHD), depression, and hostility found that in both boys and girls, "Internet addiction" scores were positively correlated with depression and ADHD symptoms. Boys also showed a correlation with hostility (Yen et al., 2007). Until it is clear that Internet problems

cannot adequately be explained by other preexisting psychological disorders, they probably will not be included in the *DSM*. Right now, the issue is under consideration for the soon-to-be-published *DSM-V,* with its most likely current classification being in the compulsive-impulsive spectrum (Block, 2008).

The bottom line is that Internet-related behavior that meets the criteria of being deviant, distressing, and dysfunctional also meets the standards for being a disorder. If it does not meet those criteria, it is not a disorder. Evidence suggests for a small percentage of the population, Internet-related behavior may be a disorder.

half times as likely to suffer from anxiety disorder as someone who reported no adverse childhood experiences (Anda et al., 2006).

Perry (2002) found that when children were removed from neglectful home environments at age 1 or 2 and placed in caring foster homes, the size of their brains increased dramatically. If they were removed from the neglectful environment after age 4, however, there was little increase in brain size (circumference). And if they were removed after age 5, there was almost no increase (see Figure 15.6). Thus, there is a critical period for brain growth. Generally, for a child's brain size to be anywhere near normal, the child needs regular environmental stimulation by about age 4.

FIGURE 15.6

EFFECTS OF NEGLECT AND REMOVAL FROM NEGLECTFUL ENVIRONMENTS ON CHILDREN'S BRAIN SIZE. Percentile of head circumference means the percentage of people in the population who have heads that are a particular size or smaller. So 30th percentile means that only 30% of people have that size or smaller. The younger the child is when he or she is removed from a neglectful home, the larger the brain/head size is after 1 year in a nurturing foster home. (Source: Perry, 2002)

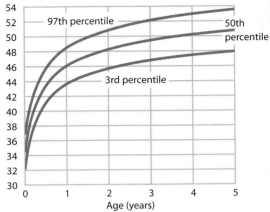

Head circumference for boys and girls (cm)

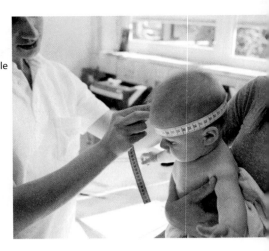

Quick Quiz 15.1: Anxiety Disorders

1. The occurrence of two or more disorders at the same time is known as
   a. bipolar disorder
   b. comorbidity
   c. dipolarity
   d. syndrome

2. Maya is preoccupied with fears of embarrassing herself in public, so much so that she avoids going shopping or out for walks in town. What disorder best describes this set of symptoms?
   a. agoraphobia
   b. specific phobia

   c. panic disorder
   d. social phobia

3. People who are prone to anxiety are deficient in receptors for _____, a major inhibitory neurotransmitter.
   a. GABA
   b. glutamate
   c. serotonin
   d. dopamine

Answers can be found at the end of the chapter.

MOOD DISORDERS

mood disorders category of psychological disorder that is characterized by disturbances in emotional behavior that inhibit normal everyday functioning.

Approximately half of the individuals who suffer from an anxiety disorder also suffer from a mood disorder (Cairney et al., 2008; Löwe et al., 2008). **Mood disorders** are disturbances in emotional behavior that prevent people from functioning effectively in everyday life. The two major forms of mood disorder are depression and bipolar disorder.

Depression and Its Causes

Like feeling anxious, occasionally feeling depressed is a normal part of everyday life. Feeling despondent after being rejected by a lover or failing an exam is a normal response to real setbacks. The clinical form of depression, however, is different and occurs in about 10% of adults in the United States at some point in their life. **Major depressive disorder**—often referred to simply as *depression*—is characterized by pervasive low mood, lack of motivation, low energy, and feelings of worthlessness and guilt that last for at least two consecutive weeks (APA, 2000). Sleep is often disturbed in depression, resulting sometimes in insomnia

major depressive disorder mood disorder characterized by pervasive low mood, lack of motivation, low energy, and feelings of worthlessness and guilt that last for at least two consecutive weeks.

Percentile of head circumference

Neglectful home

Nurturing home

	1 year	2 years	3 years	4 years	5 years
Neglectful	5%	3%	3%	2%	4%
Nurturing	28%	22%	16%	6%	5%

Age at removal from neglectful home

and sometimes hypersomnia (excessive sleep). Major depressive disorder sometimes is a single event in a person's life, but more often than not it is recurring. In either case, depression is more than just "the blues." It is a life-altering change in behavior accompanied by a lack of desire to do much of anything. It is also a major risk factor for suicide. A milder but longer lasting form of depression, however, does exist and is called **dysthymia.** Most of the symptoms are the same as in a major depressive disorder, but they are less intense in dysthymia.

Depression manifests itself differently in different people. For some, it takes the form of eating less or eating more; others alternate between intense anxiety and intense sadness; still others feel flat and have no sense of connection to other people; and many people exhibit combinations of these symptoms. The Pulitzer Prize–winning novelist William Styron, who went through a major depressive episode in his 60s, left one of the more poignant accounts of the experience in his book *Darkness Visible*. For Styron, as for many seriously depressed people, the feelings of despair reached a point at which ending his life seemed to be the only guaranteed source of relief:

> I had not as yet chosen the mode of my departure, but I knew that that step would come next, and soon, as inescapable as nightfall. . . . Late one bitterly cold night, when I knew that I could not possibly

dysthymia
form of depression that is milder in intensity, but longer in duration, than major depressive disorder.

Major depressive disorder can be a chronic, recurrent condition that robs people of the joys of living.

get myself through the following day, I sat in the living room of the house bundled up against the chill. . . . I had forced myself to watch the tape of a movie. . . . At one point in the film . . . came a contralto voice, a sudden soaring passage from the Brahms *Alto Rhapsody*.

This sound, which like all music—indeed, like all pleasure—I had been numbly unresponsive to for months, pierced my heart like a dagger, and in a flood of swift recollection I thought of all the joys the house had known; the children who had rushed through its rooms, the festivals, the love and work, the honestly earned slumber, the voices and the nimble commotion. . . . All this I realized was more than I could ever abandon. . . . I drew upon some last gleam of sanity to perceive the terrifying dimensions of the mortal predicament I had fallen into. I woke up my wife and soon telephone calls were made. The next day I was admitted to the hospital. (1990, pp. 63–67)

Depressed people are indeed at a higher risk of committing suicide than nondepressed people. Overall, however, suicide rates in the United States have actually declined slightly from 13.2 per 100,000 in 1950 to 11.3 per 100,000 in 2007 (National Center for Health Statistics, 2011). Not all people are equally at risk for suicide: In 2007 men were about 4 times as likely to commit suicide as women (18.4 versus 4.7 per 100,000), although more women attempted suicide. Race also matters when it comes to suicide. In general, European Americans are about twice as likely to commit suicide as African, Asian, and Hispanic Americans (see Figure 15.7).

Age was once a very big factor in suicide—with the elderly being most likely to carry out suicide—but more recently age has not really mattered much (National Center for Health Statistics, 2011). For instance, in 1950 those 65 and older were 5 times more likely to commit suicide than 20–24-year-olds, but by 1980 the age groups had nearly the same rates of suicide. Since 2000 suicide rates for both age groups have remained about the same. It is also interesting to note that suicide rates for 20–24-year-olds doubled from 1950 to 2007, whereas they have been cut in half in the same time period for those older than 65 (see Figure 15.8).

Depression is not often caused solely by an external life event, such as physical or sexual abuse. For some people, depression just comes on, like using a switch to turn on a light. To the extent that this is true, the reason some people and not others develop depression stems from a combination of brain chemistry and life circumstance—the diathesis–stress model again.

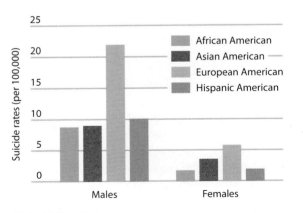

FIGURE **15.7**

SUICIDE RATES (2007) BY RACE AND GENDER. (Source: National Center for Health Statistics, 2011)

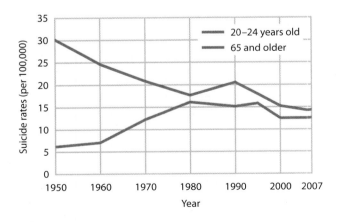

FIGURE **15.8**

SUICIDE RATES FROM 1950 TO 2007. (Source: National Center for Health Statistics, 2011)

Abusive and extremely stressful environments increase one's risk for depression later in life. Researchers studying adverse experiences found that people who reported the most adverse childhood experiences were more likely to be depressed than people who reported no adverse childhood experiences (Anda et al., 2006; Wang et al., 2010). Indeed, the role of stress in the development of depression is not trivial (Wang et al., 2010; Weinstein et al., 2010). Animal research shows that stress kills neurons in the hippocampus, which can lead to symptoms of depression (B. L. Jacobs, 2004; B. L. Jacobs, van Praag, & Gage, 2000; Kendler, Karkowski, & Prescott 1999). In humans, stressful events, especially social rejection, start a host of biological reactions, including activating the hypothalamic–pituitary–adrenal (HPA) system, which increases the likelihood of developing depression (Slavich et al., in press). Medications that make more serotonin available in the brain stimulate neural growth, which lessens the symptoms of depression (Malberg et al., 2000; Papakostos et al. 2008).

Nature&
Nurture
Different forms of the serotonin gene and stressful events work together to increase the risk of depression.

Stressful environments, however, interact with particular biological dispositions and personality traits to produce depression, especially in people who have experienced stress, trauma, and abuse (Clark, 2005; Hankin, 2010; Krueger, 1999; Uher & McGuffin, 2010). The personality traits of neuroticism and negative emotionality, for instance, are most associated with vulnerability to depression. Recall from Chapter 13 that neuroticism consists of dispositions toward anxiety, worry, sadness, guilt, and depression.

In addition, individuals with deficiencies in the neurotransmitters serotonin and neuropeptide Y (NPY) are most susceptible to depression after experiencing extremely stressful situations (Lowry et al., 2008; Morales-Medina, Dumant, & Quirion, 2010; Risch et al., 2009). For example, a meta-analysis of 34 studies found support for an interaction between differences in serotonin genes, adverse experiences, and the development of depression (Uher & McGuffin, 2010). One of the 34 studies in this meta-analysis provides a nice example of the research into the nature–nurture origins of depression; see the Research Process for this chapter (Figure 15.9).

Stressful life events, such as the death of a loved one, can trigger a major depressive episode in people who have a genetic predisposition for depression.

Connection

A person can inherit one form of a gene, or allele—say, for red hair—from one parent and a different form—maybe for brown hair—from the other parent.
See "Genes and Behavior," Chapter 3, "The Biology of Behavior," p. 77.

Bipolar Disorder and Its Causes

In some cases, periods of depression alternate with highly elevated mood and intense activity. These extreme swings of mood are symptoms of bipolar disorder. People who suffer from **bipolar disorder** experience severe mood fluctuations, cycling between very low (depressive) and very high (manic) episodes. (At one time, this disorder was called "manic depression.") **Manic episodes** typically involve increased energy, sleeplessness, euphoria, irritability, delusions of grandeur, increased sex drive, and "racing" thoughts. A useful mnemonic for remembering the symptoms of mania is D-I-G-F-A-S-T (Carlat, 1998):

D = Distractibility
I = Indiscretion
G = Grandiosity

F = Flight of ideas
A = Activity increased
S = Sleep (decreased need for)
T = Talkativeness

bipolar disorder
mood disorder characterized by substantial mood fluctuations, cycling between very low (depressive) and very high (manic) moods.

manic episode
one mood cycle in bipolar disorder, typically involving increased energy, sleeplessness, euphoria, irritability, delusions of grandeur, increased sex drive, and "racing" thoughts.

Research Process

1 Research Question

How do genetic and environmental differences interact to affect the development of depression?

2 Method

Avshalom Caspi and colleagues followed a group of nearly 1,000 people from age 3 until age 26 (Caspi, Sugden, et al., 2003). The investigators measured life events experienced by the participants at different ages. They obtained data on the presence of long and short forms of the serotonin gene in the participants' genotypes. One form (allele) comes from each parent.

3 Results

They found that people who had inherited two short forms (s/s) of the serotonin gene were more likely to exhibit depressive symptoms following stressful life events than were those who had inherited the long form (l/l). For example, in the graph shown here, we see that if people experience a few major stressful events (no more than two), their risk of having a major depressive episode does not increase, regardless of which form of the serotonin gene they carry. But if they experience three or four stressful events, the likelihood that they will have a major depressive episode nearly doubles or triples in those with the short form compared to those with the long form.

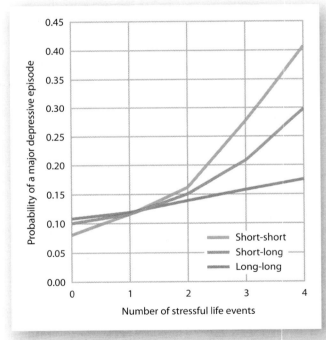

4 Conclusion

Depression is most likely in individuals who carry the short form of the gene *and* experience many severe life stressors. Neither condition by itself is likely to lead to depression.

FIGURE 15.9

GENE-ENVIRONMENT INTERACTION IN THE DEVELOPMENT OF DEPRESSION. Individuals with at least one short allele of the serotonin gene are more likely to experience depression than those with two long alleles. Those with two short forms of the gene are most vulnerable to depression if they experience at least three stressful life events. Source: "Influence of Life Stress on Depression: Moderation by a Polymorphism in the 5-HTT Gene," by A. Caspi, K. Sugden, T. E. Moffitt, A. Taylor, I. W. Craig, H. Harrington, . . . Poulton, R., 2003, *Science, 301*, 386–389.

Major symptoms	Behaviors	
major depressive disorder	Low mood, lack of motivation, low energy, feelings of worthlessness and guilt that last for at least two weeks	Change in eating behavior, intense anxiety or sadness, feeling of being disconnected, and/or inability to take pleasure in enjoyable experiences
bipolar disorder	Extreme swings in mood between depressive and manic episodes	Manic episodes characterized by distractibility, increased activity, euphoria, grandiosity, decreased need for sleep, talkativeness, flight of ideas, and indiscretion

FIGURE 15.10
MAJOR SYMPTOMS AND BEHAVIORS OF MOOD DISORDERS. (Source: APA, 2000)

People with bipolar disorder often find the initial onset of the manic phase pleasant, especially compared to the dullness and despair of the depressive phase. Unfortunately, the symptoms quickly become quite unpleasant and frightening. The manic upswing spirals out of control, often leading to frenetic activity, excessive energy, and grandiose thinking, in which sufferers think they have relationships with important people or expertise in areas where they have none. Indiscretion occurs when a person says things that are somewhat inappropriate or gets involved in promiscuous sexual relationships. Figure 15.10 lists the characteristics and symptoms of depression and bipolar disorder.

Virginia Woolf, the groundbreaking early-20th-century novelist, suffered from bipolar disorder. She dealt with bouts of severe depression and frenetic mania, which ultimately led to her suicide in 1941. Virginia's husband, the writer Leonard Woolf, offered revealing descriptions of her condition while manic:

"She talked almost without stopping for two or three days, paying no attention to anyone in the room or anything said to her. For about a day when she was coherent, the sentences meant something, though it was nearly all wildly insane. Then gradually it became completely incoherent, a mere jumble of dissociated words." (quoted in Jamison, 1993, p. 29)

Bipolar disorder affects men and women in roughly equal proportions. The manic episodes are less frequent than the depressive episodes, and the nature and frequency of the manic episodes vary considerably (APA, 2000). In a milder but longer lasting form of bipolar disorder called **cyclothymia,** both the manic and depressive episodes are less severe than they are in bipolar disorder.

cyclothymia
a relatively mild but long lasting form of bipolar disorder.

What causes bipolar disorder? Clearly, in this case, as is true for other psychological disorders, multiple biological and environmental factors interact in ways scientists are only beginning to understand. The dynamic relationship between the environment and brain in bipolar disorder may be seen as early as prenatal development. Fetuses exposed to large amounts of alcohol may suffer permanent effects, including increased risks for bipolar disorder as well as depression, schizophrenia, alcoholism, mental retardation, and drug abuse (Famy, Streissguth, & Unis, 1998; O'Conner & Paley, 2006).

Bipolar disorder also has a genetic component, but the genetics of the disorder are complex. Many variations of genes appear to play a role in the development of the disorder, the specifics of which are only beginning to be understood (Comer, 2007; Luykx et al., 2010; Shastry, 2005). Twin studies also point to a role for genetics in bipolar disorder. If one identical twin develops bipolar disorder, there is a 40%–70% chance that the other twin will also develop the disorder (Müller-Oerlinghausen, Berghöfer, & Bauer, 2002; Shastry, 2005). But even if the chance is 70% that both twins will have the disorder, that still suggests that life events, such as stress and trauma, also play a role in the development of bipolar disorder (Müller-Oerlinghausen et al., 2002; Shastry, 2005).

Abnormalities in the brains of people who suffer from bipolar disorder may be a cause or result of the biochemical, genetic, and environmental elements that contribute to the disorder. The prefrontal cortex, the amygdala, the hippocampus, and the basal ganglia all may play a role (Müller-Oerlinghausen et al., 2002; Shastry, 2005). Overactivity in many of these regions is evident in the PET scan images displayed in Figure 15.11, showing up as red areas compared to the blue regions that indicate depressed mood. There may also be problems in the connectivity among key regions involved in emotional processing, such as the prefrontal cortex and amygdala (Chepenik et al., 2010).

Neurochemistry is also important to bipolar disorder. In both the manic and depressed phases, serotonin levels are low, but low serotonin may be coupled with high levels of norepinephrine in the manic phase and with low levels in the depressed phase (Comer, 2007; Müller-Oerlinghausen et al., 2002). In addition, thyroid hormones, which control metabolism, are sometimes present in either

FIGURE **15.11**

THE BIPOLAR BRAIN. PET scan images show the brain of someone with bipolar disorder over the course of 10 days. Blue and green indicate low levels of brain activity, and red and yellow indicate high levels of brain activity. The top and bottom images show the low activity of depression, whereas the middle images show an increased level of brain activity during mania. Note how quickly this person cycled in and then out of the manic phase (10 days).

abnormally high or low levels in people with bipolar disorder (Bauer & Why-brow, 2001; Müller-Oerlinghausen et al., 2002).

Quick Quiz 15.2: Mood Disorders

1. Latresha is not hungry, is extremely tired, and doesn't feel like doing much of anything. She might be coming down with a cold, or she might be suffering from which mood disorder?
   a. generalized anxiety disorder
   b. bipolar disorder
   c. major depressive disorder
   d. obsessive–compulsive disorder

2. David went home for Christmas break, and he found that his mother, who was usually depressed, had just purchased dozens of bird houses from a local gift store. She'd had each custom wrapped and was planning to give them to all extended members of the family and all her neighbors, whom she claimed to love like family. She had spent thousands of dollars. What might be going on with David's mom?
   a. She won the lottery.
   b. She has bipolar disorder.
   c. She has an overactive hypothalamus.
   d. She is just depressed.

3. Which neurotransmitter is reduced in both the manic and depressive phases of bipolar disorder?
   a. acetylcholine
   b. dopamine
   c. norepinephrine
   d. serotonin

Answers can be found at the end of the chapter.

SCHIZOPHRENIA

psychotic disorders
psychological disorders of thought and perception, characterized by inability to distinguish between real and imagined perceptions.

Mood and anxiety disorders are mainly impairments of affect. In contrast, the **psychotic disorders** are primarily disorders of thought and perception, and are characterized by an inability to distinguish real from imagined perceptions. One very serious psychotic disorder is **schizophrenia,** which involves profound disturbances in thought and emotion—in particular, impairments in perception, such as hallucinations. Emil Kraepelin, who coined the term schizophrenia (literally "split mind") in the 1890s, viewed the disorder as a split from reality, not a split attitude or split personality as is sometimes mistakenly assumed. According to the National Institute of Mental Health (NIMH, 2007), approximately 1% of the American population is afflicted with this disorder at any given time, making schizophrenia much less common than depression. Genetically, however, if a first-degree relative (biological parent, sibling, or child) has the disorder, the odds of a person having the disorder rise to 10% (NIMH, 2007).

schizophrenia
psychotic disorder characterized by significant disturbances in thought and emotion, specifically problems with perception, including hallucinations.

Major Symptoms of Schizophrenia

For a diagnosis of schizophrenia, at least one of the following symptoms must persist for 6 months, and at least two must be present sometime during those 6 months (APA, 2000):

- delusions
- hallucinations
- disorganized speech, grossly disorganized behavior, or catatonic behavior (immobile and unresponsive, though awake)
- negative symptoms (such as not speaking or being unable to experience emotion)

FIGURE 15.12
INABILITY TO PERCEIVE FRAGMENTS IN SCHIZOPHRENIA. Perceiving fragments as parts of a whole can be difficult for people with schizophrenia. When normal subjects view fractured images like those above in sequence, they identify the object quickly, but individuals with schizophrenia often cannot make that leap swiftly. (Source: Javitt & Coyle, 2004)

Symptoms of schizophrenia fall into three major categories: positive, negative, and cognitive. Note that "positive" and "negative" in this context do not mean "good" and "bad" but rather "presence" and "absence" of behaviors. The bizarre perceptual experiences associated with schizophrenia are known as **positive symptoms.** These include hallucinations, delusional thinking, and disorganized thought and speech. Typically, perception is poorly integrated as well. Look, for instance, at the pictures of watches in Figure 15.12. People with schizophrenia have trouble putting the fragmented image together and perceiving it as a watch.

Hallucinations are convincing sensory experiences that occur in the absence of an external stimulus—in other words, the brain receives false sensory input. Auditory hallucinations are the most common form of hallucination in schizophrenia, typically taking the form of hearing voices in one's head. The following account from a person with schizophrenia describes an auditory hallucination:

Recently my mind has played tricks on me, creating The People inside my head who sometimes come out to haunt me and torment me. They surround me in rooms, hide behind trees and under the snow outside. They taunt me and scream at me and devise plans to break my spirit. The voices come and go, but The People are always there, always real. ("I Feel I Am Trapped")

The important point about hallucinations is that patients experience them as real. It is not as if someone is talking to them; rather, they hear voices and are convinced that someone is living inside them. Indeed, this is a defining feature of psychosis (Nolen-Hoeksema, 2007). Similar to but distinct from hallucinations, **delusions** are false beliefs, often exaggerated claims, that a person holds in spite of evidence to the contrary, such as the idea that one is Jesus Christ.

Other patients experience less flamboyant, but no less disabling, symptoms that are characterized by an absence of what would be considered appropriate behavior. These **negative symptoms** include nonresponsiveness, emotional flatness, immobility or the striking of strange poses (catatonia), reduction of speaking, and inability to complete tasks. Traditionally, negative symptoms have been harder to diagnose and treat than positive symptoms.

The **cognitive symptoms** exhibited by people with schizophrenia include problems with working memory, attention, verbal and visual learning and memory, reasoning and problem solving, speed of processing, and disordered speech (Barch, 2005). For example, the speech of a person with schizophrenia often follows grammatical rules, but the content makes little sense. Such utterances are referred to as **word salad.** Similarly, patients sometimes make up new words. In the following example, a woman who believed she was the only female professor at the "University of Smithsonian" (no such place) in England uses new words to produce a word salad.

I am here from a foreign university. . . . and you have to have a "plausity" of all acts of amendment to go through for the children's code . . . and it is no mental disturbance or "putenance." . . . it is an "amorition" law. . . . It is like their "privatilinia" and the children have to have this "accentuative" law so they don't go into the "mortite" law of the church. (Vetter, 1968, p. 306)

positive symptoms (of schizophrenia) the perceptual experiences associated with schizophrenia, including hallucinations, delusional thinking, and disorganized thought and speech.

hallucinations convincing sensory experiences that occur in the absence of an external stimulus.

delusion one of the symptoms of schizophrenia: a false belief or exaggeration held despite evidence to the contrary, such as the idea that one is a famous person.

cognitive symptoms (of schizophrenia) problems with working memory, attention, verbal and visual learning and memory, reasoning and problem solving, processing, and speech.

negative symptoms (of schizophrenia) symptoms that include nonresponsiveness, emotional flatness, immobility, catatonia, problems with speech, and inability to complete tasks.

word salad term for the speech of people with schizophrenia, which may follow grammatical rules but be nonsensical in terms of content.

Nature and Nurture Explanations of Schizophrenia

Schizophrenia offers a perfect, though tragic, illustration of the dynamic interplay between biology and experience in the development of a psychological disorder. Some researchers describe the diathesis–stress interaction between biological dispositions and environmental forces as a two-stage model (Kandel, 2000a; Lewis & Levitt, 2002). Stage one is the biological–genetic foundation, or disposition, and stage two is an environmental event that occurs at some point after conception, such as maternal infection, chronic stress, or using certain drugs (such as marijuana or amphetamines) at certain critical points in development (Fergusson, Horwood, & Ridder, 2005).

Although genetic factors play an important role in the development of schizophrenia, they do not make it inevitable. The heritability rates are 80% to 85%, suggesting the disorder is due largely to genetic influences (Cardno & Gottesman, 2000; Harrison & Owen, 2003; Kandel, 2000a; Lewis & Levitt, 2002; Vyas et al., 2010). Scientists have identified as many as 19 genes that contribute to schizophrenia, but the mechanisms they regulate have only recently been understood by neuroscientists (Harrison & Owen, 2003; Harrison & Weinberger, 2005; Mei & Xiong, 2008; Stefansson et al., 2009). The fact that one identical twin can develop schizophrenia while the other, genetically identical, twin may not develop it indicates that genes alone do not cause schizophrenia. Instead, genes are turned on or off by environmental experiences during brain development to produce the disorder (A. W. Grossman et al., 2003; Moffitt et al., 2005; Petronis, 2004).

The more abuse and neglect (adverse experiences) children experience in their early home life, the more likely they are to suffer from schizophrenia later in life (Edwards et al., 2003; Whitfield et al., 2005). In fact, results from the adverse childhood experiences study show how adverse experiences affect not only mental health outcomes but also the brain. Adverse experiences, in the form of abuse and neglect often happen during the critical periods of brain growth and development. There are few more concrete examples of how abuse and neglect shape the brain than the images shown in Figure 15.13 from ACE researcher Bruce Perry (2002). In the child who suffered extreme neglect, notice the much smaller overall brain size as well as the enlarged ventricles (butterfly shapes) in the middle of the brain. These features are two of the major brain abnormalities characteristic of schizophrenia. Indeed, one of the oldest findings on the brain and schizophrenia is the tendency of people with schizophrenia to have enlarged ventricles (the fluid-filled spaces in the brain) (Lieberman et al., 2001).

Although we may not yet know their causes or how exactly they interact with environmental forces, certain biological and brain abnormalities are hallmarks of schizophrenia. We consider some of the better-known ones: maternal infection, dysfunctional prefrontal and hippocampus activity, enlarged ventricles, an excess of dopamine activity in the basal ganglia, and a deficiency in the neurotransmitter glutamate.

FIGURE **15.13**

EFFECT OF EXTREME NEGLECT ON BRAIN DEVELOPMENT. These MRI images show the brain of a typically developing 3-year-old child who has had a normal amount of cognitive, social, and linguistic stimulation (left), and that of a 3-year-old child who was deprived of regular social, linguistic, tactile, or cognitive stimulation (right). Growth is clearly stunted in the child who suffered from extreme neglect. Additionally, the dark butterfly-shaped structures (ventricles) are much larger in the child who suffered from extreme neglect. Enlarged ventricles are common in people with schizophrenia. (Source: Perry, 2002)

Connection

During the first 6 months of fetal development, the brain is extremely vulnerable to all kinds of toxins.

See "Environmental Influences on Fetal Development," Chapter 5, "Human Development," p. 175.

Maternal Infections and Schizophrenia During fetal development, neural growth can occur at a rate of 250,000 new neurons per minute and peak at approximately *3 million* per minute (Purves & Lichtman, 1985)! Consequently, what happens to both the mother and the fetus is crucially important; any kind of disease or toxic substance experienced by the mother may dramatically affect neural growth in the fetus. If a woman contracts an infection during pregnancy, the risk of the child's developing schizophrenia later in life increases dramatically (A. S. Brown, 2006; Koenig, 2006). Prenatal exposure to infections and diseases such as influenza, rubella, toxoplasmosis, and herpes has been linked to increased risk of schizophrenia (A. S. Brown, 2006; Buka et al., 2001) and deficits in brain development (Short et al., 2010).

Schizophrenia and the Brain Abnormal brain development before birth may be responsible for many of the brain dysfunctions that are characteristic of schizophrenia (Lewis & Levitt, 2002). One mechanism by which maternal infections, for instance, may increase the risk of schizophrenia is by affecting the path neurons take when they migrate during fetal brain growth (Kandel, 2000a; Koenig, 2006). One of the most widely recognized brain abnormalities is a dysfunctional prefrontal cortex and its working memory; in people with schizophrenia, there is evidence of both reduced and excessive activity in that area (Andreasen et al., 1997; Barch, 2005; Goldman-Rakic, 1999; D. R. Weinberger et al., 2001; Vyas et al., 2010). Moreover, the genes in the prefrontal cortex that regulate how synapses function are dysfunctional in people with schizophrenia compared to those without the disease (Mirnics et al., 2000). Considerable research also has found that the hippocampus is smaller in people with schizophrenia, compared to those without the disorder (Barch, 2005; Harrison, 2004). See Figure 15.14 for an overview of these and other areas of the brain affected by schizophrenia, which might play a role in emotional deficits that mark the disorder.

The brain problems in schizophrenia may not be simply a function of abnormalities in certain structures, but may also stem from problems in the communications among groups of neurons. In people without schizophrenia, neural networks are efficiently clustered in close groups and move in and out of orderly and chaotic patterns of firing (Bassett et al., 2008). This process is essential for learning and memory. In people with schizophrenia, however, these networks are less clustered, less efficient and more disorderly, especially in the frontal lobes (Bassett et al., 2008). So there is disorder in all brains, but it is the kind of disorder that matters for schizophrenia.

An obvious positive symptom of schizophrenia is hallucinations. What is going on in the brain during a hallucination? Brain imaging studies show that hallucinations activate the brain in ways similar, but not identical, to real external stimulation (Shergill et al., 2000; Shergill et al., 2003; Silbersweig et al., 1995). For example, activity in the auditory cortex of the temporal lobe and the visual cortex of the occipital lobe during visual and auditory hallucinations shows striking similarities to the kind of brain activity that occurs when visual and auditory stimuli are present. Also noteworthy, however, is the lack of activity in the frontal lobes during the hallucination, which suggests that the person is unable to monitor and determine the source of the images or sounds (Shergill et al., 2003).

Frontal lobe

Critical to problem solving, insight, and other high-level reasoning. Disturbances in schizophrenia lead to difficulty in planning actions and organizing thoughts.

Basal ganglia

Involved in movement and emotions and in integrating sensory information. Abnormal functioning in schizophrenia is thought to contribute to paranoia and hallucinations.

Auditory system

Enables humans to hear and understand speech. In schizophrenia, overactivity of Wernicke's area (speech comprehension) can create auditory hallucinations.

Limbic system

Involved in emotion. Disturbances are thought to contribute to the agitation frequently seen in schizophrenia.

Occipital lobe

Processes visual sensations. People with schizophrenia rarely have full-blown visual hallucinations, but disturbances in this area contribute to such difficulties as interpreting complex images, recognizing motion, and reading emotions on others' faces.

Hippocampus

Mediates learning and memory formation, intertwined functions that are impaired in schizophrenia.

FIGURE **15.14**

AREAS OF THE BRAIN IMPAIRED BY SCHIZOPHRENIA. The structures highlighted here do not function normally in people with schizophrenia. Limbic system structures not shown here are the hypothalamus, amygdala, and cingulate gyrus. (Source: Javitt & Coyle, 2004)

Neurochemistry of Schizophrenia In addition to structural differences in the brain, the brains of people with and without schizophrenia show neurochemical differences. For decades, the prevailing view on the neurochemistry of schizophrenia was the *dopamine hypothesis*, which states that people with schizophrenia have an excess of dopamine activity in certain areas of the brain (Javitt & Coyle, 2004; Kegeles et al., 2010). The dopamine hypothesis was based on two findings. First, Nobel laureate Arvid Carlsson discovered that amphetamines stimulate dopamine release and therefore may mimic the hallucinations and delusions of schizophrenia (Javitt & Coyle, 2004). Second, early antipsychotic drugs that block dopamine receptors were somewhat effective at treating positive symptoms.

Breaking New Ground

The Discovery of Dopamine

Before 1952, no one knew that dopamine was a neurotransmitter. The belief at the time was that dopamine was merely a precursor of epinephrine (Yeragani et al., 2010). Moreover, most scientists were convinced that dopamine had no role to play in brain function (Carlsson, 1987). We now know, partly due to Arvid Carlsson's discoveries, that dopamine not only is involved in controlling our muscle movement and with the basic feelings of reward and pleasure but also is one of the main neurotransmitters involved in the development of schizophrenia. Indeed, dopamine research surpasses all other areas of research in importance in biological psychiatry (Iversen & Iversen, 2007). The person who made the seminal discovery of dopamine and identified some of its key functions was Arvid Carlsson from Sweden.

Arvid Carlsson

Even though he made important progress as a young researcher, Carlsson was denied tenure as a professor and for a while wondered whether to continue his research. He did continue, however, and his persistence paid off. A few years later, in the early 1950s, he did the work on dopamine and its role in schizophrenia and Parkinson's disease that led to his Nobel Prize in 2000 (Benes, 2001).

Yet, nearly 10 years after his groundbreaking work on dopamine, many neuroscientists could not accept that it was a neurotransmitter, because they still believed neurotransmitters had to be electrical rather than chemical (Iversen & Iversen, 2007). Although the first drug treatments for schizophrenia were discovered by others, Carlsson's work helped support the view that schizophrenia is at least partly caused by excessive amounts of dopamine in the brain—a view now known as the dopamine hypothesis (Iversen & Iversen, 2007). Due to the central role that dopamine plays in schizophrenia, Parkinson's disease, and even ADHD, it is fair to say that the field of psychopharmacology would not be the same today without the early pioneering work of Arvid Carlsson.

There are, however, some problems with the dopamine hypothesis. As we discuss in more detail in the next chapter, dopamine-specific medications (major tranquilizers) effectively treat only positive symptoms and even then are not entirely effective. In addition, only a minority of the people who receive the traditional drug treatment find it effective in managing their symptoms (Javitt & Coyle, 2004). When researchers became aware that another set of recreational drugs led to schizophrenia-like symptoms that did not directly involve dopamine, they turned their attention to these drugs. These drugs, PCP ("angel dust") and ketamine (an animal anesthetic, used recreationally as "Vit K" or "Special K"), do not affect dopamine production; instead, they impair the functioning of a different neurotransmitter, glutamate, and one of its receptors, NMDA. Glutamate is a major excitatory neurotransmitter that regulates the release of dopamine. PCP and ketamine block the action of glutamate, thus producing the same kinds of disturbances that we see in schizophrenia (Harrison & Owen, 2003; Moghaddam, 2003). Glutamate deficiencies, then, may also explain many of the symptoms of schizophrenia (Javitt & Coyle, 2004). A gene related to glutamate plays a role in prefrontal cortex functioning in schizophrenics, which further supports a role for glutamate in the disorder (Fallgatter et al., 2010).

These findings stimulated researchers to explore the role of glutamate in schizophrenia more fully. Not only is it crucial in learning, memory, neural processing, and brain development, but it also amplifies certain neural signals, making some stimuli more important than others (Goff & Coyle, 2001; Javitt & Coyle, 2004; Mayer, 2004). This process is crucial to selective attention—that is, focusing attention on some items of information while ignoring others. Thus, dysfunction in glutamate action would explain why people with schizophrenia have trouble with selective attention, cognitive control, and working memory.

Quick Quiz 15.3: Schizophrenia

1. Which of the following is a negative symptom of schizophrenia?
   a. hallucinations
   b. delusions of grandeur
   c. catatonia
   d. fatigue

2. The heritability rate for schizophrenia is roughly
   a. 100%
   b. 60%
   c. 80%
   d. 25%

3. Low levels of the neurotransmitter _____ might explain why people with schizophrenia have trouble with selective attention, cognitive control, and working memory.
   a. acetylcholine
   b. glutamate
   c. norepinephrine
   d. GABA

Answers can be found at the end of the chapter.

DISSOCIATIVE DISORDERS

dissociative disorders psychological disorders characterized by extreme splits or gaps in memory, identity, or consciousness.

Daydreaming and being caught up in a great novel or movie are common everyday experiences in which we may lose our sense of time, space, and ourselves. **Dissociative disorders** magnify this effect: They produce extreme splits or gaps in memory, identity, or consciousness. These disorders lack a clear physical cause, such as brain injury, and often stem from extreme stress or abusive experiences, especially during childhood. We focus on the most dramatic dissociative disorder, dissociative identity disorder.

Dissociative Identity Disorder

dissociative identity disorder (DID) dissociative disorder in which a person develops at least two distinct personalities, each with its own memories, thoughts, behaviors, and emotions. Some psychiatrists question the legitimacy of the disorder.

People with **dissociative identity disorder (DID)** develop at least two distinct personalities, each with a unique set of memories, behaviors, thoughts, and emotions. Consider the case of Eric, 29, who was found wandering around a shopping mall in Daytona Beach, Florida:

> Eric began talking to doctors in two voices: the infantile rhythms of "young Eric," a dim and frightened child, and the measured tones of "older Eric," who told a tale of terror and child abuse. According to "older Eric," after his immigrant German parents died, a harsh stepfather and his mistress took Eric from his native South Carolina to a drug dealers' hideout in a Florida swamp. Eric said he was raped by several gang members and watched his stepfather murder two men. (quoted in Comer, 2007, p. 208)

Eric had 27 distinct personalities, three of whom were female. Among these personalities were Dwight, who was middle-aged and quiet; Michael, an arrogant jock; Phillip, an argumentative lawyer; and Jeffrey, who was blind and mute and rather hysterical.

Eric is a classic example of what used to be called "multiple personality disorder" but is now referred to as dissociative identity disorder. Although it may not be diagnosed until adolescence, DID often first develops in childhood (Comer, 2007). Women are about 3 times more likely to suffer from DID than are men (APA, 2000). In one study, more than 90% of people with DID reported having been either sexually or physically abused (Ellason, Ross, & Fuchs, 1996).

Symptoms of dissociative identity disorder include amnesia, self-destructive behaviors, and auditory hallucinations. People with dissociative identity disorder may not remember anything about an experience or a particular period of their life, may cut themselves or attempt suicide, and sometimes hear voices giving them orders that they feel compelled to obey. The diagnosis of DID is somewhat controversial, with some psychiatrists claiming the diagnosis is not real but rather is produced unintentionally by therapists themselves (Putnam & McHugh, 2005). In one survey, a majority of psychiatrists said they believed DID should be included in the *DSM* only with reservations and have questioned the scientific evidence for the diagnosis (Lalonde et al., 2001).

Causes of Dissociative Disorders

People who suffer from dissociative disorders have one characteristic in common: They lived through a highly traumatic experience. They may have suffered sexual or physical abuse or survived a terrible accident or natural disaster in which a loved one was killed. Most explanations of dissociative disorder view it as a coping strategy that has gone awry (Putnam, 2006). The experience was so traumatic that the individual disconnects or dissociates the self from the event as a way of having it happen not to "him" or "her" but rather to "someone else." Yet not everyone who experiences traumatic events develops a dissociative disorder. Some theorists, therefore, argue that particular personality traits, such as susceptibility to hypnotism, make some people more likely to develop dissociative disorders (Kihlstrom, 2005).

SOMATOFORM DISORDERS

somatoform disorders
psychological disorders that take bodily or physical form and mimic physical diseases, but have no known physical cause or medical basis.

Some disorders take bodily or physical form and mimic physical diseases, but have no known physical cause or medical basis. The general term for these disorders is **somatoform disorders.** As you may recall from our discussion of the neuron, *soma* means "body"; and hence the term *somatoform* means "taking bodily form." The DSM lists seven different somatoform disorders, and we will briefly describe two of these seven.

Somatization Disorder

Somatization disorder occurs when a person complains of multiple physical disorders that have no known medical or physical basis. This disorder has the following criteria (APA, 2000):

somatization disorder
psychological disorder in which a person complains of multiple physical disorders that have no known medical or physical basis.

- a history of physical complaints prior to the age of 30 that occur over several years
- pain in at least four different sites on the body, such as the head, joints, or back
- two gastrointestinal problems other than pain, such as vomiting or diarrhea
- one sexual symptom, such as lack of interest or erectile dysfunction
- one pseudoneurological symptom, such as fainting or blindness

Somatization disorder is rather rare, but occurs more frequently in women (up to 2%) than men (less than 0.2%; APA, 2000). In the early 1900s, doctors believed this disorder—then known as "hysteria"—could only afflict women. Indeed, the term *hysteria* refers to a "wandering womb," which obviously only women could have.

Hypochondriasis

hypochondriasis
pervasive and debilitating fear of suffering from serious physical illness although none is found by a medical professional.

Hypochondriasis is the pervasive and debilitating fear of suffering from some kind of serious physical illness when none can be found by a medical professional. A person suffering from hypochondriasis misperceives, exaggerates, and becomes obsessively concerned with physical symptoms of a disease. The preoccupation with and exaggeration of the perceived illness must continue for at least 6 months. Hypochondriasis tends to be a very long-term, persistent problem, taking on a personality-trait-like quality and often involves self-diagnosis and extreme skepticism with doctors' diagnoses. Hypochondriasis affects between 1% and 5% of the population (APA, 2000).

With the Internet and easy access to medical information, more and more people are self-diagnosing without evidence of real symptoms and without professional evaluations. People who self-diagnose primarily from information found on the Internet are referred to informally as *cyberchondriacs* (White & Horvitz, 2009).

Somatization disorder and hypochondriasis have both similarities and differences. Excessive concern with physical health in the absence of actual medical symptoms occurs in both types of disorders. The main difference between somatization disorder and hypochondriasis, however, is that the former involves recurrent and frequently changing physical symptoms, whereas the latter involves excessive and irrational worry about a particular disease. Somatization disorder also often concerns relatively minor to moderate symptoms or illnesses, such as joint or back pain or excessive gas, whereas hypochondriasis often involves the belief that one has more serious diseases, such as brain tumors or cancer.

Quick Quiz 15.4: Dissociative and Somatoform Disorders

1. _____ produce extreme splits or gaps in memory, identity, or consciousness.
   a. Dissociative disorders
   b. Bipolar disorders
   c. Mood disorders
   d. Cognitive disorders

2. Years ago this disorder was known as multiple personality disorder:
   a. schizophrenia
   b. schizoid disorder
   c. schizotypal disorder
   d. dissociative identity disorder

3. The primary difference between somatization disorder and hypochondriasis is
   a. somatization disorder involves recurrent and frequently changing physical symptoms, whereas hypochondriasis involves excessive and irrational worry about a particular disease.
   b. somatization disorder involves excessive and irrational worry about a particular disease, whereas hypochondriasis involves recurrent and frequently changing physical symptoms.
   c. Only hypochondriasis involves excessive concern with physical health in the absence of actual medical symptoms.
   d. Only somatization disorder involves excessive concern with physical health in the absence of actual medical symptoms.

Answers can be found at the end of the chapter.

PERSONALITY DISORDERS

personality disorders

patterns of cognition, emotion, and behavior that develop in late childhood or adolescence and are maladaptive and inflexible; they are more consistent than clinical disorders.

As we saw in Chapter 13, personality consists of an individual's unique, long-term behavior patterns. **Personality disorders** are maladaptive and inflexible patterns of cognition, emotion, and behavior that generally develop in late childhood or adolescence and continue into adulthood; they are more consistent than clinical disorders such as schizophrenia, depression, and bipolar disorder. The distinction between clinical and personality disorders is somewhat arbitrary, however, and many people with personality disorders also suffer from clinical disorders. The *DSM* places the personality disorders on Axis II, meaning they are relatively permanent, may show early signs in childhood, and are viewed by the person as consistent with their personality and therefore do not cause much subjective distress. There are three distinct clusters of personality disorders: odd–eccentric, dramatic–emotional, and anxious–fearful (see Figure 15.15). Almost 10% of the general adult population (older than 18) and 20% of the young adult population (ages 18–25) suffer from some form of personality disorder (Blanco et al., 2008; Lenzenweger et al., 2007).

Odd–Eccentric Personality Disorders

schizoid personality disorder

odd–eccentric personality disorder characterized by a desire to avoid close relationships as well as by emotional aloofness, reclusivity, and a lack of humor.

The three major forms of odd–eccentric personality disorder are schizoid, schizotypal, and paranoid (APA, 2000). A person with **schizoid personality disorder** does not want close relationships; is emotionally aloof, reclusive, and humorless; and wants to live a solitary life. Similarly, a person with **schizotypal personality disorder** is also isolated and asocial, but in addition has very odd thoughts and beliefs. For instance, people with schizotypal personality disorder may believe that stories on TV or in the newspaper were written directly about them. A person with **paranoid personality disorder** is extremely suspicious

schizotypal personality disorder

odd–eccentric personality disorder characterized by a desire to live an isolated and asocial life, but also by the presence of odd thoughts and beliefs.

paranoid personality disorder

odd–eccentric personality disorder characterized by extreme suspicions and mistrust of others in unwarranted and maladaptive ways.

FIGURE **15.15**

THREE CLUSTERS OF PERSONALITY DISORDERS AND THEIR MAJOR SYMPTOMS.

(Source: APA, 2000)

Cluster	Major symptoms	Personality disorders
Odd–eccentric	Lack of interest in social relationships, inappropriate or flat emotion, thought, and coldness	Schizoid
	Isolated, odd, and bizarre thoughts and beliefs	Schizotypal
	Extreme, unwarranted, and maladaptive suspicion	Paranoid
Dramatic–emotional	Wild, exaggerated behaviors, extreme need for attention, suicidal, seductive, unstable relationships, shifting moods	Histrionic
	Shifting moods, dramatic, impulsive, self-injury (e.g., cutting)	Borderline
	Grandiose thoughts and sense of one's importance, exploitative, arrogant, lack of concern for others	Narcissistic
	Impulsive, violent, deceptive, and criminal behavior; no respect for social norms, ruthless	Antisocial
Anxious–fearful	Anxious and worrying, sense of inadequacy, fear of being criticized, nervousness, avoids social interaction	Avoidant
	Pervasive selflessness, need to be cared for, fear of rejection, total dependence on and submission to others	Dependent
	Extreme perfectionism and anxiety over minor disruption of routine, very rigid activities and relationships, pervades most aspects of everyday life	Obsessive–compulsive

and mistrustful of other people, in ways that are both unwarranted and not adaptive. They may often test the loyalty of their friends and lovers because they regularly believe other people are trying to harm them. If someone does slight them, they hold a grudge for an unusually long time. For example, if someone with this type of personality disorder discovers that a colleague has just been promoted to a position she had wanted, she might conclude that the boss does not appreciate her and is actively trying to sabotage her career. When she sees coworkers talking later that day, she might assume that they are talking about her in a disparaging manner.

Dramatic–Emotional Personality Disorders

histrionic personality disorder
dramatic–emotional personality disorder characterized by the desire to be the center of attention and by dramatic, seductive, flamboyant and exaggerated behaviors.

narcissistic personality disorder
dramatic–emotional personality disorder characterized by having an extremely positive and arrogant self-image and being extraordinarily self-centered; other symptoms are an exaggerated sense of self-importance and grandiosity.

Another class of Axis II disorders involves dramatic and emotional disorders, of which there are four (APA, 2000). People with **histrionic personality disorder** want very much to be the center of attention and often behave in very dramatic, seductive, flamboyant, and exaggerated ways. They can also be very emotional, intense, self-centered, and shallow in their emotions and relationships. Those with **borderline personality disorder** have out-of-control emotions, are very afraid of being abandoned by others, and vacillate between idealizing and despising those who are close to them. They are more likely than most to hurt themselves (cutting, burning, or attempting suicide) or suffer from eating disorders or substance abuse. Individuals with **narcissistic personality disorder** have an extremely positive and arrogant self-image, and most of their time and attention is self-focused. They have an exaggerated sense of self-importance and are grandiose. As a result, they often make unrealistic and unreasonable demands of others and ignore others' needs or wishes. They may be quite successful and climb the career ladder very quickly, but their narcissism often isolates them from others.

To many students, the most captivating and intriguing of all personality disorders is antisocial personality. Formerly known as "sociopathic" or "psychopathic" personality, **antisocial personality disorder** is marked by extremely impulsive, deceptive, violent, ruthless, and callous behaviors. People with antisocial personality disorder are most likely to engage in criminal, deceptive, and violent behaviors. Indeed, although only about 3% of the population has this disorder, between 45% and 75% of male prison inmates are diagnosed with the disorder (Fazel & Danesh, 2002; Hare, 1993). Only about 20% of female prisoners are diagnosed with antisocial personality disorder (Fazel & Danesh, 2002). Do not confuse *antisocial* with *asocial*. Antisocial personality is a serious and potentially dangerous disorder, whereas being asocial simply means being shy and not enjoying social situations. Indeed, the case of the serial killer Ted Bundy, with whom we opened the chapter, is an extreme example of someone suffering from antisocial personality disorder.

Anxious–Fearful Personality Disorders

avoidant personality disorder
anxious–fearful personality disorder characterized by extreme fear of being criticized, low self-esteem, and avoidance of social interaction.

The third cluster of personality disorders consists of the avoidant, dependent, and obsessive–compulsive personality disorders. Each of these is characterized by persistent high levels of anxiety, nervousness, and fear.

People with **avoidant personality disorder** are so afraid of being criticized that they avoid interacting with others and become socially isolated. They often feel inadequate and have low self-esteem and therefore tend to choose professions that allow them to be alone. People with **dependent personality disorder** fear being rejected and have such a strong need to be cared for that

borderline personality disorder
dramatic–emotional personality disorder characterized by out-of-control emotions, fear of being abandoned by others, and a vacillation between idealizing and despising people who are close to the person with the disorder.

antisocial personality disorder
dramatic–emotional personality disorder characterized by extremely impulsive, deceptive, violent, ruthless, and callous behaviors; a serious and potentially dangerous disorder.

dependent personality disorder
anxious–fearful personality disorder characterized by fear of being rejected and having a strong need to be cared for.

they form clingy and dependent relationships with others. They feel safe only in relationships with others; ironically, however, they tend to drive others away because they are so demanding. People with **obsessive–compulsive personality disorder** are very rigid in their habits and extremely perfectionistic. This personality disorder is similar to the clinical disorder with the same name but is more general. For example, OCD is usually focused only on cleanliness or checking, whereas obsessive–compulsive personality disorder is focused on all aspects of a person's life, as illustrated in the following case study of a 32-year-old accountant:

> For many years he has maintained an almost inviolate schedule. On weekdays he arises at 6:47, has two eggs soft-boiled for 2 minutes, 45 seconds, and is at his desk at 8:15. Lunch is at 12:00, dinner at 6:00, bedtime at 11:00. He has separate Saturday and Sunday schedules, the latter characterized by a methodical and thorough trip through the *New York Times*. Any change in schedule causes him to feel varying degrees of anxiety, annoyance, and a sense that he is doing something wrong and wasting his time. . . . [His] major problems are with women and follow the same repetitive pattern. At first, things go well. Soon, however, he begins to resent the intrusion upon his schedule a woman inevitably causes. This is most strongly illustrated in the bedtime arrangements. He must spray his sinuses, take two aspirin, straighten the apartment, do 35 sit-ups and read two pages of the dictionary. (Spitzer and colleagues, quoted in Nolen-Hoeksema, 2007, pp. 451–452)

Nature and Nurture Explanations of Personality Disorders

Because we have already discussed causes of the Axis I disorders that are similar to the schizotypal and obsessive–compulsive personality disorders, and less is known about the causes of dramatic–emotional disorders, in this section we focus on antisocial personality disorder.

Research on murderers has identified a cluster of traits possessed by most of these violent criminals: being male, coming from abusive and neglectful households, having at least one psychological disorder (often antisocial personality disorder), and having suffered some kind of injury to the head or brain (Pincus, 1999, 2001; Strueber, Lueck, & Roth, 2006–2007). Just being abused or having a psychological disorder or suffering a brain injury is not enough. To become antisocial and violent, a person usually has to experience all of these conditions.

Moreover, as a result of head injuries or living in a constant state of fear and abuse, or both, murderers almost always have moderate to severe problems of impulse control, social intelligence, working memory, and attention (Strueber et al., 2006–2007). Recall the principle of neuroplasticity from Chapter 3. Research on brain development suggests that living under a constant threat of abuse and stress changes the neural connectivity in the brain, making it less likely to develop many complex synaptic connections, especially in the frontal lobes. Being in a constant state of fear often

In the film *Monster*, Charlize Theron (below) portrayed Aileen Wuornos, a prostitute who confessed to killing several men. Abandoned by her parents in childhood, Wuornos later ran away from her grandparents' home and turned to prostitution to support herself. At one of her trials, a psychiatrist testified that she was mentally ill with borderline personality disorder. Nevertheless, she was convicted of murder and later executed.

Connection

Neuroplasticity occurs when neurons and hence brain structure and function change as a result of input from the environment.

See "Brain Plasticity and Neurogenesis," Chapter 3, "The Biology of Behavior," p. 106.

leads to neural systems that are primed for unusually high levels of anxiety, impulsive behavior, and a state of constant alertness. These are all conditions that might lead to violent or criminal behaviors.

Finally, genetics interact with abusive experience to create psychological disorders. Different forms of one particular gene, for instance, when coupled with being abused as a child, make violent and antisocial behavior in adulthood more likely (Caspi et al., 2002).

Quick Quiz 15.5: Personality Disorders

1. People with this personality disorder are so afraid of being criticized that they stay away from others and become socially isolated.
   a. borderline
   b. avoidant
   c. dependent
   d. psychopathic

2. Individuals with which kind of personality disorder are most likely to commit crimes and end up in jail?
   a. asocial
   b. narcissistic
   c. antisocial
   d. avoidant

Answers can be found at the end of the chapter.

CHILDHOOD DISORDERS

Although most clinical diagnoses are reserved for adults (older than 18), a number of disorders first show up in childhood. We discuss two of them: attention deficit hyperactivity disorder (ADHD) and autism. See Figure 15.16 for an overview of these two disorders.

Subtypes of Childhood Disorders

Jade seldom can work more than a few minutes on any given task, whether it is homework, reading, or even watching television. At school, she is constantly fidgeting in her chair and blurts out whatever she is thinking. Jade's teacher regularly has to ask her to be quiet and stop disrupting others. Her homework is full of careless mistakes, even though she usually knows the answers. With these symptoms, psychologists would probably diagnose Jade as suffering from **attention deficit hyperactivity disorder (ADHD).** To receive the diagnosis of ADHD, the child must have displayed these symptoms before age 7. Between 5% and 10% of American school-age children, 8% of children in the United Kingdom, and 3%–5% of children worldwide meet the diagnostic criteria of ADHD (Alloway, Elliott, & Holmes, 2010; Kessler et al., 2005; Polanczyk et al., 2007).

In his first year of life, Antoine behaved relatively normally. At the end of that year, however, subtle signs indicated that his development wasn't typical: He didn't babble or point to objects, he made very little eye contact, and he was hardly speaking at 18 months. When he did speak he often simply repeated what someone else said, and later he would say "you" when he meant "I." Moreover, he would regularly flap his hands. Finally, he became very interested in the details and sensory experience of objects. He often would smell and taste toys. Psychologists would diagnose Antoine with **autistic syndrome disorder,** or **autism** (from *autos,* meaning "self"). Autism is characterized by severe language and

attention deficit hyperactivity disorder (ADHD) childhood disorder characterized by inability to focus attention for more than a few minutes, to remain still and quiet, to do careful work.

autistic syndrome disorder, or **autism** childhood disorder characterized by severe language and social impairment along with repetitive habits and inward-focused behaviors.

Disorder	Major symptoms	Behaviors
Attention deficit hyperactivity (ADHD)	Inattention	Often fails to give close attention to details or makes careless mistakes, cannot sustain attention, does not listen when spoken to, does not follow through on instructions
	Hyperactivity	Fidgets with hands or feet, leaves seat in classroom when sitting is expected, inappropriate and excessive running or climbing, talks excessively
	Impulsivity	Blurts out answers before question is complete, cannot wait turn, often intrudes or interrupts others
Autism	Impaired social interaction	Has impaired eye-to-eye gaze and facial expressions, fails to develop peer relationships, lacks sharing interests
	Impaired communication	Has impaired or severely delayed speech; language use is stereotypic or repetitive
	Repetitive and stereotypic behaviors	Shows preoccupation and repetitive interests or behaviors (such as finger or hand flapping), inflexible routines or rituals

social impairment combined with repetitive habits and inward-focused behaviors. Evidence suggests that people with autism have an oversensitivity to sensory stimulation or trouble integrating multiple sources of sensory information, such as sight, sound, and touch (Iarocci & McDonald, 2006; Reynolds & Lane, 2008). Compared to children without autism, those with autism also have difficulty with joint attention and are more interested in things and inanimate objects than in people and social activities (Baron-Cohen et al., 2001). **Joint attention** is the ability to make eye contact with others and to look in the same direction that someone else is looking. For instance, if a mother points in one direction at something she is interested in, a child with autism typically will not look in that direction. He or she has difficulty with joint attention. In fact, researchers who were not aware of diagnoses and who closely examined eye contact made by autistic and nonautistic children on their first-birthday home videos were able to correctly classify children as autistic or not 77% of the time (Osterling & Dawson, 1994). Historically, approximately 5 to 6 children in 1,000 met the criteria for autism, but during the 1990s and first decade of this century the rate increased at least 10 times to 60 per 1,000 (Rice, 2007). Some researchers believe the disorder may be overdiagnosed; however, the evidence suggests the rise is mostly due to increased awareness of the disorder (Rutter, 2005; Wing & Potter, 2002).

Autism is a spectrum of disorders, ranging from severe disability to high functioning. On the high-functioning end is **Asperger's syndrome.** The fifth edition of the *DSM* is considering discarding the term *Asperger's syndrome*

joint attention
ability to make eye contact with others and to look in the same direction that someone else is looking.

Asperger's syndrome
a childhood disorder at the high-functioning end of the autistic spectrum; characterized by impaired social interest and skills and restricted interests; intelligence is usually above average and language is not delayed or deficient.

and using "high-functioning autism" or "being on the spectrum" ("Asperger's Disorder," n.d.). Children with Asperger's syndrome have impaired social interest and skills and restricted interests, but are not at all delayed or deficient in language and often have above-average intelligence (APA, 2000). In fact, they often are quite advanced in their speech. Children with Asperger's syndrome, for instance, may engage adults in long-winded and "professorial" discussions on one rather narrow topic. The man after whom the disorder is named, Hans Asperger, referred to these children as "little professors" (Asperger, 1944/1992).

Causes of Childhood Disorders

As is true of many psychological disorders, childhood disorders stem from genetic factors but often remain latent unless triggered by some environmental condition (Howe, 2010; Larsson, Larsson, & Lichtenstein, 2004). For ADHD, one of the environmental factors is whether the mother smokes while pregnant. Yet, even smoking while pregnant leads to conduct and impulse problems only if the child has one form of a dopamine gene but not another (Kahn et al., 2003). Neither prenatal smoke exposure alone nor the dopamine genotype alone is significantly associated with increased behavior disorders. One environmental factor, long suspected by many parents to cause ADHD, was the child's consuming excessive amounts of sugar (Bussing et al., 2007). Controlled clinical studies, however, do not bear out this belief (Krummel, Seligson, & Guthrie, 1996; Whalen & Henker, 1998).

People at the high-functioning end of the spectrum of autistic disorders may have independent, productive lives in spite of their social impairments and narrow interests. One such individual is Temple Grandin, who earned a PhD in animal science and became a professor at Colorado State University. A leading animal rights advocate, Grandin has designed humane facilities for livestock and written and spoken extensively about animal rights.

One consistent finding regarding brain activity of those with ADHD is low levels of activation in various areas. Brain activity in general is less pronounced in people with ADHD than in those without it (Zametkin et al., 1990; Zang et al., 2005). An understimulated brain explains the "paradoxical" effects of giving children with ADHD a stimulant to calm them down. The stimulant elevates their abnormally low nervous system activity and they require less stimulation and activity from the outside.

In autism, the brain is smaller than normal at birth but grows much faster during the first few years of life than the brains of nonautistic children (Courchesne, Campbell, & Solso, 2010). The brain of a 5-year-old with autism is the same size as that of a typical 13-year-old (Blakeslee, 2005). Head size, therefore, is a marker of possible autism. Although we do not yet know which genes are involved, this abnormal rate of brain growth is almost certainly due to genetic influences. In addition, the frontal lobes, where much processing of social information occurs, are less well connected in children with autism than in normal children (Belmonte et al., 2004). Finally, recent evidence shows that the amygdala in children with autism is 13% larger than in children without the disorder (Bachevalier, 2011; Mosconi et al., 2009). The size of the amygdala is associated with the ability to share attention with other people, one of the major deficits seen in people with autism.

A promising theory about the origins of autism is based on the mirror neurons (Ramachandran & Oberman, 2006). As we saw in earlier chapters, mirror neurons fire both when a person performs a particular behavior (such as reaching for an object) and when he or she simply watches someone else performing the same behavior. Mirror neurons are thought to be involved in many, if not most, social behaviors, such as observational learning, imitation, and even language learning. Because children with autism are deficient in these skills, neuroscientists predicted that mirror neurons malfunction in autistic children; research results show that this is indeed the case (Ramachandran & Oberman, 2006).

to Real Life

Psychological disorders are more common than many people think. Nearly half (46%) of all adults will suffer some kind of disorder at some point in their lives.

Connecting Psychology to Your Life: Now that you have some understanding of the major disorders,

- Do you know anyone who suffers from a psychological disorder, such as depression, anxiety, obsessive-compulsive disorder, schizophrenia, or a personality disorder?
- If so, how has it affected their lives?
- How does the disorder affect your relationship with this person?

Quick Quiz 15.6: Childhood Disorders

1. Jolo is a 5-year-old boy who does not speak, waves his arms around a lot, does not make eye contact, and does not seem to connect with other kids or adults. Jolo may have which disorder?
   a. autistic disorder
   b. ADHD
   c. childhood depression
   d. theory of mind

2. Kelly fidgets a lot, blurts out what she is thinking, and makes many careless mistakes in her homework, even when she knows the answers. Kelly most likely would be diagnosed with which childhood disorder?
   a. low IQ
   b. autism
   c. Asperger's
   d. ADHD

Answers can be found at the end of the chapter.

Bringing It All Together
Making Connections in Psychological Disorders
Creativity and Mental Health

For thousands of years, people have associated "madness" and "genius." Many of the world's most creative people have been touched by more than their fair share of mental instability, if not outright "madness." Perhaps, some have argued, that is just the price of greatness (Ludwig, 1995). Amadeus Mozart, Ludwig von Beethoven, Robert Schumann, Vincent Van Gogh, Virginia Woolf, Ernest Hemingway, William Styron, Jackson Pollock, Howard Hughes, Sylvia Plath, Salvador Dalí, and the Nobel Prize–winning mathematician John F. Nash, Jr., are just some of the creative geniuses who have suffered

from a psychological disorder. So many creative individuals have experienced some psychological condition that many people think creativity and disorders of the mind are connected. The term *mad genius* reflects this belief. To be clear, however: Suffering from psychological disorders is not necessary to be creative. Many creative people have not suffered from disorders, and not all who suffer from disorders are creative. There are, however, at least in art, literature, poetry, and music, higher rates of disorders than in the general population (Ludwig, 1995).

Exploring the connection between psychological disorders and creativity offers an opportunity to look again at the topics discussed in this chapter. We address two questions: (1) What is the evidence that creative people suffer from psychological disorders at a higher rate than the rest of the population? (2) Which disorders are more likely to be linked with creativity?

Evidence for a Relationship Between Creativity and Psychological Disorders

To help us answer the first question, we can look at an impressive study of creativity and psychological disorder conducted by Arnold Ludwig. In a biographical study of 1,005 eminent people in 16 professions, Ludwig (1995) examined the lifetime rates of psychological disorder across the professions and over lifetimes. Lifetime rate is the likelihood that a person will suffer a disorder at some point in her or his lifetime. Lifetime rates for any psychiatric illness are remarkably high for people in the arts: 87% of poets, 77% of fiction writers, 74% of actors, 73% of visual artists, 72% of nonfiction writers, 68% of musical performers, and 60% of musical composers (see Figure 15.17). Compare these figures with the

46% lifetime rate in the general population for any disorder (Kessler et al., 2005). The data from this large-scale study clearly indicate a higher prevalence of disorder in creative artists than in the general population.

Which Disorders Affect Creative Individuals?

Not all disorders are associated with creative ability. There is evidence, however, for a connection between creativity and many of the disorders we discussed in this chapter.

Psychotic Symptoms and Creativity

Having unusual thoughts is common to both creative people and those with schizophrenia. For instance, much of the art of Salvador Dalí, who claimed to be psychotic, consists of bizarre, dreamlike images—bordering on the kinds of delusions experienced by people with schizophrenia. John F. Nash, Jr., the mathematician made famous by the book and movie *A Beautiful Mind,* is a creative person who also has schizophrenia (Nasar, 1998). He was creative despite, rather than because of, the psychotic episodes he experienced; all of his creative work preceded his schizophrenic symptoms and stopped after they began.

It is the milder psychotic symptoms, however, that are most strongly associated with creativity (Kinney et al., 2000–2001; Nettle & Clegg, 2006; Schuldberg, 2000–2001). Each of the following groups manifest unusual thought processes that are milder than those of schizophrenia: first-degree relatives of individuals with schizophrenia, people with schizotypal personality disorder, and those who score high on the normal personality dimension of psychoticism (see Chapter 13). People in these groups are more likely to have unusual thought processes that develop into creative achievements that other people recognize to be significant (Burch et al., 2006; Fisher et al., 2004). Having a lot of ideas come to mind quickly can lead to many unusual associations that may be creative, but they may also be so unusual as to be similar to the bizarre associations seen in people with schizophrenia (Carson, Peterson, & Higgins, 2003; Eysenck, 1995).

> Connection
> **Creative thinking requires novelty and connections among ideas.**
> See "What Is Creativity?" Chapter 10, "Intelligence, Problem Solving, and Creativity," p 412.

Depression and Creativity

Emotional distress is a familiar companion to creative people. Many highly creative people have suffered from major depression (Ludwig, 1995). Across the 16 professions identified in Figure 15.17, the lifetime rate of depression was 30%, with poets (77%), fiction writers (59%), and visual artists (50%) having the highest rates. In addition, poets are 20 times more likely to commit suicide, a key indicator for depression, than

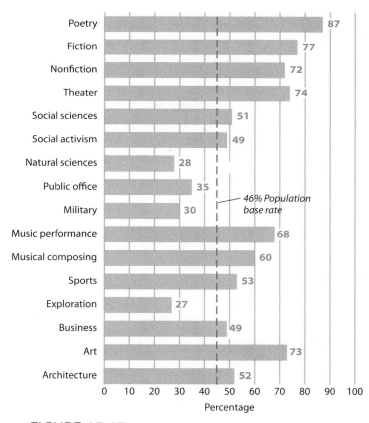

FIGURE **15.17**
LIFETIME RATES OF PSYCHOLOGICAL DISORDERS IN FAMOUS PEOPLE IN 16 DIFFERENT PROFESSIONS. (Source: Ludwig, 1995)

most people (Ludwig, 1995). One recent study in fact found that social rejection (a common experience in depression) combined with a biological disposition toward depression enhanced participants' artistic creativity (Akinola & Mendes, 2008). In less creative populations, we should note, there is often only a weak relationship between depression and creativity (Silvia & Kimbrel, 2010).

Although highly creative artists and writers may have a higher rate of depression than the general population, depressive episodes themselves do not generate much creative output. Recall that a complete lack of motivation is a common symptom of depression, so lower productivity would follow. Still, the experiences one has while depressed might inspire and motivate the creation of works of art as a way of understanding it.

Bipolar Disorder and Creativity

For more than three decades, studies of the relationship between psychological disorder and creativity have devoted more attention to bipolar illness than to any other condition (Andreasen & Glick, 1988; Bowden, 1994; Fodor & Laird, 2004; Jamison, 1993; Ludwig, 1995). Actors (17%), poets (13%), architects (13%), and nonfiction writers (11%) all exceed a 10% lifetime rate of bipolar disorder—10 times the rate in the general population (Ludwig, 1995). There is a positive relationship between bipolar disorder and creative thought. For instance, some studies show that highly creative people are more likely than noncreative people to have bipolar disorder (Andreasen, 1987, 2006; Jamison, 1993; Jamison et al., 1980; Richards, 1994). Others report the other side of the coin: People with bipolar disorder are likely to be more creative than those without this condition (Fodor & Laird, 2004; Richards, 1994; Richards & Kinney, 1990). Indeed, many creative individuals throughout history have been bipolar (Jamison, 1993).

The manic phase is more likely than the depressive phase to generate creative behavior (Andreasen & Glick, 1988; Jamison et al., 1980). Few artists and writers are creative during their depressed phases; rather, they are creatively inspired during a milder form of mania, known as the hypomanic phase. A tragic example is the composer Robert Schumann whose output and episodes of mania and depression are graphed in Figure 15.18.

Autism and Creativity

Some people who have autism or Asperger's syndrome are extremely gifted in one domain, such as music or math, a phenomenon known as savant syndrome (see Chapter 10). Most autistic savants do not produce great works of original genius because their amazing feats of calculation and recall are not original. Yet some savants do produce truly creative works of art, usually math analyses, musical compositions, drawings, or paintings (Fitzgerald, 2004). One of the 20th century's greatest mathematicians, Srinivasa Ramanujan, showed clear signs of childhood autism (Fitzgerald, 2004). Composer Wolfgang Amadeus Mozart also may have been such a savant. A contemporary creative savant is Matt Savage (born in 1992), who was diagnosed with autism at the age of 3. He is a professional jazz musician and composer who recorded three CDs by the time he was 14.

Asperger's syndrome has been associated with creative ability in science, math, and engineering (Austin, 2005; Baron-Cohen et al., 2001). Baron-Cohen and his colleagues report that engineers, mathematicians, and physical scientists score much higher than nonscientists on measures of high-functioning autism and Asperger's syndrome and score higher than social scientists on a nonclinical measure of autism. Lastly, children with Asperger's are more than twice as likely as normal children to have a father or grandfather

FIGURE **15.18**
BIPOLAR DISORDER AND CREATIVITY IN THE WORK OF ROBERT SCHUMANN. The composer's creative output coincided directly with the highs and lows of his disorder. His most productive years (1840 and 1849) were marked by his most hypomanic periods. (Source: Slater & Meyer, 1959)

who was an engineer (Baron-Cohen et al., 1997; Baron-Cohen et al., 1998; Baron-Cohen et al., 2001).

Quick Quiz 15.7: Bringing It All Together: Making Connections in Psychological Disorders

1. Research shows which psychotic disorder to be most strongly associated with creativity?
   a. schizophrenia
   b. schizotypal
   c. schizoid
   d. split-personality

2. With respect to the relationship between bipolar disorder and creativity, the _____ phase is more likely to produce creative behavior than the _____ phase.
   a. depressive; manic
   b. cognitive; depressive
   c. manic; depressive
   d. manic; affective

Answers can be found at the end of the chapter.

Chapter **Review**

DEFINING PSYCHOLOGICAL DISORDERS

- Psychologists agree on three general criteria for a psychological disorder: deviant, distressing, and dysfunctional.

- A major tool for diagnosing disorders is the *Diagnostic and Statistical Manual (DSM)*. Axis I disorders, the clinical syndromes, tend to develop after adolescence, come and go, and are not permanent. Axis II disorders tend to be lifelong and relatively permanent.

ANXIETY DISORDERS

- Anxiety disorders occur when fears and worrying are out of proportion to the situation and interfere with everyday functioning. Generalized anxiety disorder, a pervasive state of anxiety lasting at least 6 months, consists of excessive worrying about relatively minor events of daily life. Panic disorder is extreme anxiety about having a panic attack. Social anxiety disorder, a pronounced fear of humiliation in the presence of others, is marked by severe self-consciousness about appearance, behavior, or both.

- Specific phobias involve an intense fear when confronted with particular situations or objects, such as spiders or

heights. Obsessive–compulsive disorder is an anxiety disorder of thought and behavior. Compulsions are repetitive behaviors, which are often rituals that people have developed to control the anxiety created by the obsessions. Obsessions are anxiety-producing thoughts that can preoccupy a person throughout the day and are beyond the person's control.

MOOD DISORDERS

- Mood disorders are disturbances in emotional behavior that prevent people from functioning normally. People with major depressive disorder experience a pervasive low mood, lack of motivation, low energy, and feelings of worthlessness and guilt. Bipolar disorder, on the other hand, involves substantial mood fluctuation between depressive and manic episodes.

SCHIZOPHRENIA

- Schizophrenia is a psychotic disorder of profound disturbances in thought and emotion. Positive symptoms of schizophrenia include hallucinations, delusional thinking, and disorganized thought and speech. Negative symptoms of schizophrenia include nonresponsiveness, flattened affect, immobility or strange poses, reduction of speaking, and inability to complete tasks. Cognitive symptoms of schizophrenia include disordered thinking, including impaired attention and profound difficulty in monitoring conflicting sources of information.

DISSOCIATIVE DISORDERS

- Dissociative disorders entail the loss of a sense of time and space but also involve extreme gaps in memories, identity, or consciousness. People with dissociative identity disorder (DID) develop at least two distinct personalities, each of whom has a unique set of memories, behaviors, thoughts, and emotions. Some experts have reservations about classifying DID as a disorder.

SOMATOFORM DISORDERS

- Somatoform disorders take bodily or physical form and mimic physical diseases, but have no known physical cause or medical basis. These include somatization disorder, which occurs when a person complains of multiple physical disorders that have no known or medical physical basis, and hypochondriasis, the pervasive and debilitating fear of suffering from some kind of serious physical illness when none can be found by a medical professional.

PERSONALITY DISORDERS

- Personality disorders differ from clinical disorders in being generally a more consistent part of a person's personality than the clinical disorders (e.g., schizophrenia, depression, and bipolar disorder). The schizoid personality is very emotionally cold, reclusive, humorless, or uninteresting; someone with schizotypal personality disorder expresses very odd thoughts and behavior, is socially isolated, and has a restricted range of emotions. Paranoid personality disorder is marked by extreme suspiciousness and mistrust of other people, in ways that are both unwarranted and not adaptive.

- Those with borderline personality disorder suffer from out-of-control emotions, are very afraid of being abandoned by others, and vacillate between idealizing those close to them and despising them. People with dependent personality disorder fear rejection and have such a strong need to be cared for that they form very clingy relationships with others. Antisocial personality disorder is marked by extremely impulsive, deceptive, violent, and ruthless behaviors.

CHILDHOOD DISORDERS

- The most common disorders to affect children are attention deficit hyperactivity disorder (ADHD) and autism. ADHD consists of severe inattention, hyperactivity, and impulsivity. Children with autism show very inward-focused behaviors, with severe language and social impairment combined with repetitive habits and behaviors. They also have serious deficits in understanding other people's thoughts, feelings, and intentions. Asperger's syndrome is characterized by many of the same symptoms, with no impairments of language or intelligence.

BRINGING IT ALL TOGETHER: MAKING CONNECTIONS IN PSYCHOLOGICAL DISORDERS

- Creativity and psychological disorder are related, especially in the arts. Disorders such as depression, bipolar disorder, anxiety disorders, substance abuse, and suicide occur at higher rates in creative artists than in members of other professions and in the general population.

Key Terms

Quick Quiz **Answers**

Quick Quiz 15.1:   1. b   2. d   3. a
Quick Quiz 15.2:   1. c   2. b   3. d
Quick Quiz 15.3:   1. c   2. c   3. b
Quick Quiz 15.4:   1. a   2. d   3. a
Quick Quiz 15.5:   1. b   2. c
Quick Quiz 15.6:   1. a   2. d
Quick Quiz 15.7:   1. b   2. c

Challenge Your Assumptions **Answers**

- Most people who suffer from mental illness are dangerous. **False. See p. 589.**
- Panic attacks often include heart palpitations. **True. See p. 593.**
- Extreme stress can make you depressed. **True. See p. 603.**
- Schizophrenia is a disorder of split personalities. **False. See p. 607.**
- All the great artists in history can be viewed as psychologically disturbed. **False. See p. 622.**

Treatment of Psychological Disorders

Chapter Outline

Challenge *Your Assumptions*

TRUE OR FALSE?

- Depression has been turned on "like a switch" in some people using deep brain stimulation.

- Talk therapy might make people feel better, but it does not change the brain.

- People can learn to not be afraid of flying.

- Shock therapy is never effective and is no longer used.

Answers can be found at the end of the chapter.

Sometime in the year 2000 Deanna's world began to shut down. For no apparent reason, she suddenly fell into a severe and enduring depression: She felt no sense of emotional connection to anyone, utter despair, and ultimately, an enduring emotional numbness. Deanna said it felt like all the color drained out of her life (Dobbs, 2006, July 30). She tried everything, including psychotherapy, a vast array of medications, electroconvulsive therapy—nothing helped end her misery in any lasting way. She often thought about suicide.

Then Deanna volunteered for an innovative and risky experimental treatment under the leadership of a psychiatrist by the name of Helen Mayberg. Deanna had an electrode implanted deep in her brain to stimulate areas thought to be involved in the neurocircuitry of depression. Immediately after the electrode was activated, the colors seeped back into her life. How could deep brain stimulation turn off depression like a switch? Was this momentary relief or a permanent cure?

In this chapter we discuss not only Mayberg's innovative discovery of brain stimulation for the treatment of severe depression, but also more mainstream therapies—such as how restructuring thoughts can alleviate depression, panic disorder, and simple phobias. Moreover, we examine the various drug treatments for psychological disorders, describe their features, and look at how well they work, as well as consider less traditional approaches that make use of combined therapies, meditation, or even virtual reality. The multitude of approaches reflects the ongoing challenge of treating psychological disorders.

Nowhere is the complex interaction between biology and environment on more profound display than in the development and treatment of psychological disorders. Although we begin by discussing biological treatments and psychological treatments separately for clarity, we must bear in mind that both categories of treatment work together in modifying the brain, thought, feeling, and behavior. ∎

BIOLOGICAL TREATMENTS FOR PSYCHOLOGICAL DISORDERS

Mental health professionals rely on three major forms of treatment to help alleviate the symptoms of—and sometimes cure—psychological disorders: biological, psychological, and integrative therapies (see Figure 16.1). While most mental health professionals rely on all three, each practitioner works from a perspective based on training, personal interest, and experience. In other words, the same disorder can be treated in different ways depending on the clinician. People seeking treatment should bear these differences in perspective in mind when selecting someone to help because different clinician backgrounds don't always lead to the same clinical outcome (see "Psychology in the Real World," p. 658).

The biological approaches comprise drugs, surgical treatments, and electric and magnetic treatments. The psychological therapies include psychoanalytic/psychodynamic, humanistic, cognitive, and behavioral therapies. The integrative therapies combine either drugs and psychotherapies or different variations of psychotherapy; or they might combine less traditional approaches, such as meditation, with other more traditional techniques. Let's first consider the biological treatments, starting with the most widely used—drug therapies.

FIGURE **16.1**
THREE MAJOR APPROACHES TO THE TREATMENT OF PSYCHOLOGICAL DISORDERS.

Drug Therapies

Numerous pharmaceutical drugs are available for the treatment of psychological disorders. Drugs can be used to treat, but usually not cure, everything from mild anxiety to schizophrenia.

Drug Treatments for Mood and Anxiety Disorders

Six major categories of drugs are used to treat mood and anxiety disorders: monoamine oxidase (MAO) inhibitors, tricyclic antidepressants, selective serotonin reuptake inhibitors (SSRIs), benzodiazepines, barbiturates, and lithium.

monoamine oxidase (MAO) inhibitors
class of drugs used to treat depression; they slow the breakdown of monoamine neurotransmitters in the brain.

The **monoamine oxidase (MAO) inhibitors** were among the first pharmaceuticals used to treat depression (Burgess, 2009). These drugs reduce the action of the enzyme monoamine oxidase, which breaks down monoamine neurotransmitters (including norepinephrine, epinephrine, dopamine, and serotonin) in the brain. By inhibiting the action of this enzyme, MAO inhibitors allow more of these neurotransmitters to stay active in the synapse for a longer time, which presumably improves mood. Brand names include Marplan, Nardil, and Parnate. Unfortunately, MAO inhibitors interact with many foods and common over-the-counter drugs such as antihistamines to produce undesirable, even dangerous, side effects, such as life-threatening increases in blood pressure. At present, therefore, they are not often prescribed for depression (Fiedorowicz & Swartz, 2004; Yamada & Yasuhara, 2004). A new transdermal patch, which allows administration of an MAO inhibitor without its having to enter the digestive tract, may provide for some of the benefits of these drugs without the risks caused by their interactions with foods (Pae et al., 2007).

tricyclic antidepressants
drugs used for treating depression as well as chronic pain and ADHD.

Tricyclic antidepressants such as imipramine and amitriptyline, marketed under the trade names Elavil and Anafranil, are still popular for treating depression. They are also used in chronic pain management, to treat attention deficit hyperactivity disorder (ADHD), and as a treatment for bedwetting. These drugs appear to work by blocking the reuptake of serotonin and norepinephrine

"Discouraging data on the antidepressant."

© 1997 Mike Twohy/The New Yorker Collection/www.cartoonbank.com

selective serotonin reuptake inhibitors (SSRIs) drugs prescribed primarily for depression and some anxiety disorders that work by making more serotonin available in the synapse.

almost equally. Hence, they make more of these neurotransmitters available in the brain. However, the tricyclics produce unpleasant side effects such as dry mouth, weight gain, irritability, confusion, and constipation (Zeino, Sisson, & Bjarnason, 2010).

Many of the unpleasant side effects of the tricyclic antidepressants come from their effects on norepinephrine. People with depression have serotonin deficiencies (Delgado et al., 1994; Drevets et al., 1999). Therefore, the development of drugs that target only serotonin offered hope for treatment with fewer side effects. One class of drugs brought to the market in the 1990s, the **selective serotonin reuptake inhibitors (SSRIs),** make more serotonin available in the synapse. Prozac (fluoxetine), Zoloft (sertraline), Paxil (paroxetine), and Celexa (citalopram) are some of the more widely used SSRIs and are among the most widely prescribed psychotherapeutic drugs in the United States today.

Here is how SSRIs work: Serotonin, like all neurotransmitters, is released from the presynaptic neuron into the synapse. It then binds with serotonin-specific receptor sites on the postsynaptic neuron to stimulate the firing of that neuron. Normally, neurotransmitters that do not bind with the postsynaptic neuron will either be taken back up into the presynaptic neuron, in a process called *reuptake,* or be destroyed by enzymes in the synapse. The SSRIs inhibit the reuptake process, thereby allowing more serotonin to bind with the postsynaptic neuron (Murphy, 2010); see Figure 16.2. By allowing more serotonin to be used, the SSRIs alleviate some of the symptoms of depression. Drugs that affect both serotonin and norepinephrine activity are also available, but may produce some undesirable side effects that the serotonin-only drugs do not (Cipriani et al., 2010).

SSRI medications create far fewer unpleasant side effects than do tricyclic antidepressants. For this reason they have become popular, even among people who are not particularly ill but want to feel happier. Although these drugs are prescribed primarily for depression, they are also prescribed for the treatment of certain anxiety disorders, especially OCD, as well as disorders of impulse control such as compulsive gambling (Vaswani, Linda, & Ramesh, 2003). SSRIs, however, can have some side effects, such as agitation, insomnia, nausea, and difficulty in achieving orgasm. This last side effect has led some physicians to prescribe SSRIs to treat premature ejaculation (Waldinger et al., 2004). Another highly publicized but infrequent side effect of SSRI is an increased likelihood of attempting suicide compared to other treatments for depression (Fergusson et al., 2005). The recently publicized cases of teens on SSRIs committing suicide often neglect to report that adolescents are usually in severely depressed states when they are prescribed SSRIs, which suggests that they would be more likely to attempt or to commit suicide no matter which drug they were prescribed (Wessely & Kerwin, 2004). In fact, widespread antidepressant use may be associated with a decrease in suicide rates worldwide, but the nature of that relationship is a matter of debate (Isacsson et al., 2010).

Connection

Deficiencies in either the amount or the utilization of serotonin in certain parts of the brain are often found in people with depression.

See "Depression and Its Causes," Chapter 15, "Psychological Disorders," p. 600.

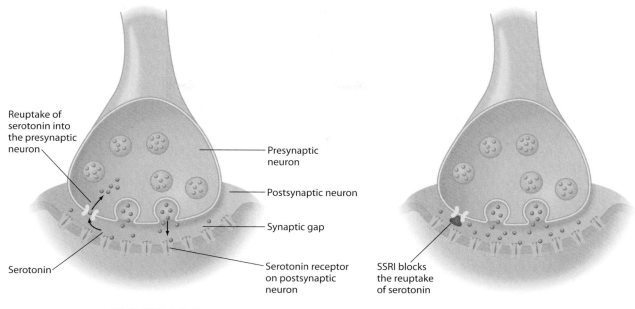

Reuptake of serotonin into the presynaptic neuron

Serotonin

Presynaptic neuron

Postsynaptic neuron

Synaptic gap

Serotonin receptor on postsynaptic neuron

SSRI blocks the reuptake of serotonin

FIGURE 16.2

THE EFFECT OF SSRIs ON REUPTAKE OF SEROTONIN. SSRIs increase serotonin levels by blocking the reuptake of serotonin into the presynaptic neuron. As a result, more serotonin stays in the synaptic cleft, where it can bind with receptors on the postsynaptic neuron.

bupropione
a widely used antidepressant that inhibits the reuptake of norepinephrine and dopamine.

benzo-diazepines
a class of anxiety-reducing drugs that can be addictive, but are less dangerous than barbiturates.

barbiturates
a class of anxiety-reducing sedatives that can be addictive and carry a risk of overdose.

lithium
a salt that is prescribed for its ability to stabilize the mania associated with bipolar disorder.

Bupropione (trade name Wellbutrin) is another widely used antidepressant that is chemically unrelated to the tricyclics, MAO inhibitors, and SSRIs. It inhibits the reuptake of norepinephrine and dopamine, both of which are excitatory neurotransmitters involved in arousal and positive emotion. Bupropione is also marketed under the trade name of Zyban as a smoking cessation aid.

Two major classes of drugs, the **benzodiazepines** (Valium, Librium) and the **barbiturates,** are prescribed for anxiety. Both have calming effects and can be addictive, but barbiturates have the higher risk of overdose. People with anxiety disorders often take SSRIs as well. We will discuss the drug treatment of anxiety disorders in more detail later in this chapter's "Bringing It All Together" section.

The treatment of bipolar disorder presents many challenges, as the manic episodes have to be regulated, the depressive episodes prevented, and the shifts from one type of episode to the other controlled. Because no one drug can manage all these effects, treatment often consists of a combination of drug therapies. **Lithium** has long been prescribed for its ability to stabilize the mania associated with bipolar disorder. We do not know how lithium works, although it appears to influence many neurotransmitter systems in the brain, including glutamate, the major excitatory neurotransmitter in the brain, which appears to play a substantial role in schizophrenia (Chuang, 2004; Jope, 1999). Taking lithium can be

Actor Robert Downey, Jr., has struggled with symptoms of bipolar disorder and drug abuse for a number of years. Treating bipolar disorder is challenging and typically involves a combination of drugs to control mania and prevent depression. Lithium effectively regulates mania, but its use must be monitored carefully to avoid harmful side effects.

Connection

Do you need a caffeinated beverage to get you going in the morning—and more throughout the day to stay alert? People who require more and more caffeine or other drugs, including prescription drugs, have developed a drug tolerance.
See "Altering Consciousness With Drugs," Chapter 6, "Consciousness," p. 252.

unpleasant and dangerous, as it can cause diarrhea, nausea, tremors, cognitive problems, kidney failure, brain damage, and even adverse cardiac effects (Aichorn et al., 2006). Also, because the amount of lithium required for effective treatment is not very different from the amount that can cause harm, it is difficult to determine the effective dosage. In addition, some people develop tolerance to lithium after years of treatment, making the drug less effective (Post et al., 1998). For these reasons, physicians need to monitor their patients' lithium levels carefully by regularly testing their blood.

Due to toxicity concerns, physicians often favor other drugs to treat the mania phase, including drugs prescribed to prevent convulsions, either alone or in combination with lithium. Currently, the most commonly used drugs for managing mania are the atypical antipsychotics (such as olanzapine, trade name Zyprexa) and valproate (marketed as Depakote or Depacon) (Malhi, Adams, & Berk, 2010).

Drug Treatments for Schizophrenia

Today, drug therapies are typically the first choice for schizophrenia. But prior to the 1950s, there were no drugs to treat the disorder. In 1952, the French physician Henri Laborit discovered that a class of drugs, the **phenothiazines,** helped diminish hallucinations, confusion, agitation, and paranoia in people with schizophrenia. He made this discovery by accident, after looking for a way to reduce the shock that sometimes occurs after major surgery (shock results when the body does not receive enough blood, and tissues are therefore deprived of oxygen) ("Drug for Treating Schizophrenia," 1998).

Connection

Schizophrenia and other disorders can be caused in part by genes that are expressed only under specific environmental circumstances.
See "Nature and Nurture Explanations of Schizophrenia," Chapter 15, "Psychological Disorders," p. 609.

phenothiazines drugs used to treat schizophrenia; help diminish hallucinations, confusion, agitation, and paranoia, but also have adverse side effects.

Phenothiazines block dopamine receptors in the brain. As you read in Chapter 15, the prevailing view for decades was that schizophrenia resulted from an excess of dopamine in the brain—a view dubbed the *dopamine hypothesis*. Although the dopamine hypothesis has come into question, the major drugs for schizophrenia are still those that reduce the availability of dopamine in the brain (Javitt & Coyle, 2004).

The best-known phenothiazine is chlorpromazine (marketed as Thorazine in the United States). Another drug, haloperidol (Haldol), discovered at about the same time, showed similar effects on schizophrenic symptoms. The phenothiazines and haloperidol are known as **traditional antipsychotics,** because they were the first medications used to manage psychotic symptoms. Unfortunately, they have many unpleasant side effects. These include fatigue, visual impairments, and a condition called **tardive dyskinesia,** which consists of repetitive, involuntary movements of jaw, tongue, face, and mouth (such as grimacing and lip smacking), and body tremors. Tardive dyskinesia is particularly problematic, as the effects often continue for months after the drugs are discontinued (Trugman, 1998).

traditional antipsychotics historically, the first medications used to manage psychotic symptoms.

Some newer antipsychotic drugs, called **atypical antipsychotics,** do not have these side effects. Clozapine (Clozaril), olanzapine (Zyprexa), and risperidone (Risperdal) are examples of atypical antipsychotics. Many physicians now consider the atypical antipsychotics the first line of treatment for schizophrenia. These drugs preferentially block a different type of dopamine receptor than the traditional antipsychotics do, which makes them less likely to create tardive dyskinesia (Potkin et al., 2003). Atypical antipsychotics also affect the activity of

atypical antipsychotics newer antipsychotic drugs, which do not create tardive dyskinesia.

tardive dyskinesia repetitive, involuntary movements of jaw, tongue, face, and mouth resulting from the extended use of traditional antipsychotic drugs.

FIGURE **16.3**

Disorder	Class of drug treatment	Drug name	Side effects
Anxiety	SSRIs	Paxil, Prozac Zoloft, Celexa	Agitation, insomnia, nausea, difficulty achieving orgasm; rare cases of increased risk for suicide
	Benzodiazepines	Valium Librium	Can be addictive
	Barbiturates	Pentobarbital	Slows breathing and heart rate; can lead to overdose
Depression	MAO inhibitors	Nardil Parnate	Dangerous increases in blood pressure
	Tricyclic antidepressants	Elavil Anafranil	Dry mouth, weight gain, irritability, confusion, constipation
	SSRIs	Paxil, Prozac Zoloft, Celexa	Agitation, insomnia, nausea, difficulty achieving orgasm; rare cases of increased risk for suicide
	Bupropione	Wellbutrin	Weight loss, dry mouth, headaches
Bipolar disorder	Lithium	Lithobid	Diarrhea, nausea, tremors, kidney failure, cognitive effects, adverse cardiac effects
Schizophrenia	Chlorpromazine	Thorazine	Fatigue, visual impairment, tardive dyskinesia
	Haloperidol	Haldol	Fatigue, visual impairment, tardive dyskinesia
	Clozapine	Clozaril	Weight gain, increased risk of diabetes, reduction of white blood cells
	Risperidone	Risperdal	Weight gain, increased risk of diabetes, reduction of white blood cells

SUMMARY OF DRUGS USED TO TREAT PSYCHOLOGICAL DISORDERS. Most of the major psychological disorders can be treated with some form of medication, to varying degrees of effectiveness and with various side effects.

other neurotransmitters in the brain. In rare cases, an excess of serotonin occurs, which can lead to tremor, diarrhea, delirium, neuromuscular rigidity, and high body temperature (Dvir & Smallwood, 2008). Unfortunately, even these medications can produce some unpleasant or dangerous side effects, such as major weight gain, increased risk of diabetes, a reduction in the number of certain white blood cells, and, rarely, a particular kind of cancer (Javitt & Coyle, 2004; Lieberman et al., 2005; Young et al., 2010). Figure 16.3 summarizes the major drug therapies, the names of the medications that are used to treat specific disorders, and the various side effects of each medication.

Psychosurgery

Recall from Chapter 1 the evidence from very early human history of attempts to cure insanity by trephining, which is drilling a hole in the skull to allow evil spirits to escape. Although psychological disorders are not now usually treated by surgical means, in the early 20th century physicians experimented with the use of surgery to disrupt the transmission of brain signals in people suffering from psychosis. In a procedure known as **prefrontal lobotomy,** they severed connections between the prefrontal cortex and the lower portion of the brain. Because the prefrontal cortex is involved in thinking (and, we now know, is crucial for working memory and planned action), and the lower areas are more concerned with emotion, they believed the surgery would have the effect of modifying behavior and possibly disengaging disruptive thought patterns involved in hallucinations and confused thinking. Typically, however, prefrontal lobotomies produced profound personality changes, often leaving the patient listless

prefrontal lobotomy
a form of psychosurgery in which the connections between the prefrontal cortex and the lower portion of the brain are severed; no longer in use.

or subject to seizures; some patients were even reduced to a vegetative state (Mashour, Walker, & Martuza, 2005).

Rosemary Kennedy, younger sister to John F. Kennedy, underwent a lobotomy when she was 23 years old to treat her erratic, often violent mood swings. Instead of producing the desired calming effect, the lobotomy left Rosemary mentally incapacitated. She would stare blankly at walls for hours on end and lost the ability to speak coherently (Lerner, 1996).

After the introduction of the traditional antipsychotic medications, lobotomy fell out of favor. Moreover, the practice was widely regarded as cruel and inhumane. Today a very few, highly constrained forms of brain surgery are occasionally performed, but only as a last resort after other forms of treatment have been unsuccessful (Mashour et al., 2005).

Electric and Magnetic Therapies

Although brain surgery for psychological disorders is rare, there are other ways to stimulate or decrease brain activation. Bizarre as it seems, electrical current can be used to help ease the suffering caused by certain psychological disorders. The application of electrical current as a medical practice goes back centuries: Apparently the ancient Romans used electric fish to treat headaches (Abrams, 1997). As we saw in the chapter opening, one of the more innovative applications of electrical stimulation may well hold the key to unlocking the mystery of depression.

Electroconvulsive Therapy

The notion of "shock therapy" conjures up images of barbaric torture of psychiatric patients. Yet electroconvulsive therapy is still used and can be effective for severe cases of depression in people who have not responded to other therapies (Fink, 2006). **Electroconvulsive therapy (ECT)** involves passing an electrical current through a person's brain

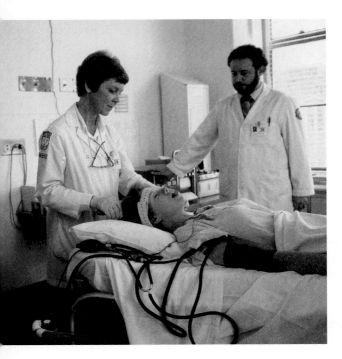

in order to induce a seizure. The origins of ECT stem from the observation that people who have seizures become calm after they have them (Abrams, 1997). Physicians thought that ECT could be an effective treatment for schizophrenia because the induced seizures would calm the patient. Research eventually demonstrated, however, that ECT did not treat the symptoms of schizophrenia effectively at all, and it disappeared as a viable therapy for years. It resurfaced later as a treatment for people with severe cases of depression.

Today, ECT is administered by connecting electrodes to the patient's head and passing an electric current (ranging from 60 to 140 volts) through the brain for one-third to one-half second. The voltage is not lethal because it is administered only to the head—indeed, the same voltage to the chest would be lethal. The treatment is called electro*convulsive* because the procedure produces a brief seizure,

electroconvulsive therapy (ECT) treatment of last resort for severe depression that involves passing an electrical current through a person's brain in order to induce a seizure.

including bodily convulsions. To minimize the convulsions, patients today are given an anesthetic and muscle relaxant prior to ECT. Standard ECT treatment involves up to 12 sessions over the course of several weeks. Some people report immediate relief of their depressive symptoms after treatment, although scientists do not fully understand how ECT works to relieve them (Nolen-Hoeksema, 2007). The downside to ECT is that it creates some permanent memory loss and other types of cognitive damage because it actually destroys some brain tissue. Using ECT on one side of the brain rather than both appears to reduce the risk of memory loss (Squire, 1977).

Repetitive Transcranial Magnetic Stimulation

The idea of somehow stimulating or manipulating brain activity with an external application of energy has enduring appeal. Some practitioners have tried to find a way to do this without creating more harm. ECT was a good idea in some respects, but as just mentioned, it leaves people with memory damage and other negative effects. In **repetitive transcranial magnetic stimulation,** physicians expose particular brain structures to bursts of high-intensity magnetic fields instead of electricity. Like ECT, repetitive transcranial magnetic stimulation (TMS) is usually reserved for people with severe depression who have not responded well to other forms of therapy. Although some people experience relief from this therapy, it is not yet clear how much magnetic stimulation is optimal and for what length of time (P. B. Fitzgerald et al., 2006; Turner-Shea, Bruno, & Pridmore, 2006). TMS has also shown preliminary success in treating the negative symptoms of schizophrenia (Brunelin et al., 2010).

Innovative breakthroughs in neurology and psychiatry have led to the development of a very promising treatment for depression. This revolutionary approach has roots in both neurosurgery and the use of electricity to treat psychological disorders. We examine how it was discovered and how it works in "Breaking New Ground."

repetitive transcranial magnetic stimulation treatment for severe depression involving exposure of specific brain structures to bursts of high-intensity magnetic fields instead of electricity.

Repetitive transcranial magnetic stimulation exposes specific areas of the brain to bursts of high-intensity magnetic fields and may be used to treat people with severe depression when other options have failed.

Deep Brain Stimulation for the Treatment of Severe Depression

The treatment of depression remains a major challenge. Few people are cured, although many obtain some relief from drugs, psychotherapy, repetitive transcranial magnetic stimulation, or ECT. Others, however, find no relief in any of these treatments. For them, depression is severe, unrelenting, and debilitating.

Helen Mayberg

But there is hope. In her quest to understand the brain circuitry of depression, neurologist Helen Mayberg discovered what appears to be a neural switch that activates depression. In the process, she came upon a strikingly effective treatment for the disorder. The path that led Mayberg to discover how a brain region called Brodmann's Area 25 (we'll call it Area 25) may control depression is an interesting story of how scientific discovery depends on luck, tenacity, creativity, vision, and hard work.

From the start of her career, Helen Mayberg deviated from the traditional focus on drug and surgical therapies as a biological treatment for depression. As a young scientist, she trained with a neurologist who studied how various areas of the human brain work together. Her early training helped her see the brain in terms of the interactions among various areas rather than in terms of their individual functions alone. During this time, Mayberg studied depression in people with Parkinson's disease. Using PET imaging of brain activation, she and her colleagues found that these patients had reduced activity in both frontal cortex thinking areas and limbic emotional areas (Drevets et al., 1997; Mayberg, 2003; Shestyuk et al., 2005).

But she and her colleagues also stumbled on a surprising phenomenon: Area 25 was actually *hyperactive* in these patients! Rather than discounting this unexpected finding, Mayberg tested it further. She found this same pattern of overactivation in Area 25 in depressed people with Alzheimer's, epilepsy, and Huntington's disease (Mayberg, 1997). Perhaps it played a role in depression more generally.

Finding overactivation in any brain area of depressed people was surprising, since many researchers have found that depression is related to underactivity rather than overactivity of certain cortical areas (Shestyuk et al., 2005). But Mayberg found depressed activity in frontal cortex areas, which fit with current models of depression, along with overactivity in Area 25.

Area 25 is located in the cingulate region of the prefrontal cortex, and it is surrounded by the limbic system. As such, it has connections with emotional and memory centers of the brain (see Figure 16.4). Mayberg reasoned that if Area 25 plays a key role in sustaining depressive thinking, one would see a reduction in activity in this area after successful treatment for the disorder. This in fact is what she and her colleagues found (Goldapple et al., 2004; Kennedy et al., 2001). Mayberg also found activity in Area 25 when otherwise healthy people recalled sad memories (Mayberg et al., 1999).

Eventually, Mayberg and her colleagues amassed evidence that an overactive Area 25 is a general feature of depression. Moreover, successful treatment by an SSRI or cognitive–behavioral therapy reduced Area 25 activation. What seems most important about Area 25 is its connections with thinking areas of the prefrontal cortex and limbic

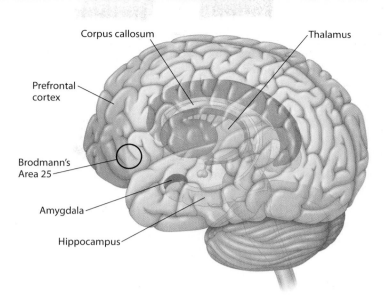

FIGURE **16.4**

BRODMANN'S AREA 25, THE PRE-FRONTAL CORTEX, AND THE LIMBIC SYSTEM. Brodmann's Area 25 is located in the cingulate region of the prefrontal cortex, where it is surrounded by the corpus callosum and structures of the limbic system (amygdala, hippocampus, thalamus). The limbic system is important in regulating emotion and motivation.

Corpus callosum

Thalamus

Prefrontal cortex

Brodmann's Area 25

Amygdala

Hippocampus

structures involved in emotion (which are connected to each other). Area 25 thus may be a gateway between thinking and emotion. An overactive Area 25 may enable the type of negative thinking that feeds depressive states. Mayberg reasoned that if it were possible to close this gate, depression might cease. But how?

Mayberg was working with colleagues who were pioneers in implanting electrodes deep in the brains of people with Parkinson's disease to regulate activity in an area of the brain that produces the tremors (shaking) associated with that disease. No one ever thought about applying this technique to depressed brain regions. But in a stroke of creative insight, Mayberg did. She figured that she could apply the same technology, known as *deep brain stimulation,* to Area 25 (Dobbs, 2006, July 30). She tried it with 12 patients whose severe depression had failed to respond to anything else. She and her colleagues implanted electrodes in Area 25 and delivered voltage to that area from an external stimulator. For 11 of the patients, the depression ceased almost immediately (Mayberg et al., 2005). Shortly after activation of the electrodes, these patients said that they felt "sudden calmness or lightness," "disappearance of the void," or "connectedness." One of them described heightened awareness and greater perception of visual details and colors in the room.

Figure 16.5 illustrates the location of the implanted electrodes and the wearable pacemaker for stimulating them. Note that the treatment involves brain stimulation in the operating room as well as a method for stimulating the implants in daily life. Patients wear an external pacemaker that controls the delivery of electrical stimulation to Area 25.

FIGURE **16.5**

DEEP BRAIN ELECTRODES AND STIMULATOR FOR STIMULATION OF AREA 25 IN DEPRESSED PATIENTS. A pacemaker implanted in the person's chest sends electrical impulses to electrodes projecting down into Area 25 of the frontal cortex.

In the following passage, Mayberg describes what happened when the stimulator was turned on to activate the electrode just implanted in Area 25 in the brain of Deanna, the woman described in the chapter opening. As the electrodes were being implanted in Area 25, Mayberg sat by Deanna's side and asked her to report, throughout the surgery, whatever she felt, however minor it might seem. What follows is Mayberg's account of what Deanna said when, unbeknownst to Deanna, the surgical team turned the stimulator on:

> "So we turn it on," Mayberg told me later, "and all of a sudden she says to me, 'It's very strange,' she says, 'I know you've been with me in the operating room this whole time. I know you care about me. But it's not that. I don't know what you just did. But I'm looking at you, and it's like I just feel suddenly more connected to you.'"
>
> Mayberg, stunned, signaled with her hand to the others, out of Deanna's view, to turn the stimulator off.
>
> "And they turn it off," Mayberg said, "and she goes: 'God, it's just so odd. You just went away again. I guess it wasn't really anything.'
>
> "It was subtle like a brick," Mayberg told me. "There's no reason for her to say that. Zero. And all through those tapes I have of her, every time she's in the clinic beforehand, she always talks about this disconnect, this closeness and sense of affiliation she misses, that was so agonizingly painful for her to lose. And there it was. It was back in an instant." (Excerpt from Dobbs, D. 2006, April 2. A depression switch? *New York Times*, p. 50. © 2006 The New York Times. All rights reserved. Used by permission and protected by the copyright laws of the United States. The printing, copying, redistribution, or retransmission of this content without express written permission is prohibited.)

Although most people who have had the procedure experience dramatic improvements or complete elimination of their depression, a few do not. Large-scale clinical trials are underway in which Mayberg and others are studying the effects of stimulation of Area 25 on larger groups of people with treatment-resistant depression. Initial findings suggest deep brain stimulation offers relief for the symptoms of severe depression without impairing cognitive function (Mayberg, 2009; Rizvi et al., 2009).

■ ■ ■

Effectiveness of Biological Treatments

Therapies are only as good as they are effective. At the end of each section discussing specific forms of therapy, we evaluate the current evidence for how effective this type of therapy is.

The SSRIs and tricyclics show comparable effectiveness in the treatment of depression (Kendrick et al., 2006). Both do a reasonable job of regulating depression and are preferable to the MAO inhibitors, given the undesirable, possibly dangerous, side effects of the latter. Of the various classes of antidepressants, the SSRIs have the fewest adverse side effects, and people seem to tolerate them better for long-term use (Nemeroff, 2007). Still, these drugs can take up to 4 weeks to take effect. Presumably, this is how long it takes synapses to produce enough new receptor sites to make use of the increased amounts of serotonin made available by SSRIs.

Recent studies, however, suggest that some of the more popular drugs for depression might not be as effective as was once thought. A study by Turner and colleagues (2008), for example, suggests that the medical journals were biased in their publications of findings on the effectiveness of antidepressants. Specifically, nearly one third of all FDA studies—most of which reported negative results on antidepressants—were not published. As a result, for over a decade the impression of effectiveness of these medications was overestimated (94% versus the more modest and more representative 51%). In addition, according to a large-scale meta-analysis, most widely used prescription antidepressants may be no better than placebos for people with mild to moderate depression. For those with severe depression, they are beneficial when compared to placebos (Fournier et al., 2010). The SSRI fluoxetine (Prozac) actually can harm certain kinds of neural growth and block synapse formation (Xu et al., 2010). Finally, a large, randomized trial in Romania compared the effectiveness and cost-effectiveness of drug treatment with Prozac and two kinds of psychotherapy (cognitive therapy and rational emotive therapy) . They measured depression scores before, twice during, and 6 months after a 14-week treatment course. The psychological therapies were more effective than Prozac and also more cost-effective. It is not clear whether the same results would hold in the United States (Sava et al., 2008).

Lithium is still widely used for treatment of mania. Lithium does appear to have long-term effectiveness in treating bipolar disorder (Berghöfer et al., 2008). The evidence, however, for lithium's effectiveness in treating "acute" phases of mania is weak in spite of its regular use for this purpose in the United States (Reed et al., 2009). Lithium does not appear to be superior to anticonvulsant or antipsychotic medications, or both, in regulating manic episodes. Moreover, these other medications have fewer toxic side effects than does lithium. Some research indicates that lithium may be most effective in preventing relapse and suicide in people with bipolar disorder, but many providers are not aware of this benefit (Carney & Goodwin, 2005).

The treatment of schizophrenia still presents a huge problem for mental health professionals. Both traditional and atypical antipsychotic drugs work best on the positive symptoms of schizophrenia, such as hallucinations and delusions, but are generally less effective on the negative symptoms, such as flattened affect, and the cognitive confusion that is characteristic of the disorder (Javitt & Coyle, 2004). One atypical antipsychotic, clozapine (Clorazil), does appear to be somewhat effective in treating the negative symptoms, but it also has a potentially serious side effect: diabetes (Javitt & Coyle, 2004). One of the major problems in treating schizophrenia, however, is persuading patients to continue taking the medication. Because of the unpleasant and often dangerous side effects of these drugs, patients often stop taking them. Up to 74% of people using traditional and atypical antipsychotics discontinue treatment (Lieberman et al., 2005; McEvoy et al., 2006). Recent evidence that glutamate may drive the neurotransmitter system in schizophrenia offers hope for the development of more effective, less aversive drug therapies for the disorder (Patil et al., 2007).

ECT is regarded as a treatment of last resort for severely depressed people who have not responded to any other therapy. Although many patients report immediate relief with ECT treatment, its benefits usually last only as long as the treatments are maintained. Also, ECT can have severe side effects, including memory loss and confusion. ECT treatment to one hemisphere of the brain appears to work better than treatment to both hemispheres and creates fewer cognitive side effects (Sackheim et al., 1993). A controlled trial found that ECT and pharmacological therapy for depression were about equally effective in preventing relapse in people with major depressive disorder, but each form of treatment helped only about half the people studied (Kellner et al., 2006).

Quick Quiz 16.1: Biological Treatments

1. The antidepressant medications known as the SSRIs work by
   a. inhibiting monoamine oxidase
   b. decreasing serotonin levels by inhibiting the reuptake of serotonin into the presynaptic neuron
   c. increasing serotonin levels by inhibiting the reuptake of serotonin into the presynaptic neuron
   d. reducing the activity of the neurotransmitter glutamate

2. Your Aunt Julia has been in treatment for years for schizophrenia. She often has jerky spastic movements, which she tells you are from her medication, not the disorder itself. What side effect is she experiencing?
   a. intolerance
   b. reactive dysphoria
   c. tardive dyskinesia
   d. insomnia

3. Electroconvulsive therapy (ECT) is still in limited use for people with which disorder?
   a. schizophrenia
   b. obsessive-compulsive disorder
   c. generalized anxiety disorder
   d. major depressive disorder

4. Helen Mayberg was surprised to find that brain images of Area 25 showed _____ in people with severe depression and helped devise a way to treat them with deep brain stimulation.
   a. reduced activity
   b. overactivity
   c. tumors
   d. reduced blood flow

5. Both traditional and atypical antipsychotic drugs work best on the _____ symptoms of schizophrenia, but are generally less effective on the _____ symptoms. (Pick the best pair of words to fill in the blanks.)
   a. negative; positive
   b. positive; negative
   c. cognitive; emotional
   d. emotional; cognitive

Answers can be found at the end of the chapter.

PSYCHOLOGICAL TREATMENTS FOR PSYCHOLOGICAL DISORDERS

psychotherapy
the use of psychological techniques to modify maladaptive behaviors or thought patterns, or both, and to help patients develop insight into their own behavior.

psychoanalytic therapy
based on Freud's ideas, therapeutic approach oriented toward major personality change with a focus on uncovering unconscious motives, especially through dream interpretation.

A number of psychological therapies have developed alongside the various medications and biologically based techniques for treating psychological disorders. **Psychotherapy** is the use of psychological techniques to modify maladaptive behaviors or thought patterns, or both, and to help patients develop insight into their own behavior. In psychotherapy a therapist and a client work together, or a therapist works with a group of people.

People may engage in psychotherapy for self-development as well as for the treatment of psychological disorders. In this chapter, we will focus on the use of psychotherapeutic techniques in treating disorders. The several types of psychotherapeutic approaches are outlined in Figure 16.1: psychoanalytic/psychodynamic therapy, humanistic–positive therapy, behavioral treatments, cognitive treatments, and cognitive–behavioral treatments. Each type of psychotherapy has its own explanation of what causes different disorders as well as how they should be treated.

Psychoanalytic/Psychodynamic Therapy

The oldest and most direct lineage to Freudian therapy is known as *psychoanalytic therapy*. Based on Sigmund Freud's own practices, **psychoanalytic**

therapy is the original form of "talk therapy" and is oriented toward major personality change with a focus on uncovering unconscious motives, especially through dream interpretation. It tends to require meeting three to five times a week. Currently classical, or Freudian, psychoanalysis is relatively rare. Freudian psychoanalysis, so innovative in its day, is today influential in how it inspires various perspectives in talk therapy, many of which have taken off in very different directions from where Freud started.

An offshoot of psychoanalytic therapy, known as psychodynamic therapy, is more often practiced. Compared to psychoanalytic therapy, **psychodynamic therapy** focuses more on symptom relief than major personality change and usually requires meeting once or twice a week (Shedler, 2010). Like psychoanalytic therapy, psychodynamic therapy aims to explore aspects of the self and motives that are unconscious (Shedler, 2010). Other key ideas of psychodynamic therapy are a focus on emotion and past experiences as well as how the person defends and avoids distressing thoughts and feelings. Moreover, the relationship between therapist and client in psychodynamic psychotherapy is that of a supportive partnership, in which the therapist listens to the client in a nonjudgmental manner. The therapist's role is to help the client gain insight into the unconscious influences behind unwanted behaviors. To help the client access these unconscious influences, the therapist may use techniques such as free association or examine processes that might reveal unconscious motives, such as transference and repression.

Classic psychoanalytic therapy often involves accessing the unconscious through dream interpretation. Indeed, Sigmund Freud argued that "dreams are the royal road to the unconscious" (Freud, 1900/1953, p. 608). Freud's two major techniques for interpreting dreams in order to uncover their unconscious content were free association and symbols. In **free association,** the client recounts the dream and then tries to take one image or idea and say whatever comes to mind, regardless of how threatening, disgusting, or troubling it may be. After this has been done with the first image, the process is repeated until the client has made associations with all the recalled dream images. Ideally, somewhere in the chain of free associations is a connection that unlocks the key to the dream. The second technique for interpreting dreams is through *symbols;* that is, dream images are thought of as representing or being symbolic of something else. Classic examples of symbols are a snake symbolizing a penis and a cave representing a vagina. If the techniques just described are successful, the patient becomes aware of the disturbing thoughts in her or his unconscious, and the problematic symptoms decrease.

In the process of **transference,** the client unconsciously reacts to someone in a current relationship as though that person were someone from the client's past. While the client is in therapy, that person is the therapist, but it can be anyone in the person's present life circumstances. For example, a woman whose father was verbally abusive to her might find herself shirking her job responsibilities because she experiences extreme fear when her older male supervisor at work speaks with even a slightly raised voice. The supervisor thinks this is an overreaction, but he does not realize that the woman's response stems from her relating to him as if he were her father. If these reactions occur during a therapy session, as they often do, the therapist can use the transference to help the client understand how her behavior and emotions in current relationships are influenced by her relationship with her father. By working through the unconsciously transferred feelings in the therapeutic setting, a client might be freed from their powerful grip in other settings. Contemporary psychoanalysis relies heavily on analyzing both the real and transferred relationship between analyst and patient.

defense mechanisms unconscious strategies the mind uses to protect itself from anxiety by denying and distorting reality in some way.

Like transference, defense mechanisms are also central to psychodynamic theory and therapy. Freud and his daughter Anna (who was also a noted psychoanalyst) described many different **defense mechanisms,** all of which operate unconsciously and involve defending against anxiety and threats to the ego. The most basic one is **repression,** which involves forcing threatening feelings, ideas, or motives into the unconscious. In psychodynamic therapy, dream interpretation and transference are used to uncover repressed defenses and unconscious wishes.

Some or all of these techniques may lead the client to catharsis. **Catharsis** is the process of releasing intense, often unconscious, emotions in a therapeutic setting.

repression the unconscious act of keeping threatening thoughts, feelings, or impulses out of consciousness.

catharsis the process of releasing intense, often unconscious, emotions in a therapeutic setting.

Humanistic–Positive Therapy

Humanistic therapies seek to help the client reach his or her greatest potential. The most prominent figure in humanistic therapy is Carl Rogers (1951), who developed **client-centered therapy.** Client-centered therapy holds that people have mental health problems because there is a gap between who they are and who they would ideally like to be. In client-centered therapy, the therapist must show unconditional positive regard— that is, genuine acceptance and empathy

Carl Rogers (far right) leads a group therapy session.

client-centered therapy a form of humanistic therapy in which the therapist shows unconditional positive regard for the patient.

for the client, regardless of what he or she has said or done. The goal is to create an atmosphere in which clients can communicate their feelings with certainty that they are being understood rather than judged. If this unconditional positive regard is effective, the client will develop a strong sense of self-worth and the confidence to strive for self-fulfillment.

More recently, positive psychology has developed its own form of psychotherapy, generally referred to as *positive psychotherapy* (Rashid, 2008; Seligman, Rashid, & Parks, 2006). These therapies focus explicitly on increasing a person's happiness, well-being, and positive emotions. Depression, for example, is treated not only by reducing helplessness, sense of worthlessness, and negative emotions, but also by actively trying to create a greater sense of well-being and sense of gratitude. Gratitude training, for instance, involves daily exercises in noticing and finding things in life for which one is grateful and thankful. People who regularly acknowledge what they have to be thankful for have a higher sense of well-being and happiness than those who do not regularly acknowledge gratitude (Emmons & McCullough, 2003).

behavior therapies therapies that apply the principles of classical and operant conditioning in the treatment of psychological disorders.

Behavioral Treatments

In **behavior therapies,** therapists apply the principles of classical and operant conditioning to treat psychological disorders. They focus on changing behavior, rather than thoughts, feelings, or motives. The idea is to help clients eliminate undesirable behaviors and increase the frequency of desirable ones.

Behavioral therapists employ the basic principles of operant conditioning through the use of **token economies** to treat maladaptive behaviors. This

token economies a behavioral technique in which desirable behaviors are reinforced with a token, such as a small chip or fake coin, which can be exchanged for privileges.

technique is based on a simple principle: Desirable behaviors are reinforced with a token, such as a small chip or fake coin, which the client can then exchange for privileges. Parents can use this approach with their children—if their room is messy and they clean it, they get a token. The kids can turn in five tokens for candy or a toy. The more this happens, the more likely they are to clean their rooms, or so the logic goes. In the realm of mental health, the technique was used with some success in the 1950s and 1960s to reduce undesirable psychotic behaviors in patients in mental institutions (Nolen-Hoeksema, 2007). Recent uses include treatment of substance abuse by people with schizophrenia. Each time the patients did not use drugs, they were rewarded with small amounts of money. Coupled with problem-solving and social-skills training, this token system helped control substance abuse in hospitalized patients with schizophrenia, who are generally very hard to treat (Bellack et al., 2006). Also, use of token economies may encourage socially appropriate behaviors and enhance life skills in children with autism (Matson & Boisjoli, 2009).

Systematic desensitization is a widely used application of behavioral treatment that is especially effective for treating simple phobias (Tyron, 2005). Systematic desensitization pairs relaxation with gradual exposure to a phobic object. First, the therapist generates a hierarchy of increasing contact with the feared object, ranging from mild to extreme. Figure 16.6 on page 646 shows a possible hierarchy for a person with arachnophobia (a fear of spiders). In addition to increasing exposure, the therapist helps the client learn relaxation techniques that he or she can use when experiencing anxiety, especially anxiety related to the phobic object. The therapist works to help the client relax and then exposes the client to the phobic stimulus at gradually increasing levels of intensity. The idea is a clever one—to pair two incompatible body responses, relaxation and anxiety. People cannot be both relaxed and anxious at the same time. And it works! Systematic desensitization often successfully treats phobias and some other anxiety disorders (Tryon, 2005).

Connection

Principles of classical and operant conditioning, including the powerful effect of reinforcement on learning, are the foundation of many behavioral therapies.

See "Conditioning Models of Learning," Chapter 8, "Learning," p. 307.

Systematic desensitization involves three levels of exposure to a phobic object: imagined, virtual, and real. In imagined exposure, people simply imagine contact with the phobic object. The next level is virtual reality exposure. At this stage, the individual may be shown photographs or exposed to a virtual reality computer simulation. For instance, one type of virtual reality software allows clients to simulate flying during treatment for flying phobia, as depicted in Figure 16.7 on page 647 (Wiederhold & Wiederhold, 2005). The most realistic level of exposure is in vivo exposure, in which the client makes real-life contact with the phobic object.

Implosion therapy, or **flooding,** is an extreme form of in vivo exposure in which the client experiences extreme exposure to the phobic object, such as when a person who is arachnophobic is asked to hold three hairy tarantulas at once. Flooding, in this sense, is very different from systematic desensitization. Flooding involves heavy exposure to the feared object, whereas systematic desensitization involves gradually making the person less sensitive to the feared object, one step at a time.

systematic desensitization a behavioral therapy technique, often used for phobias, in which the therapist pairs relaxation with gradual exposure to a phobic object, generating a hierarchy of increasing contact with the feared object.

flooding an extreme form of in vivo exposure in which the client experiences extreme exposure to the phobic object.

cognitive therapy any type of psychotherapy that works to restructure irrational thought patterns.

Cognitive and Cognitive–Behavioral Treatments

Any type of psychotherapy that works to restructure irrational thought patterns is known as **cognitive therapy.** Typically, in cognitive therapy the therapist helps the client identify irrational thought patterns and then challenges these thoughts.

Cognitive therapy (CT) is structured and problem-oriented, with the primary goal of fixing erroneous thought patterns, as we will illustrate with an example shortly. It is also time-limited and involves a collaborative effort by the therapist and the client. In using cognitive therapy, the therapist relies on what is known as the Socratic method: The therapist poses questions that help the client recognize erroneous logic that may support problematic thinking (Beck & Emery, 1985).

Let's consider the real-life case of Carlos, a 39-year-old man suffering from major depressive disorder. Carlos had tried several medications for his depression and had undergone one voluntary hospitalization, without satisfactory effects. His general practitioner (Dr. Hsu) recommended him for cognitive therapy. Many therapists believe that depressed people perceive events in such a way that they see only potentially adverse outcomes. Cognitive therapy for depression aims to point out the negative bias in such depressive thinking. Consider the following exchange between Carlos and his therapist, Dr. Walden (Gorenstein & Comer, 2002, pp. 54–55):

> **DR. WALDEN:** You say you are a "basket case" and can barely function. What leads you to those conclusions?
>
> **CARLOS:** Well, I've been hospitalized. That's how bad it's been. I just can't believe it.
>
> **DR. WALDEN:** . . . Tell me again what led to the hospitalization.
>
> **CARLOS:** I sort of panicked when the medicine didn't help, and I stopped going to work or anything else. Dr. Hsu figured that as long as I wasn't working, I might as well go into the hospital where I could try different drugs without having to manage all the side effects on my own. I also was pretty miserable at the time. I told Dr. Hsu my family might be better off without me.
>
> **DR. WALDEN:** Do you think they would be better off?
>
> **CARLOS:** I don't know. I'm not doing them much good.
>
> **DR. WALDEN:** What would life be like for them without you?
>
> **CARLOS:** It would be terrible for them. I suppose saying they'd be better off without me is going too far. As bad off as I am, I'm still able to do a few things.

1 Hearing the word "spider"

2 Seeing the word "spider" in print

3 Imagining a spider

4 Seeing a photograph of a spider in a glass jar

5 Seeing a photograph of a spider in someone's hand

6 Seeing a real spider in a jar across the room

FIGURE 16.6
HIERARCHY OF EXPOSURE TO SPIDERS (THE PHOBIC OBJECT) IN PATIENT WITH ARACHNOPHOBIA.

FIGURE **16.7**
SYSTEMATIC DESENSITIZATION IN TREATMENT OF FLYING PHOBIA. Because it is impractical and expensive to do therapy while on an actual airplane, simulating flying in a virtual reality format is an effective and cost-efficient way of systematically desensitizing people who are afraid of flying.

DR. WALDEN: What are you able to do?

CARLOS: Well, I'm not in the hospital anymore. And I don't think I will be back either. . . . I mainly went in because I thought I could get better treatment or whatever. But it didn't pan out, so what would be the point of going back in?

DR. WALDEN: So the fact that you were in the hospital isn't really a sign that you are now or were ever a "basket case," which I take to mean someone who is completely helpless and cannot function.

CARLOS: . . . In looking back on it now, it was all basically voluntary. But that doesn't erase the fact that I am still a mess.

DR. WALDEN: How much of a mess are you?

CARLOS: I can't work, I can't help out at home. I can't even watch a television show. How much else do you want to know?

DR. WALDEN: A couple of minutes ago you said you were still able to do a few things. What are those?

CARLOS: I can drive to work and . . . I guess it's an exaggeration to say that I can't work at all. There are a few things I can do at the office.

DR. WALDEN: Like what?

7 Seeing a real spider in a person's hand across the room

8 Holding a real spider in a glass jar

9 Holding a real spider in one's own hand

Cognitive–behavioral therapy focuses on changing a client's way of thinking in order to avoid irrational thoughts. Asking the client to break down problems into steps that can be tackled one at a time illustrates this approach.

Notice how Dr. Walden helps Carlos use his own logic to point out errors in the thinking that supports his notion of being worthless. For instance, Dr. Walden helps Carlos see that in spite of being hospitalized for depression, he was neither useless to his family nor totally unable to do things. Carlos came to realize that he really wasn't a "basket case" after all (Gorenstein & Comer, 2002, pp. 54–55).

Often therapists integrate cognitive techniques for restructuring irrational thoughts with behavioral techniques to shape desirable behaviors in what is known as **cognitive–behavioral therapy (CBT).** As the name implies, the focus of CBT is to change both thoughts and behavior. CBT entails restructuring thoughts, loosening the client's belief in irrational thoughts that may perpetuate the disorder, and offering incentives for acquiring more adaptive thought and behavior patterns. Cognitive–behavioral therapy is a short-term psychological treatment that has been successfully applied to disorders as varied as depression, phobias, post-traumatic stress disorder (PTSD), obsessive–compulsive disorder, eating disorders, and substance abuse. One way to conceptualize CBT is to think of it as a tool for teaching skills that curtail *depressogenic thinking*, or thinking that tends to help generate depressed moods. CBT has revolutionized the treatment of many psychological disorders.

cognitive–behavioral therapy an approach to treating psychological disorders that combines techniques for restructuring irrational thoughts with operant and classical conditioning techniques to shape desirable behaviors.

CBT helps clients change the way they evaluate potential emotional threats. To do this, CBT encourages reappraisal, which entails reexamining a situation that was previously seen as stressful. Through problem solving, clients can learn to adopt a new outlook on a situation. For example, people who are depressed often hold the depressogenic thought that they can't do anything because all tasks seem insurmountable. A problem-solving approach to this kind of thinking would be to list the various steps in a given task and then work on each step until the task is completed. Not only will the client successfully accomplish the task, but that accomplishment may also have the further benefit of improving mood. Research on the cognitive processes involved in CBT in relation to treatment effectiveness shows that people who engage in more problem solving during CBT reap more benefits (Chen, Jordan, & Thompson, 2006).

Group Therapies

group therapy therapeutic settings in which several people who share a common problem all meet regularly with a therapist to help themselves and one another.

In **group therapy,** several people who share a common problem all meet regularly with a therapist to help themselves and one another; the therapist acts as a facilitator. Group therapies often follow a structured process with clear treatment goals. The group serves as both a source of support and an aid to the therapeutic process, by allowing several people with a common problem to listen, discuss, and criticize one another. The interactions among participants become as much a part of the treatment as people's individual comments. These relationships become real-life contexts in which the various issues play out in front of the group. The presence of other people with the same problem also helps remove feelings of isolation. Groups can be very structured, as are groups that offer training in learning to overcome social anxiety disorder and groups that use CBT to treat eating disorders.

Groups can offer less structured therapeutic contexts as well. **Support groups** are meetings of people who share a common situation, be it a disorder, a disease, or coping with an ill family member. They meet regularly to share experiences, usually without programmatic treatment goals. They usually have a facilitator, a regular meeting time, and an open format. Support groups offer a sense of community, a forum for information exchange, and a place to share feelings for people who may have felt isolated by their situation. Support groups are widely available for people with all types of psychological disorders, as well as those living with chronic illnesses, such as diabetes and cancer.

Groups can be categorized in terms of their focus, such as eating disorders, substance abuse, treatment of OCD, or coping with bereavement and may be time-limited or ongoing. Time-limited groups run for a set number of sessions, tend to follow a program of treatment, and usually do not add members after the first few meetings. Ongoing groups, in contrast, welcome new members as they appear. Alcoholics Anonymous and other substance abuse groups that follow AA's 12-step approach are examples of ongoing groups. Also in this category are "life support groups" offered by churches, where people who are coping with, say, a spouse with a brain tumor or a son with major depressive disorder can meet and share their feelings about what they are going through.

Psychological treatments have been used not only to alleviate psychological disorders but also to help prevent the development of such disorders. Given the difficulties in treating many psychological disorders and the costs to individuals and society of the large numbers of people suffering from such conditions, prevention programs are an increasing area of effort in psychology and medicine (see the "Preventing Disorders" section later in this chapter). Figure 16.8 summarizes the psychotherapies that we have discussed in this section. It lists what each therapy addresses as the causes of a disorder, as well as the therapy's treatment goals and techniques.

Therapy	Cause of problem	Goal of therapy	Techniques
Psychodynamic	Disorders are symptoms of unconscious and repressed thoughts, feelings, and motives.	Work to uncover repressed and unconscious thoughts, feelings, and motives (defense mechanisms).	Dream interpretation, free association, transference; Catharsis
Humanistic	Conditions are blocking personal growth.	Create conditions for optimal growth.	Unconditional positive regard, empathic listening
Behavioral	Maladaptive behavior has been reinforced and rewarded.	Change reinforcers and rewards to change maladaptive behavior.	Classical and operant conditioning; token economies; systematic desensitization
Cognitive	Irrational thoughts lead to disordered behaviors.	Change emotions/irrational thoughts.	Critical questioning (Socratic method)
Cognitive–behavioral	Maladaptive behaviors have been reinforced and irrational thoughts have developed.	Change thoughts and behavior.	Restructure thoughts and offer incentives for acquiring more adaptive thoughts and behaviors; reappraisal
Group	Being isolated and unsupported makes disorders worse.	Facilitate support groups and sense of community so person realizes he or she is not alone.	Support groups; 12-step programs

FIGURE **16.8**
CAUSES, GOALS, AND TECHNIQUES OF PSYCHOLOGICAL THERAPIES.
Each major psychological perspective has its own theory of what causes psychological disorders, as well as distinct goals and techniques of treatment.

Effectiveness of Psychological Treatments

An increasingly prevalent view is that we need to make treatment choices based on the empirical evidence of their efficacy—that is, they need to be **evidence-based therapies** (APA Presidential Task Force, 2006). Yet very little research has addressed the issue of which psychotherapies work best for various disorders. Years ago, a review of the literature on the effectiveness of various types of psychotherapies showed that people who received any kind of therapy were better off on a number of outcomes relevant to mental status than most people who did not receive therapy (M. Smith & Glass, 1977). The study revealed no significant differences between behavioral therapies and psychodynamic ones. Current meta-analyses of the effectiveness of psychotherapy continue to show that most forms of therapy are effective and few significant differences exist in effectiveness among general psychotherapy, cognitive–behavioral therapy, and psychodynamic therapy (Shedler, 2010). This conclusion is sometimes referred to as the **dodo bird verdict,** after the dodo bird in Alice in Wonderland (Luborsky, Singer, & Luborsky, 1975). The dodo bird proclaims, "everybody has won, and must have prizes." The idea is that psychotherapy tends to work, but which kind of therapy one has appears not to matter too much.

However, this assessment does not mean there are no differences at all in effectiveness. In some cases, the usefulness of psychotherapy depends on the nature of the disorder being treated and the state of the patient's mental health. Some conditions are more responsive to psychological intervention than others. Personality disorders are best helped with psychodynamic psychotherapy (Shedler, 2010), phobias with behavioral therapy (Tryon, 2005), and schizophrenia with drug therapy (Javitt & Coyle, 2004).

For instance, people with schizophrenia experience such disordered thinking that it may be very difficult to teach them to work with their feelings and thoughts in order to change their behavior. That said, long-term group therapy appears to improve the basic life skills of people with schizophrenia (Sigman & Hassan, 2006).

People experiencing mood disorders are much more responsive to psychological approaches than are people suffering from schizophrenic disorders. But the approach needs to be matched up carefully with the disorder. Systematic desensitization, for example, is quite effective for treating a simple phobia but is inappropriate for treating depression. Length of treatment matters as well. As therapy continues, effectiveness declines (Howard et al., 1986; Kopta, 2003). Perhaps the potency of a psychological treatment begins to wear out after a certain point, or maybe only the harder-to-treat cases stay in therapy longer (Barkham et al., 2006).

Effective psychotherapy changes the brain without drugs.

Cognitive therapy and cognitive–behavioral therapy have shown perhaps the greatest effectiveness of any form of psychotherapy for treating various psychological disorders, but they are especially effective for certain cases of depression and anxiety disorders (Kehle, 2008; Tolin, 2010; Venning et al., 2009). Recent data suggest that cognitive therapy is as effective as antidepressants in treating severe depression (Hollon et al., 2005). In one study, depicted in the Research Process for this chapter (Figure 16.9), experimental groups of individuals diagnosed with depression received either cognitive therapy or drug therapy while a control group was treated with a placebo. Cognitive therapy was as effective as drug therapy in treating depression, with fewer risks (DeRubeis et al., 2005). In the treatment of obsessive–compulsive disorder, CBT slows metabolism

Research Process

1 Research Question

Is cognitive therapy as effective as the more expensive anti-depressant medication in treating people with depression?

2 Method

Two hundred forty patients with moderate to serious depression participated in a 16-week experimental study. Half of them were randomly assigned to the anti-depressant medication condition, and the other half were randomly assigned to either the cognitive therapy or placebo pill condition. The medication group received Paxil (paroxetine) for 16 weeks and no psychotherapy. The cognitive therapy group received individualized cognitive psychotherapy on a regular basis for 16 weeks. Those in the placebo pill condition received the placebo for 8 weeks and Paxil for the final 8 weeks.

Depression scores were measured twice a week for all 16 weeks using a standard depression questionnaire, the Hamilton Depression Rating Scale. A score of 12 and above is representative of depression. Participants had to have initial scores of 20 or higher to be included in the study.

3 Results

The criterion for the absence of depression was a score lower than 12 on the Hamilton Depression Rating Scale. After 8 weeks, 50% of the medication group, 43% of the cognitive therapy group, and 25% of the placebo group were no longer depressed, as the graph shows. After 16 weeks, 58% of both the medication and cognitive therapy groups were no longer depressed.

4 Conclusion

After 16 weeks of treatment, cognitive therapy and drug therapy had been equally effective in treating depression, and both were superior to a placebo condition.

FIGURE 16.9

COMPARING COGNITIVE THERAPY AND DRUG THERAPY IN TREATMENT OF DEPRESSION.
A controlled experiment shows that cognitive therapy can be as effective as medications in treating major depression without the possible side effects of medication. In practice, cognitive therapy and drug therapy are often combined effectively to treat depression. Source: "Cognitive Therapy vs Medications in the Treatment of Moderate to Severe Depression," by R. J. DeRubeis, S. Hollon, J. Amsterdam, R. Shelton, P. Young, R. Salomon ... R. Gallop, 2005, *Archives of General Psychiatry, 62,* 409–416.

in the caudate nucleus, an area of the brain that is overactive in people suffering from this disorder (Linden, 2006). In short, psychotherapy can change the brain.

Behavioral treatments such as systematic desensitization, are very effective for treatment of certain anxiety disorders, especially simple phobias, including performance anxiety and public speaking (Lazarus & Abramovitz, 2004; Tryon, 2005). In vivo exposure appears to offer the most effective treatment of simple phobias such as snake phobia, but people are more likely to drop out of such therapies than are people undergoing other forms of systematic desensitization (Buchanan & Houlihan, 2008; Choy, Fyer, & Lipsitz, 2007).

Quick Quiz 16.2: Psychological Treatments

1. José's therapist asks to hear about José's week. José tells him about some difficulty he is having with his wife and how he feels worthless in his marriage. The therapist expresses his empathy and understanding. He tells José he knows what it feels like to feel worthless and how uncomfortable that feeling is. What therapeutic approach is José's therapist taking?
   a. humanistic
   b. cognitive–behavioral
   c. cognitive
   d. psychodynamic

2. Which of the following methods is widely used for effective treatment of simple phobias?
   a. implosion therapy or flooding
   b. token economies
   c. client-centered therapy
   d. systematic desensitization

3. Often therapists integrate cognitive techniques for restructuring irrational thoughts with behavioral techniques to shape desirable behaviors in what is known as cognitive–
   a. behavioral therapy
   b. humanistic therapy
   c. psychodynamic therapy
   d. behavior modification

4. What is the safest and best form of treatment for depression?
   a. Paxil
   b. prevention
   c. group therapy
   d. cognitive therapy

Answers can be found at the end of the chapter.

TECHNOLOGY-BASED TREATMENTS FOR PSYCHOLOGICAL DISORDERS

technology-based therapy category of therapy that makes use of technology or the Internet to complement current therapies or make psychotherapeutic techniques available to more people.

A number of new therapies make use of technology or the Internet to complement current therapies or make psychotherapeutic techniques available to people who might otherwise not have access to therapy or seek it out. These are the **technology-based therapies.**

In **virtual reality therapies,** virtual (digital simulation) environments create therapeutic situations that might be hard to create otherwise. For instance, virtual reality therapy has been used for treatment of phobias such as fear of flying (as we saw in the section on desensitization) or PTSD by re-creating a traumatic situation (McLay et al., 2010; Ready et al., 2010; Riva, 2009). Both of these situations would be either costly or nearly impossible to replicate in real-life therapy (Cukor et al., 2009).

The Internet can be used as an online therapeutic environment as well. The virtual world known as Second Life provides a place for people to meet, interact, and develop a social milieu. Second Life, an online program that has been downloaded by 15 million users around the world, is a virtual environment where people interact in real time with others. It is mostly used recreationally,

virtual reality therapies category of therapies that use virtual (digital simulation) environments to create therapeutic situations that would be hard to create otherwise.

but increasingly commercially and therapeutically (Lisetti et al., 2009). Therapeutically, participants include patients and therapists, each of whom has an avatar (hence the name *avatar therapy*). Both people can talk through a headset to give their avatar a voice, or they can chat by text written on screen. Each participant can walk, fly, travel to different locations, and manipulate his or her own facial expressions and body language. As with other online games, participants encounter other avatars and interact with them.

Effectiveness of Technology-Based Therapy

James Herbert at Drexel University is studying the effectiveness of Second Life treatment for social anxiety disorder. His group offers CBT in Second Life, in 12 weekly sessions. The client (as avatar) meets with a therapist (as avatar) in a private, secure room. Clients learn new techniques and get opportunities to practice. Second Life offers people with social anxiety—who avoid therapy that requires them to get out of the house and go to a new environment—a "safe" form of psychotherapy, because they are not directly observed or exposed to ridicule and embarrassing situations. Research on the effectiveness of Second Life is still ongoing (Gorrindo & Groves, 2009; Ku et al., 2005; Yuen et al., 2009). Drawbacks to technology-based therapy, however, include its difficulty in ensuring confidentiality and in intervening if the patient becomes an immediate danger to him- or herself or to others.

Other digital therapeutic techniques make direct use of the Internet for both access to materials and creation of online environments in which treatment can occur. Titov and colleagues (2010), for example, administered treatment programs (e.g., CBT) online to people with a variety of anxiety disorders. Evidence indicates that electronic distribution can work effectively for certain anxiety symptoms, including measures of panic disorder (Wims et al., 2010).

COMBINED APPROACHES

Some integrative approaches combine different types of psychotherapy or combine nontraditional practices with traditional approaches. Sometimes the optimal treatment for a psychological disorder may be to combine drugs with psychotherapy. We will look at several combined approaches: drugs and psychotherapy, integrative psychotherapy, and mindfulness training and psychotherapy.

Drugs and Psychotherapy

Given the dynamic interplay between biological and psychological influences in many psychological disorders, combined treatments might work better than either alone (Ganasen, Ipser, & Stein, 2010). The drugs can modify some of the debilitating effects of a disorder enough so that the patients can function sufficiently well to learn techniques that might help in changing their problematic thinking and behavior. This approach works best for mood and anxiety disorders, in which thinking is not severely impaired. For example, CBT combined with drugs has been used most effectively to manage depression. The drugs help manage the depressive state, and the CBT helps clients recognize and control the thought patterns that may push them into depressive states (Cuijpers et al., 2010; J. D. Teasdale et al., 2000).

Nature & Nurture

Treatments that combine biological and psychotherapeutic approaches are often more effective than those based on a single approach.

Integrative Therapies

Some therapists take an *eclectic* approach to psychotherapy, which means that they draw on numerous techniques in their work with clients. These clinicians are typically trained in many methods and use those that seem most appropriate given the situation. They are not loyal to any particular orientation or treatment, but rather draw on those that seem most appropriate given the situation. This approach is known as **integrative therapy** (Norcross, Bike, & Evans, 2009; Prochaska & Norcross, 2007). For example, a client may show symptoms of simple phobia, which would argue for a behavioral therapy, but may also suffer from depression, which would best be treated by cognitive techniques. Problems of self-esteem might best be treated with a humanistic approach.

The vast majority of clinical psychologists practicing in the United States today say they take an integrative-eclectic approach to treating disorders (Norcross et al., 2009; Norcross, Karpiak, & Lister, 2005). These practitioners share the experience that no one therapeutic approach is effective for all psychological disorders.

Prolonged exposure therapy is an integrative treatment program for people who have post-traumatic stress disorder (PTSD) (Foa et al., 2005; Powers et al., 2010). It combines CBT with the imagined exposure form of systematic desensitization and relaxation. For clients with PTSD, this involves a course of individual therapy in which clients directly process traumatic events and thus reduce trauma-induced psychological disturbances. So a person with combat-related PTSD might revisit traumatic war scenes (such as the death of a compatriot) in her mind and also engage in cognitive approaches with the therapist to reduce irrational thinking about her role in that event (she could not have saved him). This technique has been used effectively for the treatment of combat- and rape-related PTSD (Cahill et al., 2006; Foa et al., 1999, 2005; Nacash et al., 2007; Powers et al., 2010). Sometimes drugs prescribed for anxiety disorders are used in combination with prolonged exposure therapy to treat PTSD (Rothbaum et al., 2006).

integrative therapy
an eclectic approach in which the therapist draws on different treatment approaches and uses those that seem most appropriate for the situation.

Mindfulness Training and Psychotherapy

Some newer therapies integrate the nontraditional practice of mindfulness meditation with psychotherapeutic techniques to treat psychological disorders (Chiesa, Brambilla, & Serretti, 2010; Farb et al., 2010). In mindfulness meditation, the meditator is trained to calm the body and the mind and notice the thoughts or feelings that might draw one's attention, without getting pulled around by them, without clinging to them. These skills help people keep thoughts or emotions in perspective. We will explore two combined approaches in this vein: mindfulness-based cognitive therapy and dialectical behavior therapy.

John Teasdale and his colleagues applied mindfulness meditation to the treatment of major depressive disorder (Segal, Williams, & Teasdale, 2002; Teasdale et al., 2000). Their approach combines elements of CBT with mindfulness meditation to create a treatment known as **mindfulness-based cognitive therapy (MBCT).** Both mindfulness meditation and cognitive therapy involve restructuring

Connection

Mindfulness meditation practices help people become aware of everything that occurs in the mind and recognize it for what it is: a thought, an emotion, or a sensation that will arise and dissipate.

See "Meditation and Conscious Experience," Chapter 6, "Consciousness," p. 236.

mindfulness-based cognitive therapy (MBCT)
an approach that combines elements of CBT with mindfulness meditation to help people with depression learn to recognize and restructure negative thought patterns.

Nature & Nurture

By restructuring thoughts, MBCT actually restructures synaptic connections involved in learning, memory, and emotion. Meditation restructures the brain.

one's thoughts. Standard cognitive therapy helps depressed people recognize their depressogenic thought patterns and has been very effective in reducing relapse when administered during depressive episodes. Mindfulness meditation develops skills for approaching thoughts nonjudgmentally and enhances people's ability to realize that they are neither bound by their thoughts nor defined by them.

To the extent that depression stems from recursive "negative" thought patterns in which the person becomes caught in a feedback loop that is reinforced by repeated episodes of depression, mindfulness meditation might help the patient break out of these loops (Farb et al., 2010; J. D. Teasdale et al., 1995).

Meditation-based therapies have been used with some success in the treatment of both positive and negative symptoms of schizophrenia. A general goal in mindfulness meditation is for a person to gain perspective on one's own thoughts and feelings and, ultimately, change one's relationships with them. A person with schizophrenia has the choice of accepting hallucinations as real or learning to live with them, while acknowledging that they are not real. The most common treatment for the positive symptoms of schizophrenia is to try to reduce hallucinations (usually voices) by the use of tranquilizers that ultimately sedate the mind. The downside of such treatment is cognitive dulling—lots of unpleasant side effects. As a result, many people choose not to take their drugs.

But what if people with schizophrenia could learn to live more easily with these symptoms and not be defined and utterly controlled by them? A new approach in the treatment of schizophrenic symptoms focuses on changing the relationship with the voices rather than trying to make them go away. Mindfulness training for schizophrenia takes this novel approach.

A regular regimen of several brief sessions of mindfulness meditation may help people with schizophrenia keep their "voices" or auditory hallucinations in perspective and not believe them to be real. Initial controlled and case studies indicate that people with schizophrenia experience less distress and improved functioning after such training (Chadwick et al., 2009; Taylor, Harper, & Chadwick, 2009). Another type of meditation (loving-kindness meditation, which helps cultivate a sense of caring for self and others) may offer promise in the treatment of negative symptoms of schizophrenia (Johnson et al., 2009).

dialectical behavior therapy (DBT) treatment that integrates elements of CBT with exercises aimed at developing mindfulness without meditation and is used to treat borderline personality disorders.

Another combined treatment involving mindfulness is **dialectical behavior therapy (DBT),** a program developed for the treatment of borderline personality disorder (Linehan, 1993). DBT integrates elements of CBT with exercises aimed at developing mindfulness without meditation. The training, which involves individual as well as group therapy, is designed to help clients develop a nonjudgmental attitude toward their emotions and to accept their current behavior. These skills and attitudes form the cornerstone of personality change, enabling the patient to learn how to regulate his or her own emotions (Linehan et al., 1991).

Effectiveness of Combined Approaches

In spite of the logic for combining drugs with cognitive–behavioral therapy for both the treatment and the prevention of depression (Nolen-Hoeksema, 2007), few studies have systematically examined the relative benefits of drugs, psychotherapy, and the combination of the two. However, a 14-month study of mental health in more than 500 children examined the relative effectiveness of medication, behavioral treatment, and the combination of the two approaches in treating a variety of disorders. For ADHD, for example, the combination of drugs and behavioral therapy was superior to behavioral intervention and better than medication alone for most outcome measures (Edwards, 2002). Other research has reported that combining psychosocial intervention with atypical antipsychotic medication effectively reduces relapse rates and increases general functioning in those suffering from schizophrenia for up to 12 months after treatment (Kim et al., 2008).

Clinical research shows that prolonged exposure therapy (an integrative CBT approach) is effective, substantially reducing symptoms of PTSD over extended periods of up to 18 months after treatment is complete (Foa et al., 1999). Also, prolonged exposure therapy shows substantial benefits compared to no therapy, supportive counseling, and other procedures designed to reduce stress, although it has still not been widely adopted by clinicians (Cahill et al., 2006).

The advantage of mindfulness-based cognitive therapy compared with standard cognitive therapy is that it works when the person is in a nondepressive state, and so it might help prevent relapse. One study shows that MBCT can prevent relapse in people who have had at least three previous depressive episodes. All participants had recently completed successful drug therapy for their most recent bout of depression. They were then randomly assigned to participate in MBCT or to continue with the treatment they otherwise would have received (treatment as usual), which included seeking help from other sources, such as family or doctor (Segal, Williams, & Teasdale, 2002). Figure 16.10 shows that those who practiced MBCT relapsed into depression only about half as often as those who received treatment as usual (J. D. Teasdale et al., 2000).

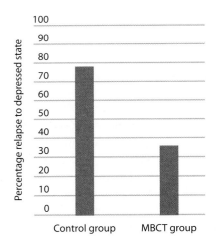

FIGURE **16.10**

EFFECTIVENESS OF MINDFULNESS-BASED COGNITIVE THERAPY (MBCT) FOR DEPRESSION. When people with depression were treated with mindfulness-based cognitive therapy, they were much less likely to experience a relapse compared to a comparison group of people with depression who received treatment as usual. (Source: Teasdale et al., 2000)

Borderline personality disorder has long been considered nearly untreatable, but dialectical behavior therapy became the first treatment effective in reducing the symptoms of this disorder (Soler et al., 2009). DBT reduces self-inflicted harmful behaviors, lowers scores on depression questionnaires, decreases dysfunctional patterns associated with substance abuse, and increases the likelihood of staying in treatment (Koerner & Linehan, 2000; Kröger et al., 2006; Linehan, Heard, & Armstrong, 1993). Most important, DBT reduces the risk of suicide attempts—the most disastrous risk associated with borderline personality disorder—much more than does nonbehavioral psychotherapy (Linehan et al., 2006). Not only is DBT effective in treating borderline personality disorder, but it has also been adapted to treat eating disorders, conduct disorders, and domestic violence (Kristeller, Baer, & Quillian-Wolever, 2006; Nelson-Gray et al., 2006; Rathus, Cavuoto, & Passarelli, 2006).

Quick Quiz 16.3: Combined Approaches

1. Dr. Feelgood believes that different disorders require different techniques and strategies for treatment. She is most likely a practitioner of
   a. psychoanalysis
   b. positive psychotherapy
   c. mindfulness meditation
   d. integrative therapy

2. Combining drugs with psychotherapy works well for which of the following disorders?
   a. mood disorders
   b. anxiety disorders
   c. both a and b
   d. neither a nor b

3. Dialectical behavior therapy (DBT) is a combined treatment program developed for the treatment of
   a. schizophrenia
   b. borderline personality disorder
   c. bipolar disorder
   d. panic disorder

Answers can be found at the end of the chapter.

Research to **Real Life**

Behavioral and cognitive therapies rely on recognizing certain patterns and implementing a program (reinforcement, etc.) to try to change that pattern. It is very difficult to change behavior. Therapists set up such schedules and exercises to help people stop maladaptive behaviors. Do you have a habit—however minor—that you would like to change? For example:

- Nail biting
- Hair twisting
- Too much snacking
- Smoking
- Too much diet soda
- Too much Internet/texting

Connecting Psychology to Your Life: Consider an experiment in trying to change that habit. Let's say, for example, your problem habit is nail biting.

First: Attend to it. See if you can notice

- how often you do it
- the situations in which you do it
- the feelings/emotions immediately before, during, and after you bite your nails

Second: Try setting up a system of reinforcement for not biting your nails (with a modest goal, such as reducing the number of times per day you do it, rather than trying to eliminate it altogether). For instance, if I can get through this chapter without biting my nails, then I get to do _____ (fill in the blank: take a coffee break, take a walk, go on Facebook, etc.).

Third: Keep a record of how often you follow your own advice. Pay attention to what you do, notice the thoughts and feelings associated with the behavior, and set up environmental contingencies (e.g., your reward for the desired behavior), which can all be important components in changing unwanted habits and behaviors.

How to Choose a Therapist

Nearly 50% of the adult population at some point in their life will suffer from some form of psychological disorder, whether it is a simple phobia, depression, anxiety, schizophrenia, or something else (Kessler et al., 2005). But only a subset of those who need therapy seek it out or receive it (*Mental health*, 2001). Why? One reason has to do with the stigma of "seeing a shrink"—many people do not want their friends, family, or coworkers and bosses to know they are seeing a therapist. There is a stigma attached to the need for mental health treatment (*Mental health*, 2001). Moreover, people often think they have friends and family who can help them, so they don't need a therapist. In fact, therapists are trained professionals who have more knowledge, understanding, and training to deal with a whole range of mental health concerns than family and friends. These two forms of help, of course, are not mutually exclusive and in fact should both be sought in unison.

Indeed, research on the effectiveness of treatment shows consistently that treatment is better than no treatment. Treatment usually works. Suppose that you or a friend or family member is showing signs of difficulty coping or adjusting and would like to find a good therapist? How would you go about doing that?

First, you need to understand the different types of therapists and what they can and cannot do. As we briefly described in Chapter 1, most therapists fall into the following five groups:

- **Psychiatrists** are medical doctors who specialized in psychiatry. They are typically the only therapists who can prescribe medications. They often treat the most severe psychological disorders.

- **Clinical psychologists** are trained to help people with moderate to severe psychological disorders that interfere with everyday functioning. They assess, diagnose, and treat people with disorders. They are often trained in PhD (doctorate of philosophy) programs, but also in PsyD programs (doctorate of psychology). Clinical psychologists often focus on past experiences as the causes of current problems.

- **Counselors** work in social settings and help people adjust to normal work- and family-related difficulties. They focus on the present rather than the past. Counselors are often trained in education departments and receive either a doctorate of education (EdD) or a master's degree in counseling.

- **Social workers** have a master's degree in social work (MSW) and also are trained in clinical practice. Once they pass the licensing exam, they are licensed clinical social workers (LCSW).

- **Marriage and family therapists (MFT)** are people who receive a master's degree in clinical psychology; they have many hours of supervised training and pass

PREVENTING DISORDERS

The best and safest form of treatment for psychological disorders is prevention. *Prevention* focuses on identifying risk factors for disorders, targeting at-risk populations, and offering training programs that decrease the likelihood that disorders will occur. Many prevention efforts are underway in this country, but the majority focus on the prevention of depression, the number one mental health concern in the United States (Kessler et al., 2005).

Just as a healthy diet and exercise program can help prevent heart disease, certain behaviors or coping skills may help stave off depression and other psychological disorders. Prevention programs train people to behave in ways that make depression less likely to develop. Preventing depression in at-risk groups, the licensing exam. As the name implies, MFTs specialize in helping couples and families deal with conflict or difficulties.

A therapist's experience is important (Saisan, Smith, & Segal, 2010). You should look for someone who is trained and has experience in the particular area in which you are having difficulty. For instance, if you are experiencing obsessive–compulsive disorder, ideally your therapist would have experience helping people with this disorder.

Note that each of these specialists is not qualified to practice therapy just because they earned their primary degree (e.g., MD, PhD, PsyD, MSW). In addition, they must undergo up to 1,500 hours of supervised training and pass a licensing exam before they can practice therapy. Therefore, at a minimum you want to make sure the therapist you are considering is licensed and in good standing. Each state has a regulatory board that can tell you whether complaints have been filed against the therapist. Some regulatory websites are dedicated to particular kinds of therapists, such as MFTs (see, for example, http://www.amftrb.org/).

In finding a therapist, trusting your gut feeling is important. Relationships with therapists, after all, *are* relationships. Some work and some do not. You have to feel comfortable with and trustful of your therapist. You should feel comfortable with setting up a trial period of perhaps five or six sessions and then determining whether you want to continue or not. All good therapists will respect your decision to go elsewhere if therapy is not working for you and won't try to make you feel guilty or try to convince you to stay. If they do, that is a red flag (Saisan, Smith, & Segal, 2010).

The approach and orientation of the therapist may matter to you. Some approaches are very short-term and targeted, and others are very long-term and general. You have to decide which is right for you. Two of the more common approaches are cognitive–behavioral therapy (CBT) and psychoanalytic/psychodynamic. Most therapists will take an eclectic or integrative approach, even if they were trained in a particular orientation. Even those trained in a particular orientation, such as psychodynamic or cognitive–behavioral, may sometimes use techniques from different orientations if they feel that they will work best for a particular person.

Finally, once you make all of these decisions, you still need to find therapists who fit your needs. The most common resources for assisting in finding a therapist are your family doctors, family and friends, providers listed by your insurance plan, and mental health associations. So ask a doctor or a friend when you are beginning to search for a therapist. Get advice from multiple sources and see whether there is any overlap.

for instance, has decreased the onset of depression by as much as 25% (Beekman et al., 2010). This rate compares well to the success rate for those who receive therapy. Many prevention programs focus on children, because interventions earlier in life increase the likelihood of making a difference. Also, teen depression is a growing problem and the major cause of suicide in young people (Wessely & Kerwin, 2004).

Van Voorhees and colleagues (2008) conducted a large-scale study of risk factors for adolescent depression. They conducted face-to-face interviews of teens in grades 7–12 in the home, obtained parent surveys, and measured depressive symptoms using a questionnaire. Several characteristics put teens at risk for a depressive episode: being female, being of a non-White race–ethnicity, having low-income status, being in poor health, and experiencing parental conflict. Teens who felt a connection among family members, warmth from their parents, and peer acceptance; who did better in school; and who participated in religious activities were less likely to have a depressive episode than others (Van Voorhees et al., 2008). Research on elementary school children reports similar findings (Dallaire et al., 2008). A recent meta-analysis of more than 30 different intervention programs aimed at preventing depression in teens found that shorter interventions and those that involved homework were most effective (Stice et al., 2009).

In addition to poverty and unemployment, psychosocial factors increase the risk of depression, especially life stress and having a pessimistic outlook on life (Southwick, Vythilingam, & Charney, 2005). For this reason, some intervention programs for teens focus on teaching them skills for dealing with stress, including developing a more optimistic outlook. One after-school program for teens at risk for developing depression is based on CBT. Participants had already experienced mild to moderate symptoms of the disorder. This program involved retraining in ways of thinking about adversity in life. Compared to those who did not receive the training, those who had the training were significantly less likely to become clinically depressed 18 months later (Clarke et al., 1995).

Another program, the Penn Resiliency Program (PRP), is designed to prevent depression and other psychological disorders by teaching resilience and skills for coping with stress, problem solving (flexibility in the face of adverse or challenging circumstances), and cognitive restructuring (learning to change one's perspective on events). In a meta-analysis of 17 interventions on nearly 2,500 teenagers, PRP participants reported fewer depressive symptoms at postintervention and both follow-up assessments compared with youths receiving no intervention (Brunwasser, Gillham, & Kim, 2009). More specifically, in a large-scale study of 697 middle

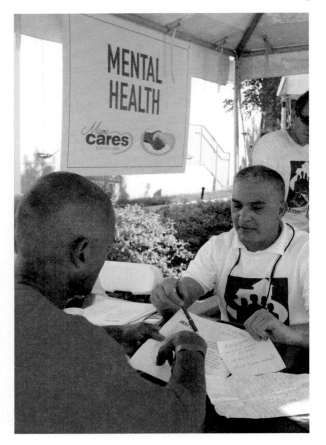

school children, the PRP was administered in weekly 90-minute sessions over a 12-week period (Gillham et al., 2007). PRP significantly reduced depressive symptoms at follow-up compared to a control group and to another intervention, which was not aimed at resiliency, in two of the three schools. In a similar prevention program, students were assigned to a control group or to an 8-week training program, which consisted of a weekly, 90-minute workshop based on PRP. The group in the training program reported significantly fewer symptoms of anxiety and depression and significantly greater well-being than the control group. There were no differences between groups on depressive episodes 6 months later, however (Seligman, Schulman, & Tryon, 2007).

What is notable is that, compared to the control group, the students in the workshop group increased their ability to achieve an optimistic outlook (Seligman et al., 2007). This is a crucial skill, because depressive thinking is characterized by a tendency to see the negative in any given situation. For example, if a glass is filled halfway, someone who is thinking negatively sees the glass as half empty. So helping people to look at things differently, in this case seeing the glass as half full, should help prevent the relapse into depression (J. D. Teasdale et al., 2000). Outlooks ingrained early in life ought to help prevent a lifetime of depression.

Bringing It All Together
Making Connections in the Treatment of Psychological Disorders
Approaches to the Treatment of Anxiety Disorders

The anxiety disorders are a diverse group of conditions, and although they share the core symptoms of fear and anxiety, they differ in many ways. Because they are so diverse, mental health practitioners employ a wide variety of treatment strategies to help people with these disorders. Because of this diversity in symptoms and treatment, the anxiety disorders offer a useful context in which to illustrate the application of treatments discussed in this chapter.

Drug Therapies

Drug therapies play a major role in the management and treatment of anxiety disorders. The main categories of medications used for anxiety disorders include the antidepressants and the antianxiety drugs.

Antidepressants

Many doctors prescribe SSRIs for the treatment of anxiety disorders, especially for OCD, social phobia, post-traumatic stress disorder (PTSD), and panic disorder. People who take SSRIs for anxiety disorders report that these medications help them avoid getting caught up in certain thoughts that otherwise would snowball into anxiety. These drugs appear to help people disengage from the repetitive cycle of anxiety-provoking thoughts or simply not care as much about such thoughts. As a result, the SSRIs have been helpful to people with OCD and may aid in changing patterns of thinking when combined with the thought restructuring produced by CBT. As mentioned earlier, the drugs help loosen the grip of anxious thinking, allowing the patient to apply cognitive techniques to learn how to think differently. Recent findings that people with OCD who take SSRIs often relapse suggest that combining these drugs with psychological treatments might be more effective than the drugs alone (Catapano et al., 2006). The SSRIs are also considered the first line of treatment for generalized anxiety disorder (Baldwin & Polkinghorn, 2005).

Other antidepressants are prescribed for anxiety disorders, but much less often. Most tricyclic antidepressants apparently do not work for people with OCD, for example, but do work for other anxiety disorders. One tricyclic, CMI, however, is most effective on norepinephrine synapses and actually reduces symptoms of OCD. Because tricyclics have numerous side effects, medical professionals tend to prescribe SSRIs instead (Bleier, Habib, & Flament, 2006).

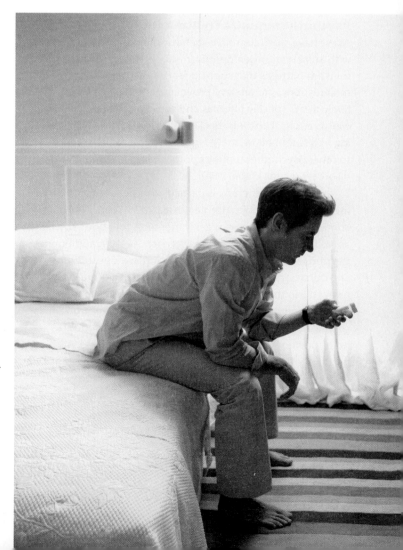

Antianxiety Medications

Drugs that soothe the agitation of anxiety are used to treat anxiety disorders, especially for people who suffer from panic attacks. Occasionally physicians prescribe beta-blockers—drugs that block the action of neurotransmitters such as norepinephrine—to quickly calm the aroused sympathetic nervous system. One such drug is propanolol, which is often used to treat high blood pressure and other cardiovascular conditions. These medications calm the physiological symptoms of anxiety by bringing down heart rate, blood pressure, and rate of breathing. The benzodiazepines (for example, Valium) also calm the physiological arousal caused by anxiety and are widely prescribed for social phobias, panic disorder, and generalized anxiety disorder. They can also treat or prevent panic attacks in high-anxiety situations. Unfortunately, when regular users discontinue use of benzodiazepines, they experience withdrawal symptoms such as insomnia, tremors, increased anxiety, tachycardia (rapid heartbeat), and sweating. Hence, the benzodiazepines are best used only occasionally. Newer antianxiety medications, such as a drug used for generalized anxiety disorder known as buspirone, are less likely to create withdrawal symptoms, but they require longer continuous usage to be effective. The newer selective norepinephrine reuptake inhibitors, as well as SSRIs, are also used in the treatment of anxiety disorders (Dell' Osso et al., 2009).

Psychotherapeutic Treatments

As we have seen, cognitive–behavioral therapy helps people with anxiety disorder identify irrational thoughts and undo thinking patterns that support fear; it also helps them modify their responses to anxiety-provoking situations. CBT effectively treats specific phobias and social phobias in children as well as adults (Hirshfeld-Becker et al., 2010). In fact, according to a recent meta-analysis, CBT appears to be superior to other psychotherapeutic approaches in treating anxiety disorders overall (Tolin, 2010).

Group CBT therapy is particularly effective for the treatment of social phobia (Hofman et al., 2006; Tolin, 2010). Such contexts usually involve weekly meetings for about 12 weeks, as well as homework assignments each week. In addition to the normal benefits of CBT for reducing anxious thoughts and behaviors, the social factors involved in a group play a key role in the therapy's effectiveness. The group offers social support: All the participants have gone through similar situations and can share their experiences. This support helps prevent feelings of isolation and helplessness. Also, group members provide examples of success. For instance, if someone in a social phobia group managed to go to a deli, order a sandwich, and pay the cashier (simple social transactions) and it went well, this provides an example that it really can be done. Other group members might be inspired to try it themselves. Avatar therapy, with virtual reality group

CBT, is now being used to treat social anxiety disorder as well (Riva, 2009).

Traditional psychodynamic therapies for anxiety disorders viewed anxiety as the main symptom of what was then commonly called neurosis. Neuroses, according to Freud, most often stemmed from repressed thoughts, feelings, and impulses that usually originated in childhood experiences. Therefore, the main approach to treatment is to uncover the unconscious thoughts, feelings, and impulses that lead to neurotic symptoms. Most commonly, this is achieved through dream interpretation, free associations, uncovering defense mechanisms, and catharsis. Relieving neurotic symptoms requires insight, and insight requires emotional release of repressed feelings.

We have already discussed the use of systematic desensitization for the treatment of specific phobias. This process couples relaxation training with gradual exposure to the feared object and is very effective for the treatment of specific phobias such as fears of animals, flying, and heights (Aitken & Benson, 1984; Wiederhold & Wiederhold, 2005).

Combined and Integrative Therapies and Anxiety

As we have seen, sometimes medication can help people get "over the hump" of crippling symptoms so that a nondrug therapy has a chance to work. Such is the case with the combination of either antidepressants or antianxiety medications and CBT or systematic desensitization. Often the course of medication treatment is short term, until the psychotherapeutic training begins to take effect. Alternatively, the medication may be decreased slowly during the course of psychological treatment.

Combining drug therapy and psychotherapy offers some real hope for treating anxiety disorders, in particular OCD. For example, in a review of the literature on children and teens who suffer from obsessive–compulsive disorder, Kaiser and Bouvard (2009) found that combining drug therapy with CBT was almost always as effective and sometimes more effective than either one alone at alleviating OCD symptoms. Although many people recommend combined therapies, a review of the treatment efficacy of combined therapies versus single therapy for anxiety disorders yielded little consistent evidence that combined therapy works better (Black, 2006). In fact, drug mechanisms in some cases may inhibit thought processes necessary to make a cognitive or behavioral therapy work, as may be the case with combined drug–exposure therapy for the treatment of anxiety disorders (Otto, McHugh, & Kantak, 2010).

There is evidence that integrative psychotherapeutic approaches offer potential relief from a range of anxiety disorders. As already noted, OCD may be treated with mindfulness meditation practices and cognitive therapy. Mindfulness-based cognitive therapy shows promise in the treatment of generalized anxiety disorder (D. L. Evans et al., 2008). Also, dialectical behavior therapy (DBT), which was developed to treat borderline personality disorder, has been used effectively to treat post-traumatic stress disorder (Wagner & Linehan, 2006).

Quick Quiz 16.4: Bringing It All Together: Making Connections in the Treatment of Psychological Disorders

1. These drugs appear to help people with OCD disengage from the repetitive cycle of anxiety-provoking thoughts:
   a. SSRIs
   b. MAO inhibitors
   c. benzodiazepines
   d. lithium salts

2. Group CBT therapy is very effective for the treatment of which anxiety disorder?
   a. generalized anxiety disorder
   b. social phobia
   c. panic disorder
   d. simple phobias

Answers can be found at the end of the chapter.

Chapter **Review**

BIOLOGICAL TREATMENTS FOR PSYCHOLOGICAL DISORDERS

- Both biological and psychological approaches are used to treat psychological disorders. Drugs are the most commonly used biological treatment.

- Many different drugs are used to treat depression. The older antidepressants include the monoamine oxidase (MAO) inhibitors and the tricyclic antidepressants. The selective serotonin reuptake inhibitors (SSRIs) reduce reuptake of serotonin at the synapse and create far fewer unpleasant side effects than the older antidepressants.

- Lithium is prescribed to stabilize the mania associated with bipolar disorder. Due to the toxicity of lithium, medical professionals often prescribe other drugs to regulate manic episodes.

- Drug therapies for schizophrenia include the traditional antipsychotics, which are rarely prescribed these days due to their adverse side effects, and the atypical antipsychotics. The atypical antipsychotics do not lead to tardive dyskinesia, and they are somewhat better at treating negative symptoms.

- Psychosurgery is brain surgery performed to treat psychological disorders. Prefrontal lobotomy was once used to reduce psychotic behavior, but it is now considered an outdated and cruel procedure.

- Electroconvulsive therapy (ECT) involves passing electrical current through the brain to induce a seizure. Because ECT can lead to memory loss, the only currently acceptable clinical application of ECT is for cases of severe depression that fail to respond to any other treatment.

- Helen Mayberg discovered what may be a neural switch for depression, known as Area 25. Deep brain stimulation of Area 25 can provide sudden relief from depression in people who have failed to respond to any other treatment.

- The SSRIs and tricyclics are equally effective in the treatment of depression. The SSRIs have the fewest adverse side effects, and seem to be tolerated better for long-term use.

- The evidence for lithium's effectiveness in treating bipolar disorder is weak in spite of its regular use for this purpose in the United States. It does not appear to be superior to less toxic anticonvulsants or antipsychotics in regulating manic episodes.

- Both traditional and atypical antipsychotic drugs work best on the positive symptoms of schizophrenia. Certain atypical antipsychotic drugs may relieve the negative symptoms.

- Although many patients report immediate relief with ECT, usually it is effective only as long as treatments are maintained. Also, the adverse effects of ECT on memory can be fairly severe.

PSYCHOLOGICAL TREATMENTS FOR PSYCHOLOGICAL DISORDERS

- Psychotherapy is the use of psychological techniques to modify maladaptive behaviors or thought patterns, or both, and develop insight into the patient's behavior.

- Psychodynamic therapies aim to uncover unconscious conflicts, motives, or other underlying psychological difficulties. Psychodynamic therapists use several techniques, such as free association, to access the unconscious.

- Humanistic therapy, such as client-centered therapy, helps clients realize their full potential. Therapists create an atmosphere in which clients can communicate their feelings with the certainty that they are being understood rather than judged.

- Behavior therapies apply the principles of conditioning to the treatment of disorders. Systematic desensitization, a widely used behavioral method, pairs relaxation with gradual exposure to a phobic object.

- Cognitive therapies work to restructure irrational thought patterns. Often therapists combine cognitive techniques for changing irrational thoughts with behavioral techniques to shape desirable behaviors in what is known as cognitive–behavioral therapy (CBT). CBT is a short-term psychological treatment that has been successfully applied to many disorders.

- Psychotherapy is more effective for certain disorders than for others. CBT may be the most effective form of psychotherapy, especially for certain cases of depression and anxiety disorders.

TECHNOLOGY-BASED TREATMENTS FOR PSYCHOLOGICAL DISORDERS

- A number of new therapies make use of technology or the Internet to complement current therapies or make psychotherapeutic techniques available to people who might otherwise not have access to it or seek it out.

- Virtual reality therapies, a subset of which is known as "avatar therapy," use virtual (digital simulation) environments that create therapeutic situations that might be hard to create otherwise.

COMBINED APPROACHES

- Combined treatments are increasingly common in practice. These include methods that combine drugs with psychotherapy or combine various forms of psychotherapy with each other. Mindfulness practices have also been added to traditional treatments.

- Many treatments, including CBT, are administered as group therapy. Group contexts serve both as a source of support and as an aid to the therapeutic process, allowing several people with similar problems to listen, discuss, and criticize one another.

- In some cases, the most effective treatments for many psychological disorders integrate one form of treatment with another.

PREVENTING DISORDERS

- Prevention focuses on identifying risk factors for disorders, targeting at-risk populations, and offering training programs that decrease the likelihood of disorders occurring.

- Many prevention efforts are underway in this country, but the majority focus on the prevention of depression, the number one mental health concern in the United States.

BRINGING IT ALL TOGETHER: MAKING CONNECTIONS IN THE TREATMENT OF PSYCHOLOGICAL DISORDERS

- The treatment of anxiety disorders illustrates how diverse approaches may be used to treat psychological disorders. Both psychological and biological therapies have been used, alone and together, to treat anxiety disorders.

Key **Terms**

atypical antipsychotics, p. 634

barbiturates, p. 633

behavior therapies, p. 644

benzodiazepines, p. 633

bupropione, p. 633

catharsis, p. 644

client-centered therapy, p. 644

cognitive–behavioral therapy, p. 648

cognitive therapy, p. 645

defense mechanisms, p. 644

dialectical behavior therapy (DBT), p. 655

dodo bird verdict, p. 650

electroconvulsive therapy (ECT), p. 636

evidence-based therapies, p. 650

flooding, p. 645

free association, p. 643

group therapy, p. 648

integrative therapy, p. 654

lithium, p. 633

mindfulness-based cognitive therapy (MBCT), p. 654

monoamine oxidase (MAO) inhibitors, p. 631

phenothiazines, p. 634

prefrontal lobotomy, p. 635

psychoanalytic therapy, p. 642

psychodynamic therapy, p. 643

psychotherapy, p. 642

repetitive transcranial magnetic stimulation, p. 637

repression, p. 644

selective serotonin reuptake inhibitors (SSRIs), p. 632

Quick Quiz **Answers**

Quick Quiz 16.1: 1. b   2. c   3. d   4. b   5. b
Quick Quiz 16.2: 1. a   2. d   3. a   4. b
Quick Quiz 16.3: 1. d   2. c   3. b
Quick Quiz 16.4: 1. a   2. b

Challenge Your Assumptions **Answers**

- Depression has been turned on "like a switch" in some people using deep brain stimulation. **True. See pp. 630 and 638–640.**
- Talk therapy might make people feel better, but it does not change the brain. **False. See p. 652.**
- People can learn to not be afraid of flying. **True. See p. 645.**
- Shock therapy is never effective and is no longer used. **False. See pp. 636–637.**

Glossary

absent-mindedness a form of forgetfulness that results from inattention.

absolute threshold the lowest intensity level of a stimulus a person can detect half of the time.

accommodation the process by which the muscles control the shape of the lens to adjust to viewing objects at different distances.

acetylcholine (ACh) a neurotransmitter that controls muscle movement and plays a role in mental processes such as learning, memory, attention, sleeping, and dreaming.

achievement motivation a desire to do things well and overcome obstacles.

acquired immunity immunity provided by antibodies produced in the body in response to specific antigens.

action potential the impulse of positive charge that runs down an axon.

adaptations inherited solutions to ancestral problems that have been selected for because they contribute in some way to reproductive success.

adaptive behavior adjustment to and coping with everyday life.

addiction condition that results from habitual use or physical and psychological dependence on a substance.

adolescence the transition period between childhood and adulthood.

adrenal glands endocrine structures that release hormones important in regulating the stress response and emotions.

adrenal-medullary system a major neuro-endocrine pathway stimulated during stress, in which the hypothalamus activates the sympathetic nervous system.

affective traits stable predispositions toward certain types of emotional responses.

afterimages visual images that remain after removal of or looking away from the stimulus.

aggression violent behavior that is intended to cause psychological or physical harm, or both, to another being.

agoraphobia an anxiety disorder involving fear of being in places from which escape

might be difficult or in which help might not be available should a panic attack occur.

AIM three biologically based dimensions of consciousness—activation, input, and mode.

alarm stage the phase of the general adaptation syndrome in which all of the body's resources respond to a perceived threat.

algorithms a step-by-step procedure or formula for solving a problem.

all-or-none principle the idea that once the threshold has been crossed, either an action potential fires or it does not.

alleles different forms of a gene.

allostasis process by which the body achieves stability through physiological change.

alpha waves pattern of brain activity when one is relaxed and drowsy; slower, higher-energy waves than beta waves.

altruism selfless attitudes and behavior toward others.

Alzheimer's disease a degenerative disease marked by progressive cognitive decline and characterized by a collection of symptoms, including confusion, memory loss, mood swings, and eventual loss of physical function.

amnesia memory loss due to brain injury or disease.

amygdala small, almond-shaped structure located directly in front of the hippocampus; has connections with many important brain regions and is important for processing emotional information, especially that related to fear.

anima according to Jung, the female part of the male personality.

animistic thinking belief that inanimate objects are alive.

animus according to Jung, the male part of the female personality.

anorexia nervosa an eating disorder in which people cannot maintain 85% of their ideal body weight for their height, have an intense fear of eating, and have a distorted body image.

antecedent event a situation that may lead to an emotional response.

anterograde amnesia the inability to remember events and experiences that occur after an injury or the onset of a disease.

antigen any foreign substance that triggers an immune response.

antisocial personality disorder dramatic–emotional personality disorder characterized by extremely impulsive, deceptive, violent, ruthless, and callous behaviors; a serious and potentially dangerous disorder.

aphasia deficit in the ability to speak or comprehend language.

appraisal the evaluation of a situation with respect to how relevant it is to one's own welfare; drives the process by which emotions are elicited.

arborization the growth and formation of new dendrites.

archetypes ancient or archaic images that result from common ancestral experiences.

Asperger's syndrome a childhood disorder at the high-functioning end of the autistic spectrum; characterized by impaired social interest and skills and restricted interests; intelligence is usually above average and language is not delayed or deficient.

association process by which two pieces of information from the environment are repeatedly linked so that we begin to connect them in our minds.

associative network a chain of associations between related concepts.

asylums facilities for treating the mentally ill in Europe during the Middle Ages and into the 19th century.

attachment the strong emotional connection that develops early in life between infants and their caregivers.

attention the limited capacity to process information that is under conscious control.

attention deficit hyperactivity disorder (ADHD) childhood disorder characterized by inability to focus attention for more than a few minutes, to remain still and quiet, to do careful work.

attitudes an individual's favorable or unfavorable beliefs, feelings, or actions toward an object, idea, or person.

attributions inferences made about the causes of other people's behavior.

atypical antipsychotics newer antipsychotic drugs, which do not create tardive dyskinesia.

auditory nerve the nerve that receives action potentials from the hair cells and transmits auditory information to the brain.

autism childhood disorder characterized by severe language and social impairment along with repetitive habits and inward-focused behaviors.

automatic processing encoding of information that occurs with little effort or conscious attention to the task.

autonomic nervous system (ANS) all the nerves of the peripheral nervous system that serve involuntary systems of the body, such as the internal organs and glands.

availability heuristic a device we use to make decisions based on the ease with which estimates come to mind or how available they are to our awareness.

avoidant personality disorder anxious–fearful personality disorder characterized by extreme fear of being criticized, low self-esteem, and avoidance of social interaction.

awareness monitoring of information from the environment and from one's own thoughts.

Axis I disorders in the *DSM-IV-TR*, the major clinical syndromes that cause significant impairment.

Axis II disorders in the *DSM-IV-TR*, the more long-standing personality disorders as well as mental retardation.

axon long projection that extends from a neuron's soma; it transmits electrical impulses toward the adjacent neuron and stimulates the release of neurotransmitters.

babbling sounds made as a result of the infant's experimentation with a complex range of phonemes, which include consonants as well as vowels; starts around 5–6 months.

barbiturates a class of anxiety-reducing sedatives that can be addictive and carry a risk of overdose.

basal ganglia a collection of structures surrounding the thalamus involved in voluntary motor control.

basic emotions set of emotions that are common to all humans; includes anger, disgust, fear, happiness, sadness, and surprise.

basic tendencies the essence of personality: the Big Five personality dimensions as well as talents, aptitudes, and cognitive abilities.

basilar membrane a membrane that runs through the cochlea; contains the hair cells.

behavior modification principles of operant conditioning used to change behavior.

behavior therapies therapies that apply the principles of classical and operant conditioning in the treatment of psychological disorders.

behavioral genetics the scientific study of the role of heredity in behavior.

behavioral measures measures based on systematic observation of people's actions either in their normal environment or in a laboratory setting.

behavioral neuroscience study of the links among brain, mind, and behavior.

behavioral thresholds the point at which a person moves from not having a particular response to having one.

behaviorism a school of psychology which proposed that psychology can be a true science only if it examines observable behavior, not ideas, thoughts, feelings, or motives.

benzodiazepines a class of anxiety-reducing drugs that can be addictive, but are less dangerous than barbiturates.

beta waves pattern of brain activity when one is awake; a rapid, low-energy wave.

Big Five or **five-factor model** a theory of personality that includes the following five dimensions: openness to experience, conscientiousness, extraversion, agreeableness, and neuroticism (OCEAN).

binocular depth cues aids to depth perception that rely on input from both eyes.

biological constraint model a view on learning which proposes that some behaviors are inherently more likely to be learned than others.

biological psychology the study of the relationship between bodily systems and chemicals and how they influence behavior and thought.

bipolar disorder mood disorder characterized by substantial mood fluctuations, cycling between very low (depressive) and very high (manic) moods.

blocking the inability to retrieve some information once it is stored.

bodily senses the senses based in the skin, body, or any membrane surfaces.

borderline personality disorder dramatic–emotional personality disorder characterized by out-of-control emotions, fear of being abandoned by others, and a vacillation between idealizing and despising

people who are close to the person with the disorder.

bottom-up processing idea that perception is a process of building a perceptual experience from smaller pieces.

broad intelligence one of Carroll's three levels of intelligence that includes abilities such as crystallized and fluid intelligence, as well as memory, learning, and processing speed.

broaden-and-build model Fredrickson's model for positive emotions, which posits that they widen our cognitive perspective and help us acquire useful life skills.

Broca's area area in the left frontal lobe responsible for the ability to produce speech.

bulimia nervosa an eating disorder characterized by binge eating and a perceived lack of control during the eating session.

bupropione a widely used antidepressant that inhibits the reuptake of norepinephrine and dopamine.

bystander effect phenomenon in which the greater the number of bystanders who witness an emergency, the less likely any one of them is to help.

cardiovascular reactivity (CVR) model hypothesis that hostility can increase the likelihood of heart disease through at least two different causal routes.

cardiovascular system the heart, blood, and all the blood vessels.

case study a study design in which a psychologist, often a therapist, observes one person over a long period of time.

catecholamines chemicals released from the adrenal glands that function as hormones and as neurotransmitters to control ANS activation.

category a concept that organizes other concepts around what they all share in common.

catharsis the process of releasing intense, often unconscious, emotions in a therapeutic setting.

causal inferences judgments about causation of one thing by another.

cellular immunity the immune response that occurs when the T lymphocytes (T cells) fight antigens.

central nervous system (CNS) the part of the nervous system that comprises the brain and spinal cord.

cerebellum a hindbrain structure involved in body movement, balance, coordination, fine-tuning motor skills, and cognitive activities such as learning and language.

cerebral cortex thin outer layer of the cerebrum, in which much of human thought, planning, perception, and consciousness takes place.

cerebrum each of the large halves of the brain that are covered with convolutions, or folds.

child-directed speech changes in adult speech patterns—apparently universal—when speaking to young children or infants; characterized by higher pitch, changes in voice volume, use of simpler sentences, emphasis on the here and now, and use of emotion to communicate messages.

chromosome a coiled-up thread of DNA.

chunking the process of breaking down a list of items to be remembered into a smaller set of meaningful units.

cingulate gyrus beltlike structure in the middle of the brain that plays an important role in attention and cognitive control.

circadian rhythms the variations in physiological processes that cycle within approximately a 24-hour period, including the sleep–wake cycle.

classical conditioning form of associative learning in which a neutral stimulus becomes associated with a stimulus to which one has an automatic, inborn response.

client-centered therapy a form of humanistic therapy in which the therapist shows unconditional positive regard for the patient.

clinical psychology the treatment of mental, emotional, and behavioral disorders and the promotion of psychological health.

cochlea a bony tube of the inner ear, which is curled like a snail's shell and filled with fluid.

cognition mental processes involved in acquiring, processing, and storing knowledge.

cognitive–behavioral therapy an approach to treating psychological disorders that combines techniques for restructuring irrational thoughts with operant and classical conditioning techniques to shape desirable behaviors.

cognitive dissonance the feeling of discomfort caused by information that is different from a person's conception of himself or herself as a reasonable and sensible person.

cognitive psychology the study of how people perceive, remember, think, speak, and solve problems.

cognitive symptoms (of schizophrenia) problems with working memory, attention, verbal and visual learning and memory, reasoning and problem solving, processing, and speech.

cognitive therapy any type of psychotherapy that works to restructure irrational thought patterns.

collective unconscious according to Jung, form of consciousness that consists of the shared experiences of our ancestors—God, mother, life, death, water, earth, aggression, survival—that have been passed down from generation to generation.

coma a state of consciousness in which the eyes are closed and the person is unresponsive and unarousable.

comorbidity occurrence of two or more disorders at the same time.

compulsion a repetitive behavior performed in response to uncontrollable urges or according to a ritualistic set of rules.

concept a mental grouping of objects, events, or people.

concept hierarchy arrangement of related concepts in a particular way, with some being general and others specific.

concrete operational stage Piaget's third stage of cognitive development, which spans ages 6–11, during which the child can perform mental operations—such as reversing—on real objects or events.

conditioned response (CR) a behavior that an organism learns to perform when presented with the CS.

conditioned stimulus (CS) a previously neutral input that an organism learns to associate with the UCS.

conditioned taste aversion the learned avoidance of a particular taste or food.

conditioning a form of associative learning in which behaviors are triggered by associations with events in the environment.

cones photoreceptors that are responsible for color vision and are most functional in conditions of bright light.

confirmation bias the tendency to selectively attend to information that supports one's general beliefs while ignoring information or evidence that contradicts one's beliefs.

conformity tendency of people to adjust their behavior to what others are doing or to adhere to the norms of their culture.

confounding variable variable whose influence on the dependent variable cannot be separated from the independent variable being examined.

conjunction fallacy error in logic that occurs when people say the combination of two events is more likely than either event alone.

consciousness an awareness of one's surroundings and of what's in one's mind at a given moment; includes aspects of being awake and aware.

conservation recognition that when some properties (such as shape) of an object change, other properties (such as volume) remain constant.

consolidation the process of establishing, stabilizing, or solidifying a memory; the second stage of long-term memory formation.

construct validity the degree to which a test measures the concept it claims to measure, such as intelligence.

continuity Gestalt law that says we see points or lines in such a way that they follow a continuous path.

continuous reinforcement reinforcement of a behavior every time it occurs.

control group a group of research participants who are treated in exactly the same manner as the experimental group, except that they do not receive the independent variable, or treatment.

conventional level the second level in Kohlberg's theory of moral reasoning, during which the person values caring, trust, and relationships as well as the social order and lawfulness.

convergent thinking problems problems that have known solutions and require analytic thinking and the use of learned strategies and knowledge to come up with the correct answer.

cooing the first sounds humans make other than crying, consisting almost exclusively of vowels; occurs during first 6 months of life.

coping act of dealing with stress or emotions.

cornea the clear hard covering that protects the lens of the eye.

corpus callosum nerve fibers that connect the two hemispheres of the brain.

correlation coefficient a statistic that ranges from −1.0 to +1.0 and assesses the strength and direction of association between two variables.

correlational designs studies that measure two or more variables and their relationship to one another; not designed to show causation.

cortical arousal level of activation in the brain.

cortisol stress hormone produced by the body to ensure that the body gets enough fuel during emotional arousal and stress.

creativity thinking and/or behavior that is both novel—original and useful—and adaptive.

critical thinking process by which one analyzes, evaluates, and forms ideas.

crystallized intelligence the kind of knowledge that one gains from experience and learning, education, and practice.

cult an extremist group led by a charismatic, totalitarian leader in which coercive methods are used to prevent members from leaving the group.

cultural test bias hypothesis the notion that group differences in IQ scores are caused by different cultural and educational backgrounds, not by real differences in intelligence.

cyberbullying the willful and repeated harm inflicted through the medium of electronic text.

cyclothymia a relatively mild form of bipolar disorder.

dark adaptation process of adjustment to seeing in the dark.

debriefing the explanation of the purposes of a study following data collection.

deductive reasoning reasoning from general statements of what is known to specific conclusions.

defense mechanisms unconscious strategies the mind uses to protect itself from anxiety by denying and distorting reality in some way.

delta waves type of brain activity that dominates Stage 3 sleep; higher energy than theta wave.

delusion one of the symptoms of schizophrenia: a false belief or exaggeration held despite evidence to the contrary, such as the idea that one is a famous person.

dementia a loss of mental function, in which many cognitive processes are impaired, such as the ability to remember, reason, solve problems, make decisions, and use language.

dendrites fingerlike projections from a neuron's soma that receive incoming messages from other neurons.

dependent personality disorder anxious–fearful personality disorder characterized by fear of being rejected and having a strong need to be cared for.

dependent variable in an experiment, the outcome or response to the experimental manipulation.

depressants substances that decrease or slow down central nervous system activity.

depth perception the ability to see things in three dimensions and to discriminate what is near from what is far.

descriptive designs study designs in which the researcher defines a problem and variable of interest but makes no prediction and does not control or manipulate anything.

descriptive statistics measures used to describe and summarize research.

developmental psychology study of how thought and behavior change and remain stable across the life span.

dialectical behavior therapy (DBT) treatment that integrates elements of CBT with exercises aimed at developing mindfulness without meditation and is used to treat borderline personality disorders.

diathesis–stress model explanation for the origin of psychological disorders as a combination of biological predispositions (diathesis) plus stress or an abusive environment.

difference threshold the smallest amount of change between two stimuli that a person can detect half of the time.

discrimination preferential treatment of certain people, usually driven by prejudicial attitudes.

display rules learned norms or rules, often taught very early, about when it is appropriate to express certain emotions and to whom one should show them.

dissociative disorders psychological disorders characterized by extreme splits or gaps in memory, identity, or consciousness.

dissociative identity disorder (DID) dissociative disorder in which a person develops at least two distinct personalities, each with its own memories, thoughts, behaviors, and emotions. Some psychiatrists question the legitimacy of the disorder.

divergent thinking problems problems that have no known solutions and require novel solutions.

DNA (deoxyribonucleic acid) a large molecule that contains genes.

dodo bird verdict the finding that most forms of therapy are effective and few significant differences exist in effectiveness among standard therapies.

dominant genes genes that show their effect even if there is only one allele for that trait in the pair.

dopamine a neurotransmitter released in response to behaviors that feel good or are rewarding to the person or animal; also involved in voluntary motor control.

double-blind studies studies in which neither the participants nor the researchers administering the treatment know who has been assigned to the experimental or control group.

Down syndrome a chromosomal disorder characterized by mild to profound mental retardation.

dreams images, thoughts, and feelings experienced during sleep.

drives the perceived states of tension that occur when our bodies are deficient in some need, creating an urge to relieve the tension.

Duchenne smile a smile that expresses true enjoyment, involving both the muscles that pull up the lip corners diagonally and those that contract the band of muscles encircling the eye.

dysthymia form of depression that is milder in intensity than major depressive disorder.

educational psychology the study of how students learn, the effectiveness of particular teaching techniques, the social psychology of schools, and the psychology of teaching.

effect size a measure of the strength of the relationship between two variables or the extent of an experimental effect.

effortful processing encoding of information that occurs with careful attention and conscious effort.

ego one of Freud's provinces of the mind; a sense of self; the only part of the mind that is in direct contact with the outside world: operates on the "reality principle."

egocentrism viewing the world from one's own perspective and not being capable of seeing things from another person's perspective.

electroconvulsive therapy (ECT) treatment of last resort for severe depression that involves passing an electrical current through a person's brain in order to induce a seizure.

electroencephalography (EEG) a method for measuring brain activity in which the electrical activity of the brain is recorded from electrodes placed on a person's scalp.

embryo the term for the developing organism from 2 weeks until about 8 weeks after conception.

embryonic stage the second prenatal stage, from 2 weeks to 8 weeks after conception, when all of the major organs form.

emerging adulthood the transitional phase between adolescence and young adulthood; includes ages 18–25 years.

emotion-focused coping way of dealing with stress that aims to regulate the experience of distress.

emotion regulation the cognitive and behavioral efforts people make to modify their emotions.

emotional competence the ability to control emotions and know when it is appropriate to express certain emotions.

emotional disclosure way of coping with stress through writing or talking about the situation.

emotional intelligence the ability to recognize emotions in oneself and others, empathic understanding, and skills for regulating emotions in oneself and others.

emotional response the physiological, behavioral/expressive, and subjective changes that occur when emotions are generated.

emotions brief, acute changes in conscious experience and physiology that occur in response to a personally meaningful situation.

empathy the ability to share the feelings of others and understand their situations.

empathy–altruism hypothesis the idea that people help others selflessly only when they feel empathy for them.

empirical method a method for developing questionnaire items that focuses on including questions that characterize the group the questionnaire is intended to distinguish.

empiricism the view that all knowledge and thoughts come from experience.

enactive learning learning by doing.

encoding the process by which the brain attends to, takes in, and integrates new information; the first stage of long-term memory formation.

endocannabinoids natural, marijuana-like substances produced by the body.

endocrine system system of glands that secrete and regulate hormones in the body.

enzymatic degradation a way of removing excess neurotransmitter from the synapse in which enzymes specific for that neurotransmitter bind with the neurotransmitter and destroy it.

epigenetics study of changes in the way genes are turned on or off without a change in the sequence of DNA.

epinephrine also known as adrenaline, a neurotransmitter that arouses bodily systems (such as increasing heart rate).

episodic memory form of memory that recalls the experiences we have had.

ethics the rules governing the conduct of a person or group in general or in a specific situation—or more simply, standards of right and wrong.

ethology the scientific study of animal behavior.

Eureka insight or **insight solutions** sudden solutions that come to mind in a flash.

event-related potential (ERP) a special technique that extracts electrical activity from raw EEG data to measure cognitive processes.

evidence-based therapies treatment choices based on empirical evidence that they produce the desired outcome.

evolutionary psychology the branch of psychology that studies human behavior by asking what adaptive problems it may have solved for our early ancestors.

exhaustion stage the phase of the general adaptation syndrome when all resources for fighting the threat have been depleted and illness is more likely.

experiment a research design that includes independent and dependent variables and random assignment of participants to control and experimental groups or conditions.

experimental group a group consisting of those participants who will receive the treatment or whatever is predicted to change behavior.

experimenter expectancy effects result that occurs when the behavior of the participants is influenced by the experimenter's knowledge of who is in the control group and who is in the experimental group.

explicit memory knowledge that consists of the conscious recall of facts and events; also known as declarative memory.

expressive suppression a response-focused strategy for regulating emotion that involves the deliberate attempt to inhibit the outward manifestation of an emotion.

extinction the weakening and disappearance of a conditioned response in the absence of reinforcement.

extrinsic motivation motivation that comes from outside the person and usually involves rewards and praises.

Facial Action Coding System (FACS) a widely used method for measuring all observable

muscular movements that are possible in the human face.

false memories memories for events that never happened, but were suggested by someone or something.

feature detectors neurons in the visual cortex that analyze the retinal image and respond to specific aspects of shapes, such as angles and movements.

fetal alcohol spectrum disorder a consequence of prenatal alcohol exposure that causes multiple problems, notably brain damage.

fetal stage the third prenatal stage, which begins with the formation of bone cells 8 weeks after conception and ends at birth.

fixation the inability to break out of a particular mind-set in order to think about a problem from a fresh perspective.

fixed interval (FI) schedule pattern of intermittent reinforcement in which responses are always reinforced after a set period of time has passed.

fixed ratio (FR) schedule pattern of intermittent reinforcement in which reinforcement follows a set number of responses.

flashbulb memories detailed, especially vivid memories of very specific, highly charged events.

flexibility of thought the ability to come up with many different categories of ideas and think of other responses besides the obvious one.

flooding an extreme form of in vivo exposure in which the client experiences extreme exposure to the phobic object.

fluid intelligence raw mental ability, pattern recognition, abstract reasoning that can be applied to a problem one has never confronted before.

forensic psychology field that blends psychology, law, and criminal justice.

forgetting the weakening or loss of memories over time.

forgetting curve a graphic depiction of how recall steadily declines over time.

formal operational stage Piaget's final stage of cognitive development, from age 11 or 12 on through adulthood, when formal logic is possible.

fovea spot on the back of the retina that contains the highest concentration of cones in the retina; place of clearest vision.

fraternal twins twins that develop from two different eggs fertilized by two different sperm.

free association a psychotherapeutic technique in which the client takes one image or idea from a dream and says whatever comes to mind, regardless of how threatening, disgusting, or troubling it may be.

frequency the number of times a particular score occurs in a set of data.

functional fixedness mind-set in which one is blind to unusual uses of common everyday things or procedures.

functional magnetic resonance imaging (fMRI) brain imaging technique that uses magnetic fields to produce detailed images of activity in areas of the brain and other soft tissues.

functionalism 19th-century school of psychology that argued it was better to look at why the mind works the way it does than to describe its parts.

fundamental attribution error the tendency to explain others' behavior in dispositional rather than situational terms.

g-factor theory Spearman's theory that intelligence is a single general (g) factor made up of specific components.

GABA (gamma-aminobutyric acid) major inhibitory neurotransmitter in the brain that tells postsynaptic neurons *not* to fire; it slows CNS activity and is necessary to regulate and control neural activity.

gate control theory of pain idea that the spinal cord regulates the experience of pain by either opening or closing neural channels, called *gates*, that transmit pain sensations to the brain.

gene-by-environment interaction research method of studying heritability by comparing genetic markers; allows researchers to assess how genetic differences interact with environment to produce certain behaviors in some people but not in others.

general adaptation syndrome (GAS) as defined by Hans Selye, a generalized, nonspecific set of changes in the body that occur during extreme stress.

generalized anxiety disorder (GAD) state of pervasive and excessive anxiety lasting at least 6 months.

generativity a term Erik Erikson used to describe the process in adulthood of creating new ideas, products, or people.

genes small segments of DNA that contain information for producing proteins.

genius high intelligence combined with creative accomplishments that have a tremendous impact on a given field.

genome all the genetic information in DNA.

genotype the entire genetic make-up of an organism.

germinal stage the first prenatal stage of development, which begins at conception and lasts two weeks.

Gestalt psychology a theory of psychology that maintains that we perceive things as wholes rather than as a compilation of parts.

glial cells central nervous system cells that provide structural support, promote efficient communication between neurons, and serve as scavengers, removing cellular debris.

glucocorticoids hormones responsible for maintaining the activation of physiological systems during emergencies.

glucose a simple sugar that provides energy for cells throughout the body, including the brain.

glutamate a major excitatory neurotransmitter in the brain that increases the likelihood that a postsynaptic neuron will fire; important in learning, memory, neural processing, and brain development.

graded potentials small changes in membrane potential that by themselves are insufficient to trigger an action potential.

grammar the entire set of rules for combining symbols and sounds to speak and write a particular language.

group therapy therapeutic settings in which several people who share a common problem all meet regularly with a therapist to help themselves and one another.

groupthink situation in which the thinking of the group takes over, so much so that group members forgo logic or critical analysis in the service of reaching a decision.

hair cells inner ear sensory receptors for sound that transduce sound vibrations into neural impulses.

hallucinations convincing sensory experiences that occur in the absence of an external stimulus.

hallucinogens substances that create distorted perceptions of reality ranging from mild to extreme.

health behavior approach explanation for illness or health that focuses on the role of behaviors such as diet, exercise, or substance abuse.

health psychology the study of the role psychological factors play in regard to health and illness.

heritability the extent to which a characteristic is influenced by genetics.

heuristics mental shortcuts; methods for making complex and uncertain decisions and judgments.

hierarchies a way of organizing related pieces of information from the most specific feature they have in common to the most general.

hippocampus a limbic structure that wraps itself around the thalamus; plays a vital role in learning and memory.

histrionic personality disorder dramatic–emotional personality disorder characterized by the desire to be the center of attention and by dramatic, seductive, flamboyant, and exaggerated behaviors.

homeostasis the process by which all organisms work to maintain physiological equilibrium or balance around an optimal set point.

hormones chemicals, secreted by glands, that travel in the bloodstream and carry messages to tissues and organs all over the body.

human development the study of change and continuity in the individual across the life span.

human language a communication system specific to *Homo sapiens;* it is open and symbolic, has rules of grammar, and allows its users to express abstract and distant ideas.

humanistic psychology a theory of psychology that focuses on personal growth and meaning as a way of reaching one's highest potential.

hypersomnia sleep difficulty characterized by sleeping more than 10 hours a day for 2 weeks or more; includes urge to nap during inappropriate times.

hypnosis state characterized by focused attention, suggestibility, absorption, lack of voluntary control over behavior, and suspension of critical faculties; occurs when instructed by someone trained in hypnosis; may be therapeutic.

hypochondriasis pervasive and debilitating fear of suffering from serious physical illness although none is found by a medical professional.

hypothalamic-pituitary-adrenal (HPA) axis a major neuroendocrine pathway relevant to the stress response involving the hypothalamus, pituitary gland, and the adrenal cortex.

hypothalamus a limbic structure; the master regulator of almost all major drives and motives we have, such as hunger, thirst, temperature, and sexual behavior; also controls the pituitary gland.

hypothesis a specific, informed, and testable prediction of the outcome of a particular set of conditions in a research design.

id one of Freud's provinces of the mind; the seat of impulse and desire; the part of our personality that we do not yet own; it owns or controls us.

ideational fluency the ability to produce many ideas.

identical twins twins that develop from a single fertilized egg that splits into two independent cells.

idioms expressions unique to a particular language; usually their meaning cannot be determined by decoding the individual meanings of the words.

implicit memory kind of memory made up of knowledge based on previous experience, such as skills that we perform automatically once we have mastered them; resides outside conscious awareness.

imprinting the rapid and innate learning of the characteristics of a caregiver very soon after birth.

impulse control disorder an anxiety disorder related to obsessive–compulsive disorder in which a person feels an intense, repetitive desire to perform certain behaviors.

in-group/out-group bias tendency to show positive feelings toward people who belong to the same group as we do, and negative feelings toward those in other groups.

incentive any external object or event that motivates behavior.

independent variable a property that is manipulated by the experimenter under controlled conditions to determine whether it causes the predicted outcome of an experiment.

individuation the process of a person's personality becoming whole and full.

inductive reasoning reasoning to general conclusions from specific evidence.

industrial/organizational (I/O) psychology application of psychological concepts and questions to work settings.

inferential statistics analyses of data that allow us to test hypotheses and make an inference as to how likely a sample score is to occur in a population.

inferiority complex an unhealthy need to dominate or upstage others as a way of compensating for feelings of deficiency.

informational social influence conformity to the behavior of others because one views them as a source of knowledge about what one is supposed to do.

insomnia a sleep difficulty characterized by difficulty falling and staying asleep, as well as not feeling rested.

instinctive drift learned behavior that shifts toward instinctive, unlearned behavior tendencies.

institutional review boards (IRBs) organizations that evaluate research proposals to make sure research involving humans does not cause undue harm or distress.

insula small structure inside the cerebrum that plays an important role in the perception of bodily sensations, emotional states, empathy, and addictive behavior.

integrative therapy an eclectic approach in which the therapist draws on different treatment approaches and uses those that seem most appropriate for the situation.

intelligence a set of cognitive skills that include abstract thinking, reasoning, problem solving, and the ability to acquire knowledge.

interference disruption of memory because other information competes with the information we are trying to recall.

intermittent reinforcement reinforcement of a behavior—but not after every response.

internal reliability characteristic of intelligence test in which questions on a given subtest tend to correlate very highly with other items on the subtest.

interneurons neurons that communicate only with other neurons.

inter-rater reliability measure of how much agreement there is in ratings when using two or more raters or coders to rate personality or other behaviors.

intimacy as defined by Erikson, the ability to fuse one's identity with another's without the fear of losing it.

intrinsic motivation motivation that comes from within a person and includes the elements of challenge, enjoyment, mastery, and autonomy.

introspection the main method of investigation for structuralists; it involves looking into one's own mind for information about the nature of conscious experience.

ions chemically charged particles that predominate in bodily fluids; found both inside and outside cells.

iris the muscle that forms the colored part of the eye; it adjusts the pupil to regulate the amount of light that enters the eye.

James-Lange theory of emotion the idea that it is the perception of the physiological changes that accompany emotions that produces the subjective emotional experience.

joint attention ability to make eye contact with others and to look in the same direction that someone else is looking.

kin selection the evolutionary favoring of genes that prompt individuals to help their relatives or kin.

language acquisition device (LAD) an innate, biologically based capacity to acquire language, proposed by Noam Chomsky as part of his nativist view of language.

latent learning learning that occurs in the absence of reinforcement and is not demonstrated until later, when reinforcement occurs.

latent level Freud's deeper, unconscious level of dreams; their meaning is found at this level.

law of closure The tendency to perceive a whole object in the absence of complete information.

law of effect the consequences of a behavior increase (or decrease) the likelihood that the behavior will be repeated.

learning enduring changes in behavior that occur with experience.

lens the structure that sits behind the pupil; it bends the light rays that enter the eye to focus images on the retina.

levels of processing the concept that the more deeply people encode information, the better they will recall it.

life satisfaction the overall evaluation we make of our lives and an aspect of subjective well-being.

linguistic determinism hypothesis the proposition that our language determines our way of thinking and our perceptions of the world; the view taken by Sapir and Whorf.

lithium a salt that is prescribed for its ability to stabilize the mania associated with bipolar disorder.

long-term memory the part of memory that has the capacity to store a vast amount of information for as little as 30 seconds and as long as a lifetime.

long-term potentiation strengthening of a synaptic connection that results when synapse of one neuron repeatedly fires and excites another neuron.

magnetic resonance imaging (MRI) brain imaging technique that uses magnetic fields to produce detailed images of the structure of the brain and other soft tissues.

major depressive disorder mood disorder characterized by pervasive low mood, lack of motivation, low energy, and feelings of worthlessness and guilt that last for at least two consecutive weeks.

manic episode one mood cycle in bipolar disorder, typically involving increased energy, sleeplessness, euphoria, irritability, delusions of grandeur, increased sex drive, and "racing" thoughts.

manifest level Freud's surface level of dreams, recalled upon waking.

mean the arithmetic average of a series of numbers.

measures the tools and techniques used to assess thought or behavior.

mechanoreceptors receptor cells in the skin that are sensitive to different tactile qualities, such as shape, grooves, vibrations, and movements.

median the score that separates the lower half of scores from the upper half.

meditation practices that people use to calm the mind, stabilize concentration, focus attention, and enhance awareness of the present moment.

medulla a hindbrain structure that extends directly from the spinal cord; regulates breathing, heart rate, and blood pressure.

memory the ability to store and use information; also the store of what has been learned and remembered.

menarche the first menstrual period.

mental age the equivalent chronological age a child has reached based on his or her performance on an IQ test.

mental representation a structure in our mind—such as an idea or image—that stands for something else, such as an external object or thing sensed in the past or future, not the present.

mental retardation significant limitations in intellectual functioning as well as in everyday adaptive behavior, which start before age 18.

mental rotation process of imagining an object turning in three-dimensional space.

mental set a tendency to continue to use problem-solving strategies that have worked in the past, even if better solutions are available.

meta-analysis research technique for combining all research results on one question and drawing a conclusion.

metacognitive thinking process that includes the ability first to think and then to reflect on one's own thinking.

mindfulness a heightened awareness of the present moment, whether of events in one's environment or in one's own mind.

mindfulness-based cognitive therapy (MBCT) an approach that combines elements of CBT with mindfulness meditation to help people with depression learn to recognize and restructure negative thought patterns.

mirror neurons nerve cells that are active when we observe others performing an action as well as when we are performing the same action.

mnemonic device a method devised to help remember information, such as a rhyme or acronym.

mode a statistic that represents the most commonly occurring score or value.

modeling the imitation of behaviors performed by others.

monoamine oxidase (MAO) inhibitors class of drugs used to treat depression; they slow the breakdown of monoamine neurotransmitters in the brain.

monocular depth cues aids to depth perception that do not require two eyes.

monogenic transmission the hereditary passing on of traits determined by a single gene.

mood disorders category of psychological disorder that is characterized by disturbances in emotional behavior that inhibit normal everyday functioning.

moods affective states that operate in the background of consciousness and tend to last longer than most emotions.

moral treatment 19th-century approach to treating the mentally ill with dignity in a caring environment.

motivation the urge to move toward one's goals; to accomplish tasks.

motor neurons nerve cells that carry commands for movement from the brain to the muscles of the body.

multiple-factor theory of intelligence idea that intelligence consists of distinct dimensions and is not just a single factor.

myelin sheath the fatty substance wrapped around some axons, which insulates the axon, making the nerve impulse travel more efficiently.

narcissistic personality disorder dramatic–emotional personality disorder characterized by having an extremely positive and arrogant self-image and being extraordinarily self-centered; other symptoms are an exaggerated sense of self-importance and grandiosity.

narcolepsy sleep disorder characterized by excessive daytime sleepiness and weakness in facial and limb muscles.

narrow intelligence one of Carroll's three levels of intelligence that includes many distinct abilities.

nativist view of language the idea that we discover language rather than learn it, that language development is inborn.

natural immunity form of immunity that is the first response to antigens.

natural selection a feedback process whereby nature favors one design over another because it has an impact on reproduction.

naturalistic observation a study in which the researcher unobtrusively observes and records behavior in the real world.

nature through nurture the position that the environment constantly interacts with biology to shape who we are and what we do.

needs inherently biological states of deficiency (cellular or bodily) that compel drives.

negative punishment the removal of a stimulus to decrease behavior.

negative reinforcement removal of a stimulus after a behavior to increase the frequency of that behavior.

negative symptoms (of schizophrenia) symptoms that include nonresponsiveness, emotional flatness, immobility, catatonia, problems with speech, and inability to complete tasks.

neural migration the movement of neurons from one part of the fetal brain to their more permanent destination; occurs during months 3–5 of the fetal stage.

neurocultural theory of emotion Ekman's explanation that some aspects of emotion, such as facial expressions and physiological changes associated with emotion, are universal and others, such as emotion regulation, are culturally derived.

neuroendocrine system the hormonal systems involved in emotions and stress.

neurogenesis the development of new neurons.

neurons the cells that process and transmit information in the nervous system.

neuroplasticity the brain's ability to adopt new functions, reorganize itself, or make

new neural connections throughout life, as a function of experience.

neuropsychoanalysis a new scientific movement started in the late 1990s that combined Freudian ideas with neuroscientific methods.

neurotransmitters chemicals that transmit information between neurons.

night terrors state that occurs occur when a person walks around, speaks incoherently, and ultimately awakens, terrified, from sleep.

non-REM form of sleep with few eye movements, which are slow rather than fast.

norepinephrine a neurotransmitter that activates the sympathetic response to stress, increasing heart rate, rate of respiration, and blood pressure in support of rapid action.

normal distribution bell curve; a plot of how frequent data are that is perfectly symmetrical, with most scores clustering in the middle and only a few scores at the extremes.

normative social influence conformity to the behavior of others in order to be accepted by them.

obedience a type of conformity in which a person yields to the will of another person.

object permanence the ability to realize that objects still exist when they are not being sensed.

observational learning learning by watching the behavior of others.

obsession an unwanted thought, word, phrase, or image that persistently and repeatedly comes into a person's mind and causes distress.

obsessive–compulsive disorder (OCD) an anxiety disorder in which obsessive thoughts lead to compulsive behaviors.

obsessive–compulsive personality disorder anxious–fearful personality disorder characterized by rigid habits and extreme perfectionism; more general than obsessive–compulsive disorder.

olfactory bulb a forebrain structure that sends information either directly to the smell processing areas in the cortex or indirectly to the cortex by way of the thalamus.

olfactory sensory neurons the sensory receptors for smell that reside high up inside the nose.

one-word utterances single words, such as "mama," "dada," "more," or "no!"; occurs around 12 months of age.

operant conditioning the process of changing behavior by manipulating the consequences of that behavior.

opponent-process theory the theory that color vision results from cones linked together in three pairs of opposing colors, so that activation of one member of the pair inhibits activity in the other.

optic chiasm the point at which strands of the optic nerve from half of each eye cross over to the opposite side of the brain.

optic nerve structure composed of the axons of ganglion cells from the retina that carry visual information from the eye to the brain.

originality the ability to come up with unusual and novel ideas.

out-group homogeneity the tendency to see all members of an out-group as the same.

pain a complex emotional and sensory experience associated with actual or potential tissue damage.

panic attacks an anxiety disorder; associated with perceptions of threat and occurring because of fear of danger, inability to escape, embarrassment, or specific objects, for example.

panic disorder an anxiety disorder characterized by panic attacks and persistent anxiety about having more attacks.

papillae textured structures on the surface of the tongue; contain thousands of taste buds.

paranoid personality disorder odd–eccentric personality disorder characterized by extreme suspicions and mistrust of others in unwarranted and maladaptive ways.

parasympathetic nervous system the branch of the autonomic nervous system that usually relaxes or returns the body to a less active, restful state.

perceived organizational support employees' beliefs about how much the organization appreciates and supports their contributions and well-being.

perception a psychological process: the act of organizing and interpreting sensory experience.

perceptual constancy the ability of the brain to preserve perception of objects in spite of changes in retinal image when an object changes in position or distance from the viewer.

perceptual set the effect of frame of mind on perception; a tendency to perceive stimuli in a certain manner.

peripheral nervous system the part of the nervous system that comprises all the nerve cells in the body outside the central nervous system.

personal unconscious according to Jung, form of consciousness that consists of all our repressed and hidden thoughts, feelings, and motives.

personality the unique and relatively enduring set of behaviors, feelings, thoughts, and motives that characterize an individual.

personality disorders patterns of cognition, emotion, and behavior that develop in late childhood or adolescence and are maladaptive and inflexible; they are more stable than clinical disorders.

personality psychology the study of what makes people unique and the consistencies in people's behavior across time and situations.

personality questionnaires self-report instruments on which respondents indicate the extent to which they agree or disagree with a series of statements as they apply to their personality.

persuasion the act of attempting to change the opinions, beliefs, or choices of others by explanation or argument.

phenothiazines drugs used to treat schizophrenia; help diminish hallucinations, confusion, agitation, and paranoia, but also have adverse side effects.

phenotype the organism's observed characteristics.

phobia an anxiety disorder: an ongoing and irrational fear of a particular object, situation, or activity.

photoreceptors cells in the retina (called rods and cones) that convert light energy into nerve energy.

physiological measures measures of bodily responses, such as blood pressure or heart rate, used to determine changes in psychological state.

physiological reactivity model explanation for the causal role of stress-related bodily changes in illness.

pituitary gland the master endocrine gland of the body that controls the release of hormones from glands throughout the body.

placebo a substance or treatment that appears identical to the actual treatment but lacks the active substance.

polygenic transmission the process by which many genes interact to create a single characteristic.

pons a hindbrain structure that serves as a bridge between lower brain regions and higher midbrain and forebrain activity.

population the entire group a researcher is interested in; for example, all humans, all adolescents, all boys, all girls, all college students.

positive psychology scientific approach to studying, understanding, and promoting healthy and positive psychological functioning.

positive punishment the addition of a stimulus that decreases behavior.

positive reinforcement the presentation or addition of a stimulus after a behavior occurs that increases how often that behavior will occur.

positive symptoms (of schizophrenia) the perceptual experiences associated with schizophrenia, including hallucinations, delusional thinking, and disorganized thought and speech.

positron emission tomography (PET) brain imaging technique that measures blood flow to active areas in the brain.

postconventional level the third level in Kohlberg's theory of moral reasoning, in which the person recognizes universal moral rules that may trump unjust or immoral local rules.

post-traumatic stress disorder (PTSD) a type of anxiety disorder triggered by exposure to a catastrophic or horrifying event that poses serious harm or threat.

preconventional level the first level in Kohlberg's theory of moral reasoning, focusing on avoiding punishment or maximizing rewards.

predictive validity the degree to which intelligence test scores are positively related to real-world outcomes, such as school achievement or job success, and thus have predictive value.

prefrontal cortex the frontmost region of the frontal lobes that plays an important role in attention, appropriate social behavior, impulse control, and working memory.

prefrontal lobotomy a form of psychosurgery in which the connections between the prefrontal cortex and the lower portion of the brain are severed; no longer in use.

prejudice a biased attitude toward a group of people or an individual member of a group based on unfair generalizations about what members of that group are like.

prenatal programming the process by which events in the womb alter the development of physical and psychological health.

preoperational stage the second major stage of cognitive development (ages 2–5), which begins with the emergence of symbolic thought.

primary appraisal quick assessment of the meaning of a given environmental event for the individual.

primary reinforcers innate, unlearned reinforcers that satisfy biological needs (such as food, water, or sex).

priming a kind of implicit memory that arises when recall is improved by earlier exposure to the same or similar stimuli.

proactive interference disruption of memory because previously learned information interferes with the learning of new information.

problem-focused coping way of dealing with stress that aims to change the situation that is creating stress.

procedural memory kind of memory made up of implicit knowledge for almost any behavior or physical skill we have learned.

prodigy a young person who is extremely gifted and precocious in one area and at least average in intelligence.

projection a defense mechanism in which people deny particular ideas, feelings, or impulses and project them onto others.

projective tests personality assessment in which the participant is presented with a vague stimulus or situation and asked to interpret it or tell a story about what they see.

prosocial behavior action that is beneficial to others.

protolanguage very rudimentary language; also known as pre-language; used by earlier species of *Homo*.

prototypes the best-fitting examples of a category.

proximity Gestalt law that says we tend to group objects together that are near one another.

pruning the degradation of synapses and dying off of neurons that are not strengthened by experience.

pseudoscience claims presented as scientific that are not supported by evidence obtained with the scientific method.

psychoactive drugs naturally occurring or synthesized substances that, when ingested or otherwise taken into the body, reliably produce qualitative changes in conscious experience.

psychoanalysis a clinically based approach to understanding and treating psychological disorders; assumes that the unconscious mind is the most powerful force behind thought and behavior.

psychoanalytic therapy based on Freud's ideas, therapeutic approach oriented toward major personality change with a focus on uncovering unconscious motives, especially through dream interpretation.

psychodynamic psychotherapy therapy aimed at uncovering unconscious motives that underlie psychological problems.

psychology the scientific study of thought and behavior.

psychoneuroimmunology (PNI) the science of how psychological factors relate to changes in the immune system.

psychophysics the study of how people psychologically perceive physical stimuli such as light, sound waves, and touch.

psychosomatic theory the idea that emotional factors can lead to the occurrence or worsening of illness.

psychotherapy the use of psychological techniques to modify maladaptive behaviors or thought patterns, or both, and to help patients develop insight into their own behavior.

psychotic disorders psychological disorders of thought and perception, characterized by inability to distinguish between real and imagined perceptions.

puberty the period when sexual maturation begins; it marks the beginning of adolescence.

punishment stimulus that decreases the frequency of a behavior.

pupil the opening in the iris through which light enters the eye.

quantitative trait loci (QTL) approach a technique in behavioral genetics that looks for the location on genes that might be associated with particular behaviors.

quasi-experimental design research method similar to an experimental design except that it makes use of naturally occurring groups rather than randomly assigning subjects to groups.

random assignment the method used to assign participants to different research conditions so that all participants have the same chance of being in any specific group.

rapid eye movements (REM) quick movements of the eye that occur during sleep, thought to mark phases of dreaming.

rational (face valid) method a method for developing questionnaire items that involves using reason or theory to come up with a question.

reaction formation a defense mechanism that occurs when an unpleasant idea, feeling, or impulse is turned into its opposite.

reaction range for a given trait, such as IQ, the genetically determined range of responses by an individual to his or her environment.

reappraisal an emotion regulation strategy in which one reevaluates an event so that a different emotion results.

reasoning the process of drawing inferences or conclusions from principles and evidence.

recessive genes genes that show their effects only when both alleles are the same.

reciprocal altruism the act of helping others in the hope that they will help us in the future.

recovered memory a memory from a real event that was encoded, stored, but not retrieved for a long period of time until some later event brings it suddenly to consciousness.

reflexes inborn and involuntary behaviors—such as coughing, swallowing, sneezing, or vomiting—that are elicited by very specific stimuli.

refractory period the span of time, after an action potential has been generated, when the neuron is returning to its resting state and the neuron cannot generate an action potential.

rehearsal the process of repeatedly practicing material so that it enters long-term memory.

reinforcer an internal or external event that increases the frequency of a behavior.

reliability consistency of a measurement, such as an intelligence test.

repetitive transcranial magnetic stimulation treatment for severe depression involving exposure of specific brain structures to bursts of high-intensity magnetic fields instead of electricity.

replication the repetition of a study to confirm the results; essential to the scientific process.

representative sample a research sample that accurately reflects the population of people one is studying.

representativeness heuristic a strategy we use to estimate the probability of one event based on how typical it is of another event.

repression the unconscious act of keeping threatening thoughts, feelings, or impulses out of consciousness.

research design plans of action for how to conduct a scientific study.

resistance stage in the general adaptation syndrome, extended effort by the body to deal with a threat.

resting potential the difference in electrical charge between the inside and outside of the axon when the neuron is at rest.

reticular formation a network of nerve fibers that runs up through both the hindbrain and the midbrain; it is crucial to waking up and falling asleep.

retina the thin layer of nerve tissue that lines the back of the eye.

retrieval the recovery of information stored in memory; the fourth stage of long-term memory.

retroactive interference disruption of memory because new experiences or information cause people to forget previously learned experiences or information.

retrograde amnesia an inability to recall events or experiences that happened before the onset of a disease or injury.

reuptake a way of removing excess neurotransmitter from the synapse, in which excess neurotransmitter is returned to the sending, or presynaptic, neuron for storage in vesicles and future use.

rods photoreceptors that function in low illumination and play a key role in night vision; responsive to dark and light contrast.

Rorschach Inkblot Test a projective test in which the participant is asked to respond to a series of ambiguous inkblots.

samples subsets of the population studied in a research project.

savant syndrome a very rare condition in which people with serious mental handicaps also show isolated areas of ability or brilliance.

schedules of reinforcement patterns of intermittent reinforcement distinguished by whether reinforcement occurs after a set number of responses or after a certain amount of time has passed since the last reinforcement.

schemas mental frameworks that develop from our experiences with particular people, objects, or events.

schizoid personality disorder odd–eccentric personality disorder characterized by a desire to avoid close relationships as well as by emotional aloofness, reclusivity, and a lack of humor.

schizophrenia psychotic disorder characterized by significant disturbances in thought and emotion, specifically problems with perception, including hallucinations.

schizotypal personality disorder odd–eccentric personality disorder characterized by a desire to live an isolated and asocial life, but also by the presence of odd thoughts and beliefs.

scientific method the procedures by which scientists conduct research, consisting of five basic processes: observation, prediction, testing, interpretation, and communication.

scientific thinking process using the cognitive skills required to generate, test, and revise theories.

secondary (or conditioned) reinforcers reinforcers that are learned by association, usually via classical conditioning (such as money, grades, and peer approval).

secondary appraisal self-assessment of the resources available to cope with stress.

secure attachment attachment style characterized by infants who will gradually explore new situations when the caregiver leaves and initiate contact when the caregiver returns after separation.

selective attention the ability to focus awareness on specific features in the environment while ignoring others.

selective serotonin reuptake inhibitors (SSRIs) drugs prescribed primarily for depression and some anxiety disorders that work by making more serotonin available in the synapse.

self-actualization the inherent drive to realize one's full potential.

self-conscious emotions types of emotion that require a sense of self and the ability to reflect on actions; they occur as a function of meeting expectations (or not) and abiding (or not) by society's rules.

self-fulfilling prophecy a statement that affects events to cause the prediction to become true.

self-reports written or oral accounts of a person's thoughts, feelings, or actions.

self-serving bias the tendency to make situational attributions for our failures but dispositional attributions for our successes.

semantic memory form of memory that recalls facts and general knowledge, such as what we learn in school.

semicircular canals structure of the inner ear involved in maintaining balance.

sensation a physical process: the stimulation of our sense organs by features of the outer world.

sensorimotor stage Piaget's first stage of cognitive development (ages 0–2), when infants learn about the world by using their senses and by moving their bodies.

sensory adaptation the process by which our sensitivity diminishes when an object constantly stimulates our senses.

sensory memory the part of memory that holds information in its original sensory form for a very brief period of time, usually about half a second or less.

sensory neurons nerve cells that receive incoming sensory information from the sense organs (eye, ear, skin, tongue, nose).

sentence phase stage when children begin speaking in fully grammatical sentences; usually age 2½ to 3.

separation anxiety the distress reaction shown by babies when they are separated from their primary caregiver (typically shown at around 9 months of age).

serial-position effect the tendency to have better recall for items in a list according to their position in the list.

serotonin a neurotransmitter with wide-ranging effects: involved in dreaming and in controlling emotional states, especially anger, anxiety, and depression.

set point the ideal fixed setting of a particular physiological system, such as internal body temperature.

sexual behavior actions that produce arousal and increase the likelihood of orgasm.

sexual orientation the disposition to be attracted to either the opposite sex (heterosexual), the same sex (homosexual), or both sexes (bisexual).

sexual strategies theory the idea that men and women face different problems when they seek out mates, and so they often approach relationships in very different ways.

shadow according to Jung, the dark and morally objectionable part of ourselves.

shamans medicine men or women who treat people with mental problems by driving out their demons with elaborate rituals, such as exorcisms, incantations, and prayers.

short-term memory the part of memory that temporarily (for 2 to 30 seconds) stores a limited amount of information before it is either transferred to long-term storage or forgotten.

signal detection theory the viewpoint that both stimulus intensity and decision-making processes are involved in the detection of a stimulus.

similarity Gestalt law that says we tend to group like objects together in visual perception.

single-blind studies studies in which participants do not know the experimental condition (group) to which they have been assigned.

sleepwalking sleep difficulty characterized by activities occurring during non-REM sleep that usually occur when one is awake, such as walking and eating.

social desirability bias the tendency toward favorable self-presentation that could lead to inaccurate self-reports.

social exchange theory the idea that we help others when we understand that the benefits to ourselves are likely to outweigh the costs.

social facilitation phenomenon in which the presence of others improves one's performance.

social learning theory a description of the kind of learning that occurs when we model or imitate the behavior of others.

social loafing phenomenon in which the presence of others causes one to relax one's standards and slack off.

social norms rules about acceptable behavior imposed by the cultural context in which one lives.

social phobia (social anxiety disorder) an anxiety disorder: fear of humiliation in the presence of others, characterized by intense self-consciousness about appearance or behavior or both.

social psychology the study of how living among others influences thought, feeling, and behavior.

social referencing the ability to make use of social and emotional information from another person—especially a caregiver—in an uncertain situation.

softwiring in contrast to hardwiring, means that biological systems—genes, brain structures, brain cells—are inherited but open to modification from the environment.

soma the cell body of the neuron.

somatic nervous system nerve cells of the peripheral nervous system that transmit sensory information to the central nervous system (CNS) and those that transmit information from the CNS to the skeletal muscles.

somatization disorder psychological disorder in which a person complains of multiple physical disorders that have no known medical or physical basis.

somatoform disorders psychological disorders that take bodily or physical form and mimic physical diseases, but have no known physical cause or medical basis.

spermarche the first ejaculation.

spontaneous recovery the sudden reappearance of an extinguished response.

sports psychology the study of psychological factors in sports and exercise.

stagnation situation where the adult becomes more self-focused than oriented toward others and does not contribute in a productive way to society or family.

standard deviation a statistical measure of how much scores in a sample vary around the mean.

statistics collection, analysis, interpretation, and presentation of numerical data.

stereotypes schemas of how people are likely to behave based simply on groups to which they belong.

stimulants substances that activate the nervous system.

stimulus discrimination restriction of a CR (such as salivation) to only the exact CS to which it was conditioned.

stimulus generalization extension of the association between UCS and CS to include a broad array of similar stimuli.

storage the retention of memory over time; the third stage of long-term memory formation.

stress a response elicited when a situation overwhelms a person's perceived ability to meet the demands of a situation.

stressors events that trigger a stress response.

striving for superiority according to Adler, the major drive behind all behavior, whereby humans naturally strive to overcome their inherent inferiorities or deficiencies, both physical and psychological.

Stroop effect delay in reaction time when color of words on a test and their meaning differ.

structuralism 19th-century school of psychology that argued that breaking down experience into its elemental parts offers the best way to understand thought and behavior.

subjective experience of emotion the changes in the quality of our conscious experience that occur during emotional responses.

subjective well-being state that consists of life satisfaction, domain satisfactions, and positive and negative affect.

sublimation a defense mechanism that involves expressing a socially unacceptable impulse in a socially acceptable way.

successful intelligence according to Sternberg, an integrated set of abilities needed to attain success in life.

suggestibility problem with memory that occurs when memories are implanted in our minds based on leading questions, comments, or suggestions by someone else or some other source.

superego one of Freud's provinces of the mind; the part of the self that monitors and controls behavior; "stands over us" and evaluates actions in terms of right and wrong; hence, our conscience.

support groups meetings of people who share a common situation, be it a disorder, a disease, or coping with an ill family member.

sustained attention the ability to maintain focused awareness on a target or idea.

sympathetic nervous system the branch of the autonomic nervous system that activates bodily systems in times of emergency.

synapse the junction between an axon and the adjacent neuron, where information is transmitted from one neuron to another.

synaptic vesicles tiny sacs in the terminal buttons that contain neurotransmitters.

synaptogenesis the formation of entirely new synapses or connections with other neurons.

syndromes groups or clusters of related symptoms that are characteristic of a disorder.

synesthesia an unusual sensory experience in which a person experiences sensations in one sense when a different sense is stimulated.

syntax the rules for arranging words and symbols to form sentences or parts of sentences in a particular language.

systematic desensitization a behavioral therapy technique, often used for phobias, in which the therapist pairs relaxation with gradual exposure to a phobic object, generating a hierarchy of increasing contact with the feared object.

tardive dyskinesia repetitive, involuntary movements of jaw, tongue, face, and mouth resulting from the extended use of traditional antipsychotic drugs.

taste buds structures inside the papillae of the tongue that contain the taste receptor cells.

taste receptor cells sensory receptors for taste that reside in the taste buds.

technology-based therapy category of therapy that makes use of technology or the Internet to complement current therapies or make psychotherapeutic techniques available to more people.

telomerase an enzyme that adds DNA sequences to telomeres.

temperament the biologically based tendency to behave in particular ways from very early in life.

teratogens substances that can disrupt normal prenatal development and cause lifelong deficits.

terminal buttons little knobs at the end of the axon that contain tiny sacs of neurotransmitters.

test bias characteristic of a test that produces different outcomes for different groups.

test fairness judgment about how test results are applied to different groups based on values and philosophical inclinations.

test–retest reliability consistency of scores on a test over time.

thalamus a forebrain structure that receives information from the senses and relays it to the cerebral cortex for processing.

theory a set of related assumptions from which scientists can make testable predictions.

theory of mind ideas and knowledge about how other people's minds work.

theta waves pattern of brain activity during Stage 1 sleep; slower, lower-energy waves than alpha waves.

thinking outside the box approach to problem solving that requires breaking free of self-imposed conceptual constraints and thinking about a problem differently in order to solve it.

three-stage model of memory classification of memories based on duration as sensory, short-term, and long-term.

token economies a behavioral technique in which desirable behaviors are reinforced with a token, such as a small chip or fake coin, which can be exchanged for privileges.

top-down processing perception of the whole based on our experience and expectations, which guide our perception of smaller elemental features of a stimulus.

traditional antipsychotics historically, the first medications used to manage psychotic symptoms.

trait a disposition to behave consistently in a particular way.

transduction the conversion of physical into neural information.

transference process in psychotherapy in which the client reacts to a person in a present relationship as though that person were someone from the client's past.

triangular theory of love Sternberg's idea that three components (intimacy, passion, and commitment), in various combinations, can explain all the forms of human love.

triarchic theory of intelligence Sternberg's three-part model of intelligence, including analytic, creative, and practical intelligence.

trichromatic color theory the theory that all color that we experience results from a mixing of three colors of light (red, green, and blue).

tricyclic antidepressants drugs used for treating depression as well as chronic pain and ADHD.

t-test statistic that compares two means to see whether they could come from the same population.

twin-adoption studies research into hereditary influence on twins, both identical and fraternal, who were raised apart (adopted) and who were raised together.

two-word utterances phrases children put together, starting around 18 months, such as "my ball," "mo wawa," or "go way."

tympanic membrane the eardrum.

Type A Behavior Pattern a way of responding to challenge or stress, characterized by hostility, impatience, competitiveness, and time urgency.

unconditional positive regard acceptance of another person regardless of his or her behavior.

unconditioned response (UCR) the natural automatic, inborn reaction to a stimulus.

unconditioned stimulus (UCS) the environmental input that always produces the same unlearned response.

unconscious one of Freud's three levels of consciousness; it contains all the drives, urges, or instincts that are outside awareness but nonetheless motivate most of our speech, thoughts, feelings, or actions.

universal term referring to something that is common to all human beings and can be seen in cultures all over the world.

validity the degree to which a test accurately measures what it purports to measure, such as intelligence, and not something else, and the degree to which it predicts real-world outcomes.

variable a characteristic that changes or "varies," such as age, gender, weight, intelligence, anxiety, and extraversion.

variable interval (VI) schedule a pattern of intermittent reinforcement in which responses are reinforced after time periods of different duration have passed.

variable ratio (VR) schedule a pattern of intermittent reinforcement in which the number of responses needed for reinforcement changes.

vegetative state state of minimal consciousness in which the eyes might be open, but the person is otherwise unresponsive.

virtual reality therapies category of therapies that use virtual (digital simulation) environments to create therapeutic situations that would be hard to create otherwise.

visual acuity the ability to see clearly.

visual imagery visual representations created by the brain after the original stimulus is no longer present.

wakefulness degree of alertness reflecting whether a person is awake or asleep.

Weber's law the finding that the size of a just noticeable difference is a constant fraction of the intensity of the stimulus.

Wernicke's area an area deep in the left temporal lobe responsible for the ability to speak in meaningful sentences and to comprehend the meaning of speech.

word salad term for the speech of people with schizophrenia, which may follow grammatical rules but be nonsensical in terms of content.

working memory the part of memory required to attend to and solve a problem at hand; often used interchangeably with short-term memory.

Yerkes–Dodson law the principle that moderate levels of arousal lead to optimal performance.

young adulthood development stage that usually happens by mid-20s when people complete the key developmental tasks of emerging adulthood.

zone of proximal development the distance between what a child can learn alone and what that child can learn assisted by someone else, usually an adult.

zygote single cell that results when a sperm fertilizes an egg.

References

Aamodt, M. G. (2010). *Industrial/organizational psychology: An applied approach* (6th ed.). Belmont, CA: Wadsworth.

Abbate-Daga, G., Gramaglia, C., Amianto, F., Marzola, E., & Fassino, S. (2010). Attachment insecurity, personality, and body dissatisfaction in eating disorders. *Journal of Nervous and Mental Disease, 198,* 520–524.

Aberg, M. A. I., Pedersen, N. L., Torén K., Svartengrenf, M., Backstrand, B., Johnsson, T., . . . Kuhn, H. G. (2009). Cardiovascular fitness is associated with cognition in young adulthood. *Proceedings of the National Academy of Sciences, 106,* 20906–20911. doi: 10.1073/pnas.0905307106

Aboujaoude, E., Koran, L. M., Gamel, N., Large, M. D., & Serpe, R. T. (2006). Potential markers for problematic Internet use: A telephone survey of 2,513 adults. *CNS Spectrum: The International Journal of Neuropsychiatric Medicine, 11,* 750–755.

Abrams, R. (1997). *Electroconvulsive therapy* (3rd ed.). New York, NY: Oxford University Press.

Achter, J. A., Lubinski, D., Benbow, C. P., & Eftekhari-Sanjani, H. (1999). Assessing vocational preferences among intellectually gifted adolescents adds incremental validity to abilities: A discriminant analysis of educational outcomes over a 10-year interval. *Journal of Educational Psychology, 91,* 777–786.

Ackerman, D. (1990). *A natural history of the senses.* New York, NY: Vintage Books.

Adam, T. C., & Epel, E. S. (2007). Stress, eating and the reward system. *Physiology & Behavior, 91,* 449–458.

Adams, L., & Szaluta, J. (1996). *Psychoanalysis and the humanities.* Philadelphia, PA: Brunner/Mazel.

Adamson, L., & Bakeman, R. (1985). Affect and attention: Infants observed with mothers and peers. *Child Development, 56,* 582–593.

Ader, R., & Cohen, N. (1975). Behaviorally conditioned immunosuppression. *Psychosomatic Medicine, 37,* 333–340.

Adler, A. (1931). *What life should mean to you.* New York, NY: Capricorn Books.

Adler, A. (1956). *The individual psychology of Alfred Adler: A systematic presentation in selections from his writings* (H. L. Ansbacher & R. R. Ansbacher, Eds.). New York, NY: Norton.

Adler, J. (Ed.). (2004). *Forensic psychology: Concepts, debates and practice.* Cullupton, England: Willan.

Adolphs, R., Cahill, L., Schul, R., & Babinsky, R. (1997) Impaired declarative memory for emotional material following bilateral amygdala damage in humans. *Learning and Memory, 4,* 291–300.

Adolphs, R., Gosselin, F., Buchanan, T. W., Tranel, D., Schyns, P., & Damasio, A. R. (2005). A mechanism for impaired fear recognition after amygdala damage. *Nature, 433,* 68–72.

Adolphs, R., Tranel, D., & Buchanan, T. W. (2005). Amygdala damage impairs emotional memory for gist but not details of complex stimuli. *Nature Neuroscience, 8,* 512–518.

Adolphs, R., Tranel, D., & Damasio, A. R. (1998, June 4). The human amygdala in social judgment. *Nature, 393,* 470–474.

Adolphs, R., Tranel, D., Damasio, H., & Damasio, A. R. (1994, December 15). Impaired recognition of emotion in facial expressions following bilateral damage to the human amygdala. *Nature, 372,* 669–672.

Aichorn, W., Huber, R., Stuppaeck, C., & Whitworth, A. B. (2006). Cardiomyopathy after long-term treatment with lithium—more than a coincidence? *Journal of Psychopharmacology, 20,* 589–591.

Ainsworth, M. D. S., Blehar, M. C., Waters, E., & Wall, S. (1978). *Patterns of attachment: A psychological study of the Strange Situation.* Hillsdale, NJ: Erlbaum.

Aitken, J. R., & Benson, J. W. (1984). The use of relaxation/desensitization in treating anxiety associated with flying. *Aviation Space and Environmental Medicine, 55,* 196–199.

Akaike, A. (2006). Preclinical evidence of neuroprotection by cholinesterase inhibitors. *Alzheimer Disease and Associated Disorders, 20*(Suppl. 1), S8–S11.

Akinola, M., & Mendes, W. B. (2008). The dark side of creativity: Biological vulnerability and negative emotions lead to greater artistic creativity. *Personality and Social Psychological Bulletin, 34,* 1677–1686.

Al-Atiyyat, N. M. H. (2009). Cultural diversity and cancer pain. *Journal of Hospice & Palliative Nursing, 11,* 154–164.

Albert, R. S., & Runco, M. A. (1989). Independence and the creative potential of exceptionally gifted boys. *Journal of Youth and Adolescence, 18,* 221–230.

Allemand, M., Zimprich, D., & Hendriks, A. A. J. (2008). Age differences in five personality domains across the life span. *Developmental Psychology, 44,* 758–770.

Allen, D. G., Shore, L. M., & Griffeth, R. W. (2003). The role of perceived organizational support and supportive human resource practices in the turnover process. *Journal of Management, 29,* 99–118.

Allen, L., & Gorski, R. (2007). *Sex differences in the bed nucleus of the stria terminalis of the human brain* [e-book]. Cambridge, MA: MIT Press.

Allison, D. B., Heshka, S., Neale, M. C., Lykken, D. T., & Heymsfield, S. B. (1994). A genetic analysis of relative weight among 4,020 twin pairs, with an emphasis on sex effects. *Health Psychology, 13,* 362–365.

Alloway, T., Elliott, J., & Holmes, J. (2010). The prevalence of ADHD-like symptoms in a community sample. *Journal of Attention Disorders, 14,* 52–56. doi:10.1177/1087054709356197

Allport, G. W. (1937). *Personality: A psychological interpretation.* New York, NY: Holt, Rinehart & Winston.

Allport, G. W. (1954). *The nature of prejudice.* Cambridge, MA: Addison-Wesley.

Allport, G. W., & Odbert, H. W. (1936). Trait-names: A psycho-lexical study. *Psychological Monographs, 47,* 1–171.

Alt, K. W., Jeunesse, C., Buritrago-Tellez, C. H., Wächter, R., Boes, E., & Pichler, S. L. (1997, May 22). Evidence for stone-age cranial surgery. *Nature, 387,* 360.

Alterovitz, S., & Mendelsohn, G. A. (2009). Partner preferences across the life span: Online dating by older adults. *Psychology and Aging, 24,* 513–517. doi:10.1037/a0015897

Altman, J., & Das, G. D. (1966). Autoradiographic and histological studies of postnatal neurogenesis. I. A longitudinal investigation of the kinetics, migration and transformation of cells incorporating tritiated thymidine in neonate rats, with special reference to postnatal neurogenesis in some brain regions. *Journal of Comparative Neurology, 126,* 337–389.

Alzheimer's Association. (2008). *What is Alzheimer's?* Retrieved March 10, 2008, from http://www.alz.org/alzheimers_disease_what_is_alzheimers.asp#plaques

Amabile, T. M. (1996). *Creativity in context.* Boulder, CO: Westview.

Amabile, T. M., Hill, K. G., Hennessey, B. A., & Tighe, E. M. (1994). The Work Preference Inventory—Assessing intrinsic and extrinsic motivational orientations. *Journal of Personality and Social Psychology, 66,* 950–967.

Amabile, T. M., & Khaire, M. (2008, October). Creativity and the role of the leader. *Harvard Business Review,* 1–11.

Amabile, T. M., & Kramer, S. J. (2007, May). Inner work life: Understanding the subtext of business performance. *Harvard Business Review,* 1–13.

Amaral, D. (2000). The anatomical organization of the central nervous system. In E. R. Kandel, J. H. Schwartz, & T. M. Jessell

(Eds.), *Principles of neural science* (4th ed., pp. 317–336). New York, NY: McGraw-Hill.

Amedi, A., Merabet, L. B., Bermpohl, F., & Pascual-Leone, A. (2005). The occipital cortex in the blind. *Current Directions in Psychological Science, 14,* 306–311.

American Association on Mental Retardation (AAMR). (2002). *Mental retardation: Definition, classification, and systems of support* (10th ed.). Alexandria, VA: Author.

American Heart Association (2005). *Heart disease and stroke statistics—2005 update.* Dallas, TX: American Heart Association.

American Heart Association. (2010). Cigarette smoking rates. Retrieved from http://www.americanheart.org/presenter.jhtml?identifier=4559

American Psychiatric Association. (2000). *Diagnostic and statistical manual of mental disorders* (4th ed.). Washington, DC: Author.

Amichai-Hamburger, Y., & Vinitzky, G. (2010). Social network use and personality. *Computers in Human Behavior, 26,* 1289–1295.

Anda, R. F., Felitti, V. J., Bremner, J. D., Walker, J. D., Whitfield, C., Perry, B. D., . . . Giles, W. H. (2006). The enduring effects of abuse and related adverse experiences in childhood: A convergence of evidence from neurobiology and epidemiology. *European Archives of Psychiatry and Clinical Neuroscience, 256,* 174–186.

Anderson, C. A., Shibuya, A., Ihori, N., Swing, E. L., Bushman, B. J., Sakamoto, A., . . . Saleem, M. (2010). Violent video game effects on aggression, empathy, and prosocial behavior in Eastern and Western countries. *Psychological Bulletin, 136,* 151–173.

Anderson, N. D., Lau, M. A., Segal, Z. V., & Bishop, S. R. (2007). Mindfulness-based stress reduction and attentional control. *Clinical Psychology and Psychotherapy, 14,* 449–463.

Andreasen, N. C. (1987). Creativity and psychological disorder: Prevalence rates in writers and their first-degree relatives. *American Journal of Psychiatry, 144,* 1288–1292.

Andreasen, N. C. (2006). *The creative brain.* New York, NY: Penguin.

Andreasen, N. C., & Glick, I. D. (1988). Bipolar affective disorder and creativity: Implications and clinical management. *Comprehensive Psychiatry, 29,* 207–216.

Andreasen, N. C., O'Leary, D. S., Flaum, M., Nopoulos, P., Watkins, G. L., Ponto, L. L. B., et al. (1997). Hypofrontality in schizophrenia: Distributed dysfunctional circuits in neuroleptic-naïve patients. *The Lancet, 349,* 1730–1734.

Anson, K., & Ponsford, J. (2006). Coping and emotional adjustment following traumatic brain injury. *Journal of Head Trauma Rehabilitation, 21,* 248–259.

Anthonisen, N. R., Skeans, M. A., Wise, R. A., Manfreda, J., Kanner, R. E., & Connett, J. E. (Lung Health Study Research Group). (2005). The effects of a smoking cessation intervention on 14.5-year mortality: A randomized clinical trial. *Annals of Internal Medicine, 142,* 233–239.

Aouizerate, B., Guehl, D., Cuny, E., Rougier, A., Bioulac, B., Tignol, J., & Burbaud, P. (2004). Pathophysiology of obsessive-compulsive disorder: A necessary link between phenomenology, neuropsychology, imagery and physiology. *Progress in Neurobiology, 72,* 195–221.

APA Presidential Task Force on Evidence-Based Practice, US. (2006). Evidence-based practice in psychology. *American Psychologist, 61,* 271–285.

Apsche, J. (1993). *Probing the mind of a serial killer.* Morrisville, PA: International Information Associates.

Arbib, M., Liebal, K., & Pika, S. (2008). Primate vocalization, gesture, and the evolution of human language. *Current Anthropology, 49,* 1053–1063. doi:10.1086/593015

Argyle, M. (2001). *The psychology of happiness* (2nd ed.). New York, NY: Routledge.

Arling, G. L., & Harlow, H. F. (1967). Effects of social deprivation on maternal behavior of rhesus monkeys. *Journal of Comparative and Physiological Psychology, 64,* 371–377.

Arnett, J. J. (2004). *Emerging adulthood: The winding road from the late teens to the twenties.* New York, NY: Oxford University Press.

Arnett, J. J. (2006). Emerging adulthood: Understanding the new way of coming of age. In J. J. Arnett and J. L. Tanner (Eds.), *Emerging adults in America: Coming of age in the 21st century* (pp. 3–19). Washington, DC: American Psychological Association.

Arnold, M. B. (1960). *Emotion and personality: Vol. 1. Psychological Aspects.* New York, NY: Columbia University Press.

Arseneault, L., Cannon, M., Witton, J., & Murray, R. M. (2004). Causal association between cannabis and psychosis: Examination of the evidence. *British Journal of Psychiatry, 184,* 110–117.

Arseneault, L., Moffitt T. E., Caspi A., Taylor, A., Rijsdijik F., Jaffee, S. R., . . . Measelle, J. (2003). Strong genetic effects on cross-situational antisocial behaviour among 5-year-old children according to mothers, teachers, examiner-observers, and twins' self-reports. *Journal of Child Psychology and Psychiatry, 44,* 832–848.

Artola, A. (2008). Diabetes-, stress- and ageing-related changes in synaptic plasticity in hippocampus and neocortex—The same metaplastic process? *European Journal of Pharmacology, 585,* 153–162.

Asch, S. E. (1951). Effects of group pressure on the modification and distortion of judgments. In H. Guetzkow (Ed.), *Groups, leadership and men.* Pittsburgh, PA: Carnegie Press.

Asch, S. E. (1952). *Social psychology.* New York, NY: Prentice-Hall.

Aserinsky, E. (1996). Memories of famous neuropsychologists: The discovery of REM sleep. *Journal of the History of the Neurosciences, 5,* 213–227.

Asperger, H. (1991). "Autistic psychopathy" in childhood (U. Frith, Trans.). In U. Frith (Ed.), *Autism and Asperger syndrome* (pp. 37–62). New York, NY: Cambridge University Press. (Original work published 1944)

Asperger's disorder. (n.d.). Retrieved from http://www.dsm5.org/ProposedRevisions/Pages/proposedrevision.aspx?rid=97#

Assouline, M., & Meir, E. I. (1987). Meta-analysis of the relationship between congruence and well-being measures. *Journal of Vocational Behavior, 31,* 319–332.

Atkinson, G., Reilly, T., & Waterhouse, J. (2007). Chronobiological aspects of the sleep-wake cycle and thermoregulation. *Physiology & Behavior, 90*(2), 189.

Atkinson, J. W. (1964). *An introduction to motivation.* New York, NY: Van Nostrand.

Atkinson, R. C., & Shiffrin, R. M. (1971). The control of short-term memory. *Scientific American, 225,* 82–90.

Austin, E. J. (2005). Personality correlates of the broader autism phenotype as assessed by the Autism Spectrum Quotient (AQ). *Personality and Individual Differences, 38,* 451–460.

Austin, M., Hadzi-Pavlovic, D., Leader, L., Saint, K., & Parker, G. (2004). Maternal trait anxiety, depression, and life-event stress in pregnancy: Relationships with infant temperament. *Early Human Development, 81,* 183–190.

Azizian, A., & Polich, J. (2007). Evidence for attentional gradient in the serial position memory curve from event-related potentials. *Journal of Cognitive Neuroscience, 19,* 2071–2081.

Baars, B. J. (1997). In the theatre of consciousness: Global workspace theory, a rigorous scientific theory of consciousness. *Journal of Consciousness Studies, 4,* 292–309.

Baars, B. J., & Franklin, S. (2003). How conscious experience and working memory interact. *TRENDS in Cognitive Sciences, 7,* 166–172.

Babson, K. A., Feldner, M. T., & Badour, C. L. (2010). Cognitive behavioral therapy for sleep disorders. *Psychiatric Clinics of North America, 33,* 629–640.

Bach, P., & Hayes, S. C. (2002). The use of acceptance and commitment therapy to prevent the rehospitalization of psychotic patients: A randomized controlled trial. *Journal of Consulting and Clinical Psychology, 70,* 1129–1139.

Bachevalier, J. (2011). The amygdala in autism spectrum disorders. In E. Hollander, A. Kolevzon, & J. T. Coyle (Eds.), *Textbook of autism spectrum disorders* (pp. 363–374). Arlington, VA: American Psychiatric Publishing.

Bachorowski, J. (1999). Vocal expression and perception of emotion. *Current Directions in Psychological Science, 8,* 53–57.

Bachorowski, J., & Owren, M. J. (2001). Not all laughs are alike: Voiced but not unvoiced laughter readily elicits positive affect. *Psychological Science, 12,* 252–257.

Bachorowski, J., Smoski, M. J., & Owren, M. J. (2001). The acoustic features of human laughter. *Journal of the Acoustical Society of America, 110,* 1581–1597.

Back, M. D., Stopfer, J. M., Vazire, S., Gaddis, S., Schmukle, S. C., Egloff, B., & Gosling, S. D. (2010). Facebook profiles reflect actual personality, not self-idealization. *Psychological Science, 21,* 372–374.

Baddeley, A. D. (1998). The central executive: A concept and some misconceptions. *Journal of the International Neuropsychological Society, 4,* 523–526.

Baddeley, A. D. (2003). Working memory: Looking back and looking forward. *Nature Reviews Neuroscience, 4,* 829–839.

Baddeley, A. D. (2007). *Working memory, thought, and action.* New York, NY: Oxford University Press.

Baer, R. A., Smith, G. T., Hopkins, J., Krietemeyer, J., & Toney, L. (2006). Using self-report assessment methods to explore facets of mindfulness. *Assessment, 13,* 27–45.

Bagwell, C. L., Newcomb, A. F., & Bukowski, W. M. (1998). Preadolescent friendship and rejection as predictors of adult adjustment. *Child Development, 69,* 140–153.

Baier, B., Karnath, H., Dieterich, M., Birklein, F., Heinze, C., & Müller, N. G. (2010). Keeping memory clear and stable—The contribution of human basal ganglia and prefrontal cortex to working memory. *Journal of Neuroscience, 30,* 9788–9792. doi:10.1523/JNEUROSCI.1513–10.2010

Bailey, D. S. (2004). Why accreditation matters. *gradPSYCH, 2.* Retrieved from http://gradpsych.apags.org/apr04/accreditation.cfm

Bailey, M. J., Dunne, M. P., & Martin, N. G. (2000). Genetic and environment effects on sexual orientation and its correlates in an Australian twin sample. *Journal of Personality and Social Psychology, 78,* 524–536.

Bailey, M. J., Kirk, K. M., Zhu, G., Dunne, M. P., & Martin, N. G. (2000). Do individual differences in sociosexuality represent genetic or environmentally contingent strategies? Evidence from the Australian twin registry. *Journal of Personality and Social Psychology, 78,* 537–545.

Bailey, M. J., & Zucker, K. J. (1995). Childhood sex-typed behavior and sexual orientation: A conceptual analysis and quantitative review. *Developmental Psychology, 31,* 43–55.

Bailey, N. W., & Zuk, M. (2009). Same-sex sexual behavior and evolution. *Trends in Ecology & Evolution, 24,* 439–446.

Baillargeon, R., & DeVos, J. (1991). Object permanence in young infants: Further evidence. *Child Development, 62,* 1227–1246.

Baird, J. C., Wagner, M., & Fuld, K. (1990). A simple but powerful theory of the moon illusion. *Journal of Experimental Psychology: Human Perception and Performance, 16,* 675–677.

Baldwin, D. S., & Polkinghorn, C. (2005). Evidence-based pharmacotherapy of generalized anxiety disorder. *International Journal of Neuropsychopharmacology, 8,* 293–302.

Ball, K., Berch, D. B., Helmers, K. F., Jobe, J. B., Leveck, M. D., Marsiske, M., . . . Willis, S. (2002). Effects of cognitive training interventions with older adults: A randomized control trial. *Journal of the American Medical Association, 288,* 2271–2281.

Ball, K., Crawford, D., & Kenardy, J. (2004). Longitudinal relationships among overweight, life satisfaction, and aspirations in young women. *Obesity Research, 12,* 1019–1030.

Ballanyi, K., Panaitescu, B., & Ruangkittisakul, A. (2010). Control of breathing by "Nerve Glue." *Science Signaling, 3*(147), pe41. doi:10.1126/scisignal.3147pe41

Balsis, S., Carpenter, B., & Storandt, M. (2005). Personality change precedes clinical diagnosis of dementia of the Alzheimer type. *The Journals of Gerontology: Series B: Psychological Sciences and Social Sciences, 60B,* P98–P101.

Baltes, P. B., Reuter-Lorenz, P. A., & Rösler, F. (Eds.). (2006). *Lifespan development and the brain: The perspective of biocultural co-constructivism.* New York, NY: Cambridge University Press.

Baltes, P. B., & Smith, J. (2008). The fascination of wisdom: Its nature, ontogeny, and function. *Perspectives on Psychological Science, 3,* 56–64.

Banaji, M. R. (2007). Unraveling beliefs. Retrieved from http://www.edge.org/q2007/q07_13.html

Banaji, M. R., & Greenwald, A. G. (1995). Implicit gender stereotyping in judgments of fame. *Journal of Personality and Social Psychology, 68,* 181–198.

Bandura, A. (1969). *Principles of behavior modification.* New York, NY: Holt, Rinehart & Winston.

Bandura, A. (1986). *Social foundations of thought and action: A social cognitive theory.* Englewood Cliffs, NJ: Prentice-Hall.

Bandura, A. (1997). *Self-efficacy: The exercise of control.* New York, NY: Freeman.

Bandura, A. (2006). Autobiography. In M G. Lindzey & W. M. Runyan (Eds.), *A history of psychology in autobiography* (Vol. 9; pp. 43–75) Washington, DC: American Psychological Association.

Bandura, A., Ross, D., & Ross, S. A. (1961). Transmission of aggression through imitation of aggressive models. *Journal of Abnormal and Social Psychology, 63,* 575–582.

Bandura, A., Ross, D., & Ross, S. A. (1963). Vicarious reinforcement and imitative learning. *Journal of Abnormal & Social Psychology, 67,* 601–608.

Banks, M. S., & Salapatek, P. (1983). Infant visual perception. In P. H. Mussen (Ed.), *Handbook of child psychology* (4th ed., Vol. 2). New York, NY: Wiley.

Bar-On, R. (2004). The Bar-On Emotional Quotient Inventory (EQ-i): Rationale, description, and summary. In G. Geher (Ed.), *Measuring emotional intelligence: Common ground and controversy* (pp. 111–142). Hauppauge, NY: Nova Science.

Barbazanges, A., Piazza, P. V., Le Moal, M., & Maccari, S. (1996). Maternal glucocorticoid secretion mediates long-term effects of prenatal stress. *Journal of Neuroscience, 16,* 3943–3949.

Barber, L. K., Munz, D. C., Bagsby, P. G., & Powell, E. D. (2010). Sleep consistency and sufficiency: Are both necessary for less psychological strain? *Stress and Health, 26,* 186–193.

Barbour, K. A., Edenfield, T. M., & Blumenthal, J. A. (2007). Exercise as a treatment for depression and other psychiatric disorders. *Journal of Cardiopulmonary Rehabilitation and Prevention, 27,* 359–367.

Barch, D. M. (2005). The cognitive neuroscience of schizophrenia. *Annual Review of Clinical Psychology, 1,* 321–353.

Bargh J. A. (1997). The automaticity of everyday life. In R. S. Wyer, Jr. (Ed.), *The automaticity of everyday life: Advances in social cognition* (pp. 1–61). Mahwah, NJ: Erlbaum.

Barkham, M., Connell, J., Stiles, W. B., Miles, J. N. V., Margison, F., Evans, C., & Mellor-Clark, J. (2006). Dose-effect relations and responsive regulation of treatment duration: The good enough level. *Journal of Consulting and Clinical Psychology, 74,* 160–167.

Barlow, D. H. (2004). Psychological treatments. *American Psychologist, 59,* 869–878.

Barlow, J. H., Powell, L. A., Gilchrist, M., & Fotiadou, M. (2008). The effectiveness of the Training and Support Program for parents of children with disabilities: A randomized controlled trial. *Journal of Psychosomatic Research, 64,* 55–62.

Baron, A., & Galizio, M. (2006). The distinction between positive and negative reinforcement: Use with care. *Behavior Analyst, 296,* 141–151.

Baron-Cohen, S., Bolton, P., Wheelwright, S., Scahill, V., Short, L., Mead, G., & Smith, A. (1998). Autism occurs more often in families of physicists, engineers, and mathematicians. *Autism, 2,* 296–301.

Baron-Cohen, S., Wheelwright, S., Skinner, R., Martin, J., and Clubley, E. (2001). The Autism-Spectrum Quotient (AQ): Evidence from Asperger syndrome/high-functioning autism, males and females, scientists and mathematicians. *Journal of Autism & Developmental Disorders, 31,* 5–17.

Baron-Cohen, S., Wheelwright, S., Stott, C., Bolton, P., & Goodyer, I. (1997). Is there a link between engineering and autism? *Autism, 1,* 101–109.

Barr, C. L., Kroft, J., Feng, Y., Wigg, K., Roberts, W., Malone, M., . . . Kennedy, J. L. (2002). The norepinephrine transporter gene and attention-deficit hyperactivity disorder. *American Journal of Medical Genetics, 114,* 255–259.

Barrett, L. F., Lane, R. D., Sechrest, L., & Schwartz, G. E. (2000). Sex differences in emotional awareness. *Personality and Social Psychology Bulletin, 26,* 1027–1035.

Barrett, L. F., Ochsner, K. N., & Gross, J. J. (2007). On the automaticity of emotion. In J. Bargh (Ed.), *Social psychology and the unconscious: The automaticity of higher mental processes* (pp. 173–217). New York, NY: Psychology Press.

Barth, J., Schumacher, M., & Herrmann-Lingen, C. (2004). Depression as a risk factor for mortality in patients with coronary heart disease: A meta-analysis. *Psychosomatic Medicine, 66,* 802–813.

Bartholow, B. D., Bushman, B. J., & Sestir, M. A. (2006). Chronic violent video game exposure and desensitization to violence: Behavioral and event-related brain potential data. *Journal of Experimental Social Psychology, 42,* 532–539.

Basak, C., Boot, W. R., Voss, M. W., & Kramer, A. F. (2008). Can training in a real-time strategy video game attenuate cognitive decline in older adults? *Psychology and Aging, 23,* 765–777.

Basbaum A. L., & Jessell, T. M. (2000). The perception of pain. In E. R. Kandel, J. H. Schwartz, & T. M. Jessell (Eds.), *Principles of neural science* (4th ed., pp. 472–491). New York, NY: McGraw-Hill.

Bassett, E. B., Verchinski, B. A., Mattay, V. S., Weinberger, D. R., & Meyer-Lindenberg, A. (2008). Hierarchical organization of human cortical networks in health and schizophrenia. *The Journal of Neuroscience, 28,* 9239–9248.

Basson, R. (2000). The female sexual response: A different model. *Journal of Sex & Marital Therapy, 26,* 51–65.

Batey, M., & Furnham, A. (2008). Creativity, intelligence, and personality: A critical review of the scattered literature. *Genetic, Social, and General Psychology Monographs, 132,* 355–429.

Batson, C. D. (1991). *The altruism question: Toward a social psychological answer.* Hillsdale, NJ: Erlbaum.

Batson, C. D., Fultz, J., & Schoenrade, P. A. (1987). Distress and empathy: Two qualitatively distinct vicarious emotions with different motivational consequences. *Journal of Personality, 55,* 19–39.

Bauer, B. A., Cutshall, S. M., Wentworth, L. J., Engen, D., Messner, P. K., Wood, C. M. . . . Sundt, T. M. (2010). Effects of massage therapy on pain, anxiety, and tension after cardiac surgery: A randomized study. *Complementary Therapies in Clinical Practice, 16,* 70–75.

Bauer, F., Korpert, K., Neuberger, M., Raber, A., & Schwetz, F. (1991). Risk factors for hearing loss at different frequencies in a population of 47388 noise-exposed workers. *Journal of Acoustic Society of America, 6,* 3086–3098.

Bauer, M., & Whybrow, P. C. (2001). Thyroid hormone, neural tissue and mood modulation. *World Journal of Biological Psychiatry, 2,* 57–67.

Bauer, M. S., & Mitchner, L. (2004). What is a "mood stabilizer"? An evidence-based response. *American Journal of Psychiatry, 161,* 3–18.

Baumeister, R. F., & Leary, M. (1995). The need to belong: Desire for interpersonal attachments as a fundamental human motivation. *Psychological Bulletin, 117,* 497–529.

Baumeister, R. F., & Masicampo, E. J. (2010). Conscious thought is for facilitating social and cultural interactions: How mental simulations serve the animal–culture interface. *Psychological Review, 117,* 945–971.

Baumeister, R. F., Masicampo, E. J., & Vohs, K. D. (2011, in press for). Do conscious thoughts cause behavior? *Annual Review of Psychology.*

Baumrind, D. (1964). Some thoughts on ethics of research: After reading Milgram's "Behavioral study of obedience." *American Psychologist, 19,* 421–423.

Bavelier, D., Tomann, A., Hutton, C., Mitchell, T., Corina, D., Liu, G., et al. (2000). Visual attention to the periphery is enhanced in congenitally deaf individuals. *Journal of Neuroscience, 20,* 1–6.

Beadle-Brown, J., Murphy, G., & Wing, L. (2006). The Camberwell cohort 25 years on: Characteristics and changes in skills over time. *Journal of Applied Research in Intellectual Disabilities, 19,* 317–329.

Beauchamp, G. K., & Mennella, J. A. (2009). Early flavor learning and its impact on later feeding behavior. *Journal of Pediatric Gastroenterology & Nutrition, 48,* S25–S30. doi: 10.1097/MPG.0b013e31819774a5

Beck, A. T., & Emery, G. (1985). *Anxiety disorders and phobias.* New York, NY: Basic Books.

Beebe, D. W., Rose, D., & Amin, R. (2010). Attention, learning, and arousal of experimentally sleep-restricted adolescents in a simulated classroom. *Journal of Adolescent Health, 47,* 523–525. doi:10.1016/j.jadohealth.2010.03.005

Beede, K. E., & Kass, S. J. (2006). Engrossed in conversation: The impact of cell phones on simulated driving performance. *Accident Analysis and Prevention, 38,* 415–421.

Beekman, A. T. F., Smit, F., Stek, M. L., Reynolds, C. F., & Cuijpers, P. C. (2010). Preventing depression in high-risk groups. *Current Opinion in Psychiatry, 23,* 8–11.

Beeman, M. J., & Bowden, E. M. (2000). The right hemisphere maintains solution-related activation for yet-to-be solved insight problems. *Memory & Cognition, 28,* 1231–1241.

Beever, T. G., & Chiarello, R. J. (2009). Cerebral dominance in musicians and non-musicians. *Science, 185,* 537–539.

Begley, S. (2007). *Train your mind, change your brain.* New York, NY: Ballantine Books.

Begley, S. (2009, July 9). What's in a word? *Newsweek.* Retrieved from http://www.newsweek.com

Belisle, P., & Chapais, B. (2001). Tolerated co-feeding in relation to degree of kinship in Japanese macaques. *Behaviour, 138,* 487–509.

Bell, A. P., Weinberg, M. S., & Hammersmith, S. K. (1981). *Sexual preference: Its development in men and women.* Bloomington: Indiana University Press.

Bellack, A. S., Bennett, M. E., Gearon, J. S., Brown, C. H., & Yang, Y. (2006). A randomized clinical trial of a new behavioral treatment for drug abuse in people with severe and persistent mental illness. *Archives of General Psychiatry, 63,* 426–432.

Belmonte, M. K., Allen, G., Beckel-Mitchener, A., Boulanger, L. M., Carper, R. A., & Webb, S. J. (2004). Autism and abnormal development of brain connectivity. *Journal of Neuroscience, 24,* 9228–9231.

Bem, D. J., & Horonton, C. (1994). Does psi exist? Replicable evidence for an anomalous process of information transfer. *Psychological Bulletin, 115,* 4–18.

Benes, F. M. (2001). Carlsson and the discovery of dopamine. *Trends in Pharmacological Sciences, 22,* 46–47.

Benet-Martinez, V., & Oishi, S. (2008). Culture and personality. In O. P. John, R. W. Robins, & L. A. Pervin (Eds.), *Handbook of personality: Theory and research* (pp. 542–567). New York, NY: Guilford Press.

Benjamin, J., Li, L., Patterson, C., Greenburg, B. D., Murphy, D. L., & Hamer, D. H. (1996). Population and familial association between the D4 dopamine receptor gene and measures of novelty seeking. *Nature Genetics, 12,* 81–84.

Benjamin, L. T., Jr. (2007). *A brief history of modern psychology.* Malden, MA: Blackwell.

Bennett, C. M., & Baird, A. A. (2006). Anatomical changes in the emerging adult brain: A voxel-based morphometry study. *Human Brain Mapping, 27,* 766–777.

Bennett, E. L., Diamond, M. C., Krech, D., & Rosenzweig, M. R. (1964). Chemical and anatomical plasticity of brain. *Science, 146,* 610–619.

Bennett, P. J., Sekuler, R., & Sekuler, A. B. (2007). The effects of aging on motion detection and direction identification. *Vision Research, 47,* 799–809.

Berenbaum, S. A., Korman, K., & Leveroni, C. (1995). Early hormones and sex differences in cognitive abilities. *Learning and Individual Differences, 7,* 303–321.

Berger, J. (1994). *The young scientists: America's future and the winning of the Westinghouse.* Reading, MA: Addison-Wesley.

Berghöfer, A., Alda, M., Adli, M., Baethge, C., Bauer, M., Bschor, T., . . . Pfennig, A. (2008). Long-term effectiveness of lithium in bipolar disorder: A multicenter investigation of patients with typical and atypical features. *Journal of Clinical Psychiatry, 69,* 1860–1868. doi:10.4088/JCP.v69n1203

Berkman, L. F., & Glass, T. (2000). Social integration, social networks, social support and health. In L. F. Berkman & I. Kawachi (Eds.), *Social epidemiology* (pp. 137–173). New York, NY: Oxford University Press.

Berlyne, D. (1960). *Conflict, arousal, and curiosity.* New York, NY: McGraw-Hill.

Berna, C., Leknes, S., Holmes, E. A., Edwards, R. R., Goodwin, G., & Tracey, I. (2010). Induction of depressed mood disrupts emotion regulation neurocircuitry and enhances pain unpleasantness. *Biological Psychiatry, 67,* 1083–1090.

Bernat, J. (2006). Chronic disorders of consciousness. *Lancet, 367,* 1181–1192.

Bernier, A., Carlson, S. M., Bordeleau, S., & Carrier, J. (2010). Relations between physiological and cognitive regulatory systems: Infant sleep regulation and subsequent executive functioning. *Child Development, 81,* 1739–1752. doi:10.1111/j.1467-8624.2010.01507.x

Bernier, R., & Dawson, G. (2009). The role of mirror neuron dysfunction in autism. In J. A. Pineda (Ed.), *Mirror neuron systems: The role of mirroring processes in social cognition* (pp. 261–286). Totowa, NJ: Humana Press.

Berridge, K. C. (2004). Motivation concepts in behavioral neuroscience. *Physiology and Behavior, 81,* 179–209.

Berry, C. M., Ones, D. S., & Sackett, P. R. (2007). Interpersonal deviance, organizational deviance, and their common correlates: A review and meta-analysis. *Journal of Applied Psychology, 92,* 410–424.

Berthoud, H. R. (2002). Multiple neural systems controlling food intake and body weight. *Neuroscience and Biobehavioral Reviews, 26,* 393–428.

Bexton, W. H., Heron, W., & Scott, T. H. (1954). Effects of decreased variation in the sensory environment. *Canadian Journal of Psychology, 8,* 70–76.

Bialystok, E., & Craik, F. I. M. (2010). Cognitive and linguistic processing in the bilingual mind. *Current Directions in Psychological Science, 19,* 19–23.

Bialystok, E., Craik, F. I. M., & Ryan, J. (2006). Executive control in a modified antisaccade task: Effects of aging and bilingualism. *Journal of Experimental Psychology: Learning, Memory, & Cognition, 32,* 1341–1354.

Bickerton, D. (1995). *Language and human behavior.* Seattle: University of Washington Press.

Binder, E., Droste, S. K., Ohl, F., & Reul, J. M. (2004). Regular voluntary exercise reduces anxiety-related behavior and impulsiveness in mice. *Behavioural Brain Research, 155,* 197–206.

Biography, Esref Armagan. (n.d.). Retrieved October 23, 2007, from http://www.esrefarmagan.com/bio.html

Birch, L. L., & Fisher, J. A. (1996). The role of experience in the development of children's eating behavior. In E. D. Capaldi (Ed.), *Why we eat what we eat: The psychology of eating* (pp. 113–141). Washington, DC: American Psychological Association.

Birch, L. L., & Marlin, D. W. (1982). I don't like it; I never tried it: Effects of exposure on two-year-old children's food preferences. *Appetite, 3,* 353–360.

Birdsong, D. (2005). Interpreting age effects in second language acquisition. In J. F. Kroll & A. M. B. de Groot, (Eds.), *Handbook of bilingualism: Psycholinguistic approaches* (pp. 109–127). New York, NY: Oxford University Press.

Birdsong, D. (2006). Age and second language acquisition and processing: A selective overview. *Language Learning, 56,* 9–49.

Bishop, S. J. (2007). Neurocognitive mechanisms of anxiety: An integrative account. *Trends in Cognitive Sciences, 11,* 307–316.

Bjork, R. A. (2001, March). How to succeed in college: Learn how to learn. *American Psychological Society Observer, 14,* 3, 9.

Black, D. W. (2006). Efficacy of combined pharmacotherapy and psychotherapy versus monotherapy in the treatment of anxiety disorders. *CNS Spectrums, 11,* 29–33.

Blais, A., Gidengil, E., Fourneir, P., Nevitte, N., Everit, J., & Kim, J. (2010). Political judgments, perceptions of facts, and partisan effects. *Electoral Studies, 29,* 1–12.

Blais, J., Craig, W., Pepler, D., & Connolly, J. (2008). Adolescents online: The importance of Internet activity choices to salient relationships. *Journal of Youth and Adolescence, 37,* 522–536.

Blakeslee, S. (2005, February 8). Focus narrows in search for autism's cause. *The New York Times.* Retrieved from http://www.nytimes.com

Blakeslee, S., & Blakeslee, M. (2007). *The body has a mind of its own.* New York, NY: Random House.

Blanco, C., Okuda, M., Wright, C., Hasin, D., Grant, B., Liu, S., & Olfson, M. (2008). Mental health of college students and their non-college-attending peers: Results from the National Epidemiologic Study on Alcohol and Related Conditions. *Archives of General Psychiatry, 65,* 1429–1437. doi:10.1001/archpsyc.65.12.1429

Blass, T. (2004). *The man who shocked the world: The life and legacy of Stanley Milgram.* New York, NY: Basic Books.

Bleier, P., Habib, R., & Flament, M. F. (2006). Pharmacotherapies in the management of obsessive-compulsive disorder. *Canadian Journal of Psychiatry, 51,* 417–430.

Block, J., Block, J. H., & Keyes, S. (1988). Longitudinally foretelling drug usage in adolescence: Early childhood personality and environmental precursors. *Child Development, 59,* 336–355.

Block, J. J. (2008). Issues for *DSM-V:* Internet addiction. *American Journal of Psychiatry, 165,* 306–307.

Blonigen, D. M., Hicks, B. M., Krueger, R. F., Patrick, C. J., & Iacono, W. G. (2006). Continuity and change in psychopathic traits as measured via normal-range personality: A longitudinal–biometric study. *Journal of Abnormal Psychology, 115,* 85–95.

Bocchieri Riccardi, L. (2007). Psychological well-being and relationship changes in women after gastric bypass surgery. *Dissertation Abstracts International: Section B: The Sciences and Engineering, 67*(7-B), 4091.

Bollen, E., & Wojciechowski, F. L. (2004). Anorexia nervosa subtypes and the Big Five personality factors. *European Eating Disorders Review, 12,* 117–121.

Bolour, S., & Braunstein, G. (2005). Testosterone therapy in women: A review. *International Journal of Impotence Research, 17,* 399–408.

Bond, R., & Smith, P. B. (1996). Culture and conformity: A meta-analysis of studies using Asch's (1952b, 1956) line judgment task. *Psychological Bulletin, 119,* 111–137.

Boneva, B. S., Quinn, A., Kraut, R. E., Kiesler, S., & Shklovski, I. (2006). Teenage communication in the instant messaging era. In R. Kraut, M. Brynin, & S. Kiesler (Eds.), *Information technology at home* (pp. 612–672). New York, NY: Oxford University Press.

Bonnet, M., Decety, J., Jeannerod, M., & Requin, J. (1997). Mental simulation of an action modulates the excitability of spinal reflex pathways in man. *Cognitive Brain Research, 5,* 221–228.

Boorboor, S. (2002). Integrating the incompatible: The rise of the incorporated immune system. [University of Rochester] *Journal of Undergraduate Research, 1,* 10–26.

Boroditsky, L. (2001). Does language shape thought? Mandarin and English speakers' conceptions of time. *Cognitive Psychology, 43,* 1–22. doi:10.1006/cogp.2001.0748

Boska, P. (2008). Maternal infection during pregnancy and schizophrenia. *Journal of Psychiatry and Neuroscience, 33,* 183–185.

Botvinick, M. M., Cohen, J. D., & Carter, C. S. (2004). Conflict monitoring and anterior cingulate cortex: An update. *Trends in Cognitive Sciences, 8,* 539–546.

Botwin, M. M., Buss, D. M., & Shackelford, T. K. (1997). Personality and mate preferences: Five factors in mate selection and marital satisfaction. *Journal of Personality and Social Psychology, 65,* 107–136.

Bouchard, T. J., Jr., & Loehlin, J. C. (2001). Genes, evolution, and personality. *Behavioral Genetics, 31,* 243–273.

Bourgeois, S., & Johnson, A. (2004). Preparing for dying: Meaningful practices in palliative care. *Omega: Journal of Death and Dying, 49,* 99–107.

Bouso, J. C., Doblin, R., Farré, M., Alcázar, M. A., & Gómez-Jarabo, G. (2008). MDMA-assisted psychotherapy using low doses in a small sample of women with chronic posttraumatic stress disorder. *Journal of Psychoactive Drugs, 40,* 225–236.

Bouton, M. E., Mineka, S., & Barlow, D. H. (2001). A modern learning theory perspective on the etiology of panic disorder. *Psychological Review, 108,* 4–32.

Bowden, C. L. (1994). Bipolar disorder and creativity. In M. P. Shaw & M. A. Runco (Eds.), *Creativity and affect* (pp. 73–86). Norwood, NJ: Ablex.

Bowden, E. M., & Jung-Beeman, M. (2003). Aha! Insight experience correlates with solution activation in the right hemisphere. *Psychonomic Bulletin & Review, 10,* 730–737.

Bowden, E. M., Jung-Beeman, M., Fleck, J., & Kounios, J. (2005). New approaches to demystifying insight. *Trends in Cognitive Sciences, 9,* 322–328.

Bower, B. (2005, December 10). The Piraha challenge: An Amazonian tribe takes grammar to a strange place. *Science News, 168*(24). Retrieved from http://www.sciencenews.org

Bowlby, J. (1969). *Attachment and loss: Vol. 1. Attachment.* New York, NY: Basic Books.

Bowlby, J. (1973). *Attachment and loss: Vol. 2. Separation, anxiety, and anger.* New York, NY: Basic Books.

Bowlby, J. (1980). *Attachment and loss: Vol. 3. Loss, sadness, and depression.* New York, NY: Basic Books.

Bowman, L. L., Levine, L. E., Waite, B. M., & Gendron, M. (2010). Can students really multitask? An experimental study of instant messaging while reading. *Computers and Education, 54,* 927–931.

Boyack, K. W., Klavans, R., & Börner, K. (2005). Mapping the backbone of science. *Scientometrics, 64,* 351–374.

Boyd, D. (2007). Why youth (heart) Social Network Sites: The role of networked publics in teenage social life. In D. Buckingham (Ed.), *MacArthur Foundation Series on Digital Learning—Youth, Identity, and Digital Media Volume* (pp. 1–26). Cambridge, MA: MIT Press.

Bradberry, C. W. (2007). Cocaine sensitization and dopamine mediation of cue effects in rodents, monkeys, and humans: Areas of agreement, disagreement, and implications for addiction. *Psychopharmacology, 191,* 705–717.

Bradley, R. M. (1972). Development of the taste bud and gustatory papillae in human fetuses. In J. F. Bosma (Ed.), *The third symposium on oral sensation and perception: The mouth of the infant.* Springfield, IL: Thomas.

Brain, Marshall. (2003). How 3-D glasses work. Retrieved from http://science .howstuffworks.com/3-d-glasses2.htm

Brand, G., & Millot, J-L. (2001). Sex differences in human olfaction: Between evidence and enigma. *The Quarterly Journal of Experimental Psychology B: Comparative and Physiological Psychology, 54B,* 259–270.

Brand, S., Gerber, M., Beck, J., Hatzinger, M., Pühse, W., & Holsboer-Trachsler, M. (2010). High exercise levels are related to favorable sleep patterns and psychological functioning in adolescents: A comparison of athletes and controls. *Journal of Adolescent Health, 46,* 133–141.

Brandtzæg, P. B., Lüders, M., & Skjetne, J. H. (2010). Too many Facebook "friends"? Content sharing and sociability versus the need for privacy in social network sites. *International Journal of Human-Computer Interaction, 26,* 1006–1030.

Braver, T. S., & Barch, D. M. (2002). A theory of cognitive control, aging, cognition, and neuromodulation. *Neuroscience and Biobehavioral Reviews, 26,* 809–817.

Breiter, H. C., Etcoff, N. L., Whalen, P. J., Kennedy, W. A., Rauch, S. L., Buckner, R. L., . . . Rosen, B. R. (1996). Response and habituation of the human amygdala during visual processing of facial expressions. *Neuron, 17,* 875–887.

Breland, K., & Breland, M. (1961). The misbehavior of organisms. *American Psychologist, 16,* 681–684.

Brennan, P. A. (2010). On the scent of sexual attraction. *BMC Biology, 8,* 71–74.

Breugelmans, S. M., Poortinga, Y. H., Ambadar, Z., Setiadi, B., Vaca, J. B., Widiyanto, B., et al. (2005). Body sensations associated with emotions in Rarámuri Indians, rural Javanese, and three student samples. *Emotion, 5,* 166–174.

Brewer, M. B., & Caporael, L. R. (2006). An evolutionary perspective on social identity: Revisiting groups. In M. Schaller, D. T. Kenrick, & J. A. Simpson (Eds.), *Evolution and social psychology* (pp. 143–161). New York, NY: Psychology Press.

Bridges, K. (1932). Emotional development in infancy. *Child Development, 3,* 324–341.

Briggs, C. (2005). Allen uses films to avoid anxiety. *BBC News-Online.* Retrieved July 3, 2008, from http://news.bbc.co.uk/2/hi/entertainment/4539493.stm

Brivic, S. (1980). *Joyce between Freud and Jung.* Port Washington, NY: Kennikat Press.

Broadbent, D. E. (1954). The role of auditory localization in attention and memory span. *Journal of Experimental Psychology, 44,* 51–55.

Broekman, B. F. P., Chan, Y-H., Chong, Y-S., Quek, S-C., Fung, D., Low, Y-L. . . . Saw, S-M. (2009). The influence of birth size on intelligence in healthy children. *Pediatrics, 123,* e1011–e1016.

Broude G., & Greene, S. (1980). Cross-cultural codes on 20 sexual attitudes and practices. In H. Barry & A. Schlegel (Eds.), *Cross-cultural samples and codes* (pp. 313–333). Pittsburgh, PA: University of Pittsburgh Press.

Brown, A. S. (2006). Prenatal infection as a risk factor for schizophrenia. *Schizophrenia Bulletin, 32,* 200–202.

Brown, K. W., & Ryan, R. M. (2003). The benefits of being present: Mindfulness and its role in psychological well-being. *Journal of Personality and Social Psychology, 84,* 822–848.

Brown, R., & Kulik, J. (1977). Flashbulb memories. *Cognition, 5,* 73–99.

Brown, R. T., Reynolds, C. R., & Whitaker, J. S. (1999). Bias in mental testing since Jensen's "Bias in Mental Testing." *School Psychology Quarterly, 14,* 208–238.

Brown, T. S., & Wallace, P. (1980). *Physiological psychology.* New York, NY: Academic Press.

Brown/grizzly bear facts. (n.d.). Retrieved November 5, 2007 from http://www.bear.org/Grizzly/Grizzly_Brown_Bear_Facts.html

Brunelin, J., Poulet, E., Bor, J., Rivet, A., Eche, J., d'Amato, T., & Saoud, M. (2010). Transcranial magnetic stimulation (rTMS) and negative symptoms of schizophrenia. *Annales Médico-Psychologiques, 168,* 422–427.

Bruner, J. S., & Minturn, A. L. (1955). Perceptual identification and perceptual organization. *Journal of General Psychology, 53,* 21–28.

Brunetti, M., Babiloni, C., Ferretti, A., Del Gratta, C., Merla, A., Olivetti, M., . . . Romani, G. L. (2008). Hypothalamus, sexual arousal and psychosexual identity in human males: A functional magnetic resonance imaging study. *European Journal of Neuroscience, 27,* 2922–2927.

Brunwasser, S. M., Gillham, J. E., & Kim, E. S. (2009). A meta-analytic review of Penn Resiliency Program's effect on depressive symptoms. *Journal of Consulting and Clinical Psychology, 77,* 1042–1054.

Bryans, W. A. (1959). Mitotic activity in the brain of the adult white rat. *Anatomical Record, 133,* 65–71.

Buboltz, W. C., Loveland, J., Jenkins, S. M., Brown, F., Soper, B., & Hodges, J. (2006). College student sleep: Relationship to health and academic performance. In M. V. Landow (Ed.), *College students: Mental health and coping strategies* (pp. 1–39). Hauppauge, NY: Nova Science.

Buchanan, J., & Houlihan, D. (2008). The use of in vivo desensitization for the treatment of a specific phobia of earthworms. *Clinical Case Studies, 7,* 12–24. doi:10.1177/1534650107300863

Buchanan, T. W., Denburg, N. L., Tranel, D., & Adolphs, R. (2001). Verbal and nonverbal emotional memory following unilateral amygdala damage. *Learning & Memory, 8,* 326–335. doi:10.1101/lm.40101

Buchanan, T. W., & Tranel, D. (2008). Stress and emotional memory retrieval: Effects of sex and cortisol response. *Neurobiology of Learning and Memory, 89,* 134–141.

Buck, L. B. (2000). Smell and taste: The chemical senses. In E. R. Kandel, J. H. Schwartz, & T. M. Jessell (Eds.), *Principles of neural science* (4th ed., pp. 625–647). New York, NY: McGraw-Hill.

Buckley, C. (2007, January 3). Man is rescued by stranger on subway tracks. *The New York Times.* Retrieved from http://www .nytimes.com

Buka, S. L., Tsuang, M. T., Torrey, E. F., Klebanoff, M. A., Bernstein, D., & Yolken, R. H. (2001). Maternal infections and subsequent psychosis among offspring. *Archives of General Psychiatry, 58,* 1032–1037.

Bukowski, W. M., & Sippola, L. K. (2001). Groups, individuals, and victimization: A view of the peer system. In J. Juvonen & S. Graham (Eds.), *Peer harassment in school: The plight of the vulnerable and victimized* (pp. 355–377). New York: Guilford.

Bulik, C. M., Sullivan, P. F., Tozzi, F., Furberg, H., Lichtenstein, P., & Pedersen, N. L. (2006). Prevalence, heritability, and prospective risk factors for anorexia nervosa. *Archives of General Psychiatry, 63,* 305–312.

Bulkeley, K. (1997). *An introduction to the psychology of dreaming.* Westport, CT: Praeger.

Bullivant, S. B., Sellergren, S. A., Stern, K. Spencer, N. A., Jacob, S., Mennella, J. A., & McClintock, M. K. (2004). Women's sexual experience during the menstrual cycle: Identification of the sexual phase by noninvasive measurement of luteinizing hormone. *Journal of Sex Research, 41,* 82–93.

Burch, G., Pavelis, C., Hemsley, D. R., & Corr, P. J. (2006). Schizotypy and creativity in visual artists. *British Journal of Psychology, 97*, 177–190.

Burchell, A. N., Calzavara, L. M., Myers, T., Remis, R. S., Raboud, J., Corey, P., & Swantee, C. (2010). Stress and increased HIV infection risk among gay and bisexual men. *AIDS, 24*, 1757–1764.

Burd, L., Roberts, D., Olson, M., & Odendaal, H. (2007). Ethanol and the placenta: A review. *The Journal of Maternal-Fetal and Neonatal Medicine, 20*, 361–375.

Burgess, W. (2009). *The depression answer book*. Naperville, IL: Sourcebooks.

Burnett, G. B., Moll, J., Frith, C., & Blakemore, S-J. (2008). Development during adolescence of the neural processing of social emotion. *Journal of Cognitive Neuroscience 21*, 1736–1750.

Burnstein, E., Crandall, C., & Kitayama, S. (1994). Some neo-Darwinian decision rules for altruism: Weighing cues for inclusive fitness as a function of the biological importance of the decision. *Journal of Personality and Social Psychology, 67*, 773–789.

Burt, K. B., & Masten, A. S. (2010). Development in the transition to adulthood: Vulnerabilities and opportunities. In J. E. Grant & M. N. Potenza (Eds.), *Young adult mental health* (pp. 5–18). New York, NY: Oxford University Press.

Burton, C. M., & King, L. A. (2009). The health benefits of writing about positive experiences: The role of broadened cognition. *Psychology & Health, 24*, 867–879.

Busch, N., Fründ, I., & Herrmann, C. (2009). Electrophysiological evidence for different types of change detection and change blindness. *Journal of Cognitive Neuroscience, 22*, 1852–1869.

Bushman, B. J., & Anderson, C. A. (2001). Media violence and the American public: Scientific facts versus media misinformation. *American Psychologist, 56*, 477–489.

Buss, A. H., & Plomin, R. (1984). Temperament: Early personality traits. Hillsdale, NJ: Erlbaum.

Buss, D. M. (1999). *Evolutionary psychology: The new science of the mind*. New York, NY: Allyn & Bacon.

Buss, D. M. (2003). *The evolution of desire: Strategies of human mating* (Rev. ed.). New York, NY: Basic Books.

Buss, D. M. (2004). Sex differences in human mate preferences. In H. T. Reis & C. E. Rusbult (Eds.), *Close relationships: Key readings* (pp. 135–151). Philadelphia: Taylor & Francis.

Buss, D. M. (2008). Human nature and individual differences: Evolution of human personality. In O. P. John, R. W. Robins, & L. A. Pervin (Eds.), *Handbook of personality: Theory and research* (pp. 29–60). New York, NY: Guilford Press.

Buss, D. M., & Greiling, H. (1999). Adaptive individual differences. *Journal of Personality, 67*, 209–243.

Buss, D. M., & Schmitt, D. P. (1993). Sexual strategies theory: An evolutionary perspective on human mating. *Psychological Review, 100*, 204–232.

Bussing, R., Gary, F. A., Mills, T. L., & Wilson Garvan, C. (2007). Cultural variations in parental health beliefs, knowledge, and information sources related to attention-deficit/hyperactivity disorder. *Journal of Family Issues, 28*, 291–318. doi:10.1177/0192513X06296117

Cacioppo, J. T., Fowler, J. H., & Christakis, N. A. (2009). Alone in the crowd: The structure and spread of loneliness in a large social network. *Journal of Personality and Social Psychology, 97*, 977–991.

Cahill, S. P., Foa, E. B., Hembree E. A., Marshall, R. D., & Nacash, N. (2006). Dissemination of exposure therapy in the treatment of posttraumatic stress disorder. *Journal of Traumatic Stress, 19*, 597–610.

Cairney, J., Corna, L., Veldhuizen, S., Herrmann, N., & Streiner, D. (2008). Comorbid depression and anxiety in later life: Patterns of association, subjective well-being, and impairment. *American Journal of Geriatric Psychiatry, 16*(3), 201–208.

Calaprice, A. (Ed.). (2005). *The new quotable Einstein*. Princeton, NJ: Princeton University Press.

Calkins, M. W. (1898). Short studies in memory and in association from the Wellesley College Psychological Laboratory. I.: A study of immediate and delayed recall of the concrete and of the verbal. *Psychological Review, 5*, 451–456.

Calvert, S. L., Rideout, V. J., Woolard, J. L., Barr, R. F., & Strouse, G. A. (2005). Age, ethnicity, and socioeconomic patterns in early computer use. *American Behavioral Scientist, 48*, 590–607.

Cameron, K., Salazar, L., Bernhardt, J., Burgess-Whitman, N., Wingood, G., & DiClemente, R. (2005). Adolescents' experience with sex on the Web: Results from online focus groups. *Journal of Adolescence, 28*(4), 535–540. doi:10.1016/j.adolescence.2004.10.006

Campbell, A. (2008). Attachment, aggression and affiliation: The role of oxytocin in female social behavior. *Biological Psychology, 77*, 1–10.

Campbell, F. A., & Ramey, C. T. (1995). Cognitive and school outcomes for high-risk African-American students at middle adolescence: Positive effects of early intervention. *American Educational Research Journal, 32*, 743–772.

Campbell, F. A., Ramey, C. T., Pungello, E. P., Sparling, J., & Miller-Johnson, S. (2002). Early childhood education: Young adult outcomes from the Abecedarian Project. *Applied Developmental Science, 6*, 42–57.

Campos, J. J., & Stenberg, C. (1981). Perception, appraisal, and emotion: The onset of social referencing. In M. E. Lamb & L. R. Sherrod (Eds.), *Infant social cognition: Empirical and theoretical considerations* (pp. 273–314). Hillsdale, NJ: Erlbaum.

Camras, L. A., Oster, H., Bakeman, R., Meng, Z., Ujiie, T., & Campos, J. J. (2007). Do infants show distinct negative facial expressions for fear and anger? Emotional expression in 11-month-old European American, Chinese, and Japanese infants. *Infancy, 11*, 131–155.

Cannon, W. B. (1929). *Bodily changes in pain, hunger, fear, and rage: An account of recent researches into the function of emotional excitement*. New York, NY: Appleton.

Cannon, W. B. (1939). *The wisdom of the body*. New York, NY: W. W. Norton.

Cannon, W. B., & Washburn, A. L. (1912). An explanation of hunger. *American Journal of Physiology, 29*, 441–454.

Canter, R. R., & Hirsch, J. (1955). An experimental comparison of several psychological scales of weight. *American Journal of Psychology, 68*, 645–649.

Cappuccio, F. P., D'Elia, L., Strazzullo, P., & Miller, M. A. (2010). Sleep duration and all-cause mortality: A systematic review and meta-analysis of prospective studies. *Sleep, 33*, 585–592.

Capri, M., Salvioli, T., Sevini, F., Valensin, S., Celani, L., Monti, D., . . . Franceschi, C. (2006). The genetics of human longevity. *Annals of the New York Academy of Sciences, 1067*, 252–263.

Caramagno, T. C. (1992). *The flight of the mind: Virginia Woolf's art and manic-depressive illness*. Berkeley: University of California Press.

Cardno, A. G., & Gottesman, I. I. (2000). Twin studies of schizophrenia: From bow-and-arrow concordances to Star Wars Mx and functional genomics [Review]. *American Journal of Medical Genetics, 97*, 12–17.

Carew, T. J., & Kandel, E. R. (1973). Acquisition and retention of long-term habituation in *Aplysia*: Correlation of behavioral and cellular processes. *Science, 182*, 1158–1160.

Carey, B. (2008, December 4). H. M., an unforgettable amnesiac, dies at 82. *The New York Times*. Retrieved from http://www.nytimes.com

Carlat, D. J. (1998). The psychiatric review of symptoms: A screening tool for family physicians. *American Family Physician, 58*, 1617–1624.

Carless, S. A. (1999). Career assessment: Holland's vocational interests, personality characteristics, and abilities. *Journal of Career Assessment, 7*, 125–144.

Carlo, G. (2006). Care-based and altruistically based morality. In M. Killen & J. G. Smetana (Eds.), *Handbook of moral development* (pp. 551–579). Mahwah, NJ: Erlbaum.

Carlsson, A. (1987). Perspectives on the discovery of central monoaminergic neurotransmission. *Annual Review of Neuroscience, 10*, 19–40.

Carlsson, A. (1993). Thirty years of dopamine research. *Advances in Neurology, 60*, 1–10.

Carlsson, A. (2000). Nobel Prize autobiography. Retrieved from http://nobelprize.org/nobel_prizes/medicine/laureates/2000/carlsson-autobio.html

Carlsson, I. (2002). Anxiety and flexibility of defense related to high or low creativity. *Creativity Research Journal, 14,* 341–349.

Carlsson, I., Wendt, P., & Risberg, J. (2000). On the neurobiology of creativity: Differences in frontal activity between high and low creative subjects. *Neuropsychologia, 38,* 873–885.

Carnagey, N. L., Anderson, C. A., & Bushman, B. J. (2007). The effect of video game violence on physiological desensitization to real-life violence. *Journal of Experimental Social Psychology, 43,* 489–496.

Carney, S. M., & Goodwin, G. M. (2005). Lithium—a continuing story in the treatment of bipolar disorder. *Acta Psychiatrica Scandinavica, 111*(Suppl. 426), 7–12.

Carrion, V. G., Hass, B. W., Garrett, A., Song, S., & Rice, A. L. (2010). Reduced hippocampal activity in youth with post-traumatic stress symptoms: An fMRI study. *Journal of Pediatric Psychology, 35,* 559–569.

Carroll, J. B. (1993). *Human cognitive abilities.* New York, NY: Cambridge University Press.

Carroll, J. L., & Rest, J. (1981, December). Development in moral judgment as indicated by rejection of lower-stage statements. *Journal of Research in Personality, 15*(4), 538–544.

Carskadon, M. A., & Davis, S. S. (1989). Sleep-wake patterns in the high-school-to-college transition: Preliminary data. *Sleep Research, 18,* 113.

Carson, S. H., Peterson, J. B., & Higgins, D. M. (2003). Decreased latent inhibition is associated with increased creative achievement in high-functioning individuals. *Journal of Personality and Social Psychology, 85,* 499–506.

Carstensen, L. L. (2006). The influence of a sense of time on human development. *Science, 312,* 1913–1915.

Carstensen, L. L., Fung, H. H., & Charles, S. T. (2003). Socioemotional selectivity theory and the regulation of emotion in the second half of life. *Motivation and Emotion, 27,* 103–123.

Carter, C. S., Mintun, M., Nichols, T. N., & Cohen, J. D. (1997). Anterior cingulate gyrus dysfunction and selective attention deficits in schizophrenia: [15O]H2O PET study during single-trial Stroop task performance. *American Journal of Psychiatry, 154,* 1670–1675.

Caruso, E. M., Mead, N. L., & Balcetis, E. (2009). Political partisanship influences perception of biracial candidates' skin tone. *Proceedings of the National Academy of Sciences, 106,* 20168–20173.

Carver, C. S., Scheier, M. F., & Segerstrom, S. C. (2010). Optimism. *Clinical Psychology Review, 30,* 879–889.

Casey, B. J., Davidson, M., & Rosen, B. (2002). Functional magnetic imaging: Basic principles of and application to developmental science. *Developmental Science, 5,* 301–309.

Caspi, A. (2000). The child is father of the man: Personality continuities from childhood to adulthood. *Journal of Personality and Social Psychology, 78,* 158–172.

Caspi, A., Elder, G. H., & Bem, D. H. (1988). Moving away from the world: Life-course patterns of shy children. *Developmental Psychology, 24,* 824–831.

Caspi, A., McClay, J., Moffitt, T. E., Mill, J., Martin, J., Craig, I. W., et al. (2002). Role of genotype in the cycle of violence in maltreated children. *Science, 297,* 851–853.

Caspi, A., Roberts, B. W., & Shiner, R. L. (2003). Personality development: Stability and change. *Annual Review of Psychology, 56,* 453–484.

Caspi, A., Sugden, K., Moffitt, T. E., Taylor, A., Craig, I. W., Harrington, H., . . . Poulton, R. (2003). Influence of life stress on depression: Moderation by a polymorphism in the 5-HTT gene. *Science, 301,* 386–389.

Cassidy, T. (2006). *Birth: The surprising history of how we are born.* New York: Atlantic Monthly Press.

Castelli, D. M., Hillman, C. H., Buck, S. M., & Erwin, H. (2007). Physical fitness and academic achievement in third- and fifth-grade students. *Journal of Sport & Exercise Psychology, 29,* 239–252.

Catapano, F., Perris, F., Masella, M., Rossano, F., Cigliano, M., Magliano, L., . . . Maj, M. (2006). Obsessive–compulsive disorder: A 3-year prospective follow-up study of patients treated with serotonin reuptake inhibitors. *Journal of Psychiatric Research, 40,* 502–510.

Cavallero, C., & Foulkes, D. (Eds.). (1993). *Dreaming as cognition.* New York, NY: Harvester-Wheatsheaf.

CBS News. (2007, January 3). Bystander pulls off daring subway rescue. Retrieved from http://www.cbsnews.com/stories/2007/01/03/national/main2324961.shtml?source=search_story

Ceci, S. J., & Williams, W. M. (2007). *Why aren't more women in science? Top researchers debate the evidence.* Washington, DC: American Psychological Association.

Ceci, S. J., & Williams, W. M. (2010). *The mathematics of sex: How biology and society conspire to limit talented women and girls.* New York, NY: Oxford University Press.

Centers for Disease Control and Prevention (CDC). (2001). *Cigarette-smoking related mortality.* Retrieved March 26, 2007, from http://www.cdc.gov/tobacco/research_data/health_consequences/mortali.htm

Centers for Disease Control and Prevention (CDC). (2005). *Sexual behavior and selected health measures: Men and women 15–44 years of age, United States, 2002.* Retrieved March 12, 2008, from http://www.cdc.gov/nchs/data/ad/ad362.pdf

Centers for Disease Control and Prevention (CDC). (2007, August 8). *Smoking during pregnancy.* Retrieved February 23, 2008, from http://www.cdc.gov/tobacco/health_effects/pregnancy.htm

Centers for Disease Control and Prevention. (2009). Healthy eating for a healthy weight. Retrieved from http://www.cdc.gov/healthyweight/healthy_eating/index.html

Ceyhan, A. A., & Ceyhan, E. (2008). Loneliness, depression, and computer self-efficacy as predictors of problematic Internet use. *Cyberpsychology & Behavior, 11,* 699–701.

Chadwick, P., Hughes, S., Russell, D., Russell, I., & Dagnan, D. (2009). Mindfulness groups for distressing voices and paranoia: A replication and randomized feasibility trial. *Behavioral and Cognitive Psychotherapy, 37,* 403–412.

Chaffee, J. (1999). *The thinker's guide to college success* (2nd ed.). Boston, MA: Houghton Mifflin.

Chan, C., Brandone, A., & Tardif, T. (2009). Culture, context, or behavioral control?: English- and Mandarin-speaking mothers' use of nouns and verbs in joint book reading. *Journal of Cross-Cultural Psychology, 40,* 584–602. doi:10.1177/0022022109335184

Chance, P. (1986). *Thinking in the classroom: A survey of programs.* New York, NY: Teachers College, Columbia University.

Chandra, A., Martinez, G. M., Mosher, W. D., Abma, J. C., & Jones, J. (2005). Fertility, family planning, and reproductive health of U.S. women: Data from the 2002 National Survey of Family Growth. National Center for Health Statistics. *Vital Health Statistics, 23,* 1–160.

Chang, E. C. (1998). Dispositional optimism and primary and secondary appraisal of a stressor: Controlling for confounding influences and relations to coping and psychological and physical adjustment. *Journal of Personality and Social Psychology, 74,* 1109–1120.

Chapman, B. P., & Moynihan, J. (2009). The brain–skin connection: Role of psychosocial factors and neuropeptides in psoriasis. *Expert Review of Clinical Immunology, 5,* 623–627.

Chappell, M., & Humphreys, M. S. (1994). An auto-associative neural network for sparse representations: Analysis and application to models of recognition and cued recall. *Psychological Review, 101,* 103–128.

Charil, A., Laplante, D. P., Vaillancourt, C., & King, S. (2010). Prenatal stress and brain development. *Brain Research Reviews, 65,* 56–79.

Charney, D. S. (2004). Psychological mechanisms of resilience and vulnerability: Implications for successful adaptation to extreme stress. *American Journal of Psychiatry, 161,* 195–216.

Chatterjee, A., Strauss, M. E., Smyth, K. A., & Whitehouse, P. J. (1992). Personality changes in Alzheimer's disease. *Archives of Neurology, 49,* 486–491.

Cheah, C. S. L., & Nelson, L. (2004). The role of acculturation in the emerging adulthood of aboriginal college students. *International Journal of Behavioral Development, 28,* 494–507.

Chechik, G., Meilijson, I., & Ruppin, E. (1999). Neuronal regulation: A mechanism for synaptic pruning during brain maturation. *Neural Computation, 11,* 2151–2170.

Cheetham, C. E. J., Hammond, M. S. L., Edwards, C. J., & Finnerty, G. T. (2007). Sensory experience alters cortical connectivity and synaptic function site specifically. *The Journal of Neuroscience, 27,* 3456–3465.

Chen, S. Y., Jordan, C., & Thompson, S. (2006). The effect of cognitive behavioral therapy (CBT) on depression: The role of problem-solving appraisal. *Research on Social Work Practice, 16,* 500–510.

Chepenik, L. G., Raffo, M., Hampson, M., Lacadie, C., Wang, F., Jones, M. M., . . . Blumberg, H. P. (2010). Functional connectivity between ventral prefrontal cortex and amygdala at low frequency in the resting state in bipolar disorder. *Psychiatry Research: Neuroimaging, 182,* 207–210.

Chess, S., & Thomas, A. (1996). *Temperament: Theory and research.* New York, NY: Brunner/Mazel.

Cheyne, J., Carriere, J., & Smilek, D. (2006). Absent-mindedness: Lapses of conscious awareness and everyday cognitive failures. *Consciousness and Cognition: An International Journal, 15,* 578–592. doi:10.1016/j.concog.2005.11.009

Chia, E., Wang, J. J., Rochtchina, E., Cumming, R. R., Newall, P., & Mitchell, P. (2007). Hearing impairment and health-related quality of life: The Blue Mountains Hearing Study. *Ear & Hearing, 28,* 187–195.

Chiesa, A., Brambilla, P., & Serretti, A. (2010). Functional neural correlates of mindfulness meditations in comparison with psychotherapy, pharmacotherapy and placebo effect. Is there a link? *Acta Neuropsychiatrica, 22,* 104–117. doi:10.1111/j.1601-5215.2010.00460.x

Choi, I., Nisbett, R. E., & Norenzayan, A. (1999). Causal attribution across cultures: Variation and universality. *Psychological Bulletin, 125,* 47–65.

Chomsky, N. (1972). *Language and mind* (2nd ed.). New York, NY: Harcourt Brace Jovanovich.

Chomsky, N. (1986). *Knowledge of language: Its nature, origins, and use.* New York, NY: Praeger.

Chomsky, N. (2000). *New horizons in the study of language and the mind.* Cambridge, England: Cambridge University Press.

Chow, T. W., & Cummings, J. L. (1999). Frontal-subcortical circuits. In B. L. Miller & J. L. Cummings (Eds.), *The human frontal lobes: Functions and disorders* (pp. 3–26). New York, NY: Guilford Press.

Choy, Y., Fyer, A. J., & Lipsitz, J. D. (2007). Treatment of specific phobia in adults. *Clinical Psychology Review, 27*(3), 266–286. Advance online publication. doi:10.1016/j.cpr.2006.10.002

Christakis, D., Zimmerman, F., DiGiuseppe, D., & McCarty, C. (2004). Early television exposure and subsequent attentional problems in children. *Pediatrics, 113,* 708–713.

Christakis, N. A., & Fowler, J. H. (2007). The spread of obesity in a large social network over 32 years. *New England Journal of Medicine, 357,* 370–379.

Christakis, N. A., & Fowler, J. H. (2008). The collective dynamics of smoking in a large social network. *New England Journal of Medicine, 358,* 2249–2258.

Christakis, N. A., & Fowler, J. H. (2009). *Connected: The surprising power of our social networks and how they shape our lives.* New York, NY: Little Brown.

Christakis, N. A., & Fowler, J. H. (2010). Social network sensors for early detection of contagious outbreaks. *PLoS ONE, 5*(1–8), e12948. doi:10.1371/journal.pone.0012948

Christensen, K., Herskind, A. M., & Vaupel, J. W. (2006). Why Danes are smug: Comparative study of life satisfaction in the European Union. *British Medical Journal, 333,* 1289–1291.

Christiansen, M., Onnis, L., & Hockema, S. (2009). The secret is in the sound: From unsegmented speech to lexical categories. *Developmental Science, 12,* 388–395. doi:10.1111/j.1467-7687.2009.00824.x

Chuang, D. M. (2004). Lithium protection from glutamate excitotoxicity: Therapeutic implications. *Clinical Neuroscience Research, 4,* 243–252.

Cicchetti, D. (2001). How a child builds a brain. In W. W. Hartup & R. A. Weinberg (Eds.), *Child psychology in retrospect and prospect.* Mahwah, NJ: Erlbaum.

Cipriani, A., La Ferla, T., Furukawa, T. A., Signoretti, A., Nakagawa, A., Churchill, R., . . . Barbui, C. (2010). Sertraline versus other antidepressive agents for depression [Review]. *Cochrane Database of Systematic Reviews,* Issue 4.

Clancy, P. M. (1985). The acquisition of Japanese. In D. Slobin (Ed.), *The cross-linguistic study of language acquisition: Vol. 1. The data.* Hillsdale, NJ: Erlbaum.

Clark, A. E., Georgellis, Y., Lucas, R. E., & Diener, E. (2004). Unemployment alters the set point for life satisfaction. *Psychological Science, 15,* 8–15.

Clark, A. S., & Schneider, M. L. (1997). Effects of prenatal stress on behavior in adolescent rhesus monkey. *Annals of the New York Academy of Sciences, 807,* 490–491.

Clark, L. A. (2005). Temperament as a unifying basis for personality and psychopathology. *Journal of Abnormal Psychology, 114,* 505–521.

Clark, L. A., Watson, D., & Leeka, J. (1989). Diurnal variation in the positive affects. *Motivation and Emotion, 13,* 205–234.

Clark, L., Bosworth, H., Welsh-Bohmer, K., Dawson, D., & Siegler, I. (2000). Relation between informant-rated personality and clinician-rated depression in patients with memory disorders. *Neuropsychiatry, Neuropsychology, & Behavioral Neurology, 13,* 39–47.

Clark, R. D., III, & Hatfield, E. (1989). Gender differences in willingness to engage in casual sex. *Journal of Psychology and Human Sexuality, 2,* 39–55.

Clark, R. D., III, & Hatfield, E. (2003). Love in the afternoon. *Psychological Inquiry, 14,* 227–231.

Clark, W. R., & Grunstein, M. (2000). *Are we hardwired? The role of genes in human behavior.* New York, NY: Oxford University Press.

Clarke, G. N., Hawkins, W., Murphy, M., Sheeber, L. B., Lewinsohn, P. M., & Seeley, J. R. (1995). Targeted prevention of unipolar depressive disorder in an at-risk sample of high school adolescents: A randomized trial of group cognitive intervention. *Journal of the American Academy of Child & Adolescent Psychiatry, 34,* 312–321.

Cobb, J. M., Fluster, Z., Leder, G., Seaver, A., Hendrick, J. L., & Hokanson, J. F. (2010). Information processing demands while texting on a simulated driving task. *Journal of Sport & Exercise Psychology, 32,* S72.

Coe, C. L., & Lubach, G. R. (2008). Fetal programming: Prenatal origins of health and illness. *Current Directions in Psychological Science, 17,* 36–41.

Cohen, J. (2010, April 2). Boxed about the ears, ape language research still standing. *Science, 328,* 38–39.

Cohen, J. D. (2005). The vulcanization of the human brain. *Journal of Economic Perspectives, 19,* 3–24.

Cohen, K. M. (2002). Relationships among childhood sex-atypical behavior, spatial ability, handedness, and sexual orientation in men. *Archives of Sexual Behavior, 31,* 129–143.

Cohen, S. (2004). Social relationships and health. *American Psychologist, 59,* 676–684.

Cohen, S., Alper, C. M., Doyle, W. J., Adler, N., Treanor, J. J., & Turner, R. B. (2008). Objective and subjective socioeconomic status and susceptibility to the common cold. *Health Psychology, 27,* 268–274.

Cohen, S., Doyle, W. J., Turner, R. B., Alper, C. M., & Skoner, D. P. (2003). Sociability and susceptibility to the common cold. *Psychological Science, 14,* 389–395.

Cohen, S., Tyrrell, D. A. J., & Smith, A. P. (1993). Negative life events, perceived stress, negative affect, and susceptibility to the common cold. *Journal of Personality and Social Psychology, 64,* 131–140.

Cohen, S., & Wills, T. A. (1985). Stress, social support, and the buffering hypothesis. *Psychological Bulletin, 98,* 310–357.

Colcombe, S. J., Erickson, K. I., Scalf, P. E., Kim, J. S., Praskash, R., McAuley, E., . . . Kramer, A. F. (2006). Aerobic exercise training increases brain volume in aging humans. *Journal of Gerontology, 61,* 1166–1170.

Colcombe, S. J., & Kramer, A. F. (2003). Fitness effects on the cognitive function of older adults: A meta-analytic study. *Psychological Science, 14,* 125–130.

Cole, S. W. (2009). Social regulation of human gene expression. *Current Directions in Psychological Science, 18,* 132–137.

Cole, S. W. (2010). Elevating the perspective on human stress genomics. *Psychoneuroendocrinology, 35,* 955–962.

Cole, S. W., Arevaloa, J. M. G., Takahashia, R., Sloan, E. K., Lutgendorf, S. K., Sood,

A. K., . . . Seeman, T. E. (2010). Computational identification of gene–social environment interaction at the human IL6 locus. *Proceedings of the National Academy of Sciences, 107,* 5681–5686.

Cole, S. W., Hawkley, L. C., Arevalo, J. M., Sung, C. Y., Rose, R. M., & Cacioppo, J. T. (2007). Social regulation of gene expression in human leukocytes. *Genome Biology, 8,* R189.1–R189.13.

Collignon, O., Girard, S., Gosselin, F., Saint-Amour, D., Lepore, F., & Lassonde, M. (2010). Women process multisensory emotion expressions more efficiently than men. *Neuropsychologia, 48,* 220–225.

Collins, A., & Loftus, E. F. (1975). A spreading activation theory of semantic processing. *Psychological Review, 82,* 407–428.

Collinson, S. L., Meyyappan, A., & Rosenfeld, J. V. (2009). Injury and recovery: Severe traumatic brain injury. *Brain Injury, 23,* 71–76. doi:10.1080/02699050802649647

Colom, R., Haier, R., Head, K., Álvarez-Linera, J., Quiroga, M., Shih, P., & Jung, R. E. (2009). Gray matter correlates of fluid, crystallized, and spatial intelligence: Testing the P-FIT model. *Intelligence, 37*(2), 124–135.

Comer, R. J. (2007). *Abnormal psychology* (6th ed.). New York, NY: Worth.

Comery, T. A., Stamoudis, C. X., Irwin, S. A., & Greenough, W. T. (1996). Increased density of multiple-head dendritic spines on medium-sized spiny neurons of the striatum in rats reared in a complex environment. *Neurobiology of Learning and Memory, 66,* 93–96.

Conduct Problems Prevention Research Group (1999a). Initial impact of the Fast Track prevention trial for conduct problems: I. The high-risk sample. *Journal of Consulting and Clinical Psychology, 67,* 631–647.

Conduct Problems Prevention Research Group (1999b). Initial impact of the Fast Track prevention trial for conduct problems: II. Classroom effects. *Journal of Consulting and Clinical Psychology, 67,* 648–657.

Corporate jobs without the corporate. (n.d.). Retrieved from http://www.apple.com/jobs/us/corporate.html

Costa, P. T. (1996). Work and personality: Use of the NEO–PI–R in industrial/organizational psychology. *Applied Psychology: An International Review, 45,* 225–241.

Costa, P. T., Herbst, J. H., McCrae, R. R., & Siegler, I. C. (2000). Personality at midlife: Stability, intrinsic maturation, and response to life events. *Assessment, 7,* 365–378.

Costa, P. T., & McCrae, R. R. (1976). Age differences in personality structure: A cluster analytic approach. *Journal of Gerontology, 31,* 564–570.

Costa, P. T., & McCrae, R. R. (1980). Influences of extraversion and neuroticism on subjective well-being. *Journal of Personality and Social Psychology, 38,* 668–678.

Costa, P. T., & McCrae, R. R. (1992). *NEO PI-R professional manual.* Odessa, FL: Psychological Assessment Resources.

Cotman, C. W., Berchtold, N. C., & Christie, L. A. (2007). Exercise builds brain health: Key roles of growth factor cascades and inflammation. *Trends in Neurosciences, 30,* 464–472.

Couch, D., & Liamputtong, P. (2008). Online dating and mating: The use of Internet to meet sexual partners. *Qualitative Health Research, 18,* 268–279.

Courchesne, E., Campbell, K., & Solso, S. (2010). Brain growth across the life span in autism: Age-specific changes in anatomical pathology. *Brain Research.* doi:10.1016/j.brainres.2010.09.101

Craik, F. I. M. (1979). The structure and organization of memory. *Annual Review of Psychology, 30,* 63–102.

Craik, F. I. M., & Lockhart, R. S. (1972). Levels of processing: A framework for memory research. *Journal of Verbal Learning and Verbal Behavior, 11,* 671–684.

Craik, F. I. M., & Tulving, E. (1975). Depth of processing and the retention of words in episodic memory. *Journal of Experimental Psychology: General, 104,* 268–294.

Crawford, S. E., & Alaggia, R. (2008). The best of both worlds? Family influences on mixed race youth identity development. *Qualitative Social Work, 7,* 81–98.

Crews, F. (1998). *Unauthorized Freud: Doubters confront a legend.* New York, NY: Viking.

Crook, T. H., Youngjohn, J. R., Larrabee, G. J., & Salama, M. (1992). Aging and everyday memory: A cross-cultural study. *Neuropsychology, 6,* 123–136.

Cross, S. E., & Markus, H. (1999). The cultural constitution of personality. In L. A. Pervin & O. P. John (Eds.), *Handbook of personality theory and research* (pp. 378–396). New York, NY: Guilford Press.

Crump, T. (2001). *A brief history of science.* New York, NY: Carroll & Graf.

Crystal, J. D., Maxwell, K. W., & Hohmann, A. G. (2003). Cannabinoid modulation of sensitivity to time. *Behavioural Brain Research, 144,* 57–66.

Csikszentmihalyi, M. (1990). *Flow: The psychology of optimal experience.* New York, NY: HarperPerennial.

Csikszentmihalyi, M. (1996). *Creativity: Flow and the psychology of discovery and invention.* New York, NY: HarperCollins.

Cuijpers, P., van Straten, A., Hollon, S., & Andersson, G. (2010). The contribution of active medication to combined treatments of psychotherapy and pharmacotherapy for adult depression: A meta-analysis. *Acta Psychiatrica Scandinavica, 121,* 415–423. doi:10.1111/j.1600-0447.2009.01513.x

Cukor, J., Spitalnick, J., Difede, J., Rizzo, A., & Rothbaum, B. O. (2009). Emerging treatments for PTSD. *Clinical Psychology Review, 29,* 715–726.

Culvers, J. (2010, April 17). 7 Tips for improving the effectiveness of your diet. Retrieved from http://ezinearticles.com/?7-Tips-For-Improving-the-Effectiveness-of-Your-Diet&id=4128679

Cummings, J. H., Bingham, S. A., Heaton, K. W., & Eastwood, M. A. (1992). Fecal weight, colon cancer risk, and dietary intake of nonstarch polysaccharides (dietary fiber). *Gastroenterology, 103,* 1783–1789.

Cunningham, W. A., & Zelazo, P. D. (2006). Attitudes and evaluations: A social cognitive neuroscience perspective. *Trends in Cognitive Sciences, 11,* 97–104.

Curley, J. P., Jensen, C. L, Mashoodh, R., & Champagne, F. A. (in press). Social influences on neurobiology and behavior: Epigenetic effect during development. *Psychoneuroendocrinology.* doi:10.1016/j.psyneuen.2010.06.005

Curtiss, S. (1977). *Genie: A psycholinguistic study of a modern-day wild child.* New York, NY: Academic Press.

Cussler, E. C., Going, S. B., Houtkooper, L. B., Stanford, V. A., Blew, R. M., Flint-Wagner, H. G., . . . Lohman, T. G. (2005). Exercise frequency and calcium intake predict 4-year bone changes in postmenopausal women. *Osteoporosis International, 16,* 2129–2141.

Cutting, A. L., & Dunn, J. (2002). The cost of understanding other people: Social cognition predicts young children's sensitivity to criticism. *Journal of Child Psychology and Psychiatry, 43,* 849–860.

Cytowic, R. E. (1989). *Synaesthesia: A union of the senses.* New York, NY: Springer-Verlag.

Czech, C., & Adessi, C. (2004). Disease modifying therapeutic strategies in Alzheimer's disease targeting the amyloid cascade. *Current Neuropharmacology, 2,* 295–307.

D'Anglejan, A. (1979). Solving problems in deductive reasoning: Three experimental studies of adult second language learners. *Working Papers on Bilingualism, No. 17.*

D'Ausilio, R. (2008, September 10). What motivates your employees? Intrinsic vs. extrinsic rewards. Retrieved from http://www.tmcnet.com/channels/performance-management/articles/39417-what-motivates-employees-intrinsic-vs-extrinsic-rewards.htm

Dabbs, J. M., Jr., Carr, T. S., & Frady, R. L. (1995). Testosterone, crime, and misbehavior among 692 male prison inmates. *Personality and Individual Differences, 18,* 627–633.

Dabbs, J. M., Jr., & Hargrove, M. F. (1997). Age, testosterone, and behavior among female prison inmates. *Psychosomatic Medicine, 59,* 477–480.

Dabbs, J. M., Jr., & Mohammed, S. (1992). Male and female salivary testosterone concentrations before and after sexual activity. *Physiology & Behavior, 52,* 195–197.

Dale, P. S., Dionne, G., Eley, T. C., & Plomin, R. (2000). Lexical and grammatical development: A behavioural genetic perspective. *Journal of Child Language, 27,* 619–642.

Dalgleish, T. (2004). The emotional brain. *Nature Reviews Neuroscience, 5,* 583–589.

Dallaire, D. H., Cole, D. A., Smith, T. M., Ciesla, J. A., LaGrange, B., Jacquez, F. M., . . . Folmer, A. S. (2008). Predicting children's depressive symptoms from community and individual risk factors. *Journal of Youth and Adolescence, 37,* 830–846.

Dallman, M. F., Pecoraro, N. C., & la Fleur, S. E. (2005). Chronic stress and comfort foods: Self-medication and abdominal obesity. *Brain, Behavior, and Immunity, 19,* 275–280.

Dalrymple, K. L., & Herbert, J. D. (2007). Acceptance and commitment therapy for generalized social anxiety disorder—A pilot study. *Behavior Modification, 31,* 543–568.

Damasio, A. R., (2000). *The feeling of what happens: Body and emotion in the making of consciousness.* Chicago, IL: Harcourt.

Danhauer, J. L., Johnson, C. E., Byrd, A., DeGood, L., Meuel, C., Pecile, A., & Koch, L. L. (2009). Survey of college students on iPod use and hearing health. *Journal of the American Academy of Audiology, 20,* 5–27.

Darke, P. R., & Ritchie, R. J. B. (2007). The defensive consumer: Advertising deception, defensive processing, and distrust. *Journal of Marketing Research, 44,* 114–127.

Darley, J. M., & Batson, C. D. (1973). "From Jerusalem to Jericho": A study of situational and dispositional variables in helping behavior. *Journal of Personality and Social Psychology, 27,* 100–108.

Darley, J. M., & Latané, B. (1968). Bystander intervention in emergencies: Diffusion of responsibility. *Journal of Personality and Social Psychology, 8,* 377–383.

Darwin, C. (1998). *The expression of the emotions in man and animals.* New York, NY: Oxford University Press. (Original work published 1872)

Dasgupta, N., McGhee, D. E., Greenwald, A. G., & Banaji, M. R. (2000). Automatic preference for White Americans: Eliminating the familiarity explanation. *Journal of Experimental Social Psychology, 36,* 316–328.

Davidson, R. J. (1994). On emotion, mood, and related affective constructs. In P. Ekman & R. J. Davidson (Eds.), *The nature of emotion: Fundamental questions* (pp. 51–55). New York, NY: Oxford University Press.

Davidson, R. J. (2001). Toward a biology of personality and emotion. *Annals of the New York Academy of Sciences, 935,* 191–207.

Davidson, R. J. (2004). What does the pre-frontal cortex "do" in affect?: Perspectives on frontal EEG asymmetry research. *Biological Psychology, 67,* 219–233.

Davidson, R. J., Ekman, P., Saron, C., Senulis, J., & Friesen, W. V. (1990). Approach-withdrawal and cerebral asymmetry: Emotional expression and brain physiology I. *Journal of Personality and Social Psychology, 58,* 330–341.

Davidson, R. J., Kabat-Zinn, J., Schumacher, J., Rosenkranz, M., Muller, D., Santorelli, S. F., . . . Sheridan, J. F. (2003). Alterations in brain and immune function produced by mindfulness meditation. *Psychosomatic Medicine, 65,* 564–570.

Davis, K. (2010). Coming of age online: The developmental underpinnings of girls' blogs. *Journal of Adolescent Research, 25,* 145–171.

Dawkins, R. (1989). *The selfish gene* (New ed.). New York, NY: Oxford University Press.

Day, H. I. (1982). Curiosity and the interested explorer. *Performance and Instruction, 21,* 19–22.

De Fruyt, F., & Murvielde, I. (1999). RAISEC types and Big Five traits as predictors of employment status and nature of employment. *Personnel Psychology, 52,* 701–727.

de Graaf-Peters, V. B., & Hadders-Algra, M. (2006). Ontogeny of the human central nervous system: What is happening when? *Early Human Development, 82,* 257–266.

De Lisi, R., & Wolford, J. L. (2002). Improving children's mental rotation accuracy with computer game playing. *The Journal of Genetic Psychology, 163,* 272–282.

De Neys, W., Vartanian, O., & Goel, V. (2008). Smarter than we think: When our brains detect that we are biased. *Psychological Science, 19,* 483–489.

de Waal, F. B. M., & Suchak, M. (2010). Prosocial primates: Selfish and unselfish motivations. *Philosophical Transactions of the Royal Society of London B, 365,* 2711–2722.

de Win, M. M. L., Reneman, L., Reitsma, J. B., den Heeten, G. J., Booij, J., & van den Brink, W. (2004). Mood disorders and serotonin transporter density in ecstasy users—The influence of long-term abstention, dose, and gender. *Psychopharmacology, 173,* 376–382.

Deacon, T. (1997). *Symbolic species: Co-evolution of language and the brain.* New York, NY: Norton.

Deary, I. J., Graham, T., Wilson, V., Starr, J. M., & Whalley, L. J. (2003). Population sex differences in IQ at age 11: The Scottish mental survey 1932. *Intelligence, 31,* 533–542.

Debes, R. (2010). Which empathy? Limitations in the mirrored "understanding" of emotion. *Synthese, 175,* 219–239.

DeCasper, A. J., & Fifer, W. (1980). Of human bonding: Newborns prefer their mothers' voices. *Science, 208,* 1174–1176.

DeCasper, A. J., & Spence, M. J. (1986). Prenatal maternal speech influences newborns' perception of speech sounds. *Infant Behavior & Development, 9,* 133–150.

Deci, E., Koestner, R., & Ryan, R. (1999). A meta-analytic review of experiments examining the effects of extrinsic rewards on intrinsic motivation. *Psychological Bulletin, 125*(6), 627–668.

Deci, E. L., & Ryan, R. M. (1985). *Intrinsic motivation and self-determination in human behavior.* New York, NY: Plenum.

Declerck, C. H., Boone, C., & Kiyonari, T. (2010). Oxytocin and cooperation under conditions of uncertainty: The modulating role of incentives and social information. *Hormones and Behavior, 57,* 368–374.

Delgado, P. L., Price, L. H., Miller, H. L., Salomon, R. M., Aghajanian, G. K., Heninger, G. R., & Charney, D. S. (1994). Serotonin and the neurobiology of depression—Effects of tryptophan depletion in drug-free depressed patients. *Archives of General Psychiatry, 51,* 865–874.

DeLisi, M., Umphress, Z. R., & Vaughn, M. G. (2009). The criminology of the amygdala. *Criminal Justice and Behavior, 36,* 1241–1252.

Dell' Osso, B., Buoli, M., Baldwin, D. S., & Altamura, A. C. (2009). Serotonin norepinephrine reuptake inhibitors (SNRIs) in anxiety disorders: A comprehensive review of their clinical efficacy. *Human Psychopharmacology: Clinical & Experimental, 25,* 17–29.

DeLongis, A., Folkman, S., & Lazarus, R. S. (1988). The impact of daily stress on health and mood: Psychological and social resources as mediators. *Journal of Personality and Social Psychology, 54,* 486–495.

Dement, W. (1999). *The promise of sleep.* New York, NY: Delacorte Press.

Demir, E., & Dickson, B. J. (2005). *fruitless* splicing specifies male courtship behavior in *Drosophila. Cell, 121,* 785–794.

Derbyshire, S. W. G., Whalley, M. G., Stenger, A., & Oakley, D. A. (2004). Cerebral activation during hypnotically induced and imagined pain. *NeuroImage, 23,* 392–401.

Derry, G. (1999). *What science is and how it works.* Princeton: Princeton University Press.

Derryberry, D., & Tucker, D. M. (1994). Motivating the focus of attention. In P. M. Niedenthal & S. Kitayama (Eds.), *The heart's eye: Emotional influences in perception and attention* (pp. 167–196). San Diego, CA: Academic Press.

DeRubeis, R. J., Hollon, S., Amsterdam, J., Shelton, R., Young, P., Salomon, R., . . . Gallop, R. (2005). Cognitive therapy vs medications in the treatment of moderate to severe depression. *Archives of General Psychiatry, 62*(4), 409–416.

Devine, P. (1989). Stereotypes and prejudice: Their automatic and controlled components. *Journal of Personality and Social Psychology, 56,* 5–18.

DeWall, C. N., MacDonald, G., Webster, G. D., Masten, C. L., Baumeister, R. F., Powell, C., . . . Eisenberger, N. I. (2010). Acetaminophen reduces social pain: Behavioral and neural evidence. *Psychological Science, 21,* 931–937.

DeYoung, C., Shamosh, N., Green, A., Braver, T., & Gray, J. (2009). Intellect as distinct from openness: Differences revealed by fMRI of working memory. *Journal of Personality and Social Psychology, 97,* 883–892.

Diamond, L. M. (2008). Female bisexuality from adolescence to adulthood: Results from a 10-year longitudinal study. *Developmental Psychology, 44,* 5–14.

Diego, M., Field, T., Hernandez-Reif, M., Deeds, O., Ascencio, A., & Begert, G. (2007). Preterm infant massage elicits consistent increases in vagal activity and gastric motility that are associated with greater weight gain. *Acta Paediatrica, 96,* 1588–1591.

Diekelmann, S., Wilhelm, I., & Born, J. (2009). The whats and whens of sleep-dependent memory consolidation. *Sleep Medicine Reviews, 13*, 309–321.

Diener, E., & Seligman, M. E. P. (2004). Beyond money toward an economy of well-being. *Psychological Science, 5*, 1–31.

Diener, E., Suh, E. M., Lucas, R. E., & Smith, H. L. (1999). Subjective well-being: Three decades of progress. *Psychological Bulletin, 125*, 276–302.

Dietrich, K., Succop, P., Berger, O., & Hammond, P. (1991). Lead exposure and the cognitive development of urban preschool children: The Cincinnati Lead Study cohort at age 4 years. *Neurotoxicology and Teratology, 13*(2), 203–211.

Digman, J. M. (1990). Personality structure: Emergence of the Five-Factor Model. *Annual Review in Psychology, 41*, 417–440.

Dingemanse, N. J., Both, C., Drent, P. J., Van Oers, K., & Van Noordwijk, A. J. (2002). Repeatability and heritability of exploratory behaviour in great tits from the wild. *Animal Behaviour, 64*, 929–938.

Dinn, W. M., Aycicegi, A., & Harris, C. L. (2004). Cigarette smoking in a student sample: Neurocognitive and clinical correlates. *Addictive Behaviors, 29*, 107–126.

DiPietro, J. A., Hodgson, D. M., Costigan, K. A., & Johnson, T. R. B. (1996). Fetal antecedents of infant temperament. *Child Development, 67*, 2568–2583.

Dobbs, D. (2006, April 2). A depression switch? *New York Times Magazine.* Retrieved from http://www.nytimes.com

Dobbs, D. (2006, July 30). Turning off depression. *Scientific American Mind, 17*, 26–31.

Dockray, S., & Steptoe, A. (2010). Positive affect and psychobiological processes. *Neuroscience and Biobehavioral Reviews, 35*, 69–75.

Doetsch, F., & Scharff, C. (2001). Challenges for brain repair: Insights from adult neurogenesis in birds and mammals. *Brain, Behavior & Evolution, 58*, 306–322.

Dolcos, F., LaBar, K. S., & Cabeza, R. (2005). Remembering one year later: Role of the amygdala and the temporal lobe memory system in retrieving emotional memories. *Proceedings of the National Academy of Sciences, 102*, 2626–2631.

Dolinoy, D., & Jirtle, R. L. (2008). Environmental epigenomics in human health and disease. *Environmental and Molecular Mutagenesis, 49*, 4–8.

Doll, R., Peto, R., Boreham, J., & Sutherland, I. (2004). Mortality in relation to smoking: 50 years' observations on male British doctors. *British Medical Journal, 328*, 1519–1528.

Domes, G., Schulze, L., Böttger, M., Grossmann, A., . . . Herpertz, S. C. (2010). The neural correlates of sex differences in emotional reactivity and emotion regulation. *Human Brain Mapping, 31*, 758–769.

Domhoff, G. W. (2001). A new neuro-cognitive theory of dreams. *Dreaming, 11*, 13–33.

Dominguez, J. M., & Hull, E. M. (2005). Dopamine, the medial preoptic area, and male sexual behavior. *Physiology and Behavior, 86*, 356–368.

Donn, J. E., & Sherman, R. C. (2002). Attitudes and practices regarding the formation of romantic relationships on the Internet. *CyberPsychology & Behavior, 5*, 107–122.

Doty, R. L., Applebaum, S., Zusho, H., & Settle, R. G. (1985). Sex differences in odor identification ability: A cross-cultural analysis. *Neuropsychologia, 23*, 667–672.

Drevets W. C., Frank, E., Price, J. C., Kupfer, D. J., Holt, D., Greer, P. J., . . . Mathis, C. (1999). PET imaging of serotonin 1A receptor binding in depression. *Biological Psychiatry, 46*, 1375–1387.

Drevets, W. C., Price, J. L., Simpson, J. R., Todd, R. D., Reich, T., Vannier, M., & Raichle, M. (1997). Subgenual prefrontal cortex abnormalities in mood disorders. *Nature, 386*, 824–827.

Drug for treating schizophrenia identified. (1998). Retrieved from http://www.pbs.org/wgbh/aso/databank/entries/dh52dr.html

Dubai, Y. (2004). The neurobiology of consolidations, or, How stable is the engram? *Annual Review of Psychology, 55*, 51–86.

Due, P., Holstein, B. E., Ito, H., & Groth, M. V. (1991). Diet and health behavior in Danish children aged 11–15 years. *Tandlaegernes Tidsskr, 6*(8), 232–237.

Duke, L. M., & Vasterling, J. J. (2005). Epidemiological and methodological issues in neuropsychological research on PTSD. In J. Vasterling & C. Brewin (Eds.)., *Neuropsychology of PTSD* (pp. 3–24). New York, NY: Guilford Press.

Dunbar, R. I. M. (1996). *Grooming, gossip and the evolution of language.* London, England: Faber & Faber.

Dunbar, R. I. M. (2001). Brains on two legs: Group size and the evolution of intelligence. In F. B. M. deWaal (Ed.), *Tree of origin: What primate behavior can tell us about human social evolution* (pp. 173–191). Cambridge, MA: Harvard University Press.

Duncan, J., Seitz, R. J., Koldny, J., Bor, D., Herzog, H., Ahmed, A., . . . Emslie, H. (2000, July 21). A neural basis for general intelligence. *Science, 289*, 457–460.

Duncan, S. C., Duncan, T. E., & Strycker, L. A. (2006). Alcohol use from ages 9 to 16: A cohort-sequential latent growth model. *Drug and Alcohol Dependence, 81*, 71–81.

Duncker, K. (1945). On problem-solving. *Psychological Monographs, 58*, ix. (Whole No. 270).

Dunham, Y., Baron, A. S., & Banaji, M. R. (2006). From American city to Japanese village: A cross-cultural investigation of implicit race attitudes. *Child Development, 77*, 1268–1281.

Dunn, E. W., Aknin, L. B., & Norton, M. I. (2008). Spending money on others promotes happiness. *Science, 319*, 1687–1688.

Durlak, J. A., Taylor, R. D., Kawashima, K., Pachan, M. K., DuPre, E. P., Celio, C. I., . . . Weissberg, R. P. (2007). Effects of positive youth development programs on school, family, and community systems. *American Journal of Community Psychology, 39*, 269–286.

Dvir, Y., & Smallwood, P. (2008). Serotonin syndrome: A complex but easily avoidable condition. *General Hospital Psychiatry, 30*, 284–287.

Dye, M. W. G., & Bavelier, D. (2004). Playing video games enhances visual attention in children. *Journal of Vision, 4*, 40A.

Eagly, A. H., & Chaiken, S. (1998). Attitude structure and function. In D. T. Gilbert, S. T. Fiske, & G. Lindzey (Eds.), *The handbook of social psychology* (4th ed., Vol. 1, pp. 269–322). New York, NY: McGraw-Hill.

Ebstein, R. P. (2006). The molecular genetic architecture of human personality: Beyond self-report questionnaires. *Molecular Psychiatry, 11*, 427–445.

Ebstein, R. P., Israel, S., Chew, S. H., Zhong, S., & Knafo, A. (2010). Genetics of human social behavior. *Neuron, 65*, 831–844.

Ebstein, R. P., Novick, O., Umansky, R., Priel, B., Osher, Y., Blaine, D., . . . Belmaker, R. H. (1996). Dopamine D4 receptor D4DR exon III polymorphism associated with the human personality trait of novelty seeking. *Nature Genetics, 12*, 78–80.

Edelman, S., Lemon, J., Bell, D. R., & Kidman, A. D. (1999). Effects of group CBT on the survival time of patients with metastatic breast cancer. *Psychooncology, 8*, 474–481.

Eder, P., & Eisenberger, R. (2008). Perceived organizational support: Reducing the negative influence of coworker withdrawal behavior. *Journal of Management, 34*, 55–68.

Edmonds, C. V., Lockwood, G. A., & Cunningham, A. J. (1999). Psychological response to long-term therapy: A randomized trial with metastatic breast cancer patients. *Psychooncology, 8*, 74–91.

Edwards, J. H. (2002). Evidenced-based treatment for child ADHD: "Real-world" practice implications. *Journal of Mental Health Counseling, 24*, 126–139.

Edwards, V. J., Holden, G. W., Felitti, V. J., & Anda, R. F. (2003). Relationship between multiple forms of childhood maltreatment and adult mental health in community respondents: Results from the adverse childhood experiences study. *American Journal of Psychiatry, 160*, 1453–1460.

Eichenbaum, H. (2010). Memory systems. *WIREs Cognitive Science, 1*, 478–490.

Eisenberger, N. I., Jarcho, J. M., Lieberman, M. D., & Naliboff, B. D. (2006). An experimental study of shared sensitivity to physical pain and social rejection. *Pain, 126*, 132–138.

Eisenberger, N. I., Lieberman, M. D., & Williams, K. D. (2003). Does rejection hurt? An fMRI study of social exclusion. *Science, 203*, 290–292.

Eisenberger, R., & Cameron, J. (1996). Detrimental effects of reward: Reality or myth? *American Psychologist, 51*, 1153–1166.

Eisenberger, R., Rhoades, L., & Cameron, J. (1999). Does pay for performance increase or decrease perceived self-determination and intrinsic motivation? *Journal of Personality and Social Psychology, 77,* 1026–1040.

Eisenberger, R., & Shanock, L. (2003). Rewards, intrinsic motivation and creativity: A case study of methodological and conceptual isolation. *Creativity Research Journal, 15,* 121–130.

Eisenberger, R., Stinglhamber, F., Vandenberghe, C., Sucharski, I., & Rhoades, L. (2002). Perceived supervisor support: Contributions to perceived organizational support and employee retention. *Journal of Applied Psychology, 87,* 565–573.

Ekman, P. (1972). Universals and cultural differences in facial expressions of emotion. In J. Cole (Ed.), *Nebraska Symposium on Motivation 1971, Vol. 19* (pp. 207–283). Lincoln: University of Nebraska Press.

Ekman, P. (1973). Cross-cultural studies of facial expression. In *Darwin and facial expression: A century of research in review* (pp. 169–222). New York, NY: Academic Press.

Ekman, P. (1984). Expression and the nature of emotion. In K. R. Scherer & P. Ekman (Eds.), *Approaches to emotion* (pp. 319–343). Hillsdale, NJ: Lawrence Erlbaum.

Ekman, P. (1992). An argument for basic emotions. *Cognition & Emotion, 6,* 169–200.

Ekman, P. (2003). *Emotions revealed.* New York, NY: Holt.

Ekman, P., Davidson, R. J., & Friesen, W. V. (1990). The Duchenne smile: Emotional expression and brain physiology II. *Journal of Personality and Social Psychology, 58,* 342–353.

Ekman, P., & Friesen, W. V. (1969). The repertoire of nonverbal behavior—Categories, origins, usage, and coding. *Semiotica, 1,* 49–98.

Ekman, P., & Friesen, W. V. (1971). Constants across cultures in the face and emotion. *Journal of Personality and Social Psychology, 17,* 124–129.

Ekman, P., & Friesen, W. V. (1978). *The Facial Action Coding System.* Palo Alto, CA: Consulting Psychologists Press.

Ekman, P., Friesen, W. V., & Hager, J. (2002). *The Facial Action Coding System* (2nd ed.). Salt Lake City, UT: Research Nexus.

Ekman, P., Friesen, W. V., O'Sullivan, M., Chan, A., Diacoyanni-Tarlatzis, I., Heider, K., et al. (1987). Universals and cultural differences in the judgments of facial expressions of emotion. *Journal of Personality and Social Psychology, 53,* 712–717.

Ekman, P., Levenson, R. W., & Friesen, W. V. (1983). Autonomic nervous system activity distinguishes among emotions. *Science, 221,* 1208–1210.

Ekman, P., & O'Sullivan, M. (1991). Who can catch a liar? *American Psychologist, 46,* 913–920.

Ekman, P., O'Sullivan, M., & Frank, M. G. (1999). A few can catch a liar. *Psychological Science, 10,* 263–266.

Ekman, P., & Rosenberg, E. L. (Eds.). (2005). *What the face reveals: Basic and applied studies of spontaneous facial expression using the Facial Action Coding System (FACS)* (2nd ed.). New York, NY: Oxford University Press.

Ekman, P., Sorenson, E. R., & Friesen, W. V. (1969). Pan-cultural elements in facial displays of emotion. *Science, 164,* 86–88.

Elbert, T., Pantev, C., Wienbruch, C., Rockstroh, B., & Taub, E. (1995). Increased cortical representation of the fingers of the left hand in string players. *Science, 270,* 305–307.

Elias, M. (2009, January 28). MRIs reveal possible source of woman's super-memory. *USA Today.* Retrieved from http://www.usatoday.com

Ellason, J. W., Ross, C. A., & Fuchs, D. L. (1996). Lifetime Axis I and Axis II comorbidity and childhood trauma history in dissociative identity disorder. *Psychiatry, 59,* 255–266.

Ellenbogen, J. M., Hu, P. T., Payne, J. D., Titone, D., & Walker, M. P. (2007). Human relational memory requires time and sleep. *Proceedings of the National Academy of Sciences, 104,* 7723–7728.

Ellickson, P. L., Orlando, M., Tucker, J. S., & Klein, D. J. (2004). From adolescence to young adulthood: Racial/ethnic disparities in smoking. *American Journal of Public Health, 94,* 293–299.

Ellickson, P. L., Tucker, J. S., & Klein, D. J. (2001). Sex differences in predictors of adolescent smoking cessation. *Health Psychology, 20,* 186–195.

Ellis, E., & Ames, M. A. (1987). Neurohormonal functioning and sexual orientation: A theory of heterosexuality–homosexuality. *Psychological Bulletin, 101,* 233–258.

Ellsworth, P. C., & Scherer, K. R. (2003). Appraisal processes in emotion. In R. J. Davidson, K. R. Scherer, & H. Goldsmith (Eds.), *Handbook of affective sciences* (pp. 572–595). New York, NY: Oxford University Press.

Elman, J. L., Bates, E. A., Johnson, M. H., Karmiloff-Smith, A., Parisi, D., & Plunkett, K. (1996). *Rethinking innateness: A connectionist perspective on development.* Cambridge, MA: MIT Press.

Elms, A. (1993). *Uncovering lives: The uneasy alliance between biography and psychology.* New York, NY: Oxford University Press.

Emery, R. A. (2006). Holland codes, careers, and college majors. Retrieved from http://www.hollandcodes.com/support-files/su-careers-majors-and-model.pdf

Emmons, R. A., & McCullough, M. E. (2003). Counting blessings versus burdens: An experimental investigation of gratitude and subjective well-being in daily life. *Journal of Personality and Social Psychology, 84,* 377–389. doi:10.1037/0022-3514.84.2.377

Empana, J. P., Sykes, D. H., Luc, G., Juhan-Vague, I., Arveiler, D., Ferrieres, J., . . . Ducimetiere, P. (2005). Contributions of depressive mood and circulating inflammatory markers to coronary heart disease in healthy European men: The Prospective Epidemiological Study of Myocardial Infarction (PRIME). *Circulation, 111,* 2299–2305.

Engel, A. K., Debener, S., & Kranczioch, C. (2006, August). Coming to attention. *Scientific American Mind, 17,* 46–53.

The engineer's life at Google. (n.d.). Retrieved from http://www.google.com/intl/en/jobs/lifeatgoogle/englife/index.html

Enzinger, C., Fazekas, F., Matthews, P. M., Ropele, S., Schmidt, H., Smith, S., & Schmidt, R. (2005). Risk factors for progression of brain atrophy in aging: Six-year follow-up of normal subjects. *Neurology, 64,* 1704–1711.

Epel, E. S., Blackburn, E. H., Lin, J., Dhabhar, F. S., Adler, N. E., & Morrow, J. D. (2004). Accelerated telomere shortening in response to life stress. *Proceedings of the National Academy of Sciences, 101,* 17312–17315.

Epel, E. S., Lin, J., Wilhelm, F. H., Wolkowitz, O. M., Cawthon, R., Adler, N. E., . . . Blackburn, E. H. (2006). Cell aging in relation to stress arousal and cardiovascular disease risk factors. *Psychoneuroendocrinology, 31,* 277–287.

Epel, E. S., McEwen, B., Seeman, T., Matthews, K., Castellazzo, G., Brownell, K. D., . . . Ickovics, J. R. (2000). Stress and body shape: Stress-induced cortisol secretion is consistently greater among women with central fat. *Psychosomatic Medicine, 62,* 623–632.

Erdelyi, M. (2010). The ups and downs of memory. *American Psychologist, 65,* 623–633. doi:10.1037/a0020440

Erikson, E. H. (1963). *Childhood and society.* New York, NY: Norton.

Erikson, E. H. (1968). *Identity: Youth and crisis.* New York, NY: Norton.

Erikson, E. H. (1982). *The life-cycle completed: A review.* New York, NY: Norton.

Eriksson, P. S., Perfilieva, E., Bjork-Eriksson, T., Alborn, A. M., Nordborg, C., Peterson, D. A., . . . Gage, F. H. (1998). Neurogenesis in the adult human hippocampus. *Nature Medicine, 4,* 1313–1317.

Eroglu, C., & Barres, B. A. (2010, 11 November). Regulation of synaptic connectivity by glia. *Nature, 468,* 223–231.

Etcoff, N. (1999). *Survival of the prettiest.* New York, NY: Anchor Books.

Evans, D. L., Ten Have, T. R., Douglas, S. D., Gettes, D. R., Morrison, M., Chiappini, M. S., . . . Petitto, J. M. (2002). Association of depression with viral load, CD8 T lymphocytes, and natural killer cells in women with HIV infection. *American Journal of Psychiatry, 159,* 1752–1759.

Evans, L. M., Akiskal, H. S., Greenwood, T. A., Nievergelt, C. M., Keck, P. E., McElroy, S. L., . . . Kelso, J. R. (2007). Suggestive linkage of a chromosomal locus on 18p11 to cyclothymic temperament in bipolar disorder families. *American Journal of Medical Genetics, 147B,* 326–332.

Evans, S., Ferrando, S., Findler, M., Stowell, C., Smart, C., & Haglin, D. (2008). Mindfulness-based cognitive therapy for generalized anxiety disorder. *Journal of Anxiety Disorders, 22,* 716–721.

Everett, D. L. (2005). Cultural constraints on grammar and cognition in Piraha: Another look at the design features of human language. *Current Anthropology, 46,* 621–646.

Exaptations. (2006). Retrieved November 28, 2007, from http://evolution.berkeley.edu/evosite/evo101/IIIE5cExaptations.shtml

Exner, J. E., Jr. (1974). *The Rorschach: A comprehensive system.* New York, NY: Wiley.

Extraordinary people—The boy who sees without eyes. (2007, May 7).[Video file]. From the 2003 television series *Extraordinary People.* Retrieved from http://www.youtube.com/watch?v=qLziFMF4DHA

Eysenck, H. J. (1947). *Dimensions of personality.* London, England: Routledge & Kegan Paul.

Eysenck, H. J. (1980). *The causes and effects of smoking.* London, England: Temple Smith.

Eysenck, H. J. (1982). *Personality, genetics, and behavior: Selected papers.* New York, NY: Praeger.

Eysenck, H. J. (1990). Biological dimensions of personality. In L. A. Pervin (Ed.), *Handbook of personality: Theory and research* (pp. 244–276). New York, NY: Guilford Press.

Eysenck, H. J. (1995). *Genius: The natural history of creativity.* Cambridge, England: Cambridge University Press.

Eysenck, H. J. (1997). Personality and experimental psychology: The unification of psychology and the possibility of a paradigm. *Journal of Personality and Social Psychology, 73,* 1224–1237.

Facione, P. A. (1990). *Critical thinking: A statement of expert consensus for purposes of educational assessment and instruction— The Delphi report.* Millbrae, CA: California Academic Press.

Fallgatter, A. J., Ehlis, A-C., Herrmann, M. J., Hohoff, C., Reif, A., Freitag, C. M., & Deckert, J. (2010). DTNBP1 (dysbindin) gene variants modulate prefrontal brain function in schizophrenic patients—Support for the glutamate hypothesis of schizophrenias. *Genes, Brain and Behavior, 9,* 489–497.

Famy, C., Streissguth, A. P., & Unis, A. S. (1998). Psychological disorder in adults with fetal alcohol syndrome or fetal alcohol effects. *Journal of Pediatric Psychology, 155,* 552–554.

Fancher, R. E. (1985). *The intelligence men: Makers of the IQ controversy.* New York, NY: Norton.

Fancher, R. E. (1996). *Pioneers of psychology* (3rd ed.). New York, NY: Norton.

Fantz, R. L. (1963). Pattern vision in newborn infants. *Science, 140,* 296–297.

Farb, N., Anderson, A., Mayberg, H., Bean, J., McKeon, D., & Segal, Z. (2010). Minding one's emotions: Mindfulness training alters the neural expression of sadness. *Emotion, 10,* 25–33. doi:10.1037/a0017151

Farber, N. B., & Olney, J. W. (2003). Drugs of abuse that cause developing neurons to commit suicide. *Developmental Brain Research, 147,* 37–45.

Fazel, S., & Danesh, J. (2002). Serious mental disorder in 23,000 prisoners: A systematic review of 62 surveys. *Lancet, 359,* 545–550.

Feist, G. J. (1993). A structural model of scientific eminence. *Psychological Science, 4,* 366–371.

Feist, G. J. (1998). A meta-analysis of the impact of personality on scientific and artistic creativity. *Personality and Social Psychological Review, 2,* 290–309.

Feist, G. J. (1999). Personality in scientific and artistic creativity. In R. J. Sternberg (Ed.), *Handbook of human creativity* (pp. 273–296). Cambridge, England: Cambridge University Press.

Feist, G. J. (2004). Creativity and the frontal lobes. *Bulletin of Psychology and the Arts, 5,* 21–28.

Feist, G. J. (2006). The development of scientific talent in Westinghouse finalists and members of the National Academy of Sciences. *Journal of Adult Development, 13,* 23–35.

Feist, G. J. (2006). *The psychology of science and the origins of the scientific mind.* New Haven, CT: Yale University Press.

Feist, G. J., & Barron, F. X. (2003). Predicting creativity from early to late adulthood: Intellect, potential and personality. *Journal of Research in Personality, 37,* 62–88.

Feist, G. J., Bodner, T. E., Jacobs, J. F., Miles, M., & Tan, V. (1995). Integrating top-down and bottom-up structural models of subjective well-being: A longitudinal investigation. *Journal of Personality and Social Psychology, 68,* 138–150.

Feist, J., & Feist, G. J. (2009). *Theories of personality* (7th ed.). New York, NY: McGraw-Hill.

Feldman, D. H. (2004). Child prodigies: A distinctive form of giftedness. In R. J. Sternberg (Ed.), *Definition and conceptions of giftedness* (pp. 133–144). Thousand Oaks, CA: Corwin Press.

Feldman-Barrett, L., Tugade, M. M., & Engle, R. W. (2004). Individual differences in working memory capacity and dual-process theories of mind. *Psychological Bulletin, 130,* 553–573.

Feng, X., Shaw, D. S., Kovacs, M., Lane, T., O'Rourke, F. E., & Alarcon, J. H. (2008). Emotion regulation in preschoolers: The roles of behavioral inhibition, maternal affective behavior, and maternal depression. *Journal of Child Psychology and Psychiatry, 49,* 132–141.

Feng, Z., Hu, W., Hu, Y., & Teng, M. (2006). Acrolein is a major cigarette-related lung cancer agent: Preferential binding at *p53* mutational hotspots and inhibition of DNA repair. *Proceedings of the National Academy of Sciences, 103,* 15404–15409.

Fenson, L., Dale, P., Reznick, J. S., Bates, E., Thal, D. J., & Pethick, S. (1994). Variability in early communicative development.

Monographs of the Society for Research in Child Development, 59 (5, Serial No. 242).

Ferguson, C. J., & Kilburn, J. (2009). The public health risks of media violence: A meta-analytic review. *The Journal of Pediatrics, 154,* 759–763.

Ferguson, C. J., & Kilburn, J. (2010). Much ado about nothing: The misestimation and overinterpretation of violent video game effects in Eastern and Western nations: Comment on Anderson et al. (2010). *Psychological Bulletin, 136,* 174–178.

Fergusson, D., Doucette, S., Glass, K. C., Shapiro, S., Healy, D., Hebert, P., et al. (2005). Association between suicide attempts and selective serotonin reuptake inhibitors: Systematic review of randomized controlled trials. *British Medical Journal, 330,* 396–402.

Fergusson, L., Horwood, J., & Ridder, E. M. (2005). Tests of causal linkages between cannabis use and psychotic symptoms. *Addiction, 100,* 354–366.

Fernald, A. (1992). Human maternal vocalizations to infants as biologically relevant signals: An evolutionary perspective. In J. Barkow, L. Cosmides, & J. Toody (Eds.), *The adapted mind: Evolutionary psychology and the generation of culture* (pp. 391–428). New York, NY: Oxford University Press.

Fernald, A., & Morikawa, H. (1993). Common themes and cultural variations in Japanese and American mothers' speech to infants. *Child Development, 64,* 637–656.

Ferster, C. B., & Skinner, B. F. (1957). *Schedules of reinforcement.* Englewood Cliffs, NJ: Prentice-Hall.

Festinger, L. (1957). *A theory of cognitive dissonance.* Stanford, CA: Stanford University.

Festinger, L., & Carlsmith, J. M. (1959). Cognitive consequences of forced compliance. *Journal of Abnormal and Social Psychology, 58,* 203–210.

Fetz, E. E. (2007). Volitional control of neural activity: Implications for brain–computer interfaces. *Journal of Physiology, 579,* 571–579.

Fiedorowicz, J., & Swartz, K. (2004). The role of monoamine oxidase inhibitors in current psychiatric practice. *Journal of Psychiatric Practice, 10,* 239–248.

Field, T. M., Hernandez-Reif, M., Diego, M., Feijo, L., Vera, Y., & Gil, K. (2004). Massage therapy by parents improves early growth and development. *Infant Behavior and Development, 27,* 435–442.

Field, T. M., Schanberg, S. M., Scafidi, F., Bauer, C. R., Vega-Lahr, N., Garcia, R., . . . Kuhn, C. M. (1986). Tactile/kinesthetic stimulation effects on preterm neonates. *Pediatrics, 77,* 654–658.

Fields, H. L. (2005). *Pain: Mechanisms and management.* New York, NY: McGraw-Hill.

Fields, H. L. (2009, September/October). The psychology of pain. *Scientific American Mind,* 42–49.

Fields, R. D. (2005). Making memories stick. *Scientific American, 292,* 75–81.

Fields, R. D. (2008). White matter matters. *Scientific American, 298*, 54–61.

15 Google interview questions that will make you feel stupid. (2009, November). Retrieved from http://www.businessinsider.com/15-google-interview-questions-that-will-make-you-feel-stupid-2009-11#

Filimon, F., Nelson, J. D., Hagler, D. J., & Sereno, M. I. (2007). Human cortical representations for reaching: Mirror neurons for execution, observation, and imagery. *Neuro-Image, 37*, 1315–1328.

Finger, S. (1994). *Origins of neuroscience: A history of explorations into brain function.* New York, NY: Oxford University Press.

Fink, M. (2006). ECT in therapy-resistant mania: Does it have a place? *Bipolar Disorders, 8*, 307–309.

Finke, R. A., Ward, T. B., & Smith, S. M. (1992). *Creative cognition: Theory, research and applications.* Cambridge, MA: MIT Press.

Finkelstein, E. A., Trogdon, J. G., Cohen, J. W., & Dietz, W. (2009). Annual medical spending attributable to obesity: Payer-and service-specific estimates. *Health Affairs (Millwood), 28*(5), w822–w831.

Finnerty, G. T., Roberts, L. S. E., & Connors, B. W. (1999). Sensory experience modifies the short-term dynamics of neocortical synapses. *Nature, 400*, 367–371.

Fischer, A. H., & Manstead, A. S. R. (2000). Gender differences in emotion across cultures. In A. H. Fischer (Ed.), *Emotion and gender: Social psychological perspectives* (pp. 91–97). London, England: Cambridge University Press.

Fischer, G. G. (2004). Should I order an EEG? An overview of electroencephalography in the hospital setting at Gundersen Lutheran Medical Center. *Gundersen Lutheran Medical Journal, 3*, 26–29.

Fisher, J. E., Mohanty, A., Herrington, J. D., Koven, N. S., Miller, G. A., & Heller, W. (2004). Neuropsychological evidence for dimensional schizotypy: Implications for creativity and psychopathology. *Journal of Research in Personality, 38*, 24–31.

Fitzgerald, K. D., Welsh, R. C., Gehrig, W. J., Abelson, J. L., Himle, J. A., Liberzon, I., & Taylor, S. F. (2005). Error-related hyperactivity of the anterior cingulate cortex in obsessive-compulsive disorder. *Biological Psychiatry, 57*, 287–294.

Fitzgerald, M. (2004). *Autism and creativity.* Hove, England: Brunner-Routledge.

Fitzgerald, P. B., Benitez, J., de Castella, A. R., Daskalakis, Z. J., & Kulkarni, J. (2006). Naturalistic study of the use of transcranial magnetic stimulation in the treatment of depressive relapse. *Australian and New Zealand Journal of Psychiatry, 40*, 764–768.

Flaherty, M. (2005). Gender differences in mental rotation ability in three cultures: Ireland, Ecuador and Japan. *Psychologia: An International Journal of Psychology in the Orient, 48*, 31–38.

Flammer, E., & Bongartz, W. (2003). On the efficacy of hypnosis: A meta-analytic study. *Contemporary Hypnosis, 20*, 179–197.

Flegal, K. M., Carroll, M. D., Ogden, C. L., & Curtain, L. R. (2010). Prevalence and trends in obesity among US adults, 1999–2008. *Journal of the American Medical Association, 303*, 235–241.

Flege, J. E. (1999). Age of learning and second language speech. In D. Birdsong (Ed.), *Second language acquisition and the critical period hypothesis* (pp. 101–131). Mahwah, NJ: Erlbaum.

Flege, J. E., Munro, M. J., & MacKay, I. R. A. (1995). Effects of age of second-language learning on the production of English consonants. *Speech Communication, 16*, 1–26.

Flege, J. E., Munro, M. J., & MacKay, I. R. A. (1995). Factors affecting strength of perceived foreign accent in a second language. *Journal of the Acoustical Society of America, 97*, 2540–2551.

Fleischer, J., Breer, H., & Strotmann, J. (2009). Mammalian olfactory receptors. *Frontiers in Cellular Neuroscience, 3*, 1–10.

Foa, E. B., Dancu, C. V., Hembree, E. A., Jaycox, L. H., Meadows, E. A., & Street, G. P. (1999). A comparison of exposure therapy, stress inoculation training, and their combination for reducing posttraumatic stress disorder in female assault victims. *Journal of Consulting and Clinical Psychology, 67*, 194–200.

Foa, E. B., Hembree, E. A., Cahill, S. P., Rauch, S. A., Riggs, D. S., Feeny, N. C., & Yadin, E. (2005). Randomized trial of prolonged exposure for PTSD with and without cognitive restructuring: Outcome at academic and community clinics. *Journal of Consulting and Clinical Psychology, 73*, 953–964.

Fodor, E. M., & Laird, B. A. (2004). Therapeutic intervention, bipolar inclination, and literary creativity. *Creativity Research Journal, 16*, 149–161.

Foerde, K., Knowlton, B., &. Poldrack, R. (2006). Modulation of competing memory systems by distraction. *Proceedings of the National Academy of Sciences, 103*, 11778–11783.

Fogassi, L., & Ferrari, P. F. (2006). Mirror neurons and the evolution of embodied language. *Current Directions in Psychological Science, 16*, 136–141.

Folkman, S. (1997). Positive psychological states and coping with severe stress. *Social Science and Medicine, 45*, 1207–1221.

Folkman, S., & Moskowitz, J. T. (2000). Positive affect and the other side of coping. *American Psychologist, 55*, 647–654.

Folley, B. S., & Park, S. (2005). Verbal creativity and schizotypal personality in relation to prefrontal hemispheric laterality: A behavioral and near-infrared optical imaging study. *Schizophrenia Research, 80*, 271–282.

Fombonne, E. (2003). The prevalence of autism. *Journal of the American Medical Association, 289*, 87–89.

Fong-Torres, B. (2010, April 25). Tom Petty: "Go after what you love." An interview. *Parade Magazine.*

Fonteille, V., & Stoleru, S. (in press). The cerebral correlates of sexual desire: Functional neuroimaging approach. *Sexologies.* doi: 10.1016/j.sexol.2010.03.011

Ford, C., & Beach, F. (1951). *Patterns of sexual behavior.* New York, NY: Harper & Row.

Ford, D. (2008). Intelligence testing and cultural diversity: The need for alternative instruments, policies, and procedures. In J. L. VanTessa-Baska (Ed.), *Alternative assessments with gifted and talented students* (pp. 107–128). Waco, TX: Prufrock Press.

Forgeard, M., Winner. E., Norton, A., & Schlaug, G. (2008). Practicing a musical instrument in childhood is associated with enhanced verbal ability and nonverbal reasoning. *PLoS One, 3*, e3566.

Forsten, B. L., Scotti, J. R., Chen, Y-C, Malone, J., & Del Ben, K. S. (2007). Internet use, abuse, and dependence among students at a southeastern regional university. *Journal of American College Health, 56*, 137–144.

Foulkes, D. (1996). Dream research: 1953–1993. *Sleep: Journal of Sleep Research & Sleep Medicine, 19*, 609–624.

Fournier, J. C., DeRubeis, R. J., Hollon, S. D., Dimidjian, S., Amsterdam, J. D., Shelton, R. C., & Fawcett, I. (2010). Antidepressant drug effects and depression severity: Patient-level meta-analysis. *Journal of the American Medical Association, 303*, 47–53.

Fouts, R. S. (1997). *Next of kin: My conversations with chimpanzees.* New York, NY: Avon.

Fouts, R. S., Fouts, D. H., & Schoenfeld, D. (1984). Sign language conversational interaction between chimpanzees. *Sign Language Studies, 42*, 1–12.

Fowler, J. H., & Christakis, N. A. (2008). The dynamic spread of happiness in a large social network. *British Medical Journal, 337*, a2338.

Fowler, J. H., & Christakis, N. A. (2010). Cooperative behavior cascades in human social networks. *Proceedings of the National Academy of Sciences, 107*, 5334–5338.

Franco, O. H., de Laet, C., Peeters, A., Jonker, J., Mackenbach, J., & Nusselder, W. (2005). Effects of physical activity on life expectancy with cardiovascular disease. *Archives of Internal Medicine, 165*, 2355–2360.

Frank, M. G., & Ekman, P. (1997). The ability to detect deceit generalizes across different types of high stakes lies. *Journal of Personality and Social Psychology, 72*, 1429–1439.

Fratiglioni, L., Winblad, B., & von Strauss, E. (2007). Prevention of Alzheimer's disease and dementia. Major findings from the Kungsholmen Project. *Physiology & Behavior, 92*, 98–104.

Fredrickson, B. L. (1998). What good are positive emotions? *Review of General Psychology, 2*, 300–319.

Fredrickson, B. L. (2001). The role of positive emotions in positive psychology: The broaden-and-build theory of positive emotions. *American Psychologist, 56*, 218–226.

Fredrickson, B. L., & Branigan, C. (2005). Positive emotions broaden the scope of attention and thought-action repertoires. *Cognition & Emotion, 19*, 313–332.

Fredrickson, B. L., & Joiner, T. (2002). Positive emotions trigger upward spirals toward emotional well-being. *Psychological Science, 13*, 172–175.

Fredrickson, B. L., & Levenson, R. W. (1998). Positive emotions speed recovery from the cardiovascular sequelae of negative emotions. *Cognition & Emotion, 12*, 191–220.

Fredrickson, B. L., Tugade, M. M., Waugh, C. E., & Larkin, G. R. (2003). What good are positive emotions in crises? A prospective study of resilience and emotions following the terrorist attacks on the United States on September 11th, 2001. *Journal of Personality & Social Psychology, 84*, 365–376.

French-Belgian Collaborative Group. (1982). Ischemic heart disease and psychological patterns: Prevalence and incidence studies in Belgium and France. *Advances in Cardiology, 29*, 25–31.

French, S. E., Seidman, E., Allen, L., & Aber, J. L. (2006). The development of ethnic identity during adolescence. *Developmental Psychology, 42*, 1–10.

Freud, A. (1946). *The ego and the mechanisms of defense.* New York, NY: International Universities Press.

Freud, S. (1953). *The interpretation of dreams.* In J. Strachey (Ed. & Trans.), *The standard edition of the complete works of Sigmund Freud* (Vols. 4 & 5). London, England: Hogarth Press. (Original work published 1900)

Freud, S. (1959). *Inhibitions, symptoms, and anxiety.* In J. Strachey (Ed. & Trans.), *Standard edition of the complete works of Sigmund Freud* (Vol. 20). London, England: Hogarth Press. (Original work published 1926)

Freud, S. (1960). *Psychopathology of everyday life.* In J. Strachey (Ed. & Trans.), *Standard edition of the complete works of Sigmund Freud* (Vol. 6). London, England: Hogarth Press. (Original work published 1901)

Freud, S. (1964). *New introductory lectures on psychoanalysis.* In J. Strachey (Ed. & Trans.), *The Standard edition of the complete works of Sigmund Freud* (Vol. 22). London, England: Hogarth Press. (Original work published 1933)

Freund, A., & Ritter, J. (2009). Midlife crisis: A debate. *Gerontology, 55*, 582–591. doi:10.1159/000227322

Friesen, W. V. (1972). *Cultural differences in facial expressions in a social situation: An experimental test of the concept of display rules.* Unpublished doctoral dissertation, University of California, San Francisco.

Frijda, N. H. (1986). *The emotions.* Cambridge, England: Cambridge University Press.

Frith, U., & Frith, C. (2010). The social brain: Allowing humans to boldly go where no other species has been. *Philosophical Translations of the Royal Society B: Biological Sciences, 365*, 165–176.

Froh, J. J., Sefick, W. J., & Emmons, R. A. (2008). Counting blessings in early adolescents: An experimental study of gratitude and subjective well-being. *Journal of School Psychology, 46*, 213–233.

Frokjaer, V. B., Vinberg, M., Erritzoe, D., Svarer, C., Baare, W., Budtz-Joergensen, E., . . . Knudsen, G. M. (2009). High familial risk for mood disorder is associated with low dorsolateral prefrontal cortex serotonin transporter binding. *NeuroImage, 46*, 360–366.

Frost, R. O., & Steketee, G. (2010). *Stuff: Compulsive hoarding and the meaning of things.* Boston, MA: Houghton Mifflin.

Fruntes, V., & Limosin, F. (2008). Schizophrenia and viral infection during neurodevelopment: A pathogenesis model? *Medical Science Monitor, 14*, RA71–RA77.

Fuller, J. L., & Thompson, W. R. (1960). *Behavior genetics.* New York, NY: Wiley.

Furster, J. M. (1999). Cognitive functions of the frontal lobes. In B. L. Miller & J. L. Cummings (Eds.), *The human frontal lobes: Functions and disorders* (pp. 187–195). New York, NY: Guilford Press.

Furuichi, T. (1983). Interindividual distance and influence of dominance on feeding in a natural Japanese macaque troop. *Primates, 24*, 445–455.

Furumoto, L. (1981). Mary Whiton Calkins (1863–1930). *Psychology of Women Quarterly, 5*, 55–68. doi: 10.1111/j.1471-6402.1981.tb01033.x

Fuster, J. M. (2002). Frontal lobe and cognitive development. *Journal of Neurocytology, 31*, 373–385.

Gaab, N., Paetzold, M., Becker, M., Walker, M. P., & Schlaug, G. (2004). The influence of sleep on auditory learning—A behavioral study. *NeuroReport, 15*, 731–734.

Gage, F. H. (2002). Neurogenesis in the adult brain. *The Journal of Neuroscience, 22*, 612–613.

Gage, F. H., Kemperman, G., & Song, H. (Eds.). (2008). *Adult neurogenesis.* Cold Spring Harbor, NY: Cold Spring Harbor Laboratory Press.

Galanter, E. (1962). Contemporary psychophysics. In R. Brown (Ed.), *New directions in psychology* (pp. 87–157). New York, NY: Holt, Rinehart & Winston.

Gale, A. (1983). Electroencephalographic studies of extraversion–introversion: A case study in the psychophysiology of individual differences. *Personality and Individual Differences, 4*, 371–380.

Galin, D. (1994). The structure of awareness: Contemporary applications of William James' forgotten concept of "The Fringe." *The Journal of Mind and Behavior, 15*, 375–402.

Gallagher, A. M., & Kaufman, J. C. (2005). *Gender differences in mathematics: An integrative psychological approach.* New York, NY: Cambridge University Press.

Gallagher, M., & Lopez, S. (2007). Curiosity and well-being. *Journal of Positive Psychology, 2*(4), 236–248.

Gallagher, R. M., & Rosenthal, L. J. (2008). Chronic pain and opiates: Balancing pain control and risks in long-term opioid treatment. *Archives of Physical Medicine and Rehabilitation, 89*(Suppl. 1), S77–S82.

Galletti, C., & Fattori, P. (2003). Neuronal mechanisms for detection of motion in the field of view. *Neuropsychologia, 41*, 1717–1727.

Ganasen, K., Ipser, J., & Stein, D. (2010). Augmentation of cognitive behavioral therapy with pharmacotherapy. *Psychiatric Clinics of North America, 33*, 687–699. doi:10.1016/j.psc.2010.04.008

Ganis, G., Thompson, W., & Kosslyn, S. (2009). Visual mental imagery: More than "seeing with the mind's eye." In J. R. Brockmole (Ed.), *The visual world in memory* (pp. 215–249). New York, NY: Psychology Press.

Garcia, J. (2003). Psychology is not an enclave. In R. J. Sternberg (Ed.), *Defying the crowd: Stories of those who battled the establishment and won* (pp. 67–77). Washington, DC: American Psychological Association.

Garcia, J., Ervin, F. R., & Koelling, R. (1966). Learning with a prolonged delay of reinforcement. *Psychonomic Science, 5*, 121–122.

Garcia, J., Kimeldorf, D. J., & Koelling, R. A. (1955). A conditioned aversion towards saccharin resulting from exposure to gamma radiation. *Science, 122*, 157–159.

Garcia, J., & Koelling, R. A. (1966). The relation of cue to consequence in avoidance learning. *Psychonomic Science, 4*, 123–124.

Garcia, J., McGowan, B. K., & Green, K. F. (1972). Biological constraints on conditioning. In A. H. Black & W. F. Prokasy (Eds.), *Classical conditioning II: Current research and theory* (pp. 3–27). New York, NY: Appleton-Century-Crofts.

Garcia-Bailo, B., Toguri, C., Eny, K. M., & El-Sohemy, A. (2009). Genetic variation in taste and its influence on food selection. *OMICS: A Journal of Integrative Biology, 13*, 69–80.

Gardner, H. (1980). *Artful scribbles: The significance of children's drawings.* New York, NY: Basic Books.

Gardner, H. (1983). *Frames of mind: The theory of multiple intelligences.* New York, NY: Basic Books.

Gardner, H. (1987). *The mind's new science: A history of the cognitive revolution.* New York, NY: Basic Books.

Gardner, H. (1993). *Frames of mind: The theory of multiple intelligences* (2nd ed.). New York, NY: Basic Books.

Gardner, H. (1999). *Intelligence reframed: Multiple intelligences for the 21st century.* New York, NY: Basic Books.

Gardner, R. A., Gardner, B. T., & Van Cantfort, T. E. (Eds.). (1989). *Teaching *sign language to chimpanzees.* Albany, NY: SUNY Press.

Garrett, R. K., & Danziger, J. N. (2008). IM = Interruption management? Instant messaging and disruption in the workplace. *Journal of Computer-Mediated Communication, 13,* 23–42.

Gass, S. (1984). A review of interlanguage syntax: Language transfer and language universals. *Language Learning, 34,* 115–132.

Gates, M. F., & Allee, W. C. (1933). Conditioned behavior of isolated and grouped cockroaches on a simple maze. *Journal of Comparative Psychology, 15,* 331–358.

Gathercole, V. C. M., & Hoff, E. (2007). Input and the acquisition of language: Three questions. In E. Hoff & M. Shatz (Eds.), *The handbook of language development* (pp. 107–127). Oxford, England: Blackwell.

Gaudiano, B. A., & Herbert, J. D. (2006). Believability of hallucinations as a potential mediator of their frequency and associated distress in psychotic inpatients. *Behavioral and Cognitive Psychotherapy, 34,* 497–502.

Gazdzinski, S., Durazzo, T. C., & Meyerhoff, D. J. (2005). Temporal dynamics and determinants of whole brain tissue volume changes during recovery from alcohol dependence. *Drug and Alcohol Dependence, 78,* 263–273.

Geary, D., & DeSoto, M. C. (2001). Sex differences in spatial abilities among adults in the United States and China. *Evolution and Cognition, 7,* 172–177.

Geerlings, S. W., Beekman, A., Deeg, D., Twisk, J., & van Tilburg, W. (2002). Duration and severity of depression predict mortality in older adults in the community. *Psychological Medicine, 32,* 609–618.

Georges, E. (1995). A cultural and historical perspective on confession. In J. W. Pennebaker (Ed.), *Emotion, disclosure, and health* (pp. 11–22). Washington, DC: American Psychological Association.

Georgiadis, J. R., Kortekaas, R., Kuipers, R., Nieuwenburg, A., Pruim, J., Simone Reinders, A. A. T., & Holstege, G. (2006). Regional cerebral blood flow changes associated with clitorally induced orgasm in healthy women. *European Journal of Neuroscience, 24,* 3305–3316.

Gershberg, F. B., & Shimamura, A. P. (1995). The role of the frontal lobes in the use of organizational strategies in free recall. *Neuropsychologia, 13,* 1305–1333.

Gibson, E., & Walk, R. (1960). The visual cliff. *Scientific American, 202,* 64–71.

Gibson, J. J. (1950). *The perception of the visual world.* Boston, MA: Houghton Mifflin.

Gibson, J. J. (1966). *The senses considered as perceptual systems.* Boston, MA: Houghton Mifflin.

Giedd, J. N., Blumenthal, J., Jeffries, N. O., Castellanos, F. X., Liu, H., Zijdenbos, A., Paus, T., Evans, A. C., & Rapoport, J. L. (1999). Brain development during childhood and adolescence: A longitudinal MRI study. *Nature Neuroscience 2,* 861–863.

Gil, S. (2007). Body-image, well-being and sexual satisfaction: A comparison between heterosexual and gay men. *Sexual and Relationship Therapy, 22*(2), 237–244.

Gilbert, S. P., & Weaver, C. C. (2010). Sleep quality and academic performance in university students: A wake-up call for college psychologists. *Journal of College Student Psychotherapy, 24,* 295–306. doi:10.1080/87568225.2010.509245

Gillham, J. E., Reivich, K. J., Freres, D. R., Chaplin, T. M., Shatté, A. J., Samuels, B., . . . Martin, E. P. (2007). School-based prevention of depressive symptoms: A randomized controlled study of the effectiveness and specificity of the Penn Resiliency Program. *Journal of Consulting and Clinical Psychology, 75,* 9–19.

Gilligan, C. (1982). *In a different voice.* Cambridge, MA: Harvard University Press.

Givón, T. (2002). The visual information-processing system as an evolutionary precursor of human language. In T. Givón & B. F. Malle (Eds.), *The evolution of language out of pre-language* (pp. 3–50). Amsterdam, Netherlands: John Benjamins.

Givón, T., & Malle, B. F. (Eds.). *The evolution of language out of pre-language.* Amsterdam, Netherlands: John Benjamins.

Gjerde, P. F., & Cardilla, K. (2009). Developmental implications of openness to experience in preschool children: Gender differences in young adulthood. *Developmental Psychology, 45,* 1455–1464.

Glaser, R., & Kiecolt-Glaser, J. K. (2005). Stress-induced immune dysfunction: Implications for health. *Nature Reviews Immunology, 4,* 243–251.

Glasper, E. R., Leuner, B., & Gould, E. (2008). Adult neurogenesis finds its niche. *Nature Neuroscience, 11,* 708–731.

Glassman, A., & Shapiro, P. (1998). Depression and the course of coronary artery disease. *American Journal of Psychiatry, 155,* 4–11.

Gluckman, P. D., & Hanson, M. A. (2008). Developmental and epigenetic pathways to obesity: An evolutionary-developmental perspective: Developmental and epigenetic pathways to obesity. *International Journal of Obesity, 32,* S62–S71. doi:10.1038/ijo.2008.240

Goel, V., & Vartanian, O. (2005). Dissociating the roles of right ventral lateral and dorsal lateral prefrontal cortex in generation and maintenance of hypotheses in set-shift problems. *Cerebral Cortex, 15,* 1170–1177.

Goff, D. C., & Coyle, J. T. (2001). The merging role of glutamate in the pathophysiology and treatment of schizophrenia. *American Journal of Psychiatry, 158,* 1367–1377.

Goldapple, K., Segal, Z., Garson, C., Lau, M., Bieling, P., Kennedy, S., & Mayberg, H. (2004). Modulation of cortical-limbic pathways in major depression. *Archives of General Psychiatry, 61,* 34–41.

Goldfield, B. A. (2000). Nouns before verbs in comprehension vs. production: The view from pragmatics. *Journal of Child Language, 27,* 501–520.

Goldin, P., McRae, K., Ramel, W., & Gross, J. J. (2008). The neural bases of emotion regulation: Reappraisal and suppression of negative emotion. *Biological Psychiatry, 63,* 577–586.

Goldman-Rakic, P. S. (1999). The physiological approach: Functional architecture of working memory and disordered cognition in schizophrenia. *Biological Psychiatry, 46,* 650–661.

Goldsmith, T. H. (2006). What birds see. *Scientific American, 295,* 69–75.

Goldstein, E. B. (2007). *Sensation and perception* (7th ed.). Belmont, CA: Thomson-Wadsworth.

Goldstein, T., Bridge, J., & Brent, D. (2008). Sleep disturbance preceding completed suicide in adolescents. *Journal of Consulting and Clinical Psychology, 76*(1), 84–91.

Goleman, D. P. (1995). *Emotional intelligence: Why it can matter more than IQ for character, health and lifelong achievement.* New York, NY: Bantam Books.

Gonzalez, V., and Mark, G. (2004). "Constant, constant, multi-tasking craziness": Managing multiple working spheres. *Proceedings of ACM CHI'04,* 113–120.

Goodwin, P., McGill, B., & Chandra A. (2009). *Who marries and when? Age at first marriage in the United States, 2002.* NCHS data brief No. 19. Hyattsville, MD: National Center for Health Statistics.

Goodwin, P. J. (2004). Support groups in breast cancer: When a negative result is positive. *Journal of Clinical Oncology, 22,* 4244–4246.

Goodwin, P. J., Leszcz, M., Ennis, M., Koopmans, J., Vincent, L., Guther, H., . . . Hunter, J. (2001). The effect of group psychosocial support on survival in metastatic breast cancer. *New England Journal of Medicine, 345,* 1719–1726.

Gopnik, A. (2009). *The philosophical baby.* New York, NY: Farrar, Straus & Giroux.

Gopnik, A., Meltzoff, A. N., & Kuhl, P. K. (1999). *The scientist in the crib: Minds, brains, and how children learn.* New York, NY: Morrow.

Gordon, P. (2004). Numerical cognition without words: Evidence from Amazonia. *Science, 306,* 496–499.

Gorenstein, E. E., & Comer, R. J. (2002). *Case studies in abnormal psychology.* New York, NY: Worth.

Gorrindo, T., & Groves, J. E. (2009). Computer simulation and virtual reality in the diagnosis and treatment of psychiatric disorders. *Academic Psychiatry, 33,* 413–417.

Gosling, S. D. (1998). Personality differences in spotted hyenas (*Crocuta crocuta*). *Journal of Comparative Psychology, 112,* 107–118.

Gosling, S. D., & John, O. P. (1999). Personality dimensions in non-human animals: A cross-species review. *Current Directions in Psychological Science, 8,* 69–75.

Goto, H. (1971). Auditory perception by normal Japanese adults of the sounds "l" and "r." *Neuropsychologia, 9,* 317–323.

Gottfredson, L. (1997). Mainstream science on intelligence: An editorial with 52 signatories, history, and bibliography. *Intelligence, 24,* 13–23.

Gottlieb, N. H., & Green, L. W. (1984). Life events, social network, life-style, and health: An analysis of the 1979 National Survey of Personal Health Practices and Consequences. *Health Education Quarterly, 11,* 91–105.

Gottschalk, S. (2010). The presentation of avatars in Second Life: Self and interaction in social virtual spaces. *Symbolic Interaction, 33,* 501–525.

Gough, H. G., & Bradley, P. (1996). *California Psychological Inventory Manual* (3rd ed.). Palo Alto, CA: Consulting Psychologists Press.

Gould, E., Vail, N., Wagers, M., & Gross, C. G. (2001). Adult-generated hippocampal and neocortical neurons in macaques have a transient existence. *Proceedings of the National Academy of Sciences, 98,* 10910–10917.

Gould, S. J., & Vrba, E. S. (1982). Exaptation: A missing term in the science of form. *Paleobiology, 8,* 4–15.

Governors Highway Safety Association. (2008). *Cell phone driving laws.* Retrieved April 1, 2008, from http://www.ghsa.org/html/stateinfo/laws/cellphone_laws.html

Gow, A., Whiteman, M., Pattie, A., Whalley, L., Starr, J., & Deary, I. (2005). Lifetime intellectual function and satisfaction with life in old age: Longitudinal cohort study. *BMJ: British Medical Journal, 331*(7509), 141–142. doi:10.1136/bmj.38531.675660.F7

Graff, J., & Mansuy, I. M. (2008). Epigenetic codes in cognition and behavior. *Behavioural Brain Research, 192,* 70–87.

Grafman, J., Schwab., K., Warden, D., Pridgeon, A., Brown, H. R., & Salazar, A. M. (1996). Frontal lobe injuries, violence, and aggression: A report of a Vietnam head injury study. *Neurology, 46,* 1231–1238.

Graham, S., & Lowery, B. S. (2004). Priming unconscious racial stereotypes about adolescent offenders. *Law and Human Behavior, 28,* 483–504.

Grant, B. F., Hasin, D. S., Stinson, F. S., Dawson, D. A., Goldstein, R. B., Smith, S., . . . Saha, T. D. (2006). The epidemiology of *DSM-IV-TR* panic disorder and agoraphobia in the United States: Results from the National Epidemiologic Survey on Alcohol and Related Conditions. *Journal of Clinical Psychiatry, 67,* 363–374.

Grant, J. A., Courtemanche, J., Duerden, E. G., Duncan, G. H., & Rainville, P. (2010). Cortical thickness and pain sensitivity in Zen meditators. *Emotion, 10,* 43–53.

Gray, J. L., & Thompson, P. (2004). Neurobiology of intelligence: Science and ethics. *Nature Reviews: Neuroscience, 5,* 471–482.

Green, D., & Swets, J. (1974). *Signal detection theory and psychophysics.* Melbourne, FL: Krieger.

Green, V. A., & Cillessen, A. H. N. (2008). Achievement versus maintenance of control in six-year-old children's interactions with peers: An observational study. *Educational Psychology, 28,* 161–180

Greenberg, L. (1979). Genetic component of bee odor in kin recognition. *Science, 206,* 1095–1097.

Greenberg, M. T., & Kusché, C. A. (1998). *Promoting alternative thinking strategies.* Boulder: Institute of Behavioral Sciences, University of Colorado.

Greenfield, P., & Yan, Z. (2006). Children, adolescents, and the Internet: A new field of inquiry in developmental psychology. *Developmental Psychology, 42,* 391–394.

Greenough, W. T., Volkmar, F. R., & Juraska, J. M. (1973). Effects of rearing complexity on dendritic branching in fronto-lateral and temporal cortex of the rat, *Experimental Neurology, 41,* 371–378.

Greenwald, A. G. (2009, March). Interview by ScienceWatch [Web]. Retrieved from http://sciencewatch.com/inter/aut/2009/09-mar/09marGreen/

Greenwald, A. G., & Banaji, M. R. (1995). Implicit social cognition: Attitudes, self-esteem, and stereotypes. *Psychological Review, 102,* 4–27.

Greenwald, A. G., McGhee, D. E., & Schwartz, J. L. K. (1998). Measuring individual differences in implicit cognition: The implicit association test. *Journal of Personality and Social Psychology, 74,* 1464–1480.

Greenwald, A. G., Poehlman, T., Uhlmann, E., & Banaji, M. R. (2009). Understanding and using the Implicit Association Test: III. Meta-analysis of predictive validity. *Journal of Personality and Social Psychology, 97,* 17–41. doi:10.1037/a0015575

Gregory, R. J. (2007). *Psychological testing* (5th ed.). New York, NY: Allyn & Bacon.

Griffiths, R. R., Richards, W. A., Johnson, M. W., McCann, U. D., & Jesse, R. (2008). Mystical-type experiences occasioned by psilocybin mediate the attribution of personal meaning and spiritual significance 14 months later. *Psychopharmacology, 22,* 621–632.

Griffiths, R. R., Richards, W. A., McCann, U., & Jesse, R. (2006). Psilocybin can occasion mystical-type experiences having substantial and sustained personal meaning and spiritual significance. *Psychopharmacology, 187,* 268–283.

Grigorenko, E. (2000). Heritability and intelligence. In R. J. Sternberg (Ed.), *Handbook of intelligence* (pp. 53–91). New York, NY: Cambridge University Press.

Grolnick, W. S., McMenamy, J. M., & Kurowski, C. O. (2006). Emotional self-regulation in infancy and toddlerhood. In L. Balter & C. S. Tamis-LeMonda (Eds.), *Child psychology: A handbook of contemporary issues* (2nd ed., pp. 3–25). New York, NY: Psychology Press.

Groome, L., Mooney, D., Holland, S., Smith, Y., Atterbury, J., & Dykman, R. (2000). Temporal pattern and spectral complexity as stimulus parameters for eliciting a cardiac orienting reflex in human fetuses. *Perception and Psychophysics, 62*(2), 313–320.

Gross, C. G. (2000). Neurogenesis in the adult brain: Death of a dogma. *Nature Reviews Neuroscience, 1,* 67–73.

Gross, J. J. (1998). The emerging field of emotion regulation: An integrative review. *Review of General Psychology, 2,* 271–299.

Gross, J. J., & John, O. (1998). Mapping the domain of expressivity: Multimethod evidence for a hierarchical model. *Journal of Personality and Social Psychology, 74,* 170–191.

Gross, J. J., & Levenson, R. W. (1993). Emotional suppression—Physiology, self-report, and expressive behavior. *Journal of Personality and Social Psychology, 64,* 970–986.

Gross, J. J., & Levenson, R. W. (1997). Hiding feelings: The acute effects of inhibiting positive and negative emotions. *Journal of Abnormal Psychology, 106,* 95–103.

Gross, J. J., Richards, J. M., & John, O. P. (2006). Emotion regulation in everyday life. In D. K. Snyder, J. A. Simpson, & J. N. Hughes (Eds.), *Emotion regulation in families: Pathways to dysfunction and health* (pp. 13–35). Washington, DC: American Psychological Association.

Grossberg, S., & Vladusich, T. (2010). How do children learn to follow gaze, share joint attention, imitate their teachers, and use tools during social interactions? *Neural Networks, 23,* 940–965.

Grossman, A. W., Churchill, J. D., McKinney, B. C., Kodish, I. M., Otte, S. L., & Greenough, W. T. (2003). Experience effects on brain development: Possible contributions to psychopathology. *Journal of Child Psychology and Psychiatry, 44,* 33–63.

Grossman, P., Kappos, L., Gensicke, H., D'Souza, M., Mohr, D. C., Penner, I. K., & Steiner, C. (2010). MS quality of life, depression, and fatigue improve after mindfulness training. *Neurology, 75,* 1141–1149.

Grossman, T., Striano, T., & Friederici, A. D. (2006). Crossmodal integration of emotional information from face and voice in the infant brain. *Developmental Science, 9,* 309–315.

Guarnaccia, V., Dill, C. A., Sabatino, S., & Southwick, S. (2001). Scoring accuracy using the comprehensive system for the Rorschach. *Journal of Personality Assessment, 77,* 464–474.

Guarraci, F. A., & Benson, A. (2005). "Coffee, Tea and Me": Moderate doses of caffeine affect sexual behavior in female rats. *Pharmacology, Biochemistry and Behavior, 82,* 522–530.

Guehl, D., Benazzouz, A., Aouizerate, B., Cuny, E., Rotgé, J.-Y., Rougier, A., et al. (2008). Neuronal correlates of obsessions in the caudate nucleus. *Biological Psychiatry, 63,* 557–562.

Guilford, J. P. (1967). *The nature of human intelligence.* New York, NY: McGraw-Hill.

Guillem, K., & Peoples, L. (2010). Progressive and lasting amplification of accumbal nicotine-seeking neural signals. *The Journal of Neuroscience, 30,* 276–286.

Guilleminault, C., Kirisoglu, C., Bao, G., Arias, V., Chan, A., & Li, K. K. (2005). Adult chronic sleepwalking and its treatment based on polysomnography. *Brain, 128,* 1062–1069.

Guiraud, A., deLorgeril, M., Zeghichi, S., Laporte, F., Salen, P., Saks, V., et al. (2008, April 29). Interactions of ethanol drinking with n-3 fatty acids in rats: Potential consequences for the cardiovascular system. *British Journal of Nutrition*, 1–8. Advance online publication. Retrieved July 10, 2008. doi:10.1017/S0007114508981472

Gunderson, E., Moline, J., & Catalano, P. (1997). Risks of developing noise-induced hearing loss in employees of urban music clubs. *American Journal of Industrial Medicine*, 31, 75–79.

Gupta, S., Agarwal, A., Banerjee, J., & Alvarez, J. G. (2007). The role of oxidative stress in spontaneous abortion and recurrent pregnancy loss: A systematic review. *Obstetrical, Gynecological Survey*, 62, 335–347.

Gutteling, B. M., de Weerth, C., Willemsen-Swinkels, S. H. N., Huizink, A. C., Mulder, E. J. H., Visser, G. H. A., & Buitelaar, J. K. (2005). The effects of prenatal stress on temperament and problem behavior of 27-month-old toddlers. *European Child and Adolescent Psychiatry*, 14, 41–51.

Guzman-Marin, R., Suntsova, N., Methippara, M., Greiffenstein, R., Szymusiak, R., & McGinty, D. (2003). Sleep deprivation suppresses neurogenesis in the adult hippocampus of rats. *European Journal of Neuroscience*, 22, 2111–2116.

Habermas, T., Meier, M., & Mukhtar, B. (2009). Are specific emotions narrated differently? *Emotion*, 9, 751–762.

Hafetz, J. S., Jacobsohn, L. S., García-España, J., Curry, A. E., & Winston, F. K. (2010). Adolescent drivers' perceptions of the advantages and disadvantages of abstention from in-vehicle cell phone use. *Accident Analysis and Prevention*, 42(6), 1570–1576. doi:10.1016/j.aap.2010.03.015

Haier, R. J., Jung, R. E., Yeo, R. A., Head, K., & Alkire, M. T. (2004). Structural brain variation and general intelligence. *NeuroImage*, 23, 425–433.

Hakuta, K., Bialystok, E., & Wiley, E. (2003). Critical evidence: A test of the critical-period hypothesis for second-language acquisition. *Psychological Science*, 14, 31–38.

Hale, B., Seiser, L., & McGuire, E. J. (2005). Mental imagery. In J. Taylor & J. Wilson (Eds.), *Applying sport psychology: Four perspectives* (pp. 117–135). Champaign, IL: Human Kinetics.

Hall, J. A., & Matsumoto, D. (2004). Gender difference in the judgment of multiple emotions from facial expression. *Emotion*, 4, 201–206.

Halpern, D. (2004). A cognitive-process taxonomy for sex differences in cognitive abilities. *Current Directions in Psychological Science*, 13, 135–139.

Halpern, J. H., Pope, H. G., Sherwood, A. R., Barry, S., Hudson, J. I., & Yurgelun-Todd, D. (2004). Residual neuropsychological effects of illicit 3,4-methylenedioxymethamphetamine (MDMA) in individuals with minimal exposure to other drugs. *Drug and Alcohol Dependence*, 75, 135–147.

Hamann, S., Herman, R. A., Nolan, C. L., & Wallen, K. (2004). Men and women differ in amygdala response to visual sexual stimuli. *Nature Neuroscience*, 7, 411–416.

Hamer, D., & Copeland, P. (1998). *Living with our genes*. New York, NY: Anchor Books.

Hamilton, W. D. (1964). The genetical evolution of social behaviour I and II. *Journal of Theoretical Biology*, 7, 1–16, 17–52.

Hammer, A. L., & Macdaid, G. P. (1992). *Career report manual*. Palo Alto, CA: Consulting Psychologists Press.

Han, J. (2004). Acupuncture and endorphins. *Neuroscience Letters*, 361, 258–261.

Haney, C., Banks, W. C., & Zimbardo, P. G. (1973). Interpersonal dynamics in a simulated prison. *International Journal of Criminology and Penology*, 1, 69–97.

Hankin, B. L. (2010). Personality and depressive symptoms: Stress generation and cognitive vulnerabilities to depression in a prospective daily diary study. *Journal of Clinical and Social Psychology*, 29, 369–401.

Hannigan, T. P. (1995). Body odor: The international student and cross-cultural communication. *Culture & Psychology*, 1, 497–503.

Hansen, R. A., Gartiehner, G., Lohr, K. N., & Daufer, D. (2007). Functional outcomes of drug treatment in Alzheimer's disease: A systematic review and meta-analysis. *Drugs & Aging*, 24(2), 155–167.

Hanson, D. J. (n.d.). Candy Lightner. Retrieved from http://www2.potsdam.edu/hansondj/controversies/1119636699.html

Harackiewicz, J. M., & Sansone, C. (1991). Goals and intrinsic motivation: You can get there from here. In M. L. Maehr & P. R. Pintrich (Eds.), *Advances in motivation and achievement: Goals and self regulatory processes* (Vol. 7, pp. 21–49). Greenwich, CT: JAI Press.

Hare, R. D. (1993). *Without conscience: The disturbing world of the psychopaths among us*. New York, NY: Pocket Books.

Hargittai, E. (2008). Whose space? Differences among users and non-users of social network sites. *Journal of Computer-Mediated Communication*, 13, 276–297.

Hargrave, G. E., & Hiatt, D. (1989). Use of the California Psychological Inventory in law enforcement officer selection. *Journal of Personality Assessment*, 53, 267–277.

Harkins, S. G. (1987). Social loafing and social facilitation. *Journal of Experimental Social Psychology*, 23, 1–18.

Harlow, H. (1958). The nature of love. *American Psychologist*, 13, 573–685.

Harmon, D. (2006). Free-radical theory of aging: An update. *Annals of the New York Academy of Sciences*, 1067, 10–21.

Harmon-Jones, E. (2003). Clarifying the emotive functions of asymmetrical frontal cortical activity. *Psychophysiology*, 40, 838–848.

Harris, J. R. (1998). *The nurture assumption: Why children turn out the way they do*. New York, NY: Free Press.

Harris, M. B. (1974). Mediators between frustration and aggression in a field

experiment. *Journal of Experimental Social Psychology*, 10, 561–571.

Harrison, P. J. (2004). The hippocampus in schizophrenia: A review of the neuropathological evidence and its pathophysiological implications. *Psychopharmacology*, 174, 151–162.

Harrison, P. J., & Owen, M. (2003). Genes for schizophrenia? Recent findings and their pathophysiological implications. *The Lancet*, 361, 417–419.

Harrison, P. J., & Weinberger, D. R. (2005). Schizophrenia genes, gene expression, and neuropathology: On the matter of their convergence. *Molecular Psychiatry*, 10, 40–68.

Hasher, L., & Zacks, R. T. (1979). Automatic and effortful processes in memory. *Journal of Experimental Psychology: General*, 108, 356–388.

Hauser, M. D., Chomsky, N., & Fitch, W. T. (2002). The faculty of language: What is it, who has it, and how did it evolve? *Science*, 298, 1569–1579.

Hayes, B. D., Klein-Schwartz, W., & Doyon, S. (2008). Toxicity of buprenorphine overdoses in children. *Pediatrics*, 121, 782–786.

Haynes, S. G., Levine, S., Scotch, N., Feinleib, M., & Kannel, W. B. (1978). The relationship of psychosocial factors to coronary heart disease in the Framingham study. I. Methods and risk factors. *American Journal of Epidemiology*, 107, 362–383.

Hazan, C., & Shaver, P. (1987). Romantic love conceptualized as an attachment process. *Journal of Personality and Social Psychology*, 52, 511–524.

Headey, B. (2008). Life goals matter to happiness: A revision of set-point theory. *Social Indicators Research*, 86, 213–231.

Health and Human Services. (2004). *New surgeon general's report expands the list of diseases caused by smoking*. Retrieved August 19, 2008, from http://www.hhs.gov/news/press/2004pres/20040527a.html

Heath, R. G. (1975). Brain function and behavior. *Journal of Nervous and Mental Disease*, 160, 159–175.

Hebb, D. O. (1949). *The organization of behavior: A neuropsychological theory*. New York, NY: Wiley.

Hedden, T., & Gabrieli, J. D. E. (2004). Insights into the ageing mind: A view from cognitive neuroscience. *Nature Reviews Neuroscience*, 5, 87–96.

Hedges, L., & Nowell, A. (1995). Sex differences in mental test scores, variability, and numbers of high-scoring individuals. *Science*, 269, 41–45.

Hedges, S. M., Jandorf, L., & Stone, A. A. (1985). Meaning of daily mood assessments. *Journal of Personality and Social Psychology*, 48, 428–434.

Hegelson, V. S., & Taylor, S. E. (1993). Social comparisons and adjustment among cardiac patients. *Journal of Applied Social Psychology*, 23, 1171–1195.

Heider, F. (1958). *The psychology of interpersonal relations*. New York, NY: Wiley.

Hennessey, B. A., & Amabile, T. M. (1998). Reward, intrinsic motivation and creativity. *American Psychologist, 53,* 674–675.

Herbert, A., & Rich, A. (1999). RNA processing in evolution: The logic of soft-wired genomes. *Annals of the New York Academy of Sciences, 870,* 119–132.

Hering, E. (1878). *Zur Lehre vom Lichtsinn.* Vienna, Austria: Gerold.

Hernandez-Reif, M., Field, T., Largie, S., Diego, M., Manigat, N., Seoanes, J., & Bornstein, J. (2005). Cerebral palsy symptoms in children decreased following massage therapy. *Early Child Development and Care, 175,* 445–456.

Heron, W. (1957). The pathology of boredom. *Scientific American, 196,* 52–56.

Herrnstein, R. J., & Murray, C. (1994). *The bell-curve: Intelligence and class structure in American life.* New York, NY: Free Press.

Herz, R. (2004). A naturalistic analysis of autobiographical memories triggered by olfactory visual and auditory stimuli. *Chemical Senses, 29,* 217–224.

Hesse, E., & Main, M. (2006). Frightened, threatening, and dissociative parental behavior in low-risk samples: Description, discussion, and interpretations. *Development and Psychopathology, 18,* 309–343.

Hettema, J. M., Neale, M. C., & Kendler, K. S. (2001). A review and meta-analysis of the genetic epidemiology of anxiety disorders. *American Journal of Psychiatry, 158,* 1568–1578.

Hien, D. A., & Miele, G. M. (2003). Emotion-focused coping as a mediator of maternal cocaine abuse and antisocial behavior. *Psychology of Addictive Behaviors, 17,* 49–55.

Hilgard, E. (1965). *Hypnotic susceptibility.* New York, NY: Harcourt, Brace, & World.

Hilgard, E. (1977). *Divided consciousness: Multiple controls in human thought and action.* New York, NY: Wiley.

Hillman, C. H., Buck, S. M., Themanson, J. R., Pontifex, M. B., & Castelli, D. M. (2009). Aerobic fitness and cognitive development: Event-related brain potential and task performance indices of executive control in preadolescent children. *Developmental Psychology, 45,* 114–129.

Hillman, C. H., Erickson, K. I., & Kramer, A. F. (2008). Be smart, exercise your heart: Exercise effects on brain and cognition. *Nature Reviews Neuroscience, 9,* 58–65.

Hinduja, S., & Patchin, J. W. (2008). Cyberbullying: An exploratory analysis of factors related to offending and victimization. *Deviant Behavior, 29,* 129–156.

Hines, L. M., & Rimm, E. B. (2001). Moderate alcohol consumption and coronary heart disease: A review. *Postgraduate Medical Journal, 77,* 747–752.

Hines, M., Fane, B., Pasterski, V., Matthews, G., Conway, G., & Brook, C. (2003). Spatial abilities following prenatal androgen abnormality: Targeting and mental rotations performance in individuals with congenital adrenal hyperplasia. *Psychoneuroendo-crinology, 28,* 1010–1026. doi:10.1016/S0306-4530(02)00121-X

Hirshfeld-Becker, D. R., Masek, B., Henin, A., Blakely, L. R., Pollock-Wurman, R. A., McQuade, J., . . . Biederman, J. (2010). Cognitive behavioral therapy for 4- to 7-year-old children with anxiety disorders: A randomized clinical trial. *Journal of Consulting and Clinical Psychology, 78,* 498–510.

Ho, Y-C, Cheung, M-C, & Chan, A. S. (2003). Music training improves verbal but not visual memory: Cross-sectional and longitudinal explorations in children. *Neuropsychology, 17,* 439–450.

Hoare, J., Fouche, J-P., Spottiswoode, B., Joska, J. A., Schoeman, R., Stein, D. J., & Carey, P. (2010). White matter correlates of apathy in HIV-positive subjects: A diffusion tensor imaging study. *Journal of Neuropsychiatry & Clinical Neuroscience, 22,* 313–320.

Hobson, J. A. (2001). *The dream drugstore: Chemically altered states of consciousness.* Cambridge, MA: MIT Press.

Hobson, J. A. (2002). *Dreaming: An introduction to the science of sleep.* New York, NY: Oxford University Press.

Hochberg, L. R., Serruya, M. D., Friehs, G. M., Mukand, J. A., Saleh, M., Caplan, A. H., . . . Donoghue, J. P. (2006). Neuronal ensemble control of prosthetic devices by a human with tetraplegia. *Nature, 442,* 164–171. doi:10.1038/nature04970

Hodgetts, W., Szarko, R., & Rieger, J. (2009). What is the influence of background noise and exercise on the listening levels of iPod users? *International Journal of Audiology, 48,* 825–832.

Hoff, E. (2006). How social contexts support and shape language development. *Developmental Review, 26,* 55–88.

Hoffmann, H., Kessler, H., Eppel, T., Rukavina, S., & Traue, H. C. (2010). Expression intensity, gender and facial emotion recognition: Women recognize only subtle facial emotions better than men. *Acta Psychologica, 135,* 278–283.

Hofman, S. G., Schulz, S. M., Meuret, A. F., Moscovitch, D. A., & Suvak, M. (2006). Sudden gains during therapy of social phobia. *Journal of Consulting and Clinical Psychology, 74,* 687–697.

Hofstede, G. (2001). *Culture's consequences: Comparing values, behaviors, institutions, and organizations across nations* (2nd ed.). Thousand Oaks, CA: Sage.

Hogan, M. J., Parker, J. D. A., Wiener, J., Watters, C., Wood, L. M., & Oke, A. (2010). Academic success in adolescence: Relationships among verbal IQ, social support and emotional intelligence. *Australian Journal of Psychology, 62,* 30–41.

Hogan, T. P. (2007). *Psychological testing: A practical introduction* (2nd ed.). New York, NY: John Wiley.

Hogeboom, D. L., McDermott, R. J., Perrin, K. M., Osman, H., & Bell-Ellison, B. A. (2010). Internet use and social networking among middle aged and older adults. *Educational Gerontology, 36*(2), 93–111. doi:10.1080/03601270903058507

Hohmann, A. G., Suplita, R. L., Bolton, N. M., Neely, M. H., Fegley, D., Mangieri, R., . . . Piomelli, D. (2005). An endocannabinoid mechanism for stress-induced analgesia. *Nature, 435,* 1108–1112.

Holder, M., Coleman, B., & Wallace, J. (2010). Spirituality, religiousness, and happiness in children aged 8–12 years. *Journal of Happiness Studies, 11,* 131–150.

Holland, J. L. (1985). *Making vocational choices: A theory of vocational personalities and work environments.* Englewood Cliffs, NJ: Prentice Hall.

Hollon, S. D., DeRubeis, R. J., Shelton, R. C., Amsterdam, J. D., Salomon, R. M., O'Reardon, J. P., . . . Gallop, R. (2005). Prevention of relapse following cognitive therapy vs medications in moderate to severe depression. *Archives of General Psychiatry, 62,* 417–422.

Holmes, J., Gathercole, S. E., & Dunning, D. L. (2009). Adaptive training leads to sustained enhancement of poor working memory in children. *Developmental Science, 12,* F9–F15.

Holmes, T. H., & Rahe, R. H. (1967). The social readjustment rating scale. *Journal of Psychosomatic Research, 11,* 211–218.

Holstege, G., Georgiadis, J., Paans, A., Meiners, L., van der Graaf, F., & Reinders, A. (2003). Brain activation during human male ejaculation. *Journal of Neuroscience, 23*(27), 9185–9193.

Hölzel, B. K., Carmody, J., Vangel, M., Congleton, C., Yerramsetti, S. M., Gard, T., & Lazar, S. (in press). Mindfulness practice leads to increases in regional brain gray matter density. *Psychiatry Research: Neuroimaging.* doi:10.1016/j.pscychresns.2010.08.006

Hopfield, J. J. (1982). Neural networks and physical systems with emergent collective computational abilities. *Proceedings of the National Academy of Sciences, 79,* 2554–2558.

Hopson, J. L. (1998, September/October). Fetal psychology. *Psychology Today, 31,* 44. Retrieved from http://www.leaderu.com/orgs/tul/psychtoday9809.html

Horn, J. L., & Cattell, R. B. (1966). Refinement and test of the theory of fluid and crystallized general intelligences. *Journal of Educational Psychology, 57,* 253–270.

Horne, J. A., & Foster, S. C. (1995). Can exercise overcome sleepiness? *Sleep Research, 24A,* 437.

Horney, K. (1945). *Our inner conflicts: A constructive theory of neurosis.* New York, NY: Norton.

Horney, K. (1950). *Neurosis and human growth: The struggle toward self-realization.* New York, NY: Norton.

Horrey, W. J., & Wickens, C. D. (2006). Examining the impact of cell phone conversations on driving using meta-analytic techniques. *Human Factors, 48,* 196–205.

Hosking, S., Young, K., & Regan, M. (2006). The effects of text messaging on young novice driver performance: Monash University Accident Research Centre, Report

No. 246. Retrieved from http://www.monash.edu.au/muarc/reports/muarc246.pdf

Hoss, R. A., & Langlois, J. H. (2003). Infants prefer attractive faces. In O. Pascalis & A. Slater (Eds.), *The development of face processing in infancy and early childhood: Current perspectives* (pp. 27–38). New York, NY: Nova Science.

Houlihan, A. E., Gibbons, F. X., Gerrard, M., Yeh, H., & Reimer, R. A. (2008). The impact of early sexual onset on the self-concept and subsequent risky behavior of African American adolescents. *The Journal of Early Adolescence, 28,* 70–91.

How a Swiss inventor hooked the world. (2007, January 4). Retrieved September 16, 2007, from http://www.swissinfo.org/eng/ search/detail/How a_Swiss_invention _hooked_the_world.html?siteSect=881&sid =7402384&cKey=1167927120000

Howard, K. I., Kopta, S. M., Krause, M. S., & Orlinsky, D. E. (1986). The dose-effect relationship in psychotherapy. *American Psychologist, 41,* 159–164.

Howe, D. (2010). ADHD and its comorbidity: An example of gene–environment interaction and its implications for child and family social work. *Child & Family Social Work, 15,* 265–275. doi:10.1111/j.1365-2206.2009.00666.x

Howell, A. J., Jahrig, J. C., & Powell, R. A. (2004). Sleep quality, sleep propensity and academic performance. *Perceptual and Motor Skills, 99,* 525–535. doi:10.2466/ PMS.99.5.525-535

Howes, C., & Matheson, C. C. (1992). Sequences in the development of competent play with peers: Social and social pretend play. *Developmental Psychology, 28,* 961–974.

Hu, S.-H., Wei, N., Wang, Q.-D., Yan, L.-Q., Wei, E.-Q., Zhang, M.-M., . . . Xu, Y. (2008). Patterns of brain activation during visually evoked sexual arousal differ between homosexual and heterosexual men. *American Journal of Neuroradiology, 29,* 1890–1896.

Hua, K., Oishi, K., Zhang, J., Wakana, S., Yoshioka, T., Zhang, W., . . . Mori, S. (2009). Mapping of functional areas in the human cortex based on connectivity through association fibers. *Cerebral Cortex, 19,* 1889–1895.

Hubbard, E. M., & Ramachandran, V. S. (2005). Neurocognitive mechanisms of synesthesia. *Neuron, 48,* 509–520.

Hubel, D., & Wiesel, T. (1962). Receptive fields, binocular interaction and functional architecture in the cat's visual cortex. *Journal of Physiology of London, 160,* 106–154.

Hubel, D., & Wiesel, T. (1979). Brain mechanisms of vision. *Scientific American, 241,* 130–144.

Hudson, W. (1960). Pictorial depth perception in subcultural groups in Africa. *Journal of Social Psychology, 52,* 183–208.

Huesmann, L. R., Moise-Titus, J., & Podolski, C. (2003). Longitudinal relations between children's exposure to TV violence and their aggressive and violent behavior in young adulthood: 1977–1992. *Developmental Psychology, 39,* 201–221.

Huff, D. (1954). *How to lie with statistics.* New York, NY: Norton.

Huffaker, D. A., & Calvert, S. L. (2005). Gender, identity, and language use in teenage blogs. *Journal of Computer-Mediated Communication, 10,* Article 1. Retrieved from http://jcmc.indiana.edu/vol10/issue2/ huffaker.html

Hull, C. L. (1943). *Principles of behavior: An introduction to behavior theory.* New York, NY: Appleton-Century.

Hunter, J. E., & Schmidt, F. L. (2000). Racial and gender bias in ability and achievement tests: Resolving the apparent paradox. *Psychology, Public Policy and Law, 6,* 151–158.

Huston, A. C., Wright J. C., Marquis J., & Green S. B. (1999). How young children spend their time: Television and other activities. *Developmental Psychology, 35,* 912–925.

Hutchinson, S., Lee, L. H., Gaab, N., & Schlaug, G. (2003). Cerebellar volume of musicians. *Cerebral Cortex, 13,* 943–949.

Huttenlocher, J., Vasilyeva, M., Cymerman, E., & Levine, S. (2002). Language input at home and at school: Relation to child syntax. *Cognitive Psychology, 45,* 337–374.

Hyde, J. S. (1990). Meta-analysis and the psychology of gender differences. *Signs: Journal of Women in Culture & Society, 16,* 53–73.

Hyde, J. S. (2005). The genetics of sexual orientation. In J. S. Hyde (Ed.), *Biological substrates of human sexuality* (pp. 9–20). Washington, DC: American Psychological Association.

Hyde, K. L., Lerch, J., Norton, A., Forgeard, M., Winner, E., Evans, A. C., & Schlaug, G. (2009). Musical training shapes structural brain development. *The Journal of Neuroscience, 29,* 3019–3025.

Hyde, T. S., & Jenkins, J. J. (1973). Recall for words as a function of semantic, graphic, and syntactic orienting tasks. *Journal of Verbal Learning and Verbal Behavior, 12,* 471–480.

Hyman, S. E. (2005). Neurotransmitters. *Current Biology, 15,* R154–R158.

I feel I am trapped inside my head, banging against its walls, trying desperately to escape. (1986, March 18). *The New York Times.* Retrieved from http://www.nytimes.com

Iacoboni, M., & Mazziotta, J. C. (2007). Mirror neuron system: Basic findings and clinical applications. *Annals of Neurology, 62,* 213–218.

Iacoboni, M., Woods R. P., Brass, M., Bekkering, H., Mazziotta, J. C., & Rizzolatti, G. (1999). Cortical mechanisms of human imitation. *Science, 286,* 2526–2528.

Iarocci, G., & McDonald, J. (2006). Sensory integration and the perceptual experience of persons with autism. *Journal of Autism and Developmental Disorders, 36,* 77–90.

Implicit Association Test: A talk with Mahzarin Banaji and Anthony Greenwald. (2008, February 12). *Edge: The Third Culture.* Retrieved from http://www.edge.org/3rd_culture/banaji_greenwald08/ banaji_greenwald08_index.html

Inhelder, B., & Piaget, J. (1958). *The growth of logical thinking: From childhood to adolescence.* New York, NY: Basic Books.

Intel Science Talent Search 2010 Winners announced. (2010, March 16). Retrieved from http://www.intel.com/pressroom/ archive/releases/20100316edu.htm

Ironson, G., O'Cleirigh, C., Fletcher, M. A., Laurenceau, J. P., Balbin, E., Klimas, N., . . . Solomon, G. (2005). Psychosocial factors predict CD4 and viral load change in men and women with human immunodeficiency virus in the era of highly active antiretroviral treatment. *Psychosomatic Medicine, 67,* 1013–1021.

Isacsson, G., Rich, C., Jureidini, J., & Raven, M. (2010). The increased use of antidepressants has contributed to the world-wide reduction in suicide rates. *The British Journal of Psychiatry, 196,* 429–433.

Isen, A. M., Daubman, K. A., & Nowicki, G. P. (1987). Positive affect facilitates creative problem solving. *Journal of Personality and Social Psychology, 52,* 1122–1131.

Itri, J., Michel, S., Waschek, J., & Colwell, C. (2004). Circadian rhythm in inhibitory synaptic transmission in the mouse suprachiasmatic nucleus. *Journal of Neurophysiology, 92*(1), 311–319.

Iversen S. D., & Iversen L. L. (2007). Dopamine: 50 years in perspective. *Trends in Neurosciences, 30,* 188–193.

Iyengar, S. S., & DeVoe, S. E. (2003). Rethinking the value of choice: Considering cultural mediators of intrinsic motivation. In V. Murphy Berman & J. J. Berman (Eds.), *Cross-cultural differences in perspectives on the self. Nebraska Symposium on Motivation, 49,* 129–174.

Izard, C. E. (1969). The emotions and emotion constructs in personality and culture research. In R. B. Cattell (Ed.), *Handbook of modern personality theory.* Chicago, IL: Aldine Press.

Izard, C. E., Trentacosta, C. J., King, K. A., & Mostow, A. J. (2004). An emotion-based prevention program for Head Start children. *Early Education & Development, 15,* 407–422.

Jablensky, A., & Woodbury, M. A. (1995). Dementia praecox and manic-depressive insanity in 1908: A Grade of Membership analysis of the Kraepelinian dichotomy. *European Archives of Psychiatry and Clinical Neuroscience, 245,* 202–209.

Jackson, K. M. (2008). Heavy episodic drinking: Determining the predictive utility of five or more drinks. *Psychology of Addictive Behaviors, 22,* 68–77.

Jackson, L. A., von Eye, A., Biocca, F. A., Barbatsis, G., Zhao, Y., & Fitzgerald, H. E. (2006). Does home Internet use influence the academic performance of low-income children? *Developmental Psychology, 42,* 429–435.

Jackson, L. A., von Eye, A., Fitzgerald, H. E., Zhao, Y., & Witt, E. A. (2010). Self-concept, self-esteem, gender, race and information technology use. *Computers in Human Behavior, 26,* 323–332.

Jacobs, B. L. (2004). Depression: The brain finally gets into the act. *Current Directions in Psychological Science, 13,* 103–106.

Jacobs, B. L., van Praag, H., & Gage, F. H. (2000). Adult brain neurogenesis and psychiatry: A novel theory of depression. *Molecular Psychiatry, 5,* 262–269.

Jacobs, D. R., Jr., Adachi, H., Mulder, I., Kromhout, D., Menotti, A., Nissinen, A., & Blackburn, H. (1999). Cigarette smoking and mortality risk: Twenty-five-year follow-up of the Seven Countries Study. *Archives of Internal Medicine, 159,* 733–740.

Jacobs, G. H., & Nathans, J. (2009). The evolution of primate color vision. *Scientific American, 300,* 56–63.

Jacobs, T. L., Epel, E. S., Lin, J., Blackburn, E. H., Wolkowitz, O. M., Bridwell, D. A., . . . Saron, C. D. (2010). Intensive meditation training, immune cell telomerase activity, and psychological mediators. *Psychoneuroendocrinology.* Published online ahead of print. doi:10.1016/j.psyneuen.2010.09.010

Jacobsen, L. K., Krystal, J. H., Mencl, E., Westerveld, M., Frost, S. J., & Pugh, K. R. (2005). Effects of smoking and smoking abstinence on cognition in adolescent tobacco smokers. *Biological Psychiatry, 57,* 56–66.

Jacobson, A. L. (1963). Learning in flatworms and annelids. *Psychological Bulletin, 60,* 74–94.

Jacobson, L. H., Kelly, P. H., Bettler, B., Kaupmann, K., & Cryan, J. F. (2006). GABAB(1) receptor isoforms differentially mediate the acquisition and extinction of aversive taste memories. *Journal of Neuroscience, 26,* 8800–8803.

Jacobson, S., & Jacobson, J. (2000). *Teratogenic insult and neurobehavioral function in infancy and childhood.* Mahwah, NJ: Erlbaum.

Jacoby, L. L., Hessels, S., & Bopp, K. (2001). Proactive and retroactive effects in memory performance: Dissociating recollection and accessibility bias. In H. Roediger, J. S. Nairne, I. Neath, & A. M. Suprenant (Eds.), *The nature of remembering: Essays in honor of Robert G. Crowder* (pp. 35–54). Washington, DC: American Psychological Association.

Jain, S., Dharap, S. B., & Gore, M. A. (2008). Early prediction of outcome in very severe closed head injury. *Injury: International Journal of the Care of the Injured, 39,* 598–603.

James, W. (1884). What is an emotion? *Mind, 9,* 188–205.

Jamison, K. R. (1993). *Touched with fire: Manic-depressive illness and the artistic temperament.* New York, NY: Free Press.

Jamison, K. R., Gerner, R. H., Hammen, C., & Padesky, C. (1980). Clouds and silver linings: Positive experiences associated with primary affective disorders. *American Journal of Psychiatry, 137,* 198–202.

Jan, J. E., Reiter, R. J., Bax, M. C. O., Ribary, U., Freeman, R. D., & Wasdell,

M. B. (2010). Long-term sleep disturbances in children: A cause of neuronal loss. *European Journal of Pediatric Neurology, 14,* 380–390.

Janeck, A. S., Calamari, J. E., Riemann, B. C., & Heffelfinger, S. K. (2003). Too much thinking about thinking? Metacognitive differences in obsessive–compulsive disorder. *Journal of Anxiety Disorders, 17,* 181–195.

Janis, I. L. (1983). *Groupthink* (2nd ed., rev.). Boston, MA: Houghton-Mifflin.

Javitt, D. C., & Coyle, J. T. (2004). Decoding schizophrenia. *Scientific American, 290,* 48–55.

Jeannerod, M. (1995). Mental imagery in the motor context. *Neuropsychologia, 33,* 1419–1432.

Jenkins, W. M., Merzenich, M. M., Ochs, M. T., Allard, T., & Guic-Roble, E. (1990). Functional reorganization of primary somatosensory cortex in adult owl monkeys after behaviorally controlled tactile stimulation. *Journal of Neurophysiology, 63,* 82–104.

Jennifer Aniston talks about her flying ritual. (2009). Retrieved from http:// www.imnotobsessed.com/2009/09/30/ jennifer-aniston-talks-about-her-flying-ritual

Jensen, A. R. (1969). How much can we boost IQ and scholastic achievement? *Harvard Educational Review, 39,* 1–23.

Jerison, H. J. (2000). The evolution of intelligence. In R. J. Sternberg (Ed.), *The handbook of intelligence* (pp. 216–244). New York, NY: Cambridge University Press.

Jha, A. P., Krompinger, J., & Baime, M. J. (2007). Mindfulness training modifies subsystems of attention. *Cognitive, Affective, & Behavioral Neuroscience, 7,* 109–119.

Ji, D., & Wilson, M. A. (2007). Coordinated memory replay in the visual cortex and hippocampus during sleep. *Nature Neuroscience, 10,* 100–107.

Ji, Y. G., Hwangbo, H., Yi, J. S., Rau, P. L. P., Fang, X., & Ling, C. (2010). The influence of cultural differences on the use of social network services and the formation of social capital. *International Journal of Human–Computer Interaction, 26,* 1100–1121.

Jimenez, R. T., Garcia, G. E., & Pearson, P. D. (1994). *The metacognitive strategies of Latina/o students who read Spanish and English.* Center for the Study of Reading, Technical Report No. 601. Urbana-Champaign, IL: College of Education.

John, O. P., & Srivastava, S. (1999). The Big Five trait taxonomy: History, measurement, and theoretical perspectives. In L. A. Pervin & O. P. John (Eds.), *Handbook of personality theory and research* (pp. 102–138). New York, NY: Guilford Press.

Johnson, D. P., Penn, D. L., Fredrickson, B. L., Meyer, P. S. , Kring, A. M., & Brantley, M. (2009). Loving-kindness meditation to enhance recovery from negative symptoms of schizophrenia. *Journal of Clinical Psychology, 65,* 499–509.

Johnson, G. (1998). Lithium—Early development, toxicity, and renal function. *Neuropsychopharmacology 19,* 200–205.

Johnson, R. E., Fudala, P. J., & Payne, R. (2005). Buprenorphine: Considerations for pain management. *Journal of Pain and Symptom Management, 29,* 297–326.

Johnston, J. C., & McClelland, J. L. (1974). Perception of letters in words: Seek not and ye shall find. *Science, 184,* 1192–1994.

Jokela, M., Hintsa, T., Hintsanen, M., & Keltikangas-Jarvinen, L. (2010). Adult temperament and childbearing over the life course. *European Journal of Personality, 24,* 151–166.

Jones, S. A., & Wilson, A. E. (2009). The horizon line, linear perspective, interposition, and background brightness as determinants of the magnitude of the pictorial moon illusion. *Attention, Perception, & Psychophysics, 71,* 131–142.

Jope, R. S. (1999). Anti-bipolar therapy: Mechanism of action of lithium. *Molecular Psychiatry, 4,* 117–128.

Jordahl, T., & Lohman, B. J. (2009). A bioecological analysis of risk and protective factors associated with early sexual intercourse of young adolescents. *Children and Youth Services Review, 31,* 1272–1282.

Joseph, R. (n.d.) Charles Whitman: The amygdala and mass murder. Retrieved from http://BrainMind.com/Case5.html

Judd, T., & Kennedy, G. (2010). A five-year study of on-campus Internet use by undergraduate biomedical students. *Computers & Education, 55,* 1564–1571.

Juliano, L. M., & Griffiths, R. R. (2004). A critical review of caffeine withdrawal: Empirical validation of symptoms and signs, incidence, severity, and associated features. *Psychopharmacology, 176,* 1–29.

Jump, V. K., Fargo, J. D., & Akers, J. F. (2006). Impact of massage therapy on health outcomes among orphaned infants in Ecuador: Results of a randomized clinical trial. *Family & Community Health, 29,* 314–319.

Jung, C. G. (1918/1964). The role of the unconscious. In *Collected works* (Vol. 10, Trans. R. F. C. Hull). New York, NY: Bollingen Foundation.

Jung, C. G. (1931/1960). The stages of life. In H. Read, M. Fordham, & G. Adler (Eds.) & R. F. C. Hull (Trans.), *The collected works of C. G. Jung* (Vol. 8). New York, NY: Pantheon.

Jung, R. E., & Haier, R. J. (2007). The parieto-frontal integration theory (P-FIT) of intelligence: Converging neuroimaging evidence. *Behavioral and Brain Sciences, 30,* 135–187.

Jung, R. E., Gasparovic, C., Chavez, R. S., Flores, R. A., Smith, S. M., Caprihan, A., & Yeo, R. A. (2009). Biochemical support for the "threshold" theory of creativity: A magnetic resonance spectroscopy study. *The Journal of Neuroscience, 29,* 5319–5325.

Jung, R. E., Segal, J. M., Bockholt, H. J., Flores, R. A., Smith, S. M., Chavez, R. S., & Haier, R. J. (2010). Neuroanatomy of creativity. *Human Brain Mapping, 31,* 398–409.

Jung, Y.-H., Kang, D-H., Jang, J. H., Park, H. Y., Byun, M. S., Kwon, S. J., . . . Kwon, J. S. (2010). The effects of mind–body training on stress reduction, positive affect, and plasma catecholamines. *Neuroscience Letters, 479,* 138–142.

Jusczyk, P. W. (1997). *The discovery of spoken language.* Cambridge, MA: MIT Press.

Jussim, L., & Harber, K. D. (2005). Teacher expectations and self-fulfilling prophecies: Knowns and unknowns, resolved and unresolved controversies. *Personality and Social Psychology Review, 9,* 131–155.

Just, M. A., Keller, T. A., & Cynkar, J. (2008). A decrease in brain activation associated with driving when listening to someone speak. *Brain Research, 1205,* 70–80.

Juster, R-P., McEwen, B. S., & Lupien, S. J. (2010). Allostatic load biomarkers of chronic stress and impact on health and cognition. *Neuroscience and Biobehavioral Reviews, 35,* 2–16.

Kabat-Zinn, J. (1990). *Full catastrophe living.* New York, NY: Delta.

Kabat-Zinn, J., Lipworth, L., & Burney, R. (1985). The clinical use of mindfulness meditation for the self-regulation of chronic pain. *Journal of Behavioral Medicine, 8,* 163–190.

Kabat-Zinn, J., Massion, A. O., Kristeller, J., Peterson, L. G., Fletcher, K. E., Pbert, L., . . . Santorelli, S. F. (1992). Effectiveness of a meditation–based stress reduction program in the treatment of anxiety disorders. *American Journal of Psychiatry, 149,* 936–943.

Kabat-Zinn, J., Wheeler, E., Light, T., Skillings, A., Scharf, M. J., Cropley, T. G., . . . Bernhard, J. D. (1998). Influence of a mindfulness meditation-based stress reduction intervention on rates of clearing in patients with moderate to severe psoriasis undergoing phototherapy (UVB) and photochemotherapy (PUVA). *Psychosomatic Medicine, 60,* 625–632.

Kagan, J. (2003). Biology, context, and developmental inquiry. *Annual Review of Psychology, 54,* 1–23.

Kahan, T. L. (2001). Consciousness in dreaming. A metacognitive approach. In T. Bulkeley (Ed.), *Dreams: A reader on religious, cultural, and psychological dimensions of dreaming* (pp. 333–360). New York, NY: Palgrave Macmillan.

Kahan, T. L., & LaBerge, S. (1994). Lucid dreaming as metacognitions: Implications for cognitive science. *Consciousness and Cognition, 3,* 246–264.

Kahn, R. S., Khoury, J., Nichols, W. C., & Lanphear, B. P. (2003). Role of dopamine transporter genotype and maternal prenatal smoking in childhood hyperactive-impulsive, inattentive, and oppositional behaviors. *The Journal of Pediatrics, 143,* 104–110.

Kahneman, D. (2002). Autobiography—Nobel Prize for 2002 in Economics. Retrieved from http://nobelprize.org/nobel_prizes/economics/laureates/2002/kahneman.html

Kahneman, D., & Tversky, A. (1972). Subjective probability: A judgment of representativeness. *Cognitive Psychology, 3,* 430–454.

Kahneman, D., & Tversky, A. (1979.) Prospect theory: An analysis of decision under risk. *Econometrica, 47,* 263–292.

Kahn-Greene, E. T., Killgore, D. B., Kamimori, G. H., Balkin, T. J., & Killgore, W. D. S. (2007). The effects of sleep deprivation on symptoms of psychopathology in healthy adults. *Sleep Medicine, 8,* 215–221.

Kaiser, B., & Bouvard, M. (2009). Obsessive–compulsive disorder in children and adolescents: Efficacy of combined treatment. *Clinical Neuropsychiatry: Journal of Treatment Evaluation, 6,* 94–100.

Kaiser Family Foundation. (2003). *Zero to six: Media use in the lives of infants, toddlers, and preschoolers.* Menlo Park, CA: Kaiser Family Foundation.

Kalat, J. W. (2007). *Biological Psychology* (9th ed). Belmont, CA: Wadsworth.

Kam, C. M., Greenberg, M. T., & Kusché, C. A. (2004). Sustained effects of the PATHS curriculum on the social and psychological adjustment of children in special education. *Journal of Emotional and Behavioral Disorders, 12,* 66–78.

Kaminsky, Z., Petronis, A., Wang, S-C., Levine, B., Ghaffar, O., Floden, D., & Feinstein, A. (2008). Epigenetics of personality traits: An illustrative study of identical twins discordant for risk-taking behavior. *Twin Research and Human Genetics, 11,* 1–11.

Kammrath, L. K., Mendoza-Denton, R., & Mischel, W. (2005). Incorporating *if . . . then . . .* personality signatures in person perception: Beyond the person–situation dichotomy. *Journal of Personality and Social Psychology, 88,* 605–618.

Kanarek, R. B. (1994). Does sucrose or aspartame cause hyperactivity in children? *Nutrition Reviews, 52,* 173–175.

Kanayama, G., Rogowska, J., Pope, H. G., Gruber, S. A., & Yurgelun-Todd, D. A. (2004). Spatial working memory in heavy cannabis users: A functional magnetic resonance imaging study. *Psychopharmacology, 176,* 239–247.

Kandel, E. R. (2000a). Disorders of thought and volition: Schizophrenia. In E. R. Kandel, J. H. Schwartz, & T. M. Jessell (Eds.), *Principles of neural science* (4th ed., pp. 1188–1208). New York, NY: McGraw-Hill.

Kandel, E. R. (2000b). Nerve cells and behavior. In E. R. Kandel, J. M. Schwartz, & T. M. Jessell (Eds.), *Principles of neural science* (4th ed., pp. 19–35). New York, NY: McGraw-Hill.

Kandel, E. R. (2001). The molecular biology of memory storage: A dialogue between genes and synapses. *Science, 294,* 1030–1038.

Kandel, E. R. (2006). *In search of memory: The emergence of a new science of mind.* New York, NY: Norton.

Kandel, E. R., Kupfermann, I., & Iversen, S. (2000). Learning and memory. In E. R. Kandel, J. H. Schwartz, & T. M. Jessell (Eds.), *Principles of neural science* (4th ed., pp. 1227–1246). New York, NY: McGraw-Hill.

Kanner, A. D., Coyne, J. C., Schaefer, C., & Lazarus, R. S. (1981). Comparison of two modes of stress measurement: Daily hassles and uplifts versus major life events. *Journal of Behavioral Medicine, 4,* 1–39.

Kanwisher, N. (2000). Domain specificity in face perception. *Nature Neuroscience, 3,* 759.

Karama, S., Lecours, A. R., Leroux, J-M., Bourgouin, P., Beaudoin, G., Joubert, S., . . . Beauregard, M. (2002). Areas of brain activation in males and females during viewing of erotic film excerpts. *Human Brain Mapping, 16,* 1–13.

Karni, A., Tanne, D., Rubenstein, B. S., Askenasy, J. J. M., & Sagi, D. (1994). Dependence on REM sleep of overnight improvement of a perceptual skill. *Science, 265,* 679–682.

Kasai, T., Kawai, S., Kawanishi, M., & Yahagi, S. (1997). Evidence for facilitation of motor evoked potentials (MEPs) induced by motor imagery. *Brain Research, 744,* 147–150.

Kathami, M. (2009). Inflammation, aging, and cancer: Tumoricidal versus tumorigenesis of immunity. *Cell Biochemistry and Biophysics, 55,* 55–79.

Kaufman, A. S. (1979). *Intelligent testing with the WISC-R.* New York, NY: Wiley.

Kaufman, A. S., & Kaufman, N. L. (1983). *K-ABC interpretative manual.* Circle Pines, MN: American Guidance Service. (2nd ed., 2004, KABC-II).

Kaul, P., Passafiume, J., Sargent, R. C., & O'Hara, B. F. (2010). Meditation acutely improves psychomotor vigilance, and may decrease sleep need. *Behavioral and Brain Functions, 6,* doi:10.1186/1744-9081-6-47

Kawamura, Y., & Kare, M. R. (1987). *Umami: A basic taste.* New York, NY: Marcel Dekker.

Kay, L. M., & Sherman, S. M. (2007). An argument for an olfactory thalamus. *Trends in Neurosciences, 30,* 47–53.

Kaye, G. T. (2001). *Celebrating 60 years of science.* Intel Corporation.

Keel, P. K., & Klump, K. L. (2003). Are eating disorders culture-bound syndromes? Implications for conceptualizing their etiology. *Psychological Bulletin, 129,* 747–767.

Keeler, R. F. (1983). Naturally occurring teratogens from plants. In R. F. Keeler & A. T. Tu (Eds.), *Handbook of natural toxins: Vol. 1. Plant and fungal toxins* (pp. 161–191). New York, NY: Marcel Dekker.

Keenan, R. M., Jenkins, A. J., Cone, E. J., & Henningfield, J. E. (1994). Smoked and IV nicotine, cocaine and heroin have similar abuse liability. *Journal of Addictive Diseases, 13,* 259–269.

Kegeles, L. S., Abi-Dargham, A., Frankle, W. G., Gil, R., Cooper, T. B. Slifstein, M., . . . Laruelle, M. (2010). Increased synaptic dopamine function in associative regions of the striatum in schizophrenia. *Archives in General Psychiatry, 67,* 231–239.

Kehle, S. (2008). The effectiveness of cognitive behavioral therapy for generalized anxiety disorder in a frontline service setting. *Cognitive Behaviour Therapy, 37,* 1–7. doi:10.1080/16506070802190262

Keitner, D. (1995). Signs of appeasement: Evidence of distinct displays of embarrassment, amusement, and shame. *Journal of Personality and Social Psychology, 68,* 441–454.

Keller, M. C., Thiessen, D., & Young, R. K. (1996). Mate assortment in dating and married couples. *Personality and Individual Differences, 21,* 217–221.

Kellerman, E. (1979). Transfer and non-transfer: Where we are now. *Studies in Second Language Acquisition, 2,* 37–57.

Kelley, H. H., & Michela, J. L. (1980). Attribution theory and research. *Annual Review of Psychology, 31,* 457–501.

Kellman, P. J., & Arterberry, M. E. (2006). Infant visual perception. In D. Kuhn & R. Siegler (Eds.), *Handbook of child psychology: Vol. 2. Cognition, perception, and language* (6th ed., 109–160). Hoboken, NJ: Wiley.

Kellner, C. H., Knapp, R. G., Petrides, G., Rummans, T. A., Husain, M. M., Rasmussen, K., . . . Fink, M. (2006). Continuation electro-convulsive therapy vs pharmacotherapy for relapse prevention in major depression. *Archives of General Psychiatry, 63,* 1337–1344.

Keltner, D. (1995). Signs of appeasement: Evidence of distinct displays of embarrassment, amusement, and shame. *Journal of Personality and Social Psychology, 68,* 441–454.

Kemeny, M., Weiner, H., Taylor, S., Schneider, S., Visscher, B., & Fahey, J. (1994). Repeated bereavement, depressed mood, and immune parameters in HIV seropositive and seronegative gay men. *Health Psychology, 13,* 14–24.

Kempermann, G. (2006). Adult neurogenesis. In P. B. Baltes, P. A. Reuter-Lorenz, & F. Rösler (Eds.), *Lifespan development and the brain: The perspective of biocultural co-constructivism* (pp. 82–107). New York, NY: Cambridge University Press.

Kempermann, G., & Gage, F. H. (1999). Experience-dependent regulation of adult hippocampal neurogenesis: Effects of long-term stimulation and stimulus withdrawal. *Hippocampus, 9,* 321–332.

Kendler, K. S. (2005). "A gene for . . .": The nature of gene action in psychiatric disorders. *American Journal of Psychiatry, 162,* 1243–1252.

Kendler, K. S., Karkowski, L. M., & Prescott, C. A. (1999). Causal relationship between stressful life events and the onset of major depression. *American Journal of Psychiatry, 156,* 837–841.

Kendler, K. S., Kuhn, J. W., Vittum, J., Prescott, C. A., & Riley, B. (2005). The interaction of stressful life events and a serotonin transporter polymorphism in the prediction of episodes of major depression. *Archives of General Psychiatry, 62,* 529–535.

Kendrick, T., Peveler, R., Logworth, L., Baldwin, D., Moore, M., Chatwin, J., . . . Thompson, C. (2006). Cost-effectiveness and cost-utility of tricyclic antidepressants, selective serotonin reuptake inhibitors and lofepramine: Randomized controlled trial. *The British Journal of Psychiatry, 188,* 337–345.

Kennedy, J. M., & Juricevic, I. (2006). Blind man draws using diminution in three dimensions. *Psychonomic Bulletin & Review, 13,* 506–509.

Kennedy, S. H., Evans, K. R., Krüger, S., Mayberg, H. S., Meyer, J. H., McCann, S., . . . Vaccarino, F. J. (2001). Changes in regional brain glucose metabolism measured with positron emission tomography after paroxetine treatment of major depression. *American Journal of Psychiatry, 158,* 899–905.

Kensinger, E. A., Garoff-Eaton, R. J., & Schacter, D. L. (2007). How negative emotion enhances the visual specificity of a memory. *Journal of Cognitive Neuroscience, 19,* 1872–1887.

Keppel, R. (2005). *The riverman: Ted Bundy and I hunt for the Green River killer.* New York, NY: Pocket Books.

Kerig, P., & Wenar, C. (2006). *Developmental psychology: From infancy through adolescence* (5th ed.). New York, NY: McGraw-Hill.

Kessler, R. C., Berglund, P., Demler, O., Jin, R., Merikangas, K. R., & Walters, E. E. (2005). Lifetime prevalence and age-of-onset distributions of *DSM-IV* disorders in the National Comorbidity Survey replication. *Archives of General Psychiatry, 62,* 593–602.

Kessler, R. C., Chiu, W. T., Demler, O., & Walters, E. E. (2005). Prevalence, severity, and comorbidity of twelve-month *DSM-IV-TR* disorders in the National Comorbidity Survey Replication (NCS-R). *Archives of General Psychiatry, 62,* 617–627.

Key Learning Community. (n.d.). Retrieved July 13, 2007, from http://www.ncrel.org/sdrs/areas/issues/methods/assment/as7key.htm

Kiecolt-Glaser, J. K., Marucha, P. T., Malarkey, W. B., Mercado, A. M., & Glaser, R. (1995). Slowing of wound healing by psychological stress. *Lancet, 346,* 1194–1196.

Kihlstrom, J. F. (2005). Dissociative disorders. *Annual Review of Clinical Psychology, 1,* 227–253.

Kim, B., Lee, S., Choi, T., Suh, S., Kim, Y., Yook, K., & Lee, E. H. (2008). Effectiveness of a combined therapy of long-acting injectable risperidone and psychosocial intervention for relapse prevention in patients with schizophrenia. *Clinical Psychopharmacology and Neuroscience, 6,* 31–37.

Kim, H. K. (2005). Can only intelligent people be creative? A meta-analysis. *Journal of Secondary Gifted Education, 16,* 57–66.

Kim, K. H. S., Relkin, N. R., Lee, K. M., & Hirsch, J. (1997). Distinct cortical areas associated with native and second languages. *Nature, 388,* 171–174.

Kim, S., & Hasher, L. (2005). The attraction effect in decision making: Superior performance by older adults. *Quarterly Journal of Experimental Psychology, 58A,* 120–133.

Kim, S-E., Ko, I-G., Kim, B-K., Shin, M-S., Cho, S., Kim, C-J., . . . Jee, Y-S. (2010). Treadmill exercise prevents aging-induced failure of memory through an increase in neurogenesis and suppression of apoptosis in rat hippocampus. *Experimental Gerontology, 45,* 357–365.

Kimball, J. (2003). *Joyce and the early Freudians.* Gainesville: University Press of Florida.

Kimura, D. (2007). "Underrepresentation" or misinterpretation? In S. J. Ceci & W. M. Williams (Eds.), *Why aren't more women in science?: Top researchers debate the evidence* (pp. 39–46). Washington, DC: American Psychological Association.

King, D. E., Mainous, A. G. III, & Geesey, M. E. (2008). Adopting moderate alcohol consumption in middle age: Subsequent cardiovascular events. *The American Journal of Medicine, 121,* 201–206.

King, L. A., Hicks, J. A., Krull, J. L., Del Gaiso, & A. K. (2006). Positive affect and the experience of meaning in life. *Journal of Personality and Social Psychology, 90,* 179–196.

Kinney, D. K., Richards, R., Lowing, P. A., LeBlanc, D., Zimbalist, M. E., & Harlan, P. (2000–2001). Creativity in offspring of schizophrenic and control parents: An adoption study. *Creativity Research Journal, 13,* 17–26.

Kinsey, A. C., Pomeroy, W. B., & Martin, C. E. (1948). *Sexual behavior in the human male.* Philadelphia: Saunders.

Kinsey, A. C., Pomeroy, W. B., Martin, C. E., & Gebhard, P. H. (1953). *Sexual behavior in the human female.* Philadelphia: Saunders.

Kirkham, T. C. (2005). Endocannabinoids in the regulation of appetite and body weight. *Behavioral Pharmacology, 16,* 297–313.

Kirkpatrick, L. A. (2005). *Attachment, evolution, and the psychology of religion.* New York, NY: Guilford Press.

Kirsh, S. J. (2006). Cartoon violence and aggression in youth. *Aggression and Violent Behavior, 11,* 547–557.

Kisilevsky, B. S., Muir, D. W., & Low, J. A. (1992). Maturation of human fetal responses to vibroacoustic stimulation. *Child Development, 63,* 1497–1508.

Klahr, D. (2000). *Exploring science: The cognition and development of discovery processes.* Cambridge, MA: MIT Press.

Klein, H. S. (2004). *A population history of the United States.* New York, NY: Cambridge University Press.

Klein, R. G. (1999). *The human career: Human biological and cultural origins* (2nd ed.). Chicago, IL: University of Chicago Press.

Kloosterman, K. (2009, August 13). Teaching the blind to see through sound. Retrieved from http://www.israel21c.org/

Klopfer, P. H. (1958). Influence of social interaction on learning rates in birds. *Science, 128,* 903.

Klucharev, V., Hytonen, K., Rijpkema, M., Smidts, A., & Fernandez, G. (2009). Reinforcement learning signal predicts social conformity. *Neuron, 61,* 140–151.

Klüver, H., & Bucy, P. (1939). Preliminary analysis of functioning of the temporal lobes in monkeys. *Archives of Neurology and Psychiatry, 42,* 979–1000.

Knox, R. (2007, April 26). Kids' use of earbuds worries hearing experts. Retrieved from http://www.npr.org/templates/story/story.php?storyId=9797364

Kobayashi, M., Saito, S., Kobayakawa, T., Deguchi, Y., & Costanzo, R. M. (2006). Cross-cultural comparison of data using the odor stick identification test for Japanese (OSIT-J). *Chemical Senses, 31,* 335–342.

Koenig, J. I. (2006). Schizophrenia: A unique translational opportunity in behavioral neuroendocrinology. *Hormones and Behavior, 50,* 602–611.

Koerner, K., & Linehan, M. M. (2000). Research on dialectical behavior therapy for patients with borderline personality disorder. *Psychiatric Clinics of North America, 23,* 151–167.

Koh, J. S., Kang, H., Choi, S. W., & Kim, H. O. (2002). Cigarette smoking associated with premature facial wrinkling: Image analysis of facial skin replicas. *International Journal of Dermatology, 41,* 21–27.

Kohlberg, L. (1981). *Essays on moral development: Vol. I. The philosophy of moral development.* New York, NY: Harper & Row.

Kohn, P. M., Lafreniere, K., & Gurevich, M. (1991). Hassles, health, and personality. *Journal of Personality and Social Psychology, 61,* 478–482.

Kokko, K., Pulkkinen, L., & Mesiäinen, P. (2009). Timing of parenthood in relation to other life transitions and adult social functioning. *International Journal of Behavioral Development, 33,* 356–365.

Komar, V., & Melamid, A. (2000). *When elephants paint: The quest of two Russian artists to save the elephants of Thailand.* New York, NY: Harper.

Kopell, B. H., Rezai, A. R., Chang, J. W., & Vitek, J. L. (2006). Anatomy and physiology of the basal ganglia: Implications for deep brain stimulation for Parkinson's disease. *Movement Disorders, 21,* S238–S246.

Kopta, S. M. (2003). The dose-effect relationship in psychotherapy: A defining achievement for Dr. Kenneth Howard. *Journal of Clinical Psychology, 59,* 727–733.

Korkeila, M., Kaprio, J., Rissanen, A., Koshenvuo, M., & Sorensen, T. L. (1998). Predictors of major weight gain in adult Finns: Stress, life satisfaction and personality traits. *International Journal of Obesity Related Metabolic Disorders, 22*(10), 949–957.

Kornell, N., & Bjork, R. A. (2007). The promise and perils of self-regulated study. *Psychonomic Bulletin & Review, 14,* 219–224.

Kornell, N., Castel, A., Eich, T., & Bjork, R. (2010). Spacing as the friend of both memory and induction in young and older adults. *Psychology and Aging, 25,* 498–503. doi:10.1037/a0017807

Kornhaber, M. L., Fierros, E., & Veenema, S. (2004). *Multiple intelligences: Best ideas from research and practice.* Boston, MA: Pearson.

Koslowski, B. (1996). *Theory and evidence: The development of scientific reasoning.* Cambridge, MA: MIT Press.

Kosslyn, S. M. (2002, July 15). What shape are a German shepherd's ears?: A talk with Stephen Kosslyn. *Edge.* Retrieved from http://www.edge.org/3rd_culture/kosslyn/kosslyn_index.html

Kosslyn, S. M. (2005). Mental images and the brain. *Cognitive Neuropsychology, 22,* 333–347.

Kosslyn, S. M., Van Kleeck, M. H., & Kirby, K. N. (1990). A neurologically plausible model of individual differences in visual mental imagery. In P. J. Hampson, D. F. Marks, & J. T. E. Richardson (Eds.), *Imagery: Current developments* (pp. 39–77). Florence, KY: Taylor & Frances/Routledge.

Kottke, J. L., & Sharafinski, C. E. (1988). Measuring perceived supervisory and organizational support. *Educational and Psychological Measurement, 48,* 1075–1079.

Kounios, J., Frymiare, J. L., Bowden, E. M., Fleck, J. I., Subramaniam, K., Parrish, T. B., & Jung-Beeman, M. (2006). The prepared mind: Neural activity prior to problem presentation predicts subsequent solution by sudden insight. *Psychological Science, 17,* 882–890.

Kraaj, V., van der Veek, S. M. C., Garnefski, N., Schroevers, M., Witlox, R., & Maes, S. (2008). Coping, goal adjustment, and psychological well-being in HIV-infected men who have sex with men. *AIDS Patient Care and STDs, 22,* 395–402.

Kramarik, A. (2006). *Akiane: Her life, her art, her poetry.* Nashville, TN: W Publishing Group.

Kramer, P. D. (1993). *Listening to Prozac.* New York, NY: Penguin Books.

Kranczioch, C., Debener, S., Schwarzbach, J., Goebel, R., & Engel, A. K. (2005). Neural correlates of conscious perception in the attentional blink. *NeuroImage, 24,* 704–714.

Kremer, S., Bult, J. H., Mojet, J., & Kroeze, J. H. (2007). Food perception with age and its relationship to pleasantness. *Chemical Senses, 32,* 591–602.

Kristeller, J. L., Baer, R. A., & Quillian-Wolever, R. (2006). Mindfulness-based approaches to eating disorders. In R. A. Baer (Ed.), *Mindfulness-based treatment approaches: Clinician's guide to evidence base and applications* (pp. 75–91). San Diego, CA: Elsevier Academic Press.

Kristenson, H. (1995). How to get the best out of Antabuse. *Alcohol and Alcoholism, 30,* 775–783.

Kristjansson, A. L., Sigfusdottir, I. D., James, J. E., Allegrante, J. P., & Helgason, A. R. (2010). Perceived parental reactions and peer respect as predictors of adolescent cigarette smoking and alcohol use. *Addictive Behaviors, 35,* 256–259.

Kristof-Brown, A. L., Zimmerman, R. D., & Johnson, E. C. (2005). Consequences of individuals' fit at work: A meta-analysis of person–job, person–organization, person–group, and person–supervisor fit. *Personnel Psychology, 58,* 281–342.

Kroeber, A. L. (1948). *Anthropology.* New York, NY: Harcourt Brace Jovanovich.

Kröger, C., Schweiger, U., Sipos, V., Arnold, R., Kahl, K. G., Schunert, T., . . . Reinecker, H. (2006). Effectiveness of dialectical behavior therapy for borderline personality disorder in an inpatient setting. *Behaviour Research and Therapy, 44,* 1211–1217.

Krueger, R. F. (1999). Personality traits in late adolescence predict mental disorders in early adulthood: A prospective-epidemiological study. *Journal of Personality, 67,* 39–65.

Krueger, R. F., & Johnson, W. (2008). Behavioral genetics and personality: A new look at the integration of nature and nurture. In O. P. John, R. W. Robins, & L. A. Pervin (Eds.), *Handbook of personality: Theory and research* (pp. 287–310). New York, NY: Guilford Press.

Krummel, D., Seligson F., & Guthrie, H. (1996). Hyperactivity: Is candy causal? *Critical Review of Food Science and Nutrition, 36,* 31–47.

Krystal, A. D. (2005). The effect of insomnia definitions, terminology, and classifications on clinical practice. *Journal of American Geriatrics Society, 53,* S255–S263.

Ku, J., Kim, J., Jang, H., Park, S., Kim, S., Kim, C., . . . Kim, S. I. (2005). Relationship between social response to virtual avatar and symptom severity of patients with schizophrenia. *Annual Review of CyberTherapy and Telemedicine, 3,* 3143–3149.

Kübler-Ross, E. (1969). *On death and dying.* New York, NY: Macmillan.

Kubota, M., Nakazaki, S., Hirai, S., Saeki, N. Yamaura, A., & Kusaka, T. (2001). Alcohol consumption and frontal lobe shrinkage: Study of 1432 non-alcoholic subjects. *Journal of Neurology, Neurosurgery, and Psychiatry, 71,* 104–106.

Kubzansky, L. D., Sparrow, D., Vokonas, P., & Kawachi, I. (2001). Is the glass half empty or half full? A prospective study of optimism and coronary heart disease in the Normative Aging Study. *Psychosomatic Medicine, 63,* 910–916.

Kuhl, P. K., & Meltzoff, A. N. (1997). Evolution, nativism, and learning in the development of language and speech. In M. Gopnik (Ed.), *The inheritance and innateness of grammars* (pp. 7–44). New York, NY: Oxford University Press.

Kuhl, P. K., Stevens, E., & Hayashi, A. (2006). Infants show a facilitation effect for native language phonetic perception between 6 and 12 months. *Developmental Science, 9,* F13–F21.

Kuhl, P., & Rivera-Gaxiola, M. (2008). Neural substrates of language acquisition. *Annual Review of Neuroscience, 31,*

511–534. doi:10.1146/annurev.neuro.30.051606.094321

Kuhn, D. (1993). Connecting scientific and informal reasoning. *Merrill-Palmer Quarterly, 39,* 74–103.

Kuhn, D., Amsel, E., & O'Loughlin, M. (1988). *The development of scientific thinking skills.* Orlando, FL: Academic Press.

Kuhn, D., & Pearsall, S. (2000). Developmental origins of scientific thinking. *Journal of cognition and development, 1,* 113–129.

Kunkel, C. (2009). Schooling built on multiple intelligences. *School Administrator, 66,* 24–25.

Kuo, L. E., Kitlinska, J. B., Tilan, J. U., Li, L., Baker, S. B., Johnson, M. D., . . . Zukowska, Z. (2007). Neuropeptide Y acts directly in the periphery on fat tissue and mediates stress-induced obesity and metabolic syndrome. *Nature Medicine, 13,* 803–811.

Kupfermann, I., Kandel, E. R., & Iversen, S. (2000). Motivational and addictive states. In E. R. Kandel, J. H. Schwartz, & T. M. Jessell (Eds.), *Principles of neural science* (4th ed., pp. 998–1013). New York, NY: McGraw-Hill.

Kuriyama, K., Stickgold, R., & Walker, M. P. (2004). Sleep-dependent learning and motor skill complexity. *Learning & Memory, 11,* 705–713.

Kurson, R. (2007). *Crashing through: The true story of risk, adventure and the man who dared to see.* New York, NY: Random House.

Kusché, C. A., & Greenberg, M. T. (1994). *The PATHS Curriculum.* Seattle, WA: Developmental Research and Programs.

Kwon, Y., & Lawson, A. E. (2000). Linking brain growth with the development of scientific reasoning ability and conceptual change during adolescence. *Journal of Research in Science Teaching, 37,* 44–62.

La Precious, H., Ware, C., Mason, J., McGuire, E., Lewis, D. W., Pagano, L., & Alley, W. (2009, May 2). *The distracted teenage driver.* Paper presented at Pediatric Academic Societies Annual Meeting, Baltimore, MD.

LaBerge, S. (1985). *Lucid dreaming.* Los Angeles, CA: Tarcher.

LaFrance, M., Hecht, M. A., & Paluk, B. L. (2003). The contingent smile: A meta-analysis of sex differences in smiling. *Psychological Bulletin, 129,* 305–334.

Lagopoulos, J. (2007). Functional MRI: An overview. *Acta Neuropsychiatrica, 19,* 64–65.

Lalonde, J., Hudson, J., Gigante, R., & Pope, H. (2001). Canadian and American psychiatrists' attitudes toward dissociative disorders diagnoses. *The Canadian Journal of Psychiatry / La Revue canadienne de psychiatrie, 46(5),* 407–412.

Lamb, R. J., Morral, A. R., Kirby, K. C., Iguchi, M. Y., & Galbicka, G. (2004). Shaping smoking cessation using percentile schedules. *Drug and Alcohol Dependence, 76,* 247–259.

Lamp, R., & Krohn, E. (2001). A longitudinal predictive validity investigation of the SB:FE and K-ABC with at-risk children. *Journal of Psychoeducational Assessment, 19,* 334–349.

Lanciano, T., Curci, A., & Semin, G. R. (2010). The emotional and reconstructive determinants of emotional memories: An experimental approach to flashbulb memory investigation. *Memory, 18,* 473–485.

Landry, R. G. (1973). The relationship of second language learning and verbal creativity. *Modern Language Journal, 57,* 110–113.

Lang, E., Berbaum, K., Faintuch, S., Hatsiopoulou, O., Halsey, N., Li, X., Berbaum, M., . . . Baum, J. (2006). Adjunctive self-hypnotic relaxation for outpatient medical procedures: A prospective randomized trial with women undergoing large core breast biopsy. *Pain, 126,* 155–164.

Lange, C. (1922). *The emotions* (I. A. Haupt, Trans.). Baltimore, MD: Williams & Wilkins. (Original work published 1885)

Lange, P. G. (2008). Publicly private and privately public: Social networking on YouTube. *Journal of Computer-Mediated Communication, 13,* 361–380.

Langlois, J. H., & Roggman, L. A. (1990). Attractive faces are only average. *Psychological Science, 1,* 115–121.

Langlois, J. H., Roggman, L. A., & Musselman, L. (1994). What is average and what is not average about attractive faces? *Psychological Science, 5,* 214–220.

Lapsley, D. K. (2006). Moral stage theory. In M. Killen & J. G. Smetana (Eds.), *Handbook of moral development* (pp. 37–66). Mahwah, NJ: Erlbaum.

Larson, L., Wu, T., Bailey, D., Gasser, C., Bonitz, V., & Borgen, F. (2010). The role of personality in the selection of a major: With and without vocational self-efficacy and interests. *Journal of Vocational Behavior, 76,* 211–222.

Larsson, J., Larsson, H., & Lichtenstein, P. (2004). Genetic and environmental contributions to stability and change of ADHD symptoms between 8 and 13 years of age: A longitudinal twin study. *Journal of American Academy of Child and Adolescent Psychiatry, 43,* 1267–1275.

Lasagabaster, D. (2000). The effects of three bilingual education models on linguistic creativity. *International Review of Applied Linguistics in Language Teaching, 38,* 213–228.

Laschet, J., Kurcewicz, I., Minier, F., Trottier, S., Khallou-Laschet, J., Louvel, J., . . . Pumain, R. (2007). Dysfunction of GABA-sub(A) receptor glycolysis-dependent modulation in human partial epilepsy. *Proceedings of the National Academy of Sciences, 104(9),* 3472–3477. doi:10.1073/pnas.0606451104

Laumann, E., Paik, A., Glasser, D., Kang, J., Wang, T., Levinson, B., . . . Gingell, C. (2006). A cross-national study of subjective sexual well-being among older women and men: Findings from the global study of sexual attitudes and behaviors. *Archives of Sexual Behavior, 35(2),* 145–161. doi:10.1007/s10508-005-9005-3

Laureys, S. (2007). Eyes open, brain shut. *Scientific American, 296,* 84–89.

Lavelli, M., & Fogel, A. (2005). Developmental changes in the relationship between the infant's attention and emotion during early face-to-face communication: The 2-month transition. *Developmental Psychology, 41,* 265–280.

Lavie, N. (2007). The role of perceptual load in visual awareness. *Brain Research, 1080,* 91–100.

Lavie, N., Hirst, A., De Fockert, J. W., & Viding, E. (2004). Load theory of selective attention and cognitive control. *Journal of Experimental Psychology: General, 133,* 339–354.

Lawless, H. T., Schlake, S., Smythe, J., Lim, J., Yang, H., Chapman, K., & Bolton, B. (2004). Metallic taste and retronasal smell. *Chemical Senses, 29,* 25–33. doi:10.1093/chemse/bjh003

Lazar, S. W., Kerr, C., Wasserman, R. H., Gray, J. R., Greve, D., Treadway, M. T., . . . Fischl, B. (2005). Meditation experience is associated with increased cortical thickness. *NeuroReport, 216,* 1893–1897.

Lazarus, A. A., & Abramovitz, A. (2004). A multimodal behavioral approach to performance anxiety. *Journal of Clinical Psychology, 60,* 831–840.

Lazarus, R. S. (1991). *Emotion and adaptation.* New York, NY: Oxford University Press.

Lazarus, R. S. (1993). From psychological stress to the emotions: A history of changing outlooks. *Annual Review of Psychology, 44,* 1–21.

Lazarus, R. S., & Folkman, S. (1984). *Stress, appraisal, and coping.* New York, NY: Springer.

Lazarus, R. S., Kanner, A. A., & Folkman, S. (1980). Emotions: A cognitive–phenomenological analysis. In R. Plutchik & H. Kellerman (Eds.), *Emotion: Theory, research, and experience: Vol. 1. Theories of emotion* (pp. 189–217). New York, NY: Academic Press.

Le Bars, P. L., Katz, M. M., Berman, N., Itil, T. M., Freedman, A. M., & Schatzberg, A. F. (1997). A placebo-controlled, double-blind, randomized trial of an extract of ginkgo biloba for dementia. North American EGb Study Group. *Journal of the American Medical Association, 278,* 1327–1332.

Leary, M. R., Kowalski, R. M., Smith, L., & Phillips, S. (2003). Teasing, rejection, and violence: Case studies of the school shootings. *Aggressive Behavior, 29,* 202–214.

Leary, M. R., Twenge, J. M., & Quinlivan, E. (2006). Interpersonal rejection as a determinant of anger and aggression. *Personality and Social Psychology Review, 10,* 111–132.

LeDoux, J. (1996). *The emotional brain: The mysterious underpinnings of emotional life.* New York, NY: Simon & Schuster.

LeDoux, J. (2003). *Synaptic self.* New York, NY: Penguin.

LeDoux, J. E. (2000). Emotion circuits in the brain. *Annual Review of Neuroscience, 23,* 155–184.

LeDuc, P. A., Caldwell, J. A., & Ruyak, P. S. (2000). The effects of exercise as a countermeasure for fatigue in sleep-deprived aviators. *Military Psychology, 12,* 249–266.

Lee, H., Macbeth, A. H., Pagani, J. H., & Young, S. W. (2009). Oxytocin: The great facilitator of life. *Progress in Neurobiology, 88,* 127–151.

Lee, K. A. (2006). Sleep dysfunction in women and its management. *Current Treatment Options in Neurology, 8,* 376–386.

Leiblum, S. R., & Hamer, R. (1998). Life after infertility treatment: A long-term investigation of marital and sexual function. *Human Reproduction, 13,* 3569–3574.

Lemay, E. P., Jr., & Ashmore, R. D. (2004). Reactions to perceived categorization by others during the transition to college: Internalization and self-verification processes. *Group Processes & Intergroup Relations, 7,* 173–187.

Lenhart, A. (2009). *Teens and mobile phones over the past five years: Pew Internet looks back.* Washington, DC: Pew Internet & American Life Project. Retrieved from http://www.pewinternet.org/Reports/2009/14--Teens-and-Mobile-Phones-Data-Memo.aspx

Lenhart, A., Purcell, K., Smith, A., & Zickuhr, K. (2010). *Social media and young adults: Social media and mobile Internet use among teens and young adults.* Washington, DC: Pew Internet & American Life Project. Retrieved from http://pewinternet.org/Reports/2010/Social-Media-and-Young-Adults.aspx

Lenneberg, E. (1967). *The biological foundations of language.* New York, NY: Wiley.

Lennie, P. (2000). Color vision. In E. R. Kandel, J. H. Schwartz, & T. M. Jessell (Eds.), *Principles of neural science* (4th ed., pp. 572–589). New York, NY: McGraw-Hill.

Lenzenweger, M. F., Lane, M. C., Loranger, A. W., & Kessler, R. C. (2007). DSM-IV personality disorders in the National Comorbidity Survey Replication. *Biological Psychiatry, 15,* 553–564.

Lepage, J-F., & Théoret, H. (2007). The mirror neuron system: Grasping others' actions from birth? *Developmental Science, 10,* 513–523.

Lerner, L. (1996). *The Kennedy women: The saga of an American family.* New York, NY: Random House.

Lesch, K. P., Bengel, D., Heils, A., Sabol, S. Z., Greenburg, B. D., Petri, S., . . . Murphy, D. L. (1996). Association of anxiety-related traits with a polymorphism in the serotonin transporter gene regulatory region. *Science, 274,* 1527–1531. doi:10.1126/science.274.5292.1527

Leserman, J., Jackson, E. D., Petitto, J. M., Golden, R. N., Silva, S. G., Perkins, D. O., . . . Evans, D. L. (1999). Progression to AIDS: The effects of stress, depressive symptoms, and social support. *Psychosomatic Medicine, 61,* 397–406.

Leserman, J., Petitto, J. M., Golden, R. N., Gaynes, B. N., Gu, H., Perkins, D. O., . . . Evans, D. L. (2000). Impact of stressful life events, depression, social support, and cortisol on progression to AIDS. *American Journal of Psychiatry, 157,* 1221–1228.

Lethbridge-Cejku, M., & Vickerie, J. (2005). Summary health statistics for U.S. adults: National Health Interview Survey, 2003. National Center for Health Statistics, *Vital Health Statistics,* 10.

Leuner, B., Glasper, E. R., & Gould, E. (2010). Sexual experience promotes adult neurogenesis in the hippocampus despite an initial elevation in stress hormones. *PLoS ONE, 5,* 1–8. doi:10.1371/journal.pone.0011597

Leuner, B., & Gould, E. (2010). Structural plasticity and hippocampal function. *Annual Review of Psychology, 61,* 111–140.

LeVay, S. (1991). A difference in hypothalamic structure between heterosexual and homosexual men. *Science, 253,* 1034–1037.

LeVay, S., & Hamer, D. (1994). Evidence for a biological influence in male homosexuality. *Scientific American, 270,* 44–49.

Levenson, R. W. (1988). Emotion and the autonomic nervous system: A prospectus for research on autonomic specificity. In H. Wagner (Ed.), *Social psychophysiology and emotion: Theory and clinical applications* (pp. 17–42). London, England: Wiley.

Levenson, R. W. (1994). Human emotion: A functional view. In P. Ekman & R. J. Davidson (Eds.), *The nature of emotion* (pp. 123–126). New York, NY: Oxford University Press.

Levenson, R. W. (2003). Blood, sweat, and fears: The autonomic architecture of emotion. *Annals of the New York Academy of Sciences, 1000,* 348–366.

Levenson, R. W., Carstensen, L. L., & Gottman, J. M. (1994). The influence of age and gender on affect, physiology, and their interactions: A study of long-term marriages. *Journal of Personality & Social Psychology, 67,* 56–68.

Levenson, R. W., Ekman, P., & Friesen, W. V. (1990). Voluntary facial action generates emotion-specific autonomic nervous system activity. *Psychophysiology, 27,* 363–384.

Levenson, R. W., Ekman, P., Heider, K., & Friesen, W. V. (1992). Emotion and autonomic nervous system activity in the Minangkabau of West Sumatra. *Journal of Personality & Social Psychology, 62,* 972–988.

Levy, B., Kuhl, B., & Wagner, A. (2010). The functional neuroimaging of forgetting. In S. Della Sala (Ed.), *Forgetting* (pp. 135–163). New York, NY: Psychology Press.

Lewin, T. (2009, October 23). No Einstein in your crib? Get a refund. *New York Times online.* Retrieved from http://www.nytimes.com.

Lewis, D., & Levitt, P. (2002). Schizophrenia as a disorder of neurodevelopment. *Annual Review of Neuroscience, 25,* 409–432. doi:10.1146/annurev.neuro.25.112701.142754

Lewis, G. D., Farrell, L., Wood, M. J., Martinovic, M., Arany, Z., Rowe, G. C., . . . Gerszten, R. E. (2010). Metabolic signatures of exercise in human plasma. *Science Translational Medicine, 2,* 33ra37.

Lidz, J., & Gleitman, L. R. (2004). Argument structure and the child's contribution to language learning. *Trends in Cognitive Sciences, 8,* 157–161.

Lieberman, J. A., Chakos, M., Wu, H., Alvir, J., Hoffman, E., Robinson, D., & Bilder, R. (2001). Longitudinal study of brain morphology in first episodes of schizophrenia. *Biological Psychiatry, 49,* 487–499.

Lieberman, J. A., Stroup, T. S., McEvoy, J. P., Swartz, M. S., Rosenheck, R. A., Perkins, D. O., . . . Hsiao, J. K. (2005). Effectiveness of anti-psychotic drugs in patients with chronic schizophrenia. *New England Journal of Medicine, 353,* 1209–1223.

Liebert, R. M., & Baron, R. A. (1972). Some immediate effects of televised violence on children's behavior. *Developmental Psychology, 6,* 469–475.

Liehr, P., Marcus, M. T., Carroll, D., Granmayeh, L. K., Cron, S. G., & Pennebaker, J. W. (2010). Linguistic analysis to assess the effect of a mindfulness intervention on self-change for adults in substance use recovery. *Substance Abuse, 31,* 79–85.

Lightner, C., & Hathaway, N. (1990). *Giving sorrow words: How to cope with grief and get on with your life.* New York, NY: Warner Books.

Lihoreau, M., Brepson, L., & Rivault, C. (2009). The weight of the clan: Even in insects, social isolation can induce a behavioural syndrome. *Behavioural Processes, 82,* 81–84.

Linden, D. E. J. (2006). How psychotherapy changes the brain—the contribution of functional neuroimaging. *Molecular Psychiatry, 11,* 528–538.

Lindsay, D. S., Hagen, L., Read, J. D., Wade, K. A., & Garry, M. (2004). True photographs and false memories. *Psychological Science, 15,* 149–154.

Linehan, M. M. (1993). *Skills training manual of treating borderline personality disorder.* New York, NY: Guilford Press.

Linehan, M. M., Armstrong, H. E., Suarez, A., Allmon, D., & Heard, H. L. (1991). Cognitive–behavioral treatment of chronically parasuicidal borderline patients. *Archives of General Psychiatry, 48,* 1060–1064.

Linehan, M. M., Comtois, K. A., Murray, A. M., Brown, M. Z., Gallop, R. J., Heard, H. L., . . . Lindenboim, N. (2006). Two-year randomized controlled trial and follow-up of dialectical behavior therapy vs therapy by experts for suicidal behaviors and borderline personality disorder. *Archives of General Psychiatry, 63,* 757–766.

Linehan, M. M., Heard, H. L., & Armstrong, H. E. (1993). Naturalistic follow-up of a behavioral treatment for chronically parasuicidal borderline patients. *Archives of General Psychiatry, 50,* 971–974.

Ling, R. (2010). Texting as a life phase medium. *Journal of Computer-Mediated Communication, 15,* 277–292.

Lipkus, I. M., Barefoot, J. C., Williams, R. B., & Siegler, I. C. (1994). Personality measures as predictors of smoking initiation and cessation in the UNC alumni heart study. *Health Psychology, 13,* 149–155.

Lippa, R. (1994). *Introduction to social psychology.* Pacific Grove, CA: Brooks/Cole.

Lisetti, C., Pozzo, E., Lucas, M., Hernandez, F., Selverman, W., Kurtines, B., & Pasztor, A. (2009). Second Life, bio-sensors, and exposure therapy for anxiety disorders. *Annual Review of CyberTherapy and Telemedicine, 7,* 19–21.

Liu, H., Elliott, S., & Umberson, D. (2009). Marriage in young adulthood. In J. E. Grant & M. N. Potenza (Eds.), *Young adult mental health* (pp. 169–280). New York, NY: Oxford University Press.

Locke, J. (1959). *An essay concerning human understanding: Vol. 1.* New York, NY: Dover. (Original work published 1690)

Lockhart, R. S., & Craik, F. I. M. (1990). Levels of processing: A retrospective commentary on a framework for memory research. *Canadian Journal of Psychology, 44,* 77–112.

Lodi-Smith, J., Geise, A., Roberts, B., & Robins, R. (2009). Narrating personality change. *Journal of Personality and Social Psychology, 96,* 679–689.

Loehlin, J. C., McCrae, R. R., Costa, P. T., & John, O. P. (1998). Heritabilities of common and measure specific components of the Big Five personality factors. *Journal of Research in Personality, 32,* 431–453.

Loeser, J. D., & Melzack, R. (1999). Pain: An overview. *Lancet, 353,* 1607–1609.

Loftus, E. (1996). *Eyewitness testimony.* Cambridge, MA: Harvard University Press.

Loftus, E. (2003). Make-believe memories. *American Psychologist, 58,* 864–873.

Loftus, E. F. (1997). Creating false memories. *Scientific American, 277,* 70–75.

Loftus, E. F., & Pickrell, J. E. (1995). The formation of false memories. *Psychiatric Annuals, 25,* 720–725.

Logothetis, N. K., Pauls, J., Augath, M., Trinath, T., & Oeltermann, A. (2001). Neurophysiological investigation of the basis of the fMRI signal. *Nature, 412,* 150–157.

Long, M. (1990). Maturational constraints on language development. *Studies in Second Language Acquisition, 12,* 251–285.

Lorenz, K. (1935). Der Kumpan in der Umwelt des Vogels. *Journal of Ornithology, 83,* 137–215.

Lorenz, K. (1937). The companion in the bird's world. *Auk, 54,* 245–273.

Lovaas, O. I. (1987). Behavioral treatment and normal educational and intellectual functioning in young autistic children. *Journal of Consulting and Clinical Psychology, 55,* 3–9.

Lovett, R. (2005, September 24). Coffee: The demon drink? *New Scientist.*

Löwe, B., Spitzer, R., Williams, J., Mussell, M., Schellberg, D., & Kroenke, K. (2008). Depression, anxiety and somatization in primary care: Syndrome overlap and functional impairment. *General Hospital Psychiatry, 30*(3), 191–199.

Lowry, C. A., Hale, M. W, Evans, A. K., Keerkens, J., Staub, D. R., Gasser, P. J., & Shekhar, A. (2008). Serotonergic systems, anxiety, and affective disorder focus on the dorsomedial part of the dorsal raphe nucleus. *Annals of the New York Academy of Sciences, 1148,* 86–94.

Lubben, J., & Gironda, M. (1996). Assessing social support networks among older people in the United States. In H. Litwin (Ed.), *The social networks of older people: A cross-national analysis.* London, England: Praeger.

Lubinski, D., & Benbow, C. P. (2006). Study of mathematically precocious youth after 35 years: Uncovering antecedents for the development of math-science expertise. *Perspectives on Psychological Science, 1,* 316–345.

Lubinski, D., Benbow, C. P., Webb, R. M., & Bleske-Rechek, A. (2006). Tracking exceptional human capital over two decades. *Psychological Science, 17,* 194–199.

Luborsky, L., Singer, B., & Luborsky, L. (1975). Comparative studies of psychotherapy. *Archives of General Psychiatry, 32,* 995–1008.

Luchins, A. S., & Luchins, E. H. (1970). *Wertheimer's seminars revisited: Problem solving and thinking.* Albany, NY: SUNY Press.

Ludwig, A. M. (1995). *The price of greatness.* New York, NY: Guilford Press.

Lukse, M. P., & Vacc, N. A. (1999). Grief, depression, and coping in women undergoing infertility treatment. *Obstetrics and Gynecology, 2,* 245–251.

Lutman, M. E., & Spencer, H. S. (1991). Occupational noise and demographic factors in hearing. *Acta Otolaryngologica, Suppl. 476,* 74–84.

Lutz, A., Slagter, H. A., Rawlings, N. B., Francis, A. D., Greischar, L. L., & Davidson, R. J. (2009). Mental training enhances attentional stability: Neural and behavioral evidence. *The Journal of Neuroscience, 29,* 13418–13427.

Luykx, J. J., Boks, M. P. M., Terwindt, A. P. R., Bakker, S., Kahn, R. S. & Ophoff, R. A. (2010). The involvement of GSK3β in bipolar disorder: Integrating evidence from multiple types of genetic studies. *European Neuropsychopharmacology, 20,* 357–368.

Lynn, R. (2006). *Race differences in intelligence: An evolutionary analysis.* Augusta, GA: National Summit.

Lyons, D. E. (2009). The rational continuum of human imitation. In J. A. Pineda (Ed.), *Mirror neuron systems: The role of mirroring processes in social cognition* (pp. 77–103). Totowa, NJ: Humana Press.

Lyons, D. M., Buckmaster, P. S., Lee, A. G., Wu, C., Mitra, R., Duffey, L. M., . . . Schatzberg, A. F. (2010). Stress coping stimulates hippocampal neurogenesis in adult monkeys. *Proceedings of the National Academy of Sciences, 107,* 14823–14827.

Maas, J. (1998). *Power sleep.* New York, NY: Villard.

Macaskill, M. (2008, February 10). Blind taught to "see" like a bat. *The Sunday Times.* Retrieved from http://www.timesonline.co.uk

Maccoby, E. E. (2000). Perspectives on gender development. *International Journal of Behavioral Development, 24,* 398–406.

Maccoby, E. E., & Jacklin, C. N. (1974). *The psychology of sex differences.* Stanford, CA: Stanford University Press.

Maccoby, E. E., & Jacklin, C. N. (1987). Gender segregation in childhood. In H. Reese (Ed.), *Advances in child behavior and development.* New York, NY: Academic Press.

MacDonald, G., Kingsbury, R., & Shaw, S. (2005). *Adding insult to injury: Social pain theory and response to social exclusion.* New York, NY: Psychology Press.

MacDonald, G., & Leary, M. R. (2005). Why does social exclusion hurt? The relationship between social and physical pain. *Psychological Bulletin, 131,* 202–223.

MacKinnon, D. W. (1970). Creativity: A multi-faceted phenomenon. In J. Roslansky (Ed.), *Creativity* (pp. 19–32). Amsterdam: North-Holland.

MacKinnon, D. W., & Hall, W. (1972). Intelligence and creativity. *Proceedings of the XVIIth International Congress of Applied Psychology,* Liege, Belgium (Vol. 2, pp. 1883–1888). Brussels: EDITEST.

MacLane, C. N., & Walmsley, P. T. (2010). Reducing counterproductive work behavior through employee selection. *Human Resource Management Review, 20,* 62–72.

MacLean, K. A., Ferrer, E., Aichele, S., Bridwell, D. A., King, B. G., Jacobs, T. L., . . . Saron, C. D. (2010). Intensive meditation training leads to improvements in perceptual discrimination and sustained attention. *Psychological Science, 21,* 829–839.

Macmillan, M. (2000). *An odd kind of fame: Stories of Phineas Gage.* Cambridge, MA: MIT Press.

MacWhinney, B. (1999). *The emergence of language.* Mahwah, NJ: Erlbaum.

Madden, M., & Lenhart, A. (2006). *Online dating.* Washington, DC: Pew Internet & American Life Project. Retrieved from http://www.pewtrusts.org/uploadedFiles/wwwpewtrustsorg/Reports/Society_and_the_Internet/PIP_Online_Dating_0306.pdf

Madigan, S., & O'Hara, R. (1992). Short-term memory at the turn of the century: Mary Whiton Calkins's memory research. *American Psychologist, 47,* 170–174.

Maes, H. M. M., Neale, M. C., & Eaves, L. J. (1997). Genetic and environmental factors in relative body weight and human adiposity. *Behavior Genetics, 27,* 325–351.

Maestripieri, D., Higley, J. D., Lindell, S. G., Newman, T. K., McCormack, K. M., & Sanchez, M. M. (2006). Early maternal rejection affects the development of monoaminergic systems and adult abusive parenting in rhesus macaques (*Macaca mulatto*). *Behavioral Neuroscience, 120,* 1017–1024.

Maguire, E. A., Woollett, K., & Spiers, H. J. (2006). London taxi drivers and bus drivers:

A structural MRI and neuropsychological analysis. *Hippocampus, 16,* 1091–1101.

Maier, N. R. F. (1931). Reasoning in humans: II. The solution of a problem and its appearance. *Journal of Comparative and Physiological Psychology, 12,* 181–194.

Main, M., & Hesse, E. (1990). Lack of resolution of mourning in adulthood and its relationship to infant disorganization: Some speculations regarding causal mechanisms. In M. Greenberg, D. Cicchetti, & E. M. Cummings (Eds.), *Attachment in the preschool years* (pp. 161–184). Chicago, IL: University of Chicago Press.

Main, M., & Solomon, J. (1990). Procedures for identifying infants as disorganized/disoriented during the Ainsworth Strange Situation. In M. Greenberg, D. Cicchetti, & E. M. Cummings (Eds.), *Attachment in the preschool years* (pp. 121–160). Chicago, IL: University of Chicago Press.

Malberg, J. E., Eisch, A. J., Nestler, E. J., & Duman, R. S. (2000). Chronic antidepressant treatment increases neurogenesis in adult rat hippocampus. *Journal of Neuroscience, 20,* 9104–9110.

Malhi, G. S., Adams, D., & Berk, M. (2010). The pharmacological treatment of bipolar disorder in primary care. *Medical Journal of Australia, 193,* S24–S30.

Malta, M., Magnanini, M. M. F., Strathdee, S. A., & Bastos, F. I. (2010). Adherence to antiretroviral therapy among HIV-infected drug users: A meta-analysis. *AIDS Behavior, 14,* 731–747.

Maner, J. K., Miller, S. L., Schmidt, N. B., & Eckel, L. A. (2010). The endocrinology of exclusion: Rejection elicits motivationally tuned changes in progesterone. *Psychological Science, 21,* 581–588.

Mangels, J. A., Gershberg, F. B., Shimamura, A. P., & Knight, R. T. (1996). Impaired retrieval from remote memory in patients with frontal lobe damage. *Neuropsychology, 10,* 32–41.

Mann, T., Tomiyama, A. J., Westling, E., Lew, A-M., Samuels, B., & Chatman, J. (2007). Medicare's search for effective obesity treatments: Diets are not the answer. *American Psychologist, 62,* 220–233.

The many facets of Facebook. (2011, January 1). *San Francisco Chronicle,* D-1.

Marais, L., Stein, D. J., & Daniels, W. M. U. (2009). Exercise increases BDNF levels in the striatum and decreases depressive-like behavior in chronically stressed rats. *Metabolic Brain Disease, 24,* 587–597.

Marek, G. J., & Aghajanian, G. K. (1996). LSD and the phenethylamine hallucinogen DOI are potent partial agonists at 5-HT2A receptors on interneurons in the rat piriform cortex. *Journal of Pharmacology and Experimental Therapeutics, 278,* 1373–1382.

Marijuana research. (2004, December 8). [Editorial]. *Scientific American, 291,* 8.

Mark, G., Gudith, D., & Klocke, U. (2008). The cost of interrupted work: More speed and stress. *CHI '08: Proceeding of the twenty-sixth annual SIGCHI conference on human factors in computing systems.* New York, NY: ACM.

Marker, C. D., Calamari, J. E., Woodard, J. L., & Riemann, B. C. (2006). Cognitive self-consciousness, implicit learning, and obsessive–compulsive disorder. *Journal of Anxiety Disorders, 20,* 389–407.

Marks, B. L., Madden, D. J., Burcur, B., Provenzale, J. M., White, L. E., Cabeza, R., & Huettel, S. A. (2007). Role of aerobic fitness and aging in cerebral white matter integrity. *Annals of the New York Academy of Sciences, 1097,* 171–174.

Marks, R. (2006). The superlative, sensitive shark. Retrieved from http://www.pbs.org/kqed/oceanadventures/episodes/sharks/indepth-senses.html

Markus, H., & Kitayama, S. (1991). Culture and the self: Implications for cognition, emotion, and motivation. *Psychological Review, 98,* 224–253.

Maron, E., Hettema, J. M., & Shlik, J. (2010). Advances in molecular genetics of panic disorder. *Molecular Psychiatry, 15,* 681–701.

Marsh, A. A., Yu, H. H., Pine, D. S., & Blair, R. J. R. (2010). Oxytocin improves specific recognition of positive facial expressions. *Psychopharmacology, 209,* 225–232.

Martindale, C. (1999). Biological bases of creativity. In R. J. Sternberg (Ed.), *Handbook of creativity* (pp. 137–152). Cambridge, England: Cambridge University Press.

Martindale, C. (2005, October 2). One face, one neuron. *Scientific American, 293,* 22–23.

Maschi, S., Clavenna, A., Campi, R., Schiavetti, B., Bernat, M., & Bonati, M. (2008). Neonatal outcome following pregnancy exposure to antidepressants: A prospective controlled cohort study. *BJOG—An International Journal of Obstetrics and Gynaecology, 115,* 283–289.

Mash, E. J., & Wolf, D. A. (2010). *Abnormal child psychology* (4th ed.). Belmont, CA: Wadsworth.

Mashour, G. A., Walker, E. E., & Martuza, R. L. (2005). Psychosurgery: Past, present, and future. *Brain Research Reviews, 48,* 409–419.

Masling, J. M., & Bornstein, R. F. (2005). *Scoring the Rorschach: Retrospect and prospect.* Mahwah, NJ: Erlbaum.

Maslow, A. (1968). *Toward a psychology of being* (2nd ed.). New York, NY: Van Nostrand.

Maslow, A. (1970). *Motivation and personality* (2nd ed.). New York, NY: Harper & Row.

Mason, J. W. (1971). A re-evaluation of the concept of "non-specificity" in stress theory. *Journal of Psychiatric Research, 8,* 323–333.

Mason, J. W. (1975). A historical view of the stress field. *Journal of Human Stress, 1,* 6–12.

Masten, C. L., Eisenberger, N. I., Borofsky, L. A., Pfeifer, J. H., McNealy, K., Mazziotta, J. C., & Dapretto, M. (2009). Neural correlates of social exclusion during adolescence: Understanding the distress of peer rejection.

Social Cognitive Affective Neuroscience, 4, 143–157. doi:10.1093/scan/nsp007

Masters, J., & Barr, S. (2010). Young children online: E-learning in a social networking context. *Knowledge Management & E-Learning: An International Journal, 1,* 295–304.

Masters, W. H., & Johnson, V. E. (1966). *The human sexual response.* Boston, MA: Little & Brown.

Masters, W. H., Johnson, V. E., & Kolodny, R. C. (1986). *Masters and Johnson on sex and human loving.* Boston, MA: Little & Brown.

Masuda, A., & Wendell, J. W. (2010). Mindfulness mediates the relation between disordered eating–related cognitions and psychological distress. *Eating Behaviors, 11,* 293–296.

Masuda, T., & Nisbett, R. E. (2001). Attending holistically versus analytically: Comparing the context sensitivity of Japanese and Americans. *Journal of Personality and Social Psychology, 81,* 922–934.

Mateo, Y., Budygin, E. A., John, C. E., & Jones, S. R. (2004). Role of serotonin in cocaine effects in mice with reduced dopamine transporter function. *Proceedings of the National Academy of Sciences, 101,* 372–377.

Mathiak, K., & Weber, R. (2006). Toward brain correlates of natural behavior: fMRI during violent video games. *Human Brain Mapping, 27,* 948–956.

Mathias, J. L., & Wheaton, P. (2007). Changes in attention and information-processing speed following severe traumatic brain injury: A meta-analytic review. *Neuropsychology, 21,* 212–223.

Mathiesen, B. B., Förster, P. L. V., & Svendsen, H. A. (2004). Affect regulation and loss of initiative in a case of orbitofrontal injury. *Neuropsychoanalysis, 6,* 47–62.

Maticka-Tyndale, E., Harold, E. S., & Opperman, M. (2003). Casual sex among Australian schoolies. *The Journal of Sex Research, 40,* 158–169.

Matson, J. L., & Boisjoli, J. A. (2009). The token economy for children with intellectual disability and/or autism: A review. *Research in Developmental Disabilities, 30,* 240–248.

Matsumoto, D., & Juang, L. (2004). *Culture and psychology* (3rd ed.). Belmont, CA: Thomson-Wadsworth.

Matsumoto, D., & Willingham, B. (2006). The thrill of victory and the agony of defeat: Spontaneous expressions of medal winners of the 2004 Athens Olympic Games. *Journal of Personality and Social Psychology, 91,* 568–581.

Matsumoto, D., Yoo, S. H., & Fontaine, J. (2008). Mapping expressive differences around the world: The relationship between emotional display rules and invidualism versus collectivism. *Journal of Cross-Cultural Psychology, 39,* 55–74. doi:10.1177/0022022107311854

Matthews, K. A., Glass, D. C., Rosenman, R. H., & Bortner, R. W. (1977). Competitive drive, Pattern A, and coronary heart disease:

A further analysis of some data from the Western Collaborative Group Study. *Journal of Chronic Diseases, 30,* 489–498.

Mauss, I. B., Levenson, R. W., McCarter, L., Wilhelm, F. H., & Gross, J. J. (2005). The tie that binds? Coherence among emotion experience, behavior, and physiology. *Emotion, 5,* 175–190.

Max, J. E., Levin, H. S., Schachar, R. J., Landis, J., Saunders, A. E., Ewing-Cobbs, L., . . . Dennis, M. (2006). Predictors of personality change due to traumatic brain injury in children and adolescents six to twenty-four months after injury. *Journal of Neuropsychiatry and Clinical Neurosciences, 18,* 21–32. doi:10.1176/appi.neuropsych.18.1.21

Max, J. E., Robertson, B. A. M., & Lansing, A. E. (2001). The phenomenology of personality change due to traumatic brain injury in children and adolescents. *Journal of Neuropsychiatry and Clinical Neurosciences, 13,* 161–170.

May, P. A., & Gossage, J. P. (2001). Estimating the prevalence of fetal alcohol syndrome. A summary. *Alcohol Research & Health, 25,* 159–167.

Mayberg, H. S. (1997). Limbic-cortical dysregulation: A proposed model of depression. *Journal of Neuropsychiatry and Clinical Neuroscience, 9,* 471–481.

Mayberg, H. S. (2003). Modulating dysfunctional limbic-cortical circuits in depression: Towards development of brain-based algorithms for diagnosis and optimized treatment. *British Medical Bulletin, 65,* 193–207.

Mayberg, H. S. (2009). Targeted electrode-based modulation of neural circuits for depression. *The Journal of Clinical Investigation, 119,* 717–725.

Mayberg, H. S., Liotti, M., Brannan, S. K., McGinnis, S., Mahurin, R. K., Jerabek, P. A., . . . Fox, P. T. (1999). Reciprocal limbic-cortical function and negative mood: Converging PET findings in depression and normal sadness. *American Journal of Psychiatry, 156,* 675–682.

Mayberg, H. S., Lozano, A. M., Voon, V., McNeely, H. E., Seminowicz, D., Hamani, C., et al. (2005). Deep brain stimulation for treatment-resistant depression. *Neuron, 45,* 651–660.

Mayer, J. D., Salovey, P., Caruso, D. R., & Sitarenios, G. (2003). Measuring emotional intelligence with MSCEIT V.2.0. *Emotion, 3,* 97–105.

Mayer, M. (2004). Structure and function of glutamate receptors in the brain. *Annals of the New York Academy of Sciences, 1038,* 125–130.

Mayne, T. J., Vittinghoff, E., Chesney, M. A., Barrett, D. C., & Coates, T. J. (1996). Depressive affect and survival among gay and bisexual men infected with HIV. *Archives of Internal Medicine, 156,* 2233–2238.

McArdle, J. J., & Prindle, J. J. (2008). A latent change score analysis of a randomized clinical trial in reasoning training. *Psychology and Aging, 23,* 702–719.

McCabe, C., & Rolls, E. T. (2007). Umami: A delicious flavor formed by convergence of taste and olfactory pathways in the human brain. *European Journal of Neuroscience, 25,* 1855–1864.

McClain, C. S., Rosenfeld, B., Breitbart, W. (2003). Effect of spiritual well-being on end-of-life despair in terminally-ill cancer patients. *Lancet, 361,* 1603–1607.

McClelland, D. C. (1985). How motives, skills, and values determine what people do. *American Psychologist, 40,* 812–825.

McClelland, J. L. (1988). Connectionist models and psychological evidence. *Journal of Memory and Language, 27,* 107–123.

McClelland, J. L., & Rogers, T. (2003). The parallel distributed processing approach to semantic knowledge. *Nature Reviews Neuroscience, 44,* 310–322.

McClelland, J. L., & Rumelhart, D. (1985). Distributed memory and the representation of general and specific information. *Journal of Experimental Psychology: General, 114,* 159–188.

McCrae, R. R. (2002). NEO-PI-R data from 36 cultures: Further intercultural comparisons. In R. R. McCrae & J. Allik (Eds.), *The Five-Factor Model of personality across cultures* (pp. 105–125). New York, NY: Kluwer Academic/Plenum.

McCrae, R. R., & Allik, J. (Eds.). (2002). *The Five-Factor Model of personality across cultures.* New York, NY: Kluwer Academic/Plenum.

McCrae, R. R., & Costa, P. T. (1996). Toward a new generation of personality theories: Theoretical contexts for the Five-Factor model. In J. S. Wiggins (Ed.), *The Five-Factor model of personality: Theoretical perspectives* (pp. 51–87). New York, NY: Guilford Press.

McCrae, R. R., & Costa, P. T. (1997). Personality trait structure as a human universal. *American Psychologist, 52,* 509–516.

McCrae, R. R., & Costa, P. T. (1999). A Five-Factor theory of personality. In L. A. Pervin & O. P. John (Eds.), *Handbook of personality theory and research* (pp. 139–153). New York, NY: Guilford Press.

McCrae, R. R., & Costa, P. T. (2003). *Personality in adulthood: A Five-Factor theory perspective* (2nd ed.). New York, NY: Guilford.

McCrae, R. R., & Costa, P. T., Jr. (2008). The Five-Factor theory of personality. In O. P. John, R. W. Robins, & L. A. Pervin (Eds.), *Handbook of personality: Theory and research* (pp. 159–181). New York, NY: Guilford Press.

McEvoy, J. P., Lieberman, J. A., Stroup, T. S., Davis, S. M., Meltzer, H. Y., Rosenheck, R. A., . . . Hsiao, J. (2006). Effectiveness of clozapine versus olanzapine, quetiapine, and risperidone in patients with chronic schizophrenia who did not respond to prior atypical antipsychotic treatment. *American Journal of Psychiatry, 163,* 600–610. doi:10.1176/appi.ajp.163.4.600

McEwen, B. S., De Kloet, E. R., & Rostene, W. (1986). Adrenal steroid receptors and actions in the nervous system. *Physiological Review, 66,* 1121–1188.

McGaugh, J. L. (2000). Memory—a century of consolidation. *Science, 287,* 248–251.

McKenna, B. S., Meloy, M. J., Wetherell, L., Stricker, J., & Drummond, S. P. A. (in press). Change in neural networks following total sleep deprivation and recovery sleep. *Sleep.*

McKinley, M., Cairns, M., Denton, D., Egan, G., Mathai, M., Uschakov, A., . . . Oldfield, B. J. (2004). Physiological and pathophysiological influences on thirst. *Physiology & Behavior, 81*(5), 795–803. doi:10.1016/j.physbeh.2004.04.055

McLay, R. N., McBrien, C., Wiederhold, M. D., & Wiederhold, B. K. (2010). Exposure therapy with and without virtual reality to treat PTSD while in combat theater: A parallel case series. *Cyberpsychology, Behavior, and Social Networking, 13,* 37–42. doi:10.1089/cyber.2009.0346

McTiernan, A. (2005). Obesity and cancer: The risks, science, and potential management strategies. *Oncology (Williston Park), 19,* 871–881.

Meaney, M. J. (2010). Epigenetics and the biological definition of gene × environment interactions. *Child Development, 81,* 41–79.

Mechelli, A., Crinion, J. T., Noppeney, U., O'Doherty, J, Ashburner, J., Frackowiak, R. S., & Price, C. J. (2004). Neurolinguistics: Structural plasticity in the bilingual brain. *Nature, 431,* 757. doi:10.1038/431757a

Mechtcheriakov, S., Brenneis, B., Koppelstaetter, F., Schocke, M., & Marksteiner, J. (2007). A widespread distinct pattern of cerebral atrophy in patients with alcohol addiction revealed by voxel-based morphometry. *Journal of Neurology, Neurosurgery, and Psychiatry, 78,* 610–614.

Medina, A. E., & Krahe, T. E. (2008). Neocortical plasticity deficits in fetal alcohol spectrum disorders: Lessons from barrel and visual cortex. *Journal of Neuroscience Research, 86,* 256–263.

Mednick, S. A., & Mednick, M. T. (1967). *Remote Associates Test: Experimenter's manual.* Boston, MA: Houghton Mifflin.

Mednick, S. C., & Ehman, M. (2006). *Take a nap! Change your life.* New York, NY: Workman.

Mednick, S. C., Makovski, T., Cai, D. J., & Jiang, Y. V. (2009). Sleep and rest facilitate implicit memory in a visual search task. *Vision Research, 49,* 2557–2565.

Mednick, S. C., Nakayama, K., & Stickgold, R. (2003). Sleep-dependent learning: A nap is as good as a night. *Nature Neuroscience, 6,* 697–698.

Medvec, V., Madey, S., & Gilovich, T. (1995, October). When less is more: Counterfactual thinking and satisfaction among Olympic medalists. *Journal of Personality and Social Psychology, 69*(4), 603–610.

Meerkerk, G., van den Eijnden, R. J. J. M., & Garretsen, H. F. L. (2006). Predicting compulsive Internet use: It's all about sex! *CyberPsychology and Behavior, 9,* 95–103.

Megan Fox makes 10 celebrities with OCD. (n.d.). Retrieved from http://abcnews.go.com/Entertainment/Media/celebrities-obsessive-compulsive-disorders-hollywood-stars-ocd/story?id=10689626&page=4

Mei, J., Green, R., Henley, T., & Masten, W. (2009). Acculturation in relation to the acquisition of a second language. *Journal of Multilingual & Multicultural Development, 30,* 481–492. doi:10.1080/01434630903147898

Mei, L., & Xiong, W.-C. (2008). Neuregulin 1 in neural development, synaptic plasticity and schizophrenia. *Nature Reviews Neuroscience, 9,* 437–452.

Melis, A. P., & Semmann, D. (2010). How is human cooperation different? *Philosophical Transactions of the Royal Society of London B, 365,* 2663–2674.

Melis, M. R., & Argiolis, A. (1995). Dopamine and sexual behavior. *Neuroscience and Biobehavioral Reviews, 19,* 19–38.

Mell, J. C., Howard, S. M., & Miller, B. L. (2003). Art and the brain: The influence of frontotemporal dementia on an accomplished artist. *Neurology, 60,* 1707–1710.

Meltzoff, A. N., & Moore, M. K. (1977). Imitation of facial and manual gestures by human neonates. *Science, 198,* 75–78.

Meltzoff, A. N., & Moore, M. K. (1983). Newborn infants imitate adult facial gestures. *Child Development, 54,* 702–709.

Melzack, R., & Wall, P. D. (1965). Pain mechanisms: A new theory. *Science, 150,* 971–979.

Melzack, R., & Wall, P. D. (1988). *The challenge of pain* (revised edition). New York, NY: Penguin.

Mendelsohn, A., Furman, O., & Dudai, Y. (2010). Signatures of memory: Brain coactivations during retrieval distinguish correct from incorrect recollection. *Frontiers in Behavioral Neuroscience, 4,* 1–12.

Mennella, J. A., & Beauchamp, G. K. (1996). The early development of human flavor preferences. In E. D. Capaldi (Ed.), *Why we eat what we eat: The psychology of eating* (pp. 83–112). Washington, DC: APA Books.

Mennella, J. A., Johnson, A., & Beauchamp, G. K. (1995). Garlic ingestion by pregnant women alters the odor of amniotic fluid. *Chemical Senses, 20,* 207–209.

Mental health: A report of the Surgeon General. (2001). Retrieved from http://www.surgeongeneral.gov/library/mentalhealth/home.html

Merskey, H., & Bogduk, N. (1994). *Classification of chronic pain.* Seattle, WA: International Association for the Study of Pain Press.

Merten, J. (2005). Culture, gender and the recognition of the basic emotions. *Psychologia, 48,* 306–316.

Meunier, M., & Bachevalier, J. (2002). Comparison of emotional responses in monkeys with rhinal cortex or amygdala lesions. *Emotion, 2,* 147–161.

Miao, C. F., Lund, D. J., & Evan, K. R. (2009). Reexamining the influence of career stages on salesperson motivation: A cognitive and affective perspective. *Journal of Personal Selling and Sales Management, 29,* 243–255.

Michael, J. (1975). Positive and negative reinforcement, a distinction that is no longer necessary; or a better way to talk about bad things. *Behaviorism, 3,* 33–45.

Miczek, K. A., de Almeida, R. M. M., Kravitz, E. A., & Rissman E. F. (2007). Neurobiology of escalated aggression and violence. *Journal of Neuroscience, 27,* 11803–11806.

Mikolajczak, M., & Luminet, O. (2008). Trait emotional intelligence and the cognitive appraisal of stressful events: An exploratory study. *Personality and Individual Differences, 44,* 1445–1453.

Milgram, S. (1963). Behavioral study of obedience. *Journal of Abnormal and Social Psychology, 67,* 371–378.

Milgram, S. (1974). *Obedience to authority: An experimental view.* New York, NY: Harper.

Mill, J., & Petronis, A. (2008). Pre- and perinatal environmental risks for attention-deficit hyperactivity disorder (ADHD): The potential role of epigenetic processes in mediating susceptibility. *Journal of Child Psychology and Psychiatry, 49,* 1020–1030.

The Millennials: Confident. Connected. Open to change. (2010). Washington, DC: Pew Research Center. Retrieved from http://pewresearch.org/pubs/1501/millennials-new-survey-generational-personality-upbeat-open-new-ideas-technology-bound

Miller, A. (1996). *Insights of genius: Imagery and creativity in science and art.* New York, NY: Springer Verlag.

Miller, A. H., Capuron, L., & Raison, C. L. (2005). Immunologic influences on emotion regulation. *Clinical Neuroscience Research, 4,* 325–333.

Miller, A. S., & Kanazawa, S. (2000). *Order by accident: The origins and consequences of conformity in contemporary Japan.* Boulder, CO: Westview Press.

Miller, B. L., & J. L. Cummings (Eds.). (1999). *The human frontal lobes: Functions and disorders.* New York, NY: Guilford Press.

Miller, G. A. (1956). The magical number seven, plus or minus two: Some limits on our capacity for processing information. *Psychological Review, 63,* 81–97.

Miller, G. E., Chen, E., Fok, A. K., Walker, H., Lim, A., Nicholls, E. F., Cole, S., & Kobor, M. S. (2009). Low early-life social class leaves a biological residue manifested by decreased glucocorticoid and increased proinflammatory signaling. *Proceedings of the National Academy of Sciences, 106,* 14716–14721.

Miller, G. F. (2000). *The mating mind: How sexual choice shaped the evolution of human nature.* New York, NY: Doubleday.

Miller, L. A., & Tippett, L. J. (1996). Effects of focal brain lesions on visual problem-solving. *Neuropsychologia, 34,* 387–398.

Miller, N., & Dollard, J. (1941). *Social learning and imitation.* New Haven, CT: Yale University Press.

Miller, S. L., & Maner, J. K. (2010). Scent of a woman: Men's testosterone responses to olfactory ovulation cues. *Psychological Science, 21,* 276–283.

Milner, B. (1962). Les troubles de la mémoire accompagnant des lésions hippocampiques bilatérales. In *Physiologie de l'hippocampe* (pp. 257–272). Paris: Centre National de la Recherche Scientifique. English translation: P. M. Milner & S. Glickman (Eds.). (1965). *Cognitive processes and the brain: An enduring problem in psychology. Selected readings* (pp. 97–111). Princeton: Van Nostrand.

Milner, B., Corkin, S., & Teuber, H. L. (1968). Further analysis of the hippocampal amnesic syndrome: 14-year follow-up study of H. M. *Neuropsychologia, 6,* 215–234.

Min, B-K., Marzelli, M. J., & Yoo, S-S. (2010). Neuroimaging-based approaches in the brain–computer interface. *Trends in Biotechnology, 28,* 552–560.

Mirescu, C., & Gould, E. (2006). Stress and adult neurogenesis. *Hippocampus, 16,* 233–238.

Mirescu, C., Peters, J. D., Noiman, L., & Gould, E. (2006). Sleep deprivation inhibits adult neurogenesis in the hippocampus by elevating glucocorticoids. *Proceedings of the National Academy of Sciences, 103,* 19170–19175. doi:10.1073/pnas.0608644103

Mirnics, K., Middleton, F. A., Marquez, A., Lewis, D. A., & Levitt, P. (2000). Molecular characterization of schizophrenia viewed by microarray analysis of gene expression in prefrontal cortex. *Neuron, 28,* 53–67.

Mischel, W. (2009). From personality and assessment (1968) to personality science, 2009. *Journal of Research in Personality, 43,* 282–290.

Mischel, W., & Shoda, Y. (1995). A cognitive-affective system theory of personality: Re-conceptualizing situations, dispositions, dynamics, and invariance in personality structure. *Psychological Review, 102,* 246–268.

Mischel, W., & Shoda, Y. (1999). Integrating dispositions and processing dynamics within a unified theory of personality: The cognitive-affective personality system. In L. A. Pervin & O. P. John (Eds.), *Handbook of personality: Theory and research* (pp. 197–218). New York, NY: Guilford Press.

Miyake, A., Friedman, N. P., Emerson, M. J., Witzki, A. H., & Howerter, A. (2000). The unity and diversity of executive functions and their contributions to complex "frontal lobe" tasks: A latent variable approach. *Cognitive Psychology, 41,* 49–100.

Miyashita, T., Kubik, S., Lewandowski, G., & Guzowski, J. F. (2008). Networks of neurons, networks of genes: An integrated view of memory consolidation. *Neurobiology of Learning and Memory, 89,* 269–284.

Mizuno, S., Mihara, T., Miyaoka, T., Inagaki, T., & Horiguchi, J. (2005, March). CSF iron, ferritin and transferrin levels in restless legs syndrome. *Journal of Sleep Research, 14*(1), 43–47.

Moffitt, T. E., Brammer, G. L., Caspi, A., Fawcett, J. P., Raleigh, M., Yuwiler, A.,

& Silva, P. (1998). Whole blood serotonin relates to violence in an epidemiological study. *Biological Psychiatry, 43*, 446–457.

Moffitt, T. E., Caspi. A., & Rutter, M. (2005). Strategy for investigating interactions between measured genes and measured environments. *Archives of General Psychiatry, 62*, 473–481.

Moghaddam, B. (2003). Bringing order to the glutamate chaos in schizophrenia. *Neuron, 40*, 881–884.

Mokdad, A. H., Serdula, M. K., Dietz, W. H., Bowman, B. A., Marks, J. S., & Koplan, J. P. (1999). The spread of the obesity epidemic in the United States, 1991–1998. *Journal of American Medical Association, 282*, 1519–1522.

Moller, J., Hallqvist, J., Diderichsen, F., Theorell, T., Reuterwall, C., & Ahblom, A. (1999). Do episodes of anger trigger myocardial infarction? A case-crossover analysis in the Stockholm Heart Epidemiology Program (SHEEP). *Psychosomatic Medicine, 61*, 842–849.

Montague, D. P. F., & Walker-Andrews, A. S. (2001). Peekaboo: A new look at infants perception of emotion. *Developmental Psychology, 37*, 826–838.

Montgomery, G. H., DuHamel, K. N., & Redd, W. H. (2000). A meta-analysis of hypnotically induced analgesia: How effective is hypnosis? *International Journal of Clinical and Experimental Hypnosis, 48*, 138–153.

Moody, E. W., Sunsay, C., & Bouton, M. E. (2006). Priming and trial spacing in extinction: Effects on extinction performance, spontaneous recovery, and reinstatement in appetitive conditioning. *Quarterly Journal of Experimental Psychology, 59*, 809–829.

Moore, E. S., Ward, R. E., Wetherill, L. F., Rogers, J. L., Autti-Rämö, I., Fagerlund, A., . . . Foroud, T. (2007). Unique facial features distinguish fetal alcohol syndrome patients and controls in diverse ethnic populations. *Alcoholism: Clinical and Experimental Research, 31*, 1707–1713. doi:10.1111/j.1530-0277.2007.00472.x

Moore, R. Y., & Eichler, V. B. (1972). Loss of a circadian adrenal corticosterone rhythm following suprachiasmatic lesions in the rat. *Brain Research, 42*, 201–206.

Moradi, A. R., Herlihy, J., Yasseri, G., Shahraray, M., Turner, A., & Dalgleish, T. (2008). Specificity of episodic and semantic aspects of autobiographical memory in relation to symptoms of post-traumatic stress disorder (PTSD). *Acta Psychologica, 127*, 645–653.

Morales-Medina, J. C., Dumont, Y., & Quirion, R. (2010). A possible role of neuropeptide Y in depression and stress. *Brain Research, 1314*, 194–205.

Moran, E. M., Snelson, C., & Elison-Bowers, P. (2010). Image and video disclosure of substance use on social media websites. *Computers in Human Behavior, 26*, 1405–1411.

Moray, N. (1959). Attention in dichotic listening: Affective cues and the influence of instructions. *Quarterly Journal of Experimental Psychology, 11*, 56–60.

Morgenstern, N. A., Lombardi, G., & Schinder, A. F. (2008). Newborn granule cells in the ageing dentate gyrus. *Journal of Physiology, 586*, 3751–3757.

Morris, J. S., Frilt, C. D., Perrett, D. I., Rowland, D., Yong, A. N., Calder, A. J., & Dolan, R. J. (1996). A different neural response in the human amygdala in fearful and happy facial expressions. *Nature, 383*, 812–815.

Morris, M. W., & Peng, K. (1994). Culture and cause: American and Chinese attributions for social and physical events. *Journal of Personality and Social Psychology, 67*, 949–971.

Morris, N. M., Udry, J. R., Khandawood, F., & Dawood, M. Y. (1987). Marital sex frequency and midcycle female testosterone. *Archives of Sexual Behavior, 16*, 27–37.

Morris, P. L., Robinson, R. G., Raphael, B., & Hopwood, M. J. (1996). Lesion location and post-stroke depression. *Journal of Neuropsychiatry and Clinical Neurosciences, 8*, 399–403.

Morrison, R. S., Maroney-Galin, C., Kralovec, P. D., & Meier, D. E. (2005). The growth of palliative care programs in United States hospitals. *Journal of Palliative Medicine, 8*(6), 1127–1134.

Moruzzi, G., & Magoun, H. W. (1949). Brain stem reticular formation and activation of the EEG. *Electroencephalography and Clinical Neurophysiology, 1*, 455–473.

Mosconi, M., Cody-Hazlett, H., Poe, M., Gerig, G., Gimpel-Smith, R., & Piven, J. (2009). Longitudinal study of amygdala volume and joint attention in 2- to 4-year-old children with autism. *Archives of General Psychiatry, 66*, 509–516. doi:10.1001/archgenpsychiatry.2009.19

Moscovici, S. (1985). Social influence and conformity. In G. Lindzey & E. Aronson (Eds.), *The handbook of social psychology* (3rd ed., Vol. 2; pp. 347–412). New York, NY: Random House.

Moscovitch, M. (2010). Memory consolidation: Past, present and future. *Journal of Neurology, Neurosurgery, and Psychiatry, 81*, e2. doi:10.1136/jnnp.2010.217554.4

Moses-Kolko, E. L., Bogen, D., Perel, J., Bregard, A., Uhl, K., Levin, B., et al. (2005). Neonatal signs after late in utero exposure to serotonin reuptake inhibitors: Literature review and implications for clinical applications. *JAMA, 293*, 2372–2383.

Moskowitz, J. (2003). Positive affect predicts lower risk of AIDS mortality. *Psychosomatic Medicine, 65*, 620–626.

Moskowitz, J., Folkman, S., Collette, L., & Vittinghoff, E. (1996). Coping and mood during AIDS related caregiving and bereavement. *Annals of Behavioral Medicine, 18*, 49–57.

Motluk, A. (2005, January 29). Senses special: The art of seeing without sight. *New Scientist, 2484*, p. 37. Retrieved from http://www.newscientist.com

Mount, M. K., Barrick, M. R., Scullen, S. M., & Rounds, J. (2005). Higher-order dimensions of the Big Five personality traits

and the Big Six vocational interest types. *Personnel Psychology, 58*, 447–478.

Müller-Oerlinghausen, B., Berghöfer, A., & Bauer, M. (2002). Bipolar disorder. *The Lancet, 359*, 241–247.

Mulvey, T. A., & Grus, C. L. (2010, August). *What can I do with a degree in psychology?* Paper presented at Annual Convention of American Psychological Association, San Diego, CA. Retrieved from http://www.apa.org/workforce/presentations/2010-psychology-degree.pdf

Munro, G. D., Lasane, T. P., & Leary, S. P. (2010). Political partisan prejudice: Selective distortion and weighting of evaluative categories in college admissions applications. *Journal of Applied Social Psychology, 40*, 2434–2462.

Munsinger, H. (1975). The adopted child's IQ: A critical review. *Psychological Bulletin, 82*, 623–659.

Murphy, S. E. (2010). Using functional neuroimaging to investigate the mechanisms of action of Selective Serotonin Reuptake Inhibitors (SSRIs). *Current Pharmaceutical Design, 16*, 1990–1997.

Murray, H. A. (1938/1962). *Explorations in personality.* New York, NY: Science Editions.

Murray, J. (2009). Top 10 weight loss tips: Physical activity and healthy eating habits are key to losing weight. Retrieved from http://weight-loss-methods.suite101.com/article.cfm/top_10_weight_loss_tips

Myers, I. B. (1962). *Myers-Briggs Type Indicator manual.* Princeton, NJ: Educational Testing Service.

Nabi, H., Shipley, M. J., Vahtera, J., Hall, M., Korkeila, J., Marmot, M., . . . Singh-Manoux, A. (2010). Effects of depressive symptoms and coronary heart disease and their interactive associations on mortality in middle-aged adults: The Whitehall II cohort study. *Heart, 11*, 1645–1650.

Nacash, N., Foa, E. B., Fostick, L., Polliack, M., Dinstein, Y., Tzur, D., et al. (2007). Prolonged exposure therapy for chronic combat-related PTSD: A case report on five veterans. *CNS Spectrums, 12*, 690–695.

Nadarajah, B., & Parnavelas, J. (2002). Modes of neuronal migration in the developing cerebral cortex. *Nature Reviews Neuroscience, 3*, 423–432.

Nakano, S., & Watanabe, Y. (2009). The virtual doubling of Japanese Internet use: 2001–2006. *Social Indicators Research, 93*, 235–238.

Naqvi, N. H., Rudrauf, D., Damasio, H., & Bechara, A. (2007). Damage to the insula disrupts addiction to cigarette smoking. *Science, 315*, 531–534.

Nasar, S. (1998). *A beautiful mind.* New York, NY: Touchstone.

Nash, M. R., Hulsey, T. L., Sexton, M. C., Harralson, T. L., Lambert, W., & Lynch, G. V. (1993). *Adult psychopathology associated with a history of childhood sexual abuse: A psychoanalytic perspective.* Washington, DC: American Psychological Association.

National Eye Institute. (2002). *Vision problems in the U.S.: Prevalence of adult vision impairment and age-related eye disease in America, 2002.* Retrieved January 20, 2007, from http://www.nei.nih.gov/eyedata/pdf/VPUS.pdf

National Human Genome Research Institute. (2010). A brief guide to genomics. Retrieved from http://www.genome.gov/18016863

National Institute of Mental Health (NIMH). (2007). *Schizophrenia.* Washington, DC: NIMH Publication # 06-3517.

National Institute on Alcohol Abuse and Alcoholism. (2005). *Heavy episodic consumption of alcohol.* Retrieved April 4, 2008, from http://www.collegedrinkingprevention.gov/NIAAACollegeMaterials/TaskForce/HeavyEpisodic_00.aspx

National Institute on Deafness and Other Communication Disorders. (2008). *Quick statistics.* Bethesda, MD: U.S. Department of Health and Human Services. Retrieved from http://www.nidcd.nih.gov/health/statistics/quick.htm

National Science Foundation. (2002). Science and technology: Public attitudes and public understanding. In *Science and Engineering Indicators—2002* (Chapter 7). Arlington, VA: National Science Foundation.

National Sleep Foundation. (2008). *2008 Sleep in America poll.* Retrieved April 2, 2008, from http://www.sleepfoundation.org/site/c.huIXKjM0IxF/b.3933533/

Natural born copycats. (2002, December 20). *The Guardian.* Retrieved from http://www.mediaknowall.com/violence/nbk.html

Nauta, W. J. H., & Feirtag, M. (1979). The organization of the brain. *Scientific American, 241,* 88–111.

Nave, K-A. (2010, November 11). Myelination and support of axonal integrity by glia. *Nature, 468,* 244–252.

Neisser, U., Boodoo, G., Bouchard, T. J., Boykin, A. W., Brody, N., Ceci, S. J., et al. (1996). Intelligence: Knowns and unknowns. *American Psychologist, 51,* 77–101.

Nelson-Gray, R. O., Keane, S. P., Hurst, R. M., Mitchell, J. T., Warburton, J. B., Chok, J. T., et al. (2006). A modified DBT skills training program for oppositional defiant adolescents: Promising preliminary findings. *Behaviour Research and Therapy, 44,* 1811–1820.

Nemeroff, C. B. (2007). The burden of severe depression: A review of diagnostic challenges and treatment alternatives. *Journal of Psychiatric Research, 41,* 189–206.

Nemeroff, C., & Rozin, P. (1994). The contagion concept in adult thinking in the United States: Transmission of germs and of interpersonal influence. *Ethos, 22,* 158–186.

Nesbit, S. M., Conger, J. C., & Conger, A. J. (2007). A quantitative review of the relationship between anger and aggressive driving. *Aggression and Violent Behavior, 12,* 156–176.

Nettle, D., & Clegg, H. (2005). Schizotypy, creativity, and mating success in humans.

Proceedings of the Royal Society (B). doi:10.1098/rspb.2005.3349

Neuberg, S. L., & Cottrell, C. A. (2006). Evolutionary bases of prejudices. In M. Schaller, J. A. Simpson, & D. T. Kenrick (Eds.), *Evolution and social psychology* (pp. 163–187). New York, NY: Psychology Press.

Neugebauer, R., Hoek, H. W., & Susser, E. (1999). Prenatal exposure to wartime famine and development of antisocial personality disorder in early adulthood. *Journal of the American Medical Association, 282,* 455–462.

Newcomb, T. M. (1961). *The acquaintance process.* Oxford, England: Holt, Rinehart & Winston.

Newcombe, N. S., & Uttal, D. H. (2006). Whorf versus Socrates, round 10. *Trends in Cognitive Sciences, 10,* 394–396.

Newport, E. L. (2003). Language development, critical periods in. In L. Nadel (Ed.), *Encyclopedia of cognitive science* (Vol. 2, pp. 733–740). London, England: Nature Group Press.

Neyens, D. M., & Boyle, L. N. (2007). The effect of distraction on the crash types of teenage drivers. *Accident Analysis and Prevention, 39,* 206–212.

Nickerson, C., Schwarz, N., Diener, E., & Kahneman, D. (2003). Zeroing in on the dark side of the American dream: A closer look at the negative consequences of the goal for financial success. *Psychological Science, 14,* 531–536.

Nicoll, R. A., & Alger, B. E. (2004). The brain's own marijuana. *Scientific American, 291,* 69–75.

Nieman, D. C., Custer, W. F., Butterworth, D. E., Utter, A. C., & Henson, D. A. (2000). Psychological response to exercise and/or energy restriction in obese women. *Journal of Psychosomatic Research, 48(1),* 23–29.

Nikolaus, S., Antke, C., Beu, M., & Muller, H. W. (2010). Cortical GABA, striatal dopamine and midbrain serotonin as the key players in compulsive and anxiety disorders—Results from in vivo imaging studies. *Reviews in the Neurosciences, 21,* 119–139.

Nilsson, L. G. (2003). Memory function in normal aging. *Acta Neurologica Scandinavica Supplementum, 179,* 7–13.

Nisbett, R. E., Peng, K., Choi, I., & Norenzayan, A. (2001). Culture and systems of thought: Holistic versus analytic cognition. *Psychological Review, 108,* 291–301.

Nisbett, R. E., & Wilson, T. D. (1977). Telling more than we can know: Verbal reports on mental processes. *Psychological Review, 84,* 231–259.

Nishida, A., Hisaoka, K., Zensho, H., Uchitomi, Y., Morinobu, S., & Yamawaki, S. (2002). Antidepressant drugs and cytokines in mood disorders. *International Immunopharmacology, 2,* 1619–1626.

Nishino, S. (2007). Clinical and neurobiological aspects of narcolepsy. *Sleep Medicine, 8,* 373–399.

Nithianantharajah, J., & Hannan, A. (2006). Enriched environments, experience dependent plasticity and disorders of the

nervous system. *Nature Reviews Neuroscience, 7,* 697–709.

Nixon, R. D. V., Ellis, A. A., Nehmy, T .J., & Ball, S-A. (2010). Screening and predicting posttraumatic stress and depression in children following single-incident trauma. *Journal of Clinical Child & Adolescent Psychology, 39,* 588–596.

Nock, M. K., Park, J. M., Finn, C. T., Deliberto, T. L., Dour, H. J., & Banaji, M. R. (2010). Measuring the suicidal mind: Implicit cognition predicts suicidal behavior. *Psychological Science, 21,* 511–517.

Noda, H., Iso, H., Toyoshima, H., Date, C., Yamamoto, A., Kikuchi, S., et al. (2005). Walking and sports participation and mortality from coronary heart disease and stroke. *Journal of the American College of Cardiology, 46,* 1761–1767.

Nolen-Hoeksema, S. (2007). *Abnormal psychology* (4th ed). New York, NY: McGraw-Hill.

Nolte, C., & Yollin, P. (2006, April 19). Officials salute city's majestic rise from rubble of '06—and the survivors. *San Francisco Chronicle,* pp. A1, A12.

Norcross, J. C., Bike, D., & Evans, K. (2009). The therapist's therapist: A replication and extension 20 years later. *Psychotherapy: Theory, Research, Practice, Training, 46,* 32–41. doi:10.1037/a0015140

Norcross, J. C., Karpiak, C. P., & Lister, K. M. (2005). What's an integrationist? A study of self-identified integrative and (occasionally) eclectic psychologists. *Journal of Clinical Psychology, 61,* 1587–1594.

Norcross, J. C., Sayette, M. A., Mayne, T. J., Karg, R. S., & Turkson, M. A. (1998). Selecting a doctoral program in professional psychology: Some comparisons among PhD counseling, PhD clinical, and PsyD clinical psychology programs. *Professional Psychology: Research and Practice, 29,* 609–614.

Norenzayan, A., & Nisbett, R. E. (2000). Culture and causal cognition. *Current Directions in Psychological Science, 9,* 132–135.

Norine, C. S. (2010, November 23). I don't think I would volunteer for this again, but I bet you could find someone that would [Twitter post]. Retrieved from http://twitter.com/#!/csnorine/status/7143386196742144

Nottebohm, F. (1985). Neuronal replacement in adulthood. *Annals of the New York Academy of Sciences, 457,* 143–161.

Novak, M. A. (2003). Self-injurious behavior in Rhesus monkeys: New insights into its etiology, physiology, and treatment. *American Journal of Primatology, 59,* 3–19.

Nowak, M. A., & Sigmund, K. (2005, October 27). Evolution of indirect reciprocity. *Nature, 437,* 1291–1298.

Nuechterlein, K., & Parasuraman, R. (1983). Visual sustained attention: Image degradation produces rapid sensitivity decrement over time. *Science, 220,* 327–329.

O'Craven, K. M., & Kanwisher, N. N. (2000). Mental imagery of faces and places activates corresponding stimulus-specific brain regions. *Journal of Cog-*

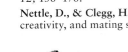

nitive Neuroscience, 12, 1013–1023. doi:10.1162/08989290051137549

O'Cleirigh, C., Ironson, G., Fletcher, M. A., & Schneiderman, N. (2008). Written emotional disclosure and processing of trauma are associated with protected health status and immunity in people living with HIV/AIDS. *British Journal of Health Psychology, 13,* 81–84.

O'Conner, M. J., & Paley, B. (2006). The relationship of prenatal alcohol exposure and the postnatal environment of child depressive symptoms. *Journal of Pediatric Psychology, 31,* 50–64.

O'Neill, J., Pleydell-Bouverie, B., Dupret, D., & Csicsvari, J. (2010). Play it again: Reactivation of waking experience and memory. *Trends in Neurosciences, 33,* 220–229. doi:10.1016/j.tins.2010.01.006

Oberman, L. M., & Ramachandran, V. S. (2007). The simulating social mind: The role of mirror neuron system and simulation in the social and communicative deficits of autism spectrum disorders. *Psychological Bulletin, 133,* 310–327.

Ochsner, K. N., Bunge, S. A., Gross, J. J., & Gabrieli, J. D. E. (2002). Rethinking feelings: A fMRI study of the cognitive regulation of emotion. *Journal of Cognitive Neuroscience, 14,* 1215–1229.

The odds of dying from. . . (2010). National Safety Council. Retrieved from http://www.nsc.org/news_resources/injury_and_death_statistics/pages/theoddsofdyingfrom.aspx

Öhman, A. (2002). Automaticity and the amygdala: Nonconscious responses to emotional faces. *Current Directions in Psychological Science, 11,* 62–66.

Ohnishi, T., Matsuda, H., Asada, T., Aruga, M., Hirakata, M., Nishikawa, M., . . . Imabayashi, E. (2001). Functional anatomy of musical perception in musicians. *Cerebral Cortex, 11,* 754–760. doi:10.1093/cercor/11.8.754

Ohno, H., Urushihara, R., Sei, H., & Morita, Y. (2002). REM sleep deprivation suppresses acquisition of classical eyeblink conditioning. *Sleep, 25,* 38–41.

Oitzl, M. S., Champagne, D. L., van der Veen, R., & de Kloet, E. R. (2010). Brain development under stress: Hypotheses of glucocorticoid actions revisited. *Neuroscience & Biobehavioral Reviews, 34,* 853–866.

Olds, J., & Milner, P. (1954). Positive reinforcement produced by electrical stimulation of septal area and other regions of rat brain. *Journal of Comparative and Physiological Psychology, 47,* 419–427.

Oliver, M. B., & Hyde, J. S. (1993). Gender differences in sexuality: A meta-analysis. *Psychological Bulletin, 114,* 29–51.

Olson, J. M., & Zanna, M. P. (1993). Attitudes and attitude change. *Annual Review of Psychology, 44,* 117–154.

Omark, D., Omark, M., & Edelman, M. (1973). Formation of dominance hierarchies in young children. In T. R. Williams (Ed.), *Physical anthropology.* The Hague, Netherlands: Mouton.

Ong, J. C., Shapiro, S. L., & Manber, R. (2008). Combining mindfulness meditation with cognitive-behavior therapy for insomnia: A treatment-development study. *Behavior Therapy, 39,* 171–182.

Onodera, A. (2003). Changes in self-concept in the transition to parenthood. *Japanese Journal of Developmental Psychology, 14,* 180–190.

Ophir, E., Nass, C. I., & Wagner, A. D. (2009). Cognitive control in media multitaskers. *Proceedings of the National Academy of Sciences, 106,* 15583–15587.

Orne, M. T. (1959). The nature of hypnosis: Artifact and essence. *Journal of Abnormal and Social Psychology, 58,* 277–299.

Oscar–Berman, M., & Marinkovic, K. (2003). Alcoholism and the brain: An overview. *Alcohol Research & Health, 27,* 125–133.

Osherow, N. (1999). Making sense of the nonsensical: An analysis of Jonestown. In E. Aronson (Ed.), *Readings about the social animal* (8th ed., pp. 71–88). New York, NY: Worth/Freeman.

Ost, J. (2009). Recovered memories. In R. Bull, T. Valentine, & T. Williamson, (Eds.), *Handbook of psychology of investigative interviewing: Current developments and future directions* (pp. 181–204). New York, NY: Wiley-Blackwell.

Oster, H. (2005). The repertoire of infant facial expressions: An ontogenetic perspective. In J. Nadel & D. Muir (Eds.), *Emotional development* (pp. 261–292). New York, NY: Oxford University Press.

Osterling, J., & Dawson, G. (1994). Early recognition of children with autism: A study of first birthday home videotapes. *Journal of Autism and Developmental Disorders, 24,* 247–257.

Ostry, D. J., Darainy, M., Mattar, A. A. G., Wong, J., & Gribble, P. L. (2010). Somatosensory plasticity and motor learning. *The Journal of Neuroscience, 30,* 5384–5393.

Ottersen, O. P. (2010). How hardwired is the brain? Technological advances provide new insight into brain malleability and neurotransmission. *Nutrition Reviews, 68,* S60-S64. doi:10.1111/j.1753-4887.2010.00350.x

Otto, M. W., McHugh, R. K., & Kantak, K. M. (2010). Combined pharmacotherapy and cognitive–behavioral therapy for anxiety disorders: Medication effects, glucocorticoids, and attenuated treatment outcomes. *Clinical Psychology: Science and Practice, 17,* 91–103.

Ouellet, M-C., & Morin, C. M. (2006). Fatigue following traumatic brain injury: Frequency, characteristics, and associated factors. *Rehabilitation Psychology, 51,* 140–149.

Ouellet, M-C., Beaulieu-Bonneau, S., & Morin, C. M. (2006). Insomnia in patients with traumatic brain injury: Frequency, characteristics, and risk factors. *Journal of Head Trauma Rehabilitation, 21,* 199–212.

Oveis, C., Horberg, E. J., & Keltner, D. (2010). Compassion, pride, and social intuitions of self-other similarity. *Journal of Personality and Social Psychology, 98,* 618–630.

Overgaard, M. (2009). How can we know if patients in coma, vegetative state or minimally conscious state are conscious? *Coma Science: Clinical and Ethical Implications, 177,* 11–19.

Owen, A. M., Coleman, M. R., Boly, M., Davis, M., Laureys, S., & Pickard, J. D. (2006). Detecting awareness in the vegetative state. *Science, 313,* 1402.

Oyama, S. (1976). A sensitive period for the acquisition of a nonnative phonological system. *Journal of Psycholinguistic Research, 5,* 261–283.

Pae, C-U., Lim, H-K., Han, C., Neena, A., Lee, C., & Patkar, A. A. (2007). Selegiline transdermal system: Current awareness and promise. *Progress in Neuro-Psychopharmacology & Biological Psychiatry, 31,* 1153–1163.

Pajares, F. (2004). Albert Bandura: Biographical sketch. Retrieved from http://des.emory.edu/mfp/bandurabio.html

Pallanti, S., Bernardi, S., & Quercoli, L. (2006). The shorter PROMIS questionnaire and the Internet addiction scale in the assessment of multiple addictions in a high school population: Prevalence and related disability. *CNS Spectrum, 11,* 966–974.

Pan, B. A., Rowe, M. L., Singer, J. D., & Snow, C. E. (2005). Maternal correlates of growth in toddler vocabulary production in low-income families. *Child Development, 76,* 763–946.

Panagopoulou, E., Montgomery, A., & Tarlatzis, B. (2010). Experimental emotional disclosure in women undergoing infertility treatment: Are drop outs better off? *Social Science & Medicine, 69,* 678–681.

Panksepp, J. (2000). Emotions as natural kinds within the mammalian brain. In M. Lewis & J. M. Haviland-Jones (Eds.), *Handbook of emotions* (2nd ed., pp. 137–156). New York, NY: Guilford.

Pantev, C., Engelien, A., Candia, V., & Elbert, T. (2001). Representational cortex in musicians: Plastic alterations in response to musical practice. In R. J. Zatorre & I. Peretz (Eds.), *The biological foundations of music: Annals of the New York Academy of Sciences* (pp. 300–314). New York, NY: New York Academy of Sciences.

Papakostos, G. I., Stahl, S. M., Krishen, A., Seifert, C., Tucker, V. L., Goodale, E. P., & Faca, M. (2008). Efficacy of bupropion and the selective serotonin reuptake inhibitors in the treatment of major depressive disorder with high levels of anxiety (anxious depression): A pooled analysis of 10 studies. *The Journal of Clinical Psychiatry, 69,* 1287–1292.

Parasuraman, R. (1998). *The attentive brain.* Cambridge, MA: MIT Press.

Paris, R., & Helson, R. (2002). Early mothering experience and personality change. *Journal of Family Psychology, 16,* 172–185.

Park, C. L., & Folkman, S. (1997). Meaning in the context of stress and coping. *Review of General Psychology, 1,* 115–144.

Parker, E. S., Cahill, L., & McGaugh, J. L. (2006). A case of unusual autobiographical remembering. *Neurocase, 12,* 35–49.

Parker, R. S. (1996). The spectrum of emotional distress and personality changes after minor head injury incurred in a motor vehicle accident. *Brain Injury, 10,* 287–302.

Parker, S. T., & McKinney, M. L. (1999). *Origins of intelligence: The evolution of cognitive development in monkeys, apes, and humans.* Baltimore, MD: Johns Hopkins University Press.

Participation in education: Undergraduate education. (n.d.). Retrieved from http://nces.ed.gov/programs/coe/2010/section1/indicator07.asp

Pascual-Leone, A. (2001). The brain that plays music and is changed by it. *Annals of the New York Academy of Sciences, 930,* 315–329.

Patchin, J. W., & Hinduja, S. (2006). Bullies move beyond the schoolyard: A preliminary look at cyberbullying. *Youth Violence and Juvenile Justice, 4,* 148–169.

Patil, S. T., Zhang, L., Martenyi, F., Lowe, S. L., Jackson, K. A., Andreev, B. V., . . . Schoepp, D. (2007). Activation of mGlu2/3 receptors as a new approach to treat schizophrenia: A randomized Phase 2 clinical trial. *Nature Medicine, 13,* 1102–1107. doi:10.1038/nm1632

Patterson, C. J. (2008). *Child development.* New York, NY: McGraw-Hill.

Patterson, D. R. (2004). Treating pain with hypnosis. *Current Directions in Psychological Science, 13,* 252–255.

Paul, E. S., Harding, E. J., & Mendl, M. (2005). Measuring emotional processes in animals: The utility of a cognitive approach. *Neuroscience and Biobehavioral Reviews, 29,* 469–491.

Paulesu, E., Frith, C. D., & Frackowiak, R. S. J. (1993). The neural correlates of the verbal component of working memory. *Nature, 362,* 342–345.

Paulozzi, L. J. (2006). Opioid analgesia involvement in drug abuse deaths in American metropolitan areas. *American Journal of Public Health, 96,* 1755–1757.

Paus, T., Keshavan, M., & Giedd, J. N. (2008). Why do many psychiatric disorders emerge during adolescence? *Nature Reviews Neuroscience, 9,* 947–957.

Pavlov, I. P. (1906). The scientific investigation of the psychical faculties or processes in the higher animals. *Science, 24,* 613–619.

Pavlov, I. P. (1928). *Lectures on conditioned reflexes: Twenty-five years of objective study of the higher nervous activity (behaviour) of animals* (W. H. Gantt, Trans.). New York, NY: Liveright.

Payne, J. D., & Kensinger, E. A. (2010). Sleep's role in the consolidation of emotional episodic memories. *Current Directions in Psychological Science, 19*(5), 290–295. doi:10.1177/0963721410383978

Payne, J. D., & Nadel, L. (2004). Sleep, dreams, and memory consolidation: The role of the stress hormone cortisol. *Learning & Memory, 11,* 671–678.

Pearson, J. D., Morrell, C. H., Gordon-Salant, S., Brant, L. J., Metter, E. J., Klein, L., & Fozard, J. L. (1995). Gender differences in a longitudinal study of age-associated hearing loss. *Journal of the Acoustical Society of America, 97,* 1197–1205. doi:10.1121/1.412231

Pearson, N. J., Johnson, L. L., & Nahin, R. L. (2006). Insomnia, trouble sleeping, and complementary and alternative medicine: Analysis of the 2002 National Health Interview Survey data. *Archives of Internal Medicine, 166,* 1775–1782.

Peckham, P. H., Keith, M. W., Kilgore, K. L., Grill, J. H., Wuolle, K. S., Thrope, G. B., . . . Wiegner, A. (2001). Efficacy of an implanted neuroprosthesis for restoring hand grasp in tetraplegia: A multicenter study. *Archives of Physical Medicine and Rehabilitation, 82,* 1380–1388.

The peculiar institution. (2002). [Editorial]. *Scientific American, 286,* 8.

Pedersen, D. M., & Wheeler, J. (1983). The Müller–Lyer illusion among Navajos. *Journal of Social Psychology, 121,* 3–6.

Peigneux, P., Laureys, S., Fuchs, S., Collette, F., Perrin, F., Reggers, J., . . . Maquet, P. (2004). Are spatial memories strengthened in the human hippocampus during slow wave sleep? *Neuron, 44,* 535–545. doi:10.1016/j.neuron.2004.10.007

Pelli, D. G., Farell, B., & Moore, D. C. (2003). The remarkable inefficiency of word recognition. *Nature, 423,* 752–756.

Penfield, W., & Milner, B. (1958). Memory deficit produced by bilateral lesions in the hippocampal zone. *Archives of Neurology & Psychiatry (Chicago), 79,* 475–497.

Pennebaker, J. W. (1995). *Emotion, disclosure, and health.* Washington, DC: American Psychological Association.

Pennebaker, J. W., Kiecolt-Glaser, J. K., & Glaser, R. (1988). Disclosure of traumas and immune function: Implications for psychotherapy. *Journal of Consulting and Clinical Psychology, 56,* 239–245.

Peper, J. S., Schnack, H. G., Brouwer, R. M., Van Baal, G. C. M., . . . Pol, H. E. H. (2009). Heritability of regional and global brain structure at the onset of puberty: A magnetic resonance imaging study in 9-year-old twin pairs. *Human Brain Mapping, 30,* 2184–2196.

Pereira, A. C. Huddleston, D. E., Brickman, A. M., Sosunov, A. A., Hen, R., McKhann, G. M. . .Small, S.A. (2007). An *in vivo* correlate of exercise induced neurogenesis in the adult dentate gyrus. *Proceedings of the National Academy of Sciences, 104,* 5638–5643.

Pérez-Álvarez, M., García-Montes, J. M., Perona-Garcelán, S., & Vallina-Fernández, O. (2008). Changing relationship with voices: New therapeutic perspectives for treating hallucinations. *Clinical Psychology and Psychotherapy, 15,* 75–85.

Perrin, J. S., Leonard, G., Perron, M., Pike, G. B., Pitiot, A., Richer, L., . . . Paus, T. (2009). Sex differences in the growth of white matter during adolescence, *NeuroImage, 45,* 1055–1066.

Perry, B. D. (2002). Childhood experience and the expression of genetic potential: What childhood neglect tells us about nature and nurture. *Brain and Mind, 3,* 79–100.

Perry, R., & Zeki, S. (2000). The neurology of saccades and covert shifts in spatial attention: An event-related fMRI study. *Brain, 123,* 2273–2288.

Persky, H., Dreisbach, L., Miller, W. R., O'Brien, C. P., Khan, M. A., Lief, H. I., . . . Strauss, D. (1982). The relation of plasma androgen levels to sexual behaviors and attitudes of women. *Psychosomatic Medicine, 44,* 305–319.

Persky, H., Lief, H. I., Strauss, D., Miller, W. R., & O'Brien, C. P. (1978). Plasma testosterone level and sexual behavior of couples. *Archives of Sexual Behavior, 7,* 157–173.

Pessoa, L. (2008). On the relationship between emotion and cognition. *Nature Reviews Neuroscience, 9,* 148–158.

Pessoa, L., Padmala, S., & Morland, T. (2005). Fate of unattended fearful faces in the amygdala is determined by both attentional resources and cognitive modulation. *NeuroImage, 28,* 249–255.

Peter, J., Valkenburg, P. M., & Schouten, A. P. (2005). Developing a model of adolescent friendship formation on the Internet. *CyberPsychology & Behavior, 8,* 423–430.

Peters, R. M., Hackeman, E., & Goldreich, D. (2009). Diminutive digits discern delicate details: Fingertip size and the sex difference in tactile spatial acuity. *The Journal of Neuroscience, 29,* 15756–15761.

Petrie, K. J., Fontanilla, I., Thomas, M. G., Booth, R. J., & Pennebaker, J. W. (2004). Effect of written emotional expression on immune function in patients with human immunodeficiency virus infection: A randomized trial. *Psychosomatic Medicine, 66,* 272–275.

Petronis, A. (2004). Schizophrenia, neurodevelopment, and epigenetics. In M. S. Keshavan, J. L. Kennedy, & R. M. Murray (Eds.), *Neurodevelopment and schizophrenia* (pp. 174–190). New York, NY: Cambridge University Press.

Petry, S., Cummings, J. L., Hill, M. A., & Shapiro, J. (1989). Personality alterations in dementia of the Alzheimer type: A three-year follow-up study. *Journal of Geriatric Psychiatry and Neurology, 2,* 203–207.

Pfrieger, F. W. (2002). Role of glia in synapse development. *Current Opinion in Neurobiology, 12,* 496–490.

Phan, K. L., Wager, T., Taylor, S. F., & Liberzon, I. (2002). Functional neuroanatomy of emotion: A meta-analysis of emotion activation studies in PET and fMRI. *NeuroImage, 16,* 331–348.

Phelps, E. A. (2006). Emotion and cognition: Insights from the study of the human amygdala. *Annual Review of Psychology, 57,* 27–53.

Phelps, E. A., & LeDoux, J. E. (2005). Contributions of the amygdala to emotional processing: From animal models to human behavior. *Neuron, 48,* 175–187.

Phelps, E. A., & Sharot, T. (2008). How (and why) emotion enhances the subjective sense of recollection. *Current Directions in Psychological Science, 17,* 147–152.

Piaget, J. (1954). *The construction of reality in the child.* New York, NY: Basic.

Piaget, J. (1962). *Plays, dreams and imitation in childhood.* New York, NY: Norton.

Piaget, J. (1972a). Intellectual evolution from adolescence to adulthood. *Human Development, 15,* 1–12.

Piaget, J. (1972b). *The child's conception of the world.* Totowa, NJ: Littlefield, Adams.

Piaget, J., & Inhelder, B. (1967). *The child's conception of space.* New York, NY: Norton.

Pierce, T. (2009). Social anxiety and technology: Face-to-face communication versus technological communication among teens. *Computers in Human Behavior, 25,* 1367–1372.

Pincus, J. H. (1999). Aggression, criminality, and the frontal lobes. In B. L. Miller & J. L. Cummings (Eds.), *The human frontal lobes: Functions and disorders* (pp. 547–556). New York, NY: Guilford Press.

Pincus, J. H. (2001). *Base instincts: What makes killers kill?* New York, NY: Norton.

Pinker, S. (1994). *The language instinct: How the mind creates language.* New York, NY: HarperPerennial.

Pinker, S. (2002). *The blank slate.* New York, NY: Viking.

Pinker, S. (2004, Fall). Why nature and nurture won't go away. *Daedalus,* 1–13.

Pinsker, H. M., Hening, W. A., Carew, T. J., & Kandel, E. R. (1973). Long-term sensitization of a defensive withdrawal reflex in *Aplysia. Science, 182,* 1039–1042.

Platsidou, M. (2010). Trait emotional intelligence of Greek special education teachers in relation to burnout and job satisfaction. *School Psychology International, 31,* 60–76.

Pliner, P. (1982). The effects of mere exposure on liking for edible substances. *Appetite, 3,* 283–290.

Plomin, R., & Caspi, A. (1999). Behavioral genetics and personality. In L. A. Pervin & O. P. John (Eds.), *Handbook of personality theory and research* (pp. 251–276). New York, NY: Guilford Press.

Plomin, R., & Petrill, S. A. (1997). Genetics and intelligence: What's new? *Intelligence, 24,* 53–77.

Plunkett, K. (1997). Theories of early language acquisition. *Trends in Cognitive Sciences, 1,* 146–153.

Pohlmeyer, E. A., Oby, E. R., Perreault, E. J., Solla, S. A. Kilgore, K. L., Kirsch, R. F., & Miller, L. E. (2009). Toward the restoration of hand use to a paralyzed monkey: Brain-controlled functional electrical stimulation of forearm muscles. *PLoS ONE, 4,* e5924. doi:10.1371/journal.pone.0005924

Polanczyk, G., de Lima, M. S., Horta, B. L., Biederman J., & Rohde, L. A. (2007). The worldwide prevalence of ADHD: A systematic review and metaregression analysis. *American Journal of Psychiatry, 164,* 942–948.

Poldrack, R. A., & Foerde, K. (2008). Category learning and the memory systems debate. *Neuroscience and Biobehavioral Reviews, 32,* 197–205.

Popper, K. (1965). *Conjectures and refutations: The growth of scientific knowledge.* New York, NY: Harper.

Porfeli, E. J., & Skorikov, V. B. (2010). Specific and diverse career exploration during late adolescence. *Journal of Career Assessment, 18,* 46–58.

Posner, M. I., & Rothbart, M. K. (2007). Research on attention networks as a model for the integration of psychological science. *Annual Review of Psychology, 58,* 1–23.

Post, R. M., Frye, M. A., Denicoff, K. D., Leverich, G. S., Kimbrell, T. A., & Dunn, R. T. (1998). Beyond lithium in the treatment of bipolar illness. *Neuropsychopharmacology, 19,* 206–219.

Potkin, S. G., Saha, A. R., Kujawa, M. J., Carson, W. H., Ali, M., Stock, E., . . . Marder, S. R. (2003). Ariprazole, an antipsychotic with a novel mechanism of action, and risperidone vs placebo in patients with schizophrenia and schizoaffective disorder. *Archives of General Psychiatry, 60,* 681–690.

Potter, J. W. (1987). Does television viewing hinder academic achievement among adolescents? *Human Communication Research, 14,* 27–46.

Powell, L. H., Kazlauskaite, R., Shima, C., & Appelhans, B. M. (2010). Lifestyle in France and the United States: An American perspective. *Journal of the American Dietetic Association, 10,* 845–847.

Powers, M., Halpern, J., Ferenschak, M., Gillihan, S., & Foa, E. (2010). A meta-analytic review of prolonged exposure for posttraumatic stress disorder. *Clinical Psychology Review, 30,* 635–641. doi:10.1016/j.cpr.2010.04.007

Prahbu, V., Sutton, C., & Sauser, W. (2008). Creativity and certain personality traits: Understanding the mediating effect of intrinsic motivation. *Creativity Research Journal, 20,* 53–66.

Preckel, F., Holling, H., & Wiese, M. (2006). Relationship of intelligence and creativity in gifted and non-gifted students: An investigation of threshold theory. *Personality and Individual Differences, 40,* 159–170.

Premack, D. (1971). Language in chimpanzees? *Science, 172,* 808–822.

Price, J. (2008). *The woman who can't forget: A memoir.* New York, NY: Free Press.

The prize in economics, 2002. (2002). Retrieved November 15, 2006, from http://nobelprize.org/nobel_prizes/economics/laureates/2002/press.html

Prochaska, J. O., & Norcross, J. C. (2007). *Systems of psychotherapy* (6th ed.). Belmont, CA: Wadsworth.

Profet, M. (1992). Pregnancy sickness as adaptation: A deterrent to maternal ingestion of teratogens. In J. Barkow, L. Cosmides, & J. Tooby (Eds.), *The adapted mind* (pp. 327–365). New York, NY: Oxford University Press.

Ptito, M., & Desgent, S. (2006). Sensory input-based adaptation and brain architecture. In P. B. Baltes, P. A. Reuter-Lorenz, & F. Rösler (Eds.), *Lifespan development and the brain: The perspective of biocultural coconstructivism* (pp. 111–133). New York, NY: Cambridge University Press.

Pugh, M. J. V., & Hart, D. (1999). Identity development and peer group participation. In J. A. McLellan & M. J. V. Pugh (Eds.), *The role of peer groups in adolescent social identity: Exploring the importance of stability and change* (pp. 55–70). San Francisco, CA: Jossey-Bass.

Pulver, C. A., & Kelly, K. R. (2008). Incremental validity of the Myers-Briggs Type Indicator in predicting academic major selection of undecided university students. *Journal of Career Assessment, 16,* 441–455.

Purves, D., & Lichtman, J. W. (1985). *Principles of neural development.* Sunderland, MA: Sinauer.

Putnam, F. W. (2006). Dissociative disorders. In D. Cicchetti & D. J. Cohen (Eds.), *Developmental psychopathology: Vol. 3. Risk, disorder, and adaptation* (pp. 657–695). Hoboken, NJ: John Wiley.

Putnam, F., & McHugh, P. (2005). Issue 3: Is multiple personality disorder a valid diagnosis? In R. P. Halgin (Ed.), *Taking sides: Clashing views on controversial issues in abnormal psychology* (3rd ed., pp. 42–53). New York, NY: McGraw-Hill.

Qiu, J., Li, H., Jou, J., Liu, J. Yeujia, L., Feng, T., . . . Zhang, Q. (2010). Neural correlates of the "aha" experiences: Evidence from an fMRI study of insight problem solving. *Cortex, 46,* 397–403.

Quiroga, R. Q., Reddy, L., Kreiman, G., Koch, C., & Fried, I. (2005). Invariant visual representation by single neurons in the human brain. *Nature, 435,* 1102–1107.

Radford, A. (1997). *Syntactic theory and the structure of English: A minimalist approach.* New York, NY: Cambridge University Press.

Raffaele, P. (2006, November). Speaking bonobo. *Smithsonian.* Retrieved from http://www.smithsonianmagazine.com

Rahman, Q. (2005). The neurodevelopment of human sexual orientation. *Neuroscience and Biobehavioral Reviews, 29,* 1057–1066.

Rahn, E. J., & Hohmann, A. G. (2009). Cannabinoids as pharmacotherapies for neuropathic pain: From the bench to the bedside. *Neurotherapeutics, 6,* 713–737.

Raij, T. T., Numminen, J., Närvänen, S., Hiltunen, J., & Hari, R. (2005). Brain correlates of subjective reality of physically and psychologically induced pain. *Proceedings of the National Academy of Sciences, 102,* 2147–2151.

Raleigh, M. J., McGuire, M. T., Brammer, G. L., Pollack, D. B., & Yuwiler, A. (1991). Serotonergic mechanisms promote dominance in adult male vervet monkeys. *Brain Research, 559,* 181–190.

Ramachandran, V. S., & Hubbard, E. M. (2003, May). Hearing colors, tasting shapes. *Scientific American, 288,* 52–59.

Ramachandran, V. S., & Oberman, L. M. (2006). Broken mirrors: A theory of autism. *Scientific American, 295,* 63–69.

Ramanathan, L., Gulyani, S., Nienhuis, R., & Siegel, J. M. (2002). Sleep deprivation decreases superoxide dismutase activity in rat hippocampus and brainstem. *Neuro-Report, 13,* 1387–1390.

Ransdell, S. (2010). Online activity, motivation, and reasoning among adult learners. *Computers in Human Behavior, 26,* 70–73. doi:10.1016/j.chb.2009.09.002

Rao, V., Spiro, J. R., Handel, S., & Onyike, C. U. (2008). Clinical correlates of personality changes associated with traumatic brain injury. *Journal of Neuropsychiatry and Clinical Neurosciences, 20,* 118–119.

Rashid, T. (2008). Positive psychotherapy. In S. J. Lopez (Ed.), *Positive psychology: Exploring the best in people, Vol. 4: Pursuing human flourishing* (pp. 188–217). Westport, CT: Praeger/Greenwood.

Rathus, J. H., Cavuoto, N., & Passarelli, V. (2006). Dialectical behavior therapy (DBT): A mindfulness-based treatment for intimate partner violence. In R. A. Baer (Ed.), *Mindfulness-based treatment approaches: Clinician's guide to evidence base and applications* (pp. 333–358). San Diego, CA: Elsevier Academic Press.

Raymaekers, L., Smeets, T., Peters, M., & Merckelbach, H. (2010). Autobiographical memory specificity among people with recovered memories of childhood sexual abuse. *Journal of Behavior Therapy and Experimental Psychiatry, 41,* 338–344. doi:10.1016/j.jbtep.2010.03.004

Raz, A., Fan, J., & Posner, M. I. (2005). Hypnotic suggestion reduces conflict in the human brain. *Proceedings of the National Academy of Sciences, 102,* 9978–9983.

Raz, A., & Shapiro, T. (2002). Hypnosis and neuroscience. *Archives of General Psychiatry, 59,* 85–90.

Raz, N. (2000). Aging of the brain and its impact on cognitive performance: Integration of structural and functional findings. In F. I. M. Craik & T. A. Salthouse (Eds.), *The handbook of aging and cognition* (pp. 1–90). Mahwah, NJ: Erlbaum.

Read, J. P., Beattie, M., Chamberlain, R., & Merrill, J. E. (2008). Beyond the "binge" threshold: Heavy drinking patterns and their association with alcohol involvement indices in college students. *Addictive Behaviors, 33,* 225–234.

Ready, D. J., Gerardi, R. J., Backscheider, A. G., Mascaro, N., & Rothbaum, B. O. (2010). Comparing virtual reality exposure therapy to present-centered therapy with 11 U. S. Vietnam veterans with PTSD. *Cyberpsychology, Behavior, and Social Networking, 13,* 49–54. doi:10.1089/cyber.2009.0239

Redmond, J., & Shulman, M. (2008). Access to psychoanalytic ideas in American undergraduate institutions. *Journal of the American Psychoanalytic Association, 56,* 391–408. doi:10.1177/0003065108318639

Reed, C., Novick, D., Gonzalez-Pinto, A., Bertsch, J., & Haro, J. (2009). Observational study designs for bipolar disorder—What can they tell us about treatment in acute mania? *Progress in Neuro-Psychopharmacology & Biological Psychiatry, 33,* 715–721. doi:10.1016/j.pnpbp.2009.03.024

Reed, G. M., Kemeny, M. E., Taylor, S. E., Wang, H. Y. J., & Visscher, B. R. (1994). Realistic acceptance as a predictor of decreased survival time in gay men with AIDS. *Health Psychology, 13,* 299–307.

Refinetti, R. (2006). *Circadian physiology* (2nd ed.). Boca Raton, FL: CRC Press.

Regier, T., & Kay, P. (2009). Language, thought, and color: Whorf was half right. *Trends in Cognitive Sciences, 13,* 439–446.

Regier, T., Kay, P., Gilbert, A., & Ivry, R. (2010). Language and thought: Which side are you on, anyway?. In B. C. Malt & P. Wolff (Eds.), *Words and the mind: How words capture human experience* (pp. 165–182). New York, NY: Oxford University Press.

Reimagining the tragic mulatto. (2010, March 2). [Radio broadcast transcript]. Retrieved from http://www.npr.org/templates/transcript/transcript.php?storyId=124244813

Remafedi, G., Resnick, M., Blum, R., & Harris, L. (1992). Demography of sexual orientation in adolescents. *Pediatrics, 89,* 714–721.

Renaud, S., & de Lorgeril, M. (1992). Wine, alcohol, platelets, and the French paradox for coronary heart disease. *Lancet, 339,* 1523–1526.

Renshaw, K. D. (2011). Working with the new generation of service members/veterans from Operations Enduring and Iraqi Freedom. *Cognitive and Behavioral Practice, 18,* 82–84. doi:10.1016/j.cbpra.2010.03.003

Retz, W., Reif, A., Freitag, C., Retz-Junginger, P., & Rösler, M. (2010). Association of a functional variant of neuronal nitric oxide synthase gene with self-reported impulsiveness, venturesomeness and empathy in male offenders. *Journal of Neural Transmission, 117,* 321–324.

Rexrode, K. M., Buring, J. E., & Manson, J. E. (2001). Abdominal and total adiposity and risk of coronary heart disease in men. *International Journal of Obesity, 25,* 1047–1056.

Rexrode, K. M., Carey, V. J., Hennekens, C. H., Walters, E. E., Colditz, G. A., Stampfer, M. J., . . . Manson, J. E. (1998). Abdominal adiposity and coronary heart disease in women. *Journal of the American Medical Association, 280,* 1843–1848. doi:10.1001/jama.280.21.1843

Reynolds, C. R. (2000). Why is psychometric research on bias in mental testing so often ignored? *Psychology, Public Policy, and Law, 6,* 144–150.

Reynolds, S., & Lane, S. J. (2008). Diagnostic validity of sensory over-responsivity: A review of the literature and case reports. *Journal of Autism and Developmental Disorders, 38,* 516–529.

Rhoades, G. K., Stanley, S. M., & Markman, H. J. (2009). The pre-engagement cohabitation effect: A replication and extension of previous findings. *Journal of Family Psychology, 23,* 107–111.

Ricciardelli, L. A. (1992). Creativity and bilingualism. *Journal of Creative Behavior, 26,* 242–254.

Rice, C. (2007). Prevalence of autism spectrum disorders: Autism and developmental disabilities monitoring network, six sites, United States, 2000. *Morbidity and Mortality Weekly Report, CDC, 56,* 1–11.

Rice, M. L. (1989). Children's language acquisition. *American Psychologist, 44,* 149–156.

Richards, J. E., Reynolds, G. D., & Courage, M. L. (2010). The neural basis of infant attention. *Current Directions in Psychological Science, 19,* 41–46.

Richards, R. L. (1994). Creativity and bipolar mood swings: Why the association? In M. P. Shaw & M. A. Runco (Eds.), *Creativity and affect* (pp. 44–72). Norwood, NJ: Ablex.

Richards, R. L., & Kinney, D. K. (1990). Mood swings and creativity. *Creativity Research Journal, 3,* 202–217.

Richardson, J. D., Huddy, W. P., & Morgan, S. M. (2008). The hostile media effect, biased assimilation, and perceptions of a presidential debate. *Journal of Applied Social Psychology, 38,* 1255–1270. doi:10.1111/j.1559-1816.2008.00347.x

Richtel, M. (2010, August 16). Outdoors and out of reach, studying the brain. *The New York Times.* Retrieved from http://www.nytimes.com

Ridley, M. (2003). *Nature via nurture: Genes, experience, and what makes us human.* New York, NY: HarperCollins.

Ries, M., & Marks, W. (2005). Selective attention deficits following severe closed head injury: The role of inhibitory processes. *Neuropsychology, 19,* 476–481.

Rinpoche, S. (1992). *The Tibetan book of living and dying.* New York, NY: HarperCollins.

Risch, N., Herrell, R., Lehner, T., Liang, K-Y., Eaves, L., Hoh, J., . . . Mirerikangas, K. R. (2009). Interaction between the serotonin transporter gene (*5-HTTLPR*), stressful life events, and risk of depression: A meta-analysis. *Journal of the American Medical Association, 301,* 2462–2471.

Riva, G. (2009). Virtual reality: An experiential tool for clinical psychology. *British Journal of Guidance & Counselling, 37,* 337–345. doi:10.1080/03069880902957056

Rizvi, S., Kennedy, S. H., McNeely, H., Giacobbe, P., Mayberg, H. S., & Lozano, A. M. (2009). Functional outcome after 12 months of deep brain stimulation for treatment resistant major depressive disorder. *European Neuropsychopharmacology, 19,* S388–S389.

Rizzolatti, G., & Arbibb, M. A. (1998). Language within our grasp. *Trends in Neuroscience, 21,* 188–194.

Rizzolatti, G., & Craighero, L. (2004). The mirror-neuron system. *Annual Review of Neuroscience, 27,* 169–192.

Rizzolatti, G., Fadiga, L., Fogassi, L., & Gallese, V. (1996). Premotor cortex and the recognition of motor actions. *Brain Research: Cognitive Brain Research, 3,* 131–141.

Roberts, B. W., & Mroczek, D. (2008). Personality trait change in adulthood. *Current Directions in Psychological Science, 17,* 31–35.

Roberts, B. W., Walton, K. E., & Viechtbauer, W. (2006). Patterns of mean-level change in personality traits across the life course: A meta-analysis of longitudinal studies. *Psychological Bulletin, 132,* 1–25.

Robertson, I. (2003). The absent mind: Attention and error. *The Psychologist, 16,* 476–479.

Robinson, D. N. (1995). *An intellectual history of psychology* (3rd ed.). Madison: University of Wisconsin Press.

Robinson, L. A., & Kleseges, R. C. (1997). Ethnic and gender differences in risk factors for smoking onset. *Health Psychology, 16,* 499–505.

Rock, A. (2004). *The mind at night: The new science of how and why we dream.* New York, NY: Basic Books.

Röder, B. (2006). Blindness: A source and case of neuronal plasticity. In P. B. Baltes, P. A. Reuter-Lorenz, & F. Rösler (Eds.), *Lifespan development and the brain* (pp. 134–157). New York, NY: Cambridge University Press.

Roederer, J. (2009). Music and the evolution of human brain function. In R. Haas & V. Brandes (Eds.), *Music that works: Contributions of biology, neurophysiology, psychology, sociology, medicine and musicology* (pp. 195–210). New York, NY: Springer-Wien. doi:10.1007/978-3-211-75121-3_14

Roehr, B. (2007). High rate of PTSD in returning Iraq War veterans. *Medscape Medical News.* Retrieved July 5, 2008, from http://www.medscape.com/viewarticle/565407

Roehrs, T., Zorick, F. J., & Roth, T. (2000). Transient and short-term insomnias. In M. H. Kryger, T. Roth, & W. C. Dement (Eds.), *Principles and practice of sleep medicine.* Philadelphia, PA: Saunders.

Rogelberg, S. G., & Gill, P. M. (2006). The growth of industrial and organizational psychology: Quick facts. Retrieved December 6, 2007, from http://www.siop.org/tip/backissues/july04/05rogelberg.aspx

Rogers, C. R. (1951). *Client-centered counseling.* Boston, MA: Houghton Mifflin.

Rogers, C. R. (1959). A theory of therapy, personality, and interpersonal relationships, as developed in the client-centered framework. In S. Koch (Ed.), *Psychology: A study of a science* (Vol. 3). New York, NY: McGraw-Hill.

Rogers, C. R. (1980). *A way of being.* Boston, MA: Houghton Mifflin.

Rogers, C. R., & Dymond, R. G. (Eds.). (1954). *Psychotherapy and personality change: Co-ordinated research studies in the client-centered approach.* Chicago, IL: University of Chicago Press.

Roid, G. H., & Pomplun, M. (2005). Interpreting the Stanford-Binet Intelligence Scales, fifth edition. In D. P. Flanagan & P. L. Harrison (Eds.), *Contemporary intellectual assessment: Theories, tests, and issues* (pp. 325–343). New York, NY: Guilford Press.

Rolland, J. P. (2002). Cross-cultural generalizability of the Five-Factor Model of personality. In R. R. McCrae & J. Allik (Eds.), *The Five-Factor Model of personality across cultures* (pp. 7–28). New York, NY: Kluwer Academic/Plenum.

Rolls, E. T. (2000). The orbitofrontal cortex and reward. *Cerebral Cortex, 10,* 284–294.

Rolls, E. T. (2004). The functions of the orbitofrontal cortex. *Brain and Cognition, 55,* 11–29.

Rolls, E. T. (2006). Brain mechanisms underlying flavour and appetite. *Philosophical Transactions of the Royal Society of London, 361,* 1123–1136.

Romain, J. (2008). Grand larceny in the first grade: Traumatic brain injury in the school-aged years. In J. N. Apps, R. F. Newby, & L. W. Roberts (Eds.), *Pediatric neuropsychology case studies: From the exceptional to the commonplace* (pp. 23–31). New York: Springer Science.

Rosch, E. (1973). Natural categories. *Cognitive Psychology, 4,* 328–350.

Rosch, E. (1975). Cognitive representations of semantic categories. *Journal of Experimental Psychology: General, 104,* 192–223.

Rose, A. J., Vegiopoulos, A., & Herzig, S. (2010). Role of glucocorticoids and the glucocorticoid receptor in metabolism: Insights from genetic manipulations. *Journal of Steroid Biochemistry & Molecular Biology, 122,* 10–20.

Rosellini, A. J., Lawrence, A. E., Meyer, J. F., & Brown, T. A. (2010). The effects of extraverted temperament on agoraphobia in panic disorder. *Journal of Abnormal Psychology, 119,* 420–426.

Roseman, I. J. (1984). Cognitive determinants of emotion: A structural theory. *Review of Personality & Social Psychology, 5,* 11–36.

Rosen, L. D., Cheever, N. A., Cummings, C., & Felt, J. (2007). The impact of emotionality and self-disclosure on online dating versus traditional dating. *Computers in Human Behavior, 24,* 2124–2157.

Rosenberg, E. L. (1998). Levels of analysis and the organization of affect. *Review of General Psychology, 2,* 247–270.

Rosenberg, E. L. (2005). The study of spontaneous facial expressions in psychology. In P. Ekman & E. L. Rosenberg (Eds.), *What the face reveals: Basic and applied studies of spontaneous expression using the Facial Action Coding System (FACS)* (2nd ed., pp. 3–17). New York, NY: Oxford University Press.

Rosenberg, E. L., & Ekman, P. (1994). Coherence between expressive and experiential systems in emotion. *Cognition & Emotion, 8,* 201–229.

Rosenberg, E. L., & Ekman, P. (2000). Emotion: Methods of study. In A. Kasdan (Ed.), *Encyclopedia of psychology* (pp. 171–175). Washington, DC: American Psychological Association and Oxford University Press.

Rosenberg, E. L., Ekman, P., Jiang, W., Coleman, R. E., Hanson, M., O'Connor, C., . . . Blumenthal, J. A. (2001). Linkages between facial expressions of anger and transient myocardial ischemia in men with coronary artery disease. *Emotion, 1,* 107–115. doi:10.1037/1528-3542.1.2.107

Rosenman, R. H., Brand, J. H., Jenkins, C. D., Friedman, M., Straus, R., & Wurm, M. (1975). Coronary heart disease in the Western Collaborative Group Study: Final follow-up experience of 8.5 years. *JAMA, 233,* 872–877.

Rosenman, R. H., Friedman, M., Straus, R., Wurm, M., Kositchek, R., Hahn, W., & Werthessen, N. T. (1964). A predictive study of coronary artery disease. *Journal of the American Medical Association, 189,* 113–124.

Rosenquist, J. N., Murabito, J., Fowler, J. H., & Christakis, N. A. (2010). The spread of alcohol consumption behavior in a large social network. *Annals of Internal Medicine, 152,* 426–433.

Rosenthal, R. (1976). *Experimenter effects in behavioral research, enlarged edition.* New York: Irvington.

Rosenthal, R. (1986). Meta-analytic procedures and the nature of replication: The debate. *Journal of Parapsychology, 50*(4), 315–336.

Rosenthal, R. (1994). On being one's own case study: Experimenter effects in behavioral research—30 years later. In W. Shadish & S. Fuller (Eds.), *The social psychology of science* (pp. 214–229). New York, NY: Guilford Press.

Rosenthal, R., & Fode, K. L. (1963). The effect of experimenter bias on the performance of the albino rat. *Behavioral Science, 8,* 183–189.

Rosenthal, R., & Rubin, D. B. (1978). Interpersonal expectancy effects: The first 345 studies. *The Behavioral and Brain Sciences, 3,* 377–386.

Rosenzweig, M. R., & Bennett, E. L. (1969). Effects of differential environments on brain weights and enzyme activities in gerbils, rats and mice. *Developmental Psychobiology, 2,* 87–95.

Rosenzweig, M. R., Krech, D., Bennett, E. L., & Diamond, M. C. (1962). Effects of environmental complexity and training on brain chemistry and anatomy: A replication and extension. *Journal of Comparative and Physiological Psychology, 55,* 429–437.

Ross, L. (1977). The intuitive psychologist and his shortcomings: Distortions in the attribution process. In L. Berkowitz (Ed.), *Advances in experimental social psychology* (Vol. 10, pp. 173–220). New York, NY: Academic Press.

Rothbaum, B. O., Cahill, S. P., Foa, E. B., Davidson, J. R. T., Compton, J., Connor, K. M., . . . Hahn, C-G. (2006). Augmentation of sertraline with prolonged exposure in the treatment of posttraumatic stress disorder. *Journal of Traumatic Stress, 19,* 625–638. doi:10.1002/jts.20170

Rothenberg, D. (2005). *Why birds sing: A journey through the mystery of bird song.* New York, NY: Basic Books.

Rowe, G., Hirsch, J. B., & Anderson, A. K. (2007). Positive affect increases the breadth of attentional selection. *Proceedings of the National Academy of Sciences, 104,* 383–388.

Rowland, N. E., Li, B-H., & Morien, A. (1996). Brain mechanisms and the physiology of feeding. In E. D. Capaldi (Ed.), *Why we eat what we eat: The psychology of eating* (pp. 173–204). Washington, DC: American Psychological Association.

Roy, M., Piché, M., Chen, J-I, Peretz, I., & Rainville, P. (2009). Cerebral and spinal modulation of pain by emotions. *Proceedings of the National Academy of Sciences, 106,* 20900–20905.

Rozin, P. (1996). Sociocultural influences on human food selection. In E. D. Capaldi (Ed.), *Why we eat what we eat: The psychology of eating* (pp. 233–263). Washington, DC: American Psychological Association.

Rozin, P., & Fallon, A. E. (1987). Perspectives on disgust. *Psychological Review, 94,* 23–41.

Rozin, P., Haidt, J., & McCauley, C. R. (2000). Disgust. In M. Lewis & J. M. Haviland-Jones (Eds.), *Handbook of emotions* (2nd ed., pp. 637–653). New York, NY: Guilford Press.

Ruan, J. (2004). Bilingual Chinese/English first-graders developing metacognition about writing. *Literacy, 38,* 106–112.

Ruff, H. (1999). Population-based data and the development of individual children: The case of low to moderate lead levels and intelligence. *Journal of Developmental & Behavioral Pediatrics, 20*(1), 42–49.

Rumbaugh, D. M., Beran, M. J., & Savage-Rumbaugh, S. (2003). Language. In D. Maestripieri (Ed.), *Primate psychology* (pp. 395–423). Cambridge, MA: Harvard University Press.

Runyan, W. M. (1981). Why did Van Gogh cut off his ear? The problem of alternative explanations in psychobiography. *Journal of Personality and Social Psychology, 40,* 1070–1077.

Runyan, W. M. (1982). *Life histories and psychobiography.* New York, NY: Oxford University Press.

Rushton, W. A. H. (1961). Rhodopsin measurement and dark adaptation in a subject deficient in cone vision. *Journal of Physiology, 156,* 193–205.

Russell, J. A. (1980). A circumplex model of affect. *Journal of Personality and Social Psychology, 39,* 1161–1178.

Rutherford, G. W., Lifson, A. R., Hessol, N. A., Darrow, W. W., O' Malley, P. M., Buchbinder, S. P., . . . Doll, L. S. (1990). Course of HIV-1 infection in a cohort of homosexual and bisexual men: An 11-year follow-up study. *British Medical Journal, 301,* 1183–1188. doi: 10.1136/bmj.301.6762.1183

Rutter, M. (2002). Nature, nurture, and development: From evangelism through science toward policy and practice. *Child Development, 73,* 1–21.

Rutter, M. (2005). Incidence of autism disorders: Changes over time and their meaning. *Acta Paediatrica, 94,* 2–15.

Rutter, M. (2006). *Genes and behavior: Nature–nurture interplay explained.* Malden, MA: Blackwell.

Ruzgis, P. M., & Grigorenko, E. L. (1994). Cultural meaning systems, intelligence and personality. In R. J. Sternberg & P. Ruzgis (Eds.), *Personality and intelligence* (pp. 248–270). New York, NY: Cambridge University Press.

Ryan, G., Baerwald, J., & McGlone, G. (2008). Cognitive mediational deficits and the role of coping styles in pedophile and ephebophile Roman Catholic clergy. *Journal of Clinical Psychology, 64,* 1–16.

Rymer, R. (1993). *Genie: A scientific tragedy.* New York, NY: HarperPerennial.

Saarni, C. (1984). An observational study of children's attempts to monitor their expressive behavior. *Child Development, 55,* 1504–1513.

Saarni, C. (1999). *The development of emotional competence.* New York, NY: Guilford Press.

Sabbagh, L. (2006, August/September). The teen brain, hard at work: No, really. *Scientific American Mind, 17,* 21–25.

Sacco, R. L., Elkind, M., Boden-Albala, B., Lin, I-F., Kargman, D. E., Hause, W. A., . . . Paik, M. C. (1999). The protective effect of moderate alcohol consumption on ischemic stroke. *Journal of American Medical Association, 281,* 53–60. doi:10.1001/jama.281.1.53

Sackeim, H. A., Greenberg, M. S., Weiman, A. L., Gur, R. C., Hungerbuhler, J. P., & Geschwind, N. (1982). Hemispheric asymmetry in the expression of positive and negative emotions: Neurologic evidence. *Archives in Neurology, 39,* 210–218.

Sackeim, H. A., Prudic, J., Devanand, D. P., Kiersky, J. E., Fitzsimons, L., Moody, B. J., et al. (1993). Effects of stimulus intensity and electrode placement on the efficacy and cognitive effects of electroconvulsive therapy. *New England Journal of Medicine, 328,* 839–846.

Sagan, C. (1987). The burden of skepticism. *Skeptical Inquirer, 12,* 38–46.

Sahdra, B. K., MacLean, K. A., Ferrer, E., Shaver, P. R., Rosenberg, E. L., Jacobs, T. L., . . . Saron, C. D. (2011). Enhanced response inhibition during intensive meditation training predicts improvements in self-reported adaptive socio-emotional functioning. *Emotion, 11,* 299–312.

Saisan, J., Smith, M., & Segal, J. (2010, May). Psychotherapy and counseling: Finding a therapist and getting the most out of therapy. Retrieved September 10, 2010 at http://www.helpguide.org/mental/psychotherapy_therapist_counseling.htm

Sakai, K. (2005). Language acquisition and brain development. *Science, 310,* 815–819.

Sallinen, M., Holm, A., Hiltunen, J., Hirvonen, K., Härmä, M., Koskelo, J., . . . Müller, K. (2008). Recovery of cognitive performance from sleep debt: Do a short rest pause and a single recovery night help? *Chronobiology International, 25,* 279–296. doi:10.1080/07420520802107106

Salovey, P., & Mayer, J. D. (1990). Emotional intelligence. *Imagination, Cognition, and Personality, 9,* 185–211.

Salthouse, T. A. (2000). Steps toward the explanation of adult differences in cognition. In T. J. Perfect & E. A. Maylor (Eds.), *Models of cognitive aging* (pp. 19–49). Oxford, England: Oxford University Press.

Sanders, L. (2009). Single brain cells selectively fire in response to specific thoughts: Thinking about her face activates "Halle Berry" neuron. *Science News, 176,* 9. doi:10.1002/scin.5591761107

Santrock, J. W. (2010). *A topical approach to life-span development* (5th ed.). New York, NY: McGraw-Hill.

Sapolsky, R. (1998). *Why zebras don't get ulcers: An updated guide to stress, stress-related disease and coping.* New York, NY: Freeman.

Sarlio-Lähteenkorva, S. (2001). Weight loss and quality of life among obese people. *Social Indicators Research, 54*(3), 329–354.

Sauter, D. A., Eisner, F., Ekman, P., & Scott, S. K. (2010). Cross-cultural recognition of basic emotions through nonverbal emotional vocalizations. *Proceedings of the National Academy of Sciences, 107,* 2408–2412.

Sava, F. A., Yates, B. T., Lupu, V., Szentagotai, A., & David, D. (2009). Cost-effectiveness and cost-utility of cognitive therapy, rational emotive behavioral therapy, and fluoxetine (Prozac) in treating depression: A randomized clinical trial. *Journal of Clinical Psychology, 65,* 36–52.

Sawyer, R. K. (2006). *Explaining creativity: The science of human innovation.* New York, NY: Oxford University Press.

Scarr, S. (1981). *Race, social class, and individual differences in I.Q.* Hillsdale, NJ: Erlbaum.

Schaal, B., Marlier, L., & Soussignan, R. (2002). Human fetuses learn odors from their pregnant mother's diet. *Chemical Senses, 25,* 729–737.

Schacter, D. L. (2001). *The seven sins of memory.* Boston, MA: Houghton Mifflin.

Schacter, D. L., & Tulving, E. (1994). *Memory systems.* Cambridge, MA: MIT Press.

Schaefer, E. J., Gleason, J. A., & Dansinger, M. L. (2005). The effects of low-fat, high-carbohydrate diets on plasma lipoproteins, weight loss, and heart disease risk reduction. *Current Atherosclerosis Reports, 7,* 421–427.

Schaie, K. W. (1996). *Intellectual development in adulthood: The Seattle Longitudinal Study.* New York, NY: Cambridge University Press.

Schellenberg, E. G. (2004). Music lessons enhance IQ. *Psychological Science, 15,* 511–514.

Schellenberg, E. G. (2006). Long-term positive associations between music lessons and

IQ. *Journal of Educational Psychology, 98,* 457–468.

Scherer, K. R., Banse, R., & Wallbott, H. G. (2001). Emotion inferences from vocal expression correlate across languages and cultures. *Journal of Cross-Cultural Psychology, 32,* 76–92.

Scherer, K. R., Banse, R., Wallbott. H. G., & Goldbeck, T. (1991). Vocal cues in emotion coding and decoding. *Motivation and Emotion, 15,* 123–148.

Scherer, K. R., Dan, E., & Flykt, A. (2006). What determines a feeling's position in affective space? A case for appraisal. *Cognition & Emotion, 20,* 92–113.

Schienle, A., Schäfer, A., & Vaitl, D. (2008). Individual differences in disgust imagery: A functional magnetic resonance imaging study. *NeuroReport, 19,* 527–530.

Schlaug, G., Jäncke, L., Huang, Y., Staiger, J. F., & Steinmetz H. (1995). Increased corpus callosum size in musicians. *Neuropsychologia, 33,* 1047–1055.

Schlehofer, M. M., Thompson, S. C., Ting, S., Ostermann, S., Nierman, A., & Skenderian, J. (2010). Psychological predictors of college students' cell phone use while driving. *Accident Analysis and Prevention, 42,* 1107–1112. doi:10.1016/j.aap.2009.12.024

Schmand, B., Smit, J., Lindeboom, J., Smits, C., Hooijer, C., Jonker, C., & Deelman, B. (1997). Low education is a genuine risk factor for accelerated memory decline and dementia. *Journal of Clinical Epidemiology, 50,* 1025–1033.

Schmidt, M. E., & Vandewater, E. A. (2008). Media and attention, cognition, and school achievement. *The Future of Children, 18,* 63–85.

Schmithorst, V. J., Holland, S. K., & Dardzinski, B. J. (2008). Developmental differences in white matter architecture between boys and girls. *Human Brain Mapping, 29,* 696–710.

Schneider, J. A., Arvanitakis, Z., Bang, W., & Bennett, D. A. (2007). Mixed brain pathologies account for most dementia cases in community-dwelling older persons. *Neurology, 69,* 2197–2204.

Schneider, L. (n.d.). Apple, Inc. Retrieved from http://jobsearchtech.about.com/od/companyprofiles/p/AppleComputer.htm

Schuldberg, D. (1990). Schizotypal and hypomanic traits, creativity, and psychological health. *Creativity Research Journal, 3,* 218–230.

Schuldberg, D. (2000–2001). Six subclinical spectrum traits in normal creativity. *Creativity Research Journal, 13,* 5–16.

Schuler, J. L. H., & O' Brien, W. H. (1997). Cardiovascular recovery from stress and hypertension risk factors: A meta-analytic review. *Psychophysiology, 34,* 649–659.

Schulkin, J. (Ed.). (2005). *Allostasis, homeostasis, and the costs of physiological adaptation.* New York, NY: Cambridge University Press.

Schultz, W. T. (2005). *Handbook of psychobiography.* New York, NY: Oxford University Press.

Schutte, C., & Hanks, R. (2010). Impact of the presence of alcohol at the time of injury on acute and one-year cognitive and functional recovery after traumatic brain injury. *International Journal of Neuroscience, 120,* 551–556.

Schutte, N. S., Malouff, J. M., Thorsteinsson, E. B., Bhullar, N., & Rooke, S. E. (2007). A meta-analytic investigation of the relationship between emotional intelligence and health. *Personality and Individual Differences, 42,* 921–933.

Schutte, N. S., Thorsteinsson, E. B., Hine, D. W., Foster, R., Cauchi, A., & Binns, C. (2010). Experiential and rational processing styles, emotional intelligence and well-being. *Australian Journal of Psychology, 62,* 14–19.

Schwartz, G. M., Izard, C. E., & Ansul, S. E. (1985). The 5-month-old's ability to discriminate facial expressions of emotion. *Infant Behavior and Development, 8,* 65–77.

Schwartz, J. H. (2000). Neurotransmitters. In E. R. Kandel, J. M. Schwartz, & T. M. Jessell (Eds.), *Principles of neural science* (4th ed., pp. 280–297). New York, NY: McGraw-Hill.

Schwartz, J. M. (1999a). A role for volition and attention in the generation of new brain circuitry: Toward a neurobiology of mental force. *Journal of Consciousness Studies, 6,* 115–142.

Schwartz, J. M. (1999b). First steps toward a theory of mental force: PET imaging of systematic cerebral changes after psychological treatment of obsessive-compulsive disorder. In S. R. Hameroff, A. W. Kaszniak, & D. J. Chalmers (Eds.), *Toward a science of consciousness III: The third Tucson discussions and debates.* Boston, MA: MIT Press.

Schwerdtfeger, A. (2007). Individual differences in auditory, pain, and motor stimulation. *Journal of Individual Differences, 28,* 165–177.

Scott, J. (2000). Rational choice theory. In G. Browning, A. Halcli, & F. Webster (Eds.), *Understanding contemporary society: Theories of the present* (pp. 126–138). New York, NY: Sage.

Scruggs, J. L., Schmidt, D., & Deutch, A. Y. (2003). The hallucinogen 1-[2,5-dimethoxy-4-iodophenyl]-2-aminopropane (DOI) increases cortical extracellular glutamate levels in rats. *Neuroscience Letters, 346,* 137–140.

Scully, J. A., Tosi, H., & Banning, K. (2000). Life event checklists: Reevaluating the social readjustment rating scale after 30 years. *Educational and Psychological Measurement, 60,* 864–876.

Sebastian, C., Viding, E., Williams, K. D., & Blakemore, S. (2010). Social brain development and the affective consequences of ostracism in adolescence. *Brain and Cognition, 72,* 134–145.

Segal, Z. V., Williams, J. M. G., & Teasdale, J. D. (2002). *Mindfulness-based cognitive therapy for depression.* New York, NY: Guilford Press.

Segerstrom, S. C., & Miller, G. E. (2004). Psychological stress and the human immune system: A meta-analytic study of 30 years of inquiry. *Psychological Bulletin, 130,* 601–630.

Segerstrom, S. C., & Sephton, S. E. (2010). Optimistic expectancies and cell-mediated immunity: The role of positive affect. *Psychological Science, 21,* 448–455.

Seifert, K. L., Hoffnung, R. J., & Hoffnung, M. (2000). *Lifespan development* (2nd ed.). Boston, MA: Houghton Mifflin.

Seigneur, C. (2010, December 18). The public isolation project: Woman talks about lessons learned from a month in a glass box. *The Oregonian.* Retrieved from http://www.oregonlive.com/oregonian/

Seligman, M. E. P., & Csikszentmihalyi, M. (2000). Positive psychology: An introduction. *American Psychologist, 55,* 5–14. doi:10.1037/0003-066X.55.1.5

Seligman, M. E. P., & Hager, J. L. (Eds.). (1972). *The biological boundaries of learning.* New York, NY: Appleton.

Seligman, M. E. P., Rashid, R., & Parks, A. C. (2006). Positive psychotherapy. *American Psychologist, 61,* 774–788.

Seligman, M. E. P., Schulman, P., & Tryon, A. M. (2007). Group prevention of depression and anxiety symptoms. *Behaviour Research and Therapy, 45,* 1111–1126.

Selkoe, D. (2002). Alzheimer's disease is a synaptic failure. *Science, 298*(5594), 789–791.

Selye, H. (1946). The general adaptation syndrome and diseases of adaptation. *The Journal of Clinical Endocrinology, 6,* 117–230.

Selye, H. (1976). *The stress of life.* New York, NY: McGraw-Hill.

Selye, H. (1982). History and present status of the stress concept. In L. Goldberger & S. Breznitz (Eds.), *Handbook of stress: Theoretical and clinical aspects* (pp. 7–20). New York, NY: Free Press.

Sen, B., & Swaminathan, S. (2007). Maternal prenatal substance use and behavior problems among children in the U.S. *The Journal of Mental Health Policy and Economics, 10,* 189–206.

Serpell, R. (1982). Measures of perception, skills, and intelligence. In W. W. Hartup (Ed.), *Review of child development research* (Vol. 6, pp. 392–440). Chicago, IL: University of Chicago Press.

Shargorodsky, J., Curhan, S. G., Curhan, G. C., & Eavey, R. (2010). Change in prevalence of hearing loss in U.S. adolescents. *Journal of the American Medical Association, 304,* 772–778.

Shastry, B. S. (2005). Bipolar disorder: An update. *Neurochemistry International, 46,* 273–279.

Shaw, P., Greenstein, D., Lerch, J. Clasen, L., Lenroot, R., Gogtay, N., . . . Giedd, J. (2006). Intellectual ability and cortical development in children and adolescents. *Nature, 440,* 676–679.

Shea, D. L., Lubinski, D., & Benbow, C. P. (2001). Importance of assessing spatial ability in intellectually talented young adolescents: A 20-year longitudinal study. *Journal of Educational Psychology, 93,* 604–614.

Shedler, J. (2010). The efficacy of psychodynamic psychotherapy. *American Psychologist, 65,* 98–109.

Shekelle, R. B., Hulley, S. B., Neston, J. D., Billings, J. H., Borboni, N. O., Gerace, T. A., et al. (1985). The MRFIT behavior pattern study: Type A behavior and incidence of coronary heart disease. *American Journal of Epidemiology, 122,* 559–570.

Shen, H., Sabaliauskas, N., Sherpa, A., Fenton, A. A., Stelzer, A., Aoki, C., & Smith, S. S. (2010). A critical role for 4β GABAA receptors in shaping learning deficits at puberty in mice. *Science, 327,* 1515–1518.

Shepard, M. (1995). Kraepelin and modern psychiatry. *European Archives of Psychiatry and Clinical Neuroscience, 245,* 189–195.

Shepard, R., & Metzler, J. (1971). Mental rotation of three-dimensional objects. *Science, 171,* 701–703.

Shergill, S. S., Brammer, M. J., Fukuda, R., Williams, S. C. R., Murray, R. M., & McGuire, P. K. (2003). Engagement of brain areas implicated in processing inner speech in people with auditory hallucinations. *British Journal of Psychiatry, 182,* 525–531.

Shergill, S. S., Brammer, M. J., Williams, S. C. R., Murray, R. M., & McGuire, P. K. (2000). Mapping auditory hallucinations in schizophrenia using functional magnetic resonance imaging. *Archives of General Psychiatry, 57,* 1033–1038.

Shermer, M. (1997). *Why people believe weird things: Pseudoscience, superstition, and other confusions of our time.* New York, NY: W. H. Freeman.

Shestyuk, A. Y., Deldin, P. J., Brand, J. E., & Deveney, C. M. (2005). Reduced sustained brain activity during processing of positive emotional stimuli in major depression. *Biological Psychiatry, 57,* 1089–1096.

Shomaker, L. B., & Furman, W. (2009). Interpersonal influences on late adolescent girls' and boys' disordered eating. *Eating Behaviors, 10,* 97–106.

Shore, L. M., & Wayne, S. J. (1993). Commitment and employee behavior: Comparison of affective commitment and continuance commitment with perceived organizational support. *Journal of Applied Psychology, 78,* 774–780.

Short, S. J., Lubach, G. R., Karasin, A. I., Olsen, C. W., Styner, M., Knickmeyer, R. C., . . . Coe, C. L. (2010). Maternal influenza infection during pregnancy impacts postnatal brain development in the rhesus monkey. *Biological Psychiatry, 67,* 965–973.

Siegman, A. W., Anderson, R., Herbst, J., Boyle, S., & Wilkinson, J. (1992). Dimensions of anger-hostility and cardiovascular reactivity in provoked and angered men. *Journal of Behavioral Medicine, 15,* 257–272.

Sigman, M., & Hassan, S. (2006). Benefits of long-term group therapy to individuals suffering schizophrenia: A prospective 7-year study. *Bulletin of the Menninger Clinic, 70,* 273–282.

Sigurdsson, T., Doyere, V., Cain, C. K., & LeDoux, J. E. (2007). Long-term potentiation in the amygdala: A cellular mechanism of fear learning and memory. *Neuropharmacology, 52,* 215–227.

Silberweig, D. A., Stern, E., Frith, C., Cahill, C., Holmes, A., Grootoonk, S., . . . R. S. J. Frackowiak (1995). A functional neuroanatomy of hallucinations in schizophrenia. *Nature, 378,* 176–179. doi:10.1038/378176a0

Silva, L. M., Cignolini, A., Warren, R., Budden, S., & Skowron-Gooch, A. (2007). Improvement in sensory impairment and social interaction in young children with autism following treatment with an original Qigong massage methodology. *American Journal of Chinese Medicine, 35,* 393–406.

Silvia, P. J. (2006). *Exploring the psychology of interest.* New York, NY: Oxford University Press.

Silvia, P. J., & Kimbrel, N. A. (2010). A dimensional analysis of creativity and mental illness: Do anxiety and depression symptoms predict creative cognition, creative accomplishments, and creative self-concepts? *Psychology of Aesthetics, Creativity and the Arts, 4,* 2–10.

Sime, J. D. (1983). Affiliative behavior during escape to building exits. *Journal of Environmental Psychology, 3,* 21–41.

Simner, J., Sagiv, N., Mulvenna, C., Tsakanikos, E., Witherby, S., Fraser, C., . . . Ward, J. (2006). Synesthesia: The prevalence of atypical cross-modal experiences. *Perception, 35,* 1024–1033.

Simon, H. A. (1978). Information-processing theory of human problem solving. In W. K. Estes (Ed.), *Handbook of learning and cognitive processes: Vol. 5. Human information processing* (pp. 271–295). Hillsdale, NJ: Erlbaum.

Simonds, J., Kieras, J. E., Rueda, M. R., & Rothbart, M. K. (2007). Effortful control, executive attention, and emotional regulation in 7–10-year-old children. *Cognitive Development, 22,* 474–488.

Simons, D. J., & Chabris, C. F. (1999). Gorillas in our midst: Sustained inattentional blindness for dynamic events. *Perception, 28,* 1059–1074.

Simon-Thomas, E. R., Keltner, D. J., Sauter, D., Sinicropi-Yao, L., & Abramson, A. (2009). The voice conveys specific emotions: Evidence from vocal burst displays. *Emotion, 9,* 838–846.

Simonton, D. K. (1984). *Genius, creativity & leadership: Historiometric inquiries.* Cambridge, MA: Harvard University Press.

Simonton, D. K. (1999). *Origins of genius.* New York, NY: Oxford University Press.

Simpson, K. (2001). The role of testosterone in aggression. *McGill Journal of Medicine, 6,* 32–40.

Singer, T., Seymour, B., O' Doherty, J. O., Kaube, H., Dolan, R. J., & Frith, C. D. (2004). Empathy for pain involves the affective but not sensory components of pain. *Science, 303,* 1157–1162.

Sirignono, S. W., & Lachman, M. E. (1985). Personality change during the transition to parenthood: The role of perceived infant temperament. *Developmental Psychology, 21,* 558–567.

Skinner, B. F. (1938). *The behavior of organisms.* New York, NY: Appleton.

Skinner, B. F. (1953). *Science and human behavior.* New York, NY: Free Press.

Skinner, B. F. (1957). *Verbal behavior.* New York, NY: Appleton-Century-Crofts.

Skinner, B. F. (1971). *Beyond freedom and dignity.* New York, NY: Knopf.

Skinner, B. F. (1979). *The making of a behaviorist.* New York, NY: Knopf.

Skinner, B. F. (1990). Can psychology be a science of mind? *American Psychologist, 45,* 1206–1210.

Slamecka, N. J., & McElree, B. (1983). Normal forgetting of verbal lists as a function of their degree of learning. *Journal of Experimental Psychology: Learning, Memory, & Cognition, 9,* 384–397.

Slater, E., & Meyer, A. (1959). Contributions to a pathography of the musicians: Robert Schumann. *Confinia Psychiatrica, 2,* 65–94.

Slavich, G. M., O'Donovan, A., Epel, E. S., & Kemeny, M. (in press). Black sheep get the blues: A psychobiological model of social rejection and depression. *Neuroscience and Biobehavioral Reviews.* doi:10.1016/j.neubiorev.2010.01.003

Sloan, P., Arsenault, L., & Hilsenroth, M. (2002). *Use of the Rorschach in the assessment of war-related stress in military personnel.* Ashland, OH: Hogrefe & Huber.

Small, G. W., Moody, T. D., Siddarth, P., & Bookheimer, S. Y. (2009). Your brain on Google: Patterns of cerebral activation during Internet searching. *American Journal of Geriatric Psychiatry, 17,* 116–126.

Smallwood, P. M., Olveczky, B. P., Williams, G. L., Jacobs, G. H., Reese, B. E., Meister, M., & Nathans, J. (2003). Genetically engineered mice with an additional class of cone photoreceptors: Implications for the evolution of color vision. *Proceedings of the National Academy of Sciences, 100,* 11706–11711. doi:10.1073/pnas.1934712100

Smith, B. D. (1998). *Psychology: Science and understanding.* New York, NY: McGraw-Hill.

Smith, C., & MacNeill, C. (1994). Impaired motor memory for a pursuit motor task following Stage 2 sleep loss in college students. *Journal of Sleep Research, 3,* 206–213.

Smith, C. A., & Ellsworth, P. C. (1987). Patterns of appraisal and emotion related to taking an exam. *Journal of Personality and Social Psychology, 52,* 475–488.

Smith, C. T., Aubrey, J. B., & Peters, K. R. (2004). Different roles for REM and stage 2 sleep in motor learning: A proposed model. *Psychologica Belgica, 44,* 81–104.

Smith, D. (2006, April 25). Harvard novelist says copying was unintentional. *New York Times.* Retrieved from http://www.nytimes.com

Smith, E. M., & Blalock, J. E. (1988). A molecular basis for interactions between the immune and neuroendocrine systems. *International Journal of Neuroscience, 38,* 455–464.

Smith, J. (2009, March 25). Number of U.S. Facebook users over 35 nearly doubles in last 60 days. Retrieved from http://www.insidefacebook.com/2009/03/25/number-of-us-facebook-users-over-35-nearly-doubles-in-last-60-days/

Smith, M., & Glass, G. (1977). Meta-analysis of psychotherapy outcome studies. *American Psychologist, 32,* 752–760.

Smith, M., & Kollock, P. (Eds). (1999). *Communities in cyberspace.* London, England: Routledge.

Smith, N., Young, A., & Lee, C. (2004). Optimism, health-related hardiness and well-being among older Australian women. *Journal of Health Psychology, 9,* 741–752.

Smyth, J. M. (1998). Written emotional expression, effect sizes, outcome types, and moderating variables. *Journal of Consulting & Clinical Psychology, 66,* 174–184.

Snarey, J. R. (1985). Cross-cultural universality of social-moral development: A critical review of Kohlbergian research. *Psychological Bulletin, 97,* 202–232.

Snyderman, M., & Rothman, S. (1987). Survey of expert opinion on intelligence and aptitude testing. *American Psychologist, 42,* 137–144.

Soler, J., Pascual, J. C., Tiana, T., Cebria, A., Barrachina, J., Campins, M. J., . . . Pérez, V. (2009). Dialectical behaviour therapy skills training compared to standard group therapy in borderline personality disorder: A 3-month randomized controlled clinical trial. *Behaviour Research and Therapy, 47,* 353–358.

Solms, M. (2000). Dreaming and REM sleep are controlled by different brain mechanisms. *Behavioral and Brain Sciences, 23,* 843–850.

Solms, M. (2004). Freud returns. *Scientific American, 290*(5), 82–88.

Solms, M., & O. Turnbull. (2002). *The brain and the inner world: An introduction to the neuroscience of subjective experience.* New York, NY: Other Press.

Solomon, P. R., Adams, F., Silver, A., Zimmer, J., & DeVeaux, R. (2002). Ginkgo for memory enhancement: A randomized controlled trial. *Journal of the American Medical Association, 288,* 835–840.

Song, S. (2006, March 27). Mind over medicine. *Time, 167,* 13.

Sorce, J. F., Emde, R. N., Campos, J., & Klinnert, M. D. (1985). Maternal emotional signaling: Its effect on the visual cliff behavior of 1-year-olds. *Developmental Psychology, 21,* 195–200.

South Korea couple starved child while raising "virtual baby." (2010, March 5). Retrieved from http://www.cnn.com/2010/WORLD/asiapcf/03/05/korea.baby.starved/index.html

Southwick, S. M., Vythilingam, M., & Charney, D. S. (2005). The psychobiology of depression and resilience to stress: Implications for prevention and treatment. *Annual Review of Clinical Psychology, 1,* 255–291.

Sowell, E. R., Thompson, P. M., Tessner, K. D., & Toga, A. W. (2001). Mapping continued brain growth and gray matter density reduction in dorsal frontal cortex: Inverse relationships during postadolescent brain maturation. *The Journal of Neuroscience, 21,* 8619–8829.

Spalding, K. L., Arner, E., Westermark, P. O., Bernard, S., Buchholz, B. A., Bergmann, O., et al. (2008, June 5). Dynamics of fat cell turnover in humans. *Nature, 453,* 783–787. doi:10.1038/nature06902

Spearman, C. (1904). "General intelligence," objectively determined and measured. *The American Journal of Psychology, 15,* 201–292.

Spearman, C. (1923). *The nature of 'intelligence' and the principles of cognition.* London, England: Macmillan.

Spector, F., & Maurer, D. (2009). Synesthesia: A new approach to understanding the development of perception. *Developmental Psychology, 45,* 175–189.

Spelke, E. (2008). Effects of music instruction on developing cognitive systems at the foundations of mathematics and science. *Learning, Arts and the Brain: The Dana Consortium Report on Arts and Cognition.* New York, NY: Dana Press.

Spencer, S. M., & Patrick, J. H. (2009). Social support and personal mastery as protective resources during emerging adulthood. *Journal of Adult Development, 16,* 191–198.

Sperry, R. W., Gazzaniga, M. S., & Bogen, J. E. (1969). Inter hemispheric relationships: The neocortical commissures: Syndromes of hemisphere disconnection. In P. J. Vinken & G. W. Bruyn (Eds.), *Handbook of clinical neurology* (pp. 273–290). Amsterdam: North-Holland.

Spiegel, D., Bloom, J. R., Kraemer, H. C., & Gottheil, E. (1989). Effect of psychosocial treatment on survival of patients with metastatic breast cancer. *Lancet, 8668,* 88–91.

Spinrad, T. L., Eisenberg, N., Cumberland, A., Fabes, R. A., Valiente, C., Shepard, S. A., et al. (2006). Relation of emotion-related regulation to children's social competence: A longitudinal study. *Emotion, 6,* 498–510.

Squire, L. (1987). *Memory and brain.* New York, NY: Oxford University Press.

Squire, L. R. (1977). ECT and memory loss. *American Journal of Psychiatry, 134,* 997–1001.

Squire, L. R. (2009). *The history of neuroscience in autobiography* (Vol. 6). New York, NY: Elsevier.

Staggs, G. D., Larson, L. M., & Borgen, F. H. (2007). Convergence of personality and interests: Meta-analysis of the multidimensional personality questionnaire and the strong interest inventory. *Journal of Career Assessment, 15,* 423–445.

Stanley, J. (1996). In the beginning: The Study of Mathematically Precocious Youth. In C. P. Benbow & D. Lubinski (Eds.), *Intellectual talent* (pp. 225–235). Baltimore, MD: Johns Hopkins University Press.

Stanton, A. L., Danoff-Burg, S., Sworowski, L. A., Rodriguez-Hanley, A., Kirk, S. B., & Austenfeld, J. L. (2002). Randomized, controlled trial of written emotional expression and benefit finding in breast cancer patients. *Journal of Clinical Oncology, 20,* 4160–4168.

Starr, C., & Taggart, R. (2004). *Biology: The unity and diversity of life* (10th ed.). Belmont, CA: Thomson–Brooks Cole.

Stefansson, H., Ophoff, R. A., Steinberg, S., Andreassen, O. A., Chicon, S., Rujescu, D., . . . Collier, D.A. (2009). Common variants conferring risks of schizophrenia. *Nature, 460,* 744–747.

Steinberg, L. (2005). Cognitive and affective development in adolescence. *Trends in Cognitive Science, 9,* 69–74.

Steinberg, L. (2010). *Adolescence* (9th ed.). New York, NY: McGraw-Hill.

Steiner, B., Wolf, S., & Kempermann, G. (2006). Adult neurogenesis and neurodegenerative disease. *Regenerative Medicine, 1,* 15–28.

Steinhausen, H., & Spohr, H. (1998). Long-term outcome of children with fetal alcohol syndrome: Psychopathology, behavior, and intelligence. *Alcoholism: Clinical and Experimental Research, 22*(2), 334–338.

Stellar, E. (1954). The physiology of motivation. *Psychological Review, 61,* 5–22.

Stenberg, C. R., Campos, J. J., & Emde, R. (1983). The facial expression of anger in seven-month-old infants. *Child Development, 54,* 178–184.

Sterling, P., & Eyer, J. (1988). Allostasis: A new paradigm to explain arousal pathology. In S. Fisher & H. S. Reason (Eds.), *Handbook of life stress, cognition and health* (pp. 629–649). New York, NY: John Wiley.

Sternberg, R. J. (1985). *Beyond IQ: A triarchic theory of human intelligence.* New York, NY: Cambridge University Press.

Sternberg, R. J. (1986). A triangular theory of love. *Psychological Review, 93,* 119–135.

Sternberg, R. J. (1995). For whom The Bell Curve tolls: A review of *The Bell Curve. Psychological Science, 6,* 257–261.

Sternberg, R. J. (1998). Principles of teaching for successful intelligence. *Educational Psychologist, 55,* 65–72.

Sternberg, R. J. (Ed.). (1999). *Handbook of human creativity.* Cambridge, England: Cambridge University Press.

Sternberg, R. J. (2000). The concept of intelligence. In. R. J. Sternberg (Ed.), *The handbook of intelligence* (pp. 3–15). Cambridge, England: Cambridge University Press.

Sternberg, R. J. (2003). A broad view of intelligence: A theory of successful intelligence. *Consulting Psychology Journal: Practice and Research, 55,* 139–154.

Sternberg, R. J. (Ed.). (2004). *Definitions and conceptions of giftedness.* Thousand Oaks, CA: Corwin Press.

Sternberg, R. J. (2005). The triarchic theory of successful intelligence. In D. P. Flanagan

& P. L. Harrison (Eds.), *Contemporary intellectual assessment: Theories, tests, and issues* (pp. 103–119). New York, NY: Guilford Press.

Sternberg, R. J. (2006a). *Cognitive psychology* (4th ed.). Belmont: CA: Thomson-Wadsworth.

Sternberg, R. J. (2006b). The Rainbow Project: Enhancing the SAT through assessments of analytical, practical, and creative skills. *Intelligence, 34,* 321–350.

Sternberg, R. J., & Detterman, D. K. (Eds.). (1986). *What is intelligence? Contemporary viewpoints on its nature and definition.* Norwood, NJ: Ablex.

Sternberg, R. J., Grigorenko, E. L., & Kidd, K. K. (2005). Intelligence, race, and genetics. *American Psychologist, 60,* 46–59.

Sternberg, R. J., & O'Hara, L. (1999). Creativity and intelligence. In R. J. Sternberg (Ed.), *Handbook of creativity* (pp. 251–272). New York, NY: Cambridge University Press.

Stevens, S. B., & Morris, T. L. (2007). College dating and social anxiety: Using the Internet as a means of connecting to others. *CyberPsychology & Behavior, 10,* 680–688.

Stewart, J. H. (2005). Hypnosis in contemporary medicine. *Mayo Clinic Proceedings, 80,* 511–524.

Stewart, R. A., Rule, A. C., & Giordano, D. A. (2007). The effect of fine motor skill activities on kindergarten attention. *Early Childhood Education Journal, 35,* 103–109.

Stewart, V. M. (1973). Tests of the "carpentered world" hypothesis by race and environment in America and Zambia. *International Journal of Psychology, 8,* 83–94.

Stice, E., Shaw, H., Bohon, C., Marti, C. N., & Rhode, P. (2009). A meta-analytic review of depression prevention programs for children and adolescents: Factors that predict magnitude of intervention effects. *Journal of Consulting and Clinical Psychology, 77,* 486–503.

Stickgold, R. (2005). Sleep-dependent memory consolidation. *Nature, 437,* 1272–1278.

Stickgold, R., & Walker, M. P. (2007). Sleep-dependent memory consolidation and reconsolidation. *Sleep Medicine, 8,* 331–343.

Storch, E. A., Abramowitz, J., & Goodman, W. K. (2008). Where does obsessive–compulsive disorder belong in DSM-V? *Depression and Anxiety, 25,* 336–347.

Strack, F., Martin, L. L., & Stepper, S. (1988). Inhibiting and facilitating conditions of the human smile: A nonobtrusive test of the facial feedback hypothesis. *Journal of Personality and Social Psychology, 54,* 768–777.

Strange, B. A., & Dolan, R. J. (2006). Anterior medial temporal lobe in human cognition: Memory for fear and the unexpected. *Neuropsychiatry, 11,* 198–218.

Strassman, R. J. (1984). Adverse reactions to psychedelic drugs. A review of the literature. *Journal of Nervous and Mental Disease, 172,* 577–595.

Strauss, M. E., Pasupathi, M., & Chatterjee, A. (1993). Concordance between observers in descriptions of personality change in Alzheimer's disease. *Psychology and Aging, 8,* 475–480.

Strayer, D. L., & Drews, F. A. (2007). Cell-phone-induced driver distraction. *Current Directions in Psychological Science, 16,* 128–131.

Strayer, D. L., & Drews, F. A. (2007). Multitasking in the automobile. In A. F. Kramer, D. A. Wiegmann, & A. Kirlik (Eds.), *Attention: From theory to practice* (pp. 121–133). New York, NY: Oxford University Press.

Strayer, D. L., Drews, F. A., & Couch, D. J. (2006). A comparison of the cell phone driver and the drunk driver. *Human Factors, 48,* 381–391.

Streissguth, A., Barr, H., Sampson, P., Darby, B., & Martin, D. (1989). IQ at age 4 in relation to maternal alcohol use and smoking during pregnancy. *Developmental Psychology, 25*(1), 3–11.

Striedter, G. (2005). *Principles of brain evolution.* Sunderland, MA: Sinauer.

Stroodley, C. J., & Schmahmann, J. D. (2009). Functional topography in the human cerebellum: A meta-analysis of neuroimaging studies. *NeuroImage, 44,* 489–501.

Stroop, J. R. (1935). Studies of interference in serial-verbal reaction. *Journal of Experimental Psychology, 18,* 643–662.

Strueber, D., Lueck, M., & Roth, G. (2006–2007). The violent brain. *Scientific American Mind, 17,* 20–27.

Styles, E. A. (2006). *The psychology of attention* (2nd ed.). Hove, England: Psychology Press.

Styron, W. (1990). *Darkness visible: A memoir of madness.* New York, NY: Vintage.

Suarez, E. C., Bates, M. P., & Harralson, T. L. (1998). The relation of hostility to lipids and lipoproteins in women: Evidence for the role of antagonistic hostility. *Annals of Behavioral Medicine, 20,* 59–63.

Suarez, E. C., Harlan, E., Peoples, M. C., & Williams, R. B., Jr. (1993). Cardiovascular reactivity and emotional responses in women: The role of hostility and harassment. *Health Psychology, 12,* 459–468.

Suarez, E. C., & Williams, R. B., Jr. (1989). Situational determinants of cardiovascular and emotional reactivity in high and low hostile men. *Psychosomatic Medicine, 51,* 404–418.

Subotnik, R. F., Duschl, R. A., & Selmon, E. H. (1993). Retention and attrition of science talent: A longitudinal study of Westinghouse Science Talent winners. *International Journal of Science Education, 15,* 61–72.

Subrahmanyam, K., & Greenfield, P. (2008). Online communication and adolescent relationships. *The Future of Children, 18,* 119–146.

Subrahmanyam, K., Greenfield, P. M., & Tynes, B. (2004). Constructing sexuality and identity in an online teen chatroom. *Journal of Applied Developmental Psychology, 25,* 651–666.

Subrahmanyam, K., Šmahel, D., & Greenfield, P. M. (2006). Connecting developmental processes to the Internet: Identity presentation and sexual exploration in online teen chatrooms. *Developmental Psychology, 42,* 1–12.

Sullivan, E. V., Harris, R. A., & Pfefferbaum, A. (2010). Alcohol's effects on brain and behavior. *Alcohol Research & Health, 33,* 127–143.

Sullivan, K. M. (2009). *The Bundy murders: A comprehensive history.* Jefferson, NC: McFarland.

Sullivan, K., Zaitchik, D., & Tager-Flusberg, H. (1994). Preschoolers can attribute second-order beliefs. *Developmental Psychology, 30,* 395–402.

Suomi, S. (2005). Genetic and environmental factors influencing the expression of impulsive aggression and serotonergic functioning in rhesus monkeys. In R. E. Tremblay, W. W. Hartup, & J. Archer (Eds.), *Developmental origins of aggression* (pp. 63–82). New York, NY: Guilford Press.

Susskind, J. M., Lee, D. H., Cusi, A., Feiman, R., Grabski, W., & Anderson, A. K. (2008). Expressing fear enhances sensory acquisition. *Nature Neuroscience, 11,* 843–850.

Sweatt, J. D. (2010, May 7). Epigenetics and cognitive aging. *Science, 328,* 701–702. doi:10.1126/science.1189968.

Swets, J. A. (1964). *Signal detection and recognition by human observers.* New York, NY: Wiley.

Syed, M., & Azmitia, M. (2010). Narrative and ethnic identity exploration: A longitudinal account of emerging adults' ethnicity-related experiences. *Developmental Psychology, 46,* 208–219.

Szaflarski, J. P., Schmithorst, V. J., Altaye, M., Byars, A. W., Ret, J., Plante, E., & Holland, S. K. (2006). A longitudinal functional magnetic resonance imaging study of language development in children 5 to 11 years old. *Annals of Neurology, 59,* 796–807. doi: 10.1002/ana.20817

Tafti, M., Dauvilliers, Y., & Overeem, S. (2007). Narcolepsy and familial advanced sleep-phase syndrome: Molecular genetics of sleep disorders. *Current Opinion in Genetics & Development, 17,* 222–227.

Takahashi, Y., Yamagata, S., Kijima, N., Shigemasu, K., Ono, Y., & Ando, J. (2007). Continuity and change in behavioral inhibition and activation systems: A longitudinal behavioral genetic study. *Personality and Individual Differences, 43*(6), 1616–1625.

Takeuchi, H., Taki, Y., Sassa, Y., Hashizume, H., Sekiguchi, A., Fukushima, A., & Kawashima, R. (2010). White matter structures associated with creativity: Evidence from diffusion tensor imaging. *NeuroImage, 51,* 11–18.

Talassi, E., Cipriani, G., Bianchetti, A., & Trabucchi, M. (2007). Personality changes in Alzheimer's disease. *Aging & Mental Health, 11,* 526–531.

Talmi, D., Grady, C. L., Goshen-Gottstein, Y., & Moscovitch, M. (2005). Neuroimaging the serial position curve: A test of single-store versus dual-store models. *Psychological Science, 16,* 717–723.

Tambs, K., Hoffman, H. J., Borchgrevink, H. M., Holmen, J., & Engdahl, B. (2006). Hearing loss induced by occupational and impulse noise: Results on threshold shifts by frequencies, age and gender from the NordTrøndelag Hearing Loss Study. *International Journal of Audiology, 45*, 309–317.

Tammet, D. (2006). *Born on a blue day: A memoir.* New York, NY: Free Press.

Tang, Z., & Orwin, R. G. (2009). Marijuana initiation among American youth and its risks as dynamic processes: Prospective findings from a national longitudinal study. *Substance Use & Misuse, 44*, 195–211.

Tangney, J. P., Stuewig, J., & Mashek, D. J. (2007). Moral emotions and moral behavior. *Annual Review of Psychology, 58*, 345–372.

Tanielian, T., & Jaycox, L. H. (Eds.). (2008). *Invisible wounds of war: Psychological and cognitive injuries, their consequences, and services to assist recovery.* Santa Monica, CA: Rand Corp.

Tao, R., Huang, X., Wang, J., Zhang, H., Zhang, Y., & Li, M. (2010). Proposed diagnostic criteria for Internet addiction. *Addiction, 105*, 556–564.

Tardif, T., Gelman, S., & Xu, F. (1999). Putting the "noun bias" in context: A comparison of English and Mandarin. *Developmental Psychology, 70*, 620–635.

Tarmann, A. (2002, May/June). Out of the closet and onto the Census long form. *Population Today, 30*, 1, 6.

Tashkin, D. (2006, May 23). *Marijuana smoking not linked to lung cancer.* Paper presented at the annual meeting of the American Thoracic Society, San Diego, CA.

Tashkin, D. R., Baldwin, G. C., Sarafian, T., Dubinett, S., & Roth, M. D. (2002). Respiratory and immunologic consequences of marijuana smoking. *Journal of Clinical Pharmacology, 42*, S71–S81.

Taylor, K. N., Harper, S., & Chadwick, P. (2009). Impact of mindfulness on cognition and affect in voice hearing: Evidence from two case studies. *Behavioral and Cognitive Psychotherapy, 37*, 397–402.

Taylor, S. E. (1989). *Positive illusions: Creative self-deception and the healthy mind.* New York, NY: Basic Books.

Taylor, S. E. (2009). *Health psychology* (7th ed.). New York, NY: McGraw-Hill.

Taylor, S. E., Kemeny, M. E., Reed, G. M., Bower, J. E., & Gruenewald, T. L. (2000). Psychological resources, positive illusions, and health. *American Psychologist, 55*, 99–109.

Teasdale, G., & Jennett, B. (1976). Assessment and prognosis of coma after head injury. *Acta Neurochirurgica, 34*, 45–55.

Teasdale, J. D., Segal, Z. V., & Williams, J. M. G. (1995). How does cognitive therapy prevent depressive relapse and why should attentional control (mindfulness) training help? *Behaviour Research and Therapy, 33*, 25–39.

Teasdale, J. D., Segal, Z., Williams, M. G., Ridgeway, V. A., Soulsby, J. M., & Lau, M. A. (2000). Prevention of relapse/recurrence in major depression by mindfulness-based cognitive therapy. *Journal of Consulting and Clinical Psychology, 68*, 615–623.

Teen scientists move to finals in prestigious competition. (2005, January 26). Retrieved August 2, 2007, from http://www.sciserv.org/sts/press/20050126.asp

Tellegen, A. (2000). *Manual for the multidimensional personality questionnaire.* Minneapolis: University of Minnesota Press.

Tellegen, A., Ben-Porath, Y. S., McNulty, J. L., Arbisi, P. A., Graham, J. R., & Kaemmer, B. (2003). *The MMPI-2 Restructured Clinical Scales: Development, validation, and interpretation.* Minneapolis: University of Minnesota Press.

Tellegen, A., Lykken, D. T., Bouchard, T. J., Wilcox, K. J., Segal, N. L., & Rich, S. (1988). Personality similarity in twins reared apart and together. *Journal of Personality and Social Psychology, 54*, 1031–1039.

Terrace, H. S. (1987). *Nim: A chimpanzee who learned sign language.* New York, NY: Columbia University Press.

Test developer profiles. (2001). Retrieved July 15, 2007, from http://www.mhhe.com/mayfieldpub/psychtesting/profiles/karfmann.htm

Thacher, P. V. (2008). University students and "the all-nighter": Correlates and patterns of students' engagement in a single night of total sleep deprivation. *Behavioral Sleep Medicine, 6*, 16–31.

Thagard, P. (2005). *Mind: An introduction to cognitive science* (2nd ed.). Cambridge, MA: MIT Press.

Thapar, A., Langley, K., Asherson, P., & Gill, M. (2007). Gene-environment interplay in attention-deficit hyperactivity disorder and the importance of a developmental perspective. *British Journal of Psychiatry, 190*, 1–3.

Thayer, S. E., & Ray, S. (2006). Online communication preferences across age, gender, and duration of Internet use. *CyberPsychology and Behavior, 9*, 432–440.

Thibaut, J. W., & Kelley, H. H. (1959). *The social psychology of groups.* New York, NY: Wiley.

Thomas, A., & Chess, S. (1977). *Temperament and development.* New York, NY: Brunner/Mazel.

Thomasius, R., Zapletalova, P., Petersen, K., Buchert, R., Andresen, B., Wartberg, L., . . . Schmoldt, A. (2006). Mood, cognition and serotonin transporter availability in current and former ecstasy (MDMA) users: The longitudinal perspective. *Journal of Psychopharmacology, 20*, 211–225. doi: 10.1177/0269881106059486

Thompson, P. M., Giedd, J. N., Woods, R. P., MacDonald, D., Evans, A. C., & Toga, A. W. (2000). Growth patterns in the developing brain using continuum mechanical tensor maps. *Nature, 404*, 190–193.

Thompson, R. F., & Madigan, S. A. (2005). *Memory: The key to consciousness.* Washington, DC: Joseph Henry Press.

Thompson, W. L., & Kosslyn, S. M. (2000). Neural systems activated during visual mental imagery. In A. W. Toga & J. C. Mazziotta (Eds.), *Brain mapping: The systems* (pp. 535–560). San Diego, CA: Academic Press, 2000.

Thorndike, E. L. (1905). *Elements of psychology.* New York, NY: Seiler.

Thornhill, R., Gangestad, S. W., Miller, R., Scheyd, G., McCollough, J. K., & Franklin, M. (2003). Major histocompatibility complex genes, symmetry, and body scent attractiveness in men and women. *Behavioral Ecology, 14*, 668–678.

Thune, I., & Furberg, A. S. (2001). Physical activity and cancer risk: Dose-response and cancer, all sites and site specific. *Medicine and Science in Sports and Exercise, 33*, S530–S550.

Thurstone, E. L. (1938). *Primary mental abilities.* Chicago, IL: University of Chicago Press.

Titov, N., Andrews, G., Johnston, L., Robinson, E., & Spence, J. (2010). Transdiagnostic Internet treatment for anxiety disorders: A randomized controlled trial. *Behavior Research and Therapy, 48*, 890–899.

Tobias, S., & Everson, H. T. (2002). *Knowing what you know and what you don't: Further research on metacognitive knowledge monitoring.* New York, NY: College Entrance Examination Board.

Tolin, D. F. (2010). Is cognitive–behavioral therapy more effective than other therapies? A meta-analytic review. *Clinical Psychology Review, 30*, 710–720.

Tolman, E. C., & Honzik, C. H. (1930). Introduction and removal of reward, and maze performance in rats. *University of California Publications in Psychology, 4*, 257–275.

Tomasello, M., & Hermann, E. (2010). Ape and human cognition: What's the difference? *Current Directions in Psychological Science, 19*, 3–8.

Tomkins, S. S. (1962). *Affect, imagery, consciousness: Vol. 1. The positive affects.* New York, NY: Springer.

Tomkins, S. S. (1981). The quest for primary motives: Biography and autobiography of an idea. *Journal of Personality and Social Psychology, 41*, 306–329.

Tomkins, S. S., & McCarter, R. (1964). What and where are the primary affects? Some evidence for a theory. *Perceptual and Motor Skills, 18*, 119–158.

Tong, E. M. W., Ellsworth, P. C., & Bishop, G. D. (2009). An S-shaped relationship between changes in appraisal and changes in emotions. *Emotion, 9*, 821–837.

Tooby, J., & Cosmides, L. (1990). The past explains the present: Emotional adaptations and the structure of ancestral environments. *Ethology and Sociobiology, 11*, 375–424.

Tooby, J., & Cosmides, L. (1992). The psychological foundations of culture. In J. H. Barkow, L. Cosmides, & J. Tooby (Eds.), *The adapted mind: Evolutionary psychology and the generation of culture* (pp. 19–136). New York, NY: Oxford University Press.

Townsend, S. S. M., Markus, H. R., & Bergsieker, H. B. (2009). My choice, your categories: The denial of multiracial identities. *Journal of Social Issues, 65,* 185–204.

Toyota, Y., Ikeda, M., Shinagawa, S., Matsumoto, T., Matsumoto, N., Hokoishi, K., . . . Tanabe, H. (2007). Comparison of behavioral and psychological symptoms in early-onset and late-onset Alzheimer's disease. *International Journal of Geriatric Psychiatry, 22*(9), 896–901. doi:10.1002/gps.1760

Tracy, J. L., & Matsumoto, D. M. (2008). The spontaneous display of pride and shame: Evidence for biologically innate nonverbal displays. *Proceedings of the National Academy of Science, 105,* 11655–11660.

Tracy, J. L., & Robins, R. W. (2007). Emerging insights into the nature and function of pride. *Current Directions in Psychological Science, 16,* 147–150.

Tracy, J. L., & Robins, R. W. (2008). The nonverbal expression of pride: Evidence for cross-cultural recognition. *Journal of Personality and Social Psychology, 94,* 516–530.

Tracy, J. L., Robins, R. W., & Tangney, J. P. (2007). *The self-conscious emotions: Theory and research.* New York, NY: Guilford Press.

Transcripts of "Secrets of the Wild Child." (1997). Retrieved from http://www.pbs.org/wgbh/nova/transcripts/2112gchild.html

Treffert, D. A. (2006). *Extraordinary people: Understanding savant syndrome.* Updated version. Lincoln, NE: iUniverse Inc.

Treffert, D. A., & Christensen, D. D. (2005). Inside the mind of a savant. *Scientific American, 293,* 108–113.

Treisman, A. (1964). Verbal cues, language and meaning in selective attention. *American Journal of Psychology, 77,* 206–209.

Tremblay, K., & Ross, B. (2007). Effects of age and age-related hearing loss on the brain. *Journal of Communication Disorders, 40,* 305–312.

Trentacosta, C. J., & Izard, C. E. (2007). Kindergarten children's emotion competence as a predictor of their academic competence in first grade. *Emotion, 7,* 77–88.

Triplett, N. (1898). The dynamogenic factors in pacemaking and competition. *American Journal of Psychology, 9,* 507–533.

Trivers, R. L. (1971). The evolution of reciprocal altruism. *Quarterly Review of Biology, 46,* 35–57.

Trivers, R. L. (1972) Parental investment and sexual selection. In B. Campbell (Ed.), *Sexual selection and the descent of man, 1871–1971* (pp. 136–179). Chicago, IL: Aldine.

Trivers, R. L. (1985). *Social evolution.* Menlo Park, CA: Benjamin/Cummings.

Troisi, A. (2003). Psychopathology. In D. Maestripieri (Ed.), *Primate psychology* (pp. 451–470). Cambridge, MA: Harvard University Press.

Tronick, E., Morelli, G. A., & Ivey, P. K. (1992). The Efe forager infant and toddler's pattern of social relationships: Multiple and simultaneous. *Developmental Psychology, 28,* 568–577.

Trucking stats and FAQ's. (n.d.). Retrieved January 20, 2007, from http://www.geocities.com/TheTropics/1608/stats.htm

True, M., Pisani, L., & Oumar, F. (2001). Infant-mother attachment among the Dogon of Mali. *Child Development, 72,* 1451–1466.

Trugman, J. M. (1998). Tardive dyskinesia: Diagnosis, pathogenesis, and management. *Neurologist, 4,* 180–187.

Tsai, J. L., Chentsova-Dutton, Y., Friere-Bebeau, L., & Przymus, D. E. (2002). Emotional expression and physiology in European Americans and Hmong Americans. *Emotion, 2,* 380–397.

Tsai, J. L., Levenson, R. W., & Carstensen, L. L. (2000). Autonomic, expressive, and subjective responses to emotional films in older and younger Chinese American and European American adults. *Psychology and Aging, 15,* 684–693.

Tsakiris, M., Hesse, M. D., Boy, C., Haggard, P., & Fink, G. R. (2007). Neural signatures of body ownership: A sensory network for bodily self-consciousness. *Cerebral Cortex, 17,* 2235–2244.

Tseng, W. S. (1973). The development of psychiatric concepts in traditional Chinese medicine. *Archives of General Psychiatry, 29,* 569–575.

Tugade, M. M., & Fredrickson, B. L. (2004). Resilient individuals use positive emotions to bounce back from negative emotional experiences. *Journal of Personality and Social Psychology, 86,* 320–333.

Tulku, T. (1984). *Knowledge of freedom.* Berkeley, CA: Dharma.

Tully, K., & Bolshakov, V. (2010). Emotional enhancement of memory: How norepinephrine enables synaptic plasticity. *Molecular Brain, 3,* 15. doi:10.1186/1756-6606-3-15

Tulving, E. (1972). Episodic and semantic memory. In E. Tulving & W. Donaldson (Eds.), *Organization of memory* (pp. 381–403). New York, NY: Academic Press.

Tulving, E. (1985). How many memory systems are there? *American Psychologist, 40,* 385–398.

Turner, E. H., Matthews, A. M., Linardatos, E., Tell, R. A., & Rosenthal, R. (2008). Selective publication of antidepressant trials and its influence on apparent efficacy. *New England Journal of Medicine, 358,* 252–260.

Turner-Shea, Y., Bruno, R., & Pridmore, S. (2006). Daily and spaced treatment with transcranial magnetic stimulation in major depression: A pilot study. *Australian and New Zealand Journal of Psychiatry, 40,* 759–763.

Tversky, A., & Kahneman, D. (1974). Judgment under uncertainty: Heuristics and biases. *Science, 185,* 1124–1131.

Tversky, A., & Kahneman, D. (1983). Extensional versus intuitive reasoning: The conjunction fallacy in probability judgment. *Psychological Review, 90,* 293–315.

Twyman, K., Saylor, C., Taylor, L. A., & Comeaux, C. (2009). Comparing children and adolescents engaged in cyberbullying to matched peers. *Cyberpsychology.* doi:10.1089/cpb.2009.0137

Tyron, W. W. (2005). Possible mechanisms for why desensitization and exposure therapy work. *Clinical Psychology Review, 25,* 67–95.

U.S. Census Bureau. (2009a). Current population survey. Retrieved from http://www.census.gov/population/socdemo/hh-fam/ms2.xls

U.S. Census Bureau. (2009b). Table 4: Annual estimates of the two or more races resident population by sex and age for the United States: April 1, 2000 to July 1, 2008 [Data file]. Retrieved from http://www.census.gov/popest/national/asrh/NC-EST2008/NC-EST2008-04-TOM.csv

U.S. Department of Health and Human Services (USDHHS). (2004). *The health consequences of smoking: A report of the Surgeon General.* Atlanta, GA: Author.

U.S. Department of Health and Human Services. (2006). *The health consequences of involuntary exposure to tobacco smoke: A report of the Surgeon General—executive summary.* Retrieved from http://www.surgeongeneral.gov/library/secondhandsmoke/report/executivesummary.pdf

U.S. Senate. (2004). Report of the Select Committee on Intelligence on the U.S. Intelligence Community's Prewar Intelligence Assessments on Iraq. Retrieved from http://www.gpoaccess.gov/serialset/creports/iraq.html

Udry, J. R., Morris, N. M., & Waller, L. (1973). Effect of contraceptive pills on sexual activity in the luteal phase of the human menstrual cycle. *Archives of Sexual Behavior, 2,* 205–214.

Uher, R., & McGuffin, P. (2010). The moderation by the serotonin transporter gene of environmental adversity in the etiology of depression: 2009 update. *Molecular Psychiatry, 15,* 18–22.

Uhlhaas, P. J., & Singer, W. (2010). Abnormal neural oscillations and synchrony in schizophrenia. *Nature Reviews Neuroscience, 11,* 100–113.

Uhlhaas, P. J., Roux, F., Singer, W., Haenschel, C., Sireteanu, R., & Rodriguez, E. (2009). The development of neural synchrony reflects late maturation and restructuring functional networks in humans. *Proceedings of the National Academy of Sciences, 106,* 9866–9871.

University of Cambridge. (2011, February 10). Extra testosterone reduces your empathy, researchers find. *ScienceDaily.* Retrieved from http://www.sciencedaily.com/-releases/2011/02/110209105556.htm

Uylings, H. B. M. (2006). Development of the human cortex and the concept of "critical" or "sensitive" periods. *Language Learning, 56,* 59–90.

Valente, M., Placid, F., Oliveira, A. J., Bigagli, A., Morghen, I., Proietti, R., & Gigli, G. L. (2002). Sleep organization pattern as a prognostic marker at the sub-acute stage of post-traumatic coma. *Clinical Neurophysiology, 113,* 1798–1805.

Valkenburg, P. M., & Peter, J. (2007a). Preadolescents' and adolescents' online communication and their closeness to friends. *Developmental Psychology, 43,* 267–277.

Valkenburg, P. M., & Peter, J. (2007b). Who visits online dating sites? Exploring some characteristics of online daters. *CyberPsychology & Behavior, 10,* 849–852.

Valkenburg, P. M., & Peter, J. (2009). Social consequences of the Internet for adolescents: A decade of research. *Current Directions in Psychological Science, 18,* 1–5.

Valkenburg, P. M., Peter, J., & Schouten, A. P. (2006). Friend networking sites and their relationship to adolescents' well-being and social self-esteem. *CyberPsychology & Behavior, 9,* 584–590.

Valois, R. F., Zullig, K. J., Huebner, E. S., & Drane, J. W. (2003). Dieting behaviors, weight perceptions, and life satisfaction among public high school adolescents. *Eating Disorders, 11,* 271–288.

Van Gerven, P., Van Boxtel, M., Meijer, W., Willems, D., & Jolles, J. (2007). On the relative role of inhibition in age-related working memory decline. *Aging, Neuropsychology, and Cognition, 14,* 95–107. doi:10.1080/138255891007038

van IJzendoorn, M., & Juffer, F. (2005). Adoption is a successful natural intervention enhancing adopted children's IQ and school performance. *Current Directions in Psychological Science, 14,* 326–330.

Van IJzendoorn, M., & Sagi, A. (1999). Cross-cultural patterns of attachment: Universal and contextual dimensions. In J. Cassidy & P. Shaver (Eds.), *Handbook of attachment* (pp. 265–286). New York, NY: Guilford Press.

van Praag, H., Kempermann, G., & Gage, F. H. (1999). Running increases cell proliferation and neurogenesis in the adult mouse dentate gyrus. *Nature Neuroscience, 2,* 266–270.

Van Rooij, A. J., Schoenmakers, T. M., van de Eijnden, R. J .J. M., & van de Mheen, D. (2010). Compulsive Internet use: The role of online gaming and other Internet applications. *Journal of Adolescent Health, 47,* 51–57.

Van Voorhees, B. W., Paunesku, D., Kuwabara, S. A., Basu, A., Gollan, J., Hankin, B. L., Reinecke, M. (2008). Protective and vulnerability factors predicting new-onset depressive episode in a representative of U.S. adolescents. *Journal of Adolescent Health, 42,* 605–616. doi:10.1016/j.jadohealth.2007.11.135

Van Wyk, P. H., & Geist, C. S. (1984). Psychosocial development of heterosexual, bisexual and homosexual behavior. *Archives of Sexual Behavior, 13,* 505–544.

Vandewater, E. A., Rideout, V. J., Wartella, E. A., Huang, X., Lee, J. H. & Shim, M. (2007). Digital childhood: Electronic media and technology use among infants, toddlers, and preschoolers. *Pediatrics, 119,* e1006–e1015.

Vandewater, E. A., Shim, M., & Caplovitz, A. G. (2004). Linking obesity and activity level with children's television and video game use. *Journal of Adolescence, 27,* 71–85.

Vanhaudenhuyse, A., Boly, M., Balteau, E., Schnakers, C., Moonen, G., Luxen, A., . . . Faymonville, M. E. (2009). Pain and non-pain processing during hypnosis: A thulium-YAG event-related fMRI study. *NeuroImage, 47,* 1047–1054.

Vaswani, M., Linda, F. K., & Ramesh, S. (2003). Role of selective serotonin reuptake inhibitors in psychiatric disorders: A comprehensive review. *Progress in Neuro-Psychopharmacology and Biological Psychiatry, 2,* 85–102.

Vaughan, W. (2009). Painless deprivation. *Science, 324*(5930), 1014.

Veith, I. (1965). *Hysteria: The history of a disease.* Chicago, IL: University of Chicago Press.

Velliste, M., Perel, S., Spalding, M., Whitford, A. S., & Schwartz, A. B. (2008, June 19). Cortical control of a prosthetic arm for self-feeding. *Nature, 453,* 1098–1101. doi:10.1038/nature06996

Venning, A., Kettler, L., Eliott, J., & Wilson, A. (2009). The effectiveness of cognitive–behavioural therapy with hopeful elements to prevent the development of depression in young people: A systematic review. *International Journal of Evidence-Based Healthcare, 7,* 15–33. doi:10.1111/j.1744-1609.2009.00122.x

Verquer, M. L., Beehr, T. A., & Wagner, S. H. (2003). A meta-analysis of relations between person–organization fit and work attitudes. *Journal of Vocational Behavior, 63,* 473–489.

Vetter, H. J. (1968). New-word coinage in the psychopathological context. *Psychiatric Quarterly, 42,* 298–312.

Villemure, C., & Schweinhardt, P. (2010). Supraspinal pain processing: Distinct roles of emotion and attention. *The Neuroscientist, 16,* 276–284.

Vinson, G. A., Connelly, B. S., & Ones, D. S. (2007). Relationships between personality and organization switching: Implications for utility estimates. *International Journal of Selection and Assessment, 15,* 118–133.

Von dem Hagaen, E. A. H., Beaver, J. D., Ewbank, M. P., Keane, J., Passamonti, L., Lawrence, A. D., & Calder, A. J. (2010). Leaving a bad taste in your mouth but not in my insula. *Social Cognitive and Affective Neurosciences, 4,* 379–386.

Vyas, N. S., Patel, N. H., Nijran, K. S., Al-Nahhas, A., & Puri, B. K. (2010). Insights into schizophrenia using positron emission tomography: Building the evidence and refining the focus. *The British Journal of Psychiatry, 197,* 3–4.

Vygotsky, L. S. (1978). *Mind and society: The development of higher psychological processes.* Cambridge, MA: Harvard University Press.

Wadlinger, H. A., & Isaacowitz, D. M. (2006). Positive mood broadens visual attention to positive stimuli. *Motivation & Emotion, 30,* 89–101.

Wagner, A. W., & Linehan, M. M. (2006). Applications of dialectical behavior therapy to posttraumatic stress disorder and related problems. In V. M. Folette & J. I. Ruzek (Eds.), *Cognitive–behavioral therapies for trauma* (2nd ed., pp. 117–145). New York, NY: Guilford Press.

Wagner, T. D., & Ochsner, K. N. (2005). Sex differences in the emotional brain. *NeuroReport, 16,* 85–87.

Wahlbeck, K., Forsen, T., Osmond, C., Barker, D. J. P., & Erikkson, J. G. (2001). Association of schizophrenia with low maternal body mass index, small size at birth, and thinness during childhood. *Archives of General Psychiatry, 58,* 48–55.

Wai, J., Lubinski, D., & Benbow, C. (2009). Spatial ability for STEM domains: Aligning over 50 years of cumulative psychological knowledge solidifies its importance. *Journal of Educational Psychology, 101,* 817–835.

Wakimoto, S., & Fujihara, T. (2004). The correlation between intimacy and objective similarity in interpersonal relationships. *Social Behavior and Personality, 32,* 95–102.

Waldinger, M. D., Zwinderman, A. H., Schweitzer, D. H., & Olivier, B. (2004). Relevance of methodological design for the interpretation of efficacy of drug treatment of premature ejaculation: A systematic review and meta-analysis. *International Journal of Impotence Research, 16,* 369–381.

Walker, M. P., Brakefield, T., Morgan, A., Hobson, J. A., & Stickgold, R. (2002). Practice with sleep makes perfect: Sleep-dependent motor skill learning. *Neuron, 35,* 205–211.

Walker, M. P., & Stickgold, R. (2006). Sleep, memory and plasticity. *Annual Review of Psychology, 57,* 139–166. doi:10.1146/annurev.psych.56091103.070307

Walker, R. W., Skowronski, J. J., & Thompson, C. P. (2003). Life is pleasant—and memory helps to keep it that way. *Review of General Psychology, 7,* 203–210.

Wallace, B. A. (2006). *The attention revolution: Unlocking the power of the focused mind.* Boston, MA: Wisdom.

Wallas, G. (1926). *The art of thought.* New York, NY: Harcourt & Brace.

Wallhagen, M. I., Strawbridge, W. J., Cohen, R. D., & Kaplan, G. A. (1997). An increasing prevalence of hearing impairment and associated risk factors over three decades of Alameda County Study. *American Journal of Public Health, 87,* 440–442.

Wamsley, E. J., Tucker, M. A, Payne, J. D., & Stickgold, R. (2010). A brief nap is beneficial for human route-learning: The role of navigation experience and EEG spectral power. *Learning & Memory, 17,* 332–336.

Wamsley, E. J., Tucker, M., Payne, J. D., Benavides, J. A., & Stickgold, R. (2010). Dreaming of a learning task is associated with enhanced sleep-dependent memory consolidation. *Current Biology, 20,* 850–855. doi:10.1016/j.cub.2010.03.027

Wang, S., Zhang, Z., Guo, Y., Teng, G., & Chen, B. (2008). Hippocampal neurogenesis and behavioural studies on adult ischemic rat response to chronic mild stress. *Behavioural Brain Research, 189,* 9–16.

Wang, Z., Inslicht, S. S., Metzler, T. J., Henn-Haase, C., McCaslin, S. E., Tong, H., . . . Marmar, C. R. (2010). A prospective study of predictors of depression symptoms in police. *Psychiatry Research, 175,* 211–216.

Warga, C. (1987). Pain's gatekeeper. *Psychology Today, 21,* 50–59.

Wason, P. C. (1960). On the failure to eliminate hypotheses in a conceptual task. *Quarterly Journal of Experimental Psychology, 12,* 129–140.

Wasserman, J. D., & Tulsky, D. S. (2005). A history of intelligence assessment. In D. P. Flanagan & P. L. Harrison (Eds.), *Contemporary intellectual assessment: Theories, tests, and issues* (pp. 3–38). New York, NY: Guilford Press.

Waterhouse, J. J., Atkinson, G. G., Edwards, B. B., & Reilly, T. T. (2007). The role of a short post-lunch nap in improving cognitive, motor, and sprint performance in participants with partial sleep deprivation. *Journal of Sports Sciences, 25,* 1557–1566.

Waterland, R., & Jirtle, R. L. (2003). Transposable elements: Targets for early nutritional effects on epigenetic gene regulation. *Molecular and Cellular Biology, 23,* 5293–5300.

Watkins, L. R., & Maier, S. F. (2003). When good pain turns bad. *Current Directions in Psychological Science, 12,* 232–236.

Watson, D., & Tellegen, A. (1985). Toward a consensual structure of mood. *Psychological Bulletin, 98,* 219–235.

Watson, J. B. (1925). *Behaviorism.* New York, NY: Norton.

Watson, J. B., & Rayner, R. (1920). Conditioned emotional reactions. *Journal of Experimental Psychology, 3,* 1–14.

Watters, E. (2006, November 22). DNA is not destiny. *Discover.* Retrieved from http://discovermagazine.com

Watters, E. (2010). *Crazy like us: The globalization of the American psyche.* New York: Free Press.

Waxenberg, S. E., Drellich, M. G., & Sutherland, A. M. (1959). The role of hormones in human behavior: I. Changes in female sexual after adrenalectomy. *Journal of Clinical Endocrinology and Metabolism, 19,* 193–202.

Way, B. M., Taylor, S. E., & Eisenberger, N. I. (2009). Variation in the μ-opioid receptor gene (OPRM1) is associated with dispositional and neural sensitivity to social rejection. *Proceedings of the National Academy of Sciences, 106,* 15079–15084.

Weaver, D. (1998). The suprachiasmatic nucleus: A 25-year retrospective. *Journal of Biological Rhythms, 13,* 100–112.

Weaver, I. C. G., Cervoni, N., & Champagne, F. A. (2004). Epigenetic programming by maternal behavior. *Nature Neuroscience, 7,* 847–854.

Weber, J., & Wahl, J. (2006). Neurological aspects of trepanations from Neolithic times. *International Journal of Osteoarchaeology, 16,* 536–545.

Wechsler, D. (1944). *Measurement of adult intelligence* (3rd ed.). Baltimore, MD: Williams & Wilkins.

Wechsler, D. (1958). *The measurement and appraisal of adult intelligence* (4th ed.). Baltimore, MD: Williams & Wilkins.

Wechsler, H. L., Lee, J. E., & Kuo, M. (2002). Trends in college binge drinking during a period of increased prevention efforts. *Journal of American College Health, 50,* 203–217.

Weil, A., & Rosen, W. (1998). *From chocolate to morphine.* New York, NY: Houghton Mifflin.

Weilund, J. D., & Humayan, M. S. (2008). Visual prosthesis. *Proceedings of the IEEE, 96,* 1076–1084.

Weinberg, R. A. (1989). Intelligence and IQ: Issues and great debates. *American Psychologist, 44,* 98–104.

Weinberg, R. S., & Gould, D. (2007). *Foundations of sport and exercise psychology* (4th ed.). Champaign, IL: Human Kinetics.

Weinberger, D. R., Egan, M. F., Bertolino, A., Callicott, J. H., Mattay, V. S., Lipska, B. K., . . . Goldberg, T. E. (2001). Prefrontal neurons and the genetics of schizophrenia. *Biological Psychiatry, 50,* 825–844.

Weinberger, M., Hiner, S. L., & Tierney, W. M. (1987). In support of hassles as a measure of stress in predicting health outcomes. *Journal of Behavioral Medicine, 10,* 19–31.

Weinhardt, L. S. (2005). Changing HIV and AIDS-related behavior: Promising approaches at the individual, group, and community levels. *Behavior Modification, 29,* 219–226.

Weinstein, A. A., Deuster, P. A., Francis, J. L., Bonsall, R. W., Tracy, R. P., & Kop, W. J. (2010). Neurohormonal and inflammatory hyper-responsiveness to acute mental stress in depression. *Biological Psychology, 84,* 228–234.

Weinstein, T. A., Capitanio, J. P., & Gosling, S. D. (2008). Personality in animals. In O. P. John, R. W. Robins, & L. A. Pervin (Eds.), *Handbook of personality: Theory and research* (pp. 328–348). New York, NY: Guilford Press.

Weisinger, R., Denton, D., McKinley, M., & Miselis, R. (1993, November). Forebrain lesions that disrupt water homeostasis do not eliminate the sodium appetite of sodium deficiency in sheep. *Brain Research, 628*(1), 166–178.

Wenden, A. L. (1998). Metacognitive knowledge and language learning. *Applied Linguistics, 19,* 515–537.

Wermke, M., Sorg, C., Wohlschläger, A. M., & Drzezga, A. (2008, February 26). A new integrative model of cerebral activation, deactivation and default mode function in Alzheimer's disease. *European Journal of Nuclear Medicine and Molecular Imaging.* Advance online publication. doi:10.1007/s00259-007-0698-5

Wertheimer, M. (1959). *Productive thinking.* New York, NY: Harper.

Wessely, S., & Kerwin, R. (2004). Suicide risk and the SSRIs. *Journal of the American Medical Association, 292,* 379–381.

Westen, D., Blagov, P. S., Harenski, K., Kilts, C., & Hamann, S. (2006). Neural bases of motivated reasoning: An fMRI study of emotional constraints on partisan political judgment in the 2004 U.S. presidential election. *Journal of Cognitive Neuroscience, 18,* 1947–1958.

Westen, D., Gabbard, G. O., & Ortigo, K. M. (2008). Psychoanalytic approaches to personality. In O. P. John, R. W. Robins, & L. A. Pervin (Eds.), *Handbook of personality: Theory and research* (pp. 61–113). New York, NY: Guilford Press.

Westlye, L. T., Walhovd, K. B., Dale, A. M., Bjornerud, A., Due-Tonnessen, P., Engvig, A. . . . Fjell, A. M. (2010). Life-span changes of the human brain white matter: Diffusion tensor imaging (DTI) and volumetry. *Cerebral Cortex, 20,* 2055–2068.

Westmaas, J. L., & Silver, R. C. (2006). The role of perceived similarity in supportive responses to victims of negative life events. *Personality and Social Psychology Bulletin, 32,* 1537–1546.

Weston, D. (1998). The scientific legacy of Sigmund Freud: Toward a psychodynamically informed psychological science. *Psychological Bulletin, 124,* 333–371.

Whalen, C. K., & Henker, B. (1998). Attention-deficit/hyperactivity disorder. In T. H. Ollendick & M. Hersen (Eds.), *Handbook of child psychopathology* (pp. 181–212). New York, NY: Plenum Press.

What causes Down syndrome? (2011). National Down Syndrome Society. Retrieved July 20, 2007, from http://www.ndss.org/index.php?option=com_content&view=article&id=60&Itemid=77

White, A. M. (2003, Spring). What happened? Alcohol, memory blackouts, and the brain. *Alcohol Research & Health,* 186–196.

White, P. (2006). A background to acupuncture and its use in chronic painful musculoskeletal conditions. *Journal of the Royal Society of Health, 126,* 219–227.

White, R. W. (1964). *The abnormal personality.* New York, NY: Ronald Press.

White, R. W., & Horvitz, E. (2009). Cyberchondria: Studies of the escalation of medical concerns in Web search. *ACM Transactions on Information Systems (TOIS), 27.* http://doi.acm.org/10.1145/1629096.1629101

Whiten, A., Horner, V., & de Waal, F. B. M. (2005). Conformity to cultural norms of tool use in chimpanzees. *Nature, 437,* 737–740.

Whitfield, C. L., Dube, S. R., Felitti, V. J., & Anda, R. E. (2005). Adverse childhood experiences and hallucinations. *Child Abuse and Neglect, 29,* 797–810.

Whiting, B., & Edwards, C. (1988). *Children of different worlds: The formation of social behavior.* Cambridge, MA: Harvard University Press.

Whitlock, J. R., Heynen, A. J., Shuler, M. G., & Bear, M. F. (2006). Learning induces long-term potentiation in the hippocampus. *Science, 313,* 1093–1097.

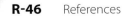

Whorf, B. L. (1956). *Language, thought, and reality: Selected writings of Benjamin Lee Whorf* (J. B. Carroll, Ed.). Cambridge, MA: MIT Press.

Wickelgren, I. (2009, September/October). I do not feel your pain. *Scientific American Mind*, 51–57.

Wickens, T. D. (2002). *Elementary signal detection theory.* New York: NY: Oxford University Press.

Wiederhold, B. K., & Wiederhold, M. D. (2005). Specific phobias and social phobia. In B. K. Wiederhold & M. D. Wiederhold (Eds.), *Virtual reality therapy for anxiety disorders: Advances in evaluation and treatment* (pp. 125–138). Washington, DC: American Psychological Association.

Wilensky, A., Schafe, G., Kristensen, M., & LeDoux, J. (2006). Rethinking the fear circuit: The central nucleus of the amygdala is required for the acquisition, consolidation, and expression of Pavlovian fear conditioning. *Journal of Neuroscience, 26*(48), 12387–12396.

Wiley, C. (1997). What motivates employees according to over 40 years of motivation surveys. *International Journal of Manpower, 18*(3), 263–280.

Wilkening, F., & Sodian, B. (2005). Scientific reasoning in young children: An introduction. *Swiss Journal of Psychology, 64,* 137–139.

Wille, B., De Fruyt, F., & Feys, M. (2010). Vocational interests and Big Five traits as predictors of job instability. *Journal of Vocational Behavior, 76,* 547–558.

Williams, A. L., & Merten, M. J. (2008). A review of online social networking profiles by adolescents: Implications for future research and intervention. *Adolescence, 43,* 253–274.

Williams, G., Cai, X. J., Elliot, J. C., & Harrold, J. A. (2004). Anabolic neuropeptides. *Physiology and Behavior, 81,* 211–222.

Williams, J. H. G., Waiter, G. D., Gilchrist, A., Perrett, D. I., Murray, A. D., & Whiten, A. (2006). Neural mechanisms of imitation and "mirror neuron" functioning in autistic spectrum disorder. *Neuropsychologia, 44,* 610–621.

Williams, K. D., & Zudro, L., (2001). Ostracism: On being ignored, excluded, and rejected. In M. R. Leary (Ed.), *Interpersonal rejection* (pp. 21–53). New York, NY: Oxford University Press.

Williams, P. A., Haertel, E. H., Hartel, G. D., & Walberg, H. J. (1982). The impact of leisure time television on school learning: A research synthesis. *American Educational Research Journal, 19,* 19–50.

Williams, R., Briggs, R., & Coleman, P. (1995). Carer-rated personality changes associated with senile dementia. *International Journal of Geriatric Psychiatry, 10,* 231–236.

Williams, R. B., Jr., Haney, T. L., Lee, K. L., Kong, Y., Blumenthal, J. A., & Whalen, R. (1980). Type A behavior, hostility, coronary atherosclerosis. *Psychosomatic Medicine, 42,* 539–549.

Willis, S. L., Tennstedt, S. L., Marsiske, M., Ball, K., Elias, J., Koepke, K. M., et al. for the ACTIVE Study Group. (2006). Long-term effects of cognitive training on everyday functional outcomes in older adults. *Journal of the American Medical Association, 295,* 2805–2814.

Wilson, M. A., & McNaughton, B. L. (1994). Reactivation of hippocampal ensemble memories during sleep. *Science, 265,* 676–679.

Wimmer, H., & Perner, J. (1983). Beliefs about beliefs: Representation and constraining function of wrong beliefs in young children's understanding of deception. *Cognition, 13,* 103–128.

Wims, E., Titov, N., Andrews, G., & Choi, I. (2010). Clinician-assisted Internet-based treatment is effective for panic: A randomized controlled trial. *Australian and New Zealand Journal of Psychiatry, 44,* 599–607.

Winawer, J., Witthoft, N., Frank, M. C., Wu, L., Wade, A. R., & Boroditsky, L. (2007). Russian blues reveal effect of language on color discrimination. *Proceedings of the National Academy of Sciences, 104,* 7780–7785.

Wing, L., & Potter, D. (2002). The epidemiology of autistic spectrum disorders: Is the prevalence rising? *Mental Retardation and Mental Disabilities Research Review, 8,* 151–161.

Wing, R., & Jeffery, R. (1999). Benefits of recruiting participants with friends and increasing social support for weight loss and maintenance. *Journal of Consulting and Clinical Psychology, 67,* 132–138.

Witelson, S. F., Kigar, D. L., Scamvougeras, A., Kideckel, D. M., Buck, B., Stanchev, P. L., Bronskill, M., & Black, S. (2008). Corpus callosum anatomy in right-handed homosexual and heterosexual men. *Archives of Sexual Behavior, 37,* 857–863.

Witkin, H. A., & Asch, S. E. (1948). Studies in space orientation. IV. Further experiments on perception of the upright with displaced visual fields. *Journal of Experimental Psychology, 38,* 762–782.

Witte, K., & Allen, M. (2000). A meta-analysis of fear appeals: Implications for effective public health campaigns. *Health Education & Behavior, 27,* 591–615.

Wolak, J., Mitchell, K., & Finkelhor, D. (2002). Close online relationships in a national sample of adolescents. *Adolescence, 37,* 441–455.

Wölfling, K., Flor, H., & Grüsser, S. M. (2008). Psychophysiological responses to drug-associated stimuli in chronic heavy cannabis use. *European Journal of Neuroscience, 27,* 976–983.

Wong, C. C. Y., Caspi, A., Williams, B., Craig, I. W., Houts, R., Ambler, A., . . . Mill, J. (2010). A longitudinal study of epigenetic variation in twins. *Epigenetics, 5,* 1–11.

Woodworth, R. S., & Schlosberg, H. (1954). *Experimental psychology* (Rev. ed.). New York, NY: Henry Holt.

Work-related hearing loss. (2001). National Institute for Occupational Safety and Health, NIOSH, Publication No. 2001-103.

Retrieved from http://www.cdc.gov/niosh/docs/2001-103/

World Health Organization. (2009). Intervention on diet and physical activity: What works: Summary Report. Retrieved from http://www.who.int/dietphysicalactivity/summary-report-09.pdf

World's greatest living polyglot. (n.d.). Retrieved May 31, 2007, from http://www.spidra.com/fazah.html

Wouters-Adriaens, M., & Westerterp, K. (2006). Basal metabolic rate as a proxy for overnight energy expenditure: The effect of age. *British Journal of Nutrition, 95,* 1166–1170.

Wurtz, R. H., & Kandel, E. R. (2000a). Central visual pathways. In E. R. Kandel, J. H. Schwartz, & T. M. Jessell. (2000). *Principles of neural science* (4th ed., pp. 523–545). New York, NY: McGraw-Hill.

Wurtz, R. H., & Kandel, E. R. (2000b). Perception of motion, depth, and form. In E. R. Kandel, J. H. Schwartz, & T. M. Jessell (Eds.), *Principles of neural science* (4th ed., pp. 548–571). New York, NY: McGraw-Hill.

Xia, M., Huang, R., Guo, V., Southall, N., Ming-Hsuang, C., Inglese, J., . . . Nirenberg, M. (2009). Identification of compounds that potentiate CREB signaling as possible enhancers of long-term memory. *Proceedings of the National Academy of Sciences, 106,* 2412–2417. doi:10.1073/pnas.0813020106

Xiang, J., Shen, H., & Li, J. (2009). Need-pressure trials of borderline personality disorder in Thematic Apperception Test. *Chinese Mental Health Journal, 23,* 340–344.

Xu, F., & Garcia, V. (2008). Intuitive statistics by 8-month-old infants. *Proceedings of the National Academy of Sciences, 105,* 5012–5015.

Xu, F., Luk, C., Richard, M. P., Zaidi, W., Farkas, S., Getz, A., . . . Syed, N. I. (2010). Antidepressant fluoxetine suppresses neuronal growth from both vertebrate and invertebrate neurons and perturbs synapse formation between *Lymnaea* neurons. *European Journal of Neuroscience, 31,* 994–1005.

Yamada, M., & Yasuhara, H. (2004). Clinical pharmacology of MAO inhibitors: Safety and future. *NeuroToxicology, 25,* 215–221.

Yang, Y., Raine, A., Han, C-B., Schug, R. A., Toga, A. W., & Narr, K. L. (2010). Reduced hippocampal and parahippocampal volumes in murderers with schizophrenia, *Psychiatry Research: Neuroimaging, 182,* 9–13.

Ybarra, M. L. (2004). Linkages between youth depressive symptomatology and online harassment. *CyberPsychology and Behavior, 7,* 247–257.

Ybarra, M. L., & Mitchell, K. J. (2004). Youth engaging in online harassment: Associations with caregiver-child relationships, Internet use, and personal characteristics. *Journal of Adolescence, 27,* 319–336.

Ybarra, M. L., & Mitchell, K. J. (2008). How risky are social networking sites? A comparison of places online where youth sexual solicitation and harassment occurs.

Pediatrics, 121, e350–e357. doi: 10.1542/peds.2007-0693

Yen, J-Y, Ko, C-H, Yen, C-F., Wu, H-Y., & Yang, M-J. (2007). The comorbid psychiatric symptoms of Internet addiction: Attention deficit and hyperactivity disorder (ADHD), depression, social phobia, and hostility. *Journal of Adolescent Health, 41,* 93–98.

Yeragani, V. K., Tancer, M., Chokka, P., & Baker, G. B. (2010). Arvid Carlsson, and the story of dopamine. *Indian Journal of Psychiatry, 52,* 87–88. Retrieved from http://www.indianjpsychiatry.org/text.asp?2010/52/1/87/58907

Yerkes, R. M., & Dodson, J. D. (1908). The relation of strength of stimulus to rapidity of habit-formation. *Journal of Comparative Neurology and Psychology, 18,* 459–482.

Yin, J. C. P., Del Vecchio, M., Zhou, H., & Tully, T. (1995). CREB as a memory modulator: Induced expression of a dCREB2 activator isoform enhances long-term memory in *Drosophila. Cell, 81,* 107–115.

Yoemans, N. D. (2011). The ulcer sleuths: The search for the cause of peptic ulcers. *Journal of Gastroenterology and Hepatology, 26,* Supplement s1, 35–41.

Yoon, J., & Thye, S. (2000). Supervisor support in the work place: Legitimacy and positive affectivity. *Journal of Social Psychology, 140,* 295–316.

Young, A. S., Niv, N., Cohen, A. N., Kessler, C., & McNagny, K. (2010). The appropriateness of routine medication treatment for schizophrenia. *Schizophrenia Bulletin, 36,* 732–739.

Young, L. C., Zaun, B. J., & VanderWerf, E. A. (2008). Successful same-sex pairing in Laysan albatross. *Biology Letters, 4,* 323–325.

Yu, A. Y., Tian, S. W., Vogel, D., & Kwok, R. C-H. (2010). Can learning be virtually boosted? An investigation of online social networking impacts. *Computers & Education, 55,* 1494–1503.

Yuen, E. K., Herbert, J. D., Forman, E. M., Comer, R., Bradley, J., Goetter, E. M., & Park, J. A. (2009, November). Virtual therapy for social anxiety disorder using Second Life: Preliminary Results. Poster presented at the conference of the Association of Behavioral and Cognitive Therapies, New York, NY.

Zajonc, R. B. (1965). Social facilitation. *Science, 149,* 269–274.

Zajonc, R. B. (1968). Attitudinal effects of mere exposure. *Journal of Personality and Social Psychology, 9,* 1–27.

Zak, P. J., Stanton, A. A., & Ahmadi, S. (2007). Oxytocin increases generosity in humans. *PLoS ONE, 2,* 1–5.

Zametkin, A. J., Nordahl, T. E., Gross, M., King, A. C., Semple, W. E., Rumsey, J., . . . Cohen, R. M. (1990). Cerebral glucose metabolism in adults with hyperactivity of childhood onset. *New England Journal of Medicine, 15,* 1361–1366.

Zang, Y. F., Jin, Z., Weng, X. C., Zhang, L., Zeng, Y. W., Yang, L., . . . Faraone, S. V. (2005). Functional MRI in attention-deficit hyperactivity disorder: Evidence for hypofrontality. *Brain Development, 27,* 544–550. doi:10.1016/j.braindev.2004.11.009

Zanna, M. P., Kiesler, C. A., & Pilkonis, P. A. (1970). Positive and negative attitudinal affect established by classical conditioning. *Journal of Personality and Social Psychology, 14,* 321–328.

Zeidan, F., Martucci, K. T., Kraft, R. A., Gordon, N. S., McHaffie, J. G., &. Coghill, R. C. (2011). Brain mechanisms supporting the modulation of pain by mindfulness meditation. *The Journal of Neuroscience, 31,* 5540–5548.

Zeino, Z., Sisson, G., & Bjarnason, I. (2010). Adverse effects of drugs on small intestine and colon. *Best Practice & Research Clinical Gastroenterology, 24,* 133–141.

Zhang, L. (2010). Do thinking styles contribute to metacognition beyond self-rated abilities? *Educational Psychology, 30,* 481–494. doi:10.1080/01443411003659986

Zhang, Y., Jin, X., Shen, X., Zhang, J., & Hoff, E. (2008). Correlates of early language development in Chinese children. *International Journal of Behavioral Development, 32,* 145–151. doi:10.1177/0165025407087213

Zhao, Y., Montoro, R., Igartua, K., & Thombs, B. D. (2010). Suicidal ideation and attempt among adolescents reporting "unsure" sexual identity or heterosexual identity plus same-sex attraction or behavior: Forgotten groups? *Journal of the American Academy of Child & Adolescent Psychiatry, 49*(2), 104–113. doi:10.1097/00004583-201002000-00004

Zigler, E. F., Finn-Stevenson, M., & Hall, N. W. (2002). *The first three years and beyond.* New Haven, CT: Yale University Press.

Zimbardo, P. G. (2007). *The Lucifer effect: Understanding how good people turn evil.* New York, NY: Random House.

Zimmer-Gembeck, M. J., & Collins, W. A. (2008). Gender, mature appearance, alcohol use, and dating as correlates of sexual partner accumulation from ages 16–26 years. *Journal of Adolescent Health, 42,* 564–572.

Zimmer, C. (2005, March 1). Looking for personality in animals, of all people. *New York Times.* Retrieved from http://www.nytimes.com

Zimmer, C. (2008, November 11). Now: The rest of the genome. *The New York Times.* Retrieved from http://www.nytimes.com

Zimmerman, C. (2007). The development of scientific thinking skills in elementary and middle school. *Developmental Review, 27,* 172–223.

Zullig, K., Pun, S., & Huebner, E. (2007). Life satisfaction, dieting behavior, and weight perceptions among college students. *Applied Research in Quality of Life, 2*(1), 17–31.

Credits

TEXT

Chapter 1

Figure 1.1: Adapted from Mulvey, T. A., & Grus, C. L. (2010, August). What can I do with a degree in psychology? Presented at Annual Convention of American Psychological Association, San Diego, CA. Retrieved online January 17, 2011 at http://www.apa.org/workforce/presentations/2010-psychology-degree.pdf.Copyright © 2010 by the American Psychological Association. Adapted with permission. No further reproduction or distribution is permitted without written permission from the American Psychological Association.

Chapter 3

Figure 3.4: (line art/text) From King, L. (2008). *The Science of Psychology: An Appreciative View,* 1st ed., Fig. 3.1, p. 68. Copyright © 2008 The McGraw-Hill Companies. Used with permission.
Figure 3.6: From King, L. (2008). *The Science of Psychology: An Appreciative View,* 1st ed., Fig. 3.2, p. 68. Copyright © 2008 The McGraw-Hill Companies. Used with permission.
Figure 3.8 b and c: From King, L. (2008). *The Science of Psychology: An Appreciative View,* 1st ed., Fig. 3.5, p. 73. Copyright © 2008 The McGraw-Hill Companies. Used with permission.
Figure 3.8 d: From Passer, M. W., & Smith, R. E. (2008). *Psychology: The Science of Mind and Behavior,* 4th ed., Fig. 4.4, p. 97. Copyright © 2008 The McGraw-Hill Companies. Used with permission.
Figure 3.10: From Passer, M. W., & Smith, R. E. (2008). *Psychology: The Science of Mind and Behavior,* 4th ed., Fig. 3.9, p. 80. Copyright © 2008 The McGraw-Hill Companies. Used with permission.
Figure 3.12: From King, L. (2008). *The Science of Psychology: An Appreciative View,* 1st ed., Fig. 3.12, p. 82. Copyright © 2008 The McGraw-Hill Companies. Used with permission.
Figure 3.18: From Passer, M. W., & Smith, R. E. (2008). *Psychology: The Science of Mind and Behavior,* 4th ed. Copyright © 2008 The McGraw-Hill Companies. Used with permission.
Figure 3.22: From O'Craven, K. M., & Kanwisher, N. (2000). Mental imagery of faces and places activates corresponding stimulus-specific brain regions. *Journal of Cognitive Neuroscience 12:6,* 1013–1023. Fig. 3, p. 1018. Used by permission of the authors.

Chapter 4

Figure 4.2: From Passer, M. W., & Smith, R. E. (2008). *Psychology: The Science of Mind and Behavior,* 4th ed., Fig. 5.4, p. 128. Copyright © 2008 The McGraw-Hill Companies. Used with permission.
Figure 4.4 a and c: From Passer, M. W., & Smith, R. E. (2008). *Psychology: The Science of Mind and Behavior,* 4th ed., Fig. 5.7, p. 133. Copyright © 2008 The McGraw-Hill Companies. Used with permission.
Figure 4.5: Published in Komischke, T. (2008). Colors and the UI. InfoQ.com. Accessed 6/7/11 at http://www.infoq.com/articles/Colors-UI. Used with permission from Tobias Komischke, Infragistics, Inc.
Figure 4.6: From Wurtz, R. H., & Kandel, E. R. (2000). Central visual pathways. In E. R. Kandel, J. H. Schwartz, and R. M. Jessell, *Principles of Neural Science,* 4th ed., pp. 548–571. © 2000 The McGraw-Hill Companies. Used with permission.
Figure 4.8: From Weiten, W. (2008). *Psychology: Themes and Variations,* 7/e, p. 103. © 2008 Wadsworth, a part of Cengage Learning, Inc. Reproduced by permission. www.cengage.com/permissions
Figure 4.9: From Kandel, E. R., Wurtz, R. H., & Jessell, R. M. (2000). *Principles of Neural Science,* 4th ed., p. 534. Copyright © 2000 The McGraw-Hill Companies. Used with permission.
Figure 4.25: From Passer, M. W., & Smith, R. E. (2008). *Psychology: The Science of Mind and Behavior,* 4th ed., Figure 5.13, p. 137. Copyright © 2008 The McGraw-Hill Companies. Used with permission.
Figure 4.26 From Ishihara's Tests for Colour Deficiency. Published by Kanehara Trading, Inc., Tokyo, Japan. Used with permission. NOTE: *Tests for colour deficiency cannot be conducted with this material. For accurate testing, the original plates should be used.*
Figure 4.28: From King, L. (2008). *The Science of Psychology: An Appreciative View,* 1st ed., Fig. 5.37, p. 188. Copyright © 2008 The McGraw-Hill Companies. Used with permission.
Figure 4.29: From Passer, M. W., & Smith, R. E. (2008). *Psychology: The Science of Mind and Behavior,* 4th ed., Fig. 5.19d, p. 141. Copyright © 2008 The McGraw-Hill Companies. Used with permission.
Figure 4.34: From Ramachandran, V. S., & Hubbard, E. M. (2003, May). Hearing colors, tasting shapes. *Scientific American, 228,* 52–59. Used with permission. Copyright © 2003 Scientific American, Inc. All rights reserved.
Figure 4.35: After Hudson, W. (1960). Pictorial depth perception in subcultural groups in Africa. *Journal of Social Psychology, 52,* 183–208. Copyright © 1960. Reprinted with permission of the Helen Dwight Reid Educational Foundation. Published by Heldref Publications, 1319 Eighteenth St., NW, Washington, DC 20036-1802.

Chapter 5

Figure 5.1: From Patterson, C. J. (2008). *Child Development,* 1st ed., p. 64. Copyright © 2008 The McGraw-Hill Companies. Used with permission.
Figure 5.2: From Hetheringon, E. M. (2006). *Child Psychology: A Contemporary Viewpoint,* 6th edition, Figure 3.2, p. 89. Copyright © 2006 The McGraw-Hill Companies. Used with permission.
Figure 5.5 (graph) : From Santrock, J. (2008). *Children,* 10th ed., Fig. 5.16. Copyright © 2008 The McGraw-Hill Companies. Used with permission.
Figure 5.13: From Baillargeon, R., & DeVos, J. (1991). Object permanence in young children: Further evidence. *Child Development, 62,* 1227–1246, Fig. 4, p. 1237. Reprinted by permission of Blackwell Publishing.
Figure 5.14: From Patterson, C. J. (2008). *Child Development,* 1st ed., Fig. 8.1, p. 286. Copyright © 2008 The McGraw-Hill Companies. Used with permission.
Figure 5.30: Reprinted with permission from www.Helpguide.org © 2001–2011. All rights reserved. For Helpguide's articles on Alzheimer's, visit www.Helpguide.org .

Chapter 6

Figure 6.1: From Laureys, S. (2007). Eyes open, brain shut. *Scientific American, 296,* 84–89. Art by Melissa Thomas, p. 87. Used with permission by Melissa Thomas.
Figure 6.2: From Teasdale, G., & Jennett, B. (1976). Assessment and prognosis of coma after head injury. *Acta Neurochirurgica, 34,* 45–55. Used with permission by Springer-Verlag.
Figure 6.7: From Monk, T. M., Folkarc, S., & Wedderburn, A. I. (1996, February). Maintaining safety and high performance on shiftwork. *Applied Ergonomics 27*(1), 317–324. Copyright © 1996 with permission from Elsevier.
Figure 6.10: Adapted from Roffwarg, H. P., Muzio, J. N., & Dement, W. C. (1966). Ontogenetic development of human dream-sleep cycle. *Science, 152,* 604, Figure 1. Reprinted with permission from the American Association for the Advancement of Science.
Figure 6.13: From Hobson, J. A. (2001). *The Dream Drugstore: Chemically Altered States of Consciousness.* Cambridge, MA: The MIT Press. © 2001 Massachusetts Institute of Technology, by permission of The MIT Press.

Chapter 7

Figure 7.5: From Thompson, R., & Madigan, S. (2007). *Memory: The key to consciousness.* Washington, DC: Joseph Henry Press, p. 30. Reprinted by permission of Princeton University Press.
Figure 7.9: Adapted from Craik, F. I. M., & Tulving, E. (1975). Depth of processing and the retention of words in episodic memory. *Journal of Experimental Psychology: General, 104,* 268–294. Used with permission from the American Psychological Association.
Figure 7.10: From Collins, A. M., & Loftus, E. F. (1975). A spreading activation theory of semantic processing. *Psychological Review, 82,* 407–428. Used with permission from the American Psychological Association.
Figure 7.11: From Eichenbaum, H. (2010, July/August). Memory systems. *WIREs Cognitive Science, 1*(4), 478–490. Copyright © 2010. Reproduced with permission of John Wiley & Sons Ltd.
Figure 7.14: From Payne, J. D., & Kensinger, E. A. (2010). Sleep's role in the consolidation of emotional episodic memories. *Current Directions in Psychological Science, 19*(5), 290–295. Figure from p. 293. © 2010 Association for Psychological Science. Reprinted by permission of Sage Publications.
Figure 7.16: From Slamecka, N. J., & McElree, B. (1983). Normal forgetting of verbal lists as a function of their degree of learning. *Journal of Experimental Psychology: Learning, Memory, and Cognition, 9,* 384–397. Used with permission from the American Psychological Association.

Chapter 8

Figure 8.3: From Feldman, R. S., (2007). *Understanding Psychology,* 8th ed., Fig. 2, p. 189. © The McGraw-Hill Companies. Used with permission of The McGraw-Hill Companies, Inc.
Figure 8.4: From King, L. (2008). *The Science of Psychology: An Appreciative View,* 1st ed., Figure 7.4, p. 256. © 2008 The McGraw-Hill Companies, Inc. All rights reserved. Used with permission of The McGraw-Hill Companies, Inc.
Figure 8.7: From Weiten, W. (2007). *School Sample Box for Weiten's Psychology: Themes and Variations (with Concept Charts),* 7th ed. © 2007 Wadsworth, a part of Cengage Learning, Inc. © 2007 Wadsworth, a part of Cengage Learning, Inc. Reproduced by permission. www.cengage.com/permissions .
Figure 8.10: From King, L. (2008). *The Science of Psychology: An Appreciative View,* 1st ed., Fig. 7.8, p. 261. © 2008 The McGraw-Hill Companies, Inc. All rights reserved. Used with permission of The McGraw-Hill Companies, Inc.
Figure 8.11: From Walker, M. P., & Stickgold, R. (2006). Sleep, memory, and plasticity. *Annual Review of Psychology, 57,* 139–166. Fig. 2, p. 145. Copyright © 2006 by Annual Reviews. All rights reserved. Used by permission.
Figure 8.14: Limits on conditioned taste aversion. From Garcia, J., & Koelling, R. A. (1966). The relation of cue to consequence in avoidance learning. *Psychonomic Science, 4,* 123–124. Used with permission.
Figure 8.15: From Bandura, A., Ross, D., & Ross, S. A. (1963). Vicarious reinforcement and imitative learning. *Journal of Abnormal Social Psychol-*

ogy, 67, 601–608. Used with permission from the American Psychological Association.
Figure 8.16: From Bandura, A., Ross, D., & Ross, S. A. (1963). Vicarious reinforcement and imitative learning. *Journal of Abnormal Social Psychology, 67*, 601–608. Used with permission from the American Psychological Association.
Figure 8.17: From Rizzolatti, G., Gadiga, L., Gallese, V., & Fogassi, L. (1996). Premotor cortex and the recognition of motor actions. *Cognitive Brain Research, 3*, 131–141. Copyright © 1996 with permission from Elsevier.

Chapter 9

Figure 9.1: From King, L. (2008). *The Science of Psychology*, 1st ed., Figure 3.18, p. 87. Copyright © 2008 The McGraw-Hill Companies. Used with permission of The McGraw-Hill Companies.
Figure 9.2: From Sakai, K. L. (2005). Language acquisition and brain development. *Science, 310*, 810–819. Reprinted with permission from the American Association for the Advancement of Science.
Figure 9.5: The Research Process: Language and Color Discrimination. Two figures from Winawer, J., et al. (2007). Russian blues reveal effect of language on color discrimination. *Proceedings of the National Academy of Sciences, 104*, 7785–7789. Used with permission.
Figure 9.6: From Shepard, R. N., & Metzler, J. (1971). Mental rotation of three-dimensional objects. *Science, 171*, 701–703. Reprinted with permission from the American Association for the Advancement of Science.
Figure 9.7: Parallel Distributed Network of the Verbal Concept "Living Thing." From McClelland, J. L., & Rogers, T. T. (2003). The parallel distributed processing approach to semantic cognition. *Nature Reviews Neuroscience, 4*(4), 310–322. Reprinted by permission from Macmillan Publishers Ltd. http://www.nature.com/nrn/index.html

Chapter 10

Figure 10.3: Adapted from Carroll, J. B. (1993). *Human cognitive abilities*. New York: Cambridge University Press. Used with the permission of Cambridge University Press.
Figure 10.9: From Grigorenko, E. (2000). Heritability and intelligence. In R. J. Sternberg (Ed.), *Handbook of Intelligence*, pp. 53–91. Cambridge University Press. Reprinted with the permission of Cambridge University Press.
Figure 10.11: From Deary, I. J., et al. (2003). Population sex differences in I.Q. at age 11: The Scottish Mental Survey 1932. *Intelligence, 31*, 533–542. Copyright © 2003 with permission from Elsevier.
Figure 10.13: From King, L. (2008). *The Science of Psychology: An Appreciative View*, 1st ed., Figs. 9.3 and 9.4, p. 330. Copyright © 2008 The McGraw-Hill Companies. Used with permission of The McGraw-Hill Companies.
Figure 10.14: From Goel, V., & Vartanian, O. (2005). Dissociating the roles of right ventral lateral and dorsal lateral prefrontal cortex in generation and maintenance of hypotheses in set-shift problems. *Cerebral Cortex, 15*, 1170–1177. Used by permission of Oxford University Press.
Figure 10.16: From Finke, R. A., Ward, T. B., & Smith, S. M. (1992). *Creative cognition: Theory, research, and applications*. Cambridge, MA: MIT Press. © 1992 Massachusetts Institute of Technology, by permission of The MIT Press.

Chapter 11

Figure 11.2: After Berridge, K. C. (2004). Motivation concepts in behavioral neuroscience. *Physiology and Behavior, 81*, 179–209. After Fig. 1, p. 181. Copyright © 2004 with permission from Elsevier.
Figure 11.3: From Smith, B. D. (1999). *Psychology: Science and Understanding*, 1st ed., McGraw-Hill. Figure 11.1 Copyright © 1998 The McGraw-Hill Companies. Used with permission of The McGraw-Hill Companies.
Figure 11.7: From Passer, M. W., & Smith, R. E. (2008). *Psychology: The Science of Mind and Behavior*, 4th ed., p. 377, Figs. 11.1 and 11.14. Copyright © 2008 The McGraw-Hill Companies. Used with permission of The McGraw-Hill Companies.

Figure 11.12: From Russell, J. A. (1980). A circumplex model of affect. *Journal of Personality & Social Psychology, 38*, 1161–1178. Used with permission from the American Psychological Association.

Chapter 12

Figure 12.1: From Holmes, T. H., & Rahe, R. H. (1967). The Social Readjustment Rating Scale. *Journal of Psychosomatic Reseearch*, Vol. 11, No. 2, pp. 213–218. Copyright © 1967 with permission from Elsevier.
Figure 12.4: From Selye, H. (1976). *The Stress of Life*, p. 476. Copyright © 1976 The McGraw-Hill Companies.
Figure 12.8: From Pereira, A. C., Huddelston, E.D., Brickman, A. M., et al. (2007). An in-vivo correlate of exercise-induced neurogenesis in the adult dentate gyrus. *Proceedings of the National Academy of Sciences, 104*, 5638–5643.

Chapter 13

Figure 13.1 (graphs): From Plomin, R., & Caspi, A. (1999). Behavioral genetics and personality. In L. A. *Pervin* & O. P. John (eds.), *Handbook of personality: Theory and research*, 2nd ed., 251–276. Used with permission of Guilford Publications, Inc.
Figure 13.2 From Feist, J., & Feist, G. J. (2006). *Theories of personality*, 6th ed. Copyright © 2006 The McGraw-Hill Companies. Used with permission of The McGraw-Hill Companies.
Figure 13.4: From Mischel, W., & Shoda, Y. (1995). A cognitive-affective system theory of personality. *Psychological Review, 102*, 246–268. Used with permission from the American Psychological Association.
Figure 13.6: From Eysenck, H. J. (1990). Biological dimensions of personality. In L. Pervin (ed.), *Handbook of personality: Theory and research*, 1st ed., 224–276. Used with permission of Guilford Publications, Inc.
Figure 13.10: From Roberts, B. W., Walton, K. E., & Viechtbauer, W. (2006). Patterns of mean-level change in personality traits across the life course. *Psychological Bulletin, 132*, 1–25. Used with permission from the American Psychological Association.

Chapter 14

Figure 14.1: From Passer, M. W., & Smith, R. E. (2008). *Psychology: The Science of Mind and Behavior*, 4th ed., Fig. 11a, p. 635. Copyright © 2008 The McGraw-Hill Companies. Used with permission of the McGraw-Hill Companies.
Figure 14.2a and b: From Milgram, S. (1974). *Obedience to Authority: An Experimental View*, 4th ed., Fig. 4., p. 28, and pp. 30–32. New York: HarperCollins Publishers. Copyright © 1974 by Stanley Milgram. Reprinted by permission of HarperCollins Publishers and Pinter & Martin Ltd.
Figure 14.3: From Milgram, S. (1974). *Obedience to Authority: An Experimental View*, 4th ed., p. 195. New York: HarperCollins Publishers. Copyright © 1974 by Stanley Milgram. Reprinted by permission of HarperCollins Publishers and Pinter & Martin Ltd.
Figure 14.9: From Sternberg, R. (1986). A triangular theory of love. *Psychological Review, 93*, 119–135. Used with permission of Dr. Robert Sternberg.

Chapter 15

Figure 15.3: From American Psychiatric Association (2000). *Diagnostic and Statistical Manual of Mental Disorders*, 4th ed., Text Revision. Arlington, VA: author. Copyright 2000, American Psychiatric Association. Reprinted with permission.
Figure 15.4: Based on information in American Psychiatric Association (2000). *Diagnostic and Statistical Manual of Mental Disorders*, 4th ed., Text Revision. Arlington, VA: author. Copyright 2000, American Psychiatric Association.
Figure 15.5: From Meerkerk, G.-J., Van Den Eijnden, R. J. J. M., & Garretsen, H. F. L. (2006). Predicting compulsive Internet use: It's all about sex. *CyberPsychology and Behavior, 9*, 95–103. Reprinted with permission by Mary Ann Liebert, Inc.
Figure 15.6: From Perry, B. D. (2002). Childhood experience and the expression of genetic potential:

What childhood neglect tells us about nature and nurture. *Brain and Mind, 3*, 94. With kind permission of Springer Science and Business Media B.V.
Figure 15.9: Interaction between Serotonin Gene and Stress to Make Depression. From Caspi, A., et al. (2003). Influence of life stress on depression: Moderation by a polymorphism in the 5-HTT gene. *Science, 301*, 386–389. Reprinted with permission from the American Association for the Advancement of Science.
Figure 15.10: Based on information in American Psychiatric Association (2000). *Diagnostic and Statistical Manual of Mental Disorders*, 4th ed., Text Revision. Arlington, VA: author. Copyright 2000, American Psychiatric Association. Reprinted with permission.
Figure 15.15: Adapted from American Psychiatric Association (2000). *Diagnostic and Statistical Manual of Mental Disorders*, 4th ed., Text Revision. Arlington, VA: author. Copyright 2000, American Psychiatric Association. Reprinted with permission.
Figure 15.16: Adapted from American Psychiatric Association (2000). *Diagnostic and Statistical Manual of Mental Disorders*, 4th ed., Text Revision. Arlington, VA: author. Copyright 2000, American Psychiatric Association. Reprinted with permission.
Figure 15.17: From Ludwig, A. M. (1995). *The Price of Greatness*. Used with permission of Guilford Publications, Inc.
Figure 15.18: From Slater, E., & Meyer, A. (1959). Contributions to a pathography of the musicians: Robert Schumann. *Confinia Psychiatrica, 2*, 65–94. Used with permission by S. Karger AG.

Chapter 16

pp. 646–647: Excerpt from Gorenstein, E. E., & Comer, R. J. (2002). *Case Studies in Abnormal Psychology*, 54–55. © 2002 by Worth Publishers. Used with permission.

PHOTOGRAPHS

Frontmatter

p. iii: © Geri Lavrov/Photographer's choice/Getty Images; p. xxvi: © Photodisc/Getty Images; p. xxix: © Image Source/Getty Images; p. xxx: © Goodshoot/PunchStock; p. xxxvii: © Micha Pawlitzki/Workbook Stock/Getty Images.

Chapter 1

p. 2: © Mango Productions/Corbis; p. 6: Sonya Farrell/Digital Vision/Getty Images; p. 9: Image Source/Getty Images; p. 10: Matthias Rietschel/AP Images; p. 12: Canadian Museum of Civilization, Artifact VII-C-1758, image S95-3306/Corbis; p. 13: SSPL /The Image Works; p. 14: Bettmann/Corbis; p. 15B: David Buffington/Blend Images/Punchstock; p. 15T: Library of Congress Prints and Photographs Division [LC-USZ62-72266]; p. 17T: © Bettmann/Corbis; p. 17B: © Bettmann/Corbis; p. 19: Petty Officer First Class Brien Aho/AP Images; p. 20TL: Hulton Archive/Getty Images; p. 20BM: iStockphoto.com/Kurt Holter; 20TM: Squared Studios/Getty Images; p. 20BL: SSPL/The Image Works; p. 20TR: © Bettmann/Corbis; p. 20BR: © Bettmann/Corbis; p. 21L: Bettmann/Corbis; p. 21B: Tetra Images/Jupiter Images; p. 21TL: Library of Congress Prints and Photographs Division [LC-USZ62-72266]; p. 21TR: Bachrach/Getty Images; p. 22B: Image Source/Getty Images; p. 22TM: iStockphoto.com/ Onur Döngel; p. 22BR: Comstock Images/Jupiter Images; p. 22TL: Bettmann/Corbis; p. 22TR: © Courtesy of Dr. Martin E. P. Seligman, University of Pennsylvania; p. 22BL: © Roger Ressmeyer/Corbis; p. 25: Ryan McVay/Getty Images; p. 26B: iStockphoto.com/arlindo71; p. 26B: iStockphoto.com/arlindo71; p. 26M: W. E. Garrett/National Geographic/Getty Images; p. 26T: Library of Congress Prints and Photographs Division [LC-DIG-ggbain-03485]; p. 27T: Frank Lukasseck/Corbis; p. 27B: iStockphoto.com/arlindo71; p. 31: ML Harris/Getty Images; p. 33: Carl De Souza/AFP/Getty Images.

Dorling Kindersley/Getty Images; p. 328: PhotoDisc/Getty Images; p. 331: Jon Brenneis/Life Magazine/Time & Life Pictures/Getty Images; p. 332: Courtesy of Albert Bandura; p. 333: © Virgo Productions/zefa/Corbis; p. 335: Nina Leen/Time & Life Pictures/Getty Images; p. 336: © Gary Salter/zefa/Corbis; p. 338T: iStockphoto.com/Paul Merrett; p. 338B: Jim Dowdalls/Photo Researchers, Inc.; p. 339: Inspirestock/PunchStock; p. 341: PhotoAlto/Alix Minde/Getty Images; p. 342: Profimedia International s.r.o./Alamy.

Chapter 9

p. 346: Mango Productions/Corbis; p. 349: Finbarr O'Reilly/X90055/Reuters/Corbis; p. 351: PhotoAlto/PunchStock; p. 352: Datacraft/Getty Images; p. 353: Richard T. Nowitz/Corbis; p. 354: David Rosenberg/Getty Images; p. 356T: China-FotoPress/Getty Images; p. 356B: Russell Monk Photography/Getty Images; p. 357: © Michael Siluk/The Image Works; p. 358: Szaflarski et al., 2006 (p. 803). Copyright Annals of Neurology; p. 360: Frans Lanting/Minden Pictures; p. 361: Courtesy of Daniel L. Everett; p. 363ML: Amos Morgan/PhotoDisc/Getty Images; p. 363R: Ross Anania/Getty Images; p. 363MR: Digital Vision/Getty Images; p. 363L: Matthieu Spohn/PhotoAlto; p. 364B: Stockbyte/PunchStock; p. 364T: Martin Poole/Getty Images; p. 365: Thiago Bernardes/Getty Images; p. 367T: Matthieu Spohn/PhotoAlto; p. 367B: BananaStock/PunchStock; p. 372: The McGraw-Hill Companies, Inc./Gary He, photographer; p. 373: The White House, Pete Souza/AP Images; p. 376B: Eileen Bach/Getty Images; p. 376T: Sean Gallup/Getty Images; p. 377: Courtesy of Stanford University News Service; p. 379T: Mark Hall/Getty Images; p. 379B: Courtesy of Joy Hirsch.

Chapter 10

p. 384: WIN-Initiative/Getty Images; p. 388: Andrew Johnson/Getty Images; p. 389: Jessica Rinaldi/Reuters/Corbis; p. 390: Michelle McLoughlin/AP Images; p. 391: Kris Connor/Getty Images; p. 393: C. W. McKeen/Syracuse Newspapers/The Image Works; p. 394: Courtesy of Nadeen & Alan Kaufman; p. 397: Commercial Eye/Getty Images; p. 399: Mika/zefa/Corbis; p. 400: Art Akiane LLC; p. 401: Steve McAlister/Getty Images; p. 402: Courtesy of John Duncan; p. 404: Somos Images/Corbis; p. 406: Royalty-free Division/Masterfile; p. 412: Mark Fellman/TM © 20th Century Fox. All rights reserved/Courtesy Everett Collection. p. 413: Brand X Pictures; p. 414L: Pixtal/Age Fotostock; p. 414ML: Popperfoto/Getty Images; p. 414M: Pixtal/Age Fotostock; p. 414MR: Sir Godfrey Kneller/The Bridgemen Art Library/Getty Images; p. 414R: Library of Congress Prints and Photographs Division [LC-USZ62-60242]; p. 415L: Time Life Pictures/Getty Images; p. 415ML: Imagno/Austrian Archives/Getty Images; p. 415M: Joseph Carl Stieler/The Bridgemen Art Library/Getty Images; p. 415MR: FPG Intl./Corbis; p. 415R: AFP/Getty Images; p. 417: Tetra Images/Getty Images; p. 419: Imagemore Co., Ltd./Getty Images; p. 420: PRNewsFoto/Intel Corp/AP Images.

Chapter 11

p. 424: Chris Fortuna/Getty Images; p. 428TM: Ryan McVay/Getty Images; p. 428BL: iStockphoto.com/Nina Shannon; p. 428BR: iStockphoto.com/Georgina Palmer; p. 429L: TRBfoto/Getty Images; p. 429L: Chris Ware/Getty Images; p. 429R: iStockphoto.com/Grzegorz Lepiarz; p. 432L: Jeffrey Ufberg/Getty Images; p. 432T: Richard Olsenius/Getty Images; p. 433T: iStockphoto.com/christine balderas; p. 433B: Dr. Fred Hossler/Getty Images; p. 434: Courtesy of Traci Mann; p. 435: Steve Cole/Corbis; p. 437: © LWA-Dann Tardif/Corbis; p. 439B: iStockphoto.com/MistikaS; p. 439T: Roberto Westbrook/

Getty Images; p. 440: Queerstock.com; p. 441: blue jean images/Getty Images; p. 442: Keystone/Sigi Tischler file/AP Images; p. 443T: Saeed Khan/AFP/Getty Images; p. 443B: Chris Ryan/Getty Images; p. 445T: Comstock Images/Jupiter Images; p. 445M: BananaStock/Punchstock; p. 445B: Jacobs Stock Photography/Jupiter Images; p. 446T: Getty Images/Image Source; p. 446B: Chris Ryan/Getty Images; p. 449: Brand X Pictures/Punch-Stock; p. 450TL: Eric Bean/Getty Images; p. 450R: Elke Van de Velde/Getty Images; p. 450BL: Ian Spanier/Getty Images; p. 451: Jeff Gross/Getty Images; p. 452: Courtesy of Dr. Lenny Kristal and Robert Kong; p. 455: Martin Barraud/Getty Images; p. 457T: Réunion des Musées Nationaux/Art Resource, NY; p. 457B: Courtesy of Erika Rosenberg; p. 458B: Ken Graham/Getty Images; p. 458T: Courtesy of Paul Ekman; p. 459T: Courtesy of Paul Ekman; p. 459B: Courtesy of Erika Rosenberg; p. 460: Everett Collection; p. 463: LWA/Getty Images; p. 464: Sadatsugu Tomizawa/AFP/Getty Images; p. 466: Jeremy Woodhouse/Getty Images; p. 467B: Sheer Photo, Inc./Getty Images; p. 467T: Joshua Sheldon/Getty Images; p. 470: Ebby May/Getty Images.

Chapter 12

p. 474: Zen Shui/Milena Boniek/Getty Images; p. 477: Masterfile; p. 478T: Peter Dazeley/zefa/Corbis; p. 478TR: iStockphoto.com/Anne de Haas; p. 478TL: Brand X Pictures/Jupiter Images; p. 478BL: iStockphoto.com/Jaroslaw Wojcik; p. 478B: iStockphoto.com/Franky De Meyer; p. 479T: Digital Vision/Getty Images; p. 479B: Mike Powell/Getty Images; p. 481TL: © iStockphoto.com/Nancy Honeycutt; p. 481TR: Image Source/Getty Images; p. 481B: iStockphoto.com; p. 483: Tom Fox/Dallas Morning News/Corbis; p. 486T: iStockphoto.com/Robert Kneschke; p. 486M: iStockphoto.com/Damir Cudic; p. 486B: iStockphoto.com/Andrea Laurita; p. 487: Darius Ramazani/zefa/Corbis; p. 488: Bob Thomas/Corbis; p. 490: Kris Timken/Getty Images; p. 491: Dirk Anschutz/Getty Images; p. 492: Steve Prezant/Corbis; p. 493: Andrew Olney/Digital Vision/PunchStock; p. 495: Diane Mcdonald/Getty Images; p. 496: Erik Dreyer/Getty Images; p. 498: Kevin Fleming/Corbis; p. 501: BananaStock/Alamy; p. 502: Duncan Smith/Getty Images; p. 503: © The McGraw-Hill Companies/Christopher Kerrigan, photographer; p. 504: iStockphoto.com/Dr. Heinz Linke; p. 504back: iStockphoto.com/Dr. Heinz Linke; p. 505: NIBSC/Photo Researchers Inc.; p. 506T: Courtesy of Susan Folkman; p. 506B: Brent Stirton/Getty Images.

Chapter 13

p. 510: Medioimages/PhotoDisc/Getty Images; p. 513T: Robert Glenn/Getty Images; p. 513B: Ingram Publishing/AGE Fotostock; p. 515: Phil Walter/Getty Images; p. 516L: © Ned Frisk/Blend Images LLC; p. 516R: RubberBall Productions; p. 517L: Steve Bly/Alamy; p. 517M: Ingram Publishing; p. 517R: Getty Images/Blend Images; p. 518: Noel Hendrickson/Getty Images; p. 519: i love images/Alamy; p. 521: Peter Aprahamian/Corbis; p. 522: Alan Bailey/Getty Images; p. 523: Lucasfilm/20th Century Fox/The Kobal Collection; p. 526: Sharon Farmer, Bill & Melinda Gates Foundation/AP Images; p. 527: Michael Rougier/Time & Life Pictures/Getty Images; p. 534TL: iStockphoto.com/Eric Isselée; p. 534ML: iStockphoto.com/Eric Isselée; p. 534BL: iStockphoto.com/Sue Mack; p. 534TR: iStockphoto.com/Andrew Johnson; p. 534TM: Digital Vision/PunchStock; p. 534BM: iStockphoto.com/Mikhail Soldatenkov; p. 534B: iStockphoto.com/Eduardo Jose Bernardino; p. 535: Ed Bock/Corbis; p. 536B: Alloy, Jacobson & Acocella, 1999; p. 536T: Imagesource/Jupiter Images; p. 539: Mario Tama/Getty Images; p. 540: Hill Street Studios/Getty Images; p. 542T: iStockphoto.

com/Scott Griessel; p. 542BR: iStockphoto.com/Scott Griessel; p. 542BM: iStockphoto.com/Scott Griessel; p. 542BL: Silverstock/Digital Vision/Getty Images.

Chapter 14

p. 546: Nisian Hughes/Getty Images; p. 550T: Anthony Plummer/Getty Images; p. 550B: Corbis Premium RF/Punchstock; p. 553: Courtesy of the Graduate Center, CUNY; p. 554: © 1968 by Stanley Milgram, copyright renewed © 1993 by Alexandra Milgram, and distributed by Penn State Media Sales; p. 556: sven hagolani/zefa/Corbis; p. 557: Photo: Patrick Wymore/© Fox/Courtesy Everett Collection; p. 558T: Mareen Fischinger/Getty Images; p. 558M: Digital Vision/Getty Images; p. 558B: Peter Dazeley/Getty Images; p. 559: Obama Presidential Campaign/AP Images; p. 560: Courtesy of Naomi Eisenberger; p. 561: © Ron Haviv/VII/Corbis; p. 562L: Courtesy of Mahzarin Banaji; p. 562R: Courtesy of Anthony Greenwald; p. 563: White Packert/Getty Images; p. 565: Jim McIsaac/Getty Images; p. 566: Tim Sloan/AFP/Getty Images; p. 567T: iStockphoto.com/Tomasz Borucki; p. 567B: iStockphoto.com/Izabela Habur; p. 568: Advertising Archive; p. 569: John Giustina/Getty Images; p. 571: Shannon Fagan/Getty Images; p. 572: NY Daily News; p. 573: Ashley Cooper/Corbis; p. 578B: George Pimentel/WireImage/Getty Images; p. 578T: Courtesy of Connor Principe and the Langlois Social Development Lab, University of Texas, Austin; p. 579: Courtesy of Connor Principe and the Langlois Social Development Lab, University of Texas, Austin; p. 581T: Bettmann/Corbis; p. 581B: Bettmann/Corbis.

Chapter 15

p. 586: Tara Moore/Getty Images; p. 589T: Erich Lessing/Art Resource, NY; p. 589B: Mitchell Funk/Getty Images; p. 591: iStockphoto.com/Richard Johnson; p. 593: Nicolas Guerin/Corbis; p. 594: G. K. & Vikki Hart/Getty Images; p. 595T: Masterfile; p. 595B: © Paul Buck/epa/Corbis; p. 600: © iStockphoto.com/Maartje van Caspel; p. 601B: Daniel Grizelj/Getty Images; p. 601L: © iStockphoto.com/Justin Allfree; p. 601ML: © iStockphoto.com/Marcel Braendli; p. 601MR: © iStockphoto.com/Maartje van Caspel; p. 601R: © iStockphoto.com/Justin Allfree; p. 603: Bob Thomas/Getty Images; p. 604: Ingram Publishing; p. 606: Courtesy of Drs. Lew Baxter & Michael Phelps, UCLA School of Medicine; p. 608: Ingram Publishing/Alamy; p. 609: Courtesy of Dr. Bruce D. Perry; p. 610: Chad Baker/Ryan McVay/Getty Images; p. 612: Pressens Bild/Henrik Montgomery/AP Images; p. 618: MDP/New Market/Gene Page/The Kobal Collection; p. 619: PhotoDisc Collection/Getty Images; p. 620: VEER Lars Topelmann/Getty Images; p. 621: Nancy Kaszerman/Corbis.

Chapter 16

p. 628: Daly and Newton/Getty Images; p. 633: Jeffrey Mayer/Getty Images; p. 636: Will & Deni McIntyre/Photo Researchers, Inc.; p. 637: Simon Fraser/University of Durham/Photo Researchers, Inc.; p. 638: Courtesy of Helen Mayberg; p. 639: Courtesy of St. Jude Medical; p. 642: Royalty-Free/Corbis; p. 644: Michael Rougier/Time-Life Pictures/Getty Images; p. 646T: iStockphoto.com/MorePixels; p. 646M: iStockphoto.com/arlindo71; p. 646B: iStockphoto.com/Linda King; p. 646B: iStockphoto.com/John Bell; p. 647T: The Charlotte Observer, Christopher A. Record/AP Images; p. 647BL: iStockphoto.com/Simone van den Berg; p. 647BR: iStockphoto.com/Jake Holmes; p. 648: Chad Johnston/Masterfile; p. 651L: Davies and Starr/Getty Images; p. 651L: Howard J. Radzyner/Phototake; p. 651R: Andrea Morini/Digital Vision/Getty Images; p. 660: Jeff Greenberg/PhotoEditInc.; p. 661: Anthony Nagelmann/Getty Images.

Name Index

A

Aamodt, M. G., 11, 443, 444
Abbate-Daga, G., 502
Abelson, J. L., 597
Aber, J. L., 208
Aberg, M. A. I., 109
Abi-Dargham, A., 611
Abma, J. C., 204, 207
Aboujaoude, E., 598
Abramovitz, A., 652
Abramowitz, J., 596
Abrams, R., 636
Abramson, A., 460
Achter, J. A., 420
Ackerman, D., 149
ACTIVE Study Group, 212, 221
Adachi, H., 500
Adam, T. C., 501
Adams, A., 386
Adams, D., 634
Adams, F., 295
Adams, L., 521
Adamson, L., 315
Ader, R., 494
Adessi, C., 91
Adler, A., 442, 522, 523
Adler, J., 11
Adler, N., 497
Adler, N. E., 490, 491
Adli, M., 641
Adolphs, R., 100, 290, 456, 462
Adrian, E. D., 89
Agarwal, A., 172
Aghajanian, G. K., 261, 632
Ahblom, A., 499
Ahmadi, S., 464
Ahmed, A., 402
Aichele, S., 236, 237
Aichorn, W., 634
Ainsworth, M. D. S., 193, 579
Aitken, J. R., 662
Akaike, A., 214
Akers, J. F., 196
Akinola, M., 624
Akiskal, H. S., 79
Aknin, L. B., 469
Alaggia, R., 208
Alarcon, J. H., 197
Al-Atiyyat, N. M. H., 164
Albert, R. S., 414
Alborn, A. M., 111, 339
Alcázar, M. A., 259
Alda, M., 641
Alger, B. E., 260, 261, 431
Ali, M., 634
Alkire, M. T., 402
Allard, T., 107, 155, 182
Allee, W. C., 549
Allegrante, J. P., 204
Allemand, M., 540, 541
Allen, D. G., 446, 447
Allen, G., 621
Allen, L., 208, 437

Allen, M., 568
Alley, W., 218
Allik, J., 517
Allison, D. B., 433
Allmon, D., 655
Alloway, T., 619
Allport, G. W., 513, 529, 562
Al-Nahhas, A., 609, 610
Alper, C. M., 488, 497
Alt, K. W., 12, 13
Altamura, A. C., 662
Altaye, M., 357, 358
Alterovitz, S., 221
Altman, J., 109
Alvarez, J. G., 172
Álvarez-Linera, J., 402
Alvir, J., 609
Alzheimer's Association, 214
Amabile, T. M., 413, 444, 445, 447, 448
Amaral, D., 97
Ambadar, Z., 461
Ambler, A., 81
Amedi, A., 119
American Association on Mental Retardation, 399
American Heart Association, 258, 497
American Psychiatric Association, 15, 16, 399, 501, 589, 590, 591, 592, 593, 594, 595, 596, 600, 605, 607, 614, 615, 616, 617, 621
American Psychological Association, 17, 68
Ames, M. A., 440
Amianto, F., 502
Amichai-Hamburger, Y., 561
Amin, R., 324
Amsel, E., 40, 201
Amsterdam, J., 650, 651
Amsterdam, J. D., 641, 650
Anda, R. E., 609
Anda, R. F., 603, 609
Anderson, A., 654, 655
Anderson, A. K., 453, 465
Anderson, C. A., 334, 571
Anderson, N. D., 236
Anderson, R., 499
Andersson, G., 653
Ando, J., 540
Andreasen, N. C., 610, 624
Andreassen, O. A., 609
Andreev, B. V., 641
Andresen, B., 259
Andrews, G., 653
Anson, K., 263
Ansul, S. E., 456
Anthonisen, N. R., 319, 342
Antke, C., 597
Aoki, C., 202
Aouizerate, B., 597
Appelhans, B. M., 501
Applebaum, S., 164, 211

Apsche, J., 559
Arany, Z., 502
Arbib, M., 350
Arbib, M. A., 354
Arbisi, P. A., 537
Archimedes, 409
Arevalo, J. M., 484
Arevalo, J. M. G., 484
Argiolis, A., 437
Argyle, M., 470
Arias, V., 247
Aristotle, 39
Arling, G. L., 195
Armagan, E., 76, 117, 118, 119
Armstrong, H. E., 655, 656
Arner, E., 433
Arnett, J. J., 206, 207, 208, 209
Arnold, M. B., 454
Arnold, R., 656
Arseneault, L., 260, 516, 536
Arterberry, M. E., 179
Artola, A., 484
Aruga, M., 182
Arvanitakis, Z., 214
Arveiler, D., 500
Asada, T., 182
Ascencio, A., 196
Asch, S. E., 550, 551
Aserinsky, E., 240, 243
Ashburner, J., 379
Asherson, P., 80
Ashmore, R. D., 203
Askenasy, J. J. M., 243, 244, 324
Asperger, H., 621
Assouline, M., 539
Atkinson, G., 240
Atkinson, G. G., 325
Atkinson, J. W., 442
Atkinson, R. C., 270, 281
Atterbury, J., 174
Aubrey, J. B., 325
Augath, M., 113
Austenfeld, J. L., 487
Austin, E. J., 624
Austin, M., 177
Autti-Rämö, I., 176
Aycicegi, A., 342
Azizian, A., 276
Azmitia, M., 208

B

Baare, W., 92
Baars, B. J., 227
Babiloni, C., 99
Babinsky, R., 290
Babson, K. A., 247
Bachevalier, J., 100, 621
Bachorowski, J., 460
Back, M. D., 32
Backscheider, A. G., 652
Backstrand, B., 109
Baddeley, A. D., 273, 274, 286
Badour, C. L., 247

Baer, R. A., 230, 236, 656
Baerwald, J., 536
Baethge, C., 641
Bagsby, P. G., 246
Bagwell, C. L., 203
Baier, B., 285
Bailey, D., 538
Bailey, M. J., 438, 440, 441
Bailey, N. W., 440
Baillargeon, R., 185, 186
Baime, M. J., 236
Baird, A. A., 206
Baird, J. C., 145
Bakeman, R., 197, 315
Baker, G. B., 611
Baker, S. B., 501
Bakker, S., 606
Balbin, E., 506
Balcetis, E., 128
Baldwin, D., 640
Baldwin, D. S., 661, 662
Baldwin, G. C., 260
Balkin, T. J., 246
Ball, K., 212, 221, 469
Ball, S.-A., 594
Ballanyi, K., 84
Balsis, S., 543
Balteau, E., 251
Baltes, P. B., 180, 212, 213
Banaji, M. R., 562, 563, 564
Bandura, A., 330, 331, 332, 333, 334, 340, 444, 571
Banerjee, J., 172
Bang, W., 214
Banks, M. S., 179
Banks, W. C., 38, 60
Banning, K., 478
Bao, G., 247
Barbatsis, G., 218
Barbazanges, A., 516
Barber, L. K., 246
Barbour, K. A., 502
Barbui, C., 632
Barch, D. M., 212, 608, 610
Barefoot, J. C., 342
Bargh, J. A., 227
Barker, D. J. P., 175
Barkham, M., 650
Barlow, D. H., 591, 594
Barlow, J. H., 196
Baron, A., 316
Bar-On, R., 467
Baron, R. A., 571
Baron-Cohen, S., 620, 624, 625
Barr, C. L., 92
Barr, H., 399, 404
Barr, R. F., 217
Barr, S., 218
Barrachina, J., 656
Barres, B. A., 84
Barrett, D. C., 506
Barrett, L. F., 454, 466
Barrick, M. R., 538

Brody, N., 386
Broekman, B. F. P., 405
Bronskill, M., 441
Brook, C., 366
Broude, G., 438
Brouwer, R. M., 181, 182
Brown, A. S., 24, 176, 610
Brown, C. H., 645
Brown, F., 324
Brown, H. R., 570
Brown, M. Z., 656
Brown, R., 290
Brown, R. T., 398
Brown, T. A., 597
Brown, T. S., 431
Brownell, K. D., 501
Brunelin, J., 637
Bruner, J. S., 128
Brunetti, M., 99
Bruno, R., 637
Brunwasser, S. M., 660
Bryans, W. A., 109
Bschor, T., 641
Buboltz, W. C., 324
Buchanan, J., 652
Buchanan, T. W., 100, 290, 291
Buchbinder, S. P., 506
Buchert, R., 259
Buchholz, B. A., 433
Buck, B., 441
Buck, L. B., 158, 159
Buck, S. M., 181
Buckley, C., 572
Buckmaster, P. S., 484
Buckner, R. L., 462, 463
Bucy, P., 100
Budden, S., 196
Budtz-Joergensen, E., 92
Budygin, E. A., 259
Buitelaar, J. K., 177
Buka, S. L., 610
Bukowski, W. M., 203, 204
Bulik, C. M., 502
Bulkeley, K., 240, 241, 248
Bullivant, S. B., 437
Bult, J. H., 211
Bunge, S. A., 463
Buoli, M., 662
Burbaud, P., 597
Burch, G., 623
Burchell, A. N., 507
Burcur, B., 325
Burd, L., 176
Burger, J., 555
Burgess, W., 631
Burgess-Whitman, N., 219
Buring, J. E., 501
Buritrago-Tellez, C. H., 12, 13
Burnett, G. B., 203
Burney, R., 503
Burnstein, E., 574
Burt, K. B., 208
Burton, C. M., 487
Busch, N., 229
Bushman, B. J., 334, 571
Buss, D. M., 25, 28, 427, 437, 438, 513, 514, 565, 577, 578
Bussing, R., 621
Butterworth, D. E., 469
Byars, A. W., 357, 358
Byrd, A., 153
Byun, M. S., 236

C

Cabeza, R., 288, 325
Cacioppo, J. T., 484, 560
Cahill, C., 610
Cahill, L., 268, 290
Cahill, S. P., 654, 656
Cai, D. J., 324
Cai, X. J., 431
Cain, C. K., 288
Cairney, J., 600
Cairns, M., 427
Calamari, J. E., 597
Calamaro, C., 246
Calaprice, A., 365
Calder, A. J., 100, 464
Caldwell, A. B., 248
Caldwell, J. A., 325
Calkins, M. W., 18, 21, 275
Callicott, J. H., 610
Calvert, S. L., 217
Calzavara, L. M., 507
Cameron, J., 444, 447
Cameron, K., 219
Campbell, A., 463
Campbell, F. A., 406
Campbell, K., 621
Campi, R., 177
Campins, M. J., 656
Campos, J., 197, 456
Campos, J. J., 197
Camras, L. A., 197
Candia, V., 155
Cannon, M., 260
Cannon, W. B., 83, 427, 431
Canter, R. R., 128
Capitanio, J. P., 533
Caplan, A. H., 104
Caplovitz, A. G., 218
Caporael, L. R., 549
Cappuccio, F. P., 244
Capri, M., 484
Caprihan, A., 414
Capuron, L., 495
Cardilla, K., 199
Cardno, A. G., 609
Carew, T. J., 291, 307, 337
Carey, B., 270
Carey, P., 506
Carey, V. J., 501
Carlat, D. J., 603
Carless, S. A., 538
Carlo, G., 192
Carlson, S. M., 324
Carlsson, A., 611, 612
Carlsson, I., 415, 416, 417
Carmody, J., 238
Carnagey, N. L., 571
Carney, S. M., 641
Carpenter, B., 543
Carpenter, L. A., 319
Carper, R. A., 621
Carr, T. S., 570
Carrier, J., 324
Carriere, J., 295, 296
Carrion, V. G., 594
Carroll, D., 503
Carroll, J. B., 388, 389
Carroll, J. L., 191
Carroll, M. D., 433
Carskadon, M. A., 324
Carson, S. H., 623
Carson, W. H., 634
Carstensen, L. L., 213, 456, 466

Carter, C. S., 100
Caruso, D. R., 467
Caruso, E. M., 128
Carver, C. S., 489
Casey, B. J., 112
Caspi, A., 23, 29, 80, 81, 92, 199, 210, 515, 516, 569, 570, 588, 604, 609, 619
Cassidy, T., 165
Castel, A., 282, 300, 301
Castellanos, F. X., 181
Castellazzo, G., 501
Castelli, D. M., 181
Catalano, P., 152
Catapano, F., 661
Cattell, R. B., 388, 389
Cauchi, A., 470
Cavallero, C., 249
Cavuoto, N., 656
Cawthon, R., 491
CBS News, 572
Cebria, A., 656
Ceci, S. J., 366, 386, 407
Celani, L., 484
Celio, C. I., 467
Centers for Disease Control and Prevention, 176, 177, 204, 258, 434, 500
Cervoni, N., 80
Ceyhan, A. A., 599
Ceyhan, E., 599
Chabris, C. F., 231
Chadwick, P., 655
Chaffee, J., 370
Chaiken, S., 568
Chakos, M., 609
Chamberlain, R., 256
Champagne, D. L., 405
Champagne, F. A., 80
Chan, A., 247, 459
Chan, A. S., 183
Chan, C., 351
Chan, Y.-H., 405
Chance, P., 370
Chandra, A., 204, 207, 209
Chang, E. C., 489
Chang, J. W., 100
Chapais, B., 574
Chaplin, T. M., 660
Chapman, B. P., 503
Chapman, K., 160
Chappell, M., 283
Charil, A., 484
Charney, D. S., 248, 596, 632, 660
Chatman, J., 434
Chatterjee, A., 542, 543
Chatwin, J., 640
Chavez, R. S., 414
Cheah, C. S. L., 208
Chechik, G., 181
Cheetham, C. E. J., 430
Cheever, N. A., 220
Chen, B., 484
Chen, E., 484
Chen, J.-I., 156
Chen, S. Y., 648
Chentsova-Dutton, Y., 456
Chepenik, L. G., 606
Chesney, M. A., 506
Chess, S., 192
Cheung, M.-C., 183
Chew, S. H., 464

Cheyne, J., 295, 296
Chia, E., 210
Chiappini, M. S., 506
Chiarello, R. J., 103
Chicon, S., 609
Chiesa, A., 654
Chiu, W. T., 591, 595, 619, 623, 658
Cho, S., 503
Choi, I., 162, 557, 653
Choi, S. W., 258
Choi, T., 656
Chok, J. T., 656
Chokka, P., 611
Chomsky, N., 355, 356, 360
Chong, Y.-S., 405
Chow, T. W., 415
Chowdhury, M., 319
Choy, Y., 652
Christakis, D., 217
Christakis, N. A., 4, 220, 434, 435, 488, 489, 560, 561
Christensen, D. D., 402
Christensen, K., 469
Christie, L. A., 212
Chuang, D. M., 633
Churchill, J. D., 609
Churchill, R., 632
Cicchetti, D., 181, 182
Ciesla, J. A., 660
Cigliano, M., 661
Cignolini, A., 196
Cillessen, A. H. N., 198
Cipriani, A., 632
Cipriani, G., 543
Clancy, P. M., 351
Clark, A. S., 516
Clark, L., 542, 543
Clark, L. A., 450, 603
Clark, R. D., III, 438, 439
Clark, W. R., 78, 79
Clarke, G. N., 660
Clasen, L., 201, 202
Clavenna, A., 177
Clegg, H., 514, 623
Clubley, E., 620, 624, 625
Coates, T. J., 506
Cobb, J. M., 235
Cody-Hazlett, H., 621
Coe, C. L., 175, 610
Coghill, R. C., 236
Cohen, A. N., 635
Cohen, J., 359, 361
Cohen, J. D., 100, 449
Cohen, K. M., 440, 441
Cohen, N., 494
Cohen, R. D., 210
Cohen, R. M., 621
Cohen, S., 488, 497
Colcombe, S. J., 213, 215
Colditz, G. A., 501
Cole, D. A., 660
Cole, S., 484
Cole, S. W., 484
Coleman, B., 470
Coleman, M. R., 229
Coleman, P., 542, 543
Coleman, R. E., 499
Collette, F., 244
Collette, L., 506
Collier, D. A., 609
Collignon, O., 466
Collins, A., 282, 283

Frady, R. L., 570
Franceschi, C., 484
Francis, A. D., 238
Francis, J. L., 603
Franco, O. H., 502
Frank, E., 632, 638
Frank, M. C., 362, 363
Frank, M. G., 557
Frankle, W. G., 611
Franklin, M., 577
Franklin, S., 227
Fraser, C., 160
Fratiglioni, L., 213, 214
Fredrickson, B. L., 453, 456, 470, 489, 490, 655
Freedman, A. M., 295
Freeman, R. D., 243
Freitag, C., 515
Freitag, C. M., 612
French, S. E., 208
French-Belgian Collaborative Group, 498
Freres, D. R., 660
Freud, A., 520, 643
Freud, S., 15, 18, 19, 21, 229, 248, 519, 520, 521, 522, 643
Freund, A., 212
Fried, I., 136
Friederici, A. D., 197
Friedman, M., 498
Friedman, N. P., 286, 463
Friehs, G. M., 104
FriereBebeau, L., 456
Friesen, W. V., 60, 456, 457, 458, 459, 462, 463, 465, 483
Frijda, N. H., 456
Frilt, C. D., 100
Frith, C., 7, 203, 610
Frith, C. D., 156, 286, 464, 575, 576
Frith, U., 7
Froh, J. J., 471
Frokjaer, V. B., 92
Frost, R. O., 588
Frost, S. J., 342
Fründ, I., 229
Fruntes, V., 24
Frye, M. A., 634
Frymiare, J. L., 100
Fuchs, D. L., 613
Fuchs, S., 244
Fudala, P. J., 257
Fujihara, T., 575
Fukuda, R., 610
Fukushima, A., 415, 416
Fukushima, D., 249
Fuld, K., 145
Fuller, J. L., 78
Fultz, J., 575
Fung, D., 405
Furberg, A. S., 502
Furberg, H., 502
Furman, O., 283
Furman, W., 204
Furnham, A., 419
Furster, J. M., 101
Furuichi, T., 574
Furukawa, T. A., 632
Furumoto, L., 18
Fuster, J. M., 201
Fyer, A. J., 652

G

Gaab, N., 71, 182, 324
Gabbard, G. O., 525
Gabrieli, J. D. E., 212, 463
Gaddis, S., 32
Gage, F. H., 110, 111, 339, 603
Galanter, E., 126
Galbicka, G., 319
Gale, A., 530
Galin, D., 229
Galizio, M., 316
Gallagher, A. M., 407
Gallagher, M., 470
Gallagher, R. M., 257
Gallagher, T. F., 249
Gallese, V., 85, 337, 338
Galletti, C., 138
Gallop, R., 650, 651
Gallop, R. J., 656
Gamel, N., 598
Ganasen, K., 653
Gangestad, S. W., 577
Ganis, G., 365
Garcia, G. E., 380
Garcia, J., 323, 326, 327, 328, 494
Garcia, R., 196
Garcia, V., 184
Garcia-Bailo, B., 159
García-España, J., 234
Gard, T., 238
Gardner, B. T., 359
Gardner, H., 20, 179, 389, 391, 393
Gardner, R. A., 359
Garnefski, N., 506
Garoff-Eaton, R. J., 288
Garretsen, H. F. L., 599
Garrett, A., 594
Garrett, R. K., 4
Garry, M., 298
Garson, C., 638
Gartiehner, G., 214
Gary, F. A., 621
Gasparovic, C., 414
Gass, S., 380
Gasser, C., 538
Gasser, P. J., 603
Gates, M. F., 549
Gates, W., 526
Gathercole, S. E., 217
Gathercole, V. C. M., 354
Gaynes, B. N., 507
Gazdzinski, S., 256
Gazzaniga, M. S., 106
Gearon, J. S., 645
Geary, D., 366
Gebhard, P. H., 49
Geerlings, S. W., 499
Geesey, M. E., 256
Gehrig, W. J., 597
Geise, A., 540
Geist, C. S., 441
Gelman, S., 351
Gendron, M., 5
Genovese, K., 47
Gensicke, H., 503
Georges, E., 487
Georgiadis, J., 437
Georgiadis, J. R., 437
Gerace, T. A., 498

Gerardi, R. J., 652
Gerber, M., 325
Gerig, G., 621
Gerner, R. H., 624
Gerrard, M., 204
Gershberg, F. B., 287
Gerszten, R. E., 502
Geschwind, N., 463
Gettes, D. R., 506
Getz, A., 641
Ghaffar, O., 81
Giacobbe, P., 640
Gibbons, F. X., 204
Gibson, E., 179
Gibson, J. J., 139
Gidengil, E., 128
Giedd, J., 201, 202
Giedd, J. N., 70, 181, 202
Gigante, R., 614
Gigli, G. L., 263
Gil, K., 196
Gil, R., 611
Gilbert, A., 362
Gilbert, S. P., 324
Gilchrist, A., 337
Gilchrist, M., 196
Giles, W. H., 603
Gill, M., 80
Gill, P. M., 11
Gillham, J. E., 660
Gilligan, C., 192
Gillihan, S., 654
Gilovich, T., 454
Gimpel-Smith, R., 621
Gingell, C., 469
Giordano, D. A., 179
Girard, S., 466
Gironda, M., 220
Givón, T., 350, 365
Gjerde, P. F., 199
Glaser, R., 496, 497
Glasper, E. R., 111, 484
Glass, D. C., 498
Glass, G., 650
Glass, K. C., 632
Glass, T., 488
Glasser, D., 469
Glassman, A., 499
Gleason, J. A., 501
Gleitman, L. R., 357
Glick, I. D., 624
Gluckman, P. D., 81
Goebel, R., 232
Goel, V., 416, 558
Goetter, E. M., 653
Goff, D. C., 612
Gogtay, N., 201, 202
Going, S. B., 502
Goldapple, K., 638
Goldbeck, T., 460
Goldberg, T. E., 610
Golden, R. N., 506, 507
Goldfield, B. A., 351
Goldin, P., 464
Goldman-Rakic, P. S., 610
Goldreich, D., 154
Goldsmith, T. H., 132
Goldstein, E. B., 126, 144, 147, 156, 158, 159, 210
Goldstein, R. B., 594
Goldstein, T., 247
Goleman, D. P., 466, 467

Gollan, J., 659, 660
Gómez-Jarabo, G., 259
Gonzalez, V., 233
Gonzalez-Pinto, A., 641
Goodale, E. P., 603
Goodall, J., 49
Goodman, W. K., 596
Goodwin, G., 156
Goodwin, G. M., 641
Goodwin, P., 209
Goodwin, P. J., 488
Goodyer, I., 625
Gopnik, A., 184, 190
Gordon, N. S., 236
Gordon, P., 361
Gordon-Salant, S., 211
Gore, M. A., 228
Gorenstein, E. E., 646, 648
Gorrindo, T., 653
Gorski, R., 437
Goshen-Gottstein, Y., 276
Gosling, S. D., 32, 532, 533, 534
Gossage, J. P., 176
Gosselin, F., 100, 466
Goto, H., 351
Gottesman, I. I., 609
Gottfredson, L., 405
Gottheil, E., 488
Gottleib, N. H., 478
Gottman, J. M., 466
Gottschalk, S., 32
Gough, H. G., 537
Gould, D., 11
Gould, E., 111, 181, 211, 339, 484
Gould, S. J., 28
Governors Highway Safety Association, 234
Gow, A., 397
Grabski, W., 465
Grady, C. L., 276
Graff, J., 81
Grafman, J., 570
Graham, J. R., 537
Graham, S., 21
Graham, T., 406, 407
Gramaglia, C., 502
Grandin, T., 621
Granmayeh, L. K., 503
Grant, B., 616
Grant, B. F., 594
Grant, J. A., 238
Gray, J., 402
Gray, J. L., 403
Gray, J. R., 238
Green, A., 402
Green, D., 127
Green, K. F., 328
Green, L. W., 478
Green, S. B., 217
Green, V. A., 198
Greenberg, L., 574
Greenberg, M. S., 463
Greenberg, M. T., 467
Greenburg, B. D., 515
Greene, S., 438
Greenfield, P., 31, 219
Greenfield, P. M., 219
Greenough, W. T., 110, 180, 609
Greenstein, D., 201, 202
Greenwald, A. G., 562, 563, 564
Greenwood, T. A., 79

Greer, P. J., 632, 638
Gregory, R. J., 397, 398
Greiffenstein, R., 243
Greiling, H., 513
Greischar, L. L., 238
Greve, D., 238
Gribble, P. L., 155
Griffeth, R. W., 446, 447
Griffiths, R. R., 258, 261
Grigorenko, E., 403
Grigorenko, E. L., 405, 407
Grill, J. H., 105
Grolnick, W. S., 197
Groome, L., 174
Grootoonk, S., 610
Gross, C. G., 109, 339
Gross, J. J., 452, 454, 455, 463, 464, 466, 486, 487
Gross, M., 621
Grossberg, S., 196
Grossman, A. W., 609
Grossman, P., 503
Grossman, T., 197
Grossmann, A., 466
Groth, M. V., 469
Groves, J. E., 653
Gruber, S. A., 260
Gruenewald, T. L., 489
Grunstein, M., 78, 79
Grus, C. L., 7
Grüsser, S. M., 260
Gu, H., 507
Guarnaccia, V., 536
Guarraci, F. A., 42
Gudith, D., 233
Guehl, D., 597
Guic-Roble, E., 107, 155, 182
Guilford, J. P., 416, 418
Guillem, K., 93
Guilleminault, C., 247
Guiraud, A., 501
Gulyani, S., 244
Gunderson, E., 152
Guo, V., 294
Guo, Y., 484
Gupta, S., 172
Gur, R. C., 463
Gurevich, M., 478
Guther, H., 488
Guthrie, H., 64, 621
Gutteling, B. M., 177
Guzman-Marin, R., 243
Guzowski, J. F., 283

H

Habermas, T., 460
Habib, R., 661
Hackeman, E., 154
Hadders-Algra, M., 206
Hadzi-Pavlovic, D., 177
Haenschel, C., 202
Haertel, E. H., 217, 218
Hafetz, J. S., 234
Hagen, L., 298
Hager, J., 60
Hager, J. L., 328
Haggard, P., 103
Hagler, D. J., 337
Hahn, C.-G., 654
Hahn, W., 498
Haidt, J., 449

Haier, R., 402
Haier, R. J., 402, 403, 414
Hakuta, K., 379
Hale, B., 365
Hale, M. W., 603
Hall, G. S., 17, 18, 21
Hall, J. A., 466
Hall, M., 500
Hall, N. W., 177
Hall, W., 420
Hallqvist, J., 499
Halpern, D., 366
Halpern, J., 654
Halpern, J. H., 259
Halsey, N., 251
Hamani, C., 41, 639
Hamann, S., 100, 525
Hamer, D., 78, 91, 432, 440, 441, 515, 597
Hamer, D. H., 515
Hamilton, W. D., 574
Hammen, C., 624
Hammer, A. L., 538
Hammersmith, S. K., 441
Hammond, M. S. L., 430
Hammond, P., 399, 404
Hampson, M., 606
Han, C., 631
Han, C.-B., 570
Han, J., 157
Handel, S., 543
Haney, C., 38, 60
Haney, T. L., 499
Hankin, B. L., 603, 659, 660
Hanks, R., 228
Hannan, A., 215
Hannigan, T. P., 162
Hansen, R. A., 214
Hanson, D. J., 426
Hanson, M., 499
Hanson, M. A., 81
Harackiewicz, J. M., 444, 447
Harber, K. D., 57
Harding, E. J., 456
Hare, R. D., 617
Harenski, K., 525
Hargittai, E., 31, 32
Hargrave, G. E., 539
Hargrove, M. F., 570
Hari, R., 252
Harkins, S. G., 549
Harlan, E., 499
Harlan, P., 623
Harlow, H., 194, 195
Harlow, H. F., 195
Härmä, M., 325
Harmon, D., 244
Harmon-Jones, E., 463
Haro, J., 641
Harold, E. S., 438
Harper, S., 655
Harralson, T. L., 499, 536
Harrington, H., 80, 92, 604
Harris, C. L., 342
Harris, J. R., 198
Harris, L., 204
Harris, M. B., 570
Harris, R. A., 256
Harrison, P. J., 609, 610, 612
Harrold, J. A., 431
Hart, D., 204
Hartel, G. D., 217, 218

Hasher, L., 212, 279
Hashizume, H., 415, 416
Hasin, D., 616
Hasin, D. S., 594
Hass, B. W., 594
Hassan, S., 650
Hatfield, E., 438, 439
Hathaway, N., 426
Hatsiopoulou, O., 251
Hatzinger, M., 325
Hause, W. A., 256
Hauser, M. D., 360
Hawkins, W., 660
Hawkley, L. C., 484
Hayashi, A., 351
Hayes, B. D., 257
Haynes, S. G., 498
Hazan, C., 194, 580
Head, K., 402
Headey, B., 469, 470
Healy, J., 632
Heard, H. L., 655, 656
Heath, R. G., 463
Heaton, K. W., 501
Hebb, D. O., 283, 291
Hebert, P., 632
Hecht, M. A., 466
Hedden, T., 212
Hedges, L., 406, 407
Hedges, S. M., 449
Heffelfinger, S. K., 597
Hegelson, V. S., 489
Heider, F., 556
Heider, K., 456, 459
Heils, A., 515
Heinze, C., 285
Helgason, A. R., 204
Heller, W., 623
Hellman, L., 249
Helmers, K. F., 221
Helmholtz, H. von, 17, 146
Helson, R., 541
Hembree, E. A., 654, 656
Hemsley, D. R., 623
Hen, R., 325, 339, 503, 504
Hendrick, J. L., 235
Hendriks, A. A. J., 540, 541
Henin, A., 662
Hening, W. A., 291, 337
Heninger, G. R., 632
Henker, B., 621
Hennekens, C. H., 501
Hennessey, B. A., 444, 445, 447
Henn-Haase, C., 603
Henningfield, J. E., 258
Henson, D. A., 469
Herbert, A., 23, 76
Herbert, J., 653
Herbert, J. D., 653
Herbst, J., 499
Herbst, J. H., 540
Hering, E., 147
Herlihy, J., 291
Herman, R. A., 100
Hermann, E., 358
Hernandez, F., 32, 653
Hernandez-Reif, M., 196
Heron, W., 429, 430
Herpertz, S. C., 466
Herrell, R., 603
Herrington, J. D., 623

Herrmann, C., 229
Herrmann, M. J., 612
Herrmann, N., 600
Herrmann-Lingen, C., 500
Herrnstein, R. J., 405, 406
Herskind, A. M., 469
Herz, R., 158
Herzig, S., 482
Herzog, H., 402
Heshka, S., 433
Hesse, E., 194
Hesse, M. D., 103
Hessels, S., 294
Hessol, N. A., 506
Hettema, J. M., 597
Heymsfield, S. B., 433
Heynen, A. J., 291
Hiatt, D., 539
Hicks, B. M., 540
Hicks, J. A., 470
Hien, D. A., 486
Higgins, D. M., 623
Higley, J. D., 12
Higuchi, S., 246
Hilgard, E., 250, 251
Hill, K. G., 445
Hill, M. A., 543
Hillman, C. H., 181, 325, 339, 502
Hilsenroth, M., 536
Hiltunen, J., 252, 325
Himle, J. A., 597
Hinduja, S., 219, 220
Hine, D. W., 470
Hiner, S. L., 478
Hines, L. M., 256
Hines, M., 366
Hintsa, T., 210
Hintsanen, M., 210
Hippocrates, 13, 20
Hirai, S., 256
Hirakata, M., 182
Hirsch, J., 128, 379, 380
Hirsch, J. B., 453
Hirshfeld-Becker, D. R., 662
Hirst, A., 232
Hirvonen, K., 325
Hisaoka, K., 495
Hitzig, E., 101
Ho, Y.-C., 183
Hoare, J., 506
Hobson, J. A., 248, 249
Hochberg, L. R., 104
Hodges, J., 324
Hodgetts, W., 153
Hodgson, D. M., 172, 177, 516
Hoek, H. W., 175
Hoff, E., 354, 357
Hoffman, E., 609
Hoffman, H. J., 152
Hoffmann, H., 466
Hoffnung, M., 187, 404
Hoffnung, R. J., 187, 404
Hofman, S. G., 662
Hofstede, G., 517
Hogan, M. J., 467, 468
Hogan, T. P., 395, 399
Hogeboom, D. L., 220
Högl, B., 247
Hoh, J., 603
Hohmann, A. G., 260, 261
Hohoff, C., 612

Hokanson, J. F., 235
Hokoishi, K., 299
Holden, G. W., 609
Holder, M., 470
Holland, J. L., 539
Holland, S., 174
Holland, S. K., 202, 357, 358
Holling, H., 414
Hollon, S., 650, 651, 653
Hollon, S. D., 641, 650
Holm, A., 325
Holmen, J., 152
Holmes, A., 610
Holmes, E. A., 156
Holmes, J., 217, 619
Holmes, T. H., 477
Holsboer-Trachsler, M., 325
Holstege, G., 437
Holstein, B. E., 469
Holt, D., 632, 638
Hölzel, B. K., 238
Honzik, C. H., 329
Hooijer, C., 296
Hopfield, J. J., 282
Hopkins, J., 230, 236
Hopson, J. L., 174, 175
Hopwood, M. J., 463
Horberg, E. J., 451
Horiguchi, J., 247
Horn, J. L., 388, 389
Horne, J. A., 325
Horner, V., 550
Horney, K., 22, 524, 525
Horonton, C., 45
Horrey, W. J., 234
Horta, B. L., 619
Horvitz, E., 615
Horwood, J., 609
Hosking, S., 235
Hoss, R. A., 577
Houlihan, A. E., 204
Houlihan, D., 652
Houtkooper, L. B., 502
Houts, R., 81
Howard, K. I., 650
Howard, S. M., 415
Howe, D., 621
Howell, A. J., 324
Howerter, A., 286, 463
Howes, C., 198
Hsiao, J. K., 635, 641
Hu, P. T., 324
Hu, S.-H., 441
Hu, W., 258
Hu, Y., 258
Hua, K., 115
Huang, R., 294
Huang, X., 217, 598
Huang, Y., 71, 182
Hubbard, E. M., 160, 161
Hubel, D., 134, 135
Huber, R., 634
Huddleston, D. E., 325, 339, 503, 504
Huddy, W. P., 128
Hudson, J., 614
Hudson, J. I., 259
Hudson, W., 162
Huebner, E., 469
Huebner, E. S., 469
Huesmann, L. R., 571
Huettel, S. A., 325
Huff, D., 64

Hughes, S., 655
Huizink, A. C., 177
Hull, C. L., 427
Hull, E. M., 437
Hulley, S. B., 498
Hulsey, T. L., 536
Humphreys, M. S., 283
Hungerbuhler, J. P., 463
Hunter, J., 488
Hunter, J. E., 398
Hurst, R. M., 656
Husain, M. M., 641
Huston, A. C., 217
Hutchinson, S., 71, 182
Huttenlocher, J., 354
Hutton, C., 108
Hwangbo, H., 561
Hyde, J. S., 366, 438, 441
Hyde, K. L., 182
Hyde, T. S., 279, 280
Hyman, S. E., 84
Hytonen, K., 552

I

Iacoboni, M., 196, 337
Iacono, W. G., 540
Iarocci, G., 620
Ickovics, J. R., 501
Igartua, K., 204
Iguchi, M. Y., 319
Ihori, N., 571
Ikeda, M., 299
Imabayashi, E., 182
Inagaki, T., 247
Inglese, J., 294
Inhelder, B., 185, 188
Inslicht, S. S., 603
Ipser, J., 653
Ironson, G., 486, 506
Irwin, S. A., 110
Isaacowitz, D. M., 453
Isacsson, G., 632
Isen, A. M., 453
Iso, H., 502
Israel, S., 464
Itil, T. M., 295
Ito, H., 469
Itri, J., 239
Iversen, L. L., 612
Iversen, S., 99, 271, 277, 286
Iversen, S. D., 612
Ivey, P. K., 49
Ivry, R., 362
Iyengar, S. S., 448
Izard, C. E., 197, 456, 458, 467

J

Jablensky, A., 15
Jacklin, C. N., 22, 198, 407, 570
Jackson, E. D., 506
Jackson, K. A., 641
Jackson, K. M., 256
Jackson, L. A., 218
Jacob, S., 437
Jacobs, B. L., 603
Jacobs, D. R., Jr., 500
Jacobs, G. H., 131, 132, 147, 148
Jacobs, J. F., 478
Jacobs, T. L., 236, 237, 490, 491
Jacobsen, L. K., 342
Jacobsohn, L. S., 234

Jacobson, J., 399, 404
Jacobson, S., 399, 404
Jacoby, L. L., 294
Jacquez, F. M., 660
Jaffee, S. R., 516
Jahrig, J. C., 324
Jain, S., 228
James, J. E., 204
James, W., 17, 18, 20, 461
Jamison, K. R., 605, 624
Jan, J. E., 243
Jäncke, L., 71, 182
Jandorf, L., 449
Janeck, A. S., 597
Jang, H., 653
Jang, J. H., 236
Janis, I. L., 551
Jarcho, J. M., 548
Jarvitt, D. C., 611, 612, 634, 635, 641, 650
Jaycox, L. H., 594, 654, 656
Jeannerod, M., 104, 365
Jee, Y.-S., 503
Jeffery, R., 435
Jeffries, N. O., 181
Jenkins, A. J., 258
Jenkins, C. D., 498
Jenkins, J. J., 279, 280
Jenkins, S. M., 324
Jenkins, W. M., 107, 155, 182
Jennett, B., 228
Jensen, A. R., 405
Jensen, C. L., 80
Jerabek, P. A., 638
Jerison, H. J., 95, 96
Jesse, R., 261
Jessell, T. M., 155
Jeunesse, C., 12, 13
Jha, A. P., 236
Ji, D., 287, 324
Ji, Y. G., 561
Jiang, W., 499
Jiang, Y. V., 324
Jimenez, R. T., 380
Jin, R., 591, 595, 619, 623, 658
Jin, X., 354
Jin, Z., 621
Jirtle, R. L., 176
Jobe, J. B., 221
John, C. E., 259
John, O., 466
John, O. P., 455, 486, 515, 529, 533, 534
Johnson, A., 174, 216
Johnson, C., 371
Johnson, C. E., 153
Johnson, D. P., 655
Johnson, E. C., 539
Johnson, L. L., 247
Johnson, M. D., 501
Johnson, M. H., 357
Johnson, M. W., 261
Johnson, R. E., 257
Johnson, T. R. B., 172, 177, 516
Johnson, V. E., 436
Johnson, W., 515, 516, 540
Johnsson, T., 109
Johnston, J. C., 145
Johnston, L., 653
Joiner, T., 470
Jokela, M., 210
Jolles, J., 296
Jones, J., 204, 207

Jones, M. M., 606
Jones, S. R., 259
Jonker, C., 296
Jonker, J., 502
Jope, R. S., 633
Jordahl, T., 207
Jordan, C., 648
Joseph, R., 463
Joska, J. A., 506
Jou, J., 100
Joubert, S., 99, 100
Juang, L., 162, 191, 296
Judd, T., 560
Juffer, F., 403
Juhan-Vague, I., 500
Juliano, L. M., 258
Jump, V. K., 196
Jung, C. G., 18, 211, 523
Jung, R. E., 402, 403, 414
Jung, Y.-H., 236
Jung-Beeman, M., 100, 416
Juraska, J. M., 180
Jureidini, J., 632
Juricevic, I., 117, 119
Jusczyk, P. W., 351
Jussim, L., 57
Just, M. A., 235
Juster, R.-P., 484

K

Kabat-Zinn, J., 230, 236, 503
Kaemmer, B., 537
Kagan, J., 199
Kahan, T. L., 241, 249
Kahl, K. G., 656
Kahn, R. S., 606, 621
Kahneman, D., 372, 374, 375, 376, 377, 378, 469
Kahn-Greene, E. T., 246
Kaiser, B., 662
Kaiser Family Foundation, 217
Kalat, J. W., 214
Kales, A., 248
Kales, J. D., 248
Kam, C. M., 467
Kamimori, G. H., 246
Kaminsky, Z., 81
Kammrath, L. K., 540
Kanarek, R. B., 64
Kanayama, G., 260
Kanazawa, S., 552
Kandel, E. R., 23, 84, 89, 99, 103, 106, 132, 134, 135, 172, 271, 277, 281, 286, 287, 288, 291, 292, 293, 294, 307, 337, 609, 610
Kang, D.-H., 236
Kang, H., 258
Kang, J., 469
Kannel, W. B., 498
Kanner, A. A., 489
Kanner, A. D., 478
Kanner, R. E., 319, 342
Kantak, K. M., 662
Kanwisher, N., 456
Kanwisher, N. N., 114
Kaplan, G. A., 210
Kappos, L., 503
Kaprio, J., 469
Karama, S., 99, 100
Karasin, A. I., 610
Kare, M. R., 159

Karg, R. S., 10
Kargman, D. E., 256
Karkowski, L. M., 603
Karmiloff-Smith, A., 357
Karnath, H., 285
Karni, A., 243, 244, 324
Karpiak, C. P., 654
Kass, S. J., 235
Katz, M. M., 295
Kaube, H., 156, 464, 575, 576
Kaufman, A. S., 394, 395
Kaufman, J. C., 407
Kaufman, N. L., 394, 395
Kaul, P., 236, 247
Kawachi, I., 489
Kawamura, Y., 159
Kawashima, K., 467
Kawashima, R., 415, 416
Kay, L. M., 98
Kay, P., 362
Kaye, G. T., 420
Kazlauskaite, R., 501
Keane, J., 464
Keane, S. P., 656
Keck, P. E., 79
Keeler, R. F., 176
Keenan, R. M., 258
Keerkens, J., 603
Kegeles, L. S., 611
Kehle, S., 650
Keith, M. W., 105
Keitner, D., 452
Keller, H., 149
Keller, M. C., 575, 577
Keller, T. A., 235
Kellerman, E., 380
Kelley, H. H., 556, 574
Kellman, P. J., 179
Kellner, C. H., 641
Kelly, K. R., 538
Kelso, J. R., 79
Keltikangas-Jarvinen, L., 210
Keltner, D., 451, 452
Keltner, D. J., 460
Kemeny, M., 506, 603
Kemeny, M. E., 489
Kempermann, G., 110, 212, 215, 339
Kenardy, J., 469
Kendler, K. S., 80, 92, 588, 597, 603
Kendrick, T., 640
Kennedy, G., 560
Kennedy, J. L., 92
Kennedy, J. M., 117, 119
Kennedy, S., 638
Kennedy, S. H., 638, 640
Kennedy, W. A., 462, 463
Kensinger, E. A., 288, 289, 324
Keppel, R., 588
Kerig, P., 400
Kerr, C., 238
Kerwin, R., 632, 659
Keshavan, M., 202
Kessler, C., 635
Kessler, H., 466
Kessler, R. C., 591, 595, 616, 619, 623, 658
Kettler, L., 650
Keyes, S., 540
Khaire, M., 445, 447, 448
Khallou-Laschet, J., 92
Khan, M. A., 437

Khandawood, F., 437
Khoury, J., 621
Kidd, K. K., 405
Kideckel, D. M., 441
Kidman, A. D., 488
Kiecolt-Glaser, J. K., 496, 497
Kieras, J. E., 198
Kiersky, J. E., 641
Kigar, D. L., 441
Kihlstrom, J. F., 614
Kijima, N., 540
Kikuchi, S., 502
Kilburn, J., 571
Kilgore, K. L., 104, 105
Killgore, D. B., 246
Killgore, W. D. S., 246
Kilts, C., 525
Kim, B., 656
Kim, B.-K., 503
Kim, C., 653
Kim, C.-J., 503
Kim, E. S., 660
Kim, H. K., 414
Kim, H. O., 258
Kim, J., 128, 653
Kim, J. S., 215
Kim, K. H. S., 379, 380
Kim, S., 212, 653
Kim, S.-E., 503
Kim, S. I., 653
Kim, Y., 656
Kimball, J., 521
Kimbrel, N. A., 624
Kimbrell, T. A., 634
Kimeldorf, D. J., 323, 326, 494
Kimura, D., 366
King, A. C., 621
King, B. G., 236, 237
King, D. E., 256
King, K. A., 467
King, L. A., 470, 487
King, S., 484
Kingsbury, R., 559, 561
Kinney, D. K., 623, 624
Kinsey, A. C., 49, 50, 438
Kirby, K. C., 319
Kirby, K. N., 365
Kirisoglu, C., 247
Kirk, K. M., 438
Kirk, S. B., 487
Kirkham, T. C., 431
Kirkpatrick, L. A., 192
Kirsch, R. F., 104, 105
Kirsh, S. J., 571
Kisilevsky, B. S., 172
Kitayama, S., 162, 574
Kitlinska, J. B., 501
Kiyonari, T., 464
Klahr, D., 201
Klavans, R., 6
Klebanoff, M. A., 610
Klein, D. A., 319
Klein, D. J., 342
Klein, H. S., 206
Klein, L., 211
Klein, R. G., 95
Klein-Schwartz, W., 257
Kleitman, N., 240, 243
Kleseges, R. C., 342
Klimas, N., 506
Klinnert, M. D., 197, 456
Klocke, U., 233

Kloosterman, K., 124
Klopfer, P. H., 549
Klucharev, V., 552
Klüver, H., 100
Knafo, A., 464
Knapp, R. G., 641
Knickmeyer, R. C., 610
Knight, R. T., 287
Knowlton, B., 5, 233
Knox, R., 153
Knudsen, G. M., 92
Ko, C.-H., 599
Ko, I.-G., 503
Kobayakawa, T., 164
Kobayashi, M., 164
Kobor, M. S., 484
Koch, C., 136
Koch, L. L., 153
Kodish, I. M., 609
Koelling, R., 327
Koelling, R. A., 323, 326, 327, 328, 494
Koenig, J. I., 176, 610
Koepke, K. M., 212, 221
Koerner, K., 656
Koestner, R., 444, 447
Koffka, K., 142
Koh, J. S., 258
Kohlberg, L., 190, 191, 192
Köhler, W., 142
Kohn, P. M., 478
Kokko, K., 209
Koldny, J., 402
Kolodny, R. C., 436
Komar, V., 306
Kong, Y., 499
Koopmans, J., 488
Kop, W. J., 603
Kopell, B. H., 100
Koplan, J. P., 433
Koppelstaetter, F., 255
Kopta, S. M., 650
Koran, L. M., 598
Korkeila, J., 500
Korkeila, M., 469
Korman, K., 366
Kornell, N., 282, 300, 301
Kornhaber, M. L., 391, 393
Korpert, K., 152
Kortekaas, R., 437
Koshenvuo, M., 469
Koskelo, J., 325
Koslowski, B., 40, 369
Kosslyn, S., 365
Kosslyn, S. M., 365
Kottke, J. L., 446
Kounios, J., 100, 416
Kovacs, M., 197
Koven, N. S., 623
Kowalski, R. M., 442
Kraaj, V., 506
Kraemer, H. C., 488
Kraepelin, E., 14, 607
Kraft, R. A., 236
Krahe, T. E., 176
Kralovec, P. D., 216
Kramarik, A., 400
Kramer, A. F., 212, 213, 215, 221, 325, 339, 502
Kramer, S. J., 445, 447
Kranczioch, C., 227, 232
Krause, M. S., 650

Kravitz, E. A., 569
Krech, D., 70, 339
Kreiman, G., 136
Kremer, S., 211
Krietemeyer, J., 230, 236
Kring, A. M., 655
Krishen, A., 603
Kristeller, J., 503
Kristeller, J. L., 656
Kristensen, M., 462
Kristjansson, A. L., 204
Kristof-Brown, A. L., 539
Kroeber, A. L., 165
Kroenke, K., 600
Kroeze, J. H., 211
Kroft, J., 92
Kröger, C., 656
Krohn, E., 397
Kromhout, D., 500
Krompinger, J., 236
Krueger, R. F., 515, 516, 540, 603
Krüger, S., 638
Krull, J. L., 470
Krummel, D., 64, 621
Krystal, A. D., 247
Krystal, J. H., 342
Ku, J., 653
Kubik, S., 283
Kübler-Ross, E., 216
Kubota, M., 256
Kubzansky, L. D., 489
Kuhl, B., 294
Kuhl, P. K., 190, 351, 354
Kuhn, C. M., 196
Kuhn, D., 40, 201, 371, 372
Kuhn, H. G., 109
Kuhn, J. W., 92
Kuipers, R., 437
Kujawa, M. J., 634
Kulik, J., 290
Kulkarni, J., 637
Kunkel, C., 393
Kuo, L. E., 501
Kuo, M., 256
Kupfer, D. J., 632, 638
Kupfermann, I., 99, 271, 277, 286
Kurcewicz, I., 92
Kuriyama, K., 324
Kurowski, C. O., 197
Kurson, R., 136
Kurtines, B., 32, 653
Kusaka, T., 256
Kusché, C. A., 467
Kuwabara, S. A., 659, 660
Kwok, R. C.-H., 560
Kwon, J. S., 236
Kwon, S. J., 236
Kwon, Y., 201

L

LaBar, K. S., 288
LaBerge, S., 249
Laborit, H., 634
Lacadie, C., 606
Lachman, M. E., 541
La Ferla, T., 632
la Fleur, S. E., 501
LaFrance, M., 466
Lafreniere, K., 478
Lagopoulos, J., 112, 113
LaGrange, B., 660
Laird, B. A., 624

Lalonde, J., 614
Lamb, R. J., 319
Lambert, W., 536
Lamp, R., 397
Lanciano, T., 290
Landis, J., 543
Landry, R. G., 381
Lane, M. C., 616
Lane, R. D., 466
Lane, S. J., 620
Lane, T., 197
Lang, E., 251
Lange, C., 461
Lange, P. G., 4, 32
Langley, K., 80
Langlois, J. H., 577
Lanphear, B. P., 621
Lansing, A. E., 543
Laplante, D. P., 484
Laporte, F., 501
La Precious, H., 218
Lapsley, D. K., 191
Large, M. D., 598
Largie, S., 196
Larkin, G. R., 470, 490
Larrabee, G. J., 296
Larson, L., 538
Larson, L. M., 538
Larsson, H., 621
Larsson, J., 621
Laruelle, M., 611
Lasagabaster, D., 381
Lasane, T. P., 128
Laschet, J., 92
Lassonde, M., 466
Latané, B., 47, 572, 573
Lau, M., 638
Lau, M. A., 236, 653, 654, 656, 661
Laumann, E., 469
Laurenceau, J. P., 506
Laureys, S., 227, 228, 229, 244, 262
Lavelli, M., 197
Lavie, N., 232
Lawless, H. T., 160
Lawrence, A. D., 464
Lawrence, A. E., 597
Lawson, A. E., 201
Lazar, S., 238
Lazar, S. W., 238
Lazarus, A. A., 652
Lazarus, R. S., 27, 449, 450, 453, 454, 478, 479, 485, 486, 489
Leader, L., 177
Leary, M., 442
Leary, M. R., 442, 559
Leary, S. P., 128
Le Bars, P. L., 295
LeBlanc, D., 623
Lecours, A. R., 99, 100
Leder, G., 235
LeDoux, J., 462
LeDoux, J. E., 99, 288, 462, 596
LeDuc, P. A., 325
Lee, A. G., 484
Lee, C., 489, 631
Lee, D. H., 465
Lee, E. H., 656
Lee, H., 463
Lee, J. E., 256
Lee, J. H., 217

Lee, K. A., 247
Lee, K. L., 499
Lee, K. M., 379, 380
Lee, L. H., 71, 182
Lee, S., 656
Leeka, J., 450
Lehner, T., 603
Leknes, S., 156
Lemay, E. P., Jr., 203
Le Moal, M., 516
Lemon, J., 488
Lenhart, A., 170, 218, 219, 220
Lenneberg, E., 353
Lennie, P., 147
Lenroot, R., 201, 202
Lenzenweger, M. F., 616
Leonard, G., 201, 202
Lepage, J.-F., 196, 337
Lepore, F., 466
Lerch, J., 182, 201, 202
Lerner, L., 636
Leroux, J.-M., 99, 100
Lesch, K. P., 515
Leserman, J., 506, 507
Leszcz, M., 488
Lethbridge-Cejku, M., 497
Leuner, B., 111, 211, 484
LeVay, S., 440, 441
Leveck, M. D., 221
Levenson, R. W., 449, 452, 453, 454, 455, 456, 462, 466, 483, 486, 487, 489
Leverich, G. S., 634
Leveroni, C., 366
Levin, B., 177
Levin, H. S., 543
Levine, B., 81
Levine, L. E., 5
Levine, S., 354, 498
Levinson, B., 469
Levitt, P., 609, 610
Levy, B., 294
Lew, A.-M., 434
Lewandowski, G., 283
Lewin, T., 217
Lewinsohn, P. M., 660
Lewis, D., 609, 610
Lewis, D. A., 610
Lewis, D. W., 218
Lewis, G. D., 502
Li, B.-H., 431
Li, H., 100
Li, J., 536
Li, K. K., 247
Li, L., 501, 515
Li, M., 598
Li, X., 251
Liamputtong, P., 32
Liang, K.-Y., 603
Liberzon, I., 463, 597
Lichtenstein, P., 502, 621
Lichtman, J. W., 172, 610
Lidz, J., 357
Liebal, K., 350
Lieberman, J. A., 609, 635, 641
Lieberman, M. D., 156, 463, 548, 559, 560
Liebert, R. M., 571
Lief, H. I., 437
Liehr, P., 503
Lifson, A. R., 506
Light, T., 236, 503
Lightner, C., 426

Lihoreau, M., 442, 561
Lim, A., 484
Lim, H.-K., 631
Lim, J., 160
Limosin, F., 24
Lin, I.-F., 256
Lin, J., 490, 491
Linardatos, E., 640
Linda, F. K., 632
Lindeboom, J., 296
Lindell, S. G., 12
Linden, D. E. J., 652
Lindenboim, N., 656
Lindsay, D. S., 298
Linehan, M. M., 655, 656, 663
Ling, C., 561
Ling, R., 219
Liotti, M., 638
Lipkus, I. M., 342
Lippa, R., 568
Lipsitz, J. D., 652
Lipska, B. K., 610
Lipworth, L., 503
Lisetti, C., 32, 653
Lister, K. M., 654
Liu, G., 108
Liu, H., 181, 209
Liu, J., 100
Liu, S., 616
Liu, Y., 246
Locke, J., 16, 20, 23
Lockhart, R. S., 279, 280, 281
Lockwood, G. A., 488
Lodi-Smith, J., 540
Loehlin, J. C., 515, 516
Loeser, J. D., 157
Loftus, E., 297, 298
Loftus, E. F., 282, 283, 298
Logothetis, N. K., 113
Logworth, L., 640
Lohman, B. J., 207
Lohman, T. G., 502
Lohr, K. N., 214
Lombardi, G., 211
Long, M., 380
Lopez, S., 470
Loranger, A. W., 616
Lorenz, K., 192, 335, 336
Louvel, J., 92
Lovaas, O. I., 319
Loveland, J., 324
Lovett, R., 257
Low, J. A., 172
Low, Y.-L., 405
Löwe, B., 600
Lowe, S. L., 641
Lowery, B. S., 21
Lowing, P. A., 623
Lowry, C. A., 603
Lozano, A. M., 41, 639, 640
Lubach, G. R., 175, 610
Lubben, J., 220
Lubinski, D., 401, 420
Luborsky, L., 650
Luc, G., 500
Lucas, M., 32, 653
Lucas, R. E., 468, 469, 470
Luchins, A. S., 410
Luchins, E. H., 410
Lüders, M., 561
Ludwig, A. M., 419, 622, 623, 624
Lueck, M., 570, 618

Luk, C., 641
Luminet, O., 468
Lund, D. J., 445, 446
Lupien, S. J., 484
Lupu, V., 641
Lutgendorf, S. K., 484
Lutman, M. E., 152
Lutz, A., 238
Luxen, A., 251
Luykx, J. J., 606
Lykken, D. T., 433, 515
Lynch, G. V., 536
Lynn, R., 403
Lyons, D. E., 337
Lyons, D. M., 484

M

Maas, J., 245
Macaskill, M., 124
Macbeth, A. H., 463
Maccari, S., 516
Maccoby, E. E., 22, 198, 407, 570
Macdaid, G. P., 538
MacDonald, D., 70
MacDonald, G., 548, 559, 561
MacKay, I. R. A., 379
Mackenbach, J., 502
MacKinnon, D. W., 413, 420
MacLane, C. N., 539
MacLean, K. A., 236, 237
Macmillan, M., 101, 541
MacNeill, C., 324
MacWhinney, B., 357
Madden, D. J., 325
Madden, M., 220
Madey, S., 454
Madigan, S., 275
Madigan, S. A., 272, 273, 275, 276, 280, 287
Maeda, A., 246
Maes, H. M. M., 433
Maes, S., 506
Maestripieri, D., 12
Magliano, L., 661
Magnanini, M. M. F., 507
Magoun, H. W., 98
Maguire, E. A., 99
Mahurin, R. K., 638
Maier, N. R. F., 409
Maier, S. F., 155
Main, M., 194
Mainous, A. G., III, 256
Maj, M., 661
Makovski, T., 324
Malarkey, W. B., 497
Malberg, J. E., 603
Malhi, G. S., 634
Malle, B. F., 350
Malone, M., 92
Malouff, J. M., 468
Malta, M., 507
Manber, R., 247
Maner, J. K., 548, 577
Manfreda, R., 319, 342
Mangels, J. A., 287
Mangieri, R., 261
Manigat, N., 196
Mann, T., 434
Manson, J. E., 501
Manstead, A. S. R., 466
Mansuy, I. M., 81

Maquet, P., 244
Marais, L., 503
Marcus, M. T., 503
Marder, S. R., 634
Marek, G. J., 261
Margison, F., 650
Marinkovic, K., 255
Mark, G., 233
Marker, C. D., 597
Markman, H. J., 209
Marks, B. L., 325
Marks, J. S., 433
Marks, R., 159
Marks, W., 262
Marksteiner, J., 255
Markus, H., 162, 517
Markus, H. R., 208
Marlier, L., 174
Marlin, D. W., 432
Marmar, C. R., 603
Marmot, M., 500
Maron, E., 597
Maroney-Galin, C., 216
Marquez, A., 610
Marquis, J., 217
Marsh, A. A., 464
Marshall, R. D., 654, 656
Marsiske, M., 212, 221
Martenyi, F., 641
Marti, C. N., 660
Martin, C. E., 49, 50, 438
Martin, D., 399, 404
Martin, E. P., 660
Martin, J., 569, 619, 620, 624,
   625
Martin, L. L., 462
Martin, N. G., 438, 440, 441
Martindale, C., 136, 416
Martinez, G. M., 204, 207
Martinovic, M., 502
Martion, E. D., 248
Martucci, K. T., 236
Martuza, R. L., 636
Marucha, P. T., 497
Marzelli, M. J., 105
Marzola, E., 502
Mascaro, N., 652
Maschi, S., 177
Masek, B., 662
Masella, M., 661
Mash, E. J., 399, 400
Mashek, D. J., 451, 452
Mashoodh, R., 80
Mashour, G. A., 636
Masicampo, E. J., 227
Masling, J. M., 536
Maslow, A., 19, 22, 290, 430,
   525, 526, 527
Mason, J., 218
Mason, J. W., 483
Mason, T. B. A., 246
Massion, A. O., 503
Masten, A. S., 208
Masten, C. L., 548, 559
Masters, J., 218
Masters, W. H., 436
Masuda, A., 503
Masuda, T., 162, 163
Mateo, Y., 259
Mathai, M., 427
Matheson, C. C., 198
Mathiak, K., 218
Mathias, J. L., 262, 263

Mathiesen, B. B., 543
Mathis, C., 632, 638
Maticka-Tyndale, E., 438
Matlin, M., 108
Matson, J. L., 645
Matsuda, H., 182
Matsumoto, D., 162, 191, 296,
   465, 466
Matsumoto, D. M., 452
Matsumoto, N., 299
Matsumoto, T., 299
Mattar, A. A. G., 155
Mattay, V. S., 610
Matthews, A. M., 640
Matthews, G., 366
Matthews, K., 501
Matthews, K. A., 498
Matthews, P. M., 212
Maurer, D., 160, 161
Mauss, I. B., 452
Max, J. E., 543
Maxwell, K. W., 260
May, P. A., 176
Mayberg, H., 638, 654, 655
Mayberg, H. S., 29, 41, 638, 639,
   640
Mayer, J. D., 467
Mayer, M., 612
Mayne, T. J., 10, 506
Mazziotta, J. C., 196, 337, 548,
   559
McArdle, J. J., 221
McAuley, E., 215
McBrien, C., 652
McCabe, C., 159
McCann, S., 638
McCann, U., 261
McCann, U. D., 261
McCarter, L., 452
McCarter, R., 458
McCarty, C., 217
McCaslin, S. E., 603
McCauley, C. R., 449
McClain, C. S., 215
McClay, J., 569, 619
McClelland, D. C., 442
McClelland, J. L., 145, 283, 367
McClintock, M. K., 437
McCollough, J. K., 577
McCormack, K. M., 12
McCrae, R. R., 514, 515, 517,
   529, 530, 537, 540
McCullough, M. E., 471, 644
McDermott, R. J., 220
McDonald, J., 620
McElree, B., 295, 296
McElroy, S. L., 79
McEvoy, J. P., 635, 641
McEwen, B., 501
McEwen, B. S., 484
McGaugh, J. L., 268, 281
McGhee, D. E., 563
McGill, B., 209
McGinnis, S., 638
McGinty, D., 243
McGlone, G., 536
McGowan, B. K., 328
McGuffin, P., 588, 603
McGuire, E., 218
McGuire, E. J., 365
McGuire, M. T., 570
McGuire, P. K., 610
McHaffie, J. G., 236

McHugh, P., 614
McHugh, R. K., 662
McKenna, B. S., 324
McKeon, D., 654, 655
McKhann, G. M., 325, 339, 503,
   504
McKinley, M., 427
McKinney, B. C., 609
McKinney, M. L., 360
McLay, R. N., 652
McMenamy, J. M., 197
McNagny, K., 635
McNaughton, B. L., 324
McNealy, K., 548, 559
McNeely, H., 640
McNeely, H. E., 41, 639
McNulty, J. L., 537
McQuade, J., 662
McRae, K., 464
McTiernan, A., 501
Mead, G., 625
Mead, N. L., 128
Meadows, E. A., 654, 656
Meaney, M. J., 80, 81
Measelle, J., 516
Mechelli, A., 379
Mechtcheriakov, S., 255
Medina, A. E., 176
Mednick, M. T., 415
Mednick, S. A., 415
Mednick, S. C., 324, 325
Medvec, V., 454
Meerkerk, G., 599
Mei, L., 609
Meier, D. E., 216
Meier, M., 460
Meijer, W., 296
Meilijson, I., 181
Meiners, L., 437
Meir, E. I., 539
Meister, M., 148
Melamid, A., 306
Melis, A. P., 549, 562
Melis, M. R., 437
Mell, J. C., 415
Mellor-Clark, J., 650
Meloy, M. J., 324
Meltzer, H. Y., 641
Meltzoff, A. N., 190, 196, 337,
   354, 456
Melzack, R., 157
Mencl, E., 342
Mendelsohn, A., 283
Mendelsohn, G. A., 221
Mendes, W. B., 624
Mendl, M., 456
Mendoza-Denton, R., 540
Meng, Z., 197
Mennella, J. A., 174, 437
Menotti, A., 500
Merabet, L. B., 119
Mercado, A. M., 497
Merckelbach, H., 298
Merikangas, K. R., 591, 595, 619,
   623, 658
Merla, A., 99
Merrill, J. E., 256
Merskey, H., 155
Merten, J., 466
Merten, M. J., 170
Merzenich, M. M., 107, 155, 182
Mesiäinen, P., 209
Messner, P. K., 4

McHugh, P., 614
Methippara, M., 243
Metter, E. J., 211
Metzler, J., 366
Metzler, T. J., 603
Meuel, C., 153
Meunier, M., 100
Meuret, A. F., 662
Meyer, A., 624
Meyer, J. F., 597
Meyer, J. H., 638
Meyer, P. S., 655
Meyerhoff, D. J., 256
Meyer-Lindenberg, A., 610
Meyyappan, A., 298
Miao, C. F., 445, 446
Michael, J., 316
Michel, S., 239
Michela, J. L., 556
Miczek, K. A., 569
Middleton, F. A., 610
Miele, G. M., 486
Mihara, T., 247
Mikolajczak, M., 468
Miles, J. N. V., 650
Miles, M., 478
Milgram, S., 66, 67, 68, 512,
   552, 553, 554, 555
Mill, J., 81, 569, 619
Miller, A., 365, 416
Miller, A. H., 495
Miller, A. L., 319
Miller, A. S., 552
Miller, B. L., 101, 201, 286, 415,
   463
Miller, G. A., 273, 623
Miller, G. E., 482, 484
Miller, G. F., 427, 514, 577
Miller, H. L., 632
Miller, L. A., 416
Miller, L. C., 104, 105
Miller, M. A., 244
Miller, N., 331
Miller, R., 577
Miller, S. L., 548, 577
Miller, W. R., 437
Miller-Johnson, S., 406
Millot, J.-L., 164
Mills, T. L., 621
Milner, B., 269, 270, 271, 291
Milner, P., 463
Min, B.-K., 105
Mineka, S., 594
Ming-Hsuang, C., 294
Minier, F., 92
Mintun, M., 100
Minturn, A. L., 128
Mirerikangas, K. R., 603
Mirescu, C., 111, 181
Mirnics, K., 610
Mischel, W., 528, 540
Miselis, R., 427
Mitchell, J. T., 656
Mitchell, K., 219
Mitchell, K. J., 32, 219, 220
Mitchell, P., 210
Mitchell, T., 108
Mitra, R., 484
Miyake, A., 286, 463
Miyaoka, T., 247
Miyashita, T., 283
Mizuno, S., 247
Moffitt, T. E., 29, 80, 92, 516,
   569, 570, 588, 604, 609, 619

Moghaddam, B., 612
Mohanty, A., 623
Mohr, D. C., 503
Moise-Titus, J., 571
Mojet, J., 211
Mokdad, A. H., 433
Molaison, H., 269, 291
Moline, J., 152
Moll, J., 203
Moller, J., 499
Montague, D. P. F., 197
Montgomery, A., 487
Montgomery, G. H., 251
Monti, D., 484
Montoro, R., 204
Moody, B. J., 641
Moody, E. W., 311
Moody, T. D., 221
Moonen, G., 251
Mooney, D., 174
Moore, D. C., 145
Moore, E. S., 176
Moore, M., 640
Moore, M. K., 196, 337, 354, 456
Moore, R. Y., 239
Moradi, A. R., 291
Morales-Medina, J. C., 603
Moran, E. M., 561
Moray, N., 231
Morelli, G. A., 49
Morgan, S. M., 128
Morgenstern, N. A., 211
Morghen, I., 263
Mori, S., 115
Morien, A., 431
Morikawa, H., 354
Morin, C. M., 263
Morinobu, S., 495
Morita, Y., 325
Morland, T., 463
Morral, A. R., 319
Morrell, C. H., 211
Morris, J. S., 100
Morris, M. W., 557
Morris, N. M., 437
Morris, P. L., 463
Morris, T. L., 31
Morrison, M., 506
Morrison, R. S., 216
Morrow, J. D., 490, 491
Moruzzi, G., 98
Mosconi, M., 621
Moscovici, S., 552
Moscovitch, D. A., 662
Moscovitch, M., 276, 281
Moses-Kolko, E. L., 177
Mosher, W. D., 204, 207
Moskowitz, J., 490, 503, 506
Moskowitz, J. T., 489, 490
Mostow, A. J., 467
Motluk, A., 117, 119
Motohashi, Y., 246
Mount, M. K., 538
Moynihan, J., 503
Mroczek, D., 512, 540
Muir, D. W., 172
Mukand, J. A., 104
Mukhtar, B., 460
Mulder, E. J. H., 177
Mulder, I., 500
Muller, D., 236
Muller, H. W., 597
Müller, K., 325

Müller, N. G., 285
Müller-Oerlinghausen, B., 606, 607
Mulvenna, C., 160
Mulvey, T. A., 7
Munro, G. D., 128
Munro, M. J., 379
Munsinger, H., 403
Munz, D. C., 246
Murabito, J., 560
Murphy, D. L., 515
Murphy, G., 319
Murphy, M., 660
Murphy, S. E., 632
Murray, A. D., 337
Murray, A. M., 656
Murray, C., 405, 406
Murray, H. A., 442
Murray, J., 434
Murray, R. M., 260, 610
Murvielde, I., 538
Mussell, M., 600
Musselman, L., 577
Myers, I. B., 538
Myers, T., 507

N

Nabi, H., 500
Nacash, N., 654, 656
Nadarajah, B., 93, 172
Nadel, L., 243, 249, 324
Nahin, R. L., 247
Nakagawa, A., 632
Nakano, S., 599
Nakayama, K., 324
Nakazaki, S., 256
Naliboff, B. D., 548
Naqvi, N. H., 103
Narr, K. L., 570
Närvänen, S., 252
Nasar, S., 623
Nash, J. F., Jr., 623
Nash, M. R., 536
Nass, C. I., 218
Nathans, J., 131, 132, 147, 148
National Center for Health Statistics, 602
National Eye Institute, 374
National Human Genome Research Institute, 82
National Institute of Deafness, 153
National Institute of Mental Health, 607
National Institute on Alcohol Abuse and Alcoholism, 256
National Safety Council, 374
National Science Foundation, 44, 45
National Sleep Foundation, 245, 246
Nauta, W. J. H., 84, 86
Nave, K.-A., 85
Neale, M. C., 433, 597
Neely, M. H., 261
Neena, A., 631
Nehmy, T. J., 594
Neisser, U., 386
Nelson, J. D., 337
Nelson, L., 208
Nelson-Gray, R. O., 656
Nemeroff, C., 449

Nemeroff, C. B., 640
Nesbit, S. M., 571
Nestler, E. J., 603
Neston, J. D., 498
Nettle, D., 514, 623
Neuberg, S. L., 548, 559, 562, 566
Neuberger, M., 152
Neugebauer, R., 175
Neville, H., 108, 109
Nevitte, N., 128
Newall, P., 210
Newcomb, A. F., 203
Newcomb, T. M., 575
Newcombe, N. S., 362
Newman, T. K., 12
Newport, E. L., 353
Neyens, D. M., 235
Nicholls, E. F., 484
Nichols, T. N., 100
Nichols, W. C., 621
Nickerson, C., 469
Nicoll, R. A., 260, 261, 431
Nieman, D. C., 469
Nienhuis, R., 244
Nierman, A., 31
Nieuwenburg, A., 437
Nievergelt, C. M., 79
Nijran, K. S., 609, 610
Nikolaus, S., 597
Nilsson, L. G., 212
Nirenberg, M., 294
Nisbett, R. E., 60, 162, 163, 557
Nishida, M., 495
Nishikawa, M., 182
Nishino, S., 247
Nissinen, A., 500
Nithianantharajah, J., 215
Niv, N., 635
Nixon, R. D. V., 594
Nock, M. K., 564
Noda, H., 502
Nogeire, C., 249
Noiman, L., 111
Nolan, C. L., 100
Nolen-Hoeksema, S., 14, 502, 608, 618, 637, 645, 655
Nolte, C., 276
Nopoulos, P., 610
Noppeney, U., 379
Norcross, J. C., 10, 654
Nordahl, T. E., 621
Nordborg, C., 111, 339
Nordberg, M., 632
Norenzayan, A., 162, 557
Norine, C. S., 4, 32
Norton, A., 182, 183
Norton, M. I., 469
Nottebohm, F., 110
Novak, M. A., 12
Novick, D., 641
Novick, O., 515
Nowak, M. A., 350
Nowell, A., 406, 407
Nowicki, G. P., 453
Nuechterlein, K., 233
Numminen, J., 252
Nusselder, W., 502

O

Oakley, D. A., 252
Obama, B., 208, 372, 559
Oberman, L. M., 337, 621, 622

O'Brien, C. P., 437
O'Brien, W. H., 499
Oby, E. R., 104, 105
Ochs, M. T., 107, 155, 182
Ochsner, K. N., 454, 463, 466
O'Cleirigh, C., 486, 506
O'Conner, M. J., 605
O'Connor, C., 499
O'Craven, K. M., 114
Odbert, H. W., 529
Odendaal, H., 176
O'Doherty, J., 379
O'Doherty, J. O., 156, 464, 575, 576
O'Donovan, A., 603
Oeltermann, A., 113
Ogden, C. L., 433
O'Hara, B. F., 236, 247
O'Hara, L., 414
O'Hara, R., 275
Ohl, F., 502
Öhman, A., 99, 462
Ohnishi, T., 182
Ohno, H., 325
Oishi, K., 115
Oishi, S., 517
Oitzl, M. S., 405
Oke, A., 467, 468
Okuda, M., 616
Oldfield, B. J., 427
Olds, J., 463
O'Leary, D. S., 610
Olfson, M., 616
Oliveira, A. J., 263
Oliver, M. B., 438
Olivetti, M., 99
Olivier, B., 632
Olney, J. W., 253
O'Loughlin, M., 40, 201
Olsen, C. W., 610
Olson, J. M., 565
Olson, M., 176
Olveczky, B. P., 148
O'Malley, P. M., 506
Omark, D., 198
Omark, M., 198
O'Neill, J., 324
Ones, D. S., 539
Ong, J. C., 247
Ono, Y., 540
Onodera, A., 541
Onyike, C. U., 543
Ophir, E., 218
Ophoff, R. A., 606, 609
Opperman, M., 438
O'Reardon, J. P., 650
Orlando, M., 342
Orlinsky, D. E., 650
Orne, M. T., 251
O'Rourke, F. E., 197
Ortigo, K. M., 525
Orwin, R. G., 204
Oscar–Berman, M., 255
Osher, Y., 515
Osherow, N., 580
Osman, H., 220
Osmond, C., 175
Ost, J., 298
Oster, H., 197
Osterling, J., 620
Ostermann, S., 31
Ostry, D. J., 155
O'Sullivan, M., 459, 557

Otte, S. L., 609
Ottersen, O. P., 23, 76
Otto, M. W., 662
Ouellet, M-C., 263
Oumar, F., 194
Oveis, C., 451
Overeem, S., 247
Overgaard, M., 229
Owen, A. M., 229
Owen, M., 609, 612
Owren, M. J., 460
Oyama, S., 379

P

Paans, A., 437
Pachan, M. K., 467
Padesky, C., 624
Padmala, S., 463
Pae, C.-U., 631
Paetzold, M., 324
Pagani, J. H., 463
Pagano, L., 218
Paik, A., 469
Paik, M. C., 256
Pajares, F., 331
Paley, B., 605
Pallanti, S., 598
Paluk, B. L., 466
Pan, B. A., 354
Panagopoulou, E., 487
Panaitescu, B., 84
Panksepp, J., 463
Pantev, C., 155, 182
Papakostos, G. I., 603
Parasuraman, R., 233
Paris, R., 541
Parisi, D., 357
Park, C. L., 490
Park, H. Y., 236
Park, J. A., 653
Park, J. M., 564
Park, S., 415, 653
Parker, E. S., 268
Parker, G., 177
Parker, J. D. A., 467, 468
Parker, S. T., 360
Parks, A. C., 644
Parks, R., 191
Parnavelas, J., 93, 172
Parrish, T. B., 100
Pascual, J. C., 656
Pascual-Leone, A., 119, 183, 212,
   336
Passafiume, J., 236, 247
Passamonti, L., 464
Passarelli, V., 656
Pasterski, V., 366
Pasupathi, M., 542, 543
Pasztor, A., 32, 653
Patchin, J. W., 219, 220
Patel, N. H., 609, 610
Patil, S. T., 641
Patkar, A. A., 631
Patrick, C. J., 540
Patrick, J. H., 207
Patterson, C., 515
Patterson, C. J., 171, 179, 187
Patterson, D. R., 251
Pattie, A., 397
Paul, E. S., 456
Paulesu, E., 286
Paulozzi, L. J., 257

Pauls, J., 113
Paunesku, D., 659, 660
Paus, T., 181, 201, 202
Pavelis, C., 623
Pavlov, I. P., 308, 309, 311
Payne, J. D., 243, 244, 249, 282,
   289, 324
Payne, R., 257
Pbert, L., 503
Pearsall, S., 201, 371
Pearson, J. D., 211
Pearson, N. J., 247
Pearson, P. D., 380
Pecile, A., 153
Peckham, P. H., 105
Pecoraro, N. C., 501
Pedersen, D. M., 161
Pedersen, N. L., 109, 502
Peek, K., 401–402
Peeters, A., 502
Peigneux, P., 244
Pelli, D. G., 145
Penfield, W., 291
Peng, K., 162, 557
Penn, D. L., 655
Pennebaker, J. W., 486, 487, 496,
   503, 507
Penner, I. K., 503
Peoples, L., 93
Peoples, M. C., 499
Peper, J. S., 181, 182
Pepler, D., 170
Pereira, A. C., 325, 339, 503, 504
Perel, J., 177
Perel, S., 105
Peretz, I., 156
Pérez, V., 656
Perfilieva, E., 111, 339
Perkins, D. O., 506, 507, 635,
   641
Perner, J., 189, 190
Perreault, E. J., 104, 105
Perrett, D. I., 100, 337
Perrin, F., 244
Perrin, J. S., 201, 202
Perrin, K. M., 220
Perris, F., 661
Perron, M., 201, 202
Perry, B. D., 107, 180, 181, 182,
   406, 599, 600, 603, 609
Perry, R., 135
Persky, H., 437
Pessoa, L., 462, 463
Peter, J., 31, 170, 219
Peters, J. D., 111
Peters, K. R., 325
Peters, M., 298
Peters, R. M., 154
Petersen, K., 259
Peterson, D. A., 111, 339
Peterson, J. B., 623
Peterson, L. G., 503
Pethick, S., 350
Petitto, J. M., 506, 507
Peto, R., 258, 500
Petri, S., 515
Petrides, G., 641
Petrie, K. J., 486, 507
Petrill, S. A., 403
Petronis, A., 81, 609
Petry, S., 543
Petty, T., 445
Peveler, R., 640

Pfefferbaum, A., 256
Pfeifer, J. H., 548, 559
Pfennig, A., 641
Pfrieger, F. W., 84
Phan, K. L., 463
Phelps, E. A., 99, 288, 289, 449,
   462
Phillips, S., 442
Piaget, J., 22, 184, 185, 188, 394
Piazza, P. V., 516
Piché, M., 156
Pichler, S. L., 12, 13
Pickard, J. D., 229
Pickrell, J. E., 298
Pierce, T., 219
Pika, S., 350
Pike, G. B., 201, 202
Pincus, J. H., 570, 618
Pine, D. S., 464
Pinel, P., 14
Pinker, S., 23, 24, 28, 103, 104,
   352, 357
Pinsker, H. M., 291, 337
Piomelli, D., 261
Pisani, L., 194
Pitiot, A., 201, 202
Piven, J., 621
Placid, F., 263
Plante, E., 357, 358
Plato, 16
Platsidou, M., 468
Pleydell-Bouverie, B., 324
Pliner, P., 432
Plomin, R., 23, 357, 403, 515,
   516
Plunkett, K., 351, 357
Podolski, C., 571
Poe, M., 621
Poehlman, T., 564
Pohlmeyer, E. A., 104, 105
Pol, H. E. H., 181, 182
Polanczyk, G., 619
Poldrack, R., 5, 233
Poldrack, R. A., 284
Polich, J., 276
Polkinghorn, C., 661
Pollack, D. B., 570
Polliack, M., 654
Pollock-Wurman, R. A., 662
Pomeroy, W. B., 49, 50, 438
Pomplun, M., 396
Ponsford, J., 263
Pontifex, M. B., 181
Ponto, L. L. B., 610
Poortinga, Y. H., 461
Pope, H., 614
Pope, H. G., 259, 260
Popper, K., 42
Porfeli, E. J., 207
Posner, M. I., 217, 251
Post, R. M., 634
Potkin, S. G., 634
Potter, D., 620
Potter, J. W., 217
Poulet, E., 637
Poulton, R., 80, 92, 604
Powell, C., 548
Powell, E. D., 246
Powell, L. A., 196
Powell, L. H., 501
Powell, R. A., 324
Powers, M., 654
Pozzo, E., 32, 653

Prahbu, V., 419
Praskash, R., 215
Preckel, F., 414
Premack, D., 359
Prescott, C. A., 92, 603
Price, C. J., 379
Price, J., 268
Price, J. C., 632, 638
Price, L. H., 632
Pridgeon, A., 570
Pridmore, S., 637
Priel, B., 515
Prindle, J. J., 221
Prochaska, J. O., 654
Profet, M., 158, 175
Proietti, R., 263
Provenzale, J. M., 325
Prudic, J., 641
Pruim, J., 437
Przymus, D. E., 456
Ptito, M., 175
Pugh, K. R., 342
Pugh, M. J. V., 204
Pühse, W., 325
Pulkkinen, L., 209
Pulver, C. A., 538
Pumain, R., 92
Pun, S., 469
Pungello, E. P., 406
Purcell, K., 170, 218, 219
Puri, B. K., 609, 610
Purves, D., 172, 610
Putnam, F., 614
Putnam, F. W., 614

Q

Qiu, J., 100
Quek, S.-C., 405
Quercoli, L., 598
Quillian-Wolever, R., 656
Quinlivan, E., 442
Quirion, R., 603
Quiroga, M., 402
Quiroga, R. Q., 136

R

Raber, A., 152
Raboud, J., 507
Radford, A., 356
Raffaele, P., 360
Raffo, M., 606
Rahe, R. H., 477
Rahman, Q., 440, 441
Rahn, E. J., 261
Raij, T. T., 252
Raine, A., 570
Rainville, P., 156, 238
Raison, C. L., 495
Raleigh, M., 570
Raleigh, M. J., 570
Ramachandran, V. S., 160, 161,
   337, 621, 622
Ramanathan, L., 244
Ramel, W., 464
Ramesh, S., 632
Ramey, C. T., 406
Ramón y Cajal, S., 84, 109
Ransdell, S., 372
Rao, V., 543
Raphael, B., 463
Rapoport, J. L., 181

Smyth, K. A., 543
Smythe, J., 160
Snarey, J. R., 191
Snelson, C., 561
Snow, C. E., 354
Snyderman, M., 386
Sodian, B., 201
Soldatos, C. R., 248
Soler, J., 656
Solla, S. A., 104, 105
Solms, M., 263, 521
Solomon, G., 506
Solomon, J., 194
Solomon, P. R., 295
Solso, S., 621
Song, H., 110
Song, S., 250, 594
Sood, A. K., 484
Soorya, L. V., 319
Soper, B., 324
Sorce, J. F., 197, 456
Sorensen, T. L., 469
Sorenson, E. R., 459
Sorg, C., 214
Sosunov, A. A., 325, 339, 503, 504
Soulsby, J. M., 236, 653, 654, 656, 661
Soussignan, R., 174
Southall, N., 294
Southwick, S., 536
Southwick, S. M., 660
Sowell, E. R., 201
Spalding, K. L., 433
Spalding, M., 105
Sparling, J., 406
Sparrow, D., 489
Spearman, C., 387
Spector, F., 160, 161
Spelke, E., 183
Spence, J., 653
Spence, M. J., 174
Spencer, H. S., 152
Spencer, N. A., 437
Spencer, S. M., 207
Sperry, R. W., 105, 106
Spiegel, D., 488
Spiers, H. J., 99
Spinrad, T. L., 197
Spiro, R. J., 543
Spitalnick, J., 652
Spitzer, R., 600
Spohr, H., 404
Spottiswoode, B., 506
Squire, L., 277
Squire, L. R., 284, 637
Srivastava, S., 529
Staggs, G. D., 538
Stahl, S. M., 603
Staiger, J. F., 71, 182
Stamoudis, C. X., 110
Stampfer, M. J., 501
Stanchev, P. L., 441
Stanford, V. A., 502
Stanley, J., 401
Stanley, S. M., 209
Stanton, A. A., 464
Stanton, A. L., 487
Starr, C., 78
Starr, J., 397
Starr, J. M., 406, 407
Staub, D. R., 603
Stefansson, H., 609
Stein, D., 653

Stein, D. J., 503, 506
Steinberg, L., 203
Steinberg, S., 609
Steiner, B., 215
Steiner, C., 503
Steinhausen, H., 404
Steinmetz, H., 71, 182
Stek, M. L., 659
Steketee, G., 588
Stellar, E., 431
Stelzer, A., 202
Stenberg, C., 197
Stenberg, C. R., 197
Stenger, A., 252
Stepper, S., 462
Steptoe, A., 490
Sterling, P., 483
Stern, E., 610
Stern, K., 437
Stern, W., 394
Sternberg, R. J., 368, 381, 386, 389, 390, 391, 405, 407, 414, 578, 579
Stevens, E., 351
Stevens, S. B., 31
Stewart, J. H., 250, 251
Stewart, R. A., 179
Stewart, V. M., 162
Stice, E., 660
Stickgold, R., 243, 244, 282, 324, 325
Stiles, W. B., 650
Stinglhamber, F., 446
Stinson, F. S., 594
Stock, E., 634
Stoleru, S., 100
Stone, A. A., 449
Stopfer, J. M., 32
Storandt, M., 543
Storch, E. A., 596
Stott, C., 625
Strack, F., 462
Strange, B. A., 288
Strassman, R. J., 261
Strathdee, S. A., 507
Straus, R., 498
Strauss, D., 437
Strauss, M. E., 542, 543
Strawbridge, W. J., 210
Strayer, D. L., 31, 218, 234, 235
Strazzullo, P., 244
Street, G. P., 654, 656
Streiner, D., 600
Streissguth, A., 399, 404
Streissguth, A. P., 605
Striano, T., 197
Stricker, J., 324
Striedter, G., 95
Stroodley, C. J., 97
Stroop, J. R., 251
Strotmann, J., 158
Stroup, T. S., 635, 641
Strouse, G. A., 217
Strueber, D., 570, 618
Strycker, L. A., 204
Stuewig, J., 451, 452
Stuppaeck, C., 634
Styles, E. A., 230, 231
Styner, M., 610
Styron, W., 601, 602
Suarez, A., 655
Suarez, E. C., 499
Subotnik, R. F., 420
Subrahmanyam, K., 31, 219

Subramaniam, K., 100
Succop, P., 399, 404
Suchak, M., 574
Sucharski, I., 446
Sugden, K., 80, 92, 604
Suh, E. M., 468, 469, 470
Suh, S., 656
Sullivan, E. V., 256
Sullivan, K., 190
Sullivan, K. M., 588
Sullivan, P. F., 502
Sumner, F. C., 18, 21
Sundt, T. M., 4
Sung, C. Y., 484
Sunsay, C., 311
Suntsova, N., 243
Suomi, S., 92
Suplita, R. L., 261
Susser, E., 175
Susskind, J. M., 465
Sutherland, A. M., 437
Sutherland, I., 258, 500
Sutton, C., 419
Suvak, M., 662
Svarer, C., 92
Svartengrenf, M., 109
Svendsen, H. A., 543
Swaminathan, S., 176
Swantee, C., 507
Swartz, K., 631
Swartz, M. S., 635, 641
Sweatt, J. D., 81
Swets, J., 127
Swets, J. A., 127
Swing, E. L., 571
Sworowski, L. A., 487
Syed, M., 208
Syed, N. I., 641
Sykes, D. H., 500
Szabo, Y., 8, 9
Szaflarski, J. P., 357, 358
Szaluta, J., 521
Szarko, R., 153
Szentagotai, A., 641
Szymusiak, R., 243

T

Tafti, M., 247
Tager-Flusberg, H., 190
Taggart, R., 78
Takahashi, Y., 540
Takahashia, R., 484
Takeuchi, H., 415, 416
Taki, Y., 415, 416
Talassi, E., 543
Talmi, D., 276
Tambs, K., 152
Tammet, D., 268, 401
Tan, V., 478
Tanabe, H., 299
Tancer, M., 611
Tang, Z., 204
Tangney, J. P., 451, 452
Tanielian, T., 594
Tanne, D., 243, 244, 324
Tao, A., 598
Tardif, T., 351
Tarlatzis, B., 487
Tarmann, A., 440
Tashkin, D., 260
Tashkin, D. R., 260
Taub, E., 182
Taylor, A., 80, 92, 516, 604

Taylor, K. N., 655
Taylor, L. A., 220
Taylor, R. D., 467
Taylor, S., 506
Taylor, S. E., 253, 489, 548
Taylor, S. F., 463, 597
Teasdale, G., 228
Teasdale, J. D., 236, 653, 654, 655, 656, 661
Tell, R. A., 640
Tellegen, A., 450, 515, 537, 538
Teng, G., 484
Teng, M., 258
Ten Have, T. R., 506
Tennstedt, S. L., 212, 221
Terman, L., 394
Terrace, H. S., 360
Terwindt, A. P. R., 606
Tessner, K. D., 201
Teuber, H. L., 291
Thacher, P. V., 324
Thagard, P., 364
Thal, D. J., 350
Thapar, A., 80
Thayer, S. E., 221
Themanson, J. R., 181
Theorell, T., 499
Théoret, H., 196, 337
Thibaut, J. W., 574
Thiessen, D., 575, 577
Thomas, A., 192
Thomas, M. G., 486, 507
Thomasius, R., 259
Thombs, B. D., 204
Thompson, C., 640
Thompson, C. P., 289
Thompson, P., 403
Thompson, P. M., 70, 201
Thompson, R. F., 272, 273, 275, 276, 280, 287
Thompson, S., 648
Thompson, S. C., 31
Thompson, W., 365
Thompson, W. L., 365
Thompson, W. R., 78
Thorndike, E. L., 312, 313
Thornhill, R., 577
Thorsteinsson, E. B., 468, 470
Thrope, G. B., 105
Thune, I., 502
Thurstone, E. L., 388
Thye, S., 446
Tian, S. W., 560
Tiana, T., 656
Tierney, W. M., 478
Tighe, E. M., 445
Tignol, J., 597
Tilan, J. U., 501
Ting, S., 31
Tippett, L. J., 416
Titchener, E., 18
Titone, D., 324
Titov, N., 653
Tobias, S., 380
Toga, A. W., 70, 201, 570
Toguri, C., 159
Tolin, D. F., 650, 662
Tolman, E. C., 329
Tomann, A., 108
Tomasello, M., 358
Tomiyama, A. J., 434
Tomkins, S. S., 449, 458
Toney, L., 230, 236
Tong, E. M. W., 454

Subject Index

Note: Page references in bold refer to definitions. Page references followed by "*f*" refer to figures.

A

AA (Alcoholics Anonymous), 649
ABA (applied behavioral analysis), 319
absent-mindedness, 295–296
absolute thresholds, **125**–127, 126*f*–127*f*
ACC. *See* anterior cingulate cortex
accommodation, **129**
ACE (Adverse Childhood Experiences) Study, 597–599, 600*f*–601*f*, 609, 609*f*
acetylcholine (ACh), **91**, 91*f*, 214
achievement motivation, **442**–443
acquired immunity, **495**–496
acquisition, 312*f*
acronyms, in encoding, 280–281
acrophobia, 13
ACTH (adrenocorticotropic hormone), 480*f*, 481
action potential, **86**–89, 88*f*, 94
adaptations, **25**
   emotions as, 452–453
   evolution and, 25–28
   to stress, 483–484
adaptive behavior, **399**
addiction, **253**, 598–599
ADHD. *See* attention deficit hyperactivity disorder
adolescence, **200**
   cognitive development in, 201–203, 202*f*, 218
   depression risk factors in, 659–660
   personality development in, 204–205, 205*f*
   physical development in, 200–201, 200*f*
   sleep in, 242*f*
   social development in, 203–205, 205*f*, 218–219
   social networking in, 170
   suicide in, 247
   technology use in, 218–220, 219*f*
adoption studies. *See* twin-adoption studies
adrenal glands, **115**
   location of, 116*f*
   stress and, 480–481, 480*f*
adrenaline (epinephrine), 91*f*, **92**, 116
adrenal-medullary system, **480**–481, 480*f*
adrenocorticotropic hormone (ACTH), 480*f*, 481
adulthood
   death and dying, 215–216
   early, 206–210, 207*f*, 209*f*, 210*f*, 220
   emerging, 206–208, 220
   late. *See* late adulthood
   middle, 210–212, 211*f*, 220–221

parenthood, 209–210, 210*f*. *See also* parenting
personality development, 210, 211–212
sleep in, 242*f*
technology and, 219–221
young, 208–210, 209*f*, 210*f*
Adverse Childhood Experiences (ACE) Study, 597–599, 600*f*–601*f*, 609, 609*f*
advertising. *See also* media
   modeling in, 332
   operant conditioning in, 316
   statistics in, 64–65
affective neuroscience, 462
affective traits, **450**
affiliation, need for, 441–442
African Americans. *See also* race–ethnicity
   implicit bias and, 562–564
   prejudicial attitudes toward, 562
   as psychologists, 18
   smoking by, 342
   suicide rates and, 602, 602*f*
afterimages, 146–147, 147*f*
aggression, **569**. *See also* anger; hostility; violence
   amygdala and, 100
   hostility *vs.*, 569
   nature and nurture of, 569–571
   serotonin and, 92
   social influences on, 570–571
   social learning theory and, 332–333, 332*f*, 333*f*
   video games and, 218, 571
aging. *See also* late adulthood
   chronic stress and, 491
   dementia and, 213–215, 214*f*
   education and, 296
   memory and, 296
   neurogenesis and, 107, 109–111, 211
   personality and, 542, 542*f*, 543
agoraphobia, **594**
agreeableness, 515–517, 517*f*
AIDS, 261, 505–507, 505*f*
AIM (activation, input, and mode), 248–249, 249*f*
alarm stage, **482**, 482*f*
alcohol
   binge drinking, 256
   bipolar disorder in offspring, 605
   blood alcohol concentration, 253–254, 255*f*
   brain changes and, 255–256, 255*f*
   driving and, 254, 255*f*, 426
   effects and risks of, 254–255, 254*f*, 255*f*, 500–501
   GABA and, 92
   operant conditioning and, 318
   in pregnancy, 176, 176*f*, 605

Alcoholics Anonymous (AA), 649
algorithms, **409**
alleles, **78**
all-or-none principle, **89**
allostasis, **483**–484
alpha waves, **240**, 240*f*, 241*f*
Alternate Uses test, 418
altruism, **573**–574
Alzheimer's disease, **214**
   acetylcholine in, 91, 214
   caregivers for, 497
   loss of identity in, 294
   memory loss in, 299
   personality change in, 542, 542*f*, 543
   signs and symptoms of, 214, 214*f*
American Journal of Psychology, 18
American Psychiatric Association (APA), 590–591
American Psychological Society (APA), 68
American Sign Language (ASL), 358–360
Ames room, 140, 141*f*
amnesia, **298**–299
amphetamines, 259
amygdala, **99**
   aggression and, 570
   autism and, 621
   emotion and, 288, 290, 462–463, 462*f*
   functions of, 99–100
   location of, 98*f*
   long-term memory and, 285, 285*f*, 287, 287*f*
Anafranil, 631
analgesics, 157
analytic intelligence, 390–391
anger. *See also* hostility
   amygdala and, 463
   bodily sensations of, 461*f*
   facial expression of, 459*f*
   heart disease and, 497–499, 499*f*
   physiological changes with, 456
anima, **523**
animal research
   on brain–machine interface, 105
   on conditioned taste aversion, 323, 323*f*, 326–328, 326*f*, 327*f*
   on emotions and the brain, 462
   ethics in, 68–70
   on immunosuppression, 494
   on imprinting, 335–336
   instinctive drift in, 328–329
   on neurogenesis, 110
   on personality, 532–534, 534*f*
   on physical contact in infancy, 194–195, 195*f*
   on sexual orientation, 440

on sign language, 358–361, 359*f*
on stress, 482–483, 484
animistic thinking, **185**
animus, **523**
anorexia nervosa, **501**
ANS. *See* autonomic nervous system
antecedent event, **453**–454, 453*f*
anterior cingulate cortex (ACC)
   emotion and, 463
   obsessive–compulsive disorder and, 597
   pain and, 156, 156*f*, 463
   violence and, 218
anterograde amnesia, **298**–299
antianxiety medications, 662
antidepressants, 631–633, 633*f*, 640–641, 661
antigens, **494**
antipsychotics, 634–635, 641
antisocial personality disorder, 175, 616*f*, **617**
anxiety, 514, 524, 524*f*
anxiety disorders
   agoraphobia, 594
   drug treatments for, 631–634, 633*f*, 635*f*, 661–662
   generalized anxiety disorder, 591, 593, 661
   nature and nurture explanations of, 596–599, 600*f*–601*f*
   obsessive–compulsive disorder. *See* obsessive–compulsive disorder
   panic disorder, 593–594
   post-traumatic stress disorder. *See* post-traumatic stress disorder
   psychotherapeutic treatments for, 662
   social phobia, 594–595
APA (American Psychiatric Association), 590–591
APA (American Psychological Society), 68
apes, sign language and, 358–360, 359*f*
aphasia, 103–104
Aplysia (sea slug), 291–293, 291*f*
apparent motion, 138
applied behavioral analysis (ABA), 319
appraisal, **454**, 463, 479
arachnophobia, 595, 645, 646*f*–647*f*
arborization, **108**
archetypes, **523**
Area 25, 638–640, 639*f*
Aricept, 294
Asch conformity studies, 551, 551*f*
Asian cultures
   anorexia nervosa in, 590

memory and, 269–270, 270f, 288
personality change after, 101–102, 110, 463, 541, 543
personality disorders and, 618
sleeping and dreaming and, 263
brain–machine interfaces, 104
brain maps, 155
BrdU, 110–111
broaden-and-build model, 453
broad intelligence, 389–390
Broca's area, 103
language learning and, 351, 351f, 358f
language production and, 103–104
second-language learning and, 380f
Brodmann's Area 25, 638–640, 639f
buffering hypothesis, 488
bulimia nervosa, 502
Bundy, Ted, 588
buprenorphine, 257
bupropione, 633
buspirone, 662
by-products, of natural selection, 28
bystander effect, 47, 572–573

C

caffeine, 257–258, 257f
California Personality Inventory (CPI), 537, 539
cancer
alcohol use and, 501
marijuana smoke and, 260
tobacco smoke and, 258, 500
Cannabis sativa, 260–261
CANOE acronym, 529, 529f
carbon monoxide, 258
cardiovascular disease
depression and, 499–500
positive emotions and, 489–490
psychological risk factors for, 497–500, 499f
stress and, 493
cardiovascular reactivity (CVR) model, 499
cardiovascular system, 493
career identity, 207
carpentered world, 161
case studies, 48
casual sex, 438, 439
cataplexy, 247
catecholamines, 115–116, 480
categories, 368
catharsis, 644
Cattell–Horn–Carroll (CHC) model of intelligence, 388–389, 389f, 396
causal inferences, 369
causation, 52–53, 53f
CBT (cognitive–behavioral therapy), 648, 654, 656, 662
CCK (cholecystokinin), 431
Celexa, 632
cell damage, sleep and, 244
cell phones
driving and, 218, 234–235, 235f

psychology research on, 31
cells, chromosomes in, 77, 77f
cellular immunity, 496
central executive, 274, 274f, 286f
central nervous system (CNS), 82, 82f
cerebellum, 97
alcohol use and, 255f
location of, 96f
long-term memory and, 284, 285f, 287, 287f
cerebral cortex, 100–103, 101f, 103f
cerebral hemispheres
communication between, 104–106, 106f
creativity and, 415, 417
epilepsy and, 105–106
functions of, 103–104
language and, 353
cerebral palsy, 196
cerebrum, 100–103, 101f, 103f
certainty effect, 378
chance mutations, 25
CHC (Cattell–Horn–Carroll) model of intelligence, 388–389, 389f, 396
chemotherapy, marijuana and, 261
child abuse
Adverse Childhood Experiences (ACE) Study, 597–599, 600f–601f, 609, 609f
language development and, 353, 354–358
neglect, 181–182, 181f, 599, 600f–601f, 609, 609f
schizophrenia and, 609
child-directed speech, 354
childbirth, cultural differences in, 165
children. See also child abuse; infancy
Adverse Childhood Experiences (ACE) Study, 597–599, 600f–601f, 609, 609f
attention deficit hyperactivity disorder. See attention deficit hyperactivity disorder
birth order of, 522–523
brain development in, 180–184, 181f, 183f, 599, 600f–601f, 609, 609f
cognitive development in, 184–190, 185f–189f
in Efe culture, 49
emotional competence of, 197–198
frontal lobes in, 101
language development in, 351–353, 352f
moral reasoning in, 190–192, 191f
motor development in, 178–179, 178f
musical training in, 182–183, 337, 339
nature–nurture debate, 23–24
neglected, 181–182, 181f, 599, 600f–601f, 609, 609f
peer interaction, 198

psychological disorders in, 619–622, 620f, 621f
sleep in, 242
socioemotional development in, 192–199, 195f, 196f
technology and, 217–218, 217f
chimpanzees, sign language and, 358–360, 359f
Chinese culture, ancient, 13
chlorpromazine (Thorazine), 634
cholecystokinin (CCK), 431
chromosomes, 77, 77f
chunking, 142, 273, 280
cigarette smoking. See tobacco use
cilia, 158, 158f
cingulate gyrus, 98f, 100
circadian rhythms, 239–240, 239f
cirrhosis, 255
CIU (Compulsive Internet Use), 598–599, 599f
civil disobedience, 191
classical conditioning, 308
conditioned taste aversion, 323, 323f, 326–328, 326f, 327f
immunosuppression and, 494
of Little Albert, 311–312, 312f–313f
operant conditioning vs., 320f
operation of, 309–311, 310f
Pavlov's dogs, 308–309, 308f
smoking and, 341, 341f
claustrophobia, 595
client-centered therapy, 644
clinical psychologists, 658
clinical psychology, 12–16, 13f, 14f, 15f
closure, 142, 142f
clozapine (Clorazil), 634, 641
CNS (central nervous system), 82, 82f
cocaine, 91, 258–259
cochlea, 151, 151f, 152f
cocktail party effect, 231, 231f
codeine, 256
cognition, 364. See also cognitive development; thinking
creative thinking and, 416, 418
exercise and, 213, 502–503, 504
cognitive–behavioral therapy (CBT), 648, 654, 656, 662
cognitive development
in adolescence, 201–203, 202f, 218
fluid vs. crystallized intelligence, 212, 213f
in infants and children, 184–190, 185f–188f, 217–218
in late adulthood, 212, 221
moral reasoning, 190–192, 191f
physical fitness and, 209
technology and, 217–219, 217f, 219f, 221
theory of mind, 189–190, 189f
cognitive dissonance, 566–567, 567f, 582
cognitive maps, 329
cognitive psychology, 8, 364
on electronic social interactions, 31

mental representation, 364–368, 366f, 367f
verbal representation, 366–368, 367f
cognitive science, 19–21
cognitive symptoms (of schizophrenia), 608
cognitive theory, on dreaming, 249
cognitive therapy (CT), 645–648, 651, 654–655
cognitivism, 19–21
collective unconscious, 523
collectivist cultures, 517, 552
college students
personality and college major, 538
sleep deprivation in, 246, 324–325, 324f
Collyer brothers, 588
color blindness, 147–148, 148f
color vision
eye structure and, 131–132, 131f
language and, 362–363, 363f
perception of color, 145–148, 146f, 147f, 148f
coma, 227, 228, 228f
commitment, 579, 579f
common cold, stress and, 497
common sense, 39
communication, in scientific method, 43f, 44
comorbidity, 591
companionate love, 579, 579f
compensation, 522
complex cells (neurons), 134–135
compulsions, 596. See also obsessive–compulsive disorder
compulsive-impulsive spectrum, 599
Compulsive Internet Use (CIU), 598–599, 599f
computers and Internet. See also social networking
brain interfaces with, 104–105, 105f
cognitive development and, 217–218
cyberbullying, 219–220
Internet addiction, 598–599, 599f
online dating services, 220
sexual material on, 219
video games, 217–218, 221, 571
virtual reality therapies, 652–653
concentration meditation, 236
concept hierarchy, 366–367
concepts, 366, 380
concrete operational stage, 185f, 188
conditioned response (CR), 309–310, 311f
conditioned stimulus (CS), 309–310, 311f
conditioned taste aversion, 323
animal studies on, 326–328, 326f
as classical conditioning, 323, 323f
immune system and, 494

FES (forearm electrical stimulation), 105, 105*f*
fetal alcohol spectrum disorder (FASD), **176**, 176*f*, 399
fetal development. *See* prenatal development
fetal stage, **172**
FFA (fusiform face area), 114, 114*f*
fidelity, **205**
fight-or-flight response, 83
figure–ground effects, 143, 143*f*
fine motor skills, 179
five-factor model, **529**–530, 529*f*
fixation, **410**
fixed interval (FI) schedule, **321**, 321*f*
fixed ratio (FR) schedule, **321**, 321*f*
flashbulb memories, **290**
flatworms, 95
flexibility of thought, **418**
float test, 13
flooding, **645**
flow, 229–230, 430
fluid intelligence, **212**, 213*f*, 388
fluoxetine (Prozac), 177, 632, 641
fMRI (functional MRI), **112**–113, 113*f*, 114, 114*f*
folk psychology, 6
food. *See* eating
foot-in-the-door technique, 581–582
forearm electrical stimulation (FES), 105, 105*f*
forebrain, 96*f*, 97*f*, 98
foreground–background perception, 163, 163*f*
forensic psychology, **11**
forgetting, **294**
    amnesia, 298–299
    Ebbinghaus's forgetting curve, 295, 296*f*
    types of, 294–298, 296*f*
forgetting curve, 295, 296*f*
formal operational stage, 185*f*, **188**–189, 201
forward conditioning, 309
fovea, 130*f*, **131**
Fragile X syndrome, 399
fraternal twins, **79**. *See also* twin-adoption studies
free association, 519, **643**
frequency, **62**, 150, 152*f*
friending, 32
frontal lobes
    in adolescence, 201
    alcohol use and, 255*f*
    creativity and, 415
    location and function of, 101, 101*f*
FR (fixed ratio) schedule, **321**, 321*f*
functional fixedness, **411**
functionalism, **18**
functional MRI (fMRI), **112**–113, 113*f*, 114, 114*f*
fundamental attribution error, **557**
fusiform face area (FFA), 114, 114*f*
The Future of Socializing (Norine), 4

G

GABA (gamma-aminobutyric acid), 89, 91*f*, **92**, 596–597
GAD (generalized anxiety disorder), **591**, 593, 661
Gage, Phineas, brain injury of, 101–102, 102*f*, 110, 463
ganglion cells, 132
Gardner's multiple intelligences, **391**, 392*f*, 393
GAS (general adaptation syndrome), **482**–483, 482*f*
gate control theory of pain, **157**
gender differences
    in adolescent brain development, 202
    in age of first marriage, 209, 209*f*
    in age-related hearing loss, 211, 211*f*
    in drive for casual sex, 438, 439
    in eating disorders, 502
    in emotion, 466
    in insomnia, 247
    in intelligence, 406–407, 406*f*
    in mental rotation tasks, 366
    in moral reasoning, 191–192
    in pain thresholds, 165
    in parenthood, 209–210, 210*f*
    in peer interactions, 198
    in personality development, 199
    in puberty, 200–201, 200*f*
    in sexual attraction and mate selection, 577–578
    in sexual response cycle, 436, 436*f*
    in smoking, 342
    in social network influences, 489
    in tactile sensitivity, 154
gene-by-environment interaction research, **80**
general adaptation syndrome (GAS), **482**–483, 482*f*
general intelligence, **388**–389. *See also* intelligence
generalized anxiety disorder (GAD), **591**, 593, 661
generativity, **211**
genes, **77**. *See also* heritability
    behavior and, 78–81, 81*f*
    chance mutations, 25
    dominant and recessive, 78
    environment and, 79–80
    epigenetics, 80–81, 81*f*
    expression of, 80–81, 81*f*
    genetic markers, 80, 515
    in the human genome, 82
    long-term memory and, 292, 292*f*
    polygenic transmission by, 78–79
    structures and mechanisms of, 77–78, 77*f*
genetic influences
    on aggression, 569–570
    on anxiety disorders, 597
    on attention deficit hyperactivity disorder, 621
    on attitudes, 565–566
    on bipolar disorder, 605–606
    on depression, 604, 604*f*
    on eating disorders, 502
    environmental forces and, 23, 80–81, 81*f*
    on intelligence, 403–404, 403*f*, 404*f*
    on language acquisition, 357–358
    on obesity, 433
    on personality, 514–516, 516*f*–517*f*, 530–531, 530*f*
    on schizophrenia, 609, 610
    on sexual orientation, 440–441
    softwiring and, 23
    on stress, 484
    twin-adoption studies and, 79–80
genetic markers, 80, 515
genius, **413**–414
genome, **77**, 77*f*, 82
genotype, **80**
Genovese, Kitty, 572–573
germinal stage, **171**
Gestalt laws of grouping, 141–145, 142*f*, 143*f*, 144*f*
Gestalt psychology, **19**–21, 20, 20*f*
g-factor theory of intelligence, **387**
ghrelin, 431
giftedness, **400**–402, 400*f*, 420
ginkgo biloba, 295
Glasgow Coma Scale, 228
glial cells, **84**–85
glucocorticoids, **480**
glucose, **431**
glutamate, **89**
    functions of, 89, 91*f*, 93
    LSD and, 261
    schizophrenia and, 612, 641
GNH (Gross National Happiness), 471
graded potentials, 89
grammar, **349**, 356
graphs, misleading, 65, 65*f*
grasping reflex, 179
gratitude training, 644
gray matter, 115, 181
Gross National Happiness (GNH), 471
group behavior. *See* social behavior
group therapy, **648**–649, 662
groupthink, 551–552

H

habituation, 307
hair cells, **151**, 151*f*, 152*f*
Halle Berry neurons, 136, 136*f*, 137*f*
hallucinations, **608**, 610
hallucinogens, 259, **260**–261
haloperidol (Haldol), 634
happiness
    basic needs and, 469
    bodily sensations of, 461*f*
    facial expression of, 459*f*
    higher needs and, 469–470
    meaning in life and, 470–471, 490
    oxytocin and, 464
    positive emotions, 489–490, 660–661
    world happiness map, 469, 469*f*
Hassles and Uplifts Scale, 478
Head Start, 406, 467
health behavior approach, **492**, 500
health psychology, **11**, **492**
    on electronic social interaction, 32
    on HIV and AIDS, 505–507, 505*f*
hearing
    auditory cortex and, 103
    brain and, 151, 153
    ear and, 150–151, 151*f*, 152*f*
    in middle adulthood, 210–212, 211*f*
    physics of sound, 149–150, 150*f*
    prenatal, 172–174, 173*f*
    psychology of, 150
    signal detection theory, 127
hearing loss, 152–153, 153*f*
heart disease. *See* cardiovascular disease
Heinz dilemma, 190–191
hemispheres, cerebral. *See* cerebral hemispheres
herbal medications for memory, 295
heritability, **79**. *See also* genes; genetic influences
    gene-by-environment interaction research, 80
    soft inheritance, 81
    twin-adoption studies, 79–80
heroes, 572
heroin, 256, 258
hertz (Hz), 150
heterosexuality, 204. *See also* sexual orientation
heuristics, **372**, 374–375
hierarchies, **282**
hierarchy of needs, 430, 430*f*
hindbrain, 96*f*, 97, 97*f*
hippocampus, **99**
    alcohol use and, 255*f*
    emotion and, 288, 462, 462*f*
    exercise and, 503
    functions of, 99, 101
    location of, 98*f*
    in long-term memory, 285, 285*f*
    memory and, 270, 271, 286–287, 286*f*
    post-traumatic stress disorder and, 594
    schizophrenia and, 610, 611*f*
    sleep and, 244
    stress and, 484
Hispanics. *See* race–ethnicity
histrionic personality disorder, 616*f*, **617**
HIV/AIDS, 261, 505–507, 505*f*
Hobson's A-I-M model, 248–249, 249*f*
homeostasis, **427**–429, 428*f*, 483
Homo erectus, 96*f*
Homo neanderthalensis, 95, 95*f*, 96*f*
homophobia, 521
Homo sapiens, 95–96, 96*f*
homosexuality, 204. *See also* sexual orientation

hormones, **115**. *See also specific*
hormones
  aggression and, 570
  functions of, 115
  hunger and, 431
  sex, 115, 200, 366, 437, 570
  stress, 479–482, 480f, 484
hospice, 216
hostile aggression, 569
hostility
  aggression *vs.*, 569
  basic, 524, 524f
  heart disease and, 498–499,
    499f
HPA axis. *See* hypothalamic-
  pituitary-adrenal (HPA) axis
hubristic pride, 451
human development, **170**
  cognitive, in adolescence,
    201–203, 202f
  cognitive, in infancy and
    childhood, 184–192,
    185f–188f, 191f, 217
  death and dying, 215–216
  in early adulthood, 206–210,
    207f, 209f, 210f
  of emotions, 197–198
  of language, 350–353, 351f,
    352f
  in late adulthood, 212–215,
    213f, 214f, 221
  in middle adulthood, 210–212,
    211f, 220–221
  of moral reasoning, 190–192,
    191f
  personality, in adolescence,
    204–205, 205f
  personality, in early adulthood,
    210
  personality, in infancy, 192
  personality, in late adulthood,
    215
  personality, in middle
    adulthood, 211–212
  physical, in adolescence,
    200–201, 200f
  physical, in infancy and
    childhood, 178–184,
    178f–181f, 183f
  prenatal, 171–175, 171f–175f
  of sleep over the life span,
    241–242, 242f
  social, in adolescence,
    203–205, 205f
  socioemotional, in infants and
    children, 192–199, 195f,
    196f, 218
  technology and, 216–221,
    217f, 219f
  of vision, 135–136
humane treatment, 69
humanistic–positive psychological
  theories
  Maslow on, 526–527
  Rogers on, 527–528
  summary of, 531f
  in treatment, 644
humanistic psychology, **19**,
  526–527
human language, **349**. *See also*
  language
human research, ethics in, 67–68
hunger
  biology of digestion, 431

food preferences and, 432
metabolism and, 430–431
thinness and obesity and,
  432–435, 433f
weight loss success, 434–435
Huntington's disease, 78, 100
hyperactivity, OCD and, 597.
  See also attention deficit
  hyperactivity disorder
hypercomplex cells, 135
hypersomnia, **247**, 263
hyperthymestic syndrome, 268
hypnosis, **250**–252, 251f
hypochondriasis, **615**
hypothalamic-pituitary-adrenal
  (HPA) axis, **481**
  depression and, 603
  eating and, 501
  stress and, 480f, 481
hypothalamus, **99**
  aggression and, 570
  alcohol use and, 255f
  emotion and, 462–463, 462f
  functions of, 99, 115
  hunger and, 431
  location of, 98f, 116f
  menstrual cycle and, 116
  sexual behavior and, 437
  sexual orientation and,
    440–441
  stress and, 480, 480f
hypothesis, **42**

I

IAT (Implicit Associations Test),
  563
iconic memory, 272
id, **519**–520, 520f
ideational fluency, **416**, 418
identical twins, **79**. *See also* twin-
  adoption studies
identity
  in Alzheimer's disease, 294
  career, 207
  dissociative identity disorder,
    613–614
  in emerging adulthood,
    206–208
  Erikson on, 205, 205f
  ethnic, 208
  peer groups and, 204
  sexual, 207
identity crisis, 205
idioms, **380**
imagery, in encoding, 280
imitation, 336–337, 354
immune system
  conditioned
    immunosuppression, 494
  HIV and, 505–507, 505f
  overview of, 495–496
  stress and, 482, 493–494,
    496–497
immunity, 495–496
implantation, 171–172, 171f, 172f
Implicit Associations Test (IAT),
  563
implicit bias, 562–564
implicit memory, **277**
  priming and, 277, 277f
  retrieval from, 283
  storage of, 285, 285f, 287, 287f
implicit prejudice, 562–564

implosion therapy, 645
imprinting, **192**, **335**–336
impulse control disorder, **596**
inattentional blindness, 231
incentives, **427**
incentive value, 443
independent variable, **53**, 55f
individualist cultures, 517, 552
individuation, 211
inductive reasoning, **369**
industrial/organizational (I/O)
  psychology, **11**. *See also*
  workplace
  congruence, 539
  employee motivation,
    443–448, 446f, 447f
  perceived organizational
    support, 446, 447f
infancy
  attachment in, 192–194
  brain development in,
    180–184, 180f, 181f, 183f
  cognitive development in,
    184–190, 185f–189f
  emotional development,
    197–198
  facial expressions and,
    196–197, 456
  imitation in, 336–337, 354
  language development in, 351
  motor development in,
    178–179, 178f
  personality development in,
    192
  physical contact in, 194–195,
    195f
  sensory development in,
    179–180, 179f, 180f
  sleep in, 241–242, 242f
  social referencing in, 197
  technology and, 217, 217f
  touch needs in, 195–196, 196f
inferential statistics, 63–65
inferior colliculus, 153
inferiority complex, **522**
inflammation, 495, 500
informational social influence,
  549–550
informed consent, 67
in-group/out-group bias, **559**
inheritance. *See* genetic
  influences; heritability
inhibitory neurotransmitters, 89
innately guided learning, 357
inner ear, 150, 151f
Inquisition, 13
insecure-avoidant attachment,
  192–193
insecure-disorganized/disoriented
  attachment, 194
insecure-resistant attachment,
  194
insight solutions, **409**
insomnia, **247**
instinctive drift, **328**–329
institutional review boards
  (IRBs), **68**, 69
instrumental aggression, 569
insula, **103**, 156, 156f, 464
insulin, 115, 431
integrative therapies, **654**
integrity, 215
intellectual honesty, 42
intelligence, **387**. *See also* IQ tests

birth weight and, 404–405
brain activation and, 402–403,
  402f
brain development and, 202,
  202f
cardiovascular fitness and, 209
Cattell–Horn–Carroll model
  of, 388–389, 389f, 396
definitions of, 386–387
emotional, 391, 466–468, 471
fluid *vs.* crystallized, 212, 213f,
  388–389
gender and, 406–407, 406f
genetic and environmental
  factors in, 403–405, 403f,
  404f, 406
genius and, 413–414
g-factor theory of, 387
giftedness, 400–402, 400f,
  420
Intel Science Talent Search, 420
mental retardation, 399–400,
  399f
modern measures of, 394–396
multiple-factor theory of, 388
multiple intelligences, 391,
  392f, 393
non-Western views of, 407
polygenic transmission of, 79
race–ethnicity and, 405–406
test bias, 397–398
test reliability and validity,
  396–397
theory summary, 387f
traditional measures of, 392,
  394
triarchic theory of, 389–391
intelligence quotient (IQ), 394.
  See also IQ tests
intelligence ratio, 394
Intel Science Talent Search, 420
interference, 294–295
intermittent reinforcement,
  319–321, 321f
internal reliability, **397**
International Flat Earth Research
  Society, 371, 371f
Internet. *See* computers and
  Internet
Internet addiction, 598–599,
  599f
interneurons, **86**
interpersonal intelligence, 391,
  392f
interpersonal relatedness, 517
interposition, 140, 140f
interpretation, 42–44, 43f
The Interpretation of Dreams
  (Freud), 248
inter-rater reliability, **535**
interviews, 49–50, 59, 536
intimacy, **210**, 579, 579f
intrapersonal intelligence, 391,
  392f
intrinsic motivation, **445**, 446f,
  447
introspection, **18**
ions, 86–87, 94
I/O psychology. *See* industrial/
  organizational (I/O)
  psychology
iPods, hearing loss and, 152–153,
  153f
IQ (intelligence quotient), 394

IQ tests
bias in, 397–398
of Binet and Simon, 392, 394
Kaufman-Assessment Battery
for Children, 394–395
normal distribution of scores,
398–399, 398f
reliability and validity of,
396–397
Stanford–Binet test, 394
of Stern, 394
Wechsler Adult Intelligence
Scale, 394, 395–396, 395f,
396f, 397
Wechsler Intelligence Scale for
Children, 394, 395–396,
396f
IRBs (institutional review
boards), 68, 69
iris, 129, 130f
iron deficiency, 247

J

James–Lange theory of emotion,
461
Japanese culture
language acquisition in,
351–352, 356
perception in, 162–164, 163f
jet lag, 240
JND (just noticeable differences),
128
jobs. See workplace
joint attention, 620
Jonestown cult, 580–582, 581f
juries, minority opinion in, 552
just noticeable differences (JND),
128

K

Kaufman-Assessment Battery for
Children (K-ABC), 394–395
K-complexes, 241
ketamine, 612
Key Learning Community, 383
kin selection, 574
Kinsey surveys, 49–50, 50f
koro, 590
Kramarik, Akiane, 400, 400f

L

LAD (language acquisition
device), 355–357
language
animals and human language,
358–361, 359f
cerebral hemispheres and,
103–106, 106f, 353
color perception and, 362–363,
363f
conditioning and learning
theory, 355
development in individuals,
350–353, 351f, 352f
evolution of, 350
metacognition and, 380–381
motherese, 465
nativist theory, 355–357
nature of, 349–350
nature vs. nurture in, 357–358,
358f

perception and, 348, 363, 363f
second, 378–381, 380f
sensitivity period in learning,
352–353, 379
sociocultural theories, 354
thought and, 361–362
vocal anatomy and, 359f
language acquisition device
(LAD), 355–357
late adulthood. See also aging;
Alzheimer's disease
dementia in, 213–215, 214f
memory and intelligence in,
212–213, 213f
personality changes in, 542,
542f, 543
sleep in, 242f
suicide rates in, 602, 602f
technology and, 221
latent learning, 329
latent level, 248
lateral geniculate nucleus (LGN),
133f, 134
laughing, 460
law of closure, 142, 142f
law of effect, 313–314
learning, 306. See also classical
conditioning; operant
conditioning
in adolescence, 202–203
association, 307
brain plasticity and, 107–109,
107f
conditioned taste aversion,
323, 323f, 326–328, 326f,
327f
by elephants, 306
enriched environments and,
339
flow and, 430
habituation and the orienting
response, 306–307
hippocampus and, 99
imitation, 336–337
imprinting, 335–336
innately guided, 357
instinctive drift and, 328–329
language, 351, 351f, 358f
latent, 329
mirror neurons and, 85–86,
336–338, 338f, 354,
621–622
neurogenesis and, 109
observational, 330–334, 332f,
333f, 334f, 338, 338f
reasons for smoking, 340–342,
341f
second languages, 378–381,
380f
sleep and, 244, 324–325, 324f
social-cognitive, 331, 528,
528f, 531f
social learning theory, 330–
334, 333f, 334f, 340, 355
socioemotional, 467
synaptic change during,
337–339, 338f
lens, 129, 130f
leptin, 431, 433
lesbian, gay, bisexual, or
transgendered (LGBT), 207.
See also sexual orientation
levels of processing, 279–280,
281f

LGN (lateral geniculate nucleus),
133f, 134
lie detectors, 557
Lie to Me, 557
Life Change Units, 477, 478f
life expectancy, tobacco use and,
258, 500
life satisfaction, 468–471
Lightner, Cari, 426
light waves, 145, 146f
Likert scale, 537
limbic system, 98–100, 98f
linear perspective, 139, 140f
linguistic determinism hypothesis,
361–362
linguistic intelligence, 391, 392f
linguistic relativism, 362
lithium, 633–634, 641
Little Albert conditioning study,
311–312, 312f
liver, alcohol use and, 254–255
lobes of the brain, 101, 101f
lobotomy, prefrontal, 635–636
logic, in science, 39
logical-mathematical intelligence,
391, 392f
long-term memory, 272
consolidation in, 281–282
cortex and, 287–288, 287f
encoding in, 278–281, 280f,
281f
genes and, 292–293, 292f
retrieval from, 283–284, 287
sensory cortexes and, 285
storage in, 282–283, 283f,
287–288, 287f
types of, 276–278, 277f
long-term potentiation (LTP),
291
love, 430, 578–580, 579f
love and belongingness needs,
430
loving-kindness meditation, 655
LSD, 261
lust, 579
lymphocytes, 495–496

M

MADD (Mothers Against Drunk
Driving), 426
magnetic resonance imaging
(MRI), 112–113, 113f
major depressive disorder, 600–
601, 605f
manic episodes, 603, 605
manifest level, 248
MAO (monoamine oxidase)
inhibitors, 631, 640
marijuana, 260–261
marriage, 209, 209f
marriage and family therapists
(MFT), 658–659
Maslow's hierarchy of needs, 430,
430f
massage therapy, 196
matchstick problem, 410, 410f
matrix reasoning, 388
Mayer–Salovey–Caruso
Emotional Intelligence Test
(MSCEIT), 467
MBCT (mindfulness-based
cognitive therapy), 654–655,
656, 656f, 662–663

MBSR (Mindfulness-Based Stress
Reduction), 503
MBTI (Myers-Briggs Type
Indicator), 538
MDMA (ecstasy), 259
mean, 62
meaning in life, 470–471, 490
measures, 58–61, 59f
mechanoreceptors, 154
media. See also advertising; social
networking
aggression and violence in,
334, 571
cognitive and brain
development and, 217, 217f
persuasion in, 568
statistics used in, 64–65, 65f
medial geniculate nucleus
(MGN), 153
medial prefrontal cortex (mPFC),
203
median, 62
meditation, 235
brain changes with, 236–238,
237f, 238f
conscious experience and,
236
for stress reduction, 503
medulla, 96f, 97
melanin, 431
melatonin, 239–240, 239f
memory, 270. See also long-
term memory; short-term
memory
acetylcholine and, 91
aging and, 212
biological memory systems,
284–285, 285f
brain and, 287–293, 287f,
289f, 292f
brain injury and, 269–270,
270f
cortisol and, 249
distorted, 296–298
emotion and, 288–291, 289f
exercise and, 503, 504
extraordinary, 268–269
forgetting, 294–299, 296f
hippocampus and prefrontal
cortex and, 99, 101, 286,
286f
medications for, 294–295
as personal reconstruction,
20–21
sensory, 270, 272, 285
short-term, 270–271,
272–276, 274f, 276f
sleep and, 243, 282, 289, 289f,
324–325, 324f
stress and, 484
studying tips, 279, 300–301
three-stage model of, 270, 272,
280f–281f
without recollection, 270, 271
men and boys. See also gender
differences
sexual response cycle in, 436,
436f
spermarche in, 201
menarche, 200–201
menstrual cycle, 116
mental age, 392, 394
mental representation, 364–368,
366f, 367f

object permanence, 185, 186, 186*f*
observation
    behavioral, 60, 535
    limits of, 39–40
    naturalistic, 48–49
    in the scientific method, 42, 43*f*
observational learning, **330–334,** 332*f,* 333*f,* 334*f,* 338
obsessions, **595–596**
obsessive–compulsive disorder (OCD), **595**
    cognitive–behavioral therapy for, 648, 650, 652
    combined therapies in, 662–663
    drug therapy for, 661
    explanations of, 597
    symptoms of, 595–596
obsessive–compulsive personality disorder, 616*f,* **618**
occipital lobes, 101*f,* 103, 286*f*
OCD. *See* obsessive–compulsive disorder
OCEAN acronym, 529, 529*f*
odd–eccentric personality disorders, 616–617, 616*f*
OFC (orbitofrontal cortex), 160
olanzapine, 634
olfaction. *See* smell
olfactory bulb, **158**
olfactory sensory neurons, **158**
one-word utterances, **351,** 352*f*
online dating services, 220
online games, 598, 599*f*
open communication systems, 349
openness, 515–516, 517, 517*f*
operant conditioning, **314**
    applications of, 319
    behavior modification, 342
    in behavior therapy, 644–645
    classical conditioning *vs.,* 320*f*
    conditioned taste aversion, 323, 323*f,* 326–328, 326*f,* 327*f*
    consequences in, 314, 314*f*
    instinctive drift and, 328–329
    law of effect in, 312–314, 313*f*
    operation of, 317–319, 318*f,* 319*f,* 320*f*
    reinforcement and punishment in, 315–317, 317*f*
    schedules of reinforcement, 319–322, 320*f,* 321*f*
    smoking and, 340–342, 341*f*
    used by oneself, 315
opioids, 157, 256–257
opponent-process theory, **147**
OPTIC, 43*f*
optic chiasm, 133*f,* **134**
optic nerve, **132,** 133*f,* 134
optimal arousal model, 429–430, 429*f*
optimism, 489, 660–661
orbitofrontal cortex (OFC), 160
orexin, 431
organizational psychology. *See* industrial/organizational (I/O) psychology
orgasm, 436–437
orienting response, 307
originality, **418**

outer ear, 150, 151*f*
out-group homogeneity, **559**
oval window, 150, 151*f*
ovaries, 116*f*
ovulation, sex drive and, 437
oxytocin, 463–464

P

pain, **155**
    anterior cingulate cortex and, 463
    cultural variation in, 164–165, 164*f*
    empathy with, 575, 576, 576*f*
    hypnosis and, 251, 252
    marijuana and, 261
    opioids and, 257
    perception of, 155–157, 156*f*
    phantom limb, 155
    social, 548, 559, 560*f*
painting
    blindness and, 76, 76*f,* 117–119, 117*f,* 118*f*
    brain and, 117–119, 118*f*
    by elephants, 306
palliative care, 216
pancreas, 115, 116*f*
panic attacks, **593–594**
panic disorder, **593–594**
papillae, 159
parahippocampal place area (PPA), 114, 114*f*
parallel distributed processing (PDP), 283, 367, 367*f*
paralysis, computers and, 104–105, 105*f*
paranoid personality disorder, **616–617,** 616*f*
parasympathetic nervous system, 82*f,* 83, 83*f,* 456
parathyroid gland, 116*f*
parental investment theory, 438, 578
parenting
    decision to become a parent, 209–210, 210*f*
    infant attachment and, 195
    Internet addiction and, 598
    language acquisition and, 354
    nature–nurture debate and, 23–24
    personality changes with, 541
parietal lobes, 101*f,* 102, 102*f*
Parkinson's disease, 97, 100, 612
passion, 579, 579*f*
passionate love, 579, 579*f*
PATHS program, 467
Pavlov's dogs, 308–309, 308*f*
Paxil, 632
PCP, 612
PDP (parallel distributed processing), 283, 367, 367*f*
Peek, Kim, 401–402
peers
    interaction with, 198, 203–204
    pressure from, 550–551, 551*f*
    smoking and, 342
Penn Resiliency Program (PRP), 660
People's Temple tragedy, 580–582, 581*f*
peptide YY (PYY), 431

perceived organizational support, **446,** 447*f*
perception, **124.** *See also* hearing; vision
    absolute thresholds of, 125–127, 126*f*–127*f*
    bottom-up and top-down processing in, 145
    of color, 145–148, 146*f,* 147*f,* 148*f*
    culture and, 161–164, 162*f,* 163*f*
    of depth, 138–140, 139*f,* 140*f,* 162, 162*f*
    difference thresholds in, 128
    foreground–background and, 163, 163*f*
    Gestalt laws of grouping, 141–145, 142*f,* 143*f,* 144*f*
    meditation training and, 237, 237*f*
    of motion, 138
    of pain, 155–157, 156*f*
    perceptual constancy, 140–141, 141*f*
    perceptual set, 128–129, 128*f*
    signal detection theory, 126–127, 127*f*
    of smell, 158–159, 158*f*
    synesthesia, 160–161, 161*f*
    of taste, 159–160, 159*f*
    of touch, 154–155
    of visual stimuli, 137–141, 139*f,* 140*f,* 141*f*
    Weber on, 17
perceptual constancy, **140–141,** 141*f*
perceptual load model, 231–232
perceptual set, **128–129,** 128*f*
Percocet, 256
performance, visual imagery and, 365, 365*f*
peripheral hearing, 108
peripheral nervous system, **82,** 82*f*
peripheral vision, 108
personality, 177, **512**
    Adler on, 522–523
    in adolescence, 204–205, 205*f*
    Alzheimer's and, 542, 542*f,* 543
    in animals, 532–534, 534*f*
    anxiety disorders and, 597
    biological theories, 530–531, 530*f,* 531*f*
    brain injury and, 541, 543
    changes across the life span, 540–541, 541*f*
    in children, 198–199
    college major and, 538
    consistency of, 540
    creative, 418–419
    culture and, 517–518, 518*f*
    definition of, 512–513
    in early adulthood, 210
    eating disorders and, 502
    evolution of traits, 514
    Eysenck on, 530, 530*f*
    Freud on, 519–522, 520*f*
    frontal lobe injury and, 102, 102*f*
    genetics and, 514–516, 516*f*–517*f*
    Horney on, 524–525, 524*f*

    in infancy, 192
    job performance and, 539
    Jung on, 523
    in late adulthood, 215
    life circumstance changes and, 541, 543
    Maslow on, 526–527
    measurement of, 535–537
    in middle adulthood, 211–212
    multiple personality disorder, 613–614
    neuropsychoanalysis, 525
    parenthood and, 209–210
    personality disorders, 616–619, 616*f*
    prenatal environment and, 177, 516
    Rogers on, 527–528
    smoking and, 342
    social–cognitive learning theories and, 528, 528*f*
    summary of approaches to, 531*f*
    trait theories, 528–530, 529*f*
    Type A Behavior Pattern, 498–499, 499*f*
personality disorders, **616**
    anxious–fearful, 616*f,* 617–618
    creativity and, 623
    dramatic–emotional, 616*f,* 617
    nature and nurture explanations of, 618–619
    odd–eccentric, 616–617, 616*f*
personality psychology, 32
personality questionnaires, **536–537**
personal unconscious, **523**
persuasion, **567–568**
pessimists, 489
PET (positron emission tomography), **113,** 115
phagocytosis, 495
phantom limb pain, 155
phenothiazines, **634**
phenotype, **81**
pheromones, 577
The Philosophical Baby (Gopnik), 184
phobias, **594**
    agoraphobia, 594
    cognitive–behavioral therapy for, 648
    social phobia, 594–595
    specific, 595
    systematic desensitization and, 645, 646*f*–647*f,* 652, 662
phonemic processing, 280
phonological loop, 274, 274*f,* 286
photoreceptors, **130,** 130*f*
physical dependence, 253
physical development
    in adolescence, 200–201, 200*f*
    in infancy and childhood, 178–184, 178*f*–181*f,* 183*f*
physical fitness, cognitive functioning and, 209
physiological measures, 59*f,* 61
physiological reactivity model, **492–493,** 493*f*
Piaget's stages of cognitive development, 184–189, 184*f,* 185*f,* 187*f,* 188*f*
pineal gland, 239
Pirahã people, 361–362, 361*f*

pituitary gland, 115
  hypothalamus and, 99
  location of, 116*f*
  stress and, 480, 480*f*
placebo, **54**
plasticity
  in the adult brain, 109–111
  learning and, 107–109, 107*f*
  neurogenesis and, 106–109, 107*f*, 214–215
play, skills from, 453
pleasure, hypothalamus and, 463
PNI (psychoneuroimmunology), **495–497**
polygenic transmission, 78–**79**
pons, 96*f*, 97
population, in research design, 47
positive psychology, **19**, 527–528, 660–661. *See also* humanistic–positive psychological theories
positive psychotherapy, 644
positive punishment, **316–317**, 317*f*
positive reinforcement, **316–317**, 317*f*
positive symptoms (of schizophrenia), **608**
positron emission tomography (PET), **113**, 115
postconventional level, **191**, 191*f*
posthypnotic suggestion, 252
postsynaptic neurons, 89, 90*f*, 94
post-traumatic stress disorder (PTSD), **594**
  cognitive–behavioral therapy for, 648
  memory and, 290–291, 290*f*
  prolonged exposure therapy for, 654, 656
  symptoms of, 594
potassium ion channels, 86–87, 88*f*, 94
PPA (parahippocampal place area), 114, 114*f*
practical intelligence, 390–391
preconscious, 229
preconventional level, **190–191**, 191*f*
prediction, 42, 43*f*
predictive validity, **397**
prefrontal cortex, **285**
  aggression and, 570
  emotion and, 463
  IQ tasks and, 402–403, 402*f*
  memory and, 285, 286, 286*f*
  recall and, 287, 287*f*
  schizophrenia and, 610, 611*f*
prefrontal lobotomy, **635–636**
pregnancy. *See also* prenatal development
  alcohol in, 176, 176*f*, 605
  nutrition during, 175–176
  parental investment theory and, 438
  schizophrenia and, 24
  tobacco use in, 176–177, 621
pregnancy sickness, 175–176
prehistoric cultures, 12–13
prejudice, **562–564**
prenatal development. *See also* pregnancy
  alcohol and bipolar disorder and, 605

of brain and sensory system, 172–175, 173*f*, 174*f*–175*f*
  of intelligence, 404
  maternal nutrition and, 175–176
  of personality, 177, 516
  schizophrenia and, 610
  stages of, 171–172, 171*f*, 172*f*, 173*f*
  of temperament, 516
  teratogens and, 176–177, 176*f*
prenatal programming, **175**
preoperational stage, **185–188**, 185*f*, 187*f*, 188*f*
presbyopia, 132
prescription drugs
  for memory improvement, 294–295
  in pregnancy, 177
presynaptic neurons, 89, 90*f*, 94
prevention programs, 658–661
pride, 451–452, 451*f*
primacy effect, 275–276, 276*f*
primary appraisal, **479**
primary motor cortex, 101, 102, 102*f*
primary olfactory cortex, 158
primary reinforcers, **315–316**
primary visual cortex, 103
primates
  brain evolution in, 95
  human language and, 358–361, 359*f*
  neurogenesis in, 110*f*, 111
priming, **277**, 277*f*, 287
privately public, 32
proactive interference, **295**
probability level, 63–64
problem-focused coping strategies, **485**, 486*f*
problem solving. *See also* decision making
  brain and, 101, 415–416
  creative, 413, 416, 418, 418*f*
  by infants, 184
  obstacles to solutions, 410–411
  solution strategies, 409–410, 409*f*, 410*f*
  types of problems, 408
procedural memory, **277**
prodigies, 400–401, 400*f*
projection, **521**
projective tests, **536**
prolonged exposure therapy, 654, 656
propanolol, 662
prosocial behavior, 572–575
prospect theory, 378
protolanguage, **350**
prototypes, **368**
proximity, **142**, 142*f*
Prozac, 177, 632, 641
PRP (Penn Resiliency Program), 660
pruning, **180–181**, 202
pseudoscience, **44–45**, 45*f*
psilocybin, 261
psoriasis, mindfulness training and, 503
psychiatrists, 658
psychoactive drugs, **252**
  alcohol. *See* alcohol
  amphetamines, 259
  caffeine, 257–258, 257*f*

cocaine, 258–259
  dependence and addiction, 253
  LSD, 261
  marijuana, 260–261
  MDMA (ecstasy), 259
  nicotine, 93, 176–177, 258, 500
  operant conditioning and, 318
  opioids, 157, 256–257
  psilocybin, 261
  sedatives, 256
psychoanalysis, **15**
psychoanalytical theory
  Adler on, 522–523
  on dreams, 248
  Freud on, 519–522, 520*f*
  Horney on, 524–525, 524*f*
  Jung on, 523
  neuropsychoanalysis, 525
  summary of, 531*f*
  in treatment of psychological disorders, 642–644
psychoanalytical therapy, **642–644**
psychobiography, 48
psychodynamic therapy, **643**
psychological dependence, 253
psychological disorders. *See also* treatment of disorders
  anxiety disorders, 591–600, 591*f*, 592*f*, 593*f*
  childhood disorders, 619–622, 620*f*, 621*f*
  choosing a therapist, 658–659
  classification of, 590–591, 591*f*
  creativity and, 622–625, 623*f*, 624*f*
  defining, 589–591
  Diagnostic and Statistical Manual, 14–15, 590–591, 591*f*, 599
  dissociative disorders, 613–614
  Internet addiction, 598–599, 599*f*
  major, 592*f*–593*f*
  mood disorders, 600–607, 602*f*, 604*f*, 605*f*
  moral treatment movement, 14
  personality disorders, 616–619, 616*f*
  prevalence of, 590–591, 591*f*
  prevention of, 658–661
  schizophrenia. *See* schizophrenia
  somatoform disorders, 614–615
psychology, 5
  critical thinking in, 28–30
  definition of, 5–6
  folk, 6
  history of clinical psychology, 12–16, 13*f*, 14*f*, 15*f*
  history of scientific psychology, 16–22
  mind–body dualism in, 24–25
  nature–nurture debate in, 23–24
  reasons for study of, 6–7, 8–9
  subdisciplines of, 7–11, 7*f*
  timeline of, 20*f*–22*f*
psychoneuroimmunology (PNI), **495–497**
psychophysics, **16–17**, 125

psychosomatic theory, 492
psychosurgery, 635–636
psychotherapy, **642**
  for anxiety disorders, 662
  behavioral treatments, 644–645
  choosing a therapist, 658–659
  cognitive and cognitive–behavioral treatments, 645–648, 651
  combined with drug therapy, 653
  effectiveness of, 650–652
  group therapy, 648–649, 662
  humanistic–positive therapy, 644
  mindfulness training and, 654–655
  psychoanalytic/psychodynamic therapy, 642–644
  summary of techniques, 649*f*
psychotic disorders, **607**
psychoticism, 517, 530
PTSD. *See* post-traumatic stress disorder
puberty, **200–201**, 200*f*
publicly private, 32
punishment, **316–317**, 317*f*
pupil, **129**, 130*f*
purity, of sound waves, 150
PYY (peptide YY), 431

Q

quantitative trail loci (QTL) approach, **514–515**
quasi-experimental design, **71**
questioning authority, 41
questionnaires, 59–60, 59*f*, 536–537

R

race–ethnicity. *See also* culture; *specific ethnic groups*
  implicit bias and, 562–564
  intelligence and, 405–406
  suicide rates and, 602, 602*f*
racism, 562
Rain Man, 401
random assignment, **53**, 55
rapid eye movements (REM), 240–243, 240*f*, 242*f*, 249
rational choice theory, 376–378
rational (face valid) method, 537
Raven's Progressive Matrices Test, 388, 388*f*
reaction formation, **520–521**
reaction range, **403–404**, 404*f*
real movement neurons, 138
reappraisal, **455**
  by AIDS caregivers, 506
  in coping strategies, 485–486
  prefrontal cortex in, 463
reasoning, 201, 368–369, 380
recall, 280, 281*f*
recency effect, 275–276, 276*f*
recessive genes, **78**
reciprocal altruism, **574**
recovered memories, 298
reflexes, 97, 179
refractory period, in neural impulse, 87, 88*f*
rehearsal, 273–275, 280, 286

reinforcement. *See also* operant
  conditioning
    positive and negative, 316–317,
      317*f*
    primary and secondary
      reinforcers, 315–316
    schedules of, 319–322, 320*f*,
      321*f*
    in social learning theory, 332
reinforcers, 315–317, 317*f*
rejection, 442, 548, 559, 561
relational view of stress, 477
relationships
    happiness and, 469–470
    love, 430, 578–580, 579*f*
    marriage, 209, 209*f*
    of self-actualizing individuals,
      527
relaxation techniques, 645
reliability, 396–397, 535
REM (rapid eye movement),
      240–243, 240*f*, 242*f*, 249
Reminyl, 294
remote association word
    problems, 415
repetitive transcranial magnetic
    stimulation, 637, 637*f*
replication, 44
representativeness heuristic, 374
representative sample, 49–50, 50*f*
repression, 296–297, 298, 520,
      644
research. *See also* animal research
    correlational studies, 50–53,
      51*f*, 52*f*, 53*f*
    descriptive studies, 47–50,
      48*f*, 50*f*
    design principles, 46–47
    ethics in, 66–70, 312, 555
    experimenter expectancy
      effects in, 56–57
    experiments, 53–57, 55*f*
    measures used in, 58–61, 59*f*
    meta-analysis, 57–58
    quasi-experimental design, 71
    scientific method in, 42–44, 43*f*
    statistics in, 52, 52*f*, 61–65,
      62*f*, 65*f*
research design, 46–47
resilience, 490
resistance stage, 482, 482*f*
resting potential, 87, 88*f*
reticular formation, 98
retina, 129, 130*f*, 133*f*
retrieval, memory, 283–284, 287
retroactive interference, 294
retrograde amnesia, 299
reuptake, 89
rewards, motivation and,
      444–445, 446–447
rhyming, 280
risperidone, 634
rods, 130, 130*f*
rooting reflex, 179
Rorschach Inkblot Test, 536, 536*f*
rubella, schizophrenia and, 24
Russian language, color
    perception and, 362–363,
    363*f*

S

sadness, 459*f*, 461, 461*f*
safe sex practices, 507

samples, in research design, 47,
      49–50, 50*f*
Samurai culture, 464–465
SAT (Scholastic Aptitude Test),
      380
savant syndrome, 401–402
scatterplots, 52, 52*f*
scent, attraction and, 577
schedules of reinforcement,
      319–322, 320*f*, 321, 321*f*
schemas, 282, 558
schizoid personality disorder,
      616, 616*f*
schizophrenia, 607
    brain and, 609–610, 609*f*,
      610*f*, 611*f*
    cingulate gyrus and, 100
    creativity and, 623
    dopamine hypothesis, 611–612
    drug treatments for, 634–635,
      635*f*, 641
    explanations of, 29
    group therapy in, 650
    major symptoms of, 607–608,
      608*f*
    marijuana and, 260
    maternal infections and, 24,
      176, 610
    maternal nutrition and, 175
    meditation-based therapies,
      655
    nature and nurture
      explanations of, 609–610,
      609*f*
    neural synchrony in, 202
    prevalence of, 607
schizotypal personality disorder,
      616, 616*f*
Scholastic Aptitude Test (SAT),
      380
school psychology, 11
science. *See also* research
    common sense and logic in, 39
    limits of observation, 39–40
    map of the sciences, 40*f*
    pseudoscience and, 44–45, 45*f*
    questioning authority in, 41
    scientific method, 42–44, 43*f*
    scientific thinking, 40–42
Science Talent Search, Intel, 420
scientific method, 42–44, 43*f*
scientific psychology
    behaviorism, 19
    cognitivism, 19–21
    empiricism, 16
    evolutionary psychology and
      behavioral neuroscience,
      21–22
    Hall and, 17–18, 17*f*
    humanistic and positive, 19
    psychophysics, 16–17
    structuralism and
      functionalism, 18
    Wundt and, 17, 17*f*, 18
scientific thinking, 40–42,
      372–373
SCN (suprachiasmatic nucleus),
      239
sea slug studies, 291–293, 291*f*
secondary appraisal, 479
secondary olfactory cortex, 158
secondary (or conditioned)
    reinforcers, 315–316
secondhand smoke, 500

second languages, 378–381, 380*f*
Second Life, 652–653
secure attachment, 193
sedatives, 256
SEL (socioemotional learning),
      467
selective attention, 230–232,
      231*f*, 232*f*, 251, 262
selective norepinephrine reuptake
    inhibitors, 662
selective serotonin reuptake
    inhibitors (SSRIs), 632, 633*f*,
      640–641, 661
self-actualization, 430, 430*f*,
      526–527
self-conscious emotions,
      450–452, 450*f*, 451*f*, 452*f*
self-esteem, social networking
    and, 219
self-fulfilling prophecy, 57
self-reports, 59–60, 59*f*
self-serving bias, 556
semantic memory, 278
semantic processing, 280
semicircular canals, 150, 151*f*
sensation, 124. *See also*
    perception; *specific senses*
    age-related decrease in,
      210–211, 211*f*
    basic processes of, 125
    culture and, 161–164, 162*f*,
      164*f*
    infant development of,
      179–180, 179*f*
    prenatal development of,
      172–175, 173*f*
    sensory cortexes, 285
sensitivity period
    in language development,
      352–353, 379
    in learning, 336
sensorimotor stage, 184–185,
      185*f*
sensory adaptation, 125
sensory deprivation, 429–430
sensory memory, 270, 272, 285
sensory neurons, 85
sentence phase, 352, 352*f*
separation anxiety, 193
serial-position effect, 275–276,
      276*f*
serotonin, 92
    aggression and, 570
    antidepressants and, 631–632,
      633*f*, 640–641
    in bipolar disorder, 606
    cocaine and, 259
    depression and, 603, 604
    Ecstasy and, 92, 93*f*
    functions of, 91*f*, 92
    LSD and, 261
    in schizophrenia, 635
set point, 427–429, 428*f*
seven-square match problem, 410,
      410*f*
sex glands, 115
sex hormones, 115, 200, 366,
      437, 570
sexism, 562
sexual behavior, 435
    in adolescence, 204
    age of first intercourse, 204
    arousal, 100, 436–437, 436*f*
    casual sex, 438, 439

creativity and, 514
    culture and, 437–438
    in emerging adulthood, 207
    happiness and, 469
    HIV/AIDS and, 507
    Internet and, 219
    Kinsey surveys on, 49–50, 50*f*
    sexual orientation, 438,
      440–441
    sexual response cycle, 436,
      436*f*
sexual identity, 207
sexual orientation, 438
    adolescence and, 204
    in animals, 440
    as continuum, 438, 440
    genetic and environmental
      factors in, 440–441
    Kinsey surveys on, 50
    sexual identity and, 207
sexual response cycle, 436, 436*f*
sexual strategies theory, 577–578
shamans, 12–13
shape constancy, 140–141, 141*f*
shaping, 19*f*, 318–319, 319*f*
shock therapy, 636–637, 636*f*,
      641
short-term memory, 270
    capacity of, 273
    hippocampus and prefrontal
      cortex and, 286, 286*f*
    operation of, 273–275, 274*f*
    serial position effect, 275–276,
      276*f*
    uses of, 272
signal detection theory, 126–127,
      127*f*
similarity, 142, 142*f*
simple cells (neurons), 134, 135*f*
single-blind studies, 56
situational attributions, 556
size constancy, 140, 141*f*, 144*f*,
      162
skepticism, in science, 41
Skinner box, 318, 318*f*
sleep
    brain and, 240–241, 240*f*, 241*f*
    brain injury and, 263
    circadian rhythms and,
      239–240, 239*f*
    depression and, 600–601
    disorders of, 246–248
    dreaming, 241, 243, 248–249,
      249*f*
    features of, 238–239
    function of, 243–244, 244*f*
    learning and, 324–325, 324*f*
    memory and, 243, 282, 289,
      289*f*
    over the life span, 241–242,
      242*f*
    reticular formation and, 98
    sleep deprivation, 243,
      244–246, 245*f*
    tips for improving, 245*f*, 246
sleep debt, 245
sleep spindles, 241
sleepwalking, 247
slow-to-warm-up child, 192
smell
    age-related decrease in, 211
    cultural variation in, 162, 164
    prenatal development of, 174
    sense of, 158–159, 158*f*

smiling, 457, 457*f*
smoking. *See* tobacco use
SMPY (Study for Mathematically Precocious Youth), 400–401
social anxiety disorder, 594–595
social behavior
  aggression. *See* aggression
  attitudes, 565–568, 565*f*, 567*f*
  attraction, 575, 577–578, 578*f*–579*f*
  attributions, 556–557
  conformity, 549–552, 551*f*, 582
  detecting deception, 557
  exclusion and inclusion, 559–561
  groupthink, 551–552
  in Jonestown cult, 580–582, 581*f*
  love, 578–580, 579*f*
  minority social influence, 552
  obedience, 552–555, 554*f*, 555*f*
  prejudice and discrimination, 562–564
  prosocial behavior, 572–575
  schemas, 558
  social facilitation *vs.* social loafing, 549
  in social networks, 560–561
  social pain, 548, 559, 560*f*
  stereotypes, 558–559
social capital, 561
social–cognitive learning, 331, 528, 528*f*, 531*f*
social desirability bias, **60**
social development
  in adolescents, 203–205, 205*f*
  in children, 192–199, 195*f*, 196*f*
  sexual orientation and, 441
social exchange theory, **574**, 575
social facilitation, **549**
Social Learning and Imitation (Miller and Dollard), 331
social learning theory, **331**
  aggression in, 571
  Bobo doll studies and, 332–334, 332*f*, 333*f*, 334*f*
  language acquisition and, 355
  modeling in, 332
  smoking and, 340, 341*f*
social loafing, **549**
social networking. *See also* computers and Internet
  in adolescence, 218–220, 219*f*
  for children, 218
  in coping, 488
  as diaries, 170
  immune system and, 497
  impact of, 4–5
  Internet addiction, 598–599, 599*f*
  in middle adulthood, 220–221
  psychology subdisciplines on, 31–32
  social psychology of, 560–561
  texting, 218, 234–235
social norms, **549**
social pain, 548, 559, 560*f*
social phobia, 594–595
social psychology, **10**, 548
  on electronic social interactions, 31–32
  on social networks, 560–561

Social Readjustment Rating Scale (SRRS), 477–478, 478*f*
social referencing, **197**
social support
  in coping, 486, 487–489
  in weight loss, 434
social support strategy, 486
social workers, 658
sociocultural theories of language, 354
socioemotional development
  in adolescence, 203–205, 205*f*, 218–219
  attachment in, 192–195, 195*f*
  in infants and children, 192–199, 195*f*, 196*f*, 218
  technology use and, 218–220, 219*f*
socioemotional learning (SEL), 467
sociopaths, 617
sodium ion channels, 86–87, 88*f*, 94
soft inheritance, 81
softwiring, 23–24, 99
soma, 84, 85*f*
somatic nervous system, **82**, 82*f*
somatization disorder, **614**–615
somatoform disorders, **614**–615
somatosensory cortex, 102, 102*f*
sound, physics of, 149–150, 150*f*
spatial ability, 366
spatial intelligence, 391, 392*f*
speech
  babbling, 351, 352*f*
  brain and, 103–104
  vocal expression, 456, 460–461
  word salad, 412–413, 608
speed (Benzedrine), 259
spermarche, **201**
spirituality, 261, 470–471
split-brain research, 106, 107*f*. *See also* cerebral hemispheres
spontaneity, 526
spontaneous recovery, **310**, 312*f*
sports psychology, 11
SRRS (Social Readjustment Rating Scale), 477–478, 478*f*
SSRIs (selective serotonin reuptake inhibitors), **632**, 633*f*, 640–641, 661
stagnation, **211**
standard deviation, **62**
Stanford–Binet test, 394, 396
Stanford Prison Experiment, 38, 66, 66*f*, 68
statistics, **61**
  in advertising, 64–65, 65*f*
  correlation coefficients, 52, 52*f*
  descriptive, 62–63, 62*f*
  inferential, 63–65
stereotypes, 21, 558–559
stimulants, **257**–259, 257*f*
stimulus discrimination, **130**
stimulus generalization, **130**
stimulus view of stress, 477–478
storage, memory, **282**–283, 283*f*, 287–288, 287*f*
strange situation, 193

stress, **476**
  adaptation to, 483–484
  aging effects from, 491
  brain and, 484
  coping strategies, 485–490, 486*f*, 506
  depression and, 499–500
  eating and, 501
  general adaptation syndrome, 482–483, 482*f*
  genes and, 484
  heart disease and, 497–499, 499*f*
  hormones, 479–482, 480*f*, 484
  immune system and, 482, 493–494, 496–497
  meaning in life and, 490
  meditation and, 503
  neurogenesis and, 111
  perceived, 497
  physiology of, 479–482, 480*f*–481*f*
  positive psychology of coping, 489–490, 506
  primary and secondary appraisal and, 479, 480*f*–481*f*
  psychoneuroimmunology, 495–497
  psychosomatic theory and, 492–493
  as stimulus, 477–478, 478*f*
  stressors, 477
stressors, **477**
striatum, 284, 285*f*, 287, 287*f*
striving for superiority, **522**
stroke, 103, 214
Stroop effect, 251–252, 251*f*
structuralism, **18**
structural processing, 280
Study for Mathematically Precocious Youth (SMPY), 400–401
studying tips, 279, 300–301, 325
subjective experience of emotion, **461**–462, 461*f*
subjective well-being, 468–471
sublimation, **521**
subsonic sounds, 150
substance abuse, 318. *See also* psychoactive drugs
success, Atkinson's model of, 442–443
suggestibility, **297**
suicide
  antidepressants and, 632
  depression and, 601, 602, 602*f*
  hypersomnia and, 247
  Jonestown cult and, 580–582, 581*f*
  operant conditioning and, 319
  rates of, 602, 602*f*
SuperClubsPLUS, 218
superego, **520**, 520*f*
support groups, 649
suprachiasmatic nucleus (SCN), 239
surprise, 459*f*, 461*f*
surveys, 49–50
sustained attention, 232–233, 233*f*
swallowing, 97*f*

symbolic communication systems, 349
sympathetic nervous system, **83**
  in emotional response, 456
  stress and, 480*f*, 481, 492
  structure of, 82*f*, 83, 83*f*
synapse, **85**
synaptic cleft, 85, 90*f*
synaptic pruning, 202
synaptic vesicles, 89, 90*f*
synaptogenesis, **108**, 337
synchronization, 232
syndromes, 590
synesthesia, **160**–161, 161*f*, 269
syntax, **349**
systematic desensitization, **645**, 646*f*–647*f*, 652, 662

T

TABP (Type A Behavior Pattern), 497–499, **498**, 499*f*
tabula rasa, 16
Tactile Dome, San Francisco, 76
Tadrart Acacus of Libya rock painting, 27*f*
Tammet, Daniel, 401
tardive dyskinesia, **634**
taste, 159–160, 159*f*, 174, 211
taste aversion. *See* conditioned taste aversion
taste buds, **159**
taste receptor cells, **159**
taxicab drivers, hippocampi of, 99
technology
  impact of use of, 4–5
  in infancy and toddlerhood, 217, 217*f*
  in therapies, 652–653
technology-based therapies, **652**–653
television. *See also* advertising; media
  aggression and violence on, 334
  cognitive and brain development and, 217, 217*f*
telomerase, **491**
temperament, **177**. *See also* personality
  in children, 198–199
  prenatal environment and, 516
temporal lobes, 101*f*, 103, 286*f*, 288
teratogens, 175, 176–177, 176*f*
terminal buttons, **85**, 85*f*, 90*f*
test bias, **398**
test fairness, **398**
testosterone
  aggression and, 570
  in puberty, 200
  sex drive and, 437
  spatial ability and, 366
test–retest reliability, 396–397
tetrahydrocannibinol (THC), 260
texting, 218, 234–235
texture gradient, 139, 140*f*
thalamus, **98**
  emotion and, 462, 462*f*
  location of, 98*f*
  vision and, 132, 133*f*, 134
THC (tetrahydrocannibinol), 260
theory, **42**